Contemporary Literary Criticism

Guide to Gale Literary Criticism Series

When you need to review criticism of literary works, these are the Gale series to use:

If the author's death date is:	You should turn to:
After Dec. 31, 1959 (or author is still living)	*CONTEMPORARY LITERARY CRITICISM* for example: Jorge Luis Borges, Anthony Burgess, William Faulkner, Mary Gordon, Ernest Hemingway, Iris Murdoch
1900 through 1959	*TWENTIETH-CENTURY LITERARY CRITICISM* for example: Willa Cather, F. Scott Fitzgerald, Henry James, Mark Twain, Virginia Woolf
1800 through 1899	*NINETEENTH-CENTURY LITERATURE CRITICISM* for example: Fedor Dostoevski, Nathaniel Hawthorne, George Sand, William Wordsworth
1400 through 1799	*LITERATURE CRITICISM FROM 1400 TO 1800 (excluding Shakespeare)* for example: Anne Bradstreet, Daniel Defoe, Alexander Pope, François Rabelais, Jonathan Swift, Phillis Wheatley
	SHAKESPEAREAN CRITICISM Shakespeare's plays and poetry
Antiquity through 1399	*CLASSICAL AND MEDIEVAL LITERATURE CRITICISM* for example: Dante, Homer, Plato, Sophocles, Vergil, the Beowulf Poet

---

Gale also publishes related criticism series:

CHILDREN'S LITERATURE REVIEW

This series covers authors of all eras who have written for the preschool through high school audience.

SHORT STORY CRITICISM

This series covers the major short fiction writers of all nationalities and periods of literary history.

POETRY CRITICISM

This series covers poets of all nationalities, movements, and periods of literary history.

DRAMA CRITICISM

This series covers dramatists of all nationalities and periods of literary history.

ISSN 0091-3421

Volume 68

Contemporary Literary Criticism

Excerpts from Criticism of the Works of Today's Novelists, Poets, Playwrights, Short Story Writers, Scriptwriters, and Other Creative Writers

Roger Matuz
EDITOR

Cathy Falk
Sean R. Pollock
David Segal
Robyn Young
ASSOCIATE EDITORS

Gale Research Inc. • DETROIT • LONDON

STAFF

Roger Matuz, *Editor*

Cathy Falk, Sean R. Pollock, David Segal,
Robyn Young, *Associate Editors*

Jennifer Brostrom, John P. Daniel, Rogene M. Fisher, Christopher Giroux,
Susan M. Peters, Bruce Walker, Debra A. Wells, Janet M. Witalec, *Assistant Editors*

Jeanne A. Gough, *Production & Permissions Manager*
Linda M. Pugliese, *Production Supervisor*
Paul Lewon, Lorna Mabunda, Maureen A. Puhl,
Camille P. Robinson, Jennifer VanSickle, *Editorial Associates*
Donna Craft, Brandy C. Johnson, Sheila Walencewicz, *Editorial Assistants*

Maureen Richards, *Research Supervisor*
Mary Beth McElmeel, *Editorial Associate*
Kathleen Jozwiak, Julie Karmazin, Tamara C. Nott, Julie Synkonis, *Editorial Assistants*

Sandra C. Davis, *Permissions Supervisor (Text)*
Maria L. Franklin, Josephine M. Keene, Denise M. Singleton,
Kimberly F. Smilay, *Permissions Associates*
Michele Lonoconus, Shelly Rakoczy, Shalice Shah, Rebecca A. Stanko, *Permissions Assistants*

Margaret A. Chamberlain, *Permissions Supervisor (Pictures)*
Pamela A. Hayes, *Permissions Associate*
Karla Kulkis, Nancy Rattenbury, Keith Reed, *Permissions Assistants*

Mary Beth Trimper, *Production Manager*
Shanna Heilveil, *External Production Associate*

Art Chartow, *Art Director*
C. J. Jonik, *Keyliner*

Library of Congress Catalog Card Number 76-38938
ISBN 0-8103-4442-4
ISSN 0091-3421

Printed in the United States of America

Published simultaneously in the United Kingdom
by Gale Research International Limited
(An affiliated company of Gale Research Inc.)

Contents

Preface

Named "one of the twenty-five most distinguished reference titles published during the past twenty-five years" by *Reference Quarterly,* the *Contemporary Literary Criticism (CLC)* series provides readers with critical commentary and general information on more than 2,000 authors now living or who died after December 31, 1959. Previous to the publication of the first volume of *CLC* in 1973, there was no ongoing digest monitoring scholarly and popular sources of critical opinion and explication of modern literature. *CLC,* therefore, has fulfilled an essential need, particularly since the complexity and variety of contemporary literature makes the function of criticism especially important to today's reader.

Scope of the Series

CLC presents significant passages from published criticism of works by creative writers. Since many of the authors covered by *CLC* inspire continual critical commentary, writers are often represented in more than one volume. There is, of course, no duplication of reprinted criticism.

Authors are selected for inclusion for a variety of reasons, among them the publication or dramatic production of a critically acclaimed new work, the reception of a major literary award, revival of interest in past writings, or the adaptation of a literary work to film or television.

The present volume of *CLC* includes E. E. Cummings, one of the most popular and widely anthologized poets of the twentieth century; Milan Kundera, whose recent novel *L'Immortalité* (*Immortality*) juxtaposes fiction with biographical reminiscence; Dorothy Parker, a literary celebrity of the 1920s best known for humorous short stories in which she satirized middle-class social mores; and Camille Paglia, a professor of humanities who has provoked critical controversy with her treatment of academic and feminist issues in *Sexual Personae: Art and Decadence from Nefertiti to Emily Dickinson.*

Perhaps most importantly, works that frequently appear on the syllabuses of high school and college literature courses are represented by individual entries in *CLC.* William Faulkner's *The Sound and the Fury* and Gabriel García Márquez's *One Hundred Years of Solitude* are examples of works of this stature appearing in *CLC,* Volume 68.

Attention is also given to several other groups of writers—authors of considerable public interest—about whose work criticism is often difficult to locate. These include mystery and science fiction writers, literary and social critics, foreign writers, and authors who represent particular ethnic groups within the United States.

Format of the Book

Each *CLC* volume contains about 500 individual excerpts—with approximately seventeen excerpts per author—taken from hundreds of book review periodicals, general magazines, scholarly journals, monographs, and books. Entries include critical evaluations spanning from the beginning of an author's career to the most current commentary. Interviews, feature articles, and other published writings that offer insight into the author's works are also presented. Students, teachers, librarians, and researchers will find that the generous excerpts and supplementary material in *CLC* provide them with vital information needed to write a term paper, analyze a poem, or lead a book discussion group. In addition, complete bibliographical citations note the original source and all of the information necessary for a term paper footnote or bibliography.

Features

A *CLC* author entry consists of the following elements:

- The **author heading** cites the form under which the author has most commonly published, followed by birth date, and death date when applicable. Uncertainty as to a birth or death date is indicated by a question mark.

- A **portrait** of the author is included when available.

- A brief **biographical and critical introduction** to the author and his or her work precedes the excerpted criticism. The first line of the introduction provides the author's full name, pseudonyms (if applicable), nationality, and a listing of genres in which the author has written. Since *CLC* is not intended to be a definitive biographical source, cross-references have been included to direct readers to these useful sources published by Gale Research: *Short Story Criticism* and *Children's Literature Review,* which provide excerpts of criticism on the works of short story writers and authors of books for young people, respectively; *Contemporary Authors,* which includes detailed biographical and bibliographical sketches of more than 98,000 authors; *Something about the Author,* which contains heavily illustrated biographical sketches of writers and illustrators who create books for children and young adults; *Dictionary of Literary Biography,* which provides original evaluations and detailed biographies of authors important to literary history; and *Contemporary Authors Autobiography Series* and *Something about the Author Autobiography Series,* which offer autobiographical essays by prominent writers for adults and those of interest to young readers, respectively. Previous volumes of *CLC* in which the author has been featured are also listed in the introduction.

• A list of **principal works,** usually divided into genre categories, notes the most important works by the author.

• The **excerpted criticism** represents various kinds of critical writing, ranging in form from the brief review to the scholarly exegesis. Essays are selected by the editors to reflect the spectrum of opinion about a specific work or about an author's literary career in general. The excerpts are presented chronologically, adding a useful perspective to the entry. All titles by the author featured in the entry are printed in boldface type, which enables the reader to easily identify the works being discussed. Publication information (such as publisher names and book prices) and parenthetical numerical references (such as footnotes or page and line references to specific editions of a work) have been deleted at the editor's discretion to provide smoother reading of the text.

• A complete **bibliographical citation** designed to help the user find the original essay or book follows each excerpt.

• A concise **further reading** section appears at the end of entries on authors for whom a significant amount of criticism exists in addition to the pieces reprinted in *CLC.* In some cases, this annotated bibliography includes references to material for which the editors could not obtain reprint rights.

Other Features

• An **Acknowledgments** section lists the copyright holders who have granted permission to reprint material in this volume of *CLC.* It does not, however, list every book or periodical reprinted or consulted during the preparation of the volume.

• A **Cumulative Author Index** lists all the authors who have appeared in the various literary criticism series published by Gale Research, with cross-references to Gale's biographical and autobiographical series. A full listing of the series referenced there appears on the first page of the indexes of this volume. Readers will welcome this cumulated author index as a useful tool for locating an author within the various series. The index, which lists birth and death dates when available, will be particularly valuable for those authors who are identified with a certain period but whose death date causes them to be placed in another, or for those authors whose careers span two periods. For example, Ernest Hemingway is found in *CLC,* yet a writer often associated with him, F. Scott Fitzgerald, is found in *Twentieth-Century Literary Criticism.*

• A **Cumulative Nationality Index** alphabetically lists all authors featured in *CLC* by nationality, followed by numbers corresponding to the volumes in which they appear.

• A **Title Index** alphabetically lists all titles reviewed in the current volume of *CLC.* Listings are followed by the author's name and the corresponding page numbers where the titles are discussed. English translations of foreign titles and variations of titles are cross-referenced to the title under which a work was originally published. Titles of novels, novellas, dramas, films, record albums, and poetry, short story, and essay collections are printed in italics, while all individual poems, short stories, essays, and songs are printed in roman type within quotation marks; when published separately (e.g., T.S. Eliot's poem *The Waste Land*), the titles of long poems are printed in italics.

• In response to numerous suggestions from librarians, Gale has also produced a **special paperbound edition** of the *CLC* title index. This annual cumulation, which alphabetically lists all titles reviewed in the series, is available to all customers and will be published with the first volume of *CLC* issued in each calendar year. Additional copies of the index are available upon request. Librarians and patrons will welcome this separate index: it saves shelf space, is easy to use, and is disposable upon receipt of the following year's cumulation.

A Note to the Reader

When writing papers, students who quote directly from any volume in the Literary Criticism Series may use the following general forms to footnote reprinted criticism. The first example pertains to material drawn from periodicals, the second to material reprinted from books:

[1]Anne Tyler, "Manic Monologue," *The New Republic* 200 (April 17, 1989), 44-6; excerpted and reprinted in *Contemporary Literary Criticism,* Vol. 58, ed. Roger Matuz (Detroit: Gale Research Inc., 1990), p. 325.

[2]Patrick Reilly, *The Literature of Guilt: From 'Gulliver' to Golding* (University of Iowa Press, 1988); excerpted and reprinted in *Contemporary Literary Criticism,* Vol. 58, ed. Roger Matuz (Detroit: Gale Research Inc., 1990), pp. 206-12.

Suggestions Are Welcome

The editors welcome the comments and suggestions of readers to expand the coverage and enhance the usefulness of the series.

Acknowledgments

The editors wish to thank the copyright holders of the excerpted criticism included in this volume, the permissions managers of many book and magazine publishing companies for assisting us in securing reprint rights, and Anthony Bogucki for assistance with copyright research. We are also grateful to the staffs of the Detroit Public Library, the Library of Congress, the University of Detroit Library, Wayne State University Purdy/Kresge Library Complex, and the University of Michigan Libraries for making their resources available to us. Following is a list of the copyright holders who granted us permission to reprint material in this volume of CLC. Every effort has been made to trace copyright, but if omissions have been made, please let us know.

COPYRIGHTED EXCERPTS IN *CLC* VOLUME 68 WERE REPRINTED FROM THE FOLLOWING PERIODICALS:

African Literature Today, n. 11, 1980. Copyright 1980 by Heinemann Educational Books Ltd. All rights reserved. Reprinted by permission of Africana Publishing Corporation, New York, NY.—***America,*** v. 155, November 18, 1986 for a review of "The War" by Frederick J. Harris. © 1986. All rights reserved. Reprinted by permission of America Press, Inc, 106 West 56th Street, New York, NY 10019.—***American Book Review,*** v. 12, September-October, 1990. © 1990 by *The American Book Review.* Reprinted by permission of the publisher.—***American Heritage,*** v. 40, February, 1989. © 1989 by American Heritage Publishing Co., Inc. All rights reserved.—***American Literature,*** v. 51, January, 1980. Copyright © 1980 Duke University Press, Durham, NC./v. 51, November, 1979. Copyright © 1979 Duke University Press, Durham, NC. Reprinted by permission of the publisher.—***The American Poetry Review,*** v. 18, January-February, 1989 for "Not Life So Proud to Be Life: Snodgrass, Rothenberg, Bell, and the Counter-Revolution" by Larry Levis. Copyright © 1989 by World Poetry, Inc. Reprinted by permission of the author.—***Arts Digest,*** v. 29, December 1, 1954 for "E. E. Cumming's Paintings and Poems (1954)" by William Carlos Williams. Copyright 1954 by The Art Digest, Inc. Renewed 1982 by William Eric Williams and Paul H. Williams. Copyright © 1978 by The Estate of Florence H. Williams. All rights reserved. Reprinted by permission of the publisher and New Directions Publishing Corporation.—***The Atlantic Monthly,*** v. 191, January, 1953 for a review of "The Devil Rides Outside" by Charles J. Rolo; v. 223, March, 1969 for "The Worlds of Jean Stafford" by Elizabeth Janeway; v. 232, July, 1973 for "Left, Right, Gonzo!" by Richard Todd. Copyright 1953, 1969, 1973 by The Atlantic Monthly Company, Boston, MA. All reprinted by permission of the respective authors.—***Belles Lettres: A Review of Books by Women,*** v. 4, Winter, 1989. Reprinted by permission of the publisher.—***The Bloomsbury Review,*** v. 8, March-April, 1988 for "Going Beyond the Limits of Language" by Barbara Loren. Copyright © by Owaissa Communications Company, Inc. 1988. Reprinted by permission of the author.—***Book World—Chicago Tribune,*** February 22, 1970. © 1970 Postrib Corp. Reprinted by courtesy of the *Chicago Tribune* and *The Washington Post.*—***Book World—The Washington Post,*** May 18, 1986; May 7, 1989; December 31, 1989; February 18, 1990; October 7, 1990; December, 1990; March 31, 1991; May 5, 1991. © 1986, 1989, 1990, 1991, *The Washington Post.* All reprinted with permission of the publisher.—***Booklist,*** v. 85, March 1, 1989. Copyright © 1989 by the American Library Association. Reprinted by permission of the publisher.—***Books,*** London, n. 3, July-August, 1991. © Gradegate Ltd. 1991. Reprinted by permission of the publisher.—***Boston Review,*** v. VIII, April, 1983 for "Tracking García Márquez: A Journey to Macondo" by Gene H. Bell-Villada. Copyright © 1983 by the Boston Critic, Inc. Reprinted by permission of the author.—***Callaloo,*** v. 13, Spring, 1990. Copyright © 1990 by Charles H. Rowell. All rights reserved. Reprinted by permission of the publisher.—***Canadian Review of American Studies,*** v. VII, Spring, 1976. © *Canadian Review of American Studies* 1976. Reprinted by permission of the publisher.—***The CEA Critic,*** v. 49, Winter 1986-Summer 1987. Copyright © 1987 by the College English Association, Inc. Reprinted by permission of the publisher.—***Chicago Tribune,*** May 20, 1956. © copyrighted 1956, renewed 1984 Chicago Tribune Company. All rights reserved. Used with permission.—***Chicago Tribune—Books,*** May 20, 1990 for "Eloquent Solitudes" by John Casey; October 28, 1990 for "More Than a Servant: Jamaica Kincaid's West Indian Au Pair Girl" by Carol Anshaw. © copyright 1990, Chicago Tribune Company. All rights reserved. Reprinted by permission of the respective author.—***Children's Literature: Annual of the Modern Language Association Seminar on Children's Literature and The Children's Literature Association,*** v. 18, 1990. © 1990 by Francelia Butler. All rights reserved. Reprinted by permission of Yale University Press.—***The Christian Century,*** v. 99, December 22-29, 1982. Copyright 1982 Christian Century Foundation.—***The Christian Science Monitor,*** August 2, 1990 for "Lives on a Short Story Roller Coaster" by Mary Warner Marien; November 26, 1990 for "Life Becomes Art" by Mary Warner Marien. © 1990 The Christian Science Publishing Society. All rights reserved. Both reprinted by permission of the respective author./ May 23, 1973. © 1973 The Christian Science Publishing Society. All rights reserved. Both reprinted by permission from *The Christian Science Monitor.*/ July 12, 1956, renewed 1984 by The Christian Science Publishing Society. All rights reserved. Reprinted by permission from *The Christian Science Monitor.*—***CLA***

Journal, v. XXI, March, 1978. Copyright, 1978 by The College Language Association. Used by permission of The College Language Association.—***The Colorado Quarterly,*** v. 12, Summer, 1963 for "Cummings, Comedy and Criticism" by John Clendenning. Copyright 1963, by the University of Colorado, Boulder, CO. Reprinted by permission of the author.—***Commentary,*** v. 83, February, 1987 for "Post-Counterculture Tristesse" by Carol Iannone. Copyright © 1987 by the American Jewish Committee. All rights reserved. Reprinted by permission of the publisher and the author.—***The Commonweal,*** v. LXXV, October 27, 1961. Copyright © 1961, renewed 1989 Commonweal Publishing Co., Inc. Reprinted by permission of Commonweal Foundation.—***Crazy Horse,*** n. 11, Summer, 1972 for an interview with Charles Simic by Philip Dacey. Copyright 1972 by University of Arkansas at Little Rock. Reprinted by permission of Charles Simic and Philip Dacey.—***The Denver Quarterly,*** v. 18, Spring, 1983 for "Jean Stafford's Western Childhood: Huck Finn Joins the Camp Fire Girls" by Melody Graulich. Copyright © 1983 by the University of Denver. Reprinted by permission of the author.—***Diacritics,*** v. I, Fall, 1971. Copyright © Diacritics, Inc., 1971. Reprinted by permission of the publisher.—***Essays in Literature,*** v. IX, Fall, 1982. Copyright 1982 by Western Illinois University. Reprinted by permission of the publisher.—***Feminist Studies,*** v. 10, Spring, 1984 for "In Quest of the Writer Ding Ling" by Yi-Tsi Mei Feuerwerker. Copyright © 1984 by Feminist Studies, Inc. Reprinted by permission of the author.—***The French Review,*** v. LVIII, April, 1985; v. LXII, December, 1988. Copyright 1985, 1988 by The American Association of Teachers of French. Both reprinted by permission of the publisher.—***The Georgia Review,*** v. XLIV, Fall, 1990. Copyright, 1990, by the University of Georgia. Reprinted by permission of the publisher.—***Harper's,*** v. 252, February, 1976. Copyright © 1976 by *Harper's Magazine.* All rights reserved. Reprinted by special permission.—***The Hudson Review,*** v. XXXV, Autumn, 1982; v. XLIV, Spring, 1991. Copyright © 1982, 1991 by The Hudson Review, Inc. Both reprinted by permission of the publisher.—***Kirkus Reviews,*** v. LIII, September 1, 1985. Copyright © 1985 The Kirkus Service, Inc. All rights reserved. Reprinted by permission of the publisher.—***The Listener,*** v. 124, September 6, 1990. © British Broadcasting Corp. 1990/ v. 84, August 20, 1970 for "Larger Than Death" by D. J. Enright; v. 123, April 5, 1990 for "Venus Genus" by Harriet Hawkins. © British Broadcasting Corp. 1970, 1990. Both reprinted by the respective authors.—***London Review of Books,*** v. 8, December 4, 1986 for "Ariel Goes to the Police" by Karl Miller; v. 13, June 13, 1991 for "Kundera's Man of Feeling" by Michael Wood. Both appear here by permission of the *London Review of Books* and the respective authors.—***Los Angeles Times Book Review,*** October 20, 1985; March 6, 1988; April 24, 1988; July 17, 1988; April 30, 1989; June 3, 1990; October 7, 1990; October 21, 1990. Copyright, 1985, 1988, 1989, 1990, *Los Angeles Times.* All reprinted by permission of the publisher.—***Mid-American Review,*** v. VIII, 1988 for "Immanent Distance: Silence and the Poetry of Charles Simic" by Bruce Bond. Reprinted by permission of the author.—***The Missouri Review,*** v. VII, 1984. Copyright © 1984 by The Curators of the University of Missouri. Reprinted by permission of the publisher.—***MLN,*** v. 99, March, 1984. © copyright 1984 by The Johns Hopkins University Press. All rights reserved. Reprinted by permission of the publisher.—***The Modern Language Review,*** v. 79, April, 1984 for "Comment Peut-on Etre Martiniquais?: The Recent Work of Edouard Glissant" by Richard D. E. Burton. © Modern Humanities Research Association 1984. Reprinted by permission of the publisher and the author.—***Ms.,*** v. VI, April, 1978 for "The Toughness of Jane Bowles" by Muriel Haynes. © 1978 Ms. Magazine. Reprinted by permission of the author.—***The Nation,*** New York, v. 182, June 2, 1956; v. 223, August 28, 1976; v. 232, June 27, 1981; v. 243, November 8, 1986; v. 250, June 25, 1990; v. 251, October 22, 1990; v. 252, June 10, 1991. Copyright 1956, 1976, 1981, 1986, 1990, 1991 *The Nation* magazine/The Nation Company, Inc. Renewed 1984 by The Nation Associates, Inc. All reprinted by permission of the publisher.—***National Review,*** New York, v. 28, March 5, 1976. © 1976 by National Review, Inc., 150 East 35th Street, New York, NY 10016. Reprinted by permission of the publisher.—***The New Criterion,*** v. IV, January, 1986 for "The Ambiguities of Milan Kundera" by Roger Kimball; v. VII, November, 1988 for "Jean Stafford's Triumph" by Bruce Bawer. Copyright © 1986, 1988 by The Foundation for Cultural Review. Both reprinted by permission of the respective authors.—***The New Leader,*** v. 72, May 15-29, 1989. © 1989 by The American Labor Conference on International Affairs, Inc. Reprinted by permission of the publisher.—***New Letters Review of Books,*** v. 3, Autumn, 1990 for "Dynamic Duo for Stage" by Deirdre Neilen. © copyright 1990 The Curators of the University of Missouri. Reprinted by permission of the publisher and the author.—***New Literary History,*** v. 21, Autumn, 1989. Copyright © 1989 by *New Literary History.* Reprinted by permission of the publisher.—***The New Republic,*** v. 178, February 11, 1978. © 1978 The New Republic, Inc. Reprinted by permission of *The New Republic.*—***New Statesman,*** v. 115, February 26, 1988. © 1988 The Statesman & Nation Publishing Co. Ltd. Reprinted by permission of the publisher.—***New Statesman & Society,*** v. 3, January 12, 1990; v. 3, March 30, 1990. © 1990 Statesman & Nation Publishing Company Limited. Both reprinted by permission of the publisher.—***Newsweek,*** v. CVII, April 28, 1986. Copyright 1986, by Newsweek, Inc. All rights reserved. Reprinted by permission of the publisher.—***New York Herald Tribune Books,*** July 15, 1928; December 16, 1928. Copyright 1928, *The Washington Post.* Both reprinted by permission of the publisher.—***New York*** Magazine, v.24, March 4, 1991 for "Woman Warrior: Sexual Philospher Camille Paglia Jousts with the Politically Correct" by Fancesca Stanfill. Copyright © 1991 by Francesca Stanfill. All rights reserved. Reprinted with the permission of the author.—***The New York Review of Books,*** v, VII, December 15, 1966; v. XIV, March 26, 1970; v. XXVIII, April 30, 1981; v. XXXVI, October 26, 1989; v. XXXVII, May 31, 1990; v. XXXVII, November 22, 1990; v. XXXVIII, May 30, 1991. Copyright © 1966, 1970, 1981, 1989, 1990, 1991 Nyrev, Inc. All reprinted with permission from *The New York Review of Books.*—***The New York Times,*** December 13, 1936; April 28, 1946; March 3, 1970; March 5, 1986; July 16, 1988; June 8, 1990; October, 1990. Copyright © 1936, 1946 © 1970, 1986, 1988, 1990 by The New York Times Company. All reprinted by permission of the publisher.—***The New York Times Book Review,*** May 9, 1943; October 26, 1952; November 23, 1952; October 4, 1959; January 29, 1967; May 6,

1973; November 30, 1975; February 19, 1978; October 6, 1985; May 4, 1986; September 13, 1987; July 10, 1988; September 3, 1989; March 4, 1990; May 20, 1990; July 22, 1990; October 7, 1990; October 28, 1990; December 23, 1990; April 28, 1991. Copyright 1943, 1952 © 1959, 1967, 1973, 1975, 1978, 1985, 1986, 1987, 1988, 1989, 1990, 1991 by The New York Times Company. All reprinted by permission of the publisher.—***The New York Times Magazine,*** October 7, 1990. Copyright © 1990 by The New York Times Company.—***The New Yorker,*** v. LXIV, May 16, 1988 for "Articles of Faith" by Terrence Rafferty. © 1988 by the author. Reprinted by permission of the publisher./ v. XIV, January 14, 1939 for "The Omelet of A. MacLeish" by Edmund Wilson. Copyright 1939, renewed 1967 by The New Yorker Magazine, Inc.; v. XX, May 20, 1944 for "A Toast and a Tear for Dorothy Parker" by Edmund Wilson. Copyright 1944 by The New Yorker Magazine, Inc. Renewed 1971 by Edmund Wilson. Both reprinted by permission of Farrar, Straus and Giroux, Inc./ v. XLIII, May 20, 1967; v. LIII, May 23, 1977. © 1967, 1977 by The New Yorker Magazine, Inc. Both reprinted by permission of the publisher.—***Novel: A Forum on Fiction,*** v. 1, Spring, 1968. Copyright © Novel Corp., 1968. Reprinted by permission of the publisher.—***Papers on English Language and Literature,*** v. 1, Winter, 1965. Copyright © 1965 by Nicholas Joost and Robert Partlow. Reprinted by permission of Southern Illinois University, publisher.—***Papers on Language & Literature,*** v. 13, Summer, 1977. Copyright © 1977 by the Board of Trustees, Southern Illinois University at Edwardsville. Reprinted by permission of the publisher.—***Paragraph: A Journal of Modern Critical Theory,*** v. 12, March, 1989. © Oxford University Press 1989. Reprinted by permission of the publisher.—***The Paris Review,*** v. 4, Spring, 1956. © 1956 The Paris Review, Inc.—***Parnassus: Poetry in Review,*** v. 16, 1990 for "Natural Selections" by William Logan. © 1990 Poetry in Review Foundation, NY. Reprinted by permission of the author./ v. 1, 1973. Copyright © 1973 Poetry in Review Foundation, NY. Reprinted by permission of the publisher.—***Partisan Review,*** v. XX, January-February, 1953 for "MacLeish and Vierreck" by Howard Nemerov. Copyright 1953 by *Partisan Review.* Reprinted by permission of the publisher and the author.—***Playboy (R),*** v. 30, February, 1983. Copyright © 1983 by *Playboy (R).* All rights reserved.—***Publishers Weekly,*** v. 237, October 19, 1990; v. 237, November 2, 1990. Copyright 1990 by Reed Publishing USA. Both reprinted from *Publishers Weekly,* published by the Bowker Magazine Group of Cahners Publishing Co., a division of Reed Publishing USA.—***Quadrant,*** v. XXXI, April, 1987.—***The Review of Contemporary Fiction,*** v. VII, Spring, 1987; v. IX, Summer, 1989. Copyright, 1987, 1989, by John O'Brien. Both reprinted by permission of the publisher.—***Salmagundi,*** Winter, 1987; Spring-Summer, 1988. Copyright © 1987, 1988 by Skidmore College. Both reprinted by permission of the publisher.—***San Francisco Review of Books,*** November-December, 1984. Copyright © by the *San Francisco Review of Books* 1984. Reprinted by permission of the publisher.—***The Saturday Review of Literature,*** v. XXVII, September 23, 1944. Copyright 1944, renewed 1971; *Saturday Review* magazine/v. 29, May 4, 1946. Copyright 1946, renewed 1973 *Saturday Review* magazine. Both reprinted by permission of the publisher.—***Science Fiction Eye,*** v. 2, February 1990. Reprinted by permission of the publisher.—***Sierra,*** v. 66, March-April, 1981 for "A Look into a Smaller Future" by Walt Anderson. Copyright © 1981 by the Sierra Club. Reprinted by permission of the author.—***Signs,*** v. 1, Autumn, 1975. © 1975 by The University of Chicago. All rights reserved.—***The South Atlantic Quarterly,*** v. 53, January, 1954. Copyright © 1954, renewed 1981 by Duke University Press, Durham, NC. Reprinted by permission of the publisher.—***The Southern Humanities Review,*** v. XXV, Winter, 1991. Copyright 1991 by Auburn University. Reprinted by permission of the publisher.—***The Southern Review,*** v. 26, July, 1990 for "Against Your Beliefs" by W. D. Snodgrass. Copyright, 1990, by the author./ v. 72, Summer, 1987. © 1987 Southern Methodist University. Reprinted by permission of the publisher.—***The Spectator,*** v. 252, March 24, 1984; v. 257, November 22, 1986. © 1984, 1986 by *The Spectator.* Both reprinted by permission of *The Spectator.*—***The Times Literary Supplement,*** n. 4561, August 31-September 16, 1990. © The Times Supplements Limited 1990./n. 3284, February 4, 1965; n. 3357, June 30, 1966; n. 3717, June 1, 1973; n. 4118, March 5, 1982; n. 4329, March 21, 1986; n. 4357, October 3, 1986; n. 4372, January 16, 1987; n. 4397, July 10, 1987; n. 4405, September 4, 1987; n. 4447, June 24-30, 1988; January 13-19, 1989; n. 4536, March 9-15, 1990; n. 4598, May 17, 1991. © The Times Supplements Limited 1965, 1966, 1973, 1982, 1986, 1987, 1988, 1989, 1990, 1991. All reproduced from *The Times Literary Supplement* by permission.—***Toronto Star,*** April 21, 1990 for "An Adventure Fantasy" by Nicholas Bradbury. Reprinted by permission of the author.—***The UNESCO Courier,*** v. 39, May-June, 1986.—***Vanity Fair,*** v. 54, May, 1991. Copyright © 1991 by The Condé Nast Publications Inc. Courtesy of *Vanity Fair.*—***Vector,*** n. 159, February-March, 1991 for "Chung Kuo 2: The Broken Wheel" by K. V. Bailey. Reprinted by permission of the author.—***The Village Voice,*** v. XXVI, August 19-25, 1981 for "Jane Bowles: Blockbusted" by Laurie Stone; v. XXXI, July 15, 1986 for "Beyond Anomie Lines: Marguerite Duras and the Art of Suffering" by Erika Munk. Copyright © News Group Publications, Inc., 1981, 1986. Both reprinted by permission of *The Village Voice* and the respective authors.—***The Virginia Quarterly Review,*** v. 52, Autumn, 1976. Copyright, 1976, by *The Virginia Quarterly Review,* The University of Virginia. Reprinted by permission of the publisher.—***VLS,*** n. 86, June, 1990 for "This Side of Parody" by Ralph Sassone; n. 83, March, 1990 for a review of "Sexual Personae: Art and Decadence from Nefertiti to Emily Dickinson" by Walter Kendrick; n. 89, October, 1990 for "Leaving Home: Jamaica Kincaid's Voyage Round Her Mother" by Jane Mendelsohn. Copyright © 1990 News Group Publications, Inc. Reprinted by permission of *The Village Voice* and the respective authors.—***The Wall Street Journal,*** October 16, 1990. © Dow Jones & Company, Inc. 1990. All rights reserved. Reprinted by permission of *The Wall Street Journal.*—***Western Humanities Review,*** v. XXV, Summer, 1971. Copyright, 1971, University of Utah. Reprinted by permission of the publisher.—***The Women's Review of Books,*** v. III, November, 1985 for "Growing Up Black" by Evelyn C. White; v. VIII, October, 1990 for "Inside Stories" by Marianne Hirsch. Copyright © 1985, 1990. All rights reserved. Both reprinted by permission of the respective authors.—***World Literature Today,*** v. 63, Summer, 1989; v. 63, Autumn, 1989. Copyright 1989 by the University of Oklahoma Press. Both reprinted by permission of the publisher.—***World Literature Written in English,*** v. 28, Autumn, 1988 for "Jamica Kincaid: 'First They Must Be Children' " by Patricia Ismond. © copyright 1988 *WLWE-World Literature Written in English.* Reprinted by permission of the publisher and the author.—***The Yale Review,*** v. LXII, March, 1973 for "Cummings: One Man Alone" by Malcolm Cowley. Copyright 1973, by Yale University. Reprinted by permission of the Estate of Malcolm Cowley.

COPYRIGHTS EXCERPTS IN *CLC,* VOLUME 68, WERE REPRINTED FROM THE FOLLOWING BOOKS:

Bell-Villada, Gene. From "Banana Strike and Military Massacre: 'One Hundred Years of Solitude' and What Happened in 1928," in ***From Dante to García Márquez: Studies in Romance Literatures and Linguistics.*** Gene H. Bell-Villada, Antonio Giménez, George Pistorius, eds. Williams College, 1987. Copyright © 1987 by The President and Trustees of Williams College. All rights reserved. Reprinted by permission of the author.—Brooks, Cleanth. From ***Modern Poetry and the Tradition.*** The University of North Carolina, 1939. Copyright, 1939, by The University of North Carolina Press. Renewed 1967 by Cleanth Brooks. Reprinted by permission of the publisher and the author.—Brotherson, Gordon. From ***The Emergence of the Latin American Novel.*** Cambridge University Press, 1977. © Cambridge University Press 1977. Reprinted with the permission of the publisher and the author.—Capron, Marion. From an interview in ***Writers at Work: The "Paris Review" Interviews.*** Edited by Malcolm Cowley. The Viking Press, 1958. Copyright © 1957, 1958, renewed 1986 by The Paris Review, Inc. Used by permission of Viking Penguin, a division of Penguin Books USA Inc.—Chace, William M. From an afterword to ***The Death of Cock Robin.*** By W. D. Snodgrass. University of Delaware Press, 1989. © 1989 by Associated University Presses, Inc. Reprinted by permission of the publisher.—Cummings, E.E. From ***i: six nonlectures.*** Cambridge, Mass.: Harvard University Press, 1953.—Duras, Marguerite. From ***The War: A Memoir.*** Translated by Barbara Bray. Pantheon Books, 1986. Translation copyright © 1986 by Barbara Bray. All rights reserved.—Faulkner, William. From ***The Sound and the Fury.*** J. Cape, 1929. Copyright 1929 and renewed 1956 by William Faulkner. Reprinted by permission of Random House, Inc.—Feuerwerker, Yi-tsi Mei. From ***Ding Ling's Fiction: Ideology and Narrative in Modern Chinese Literature.*** Cambridge, Mass.: Harvard University Press, 1982. Copyright © 1982 by the President and Fellows of Harvard College. All rights reserved. Excerpted by permission of the publishers and the author.—Geismar, Maxwell. From ***American Moderns: From Rebellion to Conformity.*** Hill and Wang, 1958. Copyright © 1958 by Maxwell Geismar. Renewed 1986 by Anne Geismar. All rights reserved. Reprinted by permission of the Literary Estate of Maxwell Geismar.—Griffin, Robert J. From "Ethical Point of View in 'The Sound and the Fury' " in ***Essays in Modern American Literature.*** Edited by Richard E. Langford. Stetson University Press, 1963. Copyright 1963 by Stetson University. All rights reserved. Reprinted by permission of the editor.—Jaffe, Dan. From "Archibald MacLeish: Mapping the Tradition," in ***The Thirties: Fiction, Poetry, Drama.*** Edited by Warren French. EverettEdwards, Inc., 1967. Copyright © 1967 by Warren French. All rights reserved. Reprinted by permission of the author.—James, Clive. From ***First Reactions: Critical Essays, 1968-1979.*** Knopf, 1980. Copyright © 1980 by Clive James. Reprinted by permission of Alfred A. Knopf, Inc. In Canada by the author.—Kundera, Milan. From ***Immortality.*** Translated by Peter Kussi. Grove Weidenfeld, 1991. Translation copyright © 1991 by Grove Press, Inc. All rights reserved.—Márquez, Gabriel García. From ***One Hundred Years of Solitude.*** Translated by Gregory Rabassa. Harper & Row Publishers, Inc., 1970. English translation © 1970 by HarperCollins Publishers, Inc. All rights reserved.—Márquez, Gabriel García. From "The Solitude of Latin America: Nobel Lecture 1982" translated by Marina Castañeda, in ***Gabriel García Márquez and the Powers of Fiction.*** Edited by Julio Ortega with Claudia Elliott. University of Texas Press, 1988. © The Nobel Foundation 1982. Reprinted by permission of The Nobel Foundation.—Márquez, García, and Rita Guibert. From an interview in ***Seven Latin American Writers Talk to Rita Guibert.*** Translated by Frances Partridge. Knopf, 1973. Copyright © 1972 by Alfred A. Knopf, Inc. All rights reserved. Reprinted by permission of Rita Guibert.—Matthews, J. H. From ***Surrealist Poetry in France.*** Syracuse University Press, 1969. Copyright © 1969 by Syracuse University Press. All rights reserved. Reprinted by permission of the publisher.—Matthews, J. H. From ***Theatre in Dada and Surrealism.*** Syracuse University Press, 1974. Copyright © 1974 by Syracuse University Press. All rights reserved. Reprinted by permission of the publisher.—Maugham, W. Somerset. From "Variations on a Theme," in ***Dorothy Parker.*** The Viking Press, 1944. Copyright 1944 by Dorothy Parker. Renewed 1972 by Lillian Hellman. Used by permission of Viking Penguin, a division of Penguin Books USA Inc.—Mizener, Arthur. From ***Twelve Great American Novels.*** New American Library, 1967. Copyright © 1967 by Arthur Mizener. All rights reserved. Used by permission of New American Library, a Division of Penguin Books USA Inc.—Olauson, Judith. From ***The American Woman Playwright: A View of Criticism and Characterization.*** The Whitson Publishing Company, 1981. Copyright 1981 Judith Olauson. Reprinted by permission of the author.—Paglia, Camille. From ***Sexual Personae: Art and Decadence from Nefertiti to Emily Dickinson.*** Yale University Press, 1990.—Stafford, Jean. From ***Boston Adventure.*** Harcourt Brace Jovanovich, 1944. Copyright, 1944 by Harcourt Brace Jovanovich, Inc. All rights reserved.—Tate, Allen. From ***Essays of Four Decades.*** The Swallow Press, Inc., 1968. Copyright © 1968, 1965, 1963, 1959 by Allen Tate. All rights reserved. Reprinted by permission of the Literary Estate of Allen Tate.—Timothy, Helen Pyne. From "Adolescent Rebellion and Gender Relations in 'At the Bottom of the River' and 'Annie John'," in ***Caribbean Women Writers: Essays from the First International Conference.*** Edited by Selwyn R. Cudjoe. Calaloux Publications, 1990. Copyright © 1990 by Calaloux Publications. All rights reserved. Reprinted by permission of the publisher.—Waggoner, Hyatt H. From ***American Poets: From the Puritans to the Present.*** Houghton Mifflin, 1968. Copyright

© 1968, renewed 1984 by Hyatt H. Waggoner. All rights reserved. Reprinted by permission of Louisiana State University Press.—Walsh, Mary Ellen Williams. From "The Young Girl in the West: Disenchantment in Jean Stafford's Short Fiction," in ***Women and Western American Literature.*** Edited by Helen Winter Stauffer and Susan J. Rosowski. The Whitson Publishing Company, 1982. Copyright 1982 Helen Winter Stauffer & Susan J. Rowsowski. Reprinted by permission of the author.—Yates, Norris W. From ***The American Humorist: Conscience of the Twentieth Century.*** Iowa State University Press, 1964. © 1964 by The Iowa State University Press. All rights reserved. Reprinted by permission of the publisher.

PHOTOGRAPHS AND ILLUSTRATIONS APPEARING IN *CLC*, VOLUME 68, WERE RECEIVED FROM THE FOLLOWING SOURCES:

The Bettmann Archive: **p. 23;** R. W. Davidson: **p. 38;** © Jerry Bauer: **pp. 70; 204; 295;** UPI/Bettmann Newsphotos: **pp. 104; 193;** Courtesy of Jill Faulkner Summers: **p. 133;** Photograph by Rodrigo Garcia Barcha: **p. 137;** AP/Wide World Photos: **pp. 169; 418;** Don Rutledge/Black Star: **p. 200;** Photograph by Aaron Manheimer: **p. 229;** Photograph by Rollie McKenna: **p. 268;** The Billy Rose Theatre Collection, The New York Public Library at Lincoln Center, Astor, Lenox and Tilden Foundations: **p. 280;** © Larry Ford, courtesy of Vintage Press: **p. 303;** Culver Pictures: **p. 321;** © Al Hirschfeld. Drawing reproduced by special arrangement with Hirschfeld's exclusive representative, The Margo Feiden Galleries Ltd., New York: **p. 339;** © Joyce Ravid: **p. 342;** UNH Publicity Office, courtesy of Charles Simic: **p. 362;** Photograph by Kathleen Snodgrass: **p. 380;** Deloss McGraw. Courtesy of W.D. Snodgrass: **p. 398;** Courtesy of Cahiers d'Art: **p. 412;** Courtesy of Blair Clark: **p. 429;** Photograph by Colin Ramsay: **p. 451.**

Jane Bowles

1917-1973

(Born Jane Sydney Auer) American novelist, short story writer, and playwright.

In her fiction, Bowles frequently portrayed women who seek unconventional lifestyles yet fear their own reckless urges. Emphasizing danger, confusion, and interdependence in female relationships, Bowles's archetypal story features two women: one, dissatisfied with society's expectations for her gender, abandons domesticity and searches for freedom and adventure in the outside world, while the other—usually a sister, companion, or lover—attempts to subdue the first's restless impulses by reinforcing her feelings of dependence. A highly respected stylist, Bowles wrote in an idiosyncratic and grotesque manner characterized by irony, wit, colloquialisms, and non sequiturs. Patricia MacManus described her writing as naturalistically surreal, wherein "reality and the absurd meet head-on and the most banal actions assume allusively dream-like connotations. Themes merge, then re-emerge to glide off in varying directions with scarcely a nod over the shoulder."

Born in New York City, Bowles went to Leysin, Switzerland in 1932 to receive treatment for tuberculosis of the knee. During her two years there she was tutored by a Frenchman and read the works of Marcel Proust, André Gide, and Louis-Ferdinand Céline, which later influenced her writing. In 1937, she met the American author and composer Paul Bowles, whom she married a year later. She began working on her first and only published novel, *Two Serious Ladies,* in 1938, and completed the work in 1941. After World War II, the Bowleses variously resided in Mexico, New York City, Paris, Ceylon, and Tangier, Morocco, their most stable address. While her husband thrived in these exotic settings, Bowles produced only seven short stories and a play. "From the first day, Morocco seemed more dreamlike than real," she commented. "I felt cut off from what I knew." In 1957, Bowles suffered a stroke that left her unable to read or write for the remainder of her life.

Bowles established her literary reputation with *Two Serious Ladies,* a novel highly praised by such noted authors as Tennessee Williams, Truman Capote, John Ashbery, and Alan Sillitoe. The latter called this work "a landmark in twentieth century American literature." Although the main characters—Christina Goering and Frieda Copperfield—meet only at the beginning and end of the book, their experiences parallel their search for self-knowledge and their struggle to escape the patriarchal restraints of bourgeois society. Christina renounces her wealth to strive for sainthood but is unaware of the pain she causes to those she cynically uses in her pursuit of salvation. In contrast, Frieda seeks sensual pleasure and excitement; while on vacation in Panama with her staid, bullying husband, she leaves him for a local prostitute named Pacifica, with whom she finds happiness. Bowles implies that the two protagonists must reject their comfortable pasts and experience suffering in order to attain true independence and contentment. The novel's witty but neutral tone and its absence of traditional plot and character motivation initially prompted mixed criticism but later scholarship has generally deemed *Two Serious Ladies* an important work of literature.

The theme of the woman's quest for autonomy coupled with the anxiety of separation also pervades Bowles's play, *In the Summer House,* and her short stories, collected in *Plain Pleasures* and *Feminine Wiles.* For example, "Camp Cataract," often considered one of her finest short stories, depicts a spinster's escape from her overprotective older sister. Devastated by her refusal to return home, the older sister commits suicide. Muriel Haynes characterized Bowles's writing: "At the center of Bowles's work is a profound sense of human separateness, the quintessential inaccessibility of individual personality. . . . Her people are displaced persons, in a perpetual quarrel with the pressures of family bonds or any form of domestic or social order. They take refuge in fantasy, self-obsession, and a goodly portion of what the normal world calls sheer nuttiness."

(See also *CLC*, Vol. 3; *Contemporary Authors*, Vols. 17-20, rev. ed., Vols. 41-44, rev. ed. [obituary]; and *Contemporary Authors Permanent Series*, Vol. 2.)

PRINCIPAL WORKS

NOVEL
Two Serious Ladies 1943

SHORT FICTION COLLECTIONS
Plain Pleasures 1966
Feminine Wiles 1976

PLAY
In the Summer House 1954

OTHER
The Collected Works of Jane Bowles 1966
My Sister's Hand in Mine: An Expanded Edition of the Collected Works of Jane Bowles 1978
Out in the World: Selected Letters of Jane Bowles, 1935-1970 [edited by Millicent Dillon] 1985

Leo Lerman

Mrs. Bowles has written and had published a first novel [***Two Serious Ladies***] whose uninhibited wit, all-inclusive psychological perception and corrosive realism will most certainly both delight and horrify many of its readers. This is definitely not a novel for cover-uppers, for those who refuse to look under the surface, or for those who prefer to take gestures at their face value. Mrs. Bowles records what she sees. And she sees clearly and in several dimensions. She is as honest and lucid as children and the just sufficiently intoxicated, and like them she speaks the truth with an astonishing, amusing and innocent clairvoyance quite regardless of consequence.

Two Serious Ladies is a novel of intellectual and psychological action. It is really two books in one, and neither book has a plot in the formal sense of the term. It records, rather than tells, the stories of the life of Miss Christian Goering and the life of Mrs. Frieda Copperfield. Miss Goering and Mrs. Copperfield meet only two or three times in these pages, but "they had met for many years at . . . parties and they occasionally had tea with each other." Parts I and III reveal Miss Goering. The long center section is concerned with Mrs. Copperfield in Panama.

Both Miss Goering and Mrs. Copperfield are ladies of a certain affluence and culture. What they do is not a matter of sophistication, but of instinct. Both are frightened creatures seeking themselves. Miss Goering is afraid of intangibles. She is conscientiously, with an intense and mortal seriousness, attempting to work out her own salvation. "As a child," we are told, "Christina had been very much disliked by other children. . . . As a grown woman Miss Goering was no better liked than she had been as a child." Some people, especially workaday people and so-called utter realists, thought her quite mad. She is little concerned with their opinions. She is energetically engaged in trying to rid herself of fear.

Mrs. Copperfield is afraid of herself, of her desire to be loved by and to love some woman—if only a dream woman. Her attempt to rid herself of this fear is more inadvertent than Miss Goering's but just as serious. She, too, spends her "life fleeing from her first fear toward her first hope," as her husband tells her. Both ladies are destined, it seems, to pass through successive hells and degradation before they embrace their feats and get anywhere in this unorthodox pursuit of peace and happiness, and both are destined to meet unusually strange people on their journeyings.

There is Miss Gamelon who comes to visit Miss Goering and never goes away. There is Arnold, middle aged and fat, who goes to an office, but would much rather do something in "the writing or painting line." And there is Arnold's father, charming, erratic, filled with "last desire." There is also Andy who had ruined his life for a beautiful blonde without arms and legs and whose mistress Miss Goering becomes. And there is Mrs. Copperfield's beloved Pacifica, sagacious, depraved, a child and a Panama whore. Both Pacifica and Peggy Gladys—aged sixteen, half Irish, half Javanese—who Mrs. Copperfield also meets in Panama, are utterly devoid of any restraint whatsoever.

These people verge on the monstrous. They wander in that vague and dubious margin between sanity and insanity. But by some magical blend of simplicity and correct proportion, Mrs. Bowles manages to preserve her own and the reader's perspective and no matter what happens her characters are more heartbreaking or amusing than monstrous. Perhaps that is because Mrs. Bowles is not concerned with the monstrous as such, for itself. Nor is she even concerned with morals or character for themselves. "No one among my friends speaks any longer of character," says Mrs. Copperfield, "and what interests us most certainly is finding out what we are like." And obviously, that is also what interests Mrs. Bowles most. Mrs. Bowles's prose is so fablelike in quality that one instinctively waits for the moral, but she draws no moral, nor does she formally conclude her novel, for there can be no formal conclusion to a record of a life save death itself.

Whether Mrs. Bowles's strange, half-mad, almost surrealistic world with its uninhibited characters who move in a breathless, hard, clear, timeless light, shocks or delights you, you will find it both compelling and thought-provoking. You will also find it illuminated by hilarious flashes of genuine satiric wit.

Leo Lerman, "Three Quite Different Spring Novels," in New York Herald Tribune Weekly Book Review, *April 25, 1943, p. 10.*

Edith H. Walton

While it is not often that one comes across a novel which makes as little sense as this one, Jane Bowles has precedents and forerunners. In an elusive way—I make the comparison very gingerly—echoes of [Ronald] Firbank,

[Carl] Van Vechten and the lost days of Dada crop up now and again in ***Two Serious Ladies,*** plus an occasional reminiscence of [William] Saroyan. To say, however, that the book is derivative would be clearly unfair. My feeling is that Mrs. Bowles has developed—and exploited—her own brand of lunacy and that she is, perhaps fortunately, unique. Certainly—to free her from the charge of plagiarism—she is nowhere near so witty as either Firbank or Van Vechten, nor do her characters, though eccentric, have the same decadent charm.

To attempt to unravel the plot of ***Two Serious Ladies*** would be to risk, I feel sure, one's own sanity. Obviously, however, I must identify this odd pair of heroines—one of whom is a wealthy spinster, Miss Goering, who suffers from obsessions; the other a feather-brained matron, Mrs. Copperfield. While the latter adventures down in Panama, acquiring a weird set of friends of very easy virtue, Miss Goering has her own startling experiences in her own austere home, where she is companioned by the sinister Miss Gamelon. Beyond the fact that they are casual acquaintances there is no visible connection between these two earnest ladies, nor do their deft stories dovetail in any important way.

What does, however, link both the ***Two Serious Ladies*** and the other characters in the book is their mad, their wayward, their bizarre aberrations, in which they indulge with so reasonable an air. Among their other eccentricities, moreover, is the naive bluntness and candor with which they all speak, the abruptness with which they move inconsequentially from one topic to another. Their world, in short, is an almost frighteningly fantastic one—the more so because its outward lineaments are so natural and so normal, because their background is so soberly realistic. Belatedly one realizes that there is hardly a character in the book who could be called really sane, unless it is the charmingly wanton and amoral Pacifica.

Two Serious Ladies is intermittently funny and certainly original, but I also felt that it strains too hard to startle and to shock and that it all too often is just merely silly. Jane Bowles undoubtedly is a clever young writer with a good deal of talent, but I feel that she has written this book with her tongue in her cheek and that it is not as irresistible as she intended it to be.

Edith H. Walton, "Fantastic Duo," in The New York Times Book Review, *May 9, 1943, p. 14.*

The Times Literary Supplement

It is difficult to see what ***Two Serious Ladies*** is about. In more or less disjointed episodes, the author follows the actions of wealthy Miss Goering, settling and unsettling houses with a few odd companions; and of Mrs. Copperfield, on holiday with her husband in Panama. There is no significant plot, no motivation in character, apparently no theme. The two serious ladies are not so much serious as peculiarly empty of any response to their surroundings or to other people. At times, it seems that the writer is examining lesbianism; but just as this idea is on the brink of confirmation, a series of liaisons with men starts up.

Perhaps it is about impotence. The book is so barren of anything alive or credible that even if the ladies are not groping towards satisfactory social and sexual relationships, then at least they should be. Miss Goering tries men, but never seems to get to bed with them; and Mrs. Copperfield is tired of her husband and seeks adventure with the prostitute Pacifica. But neither sex seems to satisfy either of the ladies. All the characters have a sense of inadequacy about them.

When a novel has to be ransacked in this way for its meaning, it has surely failed. There is nothing positive elsewhere in it which might suggest a purpose in writing, not even occasional beauties in its threadbare style. The settings are also quite empty: the stage (for all the talk of Panama, the forest, the house on the end of the island, or the train rides) is as bare as it can be without actually stripping down the curtains and dismantling the proscenium.

The impotence which the reader may scent as a possible theme is probably just an accidental impression given by a skinflint style, inconsequential actions and insignificant characters. The writer may have thought that in order to express impotence, she should write impotently. But, of course, impotence and failure are understood only in terms of power and success; and the only real and recognizable failure in the end is not that of the characters as people, but of the book as a book.

"Two Empty Ladies," in The Times Literary Supplement, *No. 3284, February 4, 1965, p. 81.*

The Times Literary Supplement

Mrs. Bowles has lived mostly in the Far East and North Africa, and these stories [in ***Plain Pleasures***] gain some of their idiosyncratic flavour from belonging nowhere—or everywhere; the characters, ranging from South American prostitutes to a Niagara summer camp to a Moslem town in North Africa, are observed with the kind of charity, and clarity, that sees all human beings as equally worthy of respect, not comic or tragic by virtue of their background. Of all American expatriate writers Mrs. Bowles is perhaps the least identifiable as an expatriate, or as an American.

Maybe this is a somewhat negative virtue—Mrs. Bowles has many positive ones. [**"Plain Pleasures"**] concerns a proud, raw widow, not given to passing her time frivolously in neighbourly gossip, who discovers over a hot potato in the tenement backyard that Mr. Drake from downstairs shares, to a momentarily perfect extent, her intense conscientiousness over the use of words and the rare value of pleasures. The plainness and restraint with which Mrs. Bowles shows us how a relationship suddenly blossoms, how two sisters meeting away from home discover the appalling strangeness of each other in the outside world, or how a sick prostitute finds, briefly, the love she needs on a picnic with fat Señor Ramirez, are not the affectations of a self-conscious stylist. It is because we are shown precisely as much as we need to see, and not a moment more, that these people retain the power to stay in our minds—there is no need even to know their names, or how they look, or where they belong.

Mrs. Bowles shares with Miss Compton-Burnett a particular pleasure and skill in what one might call the quiet bombshell utterance—often wonderfully funny; and with Miss Spark the precision of understatement, somehow suggesting that we are all busy tidying away our madness so that the world shall never laugh at us.

But comparisons do not really work in trying to convey why Mrs. Bowles deserves a belated triumph, and nor are seven short stories enough to do more than whet the appetite. Her eccentrics are lonely, hardly communicating with other people, and it is perhaps because she lends them some of the dignity of her style that to read even a little about them seems like a sort of privilege.

"A Serious Lady," in The Times Literary Supplement, *No. 3357, June 30, 1966, p. 579.*

Charles Thomas Samuels

Surrounding Mrs. Bowles's art is an effluvium of chic despair which will alienate many readers. On the other hand, her work can easily be overvalued since it combines proud idiosyncrasy with a rather startling prescience (her novel, ***Two Serious Ladies,*** published in 1943, forecast the current vogue of comic gothicism). When that book first appeared here, reviewers could damn it with a clear conscience: modernism had not yet become an obligatory mass fashion. . . . Today in the United States, where the cultivated reader feels duty-bound to be affronted, Mrs. Bowles's controlled derision is likely to seem the definitive force of civilized disgust.

Surely her indictments have an easy inclusiveness. Like her husband, Paul, Mrs. Bowles writes tight little anecdotes about the pull of bestiality, an unexpected form of self-fulfillment. Like her husband's stories, hers pit the weak against the strong, the righteous against the sensual, only to record a general rout. Though her tales lack his intellectual clarity, they have greater charm.

Two Serious Ladies follows the adventures of two wacky souls. Rich Christina Goering is one of those "fanatics who think of themselves as leaders without once having gained the respect of a single human being." Seeking salvation, she makes opportunities of other people; when her needle reaches its goal on the spiritual applause meter, her goodness abruptly stops. Fluttery Mrs. Copperfield, downtrodden by a selfish husband, nevertheless has one "sole object in life . . . to be happy, although people who had observed her behavior over a period of years would have been surprised to discover that this was all."

Out of strange charitable impulses, Christina takes a female companion, a succession of male lovers, and becomes a Samaritan of polite promiscuity. Mrs. Copperfield is dragged to Panama by her husband, where she discovers in herself a fund of willfulness to match Christina's. She installs herself in a disreputable hotel and takes up with a native prostitute. Ironically, Mrs. Copperfield gets what she has always wanted. To Christina's censorious concern in the book's last scene, she replies, with her fist meanly rapping on the table:

> "True enough . . . I have gone to pieces, which is a thing I've wanted to do for years. I know I am as guilty as I can be, but I have my happiness, which I guard like a wolf, and I have authority now and a certain amount of daring, which, if you remember correctly, I never had before."

Shocked, Christina confirms her chilling logic:

> "Certainly I am nearer to becoming a saint," reflected Miss Goering, "but is it possible that a part of me hidden from my sight is piling sin upon sin as fast as Mrs. Copperfield?" This latter possibility Miss Goering thought to be of considerable interest but of no great importance.

The book's final sentence reveals that glacial disregard for "significance" which makes ***Two Serious Ladies*** wonderfully self-possessed, but elusive. In a novel without recognizable motivation, whose characters do not so much communicate as collide, where all interstices of life and logic are effaced, the parallels in the stories of the two women are too slight to provide the structure and carry the meaning. Nor do the parallel situations support the scrutiny they seem to invite.

To be sure, there are hints of purpose scattered about. "One must allow," Christina suggests before a tryst, "that a certain amount of carelessness in one's nature often accomplishes what the will is incapable of doing." And, as Mrs. Copperfield casually asserts on another occasion, "No one among my friends speaks any longer of character . . . what interests us most . . . is finding out what we are like." But these hints never become more than hints. Too often, Mrs. Bowles is seduced by the bizarre behavior of her characters. And our wish to find life in her shadow play finally becomes mere nervous interest.

Her play, ***In the Summer House,*** is more likely to attract the uninitiated—the highlighting of drama is a distinct advantage. Christina reappears as Gertrude Eastman Cuevas, a martinet who "believes in using controls," and Mrs. Copperfield becomes Mrs. Constable, a quavery-voiced sparrow with reserves of bilious clarity. Their confrontation creates a mood of tormented longing and rough-house comedy which is one of the few native expansions of theatrical emotion. On the stage, in 1954, the play worked splendidly. . . . (pp. 38-9)

The Collected Works of Jane Bowles also include some short stories, but most of these are mere moral muckraking. The locales are exotic, the prose is distinctive and the dialogue funny; but the plots are too familiar: repressed eccentrics acknowledging the lure of the flesh. Here too, however, there is one good piece, **"A Stick of Green Candy,"** an "absurd" variation on the stock theme of awakening adolescence. (p. 39)

Charles Thomas Samuels, "Serious Ladies," in The New York Review of Books, *Vol. VII, No. 10, December 15, 1966, pp. 38-40.*

John Ashbery

With the present publication of [***The Collected Works of Jane Bowles***], which comes with an introduction by Truman Capote and blurbs by Tennessee Williams ("my favorite book"), Alan Sillitoe ("a landmark in 20th-century American literature") and others, Jane Bowles has at last surfaced. It is to be hoped that she will now be recognized for what she is: one of the finest modern writers of fiction, in any language. At the same time it should be pointed out that she is not quite the sort of writer that her imposing list of Establishment admirers seems to suggest. Her work is unrelated to theirs, and in fact it stands alone in contemporary literature, though if one can imagine George Ade and Kafka collaborating on a modern version of Bunyan's *Pilgrim's Progress* one will have a faint idea of the qualities of ***Two Serious Ladies.***

Her collected works are comprised of the novel, the play ***In the Summer House*** and seven shorter pieces. Each deals in some way with the conflict between the weak and the strong, a conflict which in Mrs. Bowles's work usually results in a draw. Her strong characters are nervous, domineering women given to ruthless but inaccurate self-analysis. They believe themselves to be idealists, and are in search of some fixed, but vague, goal. In the end they collapse, undone by their failure to take "the terrible strength of the weak" into account. The weak scarcely fare any better. They have developed organs for surviving the attacks of the strong, but, hopelessly in love with them, they rarely survive their immolation.

Sometimes a final glimmer of hope comes to them, in the form of endless vistas of despair. Mrs. Constable, alcoholic and bereft of her daughter at the end of ***In the Summer House*** achieves this negative fulfillment and emerges as the only character in the play to command our negative respect:

> They say that people can't live unless they fill their lives with petty details. That's people's way of avoiding the black pit. I'm just a weak, ordinary, very ordinary woman in her middle years, but I've been able to wipe all the petty details from my life . . . all of them. I never rush or get excited about anything. I've dumped my entire life out the window.

Two Serious Ladies tells the separate odysseys of two very different women: Christina Goering and Frieda Copperfield. Miss Goering, a "strong" character, decides she can achieve salvation only through divesting herself of her family mansion and living on less than a tenth of her income. She rents a small, uncomfortable house on what appears to be Staten Island and surrounds herself with a nondescript circle of friends, whom she regularly deserts to make mysterious night forays into a nearby town, where she takes up with Andy, a despondent barfly. Mrs. Copperfield reluctantly accompanies her husband on a trip to Panama, and finds herself perversely happy with Pacifica, a prostitute, in the seamy Hotel de las Palmas.

Only twice do the paths of the two heroines cross: at the beginning of the book and at the end, when they meet in a restaurant. Miss Goering now believes herself to be well on the way to the curious self-realization she has in mind. Mrs. Copperfield has taken a drunken "downward path to wisdom" like Mrs. Constable's in ***In the Summer House;*** she is now in love with Pacifica, who is about to marry a young man. "I can't live without her, not for a minute. I'd go completely to pieces," Mrs. Copperfield confides to Miss Goering, who replies without irony:

> "But you have gone to pieces, or do I misjudge you dreadfully?"
>
> "True enough," said Mrs. Copperfield, bringing her fist down on the table and looking very mean. "I have gone to pieces, which is a thing I've wanted to do for years. I know I am as guilty as can be, but I have my happiness, which I guard like a wolf, and I have authority now and a certain amount of daring, which, if you remember correctly, I never had before."

But the real tragedy is Miss Goering's. Mrs. Copperfield can gauge the depths to which she has sunk, but Christina in her quest for sainthood remains oblivious of the disastrous effect she has on other people, including Andy, who apparently committed suicide after she left him. With her probing but limited insight into herself she manages to perceive at the end of the novel that "hope had discarded a childish form forever," but this perception comes meshed with a further and graver delusion:

> "Certainly I am nearer to becoming a saint," reflected Miss Goering, "but is it possible that a part of me hidden from my sight is piling sin upon sin as fast as Mrs. Copperfield?" This latter possibility Miss Goering thought to be of considerable interest but of no great importance.

Mrs. Bowles's seemingly casual, colloquial prose is a constant miracle; every line rings as true as a line of poetry, though there is certainly nothing "poetic" about it, except insofar as the awkwardness of our everyday attempts at communication is poetic. This awkwardness can rise to comic heights, and in doing so evoke visions of a nutty America that we have to recognize as ours. (pp. 5, 28, 30)

In her later stories Mrs. Bowles has played down the picaresque local color she used to such effect in the novel. Especially in **"A Stick of Green Candy,"** the story which ends the book and is apparently her most recent, she achieves a new austerity that is as impressive as anything she has done. As in all her work, it is impossible to deduce the end of a sentence from its beginning, or a paragraph from the one that preceded it, or how one of the characters will reply to another. And yet the whole flows marvelously and inexorably to its cruel, lucid end; it becomes itself as we watch it. No other contemporary writer can consistently produce surprise of this quality, the surprise that is the one essential ingredient of great art. Jane Bowles deals almost exclusively in this rare commodity. (p. 30)

John Ashbery, "Up from the Underground," in The New York Times Book Review, *January 29, 1967, pp. 5, 28, 30.*

Susan Lardner

Jane Bowles is a master of the insidious effects of a short, straightforward, clean-living declarative sentence, and a very funny writer, too, so it's too bad that she seems to have gone into a slump. ***The Collected Works of Jane***

Bowles, includes a novel, a play, six stories, and a dialogue for puppets, all but three of these written in the forties and the two latest nearly ten years apart. The play, ***In the Summer House,*** was written in 1948 and produced at the end of 1953 on Broadway. . . . The earliest of the collected works is the novel, ***Two Serious Ladies*** (1943), which is really two stories tied together by a couple of meetings between the principals—resolute Christina Goering and Frieda Copperfield, whose characterization is "timid"—and by a vision the two ladies have of a dangerous land of dance halls, restaurants, bars, and travel agencies just outside the front door—an idea that runs through all Mrs. Bowles' work. "Don't you think that plain pleasures are closer to the heart of God?" asks Mrs. Perry, a widow, in the story called **"Plain Pleasures"** (1946), speaking in particular of a back-yard potato bake. Like any good Bowles lady, however, she takes her conviction in the matter as an excuse to travel and winds up, wearing jewelry borrowed from her worldly sister, on a dinner date at a restaurant, where she goes to pieces—temporarily, anyway—under the strain:

> Mrs. Perry fumbled through the contents of her purse in search of a handkerchief and, coming upon her sister's string of beads, she pulled them out and laid them in her gravy. "I am not a mashed-potato masher," she repeated, and then without warning she clambered out of the booth and lumbered down the aisle.

Mrs. Perry is typical of the Jane Bowles characters. Most of the lot are genteel, egomaniacal ladies with sisters, contending with some form of their basic geographical obsession, and as a consequence, it seems, they prefer the company of other women to that of men—which is mainly a sign of self-absorption. The Bowles pattern is laid bare in the most recent of the collected works, **"A Quarreling Pair,"** the puppet show. . . . The two puppets are sisters of opposite personalities. Harriet, the stronger puppet, is neat, small-hearted, and righteous, content to sit at home, while Rhoda is compassionate and high-strung and inclined to say things like "Sisterly love is one of the few boons in this life." "Now that's enough exaggerating," says Harriet. The argument between them, based on their contrary traits and intended by Mrs. Bowles to take place on a stage with "a rod or string dividing it down the middle to indicate two rooms," reveals a paradoxical compatibility. Harriet happens also to be the name of the high-strung sister in **"Camp Cataract"** (1949), a long story that conforms more closely than any other in the book to the pattern of **"A Quarreling Pair."** All the plots and settings, though usually more elaborate, are just as emphatically symbolic and follow pretty much the same lines to the same kind of paradox. The collected works are crowded with nomadic homebodies, cautious adventurers, doubtful aggressors, and daring cowards. Except maybe a sibylline tale called **"Everything Is Nice,"** about which it is hard to say what's going on. (p. 174)

"A Guatemalan Idyll" (1944), besides being one of the best stories in the book, is distinguished in other ways. The main character is a man, though he has no name—Mrs. Bowles refers to him as "the traveller"—and though he is decisively upstaged by a fat, ugly Latin-American lady, Señora Ramirez, who has two daughters and "very beautiful blue eyes." Her husband, by the way, appears in another story, **"A Day in the Open"** (1945), explaining to an inquiring prostitute, whom he later by mistake drops on her head in a rocky riverbed, that his family is fine. "I have sent them to a little town where they are staying in a pension," he says. "Quiet women—all three of them—the little girls and the mother." Back to Señora Ramirez. She has the distinction of being the only Bowles lady with real enthusiasm for men, even if her fantasies are not exclusively heterosexual. "You know it is my nature to love men and kissing," she explains to the traveller as she seduces him:

> Her feet stuck out into the air, and her heavy breathing filled the room. . . . According to all his standards and the standards of his friends she was not a pleasant thing to lie beside.

Confused by the experience, the traveller decides to head home to celebrate Thanksgiving with his mother, blaming his momentary excitement on the Guatemalan altitude and foreign food.

The stories written in the forties, the play, and every episode of the novel are delightful, winding so smoothly and apparently so unmethodically in the same general direction that it seems the possible variations in the pattern are endless and that each variation could have been extended indefinitely. But the last two stories, **"Everything Is Nice"** and **"A Stick of Green Candy"** (here the main character, a little girl called Mary, is a mixture of Miss Goering and Señor Ramirez), are a letdown. Stark and stylized to the point where they appear unfinished, one is cryptic but not tempting, and the other, though clear enough, is just the bare bones of a better story. And **"A Quarreling Pair"** is mainly interesting for its clues to the earlier works. The single more recent character who has some of the old liveliness is the lady in **"A Stick of Green Candy"** who wishes she had a daughter instead of a son and who says that she prefers furniture to other topics of conversation. "The only thing about furnishings that leaves me cold is curtains." I've never been crazy about puppets, myself.

The sole trouble with ***In the Summer House*** is that Mrs. Bowles suddenly gets explicit about motives and the sources of emotions, tracing the heroine's difficulties with her daughter to a childhood rivalry with her sister for her father's love. On the whole, Mrs. Bowles knows her characters so well and her control is so nearly perfect that there is no need to undercut them with explanations. Occasionally noting a clumsy gesture or a spot of grease in the corner of a mouth, referring to them politely as Miss, Mrs., Señora, Señor, she matches their coldness with detachment and counters their self-importance with humor. Her characters stand apart from most literary eccentrics—without the burden of heroism and undistorted by moral significance. It is easier to come up with a standard explanation for the behavior of mothers and daughters than it is to account for the peculiar ties between sisters, and there are three sets of mothers and daughters in the play. Maybe the demand for conventional psychology is greater among theatre audiences than among readers of stories. Otherwise, ***In the Summer House*** is a fine play, filled with vivid characters and funny, cagey scenes that weigh against the logic of the plot. (pp. 175-76)

> *Susan Lardner, "A Nice Day in the Jungle," in* The New Yorker, *Vol. XLIII, No. 13, May 20, 1967, pp. 174-76.*

James Kraft

The Collected Works of Jane Bowles includes one novel, one play, and seven short stories, which is all she has written since 1943 when she published her first and only novel. Although her publication is limited, Jane Bowles has had a small but faithful reading public, and it is not difficult to see why she excites the attention of a coterie. She is, simply, stylistically and thematically too eccentric to appeal to a larger public. She obviously relishes taking her special viewpoint and expressing it in an oddity of style. Here are the first two paragraphs of her novel, ***Two Serious Ladies:***

> Christina Goering's father was an American industrialist of German parentage and her mother was a New York lady of a very distinguished family. Christina spent the first half of her life in a very beautiful house (not more than an hour from the city) which she had inherited from her mother. It was in this house that she had been brought up as a child with her sister Sophie.
>
> As a child Christina had been very much disliked by other children. She had never suffered particularly because of this, having led, even at a very early age, an active inner life that curtailed her observation of whatever went on around her, to such a degree that she never picked up the mannerisms then in vogue, and at the age of ten was called old-fashioned by other little girls. Even then she wore the look of certain fanatics who think of themselves as leaders without once having gained the respect of a single human being.

This calculated prose, so certain of itself, seems to lean energetically forward, to move directly like Christina Goering, to express at once a compression and a thrust. "As a child Christina had been very much disliked by other children." This sentence is made deliberately suggestive to lead us to the next: "She had never suffered particularly because of this, having led, even at a very early age, an active inner life that curtailed her observation of whatever went on around her," and so forth. By this time we are caught up in this firm, clear, blunt world, which makes everything so uncertain with its peculiar, suggestive tension. We are ready for the danger that crops up in the next sentence with the word "fanatics": "Even then she wore the look of certain fanatics who think of themselves as leaders without once having gained the respect of a single human being."

This is the beginning of Mrs. Bowles' best work. It concerns first Miss Christina Goering and then Mrs. Frieda Copperfield: "Mrs. Copperfield had a sharp little face and very dark hair. She was unusually small and thin. She was nervously rubbing her bare arms and looking around the room when Miss Goering seated herself in the chair beside her. They had met for many years at Anna's parties and they occasionally had tea with each other." They meet at a party at the start of the novel and at a restaurant at the end. In between they pursue their strangely personal existences, neither with apparent success but both with some realization of what they are. The novel is about this pursuit of self against the forms that are laid down for us. These are the forms that we pick up and carry, until we throw them away—perhaps rashly or too late—trying to be what we are. Miss Goering and Mrs. Copperfield, Christina and Frieda, two different but related women, contrast two possible ways in life: the one certain, hard, and firm; the other frightened, nervous, and confused. Mrs. Copperfield's speech quickly defines her side:

> "Oh, I'm sure," said Mrs. Copperfield, "that you wouldn't want to hear about it. You can't possibly have any respect for me, but that doesn't make any difference because I have the utmost respect for you. I heard my husband say that you had a religious nature one day, and we almost had a very bad fight. Of course he is crazy to say that. You are gloriously unpredictable and you are afraid of no one but yourself. I hate religion in other people."

Mrs. Bowles' style is prosaically flat and yet richly poetic. Everything has its meaning, first for what it is, then for what it is made into, and finally for what it could become. If Christina is anything at all she is just what the opening paragraphs, moving forward, bluntly, flatly, clearly, and inexplicably, are. Every "thing" in these paragraphs is part of her, applies to her, yet nothing expresses her so much as the style that leaves possible in its clearness so much meaning. And nothing shows Mrs. Copperfield like the nervous movement of her quixotic speech. She—and not Christina—will be the unexpected.

Such a style is deliberately suggestive, and capable of much meaning. It is also limited. Mrs. Bowles writes the same story every time—with two possible exceptions that will be noted later—as if she must have a Christina-Frieda contrast in order to construct her sense of reality. Miss Goering and Mrs. Copperfield are the two warring sides of the female personality. Sometimes Mrs. Bowles makes the two women sisters, as in the story, **"Camp Cataract."** Sometimes she doubles the contrast, as in her play, ***In the Summer House,*** where the adult ladies have two daughters who reverse roles with their mothers. A short puppet play—**"A Quarreling Pair"**—involves the conversation of two antagonistic sisters. There are two women in **"A Guatemalan Idyll,"** one of whom has contrasting daughters. There are sister-like whores in **"A Day in the Open,"** again representing the Christina-Frieda difference.

In each of these contrasts one woman tries to dominate a weaker figure, but in the end emerges as strangely inadequate, oddly more insecure and dependent. Men never play a central role in this fiction. Men can save women from other women, but in doing so men also keep women from confronting what they are. The fiction is distinctly about women; men only exist to show the difference in women—the difference between power to control, which is a weakness, and the weakness of being controlled, which is really the admission of inner strength. This attitude seems distinctly feminine.

"Men never play a central role in [Bowles's] fiction. Men can save women from other women, but in doing so men also keep women from confronting what they are. The fiction is distinctly about women; men only exist to show the difference in women—the difference between power to control, which is weakness, and the weakness of being controlled, which is really the admission of inner strength."

—James Kraft

The theme of Mrs. Bowles' work is not in this contrast alone, but in where it leads the characters. Each is seeking to be free of the formal confines of the world that hold the self in place—the forms spoken of above. These forms include family love where there is no love, social conventions that do not apply, sexual attitudes that do not work, genteel manners and methods of speech that are meaningless. If this is her theme one can understand why she creates a style that moves the reader into a strange new world of personal expression. Her style expresses her theme more clearly than the retelling of any narrative could do. It is for this reason that Mrs. Bowles can bear repeated readings. Not only must her special symbols be understood—one must know that going out, to a restaurant for instance, is a sign of breaking the forms of family security and gentility—but one must read her again and again to sense the world she wants to express, for this world is in her moving style. As an example, here is perhaps the extreme point of stylistic creation in her fiction. It is a letter Frieda's husband sends just before she leaves him. What will happen in the novel is here, the movement that must take place, which the prose is trying to capture:

> I do not mean to be cruel but I shall write to you exactly what I consider to be your faults and I hope sincerely that what I have written will influence you. Like most people, you are not able to face more than one fear during your lifetime. You also spend your life fleeing from your first fear towards your first hope. Be careful that you do not, through your own wiliness, end up always in the same position in which you began. I do not advise you to spend your life surrounding yourself with those things which you term necessary to your existence, regardless of whether or not they are objectively interesting in themselves or even to your own particular intellect. I believe sincerely that only those men who reach the stage where it is possible for them to combat a second tragedy within themselves, and not the first over again, are worthy of being called mature. When you think someone is going ahead, make sure that he is not really standing still. In order to go ahead, you must leave things behind which most people are unwilling to do. Your first pain, you carry it with you like a lodestone in your breast because all tenderness will come from there. You must carry it with you through your whole life but you must not circle around it. You must give up the search for those symbols which only serve to hide its face from you. You will have the illusion that they are disparate and manifold but they are always the same. If you are only interested in a bearable life, perhaps this letter does not concern you. For God's sake, a ship leaving port is still a wonderful thing to see.

It is fair to ask where one ends with such an experiment with stylistic movement—for it ends at that: to be is to be moving, thrusting oneself forward. The "wanderlust" is one of her terms for this movement, yet as she indicates in the passage above, all her terms hide one face, all her symbols conceal and reveal one image—the movement of life. For this reason none of the endings in her works is "satisfactory"; nothing neatly finishes. In fact much goes on just as before, or perhaps even worse. Christina and Frieda are hardly better off at the end of ***Two Serious Ladies;*** but their presence as seeing selves *is* a measure of advance—even if what is seen is horribly less than they want. To have moved into a position of vision makes them "serious," and to be serious is to matter, for no other reason than that. Two serious ladies are such because they make the search for themselves, seriously, passionately. Christina tells Frieda at the end of the novel that she—Frieda—has gone to pieces. Here is Frieda's response:

> "True enough," said Mrs. Copperfield, bringing her fist down on the table and looking very mean. "I *have* gone to pieces, which is a thing I've wanted to do for years. I know I am as guilty as I can be, but I have my happiness, which I guard like a wolf, and I have authority now and a certain amount of daring, which, if you remember correctly, I never had before."

Christina is no better, no worse, in the final paragraph:

> "Certainly I am nearer to becoming a saint," reflected Miss Goering, "but is it possible that a part of me hidden from my sight is piling sin upon sin as fast as Mrs. Copperfield?" This latter possibility Miss Goering thought to be of considerable interest but of no great importance.

The last sentence epitomizes the novel's marvelous style and theme. What we would observe is so, but it is not important. The importance is in the movement, in the processes of constant observation, continually made.

This special style and theme may explain why so little has been written by Mrs. Bowles. Her field of interest is temperamentally limited to women and her ideas are limited to a particular sense of movement that is growth. All but three of her seven stories were written in the 1940s. The most recent of the three, **"A Quarreling Pair,"** continues the Christina-Frieda contrast; but the other two are slightly different. They are more static in style and poetically somewhat flat, but more important, they seem to diverge from her earlier concepts. In the first, **"Everything is**

Nice," there is one heroine only; in the second, **"A Stick of Green Candy,"** a child openly glimpses what one must call maturity. If the direction is towards a synthesis of duality and an expression of both process and the arrived state of maturity, perhaps Mrs. Bowles has been waiting in order to say better what she wants rather than repeat what she has said. Perhaps she now sees more than duality and movement and is looking for a new way to express herself.

Whatever the case, Jane Bowles is a fascinating writer whose vision remains fragmented, special, almost child-like; her work itself now needs to move and cohere. (pp. 273-76)

James Kraft, "Jane Bowles as Serious Lady," in Novel: A Forum on Fiction, *Vol. 1, No. 3, Spring, 1968, pp. 273-77.*

Millicent G. Dillon

"I am so wily and feminine that I could live by your side for a lifetime and deceive you afresh each day. But I will have no truck with feminine wiles."

With these words from ***Feminine Wiles*** we are once again in the beguiling world of Jane Bowles. A posthumous collection of last fragments: an echo, a reminder, and a new beginning. Bowles died in 1973 after many years of silence. Her underground reputation is based on one novel, ***Two Serious Ladies,*** a play, ***In the Summer House,*** and six short stories, published under the title ***Plain Pleasures.*** In 1956, at age 39, she suffered a stroke which affected her sight and speech. She died in Malaga, Spain, in a convent hospital at age 56.

Now and then, during the silence before her death, recognition came. John Ashbery, on the publication of her collected works in 1966, [see excerpt above], called her "one of the finest modern writers of fiction in any language." But the recognition did nothing to unlock her silence. It was finally not the view of others, but her own harsh judgment that deterred her. (p. 153)

These last stories, all fragments of longer works, show how she struggled in her silence. She was not by nature a confessional writer, yet her life and the times drove her to the directness of revelation, away from her own intuitive and artful indirection. In the end she came to contend with her own style and vision.

In her early published work, no matter how she may have been racked by self-doubt, her intuition was transmuted into fiction. These later stories show an artist at war with that very intuition. They show her pressed by a harsh and judging intelligence she felt not to be her own. That intelligence condemned her intuition and the art that relied on it as trickery.

In **"Emmy Moore's Journal,"** a barely disguised autobiographical fragment, a woman has come to the Hotel Henry to be alone and to write a journal. Each day she writes to her husband, Paul Moore, a kind man who has encouraged her to go to the hotel. "He wants very much for me to be happy, and worries because I am not. He knows everything about me, including how much I deplore being the feminine kind of woman that I am." Of these feminine wiles she writes to him:

> I know how they can absorb the hours of the day. Many women are delighted to sit around spinning their webs . . .
>
> I shall try to be honest with you so that I can live with you and yet won't be pitiful. Even if tossing my feminine tricks out the window means being left no better than an illiterate backwoodsman, or the bottom fish scraping along the ocean bed, I prefer to have it this way.

But after her directness, she feels bereft. "I have said nothing at all . . . I have not justified myself," Emmy Moore says to herself at the end.

In **"Andrew,"** a story of a young man who struggles to get away from his mother and is drafted into the army, Bowles deals with a character at a greater distance from herself. Once again she is concerned with judgment and with artifice. Andrew tries to rid himself of the burden of his own uniqueness. The connections he makes between things are not the connections others make: "Sometimes he wondered whether or not other people went about pretending to be logical while actually they felt as he did inside, but this was not very often, since he usually took it for granted that everyone was more honest than he."

The rational intellect that sees itself without guile is seen here as belonging only to others. Andrew is left to deceit ("With the years he was becoming more expert at travesty . . . ") or to silence.

"Going to Massachusetts," the most complete of the fragments, is a dialogue between two women, Janet and Sis, interrupted by a letter from a third, Bozoe. Like **"Camp Cataract,"** Bowles's earlier and most brilliant story, this one explores the dependencies, the secrecies, the assertiveness, the needs of women among women. Here too are feminine wiles, spun webs. At the same time, a new sense of directness is achieved in this story, particularly in the letter from Bozoe. But directness and artifice are held in controlled tension only so long. The letter from Bozoe, the urgent plea that goes unanswered, fades into silence.

"Curls and a Quiet Country Face," the final story fragment, begins in image and ends in a controlled outcry that is direct autobiographical statement. Bowles writes of the impasse she faces, of her own life in Tangiers, of being driven to write, of not writing. But that moment of directness leads her back into life as a retreat from writing.

Six letters, to her husband and friends, conclude this collection. The letter from 1949 shows Bowles as a warm, humorous, playful woman, delighting in the daily things in Morocco. But the progression of the letters is to the awareness of time passing, to the sense of her unfulfilled need to work, of the gathering silence. In the last letter to her friend Libby Holman, after she has had a stroke, Bowles faces the silence directly. Even now, she says, she cannot tell which part of the silence comes from the stroke and which from the "writer's block."

The worn opposition between wiles and honesty, between

artifice and directness that Bowles experienced was not a single dilemma. For better or worse it was her dilemma as woman and artist. We have come to see wiles in women as she saw them, a kind of cajoling based upon need, an aspect of begging both crafty and pitiful, something to be disavowed. But as to the wiles, the guile, of a writer we have no certain sense. That opposition between artifice and directness continues to be a central dilemma in much of modern fiction.

A small collection, 85 pages in all—a series of fragments. A small collection, but if it serves to send readers back to ***Two Serious Ladies,*** it is enough. In that single novel, which Alan Sillitoe has called "a landmark in Twentieth Century American literature," craft is itself honesty. (pp. 153-54)

Millicent G. Dillon, "Between Deceit and Silence," in The Nation, *New York, Vol. 223, No. 5, August 28, 1976, pp. 153-54.*

Edith Oliver

The plot [of ***In the Summer House***] is extremely complicated, skidding off the main road into any number of byways, but at its core are the attempt by Mrs. Eastman-Cuevas to dominate her daughter and the consequences of that attempt. At the outset, the daughter, half in love with her mother, yet wary of her and conscious of inherited violence within herself, spends much of her time hiding in the summer house on Mrs. Eastman-Cuevas' estate, near the sea in southern California. By the time the evening is over, she has married a young man who runs a seafood restaurant; Mrs. E.-C. has married, with some distaste, a fun-loving, catch-as-catch-can Mexican and gone off to Mexico not only with him but with his boisterous sister and a complement of gambolling female relatives; and a grabby young woman has died mysteriously on the beach, leaving her put-upon mother, a Mrs. Constable, at first grief-stricken and then, realizing that the girl never cared for her much anyway, a quite merry, sensible alcoholic. And at the very end Mrs. E.-C. has returned from Mexico to try to woo her daughter back. In all this, it is really only the characters that matter. Wolcott Gibbs wrote of the original production, "An unusual amount of intuition, intelligence, and compassion has clearly gone into the drawing of even its least happily imagined characters." Mr. Gibbs mentioned a number of faults, which didn't happen to bother me, before concluding that "to offset these disadvantages, it is often extremely funny in a rather bloodcurdling way; it rises on occasion to passages of considerable eloquence and pathos; a basic integrity of purpose is obvious." The script, within its own outlandish boundaries, is always clear, and Mrs. Bowles' writing, by and large, is of a quality we seldom hear in the theatre. Still, there is too *much* writing; the play, for all its melodramatic carapace, seems at times like a novel being acted out. (pp. 83-4)

It is an odd and fascinating play, full of enigma and foreboding and, as it turns out, afterboding. (p. 84)

Edith Oliver, "Twenty-four Years Later," in The New Yorker, *Vol. LIII, No. 14, May 23, 1977, pp. 83-4.*

Daphne Merkin

It is difficult to imagine—especially in these days of celebrity-authors—a writer who would actually *prefer* a limited readership, but then Jane Bowles is not like other writers. She is original to the point of being unnerving, and it seems entirely possible that she wrote as much with the intention to exclude as to include. She is fated to remain a specialized taste because hers goes beyond a mere idiosyncrasy of style, an identifiable semantic tic like Donald Barthelme's or William Gass's. One is tempted to make comparisons—to Ivy Compton-Burnett for the entrenched habit of irony, to Carson McCullers for the use of the grotesque—but they don't really hold up: she is both more human than the former and less sentimental than the latter. Bowles's voice is an uncompromisingly independent one and it bespeaks a vision of life so unflinching as to challenge most of our assumptions.

To read ***My Sister's Hand in Mine*** is to submit to a demanding presence. Jane Bowles is one of those writers who can truly be said to inhabit a country of her own making. Although the specific geographical location might change, the emotional terrain is characteristically depleted, and one comes away with an unsettling image of projected solitude: ". . . they descended abruptly to the muddy regions near the sea. The stone houses were completely colorless in the hot sun. All the windows were heavily grilled; there was very little sign of life anywhere." Into this airless, hostile atmosphere Bowles suspends her odd, touching characters—who effect hesitant connections with other odd, touching characters but whose deepest engagement, one suspects, is with the condition of their intractable and bewildering apartness. Bowles writes about people who haven't grown the armature of adults (this is also why her children and adult characters are interchangeable), who appear never to have fully recovered from the shock of emergence from the womb: "Such an awful, dreadful, mean thing to be alone in the world even for a minute." The men and women in her fiction are still suffering the pangs of separation-anxiety, still dangling on the other end of a metaphysical umbilical cord. . . . Bowles's interest is fixed upon extreme instances of the human predicament; her people live in "terrible cocoons," consumed by a Beckett-like desire for stasis. . . .

Bowles's fictional world makes few concessions to our easier notions about human arrangements: "I don't like long-standing relationships," says a woman in the story **"Going to Massachusetts"**; "they disagree with me. I get the blues." One would be hard-pressed to find a directly ascertainable emotion anywhere in this collection. The prevailing mood is of raging conflict; diametrically-opposed propositions are speculated upon in one and the same breath. (p. 30)

My Sister's Hand in Mine includes a novel, a play, and a group of stories. ***Two Serious Ladies*** is a startling novel about a latter-day saint, Christina Goering: "I don't like sports," she confides, "more than anything else, they give me a terrific feeling of sinning." Miss Goering is possessed of the peculiar, steely insight that one would expect of saints—"Just remember, that a revolution won is an adult who must kill his childhood once and for all." The novel is also about Mrs. Copperfield, who would qualify as a saint if she weren't so afraid of where it might lead her: "The world and the people in it had suddenly slipped beyond her comprehension and she felt in great danger of losing the whole world once and for all. . . . " Both the ladies are "serious" in the sense that they look for intangibles—happiness, salvation, identity—as though such abstractions were brightly-wrapped gifts hidden in various corners of their lives. "She stood on the street and waited to be overcome with joy and relief." Bowles had a delightfully tart wit—"She was very pretty—from a sculptural point of view"—that dilutes the profound sadness that seeps through her writing and gives an extra toughness to the poignancy of her outlook.

"Bowles writes about people who haven't grown the armature of adults . . . , who appear never to have fully recovered from the shock of emergence from the womb. . . . The men and women in her fiction are still suffering the pangs of separation-anxiety, still dangling on the other end of a metaphysical umbilical cord."

—Daphne Merkin

The play, ***In the Summer House,*** is perhaps the least satisfactory offering in the collection. It is self-consciously *sui generis*—its weirdness has been labored at—and after awhile, the inscrutable can begin to be as tiresome as the familiar. Although the play has many intriguing moments, it doesn't hint at a doomed universal pattern beyond the bizarre one it traces; it lacks the whiffs of normality that blow through the other pieces.

The stories, on the other hand, are wonderful. They suit Bowles's quixotic style exactly, and are evocative in their very impenetrability. **"Plain Pleasures"** is a delicate tale about a confirmed believer in the prosaic who is jolted into a sublime tenderness; **"Everything Is Nice"** is a haunting story whose tight-lipped tone belies its lyricism. Fat Moslem women in black dresses sprawl in low-ceilinged rooms, treating a young American visitor with sinister graciousness. The story ends on a different key than the one in which it has been told, and the disparity serves to heighten its perception of a link so fragile as to be nearly not there: "And she remembered how once she had reached out to touch the face of a clown because it had awakened some longing. It had happened at a little circus, but not when she was a child."

Jane Bowles is a capricious weaver of spells; her stories often end as though they were about to begin again somewhere else—now you see the magic, now you don't. Perhaps that is because her fiction is conceived at such a rarefied altitude; her characters are living in domesticated penal colonies—"You see, I have dubbed us all inmates," one of them says—and have, therefore only the most essential things to say to each other: "Life is tragic," remarks Gertrude in ***In the Summer House.*** "I don't want tragic," is the reply. It is precisely on account of their resistance to such unpleasant adjustments of maturity that the people in ***My Sister's Hand in Mine*** are frequently mired in primal, parent-child or sibling relationships—having failed to grasp the limits of being stuck inside their own skins. **"Camp Cataract"** is a powerful story about two sisters and their belated discovery of this most basic fact of physical estrangement; one sister it liberates, the other it destroys.

There is a persistent mystery at the heart of Jane Bowles's fiction. What is amazing, finally, is that fiction so intentionally whimsical, even perverse, should reverberate the way Bowles's does, igniting sparks of recognition on every page. (pp. 30-1)

Daphne Merkin, in a review of "My Sister's Hand in Mine," in The New Republic, *Vol. 178, No. 6, February 11, 1978, pp. 30-1.*

Francine du Plessix Gray

If there is one common denominator in [Jane] Bowles's work, it is women's relentless search for autonomy and self-knowledge, for release from all conventional structures. And a demonic, frenzied search it becomes in Mrs. Bowles's hands. In **"Camp Cataract,"** the finest short story in the new collection, [***My Sister's Hand in Mine***], a spinster who lives with her two sisters chooses to lapse into madness rather than remain in the suffocating shelter of her siblings' domesticity. Holed up in a summer camp in the company of a fat waitress whose greatest ambition is to own a garage, she reaches a dubious new level of freedom, when, on refusing to return her adoring older sister's affection, she drives her to suicide. The denouement of ***In the Summer House*** deals brutally with a woman engaged in an equally ruthless task of self-definition. The alcoholic Mrs. Constable is left bereft of her daughter, whose independence she had tried to destroy for her own selfish ends.

Two Serious Ladies, Mrs. Bowles's only finished novel, documents with extraordinary wit the decline into debauchery of two very different but equally staid women. Miss Goering is a wealthy spinster who has been made solitary since childhood by her ugliness and her severe mystical inclinations; while Mrs. Copperfield is trapped in the most respectable and prosperous sort of marriage. Miss Goering eventually sells her worldly possessions to work out "her own little idea of salvation"; she moves to a small nasty house on Staten Island and commutes to the mainland to lead a new life of bar-crawling in which she ends up as a high-class call girl. Mrs. Copperfield, a casual acquaintance of Miss Goering's, accompanies her restless, penny-pinching husband to Panama, and leaves him to take up with a band of loose women she has befriended in Colón. She eventually returns to New York with a teenage half-breed prostitute called Pacifica, admitting, in the same breath, that she has "gone to pieces" but has found a new brand of independence and happiness that she guards "like a wolf."

The theme of women's independence, and its frequent coefficients of solitude and potential destruction, have more often than not been limned with Lessingesque earnestness in a socio-realistic setting. So Mrs. Bowles's oeuvre is all the more unique because of its Grand Guignol hilarity, its constant surprises, and a blend of realism and grotesqueness that occasionally recalls Ronald Firbank. There is extraordinary tension between the sturdy, supernormal physical world she describes and the gloriously unpredictable, fantastic movements of the eccentric personages who inhabit it. These superstraight middle-aged women going to pot in their ball gowns, leaving home to make war on their inhibitions in landscapes of photographic literalness, speak, move and acquiesce to debauchery as they would in the dream freedom of a Delvaux painting. All "normal" logic of social behavior is disbanded. Total strangers decide to move into one another's houses after their first cup of tea together. Railroad conductors forbid passengers from talking to one another, under threat of calling in the police. The siblings in **"Camp Cataract"** are so unskilled at domestic niceties that they can barely get out of their dining room without crawling under tables. And Mrs. Bowles's lithe, feverish dialogue has a blend of childlike integrity, surreal candor and deadly precision often worthy of Lewis Carroll. (pp. 3, 28)

Upon reading the enthusiastic reviews that ***Two Serious Ladies*** received in 1943, I was startled to see some critics comparing it to *The Well of Loneliness,* perhaps the only novel in the English language to have previously touched on the issue of lesbianism. Mrs. Bowles's acerbic genius for the *outré* does not leave it any grounds for comparison with Radclyffe Hall's sentimental tale. Neither are her heroines' precipitous declines caused by any preference for lesbianism, for they seem as asexual as they are independent and nomadic, turning to the flesh as a symbol of independence without appearing to enjoy one moment of it. Their gloriously uninhibited carousing, their voluptuous liberation from all male discipline ("You'll get indigestion . . . good God!" Mr. Copperfield keeps saying) has much more to do with a return to the permissive sexual androgyny of juvenile bonding than with any sexual preference. It is this very childlike playfulness that gives Mrs. Bowles's work its fey power and its luminous originality, and that may disconcert readers fond of predictably "female," "mature" heroines.

The little we know about Jane Bowles's life intimates that it was as feverish and singular as that of her heroines. Left lame in her teens by a riding accident, she was married at the age of 20 to the composer and author Paul Bowles. She finished ***Two Serious Ladies*** at the age of 24, and settled in Tangiers in 1947. At the age of 40, she suffered a cerebral hemorrhage that made reading and writing impossible for her. She died in a convent hospital in Malaga, Spain, in 1973. In a recent interview in *Rolling Stone,* Paul Bowles disclosed a few more details about the last decades of Jane Bowles's life: She drank to excess, and had a passionately dependent relationship with a Moroccan woman servant who, according to Paul Bowles, is suspected of having poisoned her food over a period of years with dangerous Moroccan drugs. Millicent Dillon's biography, scheduled for publication [in 1979], is bound to shed more light on the links between Jane Bowles's singular life, the magic of her art, and her tragi-comic views of human liberation.

"If there is one common denominator in Bowles's work, it is women's relentless search for autonomy and self-knowledge, for release from all conventional structures."

—Francine du Plessix Gray

"No one among my friends speaks any more of character," Mrs. Copperfield says in ***Two Serious Ladies.*** What interests us most, certainly, is finding out what we are *like.*" In Mrs. Bowles's work, the traditional novelistic struggle between weak and strong characters ends inevitably in a draw. The rigorous pursuit of autonomy, and a rueful acceptance of its often tragic consequences, is the only heroic goal. For even the strongest are unmade by their failure to take into account "the terrible strength of the weak," and follow an equally drunken downward path to wisdom. There is a severe avoidance of all moralizing. It is left to the individual reader to determine whether Mrs. Bowles's heroines were better off in the shelter of their repressive marriages and inhibited spinsterhoods than in the anarchy of their libertinage. (p. 28)

Francine du Plessix Gray, "Jane Bowles Reconsidered," in The New York Times Book Review, *February 19, 1978, pp. 3, 28.*

Muriel Haynes

Women, often headstrong and self-involved, are the protagonists in most of Bowles's stories; her men take second place. A boorish and ineffectual lot, they are simply unequal to the highly charged female will that confronts them. For Miss Goering [in ***Two Serious Ladies***], men are the sacrificial stepping-stones by which she advances her saintly progress. In **"A Guatemalan Idyll,"** the first male tourist available is the target for Mrs. Ramirez's pent-up middle-aged sexual passion. Mrs. Eastman Cuevas, the domineering presence of the play ***In the Summer House,*** considers a husband only to gain financial security.

Clearly Bowles is not doing missionary work on the subordinate condition of women. Her outlook is actually more radical. As she pictures them, women are simply not emotionally dependent on men, who have no entry into female inner life. Love and its bitter fruits—jealousy, dependency, manipulation, and even violence—are found in women's relations with one another, as friends, mothers and daughters, sisters, lovers. Men exist as objects of physical passion, but the ravages, the theatrics, of love have their roots in another place.

At the center of Bowles's work is a profound sense of human separateness, the quintessential inaccessibility of individual personality. She observes this without a trace of sentiment and with a zestful notation of every quirk and strange "humour"—as they were once called. "I would love to read but I have trouble with concentration," one of her characters announces cheerily. Yet her stories are controlled by a compassion that springs from sorrow. Her people are displaced persons, in a perpetual quarrel with the pressures of family bonds or any form of domestic or social order. They take refuge in fantasy, self-obsession, and a goodly portion of what the normal world calls sheer nuttiness. A perverse slippage affects their relations with each other. No two ever arrive at the same point at the same time.

Bowles is esteemed as a superb stylist, but she cherished a loftier ambition for her prose than the phrase suggests. Dispensing with plot and character motivation in the traditional sense, she wanted to elevate language itself to a narrative force in fiction as it is in poetry. She did this by stripping language down to plain, uncolored sentences, rejecting words as the servants of action or as mediators between writer and reader, seductive, interpretive. Bowles's tone is neutral, impassive, its revelations a constant surprise. . . . (p. 35)

Jane Bowles was a deadpan tourist in the byways of a cockeyed America who caught the chill at its center. Perhaps if—but it's idle to speculate. It's already settled. What we have from her is little enough, but there is nothing else quite like it. (p. 65)

> *Muriel Haynes, "The Toughness of Jane Bowles," in* Ms., *Vol. VI, No. 10, April, 1978, pp. 33, 35, 65.*

Laurie Stone

[The works collected in ***My Sister's Hand in Mine***] are instruments for the assertion of personality. The plots seem like raw dreams (which the fantasist didn't bother to interpret), and all of the characters are spacey or desperate. Jane doesn't sound like anyone else. And her language is riveting, the way, on occasion, the ironic connections and tight puzzlings of articulate psychotics can be.

Jane considered **"Camp Cataract"** her most fully realized work. It is a fair assessment, for the story builds to a climax of emotion and meaning she rarely achieved elsewhere. It's about two middle-aged sisters: Harriet, who has made a break from the stranglehold of family by taking up residence at a rustic retreat, and Sadie, who is passionately attached to her sister and follows her. "Remember," she writes to Harriet, "the apartment is not just a row of rooms. It is the material proof that our spirits are so wedded that we have but one blessed roof over our heads."

Harriet feels superior to Sadie and hates most virulently the traits they have in common. She wants freedom but can only take mincing steps in that direction. " 'There is something intensely repulsive to me about unmarried women on their own . . . also a very shallow attitude,' " she tells Beryl, a dim young waitress who is smitten with her. " 'You may wonder how a woman can be shallow and know it at the same time, but then, there is precisely the tragedy. . . . ' " Harriet feels suffocated by Sadie's arrival, and she is enormously cruel.

The description of Sadie is at first remote and sardonic, and she seems a dull grotesque; but Sadie is humanized as the story progresses. Having journeyed to Camp Cataract, Sadie does not want to return home. And in the pivotal episode, where Sadie imagines confessing to Harriet and imagines, also, the pain of being rejected, the veils fall and character is starkly revealed: "Sadie knew then that this agony she was suffering was itself the dreaded voyage into the world—the very voyage she had always feared Harriet would make. That she herself was making it instead of Harriet did not affect her certainty that it was." Acknowledging the extent of Harriet's aversion, Sadie elects to keep her love a secret. She quietly commits suicide in the camp's thunderous waterfall.

The longer works are constructed of the same great strangeness that distinguishes **"Camp Cataract,"** but they are less jelled. ***Two Serious Ladies*** is so hallucinatory, it should come with a drug caution. Engaging and frustrating in equal measure, it details the meanderings and maunderings of Christina Goering, who thinks she must be sinless, and Frieda Copperfield, another timid lurcher after freedom.

There are some wonderfully ironic passages and vibrant sequences. In one scene, the prostitute, Pacifica, tries to teach Frieda to swim:

> Suddenly she stood up and placed both her hands firmly in the small of Mrs. Copperfield's back. Mrs. Copperfield felt happy and sick at once. She turned her face and in so doing she brushed Pacifica's heavy stomach with her cheek. She held on hard to Pacifica's thigh with the strength of years of sorrow and frustration in her hand.

There is Mr. Copperfield's cautionary letter to his wife. Jane must have shivered with apprehension when writing it:

> Like most people, you are not able to face more than one fear during your lifetime. . . . I believe sincerely that only those who reach the stage where it is possible for them to combat a second tragedy within themselves, and not the first over again, are worthy of being called mature. . . . Your first pain, you carry it with you like a lodestone in your breast because all tenderness will come from there. You must carry it with you through your whole life but you must not circle around it.

Despite the glowing patches and Jane's austere absurdism, ***Two Serious Ladies*** does not gather force, and, ultimately, we do not know what these people want. Dramatic power fizzles out in her play, too, although the characters are less shadowy and fragmented, and the surreal weirdness is sustained on a rather impressive scale.

The plot of ***In the Summer House:*** the decorous matriarch, Gertrude, rails at her mopy daughter, Molly, who has taken to dazing off for hours in the gazebo. "Sometimes I feel that you are plotting something," she tells Molly. "I think that your black hair helps me feel that way. Whenever I think of a woman going wild, I always picture her with black hair. . . . I sometimes picture little scenes where they turn evil like wolves."

Gertrude soon decides to marry Mr. Solares, a wealthy Mexican she does not love, and on the day of her wedding, Molly declares she loves her mother with unprecedented passion. Gertrude leaves anyway, and, with nowhere to turn, Molly marries Lionel, a young man who works in a restaurant called the Lobster Bowl. They live chastely and drizzle away their days playing cards, until Gertrude comes back to claim Molly. There is a struggle, but Molly finally awakens from her torpor and flings herself out of Gertrude's grasp—literally. There are also intimations of murder: earlier in the action, Molly may have killed a rival for Gertrude's affections, a wild, hungry girl named Vivian.

The dialogue is studded with Jane-non sequiturs and funny declarations of character. The plot is so archetypal, Shelagh Delaney unwittingly duplicated it in *A Taste of Honey*. ***In the Summer House*** has been successfully revived, but while Jane was writing actively, few people understood or appreciated her work. (pp. 35-6)

What is certain, however, is that Jane had only one real subject, women in relation to one another. Men hardly exist in her fiction, and when they appear, they are generally ineffectual, like Mr. Copperfield, or beefy, repulsive louts, like Bert in **"Camp Cataract."** Yet in Frieda's relationship with her husband and in Molly's with Lionel, Jane was able to depict what she had experienced with men—with Paul—in a far more complete way than she was ever able to treat her lesbian affairs.

Jane could reveal men's feelings (silly as she makes them out to be) because, most likely, the men she wrote about were friends, not lovers. When Jane said that women were "obscene," she probably meant that their sexuality was powerful—had power over her. Jane consistently chose lovers who seemed ludicrous to others—dowdy women far older than she, or the Arab women she spoiled and controlled. After her early affair with the alcoholic, Cecil, she met Helvetia Perkins (she was 45, Jane 23), and they lived together for six years. She was with Cherifa and Tetum in Tangier, then Cory, a middle-aged British woman, "Lady Frances" (not her real name) and Princess Martha Ruspoli de Chambrun. This last affair reversed Jane's pattern: Martha was the aggressor, and Jane chided her for "being like a man," by which she meant getting off quickly in sex.

Jane told Paul that she believed sex was "all in the head" and that she found her affairs "humiliating" and "abject." Martha claims that Jane was sexually frustrated during their relationship and believes that she was never able to have orgasms. In an interview, Jane described herself as "lusty," rather than "sexual," but while this may have been true—whatever it meant to her—she was also rapacious.

Jane performed like a libertine and enjoyed the mystique of promiscuity that grew around her. She loved to test her powers, to be the seducer. She was coquettish with men—sitting on laps, fiddling with ears; and flirtatious with women—long deep stares into the eyes. She got dozens of women into bed for quick affairs, and she wasn't at all closeted about her preference. She loved arriving at parties and announcing: "I am a lesbian, and this is my lover."

Jane may have liked the role of lesbian better than making love to women. Or maybe the opposite was true. Jane may have found sex humiliating, and perhaps she could not figure out how her mother (and father) fit into her sexual choices. Whatever her feelings, they clearly caused her overwhelming guilt, but the fact remains, Jane shied away from naming her experience, and it killed her art.

Despite her adventurousness, Jane was, it seems, fatally afraid of certain pieces of knowledge. (Maybe she stopped writing, at least in part, in order not to discover what her unconscious would reflexively reveal.) Surrounded by people, she never seemed to register that life is humiliating for everyone, that all people occasionally feel ashamed of some aspect of family life or their sexual tastes.

If Jane hadn't been a writer, the retreat from her psyche might have been less catastrophic for her. But Jane was not only a writer, she was obsessed with a subject she couldn't talk about. In **"Camp Cataract"** she wrote lucidly about the tragedy of knowing one's cowardice, but she could not move beyond her "first fear." And after describing it, there was nothing more she was brave enough to say. (p. 37)

Laurie Stone, "Jane Bowles: Blockbusted," in The Village Voice, *Vol. XXVI, No. 34, August 19-25, 1981, pp. 35-7.*

Judith Olauson

Bowles' plot [in ***In the Summer House***] is a mixture of events, character studies, and moods. Set at the home of Gertrude Eastman-Cuevas on the coast of Southern California, the environment suggests the disorder of Mrs. Eastman-Cuevas' life. The house is run-down and the garden is in a disarray of dead vegetation. Nothing will grow except for the heavy vines that cover the small summer house where Molly, Gertrude's eighteen-year old daughter, spends most of her time dreaming and reading comics. Gertrude, a dominating and selfish woman, has had a childhood of jealous attachment to her father who did not return her affection. After his death she had married a Spaniard who never met her high expectations based on the ideals she held of her father. When her husband died, she was forced to take in boarders at the once stylish Spanish mansion which she and her daughter now inhabit. Molly is totally dominated by her mother whose treatment of her reflects her mother's obsession to recapture the essence of her own father's power. Molly is both fascinated by her mother's strength and overwhelmed by it, thus seeks refuge in the summer house as a way of escaping her conflicting emotions. Their relationship is complicated by other individuals. Mr. Solares, a wealthy Mexican who wishes to marry Mrs. Eastman-Cuevas, arrives with five wild female family members who have little regard for Gertrude's suffering. Lionel, a young man with a gloomy background, visits frequently and becomes attached to Molly. Also, Vivian arrives to spend the summer as a boarder with her widowed mother, Mrs. Constable, in tow. Vivian is an energetic, fun-seeking teen-ager who terrorizes and dominates her mother. She attempts to appropriate Mrs. Eastman-Cuevas' affections and tries to alienate Lionel's love for Molly, but she mysteriously falls off a cliff and dies, Molly being the only witness.

Two months after Vivian's death, a double wedding has taken place. Gertrude has married Mr. Solares, has moved to Mexico, and has sold the mansion. Molly has married Lionel, and they have settled at a nearby seafood restaurant. Molly cannot shake off her bondage to her mother and dreams of the time when she will return. Her mother, finding life intolerable among the Mexicans, does return. The crisis evolves out of Gertrude's unintentional confession to a homicidal act in which the circumstances were as mysterious as Molly's involvement with Vivian's death. Gertrude then realizes that her contempt and desire for ruling over Molly, as well as the identification of herself with her father, are all she has in her life. She tries to force the girl to leave her husband and live with her again; but Mrs. Constable, who has remained at the hotel in a dipsomaniacal state since the death of her daughter, manages to make the two recognize that the force between them is destructive, and so precipitates their final break from one another.

Henry Hewes felt that the play was a memorable one when viewed as a study of neurotic unreality. But Harold Clurman found more ironic humor in the play and this feature, he felt, saved it from becoming overburdened with Freudian overtones. He remarked that ***In the Summer House*** could be called a "wryly comic lyric poem in a minor key," because the characters could be regarded as people isolated in a social world which exists statistically ("as a department store exists,") but not spiritually in a human context; and in that manner, "such people become weird—both sad and funny."

Bowles' vision of life, capsulized in the characters of the two mothers, is indeed a mixture of comedy and drama, and her chief concern is with the two women: one ruthless and dominating who despises her passive daughter; the other, gentle and self-effacing who is dominated by her aggressive, uninhibited daughter. In spite of their differences, the relationships between the pairs are strangely interdependent. Henry Hewes suggested that the play gains in interest if Mrs. Constable and Vivian, the visitors, are thought of as alter egos to the first pair, Gertrude and Molly.

Bowles approaches her main character, Gertrude, through psychoanalytical explanation. Her personality, it seems, is the complex chain of causes and effects, which Clurman attempted to summarize: the mother, being dependent on her father, has destroyed her daughter's will by re-enacting the father's role, thus causing her daughter to be mother-dependent; this explains nothing, said Clurman, but serves mainly to provide intriguing material for the playwright's exploration. The convolutions of Gertrude's personality are dominated by her suppressed fears and are expressed through her dominating and aggressive behavior. Her own insecurity has originated with her love-deprived childhood. In compensation, she bolsters herself through self-deception and lies. In moments of introspection she reveals a persistent feeling of isolation, as if she had fallen off a cliff and landed miles away. She attempts to articulate the intensity of her aloneness but, in the process, realizes that even her griefs and sorrows don't seem to belong to her. Nothing validates her existence and because this feeling frightens her, she retreats to the commonplaces of her life until her fears subside, just as her daughter finds refuge reading comics in the summer house. Rather than face her isolation, Gertrude finds a means to dismiss it.

Gertrude protests that her strength, like her father's, is her self-control. Never in her life, she claims, has she shown her feelings. Vivian's high-spirited behavior and uncontrolled emotional outbursts are despicable to her. She is even appalled by her daughter's awkward attempt to express her love for her. To Gertrude, human emotion is something dangerous. Startled by Molly's sudden flood of affection, she shows she is incapable of dealing with such feelings. This emotional aloofness is sponsored more from her deprivations than from the strength of her character. She has chosen as her model her father, who, in reality, loved her meek, frail, and delicate younger sister Ellen more than he did Gertrude. Having always sensed this betrayal, but having never faced it, she clings to the belief that he truly did love her.

But Gertrude's strength disintegrates when she loses contact with the false image of her father. Exhausted and insomnious, she returns from her disastrous Mexican honeymoon eager to free herself from the grotesquely comic Solares family. The incongruity of their credo, *joie de vivre,* which is pronounced happily by Mr. Solares with his heavy Spanish accent, is a hideous contrast to Gertrude's rules of self-control and self-denial. As a result of her chaotic life with the Solareses, she is unable to recall the standards and ideals which sustained her in the past. Again she deceives herself in believing that her life with Molly was full and happy and blames her dislocation on the Solares clan. Regaining possession of Molly is the solution to her dilemma, she thinks, but Molly's dependence on her mother's strength has been destroyed, and their relationship ends with Molly following her husband and with Gertrude's final admission to her true feelings of jealousy toward her sister and hatred for her father. The depths of the never-realized relationships between father and daughter and mother and daughter are made evident by implications that both Gertrude and Molly, out of their separate jealousies, caused the deaths of the individuals who threatened their illusions, Vivian and, presumably, Ellen.

The extraordinary effects of Bowles' psychological probing are heightened by a strong thrust of ironic humor. With this added dimension Gertrude can be seen as an eccentric character whose sharp and witty dialogue reveals the pointless and trivial aspects of her life. Thinking of marrying Mr. Solares has lead her to speculate about the behavior of Latins, those wholehearted individuals who enjoy living as much as she dislikes it. Speaking to Molly, but with her attention centered in herself, Gertrude parodies herself in a rambling continuous monologue which dominates the first ten minutes of the play. It is typical of the style which prompted Truman Capote to comment that the playwright's strange wit and sharp insight proved her to be an original, pure stylist.

Bowles' "stylistics" extended into the haunting portrayal of the secondary character, Mrs. Constable, who was described by Eric Bentley as a memorable figure, defined by the commonplaces about dipsomania, spinsterhood and lostness, "yet coming together with the force of something new." As the alter ego, Mrs. Constable is the reverse of Gertrude's dominating personality. In contrast to Gertrude, who has striking good looks and an imposing presence, Mrs. Constable is a frail, colorless individual who spends her days doing nothing because her life has been based on the pointless efforts to please an uncaring husband and demanding daughter. But, like Gertrude, she is confronted by the conflicts of gross reality and inner torment; rather than seeking to control them, however, as Gertrude does, she seeks release. After Vivian's death she speaks to Molly with a strange mixture of eloquence and pathos, telling her of the freedom she has found, but she never refers to the strange circumstances of the accident. Through alcohol she has extended and reinforced her release. Possessing the wisdom of the lost and exhibiting the uninhibited behavior of the inebriate, she provides another answer to human isolation, rebutting Gertrude's solution of finding solace in the trivial, that is, to wipe out all the petty details from her life.

Providing much of the pathos as well as "an exhilarating dash of rough comedy," Mrs. Constable serves also as a catalyst. In a compassionate attempt to save Molly from the destructive obsession she has for her mother, she confides the "secret" of her escape from the memory of her widowhood and the death of her daughter: neither her husband nor her daughter had even belonged to her because neither had ever really loved her. When Molly realizes that the strength she admired in her mother, which she interpreted as love, "never belonged" to her either, she takes Mrs. Constable's advice and leaves with her husband. (pp. 83-8)

Judith Olauson, "1950-1960: Lillian Hellman, Jane Bowles, Lorraine Hansberry," in her The American Woman Playwright: A View of Criticism and Characterization, *The Whitson Publishing Company, 1981, 77-99.*

Lewis Jones

One way and another, Jane Bowles's women are much exercised by notions of wildness. They flee from it, and it ambushes them in their dreams; they chase it, and it eludes them in the bogs of habit. They are lost, no longer able to distinguish fear from desire. So Mrs Copperfield, in ***Two Serious Ladies,*** suffers 'as much as she had ever suffered before, because she was going to do what she wanted to do.' And so Sadie, in a story from ***Plain Pleasures*** (1946), having impulsively chosen a course she is certain will lead to her ruin, awaits the consequences with blithe resignation:

> . . . if there was any problem implicit in making a decision, it lay, not in the difficulty of choosing, but in the concealment of her choice. To her, secrecy was the real absolution from guilt, so automatically she protected all of her deepest feelings and compulsions from the eyes of [others], although she had no interest in understanding or examining these herself.
>
> **"Camp Cataract"**

Nor are Jane Bowles's women the least curious about others. As another of them explains, 'I have a habit of never paying attention to whoever I am talking to.'

The dialogue, then, comprises for the most part a stylised and ironic arrangement of tangential witterings around a few obsessive clichés. It is absurd and sinister, both by turns and simultaneously—the effect recalls [T. S. Eliot's] *Sweeney Agonistes,* or [Harold] Pinter. In the novel and the short stories this is supplemented by minimal description and, occasionally, by psychoanalysis of the sort quoted above.

Jane Bowles's women 'break the bonds' (or forge them) with the traditional tools of travel and sex. In ***Two Serious Ladies,*** Mrs Copperfield goes to Panama, leaves her husband and takes up with Pacifica, a local prostitute. The remainder of the novel, the bulk of it, is set in America and concerns the progress of Miss Goering, 'a society lady'. For obscure but compelling reasons, Miss Goering first collects a group of disagreeable and peculiar dependents and then abandons them, devoting herself instead to sexual adventure in a decayed provincial resort. The two women meet at the end of the novel, Mrs Copperfield a ravaged drunk, and Miss Goering apparently a prostitute. Like most of Jane Bowles's characters, the two women are, in temperament and circumstances, practically interchangeable; though their respective stories are certainly dramatic, their juxtaposition is not; it is tempting to ask if one might not have been enough. There is more than enough, too, of the relentlessly random dialogue. After a hundred pages or so, it becomes gratingly artful—like reading an anthology of captions from old *New Yorker* cartoons. ***Two Serious Ladies*** is an accomplished exercise, but it is too loving a study of aimlessness to be an altogether satisfactory novel.

In ***Plain Pleasures,*** a collection of seven short stories, Jane Bowles is more at home in her chosen territory, more flexible and more disciplined. And the interchangeability of her characters becomes interesting. [**"Plain Pleasures"**], for example, is about Alva Perry and John Drake, longstanding neighbours, who have always been too shy to talk to one another, until he is one day emboldened to ask her out to dinner at a nearby hotel. The occasion makes Alva so nervous that she behaves rudely and drinks too much. Feigning concern, the hotel's proprietor offers her a bed for the night and then rapes her. When she wakes next morning, with only the vaguest memory of the night before, she decides that she has fallen in love with John. In **"Camp Cataract"**—the best story, I think—a woman called Sadie pays a visit to her sister, who is recovering from a nervous breakdown at a sanatorium-cum-hotel in the country. The sisters dislike one another, and the visit is not a success. Towards the end of it, Sadie finds herself attracted to a man selling souvenirs. He is apparently a Red Indian, but Sadie realises that his appearance is simply a gimmick when she notices his 'freckled, light hand'; a discovery that shocks her into an hallucinatory sexual fantasy leading to violent death.

It is the unreality of these characters that makes them so disturbing, their stories so grotesque and sad. Though they are dressed in a variety of credible quirks, they are essentially mere ciphers, unconvincing even to themselves: 'like many others she conceived of her life as separate from herself; the road was laid out always a little ahead of her.' They are shadows of their own shadows, spectres in their own gloom, and there is a horrible fascination in their wilful abdication of the will: *I don't choose to, but I do all the same.* (pp. 23-4)

From 1957 until her death in 1973 [Bowles] was unable to write, having suffered a stroke. As with Keats, it is tempting to speculate about what she might have gone on to do—but futile. What she did is remarkable enough. Her subject—negative *in*capability, as it were—makes it impossible to illustrate the felicity of her style, as it is all a matter of context. The stories, though, show that she was a master of the form, and the play puts her in the front rank of modern American dramatists. (p. 24)

> *Lewis Jones, "Singular Ladies," in* The Spectator, *Vol. 252, No. 8124, March 24, 1984, pp. 23-4.*

Robert E. Lougy

In the case of [Bowles'] fictional and dramatic characters (especially her women), isolation is known almost as an existential condition, a metaphysical given for those who must inhabit a world stripped of myth and denied its God. "It is intolerable," Bowles once suggested, "to be in this world without a myth." As far as her own isolation as an artist is concerned, it is difficult to precisely identify its causes, but it seems to have arisen, in part at least, from her particular temperament, her literary affinity with European rather than American writers, and her decision to settle in Morocco in the early 1950s. One notices in her fiction the absence of a vision grounded within a particular social or cultural context, such as we find, for example, in her contemporaries like Flannery O'Connor and Carson McCullers with their Southern sin-haunted figures or Eudora Welty and her vision of the American mid-west and its people. Leslie Fiedler recounts a comment by Faulkner that perhaps identifies the frequent nature of those bonds between the best writers and their places:

> I remember Faulkner . . . getting engaged in a conversation with a lady Montana, who cried out at one point, "Why can't So-and-so write a novel that would do for this part of the world what you have done in Mississippi? He *loves* Montana so!" To which Faulkner, of course, answered . . . "To write well about some place, you've got to hate it." A pause, and then, "The way a man hates his wife."

But while Bowles' characters are haunted by place, by the search for a home, we find in her literature neither that love nor that hate of which Faulkner speaks. Rather, her landscapes are more like those found in medieval morality plays or the landscape of Samuel Beckett and Kafka, spatial limits within which salvation is sought and sin and guilt experienced.

The absence of such identifiable landscapes, a sense within her art of a particular region or culture, is understandable, however, in terms of her life. For just as her literary characters are continually on the move, affirming by their gestures the essential rootlessness they feel, so too did Jane Bowles' own life have a peripatetic quality about it. Born in New York City on February 22, 1917, she was taught primarily by French governesses and knew French before she knew English. While in Leysin, Switzerland (1932-34) recovering from tuberculosis, she was tutored by a Frenchman, "well versed," she later confessed, "in Greek mythology and venereal disease," and under his tutelage, she read Gide, Proust, and Celine among others. In fact, she met Celine on a ship bringing her back to America from Switzerland:

> On the boat Jane was reading *Voyage au Bout de la Nuit.* A stranger came up to her and said, "I see you're reading Celine." "He is the greatest writer in the whole world," she told him. "Celine, c'est moi," he replied.

They had a long conversation about literature and after this meeting, she resolved to become a writer. Given such early readings and influences, it is perhaps appropriate that her later artistic affinities were with European rather than American writers. In one of her letters, she writes that "I think there is no point in using the word talent any longer. Certainly Carson McCullers is as talented as Sartre or Simone de Beauvoir but she is not really a serious writer." It is not that her writing is "unrelated" to that of her American contemporaries, as Ashbery suggests, but rather that its particular relationship is difficult to define. If, as Fiedler has suggested, "the vision of the truly contemporary writer is that of a world not only absurd but also chaotic and fragmentary," then Jane Bowles is truly a contemporary writer. And in so far as her writing explores the questions of sin and salvation and the essential loneliness of all human beings living in a world from which God has withdrawn, it again reminds us of her contemporaries. But her vision is seen through an artistic style that is uniquely her own. (pp. 157-59)

[If] Jane Bowles' art deserves our attention, we in turn deserve the pleasure we derive from witnessing the creation of a world by an artist so completely in control of her craft and language. It is to this world, comic, often grotesque, and at times deeply moving, that I would like to turn, in an essay that will be, I hope, an act of interpretation and admiration. I will have achieved my purpose if I can tease others to also visit this world.

I would like to begin with a scene that characterizes the rich and peculiar world of Jane Bowles' art. Christina

Goering, one of the two central figures in the novel, ***Two Serious Ladies,*** is describing a scene she recently witnessed from her sister's home:

> From my window I could see into the room of this building, as the wall opposite me had already been torn down. . . . I finally felt rather sad watching this and I was about to go away when a man came into one of these rooms and, walking deliberately over to the bed, took up a coverlet which he folded under his arm. . . . Then he walked around the room aimlessly for a bit and finally he stood at the very edge of his room looking down into the courtyard with his arms akimbo. I could see him more clearly now, and I could easily tell that he was an artist. As he stood there, I was increasingly filled with horror, very much as though I were watching a scene in a nightmare.

Like the world of a nightmare, Bowles' world is often disconnected and inexplicable, for within it her characters are always moving, either trying to flee from that which they cannot evade or attempting to overtake that which constantly eludes them. Only temporary reprieve from this condition is possible—Bowles' characters always awaken, after their fitful naps and troubled sleep, into a world that forces itself upon them while at the same time it denies them access to it. Her art depicts a world of impenetrable surfaces: hard and opaque, it permits only fleeting moments of clarity that must ultimately die, aborted perceptions untranslated into action. For some of her characters, such as Christina Goering, partial reprieve from this world seems at times possible. . . . (pp. 160-61)

Bowles' characters exist, however, not only in loneliness and homelessness, but in a perpetual state of guilt as well. The first time we encounter Christina Goering, she is a thirteen-year old girl baptising a young playmate of her sister's:

> If you don't lie down in the mud and let me pack the mud over you and then wash you in the stream, you'll be forever condemned. Do you want to be forever condemned? This is your moment to decide.

Throughout the novel, Christina Goering tries to work out her own salvation, attempting to redeem sins, the specific nature of which she cannot know. Since guilt and homelessness are for Bowles part of the human condition one can respond to them only by first acknowledging them and then, in a kind of Sadean rebellion, breaking through them by excessive indulgence, expanding the circumference of selfhood through the surfeiting of oneself within these limitations. To push these limits to their furthest extreme is to make the only gesture of freedom possible: "the idea . . . is to change first of our own volition and according to our own inner promptings, before they impose completely arbitrary changes upon us."

But those same inner promptings that make our gesture of freedom possible also urge us to accept that easeful and comfortable nature against which Bowles' great creations, such as Christina Goering and Mrs. Copperfield of ***Two Serious Ladies*** and Gertrude Eastman of ***In the Summer House*** (1953) constantly fight. For by succumbing to these promptings, we can conceal those aspects of our existence that are more terrifying and more real than most of us wish to bear:

> They say that people can't live unless they fill their lives with petty details. That's people's way of avoiding the black pit. I'm just a weak, ordinary, very ordinary woman in her middle years, but I've been able to wipe all the petty details from my life. . . .

For those who have the courage to descend into this "black pit" of which Mrs. Constable, of ***In the Summer House,*** speaks, redemption is possible; and thus Bowles' "two serious ladies" thrust themselves into it, seeking within for that God Who might be hiding at the bottom. Peace must be shunned if one is to confront God, for He is found only through suffering. "There are certain people," says Miss Gamelon, a companion of Christina Goering's, "who turn peace from the door as though it were a dragon breathing fire out of its nostrils and there are certain people who can't leave God alone either. . . . " The safety and comfort that this world offers must be shunned and fought against. As Christina Goering suggests about property:

> It gives me a comfortable feeling of safety. . . . However, in order to work out my own little idea of salvation, I really believe that it is necessary for me to live in some more tawdry place and particularly in some place where I was not born.

Bozoe Flanner, a character in **"Going to Massachusetts,"** one of Jane Bowles' unfinished stories, expresses similar sentiments to Janet, her friend and lover:

> I don't feel that I can allow you to sink into the mire of contentment and happy ambitious enterprise. It is my duty to prevent you from it as much as I do myself. . . . Don't accept social or financial security as your final aim. . . .

For Lionel, of ***In the Summer House,*** homes especially tend to create a similar and dangerous illusion of well-being: "To me, this place is a fake, I chose it for protection, and it doesn't work out." Such places entrap one and thus exclude the outside world and the chances for self-definition that it makes possible. . . . (pp. 161-62)

Bowles' major characters nevertheless search for a proper home, one that will fulfill rather than restrict self, and for a harmony between themselves and external spaces. Such quests, however, are doomed to failure:

> . . . Sometimes [says Gertrude Eastman, of ***In the Summer House***] I wake up at night with a strange feeling of isolation . . . as if I'd fallen off the cliffs and landed miles away from everything that was close to my heart. . . . Even my griefs and sorrows don't seem to belong to me. Nothing does—as if a shadow had passed over my whole life and made it dark. I try saying my name aloud, over and over again, but it doesn't hook things together.

This shadow that passes over one's life, darkening it and making it impossible to find connections and to "hook things together," is for Bowles evidence that we inhabit a world fallen from God's grace and a self fallen from the grace of childhood. In their wanderings and driftings, Bowles' various characters search for a home in a world from which God has withdrawn and, in doing so, has taken all homes with Him:

> When people believed in God they carried Him from one place to another. They carried Him through the jungles and across the Arctic Circle. God watched over everybody and all men were brothers. Now there is nothing to carry with you from one place to another, and as far as I'm concerned, these people might as well be kangaroos; yet somehow there must be someone here who will remind me of something . . . I must try to find a nest in this outlandish place.

Mrs. Copperfield looks for this nest; and by the end of the novel, she has or so she tells us, found her happiness. But it is a happiness "only a step from desperation all of the time." Befriended by a whore, Pacifica, who, as her name suggests, enjoys a serenity experienced by very few of Bowles' characters, Mrs. Copperfield enjoys Pacifica's companionship and friendship as the novel ends; but their relationship is seriously strained by Mrs. Copperfield's desperate and possessive clinging to Pacifica. Like the temporary euphoria Mrs. Copperfield seeks in gin, Pacifica both threatens and comforts. In so far as her continued presence is always in doubt, she is both a source of solace and anxiety for the woman who loves her.

But while she vacillates between fulfillment and emptiness, Mrs. Copperfield, in her attempt to live within what she calls a world of "happy moments," is able to find some brief, but intensely felt fragments of happiness. Such fragments for Bowles arise from fleeting moments of human contact and, in this respect, they resemble that particular beauty Mrs. Copperfield recalls having seen once in the face of an older woman:

> "I was once in love with an older woman," said Mrs. Copperfield eagerly. "She was no longer beautiful, but in her face I found fragments of beauty which were much more exciting to me than any beauty I have known at its height."

Her world is fragmented because of the continuously felt presence of death and time. All of her figures move toward a death they carry within themselves and because they are so acutely aware of this burden, they are, as one of Bowles' characters says, "so lost and so far away and so frightened." Moments that provide temporary reprieve—there is no escape—from this anxiety can best be described as repetitions or approximations of childhood, moments in which her characters can recreate, or have recreated for them, a sense of well-being and wholeness, enclosed within spaces that they associate with a time prior to their "voyage into the world." This voyage is, as one might expect in Bowles' art, an inevitable one—except for those few who seem to retain a childlike soul, even in the midst of suffering and degradation. Pacifica is such a person, but even her condition is threatened by her consciousness of its tenuousness:

> When you wake up in the morning and the first minute you open your eyes and you don't know who you are or what your life has been—that is beautiful. Then when you know who you are and what day in your life it is and you still think you are sailing in the air like a happy bird—that is beautiful. That is, when you don't have any worries.

She too, of course, must finally awaken into that world in which Mrs. Goering and Mrs. Copperfield live; but Pacifica has an elastic spirit, a certain resilience of soul that allows her to keep touch with her childhood. Combining the youthfulness and spontaneity of Dickens' Dora with the worldliness and sexuality of Anna Karenina, Pacifica is one of Bowles' few characters who is capable of confronting the world on its own terms.

For most of Bowles' characters, however, the voyage into the world is violent, traumatic, and wrenching, a birth into a world of knowledge and death that recapitulates our original Fall. In **"Camp Cataract,"** one of Bowles' finest short stories, Sadie, a middle-aged spinster, has been playing at being grown up throughout her life: "she constantly yearned to live in the grown-up world that her parents had established for them when they were children, but she did not understand it properly." Shortly before her death, she discovers the nature of this experience during a moment that is unanticipated and unsought:

> She opened her mouth to speak and doubled over, clutching at her stomach as though an animal were devouring her. Sweat beaded her forehead and she planted her feet wide apart on the ground as if this animal would be born.

This moment in which she gives birth to herself or to a permanently transformed perception of herself is a painful and irreversible instant of recognition: "Sadie knew then that this agony she was suffering was itself the dreaded voyage into the world—the very voyage she had always feared Harriet would make." The enclosures of her apartment and of her previous innocence collapse, and Sadie is thrown into the world by nothing more—and nothing less—than her consciousness of it. Her sister, on the other hand, is a "great admirer of the nomad, vagabond, gypsies, seafaring men . . . the old prophets [who] roamed the world . . . and most of the visionaries." Yet, by the end of the story, she is still within Camp Cataract, where she has gone "to imitate the natural roots of childhood . . . long enough so that I myself will feel: Camp Cataract is habit, Camp Cataract is life, Camp Cataract is not escape."

Those of Bowles' characters who do not retreat into themselves must reach out, thrusting themselves against a world that is cold and impenetrable, and attempting to become enfolded by a sense of their own potential grace, by a sense of themselves as part of a larger community of selves that will make it possible for them to retain or regain what they have lost, forgotten, or are fearful of never finding. Whether it be the salvation of a Christina Goering, the "nest" sought by Mrs. Copperfield, or those happy moments Lionel is afraid of having forgotten, the object of their quests lies ahead of them in a future thrown into doubt by what they know and what they feel. They exist in a state of sin, forever aware of the disparity between the dreamt-of and the real, between that which might have been and that which is. Thought only serves to make one more acutely aware of the limitations of thought, of its ineffectuality within a world and self that must remain unknowable. (pp. 162-65)

In Bowles' world sets of contexts and verbal constructions tend to go astray: they move from sense to non-sense and from the comic to the tragic and then back again, with little if any recognition by the characters of these shifts, and with no transformation or modification of the conditions that existed prior to the shift. A number of Bowles' scenes remind one of Dickens, where language is taken to its further extreme, stopping short of—while at the same time revealing—a chaos and desperation beneath it. (p. 165)

Bowles' language, like her world, consists of hard, impenetrable surfaces. Words are flat, disconnected. Trapped within a self that is isolated, apart, and frightened, Bowles' characters try to talk through those barriers that imprison them, only to be reminded by language itself of their separateness. Because her characters are entrapped by a language which is in itself entrapped by its literal and inherited meaning, monologues abound in Bowles' art, but monologues of persons whose solipsism is revealed by a torrent of words that serves only to bury them deeper within their own isolation. The insignificant phrase is picked up, the real drift or meaning is missed, and the possibility of two lonely people coming together is denied by the very attempt to express this need. Comedy is closely aligned with the grotesque and the horrible, and in Bowles' art, the comic moment stands not against the chaotic and the lonely, but rather serves to give them further definition. . . .

The grotesque in Bowles' comic vision arises from her recognition that even the most serious and solemn of human enterprises are tinged with absurdity. And like the "black pit" or shadows that threaten Bowles' characters, the grotesque also threatens to break down those barriers and enclosures that are erected to keep chaos and dread at bay. (p. 166)

Jane Bowles' world is inhabited by the lost and strayed, by derelicts, whores, misfits, the homeless and the frightened. They must live, exposed and vulnerable, within a world that is in a state of decrepitude, one that has for them lost a wholeness it probably never possessed. Yet it is within this world and this world alone that salvation must be sought: "you've got to admit," says one of her characters, "we're living in the world, unless we want to behave like crazy kids or escaped lunatics or something like that." On one hand, then, there is the world; and on the other, there is childhood, lunacy, eccentricity, and various forms of mysticism. And although happiness and salvation must be sought within it, the world stands forth as evidence of our fall from happiness, as an outrageously real and undeniable contrast to those centers of value which now exist only as pockets of memory incapable of being retrieved or lived in again. A young woman tells Miss Goering that

> what makes me happy I seem to catch out of the sky with both hands; I can only hold whatever it is that I love because that is all I can really see. The world interferes with me and my happiness but I never interfere with the world. . . .

Her political activist boyfriend believes that "it is wise to destroy yourself first; at least to keep only that part of you which can be of use to a big group of people"; for if you do not,

> you might lose sight of objective reality and so forth, and you fall plunk into the middle of a mysticism which right now would be a waste of time.

Revolution, however, the struggle against the world and its social and political values, demands that a certain price be paid. Whether this revolution occurs on a personal or social level, the victim is always childhood itself, the loss of those pockets of memory that Bowles' characters are attempting to locate. Christina Goering asks the boyfriend to remember "that a revolution won is an adult who must kill his childhood once and for all." But revolution for Bowles occurs strictly on a personal level and is a double-edged sword, an ambivalently directed gesture. For on one hand, it is a protest that carries with it, if culminated, the permanent loss of childhood. At the end of ***Two Serious Ladies,*** Christina Goering realizes that "hope . . . had discarded a childish form forever." But at the same time, it is also a rebellion in pursuit of a lost childhood, a protest against that world that demands of us a "dreaded voyage" into it. The memories of youth remain elusive, for they have become shadowy figures left behind in the pursuit of goals that cannot fill those voids created by childhood's departure. (pp. 167-68)

But most of Bowles' characters, male and female, are beset by memories, and in spite of the various configurations these memories assume, their imagery and their landscapes are similar. Perhaps one of the clearest emblems of this landscape is seen in **"Camp Cataract,"** in a statement made by Harriet, Sadie's sister:

> I will clarify my statement by calling Camp Cataract my tree house. You remember tree houses from your younger days. . . . You climb into them when you're a child and plan to run away from home once you are safely hidden among the leaves.

Her attempt, however, to "imitate the natural roots of childhood" is finally unsuccessful. She succeeds only in killing her sister's childlike innocence and divesting herself of those illusions and places in which she might hide. Such a journey into the past is for Bowles both necessary and doomed: one must attempt to make connections, to "hook things together," yet the quest must fail since those moments being sought cannot be captured. They are like that light Lionel used to see.

> when I was home I used to like looking out my window after certain storms that left a special kind of light in the sky. . . . A very brilliant light that illuminated only the most distant places, the places near the horizon. . . . It always gave me a lift, as if everything might change around me but in a wonderful way that I couldn't have guessed was possible.

One of Bowles' characters observes that "life is tragic," and the first tragedy is that we must lose this light, even while still retaining a diminished memory of it. Against this "special kind of light"—found in tree houses, childhood homes, and other pockets of memory toward which Bowles' characters reach—stand the black pit and the shadow, evidence of our fall into an awareness of our condition. We quest for unity and harmony as a protest against alienation, but we frequently undertake this search only at the cost of repressing, denying, or forgetting the very conditions under which it must be carried out. . . . [Bowles's] characters hear Wordsworth's "still, sad music of humanity," those intimations of mortality that give rise to humanity's "primal sympathy." But this "first pain" can become the "black pit" of Mrs. Constable or the shadow of Mrs. Eastman, transforming love into a paralyzing fear and tenderness into a destructive possessiveness. For most of us, this pain is unendurable, as Lionel observes:

> I dread being a minister because it brings you so close to death all the time. You would get too deep in to ever forget death and eternity again, as long as you lived—not even for an afternoon. I think that even when you were talking to your friends or eating or joking, it would be there in the back of your mind. Death, I mean . . . and eternity.

Most of her major figures are either in search of salvation from this condition or for a forgetfulness of it. The various paradises they seek, however, are illusory; there is no place in which one may hide. Mrs. Eastman of ***In the Summer House*** tries to create such a place for herself and her daughter; but her attempt fails because she tries to, as Mr. Copperfield at one point suggests, "end up in the same position in which you begin," circling around rather than confronting her condition. Mrs. Eastman's daughter, Molly, lives within a fragile dream world that is finally destroyed by her mother, the central figure of her dreams. "Molly," Mrs. Eastman observes, "is a dreamer," another of Bowles' figures of innocence and child-like simplicity. And although by the end of the play, she has murdered the woman she fears is stealing Mrs. Eastman's love, even this act does not destroy her innocence. When the play ends, however, Molly's dreams have been shattered; the world intrudes upon them and she is forced to leave that false paradise her mother created for her. At the same time, her mother turns more and more toward the enclosures of her childhood—toward her memory of an imaginary childhood in which she, not her sister, was her father's favorite daughter. (pp. 169-71)

If the loss of this childhood and its enclosures is our first tragedy, her characters also carry within them a second tragedy, for what is said of Sadie, of **"Camp Cataract,"** may be said of all of them: "her death existed now while she still lived." Fear, loneliness, and dread are givens in this world. But even though we cannot find a tree house in which to hide while we make plans to run away from the world, we can find moments of real happiness and peace, moments that approximate most closely those emotional spaces for which we seek. During such moments, the need for language ceases; silence seems to occupy the center of an erotic bond between two human beings. These moments for Bowles are more likely to occur between two women than between a man and woman. (p. 171)

Falling into a world with broken bottles and stones that inflict cuts and bruises, Bowles' characters search for mannequins who might buffer their falls and diminish that separateness that most often characterizes human relationships:

> When they died . . . nothing was left . . . no memories. . . . Everything vanished . . . all the panic . . . and the strain. . . . I hardly remember my life. They never loved me. . . . I didn't really love them. . . . My heart had fake roots . . . when the strain was over, they dried up . . . they shriveled and snapped and my heart was left empty.

Those who survive more or less intact in this world are those who manage to keep a proper perspective toward it:

> "Certainly I am nearer to becoming a saint," reflected Miss Goering, "but is it possible that a part of me hidden from my sight is piling sin upon sin as fast as Mrs. Copperfield?" This latter possibility Miss Goering thought to be of considerable interest but of no great importance.

By the end of the novel, Miss Goering comes to realize that although we must immerse ourselves in the mud, we cannot expect to have our redemption either verified or denied. The dignity and nobility of the human animal comes, or so it would seem, from the act of immersion itself, from those choices and struggles that lead up to it. Bowles' world consists of people too human not to be lost and lonely, and too honest and courageous to deny those truths they know about themselves. It is inhabited by those who are unable to be, in Mrs. Copperfield's words, "only interested in a bearable life." One might say of most of Bowles' major characters what is said of ***Two Serious Ladies'*** Miss Gamelon—that "reality was often more frightening to her than her wildest dreams." Her art is dominated by women who wander, seeking that concealed truth that might reveal itself in a moment snatched from a life moving toward eternity.

The beauty of Bowles' art both perplexes and haunts its readers. Within it, warmth and love are found in those moments in which the isolation and separateness of the individual are broken down; however, her art finally returns us to the individuality of her figures, to those who are interested in "finding out what we are like." The self is ultimately the center out of which all impulses and energies radiate: it is "always the starting point for everything: Yourself." And in the midst of her art stands its creator, Jane Bowles, aware of the horror and grotesqueness of the world she presents, yet regarding it with compassion, humor, and tenderness. In the passage from Bowles with which I began this essay, Miss Goering is asked by Mrs. Copperfield whether the artist jumped, and she replies: "No, he remained there for quite a while looking down into the courtyard with an expression of pleasant curiosity on his face." It is pleasant to imagine that in this particular scene, Bowles might be giving us an oblique glance at herself as artist and her own special way of looking at the world. For in her own art, she regards the world with an expression that is at once bemused and sympathetic, for hers is a world whose very pain and suffering seems to reaffirm the dignity of those who inhabit it. (pp. 172-73)

Robert E. Lougy, "The World and Art of Jane Bowles (1917-1973)," in The CEA Critic, *Vol. 49, Nos. 2-4, Winter 1986-Summer 1987, pp. 157-73.*

FURTHER READING

Bassett, Mark T. "Imagination, Control and Betrayal in Jane Bowles' 'A Stick of Green Candy.' " *Studies in Short Fiction* 24, No. 1 (Winter 1987): 25-9.

Analyzes autobiographical aspects in Bowles's highly regarded short story.

Dillon, Millicent. *A Little Original Sin: The Life and Work of Jane Bowles.* New York: Holt, Rinehart and Winston, 1981, 464 p.

The only book-length critical biography on Bowles. Considered a sympathetic, thoughtful portrait of its subject.

———. "Jane Bowles: Experiment as Character." In *Breaking the Sequence: Women's Experimental Fiction,* edited by Ellen G. Friedman and Miriam Fuchs, pp. 140-47. Princeton, N. J.: Princeton University Press, 1989.

Investigates Bowles's uncompleted novel *Out in the World,* which the critic contends remained unfinished partially due to her indecision over the use of traditional or fragmented narration.

E. E. Cummings

1894-1962

(Full name Edward Estlin Cummings) American poet, prose writer, essayist, and playwright.

Cummings's innovative and controversial verse places him among the most popular and widely anthologized poets of the twentieth century. While linked early in his career with the Modernist movement, Cummings more closely resembles the New England Transcendentalists and English Romantics in his championing of individuality and artistic freedom. Rejecting what he perceived as the small-mindedness of "mostpeople," Cummings celebrated the individual, as well as erotic and familial love. Conformity, mass psychology, and snobbery were frequent targets of his humorous and sometimes scathing satires. Cummings was also a painter whose interest in such modernist art forms as Cubism and Futurism led him to experiment in his verse with punctuation, idiomatic speech, compressed words, dislocated syntax, unusual typography, line division, and capitalization. Discussing Cummings's technique, Randall Jarrell explained: "Cummings is a very great expert in all these, so to speak, illegal syntactical devices: his misuse of parts of speech, his use of negative prefixes, his word-coining, his systematic relation of words that grammar and syntax don't permit us to relate—all this makes him a magical bootlegger or moonshiner of language, one who intoxicates us on a clear liquor no government has legalized with its stamp."

Cummings grew up in Cambridge, Massachusetts, where his father was a sociology professor at Harvard and a noted Unitarian clergyman. Demonstrating a strong predilection for poetry and art at an early age, Cummings enjoyed the full support and encouragement of his parents. He studied at Harvard from 1911 to 1915, wrote poems daily, and joined the editorial board of the *Harvard Monthly,* a college literary magazine, where he worked with his close friends S. Foster Damon and John Dos Passos. In his senior year, he became fascinated with various forms of avant-garde art, particularly Modernism and Cubism, and in his graduation address, "The New Art," he extolled innovative techniques practiced by Gertrude Stein, Ezra Pound, Igor Stravinsky, and Pablo Picasso. Cummings later incorporated elements of their styles into his poetry and paintings. During this period, Cummings eschewed upper-class Cambridge values and frequented circuses, bordellos, pubs, and vaudeville and burlesque shows. His affection for popular culture and his desire to achieve the modernist objective of capturing the particulars of a single movement or moment in time are reflected in Cummings's comment on his poetic technique: "I can express it in fifteen words, by quoting the Eternal Question and Immortal Answer of burlesk, viz. 'Would you hit a woman with a child?—No, I'd hit her with a brick.' Like the burlesk comedian, I am abnormally fond of that precision which creates movement." His first published poems appeared in the anthology *Eight Harvard Poets.* These pieces feature his appreciation of experimental forms and his use of the lower-case "i"—symbolizing both the humility and the uniqueness of the individual—that would become his trademark. The book's copy editor, however, mistook Cummings's stylistic innovations as typographical errors and made "corrections."

In 1917 Cummings moved to New York, where he was employed briefly at a mail-order book company, and soon began working full-time on his poetry and art. With World War I in progress, he volunteered for the Norton-Harjes Ambulance Service stationed in France. Cummings and his close friend William Slater Brown were separated from their unit when they arrived overseas, and spent five weeks in Paris because of the subsequent bureaucratic muddle. Cummings was completely charmed by the bohemian atmosphere of Paris and its abundance of art and artists. Cummings and Brown rejoined their unit but were detained three months later on suspicion of treason, a charge prompted by the pair's preference for the company of French soldiers and Brown's correspondence with American anarchist Emma Goldman. As a result, the two men were held in an internment camp in Normandy. Cummings's father, making use of his contacts in government, was able to secure his son's release after four months. Cummings's first book, *The Enormous Room,* documents his experiences in the French internment camp. Considered a classic of World War I literature, this work concerns the preservation of dignity in a degrading and dehumanizing situation. It also examines themes that Cummings would pursue throughout his career—the individual against society, government, and all forms of authority. Cummings used both French and English words to create a witty, satirical voice that lampoons what he perceived as the ludicrous nature of war. Governmental and military bureaucracy is satirized in the book's preface, which reprints his father's correspondence with American and French authorities, through which he attempted to obtain his son's release.

Shortly after Cummings returned to New York in 1918, he was drafted and stationed at Camp Danvers, Massachusetts. During the 1920s and 1930s he traveled widely in Europe, alternately living in Paris and New York, and developed parallel careers as a poet and painter. In 1931, the politically liberal Cummings visited the Soviet Union to discover how the U.S.S.R.'s system of art subsidation functioned. *Eimi,* an expanded version of his travel diary, however, expresses his profound disappointment at the regimentation and lack of personal and artistic freedom he encountered. From that time, Cummings abandoned his liberal political views and social circle, becoming conservative on social and political issues. In addition to being a prolific poet, Cummings published several collections of his art and composed miscellaneous prose pieces, dramas, and a ballet. Cummings received the Shelley Memorial Award for poetry in 1944, the Charles Eliot Norton Professorship at Harvard for 1952-53, and the Bollingen Prize for Poetry in 1958. He reached the height of his popularity during the 1940s and 1950s, giving poetry readings to college audiences across the United States until his death in 1962.

All of Cummings's poetry attests to his continual search for fresh metaphors and new means of expression through creative placement of words on the page, novel syntactical constructions, and unusual punctuation and capitalization. He had originally intended to publish his first collection as *Tulips & Chimneys,* but due to both the enormous quantity and explicit sexual content of many of the poems, was forced to publish selections from the original manuscript as three separate volumes: *Tulips and Chimneys, &,* and *XLI Poems.* The "tulips" of the first volume are free-verse lyric poems that nostalgically recall childhood. The poem "in Just-" for example, celebrates youth and spring through such playfully imaginative compounds as "mud-/luscious" and "puddle-wonderful," while "O sweet spontaneous" argues that nature can only be appreciated fully through the senses rather than through science, philosophy, or religion. The "chimneys" section comprises a sustained sonnet sequence concerning social hypocrisy, narrow-mindedness, and stagnation. The subjects of Cummings's frequently anthologized sonnet "the Cambridge ladies who live in furnished souls," for example, are "unbeautiful and have comfortable minds."

Cummings later addressed other topics while continuing his playful experiments, celebrations of love and nature, and social satires. *Is 5* includes the antiwar piece "my sweet old etcetera" and the elegy "i sing of Olaf glad and big," which concerns the death of a conscientious objector. *ViVa* contains a group of sonnets and other poems attacking uncreative thinking. This volume also features the well-known poem "somewhere I have never travelled, gladly beyond," which glorifies love, nature, individualism, imaginative freedom, and the mystery of faith. The poems in the collection *No Thanks,* inspired by his trip to the Soviet Union, argue for artistic freedom. *50 Poems* includes such popular pieces as "anyone lived in a pretty how town" and the elegy "my father moved through dooms of love." *1 x 1* presents Cummings as more optimistic and life-affirming than he had seemed during his period of personal and political disaffection in the 1930s. Structured in a pattern of darkness moving toward light, *1 x 1* begins with poems such as "a salesman is an it that stinks Excuse," which denigrate businessmen and politicians, and ends with pieces praising nature and love, including "yes is a pleasant country." In his late verse—*XAIPE: Seventy-One Poems, 95 Poems,* and the posthumously published *73 Poems*—Cummings effects a softer, more elegiac note, displaying his affinity with New England Transcendentalism and English Romanticism.

Critical opinion of Cummings's poems is markedly divided. Beginning with *Tulips and Chimneys,* reviewers described his verbal pyrotechnics and idiosyncratic arrangement of text as eccentric and self-indulgent, designed to call attention to the writing rather than to elucidate his themes. Some objected to Cummings's explicit treatment of sexuality, while others interpreted his depictions of social hypocrisy and banality as elitist. When his *Collected Poems* was published in 1938, Cummings's sharp satiric views caused some critics to accuse him of misanthropy. His later, more politically conservative poetry also came under attack for exhibiting traces of anti-Semitism, a charge that continues to be debated. Some reviewers, noting that Cummings's style did not change or develop significantly throughout his career, speculate that the poet exploited a style that suited him, while others fault Cummings for insufficient artistic growth. Many critics censured *50 Poems,* accusing Cummings of relying too much on formulaic writing and habitual stylistic mannerisms. Despite these negative assessments, Cummings remains highly esteemed for many popular and frequently anthologized poems. It has been suggested that the scarcity of formal critical attention to his work simply reflects the fact that his verse does not lend itself to traditional academic explication. Cummings is remembered for his innovative, playful style, his celebration of love and nature, his focus on the primacy of the individual and freedom of expression, and his treatment of, in his own words, "ecstasy and anguish, being and becoming; the immortality of the creative imagination and the indomitability of the human spirit."

(See also *CLC,* Vols. 1, 3, 8, 12, 15; *Contemporary Authors,* Vols. 73-76; *Dictionary of Literary Biography,* Vols. 4, 48; and *Concise Dictionary of American Literary Biography, 1929-1941.*)

PRINCIPAL WORKS

POETRY

Eight Harvard Poets [with others] 1917
Tulips and Chimneys 1923
& 1925
XLI Poems 1925
Is 5 1926
ViVa 1931
No Thanks 1935
Collected Poems 1938
50 Poems 1940
1 x 1 1944
XAIPE: Seventy-One Poems 1950
95 Poems 1958
100 Selected Poems 1959
73 Poems 1963

PLAYS

Him 1927
Tom 1935
Santa Claus—A Morality 1946

OTHER

The Enormous Room (prose) 1922
Eimi (travel diary) 1933
i: six nonlectures (lectures) 1953
Selected Letters of E. E. Cummings (correspondence) 1969

R. P. Blackmur

[*Blackmur was a leading American literary critic of the twentieth century. The following essay is considered to be the most influential early assessment of Cummings's work. Other portions of this essay appear in* CLC, *Vol. 12.*]

In his four books of verse, his play, and the autobiographical ***Enormous Room,*** Mr. Cummings has amassed a special vocabulary and has developed from it a special use of language which these notes are intended to analyse and make explicit. Critics have commonly said, when they understood Mr. Cummings' vocabulary at all, that he has enriched the language with a new idiom; had they been further interested in the uses of language, they would no doubt have said that he had added to the general sensibility of his time. Certainly his work has had many imitators. Young poets have found it easy to adopt the attitudes from which Mr. Cummings has written, just as they often adopt the superficial attitudes of Swinburne and Keats. The curious thing about Mr. Cummings' influence is that his imitators have been able to emulate as well as ape him; which is not so frequently the case with the influence of Swinburne and Keats. (p. 163)

There is one attitude towards Mr. Cummings' language which has deceived those who hold it. The typographical peculiarities of his verse have caught and irritated public attention. Excessive hyphenation of single words, the use of lower case "i," the breaking of lines, the insertion of punctuation between the letters of a word, and so on, will have a possible critical importance to the textual scholarship of the future; but extensive consideration of these peculiarities to-day has very little importance, carries almost no reference to the *meaning* of the poems. Mr. Cummings' experiments in typography merely extend the theory of notation by adding to the number, *not* to the *kind,* of conventions the reader must bear in mind, and are dangerous only because since their uses cannot readily be defined, they often obscure rather than clarify the exact meaning. No doubt the continued practice of such notation would produce a set of well-ordered conventions susceptible of general use. At present the practice can only be "allowed for," recognized in the particular instance, felt, and forgotten: as the diacritical marks in the dictionary are forgotten once the sound of the word has been learned. The poem, after all, only takes wing on the page, it persists in the ear. (pp. 167-68)

Any poetry which does not consider itself as much of an art and having the same responsibilities to the consumer as the arts of silversmithing or cobbling shoes—any such poetry is likely to do little more than rehearse a waking dream. Dreams are everywhere ominous and full of meaning; and why should they not be? They hold the images of the secret self, and to the initiate dreamer betray the nerve of life at every turn, not through any effort to do so, or because of any inherited regimen, but simply because they cannot help it. Dreams are like that—to the dreamer the maximal limit of experience. As it happens, dreams employ words and pictorial images to fill out their flux with a veil of substance. Pictures are natural to everyone, and words, because they are prevalent, seem common and inherently sensible. Hence, both picture and word, and then with a little stretching of the fancy the substance of the dream itself, seem expressible just as they occur—as things created, as the very flux of life. Mr. Cummings' poems are often nothing more than the report of just such dreams. He believes he knows what he knows, and no doubt he does. But he also believes, apparently, that the words which he encourages most vividly to mind are those most precisely fitted to put his poem on paper. He transfers the indubitable magic of his private musings from the cell of his mind, where it is honest incantation, to the realm of poetry. Here he forgets that poetry, so far as it takes a permanent form, is written and is meant to be read, and that it cannot be a mere private musing. Merely because his private fancy furnishes his liveliest images, is the worst reason for assuming that this private fancy will be approximately experienced by the reader or even indicated on the printed page.

But it is unfair to limit this description to Mr. Cummings; indeed, so limited, it is not even a description of Mr. Cummings. Take the Oxford Book of English Verse, or any anthology of poems equally well known, and turn from the poems printed therein of such widely separated poets as Surrey, Crashaw, Marvell, Burns, Wordsworth, Shelley, and Swinburne, to the collected works of these poets respectively. Does not the description of Mr. Cummings' mind at work given above apply nearly as well to the bulk of this poetry as to that of Mr. Cummings, at least on the senses' first immersion? The anthology poems being well known are conceived to be understood, to be definitely intelligible, and to have, without inspection, a precise meaning. The descent upon the collected poems of all or of any one of these authors is by and large a descent into tenuity. Most of their work, most of any poet's work, with half a dozen exceptions, is tenuous and vague, private exercises or public playthings of a soul in verse. So far as he is able, the reader struggles to reach the concrete, the solid, the definite; he must have these qualities, or their counterparts among the realm of the spirit, before he can understand what he reads. To translate such qualities from the realm of his private experience to the conventional forms of poetry is the problem of the poet; and the problem of the reader, likewise, is to come well equipped with the talent and the taste for discerning the meaning of those conventions as they particularly occur. Neither the poet's casual language nor the reader's casual interlocution is likely to be much help. There must be a ground common but exterior to each: that is the poem. The best poems take the best but not always the hardest reading; and no doubt it is so with the writing. Certainly, in neither case are dreams or simple reveries enough. Dreams are natural and are minatory or portentous; but except when by accident they fall into forms that fit the intelligence, they never negotiate the miracle of meaning between the poet and the poem, the poem and the reader.

Most poetry fails of this negotiation, and it is sometimes assumed that the negotiation was never meant, by the poet, to be made. For the poet, private expression is said to be enough; for the reader, the agitation of the senses, the perception of verbal beauty, the mere sense of stirring life in the words, are supposed sufficient. If this defence had a true premise—if the poet did express himself to his private satisfaction—it would be unanswerable; and to many it is so. But I think the case is different, and this is the real charge against Mr. Cummings, the poet does not ever express himself privately. The mind cannot understand, cannot properly know its own musings until those musings take some sort of conventional form. Properly speaking a poet, or any man, cannot be adequate to himself in terms of himself. True consciousness and true expression of consciousness must be external to the blind seat of consciousness—man as a sensorium. Even a simple image must be fitted among other images, and conned with them, before it is understood. That is, it must take a form in language which is highly traditional and conventional. The genius of the poet is to make the convention apparently disappear into the use to which he puts it.

Mr. Cummings and the group with which he is here roughly associated, the anti-culture or anti-intelligence group, persists to the contrary. Because experience is fragmentary as it strikes the consciousness it is thought to be essentially discontinuous and therefore essentially unintelligible except in the fragmentary form in which it occurred. They credit the words they use with immaculate conception and there hold them unquestionable. A poem, because it happens, must mean something and mean it without relation to anything but the private experience which inspired it. Certainly it means something, but not a poem; it means that something exciting happened to the writer and that a mystery is happening to the reader. The fallacy is double: they believe in the inexorable significance of the unique experience; and they have discarded the only method of making the unique experience into a poem—the conventions of the intelligence. As a matter of fact they do not write without conventions, but being ignorant of what they use, they resort most commonly to their own inefficient or superficial conventions—such as Mr. Cummings' flower and doll. The effect is convention without substance; the unique experience becomes a rhetorical assurance.

If we examine next, for the sake of the greatest possible contrast, one of the "tough" poems in ***Is 5,*** we will find a similar breach with the concrete. The use of vague words like "flower" in the lyrical poems as unexpanded similes, is no more an example of sentimental egoism than the use of vague conventions about villains. The distortion differs in terms but is essentially identical.

Sometimes the surface of the poem is so well constructed that the distortion is hard to discover. Intensity of process occasionally triumphs over the subject. Less frequently the subject itself is conceived directly and takes naturally the terms which the language supplies. The poem numbered **"One-XII"** in ***Is 5*** is an example in so far as the sentimental frame does not obscure the process.

> now dis "daughter" uv eve (who aint precisely
> slim) sim
> ply don't know duh meanin uv duh woid sin in
> not disagreeable contras tuh dat not exactly fat
> "father" (adjustin his robe) who now puts on his
> flat hat.

It is to be noted in this epigram, that there is no inexorable reason for either the dialect or the lapses from it into straight English. No one in particular is speaking, unless it be Mr. Cummings slumming in morals along with he-men and lady social workers, and taking it for granted that the dialect and the really refined language which the dialect exercises together give a setting. There are many other poems in ***Is 5,*** more sentimental and less successful, where the realism is of a more obvious sort; not having reference to an ideal so much as to a kind of scientific reality. That is, there is an effort to ground an emotion, or the facts which make the emotion, in the style of the character to whom the emotion happens. It is the reporter, the man with the good ear for spoken rhythms, who writes out of memory. The war poems and the poem about Bill and his chip **("One XVI")** are examples. Style in this sense (something laid on) is only an attribute; is not the man; is not the character. And when it is substituted for character, it is likely to be sentimental and melodramatic. That is, the emotion which is named in the poem (by one of its attributes) is in excess of its established source (that same attribute). There is a certain immediate protection afforded to this insufficiency by the surface toughness, by the convention of burlesque; as if by mocking oneself one made sure there was something to mock. It is a kind of trickery resulting from eager but lazy senses; where the sensation itself is an excess, and appears to have done all the work of intuition and intelligence; where sensation seems expert without incorporation into experience. As if sensation could be anything more than the idea of sensation, so far as poetry goes, without being attached to some central body of experience, genuinely understood and *formed* in the mind.

The intrusion of science into art always results in a sentimental realism and always obfuscates form when that science is not kept subordinate to the qualitative experience of the senses—as witness the run of sociological novels. The analogues of science, where conventions are made to do the work of feeling instead of crowning it, are even more dangerous. Mr. Cummings' tough guy and his hard-boiled dialects are such analogues. (pp. 173-78)

If we take a paragraph from the poem beginning on page thirty in ***Is 5,*** we will discover another terminus of the emotional habit of mind which produced the emphasis on the word "flower" in ***Tulips and Chimneys.***

> the Bar. tinking luscious jugs dint of ripe silver
> with warmlyish wetflat splurging smells waltz
> the glush of squirting taps plus slush of foam
> knocked off and a faint piddle-of-drops she says
> I ploc spittle what the lands thaz me kin in no
> sir hopping sawdust you kiddo he's a palping
> wreaths of badly Yep cigars who jim him why
> gluey grins topple together eyes pout gestures
> stickily point made glints squinting who's a wink
> bum-nothing and money fuzzily mouths take big
> wobbly foot-steps every goggle cent of it get out
> ears dribbles soft right old feller belch the chap
> hic summore eh chuckles skulch.

Now the point is that the effect of this whole paragraph has much in common with the effect of the word "flower." It is a flower disintegrated, and the parts are not component; so that by presenting an analysis of his image Mr. Cummings has not let us into its secret: the analysis is not a true analysis, because it exhibits, finally, what are still only the results, not the grounds, of his private conventions, his personal emotions. It is indubitable that the words are alive; they jostle, even overturn, the reader in the assurance of their vitality; but the notion of what their true vitality is remains Mr. Cummings' very own. The words remain emotive. They have a gusty air of being something, but they defeat themselves in the effort to say what, and come at last to a bad end, all fallen in a heap.

The easiest *explanation* of the passage would be to say that each separate little collection of words in it is a note for an image; an abstraction, very keen and lively in Mr. Cummings' mind, of something very precise and concrete. Some of the words seem like a painter's notes, some a philologist's. But they are all, as they are presented, notes, abstractions, ideas—with their concrete objects unknown—except to the most arbitrary guess. The guess must be arbitrary because of the quantity, not the quality, of the words employed. Mr. Cummings is not here overworking the individual words, but by heaping so many of them together he destroys their individuality. Meaning really residual in the word is not exhausted, is not even touched; it must remain abstract and only an emotional substitute for it can be caught. The interesting fact about emotional substitutes in poetry, as elsewhere, is their thinness, and the inadequacy resulting from the thinness. The thinness is compulsory because they can, so far as the poem is concerned, exist only as a surface; they cannot possess tentacular roots reaching into, and feeding on, feelings, because the feelings do not exist, are only present by legerdemain. Genuine emotion in poetry perhaps does not *exist* at all; though it is none the less real for that, because a genuine emotion does not need the warrant of existence: it is the necessary result, in the mind, of a convention of feelings: like the notion of divine grace.

In ***Tulips and Chimneys*** there is a poem whose first and last lines supply an excellent opposition of proper and improper distortion of language.

> the Cambridge ladies who live in furnished
>   souls . . .
>   the
> moon rattles like a fragment of angry candy.

In the context the word "soul" has the element of surprise which is surprise at *justness,* at *aptness;* it fits in and finishes off the notion of the line. "Furnished souls" is a good, if slight, conceit; and there is no trouble for the reader who wishes to know what the line means: he has merely to *extend* his knowledge slightly, just as Mr. Cummings merely extended the sense of his language slightly by releasing his particular words in this particular order. The whole work that the poet here demands of his reader is pretty well defined. The reader does not have to *guess;* he is enabled to *know.* The reader is not collecting data, he is aware of a meaning.

It would be unfair not to quote the context of the second line.

> . . . the Cambridge ladies do not care, above
> Cambridge if sometimes in its box of
> sky lavender and cornerless, the
> moon rattles like a fragment of angry candy.

We can say that Mr. Cummings is putting beauty next to the tawdry; juxtaposing the dead with the live; or that he is being sentimentally philosophical in verse—that is, releasing from inadequate sources something intended to be an emotion.

We can go on illustrating Mr. Cummings probable intentions almost infinitely. What Mr. Cummings likes or admires, what he holds dear in life, he very commonly calls flowers, or dolls, or candy—terms with which he is astonishingly generous; as if he thought by making his terms general enough their vagueness could not matter, and never noticed that the words so used enervate themselves in a kind of hardened instinct. We can understand what Mr. Cummings intended by "moon" and "candy" but in the process of understanding, the meaning of the words themselves disappears. The thrill of the association of "rattles" with "moon" and "angry" with "candy" becomes useless as a guide.

"Rattles" and "angry" can only be continued in the meaning of the line if the reader supplies them with a force, a definiteness of suggestion, with which Mr. Cummings has not endowed them.

The distortion is here not a release of observation so keen that commonplace language would not hold it; it is not the presentation of a vision so complete that words must lose their normal meanings in order to suggest it. It is, on the contrary, the distortion of the commonplace itself; and the difficulty about a commonplace is that it cannot be known, it has no character, no fate, and no essence. It is a substitute for these.

True meaning (which is here to say knowledge) can only exist where some contact, however remote, is preserved between the language, forms, or symbols in which it is given and something concrete, individual, or sensual which inspired it; and the degree in which the meaning is seized will depend on the degree in which the particular concreteness is realized. Thus the technique of "meaning" will employ distortion only in so far as the sense of this concreteness is promoted by it. When contrast and contradiction disturb the ultimate precision of the senses the distortion involved in inappropriate and destructive. Mr. Cummings' line about the moon and candy does not weld a contradiction, does not identify a substance by a thrill of novel association. It leaves the reader at a loss; where it is impossible to *know,* after any amount of effort and good will, what the words mean. If it be argued that Mr. Cummings was not interested in meaning then Mr. Cummings is not a serious poet, is a mere collector of sensations, and can be of very little value to us. And to defend Mr. Cummings on the ground that he is in the pretty good company of Swinburne, Crashaw, and Victor Hugo, is partly to ignore the fact that by the same argument all four also enjoy the companionship of Mr. Guest. Such defence would show a very poor knowledge of the verses of Mr. Cummings, who is nothing if not serious in the attempt to exhibit precise knowledge. His interest in words and in their real meaning is probably greater than that of most poets of similar dimensions. He has consciously stretched syntax, word order, and meaning in just the effort to expand knowledge in poetry; and his failure is because he has gone too far, has lost sight of meaning altogether—and because, perhaps, the experience which he attempts to translate into poetry remained always personal to him and was never known objectively as itself. By his eagerness Mr. Cummings' relation to language has become confused; he has put down what has meant much to him and can mean little to us, because for us it is not put down—is only indicated, only possibly there. The freshness and depth of his private experience is not denied; but it is certain that, so far as its meaning goes, in the poetry into which he translated it, sentimentality, empty convention, and commonplace rule. In short, Mr. Cummings' poetry ends in ideas *about* things. (pp. 179-84)

This essay has proceeded so far on the explicit assumption that the poems of Mr. Cummings are unintelligible, and that no amount of effort on the part of the reader can make them less so. We began by connecting Mr. Cummings to two schools, or groups, which are much the same essentially—the anti-culture group which denies the intelligence, and the group, not limited to writers, of which the essential attitude is most easily defined as sentimental egoism or romantic idealism. Where these schools are most obviously identical is in the poetry they nourish: the avowed interest is the relentless pursuit of the actual in terms of the immediate as the immediate is given, without overt criticism, to the ego. Unintelligibility is a necessary consequence of such a pursuit, if by the intelligible we mean something concrete, qualified, permanent, and public. Poetry, if we understand it, is not in immediacy at all. It is not given to the senses or to the free intuition. Thus, when poetry is written as if its substance were immediate and given, we have as a result a distorted sensibility and a violent inner confusion. We have, if the poet follows his principles, something abstract, vague, impermanent, and essentially private. When every sensation and every word is taken as final and perfect, the substance which sensations report and for which words must stand remain inexplicable. We can understand only by accident.

Of course there is another side to the matter. In a sense anyone can understand Mr. Cummings and his kind by the mere assertion that he does understand. Nothing else is needed but a little natural sympathy and a certain aptness for the resumption of a childish sensibility. (pp. 190-91)

So with the poetry of Mr. Cummings we might be altogether contented and pleased, were he himself content with the measure of his actual performance. But no poetry is so pretentious. No poetry ever claimed to mean more; and in making this claim it cannot avoid submitting itself, disastrously, to the criticism of the intelligence. So soon as we take it seriously, trying to discover what it really says about human destiny and the terms of love and death, we see how little material there is in this poetry except the assurance, made with continuous gusto, that the material exists. We look at the poetry. Sometimes one word, in itself vague and cloudy, is made to take on the work of an entire philosophy—like flower. Sometimes words pile themselves up blindly, each defeating the purport of the others. No feeling is ever defined. No emotion betrays a structure. Experience is its own phantoms, and flows willy-nilly. With the reality of experience the reality of language is lost. No metaphor crosses the bridge of tautology, and every simile is unexpanded. All the "thought" is metonymy, yet the substance is never assigned; so in the end we have only the thrill of substance.

Such an art when it pretends to measure life is essentially vicarious; it is a substitute for something that never was—like a tin soldier, or Peter Pan. It has all the flourish of life and every sentimental sincerity. Taken for what it is, it is charming and even instructive. Taken solemnly, as it is meant to be, the distortion by which it exists is too much for it, and it seems a kind of baby-talk. (pp. 191-92)

R. P. Blackmur, "Notes on E. E. Cummings'

Language," in The Hound & Horn, *Vol. IV, No. 2, January-March, 1931, pp. 163-92.*

Philip Horton and Sherry Mangan

[The following two excerpts appeared together in the May 1938 Partisan Review. *Philip Horton and Sherry Mangan, respectively, take opposite views of Cummings's 1938* Collected Poems.]

[Regarding E. E. Cummings' poetry represented in ***Collected Poems*** (1938), the] most general statement to be made is that it shows no technical improvement or intellectual development over a period of fifteen years. The *enfant terrible* of 1923 has become the professional *vieux gaillard* of today—a poet distinctly *manqué.* The poetry gives one an apparently inexhaustible repetition, not of ideas or even emotions, but of moods, whimsies, attitudes, prejudices—in short all the effluvia of personality; and the personality is one that has been a familiar museum-piece in the whatnots of literary parlours for the last decade. Perhaps it is the untimely resurrection of this famous *poupée* that outrages the sensibilities and leaves one after reading the book with the feeling of having been party to an indecency. Surely the baroque antiquity of such a quip as poem 299 (one of the "New Poems!")—

Q:dwo
  we know of anything which can
  be as dull as one englishman
A:to

should be locked under glass in the corner cuddy. The same is true of the notorious typography: its only virtue today lies in its quaint persistence as a historical curiosity. As for the sexires, they have multiplied, like the whimsies and typography, unchanged in kind and quality. All that needs to be said of them, once and for all, is that they are not very good on any level. They are inferior in both technique and spirit to such ballads as "Down In The Lehigh Valley" on the one hand, and on the other to popular songs like "My Handy Man." Compare, for instance, the prurient emasculation of poem 250: **"may i feel said he (i'll squeal said she"** to the epic sweep of: **"The grass was gone for miles around Where Lil's white arse had bumped the ground";** or the hackneyed double entendre of poem 134 (the breaking in of a new car) with the rich imagery and invention of "My Handy Man." Even the serious sex poems are corrupted by prurience, sicklied o'er with sentimentality. They stem not from the great stream of the tradition, but from the minor tributary of cheap burlesque; they are more concerned with exhibition than enjoyment—like the strip-teaser with one eye on the censors and the cops in the back row.

The satires, which together with the sex poems are largely responsible for Cummings' popular reputation, very rarely deserve the name. They are more often bits of sarcasm, fancy invective, and nose-thumbings. The real fun we get from reading the best of them is derived not from their success as poems, but from the exhibition of a clever (and potentially serious) poet deliberately pointing his sophistications with vulgarities, his poetic language with gutter slang. It is the bald trick of incongruity—a popular one in burlesque, and is supported by many of the common devices. . . .

Now there is no possible objection to either nonsense or doggerel when given and taken as such, though one may well dislike to have it sandwiched in with serious poems. The trouble here lies in the ambiguity. Apparently Cummings has cultivated the confusion of incongruities for so long that he himself is rarely certain to what degree or in what kind he wants to be serious. Similarly, he slips so easily into the jargon of newspaper, stage and street that he perfectly blunts the edge of what was meant to be indignation or bitterness. Thus, in one of his best and serious satires, the lines

obey says toc, submit says tic
Eternity's a Five Year Plan

give the effect of cant. The same triviality results in poem 214, a love ballad after the manner of Villon, which almost succeeds in overcoming its defects. In this case the jargon is that of musical comedy lyrics after Cole Porter or Kaufman.

i am a birdcage without any bird
a collar looking for a dog, a kiss
without lips; a prayer lacking any knees

and again

. . . a hand's impression in an empty glove
a soon forgotten tune, a house for lease.

This mingling of the trivial and serious, and the general confusion of values throughout Cummings' work, is by no means accidental. It is a result of his deliberate rejection of knowledge, whether of himself or of life at large. . . .

The consequences of Cummings' anti-intellectualism have been so carefully analyzed by R. P. Blackmur in his *Double Agent* [see excerpt above] that there is little else to be said of it. The ***Collected Poems*** merely confirms Blackmur's remarks. In the Introduction, for instance, Cummings writes: "Life, for eternal us, is now; and now is much too busy being a little more than everything to seem anything, catastrophic included.". This is a typical Cummings statement, for while appearing to embrace and affirm, it actually reduces to negation and rejection. Likewise, the more he tries in the later poems to define his beliefs, the more he resorts to negatives. He likes to describe the philistine norms by the negative prefix: "unselves," "unlives," "unhearts," "unminds," etc.; but the trick merely shows up his own impoverished and fuzzy affirmations. He praises the "whyless-soul," the "general looseness of doom," the "mystery of growing," and life—"the one undiscoverable guess." But he himself does not grow in his poetry. Having rejected knowledge, the chiefest instrument of evaluation and the essential means to maturity, he can hardly be expected to offer more than the scattered impulses of an immature personality. The most revealing of his negative statements, which strikes one with the impact and illumination of an absolute truth, are the lines in poem 214:

so that my life (which liked the sun and moon)
resembles something that has not occurred

Substituting "poetry" for "life," the statement would have had even greater pertinency. As Mr. Blackmur has pointed out, his poetry offers notes and materials for poems rather than actually achieved poems. To give Cummings his due, he has written a handful of really good love sonnets and poems, which still deserve publication in a modest volume of their own. Excepting them, nothing much in the way of poetry has occurred. (pp. 59-61)

To the predictable exasperation of all right-thinking critics, the special miracle of Cummings, even under the severe strain of a collected edition, blithely persists, viable, inextinguishable, a fact. The indignation of our literary theologians is comprehensible enough: Cummings's faults stand right out—indeed, what Eliotellus in eight years has not, for his graduation piece, permanently annihilated him? Yet his poetry lives easily through such attack; for his faults are inseparably the faults of his virtues, and in those virtues—gusto, abundance, magniloquence—he is nearly unique. (pp. 61-2)

[What] essentially is the case usually brought against Cummings? Failure in exact communication, pretentiousness, execrable taste, and limitation of subject.

The poet whose primary interest is to communicate either fails entirely or, if he succeeds, does so on a abysmal level, for which prose would have served. The poet whose primary interest is, within the fair limits of language (private and secret Humpty-Dumpty use of words strictly barred), to express with the maximal accuracy, depth, and vividness his experience, by succeeding in that expression, succeeds in communication, i.e. the perfect recreation of that experience in the reader. It is simply this paradox which Luis Cardoza y Aragón crystallizes in his brilliant dictum: "where there is no miracle, there is no poetry."

Now the miracle of Cummings is indubitably heretical, conceivably satanic. His words do not, by limiting one another, construct an exact and unmistakable impression; each word, on the contrary, explosively releases in the reader as much of its total content of meanings and emotivity as the reader is capable of supporting. Hence the poem in Cummings's mind and in the reader's mind are two quite different variants of the poem, not in any wise identical but both of great potency. It is principally for this reason that his poems practically defy paraphrase into prose. The glaring non-sequitur of our theologians is to argue that, since the miracle is heretical, there is no miracle. To attempt to argue out of existence the notorious fact of Cummings's poetic power merely by (quite correctly) alleging that it is not canonical, is a petulant absurdity.

Similarly self-deceptive is the contention that Cummings is discredited by his pretentiousness. That timidity of opinion of which *New-Yorker*ism is the perfect flower may chidingly deprecate as bumptious the classic poetic quality of iactantia; but, whether one likes it or not, "exegi monumentum" happens to have proved itself a historically correct statement. It would not wholly amaze, though it might equally displease, if

> the harder the wind blows the
> taller i am

proved equally so.

Cummings's taste is more difficult to defend; indeed, it is often quite indefensible. The retention of, for example, 43, **"it may not always be so; and i say . . . "**, is certainly a triumph more of courage than of prudence, though one cannot but admire the honest temerity of a récolte that is truly a collection, and not a selection; and in 47, "notice the convulsed orange inch of moon . . . ", the bathos of the last line is all too characteristic. These are not merely youthful lapses: examples could be multiplied from the poems, and the Introduction's self-identification with the aging Renoir faintly and frailly stinks. Yet the basic antithesis of today is less that of good *v* bad taste than that of taste *v* no-taste. Cummings, like the Italians, has, admirably, *a lot of* taste; it is merely regrettable that some of it is bad. But the bad is quite compensated for by a complete absence of the fashionable "perfect gray."

The accusation of undue limitation of subject, however, begins, by 1938, to carry much more weight. True enough, spring, love and death are large and universal subjects; but to make them a complete universe of discourse begins to suggest, after some sixteen years, a certain lack of sensibility, imagination, and courage. Especially in the bulk of a collected volume, there becomes apparent a cloying quality, a monotony of mere lusciousness, however spectacularly successful. It is yet somewhat early to assume, however, that Cummings's interests will never as consciously expand beyond this frame as they have to date been deliberately confined within it. One's ***Collected Poems*** often signalize the termination of a period. If at his present age he does not break through this eggshell into the world, he will remain, regrettably, a magnificent but minor singer; it is not impertinent to hope, however, that his present maturity will produce, with the impact of broader (and, after all, somewhat more interesting) experience upon this alert, sinewed and lusty talent, some further and deeper conclusion, beyond love-is-enough. (pp. 62-3)

Philip Horton and Sherry Mangan, "Two Views of Cummings," in Partisan Review, *Vol. IV, No. 6, Spring, 1938, pp. 58-63.*

"Gertrude Stein who had been much impressed by *The Enormous Room* said that Cummings did not copy, he was the natural heir of the New England tradition with its aridity and its sterility, but also with its individuality."

—The Autobiography of Alice B. Toklas

Babette Deutsch

> :dearmrcummings it is

late
r than you th
ink ;printersink s
print
ingdownand sp (o)
ill
ing(
ver)
the
page doesnt
excite or delight us
the same way anymore ;not
that we ask you to
stop (look Listen)
drinking
at the pierian sp
ring(aroundarosie)
;but you must be
careful or you will get
all
!wet
we also admire
win-
tree trunk leaf sky & sn
wfl
akes ;prettygirls littlechildr
en-
during moons sl
O wtwi
lights flowers & loves brief
mercies
;and we like your
impudent balla
dry
;but
it is
nineteenfortyone mrcummings
,and you must forgive us
if we sometimes
y
aaaw
n
;because it is
appallingly
late.
hell is a thirsty place
and only
a draught from the top of
helicon will do ;we are not asking you for
something new ,simply
few
and (er
)or better
?poems

Babette Deutsch, "e. e. cummingsesq," in The Nation, *New York, Vol. 152, No. 20, May 17, 1941, p. 591.*

S. V. Baum

Since the publication of his first book of poems, ***Tulips and Chimneys,*** in 1923, E. E. Cummings has served as the indispensable whipping boy for those who are outraged by the nature of modern poetry. Each time a protest becomes necessary, several lines are wrenched from a poem by Cummings to furnish conclusive proof that his is the work of a trickster who delights in offending sense; the poetic sample offered for examination is invariably a jumble of disjointed words and scattered punctuation. The accusers contend on the basis of such evidence that Cummings must bow to punishment and that with him must bow the rest of the "obscurantists."

The difficulty in judging the whole output of a poet by a fragment of a part does not seem to discourage castigations directed against Cummings in particular. He has been singled out for attack again and again. A glance at any Cummings volume suggests the advantages of using him in preference to any of his so-called confreres. Each printed page discloses such violation of order that the reader is shocked: words are stretched out vertically and horizontally; capital letters jump up where they do not belong; punctuation marks intrude irregularly; lacunae appear within and between lines. Because order has been violated, it is concluded that meaning, its dependent variable, has been destroyed at the same time. And a poem without meaning is nonsense.

This disruption of established order, from the beginning, has been the focal point of the disapproving attitude toward Cummings. The substance of his poetry has been well understood and appreciated, but the typographic disarrangement characteristic of his writing has been condemned as extraneous to the matter involved. In reviewing ***Tulips and Chimneys,*** Harriet Monroe, at that time editor of *Poetry,* prefaced her critical reception of his poetic exuberance with: "Mr. Cummings has an eccentric system of typography which, in our opinion, has nothing to do with the poem, but intrudes itself irritatingly, like scratched or blurred spectacles, between it and the reader's mind." A later review of the same book commented:

> His typography is so perverse that the reader is scared off before he has gone very far. The puzzle of his punctuation is not even an amusing one; it certainly is not worth solving.

This attitude, which separates form from matter in Cummings's poetry, has persisted in varying degrees among critics. Yet an overall examination of Cummings's work reveals his denial of external authority in its many aspects, for from every point of view and in every style he expounds the basic idea of individualism, the ultimate value in all his writing. (pp. 70-1)

[In Cummings' poetry from ***Tulips and Chimneys*** to ***Xaipe,*** all] experience has been ordered according to his moral standard and has consequently been reduced to two groups. The first is that of the lyric affirmative, equations of IS which make for this individual joy—the bird, the bud, the love of two human beings. While asserting the truth and beauty of these qualities which total aliveness, he has also been tasked to express the falseness and evil of the sterile negatives which threaten to despoil the store of individual lyricism and so to reduce being to not-being. In this way he has set himself up in firm opposition to the negative pronunciamento of tradition, governments and political ideologies, advertising agencies—in each case challenging and violating convention and the established order. In defense of this vital quality of being, Cummings has had to evolve a manner of writing which would communicate concrete sensations and perceptions in all the immediacy with which they are experienced.

In perceiving the world with full awareness, each man stands in momentary relationship with life, for everything whirls past him in never-ending change. When the moment has passed, it will never be repeated and can never be exactly matched. The poet's responsibility is to set down without falsification this single fragment of time. The difficulty arises in the poet's grappling with the experience of the poem so as to make it as concentrated and intense as possible and yet to produce the immediacy and directness which one would draw from the experience itself. The very use of language creates an unfaithfulness, for conventional syntax is historical, that is, it is based on an arrangement of thoughts, feelings, and sensations already completed. When the poet uses words, he enters into the confinement of time, and temporal order is imposed upon the experience of the moment, destroying the simultaneity of its complex. There is no order to the momentary perception; it is a sudden explosion during which all one's senses are attacked at once. To arrange the elements of this explosion in some sort of chronological sequence would be a serious breach of honesty. Campaigning against the prosaic characteristics of existence, what he calls *un-ness,* Cummings has felt compelled to violate the conventions of language as well: the stereotypes of syntax and parts of speech, which are symbols of submission to language. Most of all, he has felt a need to put punctuation and typography to fresh use so that they fulfill a dynamic function by approximating the sensations being recorded. This manner of expressing his insights and intense feelings has become so peculiarly his own that Marianne Moore in speaking of his poetry was reminded of "the corkscrew twists, the infinitude of dots, the sumptuous perpendicular appearance of Kufic script" [see *CLC,* Vol. 12]. (pp. 72-3)

To extract "a set of well-ordered conventions" [see previous excerpt by R. P. Blackmur] from the body of Cummings's poetic mannerisms is an assignment equal to founding order within disorder. Such an attempt bears an ironic content, for of all modern poets Cummings most virulently objects to the rash intruder who weighs and measures the lines of his poetry, pointing out examples of instances. And yet the paradox exists whereby Cummings has found his greatest share of appreciation among the scrutinizers rather than among readers innocent of literary sophistication. The factor most likely bearing weight against the poet is determined resistance to his unfamiliar technique. Consequently, the only measure which can relieve this opposition is to probe the body of his poetry in search of the *how* and *why,* systematically grouping instances of violation until such disorder assumes the shape of order and regularity. (p. 74)

In his use of space alone Cummings applies the devotion of a virtuoso. Stanzaic divisions, line breakage, and word relationships are freely varied for the indication of auditory rhythms. Ordinarily, formal indentation can be either a guide to rhyming pairs of words or else a sign that the first part of a line is missing. Under Cummings's direction such indentations denote musical rests of varying value. . . .

"Each printed page discloses such violation of order that the reader is shocked: words are stretched out vertically and horizontally; capital letters jump up where they do not belong; punctuation marks intrude irregularly; lacunae appear within and between lines."

—S. V. Baum

When the purpose of his poem so demands, Cummings will isolate a word in naked exactitude and emphasis from the rest of the poem. . . .

In a discussion of Cummings's use of space one must also consider his practice of fragmentizing a word so that its parts are spread over several lines. Frequently, punctuation marks will be inserted as additional controls. The total effect of such word breaking is to slow up the tempo of reading, an application of his complex system of pauses and rests. . . .

Occasionally Cummings will use one of the word-fragments as a separate whole. In such a case, not only has the word been broken in order to serve as a time-control, but one or more of its parts stands as an independent attributive with much the same function as that of a pun. . . .

Just as Cummings has special purpose in mind when he breaks words, so, too, there is a reason for his neglecting to observe spacing. The compounding of words acts to quicken the tempo . . . where the gradation of increasing volume is expressed with the compression of time by the expedient of running words together and by making the explosion leap up in capital letters. . . .

More frequently, the use of compound words expresses telescoped imagery. It is this device which Cummings used so often in ***Eimi*** to secure the vividness of the passing scene:

> (past now float he—shes chiselled from darkness,
> slicesofnight with greyrockfaces—also)once,
> a spoolhat priest with a bellhat(all got up fit
> to, why it's . . . with redder than orange than
> redorange petticoats)bride.
>
> . . . out
> of the black this which of
> one street leaps quick
> squirmthicklying lu
>
> minous night
> mare

Sometimes this imagery is telescoped so tightly that a portmanteau word is the result, as in *untheknowndulous s/pring,* which combines *unknown spring* with the sheen and movement of *undulous spring.* (pp. 75-8)

It has been seen that when Cummings wishes to provide a major check to the tempo of his poem, he gains a long pause by spacing. The presence of punctuation marks in his poetry is important in the same sense as well. The poet has commonly been charged with punctuating his verses with a pepper shaker, but all of these marks act as minor time-controls. . . . The parallel relationship of spacing and punctuation is verified by consideration of the final two lines of:

> . . . in the battered
> bodies the odd unlovely
> souls struggle slowly and writhe
> like caught.brave:flies;

(p. 78)

One of the most important elements in Cummings's technique of immediacy is the set of parenthetical marks. Because of his extreme honesty as a poet he has been compelled to describe the complex unit of experience without the presence of falsifying temporal order. Perception of the moment involves many impressions, none complete in itself; instead, they blur and overlap one into the other. In order to catch the effect of "all-at-oneness," Cummings inserts some part of the experience within the boundaries of parentheses and so suggests the simultaneousness of imagery. . . .

Cummings ordinarily uses parentheses in pairs, but he will occasionally set down only the opening or closing mark. This incompletion creates the impression that the poem is but a recorded fragment of a larger continuum, most of which has been deliberately omitted. In this way, he brings the suggestion of the unsaid into the poem. (pp. 79-81)

Objection has frequently been made to Cummings's "indiscriminate" use of capital letters. Academic procedure obligates the poet to capitalize the initial letter in every line and the pronoun *I* wherever it may occur. Along with other modernist poets Cummings feels justified in rejecting the initial capital letter on the basis that he may not necessarily wish to give that word the poetic emphasis such capitalization implies. And if he were to observe this academic regulation, how might he emphasize the first word in a line if it had already been burdened with a capital? Hence, a capital letter is to Cummings another mark of emphasis which he may use even within the body of a word to point out part of its action and to give it new force and vigor. . . .

By rejecting the pronoun *I* Cummings assumes a casual humility. The detachment of *i* is much more to his liking; it dissociates the author from the speaker of the poem, leaving him free to assign emphasis where he feels it truly belongs. (pp. 81-2)

S. V. Baum, "E. E. Cummings: The Technique of Immediacy," in South Atlantic Quarterly, *Vol. 53, No. 1, January, 1954, pp. 70-88.*

Roy Harvey Pearce

[*Portions of the essay excerpted below were originally published in the* Yale Review *in March, 1952.*]

[E. E. Cummings's] subject has always explicitly been himself. Saluting him in 1946, William Carlos Williams wrote, "I think of Cummings as Robinson Crusoe at the moment when he first saw the print of a naked human foot in the sand. That . . . implied a new language—and a readjustment of conscience." Cummings' poetry, however, constitutes a variation on the Crusoe motif, since it is his own foot which has made that print. He said of himself in 1953: "I am someone who proudly and humbly affirms that love is the mystery-of-mysteries, and that nothing measurable matters 'a very good God damn' ".

Self-transcendence through love: the poems praise this and try to bring it about, and they despise all that would prevent it. Still, self-transcendence turns out to be only self-realization.

Their mode is for the most part hyperconsciously lyrical, and their forms are such as to save the lyrical impulse for the modern world, in spite of the modern world. Thus their construction is postulated on a simplistic, deliberately "unsophisticated" concentration upon the effects—perhaps "affects" is a better word—proper to them. The devices are well-known; they proliferate and vary mightily; yet they do not represent any large range of inventive powers, nor, I suspect, are they meant to. A reader is forced into awareness of the poems as "behaving" as poems should—in such a way as to inhibit the "normal" tendency to generalize and to predicate: to do, in fact, what the words I am now writing are intended to do. Thus the poems are made to misbehave. Typographically, they are set up on a page so as to force us to attend to the quality of an individual experience as it is occurring. One way of forcing awareness in these poems is by seeking out the anti-poetic and exhibiting the poetry immanent in it—which is to say, transcending its anti-poetry. So there are poems on supposedly degraded sexual love, self-consciously tough-tender—many, many of these; and in straining for effect, Cummings is too often like a Bret Harte come to the Village, his sentimental subject the Luck of Patchen Street. What saves the poems—for they often are saved—is Cummings' good humor, his knowledge that only the most sacred things of the self can be kidded and still remain sacred. The end of the poems is to register joy, any kind of joy; and the source of joy is always in the uniqueness of the self. So, in general, the poems are attempts to define individuated experience in such a way as to show that its only end is realization of self. (pp. 359-60)

Correspondingly, there are the poems which satirize men whose selves, in some of their postures, no man should respect. I give two short examples:

> what does little Ernest croon
> in his death at afternoon?
> (kow dow r 2 bul retoinis
> wus de woids uf lil Oinis

and:

> mr u will not be missed
> who as an anthologist
> sold the many on the few
> not excluding mr u

And there are the poems in which the health and well-being of sex is determined as it can be comically celebrated—for example:

she being Brand
yes the little fish gambol as glad as can be
(yes the mountains are dancing together)

Here language has been restored to the feeling self from which, as Cummings thinks, it has been too long absent. The poems are excessively "verbal" (as Cummings proudly declared in the prefatory note in 1926 to ***is 5,*** although I would think "structural" a better word). They move in such a way that their predictions violate (but only to extend) normal predications. (Thus: 2 X 2 is 5, if only a poem can make it so.)

There are, I think, strict limitations to what can be done with such exclusively "verbal" (or "structural") devices. The limitations are those which result from a shortening of perspective, so that the poem is meant to be autonomous in a way which it simply cannot be. Reading through the bulk of Cummings' work, one begins to feel that what he is reading is so often mere technique; and the feeling is an unhappy one, because the poems are intended to make us envisage a man who is in the process of showing us how we may avoid being victimized and manipulated, and therefore depersonalized, by "mere" technique. The poems themselves become manipulative, that is to say. Consequently, those whose experiences on which they center become only occasions for the manipulation. What results is the Harte-like sentimentalism on which I have already remarked, as here in the opening lines of a poem whose closing lines I have already quoted:

you shall above all things be glad and young.
For if you're young,whatever life you wear

it will become you;and if you are glad
whatever's living will yourself become.
Girlboys may nothing more than boygirls need:

The burden of meaning is put upon "girlboys/boygirls." But the meaning is achieved only by the oxymoronic manipulation of two words out of their regular functions in the structure of our language. At the center of the poem is not a newly created entity, but just structural-linguistic fancy-work. So the emotional import of the poem, and its "moral" too, is not defined but rather irresponsibly stimulated. So too with such inventions as "manunkind" and "nonlecture," in which the poet would transform the word by the simple device of negating it semantically. Such negation—a negation also characteristic of Cummings as comic, satiric poet—is perhaps the other side of the coin from sentimentality, since in both cases the word's intrinsic meaning, found to be humanly inadequate, is not transported into that better world the poet would make, but simply left behind, kicked into senselessness. The poet has his way utterly, and he cannot summon up even the minimal self-discipline which is necessary if he is wholly to communicate his new self-transcending (or self-realizing) insight into his world. Words are un- rather than redefined in the poems. If the medium as it exists is indeed contaminated, yet the poet's cure for it is often worse than the disease. Such are the risks run when poetics becomes a mode of linguistic anarchy. (pp. 361-65)

Still, the poetics, like the anarchy, has its viability. We can know that viability in politics when we read Cummings' prose ***Eimi, The Enormous Room,*** and even his loving introduction to a collection of *Krazy Kat* comic strips. (Cummings, of course, is all for Krazy, since she is all for love.) There are enough poems to make us know it as a purely personal viability, even as we know its ultimate irresponsibility and so will not quite entrust ourselves to it:

(While you and i have lips and voices which
are for kissing and to sing with
who cares if some oneeyed son of a bitch
invents an instrument to measure Spring with?

At least for an instant, there is self-realization, if only at the level of saying: I'm Cummings. So far he has not had it in him to say, with Emily Dickinson: "I'm Nobody! Who are you?" (pp. 365-66)

Roy Harvey Pearce, "The Modern Age (2): Talent and the Individualist Tradition," in his The Continuity of American Poetry, *Princeton University Press, 1961, pp. 335-75.*

William Carlos Williams

[*Williams was one of America's most renowned twentieth-century poets. In the essay excerpted below, originally published in* Arts Digest *on December 1, 1954, Williams offers an appreciation for Cummings's paintings and poetry.*]

The paintings of E. E. Cummings coming from a man better known as a poet you would expect to be genre, topical, more than otherwise, to be characterized as "literary" as were those of the Pre-Raphaelites for instance. That they are not is the difference between the nineteenth and twentieth centures; we know today that painting is related to paint rather than words and Cummings has emphasized that distinction among us as much as anyone. But unfortunately you have a feeling that all the paintings of this artist could as well have been expressed in a poem, that is why he has remained an amateur—thank God.

I recall a box of strawberries which if they were not addressed completely to the taste were not expressed at all, a Greekish simplicity, you could almost eat them. You do not feel, or should not, like eating a painting but looking at it, devouring it with the *eyes.* I think it is what the paintings literally *say* that is important to Mr. Cummings. That can be of no importance to a painter, only the design—and the color, the same thing, the inarticulate design. And Mr. Cummings is of all things articulate.

It is his virtue, to the very placing of a semicolon or the dotting of an i; let us make the most of it. It marks him as New England bred and a product of its schoolmasterly tradition.

The paintings offer a great variety of subjects but always (not always) on the intimate side, sensitively interpreted, what you would expect of a poet of his verbal dexterity. (p. 233)

When it comes to the poems (to say nothing of the prose, which is not considered here), Cummings presents us with a far different front from that of which until now I have been speaking. This is the work of a major artist.

The collected poems ***(Poems 1923-1954)*** which I hold in my hand is an impressive book of 468 airy looking pages with a photograph of the author, full face, on the cover grasping himself, lightly, by the throat. The expression is serious, he is looking directly at you as if he were saying that you do what he has suggested only with more effective purpose. Or you might read the poems, which prayerfully he hopes—if you lack the intelligence to absorb them—may have the indicated effect.

I have had at least five of Cummings's books on my shelves for many years. I did have a sixth but I got so mad at it that in spite of the fact that my wife had made me a present of it at my request I tore it up and burned it; at least it had that much virtue in it and I shall never, in the present mode, cut me into small pieces and feed me to the dogs, "reveal its name." One more book, a handsome one, I keep in my grandmother's trunk in the attic, ***ViVa,*** happening on it whenever I go there in search of something else. I do not have his first book of poems, ***Tulips and Chimneys,*** much to my regret.

These are the works of a lyric poet. They could well all be called "songs" for they sing themselves to the ear, for the most part, beautifully; a lyric poet with a weakness for the sonnet which (if you can recognize it) you will find scattered through all the books.

Cummings is celebrated after all for the unconventionality of his punctuation and phrasing. You cannot mistake his page to have been written in anything but the American dialect. The scenes and persons he celebrates, with a dash, are from the life he sees about him. In spite of what they say and what the Red Cross may pretend, soldiers still go to war with "trumpet clap and syphilis."

Anything which forces the eye or the voice to revalue what it contemplates on the page (as in the case of Leonardo or any other artist) is Cummings's meat. For by such maneuvers the attention is tied to what is being said or you might miss it. All very well, you say, what of it? Save that if you continue to read, you have to do PRECISELY what he wants you to do, *i.e.,* use your wits and your eyes CORRECTLY. That is all, save that you will be rewarded for your pains by a vision of loveliness and not be deceived or cheated in any way. He has a New England conscience that can be most exasperating. In fact he is a veritable Puritan with his pornography whenever he is forced to use it.

From ***1 x 1*** (***One Times One***):

nonsun blob a
cold to
skylessness
sticking fire

my are your
are birds our all
and one gone
away the they

leaf of ghosts some
few creep there
here or on
unearth

The above is quoted to make an example of it, for Cummings is said to be difficult, if you can understand one poem you can understand all.

What in the world are you to make of this poem? Because when you are a critic you are definitely not a poet. I'll show you.

It is, definitely, a composition (a conventional composition)—it has to be for the lines are arranged regularly. In fact they are arranged in the form of a quatrain: four lines followed by four lines. That is always something.

Each of these groups of four lines is followed by another to which it is similar. In what is it similar to the one that precedes it? It is like the one that precedes it in the organization of its rhythmical sequence; that is what (musically) it means. Poems are like that.

Therefore it is a poem and not for anything the lines *say.*

It is thrilling thus to have the lines reft of sense and returned to music.

It is marvelous to be so intoxicatedly loosed along the page. We (as all poets feel) are free to cut diagonally across the page as if it were a field of daisies to lie down among them when the sun is shining "to loaf at our ease."

E. E. Cummings, like Bobby Burns, is intoxicated by women as this poem attests and that is what the poem means. But his women must have the manners of quatrains and be governed by that music (not that they must always be that way) if they are to captivate him. That is my criticism of him and of his poem; great virtues.

Over and over he says the same thing, but the meaning gets lost, often, among the punctuation, try as "i" will to make it plain and try as hard as I can "i" cannot make it plainer that it doesn't mean anything what "i" say but what "i" do (on the page) that is the meaning.

Is that plain—and dancing enough?

"The play's the thing" but Cummings is not a playboy, he means what he dances: *da capo al fin.*

Oh! I forgot to say that there have been eight or ten books written since his first book ***The Enormous Room,*** a book I would have called, but for the French writer, Artaud, a masterpiece. ***Tulips and Chimneys*** began the poems memorably. We who read that will not forget it. Then came in succession: ***XLI Poems; &; is 5;*** the play—***Him;*** By E. E. Cummings (no title); ***CIOPW; ViVa; Eimi*** (prose); ***No Thanks; Tom;. . . Collected Poems; 50 Poems; 1 x 1;*** and the present volume.

Take hope, all ye who enter here, for you will certainly be lost—and amused and fascinated by much beauty. You will not have Virgil for your guide for in fact he would not fit here as Catullus might. I could not speak either for Ariel for the atmosphere smells much too earthy and Cummings himself can be earthy, if you know what I mean.

It reminds me of a story I heard recently about a very shy

young woman who when an older woman, whom she had met at a tea, was announcing how embarrassed she felt over her hands being so grimy spoke up:

> I know how you can get them clean.
> How? Inquired the lady.
> Make a pie.

(pp. 234-37)

William Carlos Williams, "E. E. Cummings's Paintings and Poems (1954)," in his A Recognizable Image: William Carlos Williams on Art and Artists, *edited by Bram Dijkstra, New Directions, 1978, pp. 233-37.*

John Clendenning

Although E. E. Cummings was certainly a modern poet, he was not, properly speaking, a modernist. The sensibility of T. S. Eliot which dominated the twenty years of Cummings' greatest productivity and which formulated the principles and themes of modernism—such as, the objective correlative, the suppression of individuality, the quest for religious certitude, and the sterility of contemporary society—failed to affect Cummings' verse in any significant respect. This failure, indeed, did not escape the attention of Eliot's followers, for if anyone might have supposed that Cummings belonged to the modernist club, no one could doubt that his membership was publicly denied by R. P. Blackmur's "Notes on E. E. Cummings' Language" [see excerpt above]. Though more than thirty years old, this essay still forces reactions from Cummings' critics, both friends and enemies. Indeed, one might say that Blackmur's essay has fared as well as Cummings' poems: the essay and the poems represent two extremes in modern poetic and critical practice. Having completely absorbed Eliot's notion about tradition and talent, Blackmur argued that Cummings is "the extreme form, in poetry, of romantic egoism." This poetry is sentimental, childish, abstract, idiosyncratic, imprecise, unique, unconventional, anti-cultural. In short, Cummings sets down the bare emotions of chaotic experiences in vague language without the attention due to the conventions which alone make human utterances meaningful.

Without wholly accepting the modernist line, one may, at the outset, agree with Blackmur on several points. Some of Cummings' lyric celebrations reveal the worst kind of sentimentality and triteness:

> you are like the snow only
> purer fleeter, like the rain
> only sweeter frailer . . .

Equally offensive is the sentimentality of some of Cummings' "Chansons Innocentes," which are occasionally displays of mere childishness:

> little tree
> little silent Christmas tree
> you are so little
> you are more like a flower
>
> who found you in the greenforest
> and were you very sorry to come away?

Certainly one may love children without calling their every remark a poem. Similarly, one may face the everyday questions of sex without gracing each vulgar sentence with the dignity of poetry. For instance, I am convinced that "squeeze your nuts and open your face" is not poetry. The same dissatisfaction can be charged to most of Cummings' so-called "tough" poems. Unless any casual statement is poetry, this is not:

> suddenly
> i feels so lonely fer duh good ole days we
> spent in '18 kicking duh guts outa dem
> doity frogeaters an humpin duh
> swell janes on
> duh boollevares . . .

Again, one may agree with Blackmur that Cummings' verse is often remarkably unintelligent. I suspect that not all scholars are rotting, not all politicians are asses, not all Englishmen are dull, not all scientists are proud, dull, or destructive. Finally, one may sometimes become justifiably impatient with Cummings' idiosyncratic devices. One of his poems, if read aloud without regard to typographical peculiarities, is "black against white sky trees which from dropped leaf a goes whirling." These twelve trivial words are given twenty lines and a sprinkling of various marks of punctuation, parentheses, and capitalization. The typography renders the poem so difficult to visualize that the pleasure that comes from reading it is dangerously like playing scrabble. And having played the game, I doubt that the reward is equal to the effort.

There are, therefore, valid grounds for Blackmur's criticism. If taken poem by poem, Cummings' work is extremely uneven; many, even most of his verses may deservedly be forgotten. But by objecting to particular poems, one does not agree with Blackmur, for he has argued from a general principle, the rule of thumb that originality leads to inferior art. I doubt the utility of this principle, which has become a cornerstone, indeed the extreme form, in critical writing, of modernism. Were the principle applied, the best American poets—Taylor, Whitman, and Emily Dickinson, for example—would deserve our scorn. I insist that Cummings' uniqueness of mind and technique has enriched American verse. Just as the most fruitful efforts in American poetry have resulted from originality, so most of Cummings' successes were accomplished through his innovations.

No one understood his differences from the modernists better than Cummings himself. Four years, in fact, before Blackmur's essay appeared, Cummings denied his adherence to the group. In the foreword to ***is 5,*** the fourth volume of his verse, he provided a statement about his technique:

> At least my theory of technique, if I have one, is very far from original; nor is it complicated. I can express it in fifteen words, by quoting the Eternal Question and Immortal Answer of burlesk, viz. "Would you hit a woman with a child?—No, I'd hit her with a brick."

Whereas complication of technique has been typical of modernist poetry, Cummings here insisted on the simplicity of his verse. To be sure, he also denied his originality, but he clearly identified his technique with the tradition of American humor, not that of English poetry. The basis of his craft, Cummings suggested, is the surprise ending, the shocking detail, the double-take. Throughout an earlier century, humorists, particularly the literary comedians, persisted with the same device. One remembers, for example, Josh Billings' quip, "i never knew an auctioneer to lie unless it was absolutely convenient." Billings fully recognized that novelty and surprise are vital in American culture: "Sumthing new, sumthing startling iz necessary for us az a people, and it don't make mutch matter what it iz. . . . " Cummings agreed. His poetic enterprise, being clearly opposed to the Eliot-Blackmur argument for tradition, was a search for a new language and a new order that will shock, startle, and awaken the reader to an immediate perception. His work, like much of American literature that has been enriched by our native humor, employs surprise—sometimes at the expense of concrete diction—to achieve the immediacy that most good poems provide.

This surprise technique can be observed most clearly when it pertains to diction. The addition of a startling word can seize the reader's attention, causing an insight otherwise impossible:

> the Cambridge ladies who live in furnished souls
> are unbeautiful and have comfortable minds

"Souls" and "minds," despite their abstract meanings, are made clear by virtue of their startling presence in this context. After "furnished" the reader expects to see "homes" or "rooms," certainly not "souls." After "comfortable" one expects "chairs" or "beds," not "minds." The surprise words ridicule the ladies' triviality, their conservatism, their materialism, their social formalism. Combination of words similar to these are common in Cummings' work; often they achieve a union of poignant lyricism and rich humor: "night gargles windows," "looked long at the sticky moon," "leap into the ripe air."

A similar, though more radical use of surprise diction is accomplished through shifting of grammatical forms. One of Cummings' early poems began, "Spring is like a perhaps hand." The comparison of spring and hand is itself a surprising one, but the addition of "perhaps" used as a noun modifier excites this line with a paradox. Hands, ordinarily, are material and present, whereas "perhaps" is tenuous and future. A "perhaps hand" is one that promises to be, or one that anticipates itself. The simile is an excellent one, for spring is precisely the time of new life and the expectation of more, the substantial accomplishment and the insubstantial desire. The compression and the arresting effect provided by this grammar shift make the complex images and ideas of the poem clear and immediate. Some of Cummings' most successful passages use the same device. For instance, by shifting adjectives, verbs, and nouns to adverbs, he described eternity with lyrical acceptance:

> little by little and was by was
>
> all by all and deep by deep
> and more by more they dream their sleep

The absence of sentimentality in these lines results from Cummings' surprising innovations in diction. Being surprised, the reader reflects as well as feels, smiles as well as comprehends Cummings' sentiment. This balancing of tone by means of juxtaposing sentiment with surprise is typical of Cummings' use of grammatical shifts. As he demonstrated, the possible shifts are profuse. . . .

In all of these innovations, the surprise technique underscores these meanings. American humorists never employed precisely these devices, but Cummings shared with them a common motive: to hit the audience with a brick.

This exploiting of native humor is not unique with Cummings' verse. Long ago, Constance Rourke in her *American Humor* demonstrated that American poets have persistently found in our native humor a source of enrichment. Richard Chase has emphasized the same point in his books on Whitman and Dickinson. No critic, however, has recognized Cummings' place in this tradition. Indeed, in their use of surprise techniques, Emily Dickinson and E. E. Cummings were remarkably similar poets. Cummings' **"perhaps hand"** was preceded by Dickinson's "Acres of Perhaps." His **"slowly./town"** was preceded by her "Dimity Convictions." His **"featherly"** was preceded by her "New Englandly." Of course, Cummings' surprises were more common and more radical; where she broke the rules, he crushed them. But though they shared a common technique, no proof of influence is necessary. He did not need her poems as models, for each learned his craft from the same source.

Most of Cummings' other technical inventions were also designed to surprise the reader. Typographical arrangements, word fusions, and capitalizations often seize the attention and produce the double-take effect. Like the nineteenth-century literary comedians, Cummings sometimes used peculiar typography for visual surprises. (pp. 44-9)

So far, I have discussed Cummings' poetic techniques as they were applied to specific words, phrases, and lines. I hope that I have demonstrated that Cummings' use of comic devices can and often does lead to brilliance. However, no poet's work can earn an ultimate defense on such a fragmentary basis. Whole poems must be considered. Unfortunately, many of Cummings' poems are structural failures: they merely evoke images, utter sentiments, lampoon some public figures. Often one doubts that Cummings was able to organize and sustain a poetic idea. On the other hand, he has written dozens of admirably developed poems, the most successful of which are his sonnets. Perhaps his formless originality needed the sonnet's disciplinary structures; perhaps the sonnet was an ideal form for his basically lyric temper. Whatever the reason, Cummings' sonnets (he wrote more than 160) are among the best, if they are not simply the best, ever written by an American poet. (p. 50)

To be sure, Blackmur identified Cummings' triteness, sentimentality, and vulgarity in particular poems. However, the modernists' doctrines have not been equal to Cummings' accomplishments, and these are considerable. A too restricted concept of tradition prevented Blackmur from acknowledging Cummings' adherence to American traditions of experiment, originality, and humor. On the other hand, critics have failed to emphasize Cummings' successful handling of conventional patterns, like the sonnet. Furthermore, Cummings' best poems show him to be neither a fool nor a sentimentalist. . . .

Cummings, in short, was a poet with sense and sensibility, with precision and innovation, and now that he is dead, like the rain, the leaves, and the sky, his poems, the many fine ones that he left, must endure and prevail over their critics. (pp. 52-3)

John Clendenning, "Cummings, comedy, and criticism," in The Colorado Quarterly, *Vol. 12, No. 1, Summer, 1963, pp. 44-53.*

Hyatt H. Waggoner

Transcendentalism seemed remote, obscure; an "impossible" view for a poet to hold, all during Cummings' lifetime. When, some twenty years after he began to write, critics discovered that Cummings was "Romantic," they used their discovery as a way of dismissing him as irrelevant, if they happened not to like his work; or else apologized for him, defending his right to be "irresponsible" if he wished, if they happened to like it. Even Norman Friedman, whose pioneering critical study of Cummings is sympathetic and helpful, felt it necessary, as we have seen, to keep on adding other adjectives after starting with "transcendental," as though "prelapsarian," "organic," and so on were not all implied by "Transcendentalism" itself [see *CLC,* Vol. 12].

What Cummings thought he was up to had been made clear first of all in ***The Enormous Room,*** in 1922, and then in five volumes of poetry between that time and the date of ***Eimi,*** and then once again more explicitly in that book, from which I shall . . . quote. In the passage that follows, a conversation is recorded between Henry Wadsworth Longfellow Dana (unnamed in the book, for obvious reasons), Boston Brahmin turned Marxist, and Cummings, Boston Unitarian speaking as a Boston Unitarian. "Q" in what follows stands for Dana, "A" for Cummings:

> Q: The whole trouble with you is that, like so many people who were brought up on religion, you can't bear the idea of anything doing away with it.
>
> A: Can't bear the idea of any what doing away with which?
>
> Q: Of science doing away with religion.
>
> A: I see: we're supposed to suppose that the new religion, science, does away with religion, the old religion—tahk.
>
> Q: (snorts): How can you be so perverse!
>
> A: I?
>
> Q: As if religion and science weren't direct opposites!
>
> A: Right you are, colonel: every coin has two sides.
>
> Q: Odear. There you go, utterly confusing the issue—

E. E. Cummings: Self-Portrait in Blue Tie. Oil on Cardboard, May 1958. R. W. Davidson Collection.

> A: Issue? We've all tried paying with one side and keeping the other side for ourselves, haven't we?
>
> Q: But, my dear chap—can't you possibly be serious?
>
> A: I'm afraid I'm being much too serious, comrade.
>
> Q: No you're not—you're being extremely trivial and very childish and rather cheaply amusing.
>
> A: And I'm quoting Emerson.
>
> Q: Emerson?
>
> A: "When me you fly, I am the wings."
>
> Q: Who said that?
>
> A: Brahma, the sage of Concord, who (inconsiderately) went to Rome and found—
>
> Q: O, of course . . . but to return to our muttons. What you can't seem to realise is this: religion imprisons the human mind, whereas science makes people free.

> A: What I can seem to realise is that I'd just as soon be imprisoned in freedom as free in a jail—if that's any help.
>
> Q: You simply won't be serious, will you.

This was in 1933. When, years later, Cummings first went to Brown University to lecture, at the behest of his classmate S. Foster Damon, and was introduced by Winfield Townley Scott as a New England poet in the unbroken line extending from Emerson and Thoreau through Dickinson and Robinson, he was particularly pleased to be called "a direct heir and descendant of the great New Englanders." No wonder, for to be so described was equivalent to being called a true son of his parents, and fidelity to *them* is the burden of the first three of the six Harvard lectures. Cummings inherited his tradition from his home and made a lifelong career out of the juggling feat of keeping intact what he had been given, while still moving on. The feat was rendered less difficult for him than it might have been by the fact that the Emersonian doctrines of self-reliance and self-transcendence were major tenets in the teaching of his father, the Reverend Edward Cummings, a highly successful, respected, and nationally known Unitarian minister.

For Cummings, being faithful to his personal past, and particularly to the much-loved father, meant continuing to believe in the future. There was no need for him to rebel against a father who taught as articles of faith the independence, freedom, and growth of the self. John Dos Passos, recalling his visits to the Cummings home on Irving Street in Cambridge in his Harvard student days, has stressed the way "the oldfashioned Cambridge household" seemed to provide a link with the past: "I've cherished my recollection of it as a link with the Jameses and all the generations of old New England back to Emerson and Thoreau . . . Cummings improvising on the piano for the edification of his admiring family. Dr. Cummings booming from the pulpit . . ." William James, Cummings tells us in the Harvard lectures, was his father's favorite neighbor— "so true a friend and so great a human being"—and the one to whom Cummings said he might be said to owe his "existence," since it was James who introduced his father to his mother.

Cummings did not say, but might have, that culturally also he owed much to James, and to the atmosphere James both symbolized and embodied. For it was William James more than anyone else in that time and that place who kept alive Emerson's chief meanings and motives, even while he subtly modified some of them as his openness to the evidence seemed to require. Cummings preferred the unmodified to the modified meanings. His poetry and prose give us the purest example of undiluted Emersonianism our century has yet provided. In his Introduction to the new poems included in ***Collected Poems*** (1938) Cummings had placed himself unequivocally in the Emersonian tradition, but there has been a subsequent failure of even his most sympathetic interpreters to understand this. The paradox must be explained by the fact that in the recent past critics young enough and "modern" enough to be interested in Cummings have had no real firsthand and extensive knowledge of Emerson. "We can never be born enough," Cummings had said. "We are human beings; for whom birth is a supremely welcome mystery, the mystery of growing: the mystery which happens only and whenever we are faithful to ourselves." He had turned, then, to the negations of scientific philosophy and its "parlour-game of real unreality," to the "neutralization of nature" (he did not use the phrase) which I have been tracing through the works of so many of his contemporaries as the "given" from which their work took its departure. Dismissing "the modern temper" sarcastically, as accepted by "mostpeople" but not worthy of consideration by those who, like himself, refused to be defined as anything less than a transcendent person, an illimitable self, sensuous, sensual, healthily *alive,* but no mere "lookiesoundiefeelietastiesmellie," or behaviorist automaton, Cummings had affirmed (whatever "science" may say) that the "self" is a "citizen of immortality." I have partially "normalized" the pointing of Cummings' words.

> Miracles are to come. With you I leave a remembrance of miracles: they are by somebody who can love and who shall be continually reborn, a human being; . . . Nothing believed or doubted; brain over heart, surface: nowhere hating or to fear; shadow, mind without soul. Only how measureless cool flames of making; only each other building always distinct selves of mutual entirely opening; only alive. Never the murdered finalities of wherewhen and yesno, impotent nongames of wrongright and rightwrong; never to gain or pause, never the soft adventure of undoom, greedy anguishes and cringing ecstasies of inexistence; never to rest and never to have: only to grow.
>
> Always the beautiful answer who asks a more beautiful question.

To anyone familiar with Emerson's "Circles," it should have been clear many years ago that there was no emphasis or attitude here, not even the refusal to put a period at the end, that had not been foreshadowed in the essay—by which I do not mean to suggest that Cummings necessarily *knew* the essay. The only reference to Emerson in Cummings that I know of is the one . . . from ***Eimi,*** where he is referring to the poetry, to "Brahma" in particular. When a biographer finally tells us what Cummings read, it may turn out that he absorbed much of his Emersonianism—the part he did not get from his father—through Whitman. If so, that fact would add another link to the many that connect him with his friend and fellow-rebel Hart Crane.

What is true of Cummings' "metaphysic" is equally true of other aspects of his stance as man and writer. His epistemology is "intuitive" precisely in the Emersonian sense, with the same suspicion of abstraction, the same unconcern for consistency and "mere logic" and "mere fact," the same hope of seeing as with a "transparent eyeball," the same method of preparing oneself to receive nature's epiphanies by relaxed "aesthetic" attention. His aesthetic is exactly as Platonic, and just as organic, as Emerson's, with the same conception of poetry as a means of suggesting what must otherwise remain incommunicable, the same belief that the "argument" (as Emerson called it) must shape the poem, and the same search for a language "of sufficient energy" (as Emerson had put it) to convey the vision.

Cummings' mystical antinomianism is a part of the same inheritance, resting on the same Protestant religious base and issuing in the same suspicion of all moral rules, especially the *don'ts,* of society's "conspiracy" against the individual; in the same belief in the betrayal of spirit involved in the *letter* of every doctrine, every dogma, every conventional ritual; in the same hostility toward business, politics, and organized reform—toward the whole "practical," work-a-day world in short; in the same preference for the innocence and instinctive wisdom of children and animals, the product of an undivided self in which body, mind, and spirit function together; in the same insistence on an unmediated relation between the Self and the Absolute. Emerson's "What I must do is all that concerns me, not what the people think," lies behind Cummings' scorn for "mostpeople." Emerson's "I would write on the lintels of the doorpost, *Whim.* I hope it is somewhat better than whim at last, but we cannot spend the day in explanation," if taken quite literally and combined with Cummings' sense of his isolation from the intellectuals of his time, would sufficiently account for the frequent belligerency of his refusal to explain himself in "mostpeople's" terms. Antinomians do not talk the same language as either "religious" or "secular" rationalists.

Apart from his poetry and prose, and the poetry of the great poets of the past whose work he said he loved, Cummings in his Harvard lectures cited only one book. Not surprisingly, that book was the Bible. He read to his audience the whole story of the woman taken in adultery, as told in the Gospel of John, 8, 1-11. He introduced the passage by calling it "this masterpoem of human perception, whose seventh verse alone exterminates all conventional morality." The key words here are "perception," implicitly defined earlier in the sentence as "feeling," as opposed to "knowing and believing and thinking"; and "conventional" before "morality," which assumes the antinomian's equation of "morality" with "moralism." Truth, he implies, is related always to the concrete, the individual, the empiric; it must be "perceived" (Cummings usually said "felt") in the response of the total self to an always-novel experience. To follow "feeling" is thus to run the risk of coming into conflict with the "rules" of "conventional" (read "unperceptive," "unfeeling," "closed" and "rationalistic") morality.

"He who would gather immortal palms must not be hindered by the name of goodness [that is, what *society* calls or names "goodness," the "goodness" of conventional morality], but must explore if it be goodness," Emerson had written in "Self-Reliance" in the middle of a discussion of how far it might be necessary to go to preserve the integrity of the self. When a friend, years before this, had objected that "these impulses may be from below, not from above," Emerson reports himself as having replied, " 'They do not seem to me to be such; but if I am the Devil's child, I will then live from the Devil.' No law can be sacred to me but that of my nature." The *thrust* of this is against late Calvinism and its theology of the Fall, against conventional morality, against all who valued security above growth. But the *basis* of it is a positive faith, not a suspicion or hostility, a positive faith in the "Trustee" of all self-trust: "We lie in the lap of immense intelligence, which makes us receivers of its truth and organs of its activity."

I have let Emerson explain the assumptions that undergird the Transcendental faith in self-reliance because he does it more briefly and coherently than Cummings, partly perhaps because he had a better mind, partly because his stance was not, did not need to be, so defensive, and so he could speak more directly. But the religious faith that supports the self-trust is the same for both poets. Failure to recognize this has thrown more than one critic of Cummings off the track of his meaning. Several decades of having to pay for the publication of his own books and getting reviews that revealed very little comprehension of what he meant were the price Cummings had to pay for his Transcendentalism. Very probably, during the years when he could not get published, Cummings thought of Emerson's idea that, "Society is everywhere in conspiracy against the manhood of every one of its members . . . For nonconformity the world whips you with its displeasure."

If all this seems to imply that Cummings ought to be thought of as the complete and perfect exemplification of Emerson's idea of the "true poet" in the twentieth century, the implication must be denied. All that has been said so far has concerned only the *what* of the poems, not the *how;* and even the *what* has been isolated only in its larger outlines. What, in general, Cummings was saying in his poems, what the tradition of this very traditional "experimental poet" is, what kind of clarity lay behind his so often remarked obscurity—all these *whats* are a necessary preliminary to an intelligent reading of the poems, but preliminary only. They are ways of getting at his "metre-making argument."

Cummings said in the Harvard lectures that "perhaps fifteen" poems really were adequate expressions of his stance as artist and man. Surely the number is much larger than that—I should say he wrote at least twice that many highly successful and uniquely memorable short poems—but the most generous guess would put the number at a small fraction of the total number of poems he committed to print. His ***Poems, 1923-1954*** contains some six hundred poems and was followed by ***95 Poems*** and the posthumous ***73 Poems.*** If a tenth of all these should be thought worth reading by the end of the century, this self-described "failure" will have made it into the ranks of lasting poets, without ever having made any concessions to greater popularity.

Despite his dedication to growth, movement, and inventiveness, despite too his reputation as a daring experimenter in verse forms, Cummings tended to lack inventiveness. He repeated himself, writing hundreds of versions of essentially the same poem, especially in the 1930's, when he felt most deeply alienated from his culture and from most of his colleagues. He relied too much and too often on a few simple tricks to jog the imagination, to wake the reader up and make him participate in the poem. His private typography, for instance, amusing and sometimes expressive at first, became tiresome in the end, like Ezra Pound's reliance on misspelling to create the tone of his letters. His use of low dialect to create satirical effects was too easy and limited a device. His "shaped" poems only now and then benefit very much from being shaped as they are. These and other idiosyncratic stylistic tricks too often seem merely self-indulgent or worse—substitutes for fresh insight.

The chief device was more than a device, and often worked for him very well—his dislocation of syntax and breaking up and reconstituting of words—but even this, though perhaps helpful to other poets in encouraging other kinds of freedom, has not proved, in itself, an experiment from which any other poet has felt he could directly learn anything. It was "more than a device" for Cummings because, for one thing, it was expressive of his feeling that ordinary statement, subject as it is to the conventions of logic and logical syntax, could not contain the feeling-tone of even "ordinary" experience, and could not begin to suggest the sense of the miraculous that he so often wanted to convey. It was functional, for him, for another reason, too; by outraging linguistic convention, it might force that freshness of *perception* he thought was the means to illumination. When he opened a poem with the line "i thank You God for most this amazing," in which "most" modifies both what precedes and what follows—very unsatisfactorily from the point of view of logical clarity of predication—he was emphasizing the nonlogical quality of the statement by the ambiguities of the syntax. "Most" actually intensifies the whole line and also suggests the chief reason why he thanks God: It hovers over "this amazing" to make it move toward being *most* amazing. In this poem, one of his own favorites, the device works, but all too often it seems a rather easy trick.

Cummings' best poems are usually his love poems and his religious poems, both more often than not written as disguised and more or less disarranged sonnets. (Once again, to make minor personal adaptations in an old and rigid form was hardly to be a "daring" experimenter. His friend Williams could not approve.) The love poems are generally, after the 1920's, religious in tone and implication, and the religious poems very often take off from the clue provided by a pair of lovers, so that often the two subjects are hardly, if at all, separable. What makes them memorable at their best is the peculiarly Cummingsesque combination of sensuality and feeling for transcendence. Cummings had no less contempt for a "Platonism" that was not "of this earth" than he had for a "realism" that denied wish-dream. Like Emerson before him, he thought he knew that "God IS" because He could be found—sensed, *felt*—in experience. Cummings wrote some of the finest celebrations of sexual love and of the religious experience of awe and natural piety produced in our century, precisely at a time when it was most unfashionable to write such poems.

By contrast, his poems of social criticism often sound thin and petulant. They are seldom more than amusing, and often not even that. For the most part, they depend upon the stock response and elicit a stock response—not that of Philistia, of course, but that of Bohemia. **"A salesman is an it that stinks, excuse"** is likely to provide "food for thought" only to salesmen who do not read Cummings and have never reflected on the fact that to pretend heartiness and personal warmth for the sake of manipulating the potential customer and thus making a sale is to cease to function as a person and to become an embodiment of economic forces. So with most of Cummings' other satiric poems. They are likely to continue to impress only the very young and the partially read. A poet cannot afford simply to "feel" when writing satiric poems.

It is common today to deny that Cummings developed as a poet, but the denial will hold only if we accept a rigidly intellectualistic or a rigidly formalistic idea of what a poet's "development" must be. It is true that neither in ideas, nor in characteristic style, is there any *great* difference between ***Tulips and Chimneys*** in 1923 and ***73 Poems*** in 1963. There is no sudden reversal of belief such as may be seen in Eliot, no gradual shift from a dazzling impressionism to argument and abstraction, as in Stevens, no turning to another type of poem, as in Robinson. But there is "development," of just the type we ought to hope for from a poet of Cummings' type.

The development is in changing attitudes and deepening awareness, a deepened sense of what it meant to be a Transcendental poet, with a corresponding dropping away of defensive-offensive sallies into ideas and criticism. In the last poems, the old devices are used less wastefully, and the old sense of mystery finds more concrete embodiment. Cummings was always at his best when he was "rendering death and forever with each breathing," but in the end he less often depended on pure rhetoric to give content to his abstractions, his "death," "forever," "breathing." ***95 Poems*** (1958), his finest single volume, will illustrate.

The poems in the book form a loose sequence, something Cummings had often experimented with before, never so successfully, with a metaphoric use of the seasons, reversed from the order in which the "mind of winter" had conceived them, as the basic ordering principle. That is to say, they begin with Fall, go into Winter, and end with Spring. As in Thoreau's organization of *Walden,* Cummings' seasons are "seasons of the soul"—of man's life; so that the Fall poems are poems of old age and approaching death, the Winter poems the poems of death, and the Spring poems the poems of rebirth. At the same time, another organizing principle is being observed. The Fall poems are those of loneliness, of solitude, and of the separated self; the Winter poems are concerned with loss of self; and the Spring poems are concerned with a new "self" which is a "we." In this book, for the first time, Cummings really moves beyond Emerson; for Emerson was apparently never really able to re-learn what "we" means, after the shock and deprivation of the death of Waldo. (pp. 514-23)

Later poems in the volume move through **"THANKSGIVING (1956)"** (with the old brashness and anger dominant once again, as "democracy" refuses help to Hungary), through the beautiful Christmas poem, **"from spiralling ecstatically this,"** through poems of early Spring like the magnificent **"stand with your lover on the ending earth,"** to the last poem in the book, appropriately written in rhythms imitative of swinging in an old-fashioned rope swing in a tree, and in the language of a child—"if up's the word; and a world grows greener." The ideas in this last poem are the ones we have become familiar with, as we are with the poet's adoption of the attitude of the innocent child. But the development of the poet is apparent too—in the increased sense of structure which led him to arrange his book, which he expected to be his last, with this poem at the end; in the controlling metaphor of the swing, which not only orders the language and rhythms of this poem but implies that the book which has thus ended is *about* something which has not ended and will not end; and in the broadening of the appeal at the end from "just the two of us" (the lovers of the early poems) to the "we" which is the last word of the poem, and of the book, and which includes anyone who wants to be included.

Cummings' poetry is romantic, intuitive in precept and in method, and rhetorical as opposed to Imagist-Modernist. It is essentially a "poetry of statement," as Wordsworth's was and as Emerson's was—but very complex, personal, ambiguous, and dense statement, at its best, statement which challenges the reader to complete it by first participating in the making of it and then carrying it on in himself, as his own, the gift to his self of another self. New Critical techniques of analysis do not work with such verse. There is nothing that literary positivism can get hold of—just Emersonian "Primary intuitions" and despised rhetoric to help their transfer. No wonder all the New Critics ignored Cummings for thirty years, except Blackmur, who damned him for not writing the way Ransom and Eliot had taught poets to write, for using general instead of specific words, for being, in short, a "Romantic" poet instead of a Modernist.

Whether Cummings is a "major poet" or not, I should not like to venture even a guess. But that he is a poet to cherish and reread, I should like to assert as strongly as I can. He and Hart Crane were the only important poets in the 1920's and 1930's who clearly and openly continued our major poetic tradition. That Crane's life was deeply troubled and ended in suicide, and that Cummings was perhaps more nostalgic for his childhood than was good for his personal growth, and for his poetry, has nothing to do with the kind of evaluation I am trying to make. When Crane wrote "My hand/ in yours,/ Walt Whitman,/ so—" and Cummings, in his last, posthumous, volume, wrote,

> seeker of truth
>
> follow no path
> all paths lead where
>
> truth is here

both were returning to the fountain. (pp. 524-25)

Hyatt H. Waggoner, The Transcendental and Extraordinary: E. E. Cummings, in his American Poets: From the Puritans to the Present, *Houghton Mifflin Company, 1968, pp. 511-25.*

E. E. Cummings on e. e. cummings:

So ends the last lesson of a nondivisible ignoramus: a double lesson—outwardly and inwardly affirming that, whereas a world rises to fall, a spirit descends to ascend. Now our ignoramus faces the nonanswerable question "who, as a writer, am I?" with which his nonlecturing career began; and finds himself deluged by multitudinous answers. What would these multitudinous answers say if they could speak as a single answer? Possibly or impossibly this—

I am someone who proudly and humbly affirms that love is the mystery-of-mysteries, and that nothing measurable matters "a very good God damn": that "an artist, a man, a failure" is no mere whenfully accreting mechanism, but a givingly eternal complexity—neither some soulless and heartless ultrapredatory infra-animal nor any un-understandingly knowing and believing and thinking automaton, but a naturally and miraculously whole human being—a feelingly illimitable individual; whose only happiness is to transcend himself, whose every agony is to grow.

Ecstasy and anguish, being and becoming; the immortality of the creative imagination and the indomitability of the human spirit—these are the subjects of my final poetry reading: which (I devoutly hope) may not wrong a most marvellous ode by Keats, and the magnificent closing stanzas of Shelley's Prometheus Unbound.

—E. E. Cummings, in his i: six nonlectures, *1953.*

Clive James

[*The essay excerpted below was originally published in March 1969 in* The Review.

[E. E. Cumming's ***Complete Poems, 1923-1962***], will probably remain the essential compilation of the master's work. It adds ***95 Poems*** (1958) and ***73 Poems*** (1963) to what appeared in ***Poems 1923-1954,*** which ended with the last poem of ***XAIPE. . . .***

Doubless more poems will be unearthed in time, and strictly there are whole stretches of Cummings's prose (especially in ***Eimi***) which are poetry in all but name, but for the nonce this is it: the poetry collection of the year and for that matter the decade.

There is no reliable public picture of Cummings and it is doubtful if there will ever be one now. The only full-length study which existed up until the time I stopped following the secondary literature was desperately naïve, wide-eyed in worship, and as a Ph.D. subject he is too "easy": ideas-wise, he can be wrapped up in a couple of thousand words. He exists "only" as a poetic personality, in the sense that the small amount of information available concerning his life fails to enrich (i.e., contradict) the picture you get from the attitudes he strikes in his work. As a figure eating ordinary food and breathing the air of this green earth, he can be reliably caught only in age-old sketches by Edmund Wilson and a few lesser figures, sketches in which he makes momentary appearances to talk faster and more brilliantly than anyone else before abruptly departing. No argument for the essential unity of art and intellect, the compatibility of the intuitive and the considered statement and the schematic goal-achievement of an extended creative act is complete without a consideration of Cummings's ability to resist any such notions. His relevance to formal intellect was the relevance of a high-speed tap-dancer or a totally committed whore, both of whom he could admire and celebrate, with each of whom he was temperamentally at one.

As ideas, Cummings's themes lead to immobility when they don't lead to Broadway. He pushes a concept of individuality which would render civilization impossible to carry on, and his formulae for sexual spontaneity attained their apotheosis with Carol Lynley reading aloud from "Puella Mea" to her straight-arrow boy-friend in the movie version of *Under the Yum-Yum Tree.* But of course the ideas were never meant to be ideas. Like Lawrence, Cummings was extremely insistent, and often tedious, on the opposition of sexual expression and abstract thought but, unlike Lawrence's, Cummings's statements on the subject can't be picked off the page without going off in your hand. They are present in this life only as art, and rarely try to stop being art: where they do, as in his blurbs for his own books and the burlesques he once contributed to *Vanity Fair,* the hyperbole is monotonous and the conflated language tiresome.

As a poet, Cummings is not open to the accusation that he neglected to bar the way to people who might get him wrong, but it is certainly a pity that the emphasis of his work makes it easy for the superficial critical mind to line him up with the genuinely irrational writers in our time.

Cummings never proposed that intellect should be swept from the world. His retort to such a statement would have been "What world?" and his response to a further elaboration: "You call *this* a world?" As far as Cummings was concerned, the artist's responsibility to the world cannot be discussed, since it cannot even be proposed. Cummings presumed to test and report the quality of life directly, without reference to ideology of any kind. The results were not necessarily naïve. His purely artistic, wholesale rejection of the Soviet Union in the early thirties proved in the end to be personally less damaging than the piecemeal intellectual withdrawal of his contemporaries. ***Eimi*** is at least the equal of Gide's *Retour de l'U.R.S.S.* for prescience based on the creative instinct, and contains by implication everything that Cummings valued in the America he was to needle for the rest of his life. Anyone still rocking with disgusted amusement after Mr. Muggeridge's extraordinary *Observer* review of the reissue of ***The Enormous Room*** might like to compare ***Eimi*** with Mr. Muggeridge's own achievements of that period and decide whether dandies are ever right, even when they are not wrong. The two men reached the same conclusions, but look at the generosity of Cummings's book, the sweep of its pity, the prophetic urgency of its demand for the poetic in the affairs of everyday—you need to have kept your innocence to write like that. (pp. 63-5)

Cummings's poetry splits up into two main lots: poetry celebrating love, and poetry defining, satirizing and discrediting the forces trying to attack it. In the first lot, the love itself ranges from the crystal-clear concentration of a child roller-skating on a sidewalk all the way across to the titanic image of his father—

> so naked for immortal work
> his shoulders marched against the dark

—a picture of honour directly comparable with the figure of Farinata. But the bulk of this side of his work is taken up with poetry about the love between men and women, and this is the poetry most intelligent people think of when they think of Cummings. It, too, splits up: into the frankly randy and the close to holy. Almost everybody is acquainted with at least one Cummings poem of each kind. But Cummings is no nearer being two-faced here than he is anywhere else. He has no Victorian component to his mind and doesn't suffer from a pulsating pornographic vision continually bursting through to sully the serene adoration of the beloved. Nor is there any post-Victorian component: no compulsory freedom, no screwing to prove a point. It is all as unstudied, yet fully as entranced with itself, as the little girl roller-skating over the expansion strips between the slabs of cement. He simply thinks (or simply writes, if you prefer to believe he is fibbing) of a continuum between the lady lusted after as pure gash and the lady contemplated as a divine revelation: the same lady, and, in some of his really remarkable poems, at the same moment. And it seems to me that he is very successful at this, that his raunchy poems are as cleanly good as Herrick's, that his sacred ones have an affinity with the *dolce stil novo* in its most highly refined form and that he succeeded during his long creative life in joining something up which before his advent had seemed irreparably broken. In the best of the latter-day love sequences in English—Meredith's and Hardy's, to take two outstanding examples—you are given the lady on the human scale, and on the whole human scale, and are glad for the boldness. But Cummings managed something different and more difficult. Whether deeply versed in, or merely acquainted with, the sacred tradition in the love-song (I suspect deeply versed: he was well-read in several of the modern languages as well as both the classical), he succeeded in duplicating its singing voice of dedication, and produced love poems of which the greatest are comparable, even in divinity, with Dante and Petrarch. It is well known by now that Cummings's randier poems are in constant use on campuses across the English-speaking world for seducing girls. But there is a possibility, too, that his sacred poems might first seduce the seducer, making him realize that what breathes beneath him has a soul. Cummings was powerfully influenced by the figure of Beatrice and disguised as a child, a dancer or a disintegrating old slag she is in his poems often: camouflaged but not secularized. When, in **"She Being Brand,"** he describes a deflowering in the terminology of a test-drive in a Rolls, you are immediately in roaring company with the Herrick who dreamed of his own metamorphosis into a laurel and woke to find himself the proud owner of an erection and the copious results of a wet dream. But when he writes, in **"it may not always be so; and i say,"**

> Then shall i turn my face, and hear one bird
> sing terribly afar in the lost lands.

you are not far from the Dante who had pushed the thematic frontier of the *stil novo* all the way to the staggering moment when Beatrice turns her silent smile from the poet to the Godhead. Whether Cummings in real life did or did not experience this continuity of feminine matter and universal spirit I have no means of knowing (Mr. Muggeridge uniquely suggests that Cummings might have been a queer), but in the best of his love poetry his implacable creative drive towards establishing exactly that continuity ignites a cluster of stellar points numerous and radiant enough to form a Milky Way of divine goodwill. Like Yeats, he learned a good deal from Dowson about how to write majestically: majesty means pomp and pomp needs drill. Sonnet III of "Sonnets—Unrealities" in ***Tulip and Chimneys*** is a concentration of every effect in Dowson's technical book and it can be recommended as an example of how one great poet masters another's mechanics in order to be with him in spirit. Cummings turned Dowson's tone of voice away from doom towards exaltation and from frustration to fulfilment. Also he liked *big* girls. But the sense of dedication is the same.

As an example of toughly articulated benevolence, the pagan lovesong elevated to sublimity through tenderness, there is hardly anything in this century which will bear comparison with Cummings's love poetry except the very best products of Tin Pan Alley. And as his successes are Tin Pan Alley's successes—simplicity, self-definition, formal drive, the phrase pointed to revivify the words within it—so his failures are Tin Pan Alley's failures—sentimentality, self-parody, the limpidity that gels too soon. Reading Cummings through now, I skip about 60 per cent of his love poems, since they are adequately covered by the other 40. It's a failure-rate considerably smaller than that with which any song writer is content to live: eventual repetitiveness is the inevitable penalty for being plain from the beginning. In his love poetry alone he wrote himself at least seven tickets to immortality: **"when thou hast taken thy last applause, and when"**; **"it may not always be so; and i say"**; **"this is the garden: colours come and go"**; **"who's most afraid of death? thou art of him"**; **"somewhere i have never travelled, gladly beyond"**; **"you shall above all things be glad and young"** and **"hate blows a bubble of despair into."** Scores more of his poems parallel, and scores more again merely parody, these few, but that doesn't make the few vulnerable or the many extraneous. A slim selection of the best wouldn't be much help, since you need to be acquainted with a couple of hundred of the lesser poems to sort out the language difficulties in the thirty or so (counting in the satires) which are really tremendous. In short, Cummings needs real study—not the fake kind, but the kind with generosity built in. It's not enough to be able to trace Cummings's debts to Baudelaire, Flecker and *Krazy Kat,* although that helps.

Cummings's other poetry is mainly a defence of the thematic unity I have just described. Eliot once defined humour as the weapon with which intelligence defends itself: a profound statement in that it described the dynamics of the business by suggesting that humour moves always from a base. Cummings's humour (and his satire is usually funny enough to be dignified by this categorically superior word) moves from a base in his fertile territory of love, and by gruesomely specifying the enemy forces helps convince the reader that the home base is not Cloud-Cuckoo-land but the only viable actuality: you must live in love or else nowhere.

> take it from me kiddo
> believe me
> my country, 'tis of
>
> you, land of the Cluett
> Shirt Boston Garter and Spearmint
> Girl With The Wrigley Eyes (of you
> land of the Arrow Ide
> and Earl &
> Wilson
> Collars) of you i
> sing

And so on in a thousand details, all of them aimed at establishing the "real" as the false: politics, the army, the police, the academy, the science whose microscopes "deify one razor blade into a mountain range." None of this is literary news now, of course, but Cummings paved the way and nobody since has done the job better. The real objection to the bulk of the work of Ginsberg, Ferlinghetti and the rest is that the man who started it all could squeeze their scattered effects into a form and make the whole thing travel like a skilfully aimed custard-pie. The technical difference mirrors the difference in mental makeup, not to say mental intensity: Cummings isn't kidding. He really loathes what they are half in love with. His field of observation is broad enough and deep enough to get the detail right, but the detail is not *loving* detail: a concentration of Menckenese at its very best, his invective is a roar of pain. And again like Mencken's, Cummings's pain is founded on a knowledge of the past, of what has always been valuable. Cummings was superbly educated, he had his measures of excellence and he was not at sea. He knew exactly what he did not want. There is no element, in his condemnation, of complicity in what he condemns. Unlike his successors, he is deeply rational and it is only through complete trust in his own rationality that he is able to condemn intellect. There is not a trace of mysticism in him: he proposes no dualisms, but simply asserts the divine as the sole level of reality and perpetual revelation as the only mode of vision. Cummings, as well as bringing a tradition into being, was winding one up: a New England tradition, and hence a European tradition, and hence a tradition of civilization in the West. He is far closer to Catullus than he is to a man like Ginsberg. The old way was all *perizia,* and Cummings takes that to pretty near the limit. The new way is all *Dummheit:* a new start, a new rate of speaking for a world growing to look like Los Angeles—a speech clumsily spectacular, semi-constructed, half articulate, a bit thick. In this world the intensity, and above all the *velocity,* of an intelligence like Cummings's will be close to incomprehensible.

Cummings's love poetry is beautiful on the one hand, and his attacking poetry explosive on the other, because of a sense of form trained up high and punishingly maintained. He rewrote the sonnet form as a jazz solo in which the tag phrase jolts what you have been hearing into rhythmic intelligibility. Treating the whole sonnet as a rhythmic unit and using its traditional inner partitions only to lean against for a quick intake of breath, he avoided the usual caboose effect of squeaky couplets, quatrains or sestets tugged along behind. His sonnets finish so strongly that it is a fair guess to say he wrote them from the bottom up: certainly he hardly ever let the formal requirements trap him into a forced thought. Working for him always, in this and in any other form, was a strictly sensational capacity to propel a line: the special feature of Cummings's technique is not typography but kinetics. . . .

Cummings's diction was often self-indulgent (as Edmund Wilson pointed out at the beginning, Cummings overworked the long "i"), his super-precise-looking adverbs were often only padding, but the impetus of his line remained a miracle from first to last. Except for some largish poems early on, he never used a form bigger than he could control in a single rhythmic breath, but the alterations of pace within that rhythmic unit were, in the jazzman's sense of the word, ridiculous. In a sense he was *too* good. Able to move anything at any pace, he was tempted to move hunks of nothing like a rocket, and you come across fast-travelling assemblages which have velocity but no momentum.

Cummings's true technical triumphs were all sonic. Except where they freed him into new areas of audio effect, his typographical tricks—the Apollinaire-raids—were an irrelevance. They gave courage to a generation of bad poetry, they give courage to bad poetry still, but they came from the graphic, merely talented side of his mind and were very limited in their poetic usefulness. The "concrete" effects can always be related to the theme, but only mechanically. "Moon" is just as suggestive a way as "mOOn" of writing "moon." Cummings was dedicated to typographical innovation all his life and set great store by meticulously indirect layout. He will be remembered for little of this: he can no more be credited with it as an invention than held responsible for the damage it has since caused. Several of Cummings's pages of alphabet soup . . . are really exploded sonnets. Put them back together and you quickly find they are not as good as the sonnets he was careful to leave in one piece.

A more troublesome technical point concerns his syntactical effects, which are numerous enough to constitute a private language and render his poetry virtually untranslatable. . . .

Cummings is quite clear and quite consistent in his untiring use of such effects, which are misleading only if you attempt to do a prac. crit. on single poems and neglect to read him entire. The real trouble with his syntax starts when whole poems are made up of nothing but negatively or tangentially defined concepts hemming in a falsely thrilling platitude. This poem is one of the neater examples:

when god decided to invent
everything he took one
breath bigger than a circus tent
and everything began

when man determined to destroy
himself he picked the was
of shall and finding only why
smashed it into because

The circus tent saves the day for the first stanza, but it takes more than a passing acquaintance with Cummings's work to make sense of the second, and by the time you have acquired a certain familiarity you are well aware that this is the side of Cummings which needs to be left alone to die off by itself. Probably it will be pummelled to death in brainless articles for *PMLA* circa 1990. But this is an extreme example and with steady reading his use of such devices becomes perfectly clear. As it becomes clear, it tends to become tedious. Like his typography, this component in Cummings's use of language did its work by making him feel special as he slogged on. Now that he is dead its importance should very much lessen. Young poets who admire him will always betray themselves by echoing this sort of thing, but really it is a mannerism and can't be followed. Caught up in his commitment to the unique, Cummings was often a mannerist—but at least it was his own manner.

Cummings's satirical poems, with their crazy-quilt diapering of billboard slogans, campaign buttons and patriotic clichés now long forgotten, have a receptivity to the emergent American idiom which reminds us that his vital development was contemporaneous with the gradual appearance of that great repository of informal poetry, Mencken's *American Language.* As Valéry once suggested, the language itself is the real poem. As a contributor to this poem, any bus-conductor with an authentic gift for swearing has the edge on the darling of the literary society. Cummings measured himself against the anonymous contributors to the language, to joy, to the traditions of skill: balloon men, good-time girls, strippers, whores, acrobats who climb on ladders of swords, dancing elephants. Of the small amount of his poetry which is perfect we can say that it is good enough for its author's name to be forgotten in safety. Of the large amount which is less so, we can say that it needs understanding in the light of its author's manifest intentions, and that these intentions were lifegiving, basically sane, lyrically inspired and good. He also measured himself against the finest poets of the near and far past, prepared himself to join them, and is with them now. (pp. 66-73)

Clive James, "An Instrument to Measure Spring With," in his First Reactions: Critical Essays, 1968-1979, *Alfred A. Knopf, 1980, pp. 63-73.*

Malcolm Cowley

[*Cowley was a prominent American critic during much of the twentieth century. In the following excerpt, Cowley positions Cummings as a literary heir of Ralph Waldo Emerson.*]

In the years from 1923 to 1926 Cummings published four books of poetry: ***Tulips and Chimneys, &*** (he wore his titles cut short), ***XLI Poems,*** and ***Is 5.*** Many or most of the poems in all four were written either at college or during the burst of activity and experiment that followed his release from the detention barracks at La Ferté, but the first and the last book stand somewhat apart from the other two. In ***Tulips and Chimneys*** there are some of his recent experiments, but there are also earlier long pieces full of oriental or medieval color, and these seem utterly traditional in their effort to be exotic. Only one of them has life in it, **"All in green went my love riding,"** a lyrical ballad that is a gifted exercise in Preraphaelitism. The fourth book, ***Is 5,*** contains many satirical pieces written in what seems to have been a new manner for Cummings. **"Poem, or Beauty Hurts Mr. Vinal," "she being Brand-new," "workingman with hand so hairy-sturdy," "my sweet old etcetera":** these and others deal mostly with contemporary subjects, using catch phrases and advertising slogans that are strictly of the time (as note "pretty littleliverpill-hearted-Nujolneeding-There's-A-Reason americans" in the diatribe against Harold Vinal, a harmless lyric poet from Maine); yet their wit and their headlong rhythms give them an inner life that makes them nearly indestructible. Among all the books of poetry that Cummings published, ***Is 5*** is still the liveliest.

None of the first four books was a popular success. The audience for poetry was even smaller at the time than in earlier and later periods, and most of it shared Mr. Vinal's taste for conventional beauty. With Cummings the critics were severe: they condemned his fleshly realism, his experiments with typography, and his custom of using a small "i" for the first-personal pronoun. "e. e. cummings" they called him, with a visible curl of the lip. But the more his work was condemned by critics, the more it was admired by many of the younger writers and the more he was adopted as one of their spokesmen, along with Dos Passos and Hemingway. Fitzgerald had been the first spokesman, but rebels lost faith in him when he appeared too often in *The Saturday Evening Post.* Cummings too was making a keep-alive compromise, by writing prose pieces for *Vanity Fair,* but most of these were signed with a pseudonym. As for his private life, he kept it private, and that added to his prestige. (pp. 337-38)

[The second of Cummings's ***i: six nonlectures*** contains very few [passages] in which he used the pronoun "we" as referring to any group larger than the one composed of the poet and his love. Usually other groups were "they," alien and hostile. But "we," meaning his generation, were reckless persons who liked to accept a challenge, and "we" sometimes gambled with death simply "for fun" and to reaffirm our joy in being alive. That is surely a theme or feeling that pervaded the 1920's; an adolescent feeling, if you will—Cummings makes that concession to critics—but one to which he looked back in the 1950's with a continuing sense of we-ness.

The 1920's had other favorite themes and one is amazed, in rereading his early work, to find how often Cummings expressed them. Of course he was a lyric poet in the bad-boy tradition, broadly speaking, of Catullus and Villon and Verlaine. Of course he kept returning to the standard lyrical subjects of love, death, April, and the special quality of a moment. But traditional as he was on one side of his work, and determinedly unique on another, he was also a man of his generation. Much oftener than one might expect, he said what other young writers were saying at the time, or would soon be saying, and he usually said it with more ingenuity and morning freshness.

I won't revert to themes directly connected with his adventures in wartime: the feeling that death was omnipresent and life all the more to be enjoyed; the other feeling, for American ambulance drivers, that they were spectators of the greatest show on earth; and the notion that everyone in authority was stupid and that only common soldiers deserved sympathy. All this one finds in his early poems, together with other war-connected themes. More than other postwar writers, Cummings made fun of the big words, especially when spoken by politicians. Better and more amusingly than others he expressed his mistrust of almost everyone over thirty: "o the sweet & aged people who rule this world (and me and you if we're not very careful) . . . OH the bothering dear unnecessary hairless old." But Cummings also wrote poems on other themes that were popular with a whole generation of rebel writers, and here I might give a few examples.

There is first of all the revolt against Victorian standards, especially those prescribing chaste language and chaste behavior. Cummings made himself a leader in the revolt by describing, explicitly and often, the act of sex. Thus, in his second book of poems, &, there are nine rather labored sonnets recording visits to various prostitutes, including "Cecile . . . Alice . . . Loretta, cut the comedy, kid . . . Fran Mag Glad Dorothy."

There is the expatriate theme of praise for "superb and subtle" Paris, with its churches at twilight, its cafés, its streets that "turn young with rain," and its little ladies.

There is the tourist without Baedeker wandering beside his mistress among Roman ruins. "Ponder, darling, these busted statues," he tells her; but then he exhorts her to turn aside from the unimportant past and "instigate constructive horizontal business."

There is the spectator's report on New York as another such Greatest Show as the war had been. Dos Passos embodied the report in a long novel, *Manhattan Transfer,* but Cummings was more succinct:

> by god i want above fourteenth
>
> fifth's deep purring biceps, the mystic screech
> of Broadway, the trivial stink of rich
>
> frail firm asinine life.

There is the supercilious delight in advertising slogans and the habit of using them in poems. Cummings used them only for satire—"what's become of Maeterlinck / now that April's here / (ask the man who owns one / ask Dad, He knows)"—but later Hart Crane and others began to exploit them seriously.

There is the contempt for citizens who lead ordinary lives, "impersons" who accept the slogans at face value.

There is the utter scorn for conventional poets still feeding on the past:

> if we are to believe these gently O sweetly
> melancholy trillers among the thrillers
> these crepuscular violinists among my and your

skyscrapers—Helen & Cleopatra were Just Too
Lovely,
The Snail's On The Thorn enter Morn and
God's
In His andsoforth.

There is the respect for rebels of all sorts, even for Communists in those early days. Thus, in his report of a Paris demonstration broken up by the police, Cummings says that "the communists have fine eyes . . . none look alike," whereas the police, "tidiyum, are very tidiyum reassuringly similar."

There is compassion for outcasts, not excluding the drunk lying in his pool of vomit as people carefully step around him, and there is the feeling that poets are outcasts too, for all their pride. "why are these pipples taking their hets off?" Cummings asks in an idiom borrowed from Krazy Kat of his favorite comic strip. He answers:

the king & queen
alighting from their limousine
inhabit the Hotel Meurice(whereas
i live in a garret and eat aspirine)

There is finally the deep strain of anti-intellectualism that I have already mentioned. Among its manifestations is a prejudice against scientists and "prurient philosophers" who poke and prod the earth, combined with praise for a child's direct vision that sees the earth as "mud-luscious" and "puddle-wonderful."

There is, in fact, almost every theme that was to be widely treated by new writers in the 1920's, except for Hemingway's theme of giving and accepting death, and Fitzgerald's theme of the betrayed suitor for the very soul of money. Cummings spoke of money not often and then with the disdain of a barefoot friar. Besides the themes he treated, his poems embody various attitudes that lay behind them: the passion for reckless experiment in life and art, the feeling that a writer's duty was to be unique, and the simple determination to enjoy each moment and to make the most of having been born. In spite of his aloofness, it is no wonder at all that the rebel writers had come to regard him as an indispensable spokesman for their cause.

The question in the middle 1920's was what Cummings would do next.

His next work, to our surprise, was for the theatre and it was not so much a play as a brilliant vaudeville. ***Him*** (1927) was abused by the drama critics, but it was deliriously enjoyed by the younger people in the audience. Once again Cummings had spoken for them, and ***Him*** is in fact so much "of the twenties"—in the attitudes it reveals toward women, politics, Negroes (here admired for their sexual freedom), and the life of art—that it has seldom or never been revived. During the original production by the Provincetown Players, the very small auditorium was crowded every night, but the production was expensive, the Players were losing money they didn't have, and the piece had to be withdrawn after a few weeks. Cummings went back to painting and to writing verse.

A new book of poems, ***VV*** (which he also called **"Viva"**), appeared in 1931 and was a mild disappointment to his readers. Mostly the book deals with the same themes as his earlier work, but it is less exuberant than ***Is 5***—much less of a hurrah than the title promises—and it speaks less directly for the poet's generation. There is a growing bitterness in the satires directed against politicians, generals, and run-of-the-mine people. The bitterest of all has proved to be the most enduring: it is the ballad of blond Olaf, the conscientious objector who is prodded with bayonets, then beaten to death while repeating "I will not kiss your f.ing flag." As a general thing, however, the development revealed in the book is a matter much less of tone than of technique.

Although Cummings's technique is a confusing subject, one argued back and forth since his poems first appeared in *The Dial,* much of it depends on the elaboration of a few devices that are fairly simple in themselves. Too much of it so depends, a reader may end by feeling. The two principal devices employed in ***VV*** had appeared at times in his earlier work, but here he carries them both to extremes. One is the calligram—or picture writing, to use a more general term—and the other is the word scramble, which might also be called the cryptogram. Cummings's use of the two devices has been discussed more than once, and I do not propose to resume the discussion here. It is enough to say that when he combines calligram with cryptogram, as he sometimes does in ***VV,*** the result in three or four cases is something beyond my ability to decipher. Even worse, a deciphered statement may be one that Cummings has made elsewhere, in plainer words, and thus it leaves a reader with the impression that his time and the poet's have both been wasted. ***VV*** is the most ingenious of Cummings's books, but—aside from the ballad of blond Olaf, a tribute to the poet's mother, and a few other moving poems—it is by far the least successful.

On the technical side, however, ***VV*** gives more than a hint of two additional devices that the poet was to cultivate more intensively in his later books. One of these is his use of negative terms—especially those formed by the prefixes "un-," "im-," and "not-" and the suffix "-less"—to imply special shades of meaning. In **"Poem XLII,"** for instance, he speaks of an "upward deep most invincible unthing," which I should take to be a spiritual essence. **"Poem LXVII"** tells of watching "unhands perform what mimicry," and here I don't know exactly what he means, although "unhands" would be a sinister word in Cummings's idiom. In later books one finds a host of such expressions: "an undream of anaesthetized impersons," "a notalive undead too-nearishness," "unfools unfree / undeaths who live," "till unwish returns on its unself," and the adjective "whereless," one that might pass into general usage. The poet says of politicians who want to save the world, "scream, all ye screamers, till your if is up / and vanish under prodigies of un." If such prodigies do not unexist, it is because Cummings has performed them.

The other device is the game he was beginning to play with parts of speech. It is a game with elastic rules or none at all: roughly, any part of speech can be transformed into any other. Verbs, adjectives, pronouns, even some adverbs and conjunctions, are used instead of nouns. Nouns become verbs ("but if a look should *april* me"), or they become adverbs by adding "-ly," or adjectives in the superlative by adding "-est" (thus, instead of writing "most like a girl," Cummings has "girlest").

Adjectives, adverbs, and conjunctions, too, become participles by adding "-ing" ("onlying," "softlying," "whying"); participles become adverbs by adding "-ly" ("kneelingly"). Some of those practices are foreshadowed in ***VV,*** where one finds, for instance, "footprints on the sands of was"—of time, obviously, though "was" in later books becomes "the past." Also in ***VV*** one finds "the smallening World" and "laughtering blocks"—the latter a hideous phrase—as well as "togethering" and "foreverfully," both more effective. In the later books—which include ***50 Poems*** (1940), ***1 x 1*** (1944), ***XAIPE*** ("Rejoice!" 1950), and ***95 Poems*** (1958)—such coined words and transposed parts of speech come close to being a new language. An example in ***50 Poems*** is **"Poem 29"**, of which the first stanza reads:

anyone lived in a pretty how town
(with an up so floating many bells down)
spring summer autumn winter
he sang his didn't he danced his did.

A translation—omitting the second line, which means whatever it means—might be, "The poet lived year by year in an ordinary town, where he sang his negations and danced his affirmations." Need one say that Cummings's new language has a marvelous way of lending strangeness to sometimes rather commonplace statements? It also serves as a means of avoiding various words that he detested. Later in the same poem, when he says that "noone loved him more by more," it is obvious that "noone" is the poet's wife. After his second divorce, Cummings was happily married for nearly thirty years, a fact attested by some of his finest poems, but the word "wife" appears in none of them.

Any words involved in his game with parts of speech acquired a plus or a minus value. Thus, "was" as a noun is minus; "is" and "am" and "become" are plus. "Who" is plus, but "which" is minus, especially when it refers to impersons, and so is the adjective "whichful." "It," another neuter, seems to be the negative of "he" or "him" and leads to "itmaking," a term of utter condemnation. "Where" and "when" are both minus as nouns; "wherelings" and "whenlings" are pitiable people, "sons of unless and children of almost"—one might say the Jukes and Kallikaks of Cummings's world. The honorifics are "here" and "now." "beautiful most is now," he says, and elsewhere, in a fine tribute to his father,

this motionless forgetful where
turned at his glance to shining here.

All such words have become abstractions, and the meanings they imply are ethical and metaphysical. Usually ethics and ontology are fatal subjects for modern poets, but Cummings was feeling impelled to venture into them. The anti-intellectual was about to become, in limited ways, an ideologist. There had been changes in his life and they had led to a number of ideas that were partly new for him and were completely opposed at the time to those held by "mostpeople," as he called the American public. When one looks back at his career, it would seem that he had to invent his new language as the only fresh and serviceable means of expressing the ideas in poetry.

Changes in his life. . . . His father had been killed in a motor accident (at a grade crossing in a blinding snowstorm), his second marriage had broken up, and in 1931 he had made a trip to Russia. This last was a shattering experience, much on the order of Dos Passos's visit to Loyalist Spain in 1937. Cummings wrote a prose book about the trip (***Eimi,*** 1934), which is hard to read because of its pointillist style, but in which the conclusions are forthright. Russia, he reported, was a country racked by fear and suspicion. Living under the shadow of Stalin, Communists were the bigoted defenders of a system that destroys individuals. Soon the same conclusions were being stated in his poems:

every kumrad is a bit
of quite unmitigated hate
(travelling in a futile groove
god knows why
and so do i
(because they are afraid to love

Cummings was not afraid to love, but he hated, too, and his hatred (or call it his feeling of revulsion) circled out from Stalin and his "kumrads" to wider and wider social groups. First to be encompassed were politicians who abetted Communism by making appeals to the same public yearning for a better life. Cummings had always detested politicians, but now he raged against them:

a politician is an arse upon
which everyone has sat except a man

Reformers and crusaders, especially those who supported the New Deal, came next into the circle of aversion:

then up rose pride and up rose pelf
and ghibelline and guelph
and ladios and laddios
(on radios and raddios)
did save man from himself

Growing still wider, the circle was drawn about salesmen of every type: "a salesman is an it that stinks . . . whether it's in lonjewray or shrouds"—a salesman in shrouds being anyone in favor of entering the Second World War on Stalin's side. Labor unions were still another abomination:

when serpents bargain for the right to squirm
and the sun strikes to gain a living wage—
when thorns regard their roses with alarm
and rainbows are insured against old age

—then, Cummings says, "we'll believe in that incredible unanimal mankind." At this point the circle of those rejected has become so wide that it includes almost everyone living except "you and me," that is, the poet, his love, and perhaps a handful of friends.

Not since the trip to Russia had Cummings been a spokesman for his literary generation. Most of its other members—with almost all the younger writers—had been moving in an opposite direction from his. During the 1930's a dream that haunted many was that of joining forces with all the dispossessed and of moving forward shoulder to shoulder into a brighter future. Even Hemingway shared the dream for a time. *To Have and Have Not,* published during the Spanish civil war, has a hero who lives by his own law, but his dying words are "No matter how a man alone ain't got no bloody fucking chance." "It had taken him a long time to get it out," Hemingway adds in his own voice, "and it had taken him all his life to learn it." Steinbeck, a younger man, was more affirmative in *The Grapes of Wrath* (1939): he tells how the mistreated Okies in California acquired a sense of collective purpose, until each of them—as Preacher Casy prophesies before his death—was on the point of becoming only a little piece of "one big soul." Cummings had no patience with this religion of humanity, or with humanity itself. He was to write during the Second World War:

> pity this busy monster manunkind
> not. . . .
>   listen: there's a hell
> of a good universe next door; let's go

Long before that other war, his statements of opinion had begun to seem inopportune and embarrassing. ***Eimi,*** for instance, appeared at a moment when much of the book-reading public was entranced by the Russian Five Year Plan, and it proved to be a commercial disaster. Its publisher rejected Cummings's next book of poems. After extensive travels in manuscript, and with a change in title, this was finally printed at his own expense as ***No Thanks*** (1935). It was dedicated, with no thanks, to fourteen publishers. . . .Cummings's first ***Collected Poems*** (1938) had less trouble in finding a home, and the books that followed had none at all, but I can't remember that they were widely discussed. In the left-wing press, hardly anyone excoriated Cummings or pleaded with him sorrowfully, as some did with Dos Passos; the books were mostly passed over in silence, as if they were social blunders. Perhaps it was the feeling of simply not being heard that made the poet's voice too shrill in some of the later diatribes.

Most of the poems, however, didn't suffer in themselves from his changed opinions, as the later novels of Dos Passos undoubtedly suffered. . . .

Cummings took no interest in historical forces. He was essentially a lyric poet, and in the best of his later work he continued to deal with the traditional lyric themes of love and death, of springtime and the ineffable quality of moments. There was less exuberance than in the early poems, less inventiveness in spite of the game he played with parts of speech, but there was at times more depth, combined with the effort I mentioned to express a coherent attitude, almost a metaphysic.

This last was something that Dr. Edward Cummings would have understood, and indeed it represented, in some measure, a return to the father. Such returns can be traced in the lives of many writers; Dos Passos is one of them, but there are scores of examples from which to choose. How often rebellion against the father—perhaps under the sign of the mother—is revealed in early works, and how often the father's image looms behind the later career! (pp. 339-49)

[If Cummings] too, admired his father more and more, it was obviously not for the social gospel one assumes that the father preached to his congregation at the South Church, Unitarian.

It was for personal qualities: love, kindness, utter independence, and faith based on an inner rightness of feeling:

> Scorning the pomp of must and shall
> my father moved through dooms of feel;
> his anger was as right as rain
> his pity was as green as grain

The New England tradition to which the poet returned was not that of the Unitarians or of the Calvinists, much less of the Come-outers, but that preached by Emerson in the years after he left the pulpit and before he became an Abolitionist. It was the tradition of the autonomous individual standing before God (or the Oversoul), living by universal laws in harmony with nature, obeying an inner voice, and letting society take care of itself. Emerson . . . there is no record that Cummings ever read his essays, yet his ideas had once pervaded the Cambridge air, and Cummings's later poems are Emersonian in more respects than one.

Thus, Emerson in the flush of his thought was an individualist to such an extent that he could not conceive of history as a process involving social systems and masses of people. . . .

For Cummings too, history was supremely unimportant:

> all history's a winter sport or three:
> but were it five,i'd still insist that all
> history is too small for even me;
> for me and you,exceedingly too small.

Here "me and you" are of course the poet and his love, the only group to which Cummings proclaimed his loyalty. He could do so because "me and you" were really not a group; they were "wonderful one times one." For him almost every group of more than two was either mythical or malevolent, or both. "swoop (shrill collective myth) into thy grave," he exclaimed in that same poem. In other poems we read that the state is an "enormous piece of nonsense" and that its citizens (or "sitisn'ts") are a huge "collective pseudobeast / (sans either pain or joy)." Emerson wrote, and Cummings would have agreed, that "Society everywhere is in conspiracy against the manhood of every one of its members." As a rule, however, Emerson expressed less hostility to groups than Cummings did; he simply disregarded them in his scheme of things (while acknowledging the existence of "races," as he called the English and the French; of course what he meant was nations). He was interested in the moral character of each nation, but not at all in its politics. I am sure he would have assented when Cummings said:

> a state submicroscopic is
> compared with pitying terrible
> some alive individual

Cummings also wrote that "there are possible 2½ or improbably 3 individuals every several fat thousand years," and here the echo seems unmistakable. Emerson had said in "The American Scholar," "Men in history, men in the world of to-day, are bugs, are spawn, and are called 'the mass' and 'the herd.' In a century, in a millennium, one or two men; that is to say, one or two approximations to the right state of every man." I can imagine that Emerson would have nodded happily—as Whitman would have nodded too—when Cummings suggested that any man truly alive contains the universe within himself:

(his briefest breathing lives some planet's year,
his longest life's a heartbeat of some sun;
his least unmotion roams the youngest star)

Emerson was more of a mystic, in the technical sense of the word, than most critics have realized, and some of his essays refer explicitly to an "ecstatical state" in which the soul is reunited with the Oversoul. Such a state is to be understood in a famous passage near the beginning of *Nature:* "Standing on the bare ground—my head bathed in the blithe air and uplifted into infinite space—all mean egoism vanishes. I become a transparent eyeball; I am nothing; I see all; the currents of the Universal Being circulate through me; I am part and parcel of God." Time and space being abolished at such moments, the soul is bathed in a higher Reason to be distinguished from mere Understanding. The distinction in Cummings's later poems is between "know" or "because," both contemptuous nouns in his language, and "feel," which is something to be honored (**"my father moved through dooms of feel"**). As for the states of ecstasy, they are possibly foreshadowed in the early poems by Cummings's effort to render the special quality of moments. In later poems that sense of the moment, the now, is so intensified that it comes close to being a mystical vision. "ten centuries of original soon"—that is, of history—are "plunged in eternal now." "dimensionless new alls of joy" flood over the poet as he perceives the "illimitably spiralling candy of tiniest forever." "now the ears of my ears awake," another poem ends, "and now the eyes of my eyes are opened." In passages like these Cummings appears to be writing as the latest—though I suspect not the last—of the New England Transcendentalists.

The parallel can be carried too far. Where Emerson was essentially a Neoplatonist, Cummings was a scoffer in his youth, then more and more a Christian. He does not think of Christ as the most perfect man, in Emerson's way of speaking, but rather prays to him as a divine intercessor. In theological terms his God is less immanent than Emerson's and more transcendent. He says in a poem addressed to God—here I translate into prose—"How should any tasting, touching, hearing, seeing, breathing, merely human being—lifted from the no of all nothing—doubt unimaginable You?" As regards a future life, one of the subjects on which Emerson remained ambiguous, Cummings lets us infer that he believes in the resurrection of the flesh. "our now must come to then," he tells his love in a late sonnet—

our then shall be some darkness during which
fingers are without hands,and i have no
you:and all trees are(any more than each
leafless)its silent in forevering snow

—but never fear(my own,my beautiful
my blossoming)for also then's until

Other poems of the time make it clear that "until," for Cummings, was the moment when lovers shall rise from the grave.

Cummings lived into the late summer of 1962 and continued working to the last day. His career, if not his opinions, had been remarkably self-consistent. Except for his painting, carried on through the years, and except for a few lively incursions into prose—of which ***The Enormous Room*** is the most durable—he had never worked at any trade except that of writing verse. "*Peintre et poète,*" he had told a French policeman who asked his profession before arresting him; I think that was in 1923. Poet and painter—and nothing else—he remained to the end.

He wrote twelve books of poetry, including one that appeared after his death (***73 poems,*** 1963), but not including collected or selected works. The books contain 770 poems in all, an impressive output for a lyric poet and one recalling that of another New Englander, Emily Dickinson. Most of the poems are as short as hers, with perhaps one-fourth of them variations on the traditional fourteen-liner. After the early romantic pieces in ***Tulips and Chimneys,*** Cummings never ventured again into longer forms. Not all the poems are on the same level, and some of the more ingenious ones remind me that there is a drawer in our house full of kitchen gadgets made of stamped tin and wire, all vastly ingenious—U. S. patent applied for—but many of them unworkable and most of them seldom used. Cummings's inventions, too, are sometimes gimcrack and wasted, but the best of them have enriched the common language. The best of his lyrics, early and late, and not a few of the sonnets—more, it seems to me, on each rereading—have a sweep and music and underlying simplicity that make them hard to forget. And where does he stand among the poets of our time? He suffers from comparison with those who built on a larger scale—Eliot, Aiken, Crane, Auden among others—but still he is unsurpassed in his special field, one of the masters.

One may feel that in his later years, when he was groping his way back toward Emerson, Cummings wrote rather more new poems than he had new things to say. He might have been more severe with his work, and with his acolytes, but he had earned the privilege, after all, of being a little self-indulgent. He did not abuse the privilege. Except for those six nonlectures at Harvard, his only concession to the public, and to the need for earning money, was reading his poems aloud to mostly undergraduate audiences in all parts of the country. It required physical courage, for by that time he was partly crippled by arthritis, wore a brace on his back that jutted out two inches from his shoulderblades, and had to read while sitting in a straight-backed kitchen chair. After reading for half an hour, he had to rest for ten minutes; then he came back to finish the program. Nevertheless he held and charmed the audience, which was usually acquainted with his work and well prepared to listen.

He was speaking in the McCarthy years to what had come to be known as the silent generation. Sometimes he scolded the youngsters, as at Harvard, for being obsessed with security. "What is that?" he asked them. "Something negative, undead, suspicious and suspecting; an avarice and an avoidance; a self-surrendering meanness of withdrawal; a numerable complacency and an innumerable cowardice. . . . How monstrous and how feeble seems some unworld which would rather have its too than eat its cake!" The youngsters, cautious as they were at the time, liked to dream about the romantic freedom of the 1920's. They specially enjoyed his early poems, with their recklessness and brio, but they did not object to the conservative Christian anarchism of the later poems. Once again Cummings, the man stubbornly alone, found himself accepted by others as a spokesman. (pp. 349-54)

Malcolm Cowley, "Cummings: One Man Alone," in The Yale Review, *Vol. LXII, No. 3, March, 1973, pp. 332-54.*

John Bayley

A perpetual child, Cummings did like to be understood, and his charm made his friends eager to help and protect him. But in his best poems he is absorbed, like a good child in its toys, and isn't in the least concerned with understanding. The analogy is exact, for the reader must get down with the poet among the building blocks on the floor; it is no good meeting him when he is charming the grown-ups—especially the more sentimental ones—with his cute ways. Auden once wrote that "to grow up does not mean to outgrow either childhood or adolescence but to make use of them in an adult way." By this criterion Cumming's poetic techniques are designed to perpetuate adolescence, both in the poetry and the poet.

Most good poets suffer for their gift and use it to make such suffering visible—to write out the nature of it is to enhance its reality. Cummings uses the gift to retain and maximize the insulation of a happy childhood. Poetry is his toy, but not "his toy, his dream, his rest", as it was for Berryman and Lowell, the plotted and cultivated scenario of an otherwise distracted existence. It is a paradox that although Cumming's typographical dodges seem to be drawing attention to themselves they in fact come off best when they are at their least self-conscious. The poems that are admirable in ***Tulips and Chimneys*** (published in 1922, a memorable year in literary annals) are the series of "Actualities" and "Post Impressions". Sexual experience with ladies like Marj and Lil provided Cummings with the perfect subject for his format: detachment in comic physical involvement, the agilely precarious recording of experience and appearances, even as the poet lies passive in the sleazy, clumsy, but not hostile machine which he is laboriously manipulating. Experience, particularly sexual experience, is like a new American mechanism to be spryly mastered (as in that splendid poem **"she being Brand"**) and the poet in the happiest way is both operator and passive recorder.

All his life Cummings was able to write such poems, but they alternate with the winsome and folksy type which became more common as time went on. Here his best technique goes bad on him; artful verbalization emphasizes rather than remakes cliché, as it often does in the poetry or Dylan Thomas, with which Cummings's has many affinities. (p. 235)

From his Harvard days Cummings had a grounding in the classics—a considerably better one than Pound—and a good teacher had encouraged him to attempt translations, both free and exact. His technical breakthough, which still owed much to Pound and was probably not consciously arrived at, was the discovery that the same idiom would fit any situation. Joyce's grand style adapted itself deliberately to the meanest context, and Cummings's miniatures learned to do the same. A simple example is one of the "Portraits" in ***Tulips and Chimneys,* "i walked the boulevard":**

i saw a dirty child
skating on noisy wheels of joy

pathetic dress fluttering

behind her a mothermonster
with red grumbling face

cluttered in pursuit

pleasantly elephantine

while nearby the father

a thick cheerful man

with majestic bulbous lips
and forlorn piggish hands

joked to a girlish whore

with busy rhythmic mouth
and silly purple eyelids

of how she was with child

There is here the same dependence on a neat "point" which marks all Cummings's successful poetic contraptions, though the point may build up in the poem's shape and not be sprung in the last line. There are contexts like the "war" poems and the semi-political squibs where such a point will not work, and where Cummings's cute cursory innocence does not answer. But point can come in the form of an excellent descriptive conceit, like the sky in **"Impressions II"**, first resolved "by the correct fingers of April" into "a clutter of trite jewels",

now like a moth with stumbling

wings flutters and flops along the
grass collides with trees and
houses and finally
butts into the river

Himself a painter and draughtsman, though of no great originality or power, Cummings at his verbal best often suggests the painterly techniques of the Impressionists and post-Impressionists and their admiration for Japanese art. His verse in fact is at its best when it draws attention not to its own words but to the picture they are bringing into existence. That is the kind of observation that would mean nothing in connection with most poetry, but with Cummings there can be a real sense of space between the words on the page and the mental images evoked. In the best poems, and the ones that best stand re-reading, we seem to slip straight into the mental images. The zestful verbal capers, anthology pieces such as "anyone lived in a pretty how town", have a short reading life: their verbal substance is not of the kind that survives prolonged acquaintance. The poetry is at its worst when the verbal and sentimental are made to play engaging games together, as in "my father moved through dooms of love" or "sons of unless and children of almost".

This indicates a matter of great importance in relation to Joyce's verbal art. *Finnegans Wake* not only remains wholly and eerily alive but it can move us deeply in the simplest way. Joyce has in a sense found the modern way of doing what Dickens did in relation to crossing-sweepers and the deaths of children and Barkis going out with the tide and David Copperfield's vision of his mother holding up her baby in her arms. Cummings often seems to be looking for the modern way of doing such things, and not finding it. It is of course invidious to compare a great writer with a minor verbal artist, but the point is none the less a valid one. Cummings almost never moves us: he is his own child, too self-absorbed.

Almost never, but he approaches tenderness sometimes, as in the "etcetera" poem, in which the word falls through successive slots of meaning—a way of dismissing sentiment, of pushing detail impatiently aside, evading parental exhortation, shrugging off oneself and one's dreams—until it falls into its final and tenderly intimate meaning, all the more tender and intimate for being a euphemism, and earning a capital letter.

> (dreaming,
> et
>   cetera, of
> Your smile
> eyes knees and of your Etcetera)

In general, though, Cummings has none of the artist's sensitivity to the outside world and to the reality of other people and their responses. Nothing shows this more clearly than a small poem which must upset friends and fellow artists, the non-Jews, as is the way with such things, more than the Jews themselves.

> a kike is the most dangerous
> machine as yet Invented
> by even yankee ingenu
> ity (out of a jew, a few
> dead dollars and some twisted laws)
> it comes both prigged and canted

"pricked and cunted" in the original version, which had to be bowdlerized when submitted to the *Quarterly Review of Literature.* It appeared in 1950 in the collection ***Xaipe,*** published by OUP after Cummings's American publishers had declined to continue making losses on his work.

Despite remonstrances Cummings insisted on including it, whipping out his smallboy reaction and protesting that a kike was not a Jew but an American hybrid, which was the point of the poem, and citing his recent experiences in Hollywood ("a wailing wall for Christians") where he had endeared himself to no one and failed to obtain employment. Many Cummings poems, especially in the ***Xaipe*** volume, are wishfully satirical, but to be effectively bitter a satirist must be involved. Memorable open poetry is subversive in its very nature, but a closed poetry cannot go out to subvert. Shock words like "kike" and "nigger" do not quite seem quaint, however, even in our unshockable era; liberal America minded them very much, and perhaps would still do so. The real trouble is that they point to something mean—in both the American and the English sense—in the poet's satiric impulse. As his biographer [Richard S. Kennedy] shrewdly observes, Cummings could only see the world as directed at him and "emblematic" of his situation. So does everyone at times, poets particularly, but while poets like Yeats and Lowell return by this very process to the universal, Cummings remains in his own area of smallness.

Out of it come his own special effects, which are certainly like no one else's. He is a poet for do-it-yourself readers. . . .

[***Complete Poems, 1910-1962***] is austerely and beautifully produced, without notes or introduction, but these are not missed. There are felicities every few pages and once in a while a whole poem that succeeds. (p. 236)

John Bayley, "Mothermonsters and fatherfigures," in The Times Literary Supplement, *No. 4118, March 5, 1982, pp. 235-36.*

FURTHER READING

Friedman, Norman. *E. E. Cummings: The Art of His Poetry.* Baltimore: Johns Hopkins University Press, 1960, 209 p.

Respected study of Cummings's *oeuvre.*

———, ed. *E. E. Cummings: A Collection of Critical Essays.* Englewood Cliffs, N. J.: Prentice-Hall, 1972, 185 p.

Collection of seminal critical essays on Cummings and his poetry.

Kennedy, Richard S. *Dreams in the Mirror: A Biography of E. E. Cummings.* New York: Liveright, 1980, 529 p.

Biography revealing new details on Cummings's life and works.

Rotella, Guy L. *E. E. Cummings: A Reference Guide.* Boston: G. K. Hall, 1979, 212 p.

Annotated bibliography of critical writings on Cummings from 1922 to 1977.

Wegner, Robert E. *The Poetry and Prose of E. E. Cummings.* New York: Harcourt, Brace, 1965, 177 p.

Detailed critical study of Cummings's work.

Ding Ling

1904-1986

(Born Jiang Bingzhi; also transliterated as Chiang Pin-Chin; also wrote under the pseudonym Ting Ling) Chinese short story writer, novelist, editor, and essayist.

Many of Ding Ling's short stories and novels display strongly feminist interests, exploring the conflicts and oppression of women in both traditional and Communist China. The achievements of her highly political literary career include the Stalin Prize for literature, national recognition as one of China's most prominent writers and editors, and influential membership in the Chinese Communist party during its early struggle for power. Her reputation was controversial, however, because of her candid examination of female sexuality and feminist approach to Communism. During anti-intellectual purges, particularly the Cultural Revolution of the 1960s, she vanished from the public eye and was sentenced to hard labor and solitary confinement. Her books were banned—punishment for "immoral," "bourgeois," and "traitorous" elements. Critics who have reviewed her work in translation often conclude that while Ding Ling flourished during the early years of her career, her creativity was limited by harsh censorship during the Cultural Revolution.

Ding Ling was born into a formerly wealthy family in the Hunan province of China. When she was three years old, her father's death left the family with numerous debts, forcing her mother to find work as a teacher. Ding Ling often described her mother as a strong influence on her development of feminist ideas and rejection of traditional lifestyles; it was through her travels with her mother to various schools that she became an enthusiastic social activist, attending numerous student demonstrations and meetings. In 1919, she transferred to a progressive school in Changsha, where she was introduced to modern vernacular literature and Western authors and was encouraged to write. The following year, after refusing to accept an arranged marriage, Ding Ling traveled to Shanghai to attend the People's Girls School, an institute founded by leftist intellectuals. She became dissatisfied with the school, however, and decided to educate herself by studying literature and painting and living a frugal but unrestricted life. She later attended Peking University, where she met a poet named Hu Yepin, who became her common-law husband and the father of her first child. After attempting to support herself as a governess and as a private secretary while Hu Yepin struggled to gain recognition as a poet, Ding Ling impulsively decided to travel to Shanghai to become a movie actress. Although her venture into films failed, the experience became the basis for "Mengke," the short story that launched her literary career.

In "Mengke" (included in Ding Ling's collection *Zai heianzhong*), an energetic and ambitious young woman travels to Shanghai, where she is overwhelmed and demoralized by the dazzling world of filmmaking. Critics emphasized the story's theme of the social degradation and exploitation of women—a frequent motif of Ding Ling's early works. Although Mengke succeeds as a movie star, she senses that she is "selling not just her body but even her soul." The dilemmas faced by young single women is also the focus of "Shafei nüshi de riji" ("Miss Sophie's Diary," also in *Zai heianzhong*), which established Ding Ling as one of China's most celebrated and notorious women writers for its emphasis on sexuality. Intense self-examination is the pervading motif of "Miss Sophie's Diary," which focuses on a high-strung, tubercular young woman who experiences conflicting emotions toward an attractive but superficial young man: "[In] this precious, beautiful form I adore, there resides such a cheap, ordinary soul. . . . " Immersed in an internal battle of contradictory impulses, Miss Sophie feels ultimately degraded by the affair: "All in all, I have wreaked havoc on myself. If a person's enemy is himself, how, oh heavens, can he seek vengeance and indemnity for all his losses?" Many critics asserted that, like many of Ding Ling's early short stories, "Miss Sophie's Diary" highlights the isolation and vulnerability of women who have rejected institutionalized restrictions of marriage, conventional employment, or school. Ysi-tsi Mei Feuerwerker observed: "Although liberated in the sense that they have broken with traditional authority, they lack the economic means and social support needed for any genuine independence. They might be free of the institutionalized oppression of fathers or husbands, but they become all the more vulnerable to the pain of betrayal by lovers or by their own fluctuating emotions."

Although Ding Ling had been actively involved in leftist causes since the 1920s, her commitment to Communism was strengthened following the execution of Hu Yepin by the Nationalist police in 1931. She joined the Communist party, assuming editorship of its major literary journal, and her writing focused increasingly on social injustice and the socialist revolution rather than the plight of introspective and alienated individuals. In 1933, Ding Ling was kidnapped by Nationalist forces and imprisoned for three years, but managed to escape to Yanan, a Communist-controlled Border Region, by disguising herself as a Manchurian soldier. Upon her arrival in Yanan she was welcomed as a Communist hero, and she soon immersed herself in socialist cultural activities, including the Women's League and the Red Literature and Art Association. As editor of the party's newspaper, *The Liberation Daily,* she began publishing critical pieces on society, literature, and art; her essay "Sanbajie you gan" ("Thoughts on March 8") exposed the continued injustices suffered by women living under Communist control. This work was chastised by the Communist party, which increasingly dictated that all literature and art must be subject to party control. Ambiguous presentations, for example, were considered undesirable, and upbeat endings, preferably revealing the triumphs of socialism, were mandatory. Although Ding Ling promised to comply with Communist party standards, her Stalin Prize-winning novel, *Taiyang zhao zai Sangganhe shang* (*The Sun Shines on the Sanggan River*), has been praised for its relative ambiguity and complexity. Based on her involvement in leftist land reform, the work concerns the early phase of collectivization in a small village of about 200 families in northern China. Critics praised her portrayal of agrarian society in conflict, and the people's struggle to maintain traditional customs amid the fundamental changes in social structure caused by land redistribution. Edward A. Gargan stated: "[Ding Ling's] characters were not stereotypically either heroes or villains and her portraits of peasants' lives captured their confusions and frustrations as political concerns intruded into village life for the first time."

Many critics consider *The Sun Shines on the Sanggan River* to be Ding Ling's last work of literary value. The victim of an anti-intellectual campaign in 1957, she was censured for "sexual immorality," "professional failings," "ideological shortcomings," and for "traitorous conspiracy against Communism." The party expelled her, banned her works, revoked her citizenship, and exiled her to the Great Northern Wilderness for twelve years. She was subjected to increased abuse with the onset of the Cultural Revolution in 1966, and in 1970 she was placed in solitary confinement in the notorious Quincheng prison, where she remained for five years. During the late 1970s, Ding Ling was officially rehabilitated and allowed to resume her writing career. Many critics characterized her works following her years of imprisonment as timidly flattering depictions of Communism, and some younger Chinese writers, distressed by her defense of literary censorship, commonly referred to her as "Old Shameful." Others, however, steadfastly defended Ding Ling's later works, asserting that they reflect her genuine embrace of the Communist party's philosophy that the purpose of art is promotion of the common good of the people. In an essay, Ding Ling stated: "I wanted to give myself up totally to the cause of the people, to share their destiny, their cares and their sufferings, to live and die with them."

(See also *Contemporary Authors,* Vol. 118.)

PRINCIPAL WORKS

NOVELS

Wei Hu 1930
Muqin 1933
Taiyang zhao zai Sangganhe shang 1948
[*The Sun Shines on the Sanggan River,* 1954]

SHORT FICTION COLLECTIONS

Zai heianzhong 1928
Zisha riji 1929
Yige nüren 1930
Yigeren de dansheng 1931
Shui 1932
Yehui 1933
Yiwaiji 1936
Suqu de wenyi 1938
Yinian 1939
Wo zai Xiacun de shihou 1943
Shaanbei fengguang 1948
Miss Sophie's Diary and Other Stories 1985

OTHER

I Myself Am a Woman: Selected Writings of Ding Ling (anthology) 1989

Yi-tsi Mei Feuerwerker

With a few exceptions, the thirteen or fourteen stories Ding Ling wrote in 1927-1929 are about lone young women. Away from home, living unconventional lives in the amorphous semimodern city, they appeared to share certain superficial characteristics with their author. Because of this, many of her readers assumed that Ding Ling's stories mirrored in diverse ways the story of her own life—an assumption that was reinforced by the confessional mode of her writing. During this first phase Ding Ling was hardly alone in such literary introspection; indeed, she could easily qualify as a female member of what Leo Lee has called the "romantic generation of modern Chinese writers." The themes of love and sex in her stories, the frequency of patent autobiographical allusions, the focus on the alienated sensitive individual—all would seem to link her to the writers so vividly portrayed in Lee's book.

Yet in some important ways Ding Ling stands apart. Being a woman is not the least of them, particularly since her own critical attitude toward the image of the suffering female restrained her from the kind of sentimental indulgence found in the writings of suffering *male* romantic authors. In her stories the love experience is not so much an excuse for subjective effusions as an occasion for tough moral self-questioning. Characters are, to be sure, in confrontation with the world, but they must also face up to who they are themselves. Her manipulation of fictional points of view allows an interplay of complex and ironic perspectives on personal experiences even when they are drawn from real life. Furthermore her intense exploration of subjectivism in literature during this period soon led her to an exposure of its limits, so that by early 1930 she was moving away from romantic concerns and toward revolutionary commitment, ready to begin the search for a broader arena for literature.

In the three years that Ding Ling concentrated on subjective themes, she succeeded in extending the range of Chinese literature to areas of experience it had never encompassed before. She succeeded, paradoxically, because she was extremely self-centered in her early writing, recording and revealing many aspects of the sensibilities of her own young emergent generation. Our interest in that record, our recognition of its precious quality, is due to its having been, in the long perspective of Chinese literary history, a record that was possible for only a fleeting moment. Before and after the late 1920s confessional writings on the preoccupations of youth were rarely produced in China. Ding Ling's early works seem obsessed with the uncertainties and search for self-definition that characterize youth's first encounters with experience. These stories bear the unmistakable hallmarks of a young writer and are in this respect characteristic of the literature of the early May Fourth era.

Ding Ling's distinction came from the particular revelations she was making about young women. There were a few other women writers, but none achieved her reputation or popularity. A contemporary critic considered Ding Ling's first collection of short stories, ***Zai heianzhong*** (***In the Darkness***), "the best among works by women," because "in style it is different from that of women writers up till now, it points to the actual life and pain of women today, it contains delicate analyses of women's psychology, it creates bold and outspoken descriptions." It was typical of literary criticism of that time to comment on the unprecedented audacity (*dadan*) with which Ding Ling depicted the conditions and emotional states of women; her fame—or perhaps her notoriety—was based on what she was perceived to have dramatically disclosed.

As the transformation of Chinese society began to accelerate in the first decades of the twentieth century, there was a rapid and dramatic shift in the roles of youth and women. Both were becoming the vanguard of revolution in a society that had traditionally been dominated by men and those who were old. Women and youth had less to lose by turning against the world as it was. But rebelling against authority and convention in unprecedented ways, they also had to bear the brunt of violent change. It was not only the novelty of their emergence that attracted new literary attention; the particular social and psychological strains they labored under made them especially interesting subjects.

In comparison with youth, women had been relatively visible in traditional literature, but they had been presented less as subjects in their own right than as objects or images catering to the needs, desires, and projections of a preponderantly male authorship. But now both youth and women were discovered as serious subjects and were achieving sudden prominence in literary works. Among the writers, those who were young, or female, or both, were confronted with two emerging realities, that of the external world, and that of themselves within it. Their writings were a response to the struggle to define this new self-awareness.

Literature assumed an unusually personal meaning for writer and public, and that was the major reason for the extraordinary phenomenon of author-character-reader identification during the romantic generation. In a story Ding Ling wrote in 1930, a writer looking back on his career is ready to give up writing. His readers are

> students of the petty bourgeois class above high school level. They feel that the writing suits their tastes . . . perhaps the events reflect their ideals, the characters seem so lovable, partly resemble themselves. They further believe them to be reincarnations of their author, so they fall in love with the author.

(pp. 19-21)

Even though Ding Ling, in referring to the "May Fourth phase" of her work, always denied that she had been writing about herself, it was the ability to "give voice to the inner feelings" of her readers that seemed to make these repeated denials necessary. Author-character identification may have been proof of the effect she had on her readers, but it also became a burden she was condemned to bear. Almost thirty years later, after Ding Ling's writings had undergone several radical transformations, these early stories were brought back as "evidence" in the campaign against her; her own character was attacked through the characters she created. Throughout the antirightist drive of 1957, the running refrain was that Ding Ling was the incarnation (*huashen*) of her own characters, or, which is of course the same thing, that the characters were incarnations of their author. Even more damning, the image of Ding Ling as a writer/character was fixed by the productions of these first three years—if later characters were negative it was because they were found to exhibit traces of the bad prototypes. Such critically naive or politically calculated blurring of the distinction between life and literature, between autobiography and fiction, plagued Ding Ling throughout much of her literary life. (p. 21)

Ding Ling's first published story, [**"Mengke"**], issued in 1927, is about Mengke, a young woman from the provinces who comes to Shanghai and becomes a movie actress. The story takes off from an actual experience, but the heroine succeeds where her author in real life had failed. Although Ding Ling's purpose in trying out for the movies was to improve a precarious livelihood that depended on uncertain family subsidies and Hu Yepin's pitiful income as a writer, the notion was also inspired by her reading of literature.

According to Shen Congwen, the examples of three women in *La Dame aux Camélias, Madame Bovary,* and *Notre Coeur,* "before helping her write, encouraged her to go to Shanghai." Their stories led her to think, "Wouldn't it be worth it for her to go into that vast, expansive human sea to seek a brand new life in which laughter and tears were mixed together, and take a chance on testing her own destiny?" The venture failed and left Ding Ling filled with contempt for the film industry, but it did bring her for the first time "into serious contact with the realities of life." As Shen puts it:

> A film studio is not unlike a miniature society. Although she was only a spectator, from her spectator position she could learn to know the faces of various social types and their relationships. The loneliness of her position intensified the attention she paid to the conduct and behavior of other kinds of people. While the film company could not make this woman writer into a star of the silver screen, it did teach her a meaningful lesson about life.

The lesson about life becomes material for a story that centers on the struggle of the self against a harsh world, as the unworldly Mengke gradually learns what the world is like. The world humiliates and degrades; more particularly it exploits the innocence and vulnerability of the young, attractive woman, making her into an object, a commodity to satisfy its own lewd desires. The story begins and concludes with thematically parallel episodes. At the start Mengke leaves art school in indignation after trying to protect a model who had been "insulted" by a teacher. In the end she herself can make a living only as a movie star, a career that makes her feel she is "selling not just her body but even her soul."

What demoralizes her and leads eventually to such a capitulation is her stay in the modern, fashionable, affluent household of her aunt and cousins. The fatal lure of this environment, which will compromise her integrity and undermine her trust in the world, is embodied in her cousin Xiaosong, twenty-five years old. Back from France just half a year, he is a translator of foreign fiction in magazines. Fascinating as this Western connection is, it also, as often in Ding Ling's stories, signals something suspect, inauthentic, possibly corrupting. The cousin charms Mengke with talk about the museums, theaters, and restaurants of Paris, and takes her to the Ka-er-deng (Carlton?) cinema to see *Chahuanü* (*Camille*). There is much submerged sentimental eroticism in this scene (her identification with the actress also presages Mengke's own future) so that later when she finds the cousin in a hotel with a "whore-like woman" she feels betrayed. This shocking evidence of male treachery, as well as the shallowness of her cousins' lives underneath all that Western veneer precipitates Mengke's decision to flee her aunt's house. Then, without making very explicit the logic of the outcome, the story has her fall straight into the "deep pit of hell."

"Amao guniang" ("Miss Amao") likewise has as its central character a young girl who begins in innocence and is defeated by the world. While Mengke discovers the world as it is, a place where sacrifice of integrity and self-respect are the conditions of survival, Amao destroys herself because she desires to escape from the confines of her environment and then learns that escape is impossible.

When Amao leaves behind the remote, isolated valley village of her childhood, and is sent forth as a bride to live at her husband's home on a hillside by West Lake, she becomes aware of hitherto unsuspected possibilities in life. Initially these are represented by the distant but visible city of Hangchow. "As soon as it was night, from far away across the Lake, where sky and water met," the city would "shine like densely clustered stars, a large golden light reflected on the water." In the company of some neighbors she finally gets her wish to visit Hangchow, but at one point during the long walk the city seems to be much farther away than she had realized, "a mysterious place, a place which perhaps one could not reach." This pattern of expectations aroused and then thwarted is repeated throughout the story; each new experience and discovery becomes a new source of despair.

In part it is Amao's own particularly innocent outlook on the world that entraps her in this pattern of frustrated expectations. The story is told primarily through her as the center of consciousness, but the narrator constantly steps outside to place the character's "romantic" view of things into realistic perspective. When Amao and her neighbors return from the city by boat, she sighs as the lake water carries her farther and farther away.

> but as they approached home, she became very happy again; it was due to a kind of vanity. When Third Sister and Yuying pointed out their houses to her, she could see them nestling deeply in the mountain valley, which was better than all those nearby. In the valley there were also many elegant houses half hidden from view. From the lake it looked as if their houses were right on top of a Western-style storied red house. Fortunately she had forgotten that theirs were the only crude small tiled huts in the valley, built of old boards and patched everywhere with old and rusty metal plates.

Such movement in and out of the protagonist's consciousness is reminiscent of the ironic method in *Madame Bovary,* which Ding Ling is reputed to have read in translation at least ten times. More than one of her friends have testified to her fondness for the novel, but unlike Flaubert, Ding Ling is sympathetic toward the plight of her heroine. Her juxtaposition of the dual points of view is less artful but also less calculatingly cruel.

Amao's exposure to the glitter of the city and her intermittent contacts with the fashionable people who occupy the elegant houses around hers create a desire for a better life, and when, despite all her efforts, this life turns out to be beyond reach, she sinks into a deep depression, into the "sorrow of hoping without hope." Her health fails, she swallows a bunch of matches and dies in horrible pain. There is the sound of a violin from a nearby mansion. When Amao first heard this music—unseen, foreign, suggesting the unattainable, like her glimpses of the city, her dreams for a different life—she had been filled with an inexplicable sadness. After the screams of her final agony, the violin too falls silent.

Amao is the young Chinese peasant girl from the village who discovers the material wealth and mysterious culture of the city's semi-Westernized sector and is destroyed by her passionate longing for them. In another story Ding Ling writes about a lower-class victim of the modernized city who is a survivor. The prostitute Aying in "Qingyünli zhong de yijian xiaofang li" (**"A Small Room in Qingyün Lane"**), falling asleep on the wet splotchy bed after her customer leaves, dreams of being again in the arms of the lover she left in the village, but unlike Amao she knows her dreams are useless, are in fact "stupid and laughable." With the nonchalant resilience that has enabled her to survive for three years in her sordid Shanghai environment, she gets on with the preparations for the evening's work and stands on the street waiting for the two or three dollars she hopes the night will bring.

In **"Shafei nüshi de riji" ("The Diary of Miss Sophie")**, Ding Ling's best-known story, the threat of destruction comes not so much from the outside world's violation of the innocent individual as from what she finally learns about herself in her confrontation with the world. The diary form is employed to carry out a kind of intense self-examination that would not have been possible for the less sophisticated, less self-conscious peasant bride or prostitute. Miss Sophie, about twenty, away from home, and living by herself in Peking, not enrolled in the university though most of her friends are, is much more typical of the heroines in Ding Ling's early fiction. With few or attenuated family connections, these young women rarely have family or given names, but take unconventional Westernized ones like Sophie, Isa, and Lia, or poetic ones like Yecao (Wildgrass). Very often they are impoverished or in ill health, living in rented shabby back rooms (*tingzijian*) of dreary apartment buildings, surviving anonymously and precariously in the interstices of the huge city. Their insecurity and isolation come from their having broken away from the traditional social structure and conventional codes of behavior: economically perhaps, but even more morally and spiritually, they are totally on their own. They live on the fringes, away from the institutionalized restrictions of marriage, a regular job, or school. But what they often discover in their free-wheeling, anarchistic existence is that in facing the world they must also encounter themselves.

Among these early women characters Miss Sophie emerges as the most representative, or rather as the most extreme, because she receives the most extended treatment. Her emancipated way of life is carried further than most because her advanced state of tuberculosis prevents her from engaging in any regular occupation and encourages reckless behavior. She finds herself strongly attracted to Ling Jishi, a man who has the "handsome air of a medieval knight" but a despicable soul. Her diary centers on this perverse passion: while she indulges in feverish fantasies of longing for him she realizes at the same time that he is unworthy of them.

Like other objects of temptation in Ding Ling's stories—Mengke's cousin, Amao's city—Ling Jishi is both enhanced and tainted by Western connotations. (In fact, being from Singapore, he is only ambiguously Chinese.) Tall and slim, he has a white complexion, bright red and temptingly soft lips—an important focus for Sophie's fantasies—and hopelessly "Western" values.

> What does he want? Money, to entertain in his living room the young wives of his business associates, and several white and plump sons, exquisitely dressed. What is his love? To squander money in the brothel for some momentary sexual gratification, and to sit on the soft sofa clasping a scented body, a cigarette in his mouth, laughing unrestrainedly with friends, left legs over right knees . . . an enthusiast of debates, tennis matches, studying abroad at Harvard, becoming a foreign service officer or ambassador, or inheriting his father's occupation, going into the rubber business, becoming a capitalist. [She sees through him, but is hopelessly infatuated anyway]: He has so insanely stirred up my emotions . . . I know for sure, that if he would tightly hold me, let me kiss him all over, and then cast me into the ocean, into fire, I would happily close my eyes and await that death which would forever preserve this love of mine. Alas, to think that I am in love with him, all I want is for him to let me have a good death.

The see-saw battle of contradictory impulses that the story traces in detail rises to a hysterical pitch and finally climaxes in a kiss, representing for Sophie both victory and degradation. After that she sends her lover away and castigates herself in despair: "All in all, I have wreaked havoc on myself. If a person's enemy is himself, how, oh heavens, can he seek vengeance and indemnity for all his losses?"

Even as Sophie records in her diary the hysterical course of self-destruction, she is quite fully aware, on one level at least, of what she is doing. Going to hell with both eyes open is—precisely because one does see where one is going—a journey worth documenting. The author's claim here is that no matter how deserving of condemnation, she merits our attention in spite of, or even because of, what she is. This unapologetic dwelling on the self is one of the most characteristic themes of May Fourth literature, and a radically new departure in Chinese fiction. (pp. 25-9)

In **"The Diary of Miss Sophie"** the onset of love uncovers the contradictory and perverse aspects of personality. Although in the great love stories of the past (*Dream of the Red Chamber, The Peony Pavilion, The Western Chamber*) sexual passion always contained the potential for undermining rationality and the social order, it was not until the literature of the May Fourth period that love and sexual feelings became intensely problematic and capable of totally subverting the individual's sense of self. Miss Sophie is an extended example of this, but there are other stories in which moral predicaments and crises of identity and relationships are revealed through the tangles of love. While Ding Ling's bold, outspoken exploration of women's sexual feelings made her notorious among her contemporaries,

"Sophie is constantly fluctuating between the many opposites set up in the story: wholesome milk and ruinous wine, health and illness, laughter and tears, life and death, truth and deception, friendship and loneliness, regard and disgust for herself. The diary follows the shifts and turns in her experiences; nothing is settled, nothing is clarified before leading immediately to its opposite. The restless turmoil is intensified by the dominant contradiction of being in love with a man she despises; in the end the self-scrutiny this experience provokes drives her into the impasse of near-suicidal despair."

—Ysi-tsi Mei Feuerwerker

she often was able to seek access through such feelings to other aspects of the human condition.

The very early story **"Shujia zhong"** (**"Summer Vacation"**) concerns the love affairs of a group of young women school teachers, but on another level is about the sense of malaise among "progressive" individuals who feel out of time and place. It was too easy in school to "pick up knowledge outside books, forgetting what one came to school for, from morning till night to be head-over-heels involved in kissing, embracing, stealthily placing letters by pillows, in bitterness, tears." But the carefully specified time-space context of these apparently trivial activities invest them with further meaning.

The ironically named Self-Reliance Girls School (Zili nüxiao) is located in the town of Wuling, a provincial backwater. The school has been made over from a tiny dilapidated temple, its main hall appointed like an auditorium, its side rooms serving as classrooms and teachers' bedrooms. The teachers' modern way of life and occupation, like the school itself, must make their way in makeshift, uncertain fashion among the most uncongenial surroundings. After several years in town, the bobbed hair of the teachers, the light-colored blouses and short skirts they have adopted still attract "the eyes of the entire street" whenever they appear. Furthermore it is summer vacation, and whenever it is hot, "there is nothing one can do; there are few trees, few wide spaces, just densely packed houses enclosing narrow streets." These young women, idle between terms, oppressed by heat, are trapped in boredom and frustration.

Two public occasions momentarily interrupt the tedium: a variety show at a school and a "new style" wedding, each a modern event staged against the incongruous backdrop of the provincial town, each inviting leers and scandalous gossip about the teachers among the townspeople. The young women's vaunted *dushen zhuyi,* a self-sufficient but not necessarily celibate "bachelorism," sounds brave but does not enable them to rise above the tearful bickerings of futile, petty love affairs. Homosexual love may have been a salacious subject for that time; in the story it also becomes a kind of metaphor for the semiliberated, the would-be avant-garde who lack the resources to transcend the restrictive conditions of their existence.

A more sympathetic view of the hazards of sexual passion in an unforgiving environment is presented in the story **"Xiaohuolun shang"** (**"On a Small Steamboat"**). A teacher who unwisely falls in love with a married man is dismissed by the school for her conduct, only to find her lover betraying her with someone else. The story begins with Jie Dajie boarding the small steamboat and is told in flashback as she travels into an uncertain future, "gazing at the endless ranges of green mountains, the turbulent flowing water, feeling lost and adrift with no place to go."

Both stories portray women as victims—of men, institutions, conventional mores, but also of their own feelings. The dark mood of suffering and self-destruction in the writings of many other contemporary women writers like Lu Yin, Feng Yuanjun, and Xie Bingying came from the sense of oppression that women suffered and was reinforced by a concept of woman as a being imbued with extraordinary sensitivity, fragility, and capacity for pain. This image of the suffering woman was a carry-over from traditional literature. Women rarely spoke in their own voices in the past—the number of women writers in China's four-thousand-year tradition is minuscule—but male writers did often assume the personae of women in voicing complaints about rejection by their lords, separation from home, and similar painful situations. The sensitive and suffering female also existed in the Western tradition and, along with other themes of Romanticism, turned out to be one of the more congenial imports during the May Fourth period. Certainly the importance of love and marriage as *the* subject among the young writers of that time provided endless occasions for describing women crushed by marriage, or dying from blighted love. Traditional culture and Western influence both contributed the notion of the passively suffering female, one that seems to have been accepted by women as part of their self-conception when they began to write about themselves.

While focusing also on the female condition Ding Ling nevertheless struggled to counter this idea of women in many of her stories:

> In my stories of the past, the main characters were often women. This is natural because I myself am a woman and understand better the weaknesses (*ruodian*) of women. But because of this there has been much misunderstanding. Actually I strongly dislike the weaknesses in women. . . . I may not feel sympathetic towards the women in my writings, but what I write is not always in accordance with my own opinion. At the beginning the two may not be very far apart, but as I write the gap becomes wider, and at times what I write turns out to be the opposite of my intention.

This seemingly uncontrollable ambivalence, this conflict between intention and practice, sympathy and censure, stems from Ding Ling's view that women suffer not only as victims of society but also from self-defeating female weaknesses. The two stories just discussed present women in this light, but Ding Ling also wrote many more stories in which women try to be strong and hard (*qiangying*), and fight to counteract their weaknesses. For them, being in love may also be an occasion to test their strength. The young woman faced with love is therefore a variation on, or one important aspect of, the theme of the self confronting the world.

However, there are no easy victories for the strong and hard woman. Very often she fails in another way: having asserted herself, her own conscience and self-consciousness rob her of satisfaction. Miss Sophie's "victory," as she terms it, when she finally gains a kiss from the object of her infatuation, is also immediately seen as degradation.

The "Salome-type" flirt in **"Yige nüren he yige nanren" ("A Woman and a Man")** takes the initiative in arranging a rendezvous with a poet—a modern one who affects the Japanese-style name Ou Waiou—because she "wanted to see herself victorious," she could not rest until she "could see another's soul acupunctured by her and vibrating in her palm." It was like an addiction: "if she could not under conditions of danger and secrecy play with (*wan wei*) a heart she had roused, she apparently would not be able to go on living." When they are together, she does not find in her poet the satisfaction she had envisioned. But even in the middle of the "hot prickly proceedings" the heroine exhibits a certain self-awareness:

> Weidi understood also in her own heart that it was like acting in a play, but she could not bear to laugh at herself: she was very sympathetic towards her own predicament. She sighed gently, assuming a mysterious mien just recently learned from the movies, haughty, deeply expressive, and doleful.

There is a double point of view at work here: the self-consciousness of the main character and the narrator's gently ironic tone both serve to distance the reader from the action. The battle of the sexes is transformed into a comedy of play-acting and miscalculations. At the end, Weidi can't wait to get back to her husband.

"Ta zou hou" ("After He Left") focuses on the moral qualms of a girl who capriciously exercises her power over her lover by sending him home at 2:00 A.M. in the rain. The story begins after he leaves and is told entirely in flashback through the recollecting and evaluating consciousness of Lia. The process leads her to conclude that in acting as she did she has used her attractions like a prostitute. The progression of her reflections is meticulously plotted as it moves from smugness to self-criticism to self-pity: "Why was she like this? She did not understand, she wanted to know what made her this way, but was afraid that after understanding she would feel worse."

The "narrated monologue" permits the "merging of the point of view of the author and the point of view of the character":

> But in a flash, everything in her universe changed. Alas! How terrible are thoughts when given free rein: Lia had been happy; but she did not want to wallow in happiness, she wanted to coolly perceive her own good fortune, to prolong it and engrave it in her heart. Who could know that this is how misfortune is built? She thought about everything, she was happy about everything, then suddenly she began to reflect on her true feelings. And she refused to be slipshod, she was so mistrustful that she finally landed herself in misery. . . . Timidly she began to analyze herself.

This sort of "collaborative," constantly evaluating self-consciousness will not allow characters to let go of their love experiences until they have complicated them into occasions for close questioning of themselves as human beings. Such self-questioning is all the more insistent when the assertive woman, striving to counteract the image of the passively suffering weak female, finds herself caught in a moral dilemma brought on by the exercise of power. In Ding Ling's works of this period there are many lovers, many variations of the same theme, but the relentless examination of the self that each situation demands shows her to be a writer of high moral seriousness, in spite of the scandalous nature of what is going on within most of the stories.

Yet it was this focus on love and sexuality in her early writings that made her vulnerable to accusations of "immorality" later on, when she became a target of the established Chinese revolution. During the anti-rightist campaign of 1957 she was attacked for her preoccupation with sex; indulgence in the kind of sexual fantasy found in **"The Diary of Miss Sophie,"** for example, was called "a sort of opiate for youth . . . they will want to find the 'happiness' Sophie had from Ling Jishi's person and completely forget the class struggle of real life." This criticism implies that puritanism is necessary in a revolutionary society because sexual fantasies can be expected to divert or distract one from working steadfastly for collective goals. Although such literary censorship may be seen as another example of obscurantist party intervention in aesthetic matters, there is indeed the risk, as Ding Ling's stories themselves suggest, that persistent exploration of the love experience may leave the individual unsure of where he stands in relation to the external world, and this uncertainty could interfere with his ability to assume an effective social role.

The outpouring of puritanical outrage during the 1957 campaign was directed against Ding Ling's personal life as much as against her works. As an author she was held personally responsible for the sins of her characters. The gossip mills had ground out more than sufficient material concerning her own early love relationships to intimate that the "immorality" of her fictional creations mirrored her own. Such criticism, both naive and deliberate in its refusal to recognize the distinction between life and art, also points to the particular hazards of being a female writer.

The feminist concerns in Ding Ling's own life and writings belong to those of the "second generation." She did not involve herself in the primary battles against the flagrant, institutionalized forms of female oppression, such as arranged marriages, foot-binding, concubinage, female infanticide. These were largely left behind when she moved from Hunan to live the life of an emancipated woman in the semi-Westernized cities of Peking and Shanghai. She did write about women imprisoned in stultifying marriages, seduced and betrayed by faithless lovers, or forced into prostitution to survive in a society which regarded them as commodities, but more often she presented women who were no less victimized even while apparently free of such external forms of oppression. Her "liberated" women who engage in love relationships outside the pale of conventional structures give us new insight into the basic, internal contradictions of the female condition. Such women are subject, paradoxically, to the consequences both of their emotional vulnerability and of their self-conscious assertiveness. This is a source of their harsh self-criticism and despair. Ding Ling was able to achieve such insights into women's experience only because she unflinchingly dared to explore largely uncharted psychological and moral territory. Her audacity contributed much to her early literary success but also made her an easy target for attack later. (pp. 31-6)

Yi-tsi Mei Feuerwerker, in her Ding Ling's Fiction: Ideology and Narrative in Modern Chinese Literature, *Cambridge, Mass.: Harvard University Press, 1982, 196 p.*

Yi-tsi Mei Feuerwerker

Ding Ling began writing in the late 1920s, as a member of the May Fourth generation, the iconoclastic, breakaway generation that initiated the era of the new Chinese literature. Except for the period when she was silenced, she continued to write for more than fifty years. Taken together, her writings provide a telescopic history of modern Chinese literature. Her personality and temperament seem to have conspired with certain accidents of history and biography to place her constantly in the center of whatever was going on. Time and again, she has been actively involved in the literary issues and controversies of the past half-century.

Ding Ling was born in 1904 into a once wealthy gentry family in Hunan, the home province of many of China's revolutionary leaders. She was named Jiang Bingzhi and later created the pen name Ding Ling. Her paternal grandfather and great-grandfather had been officials under the Manchu dynasty. Indeed, when Ding Ling was born, there was still a Manchu emperor on the throne, a reminder that the tremendous upheavals in China have taken place only within her lifetime. By the time Ding Ling's parents were married, the family had entered a period of precipitous decline, producing, as families will at such times, a generation of degenerate males who whiled away their days in gambling, opium, and keeping fancy horses. Ding Ling's father was such a man, but he suffered from ill health and died when Ding Ling was three. Her mother was the great influence on her life, a woman, Ding Ling has often said, much greater than herself. When Ding Ling's father died leaving her mother with a host of debts and two small children—one an infant son who died soon after—the young widow moved back to her hometown Changde and took the bold step of attending a normal school to prepare herself for a teaching career. She later became a pioneer educator and founder of elementary schools.

In an unfinished novel entitled *Mother,* Ding Ling gives an account of her mother's experiences as a student, including a moving description of how her mother "let out" her bound feet, a process almost as painful as the initial binding. She soaks them daily in cold water to speed up the process and insists on enduring the pain of running in gym class, even though she could have been excused. The unbound feet become a central image in the novel, symbolic of the mother's heroic efforts to break out of the bonds of the past. With the example provided by her mother, Ding Ling became a precocious activist. When only thirteen, she was demonstrating with other female students at the Hunan Provincial Assembly demanding equal rights for women. With her mother's support she broke off an arranged marriage in a stormy confrontation with her uncle, the head of the family, later publishing an article denouncing her uncle and the whole social stratum to which he belonged. This was her "first taste of the power of the pen." She soon left home, an "exiled insurrectionist," for the semi-Westernized metropolis of Shanghai to try out the life of a liberated woman in the China of the 1920s.

Ding Ling's feminist concerns can be said to belong to those of the "second generation" in that the pioneering battles against the most flagrant institutionalized forms of oppression—arranged marriages, foot-binding, denial of education—had already been fought and won for the daughter by the mother. What she was to explore in her own life and early writings were the dilemmas of young women who had broken away from traditional social structures and conventional modes of behavior and had found themselves living on the fringes of society, up against the hostile world on their own.

In Shanghai, Ding Ling sporadically attended classes—she never finished high school—studied painting and Western literature, hobnobbed with anarchists, then moved to Peking with the idea of getting into the university. There she met a fledgling poet, Hu Yepin: a "rare person," she was to write some twenty years after he was killed, "with the most perfect qualities, yet a piece of completely uncut, unpolished jade." Soon they were living together, a life of almost idyllic young love, literary aspirations, and precarious poverty.

The story that established Ding Ling's name and made her the most famous—or notorious—woman writer of her time was **"The Diary of Miss Sophie,"** published in 1928, an account of a tubercular, high-strung woman's infatuation with a young man who has the handsome "exterior of a medieval knight" but a despicable soul. It exploded, in the words of contemporary critics, like a bombshell, shattering the quiet of the literary scene. No one in Chinese literature had ever described in such frank and impassioned terms the sexual fantasies of a young woman. Because this is Ding Ling's best-known story, she has been unfortunately identified with its central characer; a constant refrain in later political campaigns, when she was attacked for her sexual immorality, was that she was the "incarnation of Sophie." As the history of Marxist criticism in China has shown, fictional characters are an infinitely malleable source of damning evidence to use against a writer, since authors are "responsible" for what their characters do. Such critically naive or politically calculated blurring of the distinction between life and literature has plagued Ding Ling throughout much of her career.

Although Ding Ling's early stories won recognition for the unprecedented audacity and sensitivity with which she depicted the psychology of modern young women, more recent criticism has focused on the social context of the dilemmas of her characters. Although liberated in the sense that they have broken with traditional authority, they lack the economic means and social support needed for any genuine independence. They might be free of the institutionalized oppression of fathers or husbands, but they become all the more vulnerable to the pain of betrayal by lovers or by their own fluctuating emotions. Sophie uses the diary form for a relentless investigation of the self caught in this predicament; her apparent liberation from the constraints of social structures leads her to feel that she has no one to blame but herself for what she is doing or suffering. She is therefore all the more anxious to analyze and understand her own behavior. Yet as spectator and self-conscious actor in her own drama, she often catches herself playing a part, making it difficult for others to give her the true understanding that she craves, while sabotaging at the same time her own efforts to evolve an intelligible and authentic image of the self to cope with her personal crisis. By the end of the diary Sophie has become disillusioned with both herself and the diary as a means toward self-understanding. Thus the story in theme and form is a provocative inquiry into the limits of subjectivism in modern literature, and foreshadows Ding Ling's readiness to move into a broader arena for her fictional explorations.

External events also politicized Ding Ling's fiction. During the late 1920s both the Kuomintang government's persecution of writers and the radicalization of literature were proceeding apace. Shanghai, where Ding Ling and Hu Yepin were living, had become the center of intellectual life because its foreign settlements and less than totally efficient police allowed a political opposition to exist with some degree of impunity. Hu Yepin joined the League of Left-Wing Writers and became increasingly active in the Chinese Communist party. While he was busy attending meetings, Ding Ling stayed at home writing stories about the conflict between love and revolution. Their first child, a son, was born in November 1930. Two months later, on January 17, 1931, Hu Yepin was arrested while attending a meeting and on February 7, along with twenty-three or twenty-four alleged Communists, was executed in Longhua prison. The brutality of the summary executions aroused widespread protest within China and abroad, and the Five Martyrs—there were four other young writers among the victims—soon became one of the most powerful emblems of literary persecution in history.

Modern Chinese literary history is strewn with the dead bodies and broken lives of martyred writers. This heartbreaking fact is evidence of a belief in the power and seriousness of literature, a belief apparently shared by those who undertake the risk of writing and those in power who persecute them for doing so. This same belief led Ding Ling to commit herself even more fully to the cause for which her husband had been killed. She soon joined the Communist party and assumed the editorship of its major literary journal. Her own writings also took a sharp leftward turn. Instead of focusing on introspective and alienated young women, she expanded her subject matter to striking factory workers, awakened peasants, social injustice, and the coming socialist revolution.

On May 15, 1933, Ding Ling was arrested, or rather abducted, since it was an illegal operation, from her home in the International Settlement by government agents; she was imprisoned and presumed to have become another martyr. The main purpose of her arrest apparently was not to execute her but to persuade her to renounce the Communist party and to place her talents at the service of the Kuomintang government. She refused to cooperate, but as time went by the conditions of her detention ameliorated. Three years later, in September 1936, she managed a daring escape to the border regions in northwest China, where the Communist party then had its base. For part of the journey she disguised herself as a Manchurian soldier, which meant riding on horseback for the first time in her life, but she made it through the treacherous terrain and arrived to a heroine's welcome. There was a banquet, and Chairman Mao Zedong composed two poems to commemorate the occasion. Two years later her children, who had been in the care of her mother, were sent to the Border Regions to join her.

When the War of Resistance against Japan broke out in 1937, Ding Ling organized and directed the Northwest Front Service Corps and spent several months with her dramatic troupe traveling through the backward mountain villages of the area, performing plays and songs to spread the message of uniting to fight Japan. One important member of the troupe was the writer Chen Ming, twelve years her junior. Despite much criticism of their relationship, they were married in 1942.

At the time when Ding Ling arrived at the Border Regions, the Chinese Communist party did not look like much more than a bunch of stragglers who had barely escaped the encirclement campaigns of the Kuomintang and survived the Long March to reach one of the poorest and most backward areas of China. Yet it was from such an improbable base that the party carried out the most dramatic expansion of a revolutionary movement in history and established thirteen years later its government over all of China. There in Yanan the party forged the revolutionary techniques that were to carry it to power, and Mao Zedong formulated his vision of the Chinese revolution as above all a process of mass consciousness-raising. One question that was debated urgently and that directly involved Ding Ling was the role of art and literature within such an engrossing effort. Although the stories about war and revolution from her Yanan period emphasized heroic characters and positive outcomes, she did not believe that support of collective goals precluded all negative criticism. It was over this matter of whether literature should mainly underscore the "bright side" and play down the "dark side" that she came into open conflict with the party.

Ding Ling was at the time the editor of the literary page of the party's newspaper, *The Liberation Daily,* and in that capacity she called for critical essays on society, literature, and art. She published several articles that exposed the dark side of Yanan reality. She herself contributed an essay, **"Thoughts on March 8,"** published on March 9, 1942, in which she wrote that although women in the liberated areas under Communist control were much better off than women elsewhere in China, the bitter contradictions of their existence remained. They were forever the objects of attention or criticism, damned if they married or didn't, had children or didn't, stayed home or didn't. Divorce was usually initiated by the man; if the woman wanted it, "then there must be something even more immoral and it is entirely the woman who should be cursed." Then the woman grew old and lost her attractiveness, never having escaped the fate of being "backward." In traditional society she might have been considered "pitiful" or "ill-fated"; now that she was supposedly equal and had choices, if she suffered it was "her own doing," it "served her right."

> I am a woman myself, I understand women's shortcomings better than most, but I understand even more their suffering. They cannot be above their times, they are not ideal, they are not forged of steel. They are unable to resist society's temptations and silent oppressions, they all have a history of blood and tears, they have all had lofty emotions (whether they have risen or fallen, are fortunate or unfortunate, still struggling alone or have joined the crowd). To say this about women comrades who have come to Yanan is not unjust. Therefore it is with a great deal of leniency that I consider those who have sunk to become female criminals. I hope that men, especially men in high positions, and women themselves will see the shortcomings of women more as based in society.

For such criticism, Ding Ling and the several writers whose essays she had published were attacked by the party and required to confess their mistakes. Mao Zedong's famous "Talks at the Yanan Forum on Literature and Art," given in May 1942, were in large part directed against Ding Ling and other "petty bourgeois" writers who, like her, had come to join the revolution at the Border Regions. An important turning point in the history of Chinese literature, the talks state explicitly once and for all that literature and art must be subordinate to politics and claim for the party the right to direct, control, and intervene in the literary process. Although the principles stated by Mao have been applied with varying degrees of stringency, they have remained the fundamental scripture of party policy toward literature for the past forty years.

Having been responsible, in part at least, for precipitating the confrontation and bringing down on literature and art the authoritative pronouncements of Mao Zedong, Ding Ling underwent public self-criticism, worked in the party school and in the countryside, and did not write for the next two years. In 1944 she wrote several sketches of model labor or production heroes based on uplifting real-life incidents and was congratulated by Mao for embarking on this new literary path. When the People's Republic of China was established five years later, she was for a time one of the most prominent members of its cultural hierarchy, vice-chairperson of the Writers' Union, editor of important literary journals, and head of the training school for writers. For the first time in her life she traveled abroad, leading delegations to the Soviet Union, Hungary, and Czechoslovakia.

In 1951 Ding Ling was awarded the Stalin Prize in literature for her novel on land reform, ***The Sun Shines on the Sanggan River.*** The Stalin Prize may or may not in itself be a guarantee of literary excellence, but this award, along with her other honors and positions, indicates that Ding Ling was then one of the most acclaimed writers in the People's Republic of China. The events of the novel take place over about twenty-one days during the early phase of radical land reform in a small village of about two hundred families in northern China. Ding Ling managed within these limits to provide in microcosm the quintessential Chinese revolutionary experience. Although land reform was an important policy that helped win over the peasantry in the Communists' war against the Kuomintang government, its main purpose was the total destruction of the traditional structure of rural economic and political power and it took place even where landlords were not the problem. Through participation in the land reform process and the activated mass struggle, the peasants' consciousness was raised; for the first time they saw that their centuries-old poverty and oppression could indeed be lifted and their world transformed into one where hope and a new beginning were suddenly possible. Whether Ding Ling's novel is historically accurate is beside the point. As a fictionalized treatment of an ideological version of the past, it is a celebration of the dream of revolution come true at this special moment of awakening for the humble individuals in small villages.

The Sun Shines on the Sanggan River showed, in its sweeping vision of China in revolution, the vast distance, in both ideology and technique, that Ding Ling had traversed in her writing since her early stories about young women involved in lonely crises of love, sex, and identity. Although this literary development confers interest and complexity on Ding Ling's works, it did not assure her continuing status in a volatile revolutionary society. Her prestigious position lasted but a few years. In 1957 she was the prime target of the antirightist drive and denounced in a nationwide campaign. She was attacked for her superiority complex, for her sexual immorality, for ideological failings, for maligning the peasant masses in her fiction, and for traitorous conspiracy against the party. She was further charged with setting up literature in opposition to party leadership, by subscribing to the bourgeois view that the achieved literary work was an individual creation that could secure for its author profit and fame, a view referred to by her critics as her "one-bookism." The party saw it as necessary to wage the struggle against her to "protect the socialist line in art and literature."

Could her literary activities indeed have constituted such a threat? The history of political campaigns against writers in the People's Republic of China—and indeed there have been waves of them since 1949—is painful to contemplate. Factional feuds, some of which can be traced back to the 1930s in Shanghai, when vituperative debate and adroit quoting out of context became the fashion, were an important continuing impetus. The campaigns were exploited as opportunities for rivals to take over literary journals and propel themselves into high positions in the cultural bureaucracy. There were of course genuine ideological uncertainties over the latitude that should be conceded to such refractory and extravagant pursuits as literature and art under conditions of scarcity. Should not only the literature that could clearly demonstrate its usefulness for the attainment of collective goals be accepted? Utilitarianism and philistine moralism, which historically have been the enemies of art everywhere, found in revolutionary China a powerful ally in fundamentalist political ideology. In Ding Ling's case this mix of motives was reinforced by the expediency of making an example of one of China's most prestigious writers.

One suspicion often voiced is that Ding Ling was a more obvious target because she was a woman. Although this may be difficult to ascertain, once the campaign was under way it followed the familiar pattern of criticizing a woman not so much for what she writes or does, but for what she is, for what is presumed to be her personal character, which then is quickly narrowed to the question of sexual conduct. Sexual conduct becomes a relevant and inflammatory issue because the double standard makes women particularly vulnerable. Ding Ling's stories were combed for her glorification of sexual immorality; they were cited as further evidence of what were claimed to be their author's own violations of the chastity code. Her specific feminist concerns were criticized as divisive and undermining of collective goals for it was held it was the reactionary class that suppressed women's liberation, not men in general.

The sessions of mass criticism against Ding Ling went on from June 6 to September 27, 1957, but apparently she was not repentant enough and in 1958 she was expelled from the party. Information about where she was or what had happened to her did not emerge until after her official rehabilitation twenty-one years later.

She was sent to a state farm for labor reform in the Great Northern Wilderness, the northeast corner of China just south of the Heilongjiang River bordering Siberia. The first year she acquired much expertise in raising poultry while trying to adjust to the harsh climate and frontier conditions. Her situation improved somewhat when she was given the task of teaching adult literacy classes. Although there seemed little chance of publication, she did try to take up writing again. But with the onset of the Cultural Revolution in 1966, her "days of fear" began. Having been labeled a rightist, she was an available target for anyone during this period of near anarchy when ideological fanaticism held sway. Her home, a thatched hut seven meters square, was raided dozens of times by groups of Red Guards; all her manuscripts, diaries, notes, scraps of paper with a single word were taken away, torn up, irretrievably lost. During "struggle-and-criticism" sessions she suffered much physical abuse. Then she was forced to perform menial labor under the "supervision of the revolutionary masses" for up to fourteen hours a day. In 1970 she was returned to Peking in shackles and put in solitary confinement in the notorious Qincheng prison where she remained for five years. Only the day after her release in 1975 did she learn that her husband, Chen Ming, had spent that same time in the same prison, one cell away. After three more years of restricted freedom in a mountain village in Shanxi, she was allowed to return to Peking.

Official rehabilitation in 1979 finally permitted Ding Ling to resume her writing career. The ban on her books was lifted; both new and old works were again available to the public. A piece about a model heroine, written in 1966 but destroyed during the Cultural Revolution and then rewritten, was published in July 1979. It was her first work to appear since 1956. To make up for lost time, she has been very prolific, writing critical essays, a sequel to her land reform novel, and reminiscences of her friends, many of whom she discovered had died during her imprisonment. In the fall of 1981 she came to the United States for the first time, spending two months at the International Writing Program at the University of Iowa and two months touring and lecturing on college campuses. (pp. 68-77)

[Ding Ling] views her unjust persecution by the party as a temporary, although extended, aberration. Now having acknowledged its mistakes about her and other "rightists" as well, the party can be restored at last to its authentic self, as a true carrier of the revolutionary ideal. Ding Ling's adoption of this attitude, difficult as it may be for us to sympathize with, may be psychologically necessary as a way to come to terms with what happened to her, in light of her lifelong commitment to the party, a commitment that had already, in the days of her youth, required the sacrifice of her husband. Was the martyrdom of Hu Yepin and her own subsequent pain and perilous struggle to have been for nothing? Her positive stance also has much to do with her self-image as a writer and the writer's vital role in Chinese society. What became evident to me in our travels was the tremendous moral authority, inconceivable in the United States, that Ding Ling the writer radiated. She was esteemed because of her status as a writer, and even more by some for what she had been through. Yet precisely due to this special moral stature, Ding Ling considers that her primary responsibility must be to continue to reaffirm the true goals and values of the existing ideological system. There may not in any case be an alternative visible on the horizon today for China, but just as important to realize is the fact that the Chinese revolution, before it went astray, is the path to which she had long ago dedicated her life. (pp. 81-2)

Yi-tsi Mei Feuerwerker, "In Quest of the Writer Ding Ling," in Feminist Studies, *Vol. 10, No. 1, Spring, 1984, pp. 65-83.*

Edward A. Gargan

[In the following obituary reporting Ding Ling's death on March 4, 1986, Gargan chronicles the major events of her life and career.]

Ding Ling, who emerged from an obscure rural backwater to become one of China's foremost writers and her country's most articulate champion of women's rights, died yesterday in a Peking hospital of an unspecified illness, the official New China News Agency reported. She was 82 years old.

For Ding, it was the women in a rapidly changing China who absorbed her energies. From her earliest stories to her later political work—she wrote about 300 novels, short stories, plays and essays—she sought to explore the psychological tensions of women straining against the bonds of traditional society and to further the equality of women within revolutionary society.

As early as March 1942, as Mao Zedong's forces battled the Japanese occupation army in northern China, Ding was writing about the condition of women in Mao's base area of Yanan, implicitly suggesting that women were still seen in the traditional role of feminine reticence that the revolution was supposed to uproot.

After World War II, while Communist forces were still battling the Nationalists, Ding, who had been involved in various leftist causes since the 1920's and had joined the Communist Party in 1932, was sent to join a land reform team in a village in Hebel. The experience was to provide the basis for her most celebrated novel,

The Sun Shines Over the Sanggan River, which was published in 1949, and for which she was awarded the Stalin Prize for Literature in 1951. Over the following years the novel was published in English and other European languages.

Unlike most propagandistic literature, this work provided a vastly more complex picture of the Communist campaign aimed at redistribution of the land. Miss Ding wrote of agrarian society wrestling with traditional customs and mores amid the fundamental changes in social structure caused by land redistribution and new forms of local control. Her characters were not stereotypically either heroes or villains and her portraits of peasants' lives captured their confusions and frustrations as political concerns intruded into village life for the first time.

After the victory of the Communists in 1949, she assumed a number of important posts in literary and cultural organizations, and was named editor of *People's Literature,* a literary magazine. But in 1957 she was caught up in the political purges of the so-called antirightist campaign and was criticized by left-wing intellectuals. Although she resisted the attacks on herself, she was removed from the public eye and could no longer publish her work.

She was exiled to a commune in Heilongjiang, where she spent nine years organizing adult literacy classes and practicing her unheralded skills as a teller of folk stories. With the onset of the Cultural Revolution in 1966, she was attacked both verbally and physically by Red Guards, and in 1970 she was imprisoned outside Peking. Ding was exonerated in 1977, a year after Mao's death and after seven difficult years, five of which she spent in solitary confinement. She was given a prominent position in the Writers Union. In conversations with Western visitors, she described the brutality of her imprisonment but she remained adamant in her admiration for the work of Mao.

Ding was widely read throughout China until her fall from grace in 1957, but with her banishment from public life and the banning of her works, the generation of Chinese educated during the next 20 years remained largely ignorant of her writing.

Ding was named Jiang Bingzhi when she was born in 1904, in what is now Linli County in Hunan Province, into the prominent Jiang clan, which owned more than half the land in the county.

When she appeared in print for the first time, in 1927, she adopted her mother's maiden name as her pen name.

The period of the 1940's was Ding's most prolific and creative. She worked for the party in several propaganda jobs, including editing the literary pages of *Liberation Daily,* the official Communist newspaper of the Yanan period.

She lived her last years in the comfort accorded literary luminaries in China. Her conversations with foreign visitors in the last years of her life always returned to the trauma of the Cultural Revolution. Of the fierce political paranoia that pervaded those years she used to recall a favorite saying of the time: "When there are only two persons, they talk frankly. When there are three, they tell jokes. And when there are four, they speak falsehood."

"But now it is different," she always added.

Edward A. Gargan, in an obituary in The New York Times, *March 8, 1986, p. B6.*

Jonathan Mirsky

Before her death three weeks ago at the age of eighty-two, Ding Ling, author of **"Mengke," "The Diary of Miss Sophie",** ***Wei Hu*** and ***The Sun Shines over the Sanggan River,*** was thought of as the leading Chinese woman novelist of the twentieth century. In China, literature is a serious business, and few writers there have been taken more seriously than she was. Among Chinese writers she had also spent probably the longest time as a political prisoner; she was notable for having been a captive of both Chairman Mao [Zedong] and Generalissimo Chiang Kai-shek. Her official obituary, in the party's self-serving style when it wishes both to praise itself and to apologize, claimed that "despite her frustrations Ding Ling kept her faith in the Communist Party and in the people". It then listed the bleakest moments in her career:

> 1933-36—imprisoned by the Guomindang [Chiang Kai-shek's Nationalists]; 1955—wrongly charged as anti-Party [this is one of the Chinese equivalents of treason]; 1957—wrongly labelled Rightist and expelled from the party; 1966-76—during the Cultural Revolution, kept in prison and isolated; 1979—spared, rehabilitated, and restored to party membership.

The delicacy of her case is apparent in that the party did not dare to set her free until 1979, when Mao had been dead for three years. The vicissitudes of her life between 1930 and 1979 were a tremendous embarrassment to the leadership—a close look at them blurred the party's distinction between the Chiang and Mao periods; if anything, the post-revolutionary years turned out to have been worse for Ding Ling, and for writers generally, than the Guomindang period. She herself indulged in only one public moment of bitterness at the end of her twenty-two-year detention—"In the 1930s, the Guomindang banned my books. After 1958, we ourselves banned them." But in the same statement she remembered the other writers who had been "smashed", many of them old comrades no longer alive. "Did they all really deserve to be treated like dung?" The "we ourselves" were Mao and his disciples, many of them still in charge in 1979 (as they are today). But this was two years before the party's verdict on Mao's twenty-five years of "tragic errors". This was the judgment in which his old comrades were to concede that they had been involved to a limited degree. In 1979, therefore, the best that could be said about Ding Ling was that it was good that she had returned from "obscurity"; in fact every writer in China, as well as most readers, knew exactly what had befallen her. The single allegation rejected by everyone was the Gang of Four's assertion that Ding Ling had been a spy for Chiang Kai-shek.

Ding Ling on the development of her political and artistic philosophies:

I was born in 1904, at a time when the Manchu Empire was in its death throes, into a family of notables, a breeding-ground of mandarins such as described in those great classic Chinese novels *Dream of the Red Chamber,* by Cao Xueqin, and *The Scholars,* by Wu Jingzi.

My family was a replica in miniature of feudal society in decline and its history was a chequered one. The branch of the family to which my father belonged was impoverished and going rapidly downhill, and when I was four years old my father died completely ruined. My lonely childhood gave me an insight into the miserable lot of the people in Chinese society at the beginning of the twentieth century and opened my eyes to the selfish attitudes which governed relationships between one man and another. I found comfort in, and learned much from, reading the great Chinese classic novels. European Renaissance literature and foreign literature of the nineteenth century was also grist to my mill. And it was this reading that sowed in me the seed of my vocation as a writer.

I became a writer, not out of personal vanity or out of a love of art for art's sake, but to defend my fellow countrymen and help them to achieve liberty. The same objectives motivated other writers, both my contemporaries and those of the following generation, to engage in a literature of combat.

I wanted to give myself up totally to the cause of the people, to share their destiny, their cares and their sufferings, to live and die with them. During the 1920s my female characters had been petty bourgeois intellectuals in revolt: from the 1930s onwards they were based on working women and peasants.

I took part in the agrarian reform which abolished the feudal land system and redistributed the land. In the new China that had just been established I was given the task of helping in the reorganization of literary life. So absorbed was I in this task that I almost forgot that I too was a writer. It was only when this practical work was completed that I began once again to be haunted by the characters buried deep within my soul. I became eager to reveal their existence by writing them into my novels, stories and essays.

When I write, my pen follows the thread of my imagination and I stick to my first impulses, not trying to refashion the characters I have known and loved in my life and who become the heroes and heroines of my books.

Ding Ling in her essay "Self-Portrait of a Woman Writer," 1986.

In fact she had been a revolutionary from the beginning. Born in 1904, and left fatherless very young, she was brought up by her feminist mother, a teacher in a "modern" school who joined the Communist Party three years before her daughter. Ding Ling and an equally liberated school-friend, modelling themselves on Ibsen's Nora, prowled Nanking's streets at night, disguised as men or as prostitutes. Almost as if she were determined to accumulate enough material for a lifetime of novels, Ding Ling entered into scandalous romances, drank too much, and became the common-law wife of the revolutionary writer, Hu Yepin. During the late 1920s she published short stories about the sexuality of young women, so explicit for their time and place that she became instantly famous—not to say notorious. **"Mengke"** and **"Miss Sophie"** are both about "liberated Noras" and are partial attempts to deal with the question of the Chinese critic who wondered what happened to Ibsen's heroine after she leaves home.

Mengke, the daughter of rural gentry, comes to Shanghai and plunges into the glittering dangerous world of the cinema. Energetic, ambitious, unsatisfied, filled with romantic and even erotic hopes, she soon discovers that the men she meets think only of sexual conquest. Eroticism followed by disappointment is the theme, too, of **"The Diary of Miss Sophie".** The heroine is a young victim of tuberculosis who dismisses a worthy lover, preferring a sexual liaison which soon disgusts her. But Miss Sophie, who considers life "my personal plaything", looks back on her passionate affair as a valuable experience, and decides to "die quietly". In the novel, ***Wei Hu*** (1930), supposedly about the conflict between love and revolution, the activist Wei Hu gives up his lover for the cause. But Ding Ling pays far more attention to human anguish than to political circumstances. Indeed, it was her concentration on emotion in the midst of social upheaval that made Ding Ling's reputation; it was also this, though, that would eventually bring her into collision with the party.

In 1930 she joined the League of Left-wing Writers (not a communist organization, despite what is claimed today) as well as the party. The next year Hu Yepin was executed by Chiang Kai-shek's police, and Ding Ling went to prison for three years. As soon as she was freed she made her way to the north-west, to Yanan, where Mao had his guerrilla headquarters. There she was welcomed as a spectacular example of intellectual commitment to the revolution.

Once in Yanan most writers dried up. Ding Ling herself wrote little, but when she did, as in the story **"In the Hospital"** and the essay **"Thoughts on Women's Day",** she attacked the party for its male chauvinism. This was awkward; Yanan was in a deeply conservative area, and the party needed the support of the peasants, who treated their womenfolk badly. Mao, too, fancied himself as a champion of women's rights, and the Chairman expected writers to criticize his adversaries, rather than himself. In 1942, therefore, he temporarily ceased fighting the Japanese and Chiang Kai-shek in order to conduct a campaign to "rectify" ideas—the first of the great anti-intellectual drives which were to convulse China for decades. It began at what became known as the Yanan Forum on Literature and Art, during which Mao placed Ding Ling literally in the front row of the audience. Then he laid down his rules for writers.

The party has jettisoned much of Mao's thought, but his dogma on the function of revolutionary literature has never been repudiated. Writers have one great responsibility, Mao told Ding Ling and her colleagues. They were not to imagine that because they had dared to attack the Nationalists in Shanghai (where Ding Ling's husband was shot and she was arrested) they were entitled to criticize the party in Yanan. Indeed, they must praise the party and its policies, and vilify its enemies. Only two types of characters would be permitted: "bright" ones, who would be models for their readers, and dark, negative creatures, whose role, like the villain in a western musichall, was to arouse scorn. Ambiguous, grey situations are unhelpful, Mao pointed out. In fiction upbeat endings were mandatory. Ding Ling, like most of her colleagues, apologized and before long was sent north to Manchuria to observe communist land reform. From this emerged her best-known novel, ***The Sun Shines over the Sanggan River,*** which received the 1951 Stalin Prize. Even here she managed to create characters who were not merely "bright" or "dark".

She was becoming a literary star, a committee *apparatchik,* a delegate to cultural congresses abroad, and a stern disciplinarian of writers who strayed from the party line. But she also had made enemies above her in the cultural pecking order, and in 1954, as the party accelerated into a new anti-intellectual drive, Ding Ling became one of its targets. Again she apologized, but this was the beginning of the ordeal which culminated in 1957 in a mass meeting of 1,350 people; there the case against her was concluded. It is a mark of the corrupt spirit of the times that the author of *Rickshaw Boy,* the veteran writer Lao She, who would himself be harassed to death during the Cultural Revolution, found it necessary to call Ding Ling a criminal. She disappeared from sight—until 1979. (pp. 302, 315)

But Ding Ling survived, as she would survive her solitary confinement during the Cultural Revolution, when thousands of other writers and artists died. And she had learnt her lesson well. Once released, and after her bitter questions about the past, she again began to appear at great cultural occasions, wheeled out to urge younger comrades to heed the party's call. She continued to do this, even as the police were locking up the young dissidents who had clustered about Peking's Democracy Wall. She was, after all, living in Deng Xiaoping's China, and it was Deng, the new Party General Secretary in 1954, who had overseen the campaigns in which Ding Ling had become a central victim, campaigns which even after his own persecution during the Cultural Revolution, Deng would affirm had been necessary if over-zealous.

So when she was brought back from "obscurity", and her party membership was restored to her (in China this brings many perquisites), Ding Ling kept silent, even on her tours to the West, where she assured her audiences that the bad times were over. If she blamed anyone except the Gang of Four it was not in public. It was the wisest course for an elderly writer who remembered what had happened to those condemned as "anti-party". Most of her literary comrades had died, swept away in the anti-intellectual purges of the 1950s and 1960s. Like her, the few aged survivors were now greatly honoured but had written nothing for thirty years except party-praising set-pieces. As late as the Writers Conference of January 1985, authors who had endured decades of "smashing" confessed that they still lived in fear. It was understandable, then, that Ding Ling, like her own Miss Sophie, preferred to die quietly. (p. 315)

Jonathan Mirsky, "Ding Ling: Setting the Record Straight," in The Times Literary Supplement, *No. 4329, March 21, 1986, pp. 302, 315.*

Susan Brownmiller

A model of the modern emancipated woman in prerevolutionary Shanghai, and an author of scandalous romantic fiction, the Chinese writer Ding Ling joined the Communists in Yanan in the 1930's and edited the literary columns of *Liberation Daily,* the party newspaper. At a critical juncture in party affairs, she allied herself with Mao Zedong's famous dictum that all art must hasten the revolution. Despite her efforts at political rectitude, she was hounded, exiled, and periodically imprisoned from the late 1950's onward.

I Myself Am a Woman, augmented by a long interpretive essay by Tani E. Barlow, an assistant professor of history at the University of Missouri, is the most comprehensive selection of Ding Ling's work yet published in America. We now can ponder at close range the literary progression of a tempestuous rebel caught up in a revolution she believed to be necessary and good, who willingly sacrificed her ironic detachment and subtlest perceptions to the Maoist principle of "serving the people."

It is easy to see why the audacious stories from the 1920's established Ding Ling's literary reputation.

In **"A Woman and a Man"** (1928) the newly married, bored and provocative Wendy (she has dropped her Chinese name) arranges an assignation with Ouwai Ou, a pretentious, dissipated poet who has given himself a Japanese *nom de plume.* Ouwai Ou, alas, finds easier sexual satisfaction with Aijin, a back-alley prostitute who is grateful for his money. Her chastity, if not her feelings of sexual desirability, intact, Wendy returns to her husband armed with the small crumb of insight that Ouwai Ou is "afraid of me! Afraid of me!"

This delightful piece of fiction, which skewers the superficial bourgeois-intellectual circle that Ding Ling had come to detest, mixes a fine sense of place and a minute dissection of her characters' inner feelings with her inimitable signature from that era: a frisky, satirical poke at the double standard. The author of **"A Woman and a Man"** could be a spiritual sister to Jean Rhys.

In the winter of 1930, the father of Ding Ling's child and 23 other Communist activists and writers were executed by Chiang Kai-shek. Her response was swift and irrevocable: she joined the revolutionary struggle.

"Net of Law" (1932) shows the effects of her Marxist transformation. The condition of woman is still close to her heart as she attempts to enter the world of China's proletariat. Alcoholism, wife beating, even murder, are rife in the slums of Hankou, a factory town, but the enemy is plainly the viperish capitalist system. An opaque veil hangs over the inner life of her characters; she prefers to show that the masses are in motion.

"When I Was in Xia Village" (1941) demonstrates the transmogrification of Ding Ling, now a high Party functionary, into Maxim Gorky. Zhenzhen, a poor peasant raped by the Japanese, has contracted a venereal disease. When she returns to her backward village, she is ostracized by the elders. But there is hope for Zhenzhen: the Communist Party arranges for her to go to Yanan for treatment.

Innocuous on the face of it, this story was apparently a factor in Ding Ling's subsequent trouble. Ms. Barlow says that it "upset literary policy enforcers because it reverted back to Ding Ling's earlier preoccupation with sex and justice. It also placed a woman seeking social redress at the center of the plot." I would offer a slightly different emphasis. More likely, Ding Ling's specific ideological heresy lay in placing an *individual's* social redress at the plot's center; in just such hairsplitting distinctions a generation of Chinese writers was destroyed.

In any event, the details of Ding Ling's fall from grace are still murky. Her class background, stormy personal life and high visibility were sufficient grounds for suspicion. A victim of the 1957 antirightist campaign, she was exiled to Manchuria, where she managed to continue writing under the patronage of some old friends in high places. She and thousands of other intellectuals fell into the hands of the Red Guards in 1966. Ding Ling underwent the ritual humiliations of the Great Cultural Revolution—the dunce cap, the public confession—and spent most of the next decade in solitary confinement. She was rehabilitated in 1978 under the aegis of Deng Xiaoping.

"Du Wanxiang," the final story in this collection, dated 1978 but written more than 10 years earlier, is a stolid parable about the hardships of a poor, industrious peasant with minimal skills (actually they are the feminine skills of cooking and cleaning) who triumphs in her desire to serve the people in a development outpost. The last lines read, after the fashion of the day, "Du Wanxiang is our frontline soldier. We must learn from her. We must go forward with her."

Officially restored to a position of eminence, Ding Ling was granted a trip to the United States in 1981, where she visited the University of Iowa's writing program and met with Arthur Miller. A new generation of Chinese writers, impatient for change and disappointed by her continued defense of literary censorship took to calling her Old Shameful. She died a natural death in 1986. (pp. 7-8)

Susan Brownmiller, "For Her Pains, She Was Called Old Shameful," in The New York Times Book Review, *September 3, 1989, pp. 7-8.*

Jonathan Mirsky

In the admirably translated short stories and essays collected in ***I Myself Am a Woman*** (the introduction, unfortunately, is a thicket of fashionable clichés), we see [Ding Ling's] progress, over fifty-one years, from a sensitive observer of the inner lives of sophisticated Chinese to a party hack. Daughter of a self-emancipated woman who chose to educate herself rather than remain a mournful widow, Ding Ling (her pen name) became a member of the May Fourth Movement of the 1920s, which was made up largely of militantly nationalistic young intellectuals—like Mao [Zedong] and Deng Xiaoping—who blamed China's backwardness and oppression on its traditional culture and demanded changes in family and sexual relations, language, and education. During a protracted adolescence in Shanghai she frequently changed lovers, residences, and jobs before publishing, in 1928, **"Miss Sophia's Diary."**

This short story at once made her famous, at least in Shanghai's literary circles, and it remains one of the few works of twentieth-century Chinese literature one can read with pleasure, without making allowances for the isolation of Chinese writers and the difficulties under which they have suffered. It records the emotions of a young woman writer, probably very much like Ding Ling, infatuated with a beautiful, stupid young man. Certain sexually frank passages, graphic enough today, were outrageous in a country where the last emperor had been deposed only fifteen years earlier. Miss Sophia masturbates ("boils my milk")—"I'm never really sure that it suits my taste, no matter how often I do it, but it's the only thing that releases frustration on a windy day"—and she has no illusions about the object of her passion:

> When I think that in this precious, beautiful form I adore, there resides such a cheap, ordinary soul, and that for no apparent reason I've gotten intimate with him several times (but nothing even approaching what he gets at his brothel!) . . . Don't I offer myself to him for his pleasures the same as any whore?

The diary ends bleakly: "Life sneaks on. Death too. Oh, how pathetic you are Sophia." Mao would have hated Miss Sophia; he could look at such people only as coming from the enemy class: "We cannot love enemies, we cannot love social evils, our aim is to destroy them." In the pre-Communist period Chinese readers were free to see her as a weak but not unsympathetic person, and to have mixed feelings about her, as we do for Emma Bovary, upon whom, as Tani Barlow points out, Ding Ling modeled her.

Ding Ling wrote other stories about Shanghai intellectuals in which political and revolutionary themes became prominent (she had joined the underground party in 1932) but not strident, and after her husband was executed, and she had spent a year in one of Chiang Kai-shek's prisons, she escaped to Mao's enclave at Yanan. There she was greeted as a great catch by the Communists. She threw herself into campaigns to promote literacy and circulate anti-Japanese propaganda, but retained her sharp eye and tongue, for which, Mao was to say, there could be no room within the revolution. In 1942 she published the short essay **"Thoughts on March 8"** (especially well translated here by Gregor Benton) to mark International Women's Day. As Tani Barlow says,

> There was something to offend everybody in this essay. Political theorists resented her implication that the Party had an internal class system. War planners were angry because they had yet to find a policy for mobilizing women that served both family interests and the aims of the state.

Women in revolutionary Yanan, Ding Ling wrote, came under traditional pressures to get married and bear children, and they were abused if they remained single or tried to get a divorce—for which they were accused of immorality, although, as she did not say, Mao himself had no inhibitions about disposing of his wives. Ding Ling referred to women's "tragedy," to "the silent oppression they suffer here in Yanan"; she suggested that it would be "better if all Communist Party members were more responsible for their own moral conduct." Worst of all, perhaps, from the Maoist standpoint, she dared to speak not as a revolutionary but because "I myself am a woman, and I therefore understand the failings of women better than others. But I also have a deeper understanding of what they suffer."

This was unacceptable. The Party rejected the notion that women in the Liberated Area had special problems, although all the leaders knew Mao treated his own women badly. Yanan itself was in an especially backward region, where the Party leaders believed that women's liberation, particularly the concept of divorce upon women's demand, would endanger its relations with tradition-bound peasants.

Then came the long, slow tragedy. With Ding Ling in the audience, Mao at the Yan'an Forum of 1942 issued the denunciation that included her own work, and like most other urban radical writers she underwent "rectification." She was required to condemn her own work and confine herself to writings that followed the Party line. After the founding of the People's Republic in 1949, Ding Ling, now awarded a Stalin prize, became a powerful literary functionary. She took part in the anti-intellectual campaigns that began in the early 1950s and she had a hand in more purges of intellectuals than Party norms required, sometimes attacking writers for what they had said during arcane disputes in Shanghai twenty years earlier. In 1957

"From the standpoint of the control system, the primary relationship on the [Chinese] literary scene is between readers and top leadership. The whole point of literature, so viewed, is to cause readers to think what the top leadership feels it is best that they think. . . . Party theorists, borrowing a term from Stalin, explain that literature is a tool for "engineering the soul" of readers."

—Perry Link

Ding Ling's independent past caught up with her and she herself was chosen to be "smashed" by Party officials, who denounced her, using the mixture of political and sexual scandal that the Party reserves for politically fallen women.

Then came public humiliation, internal exile, solitary confinement, more humiliation during the Cultural Revolution, and, in 1978, two years after Mao's death, rehabilitation. The result, sadly, was the emergence into a relatively privileged position of a grande dame who behaved so timidly that she was soon called Old Shameful by those who had counted on her to use her reputation and position to condemn the Party for what it had done to writers. That would have required more courage than she had. By 1976, Deng Xiaoping, the Party boss during the Fifties both when Ding Ling was crushing her enemies and when she herself was purged, had become the most powerful man in China and beyond criticism.

The full measure of her shame can be seen in the story **"Du Wanxiang."** Published in 1978, the year of Ding Ling's release, it had been drafted just before the Cultural Revolution, and is so banal that it must either have been a parody of all the worst aspects of socialist realism or a desperate bid to obtain the author's freedom. As Tani Barlow says—and it takes a devoted translator to work through **"Du Wanxiang"**—the story "juxtaposes old-fashioned four-character idioms and assorted bits and pieces of 'Maospeak.' "

Du Wanxiang is a perfect Maoist heroine. Motherless and from a poor peasant family, she is unerringly cheerful, hard-working, and optimistic, even when she is sold into marriage and treated like Cinderella by her sisters-in-law, whom she soon wins over. She is such a good worker that the Party spots her and trains her to become a minor cadre:

> She was no longer a friendless, pathetic woman who only knew how to toil and how to avoid vicious, brutal scolding and abuse, . . . she was recruited into the Communist Party. She had found her real mother.

Unlike the intellectuals Ding Ling knew intimately, Du Wanxiang and her comrades are delighted to work in the freezing wastelands. "Communist Party! Brilliant and great Communist Party. You've cast such light on humankind! Given such hope, such warmth!" As for Du herself, she told her admiring comrades, "All I want is to stay under the Party's leadership forever."

What had happened to the Ding Ling who had written about Miss Sophia is what happened to most Chinese writers working under Party control after 1942: they no longer wrote for their readers. As the Princeton scholar Perry Link has explained, we "bourgeois" Westerners must first set aside our notions about the primacy of the writer if we are to understand mainland fiction:

> From the standpoint of the control system, the primary relationship on the [Chinese] literary scene is between readers and top leadership. The whole point of literature, so viewed, is to cause readers to think what the top leadership feels it is best that they think. . . . Party theorists, borrowing a term from Stalin, explain that literature is a tool for "engineering the soul" of readers.

(pp. 27-8)

Jonathan Mirsky, "Stories from the Ice Age," in The New York Review of Books, *Vol. XXXVI, No. 16, October 26, 1989, pp. 27-28, 30.*

William Wei

Larger than life, that was Ding Ling, the most distinguished female writer of pre-1949 China. After she had been physically beaten in one particularly nasty episode during the Cultural Revolution, someone said to her, "If I were you, I would die." But she had the spirit to say simply, "No, I must live." And with those words, she did, for nearly two more eventful decades.

Ding Ling began her career as a notorious anarcho-feminist who wrote **"Miss Sophia's Diary,"** an impassioned first-person meditation on sexual frustration, and ended it as a Communist writer who produced such pablum as **"Du Wanxiang,"** a parable on the socialist women in China. The deep tension between the feminist and socialist ideals that had shaped her life and her writings was finally resolved in favor of the latter. Apparently, she had made this decision as early as 1979: her life as a woman was conspicuously absent from a speech she gave that year at the National Congress for Writers and Artists. Her identity as a woman and writer was subordinated to the state ideology.

Even though Ding Ling was one of the most celebrated victims of the Chinese government's intolerance of literary dissidence, she steadfastly refused to blame the Communist Party's control of literature for her victimization, much to the disappointment of the "lost generation" of the Cultural Revolution, who had hoped that she would serve as their spokesperson. She was content to criticize implicitly China's cultural and political leaders, and to attribute her painful persecution to a social phenomenon that encompassed the entire society. She was willing to speak out for party policies and later supported the political campaign against "spiritual pollution" from the West. She seems to have survived her ordeal by believing that the Chinese Communist Party would somehow and someday rehabilitate her, as it did in 1978. How she made the transition from radical feminist to Communist hack is the central question underlying Tani Barlow's superb anthology of Ding Ling's writings, [***I Myself Am a Woman***]. . . .

Initially, Ding Ling's central preoccupation was the need for women to assert their individualism through their female condition. Often that meant liberating themselves sexually as a means of knowing themselves individually. Hence, in many of her early stories the protagonist is a young woman living a liberated life-style, struggling to attain self-awareness through the man she loves or lusts after. But by the early 1930s, after the execution of her lover Hu Yepin by the Nationalists, Ding Ling abandoned this interest in favor of revolutionary politics and produced so-called proletarian pieces centered on class rather than gender. While women and their internal struggle for self-realization were no longer the focus, women were presented as victims of discrimination in society. Later, during the Yan'an period (1937-47), she retreated even further from her early feminist orientation. However, she was still concerned with the oppression of women, especially by so-called progressive forces. In **"Thoughts on March 8,"** she expressed her concerns about the double standards being applied to women and whether the state control of literature did not prevent the needs of women writers and readers from being adequately addressed. Would the state-sanctioned literature correctly represent the experiences of women or would it reduce them to an aspect of political ideology? Ironically, her essay precipitated Mao Zedong's "Talks at the Yan'an Forum on Arts and Literature," which imposed a narrow political doctrine on cultural productions. Until this doctrine was discredited in 1983, literature was reduced to a political tool.

William Wei, "From Miss Sophia to Comrade Wanxiang," in The American Book Review, *Vol. 12, No. 4, September-October, 1990, p. 31.*

FURTHER READING

Feuerwerker, Yi-tsi Mei. *Ding Ling's Fiction: Ideology and Narrative in Modern Chinese Literature.* Cambridge, Mass.: Harvard University Press, 1982, 196 p.

Thorough analysis of Ding Ling's life and career emphasizing the influence of Chinese history and politics on her writing.

Marguerite Duras

1914-

(Born Marguerite Donnadieu) French novelist, playwright, scriptwriter, short story writer, and essayist.

Hailed as one of France's most original and controversial contemporary writers, Duras utilizes fiction, drama, and film to explore the nature of love and the existential conflicts of the individual. While her early novels were considered realistic and stylistically conventional, Duras's later experiments with form, repetition, allusive dialogue, and fragmentation led many critics to label her as one of the French *nouveaux romanciers,* or New Novelists. Juxtaposing biographical and fictitious elements within shifting time frames and questioning the reliability of memory, Duras often challenges the boundaries between fact and fiction, writer and reader. Although frequently presenting characters who become plagued by ambiguities of communication and the temporality of self-knowledge, Duras nonetheless evidences a subtle but persistent faith in love and human survival. Alfred Cismaru asserted: "[Duras] has never given in entirely to all contemporary notions on the absurdity of life and the complete absence of the possibility of happiness. Remote, hidden, hardly traceable but invigorating and restating the dignity of the human condition, hope emerges, at times, from even the most despairing situations."

Duras was born near Saigon, Vietnam, then known as French Indochina. After her father's death in 1918, her mother unwittingly bought a parcel of worthless land in Cambodia from the corrupt colonial government. Even though this purchase led to the family's financial ruin, Duras's mother managed to send her daughter to the prestigious Lycée de Saigon where she studied Vietnamese and French. At the age of seventeen Duras left Cambodia for France and eventually earned a *licence* in law and political science at the University of Paris, Sorbonne. In 1939, while working as a secretary for the Ministry of Colonial Affairs, she married Robert Antelme, an active member of the French Communist party. They divorced seven years later after Antelme returned from a German concentration camp where he was held for one year during World War II. Duras, who also joined the Communist party and was active in the Resistance movement during Germany's occupation of France, began to write fiction shortly after the outbreak of the war.

Critics often divide Duras's literary career into four distinct thematic and stylistic periods. During the first period, she produced three novels commonly described as her most realistic and conventional: *Les impudents, La vie tranquille,* and *Un barrage contre le Pacifique* (*The Sea Wall*). Although Duras was beginning to address the relationship between love and self-destruction, a prominent motif in all her works, most critics concur that her early female characters are emotionally simplistic due to their reliance on men for personal fulfillment. Neither *Les impudents* nor *La vie tranquille* achieved critical or popular success; *The Sea Wall* garnered attention as Duras's first significant novel. This work, which contains strong autobiographical elements, is set in French Indochina and focuses on an impoverished French widow who struggles to support her two young children. In chronicling the widow's attempts to save her crops from a flood by constructing a sea wall, Duras demonstrates her emerging concerns with the internal and external struggles of humankind. Germaine Brée observed: "The very title of the story suggests a dogged, unequal battle against a superhuman force. This was to remain one of Duras's basic themes: barrage against the immense solitude of human beings, barrage against the pain of all involvements, barrage against despair."

Duras's second literary period is marked by a shift from linear plots and abrupt, obscure dialogue to a more personal and ironic idiom. The primary works of this cycle—*Le marin de Gibraltar* (*The Sailor from Gibraltar*) and *Les petits chevaux de Tarquinia* (*The Little Horses of Tarquinia*)—are considered more concentrated than Duras's previous novels because they focus on fewer characters, events, and relationships. *The Sailor from Gibraltar* is the story of Anna, a rich woman who travels on her yacht throughout the Mediterranean in search of her former lover. Duras suggests that Anna's persistence gives significance to her otherwise empty and meaningless life. *The Little Horses of Tarquinia* similarly reflects Duras's increasing interest in individual characters and their varying moods and emotions. A sparse, detached account of two couples who travel to a resort in Italy and engage in "petty quarrels on nothing at all," *The Little Horses of Tarquinia* explores the metaphysics of boredom and inactivity. Alfred Cismaru explained: "As we view [this] society devoured by the solitude of togetherness and the boredom emanating from uneventful events, we are prompted to weigh our own participation in the world, to measure carefully the exact position we occupy in it."

Duras's next literary cycle includes works often described as antinovels, in which she employs minimalist techniques to accent particular experiences or emotions. Some of the better-known antinovels include *Le square* (*The Square*), *Moderato cantabile, Le ravissement de Lol V. Stein* (*The Ravishing of Lol Stein*), and *Le vice-consul* (*The Vice-Consul*). *The Square* is the account of a man and woman who, after meeting on a park bench, struggle to communicate and assert their individual identities despite their unfamiliarity. Duras never reveals the names or ages of the characters, only that the man is a traveling salesman and the woman a maid. *Moderato cantabile,* while structurally more complex than *The Square,* also suggests that individuals are limited in comprehending the emotional significance of a single moment or event. Called an "x-ray of a depression" by Julia Kristeva, *Moderato cantabile* explores negative aspects of love and the complexities of insanity. This story traces the respective reactions of Anne, the wife of a rich industrialist, and Chauvin, one of her husband's workers, after they witness a man killing his unfaithful wife. Every day for a week following the incident, the two characters meet in a café to discuss the murder and to attempt to understand the killer's motivations. Similar themes are addressed in *The Ravishing of Lol Stein,* which describes a woman's descent into madness after being rejected by her fiancé. Considered an antinovel because of its stark narrative, unreliable narrator, and fragmentary contrasts and insights, *The Ravishing of Lol Stein* has also been described as an investigation into human consciousness. *The Vice-Consul,* considered the last of Duras's antinovels, simultaneously focuses on a young Oriental girl who is abandoned by her mother after becoming pregnant and a government official who becomes involved in the glamorous diplomatic life of Calcutta, India. Containing what Alfred Cismaru calls "standard [antinovel] devices: unfinished sentences, subconversations, hidden allusions . . . [and] mysterious and unexplained situations," *The Vice-Consul* is considered one of the most abstract and impressionistic works of this period.

With *La maladie de la mort* (*The Malady of Death*), Duras entered what most critics regard as her fourth and most eclectic literary period. While writing this novel, Duras, who drank excessively throughout much of her adult life, fell into an almost continuous alcoholic stupor. Set in large type and only sixty pages in length, *The Malady of Death* was dismissed by most critics as a publicity stunt by Duras's publisher to promote as a novel what was actually a short story. A minimalist account of an asexual man who pays a prostitute to live with him for a week, this work addresses the man's overwhelming sense of isolation and his inability to love. After *The Malady of Death* was published, Duras checked herself into an alcoholic treatment center at the American Hospital in Paris. During the months of painful withdrawal that followed, she wrote *L'amant* (*The Lover*), which won the prestigious Prix Goncourt in 1984 and became the first of Duras's novels to garner international critical and popular acclaim. Critics concur that this work most effectively synthesized Duras's themes with her minimalist style. While often considered a revised version of *The Sea Wall, The Lover* explores more completely Duras's childhood experiences in French Indochina and her debilitating relationships with her overbearing mother and indolent brothers. Duras writes in the work: "I've written a good deal about the members of my family, but then they were still alive, my mother and my brothers. And I skirted around them, skirted around all these things without really touching them." *The Lover* also examines a young Frenchwoman's first sexual experience and her involvement with a Chinese millionaire. While *The Lover* is recognizably autobiographical, Duras focuses on the recollection of events and their emotional significance rather than on the events themselves, thus creating a complex structure that conveys the illusion of simplicity.

In 1985, Duras published *La douleur* (*The War: A Memoir*), a collection of six narratives believed to have been written during World War II and forgotten for forty years. In the title story, Duras recounts her experiences with the French Liberation Movement during the war. She also describes the mental agony she endured while waiting for her husband, Robert Antelme, to return from a German concentration camp: "I'd like to give him my life. I can't even give him a bit of bread. You can't call this thinking, everything's in a state of suspended animation." While *The War* was faulted for the varying quality of its individual narratives, it also won praise for its stark, honest, and original portrayal of the atrocities of armed conflict. Duras's next work, *Les yeux bleux, cheveux noirs* (*Blue Eyes, Black Hair*), is considered a reworking of *The Malady of Death.* This novel focuses on a homosexual man who pays a woman resembling the man with whom he is infatuated to sleep naked under a yellow lamp. The narrative is written as a stage play and includes a Greek chorus and dialogue reminiscent of stage direction. *Emily L.* also addresses how one's inability to love can lead to self-destruction. Introducing the text with the sentence, "IT BEGAN WITH FEAR," Duras presents the story of a couple who, while drinking in a café, speculate about the lives of another couple sitting at a nearby table. As the narrator and her lover invent a scenario that involves betrayal and unrequited love, they simultaneously delve into the fear and doubts inherent in their own relationship. Marianne Hirsch observed: "All else disappears as one story mirrors the other, as one story feeds the other's despair."

While Duras has earned an international reputation as a novelist, her films and dramas have also received attention for their unusual structures and abstract conceptions of time. Duras's first screenplay, *Hiroshima, mon amour,* a film about the atomic bombing of Hiroshima, was well-received and won several international prizes, including the New York Film Critics Award for best foreign film. Her subsequent films, however, were frequently castigated for being tedious, pretentious, and uncinematic due to periods of long silence and a lack of action. Despite the fact that Duras's films and dramas have received mixed reviews, commentators recognize her mastery of haunting dialogue and strong visual sense, which are also integral components of her fiction. Those critics who commend Duras for the diversity and experimental nature of her canon and her rejection of traditional aesthetics maintain that her open investigation of the complexities and mysteries of the human psyche is the most enduring facet of her work. Carol J. Murphy elaborated: "[The] trajectory of Duras's fictional enterprise remains firmly entrenched in desire—the desire to know how to understand and express that which continually slips away from human understanding."

(See also *CLC,* Vols. 3, 6, 11, 20, 34, 40; *Contemporary Authors,* Vols. 25-28, rev. ed.; and *Dictionary of Literary Biography,* Vol. 83.)

PRINCIPAL WORKS

NOVELS

Les impudents 1943
La vie tranquille 1944
Un barrage contre le Pacifique 1950
[*The Sea Wall,* 1952]
Le marin de Gibraltar 1952
[*The Sailor from Gibraltar,* 1966]
Les petits chevaux de Tarquinia 1953
[*The Little Horses of Tarquinia,* 1960]
Le square 1955
[*The Square,* 1959]
Moderato cantabile 1958
[*Moderato cantabile,* 1960]
Dix heures et demie du soir en été 1960
[*Ten-Thirty on a Summer Night,* 1962]
L'après-midi de Monsieur Andesmas 1962
[*The Afternoon of Monsieur Andesmas,* 1964]
Le ravissement de Lol V. Stein 1964
[*The Ravishing of Lol Stein,* 1966]
Le vice-consul 1966
[*The Vice-Consul,* 1968]
L'amante anglaise 1967
[*L'amante anglaise,* 1968]
Détruire, dit-elle 1969
[*Destroy, She Said,* 1970]
Abahn Sabana David 1970
L'amour 1971
L'homme assis dans le couloir 1980
[*The Seated Man in the Passage,* published in *Contemporary Literature,* Summer 1983]
Agatha 1981
L'homme Atlantique 1982
La maladie de la mort 1982
[*The Malady of Death,* 1986]
L'amant 1984
[*The Lover,* 1985]
La douleur 1985
[*The War: A Memoir,* 1986]
Les yeux bleux, cheveux noirs 1986
[*Blue Eyes, Black Hair,* 1988]
Emily L. 1987
[*Emily L.,* 1989]

PLAYS

Les viaducs de la Seine-et-Oise 1959
[*The Viaducts of Seine and Oise,* published in *Three Plays,* 1967]
Théâtre I: Les eaux et forêts; Le square; La musica 1965
[*The Rivers in the Forests,* 1964; *The Square,* published in *Three Plays,* 1967]
L'amante anglaise 1968
Théâtre II: Suzanna Andler; Des journées entières dans les arbres; "Yes," peut-être; Le shaga; Un homme est venu me voir 1968
[*Suzanna Andler,* 1975; *Days in the Trees,* published in *Three Plays,* 1967]
L'eden cinéma 1977
**Théâtre III: La bête dans la jungle; Les papiers d'Aspern; La danse de la Mort* 1984

SCREENPLAYS

Hiroshima, mon amour 1960
[*Hiroshima, mon amour,* 1961]
Une aussi longue absence [with Gérard Jarlot] 1961

FILMS (SCREENWRITER AND DIRECTOR)

La musica 1966
Jaune le soleil 1971
Nathalie Granger 1972
La femme du Gange 1973
India Song 1974
Baxter, Vera Baxter 1976
Son nom de Venise dans Calcutta désert 1976
Des journées entières dans les arbres 1976
Le camion 1977
Le navire night 1978
Césarée 1979
Les mains négatives 1979
Aurélia Steiner, dite Aurélia Melbourne 1979
Aurélia Steiner, dite Aurélia Vancouver 1979
Agatha ou les lectures illimitées 1981
L'homme Atlantique 1981
Dialogue de Rome 1982
Les enfants 1984

OTHER

Des journées entières dans les arbres (short stories) 1954
[*Whole Days in the Trees and Other Stories,* 1984]
Les parleuses (interviews) 1974
[*Woman to Woman,* 1987]
Outside (essays) 1981
Le vie materielle (recorded conversations) 1986
[*Practicalites: Marguerite Duras Speaks to Jérôme Beaujour,* 1990]

*Les papiers d'Aspern is adapted from Henry James's The Aspern Papers and La danse de mort is adapted from August Strindberg's The Dance of Death.

Bettina L. Knapp

Yet another fluid, facile, impressionistic work has poured forth from Duras's pen. Unfortunately, [in ***La maladie de la mort***], her poetic prose, once so moving and aesthetically captivating, has become redundant and repetitive. What had been innovative—the discovery of the feeling world, the concretization of instinct and the dream, the depiction of that fine line dividing sanity and insanity—incised so brilliantly in ***Le ravissement de Lol V. Stein*** and ***Le vice-consul*** among other works, has now been worked to *death.* Lately, Duras has made us privy to minutiae, representations revolving around well-worn themes such as the need to love and be loved, the sexual urge, and so forth. Surely, these are potent factors in life, but it is incumbent upon the artist to inject new blood, fresh perceptions into sensations and feelings—an uninvitiated *élan vital* that will empower the work to live powerfully, viscerally, and indelibly in the mind's eye. Duras seems to have reached an impasse in ***La maladie de la mort***—a *dead* spot ironically speaking.

In this her latest work, she introduces the reader to a man who longs to immerse himself in the feminine principle which would afford him a sense of completion, fulfillment—love. As he walks around a bed in the center of the room, observing the nude body of a prostitute lying on it full view, he describes her glistening form that emerges like a hierophany in the night, shedding its mysterious fascination in pulsating rhythms. Silence enfolds the couple during the love-making episodes: as mortal is transformed into immortal, the many into the one, as if Parvati and Siva had been incarnated in all of their glory. Unity, however, is followed by diversity; isolation corrodes those who have embraced; tension supplants what had been indelibly glued—bodies. Flesh has separated from flesh; each is shut up in his and her world of silence and isolation—encapsulated paradoxically in infinite blackness. The man pursues his ambulations, looks at the body in slumber as it responds evenly or spasmodically to cosmic rhythms; its silken sheen, velvety lines, supple and firm skin, become palpable like a sculpture. Suddenly she vanishes. The mythical void takes over and what had once been alive and warm is transformed into bloodless particles: "la maladie de votre vie, la maladie de la mort" is the fate meted out to one who cannot really love.

Although captivating on the surface, ***La maladie de la mort*** is simplistic. To retrieve the greatness that Duras had once offered the world, a descent into Self must be experienced. Only then will she be forced to wrestle with the *prima materia*—those cataclysmic forces inhabiting her unconscious; only then will she emerge from the rite of passage with unvitiated perceptions—the raw, fresh, neoteric experience. (pp. 751-52)

Bettina L. Knapp, in a review of "La maladie de la mort," in The French Review, *Vol. LVIII, No. 5, April, 1985, pp. 751-52.*

Walter Clemons

The international success of her affecting novel ***The Lover*** . . . has made Marguerite Duras a hot property. Her early novels are being reprinted in paperback, and Brooke Shields recently starred off-Broadway in one of her plays. The teasing mixture of fact and fiction in her work is a potent factor in its appeal. ***The Lover*** reads like a nakedly autobiographical account of an affair between a 15-year-old in prewar Indochina and a rich Chinese 12 years her senior. Yet its shrewdest American critic, Barbara Probst Solomon, warned that the tale shouldn't be swallowed literally but is better read as a parable of French colonialism and its heroine as a mythic creation.

The mythic element is strong in Duras's newest book, which is presented as a work of nonfiction. ***The War*** is an ostensible diary that Duras says she found in a cupboard and doesn't remember writing. The time is 1944. Duras works with the Resistance and awaits the return of her husband, Robert L., who had been deported to a concentration camp. Yet the diary contains historical perspectives unavailable at the time. "I can't see myself writing the diary," she says at the start. "One thing is certain: it is inconceivable to me that I could have written it while I was actually awaiting Robert L.'s return."

One's impatience with this obfuscation is lessened by the power of the narrative. It gives a tense, absorbing picture of a hectic period. Duras is scathing on French "mothball" patriots, who had put their uniforms away until it was safe to dress up for the liberation. Uniformed Gaullist ladies "wear the special smile of women who want people to see both how tired they are and what efforts they're making to conceal it."

The book's most harrowing passage describes her husband's return from Belsen, so near death from starvation that he had to be fed cautiously, lest food kill him. His heart, "grown enormous in the cave of his emaciation . . . was beating so fast you couldn't have counted its beats." He shed his fingernails and excreted a green slime "with a smell . . . of humus, of dead leaves, of dense undergrowth. It was a somber smell, dark reflection of the dark night from which he was emerging and which we would never know." The devotion with which she nursed him is so convincing that the shock to the reader is electric when she matter-of-factly reveals that as soon as Robert L. was stronger, she asked for a divorce in order to marry D., her companion in the Resistance. Robert L. "didn't ask me my reasons for leaving. I didn't tell him what they were." Nor does she tell us.

This apparently factual narrative is as artful as Lillian Hellman's reminiscences, and one mistrusts Duras when she decorates her harsh story with fancy poetic musings. She does not, however, portray herself as noble. She lacerates herself for flirting with a Gestapo agent marked for assassination by the resistance. She writes a remarkable story about her attraction to a handsome, 23-year-old collaborator without "a thought in his head, only desires; he's got a body made for pleasure, riotous living, fighting, girls." On what might be the last day of his life he gambled with his captors "with a real urge to play, the urge of someone who's going to live, no less."

This book of fragments trails off with a couple of arty stories without genuine urgency. Another recent Duras work, ***The Malady of Death,*** printed on 60 pages of huge primer type, is a wispy, abstract meditation of love and death that will make you very cross if you buy it in the hope of enjoying a story of the intensity of ***The Lover*** or the best pages of ***The War.*** Duras is a sometimes powerful, sometimes pretentious artiste. It would be a mistake to dismiss her because she's not always to be taken as seriously as she takes herself. ***The Lover,*** if you haven't yet read it, is stunning.

Walter Clemons, "Mythologies of Marguerite," in Newsweek, *Vol. CVII, No. 17, April 28, 1986, p. 74.*

Francine du Plessix Gray

[***The War: A Memoir***] is a complex and extraordinary book, a collection of six narratives, four overtly autobiographical and two fictional, set in France at the end of World War II. Its title chapter is the most powerful text I have read about that period. Marguerite Duras describes the weeks of 1945 during which she waited to know if her husband had survived imprisonment in Germany, and her struggle to save his life after he returned from Belsen. The memories it relates are so harrowing that the author claims not to recall how or when she composed it. Its original draft, she tells us, was only discovered in 1984 in a cupboard in her country house. "I found myself confronted," Miss Duras writes in her introduction, "with a tremendous chaos of thought and feeling that I couldn't bring myself to tamper with, and beside which literary work was something of which I felt ashamed." The book's original French title was ***La douleur*** (*Pain*).

Because it is equally sublime as a literary work and as an act of witness, because its style and theme so tightly encapsulate the last four decades of this admirable writer's career, the first chapter of ***The War*** needs to be fully considered on its own merit, rather than as a prelude to the less accomplished texts that follow it.

Throughout the several genres in which Miss Duras has worked—novel, film, drama—her principal concern has been the interplay of fidelity, memory and obsession, particularly as they relate to the lives of women. Her central theme is that the power of our obsessions vastly supersedes our fidelity to the remembered *object* of our obsessions. Miss Duras's characteristic heroine is driven to neurosis by her obsessive memory of a lost love (usually a feckless, inconsequential man) who might return to offer her some form of liberation, and for whom she is willing to wait indefinitely. One recalls ***Hiroshima, mon amour, The Ravishing of Lol Stein, Ten-Thirty on a Summer Night, Moderato contabile, The Sailor From Gibraltar*** and ***The Lover,*** whose motif of "love unto death" pertains equally to the male protagonist. Miss Duras's women identify so totally with the male object of their obsessions that their loyalty is ultimately a form of fidelity to the self. Their fixations far transcend any erotic longing, are almost mystical in their irrationality and fervor. And their hallucinatory, faithful waiting embodies the author's ambiguous feminist vision—woman as both passive victim and active redeemer, woman as sanctuary of mythic memory and principal interpreter of human suffering. (He: "You saw nothing in Hiroshima." She: "I saw everything in Hiroshima . . . I have wept for years about Hiroshima.")

As a committed feminist and left-wing militant, Miss Duras's insistence on the traditional themes of redemptive memory and love has set her apart from the pessimism and formalism of the "nouveau roman" school. Her firmly structured plots, her complex emotional bonds make her as different from Alain Robbe-Grillet or Claude Simon as John Updike, say, is different from John Barth or John Hawkes. And unlike many of her French contemporaries, Miss Duras has never allowed the surface of language to become the central pleasure of her texts. Her concerns have been more psychological and metaphysical. Through a diction that ranges from telegraphic terseness to incantational languor, she has sought to shape cadences that might simulate her protagonists' inevitably tormented states. "We're the only ones who are still waiting, in a suspense as old as time," Miss Duras writes in the opening chapter of ***The War,*** "that of women always, everywhere, waiting for the men to come home from the war." At no time has her theme of women's fidelity to memory been more movingly and mimetically stated than in this meditation on the horrors of World War II.

The memoir is set in Paris in April of 1945, as Allied forces begin to liberate the concentration camps, and the first full account of Nazi atrocities is being disclosed to the free world. Marguerite Duras and the war prisoner she waits for—her husband, a resistance fighter, Robert L.—had already decided before his arrest that they would separate. Miss Duras plans to divorce Robert L. to marry his best friend, D., whose child she wishes to bear. And yet: "I've chosen to wait for Robert like this, unto death." D., who becomes as fully dedicated as Miss Duras to Robert's survival, will be instrumental in saving his life; he travels to Belsen three days after its liberation to rescue the barely alive, 75-pound victim. So the memoir is infused by obsessions that far transcend the force of love or the deepest friendships, and have a quality of almost religious dedication.

Unlike ***The Lover,*** a partly masked autobiographical novel, ***The War***'s first chapters are pure memoirs and cloak none of their historical particulars. Any biographical sketch of Miss Duras makes it evident that "Robert L." refers to her first husband, the writer Robert Antelme, and that "D." is the philosopher Dionys Moscolo, father of Miss Duras's only son. The current President of France, François Mitterrand—also referred to by his underground name, Morland—is prominent in the narrative as the resistance leader who first identifies the barely recognizable Robert L. amid a heap of dead and dying men at Belsen and arranges for D.'s rescue mission.

The only autobiographical aspect of ***The War***'s first chapter that may be fictional is Miss Duras's claim, in her introduction, that she did not "tamper" with the original draft she happened to find in 1984, on the 40th anniversary of the Liberation. For one of the book's most memorable achievements is the skill with which pure pain is etched into Miss Duras's idiom, a skill never so fully evidenced in her writing of the 1950's or 60's, and rarely achieved by anyone but the most mature artist. In these pages Miss Duras's language goes beyond mimesis, loses all semblance of a stylistic device, becomes a clay into which the Nazi terror and the sorrow of waiting becomes encrusted. Her dislocated syntax and skeletal, willfully artless diction simulate as they never have before the narrator's anguish, suspense, confusion.

> I'm so afraid, I'm not waiting any more. Is it all over? Is it? Where are you? How can I tell? I don't know where he is. I don't know where I am either. I don't know where we are. What's this place called? What sort of place is it? . . . Who is this Robert L.? . . . Why should he be waited for, he rather than another? What is she really waiting for? What other waiting? . . . What's going on in that room? Who is she?

"Marguerite" so identifies with the suffering or dead prisoner that she herself comes close to starvation, unable to eat a morsel. "The bread is bread he hasn't eaten, the bread for lack of which he died." Like most of her fictional heroines, the torment of waiting leads her to hallucinate; she wanders through the city "like a sleepwalker."

"His mouth is half open. It's evening. He thought of me before he died. The pain is so great it can't breathe, it gasps for air. Pain needs room. There are far too many people in the streets; I wish I were on a great plain all alone. Just before he died he must have spoken my name."

A different phase of terror begins when the spectral prisoner is driven back from Belsen with Mr. Mitterrand's help and is carried home to his wife; he is a near-cadaver with a smile of "supernatural weariness . . . of embarrassment." His head is "gaunt but sublime, it emerged alone from that bag of bones . . . the neck was so withered and shrunken—you could circle it with one hand." Robert L. can only be fed a spoonful of gruel an hour; each feeding is quickly succeeded by excretions of "inhuman" feces, which "separated him from us more than the fever . . . the nailless fingers, the marks of SS blows." Marguerite is now submerged by her obsession to restore him to life, unable to sleep more than an hour at a time in fear of losing him in her sleep. "My identity has gone. I'm just she who is afraid when she wakes."

In the last four decades we have often been warned that human speech is too frail to bear the weight of horror forced upon us by the Holocaust, that we may have to resort to some form of "literature of silence" to narrate the Totally Inhuman. As she describes a man returned from the Beyond of Nazi camps, Miss Duras's minimal, bone-spare diction approximates this necessary zero-degree of language. The presence of death is even more concrete and harrowing in these pages than in any eyewitness account of the camps that comes to mind—Elie Wiesel's *Night,* Leon Poiakoff's *Auschwitz.* It is all the more present, perhaps, because Miss Duras does not describe the phenomenon of mass destruction that is "beyond literature," but keeps it on the scale of our perception through one individual's agony. Barbara Bray's translation is so superb that I was even more moved by her English rendering than by the original.

In time the obsessive hunger of many deportees invades Robert L., replacing his fever. "Methodically, as if performing a duty, he was doing what he had to do to live. He ate. . . . He has gone and hunger has taken his place." Robert L. also survives Marguerite's restatement of their impending divorce, and the news that his 24-year-old sister has died at Ravensbrück. A year after his return from death, when he is convalescing on a Mediterranean beach, Marguerite watches him walking, still leaning on a cane, toward the sea. "I looked at him. He saw me looking. He blinked his eyes behind his glasses and smiled at me, giving little shakes of the head, as you do when you're laughing at someone." The first chapter of ***The War*** ends with this religious image, very uncharacteristic of the left-wing, agnostic French avant-garde with which Miss Duras has been associated, the image of a resurrection achieved through obsessive fidelity and faith.

One must now deal with the more problematic narratives that succeed this brief and monumental text. Each of ***The War***'s chapters is preceded by a few italicized paragraphs discussing its degree of verity or fiction. Chapters Two through Four, all autobiographical, are also linked by the theme of reversal: Duras the victim now plays the role of executioner.

In **"Monsieur X., Here Called Pierre Rabier,"** the narrator flashes back to 1944, the last days of the Nazi occupation of Paris, when her Resistance network has ordered her to stay in touch with a Gestapo agent who is enamored of her. At the war's end, after she has testified against Rabier at his trial, a guilt-stricken Miss Duras tries to take the witness stand again to say that he once saved a Jewish family; but the courtroom of vengeful Parisians turns against her and orders his execution. **"Albert of the Capitals"** deals with another informer, whose interrogation under torture Miss Duras most brutally and efficiently conducts after the Liberation: "The more they hit and the more he bleeds, the more it's clear that hitting is necessary, right, just." The most convincing narrative of the book's middle section, it is made powerful by Miss Duras's amazing candor about her own potential for violence. And **"Ter of the Militia"** concerns a young, still more inconsequential informer who was once at her mercy, and whose execution or amnesty she is not certain of to this day.

Given the grandeur of ***The War***'s first chapter, it is hard to determine what failed in Miss Duras's artistry when composing or revising these three relatively anecdotal, coarsely crafted tales. Their principal interest is political: They document an aspect of the French Resistance that has remained taboo for four decades—the gratuitous violence that overtook many underground fighters upon the Liberation, when "some drove off every morning in hopes of still finding a fight."

Throughout these narratives one senses that Miss Duras is extremely uneasy with the theme of the Liberation's violence and suffused with self-contempt for her own participation in it. The key to her anguish may lie in an oracular sentence that comes in her introduction to **"Albert of the Capitals."** "Learn to read them properly," she tells us about these texts, "they are sacred." Questioned about the meaning of these words in a recent interview, Miss Duras answered that as executioner she stood guilty under some absolute law. So it is possible that Duras the moralist and pacifist is still coming to terms with a transgression too painful to shape into art, that it is easier for her (for any one of us) to find a language for the memory of pain than for the memory of guilt.

As for the last two texts in ***The War,*** they are wan, vaguely surreal little fictions about anomic loners musing over their fate after the armistice. It is hard to know why they were included in this collection, whose successive chapters tend to decrease in stature. Yet one ends ***The War*** without any sense of disillusionment; rather, one is enormously grateful for an initial text whose power and uniqueness fulfill a principal condition of art—to transfigure life's pain. (pp. 148-9)

Francine du Plessix Gray, "The Power of Our Obsessions," in The New York Times Book Review, *May 4, 1986, pp. 1, 48-9.*

Julian Barnes

The French *nouveau roman* has been one of the least charming literary modes of the last few centuries: 39 ways of looking at a Venetian blind, for none of which will the writer take responsibility. There is a sort of inverted boasting about it; the stance of "I don't know any better than you" seemed in its day wry and sophisticated, but now appears coy and fake-ignorant. Plot is vulgar; character is old-fashioned ("But how can we ever know what someone is *really* like?" the *nouveau romancier* feebly and self-excusingly cries); tenses and persons are fiddled with (past to present, first to third—distancing devices to keep book and writer at arm's length from the reader); above all, the tone is cool and unimpressed. While to ask about truth—how true, for instance, was Marguerite Duras' ***The Lover?***—merely displays a coarse and prelapsarian mind. Autobiography filtered through a bad memory may as well be called fiction: why not?

[***The War: A Memoir,*** a] new collection of texts (as Marguerite Duras would, and does, prefer to call them), is tricked out with typically irritating explanations of their status. "This text has remained unpublished for forty years. Now I can't remember what it's about. But it's a text that takes off on its own. It might well work in the cinema." We'll be the judge of that, the uncowed response to that final remark might be; and one is also impelled to ask how you manage to rewrite a story when you can't remember what it was about in the first place. Another chapter begins with this advertisement: "I give you the torturer along with the rest of the texts. Learn to read them properly: they are sacred." Here we are reminded that feyness can quite happily co-exist with arrogance in a writer, and that the "I can't remember composing this" line (genuine as it might be) also implies "But I certainly think it's worth publishing."

Yet pick your way past these nettles and strands of barbed wire, and Marguerite Duras' book proves forcefully interesting. Four chunks of diary or as-it-were diary (readers mustn't be too sure of the status of what they're getting) plus two very short stories evoke the paranoid reality of occupied (and just-liberated) Paris with a rich conviction enhanced by the spare, almost arid technique. The lack of drama in the prose, plus the absence of heroics or sentimentality in the tone, powerfully set off the violent reality of the subject matter.

In the title memoir [**"The War"**] (the most normally dramatic piece in the book) Duras' husband is rescued in the nick of time from Belsen (by the young Francois Mitterrand, no less) and agonizingly nursed back to life. **"Monsieur X., Here Called Pierre Rabier"** recounts the nervously symbiotic relationship between Duras the *resistante* and a Nazi collaborator, in which it rapidly becomes unclear who has power over whom (the moral world of this piece is reminiscent of Greene's *The Tenth Man*). **"Albert of the Capitals"** describes without flinching or special pleading a torture session in which Duras was the interrogator, while **"Ter of the Militia"** concerns a likable, womanizing collaborator motivated not by political belief but by a taste for action—the hardest sort of enemy to deal with, since he accepts his probable fate, and declines to bear a grudge against you, his executioners.

It is in areas like these, where the moral line blurs, where the enemy becomes understandable and human, where you get too close and the vision begins to blur, that Duras is at her strongest. If these four texts were indeed written during or just after the war and have remained largely unrevised, then they display a clarity of mind and eye remarkable in a 30-year-old. But there is a daunting chilliness there too: when Robert L., Duras' husband, returns from Belsen, he has barely got his strength back when she tells him that she is going off with a Resistance comrade called D. "I said that even if D hadn't existed I wouldn't have lived with him again. He didn't ask me my reasons for leaving. I didn't tell him what they were." Is it sentimental to feel that the fellow deserves a better explanation than this; and is it unreasonable to feel that we, as readers, deserve one too? (pp. 3, 9)

Julian Barnes, "Duras Mines Her Memories," in Book World—The Washington Post, *May 18, 1986, pp. 3, 9.*

Erika Munk

Hiroshima, mon amour was a revelation to me in my youth. So, in a period of excitement about the New Novel, was ***The Square.*** Then, for many years, I knew Marguerite Duras's work primarily through her plays, and felt no sharp desire to know more. In them, nothing was lived in the moment, everything in retrospect, and though this was a bold principle, it seemed—at least in American productions—a deadly practice. Her world was static and enervating. Her most recent book, ***The War*** is, on the contrary, moving and alive. And, by revealing what her work has lost, placing later characters and events in their true background, it explains a great deal about the particular atmosphere of her other writing.

War isn't this book's proper title: Duras called it ***La douleur,*** suffering. (Is suffering too much for American readers to deal with, while war is considered appealing to us?) Duras sees war not just antiheroically, in the *Good Soldier Schweik* worm's-eye-view grimly comic tradition, but as the violence and loss of those who stay home and those who are captive. There is the suffering of anxiety, and the suffering of the concentration camps, the suffering of the loving and the loveless, the tortured and the torturers—who aren't always whom you'd expect in a World War II story. Heroism exists, but doggedly, tiredly, without any large gestures. There are no battle scenes. ***La douleur*** is never cynical; nevertheless, it has a very strong smell of the truth.

Calling it ***The War*** does isolate—as *Suffering* would not—what makes this book so different from Duras's later prose: an intimate, clear grounding in lived history. External and internal forces clash directly, and the most passionate subjectivity is framed in familiar headlines. The Gestapo's on the street, DeGaulle's on the radio, Mitterand's on the phone. This immediacy, this density of circumstance, is in startling contrast to Duras's typical repetitions and inwardness.

In Duras's autobiographical Indochina novels—***The Sea Wall,*** 1950; ***The Lover,*** 1984—her family's suffering as poor settlers at the mercy of a cold and stupid colonial bureaucracy is central; escape is the only solution. Otherwise, most of her fiction seems unweighted, no matter how exotic the setting, by time and place; in her play ***India Song,*** exploitation and leprosy even have an unpleasantly symbolic function, as if they're present to illuminate and counterpoint the Europeans' spiritual state (despite Duras's hatred of colonialism and her active opposition to the French during the Algerian War). Judging from what's been translated, only the screenplay for ***Hiroshima, mon amour*** deals directly with the interweaving of public and private emotion that occurs when history impinges on us.

The first half of ***The War***—by far its most compelling section—is a rough journal, which Duras says she found in her country house after forgetting it for 40 years. The first part of this narrative records, with excruciating care, what it means to wait for someone you love. It is April 1945. The concentration camps are being liberated; Berlin is surrounded but has not yet fallen. Duras's husband, Robert L., has been a political prisoner in Germany for a year, and she is living through the most extreme anguish of anxiety.

Her coolest thought is, "He might come straight here and ring at the front door, 'Who's there?' 'Me.' Or he might phone from a transit center." More often, she imagines his death:

> In a ditch, face down, legs drawn up, arms outstretched, he's dying. . . . He's been dead for three weeks. Yes, that's what's happened. I'm certain of it. I walk faster. His mouth is half open. It's evening. He thought of me before he died. The pain is so great it can't breathe, it gasps for air. . . . All along the roads of Germany there are men lying like him. Thousands, tens of thousands, and him.

She isn't soft on herself; she shows the egotism of this suffering, has Robert L. speaking her name as his last word no matter what death throes she envisions. She feels singled out, persecuted. "No one has anything in common with me. The street. At this moment there are people in Paris who are laughing, especially the young. I have nothing left but enemies." She is sorry for herself: "No one can know my struggle against visions of the black ditch." Her lover, D., is frightened and annoyed at her obsessiveness: "You're sick. You're a madwoman." She agrees. "My cowardice is such that it can't be described, except by D."

But her frailty is only part of her character. If only she'd shut up about her worries, her fantasies, she would seem quite compassionate. Duras is careful to place her own waiting among all the women's waiting.

> We're starting to find out about the Jews. Madame Katz waited for six months. . . . Her daughter had died in March 1945; it took nine months to trace the name. . . . Madame Katz says (word for word), 'All her underwear is washed and mended and ironed. I've had her black coat lined and the pockets seen to . . . I've had new tips put on her shoes and darned her stockings. I don't think I've forgotten anything.' Madame Katz is challenging God.

There are many such anecdotes, precise and heartwrenching.

And whatever misery she's in, Duras conscientiously puts out a newspaper, questions returned prisoners, sets up an information network to make it easier for people to find each other. As a member of the Resistance, she is scathing about the last-minute appearance of Gaullist patriots, "the France of authority." "We wonder where these people have sprung from, and these clothes, impeccable after six months of occupation, these leather shoes, these hands, this tone of voice." (Her picture of such opportunists, and of the difficulties encountered by anyone trying to trace a deportee, is confirmed in François Maspero's *Cat's Grin,* another wonderful book about the Occupation and Liberation).

Duras has a grand contempt for those who are trying to use the suffering of the war to build a political case. "I venture to ask, 'How do you get news to the families?' . . . (A French officer) looks at me and bursts out laughing. 'You don't understand. It's not a question of news. We're collecting information about Nazi atrocities.' " She is grimly sarcastic: "On page two of *FN* (newspaper of the *Front National*) it says a thousand deportees were burned alive in a barn near Magdeburg on the morning of April 13. In *Art and War* Frédéric Noël says, 'Some people think war brings artistic revolution, but war really operates on other levels.' "

Still, no matter how carefully she reads the papers and listens to the men who've come back, nothing prepares Duras for what happened in Germany. Compared to the reality of his homecoming, her scenarios of Robert L.'s death could be clips from a movie, scenes from a war novel a hundred years old. After two generations of Holocaust imagery this innocence is almost unfathomable, and deeply illuminating. (My 13-year-old daughter could describe the condition Robert L. was likely to be in, coming back from Belsen.) "I was told later that the concierge had put decorations up in the hall to welcome him, and that as soon as he'd gone by she tore them all down and shut herself up alone in her lodge to weep." Normal human imagination, even a novelist's, has been proved inadequate, beside the point.

Duras and D. nurse Robert back to the living. The vividness of her description is astonishing, each detail of his transparent emaciation, his inhuman shit, his swollen heart a ruinous commentary on the poverty of her fantasies. "His legs look like crutches inside his trousers. When the sun shines you can see through his hands." Against all probabilities, Robert L. lives. "He crams everything down. If the dishes don't come fast enough, he sobs and says we don't understand."

He lives, but he—like the world—is changed.

> He doesn't say what he's thinking. He's hidden. He's dark. Then by the side of the road one morning that huge headline: Hiroshima. It's as if he'd like to lash out, as if he's blinded by a rage through which he has to pass before he can live again. . . . Hiroshima is perhaps the first thing outside his own life that he sees or reads about. . . . He wrote a book on what he thought he had experienced in Germany. It was called *The Human Race.* Once the book was written, finished, published, he never spoke of the German concentration camps again. Never uttered the words again. Never again. Nor the title of the book.

The relations between people in this story are intense, direct, natural, helpful: the closeness of comrades. There is self-description, but no self-analysis. The action is resolutely unpsychologized, and the short shrift given motivation can be startling. Five pages from the end of the memoir we read: "More strength came back (to Robert L.). Another day I told him we had to get a divorce, that I wanted a child by D. . . . that even if D. hadn't existed I wouldn't have lived with him again. He didn't ask me my reasons for leaving. I didn't tell him what they were."

Therapeutically minded cynics might think that the extremity of her suffering came from guilt. But this is a shallow and reductive thought, which the whole tone of the story contradicts. It's also wrong on the evidence: the diary ends with Duras, D., Robert L., a woman who seems to be Robert L.'s girlfriend, and other friends on a Mediterranean beach. The men, except Robert, are playing ball. "We can still hear the players. But Robert L.—we still can't hear him. It's in that silence that the war's still there, flowing across the sand and through the wind."

Three other autobiographical pieces and two short stories complete the volume. The latter are schematic and calculated, too easily "moving," especially in their use of child characters. The ones about herself, however, are revealing glosses on the main narrative: in **"Monsieur X., Here Called Pierre Rabier,"** Duras strings along a Gestapo agent until her Resistance comrades can identify him for the kill; in **"Albert of the Capitals,"** she takes over the interrogation of an informer who's being beaten and shows her own hatred and violence; in **"Ter of the Militia,"** she finds herself sexually attracted by another collaborator. All three stories take place before Robert comes home.

Rabier, the agent, interests Duras because of his "illusion that a person may exist solely as a dispenser of reward and punishment. An illusion that takes the place of ethics, philosophy, and morality—and not only in the police." What struck me was his extreme, inhuman loneliness, in contrast to the closeness and purpose with which she and her companions did their dangerous work. **"Albert"** shows the moral ambiguities of the Resistance once it was victorious, ambiguities from which Duras doesn't exempt herself. **"Ter"** is slight and oddly patronizing: the young fascist as a heedless, life-loving child-animal. The point of all three stories is to show the Resister as death-dealer; the problem is that Duras strikes poses. Which remain poses even when she's aware of them. The full suffering of the war didn't come home to her until the camps were opened.

The Little Horses of Tarquinia, first published in France in 1952, could be an autobiographical continuation of ***The War,*** though the voice of the writer has undergone a profound metamorphosis—from first person to third, from "diary" to fiction, from the historic to the familial—but also from passion to observation. We are on the same beach, bounded by the same river and sea and mountains, where ***The War*** ended, among a group of vacationing intellectuals who by very little stretch of the imagination might include Duras and D. (now her husband), and Robert and Ginetta (now their best friends, under new names).

They are bored, it's too hot, there's nothing to do, no one can get up the energy even for a sightseeing excursion, they complain about the food, drink a lot, squabble with their maid. Up on the mountain, a young man has died while defusing mines left over from the War, and his parents sit by a box of his fragments, refusing to give it up to the local authorities.

At the hotel, a stranger with a motorboat appears, and the narrator goes to bed with him; then she realizes her loyalty to her husband. It doesn't seem to mean much to her either way. The war is still killing without purpose, but it has also killed purpose. These are Parisians who rarely even argue about ideas, whose personal and intellectual lives are frayed. There's something they no longer know or feel, which they were fully attuned to in ***The War.*** Losing politics, and losing the immediacy of suffering, Duras seems to have settled for the minutiae of domestic life, beautifully limned, framed in a few modest moral dilemmas.

Duras's sentences here seem uttered in a void, and their overwhelming emotion is loneliness; the effect of her prose on the reading mind is like the effect of her static, repetitive stage imagery on the eye: gestures and dialogue, and suffering, take place in a cool, distanced silence. The reader sinks into this novel as into a torpid, sensual month on the water, noticing the ethical framework, watching it wash out in a sea of dispassion.

Perhaps, given her postwar experience with Stalinism, Duras was bound to move this way. There's a passage in ***The Lover:***

> Collaborators, the Fernandezes were. And I, two years after the war, I was a member of the French Communist party. The parallel is complete and absolute. The two things are the same, the same pity, the same call for help, the same lack of judgment, the superstition if you like, that consists in believing in a political solution to the personal problem.

The difficulty is that she can't find a personal solution either.

The Sailor from Gibraltar, also first published in 1952, again takes place right after the war. [The] cover quotes—on the front, "A haunting tale of strange and random passion"; on the back, "Charming . . . all sun and sea and beautiful people making love . . . a very attractive book"—entice us with their contradictions, but neither one is true. This is the tale of an exemplary alienated man who finds purpose for his life by latching on to someone else's obsession. The narrator, who has been working for years in the registry section of the Colonial Ministry, copying out birth and death certificates, takes his lover on vacation to Italy. She's defined in the book's second and third sentences—"Jacqueline made no objection. She never made any objection"—and their relationship, just as cogently, is defined a little further on: "I watched her talking, and she seemed pleased at this—perhaps she thought I was listening. I hadn't looked at her properly for I don't know how long; months."

When he does take a good look, he hates her. They're in Florence; it's too hot to go sightseeing. He takes her to a village by the sea, with a river running through it, where he ditches her after falling in love at first sight. The rest of the book is spent drifting on a yacht, at the whim of a woman who endlessly searches for her lost, criminal, great love while fucking anyone who takes her fancy. He has traded a boring, conformist, loveless alienation for an exotic—though also boring—rich, bohemian, eroticized pointlessness. This is a funny book, despite too many sentences like, "Over our heads, above the awfulness of life, the sun went on shining, blazing." But what it mainly achieves is a completely implausible answer to the dilemma of a man who was happy during the war ("It was dangerous . . . but I was happy"), and hasn't been since.

Lol Stein is a 1966 novel in which Durassians find her essence. Lol Stein, deserted by her fiancé when he falls in love at first sight—Duras really believes in this phenomenon—returns to the scene of her betrayal and becomes a voyeur (voyeuse?), peeping on a childhood friend who is adulterously carrying on with a man fascinated by Lol. Not even peeping, really; if I have the sightlines right, she can see the window of the hotel room where they meet but not inside to the bed.

Duras, however, does not intend her readers to have such vulgar thoughts. We are to meditate on memories, on repetition, on identity. The characters—brain-dead bourgeois—are over and over called by their full, improbable names: Lol Stein, Tatiana Karl, Michael Richardson, John Bedford. The writing is portentous in the extreme. "His face had tightened into the full of maturity. Pain was etched upon it, ancient, primordial pain . . . it now had to be played out to the bitter end." Not untypical. As the narrator says: "I make no effort to fight the deadly monotony of Lol's memory." If ***Lol Stein*** is indeed epitomical Duras, I admit to failing the test and finding it vacant.

It's hard to believe that ***The War*** is a found text, a genuinely forgotten old diary. (The French critics were quite skeptical about its so-timely appearance on the anniversary of the Liberation, and I'm somewhat bemused by the equally timely way Mitterand is the *deus ex machina* in the first story, and Duras saves his life in the second.) On the other hand, the intensity of its portrayal of what happened in the camps is timely in the best possible way, given the current French vogue for declaring that the Holocaust never happened. It seems equally inconceivable, however, that Duras could have written it right after she finished ***The Malady of Death*** published in France in 1982 and just released here.

The Malady of Death is, first off, a bit of a publisher's con—60 pages, each with about 75 words, huge easy-reading type, a lot of white space. [The publisher] calls it a "work of fiction" on the bookflap, to get around the fact that it's a $9.95 short story. This effrontery wouldn't matter if the work itself weren't extremely thin, almost nonexistent.

Little as it is, ***The Malady of Death*** is too long for itself. A man pays a woman to spend every night with him for a while, so that he can learn to love. She agrees. At first he just watches her sleep, then he sleeps with his face between her legs, finally he "takes" her. She goes away. But meanwhile, as the nights with him pass, she has seen that he is sick to death with lovelessness. She tells him how he's ill, but he remains unable to love.

The story is addressed to the man: "You," with "your sex," "seeking somewhere to shed its load of tears." He's not young; perhaps he is celibate, more likely homosexual. "You want to try . . . to get used to that body . . . to the risk of having children implicit in that body, to that hairless unmuscular body." When the man rebukes the woman for speaking about sex, "she asks if *they* talk about it. You say no." "She asks: Haven't you ever loved a woman? You say no, never." "You don't love anything or anyone, you don't even love the difference you think you embody. All you know is the grace of the bodies of the dead. The grace of those like yourself."

The story begins neither in the past nor the present, but conditionally. "You wouldn't have known her, you'd have seen her everywhere at once . . . You may have paid her." Then it switches quickly to the present. "And then she says: What is it you want?" Until the end, the present dominates; then the conditional returns. Perhaps the author is talking to a man, telling him of something she imagines happening to him, lecturing him through this didactic vision; "You" is certainly not the reader. Whatever, the woman's tone of moral superiority—which, if we are to understand the man as homosexual, is almost inconceivably arrogant—and her passive acquiescence, her distanced, almost inadvertent orgasms, are chilling.

As is Duras's description of the woman, naked. "The body's completely defenseless, smooth from face to feet. It invites strangulation, rape, ill usage, insult, shouts of hatred, the unleashing of deadly and unmitigated passions." Duras seems to assume that desire for a woman is always sadistic, and that this sadism is exciting. (Even her own desire: when, in ***The Lover,*** she describes a schoolmate, Hélène Lagonelle, for whom she is "worn out with desire," she says of her: "She makes you want to kill her, she conjures up a marvellous dream of putting her to death with your own hands. . . . A pleasure unto death.") The atmosphere is silent, solitary. A room, the sound of the sea outside the window. The rest of the world, beyond this couple, is an echoing blank.

I have quoted so much from this silly volume because an academic friend who specializes in things French tells me that ***Malady*** is considered feminist over there, and I hope these lines make clear that such a claim is almost as amazing as the fact that it's considered a major work of poetic prose.

An excerpt from *The War*

There are an awful lot of them. There really are huge numbers of dead. Seven million Jews have been exterminated—transported in cattle cars, then gassed in specially built gas chambers, then burned in specially built ovens. In Paris, people don't talk about the Jews yet. Their infants were handed over to female officials responsible for the strangling of Jewish babies and experts in the art of killing by applying pressure on the carotid arteries. They smile and say it's painless. This new face of death that has been discovered in Germany—organized, rationalized—produces bewilderment before it arouses indignation. You're amazed. How can anyone still be a German? You look for parallels elsewhere and in other times, but there aren't any. Some people will always be overcome by it, inconsolable. One of the greatest civilized nations in the world, the age-long capital of music, has just systematically murdered eleven million human beings with the utter efficiency of a state industry. The whole world looks at the mountain, the mass of death dealt by God's creature to his fellows. Someone quotes the name of some German man of letters who's been very upset and become very depressed and to whom these things have given much food for thought. If Nazi crime is not seen in world terms, if it isn't understood collectively, then that man in the concentration camp at Belsen who died alone but with the same collective soul and class awareness that made him undo a bolt on the railroad one night somewhere in Europe, without a leader, without a uniform, without a witness, has been betrayed. If you give a German and not a collective interpretation to the Nazi horror, you reduce the man in Belsen to regional dimensions. The only possible answer to this crime is to turn it into a crime committed by everyone. To share it. Just like the idea of equality and fraternity. In order to bear it, to tolerate the idea of it, we must share the crime.

Reading these books after reading is enormously sad. Even when the writing is graceful, evocative, and enchantingly able to recreate the elusive textures of daily life—as often in ***The Little Horses of Tarquinia,*** and more fantastically, in ***The Sailor from Gibraltar***—a great vitality has disappeared, too often replaced by self-conscious, even proud, emptiness. Even when events, however slight and inward in their movement, are engaging and illuminating, they seem, book by book, to dwindle in their import. Eroticism itself becomes something willed, bodiless, and inflated. The tightness of the focus does not increase the intensity or clarity of the vision (as it does, say, in Saurraute's novels).

The War shows precisely how the idea of suffering and our ways of imagining pain were changed forever by Auschwitz. The other four novels, better and worse, illustrate how Duras and the people she was writing about, faced with this enormity, couldn't escape its imprint. "It's in that silence that the war's still there." (pp. 47, 50)

Erika Munk, "Beyond Anomie Lines: Marguerite Duras and the Art of Suffering," in The Village Voice, *Vol. XXXI, No. 28, July 15, 1986, pp. 47, 50.*

George Craig

La douleur itself and the other, shorter texts grouped here under that name, . . . are all prompted by aspects of the experience of Marguerite Duras in Paris in 1944-45: a time of dizzying swings between hope and desolation, joy and horror, within both public and private experience. Innumerable fictional reconstructions have, over the years since then, simplified all this into an adventure. Unassumingly, unemphatically, these texts set that aside and commit us instead to something virtually—often actually—unbearable. Two of them, **"La douleur"** and **"Albert of the Capitals"**, draw the reader into a world where imaginative participation seems inexcusable, whether as intrusion or as indulgence. In **"La douleur"** the young first-person narrator chronicles first her wait for the return from Dachau of her husband, and then her awareness of every detail of his ruined body and its functions. In **"Albert of the Capitals"** we become part of the group of *Résistants* watching a young woman interrogate an elderly informer while two male colleagues torture him.

If the other pieces are less harrowing, they are hardly less disquieting. In one, the narrating "I" is picked out (she is an *intellectuelle* and her world fascinates him) for long talks in public places by a Gestapo agent, with the promise of help for her arrested husband as the bribe. Others show us a simple, spirited, handsome boy who has joined the hated Milice only so that he can get about in a car with a gun; a collaborationist feeling the full weight of his situation as the war ends; and a little Jewish girl locked away for safety in a strange limbo.

There are pointers in plenty here, and their direction seems unmistakable. There is the awfulness of the things addressed, and the specificity of detail as to people, dates and places within that. There is the location of all this within particular lives (most notably those of Marguerite

Duras herself and those closest to her). And there is the intersection of their lives with the lives of others, at least one of whom (François Mitterrand) has other claims on our attention. Taken together, all these seem to require us to see the texts as forming something like what historians call a "primary source", and, even more, what librarians and booksellers call "non-fiction". Indeed it might well seem insulting to do anything else, and especially to suggest that they had literary importance. In the fascinating short glosses she has written for the texts, Duras seems to add her support to this. ***La douleur,*** she says, is a "diary" and can't really be called "writing"—indeed she finds it "inconceivable" that she could have kept even a diary at the time. The point is clear enough: it is painful for her now to contemplate both what she wrote about and the fact of having written about it. In this light the texts are "a tremendous chaos of thought and feeling that I couldn't bring myself to tamper with, and beside which literature was something of which I felt ashamed."

It is hard to see how she would not feel that: which of us can easily spin the lies we call "fictions" about the moral and physical degrading of those near us? How, even if we could, would we face those who know literature only as a pastime, an amusement? Not for the only time in these pages one is reminded of Samuel Beckett, who dealt with related historical issues, of which he too had first-hand experience, by refusing to speak of them at all. But, however understandable and indeed admirable Duras's feelings, they do not of themselves determine the nature and value of what she has written.

There is, first, the fact that much of the charge of the texts comes from the quiet, sober writing. Elision and understatement provoke the scream or the groan in us even as they exclude them from the text (one thinks of the unheralded paragraph in **"La douleur"** in which the narrator tells her husband, when he is at last back from the dead, that she wants a divorce). When history is also now, we are no longer looking only at history. But there is something else too. There are occasional "political" patches in these texts (summary judgments on individuals, groups, classes), but the sort of easy identification that these suggest—heroes and heroines over here, villains over there—sounds as if it has been learned by heart, and is at variance with Duras's explorations of feeling and action. Not only is the "I" of ***La douleur*** more than simply she-who-waits, she is not forever different from the tough interrogator and fancier of "real men" of the texts in Part Three. Indeed, as so often in her fiction, Duras's imagination is drawn above all by the aberrant. It is to take nothing away from the actual, terrible world of Paris then to say that it has powerful echoes in what we can know, from her work as a whole, of her inner life. Just as the beautiful and moving ***L'amant*** regrouped many elements familiar from her novels, so, in their different way, do these texts. It all happened, all right; but it happened to happen to her.

George Craig, "The Horror of What Happened to Happen," in The Times Literary Supplement, *No. 4357, October 3, 1986, p. 1112.*

Maria Margaronis

[In 1986] Marguerite Duras, grand old lady of the French literary left, declared herself a Reaganite. In a conversation with her old Resistance comrade François Mitterrand, she praised her new hero: "I think he is the incarnation of a kind of primal, almost archaic, power." Such rightward migrations are more the rule than the exception now in France, but in Duras's case the passage has been political only in the most private, accidental sense. The qualities that have led her to admire Reagan are intimately and perversely linked to the ones that have made her a great writer, even a great writer of the left. Duras is a saboteur of moral conventions, a pioneer of candor, a historian of intuitions. There have been times, like May 1968, when her talents could be hitched to a heroic political engine, but she is interested in means, not ends. In her subjective universe, Reagan's anti-intellectual bluntness takes on a revolutionary spin.

For much of her long career, Duras has written extremely concentrated, stylized texts, film scripts and novels pared down to reveal the bare form of an emotional encounter. Like a set of musical variations, they recapitulate and transpose the same motifs: illicit love, betrayal, memory, loss. Many of them are set in the East, particularly in the French Indochina of her childhood, to which she has returned again and again to play out different versions of an obsessive, doomed love affair. Against a background of intense heat that bakes the plain, the rice paddies and the white colonial villas, a woman is transfigured by an irresistible passion. The long moment of her desire is fractured and multiplied by repetition and memory until it shakes her whole life, bending together liberation and destruction. The heroine of the novel ***The Ravishing of Lol Stein*** (1964) endlessly relives her first abandonment in a voyeuristic affair with the lover of her best friend. Lol's lost fiancé reappears in ***India Song*** (1973), where four contrapuntal voices reconstruct his love for an ambassador's wife. And in ***Hiroshima, mon amour,*** a film made in 1960 with Alain Resnais and the only one of Duras's more minimalist works to please American sensibilities, a night with a Japanese man unearths a French woman's memory of her first love, a German soldier occupying her country. Her desire for the new foreigner, built in the place, to use Duras's word, that death has "preserved," is a temporary unforgetting of what is permanently lost, a joy that shares its skin with destruction.

In her most recent books, ***The Lover*** and ***The War,*** Duras has turned to confession and autobiography, and to a more direct exploration of the interconnectedness of love and power. These texts—call them novels or memoirs—draw their uncanny force from Duras's refusal to submit her life to any single reading: she writes often as if she were a stranger to herself, the inquisitor of her past as well as its apologist. "The story of my life doesn't exist," she says in ***The Lover.*** "There's never any center to it. No path, no line." In fact, the landscape of her work is veined with alternate routes. The pronouns shift from "I" to "she" to "you," and we follow her obediently into a maze of love and shame and dual loyalties, seduced by her candor, repelled by her narcissism and her arrogance: "Learn to read them properly," she warns of the last texts in ***The War.*** "They are sacred." The claim is extravagant; her conviction points both to the courage that has enabled Duras to investigate the links between impulses and feelings we prefer to keep distinct, and to the solipsism that skews her view of the outside world.

The Lover is essentially a reworking of the material Duras used in ***The Sea Wall,*** a straightforward, realistic novel first published in 1950. A young French girl lives with her mother and brothers in a run-down bungalow on the flat Pacific coast of French Indochina. They are poor but not hungry, living mainly on rice and the fishy black flesh of the stilt bird. The mother is bedraggled and depressed after years of struggling to make her small concession of land bear fruit. Her main ambition is to help her daughter escape, preferably to a respectable middle-class life in France. The girl is dreamy, thin, deathly bored. Enter a Chinese man, racially "inferior," flashy and the heir to untold wealth.

The Sea Wall is about poverty experienced as corrosive failure. As the Pacific eats away the barriers Ma has labored to build and floods the fields with salt, so poverty floods desire with greed and shame, occupying and obliterating the slightest possibility of love. The family seize on the Chinese as the solution to their financial problems; coached by her mother and brother, the girl tries to get him to propose. The empty, constipated courtship of the sentimental lecher and the vain adolescent is related in excruciating detail. In the grip of her family, the girl can have no erotic instinct that does not turn into a form of prostitution. When the Chinese offers her a diamond to go away to the city with him, she has learned enough to keep the gift without paying the price. Thrilled and tormented by the "sparkler," Ma beats her daughter to get her to confess that she has slept with the man. To escape the blows, she lies and says she has.

In ***The Lover,*** the girl does sleep with the Chinese. The wall against the Pacific has collapsed more completely, and the leveling force has turned from greedy to poverty to hungry desire—the familiar torrential desire begotten by despair upon impossibility. The book is intimate, searching, oddly disjointed. "Before," writes Duras, "I spoke of clear periods, those on which the light fell. Now I'm talking about the hidden stretches of that same youth." The language itself, spare and repetitive, seems to bear the imprint of an immense pressure. We are in a no man's land between truth and fiction, where memory is stroked and shaped by longing.

The girl, in this version, is queerly beautiful, both innocent and knowing, a child and a woman; her body understands what she can't yet express. It is she who seduces the Chinese, who asks him "to do as you usually do with women. . . . to do it again and again." Their relationship is a prism where limits dissolve: tenderness meets cruelty and love embraces contempt. The girl's desire for the man is sharpened by the knowledge it brings her of loss, emptiness and shame, and by the thrill of her passive power over him, which is like her mother's power over her:

> Today I tell him it's a comfort, this sadness, a comfort to have fallen at last into a misfortune my mother has always predicted for me when she shrieks in the desert of her life. . . . I tell him one day I'll leave my mother, one day even for my mother I'll have no love left. I weep. He lays his head on me and weeps to see me weep.

The "harsh pleasure" the man gives her is close kin to the "terrible harshness" of her family, and her experience of love is illuminated until every dark facet has been revealed. It is not only her mother's despair that has seeped into the young girl's life but the tyranny of her hated elder brother, who absorbs the mother's love and pins his siblings in a shadow of fear. In his presence, the girl's desire is choked and the Chinese lover becomes "an unmentionable outrage, a cause of shame who ought to be kept out of sight"; but the brother is also there in their lovemaking, adding the sadomasochistic spice of loathing. She likes it when the Chinese "takes" her violently and with insults: "He calls me a whore, a slut, he says I'm his only love, and that's what he ought to say, and what you do say when you just let things say themselves, when you let the body alone, to seek and find and take what it likes, and then everything is right, and nothing's wasted, the waste is covered over and all is swept away in the torrent, in the force of desire." It is typical of Duras's courage that she does not stop at this, but allows her romantic image of sexual transport its full resonance with a more frightening kind of power and occupation. (pp. 493-95)

In ***The War,*** a collection of memoirs about Duras's life in the Paris Resistance in World War II, the knot of power is turned so that its dark side is uppermost. The dazzling heat haze is gone; Duras herself, a grown woman now, is a more solid figure. And the terms under direct investigation are the shadows stitched to the heels of desire in ***The Sea Wall*** and ***The Lover:*** complicity, violence, betrayal. The three main texts in the book form a kind of triptych.

The first, **"The War,"** is a harrowing story of powerlessness and need, a detailed account of Duras's vigil for her husband, Robert L., who was a prisoner in the concentration camps. The writing is splintered into tiny, sharp sentences, pointing every which way, fixed painfully in the claustrophobic space of waiting. She records every twist of anxiety, every abrupt reversal of her thoughts as she paces her apartment or stands for hours in the Gare d'Orsay collecting information about released prisoners. At one moment she is convinced her husband is dead, imagines his body lying in a ditch; at the next, she is calculating the number of days and hours until his return. There is a kind of generous love here that Duras has not often addressed.

When Robert L. eventually does return (rescued by none other than François Mitterrand), his emaciated, terrifying body replaces Duras's tortured thoughts at the center of the narrative. In her flat, relentless voice she describes the sticklike limbs, the shrunken neck, the strange, inhuman face until they seem to incarnate all the complicated horror of the war. Robert L. is a human being and yet monstrous, a thing; his perverse condition embroils everyone who loves him in a vivid nightmare. At first, to save his life, he must be denied food, just as he was in the concentration camp; as he recovers, he becomes sheer appetite:

"I used to watch him from the sitting-room door. I didn't go in. For two weeks, three, I watched him eat with unremitting pleasure. I couldn't get used to it either. Sometimes his pleasure made me weep, too. He didn't see me. He'd forgotten me." To the end he remains distant, a holy martyr; when he is well, having gone with him through the valley of death, Duras asks for a divorce so that she can have a child with his best friend. It is as if they have lived out their love to its conclusion. The skull beneath the skin can never recede, and Robert L. must always remain both more and less than human. (p. 495)

If Robert L. is a kind of sacrificial lamb, Duras herself, in the rest of the book, plays the dual role of sinner and confessor. The second piece, **"Monsieur X., Here Called Pierre Rabier,"** relates the cat-and-mouse courtship of Duras by the Gestapo agent who arrested her husband. The piece is a study in the banality of evil—Rabier is a cultured, charming man, "absolutely indifferent to human suffering in general, but indulging himself in the luxury of his own forms of squeamishness." But it is also an investigation of betrayal. Duras begins by meeting Rabier to maintain contact with the French prisoners he guards; then, because the danger is too great, she agrees to help her fellow Resistance members kill him, becoming what he might have been to her: "his policeman, the one through whom he'll die." Though the moral framework of the memoir is clear—to emphasize the difference between herself and the Nazi, Duras explains that she carefully testified at his trial about those he had spared as well as those he had sent to their death—its dramatic effect is more ambiguous. Duras fears and despises Rabier, but she also comes to understand him, to be touched by his small kindnesses and the luxuries he offers her. She is ashamed not only of dining with him but of deceiving him. Their relationship, a power struggle disguised as a courtship, where nothing can be said or done that is not tainted, is not unlike the relationship between the heroine and her Chinese suitor—also wealthy, also a ticket to material pleasures—in ***The Sea Wall.***

"Duras is a saboteur of moral conventions, a pioneer of candor, a historian of intuitions."

—Maria Margaronis

The last panel of the triptych, **"Albert of the Capitals," "Ter of the Militia,"** finds Duras unquestionably in power. Ter is a young collaborator arrested by the Resistance for whom she feels sympathy, even desire. And Albert is the contact of an informer, never named, whom Duras tortures. The description of the torture is blunt, unsparing, like the description of Robert L.'s starving body. And the complicated thoughts of Duras, the torturer, are here too, without judgment or distance: the dissociation, the concentrated attention, the anxiety, the rage, all coming up at the right moment to accomplish the work of battering a man's body until a single word is dug out, the answer to an irrelevant question, "What color was the identity card that got you into the Gestapo?"

> (She) looks at the fists falling, hears the gong of the blows, realizes for the first time that in a man's body there are layers almost impossible to pierce. Tier upon tier of deep truths difficult to reach. . . . Now it's exhausting, almost impossible. Demolition work. Blow by blow. . . . The work is going on far away, in that solitary chest of his. They hit him in the stomach. The informer howls, clutches his stomach with both hands, writhes. Albert draws closer, deals him a blow in the private parts. He covers his genitals with both hands and howls some more. He's bleeding copiously from the face.

By the end of this, you know what it is to torture a person, almost as if you had been there in the room, deciding with Duras's watching comrades whether to stay or go. As a reader, it is almost impossible not to stay. The most frightening thing about this piece of writing is the pleasure in it: if ***The Lover*** gave desire its full complement of cruelty and shame, **"Albert of the Capitals"** reveals, through the rhythms and images of the prose, the sexual undertow of torture.

It may be that the conservative in Duras intends this text to support her claim, in ***The Lover,*** that the collaborators and the French Communist Party, which formed the backbone of the Resistance, were "the same":

> The parallel is complete and absolute. The two things are the same, the same pity, the same call for help, the same lack of judgment, the same superstition if you like, that consists in believing in a political solution to the personal problem.

But the radical in her undercuts any such simplistic reading by allowing the writing its full moral complexity, refusing to let it point in any single, manageable direction.

In Duras's world, the love of power and the power of love can seem almost interchangeable: sex and torture both strike at the hinge between language and the body, and force the flesh to "ejaculate its truth." Her unsettling strength as a writer stems from her obsessive need to probe that connection and her own involvement in it; so, in a way, do her idiosyncratic politics. In her earlier, more stylized work, written under the influence of a kind of literary Maoism, Duras used erotic dissolution to suggest the revolutionary moment that would bring us back to "absolute zero" and enable us to remake the world. She showed no interest in the arrangements that might follow that moment; from the beginning, her work has been concerned with the process by which boundaries are broken and internal truths are changed. As revolution has fallen out of fashion, Duras has searched for a new catalyst for ecstasy. For her, it is the flaying intensity of the experience that counts, not its purpose or moral meaning. While she likes to cast herself as a rebel, she also loves to imagine herself in the grip of some manly force that leaves her no will, no choice, that produces an explosion of contradictory emotions. In her polymorphously perverse morality play, Ronald Reagan has slipped easily into the Janus-faced role of conqueror and seducer—a suitably subversive lover for the comrade of François Mitterrand. (pp. 495-96)

Maria Margaronis, "The Occupying Passion," in The Nation, *New York, Vol. 243, No. 15, November 8, 1986, pp. 493-96.*

Frederick J. Harris

French novelist, playwright and filmscript writer Marguerite Duras's new book, ***The War* [*La douleur*]**, is actually a collection of six different texts whose common denominator is the French experience during World War II or its immediate aftermath. . . .

"La douleur" can be translated as "pain" or "suffering"; and the main focus of the narration is on the pain or suffering of the narrator Marguerite as she awaits the return of her husband from a Nazi concentration camp during April and May of 1945. Readers of Marguerite Duras will quickly recognize the situation of people waiting, and particularly that of women waiting, actively or passively, for something to happen. This familiar situation has served the narrator well. Aside from the Resistance novel that invariably portrays the bold and often heroic exploits conducted by the Resistance against a materially superior German occupier, the more common theme in French literature concerning World War II has been that of those French who were voluntarily or involuntarily sent to Germany during the war: POW's, *résistants,* Jews and laborers of one category or another. We have here instead the perspective of a *résistante* who has stayed in France while her husband has been deported to Germany, somewhat less than a year before the time of the narration.

The largely autobiographical account is narrated in the form of a diary. However, the diary as a structuring device breaks down toward the end of the text. Marguerite experiences momentary difficulty in remembering whether François Mitterand, currently France's President but in 1945 a *résistant* like herself, had called her in April or May to inform her that her husband, Robert L., the name she uses for Robert Antelme, had been located in Dachau. From that point on, the diary structure is abandoned. This is consistent with the narrator's statement in the preface that though she had only recently found the diary in some cupboards of her house, and though she knows full well that she wrote it, she has no recollection of having written it, and it is, in fact, inconceivable to her that she could have written it while actually awaiting Robert L.'s return. Clearly the text was written at a later date.

The story of Marguerite's waiting is a very human one, filled with an anguish at times verging almost on despair, but ultimately abounding in courage, hope, generosity and love. It shares a number of elements we have come to expect in literature on World War II. Because this war broke so many precedents, moral as well as technological, people were often cast adrift, so to speak, in uncharted waters. The realities of the Nazi camps begin to unfold as the narration proceeds and as news filters back to Paris from the Allied armies advancing in Germany. People do not know what to make of the reports coming from Germany, and rumor and speculation run rampant as they try to make some sense of the atrocities they are learning about for the first time. "You look for parallels elsewhere and in other times, but there aren't any."

Irony, too, abounds as it does in so much of World War II literature. Of what good to Marguerite is the general sense of jubilation over victory when her husband may be lying dead in a ditch somewhere in Germany. Paris, the City of Light, is once again literally "lit up," but it is now without Robert L. and many other deportees: "It is a sign of death, of a tomorrow without them." What will peace mean for her under these conditions? "It's like a great darkness falling, it's the beginning of forgetting."

Perhaps the consummate irony is the fact that Marguerite and Robert L. had been planning to separate for some two years already at the time of narration, and that when Robert L. finally does return to Paris and Marguerite at the end of the text, she informs him that she fully intends to go through with the divorce and to marry his friend, one of the two Frenchmen who had actually driven posthaste to Dachau to rescue him after the camp's liberation. But this, too, will not be an unfamiliar situation to Duras's readers. She tells the reader now as she has in the past—and most recently in ***The Lover***—that a perfect union of two people cannot exist in the here and now, that a perfect union can exist only in death. And while the narrator is prepared to wait "unto death," her own death, for Robert L., and does everything in her power to secure his return and to restore his wasted skeleton to health once he does return, she ends this very powerful and often beautiful and touching memoir with the ambivalent sentence: "And I knew he knew, knew that every hour of every day I was thinking, 'He didn't die in the concentration camp.' "

The other five texts in the collection are disappointing. Two, we are told, are fictional, the others are not. They are interesting only because of the situations they describe: the narrator's flirtation with a French agent of the Gestapo in an attempt to learn something of her husband's whereabouts and condition, and later the vindictive violence of liberated France; the trial of a French informer to the Germans; the arrest of a Frenchman in the militia who, likewise, had worked for the Germans; a short fictional sketch on the outskirts of Paris in which a youngish man, possibly having had some former affiliation with the enemy, confronts two local people in the persons of an older man and a boy and, finally, another fictional tale, that of a Jewish girl whose mother had just had time to leave her in the care of a neighbor on the floor above before being arrested and taken away by the German police, never to be heard from again.

All five texts proceed in a narrative style that might be described as plodding, and none of the characters is sufficiently developed to excite the reader's interest or spark animation. Be this as it may, the first selection is fascinating reading, and it is well presented in Barbara Bray's translation. For those interested in World War II and the questions it has raised about human suffering and human morality, ***The War*** is essential. The narrator, Marguerite, expresses it quite eloquently in the first text: The crime committed by the Nazis, in particular the horror of the camps, is a collective crime. We can make sense of it and learn from it only if we accept a collective responsibility. To bear the crime and "to tolerate the idea of it," we must share it. "The only possible answer to this crime is to turn it into a crime committed by everyone." (pp. 288-90)

Frederick J. Harris, "'Even without Wars, Life Is Dangerous'," in America, *Vol. 155, No. 13, November 18, 1986, pp. 288-90.*

Jayne Pilling

Marguerite Duras's new novel comes, unusually, with a typed insert from the author, telling us that it is "l'histoire d'un amour, le plus grand et le plus térrifiant qu'il m'a été donné d'écrire". An exhortation to the reader follows, in effect a plea for perseverance in face of the novel's difficulty: a shrewd precaution by Duras, mindful perhaps of the vast new readership gained by her recent bestsellers, ***L'amant*** and ***La douleur.***

Both these autobiographically inspired books displayed a renewed force and clarity in Duras's writing. Much of her output over the preceding decade had seemed creatively exhausted, desperate even, obsessively reworking texts and ideas in books and films, seeking a language adequate to her needs. ***Les yeux bleux, cheveux noirs*** is likely to mystify and infuriate new admirers, but reward long-time Duras readers.

"Une soirée d'été, dit l'acteur, serait au cœur de l'histoire" is the first in a series of stage directions and commentary that punctuates the ensuing narrative. . . . The bizarre relationship between the unnamed protagonists is to be read by the reader of the novel and, aloud, by the actors who stand like a Greek chorus on the stage that serves a six-night performance by the couple in question.

This structure renders synopsis difficult, and the difficulty is compounded by a sense of the ridiculous in describing what happens. A man pays a woman to sleep naked under yellow lamplight every night in his room, to save him, he says, from madness, from solitude. Watching her, talking to her, he can keep alive his hopeless infatuation with another man, glimpsed fleetingly with a woman in a hotel lobby. He does not recognize that she was in fact this same woman, though her blue eyes and black hair remind him of the dark handsome stranger. As the nights go by, he reveals his inability to feel for a woman. She tries to engage him physically, via masturbation, oral sex and descriptions of violent sexual encounters with another man, but fails. They talk, sleep, cry—their only moments of intimacy. The ritual undergoes subtle variations, with moments of laughter, fear and violence. Theirs is a *voyage au bout de la nuit,* in which the impossibility of love is explored.

The sound and presence of the sea, a recurring motif in Duras's work, is constant throughout: a crushing, inexorable force whose ceaseless tidal movement mirrors her characters' desire and failure to establish connection with others. The sea also plays a large role in ***Un barrage contre le Pacifique*** (1950), Duras's third, formally quite conventional novel, published in (often over-literal and banal) English translation last year as ***The Sea Wall.*** Set in Indochina in the 1930s, it charts the struggles of a French widow to wrest a living—and a life—from the land, having to fight against nature, colonial corruption and her own son and daughter (***L'amant*** drew on the same family history). Clearly, the psychological realism of ***L'amant*** or ***Un barrage*** is absent from ***Les yeux bleux.*** A literal interpretation might seize on the apparent homosexuality of the male character, but he is in fact more of an extreme embodiment of "Duras man" in relation to "Duras woman": finally unknowable and impossible. Sexual difference, shorn of all social context, is dissected here with a use of graphic, anatomical metaphor quite new in her work. As the actor comments: "il se présenterait comme l'homme dans son absence centrale, son irréversible exteriorité".

On its own terms, the novel remains a puzzle, at best a crude psychoanalytical jigsaw. Yet as comment on and key to Duras's work it is highly illuminating. ***Les yeux bleux*** is suffused with echoes, richly refracted, from earlier work. *Dix heures et demie du soir en été* sets the time, and the place is recognizable, in detail, from the film ***Agatha.*** The implication of subject, object and reader in the voyeuristic process is haunted by ***Le ravissement de Lol V. Stein.*** Reading backwards, as it were, the novel begins to make sense. The author's transpositions of texts and themes between film, novel and play acquire new, exciting perspectives. . . .

[Duras] is condemned to perpetual struggles against the limitations of language, and of fictional forms. The experimental urge is almost palpable in the actors' commentary: doomed to a frustrating conditional imperfect. Yet there is also a sense of relief, of triumph even, in the final movement to confront head-on, in the present indicative, the nature of the problem.

Duras is now in her seventies, an age at which the past can vividly engulf the present in consciousness. Hence perhaps the power and directness of ***L'amant*** and ***La douleur,*** which, while clearly relating to enduring concerns, indicated a new direction for Duras's compulsion to write, her fiction revitalized through dealing with those onslaughts of often painful memory. ***Les yeux bleux*** seems more of a return to a former style, but a similar retrospective impulse is clearly at work. It's hard to predict how much this would mean to readers unfamiliar with her writings, but for many it could function as a near-perfect Duras handbook.

Jayne Pilling, "Puzzling at the Past," in The Times Literary Supplement, *No. 4397, July 10, 1987, p. 741.*

Nicole Ward Jouve

Marguerite Duras has been lucky. She's made it.

Her novel ***L'amant (The Lover)*** has been a bestseller, making her rich in her old age after the long lean years. In spite of her high reputation, she complains she had to eke out a living on her foreign rights sales. She was robbed of millions owing to a bad contract for the screenplay of ***Hiroshima, mon amour.***

So it's nice to see her afloat . . . even though it has all come so late. One almost thinks, at times, too late, for Duras' behaviour in the media since it all happened has been anything but discreet, to say the least: she's moved from the left to a bizarre neo-conservatism which made her support Reagan's raid on Libya. Does she mean it, one wonders, or is it deliberate provocation? Glory is hell, Duras says: "People invite you to dinner to show you off like an animal they bought and especially tamed." Better run away with the bit between your teeth?

One of the results of this late fame is a rush of Duras translations—not only of her new books, but even of the older stuff which nobody wanted at the time. So we get [***Woman to Woman***], these 1974 conversations between Duras and Xavière Gauthier, the editor of the 1970s women's review *Sorcières* and one of the first writers to be published by Des femmes. Gauthier had been asked to interview women writers by *Le Monde,* the interviews with Duras grew to book length, and Minuit published them. They have something anachronistic about them, given Duras' evolution, and the now muted state of the women's movement in France. But then, this is a phenomenon of the '80s: the new becomes obsolete at a dizzying pace, then assumes a retro charm. Nostalgia is one of the few bull-markets left around.

Yet ***Woman to Woman*** remains a fascinating book.

It's not just that the manner of the interviews is attractive and appropriate to Duras: the leisurely, meandering pace, the interruptions, the openness, the erased or lost bits, the thematic, obsessional returns. Nor just that many insights into Duras' books and films are provided. It's just that a lot of what the speakers, the "parleuses", say remains relevant: the talk about writing and desire, about the lost art of loving, the transgression there is whenever a woman writes. The hole in the afternoon of the women who stay at home, the "spaced out" activity of chores, the boredom, the suicidal tendency: "It's only in prisons that man lives woman's experiences of time, lives it, I think, completely." The vote: "What a fraud!" Someone saying to you, "choose me" when you haven't asked him for anything. The need to go through Marxist awareness, and the realisation that it cannot effect the cure: "There's a kind of schizophrenic crossing between the proletariat's knowledge and its subjection . . . it's just like a person who is mentally ill—he knows all about psychoanalysis; he can practically analyse his own case, but the illness remains. His knowledge is not enough."

Against the excess of knowledge, the exploitation of knowledge, Duras returns again and again to the virtues of silence, of passivity. The impenetrable forest of her childhood, the Indochina jungle where she wandered with her brother, where the creepers 30 metres above your head were full of fish, in suspended basins between the trees, and where so many convicts died to build a road in the Mekong Delta that it was like the Way of the Cross. From that lost, ambiguous, poor white colonial childhood so many of Duras' books have come, keep coming.

And so despite the period flavour, despite all that has happened to Duras and to us all since these interviews took place, they convey something that is essential about Duras (essential for us too?): the rich passivity, the whites, the informed silence. The capacity for excess, for turning things on their head.

An anecdote she recently told held them all. She flew to Rome airport, to work on a film. The people supposed to meet her didn't turn up, or missed her. She sat in the airport for eight hours. She was staring at a large coffee stain she'd made on her white skirt. The stain, in these interviews, already assumes an unexpected dimension. The "parleuses" are talking of Mary, mother of God, who being immaculate, must not have had periods, has no stains.

To Gauthier who suggests that means that all other women are impure, maculate, Duras replies: "That's an interpretation of nature that was distorted from the start, because you could also regard periods as a surplus of life, an excess of life." (pp. 25-6)

Nicole Ward Jouve, "Speech and Silence," in New Statesman, *Vol. 115, No. 2970, February 26, 1988, pp. 25-6.*

Barbara Loren

If the challenge of a writer is to recreate experience that goes beyond the limits of language, then Marguerite Duras is a writer par excellence. Her latest novels are among the most powerful works of fiction produced in this century. Whether or not one is familiar with Duras' fiction, the conversations between Duras and Gauthier recorded in ***Woman to Woman*** are gripping, poetic, and refreshing. While these interviews do address the questions of social change, they do so non-prescriptively. In one passage, Duras summarizes the short-comings of any literature that is *solely* political:

> Duras: But to call society into question is still to accept it. It's like movies about war: in all war movies, there's a secret adoration of war.
>
> Gauthier: Yes, so then it's not "called into question."
>
> Duras: I mean people who are involved in this, who write about a refusal of society, carry a kind of nostalgia within themselves. I'm sure they must be much less separated from it than I am. I'm absolutely sure.

The ground that Duras and Gauthier cover in their conversations is expansive. The fact that the interviews were transcribed exactly as spoken makes them all the more powerful. It allows for the gaps, silences, and incoherencies—so much a part of Duras' creative works—that occur in natural dialogue. At one point in the interview there is a notation of silence, after which Duras comments: "The mini cassette is running. (Laughter) If only we could keep the silence in the typography."

This silence recalls the silence and lack of conventional action that is a hallmark of Duras' films and novels. Duras emphasizes that her works revolve around absence and non-action:

> . . . a word moves as much as an arm . . . a gaze moves as much as a horse . . . a shift in gaze is worth the moving of a machine, they (those who adhere to convention) don't understand.

Though there is sometimes a struggle to grasp the essence of a conversation, this struggle allows the reader to participate in Duras' and Gauthier's process of discovery. Duras' words are like arrows, and they rarely fail to hit dead center. But she is constantly willing to risk being totally off the mark. She speaks of her own novels, films, and aesthetic of writing, and also addresses a broad range of topics, including gender identity, oppression, revolution, eroticism, and the problems of colonialism. While addressing these tender, potentially worn topics, neither Duras nor Gauthier rely on slogans or cliches. When speaking of the destruction of the human spirit caused by colonialism, for example, Duras explains that her novels use leprosy to embody the effects of colonialism. Leprosy, she explains, is usually only evident in the colonized peoples of these countries. (Duras spent her childhood in colonized Asian countries where leprosy was rampant.) Leprosy, like colonialism, is deadly, and simultaneously anesthetizing: the colonized, working class people in Duras' novels die of this disease.

Though ***Woman to Woman*** is a secondary text that is essential to furthering one's understanding of Duras' work, it goes far beyond this. The material in it is new, not critical, and it does not rely on any previous knowledge of Duras. In all, it is a beautiful book, secondary and primary. It has already been called "an underground classic," by some critics, but in time its classic nature will surface. (pp. 7, 10)

Barbara Loren, "Going beyond the Limits of Language," in The Bloomsbury Review, *Vol. 8, No. 2, March-April, 1988, pp. 7, 10.*

Duras on writing:

I know that when I write there is something inside me that stops functioning, something that becomes silent. I let something take over inside me that probably flows from femininity. But everything shuts off—the analytic way of thinking, thinking inculcated by college, studies, reading, experience. I'm absolutely sure of what I'm telling you now. It's as if I were returning to a wild country. Nothing is concerted. Perhaps, before everything else, before being Duras, I am—simply—a woman.

Marguerite Duras in an interview in Signs: Journal of Women in Culture and Society, *1975.*

Robert Steiner

Long recognized in Europe as a novelist specializing in psycho-sexual distress, Marguerite Duras has only recently found a wide American audience. Her novel, ***The Lover,*** received enormous acclaim in 1985, followed closely by ***The Malady of Death*** and now ***Blue Eyes, Black Hair.*** The three books retain the spare elliptical style for which Duras has long been noted, a style born in part out of her film work (***Hiroshima, mon amour***) and a brief identification with the *nouveau roman* of the '50s and '60s. One of her finest novels, ***Destroy, She Said,*** Duras turned into a film that she directed. Indeed, ***Blue Eyes, Black Hair*** most strongly resembles that book, though the earlier work kept much of the sexual anxiety suppressed in favor of a larger theme of revolutionary politics. Thematically, the new book follows a continuum begun more than 20 years ago with ***The Ravishing of Lol Stein,*** a compelling analysis of sexual self-destruction.

Blue Eyes, Black Hair dramatizes, in claustrophobic reductive scenes, the sexual suffering of an unnamed man and woman at a French seaside resort. The man is a homosexual who one summer night is awe-struck by the glimpse of a heterosexual foreigner in the company of a woman. The stranger disappears, leaving behind a rich, painful fantasy and a "sexual sadness that makes the eyes seem to have seen everything." The hero's obsession not only brings him to tears with cloying regularity but urges him to thoughts of murder and, in an attempt to suffuse his life with the foreigner's, into an "impossible" love-hate relationship with the young woman who, after three passionate days with the northern stranger, "weeps for an affair and a story that never were."

For much of the novel, the young woman lies naked in the light of a bare bulb in the man's empty seaside house, sometimes covered by a white sheet, her face by a piece of black silk, as she sleeps for him while he watches and thinks of his lost love, of murder, of loving this woman who was so close to his fantasy: "He needs her, needs her there in the room, so he can weep for the young foreigner with blue eyes, black hair." He insists on paying her to do this, though out of her sudden love for him, she would rather do it for nothing. Theirs is a nightly vigil over the body of a memorable impossibility of perfect adoration. Nothing happens, little is said. As lovers, they do not touch because what they have found in common is the death of hope. This is a minimalist picture of passion, fragments of repeated imagery and feeling that seem always to conclude a phrase too early. Were this music, it would be Webern's.

Because the young woman intends to be a writer, we are offered scenes of the relationship as though it were a stage play, with actors advised not to act but to speak the words of the novel we are reading, all as though the affair will one day become a book, a book being the fondest form of memory. This novel is a fiction of gestures rather than events, snapshots of a sexual yearning so frustrated that the idea of desire replaces desire itself. The homosexual hero desires not the woman but the fact of her proximity to the lost foreigner; she reminds him of his wasted existence, reminds him that he is "disaster personified." In her presence, his grief looms larger than the mere loss of what was already impossible in his sexual life. The reality of longing erases the world in favor of an idea of it, the way a kiss stands for a love affair. So theirs would be a tale of essences, a ritual in which the skeleton must suggest the flesh that has not yet grown to the bone.

Blue Eyes, Black Hair is one of those minor erotic fictions that contemporary French literature celebrates. One finds it in Bataille, Blanchot and Robbe-Grillet—the familiar business of sex and death at a seascape, with parched characters whose sexual obsessions are poetry and whose longing becomes mordant philosophy: "You haven't got a place, and you don't know where to find one. And it's for that that I love you and that you are lost." Indeed. The problem with this novel is that in its effort to evoke mystery, it is woefully precious and sentimental. The characters do not so much feel as wax poetic. They are in fact too immature in their passions to be dramatic for very long, and since they are more temperament than flesh, more given to tableaux than action, it is difficult to be concerned with their fates. Theirs is the sort of despair that evokes irritation rather than sympathy, boredom rather than puzzlement. The earlier Duras did it better.

Robert Steiner, "All You Need Is Loss," in Los Angeles Times Book Review, *April 24, 1988, p. 10.*

Joanne Schmidt

Like some of the other French women writers in Duras's generation, recognition was a slow and very painful process. Although [her] film ***Hiroshima, mon amour*** was a notable success in 1959, triumph was accorded director Alain Resnais, who had asked Duras to write the screenplay. Duras learned that the film world devalued writers. Even after she wrote the screenplay for a film that became a landmark in world cinema, her reputation remained marginal. That Duras suffered from alcoholism is by no means difficult to understand. She was also considered "difficult" as a writer because of her brief affiliation with the *nouveau roman,* a group that made a radical break from the linear, bourgeois French novel, and for the experimental nature of her writing. Not until the publication of ***Woman to Woman*** in 1970 did interest from French feminists help increase her popularity and, in part, her readership.

The Sailor from Gibraltar (1952) is an early novel that is still linear in its plot development. The narrator/male protagonist remains nameless throughout the novel, which connects him to the realms of the imaginary and unconscious, both important to Duras. In Part I, the narrator is vacationing in Italy with Jacqueline, his lover of two years. Between bouts of intense heat and heavy alcohol consumption, he realizes that he wants to start a new life and not return to France. He breaks up with Jacqueline after meeting the rich owner of a yacht named *Gibraltar.* Jacqueline, a sympathetic character, vents her anger because she knows there is another woman; nevertheless, he is determined to leave with the new woman and taste the "wine of freedom."

In Part II, "he" is very receptive to "her" (also nameless until later, where she is called Anna). She invites him to join her in her occupation: "I am looking for someone." That someone is a sailor from Gibraltar with whom she had a passionate affair three years earlier. He decides to join Anna in her search for the man of her obsession, while he begins to become preoccupied with her. Although Anna does have "a special fidelity" to the sailor, she realizes that this obsessive search is an end in itself. "It's strange, but I never ask myself what I'd do if I found him." The quest continues, the sailor eludes them, and the narrator continues on with Anna and her crew, making this a novel with no real closure, a technique common to the *nouveau roman.*

Already themes such as obsessive love, desire, abandonment, and loss, accompanied by narration restricted to individual situations and lack of closure, are evident in this early Duras novel.

The Ravishing of Lol Stein (1964) is, by far, the most complex of the novels considered here. Duras believes it to be a turning point in her career and one of her most frightening novels because she wrote it during a detoxification from alcohol abuse and because the theme of madness is developed. This novel is ambitious in its attempt to articulate the realm of the unconscious. Also, themes such as love, abandonment, memory, repetition of events, madness, desire, and the erotic are further explored here.

Lol Stein is the abandoned women par excellence. The narrator is Jack Hold, or the "narrator narrated," as Sharon Willis labels him. Therefore, the "I" is male and he discredits all previous accounts of Lol's life. Jack Hold begins his story by flashback to the actual abandonment scene at Town Beach casino at a dance. Lol is jilted by her fiancé, Michael Richardson, for another woman, Anne-Marie Stretter. Lol, who is known to suffer from mental illness, freezes the pain of her abandonment in her mind and becomes victim to an obsessive playback of this tragic event for the next ten years. During that time, Lol Stein marries John Bedford, a man who has a penchant for "broken-hearted women." He takes her to another city, and they have three daughters. Lol experiences a relatively calm existence until she and her husband decide to move back to the town, South Tahla, and live in her parent's house.

After returning to South Tahla, Lol reconstructs the pain of that awful memory. During one of her frequent walks, she begins spying on Tatiana Karl, her childhood friend who was present at the Town Beach casino dance, and her lover, Jack Hold. Lol "watches these lovers, she devours them with her eyes, she invents them." Lol displays a new "initiative" that surprises her husband. Seeing Tatiana again has repercussions for Lol, and she gets back in touch with her. Tatiana then invites Lol and John and Jack Hold to dinner at her house. The theme of the love triangle begins to develop after the dinner, when Lol again spies on Tatiana and Jack Hold. A complicated reversal occurs when Jack later becomes enamored of Lol and makes love to her. Lol lies to Tatiana about seeing Jack, Tatiana threatens not to see Jack again, and she calls Lol a lunatic. Now Jack is obsessed with Lol. A breakthrough occurs for Lol because her memory of the past has grown. Jack Hold agrees to travel back to Town Beach casino with Lol and witnesses Lol exploring her past. She *is* mentally ill because of attacks she has there. Tatiana was right. Lol encourages Jack to continue to see Tatiana and the novel ends with Lol staring at the two lovers from outside. As Sharon Willis proposes, love circulates in Duras's love triangles.

The Vice-Consul (1966) is in the same cycle of writing as ***The Ravishing of Lol Stein,*** with hysteria depicted in a male character. Two separate plots are artfully interwoven in this "novel within a novel" narrated by Peter Morgan, a friend of the ambassador. One is the narration of the beggar woman's exile from her homeland and her mother's house because she is pregnant and consequently an outcast. The other is the narration of the vice-consul, who is also a pariah, at the Calcutta embassy where he has been transferred.

While the story of the beggar woman frames that of the vice-consul in an atmosphere of loss and separation, of maternity, and of the force of the natural world against which the beggar woman struggles to survive, his account is localized in Calcutta. He is haunted by his "frightening" reputation at his last embassy job in Lahore. He suffers from nervous depression and fits of rage; he is described as having an unpleasant voice, common among hysterics; and "his face is blank." He becomes obsessed with Anne-Marie Stretter, the ambassador's wife, who is a recurring character from ***Lol Stein.***

The climax of the novel occurs at a reception at the ambassador's house. As the hostess, Anne-Marie Stretter must dance with all of her new male guests. The vice-consul has too much to drink. When Stretter pulls away from him while dancing, his fit of rage is heard by all present. "Don't leave me!" In Duras's novels, the cry is highly significant because in psychoanalysis it emerges from deep within the unconscious. As a character, the vice-consul is considered closer to the "feminine." He inhabits the world of the hysteric and the mad in Duras's work. His transfer is inevitable at the end of the novel.

L'amante anglaise (1967) was published one year after ***The Vice-Consul.*** This detective novel is divided into three neatly organized parts. In Part I, a savage murder committed in a small town named Viorne is close to being solved. Separate parts of a mutilated female body, found in cargo portions of trains all over France, are reassembled by police. Identification is not possible as the head is missing. The detective in charge is equipped with two tape recorders: one gives conversations in a local cafe five days after the murder, and the other records further investigation as preparation for a book about the crime. Duras's sophisticated technique of a "novel within a novel" helps unravel the crime and strips away the layers of speculative language that hide the truth. By the end of this part, Claire Lannes, known as a "harmless lunatic" who lived with Pierre, her husband, confesses to the murder of Marie-Thérèse Bousquet, her "deaf and dumb" cousin.

In Part II, information about Claire's psychology is obtained from her husband, Pierre. Her motive according to him "was just that she was mad." We also learn that Claire left her native town of Cahors after the end of a love affair, had a powerful imagination, and could be destructive around the house.

In Part III, the cross-examination of Claire takes place. She seems capable of answering lucidly, but she will not reveal the whereabouts of the head. "If I tell where the head is I'll have told everything." After all, she has revealed so much information about herself before the crime (i.e., her murderous dreams, thoughts of suicide, and the voices she hears in her head) that the only secret she has left is the location of the head. It is no accident that Duras ends her novel with Claire the madwoman keeping her only secret intact and failing to allow the detective to obtain the truth about the head. Duras calls the nature of truth itself into question in this novel. Willis thinks the headless woman's body is a metaphor for all of Duras's works combined.

Woman to Woman (1974), first published as ***Les parleuses*** or "talking women," is an extremely important book in Duras's career. French feminists claimed Duras as a foremother; her readership increased because these interviews made her more accessible to her public; and, as a result, her reputation grew. Xavière Gauthier, a writer and friend of Duras, leads the five interviews, which are uncensored and unedited.

In the first interview, Duras speaks about language in her texts. She explains her radical approach to language: "The word counts more than the syntax. . . . The grammatical tense follows, at a distance." Duras also claims she experiences hypnotic states when she writes. "I know that when I write there is something inside me that stops functioning, something that becomes silent. I let something take over inside me that probably flows from femininity." She knows that she is forgoing new territory in her writing because "silence is heard in her books" and the "force of female desire" is depicted. Among other topics discussed are her alcoholism and being psychoanalyzed by Jacques Lacan.

The remaining four interviews are filled with important information about her novels and films. Duras also reveals a great deal of autobiographical detail. One of the most painful experiences from a financial point of view for Duras was when she wrote the screenplay for ***Hiroshima, mon amour.*** Even Resnais did not alert her to the percentage clauses in the film contract. As a result, she was "robbed" of hundreds of thousands of francs in royalties. She learned to be a better businesswoman in the future.

Marguerite Duras (1976-1979) includes a collection of essays by Duras and other contributors, three interviews with Duras, and the entire shooting script, with notes, of her film ***India Song.*** This complete script will be greatly appreciated by those interested in her unique filmmaking techniques. Photographs from her films are also included.

In the seven essays by Duras, she includes film methods used in making ***India Song;*** stage directions for the theater for this script; how she managed to make films without a salary for an uninterested public ("No one sees my films"); her film ***Son nom de Venise dans Calcutta desert;*** the reactions of her pragmatic mother to one of Duras's autobiographical films, and her last visit to her mother's home before her death; her film ***Vera Baxter,*** about a woman who was burned because she was perceived as a sorceress; and, finally, her film ***Le camion*** about a woman who is happy "without a need to search for meaning."

In the three interviews with Duras, "Dispossessed" by Xavière Gauthier questions the author about the difference for her between films and writing books; "The Path of Joyful Despair" by Claire Devarrieux asks Duras to discuss the politics of ***Le camion,*** and "An Act Against All Power" by Jacques Grant and Jacques Frenais solicits Duras to analyze closely ***Vera Baxter*** and ***Le camion.***

The remaining essays fall into the category of tributes to Duras, the most notable by Jacques Lacan, the structuralist psychoanalyst, who psychoanalyzed Duras and remains one of her greatest admirers. Maurice Blanchot the writer; Dionys Mascolo, her second former husband and an author; Joel Farges; Benoit Jacquot; and others continue the tone of tribute in their essays. All these essays help in understanding Duras the filmmaker, who claims, "I make films to occupy my time. If I were strong enough to do nothing, I wouldn't do anything at all. It's because I'm not strong enough to do nothing that I make films."

Outside (1981) is a lively collection of essays written by Duras for a purely pragmatic reason. "I needed money." She explains the title: "Writing articles meant going outside like going to the movies." When she writes books she does not go outside as much.

Duras's activism and inability to ignore injustice are evident throughout as is her deep compassion and sympathy for the oppressed. One-third of these essays give opinionated responses to injustices such as racism in France, the treatment of animals in slaughterhouses, the illiterate, French bureaucracy, and the French judicial and prison systems. As a result, ample insights are given into Duras's social consciousness and political activism as a writer.

The jewels of this collection are essays on great women artists and performers such as close personal friends Jeanne Moreau, Delphine Seyrig, Madeleine Renaud, Margot Fonteyn, Leontyne Price, Melina Mercouri, Brigitte Bardot, Maria Callas, and Monique Wittig. Duras has warm exchanges with these women that indicate an easy rapport with other women. She once admitted that, when she was younger, she hated the female sex.

Other essays in this collection are as diverse in topic and as well written as befits a true literary virtuoso. It is obvious that she also considers herself a global citizen in "that every person is inevitably connected with every other."

The Malady of Death (1982) is a short novel in which Duras strips writing to bare essentials. Here the narration alternates between the male narrator's use of "you" for himself and the third person "she" for the woman in his room. The namelessness of these characters is international. "She" has been paid to be present for sexual favors and to help relieve the solitude of the male character. She is "subject" as she sleeps calmly despite the inner and outward turbulence of the male character/narrator. He suffers from the malady of death, the lack of love, and the fear of the unknown; whereas she sleeps, omniscient and powerful, through the frightening and murderous thoughts of the male. The powerful presence of the woman's body and its endless capacity for pleasure make this a powerful, erotic novel. Duras includes directions for stage adaptation at the end.

The War: A Memoir (1985), originally published under the title ***La douleur,*** meaning pain or suffering, is a fascinating firsthand account of Duras's experiences during World War II. The manuscript was found years after it was written in 1944, after Duras's friend Xavière Gauthier asked if she had any of her earlier writing available for publication. Its autobiographical nature helped Duras become better understood and accessible to her public just one year after ***The Lover*** was published. She received the Prix Goncourt in 1984 for this novel after forty years of being ignored by her peers.

The text is divided into three parts. Part I is titled **"The War."** Duras recounts the pain of waiting for news of her deported husband, Robert. As a writer, she was politically active in the French Resistance. She founded a paper called *Libres* and included a tracing service to determine the whereabouts of political prisoners. She writes about the intense pain of awaiting news of Robert's whereabouts before she learns that he is still alive. François Morland, the man who delivers the news, is actually François Mitterand both active in the same Resistance network. Despite Robert's return to safety and Duras's intense emotional release and regained will to live, she asks him for a divorce. She had met and fallen in love with Dionys Mascolo, her soon-to-be second husband with whom she had her only child, Jean Mascolo.

Part II depicts the life of Pierre Rabier, an agent of the gestapo. This true story explains the precarious situation Duras found herself in when Rabier became attracted to her. As a worker for the Resistance, she pretended ignorance to Rabier, a "creator of fear" responsible for sending people to ovens and concentration camps. Duras was protective of François Morland's whereabouts and does not give in to Rabier, who was finally shot after the war.

In Part III, four short pieces are included. In **"Albert of the Capitals,"** Duras documents the torture of an informer caught by the Resistance camp. In **"Ter of the Militia,"** a young member of the far-right French militia is depicted. **"The Crushed Nettle,"** the only invented story, is about a member of the Communist party. And finally **"Aurelia Paris"** tells the story of a little Jewish girl during the war. (pp. 12-13)

Marguerite Duras is one of the most powerful and gifted French women writers of our time, with one of the richest and most fertile intellects. She particularly challenges women as readers, writers, and critics to examine in themselves love, desire, and the erotic as a crucial step to understanding woman's connection to nature. She depicts women as an oppressed "race" in a patriarchal world. Duras paves the way to the beginnings of an understanding of ourselves that can free us and return us to the realm of "subject" where true liberation will come—when all women have the right to be "subject" in a world without an "other." (p. 13)

Joanne Schmidt, "Marguerite Duras," in

Belles Lettres: A Review of Books by Women, *Vol. 4, No. 2, Winter, 1989, pp. 12-13.*

Leslie Hill

Duras has demonstrated, throughout her work, a powerful and compelling interest in border zones, ambiguous and intermediate spaces which exist between or at the edge of identifiable domains. These margins take various forms: geographical, racial, social, psychological, or sexual. Thus, for instance, the theme of the seaboard in novels such as ***Un barrage contre le Pacifique*** or ***Moderato cantabile,*** both set in places where order is doubly threatened by forces it cannot contain; thus, too, in works like ***Le vice-consul*** and ***India Song,*** Duras's obsessive return to the twilight world of decaying Western colonialism where a desperate intensity, like 'une lèpre du cœur' (a leprosy of the heart), respecting neither race, gender, nor social class, spreads contagiously to embassy staff, society women and the invisible figure of a beggar woman from Savannakhet. Elsewhere, there is the strange no man's land, sited somewhere between grief and rapture, which Duras explores in ***Le ravissement de Lol V. Stein*** and in a series of subsequent texts, like ***L'amour*** or ***La femme du Gange,*** which offer alternative readings of characters and events; and there is the unsettling treatment of love in the context of social and nuclear catastrophe found in the script for Resnais's ***Hiroshima, mon amour,*** or the disturbing framing of sexual desire by violence and prostitution displayed in shorter narratives like ***L'homme assis dans le couloir*** or ***La maladie de la mort.***

In all these texts, whether novels, plays, or films, not only is the coherence or unity of place disturbed, but a number of other social, sexual or emotional boundaries also become blurred and their necessity questioned. Gender differences between male and female in Duras's work are maintained, even exacerbated, but they are also displaced and reframed, and the same, too, could be said of generic distinctions. Narrative fiction, theatre and cinema treat in diverse ways the crucial relationship in Duras's work between speaking and seeing and to this extent they remain incommensurate with one another. But they also begin to exchange certain fundamental properties and to address the same difficulties or impossibilities of representation. In what follows, in looking at some of Duras's more recent work, notably ***L'amant, La douleur*** and the film sequence ***Aurélia Steiner,*** I shall be considering some of Duras's texts and films in the light of those difficulties.

The effect of the preoccupation with limits and borders in Duras's work has a first consequence, which is to attribute some kind of transgressive potential to the act of writing. Duras is one of the few authors left in France, perhaps, to claim seriously, and with enthusiasm, some transcendent status for writing. In 'Les Yeux verts', the special issue of the *Cahiers du cinéma* that she compiled in 1980 to accompany the release of the two films entitled ***Aurélia Steiner,*** she asserts, for instance, here, that 'l'écrit a à voir avec Dieu' (writing has to do with God). In similar vein, in prefacing two of the fictional texts collected in ***La douleur*** (which Duras claims to be thinly disguised transpositions of real events), Duras enjoins the reader: 'Apprenez à lire: ce sont des textes sacrés' (Learn to read: these are sacred texts).

This identification of writing with the sacred and with God has, on occasion, left her work open to a charge of obscurantism and essentialism. Evidence for this comes at times from some of Duras's own remarks as expressed in interviews or some of her recent journalistic pieces. It is important, however, to distinguish between some of the terms of Duras's self-commentary and her own fictional or cinematographic texts. More pertinently, an effort must be made to read the former more as an after-hours extension of the latter and not as a privileged theoretical (or, as it more often is, anti-theoretical) discourse which might provide an adequate translation of what is at stake in Duras's fiction and films. (pp. 1-2)

If Duras endows writing or the written text ('l'écrit') with transcendent qualities, it is plainly not because literature is a vehicle for religious belief or doctrinal convictions. It is rather because, like the Biblical text itself, writing, for Duras, bears witness, in the manner of a prophecy or illumination, to the presence at the heart of language and textuality of something, an object or an experience, which cannot be described except as an interruption, as a cessation of discourse, as a moment of transgression or transcendence. The name of God serves as a possible name for that which cannot be preserved or retained within a stable frame except as a disappearing trace, and thus cannot be represented. God, in Duras, is a name for this impossibility of naming, and functions as a sign of the fundamental confusion and precariousness that exists at all boundaries and margins. Here, God is another name for catastrophe and it is no coincidence that the reference to God arises in the context of Aurélia Steiner and the name of Auschwitz, for in the shifting versions of films and writings entitled ***Aurélia Steiner*** it is the unspoken name of Auschwitz which, in turn, has to function as a possible name for something which it is not only not possible to represent but which cannot even be referred to in universal terms.

A number of Duras's later texts, from ***India Song*** to ***Emily L.,*** occupy a borderline which runs somewhere between representation and performance, event and non-event, reconstruction and fabrication, memory and invention. These texts are often staged from the point of view of a narrator who plays the part of a person involved in the spectacle but distanced from it, as therefore both actor and witness, without it being entirely clear how the two positions might be kept separate. Such, for instance, is the role of Jacques Hold in ***Le ravissement de Lol V. Stein*** or of Peter Morgan in the story of the beggar in ***Le vice-consul*** and clearly both men fabricate as much as they record the stories which they tell (which are about women).

Another model for this double role played by the narrative voice is provided, in a different register, by the so-called 'voix extérieures au récit' (voices outside the story) of ***India Song***—women's voices, says Duras, that are touched by madness, full of disembodied memories that have been forgotten and must be remembered or resurrected—who tell each other the story of Anne-Marie Stretter as though it were their own, which, by the very act of telling, it has become. In the films of the late 1970s or 1980s a similar function falls to the film-maker herself, with Duras providing her own narrative voice-over—or dramatic monologues—for ***Les mains négatives, Césarée, Aurélia Steiner,*** or ***Dialogue de Rome.*** In these last works, it is the genre of film documentary that is taken up, drafted into a mode of filmic writing that redraws the boundaries of the real and the imaginary, the documentary and the hieratic. . . . (pp. 3-4)

In both ***L'amant*** and ***La douleur,*** Duras takes this last process one step further, into the realm of literature and autobiography. Though ***L'amant,*** by winning the 1984 Prix Goncourt, was granted provisional status as a novel by the literary establishment, both it and ***La douleur*** are texts that claim to bear witness to real, historical events. In the first instance, both are based more on memories or experiences retrieved from the past than on imaginary occurrences. To this extent, both ***L'amant*** and ***La douleur,*** represent a partial abandonment of novel-writing and a shift beyond the apparent confines of fiction. In introducing the first section of ***La douleur,*** Duras describes it, in enthralled terms, as a 'Journal', a diary, which enjoys a privileged relationship with the distress it is an attempt to record. It becomes, for Duras, a direct embodiment of that grief, an absolute event that cannot be identified as a written text (as an 'écrit') or even as literature. On the contrary, it transgresses the bounds of both. Reading the text and rediscovering in it the ghostly presence of a 'désordre phénoménal de la pensée et du sentiment' (phenomenal confusion of thought and feeling), Duras avers: 'la littérature m'a fait honte' (literature filled me with shame).

The two texts, though they were published within six months of each other and pursue the same life's story, are in many ways very different. The first, ***L'amant,*** which was written in 1984, began as a commentary on an album of family photographs. Some of these photographs, to which reference is often made in the text, appear elsewhere, in *Les yeux verts,* or in Duras's book of dialogues with Michelle Porte [*Les lieux de Marguerite Duras,* 1977]. The photographs themselves were eventually omitted from the projected book, leaving a written text surrounded by an invisible photographic shadow. Made up of personal memories revolving around two alternating strings of events, Duras's relationship with her first lover, a Chinese, and her relations with her mother and two brothers, ***L'amant*** repeats, supplements, or modifies the biographic details already contained in Duras's novel of 1950, ***Un barrage contre le Pacifique*** and the 1977 play ***L'eden cinéma*** (in which, notably, both the ethnic identity of the lover and the precise nature of the daughter's relationship to him are concealed or displaced). And the intricate intertext of ***L'amant*** could also include other semi-autobiographical texts like her first novel of 1943, ***Les impudents,*** or texts like ***Des journées entières dans les arbres*** or ***Agatha.***

In the main section of ***La douleur,*** which was most likely written, for the most part, in 1946 (a fragment first appeared in 1976), Duras records some of the events of 1944 and 1945. These bear essentially on the return from Belsen of Robert Antelme, to whom she was married at the time, and who, in the book, is named, cryptically or half-fictitiously, as Robert L. Antelme himself was deported in June 1944 and was held in different concentration camps till the following year. He wrote his own account of his experiences in Nazi Germany in 1944 and 1945 in his book, *L'espèce humaine,* which first appeared in 1947, and Duras's narrative of her wait for Antelme back in France may well have been written in parallel with Antelme's text, but completed, it would seem, after the publication of *L'espèce humaine.* Duras's own memoir, in ***La douleur,*** is accompanied by a series of other pieces, some fictional, some (according to the author) based on real events, some left untouched, some rewritten for publication in 1985. (pp. 4-5)

The book came out in March, 1985, some six months after ***L'amant*** and almost exactly forty years, to the day, after the events it recalls. It functions thus as a timely memorial to the events of 1945, but, as such, raises the question of the appropriateness or the possibility of such a memorial. In the summer of 1985, it was not a solitary question. 1985 was also the year of Claude Lanzmann's *Shoah,* and ***La douleur,*** appearing against the background of the trial of Klaus Barbie in Lyon and the election campaign of 1986, provoked a series of other writings and recollections. These included a set of interviews Duras recorded in 1985 and 1986 with François Mitterrand (who, under the name François Morland, was involved with Antelme and Duras in the Resistance and instrumental in rescuing Antelme from Belsen). In 1987, Dionys Mascolo, another close associate during that period, whose name appears in the text of ***La douleur*** as D., gave a further account of how Antelme was brought back into France, and also published the text of a letter from Antelme from June 1945. In the course of a tortuous commentary on that letter, which he reads as a kind of anticipatory testament, Mascolo excavates the foundations of what, two years later, was to become *L'espèce humaine.*

In the case of both ***La douleur*** and ***L'amant,*** there is here, around lived experiences, a strange and growing proliferation of texts. What might have been a simple question of documenting the past gives way to an almost uncontrollable dispersion of textual events of disparate kinds. No two writings seem to share the same status and all—novel, play, memoir, diary, document, film script, photograph album, and interview—compete with each other as adequate representations of the past. As in the versions of ***Aurélia Steiner,*** what is centrally at issue here is a problem of representation. Both ***L'amant*** and ***La douleur*** are attempts to bear witness to powerful or catastrophic events: an illicit story of seduction, family enmities and entanglements, the imagined loss of a loved one, the unimaginable reality of the concentration camp. If the function of writing is to bear witness, then, one might well argue, it is events such as these that deserve, above all others, to be represented. But in what way is such representation possible?

In the first instance, to bear witness means speaking of exceptional events as a privileged spectator and actor, and this is the position adopted by Duras as a narrator or narrative voice in both texts. It is possible on one level to read both ***L'amant*** and ***La douleur*** as texts of remembrance, whose chief object is to piece together and reconstruct the experience of the past. The purpose of writing ***La douleur,*** Duras suggested in 1981, was to recollect: 'Je crois,' she admits, 'que je l'ai écrit pour ne pas oublier. Ce qu'un homme peut devenir, ce qu'on peut lui faire subir' (I believe I wrote it in order not to forget: what can become of a man, what he can be subjected to). But the past that the text wishes to remember in this way turns out to be strangely difficult to resurrect or make present.

A contagious aura of forgetfulness surrounds ***La douleur.*** This affects primarily the production of Duras's own text. In prefacing the diary in 1985, Duras claimed not to remember ever even writing it. (pp. 5-6)

As Duras [indicates], her forgetting has more than anecdotal value. It is symptomatic of deeper disturbances at work in the text. As Duras reviews and discounts the available choices, what she implies is that the writing of the text was itself an impossibility. No space, no time, no presence seems to have been available to collect the experience together, to recollect or remember it. Indeed, as though to echo these doubts, the text of the memoir is not stable. It begins as a diary, but so casually that one suspects this almost to be no more than a device, and it resembles a constructed retrospective narrative more than a series of discontinuous notations. The story it tells, however, remains a discontinuous one. And though it records Duras's frenetic attempts to obtain information, what it documents in reality is less a series of events than stages in the experience of fear, grief, loss.

Its main preoccupation is with imagining what, for lack of information or from fear itself, it is somehow not possible to imagine or make present. Its concern is thus with the precarious nature of representation and the language used—at times in desperation—to represent the unknown. At times it is impossible for Duras to sustain the use of the first person in her text and she begins referring to herself in the third person, as though she were a character from one of her own novels (and this rhetoric of self-dissociation, which Duras uses extensively in ***Le ravissement de Lol V. Stein,*** is a major characteristic of ***L'amant***). She becomes emptied of her own identity, which merges with that of the man she is waiting for: 'je n'ai de place nulle part ici, je ne suis pas ici, mais là-bas avec lui, dans cette zone inaccessible aux autres, inconnaissable aux autres, là où ça brûle et où on tue' (I have no place here anywhere, I'm not here, but with him, in a zone nobody else can reach or knows about, together with the burning and the killing). She observes: 'ce n'est que souffrances partout, saignement et cris, c'est pourquoi la pensée est empêchée de se faire, elle ne participe pas au chaos mais elle est constamment supplantée par ce chaos, sans moyens, face à lui' (there is just suffering everywhere, bleeding and cries, which is why thoughts are prevented from forming, they are not part of chaos but are constantly being supplanted by it, helpless in the face of it).

Seen as an account of the period from 1944 to 1945, the writing of ***La douleur*** remains without object. It has no privileged knowledge to communicate, no certainties and no knowledge of events, except what is public knowledge anyway. What the text remembers is the uncertain and the unknown, its object is to imagine the unimaginable, the absent. Duras writes that 'ce qui survient ce sont des bouleversements sans objet' (the things that occur are upheavals without an object). At the end, as the book offers the perspective of a denouement, a story rounded off and complete, a gap of silence survives, mirrored in the severely elliptical nature of the last pages, which refuse the theme of rediscovered togetherness, for as Duras informs us, she and Antelme separated immediately after, almost before his return. (This last motif is repeated in ***L'Amant,*** when Duras affirms of herself and her lover that 'un avenir commun n'est pas envisageable' [a shared future cannot be envisaged], and reminds us that desire, in Duras's texts, is more often about separation than union, about creating differences rather than striving to efface them.) The future exists as a possibility for survival, not as a time for making plans or projects. The indeterminacy of the future is echoed in Duras's note about Antelme's own silence once *L'espèce humaine* was completed. The final words of ***La douleur*** are by way of a tribute to Robert L.: 'Je savais qu'il savait, qu'il savait qu'à chaque heure de chaque jour, je le pensais: 'Il n'est pas mort au camp de concentration" ' (I knew that he knew, that he knew that at every hour in every day, the thought went through my mind: "He didn't die in the concentration camp"). (pp. 7-8)

From beginning to end, one might say, the question of the *unimaginable* haunts the work of Duras. It is confronted explicitly in ***La douleur*** and, in retrospect, two considerations arise. The first is an ethics of literature. If, as Antelme argues [in his *L'espèce humaine*], there is only one humanity, then the experience of the camps and responsibility for the camps, far from being the catastrophe or crime of a few, belong to al!. Even if it may seem 'incongru, presque indécent' (incongruous, almost indecent), as Duras puts it in 1981, to lay claim to the experience of a survivor of the camps, it is possible and necessary for writing to bear witness to that survival. The only response to the crime of the camps, for Duras, is to make it into a universal crime: 'la seule réponse à faire à ce crime,' writes ***La douleur,*** 'est d'en faire un crime pour tous. De le partager. De même que l'idée d'égalité, de fraternité' (the only response one can make to this crime is to make it a crime for everybody. To share it. In the same way as the idea of equality and fraternity). From this point on, writing, for Duras, becomes irredeemably a writing of catastrophe, of the unimaginable and unspeakable margins of language.

As well as an ethics of writing, there is here, also, a politics of writing. It is no longer, as it was for Duras in the late 1940s, when she was a member of the French Communist Party, a politics of revolution, but a politics of revulsion, based on an apocalyptic rejection of political faith, whether of the right or of the left, and on a scandalous, outrageous assertion of the mutual equivalence of the two. For Duras, all political belief systems are an attempt to elude the unrepresentable nature of the sacred. If human disaster cannot be represented, it makes little sense to establish elaborate systems of political representation, democratic or otherwise, to defend against it. On the contrary, argues Duras, it is the politics of representation itself which culminates in the unspeakable, in war and oppression. (A complete history of Duras's politics would require a more lengthy account than is possible here. It would need, for instance, to bring together: a text such as ***Abahn Sabana David***—or the film, ***Jaune le soleil***—, Duras's activities in May 1968, her association with Maurice Blanchot, her involvement (as a non-Jew) with Judaism, and her recent articles for papers like *Libération* or the short-lived *L'autre Journal.*) In ***L'amant,*** of the relation between wartime collaboration and her own membership of the P.C.F., Duras writes: 'L'équivalence est absolue, définitive. C'est la même chose, la même appel au secours, la même débilité du jugement, la même superstition disons, qui consiste à la solution politique du problème personnel' (The equivalence is absolute, definitive. It's the same thing, the same pity, the same cry for help, the same inanity, the same superstition, let us say, in believing in the political solution to the personal problem). (pp. 11-12)

When reality becomes unimaginable, writes Antelme in *L'espèce humaine,* the only recourse is to the imagination and the detour of fiction. As though to reinforce the point, the diary of ***La douleur*** surrounds itself with fictional texts. The book places itself beyond the question of whether it is document or fiction. It is a work whose purpose is not to preserve or make real what might have happened in 1945, but to testify to it by an act of language. But in this regard the position of ***La douleur*** is not unique in Duras's work. Indeed the text, though unpublished for forty years, leaves many traces elsewhere in Duras's work.

Some may be found in ***Hiroshima, mon amour,*** for instance, her first film script, delivered to Alain Resnais in 1958. Towards the end, as the French woman finishes telling of the death of the German soldier, her lover, she describes her pain and grief ('De la douleur, je me souviens encore un peu', she says [I still remember the pain a little]), and how her own identity became merged with that of the soldier's dead body ('Je ne pouvais trouver entre ce corps et le mien que des ressemblances . . . hurlantes', [Between his body and mine I could only find similarities . . . screaming at me], she says to her Japanese lover). Eventually, she escapes to Paris, and her arrival coincides with the bombing of Hiroshima: 'Quand j'arrive à Paris, le surlendemain, le nom Hiroshima est sur tous les journaux. Mes cheveux ont atteint une longueur décente' (When I arrived in Paris, two days later, the name of Hiroshima was in all the papers. My hair had grown to a respectable length). Private disaster is echoed, outstripped, overwhelmed, effaced by public catastrophe. In ***La douleur,*** the motif is the same: Antelme slowly recovers, puts on weight. The date is August 1945, and Duras notes: 'Sur le bord de la route, un matin, ce titre énorme dans un journal: Hiroshima' (By the side of the road, one morning, a huge headline in a newspaper: Hiroshima). On one side a treasonable love affair with a German soldier who is killed, on the other, the desperate rescue and survival of a husband. Like the comparison of the bombing of Hiroshima with a casual affair between a French actress and a Japanese architect, the association is scandalous. But the scandal, by transgressing the limit of what is properly imaginable, bears witness: to the unimaginable catastrophe of war and of representation.

In 1961 Duras published another script, ***Une aussi longue absence,*** shot the same year by Henri Colpi and Jasmine Chasnay. The film is a pallid and lifeless affair, but the plot has a familiar ring. Thérèse Langlois, who runs a café in Puteaux, meets a tramp who reminds her of her husband, Albert, arrested sixteen years earlier, in June 1944, and deported to Germany in July 1944. (These dates are in fact those of Robert Antelme and Thérèse is the name chosen by Duras for the female protagonist—whom she claims to be based on herself—of the stories, **"Albert des Capitales"** and **"Ter le Milicien"**, which are included in ***La douleur.***) Thérèse is convinced this tramp might be her husband, but, having been deported in the war, he has lost all memory of the past and spends his time cutting pictures from newspapers and magazines, searching perhaps for an image that might represent something of his past life. According to his papers, his name is: Robert Landais . . . (And one wonders why Antelme is named in ***La douleur*** as Robert L.)

It is curious that both works which make secret allusion to the forgotten text of ***La douleur*** should be film scripts. It is as though there is an absent film running in the background of ***La douleur,*** a film which cannot be made but which, if it could, might testify to the unspeakable past. The question occurs elsewhere in ***La douleur.*** At one point, in **"Albert des Capitales",** Thérèse, preoccupied—unspeakably—with the task of torturing a collaborator, reflects:

> "One has to be somewhere doing something," Thérèse says to herself. At this moment, this is where I am, in a darkened room, shut in with Albert and Lucien, the pair from Montluc, and this informer of Jews and Resistance workers. I'm at the cinema. She is there. Once she was on the banks of the Seine, at two in the afternoon, one summer's day and someone kissed her and told her they loved her.

There is here a scandalous and impossible image, an image of torture, and a strange sense that the impossible image, just as in ***Hiroshima, mon amour,*** has become absorbed into an amorous encounter. Thérèse becomes divided against herself, split into two competing pronouns. By an unexpected reversal, the cinema, the cavern of images, like the cellar of ***Hiroshima, mon amour,*** has become the place of an impossibility of representation. Representation has been supplanted by an absent, phantom image. So if the image becomes a means of testifying to the impossibility of representation, then film itself, whatever its value as a document, becomes an invisible ghost: 'J'ai *vu* les actualités. Je les *ai vues*' (I've *seen* the newsreels. I've *seen* them), says the French woman in ***Hiroshima, mon amour.*** 'Tu n'as rien vu,' replies her lover. 'Rien.' (You've seen nothing. Nothing).

If ***Hiroshima, mon amour,*** like ***La douleur,*** is a text traversed by a contradictory tension between the desire for an image and the knowledge that the image is impossible, the same is also true of ***L'amant.*** The initial title was *L'Image absolue* and it is clear that one absolute image commands its entire structure. That image is the image of the ferry over the Mekong river. Like a screen memory, it is shorthand for a lengthy scenario of desire and seduction. The image, however, is absent, like a phantom. It is missing from the book not only in the sense that other photographs are also missing, having been removed by the author, but in the sense that it was never there, was never present and cannot be made so. It survives as a text, an object of desire, a fantasy glimpsed in retrospect and bearing witness to the event it commemorates. And, as a text, it is possible for the image to represent the scene of desire the ferry incident enacts because, paradoxically, it represents nothing. It is the absent trace of an unrepeatable and unforeseen event. Had it existed, it would have testified to the existence of God (by the same token, were God to exist, the image would not be impossible). The image, writes Duras,

> could only have been taken if it had been possible to tell in advance what importance this event, this crossing the river, would have in my life. Yet, while the event was in progress, nobody knew it even existed. Only God knew about it. That's why the image—and it could not have been otherwise—does not exist. It was left out. It was forgotten. It wasn't taken away, removed from the collection. To this absence of it having been taken it owes its value, of representing an absolute, being, in fact, the author of it.

Though this image is non-existent, it is paradoxically also ever-present. Its absence disorganises the already tentative biographical narrative of ***L'amant*** (Duras notes from the outset that 'l'histoire de ma vie n'existe pas' [the story of my life does not exist]). But its textual double, its written negative, returns time and again, in the text of ***L'amant,*** as an inexhaustible scene, one which the narrator, as witness and actor, contemplates from afar, like a screen memory, or mirror, in which she rediscovers the secret of her own, as yet undifferentiated sexual desire: 'J'avais à quinze ans le visage de la jouissance et je ne connaissais pas la jouissance' (At the age of fifteen I had the face of pleasure and did not know pleasure). The vision of this face, before its premature ageing (which Duras sites, like the loss of innocence it is, at eighteen, when she left Indo-China), survives, indeterminable and absolute, as a token of an impossible and unreachable past. The past, like Duras's face, after leaving for France, turns into a landscape of destruction, but the devastation, as ***L'amant*** makes clear, sustains an intensity of desire which fuels the desire to write and the desire to write the intensity of desire. Writing, desire, for Duras, become names for one another.

The past exists, in ***L'amant,*** insofar as it is lost, almost forgotten. But as it disappears, it leaves traces in many places, and ***L'amant,*** like ***La douleur,*** is inhabited, as though by a ghost from the past, by another space of possible representation. It is a space somewhat akin to a cinema, in which a viewer gazes, like a voyeur, at a screen, unable to make up her mind whether she is a spectator or an actor, or whether to refer to herself in the first or third person. On that screen, for instance, is the image of her still innocent schoolfriend, Hélène Lagonelle, whom in an interview Duras the author describes, mysteriously, as a prototype for Lol V. Stein, and to whom, in ***L'amant,*** the narrator delegates her own desires, enjoying the body of her lover—and of Hélène—by the agency of Hélène Lagonelle, thus dividing herself from herself, split across the gap between her own gaze and the object of that gaze, her partner and her double. (And readers of ***Le ravissement de Lol V. Stein*** will recognize here the voyeuristic structure by which Lol stages and restages her own desire in a repetition of the scene in the ballroom at T. Beach. In turn, the gaze is repeated, by Jacques Hold, as he looks on at Lol looking on at himself, unable to decide whether he is a witness or an actor. In such situations, of course, it can be claimed that the gaze is inherently male in its reductive seizure of the female body as an object. Duras's voyeurs, though, are more often female than male, and the gaze more often corresponds to an experience of internal division and separation than one of bug-eyed fetishism.)

On the screen of ***L'amant,*** too, is the image of the viewer herself, both seducing and being seduced by her lover, in a mobile exchange of roles and desires, while all around, in the beginning darkness, the noises of 'une ville de plaisir' (a city of pleasure) resemble 'le son d'un film mis trop haut, qui assourdit' (the soundtrack of a film with the volume set deafeningly loud). On that screen is also the story of a beggar-woman, of whom it is impossible to tell whether she belongs to fiction or reality, who is transporting with her a dead child, searching for a place in a film perhaps, one like ***India Song,*** which does not pretend to represent the impossibility of her life but gives her instead an invisible speaking—chanting—part, and shows her trace like a ghost set at the edge of the cinema frame and commanding all that happens within it. On that screen, too, perhaps finally, is something resembling a family melodrama or a Hollywood morality play, a film, say, like Charles Laughton's *The Night of the Hunter,* as reinvented by Duras, in which childhood innocence fights a last battle against paternal corruption and greed, and in which a counterfeit preacher (Robert Mitchum), demonstrates how, while the right hand may speak words of love, the left can always speak of hate (and vice versa). This is what Duras forgets in ***L'amant,*** in order finally to remember it again:

> In the stories in my books relating to my childhood, all of a sudden I can no longer remember what I avoided saying, what I did say, I seem to remember mentioning the love we felt for our mother, all of us, and the hatred, too, the awful hatred, in this mutual story of ruin and death which was this family's story in any case, in the case of love as well as hatred and which is still beyond my understanding, still out of reach, hidden in the depths of flesh, as blind as a new-born baby in its first day of life.

If a film inhabits both ***La douleur*** and ***L'amant,*** what film would it be? In ***Un barrage contre le Pacifique,*** Joseph (the younger brother of ***L'amant***) tells of his mother saving money by playing the piano at the local cinema, the 'Eden'. The two children, who would go with their mother, used to fall asleep by her side as soon as the newsreels began. However, because of the position of piano and screen, 'en dix ans la mère n'avait pas pu voir un seul film' (in ten years, the mother hadn't been able to see a single film). The 'Eden' (Duras later revives it for the title of ***L'eden cinéma***) turns out to be this curious thing, a silent cinema with an invisible screen. If the cinema, true to its name, represents a Biblical Eden, it does so in a contradictory fashion. On the one hand, it speaks of a maternal world of sleep and of dream images (one which Joseph, as Madeleine Borgomano argues, strives, for his part, to rediscover by loving a woman met at the cinema). The cinema is linked to the mother in other ways, too. It may be remembered that, in ***L'eden cinéma,*** 'les yeux verts' (the green eyes), which later come to name Duras's contribution to the *Cahiers du Cinéma,* are spoken of as being the mother's. Thus Suzanne: 'On ne se souvenait pas de cette femme, notre mère, jeune, entourée d'enfants, aimée par cet inconnu, notre père. Belle. Des yeux, verts, disait-on' (We had no memory of this woman, our mother, young, surrounded by children, loved by this stranger, our father. Beautiful. Eyes, green, people said).

If the cinema names the mother, it also names her bereavement and the absence of the father. The cinema refers us to grief and loss as well as the maternal body. It also refers us to a catastrophic impossibility, that of joining together sound and image as a unified presence. The implications are significant. In ***L'eden cinéma,*** years after ***Un barrage contre le Pacifique,*** the figure of the mother is still treated according to a fundamental dichotomy. A stage direction explains the mother is to remain motionless, 'sans expression, comme statufiée, lointaine, *séparée*—comme la scène—de sa propre histoire' (expressionless, like a statue, aloof, *separated*—like the state—from her own story). The mother is split between a stage representation and her own existence which is beyond representation. The effect of the play is not to represent her story, as though that would exhaust the story, but to bear witness to her existence by having her children retell her life. The mother never speaks of herself and remains passive, an icon of her own suffering. Like Anne-Marie Stretter in ***India Song,*** she stands at the centre of the play but divided against herself, quoted rather than acted, reflected through mirrors rather than embodied in herself.

In ***Les petits chevaux de Tarquinia*** in 1953, famously, Duras wrote that 'aucun amour au monde ne peut tenir lieu de l'amour' (No love in the world can take the place of love). As with love, so with images. Duras's cinema is motivated by a desire for definitive images and much care goes into creating such a cinematographic utopia, at times with an extreme poverty of resources. But inherent in Duras's films there is, too, the knowledge that such an absolute image is necessarily absent and impossible. The cinema, then, becomes the site of an incipient catastrophe, the disaster of an image striving—failing—to represent that which is unrepresentable.

In some films, Duras dramatizes this failure by pushing the image to its limits. This is often done by using dingy artificial lighting (as in ***Son nom de Venise dans Calcutta désert*** or ***Le camion***), or shots taken in the half-light of evening or morning (as in ***Césarée,*** or ***Les mains négatives***). On occasion the process is taken to the point where the image itself is abolished or effaced (as in the latter part of ***L'homme atlantique***). More often, as in ***Les enfants,*** Duras exacerbates the theatricality of her mise-en-scène to a point of extreme hieratic implausibility or abstraction. But what Duras explores most consistently is the gap between sound and image. By the use of voice-overs spoken by invisible characters, by developing verbal commentary into a style of fictional monologue which seems almost divorced from what is shown on the image-track, Duras pulls speech and sight apart. They no longer coincide. Gone is the fantasy identification of the screen as the source of the spoken word. Representation is abandoned in favour of an inquiry into the conditions of representation and an exploration of the interval between image and speech. That interval cannot itself be represented and traces a limit within the whole system of representation. In ***India Song*** and the ***Aurélia Steiner*** films, the gap becomes like an impossible image of the unrepresentable, a failed representation of a catastrophe which cannot be made present.

Such, for instance, is the case with ***Aurélia Steiner*** (Vancouver). One of the opening shots—the second—of the film, in monochrome, is of the horizon in the distance, and shows in long shot the cloudy sky over the slightly darker sea before tilting back to study the dark sky and the sun behind the clouds. Duras's own off-screen voice seems to describe the scene (the spoken text is slightly different from that published):

> It is the middle of the day. The sky is dark. In front of me is the sea. Today it's flat, heavy, solid like iron and exhausted, it seems. Between the sky and the water there is a broad black line. It covers the entirety of the horizon, it has the regular form of a giant erasure, the unmistakable character of an unbridgeable divide.
>
> (pp. 12-19)

The film, ***Aurélia Steiner*** (Vancouver), like others in the series, turns on a name. The name refers to the dead mother of the child born in the concentration camp as well as the child and the narrator herself, thus, once again, to the figure of a spectator and an actor, viewer and viewed. But, more than this, the name also names the act of writing itself, one which here is addressed to the dead father of Aurélia Steiner, as though to remember his name, and all the ***Aurélia Steiner*** texts end with the invocation: 'Je m'appelle Aurélia Steiner [. . .] J'écris' (My name is Aurélia Steiner [. . .] I write). It also names the moment of transgression, of love, birth and death, by which the name is brought forth from within the camp. The bond of identification and desire forged between these different instances of the name gives an insight which is apocalyptic in its finality and in its revelatory intensity. Apocalyptic themes are common in Duras's work, and it is characteristic, too, that in ***Aurélia Steiner*** they are set within the dim half-light of evening and against the seashore. The film speaks of a fundamental fragility of barriers and difference. Of the sea ('la mer', but also, no doubt: 'la mère', the mother) Duras writes, at one point, that 'la différence inexistait' (difference non-existed). In this between-worlds, where writing is a continued attempt to grasp and give form to the unrepresentable, ***Aurélia Steiner,*** as film and as text, functions as a revelation, but it is a revelation without message or essence.

The name of Aurélia Steiner, in ***Aurélia Steiner*** (Vancouver), is also a number: 200095, which appears handwritten on the screen. The name is a Jewish name ('Juden,

Juden Aurélia, Juden Aurélia Steiner' says the sailor), and the films and texts that, across their differences, share the name of ***Aurélia Steiner*** can be read as an attempt to bear witness to that name. The name belongs to the narrator as well as the child and mother. What is at issue, then, is a question of representation: what does it mean to write with a Jewish name, from the perspective of a Jewish name, a name like Aurélia Steiner? (Duras herself acknowledges that she is not 'a Jew', but endeavours to divorce from religious essentialism the notion of what the term, 'a Jew', might mean, to rediscover in Judaism a cultural limit, a border which cannot be internalized as an essence, and it is this sense of Judaism as a dereliction of essence that, in turn, is at stake in the appeal to God from the margins of ***Aurélia Steiner,*** in ***Les yeux verts.***)

There is, in ***Aurélia Steiner*** (Vancouver), a central scene in the concentration camp that the rest of the text struggles to articulate and frame. It is a scene of execution, death, love and birth. The scene, necessarily, apocalyptically, can no longer be remembered by its actors, except perhaps for the child, Aurélia, who, like the messenger in the Book of Job, is in the position of being able—or obliged—to write: 'I only am escaped alone to tell thee' (Job, I, 15). The scene must be reconstructed, invented, written. Persistently, the text returns, without illustration, to the idea of 'le grand rectangle blanc de la cour de rassemblement du camp' (the great white rectangle of the camp parade ground). This rectangle is where the execution of Aurélia Steiner's parents takes place and her own birth occurs. The rectangle is an invisible stage on which the scene of death and birth is acted out. It is also, of course, at the same time, the rectangle of the film frame itself. The name appears, twice over, hand-written, as a frame within the film, and in ***Aurélia Steiner*** (Paris) it returns as a rectangle of cloth sewn inside the clothes of a rescued and abandoned child, bearing the initials: A.S. The frame draws the limits of an effort of representation with the knowledge that what should appear in that frame is in fact unrepresentable, absent, impossible. But if it is impossible to fill that frame, suggests Duras, it is at least possible to bear witness to the impossibility of doing so. (pp. 19-20)

Leslie Hill, "Marguerite Duras and the Limits of Fiction," in Paragraph: The Journal of the Modern Critical Theory Group, *Vol. 12, No. 1, March, 1989, pp. 1-22.*

Trish Deitch Rohrer

Emily L., written by the acclaimed French writer Marguerite Duras and translated by Barbara Bray, is a short and odd experimental novel—a story within a story—about a French writer and her longtime lover who sit in a cafe in a port town off the Seine and imagine the life history of an aging English couple they've never met, who are sitting across the room from them getting unhappily drunk. By the end of the novel it seems clear that the story the French writer and her lover imagine is, in some way, the story of their own life together.

What's experimental or different about ***Emily L.*** is this:

"I think that a writer ought to break rules. Without such transgressions, there is neither a writer nor writing. I do not mean that bad writing or living habits should be promoted. I simply mean that writers should be difficult.

When you read a good writer, you never know where he is taking you. It is like walking in a jungle; there is no path to follow."

Marguerite Duras, 1985

The story that's imagined, that is, the life story of the aging English couple, is a traditional love story, complete with parents who forbid the lovers to marry, poems burned in a fire, an endless and exotic journey around the world in a sailing vessel, betrayal, new, unrequited love, and then, in the end, two lovers nearing death, drunk and despondent in a cafe bar far from home in a port town off the Seine.

The story that isn't imagined—that is, the more immediate story that is being told by the French writer about an evening she and her lover spent in a cafe in a port town off the Seine imagining the life story of the drunken English couple—is not at all traditional. It's a kind of autobiographical memoir—meandering and cerebral—about Duras' feelings and thoughts *in the moment* while she sits at a table in a familiar and comfortable cafe with her mate.

What makes this book original is the melding of these two forms: the traditional, fictional narrative and what is essentially a present-tense memoir—one where the author talks about her love of a place (the cafe and its environs), her deep though ambivalent feelings about her mate, her despair (largely fueled by her early experiences growing up in the French colonies of Siam during the war) and her *raison d'etre,* her writing.

What Duras has most neatly and cleverly accomplished in writing ***Emily L.*** is a demonstration of how she—an established and well-regarded fiction writer—transforms *real* experience (that is, the thoughts, feelings, perceptions and memories written about in the non-traditional, autobiographical frame of the book) into fiction (the traditional love story about the aging English couple). Literarily—*academically*—speaking, then, ***Emily L.*** is a gem.

But if you're looking for some other—less noble—pleasure in reading, you won't find it here. I didn't find ***Emily L.*** at all entertaining. The writing is spare and economical, and it's often pretty, but it seems slow to the point of static, and convoluted. The sentences seem more often than not like conversations overheard but not quite understood. Here's an example:

> More people arrived and went straight into the hotel restaurant.

> You said, 'She must feel the power within her like a kind of lost intelligence that's no use to her anymore.
>
> And like some terrible flaw she acquired from outside her own life, she doesn't know when or how, or from whom or what?
>
> Some flaw deep inside her that she's kept silent about all her life, so as to stay where she wanted to be—in the barren regions of her love for the Captain.'

In 1950, Duras published a novel—her third—called ***The Sea Wall,*** about an impoverished and ignorant young woman living in the French colonies in Siam, who takes advantage of a rich and lonely Chinese man very much in love with her. The novel, a straight narrative with a conventional beginning, middle and end, is passionate, messy, overlong and utterly readable. And in 1984, Duras published ***The Lover*** which won the prestigious Goncourt Prize in France and was a best seller in the United States. ***The Lover*** is essentially the same story as ***The Sea Wall,*** but told from a more mature, more forgiving point of view (in ***The Lover,*** the young French woman from the colonies is as much in love with the rich Chinese man as he is with her, and the wounds that are suffered on account of their affair seem more profound and more tragic). It's a short, lean, beautiful book, economical yet fully passionate and thoughtful.

Emily L. is, in many ways, the same story told again, but this time with the maturity of Duras' 75 years behind it. It's a knowing, accepting sort of book, but its characters are weary. And there's something in that weariness that has insinuated itself into the writing, I'm afraid. Where Duras had learned an economy of craft and style in ***The Lover,*** she's now taken that economy and created a book that is so spare, and so without youthful, active passion, that it seems almost to lack a physicality, a sensuousness that helps the reader take hold of the book and hang on.

Emily L. is a lovely book in many ways—not lacking in depth, complexity, wisdom, or beauty—but it's not for everyone.

Trish Deitch Rohrer, "It Is Marguerite She Mourns For," in Los Angeles Times Book Review, *April 30, 1989, p. 9.*

Hope Hale Davis

In a 1967 *Cahiers du Cinema* interview, Marguerite Duras insists that she "can't read novels any more. Because of the sentences . . . " What she likes are fragments, stage directions, as in her novel/film ***Destroy, She Said:*** "Dusk in the hotel. The seventh day. Silence." About one long encounter in the film between two women she recalls: "Many people said to me, 'It's impossible; they exchange nothing but banalities.' But that's exactly the point . . . "

Banalities may also be the point in ***Emily L.,*** with a plot as boldly lifted from the public domain of fiction as any of Iris Murdoch's. Yet a cliché used by Duras is veiled in such mystery, such delicate conjurations as perhaps to go unrecognized. In any case, her new novel, coming more than two decades after her assertions in that interview, is composed almost entirely of complete sentences, firm as the stark opening: "IT BEGAN WITH FEAR."

A couple is spending the weekend at a quayside hotel opposite a tanker port with the cliffs of Le Havre in the distance. Like characters in other Duras novels, the two are on a terrace overlooking a scene described with a fine-penned precision that by itself creates emotion. As they sit drinking, their imagination is caught by another couple and they speculate about these strangers' lives. This dialogue, recounted later by the woman as if addressing the man, shapes the tale. The guesswork in ***Emily L.*** forms a story that gradually becomes more and more detailed, momentous and unlikely.

Before the watchers become preoccupied with the other pair, they are intent on their own parallel story (which she threatens to write) "of the affair we'd had together, the one that was still there and taking forever to die." But she is distracted by the first of two moments of fright: "It's between two landings of the ferry, while the square is empty, that fear arrives." (Is this meant to evoke the moment in Duras' 1984 erotic novel, ***The Lover,*** when the schoolgirl heroine arrives on the Saigon ferry and gets into the long black car of the Chinese stranger?)

The second fear comes with the sudden appearance of 15 people "where there shouldn't be anybody at all." They all look alike, and the narrator (who may be the only one who sees them) decides they are Koreans. In her thoughts "they're clearly murderers, but I recognize this fear, whereas I don't know anything about the one before." The Koreans play no part in the story and are dropped long before the end. Was Duras, who grew up in Indochina, simply giving visual form to some alarming memory of Asians? Is this one of her ways of achieving uncanny effects?

In her *Cahiers* interview about ***Destroy, She Said,*** Duras confesses, "I have the feeling I wrote it in a state of imbecility. And in the dark." Only as she made the film did the book come clear.

By imbecility Duras may have meant something closer to the state of an "idiot savant." Except her talents are not so narrowly focused. In the more than half century since she began writing, at age 18, she has produced fiction, plays and many film scripts, notably ***Hiroshima, mon amour.*** The scenes of historical horror in that movie gave it worldwide acceptance, despite the masochistic self-dramatization that critics see as weakening the author's work.

No one would have guessed from the early Duras novels that she would be known as a writer of brief, oblique stories, of which ***Emily L.*** is the latest. ***The Sea Wall,*** 1950, runs to 288 pages of conventional narration telling in full the family history that would be touched on in ***The Lover.*** Her 1952 fantasy of endless quest aboard a boat, ***The Sailor from Gibraltar,*** is 300 pages long, and seems longer, a labor of love and ingenuous devotion to Hemingway.

Throughout her fiction the personalities, place names, scenes and events keep reappearing. In the cryptic later novellas the characters—described by an admiring French critic quoted unadmiringly by John Simon as "figures of indifference and meaninglessness"—drift as in a dream from one story to another. Sometimes Duras points this out herself in a tone almost of bravado, other times she lets the reader wonder. Often the same crucial experiences are repeated, such as the loss of a baby girl at birth; the observers imagine this happened to the watched couple in ***Emily L.***

What attracts the narrator to the couple is the fact that they speak English. They are trapped in the tanker harbor by some problem with their boat, and the narrator soon imagines they are forced to wander the world. The man, who wears a yachting cap, becomes "The Captain." His nationality is almost inevitable, since Duras is an Anglophile. (In ***The Ravishing of Lol Stein*** the men in Lol's life are named Michael Richardson and John Bedford. In ***Blue Eyes, Black Hair*** the character who obsesses both the male and female protagonists is a man from "the North," probably Vancouver.) Over and over in ***Emily L.*** we are told that The Captain is drinking a black Pilsen and his wife a double Bourbon—to Duras, apparently, unmistakably British tipples.

The couple's imagined story is romantic, of course, and makes no show of being plausible. The father's opposition to the girl's love for the hired "captain" lasted unto death, but was incredibly tolerant. The young man was kept on for 10 years to look after a boat that seemingly was never used. The lovers, even after marriage, lived in the family's Isle of Wight boathouse.

Naturally this is not as simple as it seems. The bride in the boathouse has written poems, and without her willing it they are beginning to appear all over the world. Since her seaman husband cannot understand the poetry, his imagined reflections are remarkable in their sophistication: "Her innocence was such that she'd written the poems without realizing that their worth derived from their very obscurity. She was a child who had to be protected against herself, against an obscurity so clear to her that she took it for her own nature." Is Duras referring here to herself, to the "unremitting narcism" she has been accused of?

The novel may "really" be about writing. The narrator calls her own early ambition "sheer idiocy." Her lover (a writer too) remarks that pride is involved. She agrees, but also "It's as if it protected you from some sort of fear . . . "

This fear, running like a dark stream through all the novels, has legitimate sources. In Indochina, whether or not Duras was actually seduced by a Chinese millionaire, and whether or not her brother was a murderer—as suggested in several novels, especially the first, ***Les impudents***—she grew up in a reckless, violent family. Then, during World War II she joined the Resistance. In **"Monsieur X., Here Called Pierre Rabier,"** she recounts in terrifying detail the hazardous meetings with her Gestapo contact on the streets of occupied Paris.

That memoir is one of a collection of autobiographical pieces published in France as ***La douleur*** and in the United States as ***The War*** (1986). A long first section is offered as a newly discovered diary of an agonizing period in 1944. Duras describes her headaches and sleepless nights and desire for death while waiting for the possible return of her husband from his imprisonment as a Resistance leader. He comes back, emaciated and hardly alive. She nurses him through his slow recovery, with all its repellent physical symptoms, and finally breaks the news that she is leaving him for his best friend.

The foreword to the last memoir piece notes that the events described took place during the decade that she was a member of the Communist Party. She adds that luckily she unconsciously preserved her writing from the party's "nauseating proximity."

If all that does not suffice to account for her fears, Duras has the horrors of actual delirium tremens to remember. During the '70s she and her faithful companion, a man called Yann Andrea, literally gave themselves up to drink. In a book called *M.D.* Andrea describes their bleak alcoholic seclusion. She would start the day with red wine, try coffee, still more wine, until finally she could hold something down. She seems to have changed clothes very seldom, even at night, for fitful stupor was as close as she could come to sleep. Before she had gone quite too far, though already unable to hold a pen, she dictated a novel that is bad in every possible way, ***Malady of Death,*** published in 1982. Then there was nothing, and suddenly she took herself to the American Hospital in Paris for an excruciating cure, with Andrea holding her hand through the worst hours. When ***The Lover*** appeared in 1984, it was rated the most elegantly written of all her works.

Emily L., too, has been a best seller in France. It is easy to see why. The fantasies of an obsessed and masterful writer can be hard to resist. They compel and infuse. Wishes are fulfilled. One of the various Duras wish-fulfillment fantasies to be discerned here from earlier books, the longing for a slave-lover, has been revised appropriately by the aging author. Watching the English woman, the narrator observes that "she's appreciably older than he. And that he has caught up with her in her slowness, and won't outstrip it. And that it's been like that for years."

But there is more to a Duras best seller than borrowed fantasies and never-never-land plots, as there is always more to a dream than can ever be captured. Duras comes as close as anyone can to capturing a dream. (pp. 22-3)

Hope Hale Davis, "Fearful Fantasies," in The New Leader, *Vol. 72, No. 9, May 15-29, 1989, pp. 22-3.*

Mary Flannagan

It is difficult to define a work which the author herself cannot. Marguerite Duras's ***Practicalities*** is composed of transcribed tapes which she made with Jerome Beaujour "to pass the time". These concise meditations in the presence of another include memories, confessions, visions, essays, dreams and micro-tales. They range from the trivial to the profound, and are infused with the lyrical pessimism of her novels.

The language is a cross between written and spoken, what she calls "a free kind of writing". Yet the book is not a stream of consciousness. These highly-finished fragments have been rigorously edited by Duras, and she has imposed a satisfying rhythm in their alternations of length and subject matter.

About writing she argues, rightly I think, that a novel or story is pre-existent, present but hidden, to be discovered by instinct. It is organic and involves "the power of reading before it is written something which is still illegible to everyone else". This is perfection, though some of her reflections on her craft exist so much in the shadow of her novels as to be obscure unless you are familiar with the texts.

She has the ability to divine enormous implications in seemingly insignificant people and things. Pushing beyond the place where language stops, she gives expression to mute archaic emotions. Many of the anecdotes are small masterpieces, particularly the tragic **"The Cutter-off of Water".** A poor family who live by a high-speed rail line have their water supply shut off by an otherwise decent official in the midst of a heat wave. In despair the social rejects commit suicide by lying down on the tracks before the oncoming train.

There is the exquisite account of Duras's discovery of the woman's coraco in an old chest of drawers. The garment, lost over two hundred years before, is covered with darns that are themselves darned. The owner "must have hunted all over the place for it. Day and night. She couldn't think where it could have got to."

Some of the pieces are like diary entries: her alcoholism; her drying out and the bizarre hallucinations that followed; her affair at 65 with a young homosexual. **"Alcohol",** with its terrible resigned understanding, is especially poignant. Drink "doesn't console, it doesn't fill up anyone's psychological gap, all it replaces is the lack of God".

Her attitude to women is confusing. She admits to writing about them in order to write about herself. She is a feminist yet also a man's woman, continually in quest of new love. She believes that women are happier now than when they were domestic slaves, yet she is hard indeed on those who don't scrub their floors and keep their cupboards tidy. And she repeatedly equates women's "divinity" with the maternal archetype. Men, all of whom are homosexuals, get even shorter shrift. "You have to be very fond of them to love them. Otherwise they're simply unbearable."

She can be arrogant, self-indulgent and occasionally incomprehensible. But she is disarmingly frank about her shortcomings, and one admires the way she has transformed personal weakness into artistic strength.

Though the book may lack definition, the individual pieces never do. Duras has a unique way of extracting the pit from the fruit by balancing tough reasoning with intuition. Bravely she goes for the meaning, knowing too well her efforts may end in meaninglessness. And despite a certain didactic tone, her ideas are flexible. It is their very randomness and contradiction, coupled with her stunning insights, that make ***Practicalities*** such a delight to read.

Mary Flannagan, "The Fruit and Pit," in New Statesman & Society, *Vol. 3, No. 83, January 12, 1990, p. 36.*

Gabriel Josipovici

Throughout the autumn and winter of 1986 Marguerite Duras talked to Jérôme Beaujour about anything that took her fancy. The conversations were transcribed, then edited by Duras into a series of distinct pieces ranging from one to ten pages. [In ***Practicalities***] Beaujour is a mere ghostly presence, someone who is being talked at rather than an active questioner. "At most the book represents what I think sometimes, some days, about some things", Duras writes. In French the book was called ***La vie materielle,*** but for some reason Barbara Bray has removed the Marxist echo and given English readers the meaningless title, ***Practicalities.***

This is particularly unfortunate because the personality and life that come through are the antithesis of practical. We learn here about Duras's recurrent alcoholism; about the horrors of her periodic efforts at drying out; about her improbable love affair at sixty with an unstable young homosexual (which has been examined from his point of view in Yann Andrea's *M.D.*); about her house in the country and her flat at the seaside; about her past, her views on men, women, life, love and writing. It does not add up to much, and the personality that comes through is neither interesting nor appealing.

Duras's recent burst of memoir-writing and autobiographical fiction has raised once again the question of the relation of a writer's life to her work. In this case we have the curious phenomenon of someone who cannot write a dull sentence and yet whose comments outside fiction range from the embarrassing to the banal. The puzzle is compounded by the fact that so much of her fiction, it turns out, is autobiographical in inspiration, from her early novel about her mother, ***Un barrage contre le Pacifique,*** to her recent novel about her infatuation with Yann, ***Yeux bleux, cheveux noirs.*** Yet the point here is that for the reader it could not matter less whether these were "true" or "invented". Duras's novels create their own mood and space from the first sentence. No one else writes in the least like her; she fits into no category or school. The only thing to be said about her work is that it has the stamp of complete authenticity when it comes off, and can be excruciatingly mannered when it does not. This is because she is always prepared to take risks. And because, despite the vagaries of her private life, she continues to produce novels (and films) at an amazing rate.

Practicalities does not reveal where her best works get their power from, nor why her recent work has been so uneven. Instead it reveals a rather pathetic yet also rather smug and opinionated woman. Too much of it consists of sentences like: "I've noticed that writers who are superb at making love are much more rarely great writers than those who are scared and not so good at it." And: "There's one thing I'm good at, and that's looking at the sea." Our culture is hungry for personalities and opinions. It usually gets what it deserves.

Gabriel Josipovici, "Risking an Opinion," in The Times Literary Supplement, *No. 4536, March 9-15, 1990, p. 248.*

Marianne Hirsch

Marguerite Duras's work renegotiates the relation of the personal and the political in complicated but ultimately precarious ways. As her writing becomes more self-revealing and autobiographical, it confirms so deep an interconnection between personal and political, fictional and journalistic writing, as to raise a number of vexing questions. "I write about women in order to write about myself, about myself alone through the ages," she announces in ***Practicalities;*** she appropriates and incorporates those stories which feed her writing, typically the stories of other women. What are the politics of the static, almost paralyzing, confrontation of one woman's life with another's, which recurs throughout Duras's works? What kind of feminism does she represent now, in the eighties and nineties?

Practicalities and ***Emily L.,*** the one a series of taped and transcribed conversations, the other a novel, together suggest how Duras structures narratives out of the fragments of the everyday, and how, disturbingly, those fragments can always be led back to her own recurring preoccupations and obsessions. Disturbing because, for the feminist reader, Duras's representations of women's lives are more than the fragments of fiction, more than the elements of a personal history: they are political statements about women made by France's most renowned contemporary woman writer in a social and political climate inimical to women and to feminist concerns. Duras's political history in the resistance and the Communist Party, her present eagerness to comment on current events, her extensive journalistic practice, all encourage us in holding her thus accountable: "My role as a writer and my political role are the same. I speak from the same place, rigorously with the same style," she says in a recent interview in *Le nouvel observateur.*

Practicalities (La vie matérielle) is a series of short pieces, taped and transcribed conversations between Duras and Jérôme Beaujour about, precisely, the "materiality" of women's lives. They range from commentaries on Duras's novels, plays and films, to descriptions of Paris and her neighborhood, her other houses, certain objects and moments in her life, an article she read, a color mentioned in her novel that only she can see, family photographs, a painting she loves, the face of Lech Walesa's wife on television. This is journalistic exercise as well as the practice of proto-fiction. A number of preoccupations recur: her alcoholism and the painful detoxification process she underwent; her relationship to her young homosexual companion Yann Andréa; the act of writing for a woman, its connection to the body, to the rest of her life. "The book has no beginning and no end, and it hasn't got a middle either. If it's true that every book must have a *raison d'être,* this isn't a book at all." Duras evidently enjoys what she calls "such a free kind of writing," which "no previous or current genre could have accommodated." Although the idea of such a project may appear hopelessly self-indulgent—a measure of Duras's enormous public success—readers of her work will find gems of insight amid moments of irritation.

The primary focus is on women's lives. For Duras the feminine is a large category, undifferentiated by class or other social demarcations. The tedium of those female lives—their "materiality"—"shapes" the book's formlessness. Duras cleans out a drawer in an old chest and finds hidden behind it a woman's undergarment from 1720, lace around the neck, pink with stains of menstrual blood, that had been rinsed but not yet put through the annual wash. Duras thinks about the woman searching for the misplaced garment. She thinks about how women spend their time, live in their houses; she writes about dirt and cleanliness, about cooking and writing. "A woman's work," she boldly declares, "from the time she gets up to the time she goes to bed, is as hard as a day at war, worse than a man's working day."

The most troubling and revealing piece in the book, **"The Cutter-off of Water,"** retells a newspaper story of a "retarded" mother who killed herself along with her husband and her children by lying down on the tracks of the express train after a city employee cut off their water supply on a hot summer day. The employee later excused his action by explaining that the mother did not protest when he gave her a last chance to pay her bill. Duras tries to imagine one particular moment in the story: after the water was cut, probably after the young mother had already decided on her family's death, she went to the local café and said something to the owner, but no one remembered what. This "silence" fascinates Duras, and makes her writing possible: "I restore the silence in the story . . . I restore the profound silence of literature. That's what helps me forward, helps me get inside the story."

Duras speculates that the mother spoke about something other than her decision—maybe something about the heat. This other unknown speech is, she says, "sacred" language—language at the point of its ultimate power. It is this female language, or female silence, which provides Duras with the pre-text and provocation of her text. A woman kills her children and herself; another woman, Duras, contemplates the scene from her desk in Paris, trying to understand and needing to write, because the woman who kills—the woman who is killed—is also she, both same and different.

This fascination and identification is troubling; it recalls Duras's controversial July 1985 article in *Libération* about the Gregory case, the 1984 murder of a four-year-old boy in a Northern French village. As soon as his mother, Christine Villemin, was accused of the murder—and before the trial—Duras went to look at her house, and concluded, on the basis of her observation, without ever even trying to speak to her, that Christine was "guilty and sublime." As though Christine were a character in one of her novels, Duras "recognized" her as a woman who had to escape from her life and who chose the death of her child as the surest form of flight.

How are we to evaluate the passionate intensity Duras reveals when speaking of these crimes? How can we characterize this relation between the woman writer and the other women who occasion her writing? What is its psychology, what are its politics? What is at stake in this erasure between self and other, between fiction and journalism? ***Practicalities*** raises but does not answer these troubling questions.

Emily L. presents a familiar scene to readers of Duras: a couple—the narrator and her younger lover, barely disguised versions of Duras and Yann Andréa—at a seashore café observing another couple and eventually imagining their story, that of a lower-class British sea captain and his delicate upper-class wife, Emily L., who appears to be on the edge of death. For the narrator, the other couple's story presents the only way of writing about herself and the only way to hold on to her young lover. Her penetrating gaze is directed at Emily L., who she imagines is a poet who no longer writes. She is fascinated by what she imagines as the other woman's writing. Fifteen poems written clandestinely were given without Emily L.'s consent by her husband to her father, who had them published; her husband burned one unfinished poem because it affected him so profoundly. It is the loss of *that* poem that, in the narrator's estimation, makes it impossible for Emily L. to live or to die.

This fragmentary poem again represents that female "silence" which provokes the narrator into writing even as it paralyzes the character into immobility. In the story imagined by Duras's narrator, the young woman wrote the poem after the most painful moment of her life—the death, in childbirth, of her baby girl, a death which nearly killed her too. Again fascinated by a mother who is marked by a child's death, Duras presents her, like the mother in **"The Cutter-off of Water"** or Christine Villemin, as both perpetrator and victim of the child's death. The Captain finds the poem criminal; as he reads it, he feels "stabbed by the truth." But the poem mentions neither baby nor husband. What is its unbearable criminal transgression, then? Is it that it expresses, however indirectly, the immensity of the mother's pain at losing her child, or that it doesn't mention it, that it replaces, erases that pain by focusing on winter afternoon light? The unfinished and unfinishable section of the poem is about "an inner difference at the heart of meaning," a difference that "was reached through, and was in a way the mark of, supreme despair." The poem cannot be finished, it cannot exist, because it speaks of a pain that is absolute but that offers neither illumination nor meaning.

These lines from Emily L.'s poem are almost direct quotations from a poem actually written by Emily Dickinson, "There's a certain slant of light." Duras borrows them without any reference to Dickinson whatsoever; by attributing them to one of her characters, she is creating a complicated line of female transmission, identification and appropriation. In much the same way that the woman poet erases her husband and child in her unfinished poem, the narrator erases both Emilies: the young woman in the café to whom she attributes the poem, and Emily Dickinson who did, in fact, write it.

As the narrator and her lover watch the young woman, the scene of the despair they perceive is repeated in their own fascination: like Emily L., they become obsessed and paralyzed, although unlike her, they talk and eventually the narrator writes. All else disappears as one story mirrors the other, as one story feeds the other's despair. But as one story begins to take shape, the other recedes; the narrator's writing silences the other woman. ***Emily L.*** ends with a meditation on how to write the violence of these moments of identification and appropriation, how to write the unmitigated hopelessness revealed by the winter afternoon light without transforming its threat. The only way to write, the narrator maintains, is without correction or revision, "at one's own pace and in accordance with what one is experiencing at the time; one ought to eject what one writes . . . just leave everything as it is when it appears." Writing remains an act of extreme, narcissistic, cannibalistic self-involvement; its source, its material, its method and its destination all come back to the writer's own subjectivity.

Writing has become archival work for Duras, a kind of housecleaning and ordering of the fragments of her history and of women's history; it is, as she calls it in ***Practicalities,*** "a woman's work." Duras lives in her work, like the women she describes in "House and Home" do, "a life that seems, even to the woman herself, to have been written down and described already." She shuffles and rearranges, sometimes tries to clear everything out, sometimes acquires a number of new possessions "on sale," but ends up keeping a good deal of what she has assembled: "tidying up life, and documenting it." The objects reverberate with one another, repeat each other, like household objects, constituting a fragmentary, discontinuous history that seems endlessly to circle back on itself.

In these two works, Duras's familiar themes resonate both psychologically and politically, making her current work both rich and troubling. It is no longer possible to start afresh, to clean house, as Duras wanted to in the late 1960s. Then she wrote about emptiness and nothingness—a *tabula rasa* from which to reinvent the social. Today that emptiness, that paralysis, have a different valence. The mirroring of writer and subject, reader and author, reader and subject, the mirroring of women's material lives with one another, create a perpetual revolution, a turning in place, which is very like the endless repetition of housework. Women, Duras tells us, never emerge from it: "Ever since my son was a little boy *I've* brought the food from the kitchen and put it on the table. And when one course was finished and the next one was due, *I'd* go and fetch it without thinking, quite happily. Lots of women do it . . . With the Italians, for example, you see women of eighty serving children of sixty."

Duras maintains in ***Practicalities*** that over the centuries women's lives have remained the same: "I seriously believe that to all intents and purposes the position of women hasn't changed." To reveal this repetition in the context of feminism will continue to be deeply disquieting. It is a revelation akin to that of the winter afternoon light—oppressive, painful, irredeemable. Without the subversive possibilities and the momentum of a post-'68 feminism, the nihilism of Duras's writing—a nihilism we can read as either utterly radical or profoundly reactionary—can no longer disguise its despair. (pp. 19-20)

Marianne Hirsch, "Inside Stories," in The Women's Review of Books, *Vol. VIII, No. 1, October, 1990, pp. 19-20.*

FURTHER READING

Callander, Margaret M. "Reading Marguerite Duras's *Moderato cantabile.*" *Modern Languages* 69, No. 3 (September 1988): 160-64.

Examines the "symbolic, hallucinatory, and stylised elements" of Duras's text. Callander states that while the novel is enigmatic, the tight structure and recurring motifs provide a "strange and intense 'reading experience'."

Conley, Verena Andermatt. "Signs of Love: Duras's Minimal Ways." *L'Esprit Créateur* 29, No. 3 (Fall 1989): 101-10.

Discusses how Duras's knowledge of psychoanalysis and philosopher Georges Bataille's theories of eroticism influenced her treatment of love and passion.

DiBattista, Maria. "The Clandestine Fictions of Marguerite Duras." In *Breaking the Sequence: Women's Experimental Fiction,* edited by Ellen G. Friedman and Miriam Fuchs, pp. 284-97. Princeton: Princeton University Press, 1989.

Feminist analysis in which DiBattista asserts that the clandestine love relationships in Duras's works represent something "specifically female."

Gaensbauer, Deborah. "Trespassing and Voyeurism in the Novels of Virginia Woolf and Marguerite Duras." *Comparative Literature Studies* 24, No. 2 (1987): 192-201.

Scholarly comparative analysis.

Gilbert, Harriett. "Hard Facts." *New Statesman* 112, No. 2889 (8 August 1986): 28.

Laudatory review of *The War* in which Gilbert states that Duras's account of World War II never "reads like a confession, or a justification, or agitprop."

Hill, Leslie. "Marguerite Duras: Sexual Differences and Tales of Apocalypse." *The Modern Language Review* 84, No. 3 (July 1989): 601-14.

Examines how Duras's use of repetition and paradox creates "an effect of an underlying movement of perpetual variation" within the context of sexual identity.

Husserl-Kapit, Susan. "An Interview with Marguerite Duras." *Signs: Journal of Women in Culture and Society* 1, No. 2 (Autumn 1975): 423-34.

Interview in which Duras discusses feminism, her female protagonists, and motherhood.

Kristeva, Julia. "The Pain of Sorrow in the Modern World: The Works of Marguerite Duras." *PMLA* 102, No. 2 (March 1987): 138-52.

Academic analysis in which Kristeva examines how "human madness" is manifested in Duras's works.

McNeece, Lucy Stone. "Exile as Allegory: Marguerite Duras's *Le vice-consul.*" *Rivista di letterature moderne e comparate* XLIII, No. 4 (October-December 1990): 425-47.

Analyzes how Duras combines thematic, structural, and figurative elements to create an allegorical text about death and exile.

Michel, Sonya. "Warring Impulses." *The Women's Review of Books* IV, No. 1 (October 1986): 11-12.

Review of *The War* which examines how World War II influenced Duras's literary concerns and narrative style.

Milne, Kirsty. "Waiting for Sorrow." *The Listener* 116, No. 2974 (21 August 1986): 23.

Asserts that *The War* is "one of the most harrowing pieces of writing you could ever expect to read" due to Duras's shifts between "passionate bitterness" and "hard-eyed desperation."

O'Neill, Kevin C. "Structures of Power in Duras's *Un barrage contre le Pacifique.*" *Rocky Mountain Review of Language and Literature* 45, Nos. 1 & 2 (1991): 47-59.

In-depth analysis of Duras's early novel. O'Neill suggests that in this work the author was attempting to free herself from the restrictions placed upon her by a male-dominated world by creating a universally acceptable idiom.

Paris, Erna. "Casualties of Peace." *Maclean's* 99, No. 26 (30 June 1986): 47.

Praises *The War* for its tight, minimalist narrative, but also states that several of the collection's stories "fall short of the standards Duras's readers have come to expect."

Porte, Michelle. "The Places of Marguerite Duras." *Enclite* 7, Nos. 1 & 2 (Spring-Fall 1983): 54-62.

Transcript of a two-part interview which was broadcast on French television in May, 1976. Duras discusses her childhood in French Indochina, the differences between her novels and films, and the prevalent motifs in her works.

Reynolds, Stanley. "Under Duras." *Punch* 289, No. 7565 (11 December 1985): 79, 82.

Laudatory review of English translations of *The Little Horses of Tarquinia, The Lover,* and *The Sailor from Gibraltar.*

Schuster, Marilyn R. "Reading and Writing as a Woman: The Retold Tales of Marguerite Duras." *The French Review* LVIII, No. 1 (October 1984): 48-57.

Feminist analysis of the fluctuating roles of Duras's female protagonists.

Soloman, Barbara Probst. "Marguerite Duras: The Politics of Passion." *Partisan Review* LIV, No. 3 (1987): 415-22.

Brief personal account of the critic's encounter with Duras in 1964 and an analysis of the writer's political symbols.

Woodhull, Winifred. "Marguerite Duras and the Question of Community." *Modern Language Studies* 17, No. 1 (Winter 1987): 3-16.

Examines the relationships between speech and experience, and community and individual identity in *L'amante anglaise.*

William Faulkner

1897-1962

(Full name William Cuthbert Faulkner) American novelist, short story writer, poet, playwright, essayist, and scriptwriter.

The following entry presents criticism on Faulkner's novel *The Sound and the Fury* (1929). For discussions of Faulkner's complete career, see *CLC,* Vols. 1, 3, 6, 8, 9, 11, 14, 18, 28, and 52.

The novel that established Faulkner's reputation as a preeminent figure in American literature, *The Sound and the Fury* is often considered his most successful work. Praised for its complex structure as well as its penetrating examination of human character, *The Sound and the Fury* obscures distinctions between past and present by employing nonchronological narration, stream-of-consciousness techniques, and multiple points of view. The work focuses upon the deterioration of the Compsons, a Mississippi family destroyed by lovelessness, selfishness, and an obsession with lost Southern nobility. Robert Griffin observed: "[The Compsons] are doomed by the curse upon them, a curse of blood passed down through generations, expressing itself in feeble-mindedness, insanity, alcoholism and promiscuity and leading to the complete destruction of the family. Furthermore, they are doomed through their pride in the Compson blood, their extreme awareness of the Compson name."

Faulkner described the experience of writing *The Sound and the Fury* as one of the most exhilarating pursuits of his career. Following numerous unsuccessful attempts to publish his novel *Flags in the Dust,* he resolved to write only for himself, and so began *The Sound and the Fury:* "[One] day it suddenly seemed as if a door had clapped silently and forever to between me and all publishers' addresses and booklists and I said to myself, Now I can write. Now I can just write. Whereupon I, who had three brothers and no sisters and was destined to lose my first daughter in infancy, began to write about a little girl." The girl Faulkner first portrayed in "Twilight," a short story eventually expanded into *The Sound and the Fury,* is Caddy Compson. Forced into the role of surrogate parent because of her mother's weak, self-pitying, and callous nature, Caddy provides compassion and direction for her three brothers during their childhood. However, as an adult, she becomes the focus of their obsessive love and hatred, and the simultaneous source of both order and destruction within the family; according to Olga W. Vickery, she is "almost a symbol of the blind forces of nature." Although Caddy's viewpoint is not presented in the work, she emerges through her brothers' monologues as a strong, caring, but desperate figure who was rejected by her kin when her promiscuous behavior resulted in family dishonor.

The Sound and the Fury is composed of four sections, each with a distinct narrator who relates the events of a specific date in the Compson's history. The first section consists of a monologue by Benjy Compson, a mentally retarded man whose mind at the age of thirty-three is equivalent to that of a three-year-old child. In an interview, Faulkner vividly described Benjy's character: "Without thought or comprehension; shapeless, neuter, like something eyeless and voiceless which might have lived, existed merely because of its ability to suffer, in the beginning of life; half fluid, groping: a pallid and helpless mass of all mindless agony under sun." Although Benjy perceives his surroundings acutely and understands language, he remains locked in his own solitary world, unable to speak, interpret his emotions, or understand the passage of time. At the opening of the novel, he stands near a golf course that was once his favorite pasture, but was sold to pay for his sister Caddy's wedding and for the first year of his brother Quentin's Harvard education. As he listens to the calls of the golfers on the course, his perceptions become intermingled with intense childhood memories that he experiences as though they were occurring in the present. Through mechanical yet powerful recollections that are aroused by sounds, images, and smells, the reader discovers that Benjy's basic experience has been one of loss and neglect. His mother, who rejected him when it was discovered that he was retarded, changed his name from Maury, a family name, to Benjy, and his brothers, Quentin and Jason, perceive him only as a nuisance and a source of embarrassment.

Some critics have suggested that the Compsons' rejection of Benjy symbolizes the moral deterioration of their family as reflected by their intrinsic lack of love, denial of self, and aristocratic pride. Throughout *The Sound and the Fury,* Benjy howls with grief when remembering his beloved sister Caddy, one of the few people who had shown him compassion and understanding. Explaining Benjy's inability to understand Caddy's absence, Faulkner stated: "Benjy wasn't rational enough even to be selfish. He was an animal. He recognized tenderness and love though he could not have named them. . . . He no longer had Caddy; being an idiot he was not even aware that Caddy was missing. He knew only that something was wrong, which left a vacuum in which he grieved." Some critics have also suggested that Benjy functions in some ways as a Christ figure, his anguished wailing expressing an intense, universal suffering.

In the second section of *The Sound and the Fury* Quentin Compson recounts through first-person narration the events and turbulent emotions he experiences on the day of his suicide. Like Benjy, he is immersed in a rigidly ordered private world and vividly recalls his childhood. However, while Benjy is unaware of temporal progression and hungers for affection, Quentin is incapable of love and is virtually paralyzed by his perception of time as a destructive force—he is obsessed with the past and the only future he can imagine for himself is death. Throughout Quentin's narrative, feelings of fear, dread, and meaninglessness are emphasized by images of death-like stillness as well as exhaustive references to watches and clocks. Many critics have suggested that the watch Quentin inherits from his aristocratic grandfather, General Compson, symbolizes his inability to relinquish the outdated values of honor and purity that characterized the old South. For example, Quentin is obsessed with Caddy's sexuality; he associates her loss of virginity to a brief lover by whom she becomes pregnant with the loss of Southern nobility and pride. However, it has also been suggested that Quentin's fixation on his sister stems from his own incestuous feelings and his longing to reclaim the closeness they shared as children. Conceiving of the Compson estate as a closed Edenic paradise, Quentin refuses to accept Caddy's pregnancy and her subsequent marriage to Herbert Head, whom she weds to conceal the illegitimacy of her pregnancy. Tormented by guilt and despair, Quentin tells his father that Caddy's unborn child is his. Mr. Compson, an alcoholic fatalist who emotionally manipulates his children, rejects Quentin's story, recognizing his son's desire to preserve an impossible relationship with Caddy and to sustain the intensity of his emotions from the dissolution caused by the passing of time: "[You] cannot bear to think that someday it will no longer hurt you like this." Extensive critical discussion has focused on Quentin's suicide. David Minter summarized the range of possible motives: "Quentin kills himself in part as punishment for his forbidden desires. . . . But he also kills himself because he fears his own inconstancy. What he discovers in himself is deep psychological impotence. He is unable to play either of the heroic roles; as seducer or as avenger. . . . What he fears is that he will ultimately fail, too, in the role of the despairing lover. What he cannot abide is the prospect of a moment when Caddy's corruption no longer matters to him."

The third section of the novel is narrated by Jason Compson, whose monologue has been variously described as suspect, egocentric, and grimly satiric. Devoid of introspection, Jason's caustic wit, avarice, and harsh rationalism contrast sharply with Benjy's confused observations and Quentin's melancholy narrative. James M. Cox observed: "[Jason's] long lamentation, though a monologue, is not spoken to himself; rather it is his self-dramatization of his plight in a language devoted to reckless and exaggerated criticism of all the ills his flesh is heir to." Unlike Quentin, Jason has no reverence for his lost childhood or the irretrievable past; according to Vernon T. Hornback, time for Jason is a commodity "to be used; saved, not wasted; expended in a calculated fashion, like money or goods." While Jason is free from Quentin's excessive nostalgia and guilt, many critics have suggested that he is victimized by his own worry, fear, and suspicion associated with his utilitarian efforts to control time. Jason also contrasts with Quentin in his undisguised contempt for family members. In addition to his derision and sarcasm, Jason's habit of regularly stealing money from his family has prompted some critics to assert that his habitual cruelty indicates the moral collapse of the Compsons. At the time of his narrative, Caddy's husband has divorced her after discovering that her child is not his. Consequently, she sends her illegitimate daughter, whom she has named Quentin in honor of her brother's memory, to live at the Compson household. Acting as Miss Quentin's guardian, Jason embezzles the money Caddy entrusts to him for the child's care. He becomes the victim of his own scheme, however, when Miss Quentin, tormented by the callous treatment she has received in the Compson household and infuriated by Jason's continuous verbal abuse, breaks into his room, steals back her money as well as a substantial portion of his savings, and runs away.

The final section of *The Sound and the Fury* focuses on Dilsey, the Compson's black housekeeper. In a posthumously published introduction to *The Sound and the Fury,* Faulkner described Dilsey as a figure of endurance and stability: "There was Dilsey to be the future, to stand above the fallen ruins of the family like a ruined chimney, gaunt, patient and indomitable." This section contrasts with the three preceding monologues in that it is related from an omniscient, third-person perspective that many critics have associated with Dilsey's freedom from obsessive self-involvement. A sense of community, rather than entrapment within the self, is emphasized by the clear, objective description of characters and surroundings. A figure of strength, Christian morality, and humanistic decency, Dilsey encourages peace and order in the embittered Compson household. Her acceptance of reality is symbolized by her sensible attitude toward time; the only member of the Compson household who can tell time by the one-handed and inaccurate clock in the kitchen, she focuses predominantly on the present. Critics have also discussed the religious aspects of Dilsey's character, observing that the last section of *The Sound and the Fury* occurs on Easter Sunday and ends with Dilsey taking Benjy to church with her. Despite the objections of her fellow worshippers who are offended by the presence of a retarded white man in a black church, Dilsey states, "Tell um de good Lawd dont keer whether he bright er not." In the novel's climactic scene, she is moved to tears by a powerful sermon that many critics regard as the one meaningful act of ritual presented in *The Sound and the Fury*. Robert Griffin stated: "Dilsey represents the 'old verities' of Christianity—not Christian rites or theological dogma but the fundamental Christian ethic—forbearance and endurance and love and brotherhood."

The Sound and the Fury continues to rank among Faulkner's most frequently interpreted novels and is often regarded as one of the most significant prose works of the twentieth century. Isadore Traschen echoed the opinions of many critics and influential writers in designating *The Sound and the Fury* "the greatest American novel of the century, our prose *Waste Land*," an essentially "tragic work, comparable in its dimensions and intensity to the family tragedies of the Greeks, the houses of Atreus and Laios." This underlying sense of tragedy may lie in the grim fact that, as Arthur Mizener noted, "the sound and fury of temporal existence—whether it be Caddy's passion or Quentin's defiance or Mr. Compson's despair—signify, for all their pathos, nothing."

(See also *Short Story Criticism*, Vol. 1; *Contemporary Authors*, Vols. 81-84; *Dictionary of Literary Biography*, Vols. 9, 11, 44; *Dictionary of Literary Biography Yearbook: 1986; Dictionary of Literary Biography Documentary Series*, Vol. 2; and *Concise Dictionary of American Literary Biography, 1929-1941*.)

PRINCIPAL WORKS

NOVELS

Soldiers' Pay 1926
Mosquitoes 1927
Sartoris 1929; also published as *Flags in the Dust* [unabridged edition], 1973
The Sound and the Fury 1929
As I Lay Dying 1930
Sanctuary 1931
Light in August 1932
Pylon 1935
Absalom, Absalom! 1936
The Wild Palms 1939
The Hamlet 1940
Intruder in the Dust 1948
A Fable 1954
The Town 1957
The Mansion 1959
The Reivers 1962

SHORT STORY COLLECTIONS

These Thirteen 1931
The Unvanquished 1938
Go Down, Moses and Other Stories; also published as *Go Down, Moses*, 1942
Knight's Gambit 1949
Collected Stories of William Faulkner 1950
Uncollected Stories of William Faulkner 1979

OTHER

The Marble Faun (poetry) 1924
A Green Bough (poetry) 1933
Requiem for a Nun (play) [first publication] 1951
Essays, Speeches and Public Letters 1966

Frances Lamont Robbins

Judging from ***The Sound and the Fury,*** the first of his books which we have read, we should say that William Faulkner is [James] Joyce's most able and most consistent American disciple. He is by no means a slavish imitator of Joyce's style, and only in the second section of ***The Sound and the Fury*** does his effort to follow it seem labored and unoriginal. But the discontinuity which is the outward evidence of the Joycean viewpoint is present in Mr. Faulkner's work, and Joyce's search for a clear way to investigate and express the broken motive patterns of human behavior is Mr. Faulkner's search, too. It seems to us, however, that his work is still no more than an exciting promise. For one thing, it is overstrongly marked by a juvenile preoccupation with the *melodramatic* aspects of tragedy, and by the distrust of familiar values which characterizes the work of so many writers of the present generation and limits their understanding of life. Mr. Faulkner has strong creative talent, and is richly sensitive to poetic emotion. ***The Sound and the Fury*** is a tragedy of disintegration. A southern family of gentle blood is shown in decay, its members, petty failures, drunkards, suicides, pathological perverts and idiots. Against the rottenness of the white family is set the full-living wholeness of their Negroes. In this contrast, there is the suggestion of a second theme, too faintly expressed to be clear. An unusual method of presentation is used in telling the story. It appears at first to require a key, as *Ulysses* does; but careful reading discloses the plot. Part One presents the tragedy as seen through the eyes of Benjy, the idiot son, a grown man thrown back into childhood by any chance sight or smell. Through his broken thoughts we learn of Caddy, a beloved sister, who has run away from the hideous home and sent back an illegitimate daughter. In Benjy's mind, mother and daughter are inextricably confused. In Part Two, we move back eighteen years and witness, through the workings of his mind, the last day in the life of Quentin, brother of Benjy and Caddy, the hope of the family, who has been sent to Harvard by a great and questionable effort, and who, in love with his sister, commits suicide as a protest against her deflowering and disgrace. Part Three brings us again into the present, where we look through the mean eyes of Jason, the third brother. His version of the family collapse is colored by his cheapness, bitterness, cock-sure "realism" and jealous hatred of Caddy's memory as expressed in her daughter. We see him, half mad, pull the shred of his own life to pieces in his effort to destroy her. And in the final part of the novel, in the author's direct narrative, the spectacle of white disintegration is shown and sharpened by the emphasis thrown upon Negro solidity. ***The Sound and the Fury*** is a novel of power and of terrible sincerity. We do, however, find that the theme, dramatic and potentially moving, loses much of its force and clarity by being presented, almost wholly, through subjective analysis. It takes a stronger hand than William Faulkner's to divert the stream of consciousness into channels of perfect usefulness and beauty. (p. 268)

Frances Lamont Robbins, in a review of "The Sound and the Fury," in Outlook and Independent*, Vol. 153, No. 7, October 16, 1929, pp. 268-69.*

William Faulkner

[*The following excerpt is taken from a draft of Faulkner's 1933 introduction to* The Sound and the Fury *first published in* Mississippi Quarterly *in 1973. Although he wrote several introductions, none were published in any edition of the novel.*]

Art is no part of southern life. In the North it seems to be different. It is the hardest minor stone in Manhattan's foundation. It is a part of the glitter or shabbiness of the streets. The arrowing buildings rise out of it and because of it, to be torn down and arrow again. There will be people leading small bourgeois lives (those countless and almost invisible bones of its articulation, lacking any one of which the whole skeleton might collapse) whose bread will derive from it—polyglot boys and girls progressing from tenement schools to editorial rooms and art galleries; men with grey hair and paunches who run linotype machines and take up tickets at concerts and then go sedately home to Brooklyn and suburban stations where children and grandchildren await them—long after the descendents of Irish politicians and Neapolitan racketeers are as forgotten as the wild Indians and the pigeon. (pp. 220-21)

[In the South, we] have never got and probably will never get, anywhere with music or the plastic forms. We need to talk, to tell, since oratory is our heritage. We seem to try in the simple furious breathing (or writing) span of the individual to draw a savage indictment of the contemporary scene or to escape from it into a makebelieve region of swords and magnolias and mockingbirds which perhaps never existed anywhere. Both of the courses are rooted in sentiment; perhaps the ones who write savagely and bitterly of the incest in clayfloored cabins are the most sentimental. Anyway, each course is a matter of violent partizanship, in which the writer unconsciously writes into every line and phrase his violent despairs and rages and frustrations or his violent prophesies of still more violent hopes. That cold intellect which can write with calm and complete detachment and gusto of its contemporary scene is not among us; I do not believe there lives the Southern writer who can say without lying that writing is any fun to him. Perhaps we do not want it to be.

I seem to have tried both of the courses. I have tried to escape and I have tried to indict. After five years I look back at ***The Sound and The Fury*** and see that that was the turning point: in this book I did both at one time. When I began the book, I had no plan at all. I wasn't even writing a book. Previous to it I had written three novels, with progressively decreasing ease and pleasure, and reward or emolument. The third one was shopped about for three years during which I sent it from publisher to publisher with a kind of stubborn and fading hope of at least justifying the paper I had used and the time I had spent writing it. This hope must have died at last, because one day it suddenly seemed as if a door had clapped silently and forever to between me and all publishers' addresses and booklists and I said to myself, Now I can write. Now I can just write. Whereupon I, who had three brothers and no sisters and was destined to lose my first daughter in infancy, began to write about a little girl.

I did not realise then that I was trying to manufacture the sister which I did not have and the daughter which I was to lose, though the former might have been apparent from the fact that Caddy had three brothers almost before I wrote her name on paper. I just began to write about a brother and a sister splashing one another in the brook and the sister fell and wet her clothing and the smallest brother cried, thinking that the sister was conquered or perhaps hurt. Or perhaps he knew that he was the baby and that she would quit whatever water battles to comfort him. When she did so, when she quit the water fight and stooped in her wet garments above him, the entire story, which is all told by that same little brother in the first section, seemed to explode on the paper before me.

I saw that peaceful glinting of that branch was to become the dark, harsh flowing of time sweeping her to where she could not return to comfort him, but that just separation, division, would not be enough, not far enough. It must sweep her into dishonor and shame too. And that Benjy must never grow beyond this moment; that for him all knowing must begin and end with that fierce, panting, paused and stooping wet figure which smelled like trees. That he must never grow up to where the grief of bereavement could be leavened with understanding and hence the alleviation of rage as in the case of Jason, and of oblivion as in the case of Quentin.

I saw that they had been sent to the pasture to spend the afternoon to get them away from the house during the grandmother's funeral in order that the three brothers and the nigger children could look up at the muddy seat of Caddy's drawers as she climbed the tree to look in the window at the funeral, without then realising the symbology of the soiled drawers, for here again hers was the courage which was to face later with honor the shame which she was to engender, which Quentin and Jason could not face: the one taking refuge in suicide, the other in vindictive rage which drove him to rob his bastard niece of the meagre sums which Caddy could send her. For I had already gone on to night and the bedroom and Dilsey with the mudstained drawers scrubbing the naked backside of that doomed little girl—trying to cleanse with the sorry byblow of its soiling that body, flesh, whose shame they symbolised and prophesied, as though she already saw the dark future and the part she was to play in it trying to hold that crumbling household together.

Then the story was complete, finished. There was Dilsey to be the future, to stand above the fallen ruins of the family like a ruined chimney, gaunt, patient and indomitable; and Benjy to be the past. He had to be an idiot so that, like Dilsey, he could be impervious to the future, though unlike her by refusing to accept it at all. Without thought or comprehension; shapeless, neuter, like something eyeless and voiceless which might have lived, existed merely because of its ability to suffer, in the beginning of life; half fluid, groping: a pallid and helpless mass of all mindless agony under sun, in time yet not of it save that he could nightly carry with him that fierce, courageous being who was to him but a touch and a sound that may be heard on any golf links and a smell like trees, into the slow bright shapes of sleep.

The story is all there, in the first section as Benjy told it. I did not try deliberately to make it obscure; when I realised that the story might be printed, I took three more sections, all longer than Benjy's, to try to clarify it. But when I wrote Benjy's section, I was not writing it to be printed. If I were to do it over now I would do it differently, because the writing of it as it now stands taught me both how to write and how to read, and even more: It taught me what I had already read, because on completing it I discovered, in a series of repercussions like summer thunder, the Flauberts and Conrads and Turgenievs which as much as ten years before I had consumed whole and without assimilating at all, as a moth or a goat might. I have read nothing since; I have not had to. And I have learned but one thing since about writing. That is, that the emotion definite and physical and yet nebulous to describe which the writing of Benjy's section of ***The Sound and The Fury*** gave me—that ecstasy, that eager and joyous faith and anticipation of surprise which the yet unmarred sheets beneath my hand held inviolate and unfailing—will not return. The unreluctance to begin, the cold satisfaction in work well and arduously done, is there and will continue to be there as long as I can do it well. But that other will not return. I shall never know it again.

So I wrote Quentin's and Jason's sections, trying to clarify Benjy's. But I saw that I was merely temporising; That I should have to get completely out of the book. I realised that there would be compensations, that in a sense I could then give a final turn to the screw and extract some ultimate distillation. Yet it took me better than a month to take pen and write *The day dawned bleak and chill* before I did so. There is a story somewhere about an old Roman who kept at his bedside a Tyrrhenian vase which he loved and the rim of which he wore slowly away with kissing it. I had made myself a vase, but I suppose I knew all the time that I could not live forever inside of it, that perhaps to have it so that I too could lie in bed and look at it would be better; surely so when that day should come when not only the ecstasy of writing would be gone, but the unreluctance and the something worth saying too. It's fine to think that you will leave something behind you when you die, but it's better to have made something you can die with. Much better the muddy bottom of a little doomed girl climbing a blooming pear tree in April to look in the window at the funeral. (pp. 222-24)

> *William Faulkner, "An Introduction to 'The Sound and the Fury': 'Mississippi Quarterly' Version," in* The Sound and the Fury by William Faulkner: An Authoritative Text, Backgrounds and Contexts, Criticism, *edited by David Minter, W. W. Norton & Company, 1987, pp. 220-24.*

Olga W. Vickery

[*The essay excerpted below was originally published in* PMLA *in December, 1954.*]

The Sound and the Fury was the first of Faulkner's novels to make the question of form and technique an unavoidable critical issue. In any discussion of its structure the controlling assumption should be that there are plausible reasons for the particular arrangement of the four sections and for the use of the stream of consciousness technique in the first three and not in the fourth. Jean-Paul Sartre's comment that the moment the reader attempts to isolate the plot content "he notices that he is telling another story" indicates the need for such an assumption, not only for any light that may be thrown on ***The Sound and the Fury*** but for any insight that may emerge concerning Faulkner's method and achievement.

In connection with the interdependence of the sections it has been pointed out [by Lawrence E. Bowling in a 1948 *Kenyon Review* article] that the water-splashing episode "presents all the main characters in situations which foreshadow the main action." Equally important is the fact that the structure of the novel is paralleled by the events of the entire evening of which the water-splashing is only a part. These events reveal the typical gestures and reactions of the four children to each other and to the mysterious advent of death. They chart the range and kind of each of their responses to a new experience. In this way the evening partakes of the dual nature of the novel: primarily it is an objective, dramatic scene revealing the relations and tensions which exist among the children, but at the same time it is a study in perspective. Between the fact of Damuddy's death and the reader stands not only the primitive mind of the narrator, Benjy, but the diverse attitudes of the other children and the deliberate uncommunicativeness of the adults. The result is not needless complexity or confusion but rather, in Henry James's words [in *The Art of the Novel*, 1934], "a certain fullness of truth—truth diffused, distributed and, as it were, atmospheric."

Within the novel as a whole it is Caddy's surrender to Dalton Ames which serves both as the source of dramatic tension and as the focal point for the various perspectives. This is evident in the fact that the sequence of events is not caused by her act—which could be responded to in very different ways—but by the significance which each of her brothers actually attributes to it. As a result, the four sections appear quite unrelated even though they repeat certain incidents and are concerned with the same problem, namely, Caddy and her loss of virginity. Although there is a progressive revelation or rather clarification of the plot, each of the sections is itself static. The consciousness of a character becomes the actual agent illuminating and being illuminated by the central situation. Everything is immobilized in this pattern; there is no development of either character or plot in the traditional manner. This impression is reinforced not only by the shortness of time directly involved in each section but by the absence of any shifts in style of the kind that, for example, accompany the growing maturity of Cash Bundren in ***As I Lay Dying.***

By fixing the structure while leaving the central situation ambiguous, Faulkner forces the reader to reconstruct the story and to apprehend its significance for himself. Consequently, the reader recovers the story at the same time as he grasps the relation of Benjy, Quentin, and Jason to it. This, in turn, is dependent on his comprehension of the relation between the present and the past events with which each of the first three sections deals. As he proceeds from one section to the next, there is a gradual clarification of events, a rounding out of the fragments of scenes and conversations which Benjy reports. Thus, with respect to the plot the four sections are inextricably connected, but with respect to the central situation they are quite distinct and self-sufficient. As related to the central focus, each of the first three sections presents a version of the same facts which is at once the truth and a complete distortion of the truth. It would appear, then, that the theme of ***The Sound and the Fury,*** as revealed by the structure, is the relation between the act and man's apprehension of the act, between the event and the interpretation. This relation is by no means a rigid or inelastic thing but is a matter of shifting perspective, for, in a sense, each man creates his own truth. This does not mean that truth does not exist or that it is fragmentary or that it is unknowable; it only insists that truth is a matter of the heart's response as well as the mind's logic.

In keeping with this theme each of the first three sections presents a well demarcated and quite isolated world built around one of these splinters of truth. The fact that Benjy is dumb is symbolic of the closed nature of these worlds; communication is impossible when Caddy who is central to all three means something different to each. For Benjy she is the smell of trees; for Quentin, honor; and for Jason, money or at least the means of obtaining it. Yet these intense private dramas are taking place in a public world primarily concerned with observable behavior. Accordingly, in the fourth section we are shown what an interested but unimplicated observer would see of the Compsons. For the first time we realize that Benjy has blue eyes, that Mrs. Compson habitually wears black dressing gowns and that Jason looks somewhat like a caricature of a bartender. Moreover, since we are prevented from sharing in the consciousness and memories of the characters, Caddy is no longer an immediate center. Nevertheless, through the conflict between Jason and Miss Quentin the final repercussions of her affair penetrate into the life of Jefferson and even Mottson. And out of the Compson house, itself a symbol of isolation, one person, Dilsey, emerges to grasp the truth which much be felt as well as stated.

Out of the relation that Benjy, Quentin and Jason bear to Caddy yet another pattern emerges: a gradual progression from the completely public world of the fourth. The latter, in a sense, both reverses and repeats the former: in the one Benjy is restricted by his retarded mind to immediate facts and sensations, in the other the reader is similarly limited. But Benjy's subjectivity has been replaced presumably by the reader's objectivity. Quentin's section is very close to Benjy's, for although he performs the gestures expected of him by other people, his world is essentially as isolated and irrational as his brother's. Jason, on the other hand, moves nearer to the public world of the fourth section insofar as he is able to act effectively, if unethically, in a social situation.

Moreover, each of these shifts from the private to the public world is accompanied by a corresponding shift in the form of apprehension. With Benjy we are restricted entirely to sensation which cannot be communicated; quite appropriately therefore Benjy is unable to speak. The closed world which he builds for himself out of various sensations becomes at once the least and the most distorted account of experience. He merely presents snatches of dialogue, bits of scenes exactly as they took place. Such reproduction is not necessarily synonymous with the truth. Benjy, however, makes it his truth and his ethics, for it is in terms of sensation that he imposes a very definite order on his experience. Despite the apparent chaos of fragments, Benjy himself lives in a world which is inflexible and rigid. The extent of its inflexibility is indicated by his bellows of protest whether over a wrong turn taken by Luster, Caddy's use of perfume or her sexual promiscuity.

Quentin's world is almost as isolated and inflexible as Benjy's, but its order is based on abstractions rather than sensations. Thus, his section is filled with echoes, both literary and Biblical, phrases, names quoted out of context but falling neatly into the pattern of his thought. These echoes assume the quality of a ritual by which he attempts to conjure experience into conformity with his wishes. When Caddy's behavior disarranges his world, his protest partakes of Benjy's outrage and agony. He stands despairing before the abyss which has suddenly separated experience and his conception of what experience ought to be, and when all his efforts to coerce experience with a word, "incest," fail, he chooses death which alone can terminate his unwilling involvement in circumstance.

The third section shows a greater degree of clarity though not of objectivity. The reason for this is that Jason operates in terms of a logic which forms the basis of social communication. We may not approve the direction in which his logic takes him, but that his actions are the result of clear, orderly thinking in terms of cause and effect cannot be disputed. The steps in his reasoning follow one another naturally: since it was because of Caddy that he was deprived not only of his inheritance but of his promised job, his recompense must come from Caddy; and since Miss Quentin was the actual cause of Herbert's displeasure, it is through her that he simultaneously gains his wealth and his revenge. It is part of the general satiric intent of this section that Jason's obvious distortion of Caddy should be associated with logic and reason, for it throws a new perspective not only on the actions of the

Compsons but on Jason, the representative of the "rational" man.

The objective nature of the fourth section precludes the use of any single level of apprehension, yet it provokes the most complex response. Dilsey, almost as inarticulate as Benjy, becomes through her actions alone the embodiment of the truth of the heart which is synonymous with morality. The acceptance of whatever time brings, the absence of questioning and petty protests, enables her to create order out of circumstance rather than in defiance of it, and in so doing she gains both dignity and significance for her life. In a sense, Dilsey represents a final perspective directed toward the past and the Compsons, but it is also the reader's perspective for which Dilsey merely provides the vantage point. This fact suggests another reason for the objective narration in this section: to use Dilsey as a point of view character would be to destroy her efficacy as the ethical norm, for that would give us but one more splinter of the truth confined and conditioned by the mind which grasped it.

Our first impression of the Benjy section is that it presents a state of utter chaos for which the only possible justification is the fact that Benjy is an idiot and therefore has a right to be confused. But out of this disorder two patterns emerge: the one, completely independent of public perspective, constitutes Benjy's world, the other serves as the author's guide for enabling the reader to grasp the fragments as a comprehensible order. With respect to the latter, Lawrence Bowling has pointed out both Faulkner's use of italics to indicate shifts in time and the fact that the reasons for such shifts occurring are easily recognizable. An object, a sound, an incident may propel the mind toward some point in the past where a similar experience took place.

Equally important is the fact that there are actually very few scenes involved despite the length of time covered. The events of 7 April 1928 are easily identified because of the prominence given to Luster in them. His dogged and somewhat querulous search for the lost quarter and his single-minded preoccupation with the show run like an identifying motif in a difficult composition. Otherwise, there are but three extended episodes: one taking place some time in 1898, the day Damuddy died; the second occurring on the evening Benjy received his new name; and the last consisting of the scene of Caddy's wedding. Each of these episodes has its own principle of organization and cohesion. Benjy's other recollections create the impression of a mind confused and undiscriminating, but they are for the most part short, self-sufficient vignettes. At times these unit-episodes interlock as when Benjy's intrusion into Miss Quentin's privacy on the swing recalls a similar scene involving Caddy. In this case the recollected event is completed before we are returned to the present scene of Miss Quentin's anger and her friend's perverse humor. (pp. 293-97)

With consummate skill the repetitions and identifying sensations which are used to guide the reader are also used as the basis of Benjy's own ordering of experience. Benjy's mind works not by association which is dependent, to some extent, on an ability to discriminate as well as compare but by mechanical identification. Thus, being caught on the fence while walking with Luster does not recall an associated feeling or fact but the exact replica of the incident. More important is the fact that the three deaths in the family which Benjy senses are repetitions of each other, provoking an identical response. What he reacts to is the fact of death, or the fact of being caught on the fence. To differentiate in terms of time and circumstance is a logical matter and therefore beyond Benjy's range of apprehension.

Curiously enough, despite Benjy's prompt response to certain phenomena which disrupt his order, he regards sensations quite impersonally: "Then he fell into the flowers, laughing, and I ran into the box. But when I tried to climb onto it it jumped away and hit me on the back of the head and my throat made a sound." His report of the accident omits not only the causal nature of the sequence of events but also any consciousness of himself as a focus for the experience. The same impression is conveyed by the scene in which he burns his hand or in which Versh feeds him. Since he disassociates himself even from the sensations of which he cannot help being conscious, there is a resultant confusion of the senses themselves: "*I squatted there, holding the slipper. I couldn't see it, but my hands saw it, and I could hear it getting night, and my hands saw the slipper but I couldn't see myself, but my hands could see the slipper and I squatted there, hearing it getting dark.*" The slipper and the nightfall are not part of a single, familiar pattern and so he is forced to relate them as best he can.

Benjy's world is made up not only of sensations but of sensations to which he attributes an independent existence. This is further emphasized by his inflexible identification of one word with one object. Very seldom, for example, is the name of a speaker replaced by a pronoun in his section. Each person is freed from the multiplicity of descriptive relations which make him at once man and brother, father, Negro or white. For Benjy, he is forever fixed as simply Jason, Quentin or Luster. In the one scene where Benjy is brought into contact with Luster's friends, parts of the dialogue are consistently attributed to Luster, but the answers appear to come out of the air. Benjy does not know the names of these strangers and to give them an identity in terms of description is beyond his power. His literalism finds its sharpest illustration in the scene where the cries of the golfers are heard. "Caddy" can mean only one thing and elicit only one response.

Benjy both orders and evaluates his experience with this same rigidity. The objects he has learned to recognize constitute an inflexible pattern which he defends against novelty or change with every bellow in his overgrown body. At what time or under what circumstances the small mound of earth which Dilsey calls his graveyard was formed and marked with two empty bottles of blue glass holding withered stalks of jimson weed is unimportant. But that this arrangement, once established, should remain unchanged in the slightest detail is of the utmost importance. When Luster removes one of the bottles, Benjy is momentarily shocked into a silence which is immediately succeeded by the roar of protest. It is not that the bottle has any intrinsic value for Benjy, but merely that it forms part of the pattern which must not be disturbed. The fixed route to the graveyard is also sacred; Benjy is overwhelmed with horror and agony when Luster takes the wrong turn only to subside the minute the mistake is corrected.

Within this rigid world Caddy is at once the focus of order and the instrument of its destruction. The pasture, the fire and sleep, the three things Benjy loves most, are associated with her, as is illustrated by the recurrent phrase "Caddy smelled like trees," his refusal to go to sleep without her and his memory of her during the rainy evening. On that evening, for a brief moment, everything in his world was in its proper place. Caddy both realizes and respects his fear of change: while playing at the Branch she is quick to reassure him that she is not really going to run away; later, she washes off her perfume and gives the rest of it to Dilsey in order to reassure him. Even when she has accepted the inevitability of change for herself and is preparing to marry Herbert, she tries to bind Quentin to a promise of seeing that Benjy's life is not further disordered by his being committed to a mental institution. Yet what Benjy most expects of Caddy is the one thing she cannot give him, for his expectation is based on his complete indifference to or rather ignorance of time. As long as Caddy is in time, she cannot free either herself or his world from change. His dependence on her physical presence, her scent of trees, is subject to constant threats which he fends off to the best of his ability. Sin and perfume are equally resented as intrusions of change into his arbitrary and absolute pattern. Thus, Caddy, as in the Quentin section, is at once identified with the rigid order of Benjy's private world and with the disorder of actual experience. Depending on which of the two is dominant at the moment, Benjy moans or smiles serenely.

Since Benjy is concerned with preserving the pattern rather than any single one of its parts, there is little that he can lose. Even Caddy has no existence for him except as she forms part of that pattern. As with the blue bottle which Luster snatches from its place, so with Caddy he is reminded by the small depression in the earth or by the sound of her name that something is missing, but what it is he misses, he scarcely knows himself. Despite his moans Benjy suffers less than any other person in the book because even pain is something external to himself and because one pattern can be replaced with another. If the "bright shapes" of the fire are shut off from him, he can still look into the mirror and see there an endless panorama of shape and color reflecting reality but confining it within a frame so that it is no longer a threat but an amusement.

The parallels between the Quentin and Benjy sections are very strong, despite the widely different impression each conveys. Quentin too has constructed for himself a private world to which Caddy is essential, a world which is threatened and finally destroyed by her involvement in circumstance. His hopeless and endless brooding is but Benjy's moan become articulate though not rational. However, his order is based on emotions rather than sensations, on concepts rather than physical objects. And whereas Benjy is saved by being outside time, Quentin is destroyed by his excessive awareness of it. For the former, both the pattern and its disordering are eternally present as his alternation between moaning and smiling demonstrates; for the latter, the pattern has become a part of the past which cannot be recaptured and contentment has been replaced by despair. Quentin can neither accept nor reconcile himself to that change or to the possibility that a further change may make even his despair a thing of the past, and so he chooses death as a means of escaping the situation.

The structure of the section with its two sets of events, one past and the other present, reflects Quentin's problem. Throughout the day he can proceed quite mechanically with such chores as getting dressed, packing, writing letters and generally tidying up the loose ends of his life at Harvard. To a large extent he can even make the appropriate gestures and speak the proper words expected of him by others. Meanwhile, his mind is occupied with echoes of the past which make themselves felt with increasing intensity until they threaten to prevent even a mechanical attention to the details of living through that final day. Quentin cannot escape either his memories of the past or his involvement in the present. The Italian child who is connected with his thoughts of Sister Caddy stops him by her very presence from concentrating solely on Caddy.

His fights with Julio, the outraged brother, and with Bland constitute the two points at which past and present, the

Original dust jacket for The Sound and the Fury.

private and the public worlds, collide. In the first case, the present asserts its power, once more involving him in a situation not of his making. The irony of the scene lies not only in the fact that Quentin should be blamed for doing the one thing which it would be impossible for him to do, but that chance should involve him in a present which he has already rejected by choosing death. In the incident with Bland the past breaks into the present as Quentin's memory of Dalton Ames becomes stronger than the routine responses he is forced to make to Mrs. Bland and her guests. Significantly, in neither case does Quentin offer any resistance to the blows he receives.

The order which Quentin had once built around Caddy is as rigid and inflexible as Benjy's and it shares Benjy's fear of change and his expectation that all experience should conform to his pattern. The cause of his ineffectuality and his ultimate destruction is the fact that his system antecedes his experience and eventually is held in defiance of experience. His is an ethical order based on words, on "fine, dead sounds," the meaning of which he has yet to learn. Insofar as virginity is a concept, associated with virtue and honor, it becomes the center of Quentin's world, and since it is also physically present in Caddy, it forms a precarious link between his world and that of experience. Mr. Compson remarks that virginity is merely a transient physical state which has been given its ethical significance by men. What they have chosen to make it mean is something which is a defiance of nature, an artificial isolation of the woman. Caddy who seems almost a symbol of the blind forces of nature is an unstable guardian for that "*concept* of Compson honor precariously and . . . only temporarily supported by the minute fragile membrane of her maidenhead." Since his emotional responses center on these concepts, Quentin is quite incapable of love for any human being, even Caddy. Despite his feverish preoccupation with ethics, he is unable to perform any ethical actions himself; even his death is not so much a protest as it is simply a withdrawal. Thus, it is not the time that is out of joint but Quentin's relation to time.

Where Benjy had selected odd fragments of his actual experience to form a pattern which he endowed with expectations of eternity, Quentin attempts to coerce experience into conformity with his system. Having rejected the life around him as insufficiently meaningful, he invents instead his own play, which he regards as reality, and peoples it with creatures of his own fantasy. He begins grooming Caddy for her role from the outset, insisting on her conformity to his conception of her. At the Branch he slaps her for disregarding his orders, and periodically after that he reasserts his control, scouring her head in the grass for kissing boys and smearing her with mud for not being concerned with his behavior. But his main intention is not simply to punish her for forgetting her part but to make her understand the significance of her role as the guardian of Compson honor. Hence his pique when she refuses to bother herself about his games with Natalie.

Quentin's desire to convert Caddy's promiscuity into an act of incest is another instance of his attempt to trick experience into conformity with his pattern. In "the long diminishing parade of time" Caddy's affair is but one more event, seemingly without reason or significance, providing one more illustration of transience and change in human life. She herself places little importance on the actual Ames affair, although she is concerned with its effect on Quentin, Benjy, and her father. For Quentin, however, it means the complete collapse of his careful ethical structure which he had tried to hold beyond time. Like Benjy's, his reaction is a moan of pain and outrage which expects no answer.

His solution is to make Caddy admit that they have committed incest. In this way he hopes to make Compson honor a thing of importance and momentous significance even as he destroys it. This gesture is in contrast to Caddy's promiscuity which merely slights the honor. Moreover, incest can be used to affirm the validity of his ethical pattern. Quentin has already, in a sense, usurped the role of God by creating a paradise for himself and Caddy isolated from the world through the fact of sexual innocence. Through incest he can convert this paradise into hell, thereby maintaining the same order but in reverse. Sin instead of virtue, punishment instead of bliss, will be made everlasting. The isolation through innocence can become isolation through sin. The incest, however, is as unreal a center for Quentin's hell as his sister's sexual purity was for his paradise. It is significant that he refuses to commit the actual act. Committing incest would destroy his order completely by involving him in the terrible reality of experience. But through a lie he can circumvent experience; like the boys discussing the money they would have received and spent had they caught the fish, he makes "of unreality a possibility, then a probability, then an incontrovertible fact, as people will when their desires become words." However, his ritualistic chant of "Father, I have committed incest" has no power over "the sequence of natural events and their causes which shadows every mans [sic] brow."

The greatest enemy of Quentin's ethical system is time, the whole long diminishing parade of moments whose beginning and ending we cannot conceive. His very concern with time takes place in time. Accordingly, the inexorable passing of one moment after another gives an emotional and dramatic intensity to his brooding since we know that each instant brings him that much closer to death. His act of breaking the watch merely increases his and our awareness of time; the chiming of bells, the lengthening shadows, his own hunger, all insist that night is approaching. And irrespective of any act of his, even suicide, time will continue whether or not it is being marked off by hands on a dial or the sound of bells. Man's efforts to control even his own allotted time can only result in a mockery, as Quentin realizes when he looks in the shop window. By becoming conscious of time man puts himself in opposition to it only to find that his victories are illusions. Yet Quentin's every effort is bent toward circumventing time and achieving permanence by somehow arresting that steady succession of events which reduces everything, even sorrow and disappointment, to points in time. He would like to believe that Caddy's one act is so monstrous that it has instantaneously made of him an old man whose involvement in experience is at an end. He attempts to make first Caddy's purity and the her "sinning" everlasting, and when both attempts fail, he chooses death not so much to terminate time as to arrest it forever at one point.

Quentin cannot sever his relation to time or "the sequence of natural events and their causes." Each day weaves its own pattern of chance and circumstance, flouting his will and his desire. Time is man's misfortune and he "a gull on an invisible wire attached through space dragged." The illusion of flight, the reality of the invisible wire, the illusion of being free and in control, the reality of finding oneself after all only a dupe—that is the irony implicit in man's involvement in time. The battle against time cannot even be fought since defeat is inevitable and victory "an illusion of philosophers and fools." Ignoring the plans and dreams of one man or all men, time, working through circumstance, forms a pattern of its own in which men are only pawns. That is the fact most difficult for Quentin to accept and live with. It is especially difficult in view of Quentin's youth which tends to invest even trifles with tragic profundity. Rather than face the certainty of further change, even change toward happiness, he takes his own life.

Quentin's desire for death is, of course, bound up with his consciousness of time and more specifically of memory. Although he cannot control the course of events nor change what has already happened, he can terminate his awareness of it. It is inevitable therefore that Quentin should be enamored of death, that he should yearn for it like a lover: "A quarter hour yet. And then I'll not be. The peacefullest words. Peacefullest words. *Non fui. Sum. Fui. Non sum.*" He rings changes on the Latin words trying to probe their full meaning. In a sense, the whole history of Caddy lies in his memory and when he ceases to be, so does her betrayal of Compson honor. By declining all further participation in life he can isolate himself and his memory of Caddy from the "loud world." To watch the gradual changes in his body and yet remain untouched and unmoved, to separate himself forever from the circumstances in which he is involved, that is Quentin's vision of death and, significantly, it approximates his own description of Benjy's mirror. As Sartre points out, Quentin has almost achieved that state even before his actual suicide [see *CLC,* Vol. 9]. Certainly he seems withdrawn from and unconcerned with the meticulously performed actions of his body.

The symbols and recurrent phrases that run through Quentin's section both intensify the emotional impact and reinforce the meaning. Such names as Jesus, St. Francis, Moses, Washington, and Byron not only add a richness of historical and literary allusion but convey the nature of Quentin's world. Into that world Benjy is admitted as "Benjamin the child of mine old age held hostage into Egypt" and Caddy as Eve or Little Sister Death. Mr. Compson forces an entry not as father or friend but as a voice which can juggle words and ideas while insisting on their emptiness. As for Quentin, he sees himself as the hero of the family drama, "the bitter prophet and inflexible corruptless judge." Part of his outrage and frustration in connection with Caddy is that neither her husband nor her lover seems worthy, in his eyes, of assuming a role in his world: Herbert is obviously despicable and Ames refuses to act in terms of Quentin's preconceptions.

The heavy, choking fragrance of honeysuckle dramatizes the conflict between his order and the blind forces of nature which constantly threaten to destroy it. Honeysuckle is the rife animality of sex, the incomprehensible and hateful world for which Caddy has abandoned his paradise, and hence it is also the symbol of his defeat. Yet honeysuckle is only a sensation, just as Caddy's affair with Ames is simply a natural event. It is Quentin who makes of the one a symbol of "night and unrest" and of the other the unforgivable sin. The references to roses have a similar function in that they too are associated with sex, but they are identified with a single scene, that of Caddy's wedding. Therefore, they are at once the symbol of the world he fears and of his irrevocable betrayal by that world. Roses are Caddy's sex, her promiscuity and her "sin" made socially respectable. The validity of his world is challenged and defeated by a counter system: "Roses. Cunning and serene."

There is a parallel as well as a contrast in the symbolic value attached to scents in the first and second sections. Both Benjy and Quentin associate disorder and a threat to themselves with a particular fragrance. The difference lies in the fact that Benjy resents either the inexplicable absence of the smell of trees which belongs to Caddy or the change of one scent for another, the substitution of perfume for the tree scent. Quentin, on the other hand, resents a change in the scent itself whereby the honeysuckle which he once liked becomes something oppressive and hateful. The scent which had enveloped his games with Caddy also envelops Caddy and Ames in quite a different game. Everything seems the same, yet there has been an agonizing change which makes each familiar object or sensation a mockery of itself.

The constant references to the shadows and the mirror emphasize the barrier between Quentin and reality. It is not only Benjy but also Quentin who sees Caddy's wedding reflected in the mirror. Caddy, however, cannot be confined to its surface; she runs not only out of the mirror but out of his and Benjy's world. Similarly, Quentin sees her and Ames not as people but as silhouettes distorted against the sky. He is lost amid these shadows, feeling that they falsify the objects they pretend to reflect, yet unable to reach out beyond them. It is significant that he sees only those aspects of Caddy as shadows which he cannot incorporate into his world: it is her love affair and her marriage which he finds perverse, mocking, denying the significance they should have affirmed. The same feeling of mockery is present in his insistence that he has tricked his shadow. A man who is dead needs no shadow, but still his accompanies him throughout the day as if it were mirroring reality when in truth it is but aping another illusion.

The number of times that the shadow images are fused with images of water indicates that death by water is Quentin's way of reconciling his two worlds, of merging shadow and reality and tempering their conflict. Whatever suggestion of purification may be present, water is primarily a symbol of oblivion for Quentin. Narcissa Benbow can act as if a little water would clear her of her deed, but as

Dilsey's determined scouring of Caddy's bottom shows, the stains of one's experience are not that easily removed. Both Quentin and Caddy run to the Branch to surrender themselves to its hypnotic rhythm which, like sleep, soothes the mind into unconsciousness, blurring thought and emotion, eliminating the necessity for acting. It is in the hope of making this peace eternal that Quentin surrenders his body to the water where the hard knots of circumstance will be untangled and the roof of wind will stand forever between him and the loud world.

With Jason's section we enter into a world far different from Benjy's or Quentin's, yet related to theirs through Caddy. It represents a third possible way of reacting to experience, as distorted yet as "true" as the former two. Since Jason reacts logically rather than emotionally, his section offers no barriers to comprehension. His particular method of ordering and explaining his actions in terms of cause and effect, profit and loss, is all too familiar. Yet logic, presumably the basis of human communication and hence of society, isolates Jason as effectively as the moral abstractions of Quentin or the complete dependence on sensations of Benjy. In the midst of Jefferson or even his family, he is by necessity as well as by choice alone. And instead of being concerned, he glories in his self-sufficiency "since to him all the rest of the town and the world and the human race too except himself were Compsons, inexplicable yet quite predictable in that they were in no sense whatever to be trusted."

One of Jason's dominant characteristics, and the main source of humor, is his pride that he has no illusions about his family or himself. The humor, however, arises not from the situation but from the way in which Jason talks about it. Where Quentin sees Caddy's behavior and his own relation to it in terms of tragedy, Jason assumes the role of comic hero. He sees himself as a modern Sancho Panza who could never mistake a windmill for an army, but who has no objections to others doing so, especially if he can turn it to his own advantage. This tolerance or rather non-interference even extends to allowing Mrs. Compson to go on supporting Uncle Maury and protecting Miss Quentin against any real discipline, although he accepts as fact that the former is a wastrel and the latter a bitch.

The conviction that he alone has a firm grasp on reality results in a literalism untouched by any hint of qualification in Jason's thinking. Through it we get a new and welcome perspective on the Compsons, but it is just a perspective and not the final word that Jason makes it out to be. It is his very insistence on facing facts that causes his distorted view of Caddy, his family and the whole human race. He cannot imagine that there might be other facts, other aspects of the situation, than the ones that directly affect him; as a result, he sees certain things so clearly that all others escape him. In the process logic replaces truth, and law, justice. Caddy's affair with Ames does result in Herbert's eventual rejection of all the Compsons and that, in its turn, in his double loss since he was deprived at one stroke of both his inheritance and his job. In his reasoning the human beings involved are quite irrelevant. He is not concerned with either Caddy or her daughter except as they enter into the pattern of loss and recompense and finally loss again. In short, his is a world reduced to calculation in which no subjective claims are tolerated and no margin for error allowed.

This calculating approach to experience pervades his every act, no matter how trivial. He offers Luster a ticket for five cents and burns it rather than give it away. His promise to Caddy to allow her to see her baby is a bargain that he fulfills to the letter but no further. He never permits himself or Earl to overstep the terms of their agreement of so much work for so much pay. Even where sincere affection is apparently involved, his relationship with Lorraine gives the impression of a contract duly notarized. Two days are devoted to keeping house in a most serious and even uxorious fashion; the other five are devoted to business and into that part of his life Lorraine must not intrude by so much as a phone call at the risk of terminating their "contract." All these arrangements constitute Jason's way of protecting himself from any intrusion of the irrational. It is his method of assuming control over experience by preventing himself from becoming involved in circumstances he has not foreseen.

His control over the Compson house reveals the same tendency to think in terms of contracts. He fulfills his filial duties by supporting his mother and even her servants in much the same condition as before Mr. Compson's death. But the way in which he sacrifices "what pleasures might have been the right and just due and even the necessity of a thirty-year-old bachelor" travesties his obligations. Nevertheless, he expects to receive full value in return, not only in services but in subservience. In his own home he insists that dinner be served on time to all the members of the family even though such familial repasts become grotesque parodies of conviviality and family life. Special attention is directed to Miss Quentin, who must be made not good but discreet; Jason disclaims all concern for what she does, providing appearances are not flouted. This preoccupation with social form partakes of the nature of a ritual with which Jason would charm away disorder and placate the Player, but it is destructive of the very significance it should affirm.

Jason's concern with forms of action rather than with the actions themselves is reflected in his legalistic view of society and especially of ethics. It is on this view that the double irony of Miss Quentin's theft of his thievings hinges. He has retrieved his losses, suffered because of Caddy, at the expense of Caddy's daughter without actually breaking any law. Caddy is sending money for her daughter's support and the daughter is being supported. Mrs. Compson retains the pleasure of tearing up and burning cheques even while her account at the bank grows. Meanwhile, Jason recovers what he considers to be his own money in a legal though unethical fashion. However, with her one unpremeditated act Miss Quentin destroys the work of years; more important, she is as safe from prosecution despite her heedlessness as Jason was because of all his care. Legally, she has only stolen what already belonged to her. When Jason demands an endorsement of his just indignation from the sheriff, the latter refuses to help on the basis of the very letter of the law Jason had so carefully observed. Thus, he is effectively hoisted with his own petard and fairly defeated with his own weapons.

During his frantic pursuit of Miss Quentin the nature of the conflict in which Jason is involved becomes explicit. He realizes that his enemy is not his niece or even the man with the red tie; rather it is "the sequence of natural events and their causes which shadows every mans [sic] brow." From the first he had distrusted everything which he could not himself control. Unlike Quentin for whom reality lay in ethical concepts, Jason had learned to believe in whatever he could hold in his hands or keep in his pocket. That alone could be protected from chance and change. The money placed in a strong box, hidden in a closet, kept in a locked room is the symbol of Jason's world. Yet even that is vulnerable to circumstance, to the accidental juxtaposition in place and time of a girl's whim and a man's red tie. Hence his outrage that Miss Quentin should have taken the money more or less on impulse; had her act been deliberate, calculated, he could have foreseen it and so guarded against it. The red tie becomes for him the symbol of the irrational, the antithesis of his own careful logic.

With the car speeding toward Mottson, Jason surveys the available courses of action. But he is not able to foresee and arrange for all the possibilities; the pattern of circumstance begins to close in. The fact that he has forgotten his camphor and that there is none mislaid in the car gives the first indication of his helplessness. The main setback, however, is that Miss Quentin and the man should not be where he expected to find them. Jason is not only forced into letting the recovery of his money rest on chance but even that chance is suddenly denied him. A similar surprise awaits him in the old man whose responses he calculates quite dispassionately. He finds himself caught in an unforeseen and uncontrollable situation: the unexpected occurs and he is overwhelmed by the "fatal, furious little old man" whose strength he had so confidently discounted.

Jason is thoroughly defeated by the "rearguards of Circumstance" which he had challenged by his trip to Mottson. The contents of his inviolate strong box and Miss Quentin, together the symbol of his revenge and frustration, disappear from Jefferson, yet his world does not collapse as Quentin's does. Like Benjy, he violently protests his loss, but, also like Benjy's, his order remains intact despite the loss of certain elements. Always the practical man, Jason cuts his losses and continues in exactly the same way, discharging his obligations to the letter, slowly accumulating money for another strong box, neither asking for nor giving more than the law requires. In a sense, the final and irrevocable loss of the money is even somewhat of a relief, for it spells the end of his involvement with Caddy, who has always, even in her absence, represented the threat of the irrational and incalculable.

Still isolated and unrepentant, Jason survives while Quentin is destroyed by the events he can neither accept nor control. On the other hand, that survival is itself futile, for Jason is the last of the Compson line and a childless bachelor. That very childlessness is another indication of his deliberate rejection of any relationship which he cannot control, especially one in which emotions dominate logic and trust replaces contracts. Insofar as Jason flourishes in a world in which Quentin, a more sensitive individual, perishes, a certain amount of satire and irony is involved. But it is by no means restricted to the South or to the contemporary scene. The tendency to identify logic with truth and law with justice is not limited to twentieth century America; the Jasons of the world have been claiming an eye for an eye long before Jesus began speaking of love and forgiveness and pity and sacrifice. Furthermore, even in Snopes-infested Jefferson, Jason stands alone; he is rejected by Earl, the sheriff, and even old Job, whose Negro wisdom sums up Jason's philosophy and its flaws: " 'You's too smart fer me. Aint a man in dis town kin keep up wid you fer smartness. You fools a man whut so smart he cant even keep up wid hisself. . . . Dat's Mr. Jason Compson'."

In the last section we finally emerge from the closed world of the Compson Mile into the public world as represented by Jefferson. No longer colored by the subjectivity of a single point of view, the outward manifestations of appearance and behavior assume a new importance. We are still permitted occasional glimpses of Jason's mind but only as he reacts to experience and not as he attempts to control it. The primary result is that the whole history of the Compsons is given a wider reference. Absence and time have erased Caddy and Quentin from the scene, even if the promiscuity of the one and the suicide of the other originally had an impact beyond the family. And Caddy, at any rate, never existed in the novel except in the minds and memories of those whom she had affected. In this larger context, the sound and the fury of the family signify very little if anything.

Certain individuals such as the sheriff and Earl sense something of the situation and this influences their actions with regard to Jason. Others such as the furious, little old man and the show's manager simply react to what they see of Jason, without knowing or caring what his reasons or provocation might have been. Beyond these few people who are caught up in the last reverberations of the events set in motion by Caddy's act, larger numbers remain untouched and indifferent except for mild curiosity. Only Benjy continues to make some impression and that simply because his idiocy has its external manifestations which cannot be ignored. The Negroes are excited by his presence, especially the children who watch him "with the covertness of nocturnal animals." The whites regard him as a problem: since he is obviously white, they frown on his attendance at a Negro church, but since he is as obviously an idiot, they are unwilling to receive him into theirs. Somehow in the process, the additional fact that he is a human being is forgotten by all except Dilsey.

In this section Dilsey emerges not only as a Negro servant in the Compson household but as a human being. With nothing to judge but her actions, with no prolonged ethical or religious polemics, her very presence enables the reader to achieve a final perspective on the lives of the Compsons. Mrs. Compson's nagging self-pity, Jason's carping exactions, Miss Quentin's thoughtlessness gain a dramatic actuality lacking while they were being filtered through an individual consciousness. Various contrasts between Dilsey and the others are delineated with striking clarity. The contrast becomes actual conflict where Dilsey and Jason are concerned. It is not only that Dilsey "survives," because, for that matter, so does Jason, but that her endurance has strength to suffer without rancor as well as to resist, to accept as well as to protest. She is the only one who challenges his word in the household, who defends the absent Caddy, Miss Quentin, Benjy and even Luster from his anger. But more important, she challenges the validity and efficacy of his world by a passive and irrational resistance to which he has no counter. That someone should work without pay is so foreign to his system that he is helpless in the face of it.

There is no doubt but that Dilsey is meant to represent the ethical norm, the realizing and acting out of one's humanity; it is from this that the Compsons have deviated, each into his separate world. The mother and [Quentin and Jason] have abandoned their humanity for the sake of pride or vanity or self-pity. Both Benjy and Caddy are tests of the family's humanity, he simply because he is not fully human and she because her conduct creates a socio-moral hiatus between the family and Jefferson. Benjy's behavior is a constant trial to the family and to this extent counterpoints Caddy's lone disgracing act. Both challenge the family's capacity for understanding and forgiveness and the family fails both. Quite appropriately, the Compson Mile exists in an atmosphere not only of disintegration but of constriction. The property shrinks as the town begins "to encroach and then nibble at and into it." The only room which seems to be lived in is Dilsey's kitchen; the others are so many private mausoleums. While each of the Compsons to some extent attempts to coerce experience and to deny his involvement in the sequence of natural events and their causes, Dilsey accepts whatever time brings. She alone never suffers that moment of rejection which is equated with death.

By working with circumstance instead of against it she creates order out of disorder; by accommodating herself to change she manages to keep the Compson household in some semblance of decency. While occupied with getting breakfast, she is yet able to start the fire in Luster's inexplicable absence, provide a hot water bottle for Mrs. Compson, see to Benjy's needs and soothe various ruffled tempers. All this despite the constant interruptions of Luster's perverseness, Benjy's moaning, Mrs. Compson's complaints, and even Jason's maniacal fury. Nor is Dilsey's attitude of acceptance confined to the minor disorders of daily tasks. The same calmness is evident with regard to Caddy's affair, Quentin's suicide and the arrival of Caddy's baby. As she herself states: she has brought up Caddy and can do the same for Miss Quentin. And if it so happens that their conduct mocks all her care and love, then it is time to find another order in the subsequent confusion. Dilsey's attitude, as she lives it, is formed by her instinctive feeling that whatever happens must be met with courage and dignity in which there is no room for passivity or pessimism.

Her ability to stand steadfast without faltering "before the hopeless juggernaut of circumstance" finds further expression in her patient preoccupation with the present, which is the only possible way of living with time. This does not imply that Dilsey is cut off from the past but only that she deals with it as it is caught up in the present without attempting to perpetuate a part of it as Quentin does, or to circumvent it as Jason tries to do. In a sense, she is a living record of all that has happened to the Compsons made significant by her own strength and courage. It is a record of pain and suffering and change but also of endurance and permanence in change.

In describing Dilsey as an ethical norm it should be stressed that she propounds no system, no code of behavior or belief, and this despite the emphasis on the Easter service which she attends. Neither in her attitude nor in the service itself is there any reference to sin and punishment but only to suffering and its surcease. At no time does Dilsey judge any of the Compsons, not even Jason, though she does object at one point to those who frown on Benjy's presence in a Negro church. But her presence enables the reader to judge not systems but actions and hence to grasp the truth instinctively: "They [Negroes] come into white people's lives like that in sudden sharp black trickles that isolate white facts for an instant in unarguable truth like under a microscope." And though she does not judge, Dilsey is never deceived; her comprehension of the relations between Caddy and the rest of the family is unerring.

Dilsey's participation in the Easter service is the one meaningful ritual in the book. As she proceeds sedately from house to church, acknowledging greetings with proper reserve and dignity, she is still conscious of being, in some sense, a member of the Compson household with a certain prestige and obligations. With each member of the congregation similarly conscious of his own distinctive position in society, the Reverend Shegog begins using the magic of his voice. When he concludes, communication has been replaced by communion in which each member loses his identity but finds his humanity and the knowledge that all men are equal and brothers in their suffering.

Out of Dilsey's actions and her participation in the Easter service arise once more the simple verities of human life, "the old universal truths lacking which any story is ephemeral and doomed—love and honor and pity and pride and compassion and sacrifice." It is these truths which throw the final illumination not only on Caddy and the whole sequence of events that started with her affair but also on what each of the Compsons believed her to be. The splinters of truth presented in the first three sections reverberate with the sound and the fury signifying nothing. But out of those same events, the same disorder and confusion, come Dilsey's triumph and her peace, lending significance not only to her own life but to the book as a whole. (pp. 298-311)

Olga W. Vickery, " 'The Sound and the Fury': A Study in Perspective," in The Sound and the Fury by William Faulkner: An Authoritative Text, Backgrounds and Contexts, Criticism, *edited by David Minter, W. W. Norton & Company, 1987, pp. 293-311.*

Faulkner on the development of *The Sound and the Fury:*

[***The Sound and the Fury***] began with a mental picture. I didn't realize at the time it was symbolical. The picture was of the muddy seat of a little girl's drawers in a pear tree where she could see through a window where her grandmother's funeral was taking place and report what was happening to her brothers on the ground below. By the time I explained who they were and what they were doing and how her pants got muddy, I realized it would be impossible to get all of it into a short story and that it would have to be a book. And then I realized the symbolism of the soiled pants, and that image was replaced by the one of the fatherless and motherless girl climbing down the rainpipe to escape from the only home she had, where she had never been offered love or affection or understanding. I had already begun to tell it through the eyes of the idiot child since I felt that it would be more effective as told by someone capable only of knowing what happened, but not why. I saw that I had not told the story that time. I tried to tell it again, the same story through the eyes of another brother. That was still not it. I told it for the third time through the eyes of the third brother. That was still not it. I tried to gather the pieces together and fill in the gaps by making myself the spokesman. It was still not complete, not until 15 years after the book was published when I wrote as an appendix to another book the final effort to get the story told and off my mind, so that I myself could have some peace from it. It's the book I feel tenderest towards. I couldn't leave it alone, and I never could tell it right, though I tried hard and would like to try again, though I'd probably fail again.

Faulkner, in a 1956 interview with Jean Stein vanden Heuvel, in The Paris Review.

Robert J. Griffin

> I believe that man will not merely endure: he will prevail. He is immortal, not because he alone among creatures has an inexhaustible voice, but because he has a soul, a spirit capable of compassion and sacrifice and endurance. The poet's, the writer's, duty is to write about these things. It is his privilege to help man endure by lifting his heart, by reminding him of the courage and honor and hope and pride and compassion and pity and sacrifice which have been the glory of his past. The poet's voice need not merely be the record of man, it can be one of the props, the pillars to help him endure and prevail.
>
> Faulkner's Nobel Prize Address—Stockholm, 1949

Since his Stockholm address, critics have paid a good deal of attention to the moral content, the heart-lifting or quasi-religious "message," of William Faulkner's fiction. They have noted that probably every work contains some assertion of value. . . . Throughout is the theme of rigidity of spirit as opposed to the need for acceptance of human fallibility and the need for pity and sympathy.

But while Faulkner may often present these ironies of unrealistic religiousness, he also indicates that one may find direction, discipline, and consolations in religion. (In ***Light in August*** Byron Bunch provides the contrasting norm, as the man who committed himself to the moral life but can still admit self-doubt and demonstrate real charity.) It is this beneficial side of religion which Faulkner emphasizes in ***The Sound and the Fury.***

In her excellent analysis, "The Sound and the Fury: A Study in Perspective" [see excerpt above], Olga W. Vickery treats the four-part structure of the novel as representative of four ways of perceiving experience, dramatizing the progression from a private to a public world: Benjy's associative system of sensations, Quentin's obsessive abstractions, Jason's individualistic profit-and-loss pragmatism, and Dilsey's ability to create order out of experience through her tragic awareness of life. I should like to elaborate a little on Mrs. Vickery's analysis; where she concentrates more on the epistemological aspects of the structure, the present discussion focuses on perspectives as *ethical* perspectives, particularly in the light of relationships to Christian religion.

I want to emphasize that ***The Sound and the Fury*** is a moral book, that integral to its structure is the depiction of four distinct ethical points of view. To outline simply, one may say that the novel presents in turn an amoral report of sensations and reactions, the emotive abstractions of a moral absolutist or "idealist," the rationalizations of a moral hypocrite, and the humanistic acceptance and endurance of a moral realist; thus the progression is ethical as well as epistemological. This is not the whole of Faulkner's meaning, of course, but it does constitute so integral an element that the novel is definitely a moral book, and ultimately a sort of religious book.

To say that the Benjy section presents an ethical point of view may be a bit misleading, for the very importance of the section to this aspect of the novel is the absence of any ethical perspective. Benjy is totally amoral. His reports or remembrances of what-was and what-is are colored by no conception of what-ought-to-be; no value judgments are expressed in his section. His mind receives (and, for the novelist's convenience, gives out) mere sensations connected somehow in space and time but not mentally connected by logical or causal relationships. His thoughts proceed by simple association—generally mnemonic—rather than by an imposed interpretation. Thus he scarcely thinks at all; he does not judge. This does not mean that he has no evaluative reactions; in a sense he does. He may react favorably or unfavorably (e.g., by bellowing), but he does not conceive of his reactions to events as being evaluational. He reacts unfavorably to Caddy's perfume and favorably to her natural tree-like smell, but he does not judge, "perfume is bad." Similarly when he does wrong—molesting the little girl—he does not see it as wrong, because he does not know what wrong is. He does not know wrong from right, because he does not know the concepts *wrong* and *right.* Thus Benjy is the pure innocent, the personification of the amoral point of view.

In the second section, we find Quentin suffering from an altogether different ethical perspective. Quentin is an idealist, insofar as that term denotes one who adheres to moral absolutes or fixed principles. It is true that Quentin is the victim of his own abstractions, but it must be remembered that these are not just theoretic abstractions rationally arrived at. Quentin is very emotional about his abstractions; he is a zealot. Things are either all right or all wrong for him, and when he finds that nothing is altogether right he suffers from his conviction that everything is wrong. He notices the watches in the window of a watchmaker's shop and asks, "Are any of them right?" The watchmaker's "No" reinforces his interpretation of the universe:

> There were about a dozen watches in the window, a dozen different hours and each with the same assertive and contradictory assurance that mine had, without any hands at all. Contradicting one another.

He makes the mistake his father describes as that of "confusing sin and morality," because he believes as his mother says that "there is no halfway ground." Caddy's fiance, Herbert, tells Quentin that "a young fellow like you would consider cheating a lot more serious than you will in five years"; to which Quentin replies, "I don't know but one way to consider cheating I don't think I'm likely to learn different at Harvard." He doesn't learn that there is more than one way, and therein lies his tragedy; he never accepts his father's word that purity "is a negative state and therefore contrary to nature." This fervent, literally suicidal devotion of Quentin's to abstract absolutes Faulkner has underscored in his Appendix to the novel:

> Quentin III. Who loved not his sister's body but some concept of Compson honor. . . . Who loved not the idea of the incest which he could not commit, but some presbyterian concept of its eternal punishment: he, not God, could by that means cast himself and his sister into hell, where he could guard her forever and keep her forevermore intact amid the eternal fires.

This is the ultimate position of the moral absolutist: He sets himself up as God.

No doubt Jason realizes the folly of Quentin's idealistic perspective; Mrs. Compson has observed that Jason "is the only one of my children with any practical sense." Jason is not addicted to any absolute abstractions, nor is he emotively involved with anything other than himself. He lets neither theory nor feeling interfere with his self-interest. Caddy observes, "You never had a drop of warm blood in you." His cold-blooded selfishness is everywhere apparent, as in his business dealings. His employer says, " 'I reckon you'll never be a slave to any business,' . . . . 'Not unless it's Jason Compson's business,' [Jason] says." Jason has been characterized as a "utilitarian," and we might conclude that his ethical position is "realistic," insofar as he conducts himself in accordance with a pragmatic refusal to be hamstrung by theoretic principle or emotive attachment. But Jason does profess to adhere to a certain moral code. He claims, for instance, to care about Miss Quentin's behavior because of the family honor. But we may be sure the main reason he has for trying to prevent her escape is fear of losing the checks Caddy has been sending for her daughter's support. In Jason the "decency and pride" of the original Compsons has degenerated into "vanity and self-pity." Jason is a moral hypocrite. He wants to call in the law when his niece runs off with his money, but a large part of that money was savings from his misappropriation of Caddy's checks. He trusts no one, because he knows no one should trust him. His moral "realism" is a perverted realism—and he is, not altogether unlike his brother Quentin, the victim of an *idée fixe.* The remainder of his life is governed by his sense of being cheated out of a job in Caddy's husband's bank, and then out of the money he had misappropriated in order to make up for that original "injustice." Thus Faulkner's characterization of Jason as the "first sane Compson since before Culloden" is heavy with irony, for the fact that he is "logical," "rational," and "contained" is not enough to make him a worthwhile human being—he is too *self*-contained. (However, Jason is "sane" when compared to his two brothers, the idiot and the suicide.) Jason would seem to be an object lesson in the need for the old verities which Faulkner stressed in his Stockholm address.

"The whole tortured effort of the individual Compsons is one of uncontrolled and damning recollection. Underscored by Faulkner's stream-of-consciousness technique, the maddening, frustrating memories drive the protagonists of the tale to their respective judgments, or even comprise the punishment itself as a manifestation of the curse upon them."

—Robert J. Griffin

Dilsey represents the other side of the coin. Her ethical perspective is unblinkingly realistic. She endures because she has learned to accept life and accommodate to it; and her realistic ethic is humanistic, in contrast with Jason's perverted, selfish pragmatism. Dilsey's quiet accommodation to life is neatly synecdochized in her ability to tell time by the one-handed kitchen clock. She recognizes immediately what the distraught librarian, Melissa Meek, failed to recognize: "she knows Caddy doesn't want to be saved hasn't anything worth being saved for nothing worth being lost that she can lose." But it is not enough to say that Dilsey endures because she knows how to accept and make-the-best. Her acceptance is not stoic acceptance (Faulkner has labeled Jason "stoic"); it is Christian. The Negro Easter service in the last section represents a source of Dilsey's strength. On the way to church she exhibits Christian tolerance in the face of objections to her taking Benjy to the service: "Tell um de good Lawd dont keer whether he bright or not." In the church she exhibits Christian disdain for mere appearances: her daughter Frony expresses the general disappointment over the visiting minister's insignificant appearance, and Dilsey replies, "I've knowed de Lawd to use cuiser tools dan dat." Her premonition of the minister's effectiveness is justified, and at the end of the powerful service she sits bolt upright beside Benjy, refortified in her faith, "crying rigidly and quietly in the annealment and the blood of the remembered Lamb."

Dilsey represents in the novel the ethical norm of Christian humanism. Her fundamental Christianity is contrasted with the other characters' lack of it. When she returns home from the Easter service, Mrs. Compson asks for the Bible that has fallen from her bed.

> Dilsey crossed to the bed and groped among the shadows beneath the edge of it and found the Bible, face down. She smoothed the bent pages and laid the book on the bed again. Mrs. Compson didn't open her eyes. Her hair and the pillow were the same color, beneath the wimple of the medicated cloth she looked like an old nun praying. "Don't put it there again," she said without opening her eyes. "That's where you put it before. Do you want me to have to get out of bed to pick it up?" Dilsey reached the book across her and laid it on the broad side of the bed, "You can't see to read, noways," she said. "You want me to raise de shade a little?" "No. Let them alone. Go on and fix Jason something to eat."

Mrs. Compson is not willing to put forth any effort for her religion. She wants it nearby in case she should need it, but evidently has no awareness of needing it, or of how to use it should she sense the need.

I have already suggested the irreligious aspect of Quentin's absolutist ethical perspective: he places himself in the seat of judgment, failing to heed his father's counsel that "every man is the arbiter of his own virtues but let no man prescribe for another man's well-being." Jason is anti-religious. In the Appendix Faulkner speaks of his "thinking nothing of God one way or the other," but he thinks enough of Him to defy Him.

> From time to time (in his frantic pursuit of Miss Quentin and the stolen money) he passed churches, unpainted frame buildings with sheet iron steeples, surrounded by tethered teams and shabby motorcars, and it seemed to him that each of them was a picket-post where the rear guards of Circumstance peeped fleetingly back at him. "And damn You, too," he said, "See if You can stop me," thinking of himself, his file of soldiers with the manacled sheriff in the rear, dragging Omnipotence down from His throne, if necessary; of the embattled legions of both hell and heaven through which he tore his way and put his hands at last on his fleeing niece.

These contrasts with Dilsey's simple faith—her deriving strength from her Christianity—indicate Faulkner's approval of a kind of Christian ethic. He does not preach or openly advocate, of course; but he presents Dilsey in such a favorable light, dominating the last ("omniscient-author") section of the novel, as to clearly suggest his own sentiments. Dilsey represents the "old verities" of Christianity—not Christian rites or theological dogma but the fundamental Christian ethic—forbearance and endurance and love and brotherhood. It is significant that the only real sense of brotherhood emerges in the Negroes' Easter service: "their hearts were speaking to one another in chanting measures beyond the needs of words."

Faulkner uses this scene of the church service as a vivid antithesis to the rest of the novel. There are three elements in the scene which contrast with the elements that make up the existence of the Compsons. Instead of the doom and pointlessness of the Compsons' lives, first of all, the St. Louis preacher offers salvation and hope. He hears "de wailin of women and de evenin lamentations" (like the continual weeping of old Mrs. Compson); he sees "de darkness and de death everlastin upon de generations"; but these are superseded by the redemption and hope offered through the crucifixion and resurrection he describes, available to all "whut got de blood and de ricklickshun of de Lamb."

And here is the second set of elements contrasted with the Compson existence: the recollection and the blood. The whole tortured effort of the individual Compsons is one of uncontrolled and damning recollection. Underscored by Faulkner's stream-of-consciousness technique, the maddening, frustrating memories drive the protagonists of the tale to their respective judgments, or even comprise the punishment itself as a manifestation of the curse upon them. Benjy's recollections of Caddy cause him to break out repeatedly in his moanings. Quentin's haunting memory of his adolescence with his sister—especially the recurring scene of Caddy and him in the water—leads him finally to his suicide by drowning. Jason's most punitive memories are just beginning in the final pages of the book, just as the church scene opens. He will have to live the remainder of his life with the frustrating recollection of the robbery by his niece and with the knowledge of his impotence in the face of it. Similarly, the blood of the Compsons is that which constitutes the two-fold instrument of doom. They are doomed by the curse upon them, a curse of blood passed down through generations, expressing itself in feeble-mindedness, insanity, alcoholism and promiscuity, and leading to the complete destruction of the family. Furthermore, they are doomed through their pride in the Compson blood, their extreme awareness of the Compson name.

Juxtaposed to the recollection and blood of the Compsons is that of the religious Negroes. Recollection for them, instead of a tortured memory, becomes an ecstatic mystic experience, a remembering that is not a remembering at all but an initiation into a new depth of emotional and existential experience that sustains them where their own backgrounds and family ties are not sufficient. The blood, of course, is not the cursed blood of a family name or of inherited and damning characteristics, but the redeeming sacrificial "blood of the Lamb" that frees the sinner from obsession with himself. The third set of elements contrasts with the sound and the fury of the Compson clan: it consists of the quietness and peace paradoxically induced by the wild fervor of the religious service and expressed in the Compson idiot. Here, for the only time in the book, Benjy finds peace.

Many have noted the "Christ-figure" aspect of Benjy's role in the novel (33 years old, for instance—shades of Joe Christmas). Dilsey says, "You's de Lawd's chile," and in his unintellectualized suffering he has the inadvertent ability to express the world's suffering. His wailing "was nothing. Just sound. It might have been all time and injustice and sorrow become vocal for an instant"—Quentin's obsession with time, Jason's perverted sense of injustice, Dilsey's genuine loving sorrow. We might at first wonder why the idiot so horrified at the disruption of order in going to the left of the monument should not react similarly to the powerful goings-on of the Easter service. There, however, he is at home in the wordless communion of believers, all for the moment pure and innocent and washed in the blood of the Lamb. "In the midst of the voices and the hands Ben sat, rapt in his sweet blue gaze." Of course Benjy's kind of innocence is impotent; he is, in his total natural ignorance, necessarily areligious as well as amoral; he cannot share. But Faulkner has given us a hopeful contrast in the knowing perspective of Dilsey—loving and long-suffering and washed in the blood of humanistic understanding. (pp. 55-64)

Robert J. Griffin "Ethical Point of View in 'The Sound and the Fury'," in Essays in Modern American Literature, *edited by Richard E. Langford, Stetson University Press, 1963, pp. 55-64.*

Vernon T. Hornback, Jr.

Time and man's place in history are specifically related, for Faulkner's characters, to their collective experience as Southerners. In one way or another, each of his characters must come to terms with the meaning of Southern history. Three approaches to time and history emerge in ***The Sound and the Fury.*** The first, Quentin's, involves an obsession with, and entrapment in, the past. Quentin, as we shall see, is paralyzed, unable to act in the present, because of a commitment to a view of time which is essentially a form of cyclical determinism. Quentin's allegiance is to a dead past, the past of his archetypal culture-hero and ancestor, his grandfather General Compson. Quentin is incapable of living in the present because, for him, all the truly valuable acts were performed in the past, and the present is but a dim shadow, a poor reflection, of that past. He believes himself fated to a repetition of dead gestures and attitudes, a commitment to a dead past and an outmoded code. The second view of time, Jason's, also involves an obsession, but a radically different obsession, with time. For Jason, it is a manipulable commodity, to be used for profit, and he never quite has enough of it. For him, "time is money." His is a purely economic orientation, implying a commitment to a materialistic business ethic and a mechanistic, spatialized, naively linear concept of "progress" in its narrowest, laissez-faire sense. Jason replaces Quentin's cyclical determinism with an equally destructive linear determinism, which we shall label "progress time." The third view of time, Dilsey's, involves an acceptance of time as lived, experienced duration. It involves no determinism, but implies an existential view of time, which is also, fundamentally, the traditional Western view of history.

Because Jason Compson's attitude toward time has been most elusive for critics, we shall consider it first. Progress time was tentatively introduced into the Faulkner canon with the appearance of the first Snopes in Jefferson in ***Sartoris,*** but it is Jason who presents the first fully rounded treatment. Jason hurts or destroys others—Caddy, Benjy, his niece Quentin—as Flem Snopes will in the *Snopes* trilogy, by his rapacious exploitation of time as a commodity. While Quentin envisions time as a trap imprisoning him in the past of his dead grandfather, Jason has as little regard for his dead grandfather as for any other Compson—or for any other member of the human race: "to him all the rest of the town and the world and the human race too except himself were Compsons, inexplicable yet quite predictable in that they were in no sense whatever to be trusted." Jason has committed what James Dickey has identified as the ultimate act of alienation for a Southerner: he has given up his ancestry. Jason has escaped his past as a Southerner by isolating himself, by becoming a disciple of a naive, materialistic progress theory of history.

Jason, called ironically the "first sane Compson since before Culloden and (a childless bachelor) hence the last," is logical, rational, in the same sense in which Flem Snopes will be. He has a legalistic rather than moral attitude toward guilt, which psychologically insulates him against the implications of his condition. Neither the absurd freedom to achieve ultimately inconsequential goals, which is one side of progress time, nor the underlying fatalism implied by the fixed and mechanical course of progress time, ever occurs to Jason. Time is a commodity, not a condition. It is to be used: saved, not wasted; expended in a calculated fashion, like money or goods. Unlike Quentin, Jason feels no need to escape time. He rather feels the frustration of one who must be constantly on his guard lest he should fail to get the most for his effort and money out of time. He never quite has enough time: he is always too late to catch his niece. Time thwarts him, but in his view it does so because he fails to *use* it properly.

Jason is almost an epitome, and at the same time a caricature, of the American business ethic. In connection with his vindictiveness toward his niece Quentin, whom he unreasonably blames for the loss of the job promised him by Caddy's husband, he says:

> After she was gone I felt better. I says I reckon you'll think twice before you deprive me of a job that was promised me. I was a kid then. I believed folks when they said they'd do things. I've learned better since. Besides, like I say I guess I don't need any man's help to get along. I can stand on my own feet like I always have.

He justifies his own greed and unscrupulousness in terms of self-reliance and "business is business." He uses Quentin's illegitimacy to blackmail Caddy, he embezzles young Quentin's money, he sweats and scrimps and denies himself pleasures in order to accumulate money. He is isolated, self-sufficient, and inhuman; but he is vulnerable. His unquestioning acceptance of progress time, with its illusion of freedom, leaves him open to the very evils by which he succeeds. As the isolated self-sufficient man he can trust nobody. He cannot even trust his precious money to a bank. And so the thief is robbed by his victim, not merely of the four thousand dollars which was by rights hers, but also of the $2,840.50 which Jason had saved from the labor and sweat of his own time. Although Jason thinks himself the master of time—he can use it, save it, convert it into money—he is also the victim of time. Despite his frantic haste, which is everywhere frustrated, he cannot catch up with Quentin. He is always too late, arriving at her latest point of departure just after she has gone.

Jason's view of time lends itself to a bitingly ironic comic interpretation in ***The Sound and the Fury.*** The busy, bustling Jason is finally reduced to static, thwarted immobility.

> He sat there for some time. He heard a clock strike the half hour, then some people began to pass, in Sunday and Easter clothes. Some looked at him as they passed, at the man sitting quietly behind the wheel of a small car, with his invisible life ravelled out about him like a wornout sock.

Jason undergoes a kind of symbolic death. In one of his class sessions at the University of Virginia, Faulkner defined life as motion, and death as stasis. Jason's life is raveled out, finished. Of course he will continue to be alive, but for the moment he is figuratively dead. As Quentin Compson discovered before him, progress time is illusory. Jason will never consciously understand this lesson, because he is incapable of introspection. He will merely redouble his suspicion of every other human being, thinking that he will not be victimized again. And he will be successful until he matches wits with a man more ruthless and unscrupulous than he. In ***The Mansion*** Flem Snopes beats Jason out of the last piece of Compson land. Jason sells the land to Flem for an airport which he knows will never be built, and then discovers that Snopes intended from the first to use it for jerrybuilt housing. Commenting on Jason's reaction to being in taken by Flem, V. K. Ratliff says [in ***The Mansion***],

> That Jason may have divined, as though through some prescience bequeathed him by their mutual master, the Devil, that Flem Snopes didn't want and didn't intend to have a flying field on that property.

Jason will again learn that living as a predator has its drawbacks, particularly when another and stronger predator comes along. The jungle ethic of progress time offers a deadly kind of freedom.

While Jason believes himself radically free as a result of his rejection of the past, Quentin believes himself wholly conditioned and determined by it. His section of the novel begins, appropriately, with his own statement of his preoccupation with time: "When the shadow of the sash appeared on the curtains it was between seven and eight o'clock and then I was in time again, hearing the watch." Quentin's apprehension of time is frequently in terms of clocks and watches. For Quentin the watch or clock is the symbol of his dilemma, the neurasthenic inability to confront the meaning of his past and live in the present. With its circular dial around which the hands continually swing in an endlessly repeated cycle, it is a symbol of cyclical time. And, because his father had said, "Clocks slay time . . . time is dead as long as it is being clicked off by little wheels; only when the clock stops does time come to life," it represents the meaningless, uncontrollable force of progress time as well. The watch represents cyclical time also because "it was Grandfather's," and as a timepiece associated with that archetypal ancestor-hero, it is symbolic of the boy's obsession with the past and its hold upon him. The watch will become the ambivalent center of Quentin's irreconcilable tension between cyclical and progress time. When he received it from his father he was told, "I give you the mausoleum of all hope and desire." Time is the invincible enemy which frustrates human aspirations, the negation of freedom: "Because no battle is ever won he said. They are not even fought. The field only reveals to man his own folly and despair, and victory is an illusion of philosophers and fools." Quentin learns from his father to expect defeat as fated and inevitable. Hearing the watch, Quentin goes to the dresser, turns the watch face down, and returns to bed. Then he begins to wonder what time it is. The mechanical progression of time is as terrifying to him as the power of the past. Neither present nor past is congenial to him; yet he can escape neither.

Sartre has noted that time for Quentin Compson does not move out of the past into the future [see *CLC,* Vol. 9]. It is rather past and present confused, without expectation of future. Man is "deprived of potentiality and explained only by what he was." His obsession with the past is so radical as to deprive him of the capacity for effective action in the present, and so he cannot move into the future in any real sense. As his father tells him, "a man is the sum of his misfortunes. One day you'd think misfortune would get tired, but then time is your misfortune. . . ." Quentin defines himself as the sum of his family's past. In more than a figurative sense, he *is* his dead grandfather, but only a pale shadow of him. Not Quentin, the living grandson, but General Compson, the dead ancestor-hero, is real. The past has substance, it can be apprehended. The present is irrational, incomprehensible, terrifying. Quentin cannot cope with change, especially change in his sister Caddy. Change is a threat, for it appears to deny the efficacy of the past. He attempts to convince his father that he is guilty of incest with Caddy, for he thinks that this act will be so monstrous as to isolate him and Caddy from change. He will remove them from human time, preserve the past forever. He fails because he could not commit incest, not because it is a terrible sin, but because he is incapable of *doing* anything in the present. Even his suicide is conceived as already having taken place in the past, as a result of past actions not of his doing, but inherited with his name. As Sartre points out, Quentin does not choose his suicide, because he cannot conceive of *not* committing suicide; it is determined, inevitable, actually only a repetition of his grandfather's death. Before he leaves his Harvard dormitory room for his last walk, he invests his grandfather with a new archetypal significance:

> It used to be that I thought of death as a man something like Grandfather a friend of his a kind of private and particular friend like we used to think of Grandfather's desk not to touch it not even to talk loud in the room where it was always I thought of them as being together somewhere all the time waiting for old Colonel Sartoris to come down and sit with them waiting on a high place beyond the cedar trees Colonel Sartoris was on a still higher place looking out

> across at something and they were waiting for him to get done looking at it and come down Grandfather wore his uniform and we could hear the murmur of their voices from beyond the cedars they were always talking and Grandfather was always right.

The Grandfather archetype is invoked and identified with death. If the only valuable acts are the ones performed by the ancestor-hero, and his ultimate act was death, then Quentin must die. He must rejoin the past in which his grandfather is still present to him. Grandfather was always right: imitate Grandfather: die.

In the paragraph following this identification of the Grandfather archetype with death, Quentin begins talking of himself in the lower case "i" as if his self no longer existed. He is already dead, gone to join Colonel Sartoris and Grandfather and the other ghosts who are more real than he. At the end of the long passage, he recalls his father's words: "its not despair until time its not even time until it was."

He has already broken the crystal and torn the hands off his grandfather's watch, a symbolic rejection of both cyclical and progress time. But, "The watch ticked on." The symbolic rejection was ineffectual; one cannot escape time by denying it. The dilemma remains. The futile and bloody fight with the insufferable Gerald Bland is only a confirmation that he cannot escape the past. He has merely repeated his humiliation at the hands of Dalton Ames. And the watch keeps ticking. He cannot escape progress time either. He must commit himself to one or the other. He can live in neither. He puts the broken but still ticking watch in Shreve's room and walks to the bridge and joins his grandfather.

Set against Quentin's absorption in past time, on the one hand, and Jason's impatience with the present in order to get into the more lucrative and successful future, on the other, is Dilsey's life of duration. After Dilsey's name in the Appendix written for the *Viking Portable Faulkner,* and reprinted as the Foreword of the Modern Library edition of ***The Sound and the Fury,*** is written the simple legend, "They endured." In another context Faulkner says of her, "Dilsey, the Negro woman, she was a good human being. That she held that family together for not the hope of reward but just because it was the decent and proper thing to do." Dilsey is one of the few morally responsible human beings in the early Faulkner canon. She lives in the time of existential, experienced duration, what we shall refer to as existential time. She accepts responsibility, although as a Negro woman living in the South her freedom is limited. Yet she has won moral freedom by patience and endurance. For Dilsey, the word *endurance* takes on the double meaning that it will later have for Faulkner as a value term. It means not only fortitude, stamina, humility, and resignation, all of which it includes to some degree, but also the proper attitude toward time, which is to say, the proper attitude toward living. Dilsey is neither obsessed by time nor frustrated by it, because she can cope with it. She is never in a hurry, but she accomplishes things. She is the sole factor in the Compson household that prevents the destructive Jason from having his way. In the end she sees the Compsons destroy themselves, but it is not for lack of effort on her part to save them. Dilsey at least tries, while Quentin does not.

With respect to time, Dilsey's attitude is casual to the point of comedy. She has so little regard for the clocks that obsess Quentin and Jason in their different ways that she does not even bother to set her kitchen clock, which, anyway, has only one hand.

> On the wall above a cupboard, invisible save at night, by lamplight and even then evincing an enigmatic profundity because it had but one hand, a cabinet clock ticked, then with a preliminary sound as if it had cleared its throat, struck five times.
>
> "Eight o'clock," Dilsey said.

Mechanical progress time and cyclical time are both mocked in Dilsey's enigmatically profound clock which tells no time at all. For Quentin the watch, even stripped of its hands, remained a powerful force in his imagination, to be somehow reckoned with, or escaped in death. For Dilsey the clock is of so little consequence that its chronology and hers need not even coincide. Faulkner makes a point of repeating this motif twice again, emphasizing Dilsey's easy acceptance of lived time.

While Jason sits in the figurative death of motionlessness in Mottstown, Dilsey, Luster, and Benjy attend Easter services in the Negro church. The simple and moving sincerity of the service, and the fierce but peaceful dignity of the weeping Dilsey are a muted contrast to the furious, frantic disintegration of Jason and his final capitulation to defeat. Quentin had died on Good Friday, Caddy's daughter Quentin had fled on Holy Saturday, and on Easter Sunday Dilsey says, "I've seed de first en de last. . . . I seed de beginnin, en now I sees de endin." There is no Resurrection on Easter Sunday for the Compsons. Dilsey sees only destruction for them. Because they cannot cope with time, they are defeated, crushed by the weight of the past or deceived by the illusion of success in the future. The Compsons cannot live in the real, existential present.

As an ironic commentary on the Compson destiny, the novel closes with the one Compson who has successfully achieved peace with time, the idiot Benjy, riding past the Confederate Monument in the Jefferson city square—the monument to the past which has, in one way or another, defeated them all. Luster has driven Benjy around the square many times, and always in the same direction. This time he elects to drive in the opposite direction, a gesture, perhaps, of rebellion against the Compson world. Benjy's reaction is a predictable howl of terror and confusion. With characteristic violence, Jason reacts to the disruption of orderly progression. Fuming and exasperated as usual, he curses and strikes Luster, and reverses the direction. Benjy's idiot calm is restored, and Jason is reassured that orderly linear progress is efficacious. None of the Compsons can cope with the real world. Each attempts to escape it in some way: Quentin through suicide, his father through whisky and a cynical brand of stoicism, his mother through hypochondria and self-pity, Jason through sheer refusal to consider any alternative to his economic jungle, Caddy and Quentin III by actual physical flight. Only Benjy, an idiot, succeeds in avoiding the anguish of time, but he cannot do so on a *human* level. Of all the characters in ***The Sound and the Fury,*** only Dilsey, who, as a Negro, is also a symbol of that past which has defeated the Compsons, or, to be more precise, a symbol of the terrible burden of guilt which lies in that past and causes Quentin's obsession and Jason's rejection, only Dilsey can live in the world the Compsons have made. (pp. 51-8)

Vernon T. Hornback, Jr., "The Uses of Time in Faulkner's 'The Sound and the Fury'," in Papers on English Language and Literature, *Vol. 1, No. 1, Winter, 1965, pp. 50-8.*

"I feel that the verities which these people suffer are universal verities—that is, that man, whether he's black or white or red or yellow still suffers the same anguishes, he has the same aspirations, his follies are the same follies, his triumphs are the same triumphs. That is, his struggle is against his own heart, against—with the hearts of his fellows, and with his background."

—William Faulkner, 1957

Arthur Mizener

[Pride] is the source of heroism in Faulkner's work. His hero is characteristically a man who denies for the sake of his pride the very obligation of living itself, as does the hero produced by Faulkner's last important family, the Compsons. The story of this hero is told in ***The Sound and the Fury*** (1929), a book that also tells the story of Jason Compson, Faulkner's finest portrait of a poor white, even though his name is Compson; he is, in fact, precisely what the career of his legendary namesake suggests he is. And it has Dilsey, who was modeled with loving care on the Negro Mammy who brought up Faulkner himself and to whom he dedicated ***The Sound and the Fury;*** she is undoubtedly the most magnificent of all Faulkner's many portraits of Negroes, and she is something greater than a hero. When Faulkner wrote a set of biographical notes on the characters in ***The Sound and the Fury*** to help readers understand the genealogy of the Compsons, he headed one section of those notes: "These others were not Compsons. They were black," and the last name in this list is Dilsey's; of her Faulkner wrote simply, "They endured."

Four generations of Compsons appear in the novel, the oldest—Grandpa and Damuddy—only very briefly. The next generation consists of Jason Compson senior, his wife, Caroline Bascom Compson, and her ne'er-do-well brother, Maury Bascom. The Compsons have four children, Quentin, Candace, known in the family as Caddy, Jason, and Maury, who, when he is five, is discovered to be an idiot and is renamed Benjamin. Finally there is Caddy's illegitimate daughter whom she names Quentin for her beloved brother who is dead when Caddy's child is born. The Negroes consist of Dilsey, her husband, Roskus, their children, Versh, T. P., and Frony, and a grandchild named Luster.

The form of ***The Sound and the Fury*** is a daring experiment in the use of interior monologue; one of its main purposes is to give dramatic intensity to the narrative of a family tragedy that covers some forty years and has remoter echoes back as far as 1699. By imposing on his story the radical limitation of time required by interior monologue Faulkner reduces the present time of the novel to four days. These are, in the order in which they are presented in the novel: April 7, 1928, the day before Easter and also the thirty-third birthday of Benjy, the Compson's idiot youngest son, whose monologue covers the events of the day; June 2, 1910, which is covered by the monologue of Quentin Compson, then a student at Harvard, and is the day he commits suicide; April 6, 1928, which is covered in Jason Compson's monologue and describes his share in the family tragedy; and April 8, 1928, Easter Sunday, which is covered in the final section of the book and is the only one written in the third person; it is focused mainly on Dilsey.

Apart from these four days of the novel's present time, which the characters of course cover in detail in their monologues, their memories tend to cluster around a few dramatic occasions in the family's past history—the night Damuddy died in 1910, the few days of Caddy's disastrous love affair with Dalton Ames that left her two months pregnant when she hastily married Herbert Head in the spring of 1910; the day of that wedding, which is confused in the mind of Benjy—from whom we hear most about it—with the night of Damuddy's death (both involved large and unusual gatherings at the Compson house).

But we only gradually reconstruct for ourselves the Compson family's history, because it is presented to us only as it recurs in fragments in the memories of the characters whose interior monologues we overhear. Not only does this method of narration disrupt the order of events radically; it also presents these disordered events to us without explanation because the people who are remembering them know them too well to need to explain them to themselves; in the case of Benjy this lack of explanation goes even further, for well as he knows what he is remembering, Benjy does not understand most of it. What Faulkner gains by using this method is an uninterrupted view of his characters' innermost thoughts and feelings. In a conventional realistic novel the events of an action are presented in a temporal order; how a character knows these events, the order of the thoughts and feelings and memories which constitute his consciousness, can only be occasionally hinted at and must be largely reconstructed from such hints by the reader. In ***The Sound and the Fury***—except for the last section, which is written in the third person—the consciousnesses of the characters are presented in the order that the ebb and flow of thoughts, feelings, and memories determine; the events of the action can only be hinted at when the thoughts and memories of the characters touch on them in some psychologically plausible way, and their temporal order must be largely reconstructed from such hints by the reader. What Faulkner has done, then, is to subordinate the historical reality of the temporal order of events to the psychological reality of the affective order of the consciousness.

This subordination is particularly marked in the monologue with which the novel begins, that of Benjy, the thirty-three-year-old idiot son. Though Faulkner presents his monologue in sentences, Benjy is dumb and does not think in words. His simple but powerful feelings—his love of the Compson pasture, which is identified for him with the only happiness he has ever known, his love of his sister, Caddy, his love of firelight—these feelings govern the images that float through his mind and that are, as it were, translated into words for us by Faulkner. Benjy has no conscious conception of time, though he can suffer the losses it brings him; his mind moves freely from what is happening in the present to any incident in the past it reminds him of. His inability to conceive time is not merely a dramatic convenience for Faulkner; it is an important part of his theme.

What no Compson can endure is the outrage to his pride, the loss of dignity, imposed on him by his own time-bound nature. What Quentin will kill himself rather than endure is the temporal change that carries him and Caddy out of the timeless paradise of their childhood affection and brings Caddy to the fulfillment of her nature in her love for Dalton Ames and her pregnancy. Rather than admit that time can do that to him and Caddy, Quentin first insists that Caddy had no lover, that he and she have committed incest, and then—when Caddy does not join him in this grotesque and tragic fantasy but instead marries—he commits suicide. Throughout the day of his suicide, as if to emphasize his awareness that time is his real enemy, Quentin is obsessed by the ticking of the watch he has inherited from the past, from his grandfather. He tears off its hands and then listens sardonically to its incoherent ticking, "clicking away," as he says, "not knowing it couldn't even lie."

The reason Quentin so hates time is made clear in the conversation with his father—about his claim to have committed incest with Caddy—that he remembers just before he commits suicide.

> . . . you wouldn't [he remembers his father saying] have been driven to the expedient of telling me you have committed incest [had you not been serious] and i i wasnt lying i wasnt lying and he you wanted to sublimate a piece of human folly into a horror and then exorcise it with truth and i it was to isolate her out of the loud noise of the world so that it would have to flee us of necessity and then the sound of it would be as though it had never been and he did you try to make her do it and i i was afraid she might and then it wouldnt have done any good but if i could tell you we did it would have been so and then the others wouldnt be so and then the world would roar away and he and now this other [Quentin's threat of suicide] you are not lying now either but you are still blind to what is in yourself to that part of general truth the sequence of natural events and their causes which shadows every man's brow even benjys you are not thinking of finitude you are contemplating an apotheosis in which a temporary state of the mind will become symmetrical above the flesh and aware both of itself and of the flesh it will not quite discard you will not even be dead.

Quentin then repeats over and over his father's word "temporary," "a temporary state of the mind." That is the horror for him, that he cannot command his own nature, that what he determines on in his mind cannot, by a transcendent act of his will, "become symmetrical above the flesh," but is at the mercy of time, is "temporary." His father understands him perfectly because at bottom he feels exactly the same way about time. "was," he says, "the saddest word of all there is nothing else in the world its not despair until time its not even time until it was." (Faulkner is writing in this unpunctuated style because all this is taking place in Quentin's memory, but it may help to punctuate a difficult passage like this, which then goes, " 'Was,' the saddest word of all. There is nothing else in the world. It's not despair until time [exists]; it's not even time until 'it was.' ")

Quentin may seem next to mad in his refusal to accept the reality of what his father calls "finitude," "the sequence of natural events and their causes that is in ourselves." But Quentin sees quite clearly that it is the flow of this temporal sequence of natural events that erodes every state of thought and feeling, however passionately it is determined on; it makes all states of the mind temporary, mere alms for oblivion. Quentin's father knows this too; he is as aware as Quentin that all the sound and fury, all the eloquent thought and heroic action of man's history, signify nothing. Quentin's father has accepted that as the truth, though he finds he cannot live with this truth and quietly drinks himself to death. Quentin defies it; he would rather die at once than suffer the humiliation time is sure to put upon him. As his father says to him with understanding and sympathy, "you cannot bear to think that someday it will no longer hurt like this now."

Only for Benjy, the idiot son with the defective sense of time, is there some escape from knowing what time does to men's commitments of feeling, though as Mr. Compson says to Quentin, it shadows even his brow. He too lost Caddy when she was married in 1910 and his beloved pasture was sold to a golf club to pay for the wedding and for Quentin's year at Harvard, and it is still a grief to him. Now, in 1928, he still goes every day to hang over the fence and look at the old pasture, and every time he hears a golfer say, "caddie," he howls with grief. Nevertheless, unlike Quentin and his father, he can live with Caddy in memory almost as if the past were present—though not quite: he always remembers Caddy in the past tense.

The novel opens with Benjy's interior monologue, on the morning of April 7, 1928, Benjy's birthday, and he has as usual gone to look at the pasture under the care of Luster, Dilsey's grandchild.

> Luster came away from the flower tree and we went along the fence and they [the golfers] stopped and we stopped and I looked through the fence. . . .

> "Here, caddie." He hit. They went across the pasture. I held to fence and watched them going away.
>
> "Listen at you, now," Luster said. "Aint you something, thirty-three years old, going on that way. After I done went all the way to town to buy you that cake [which Dilsey has bought for Benjy's birthday]. Hush up that moaning." . . .
>
> We went along the fence and came to the garden fence, where our shadows were. My shadow was higher than Luster's on the fence. We came to the broken place and went through it.
>
> "Wait a minute." Luster said. "You snagged on that nail again. Cant you never crawl through here without snagging that nail."

With its defective sense of time, Benjy's mind then moves without transition to an occasion nearly thirty years earlier when he had been snagged on that same nail and Caddy had been with him.

> Caddy uncaught me and we crawled through. Uncle Maury said to not let anybody see us, so we better stoop over, Caddy said. Stoop over, Benjy. Like this, see. We stooped over and crossed the garden. . . .
>
> Keep your hands in your pockets, Caddy said. Or they'll get froze. You don't want your hands froze on Christmas, do you.

This memory of Caddy worrying over his cold hands makes Benjy's mind jump again to a time some ten years later than that Christmas.

> "It's cold out there." Versh said. "You don't want to go out doors." . . .
>
> "Let him go." Uncle Maury said. . . .
>
> We went out doors. The sun was cold and bright.
>
> "Where you heading for." Versh said. "You don't think you going to town, does you." We went through the rattling leaves. The gate was cold. "You better keep them hands in your pockets." Versh said. "You get them froze onto that gate, then what you do. Whyn't you wait for them in the house." He put my hands into my pockets. . . .
>
> Caddy was walking. Then she was running, her book satchel swinging and jouncing behind her.
>
> "Hello, Benjy." Caddy said. She opened the gate and came in and stooped down. Caddy smelled like leaves. "Did you come to meet me." She said. "Did you come to meet Caddy. What did you let him get his hands so cold for, Versh."

Then Benjy's mind is brought back to the present by Luster.

> What are you moaning about, Luster said. You can watch them again when we get to the branch. Here. Here's you a jimson weed. He gave me the flower.

In this way we are gradually made familiar with Benjy's mind and begin to recognize the extent to which his consciousness is governed by a few simple feelings, above all by his love of Caddy. He is aware only of what, in the most literal sense, happens. He experiences his love for Caddy, but he does not know it, has not sufficient powers of generalization to say to himself, "This is love." Nor does he know that it motivates his action, because his mind is incapable of thinking, "It is now time for Caddy to come home from school; I love her and want to go to the gate to meet her." He does not even know that thinking of Caddy makes him moan aloud; we learn this from what is to him the meaningless conversation of others.

In an important sense, this is the best possible kind of consciousness for Faulkner's purpose. Aware of events only as manifestations of its feelings about them—of what for Faulkner gives them their real meaning and value—and almost completely unconscious of their existence in time, it experiences what it lives by—its love—with a purity unknown to minds confused by the uncontrollable habit of looking before and after; and, since it knows almost no difference between "this now" and then, its feelings are unmodified by time. Their father is right when he tells Quentin that for him, "someday it will no longer hurt like this now." But for Benjy "this now" continues to exist forever almost as intensely as it did the moment it occurred. "Its not despair until time and its not even time until it was"; and as nearly as is possible it is never "it was" for Benjy.

These are the reasons Faulkner begins ***The Sound and the Fury*** with Benjy's interior monologue. For what is to him the significant aspect of reality, it is the most meaningful way (if, unfortunately, the most difficult one for readers to follow) of apprehending the experience the novel presents. It prepares us to understand Quentin's interior monologue which follows and which is, in content if not in appearance, more difficult than Benjy's because Quentin too can live only in the reality that Benjy lives in but knows, and therefore must fight his metaphysically complicated fight against, what Benjy is luckily barely conscious of, the meaningless temporal reality of his existence. As a consequence, Quentin's long monologue (it is almost half again as long as Benjy's), though much easier to follow in a superficial way, is more difficult to understand than Benjy's.

Quentin's monologue is followed by Jason's monologue of April 6, 1928, the day before the one covered by Benjy's opening monologue. Jason is, in his grim way, hilariously funny. He has all the egocentricity and the paranoid self-pity of his mother's side of the family combined with the stubborn pride and determination to stick to what they think right of the Compsons. His meanness and lack of scruple are equaled only by his assurance of his own rectitude and his almost heroic stoicism in the face of the universal conspiracy to make him suffer which he discovers all around him. He sees this conspiracy as impersonal, in the nature of things, and that gives him a kind of philosophic patience with it. Since Jason's feeling that things have been specially arranged to make him miserable is only an exaggerated version of what everyone feels at some time, we have a kind of reluctant sympathy with him as we watch him enduring his fate.

> I went out back to back the car out, then I had to go all the way round to the front [of the house] before I found them [the Negro servants].
>
> "I thought I told you to put that tire on the back of the car," I says.
>
> "I aint had time," Luster says. "Aint nobody to watch him [Benjy] till mammy git done in the kitchen."
>
> "Yes," I says, "I feed a whole damn kitchen full of niggers to follow around after him, but if I want an automobile tire changed, I have to do it myself."

By the spring of 1928, the time of Jason's monologue, both Quentin and his father are dead; Caddy has been divorced by Herbert Head when he discovered that her daughter—whom she names Quentin—is not his, and she has sent Quentin home to Jefferson to be brought up by Dilsey and has disappeared. She sends money regularly for Quentin, but Jason steals it and adds it to the hoard he is accumulating penny by penny from his salary as a clerk in the hardware store. He ought to have more than he does, but he has spent on an automobile the thousand dollars his mother gave him to buy a partnership in the hardware store. This automobile had become an absolute necessity to him when Herbert Head had given Caddy a car as an engagement present. It was an obvious part of the typical injustice of things that his sister, a mere woman, should have a car when he did not, and he had made up his mind on the spot to put this injustice right at the first opportunity. The first opportunity was when he had a chance to rob his mother and he had seized it with unhesitating courage.

It has made his life a good deal more difficult. He has to go through a complicated routine each month to keep his mother in ignorance, and his capital position has of course been weakened. Nonetheless, by 1928, his savings amount to $2,840.50, and with the money he has stolen from Quentin added to them, his capital comes to just short of $7,000. He keeps this money locked in his room because he is quite sure bankers are as crooked as the cotton brokers in New York who somehow manage to cheat him out of his money every time he takes a little fling on the cotton market ("Well, I reckon those eastern jews have got to live too. But I'll be damned if it hasn't come to a pretty pass when any damn foreigner that cant make a living in the country where God put him, can come to this one and take money right out of an American's pockets").

Living as he does entirely in the world as he knows it in his own consciousness, Jason is honestly unaware of the feelings of others; whatever they say or do he knows only as a part of the maddeningly unjust conspiracy to make it harder for Jason to have what he wants. He finds Quentin a special trial ("Once a bitch always a bitch, what I say"), and in his efforts to keep her in her place he overreaches himself, despite his cleverness. He makes her so miserable that in sheer desperation she climbs out of her bedroom window and around the outside of the house to the window of Jason's locked bedroom, breaks in, and steals his money. She then runs off with a man from a carnival and disappears forever. Jason's defeat is complete; he cannot even appeal effectively to the law, since he has himself stolen from Quentin better than half the money she has now stolen from him.

In his biographical notes on the Compsons, Faulkner describes Jason as "the first sane Compson since before Culloden. . . . Logical rational contained and even a philosopher in the old stoic tradition: thinking nothing of God one way or the other . . . who was using his infant niece's illegitimacy to blackmail its mother." His self-pity convinces him of the special malice of everyone he has anything to do with and makes him sure that any piece of mean cleverness his ingenious mind conceives, however unscrupulous it may be, is simply a justified defense of his rights. As a result, he is completely defeated by a seventeen-year-old girl who is not malicious at all, only driven to desperate, self-destructive rebellion by the cruelty with which Jason—never in his self-righteousness suspecting what she feels—treats her.

Faulkner's statement in his biographical note on Jason that Jason "thinks nothing of God one way or the other" is not accidental; in a quiet way quite unlike the melodramatic religiosity of much twentieth-century literature, ***The Sound and the Fury*** is a religious book. In it the sound and fury of temporal existence—whether it be Caddy's passion or Quentin's defiance or Mr. Compson's despair—signify, for all their heroism and pathos, nothing. The only significant lives in ***The Sound and the Fury*** are Benjy's and Dilsey's, and only Dilsey grasps their significance.

In the book's last section we watch Dilsey doing what she has been doing all her life, that is, keeping the Compson family in existence. It is as humble and homely a job as can be imagined. Dilsey cooks and washes, keeps Mrs. Compson as happy as her inexhaustible self-pity will allow her to be, brings up two generations of Compson children, and takes care of the idiot Benjy. It is all done with an unobtrusive love whose source we discover when Dilsey goes off to the services—it is Easter Day—at her Negro church, taking with her Benjy, who, Faulkner reminds us again, is exactly the age Jesus was when he was crucified. At the climax of the service, the eloquent, monkey-faced Negro minister slides from the correct, white man's English in which he had begun his sermon into the Negroes' own language and cries: "O breddern! I sees de doom crack en hears de golden horns shoutin down de glory, en de arisen dead whut got de blood en de ricklickshun of de Lamb!" And "in the midst of the voices and the hands, Ben sat, rapt in his sweet blue gaze. Dilsey sat bolt upright beside him, crying rigidly and quietly in the annealment and the blood of the remembered Lamb."

They are Faulkner's pure in heart, the one by inescapable innocence of the world, the other by the triumph of her faith and love over her knowledge of the world. For no one has understood better than Dilsey the tragedy of the Compsons. She has cared for them with unfaltering devotion, however little they may have deserved it, however hopeless she saw her efforts to be. Now she has seen the last of them—the seventeen-year-old Quentin—irretrievably lost, as she had seen Quentin's mother, Caddy, and her uncle Quentin and her grandfather lost before her. Only, unlike the rest of them, Dilsey has seen this family history in the light of the faith she has just so movingly renewed. Characteristically Faulkner reminds us, at the very moment he is showing us Dilsey's vision of what this history truly means, that like all the others Dilsey lives in time. He does so by surrounding this moment with the incongruous human comedy of Negro social life. Dilsey treats most of her acquaintances with a comic social scorn that expresses quite literally Faulkner's judgment of all men. "What [we] need," Dilsey says, "is a man kin put de fear of God into dese here trifling young niggers." When they address her, however respectfully—"Sis' Gibson! How you dis mawnin?"—she will not answer them unless they are quite old; her daughter Frony has to keep up the amenities—"Mammy aint feeling well dis mawnin."

When Dilsey is walking back from church, back into the unavoidable world of time that no Compson except Benjy has ever been able to endure, she continues to cry. It offends Frony's sense of the social decencies.

> "Whyn't you quit dat, mammy? Wid all dese people looking. We be passing white folks soon."
>
> "I've seed de first en de last," Dilsey said. "Never you mind me."
>
> "First en last what?" Frony said.
>
> "Never you mind," Dilsey said. "I seed de beginning, en now I sees de endin."

What Dilsey has seen is not merely the temporal, historical reality of the Compsons, whom she has known from the first to the last member of the family, but also the paradoxical reality of that history's timeless meaning. Dilsey is remembering—and believing—the promise of "I am Alpha and Omega, the beginning and the end, the first and the last." (pp. 147-59)

Arthur Mizener, "William Faulkner: 'The Sound and the Fury'," in his Twelve Great American Novels, *New American Library, 1967, pp. 120-59.*

David Minter

[*The essay excerpted below was originally published in 1979 in* American Literature.]

Early in 1928, while he was still trying to recover from Horace Liveright's rejection of ***Flags in the Dust,*** William Faulkner began writing stories about four children named Compson. A few months earlier, his spirits had been high. Confident that he had just finished the best book any publisher would see that year, he had begun designing a dust jacket for his third novel. His first book, ***The Marble Faun,*** had sold few copies, and neither of his previous novels, ***Soldiers' Pay*** and ***Mosquitoes,*** had done very well. But ***Flags in the Dust*** had given him a sense of great discovery, and he was counting on it to make his name for him as a writer. Following Liveright's letter, which described the novel as "diffuse and non-integral," lacking "plot, dimension and projection," Faulkner's mood became not only bitter but morbid. For several weeks he moved back and forth between threats to give up writing and take a job, and efforts to revise his manuscript or even re-write the whole thing. Yet nothing seemed to help—neither the threats, which he probably knew to be empty, nor the efforts, which left him feeling confused and even hopeless. Finally, he decided to re-type his manuscript and send it to Ben Wasson, a friend who had agreed to act as his agent.

The disappointment Faulkner experienced in the aftermath of Liveright's blunt rejection was intensified by the solitude it imposed. He had enjoyed sharing the modest success of his earlier books, particularly with his mother, with old friends like Phil Stone, and with his childhood sweetheart, Estelle Oldham Franklin. But he found it impossible to share failure. "Don't Complain—Don't Explain" was the motto his mother had hung in the family kitchen and imprinted on the minds of her sons. To her eldest son the experience of failure proved not only more painful but more solitary than any anticipation of it. Soon he also found himself immersed in a deep personal crisis, the contours of which remain a mystery. Several years later he spoke to Maurice Coindreau of a severe strain imposed by "difficulties of an intimate kind" ("des difficultes d'order intime"). To no one was he more specific. In a letter to his favorite aunt, he refers to a charming, shallow woman, "Like a lovely vase." "Thank God I've no money," he added, "or I'd marry her." But what if anything his intimate difficulties had to do with his new love, we do not know. What we know is that the difficulties touched much. "You know, after all," he said to an acquaintance, "they put you in a pine box and in a few days the worms have you. Someone might cry for a day or two and after that they've forgotten all about you."

As his depression deepened, Faulkner began reviewing his commitment to his vocation. Unable to throw it over, he determined to alter his attitude toward it—specifically by relinquishing hope of great recognition and reward. For several years, he had written in order to publish. After ***Soldiers' Pay*** that had meant writing with Horace Liveright before him. Yet, as his work had become more satisfying to him, it had become less acceptable to Liveright. Refusing to go back to writing things he now thought "youngly glamorous," like ***Soldiers' Pay,*** or "trashily smart," like ***Mosquitoes,*** he decided to go on even if it meant relinquishing his dream of success.

His hope faded slowly, he recalled, but fade it did. "One day I seemed to shut a door between me and all publishers' addresses and book lists. I said to myself, Now I can write"—by which he meant that he could write for himself alone. Almost immediately he felt free. Writing "without any accompanying feeling of drive or effort, or any following feeling of exhaustion or relief or distaste," he began with no plan at all. He did not even think of his manuscript as a book. "I was thinking of books, publication, only in . . . reverse, in saying to myself, I wont have to worry about publishers liking or not liking this at all."

More immediately, however, what going on and feeling free to write for himself meant was going back—not only to stories about children but to experiences from his own childhood and to characters he associated with himself and his brothers. Taking a line from "St. Louis Blues," which he had heard W. C. Handy play years before, he called the first Compson story "That Evening Sun Go Down" [later published as **"That Evening Sun"**]. The second he called **"A Justice."** In both stories children face dark, foreboding experiences without adequate support. At the end of **"A Justice"** they move through a "strange, faintly sinister suspension of twilight"—an image which provided the title for another story, which Faulkner began in early spring.

Called **"Twilight,"** the third of the Compson stories engaged him for several months, and became ***The Sound and the Fury,*** his first great novel. Through the earlier stories he had come to see the Compson children poised at the end of childhood and the beginning of awareness, facing scenes that lie beyond their powers of understanding and feeling emotions that lie beyond their powers of expression. In the second story, as twilight descends and their world begins to fade, loss, consternation, and bafflement become almost all they know.

This moment, which the stories discovered and the novel explores, possessed particular poignancy for Faulkner—a fact confirmed by scattered comments as well as by the deep resonance of the novel and the story of its making. "Art reminds us of our youth," Fairchild says in ***Mosquitoes,*** "of that age when life don't need to have her face lifted every so often for you to consider her beautiful." "It's over very soon," Faulkner remarked as he observed his daughter nearing the end of her youth. "This is the end of it. She'll grow into a woman." During the creation of the Compson children, he became not merely private but secretive. Even the people to whom he had talked and written most freely while working on ***Flags in the Dust***—his mother and aunt, Phil Stone and Estelle Franklin—knew nothing about his new work until it was finished. Although he was capable, as he once remarked, of saying almost anything in an interview, and on some subjects enjoyed contradicting himself, his comments on ***The Sound and the Fury*** remained basically consistent for more than thirty years. Even when the emotion they express is muted and the information they convey is limited, they show that the novel occupied a special place in his experience and in his memory. The brooding nostalgia which informs the novel also survived it: it entered interviews for years to come, and it dominated the "introduction" he wrote to ***The Sound and the Fury*** in the early thirties, both as emotion recalled and as emotion shared. Looking back on the painful yet splendid months of crisis during which he wrote ***The Sound and the Fury,*** Faulkner was able to discover emotions similar to those which that crisis enabled him to discover in childhood.

Like ***Flags in the Dust, The Sound and the Fury*** is set in Jefferson and recalls family history. The Compson family, like the Sartoris family, mirrors Faulkner's deepest sense of his family's story as a story of declension. But ***The Sound and the Fury*** is more bleak and more compelling. It is also more personal, primarily because the third or parental generation, which in ***Flags in the Dust*** is virtually deleted as having no story, plays a major role in ***The Sound and the Fury.*** Despite its pathos, ***Flags*** remains almost exuberant; and despite its use of family legends, it remains open, accessible. Faulkner's changed mood, his new attitude and needs, altered not only his way of working but his way of writing. A moving story of four children and their inadequate parents, ***The Sound and the Fury*** is thematically regressive, stylistically and formally innovative. If being free to write for himself implied freedom to recover more personal materials, being free of concern about publishers' addresses implied freedom to become more experimental. The novel thus represented a move back toward home, family, childhood, and a move toward the interior; but it also represented an astonishing breakthrough. Furthermore, both of its fundamental principles, the regressive and the innovative, possessed several corollaries. Its regressive principle we see, first, in the presence of the three Compson brothers, who recall Faulkner's own family configuration, and second, in the use of memory and repetition as formal principles. Faulkner possessed the three Compson brothers, as he later put it, almost before he put pen to paper. He took a central event and several germinating images from the death of the grandmother he and his brothers called Damuddy, after whose lingering illness and funeral they were sent from home so that it could be fumigated. For Faulkner, as for Gertrude Stein, memory is always repetition, being and living never repetition. ***The Sound and the Fury,*** he was fond of remarking, was a single story several times told. But memory was never for him simple repetition. He used the remembered as he used the actual: less to denominate lived events, relationships, and configurations, with their attendant attributes and emotions, than to objectify them and so be free to analyze and play with them. To place the past under the aspect of the present, the present under the aspect of the past, was to start from the regressive toward the innovative. Like the novel's regressive principle, its innovative principle possessed several corollaries, as we see, for example, in its gradual evocation of Caddy, the sister he added to memory, and in its slow progression from private toward more public worlds.

The parental generation, which exists in ***Flags in the Dust*** only for sake of family continuity, is crucial in ***The Sound and the Fury.*** Jason is aggressive in expressing the contempt he feels for his mother and especially his father. Although Benjy shares neither Jason's contempt nor the preoccupations it inspires, he does feel the vacancies his parents' inadequacies have created in his life. Although Quentin disguises his resentment, it surfaces. Like Benjy's and Quentin's obsessive attachments to Caddy, Jason's animosity toward her originates in wounds inflicted by Mr. and Mrs. Compson. In short, it is in Caddy that each brother's discontent finds its focus, as we see in their various evocations of her.

To the end of his life, Faulkner spoke of Caddy with deep devotion. She was, he suggested, both the sister of his imagination and "the daughter of his mind." Born of his own discontent, she was for him "the beautiful one," his "heart's darling." It was Caddy, or more precisely, Faulkner's feeling for the emerging Caddy, that turned a story called **"Twilight"** into a novel called ***The Sound and the Fury:*** "I loved her so much," he said, that "I couldn't decide to give her life just for the duration of a short story. She deserved more than that. So my novel was created, almost in spite of myself."

In the same statements in which Faulkner stressed the quality of his love for Caddy, he emphasized the extent to which his novel grew as he worked on it. One source of that growth derived from Faulkner's discovery of repetition as a technical principle. Having presented Benjy's experience, he found that it was so "incomprehensible, even I could not have told what was going on then, so I had to write another chapter." The second section accordingly became both a clarification and a counterpoint to the first, just as the third became both of these to the second. The story moves from the remote and strange world of Benjy's idiocy and innocence, where sensations and basic responses are all we have; through the intensely subjective as well as private world of Quentin's bizarre idealism, where thought shapes sensation and feeling into a kind of decadent poetic prose full of idiosyncratic allusions and patterns; to the more familiar, even commonsensical meanness of Jason's materialism, where rage and self-pity find expression in colloquialisms and clichés. Because it is more conventional, Jason's section is more accessible, even more public. Yet it too describes a circle of its own. Wanting to move from three peculiar and private worlds toward a more public and social one, Faulkner adopted a more detached voice. The fourth section comes to us as though from "an outsider." The story, as it finally emerged, tells not only of four children and their family, but of a larger world, itself at twilight. "And that's how that book grew. That is, I wrote that same story four times. . . . That was not a deliberate *tour de force* at all, the book just grew that way. . . . I was still trying to tell one story which moved me very much and each time I failed. . . . "

Given the novel's technical brilliance, it is easy to forget how simple and how moving its basic story is. In it we observe four children come of age amid the decay and dissolution of their family. It began, Faulkner recalled, with "a brother and a sister splashing one another in the brook" where they had been sent to play during the funeral of a grandmother they called Damuddy. From the play in the brook came what Faulkner several times referred to as the central image in the novel—Caddy's muddy drawers. As she clambers up a tree outside the Compson home to observe the funeral inside, we and her brothers see them from below. From these episodes, Faulkner got several things: his sense of the branch as "the dark, harsh flowing of time" which was sweeping Caddy away from her brothers; his sense that the girl who had the courage to climb the tree would also find the courage to face change and loss; and his sense that the brothers who waited below would respond very differently—that Benjy would feel but never understand his loss; that Quentin would seek oblivion rather than face his; and that Jason would meet his with vindictive rage and terrible ambition. The novel thus focuses not only on three brothers Faulkner possessed when he began, but also on Caddy, the figure he added to memory—which is to say, on the child whose story he never directly told as well as on those whose stories he directly tells. His decision to approach Caddy only by indirection, through the needs and demands of her brothers, was in part technical, as he repeatedly insisted. By the time he came to the fourth telling, he wanted a more detached, public voice. In addition, he thought indirection more "passionate." It was, he said, more moving to present "the shadow of the branch, and let the [reader's] mind create the tree."

But in fact Caddy grew as she is presented, by indirection—in response to needs shared by Faulkner and his characters. Having discovered Benjy, in whose idiocy he saw "the blind, self-centeredness of innocence, typified by children," he "became interested in the relationship of the idiot to the world that he was in but would never be able to cope with. . . . " What particularly agitated him was where such a one as Benjy could find "the tenderness, the help, to shield him. . . . " The answer he hit upon had nothing to do with Mr. and Mrs. Compson, and only a little to do with Dilsey. Mr. Compson is a weak, nihilistic alcoholic who toys with the emotions and needs of his children. Even when he feels sympathy and compassion, he fails to show it effectively. Mrs. Compson is a cold, self-involved woman who expends her energies worrying about her ailments, complaining about her life, and clinging to her notions of respectability. "If I could say Mother. Mother," Quentin says to himself. Dilsey, who distinctly recalls Mammy Caroline Barr, to whom Faulkner later dedicated ***Go Down, Moses,*** epitomizes the kind of Christian Faulkner most deeply admired. She is saved by a minimum of theology. Though her understanding is small, her wisdom and love are large. Living in the world of the Compsons, she commits herself to the immediate; she "does de bes' " she can to fill the vacancies left in the lives of the children around her by their loveless and faithless parents. Since, by virtue of her love and faith she is part of a larger world, she is able not only to help the children but "to stand above the fallen ruins of the family. . . . " She has seen, she says, the first and the last. But Dilsey's life combines a measure of effective action with a measure of pathetic resignation. Most of Benjy's needs for tenderness and comfort, if not help and protection, he takes to his sister. And it was thus, Faulkner said, that "the character of his sister began to emerge. . . . " Like Benjy, Quentin and Jason also turn toward Caddy, seeking to find in her some way of meeting needs ignored or thwarted by their parents. Treasuring some concept of family honor his parents seem to him to have forfeited, Quentin seeks to turn his fair and beautiful sister into a fair, unravished, and unravishable maiden. Lusting after an inheritance, and believing his parents to have sold his birthright, Jason tries to make Caddy the instrument of a substitute fortune.

The parental generation, which exists in ***Flags in the Dust*** only for the sake of continuity, thus plays a crucial if destructive role in ***The Sound and the Fury.*** Several readers have felt that Faulkner's sympathies as a fictionist lay more with men than with women. But his fathers, at least, rarely fare better than his mothers, the decisive direction of his sympathy being toward children, as we see most clearly in ***The Sound and the Fury***. . . . (pp. 378-85)

Although he is aggressive in expressing the hostility he feels for his parents, Jason is never able satisfactorily to avenge himself on them. Accordingly, he takes his victims where he finds them, his preference being for those who are most helpless, like Benjy and Luster, or most desperate, like Caddy. Enlarged, the contempt he feels for his

"In *The Sound and the Fury* [Faulkner] took possession of the pain and muted love of his childhood—its dislocations and vacancies, its forbidden needs and desires. The loss we observe in *The Sound and the Fury* is associated with parental weakness and inadequacy—with parental frigidity, judgment, and rejection."

—David Minter

family enables him to reject the past and embrace the New South, which he does without recognizing in himself vulgar versions of the materialism and self-pity that we associate with his mother. Left without sufficient tenderness and love, Quentin, Caddy, and Benjy turn toward Dilsey and each other. Without becoming aggressive, Benjy feels the vacancies his parents create in his life. All instinctively, he tries to hold fast to those moments in which Caddy meets his need for tenderness. In Quentin, we observe a very different desire: he wants to possess moments only as he would have them. Like the hero of [Ezra] Pound's *Cantos,* Quentin lives wondering whether any sight can be worth the beauty of his thought. His dis-ease with the immediate, which becomes a desire to escape time itself, accounts for the strange convolutions of his mind and the strange transformations of his emotions. In the end it leads him to a still harbor, where he fastidiously completes the logic of his father's life. Unlike her brothers, Caddy establishes her independence and achieves freedom. But her flight severs ties, making it impossible for her to help Quentin, comfort Benjy, or protect her daughter. Finally, freedom sweeps "her into dishonor and shame. . . . " Deserted by her mother, Miss Quentin is left no one with whom to learn love, and so repeats her mother's dishonor and flight without ever knowing her tenderness. If in the story of Jason we observe the near-triumph of all that is repugnant, in the stories of Caddy and Miss Quentin we observe the degradation of all that is beautiful. No modern story has done more than theirs to explore [William Butler] Yeats's terrible vision of modernity in "The Second Coming," where the "best lack all conviction," while the "worst are full of passionate intensity."

Faulkner thus seems to have discovered Caddy as he presents her—through the felt needs of her brothers. Only later did he realize that he had also been trying to meet needs of his own: that in Caddy he had created the sister he had wanted but never had and the daughter he was fated to lose, "though the former might have been apparent," he added, "from the fact that Caddy had three brothers almost before I wrote her name on paper." Taken together, the Compson brothers body forth needs Faulkner expressed through his creation of Caddy. In Benjy's need for tenderness we see something of the emotional confluence which precipitated the writing of ***The Sound and the Fury.*** The ecstasy and relief Faulkner associated with the writing of the novel as a whole, he associated particularly with the writing of Benjy's section. In Jason's preoccupation with making a fortune, we see a vulgar version of the hope Faulkner was trying to relinquish. In Quentin's Manichaean revulsion toward all things material and physical, we see both a version of the imagination Allen Tate called "angelic" and a version of the moral sensibility that Faulkner associated with the fastidious aesthete. It is more than an accident of imagery that Quentin, another of Faulkner's poets *manqués,* seeks refuge, first, in the frail "vessel" he calls Caddy, and then, in something very like the "still harbor" in which Faulkner had earlier imagined Joseph Hergesheimer submerging himself—"where the age cannot hurt him and where rumor of the world reaches him only as a far faint sound of rain."

In one of his more elaborate as well as more suggestive descriptions of what the creation of Caddy meant to him, Faulkner associated her with one of his favorite images.

> I said to myself, Now I can write. Now I can make myself a vase like that which the old Roman kept at his bedside and wore the rim slowly away with kissing it. So I, who had never had a sister and was fated to lose my daughter in infancy, set out to make myself a beautiful and tragic little girl.

The image of the urn or vase had turned up earlier in a review of Hergesheimer's fiction; in Faulkner's unpublished novel about Elmer Hodge; in ***Mosquitoes;*** and in ***Flags in the Dust.*** It had made a recent appearance in the letter to Aunt Bama describing his new love, and it would make several later appearances. It was an image, we may fairly assume, which possessed special force for Faulkner, and several connotations, at least three of which are of crucial significance.

The simplest of these, stressing desire for shelter or escape, Faulkner first associated with Hergesheimer's "still harbor" and later with "the classic and serene vase" which shelters Gail Hightower "from the harsh gale of living." In ***The Sound and the Fury*** Benjy comes to us as a wholly dependent creature seeking shelter. Sentenced to stillness and silence—"like something eyeless and voiceless which . . . existed merely because of its ability to suffer"—he is all need and all helplessness. What loss of Caddy means to him is a life of unrelieved, and for him meaningless, suffering. For Quentin, on the other hand, it means despair. In him the desire for relief and shelter becomes desire for escape. In one of the New Orleans sketches, Faulkner introduces a girl who presents herself to her lover as "Little sister Death." In an allegory written in 1926 for Helen Baird, who was busy rejecting his love, he reintroduces the figure called Little sister Death, this time in the company of a courtly knight and lover—which is, of course, one of the roles Quentin seeks to play. At first all of Quentin's desire seems to focus on Caddy as the maiden of his dreams. But as his desire becomes associated with "night and unrest," Caddy begins to merge with "Little sister Death"—that is, with an incestuous love forbidden on threat of death. Rendered impotent by that threat, Quentin comes to love, not the body of his sister, nor even some concept of Compson honor, but death itself. In the end, he ceremoniously gives himself, not to Caddy, but to the river. "The saddest thing about love," says a character in ***Soldiers' Pay,*** "is that not only the love cannot last forever, but even the heartbreak is soon forgotten." Quentin kills himself in part as punishment for his forbidden desires; in part because Caddy proves corruptible; in part, perhaps, because he decides "that even she was not quite worth despair." But he also kills himself because he fears his own inconstancy. What he discovers in himself is deep psychological impotence. He is unable to play either of the heroic roles—as seducer or as avenger—that he deems appropriate to his fiction of himself as a gallant, chivalric lover. What he fears is that he will ultimately fail, too, in the role of the despairing lover. What he cannot abide is the prospect of a moment when Caddy's corruption no longer matters to him.

Never before had Faulkner expressed anxiety so deep and diverse. In Quentin it is not only immediate failure that we observe; it is the prospect of ultimate failure. Later, Faulkner associated the writing of ***The Sound and the Fury*** specifically with anxiety about a moment "when not only the ecstasy of writing would be gone, but the unreluctance and the something worth saying too." Coming and going throughout his life, that anxiety came finally to haunt him. But as early as his creation of Quentin he saw clearly the destructive potential of the desire to escape it. If he wrote ***The Sound and the Fury*** in part to find shelter, he also wrote it knowing that he would have to emerge from it. "I had made myself a vase," he said, though "I suppose I knew all the time that I could not live forever inside of it. . . . " Having finished ***The Sound and the Fury,*** he in fact found emergence traumatic. Still, it is probably fair to say that he knew all along what awaited him. Certainly his novel possessed other possibilities than shelter and escape for him, just as the image through which he sought to convey his sense of it possessed other connotations, including one that is clearly erotic and one that is clearly aesthetic. (pp. 385-88)

"There is a story somewhere," Faulkner said,

> about an old Roman who kept at his bedside a Tyrrhenian vase which he loved and the rim of which he wore slowly away with kissing it. I had made myself a vase, but I suppose I knew all the time that I could not live forever inside of it, that perhaps to have it so that I too could lie in bed and look at it would be better; surely so when that day should come when not only the ecstasy of writing would be gone, but the unreluctance and the something worth saying too. It's fine to think that you will leave something behind you when you die, but it's better to have made something you can die with.

In this brief statement, the vase becomes both Caddy and ***The Sound and the Fury;*** both "the beautiful one" for whom he created the novel as a commodious space, and the novel in which she found protection, even privacy, as well as expression. Through its basic doubleness, the vase becomes many things: a haven or shelter into which the artist may retreat; a feminine ideal to which he gives his devotion; a work of art which he can leave behind when he is dead; and a burial urn which will contain one expression of his self as artist. If it is a mouth he may freely kiss, it is also a world in which he may find shelter; if it is a womb he may enter, it is also a space in which his troubled spirit may find both temporary rest and lasting expression.

Of all his novels, it was for ***The Sound and the Fury*** that Faulkner felt "the most tenderness." Writing it not only renewed his sense of purpose and hope; it also gave him an "emotion definite and physical and yet nebulous to describe. . . . " Caught up in it, he experienced a kind of ecstasy, particularly in the "eager and joyous faith and anticipation of surprise which the yet unmarred sheets beneath my hand held inviolate and unfailing. . . . " Such language may at first glance seem surprising. For ***The Sound and the Fury*** is, as Faulkner once noted, a "dark story of madness and hatred," and it clearly cost him dearly. Having finished it, he moved to New York, where he continued revising it. "I worked so hard at that book," he said later, "that I doubt if there's anything in it that didn't belong there." As he neared the end for which he had labored hard, he drew back, dreading completion as though it meant "cutting off the supply, destroying the source. . . . " Perhaps like Rilke and Proust, he associated "the completed" with silence. Having finished his revisions, he contrived for himself an interface of silence and pain. Happening by his flat one evening, Jim Devine and Leon Scales found him alone, unconscious, huddled on the floor, empty bottles scattered around him.

What ***The Sound and the Fury*** represented to him, however, he had anticipated in ***Mosquitoes:*** a work "in which the hackneyed accidents which make up this world—love and life and death and sex and sorrow—brought together by chance in perfect proportions, take on a kind of splendid and timeless beauty." In the years to come, he would think of his fourth novel as a grand failure. Imperfect success would always be his ideal. To continue his effort to match his "dream of perfection," he needed dissatisfaction as well as hope. If failure might drive him to despair, success might deprive him of purpose: "it takes only one book to do it. It's not the sum of a lot of scribbling, it's one perfect book, you see. It's one single urn or shape that you want. . . . "

Faulkner wanted, he once wrote Malcolm Cowley, "to be, as a private individual, abolished and voided from history." It was his aim to make his books the sole remaining sign of his life. Informing such statements is a definite need for privacy. But informing them, too, is a tacit conception of his relation to his art: that his authentic self was the self variously and nebulously yet definitely bodied forth by his fictions. It is in this deeper rather than in the usual sense that his fiction is autobiographical. It is of his self expressive, which is to say, creative. "I have never known anyone," a brother wrote,

> who identified himself with his writings more than Bill did. . . .
>
> Sometimes it was hard to tell which was which, which one Bill was, himself or the one in the story. And yet you knew somehow that the two of them were the same, they were one and inseparable.

Faulkner knew that characters, "those shady but ingenious shapes," were a way of exploring, projecting, reaffirming both the life he lived and the tacit, secret life underlying it. At least once he was moved to wonder if he "had invented the world" of his fiction "or if it had invented me. . . . "

Like indirect knowing, however, imperfect success, which implies partial completion, carries several connotations. Both the decision to approach Caddy only by indirection and the need to describe the novel as a series of imperfect acts partially completed ally it with the complex. They are in part a tribute to epistemological problems and in part a sign that beauty is difficult—that those things most worth seeing, knowing, and saying can never be directly seen, known, and said. But indirection and incompletion are also useful strategies for approaching forbidden scenes, uttering forbidden words, committing dangerous acts. For Elmer Hodge, both his sister Jo-Addie and behind her "the dark woman. The dark mother," are associated with a "vague shape [s]omewhere back in his mind"—the core for him of everything he dreads and desires. Since attainment, the only satisfying act, is not only dangerous but forbidden, and therefore both can't and must be his aim, Elmer's life and art become crude strategies of approximation. The opposite of crude, the art of ***The Sound and the Fury*** is nonetheless an art of concealment as well as disclosure—of delay, avoidance, evasion—particularly where Caddy is concerned. Beyond Faulkner's sense that indirection was more passionate lay his awareness that it was also less dangerous. For him both desire and hesitancy touched almost everything, making his imagination as illusive as it is allusive, and his art preeminently an art of surmise and conjecture.

In ***Flags in the Dust*** he had taken ingenious possession of a heritage which he proceeded both to dismember and reconstruct. In ***The Sound and the Fury*** he took possession of the pain and muted love of his childhood—its dislocations and vacancies, its forbidden needs and desires. The loss we observe in ***The Sound and the Fury*** is associated with parental weakness and inadequacy—with parental frigidity, judgment, and rejection. In the figure of Dilsey Faulkner re-created the haven of love he had found in Mammy Callie; in the figure of Caddy, he created one he knew only through longing. If the first of these figures is all maternal, the second is curiously mixed. In the figure of the sister he never had, we see not only a sister but a mother (the role she most clearly plays for Benjy) and a lover (the possibility most clearly forbidden). Like the emotion Faulkner experienced in writing it, the novel's central figure comes to us as one "definite and physical yet nebulous. . . . " Needing to conceal even as he disclosed her, Faulkner created in Caddy Compson a heroine who perfectly corresponds to her world: like it, she was born of regression and evasion, and like it, she transcends them. (pp. 389-92)

David Minter, "Faulkner, Childhood, and the Making of 'The Sound and the Fury'," in "The Sound and the Fury" by William Faulkner: An Authoritative Text, Backgrounds and Contexts, Criticism, *edited by David Minter, W. W. Norton & Company, Inc., 1987, pp. 378-92.*

May Cameron Brown

Faulkner's fourth novel, ***The Sound and the Fury,*** is probably the most widely discussed and best known of all of his works. One aspect of the novel which has especially intrigued readers for the now almost fifty years since its publication is the chaos of thought and feeling at the heart of the Compson world. It is a deteriorating world, represented symbolically by Faulkner in the physical and spiritual maladies of its inhabitants: Mrs. Compson's self-pity and hypochondria, Mr. Compson's fatal alcoholism, Benjy's idiocy, Jason's cynicism and sterility, Caddy's (and her daughter's) promiscuity, and Quentin's madness. Although almost any one of the characters of the novel might serve as a voice for this decaying aristocratic world, Quentin, the narrator of the second section, is uniquely qualified to relate this tale of a family destroyed by its own helplessness, perversion, and selfishness. As the oldest son, he is expected to become the head of the family who will continue the Compson line and preserve the tradition which is central to the Southern experience. His failure to fulfill these obligations reveals not only his own limitations but also the failure of his heritage to provide values by which he can live. The unusual blend of order and chaos in Quentin's section; the illusory, obsessive imagery; his inability to find and express a meaning in his experience—all reflect the decaying world which is at the heart of the novel.

Quentin's section encompasses his activities on the final day of his life as well as his memories of events from his past. The actions of the present, which begin in the morning and close with Quentin's final preparation for suicide, at night, are set against his reveries of key events from his past as if Quentin, aware that he is to die, is making a final examination of his life. His activities in the present are remarkable in themselves and directly related to the fixations which occupy Quentin's mind—the breaking of the watch and the visit to the jeweler's shop, events which help to establish the emphasis on time; his visits to the river, which prefigure his suicide and reflect his obsession with sexuality; his meeting with the Italian girl, who becomes his "sister," and his subsequent arrest and trial; the picnic and the fight with Gerald Bland, which becomes confused with the fight with Dalton Ames. All of these experiences establish a framework in the present and serve as vehicles for Quentin's memories of the past, memories which are central to his consciousness and which establish the special qualities of his voice—his obsessions with time and his sister, his multiple levels of association, and the complex and often fragmented structure of his thoughts.

The most significant characteristic of Quentin's mind is his fixation with time, a fixation which determines not only the language in which he speaks but also the structure of his section of the novel. All of his other obsessions are aspects of his preoccupation with time, as are the recurrent images and their associations, which create the almost constant movements of his consciousness from present to past.

For Quentin, time is painful and destructive. He lives in the past, which he attempts to reconstruct by imaginatively damning himself and Caddy to the purifying flames of

Faulkner's map of Yoknapatawpha County.

hell. His major actions in the present—caring for the Italian girl, whom he calls "sister," and fighting with Gerald Bland—are reflections of the most significant aspects of his past—caring for his real sister and defending her honor according to his distorted chivalric code. Because time is his enemy, responsible for his loss of Caddy and hence for his suffering, he seeks to destroy it by breaking his grandfather's watch and then to escape it by avoiding all instruments which record time. The more desperate he is in his efforts to avoid time, the more conscious of it he becomes. The watch continues to tick, along with the clocks in the jeweler's shop, and the Harvard bells chime every quarter hour.

Quentin cannot stop time by destroying the watch any more than he can prevent Caddy's loss of virginity by hoping to isolate her from the "loud world." What he can do and finally must do is to defeat time by destroying himself. His grandfather's watch, an object from the past given him by his father, becomes one of the key symbols in his section, and the breaking of the watch as the first action of the last day of his life represents his suicide.

In addition to the specific signals of time—the watch, the clocks, the chimes, and the sun—there are a number of interrelated images, among them mirror, water, door, shadow, and twilight, which direct his mind toward Caddy, his heritage, and death, three major aspects of his consciousness which gain meaning and focus through their association with time. These images drift from Quentin's conscious mind to his unconscious, functioning now literally, now metaphorically, joining the past and the present.

Because a large number of the images which flood Quentin's consciousness are associated with Caddy, we are continually reminded of his obsessions with the past and with virginity as the equivalent of family honor. The term "sister" with all its reverberations is one of the most common in his section. In addition to the variations of the motif "did you ever have a sister did you," which he applies to Dalton Ames, Gerald Bland, Christ, and Saint Francis, Quentin refers to the Italian child as "sister" and assumes with her the role of the older brother and protector as he has attempted to do with Caddy. Other parallels between the two relationships are worth remarking. During his time with the child Quentin tries to find her home and, failing this, to desert her, discovering only that he has run in a circle back to her. Shortly thereafter the real brother Julio accuses Quentin of sexually molesting the child and threatens to kill him, much as Quentin has threatened Dalton Ames. As he fails the Italian girl as surrogate brother in the present, so Quentin has failed Caddy as a real brother in the past. He has been unable to provide his sister with security and protection. After her loss of virginity, the only home he can conceive for her is a hell removed from the world. Instead of trying to save Caddy, he gives up life when he might have been a source of help for her and his namesake.

The specific references to Caddy gain support from the inclusion of such other images as "mirror," images which are related at key points in the Quentin section to significant events in the lives of the Compson children. Quentin uses the mirror images infrequently, either as a literal descriptive term or more significantly in relation to Caddy's loss of innocence and her marriage:

> *Only she was running already when I heard it* (Benjy's bellowing). *In the mirror she was running before I knew what it was. That quick, her train caught up over her arm she ran out of the mirror like a cloud, her veil swirling in long glints her heels brittle and fast clutching her dress onto her shoulder with the other hand, running out of the mirror the smells roses roses the voice that breathed o'er Eden.*

Notably, Quentin's first direct reference to Caddy contains the mirror image: "The month of brides, the voice that breathed *She ran right out of the mirror, out of the banked scent. Roses. Roses. . . .* " In a sense Caddy is running into reality and into sexuality which is represented by the roses, and out of the illusion which Quentin tries to maintain. The mirror seems to be a measure of his inability to regard Caddy's marriage directly; and although he can describe her movement metaphorically, he continues to try unconsciously to confine her within the mirror, the illusion of childhood purity. Thus, he often remembers her running "out of the mirror," but he cannot really allow her to step through the threshold into maturity.

A more obvious threshold is the door, which functions literally and figuratively in the past and the present of Quentin's section. One of the key references, the one with which Faulkner originally began the novel and one which parallels closely the mirror imagery, recalls Caddy's loss of virginity: *"One minute she was standing in the door. Benjy. Bellowing."* "*. . . as soon as she came in the door he began to cry.*" In addition to its literal meaning, the door, like the mirror, represents Caddy's movements into adulthood, and Benjy's reaction is characteristic of his resistance to change just as Quentin's anger is evidence of his own resistance. It is interesting to note that in spite of his desire to prevent Caddy's maturity and his own, Quentin is able to confront and pass through other thresholds. On the morning of his final day, he embarks on a series of remarkable adventures, the most important of which are introduced by doors. The bakery door with its tinkling bell signals the beginning of his relationship with the Italian child, an event which culminates in his arrest and concludes with his passing through the courthouse door. Perhaps more significant is the door of the jeweler's shop. Inside, Quentin hears the "ticking, like crickets in September grass" and observes the "assertive and contradictory assurance" of the watches in the window. When he leaves, "shutting the door upon the ticking," the imagery foreshadows his ultimate shutting of the door, the suicide which will kill time.

His earliest recollection of the door, one which corresponds to the incident in the jewelry store, is his childhood experience of getting up in the night:

> *hands can see touching in the mind shaping unseen door Door now nothing hands can see . . . yet the eyes unseeing clenched like teeth not disbelieving doubting even the absence of pain shin ankle knee the long invisible flowing of the stair-railing where a misstep in the darkness filled with sleeping Mother Father Caddy Jason Maury door I am not afraid only Mother Father Caddy Jason Maury getting so far ahead sleeping I will sleep fast when I door Door door. . . .*

This passage occurs during Quentin's final preparations for his suicide and thus serves not only as a commentary on his childhood perceptions and fears but also as a reflection of the action which he intends to take in the present. The door becomes the entrance into death, and the sleeping death itself, which will come when Quentin steps through the door of his Harvard room.

Quentin's contemplation of death and his obsession with virginity are aspects of his consciousness more fully revealed through the most common image of his imagination, water. Two central episodes of the past, Quentin's sexual play with Natalie and Caddy's loss of virginity, are associated with water. In the Natalie scene, which occurs in the rain, Quentin, discovered by Caddy, tries to atone for his behavior by jumping into the hog wallow. The hogwallow mud of Quentin's experience with Natalie becomes blurred into *"the swine of Euboeleus running coupled within how many Caddy"* as Quentin recalls Caddy's affair with Dalton Ames.

In this scene, his longest uninterrupted memory, Quentin introduces water as a purifying agent, first with Benjy's attempts to push Caddy into the bathroom to wash off the smell of sexuality. This incident leads to Quentin's memory of running in the humid darkness to the branch where he finds Caddy " . . . lying in the water her head on the sand spit the water flowing about her hips . . . her skirt half saturated flopped along her flanks to the waters motion in heavy ripples going nowhere renewed themselves of their own movement. . . . " As he contemplates killing her, Quentin associates this moment with the night of Damuddy's death: "do you remember the day damuddy died when you sat down in the water in your drawers." Caddy's muddy drawers, for which she had been scolded, represent the sexuality for which Quentin now wishes to kill her; and the sensuous water that Caddy is using to purify herself becomes the key which triggers Quentin's memory. Thus water becomes on one level the symbol of his exposure to the knowledge of good and evil which he repeatedly attempts to deny and the image through which his obsessions with death and sex are juxtaposed in his imagination.

In the present time of Quentin's section the water imagery functions in a somewhat different way. Although his death by water may be considered a kind of ritualistic purification, the water is never specifically related to sexuality. It is rather a reflection in which he views himself in the past and the present and a threshold which he contemplates and enters when no other action is left him. Water is less a regenerative force than a peaceful escape from the "loud world" and time. Although Quentin cannot perceive fully the death which he envisions, he can become one with the gentle motion of the water that will convey him to that death. Like the water, which is still and swift, moving but constant and continuous, Quentin tries to move and stand still, to exist simultaneously in both past and present. Finding that he can neither recreate the past nor exist in a meaningless present, Quentin chooses death.

On a literal level the river serves to locate Quentin's actions on his final day. The shadow, which he repeatedly observes reflected on the surface of the water, helps to fix his activities in time, the position of the shadow indicating the movement of the sun. In fact, the largest shadow group concerns the movement of time and is connected with Quentin's preoccupation with self-destruction. Wanting to assume Caddy's guilt, Quentin tries to trick or to destroy his shadow as a temporary substitute for destroying himself.

The passage from *Macbeth* which furnished the title for the novel provides further insights into Quentin's view of life, especially his attempts to maintain the illusions of the past. The speech occurs in a remarkable short scene which begins with Macbeth's display of confidence in victory and ends with his assurance of defeat as Birnam Wood advances toward Dunsinane. He has created for himself a false representation of life, and his trust in that illusion proves fatal. Between his expression of belief in the prophecy and his confrontation with the reality, Macbeth learns of the queen's death and responds in the famous lines:

> To-morrow, and to-morrow, and to-morrow,
> Creeps in this petty pace from day to day

> To the last syllable of recorded time,
> And all our yesterdays have lighted fools
> The way to dusty death. Out, out, brief candle!
> Life's but a walking shadow, a poor player
> That struts and frets his hour upon the stage
> And then is heard no more: it is a tale
> Told by an idiot, full of sound and fury,
> Signifying nothing.

Clearly Quentin's life and language echo Macbeth's words. The emphasis in the passage on mechanical "recorded time" is an obvious parallel, and Quentin's yesterdays have in a sense lighted his way to death. Walking in a shadow world, denying reality, Quentin reenacts his role as protector of women but fails in the present as surely as he has in the past (poor player). Life, motion, time—all are meaningless, and death for Quentin as for Macbeth will end the empty "sound and fury" of existence. Quentin puts it this way:

> A quarter hour yet. And then I'll not be. The peacefullest words. Peacefullest words. *Non fui. Sum. Fui. Nom* [sic] *sum* . . . I was. I am not . . . I am . . . I was not . . . I have sold Benjy's pasture and I can be dead in Harvard . . . Harvard is such a fine sound forty acres is not a high price for a fine sound. A fine dead sound we will swap Benjy's pasture for a fine dead sound.

It is Quentin's partial awareness of the emptiness of words and values which creates his despair and isolates him in a world of shadows.

His isolation is embodied in another recurrent image, twilight, which is for him both a quality of light and a quality of mind. Quentin's references to twilight in the past relate principally to Caddy's sexuality and are associated with the odors of the apple tree and of honeysuckle: ". . . *getting the odour of honeysuckle all mixed She would have told me not to let me sit there on the steps hearing her door twilight slamming . . . the curtains leaning in on the twilight upon the odour of the apple tree her head against the twilight.* . . . " His references in the present are concerned primarily with the time of day, "the sky green paling into gold," but there is a key passage which places the image on a deeper level. As he travels back to Harvard after his extraordinary day, Quentin tells us, " . . . I could see the twilight again, that quality of light as if time really had stopped for a while, with the sun hanging just under the horizon, . . . and the road going on under the twilight, into twilight and the sense of water peaceful and swift beyond." On a conscious level Quentin associates twilight with a peaceful state, with the anticipated suicide when time will cease to torture him. On an unconscious level twilight is frightening and stifling, filled with horrifying shapes of the past and odors of fecundity. The twilight state is an ambivalent one between day and night, acceptance and rejection, past and present, life and death. Quentin's use of the image emphasizes the ambivalence of his consciousness and thus serves perhaps better than any other single term to define him.

Quentin rarely uses any one of the recurrent images in isolation. Water reflects shadows; shadows recall twilight, which, in turn, suggests honeysuckle, rain, and Caddy. Because association is a principal structural device in Quentin's section, one image recalls another and the present leads to the past and back to the present in an orderly pattern. Yet in spite of this logical progression, Quentin's section is difficult for a number of stylistic reasons, among them interpolation and fragmentation, sometimes to the point of incoherence. These complexities are, of course, appropriate and necessary to the definition of Quentin's confused and disturbed mind. What Faulkner shows us is experience as it enters consciousness rather than the static experience which has been logically arranged in the mind and is subsequently presented in standard syntax.

In the Quentin section images and memories merge and expand to create a complete view of the character. The fragmented images with which Quentin begins, become, as he is further and further removed from reality, entire scenes from the past which blot out the present. Thus we are not aware of the fight with Gerald Bland until Quentin awakes from his unconscious memory about the fight with Dalton Ames and asks his friends what has happened. In the closing pages of the section, Quentin recreates in an extended passage without punctuation or capitalization the painful conversation with his father concerning incest. Mr. Compson's fatalistic comments—"even the despair or remorse or bereavement is not particularly important to the dark dicemen"—along with Faulkner's use of the lower case "i," emphasize Quentin's total despair and his loss of identity with time. The section which follows is even more frightening. Here Quentin's accelerated thoughts are absorbed entirely into his compulsive and almost ritualistic final preparations for suicide, behavior which indicates his ultimate withdrawal. Mechanical actions replace feeling.

The levels on which Quentin's mind functions account for the structural organization of his monologue. The most accessible level is that of immediate sensory impressions, usually occurring in his conscious mind and in the present. The unconscious reveries and the multiple associations within the reveries are more complicated. They are the stylistic opposite of the simple, declarative sentences which describe his mechanical actions, words used to express fragmented and strongly emotional memories:

> *the first car in town a girl Girl that's what Jason couldn't bear smell of gasoline making him sick then got madder than ever because a girl Girl had no sister but Benjamin Benjamin the child of my sorrowful if I'd just had a mother so I could say Mother Mother.*

In this example, typical of many, Faulkner's use of the cumulative appended groups of words creates the ambiguity so crucial to the characterization of Quentin and to the definition of his imprisonment. The references to the car given to Caddy by Herbert Head recall, in addition to Caddy's virginity, Jason's allergy to gasoline, the change of Benjy's name, and Mrs. Compson's utter failure to be a mother to her children. In this final plea to his mother, coupled with other memories of loss associated with her, Quentin summarizes the major incidents of his childhood. Throughout Quentin's section lack of grammatical hierarchy, unfinished syntactical units, ambiguous pronouns, and repeated images reinforce the effects of merging memories, fragmented thoughts, and unresolved tension.

Haunted by a past to which he is inadequate, dogged by a present he cannot face, and doomed to no future, Quentin, through his diction and general point of view—both what he speaks and what he thinks—dramatizes a modern yet universal sensibility. Shortly before his suicide he thinks:

> I seemed to be lying neither asleep nor awake looking down a long corridor of grey halflight where all stable things had become shadowy paradoxical all I had done shadows all I had felt suffered taking visible form antic and perverse mocking without relevance inherent themselves with the denial of the significance they should have affirmed thinking I was I was not who was not was not who.

Imprisoned by his obsessions from which his only escape is suicide, Quentin can but agree with his father that "no battle is ever won. . . . They are not even fought. The field only reveals to man his own folly and despair, and victory is an illusion of philosophers and fools." (pp. 544-53)

May Cameron Brown, "The Language of Chaos: Quentin Compson in 'The Sound and the Fury'," in American Literature, *Vol. LI, No. 4, January, 1980, pp. 544-53.*

FURTHER READING

Bassett, John. *William Faulkner: An Annotated Checklist of Criticism.* New York: David Lewis, 1972, 551p.

A comprehensive annotated list of reviews and criticism on Faulkner through 1970.

———. *Faulkner: An Annotated Checklist of Recent Criticism.* Kent, Ohio: Kent State University Press, 1983, 272 p.

An annotated compilation of criticism and scholarship on Faulkner from 1971 to 1982.

Chappell, Fred. "The Comic Structure of *The Sound and the Fury.*" *The Mississippi Quarterly* 31, No. 3 (Summer 1978): 381-86.

Argues that *The Sound and the Fury* may be interpreted as a comic novel.

Collins, Carvel. "William Faulkner: *The Sound and the Fury.*" In *The American Novel: from James Fenimore Cooper to William Faulkner,* edited by Wallace Stegner, pp. 219-80. New York: Basic Books, Inc., 1965.

Discussion of narrative structure in *The Sound and the Fury.*

Cox, James M. "Humor as Vision in Faulkner." In *Faulkner and Humor: Faulkner and Yoknapatawpha, 1984,* edited by Doreen Fowler and Ann J. Abadie, pp. 1-20. Jackson: University Press of Mississippi, 1986.

Highlights the humorous aspects of Jason Compson's narrative.

Edel, Leon. "How to Read *The Sound and The Fury.*" In *Varieties of Literary Experience,* edited by Stanley Burnshaw, pp. 241-57. New York: New York University Press, 1962.

Focuses on the reader's approach to *The Sound and the Fury,* explaining the relationship between Faulkner's complex style and themes.

Feldstein, Richard. "Faulkner's *The Sound and the Fury:* The Incest Theme." *American Imago* 42, No. 1 (Spring 1985): 85-98.

Examines the motif of incest in *The Sound and the Fury.*

Gross, Beverly. "Form and Fulfillment in *The Sound and the Fury.*"*Modern Language Quarterly* 29 (1968): 439-49.

Analysis of form in *The Sound and the Fury,* focusing particularly on the novel's last section.

Kreiswirth, Martin. "Learning as He Wrote: Re-Used Materials in *The Sound and the Fury.*" *The Mississippi Quarterly* 34, No. 3 (Summer 1981): 281-98.

Discusses the influence of Faulkner's earlier works on *The Sound and the Fury.*

Mellard, James M. "*The Sound and the Fury:* Quentin Compson and Faulkner's 'Tragedy of Passion'." *Studies in the Novel* II, No. 1 (Spring 1970): 61-75.

Discusses the tragic form of Quentin's narrative in *The Sound and the Fury.*

Messerli, Douglas. "The Problem of Time in *The Sound and the Fury:* A Critical Reassessment and Reinterpretation." *The Southern Literary Journal* 6, No. 2 (Spring 1974): 19-41.

Analysis of critical approaches to the concept of time in Faulkner's works.

Peavy, Charles D. "Faulkner's Use of Folklore in *The Sound and the Fury.*" *Journal of American Folklore* 79, No. 313 (July-September 1966): 437-44.

Explores Faulkner's integration of Southern folklore in *The Sound and the Fury.*

Radloff, Bernhard. "Time and Time-Field: The Structure of Anticipation and Recollection in the Quentin-Section of *The Sound and the Fury.*" *Dalhousie Review* 65, No. 1 (Spring 1985): 29-42.

Discusses Quentin's psyche, focusing on his obsession with time.

Wadlington, Warwick. "*The Sound and the Fury:* A Logic of Tragedy." *American Literature* 53, No. 3 (November 1981): 409-23.

Examines the role of tragedy in *The Sound and the Fury,* emphasizing the disparity between the Compsons' heroic temperament and passivity.

Wagner, Linda W., ed. *William Faulkner: Four Decades of Criticism.* East Lansing: Michigan State University Press, 1973, 374 p.

A collection of major critical essays dating from the 1930s to the early 1970s.

Wolff, Sally and Minter, David. "A 'Matchless Time': Faulkner and the Writing of *The Sound and the Fury.*" In *Writing the American Classics,* edited by James Barbour and Tom Quirk, pp. 156-76. Chapel Hill: The University of North Carolina Press, 1990.

Biographical discussion of the experiences influencing Faulkner's authorship of *The Sound and the Fury.*

Gabriel García Márquez

1928-

(Full name Gabriel José García Márquez; also wrote under the pseudonym Septimus) Colombian novelist, short story writer, journalist, critic, and scriptwriter.

The following entry presents criticism on García Márquez's novel *Cien años de soledad* (1967; *One Hundred Years of Solitude*). For discussions of García Márquez's career, see *CLC,* Vols. 2, 3, 8, 10, 15, 27, 47, 55.

After years of writing fiction without attaining significant notice, García Márquez garnered enormous popular and critical success with the publication of *One Hundred Years of Solitude.* Praised for its satirical blend of myth, historical fact, and imaginative hyperbole, this novel established him as one of the most notable authors of the "boom" in Latin American literature, a period of achievement that occurred in the 1960s and brought international recognition to García Márquez and such authors as Carlos Fuentes, Mario Vargas Llosa, and Julio Cortázar. Chronicling the history of Macondo, a fictional village based on García Márquez's hometown of Aracataca, *One Hundred Years of Solitude* traces the rise and fall of the Buendía family from its harmonious beginnings under founder José Arcadio Buendía to its increasingly chaotic decline through six generations of descendants. Considered a masterpiece of contemporary Latin American literature, the novel is widely regarded as a seminal example of magic realism, in which fantastic incidents are presented in an objective style to obscure distinctions between illusion and reality.

For the first eight years of his life, García Márquez lived in Aracataca with his grandparents. The long decline of the town, the local myths and superstitions of the townspeople, and the storytelling of his grandmother all played significant roles in shaping his imagination. According to García Márquez, "the key to writing *One Hundred Years of Solitude* was the idea of saying incredible things with a completely unperturbed face." He attributed this technique to his grandmother and her ability to tell "wild tales of the supernatural" that he tended to believe "because of her serious, deadpan facial expression. Now, as a writer, I do the same thing; I say extraordinary things in a serious tone. It's possible to get away with *anything* as long as you make it believable." While working as a journalist in South America, Europe, and the United States during the late 1940s, García Márquez began to write short stories set in the village of Macondo, whose name derived from an old banana plantation near Aracataca that García Márquez learned about from his grandparents. The village's richly imagined locale and colorful characters have elicited frequent critical comparisons to William Faulkner's mythical Yoknapatawpha County; García Márquez has readily acknowledged the influence of Faulkner's work on his fiction.

Following its appearance in South America, *One Hundred Years of Solitude* garnered immediate acclaim and became a best-seller. "I knew [the novel] would please my friends more than my other [works] had," García Márquez commented in an interview. "But when my Spanish publisher told me he was going to print eight thousand copies, I was stunned because my other books had never sold more than seven hundred. . . . [All eight thousand copies] were sold within one week in Buenos Aires." Although the novel provoked widespread debate amongst Latin American literary critics who disagreed as to whether the work presented a stereotypical portrait of South America in the manner of Latin American social realist novels of the 1940s and 1950s, most concurred that *One Hundred Years of Solitude* ranked as possibly the best Latin American novel of its era. While some initial English-speaking reviewers stated that García Márquez treated Macondo and its history as a microcosm for Latin America, others felt that the book's mythical and magic realist aspects combined to impart a more universal statement. Extensive critical commentary has since focused on many facets, particularly the novel's intertextual references and numerous allusions to biblical and classical myth.

The first sentence of *One Hundred Years of Solitude* anticipates García Márquez's ensuing treatment of time as an essentially nonlinear phenomenon in which past, present, and future are fused into a single instant: "Many years later, as he faced the firing squad, Colonel Aureliano Buendía was to remember that distant afternoon when his father took him to discover ice." Like many of Faulkner's works, *One Hundred Years of Solitude* possesses a chronological structure wherein the plot develops via cause and effect but in which the present narrative shifts backward and forward in time to relate incidents that have either occurred previously or will occur later. For example, the novel begins with Colonel Aureliano Buendía looking back on the day when "his father took him to discover ice" from a distant future perspective. A chapter later, the book shifts backward in time to explore the relationship between Aureliano's mother, Úrsula, and his father, José Arcadio Buendía.

After marrying his cousin, Úrsula Iguarán, José Arcadio finds his new bride unwilling to consummate the marriage due to her fear that such an act of incest will cause the birth of a child with a pig's tail, a deformity that previously resulted from an incestuous union in the family and which is rumored to portend the end of the Buendía line. García Márquez thus alludes to the classical myth outlined in Sophocles' *Oedipus Rex* and establishes the novel's predominant themes of guilt and inescapable fate. When a townsman, Prudencio Aguilar, insinuates that José Arcadio is impotent, the latter is driven by pride to kill Prudencio and to then assert his conjugal privilege with Úrsula. Although their child is born without the dreaded pig's tail, the couple are compelled to leave town due to the sense of guilt induced by the mournful ghost of Prudencio, who constantly follows José Arcadio complaining of the solitude of death. Throughout *One Hundred Years of Solitude,* ghosts regularly mingle with the living, functioning as literal reminders of the past and synthesizing the human impulse for history—a realistic phenomenon—with the supernatural. As José Arcadio and Ursula set off into unexplored territory to forge a new life in the wilderness, García Márquez adds a variety of biblical allusions to his blend of classical myth and magic realism. Acting as a kind of Moses, José Arcadio leads a small group of men and women away from civilization and toward a new promised land; escaping their pre-Arcadian beginnings, José Arcadio and Úrsula found the Edenic paradise of Macondo, where the couple attempt to escape the original sin implied in their flight.

At the beginning of *One Hundred Years of Solitude,* García Márquez delineates José Arcadio's myopic pursuit of knowledge in Macondo. After refining the technical aspects of the nearly ideal village community, José Arcadio is led on several illusory quests for experience, including a search for gold using a pair of magnets supplied by Melquiades, a gypsy chieftain who travels periodically with his people to the remote tropical village to entice the residents with new inventions and wonders from the outside world. These include such marvels as a giant magnifying glass, a trunk filled with ice, flying carpets, and an alchemical laboratory. After using a daguerrotype in a futile attempt to prove the existence of God, José Arcadio lapses into an insane rage, forcing his terrified family to tie him to a chestnut tree where he remains even after his death, babbling in Latin against all evidence of God's existence.

One Hundred Years of Solitude moves into the territory of the political novel when José Arcadio's son, Aureliano Buendía, reacts against his country's remote Conservative government and its gradual imposition of dictatorial laws on the village. Critics generally agree that this section parallels the historical conflict that occurred in the nineteenth century between Colombia's working-class Liberal party and its stronger, upper-class Conservative party. According to Gordon Brotherston, however, "[García Márquez] shows that he doesn't want merely to chronicle the past by his admirably constant disregard of precise ages and dates." An apolitical and solitary dreamer who was previously absorbed in the futile craft of creating little fishes out of gold, which he then sold for gold coins in order to obtain material to make more fishes, Colonel Aureliano Buendía leads his fellow Liberals into a countless series of vaguely defined and bloody revolutions during which he fathers seventeen illegitimate sons who all bear the name Aureliano. Although he finally accepts defeat after losing many battles, Aureliano Buendía publicly threatens to incite his sons to carry on the revolution when the state lionizes him as a hero. In a clear biblical allusion, all of his sons are killed in a single night except for an infant who, like Moses, is discovered floating among a river's bullrushes. The novel thus combines both biblical myth and history, offering what Ricardo Gúllon called "a parable of man's creation, man's history and human nature."

In the next section of the novel, Macondo is irrevocably changed as secular and religious officials move in and imperialism invades the village in the form of a ruthless banana company from the United States that transforms the backwater hamlet into a booming agricultural town. The company eventually enslaves the inhabitants by allowing them no say in corporate policies and paying them in script that is redeemable only at overpriced company commissaries. When one of José Arcadio's grandsons finally organizes a strike to protest the resulting dehumanization, the company lures the demonstrators and their families into a public square with promises of negotiations, arranges for a mass execution to be performed by the government's army, and then has the bodies shuttled away by train, effectively destroying all proof that the massacre ever occurred. This incident, which is based upon an actual historical event that occurred across Colombia's banana zone from Santa Marta to Aracataca, had been the subject of numerous works by earlier writers, most notably Pablo Neruda in his poem "La United Fruit Co." García Márquez commented: "[The banana strike] sequence sticks closely to the facts of the United Fruit strike of 1928, which dates from my childhood; I was born that year. The only exaggeration is in the number of dead, though it does fit the proportions of the novel. So instead of hundreds dead, I upped it to thousands." Many critics have agreed with Gene H. Bell-Villada: "The episode of the banana strike and military repression in *One Hundred Years of Solitude* constitutes the highest point in García Márquez's extensive chronicle of Macondo. It is a vivid and dramatic scene, packed with sociopolitical suspense, capped with sanguinary horror, and followed by uncanny official silence."

In a biblical allusion to the Great Flood, Macondo is next besieged by a four-year rain, referred to as "The Deluge," that plunges the town into decline. As *One Hundred Years of Solitude* proceeds, names and incidents recur with increasing frequency, confusing the identities of both the male heirs, who are usually named Aureliano or José Arcadio, as well as female descendants, who often bear the names Remedios, Amaranta, or Úrsula. The Aurelianos are solitary dreamers of small physical stature who pursue illusory quests without experiencing true revelation; the Arcadios are large, strong, adventurous men who die without leaving any effect on society. The various female characters named Amaranta and Remedios are generally virgins who unwittingly radiate danger for men who fall under their charms; a male suitor seeking the first Amaranta's hand commits suicide after being rejected, and another man suffers a cracked skull while attempting to watch Remedios the Beauty as she bathes. By contrast, many commentators have noted that the first Úrsula, who lives through most of the novel, provides a locus of unity and human dignity by administering to numerous family crises and serving as a voice of conscience to the less practical male characters.

The final section of *One Hundred Years of Solitude* chronicles the extinction of the Buendía bloodline. Aureliano Babilonia, an illegitimate member of the family who is unaware of his relation to the Buendías, lives his last days in the purely instinctual pursuit of carnal bliss with his aunt, Amaranta Úrsula. After Amaranta Úrsula dies giving birth to a baby with the fated pig's tail, Aureliano Babilonia watches as the last of the Buendía line turns into "a dry and bloated bag of skin that all the ants in the world were dragging toward their holes." Toward the end of the novel, Aureliano discovers how to decipher the prophecies of the gypsy Melquíades, who had returned earlier to stay with the Buendías and had written their entire history on parchments in a language and code inaccessible to previous family members. As Aureliano Babilonia grasps the Buendía family history in its entirety, all illusions are destroyed and *One Hundred Years of Solitude* turns in on itself, returning to the notion of past, present, and future occurring in a single instant of time. Macondo is revealed through the parchments to be a mere fictional creation; as Aureliano Babilonia, a surrogate for the reader, finishes the last sentence of Melquíades' manuscript he deciphers the manner of his own death and a whirlwind sweeps down upon Macondo, returning the town to dust. The cyclical nature of the Buendías' existence, whose end was implied in its beginning, is thus validated in the reader's mind; as Úrsula noted of the constant repetition of names and incidents in the Buendía household, "time did not pass, . . . it went around in circles."

(See also *Contemporary Authors,* Vols. 33-36, rev. ed.; *Contemporary Authors New Revision Series,* Vols. 10, 28; and *Dictionary of Literary Biography Yearbook: 1982.*)

PRINCIPAL WORKS

NOVELS

La mala hora 1962
[*In Evil Hour,* 1979]
Cien años de soledad 1967
[*One Hundred Years of Solitude,* 1970]
El otoño del patriarca 1975
[*The Autumn of the Patriarch,* 1975]
El amor en los tiempos del cólera 1985
[*Love in the Time of Cholera,* 1988]
El general en su laberinto 1989
[*The General in His Labyrinth,* 1990]

SHORT FICTION AND SHORT FICTION COLLECTIONS

La hojarasca (novella) 1955
[*Leaf Storm,* published in *Leaf Storm and Other Stories,* 1972]
El coronel no tiene quien le escriba (novella) 1961
[*No One Writes to the Colonel,* published in *No One Writes to the Colonel and Other Stories,* 1968]
**Los funerales de la Mamá Grande* 1962
No One Writes to the Colonel and Other Stories (novella and short stories) 1968
***La increíble y triste historia de la cándida Eréndira y de su abuela desalmada* 1972
Leaf Storm and Other Stories 1972
***Ojos de perro azul* 1972
Todos los cuentos de Gabriel García Márquez: 1947-1972 1975
Innocent Eréndira and Other Stories 1978
Crónica de una muerta anunciada (novella) 1981
[*Chronicle of a Death Foretold,* 1982]
Collected Stories 1985
Collected Novellas 1990

OTHER

La novela en América Latina: Diálogo [with Mario Vargas Llosa] (dialogue) 1968
†*Relato de un náufrago . . .* (journalism) 1970
[*The Story of a Shipwrecked Sailor,* 1986]
Cuando era feliz e undocumentado (journalism) 1973
Crónicas y reportajes (journalism) 1976
Periodismo militante (journalism) 1978

*The stories in this collection are published together with the novella *No One Writes to the Colonel* in *No One Writes to the Colonel and Other Stories.*

**The stories in these collections are published in *Innocent Eréndira and Other Stories.*

†This work was originally published in 1955.

I. INITIAL REVIEWS

Paul West

To put it one way: [***One Hundred Years of Solitude***] is a chronicle of the Buendía family, whose successive generations have lived and died in a mythical Latin-American town called Macondo, and its framework is a family tree (printed at the front of the book) which shows that the astounding progenitor José Arcadio Buendía married Ursula Iguarán and thus produced Colonel Aureliano Buendía (who married Remedios Moscote), that José Arcadio married Rebeca, and that—out there on a limb of her own—Amaranta married nobody at all.

But this extraordinary novel obliterates the family tree in a prose jungle of overwhelming magnificence, even to the extent of only infrequently letting the people talk in their own right. I haven't read this Colombian author in his native Spanish, but Gregory Rabassa's translation is a triumph of fluent, gravid momentum, all stylishness and commonsensical virtuosity.

Above all, García Márquez (*via* his translator) feeds the mind's eye non-stop, so much so that you soon begin to feel that never has what we superficially call the surface of life had so many corrugations and configurations, so much bewilderingly impacted detail, or men so many grandiose movements and tics, so many bizarre stances and airs. So I find it odd that the blurb points to "the simplicity, ease, and purity" of García Márquez's writing while a quoted review of his previous book, ***No One Writes to the Colonel,*** mentions its "serenity" and "understatement." That's like calling a mammoth a moth. Let it be said at once that, although this man's sentences are immaculately built, the vision they contain is violent and lurid enough to make the works of two better-known Latin-Americans, J. L. Borges and Julio Cortázar, look (respectively) mincing and pretty.

Take García Márquez at his mildest:

> He sold everything, even the tame jaguar that teased passers-by from the courtyard of his house, and he bought an eternal ticket on a train that never stopped traveling. In the postcards that he sent from the way stations he would describe with shouts the instantaneous images that he had seen from the window of his coach, and it was as if he were tearing up and throwing into oblivion some long, evanescent poem: the chimerical Negroes in the cotton fields of Louisiana, the winged horses in the bluegrass of Kentucky, the Greek lovers in the infernal sunsets of Arizona, the girl in the red sweater painting watercolors by a lake in Michigan who waved at him with her brushes, not to say farewell but out of hope, because she did not know that she was watching a train with no return passing by.

It's a prose that's always controlled, but it expresses a vision full of lunges, spurts, mild or maniacal hallucinations, preternatural heavings and bulging gargoyles. Tracing the growth of Macondo—from jungle village into a town served by a railroad and then into ghost town—García Márquez is rather like an infatuated god watching a planet seethe and bubble, settle and cool, and then develop forms of life that finally annihilate themselves. The town, of course, is made of prose, as is the ever-encroaching jungle; and, such is the prose's dense physical immediacy, you have the sense of living along with the Buendías (and the rest), in them, through them, and in spite of them, in all their loves, madnesses and wars, their alliances, compromises, dreams and deaths. The book stages a process in which naming doesn't matter so long as the characters rear up large and rippling with life against the green pressure of nature itself.

In other words, you feel magnified, anthropologically enlarged, by having to fight for air and space and sanity against: José Arcadio Buendía who, against the day when all memories have been lost, hangs a sign on the cow explaining what she's for and thinks about a spinning dictionary with a man lying along its axis; José Arcadio the giant who, with a religious medal around his bison neck, his arms and chest tattooed all over, and a belt twice the width of a horse's cinch, eats sixteen raw eggs on waking: Colonel Aureliano Buendía who organizes thirty-two armed uprisings and loses them all, who has seventeen male children by seventeen different women (and loses *them* all in one night before the eldest reaches thirty-five), who survives fourteen attempts on his life, seventy-three ambushes, one firing squad and a dose of strychnine in his coffee enough to kill a horse, and who finally draws a chalk line round himself so that no one shall come too near; a vast woman called the Elephant who at an eating contest consumes a whole side of veal without breaking a single rule of table manners and thereafter polishes off two pigs, a bunch of bananas and four cases of champagne; José Arcadio Segundo who locks himself up for six months with seventy-two chamberpots; Gaston who waits years for a small biplane from his past to arrive above the treetops; and the Aureliano, last of the line, whose newborn son has a pig's tail extending from his coccyx and, only hours after birth, is dragged away by millions of ants.

It's not often that you find a Technicolor tableau of fools which, got up as a family saga, stretches the mind by cramming it and reenacts paradise found and lost as a version of Latin America's own history as well as of (I suspect) one man's love-hate feelings for his own bombinating imagination. Knowing his material inside-out, García Márquez writes it large without losing sight of its true size or of the inexorable truths that hold good for all lives everywhere. The verbal Mardi Gras which is his mode of narrating invokes a before and an after (birth and death) which no hyperboles, his or ours, can alter. Like the jungle itself, this novel comes back again and again, fecund, savage and irresistible. (pp. 4-5)

Paul West, "A Green Thought in a Green Shade," in Book World—Chicago Tribune, *February 22, 1970, pp. 4-5.*

John Leonard

You emerge from this marvelous novel [***One Hundred Years of Solitude***] as if from a dream, the mind on fire. A dark, ageless figure at the hearth, part historian, part haruspex, in a voice by turns angelic and maniacal, first lulls to sleep your grip on a manageable reality, then locks you into legend and myth. ***One Hundred Years of Solitude*** is not only the story of the Buendía family and the Colombian town of Macondo. It is also a recapitulation of our evolutionary and intellectual experience. Macondo is Latin America in microcosm: local autonomy yielding to state authority; anticlericalism; party politics; the coming of the United Fruit Company; aborted revolutions; the rape of innocence by history. And the Buendías (inventors, artisans, soldiers lovers, mystics) seem doomed to ride a biological tragi-cycle in circles from solitude to magic to poetry to science to politics to violence back again to solitude.

Which isn't to say that the book is grimly programmatic. It is often wildly funny, and superbly translated by Gregory Rabassa. Nor does the specific get buried under the symbolic. Macondo with its rains, ghosts, priests, Indians, Arabs and gypsies, is splendidly evoked. So richly realized are the Buendías that they invite comparison with Karamazovs and Sartorises. Indeed, specificity overwhelms incredulity, setting up the reader for imagist explosions more convincing than mere data can ever be: Anything goes, and everything comes back.

Would you believe, for instance, men with machetes in search of the sea hacking their way through "bloody lilies and golden salamanders" to find in a swamp a Spanish galleon? A plague of insomnia? A stream of blood feeling its path across a city from a dying son to a grieving mother? A mule that eats sheets, rugs, bedspreads, drapes and "the canopy embroidered with gold thread and silk tassels on the episcopal bed"? A Sanskrit manuscript predicting the 100 years of Macondo, down to the very deciphering of the prediction by the last Buendía? A paterfamilias chained to a tree in the garden, muttering in Latin? Or, when that paterfamilias finally dies, this consequence:

> A short time later, when the carpenter was taking measurements for the coffin, through the window they saw a light rain of tiny yellow flowers falling. They fell on the town all through the night in a silent storm, and they covered the roofs and blocked the doors and smothered the animals who slept outside. So many flowers fell from the sky that in the morning the streets were carpeted with a compact cushion and they had to clear them away with shovels and rakes so that the funeral procession could pass by.

I believe—in the last Buendía infant born as prophesized with the tail of a pig, and eaten alive by ants. In the brothel with alligators. In the 3,000 dead strikers against the banana plantation, hauled away by silent train; and Remedios the Beauty, plucked up by the wind and flown to God as she hung up bedsheets to dry; and Melquíades, who introduces Macondo to the miracle of ice. I believe in all the Buendías, from the original José Arcadio and the original Ursula (cousins who marry and by mythic mitosis divide into generations of Arcadios and Aurelianos and Armarantas) down through "the most intricate labyrinths of blood" to the end of the family line in a room full of chamber pots in "the city of mirrors (or mirages)" as the wind comes to sweep away all memory.

Family chronicle, then, and political tour de force, and metaphysical speculation, and, intentionally, a cathedral of words, perceptions and legends that amounts to the declaration of a state of mind: solitude being one's admission of one's own mortality and one's discovery that that terrible apprehension is itself mortal, dies with you, must be rediscovered and forgotten again, endlessly. With a single bound, Gabriel García Márquez leaps onto the stage with Günter Grass and Vladimir Nabokov, his appetite as enormous as his imagination, his fatalism greater than either. Dazzling.

John Leonard, "Myth Is Alive in Latin America," in The New York Times, *March 3, 1970, p. 39.*

Jack Richardson

Since its publication in 1967, Gabriel García Márquez's ***Cien años de soledad*** [***One Hundred Years of Solitude***] has provoked throughout Latin America reactions far beyond those of ordinary critical approval. Indeed, this novel by a Colombian writer who has lived in Europe for the last fifteen years has been welcomed, written about, and discussed by Spanish readers with an almost relieved exuberance, as if to suggest that the style and sensibility of their history had at last been represented by a writer who understands their particular secrets and rhythms, by a writer who, moreover, presents these qualities with a classic lucidity and humor, and whose art is large enough to include the rough and the fastidious taste, to be epic at a time when so much of what is interesting in literature belongs to the idiosyncratic and consciously complex—certainly timely qualities for our fiction, but qualities not particularly suited to an imagination which wishes to span a century of narrative or catch the essence of an entire culture.

One has only to read a few pages of Márquez's novel to understand the response it has occasioned. Immediately, the reader senses in its style a simple audaciousness which alerts him to the premise that he is attending to something more than an ordinary chronicle of fiction, that he is being presented, rather, with a work that presumes nothing, that starts from a beginning both in literary and historical time, as if existence itself had no previous records or memories. Although ***La hojarasca (Dead Leaves)*** and ***Los funerales de la Mamá Grande (Big Mama's Funeral),*** earlier works by Márquez, used the town of Macondo and its people for their subject, ***Cien años de soledad,*** . . . while occasionally referring to events recounted in the two previous collections of stories, moves on to a new level of narrative, a level more inclusive and distant, more robust and magical, than the earlier tales about the inhabitants of this imaginary South American town.

Having examined the fictional reality of his characters in short, perceptive sketches, Márquez seems here to transport them into a literary myth, a myth which at once sets them permanently beyond the common laws of life and at the same moment dissolves them forever in a deliberate act of artistic obliteration. ***Cien años de soledad*** may indeed be a depiction of a time and a culture, but Márquez also makes it clear that his tale is more a dream of art than a collection of social and historical truths, and, at the work's end, when this dream takes on the force of a metaphor for all the cycles of human life that have vanished, one realizes that the excellence of this book lies in its victory over the quaint and anecdotal, in its sustained vision of the vanities and futile passions with which humanity tries to forestall its fate of being, in art and actuality, comically impermanent.

I emphasize the formal aspect of ***Cien años de soledad*** only so that it will not be taken by English readers for a Hispanic *Forsyte Saga,* or a regional fairy tale stuffed with Latin whimsy and emotional outrageousness. Márquez, in following the rise and decline of the Buendía family, of course makes use of themes that have turned up often before in the literature of his continent. Futile revolution, Yankee imperialism, governmental lunacy, ludicrous *machismo,* doomed passion, voracious nature—Márquez boldly makes use of all of these old concepts of South American private and political history, but his method is to extend and inflate these notions until they become so grand that the reader feels that he has been presented with final configurations of things which have been only hinted at before, that he is encountering characters whose direct antecedents have been only tentative and inchoate and whose future descendants can never be more than epigoni. In short, Márquez has not only rounded out and fixed these motifs, but, by an extension of artistic logic, has made of them symbols by which subtle patterns of life can be forever held in our memory.

Cien años de soledad, first of all, is a novel in which event and time are conjoined, where straight chronicle is mixed with memory and a linear narrative is subject to the temporal capriciousness of its author. Márquez begins his book by the evocation of a distant and Eden-like epoch:

> Many years later, as he faced the firing squad, Colonel Aureliano Buendía was to remember that distant afternoon when his father took him to discover ice. At that time Macondo was a village of twenty adobe houses, built on the bank of a river of clear water that ran along a bed of polished stones, which were white and enormous, like prehistoric eggs. The world was so recent that many things lacked names, and in order to indicate them it was necessary to point. Every year during the month of March a family of ragged gypsies would set up their tents near the village, and with a great uproar of pipes and kettle-drums they would display new inventions.

A pleasant and pristine world, but a world already shadowed by that firing squad in the first line, a world just about to be invaded by outlandish knowledge. At once, we know we are not only in the memory of a character but also in a historic and mythical moment. From this first paragraph, there is a continuous shift through time which gives the lively incidents and swaggering action in the succeeding pages the quality of seeming anticipated or mournfully recalled, and Márquez's characters appear, even at their most rambunctious, as beings dreadfully mortal if not outright ghostly. This sense of the ironies of time deepens and qualifies the ebullient, carnival moments of ***Cien años de soledad,*** making them seem, for all their lust and strength, painfully fragile tokens of all that is forever dying with great human fuss and style.

"[*Cien años de soledad*] is more a dream of art than a collection of social and historical truths, and, at the work's end, . . . one realizes that the excellence of this book lies in its victory over the quaint and the anecdotal, in its sustained vision of the vanities and futile passions with which humanity tries to forestall its fate of being, in art and actuality, comically impermanent."

—Jack Richardson

Although there are many ways of approaching the structure of this novel, it is perhaps simplest to begin with the chronicle of the Buendía family. The patriarch of the clan, José Arcadio Buendía, with some twenty other young men and their wives, founds the village of Macondo and, though discontented with his achievement, makes of its initial years a nearly perfect community. This first Buendía is like a spiritual conquistador, a man hungering for new experience and knowledge, a man for whom no fact of science will ever live up to what he imagines can be found out about the world. A fine, compassionate leader, he nevertheless dreams further perfections of this world until these visions at last drive him mad and, deep in an amiable lunacy, he spends his last years tied to a chestnut tree in his orchard, babbling in a hyperbolic, medieval Latin arguments against all the imagined proofs for the existence of God.

The son of José Arcadio, Colonel Aureliano Buendía, moves Macondo out of its isolation into political conflict. As the military leader of a progressively vague and ill-defined revolution against a nebulous dictatorial government, the Colonel fights one meaningless battle after another, slowly being brutalized out of life in the process, so that when at last peace is signed, he has the will only to cast and recast tiny golden fish, in a stultifying reenactment of his futile military campaigns. He becomes one of those heroes whom a country would rather forget, and he dies in the peculiar solitude of those men who were once adored by thousands.

With the death of the Colonel, Macondo begins to decline, battered by history. Its government's collusion with foreign imperialism begins to corrode the community, distending it unnaturally through the importation of cheap labor, and dispiriting it by handing to an insatiable banana company power over its people, who at first do not understand the company's intentions and, only too late, discover that they have been cajoled into bondage. Two grandsons of the Colonel, the twins Aureliano Segundo and José Arcadio Segundo, reflect the town's melancholy transition: the former, caught between the easeful sensuality of his mistress and the social delusions of his bourgeois wife, becomes a genial orgiast, someone always in need of company, continually arranging feasts and revels that continue for days; the latter, having witnessed an execution as a child, has a sense of human viciousness which makes him less receptive to the sportive in life. He finally becomes an organizer in a workers' strike against the banana company and is forced into a stunned and isolated retirement after government troops massacre his followers and their families in the town square. No one, except himself, will admit to having seen the slaughter or even to the fact that such an event ever took place.

The last Buendías spend their days in passionate incest. Aureliano Babilonia, an illegitimate member of the household, and his aunt Amaranta dart naked through the crumbling family house, seeking each other out in bursts of lovemaking, indifferent to the insects and plant life that are gradually reclaiming all of Macondo back from the human will that created and sustained it. These lovers live in an erotic dream that permits them to return to the pure and pleasurable life of instinct, a life without a past or a future to question the delight they discover again and again in their bodies. They produce the last Buendía, a boy, who, at the base of his spine, sprouts a small "pig's tail," a twisted, cartilaginous growth that is a sign not only of a genetic breakdown but of the terrible fulfillment of an old prophecy: that the coupling of the Buendías would produce just such a deformity. For over a hundred years, the family has struggled through aspirations, dreams, war, birth and death to avoid ending in aberration, but has at last ended with a monstrosity, the melancholy sign of all that it has created. Not a day after his birth, the ultimate Buendía is carried off and devoured by an army of ants, and the line comes to an end.

So far, I have emphasized the men of the Buendía family, for it is they who provide the extravagant action of the book. The women, however, provide the dignity, and, in the long line of their lives, hold the work together, preventing it from becoming a mere joining of fragmented incidents. The will and spirit of Úrsula, especially, the wife of the first Buendía, José Arcadio, gives structure to the entire book. Úrsula's demands in the world are small: to endure, to keep life moving on with some degree of honor and respect, to keep a natural sanity about things that can only be shaken when those she loves prove themselves brutal. Through generation after generation of her family she lives on, overcoming grand and petty calamities, growing blind and wizened, finally dwindling to nothing but a bent little toy for her great-grandchildren's amusement, yet never giving up her sensible notion that there must be some decent goal to be reached after all the frenzy and passion she has witnessed. And then there are Amaranta, Úrsula's daughter, who, because of a bad moment of love as a girl, spins out the rest of her long existence doing embroidery, held to life only by the desire to outlive the women she hates; and Pilar, the village whore, who populates Macondo with bastards fathered by the young men of three generations while waiting for the perfect man promised by her Tarot pack. It is no wonder that Márquez gives his women long lives, for they seem far more able to make a pact with life than the men. When Colonel Buendía dies, one feels the poignancy in the death of a single being; but when Úrsula is buried, one understands that life itself can be worn down to nothing.

At the heart of ***Cien años de soledad*** is its magic, a magic that moves from the simply phenomenal—a levitating priest, a flock of yellow butterflies that flit ominously about a young seducer, plants that bleed when cut, countless ghosts that are accepted as part of the natural landscape—to the core of Márquez's world. In this world, as I have said, beings shuffle back and forth in time, and the ordinary has been so clearly seen and relentlessly followed to its conclusion that the world itself becomes more than natural, becomes, instead, a wild conjuring of things which may seem to be set in reality but which slide imperceptibly into the fantastic.

As we reach the last pages of ***Cien años de soledad*** we discover, when Aureliano Babilonia deciphers a stack of old papers, that we have been reading the history of Macondo and the Buendías as recorded by one Melquíades, the chief of the gypsy band whom we encountered on the first page in the memory of Colonel Buendía. It is Melquíades who, in his skeptical, creative gypsy mind, has held the past, present, and future of Macondo as if they were but an instant of thought, he who has told the story, with wild embellishments and excesses, he who has made the magic of the whole enterprise—a magic which, once discovered, eases, allowing all the feats of imagination and sleight of hand to fade away. As a hurricane sweeps down upon the town, Aureliano reads both his own end and that of Macondo, sees, perhaps, the obliteration of the very book that created him. In a final stroke of magic and of art, Melquíades-Márquez not only ends the story of the Buendías, he eradicates it forever in one luminous moment.

In ***Cien años de soledad*** Márquez forces upon us at every page the wonder and extravagance of life, while compassionately mocking its effusions; and when the book ends with its sudden self-knowledge and its intimations of holocaust, we are left with that pleasant exhaustion which only very great novels seem to provide; for they allow us, in a moment of exquisite balance, to hold a vision—to be sure, in some fear, but also with humor—of the beginnings and ends to all the enterprises of living. Márquez, with his tale of Macondo and the Buendías, strikes such a balance and makes us feel as if we had survived his century of articulate dreams only to awaken and discover that they must finally all come true. (pp. 3-4)

Jack Richardson, "Master Builder," in The New York Review of Books, *Vol. XIV, No. 6, March 26, 1970, pp. 3-4.*

D. J. Enright

[***One Hundred Years of Solitude***] is the long, episodic, fantastic and violent story of the Buendia family who founded a town called Macondo, in the South American jungle—or out of this world. In early days Gypsies form the settlement's only link with the outside world, bringing such wonders as the magnet and the magnifying glass and (for here the mundane is for ever mingling with the miraculous) a flying carpet. Later the village loses its memory, and they must hang signs on everything, indicating, for example, that 'this is a cow. She must be milked every morning so that she will produce milk.' All this is charming and splendidly inventive, but unfortunately civil war is *de rigueur* and the realistic thud of rifle butts doesn't harmonise too well with magic. . . .

From the protracted 'revolution', with its rather hack LatinAmerican mixture of panache and squalor, it is a pleasure to turn to the Buendia women. In all innocence, Remedios the Beauty is a *femme fatale* whose perfume drives men mad. One afternoon—there are three levitations in the novel, but this is the most elevated—she rises into the sky and is seen no more. Other characters fail to disappear even after death: Macondo is full of revenants.

The seeds of ruin lie in the Titan-like Buendias themselves, but one agent of destruction is the harmless banana: when the plantation workers strike, over 3,000 of the townspeople are massacred, their bodies vanish, and the gringo boss invokes rain which lasts for five years. Time is circling back towards its beginning, and the Gypsies reappear with magnet and magnifying glass. Aunt and nephew fall savagely in love and the predicted monster is born, a child with a pig's tail. Amaranta Ursula bleeds to death, and when Aureliano, the last of that name, recovers his wits, he finds that nothing is left of the baby but 'a dry and bloated bag of skin that all the ants in the world were dragging toward their holes'. He is then able to decipher the parchments written in Sanskrit and code by the ancient Gypsy guru, Melquiades, which set forth the whole story of the family, and as he ends them, so Macondo ends, swept from the earth by a whirlwind.

The novel has been hailed in various quarters as a comic masterpiece. Comic? Colourful it certainly is, with the black of plague, the red of blood and the yellow of mysterious, magical flowers and butterflies. But the giants who populate it seldom laugh, except in drunken orgy, and the tragic and the futile far outweigh the comic. Comedy is peripheral, as when José Arcadio, founder of the line, seeks to prove the existence of God with the help of a daguerreotype.

These are no happy giants or jolly grotesques: the sense of doom thickens rapidly after the initial Adamic phase. The family achievement is that the family lasts, in despite of its own madness and destructiveness, for 100 years. The matriarch Ursula has that precarious satisfaction. And Aureliano Segundo and his concubine Petra Cotes, after years of lust and humiliation, attain in age to the only peaceful love in the book, until Aureliano Segundo dies, painfully though fairly conventionally (except that his twin brother dies at the same instant), of what seems to be cancer of the throat. But the founder ends his life tied to a tree, himself more arboreal than human, and Colonel Aureliano, dominant figure of the novel, turns from 20 years of senseless fighting to making little gold fishes which he then melts down in order to remake them. Life doesn't accommodate itself to those who are larger than life. Both the civil war and the banana company damage Macondo hideously. The giants are trapped, tied each to his own tree; they repeat their disasters until the wheel has come full circle. Before then one of the last generation is told that he takes his name from a former street—though the street was named after the Colonel. What each of them has suffered, whether a recluse like Rebeca or a man of action like the Colonel, is solitude, a word which echoes through the novel: they are all marked with 'the pox of solitude'.

The book is hardly comic. Whether it is a masterpiece is more difficult to say. Its attractions, unnaturally natural and preternatural, are obvious, and they appeal to a strong human appetite. Yet finally I think the Buendias approach just a little too closely to Charles Addams's family of ghouls. Thomas Mann's *Buddenbrooks* has the advantage in that, without impoverishment by any crude or restrictive 'realism', it concerns a family, a society and a group of individuals whom we comprehend intellectually: it is nearer to us in our waking hours, where ***One Hundred Years of Solitude*** is nearer to our dreams.

> Our revels now are ended: these our actors,
> As I foretold you, were all spirits, and
> Are melted into air, into thin air . . .

We think of these lines as the novel closes: but there is no Prospero here, even less a Miranda and Ferdinand, and no Naples to recover [as in Shakespeare's *The Tempest*]. This novel is essentially an enormous and rich rag-bag, even over-rich, a vigorous and yet slightly bloated avatar of the austere Jorge Luis Borges.

D. J. Enright, "Larger than Death," in The Listener, *Vol. 84, No. 2160, August 20, 1970, p. 252.*

II. INTERVIEWS

García Márquez [Interview with Rita Guibert]

[*The following interview was conducted in New York City on June 3, 1971.*]

[*Guibert*]: *How has the success of* **One Hundred Years of Solitude** *affected your life? I remember your saying in Barcelona, "I'm tired of being García Márquez."*

[García Márquez]: It's changed my whole life. I was once asked, I can't remember where, how my life differed before and after that book, and I said that after it "there are four hundred more people." That's to say before the book I had my friends, but now there are enormous numbers of people who want to see me and talk to me—journalists, academics, readers. It's strange . . . most of my readers aren't interested in asking questions, they only want to talk about the book. That's very flattering if you consider case by case, but added up they begin to be a problem in one's life. I would like to please them all, but as that's impossible I have to act meanly . . . you see? For instance, by saying I'm leaving a town when all I'm really doing is changing my hotel. That's how vedettes behave, something I always hated, and I don't want to play the vedette. There is, besides, a problem of conscience when deceiving people and dodging them. All the same I have to lead my own life, so the moment comes when I tell lies. Well, that can be boiled down to a cruder phrase than the one you mentioned. I say, "I've had it to the balls with García Márquez!" (pp. 310-11)

Melvin Maddocks of Life, *said of* **One Hundred Years of Solitude,** *"Is Macondo meant to be taken as a sort of surrealistic history of Latin America? Or does García Márquez intend it as a metaphor for all modern men and their ailing communities?"*

Nothing of the sort. I merely wanted to tell the story of a family who for a hundred years did everything they could to prevent having a son with a pig's tail, and just because of their very efforts to avoid having one they ended by doing so. Synthetically speaking, that's the plot of the book, but all that about symbolism . . . not at all. Someone who isn't a critic said that the interest the novel had aroused was probably due to the fact that it was the first real description of the private life of a Latin American family . . . we go into the bedroom, the bathroom, the kitchen, into every corner of the house. Of course I never said to myself, "I shall write a book that will be interesting for that reason," but now that it's written, and this has been said about it, I think it may be true. Anyway it's an interesting concept and not all that shit about a man's destiny, etc. . . .

I think the theme of solitude is a predominant one in your work.

It's the only subject I've written about, from my first book until the one I'm working on now, which is an apotheosis of the theme of solitude. Of absolute power, which I consider must be total solitude. I've been writing about that process from the first. The story of Colonel Aureliano Buendía—the wars he fought and his progress to power—is really a progress toward solitude. Not only is every member of his family solitary—as I've repeated often in the book, perhaps more than I ought—but there's also the anti-solidarity, even of people who sleep in the same bed. I think the critics who most nearly hit the mark were those who concluded that the whole disaster of Macondo—which is a telluric disaster as well—comes from this lack of solidarity—the solitude which results when everyone is acting for himself alone. That's then a political concept, and interests me as such—to give solitude the political connotation I believe it should have.

When you were writing it, were you consciously intending to convey a message?

I never think about conveying messages. My mental makeup is ideological and I can't get away from it—nor do I try or want to. Chesterton said that he could explain Catholicism starting from a pumpkin or a tramway. I think one could write ***One Hundred Years of Solitude,*** or a story about sailors, or the description of a football match, and still keep its ideological content. It's the ideological spectacles I wear that explain—not Catholicism in this case—but something else which I can't define. I have no preconceived intention to say this or the other thing in a book of mine. I'm solely interested in the behavior of the characters, not whether that behavior is exemplary or reprehensible.

Are you interested in your characters from a psychoanalytical point of view?

No, because that would need a scientific training which I don't possess. The opposite happens. I develop my characters and work on them, in the belief that I'm only making use of their poetical aspects. When a character has been assembled, some of the experts tell me that this is a psychoanalytic analysis. And I'm confronted then with a series of scientific assumptions that I don't hold and have never even dreamed of. In Buenos Aires—a city of psychoanalysts, as you know—some of them held a meeting to analyze ***One Hundred Years of Solitude.*** They came to the conclusion that it represented a well-sublimated Oedipus complex, and goodness knows what else. They discovered that the characters were perfectly coherent from a psychoanalytic point of view, they almost seemed like case histories.

And they talked about incest too.

What interested me was that the aunt should go to bed with her nephew, not the psychoanalytic origins of this event.

It still seems strange that, although machismo *is one of the typical features of Latin American society, it's the women in your books who have strong, stable characters—or, as you've said yourself, they are masculine.*

This didn't happen consciously, the critics made me see it, and set me a problem by so doing, because I now find it more difficult to work on that material. But there's no doubt that it's the power of women in the home—in society as it's organized, particularly in Latin America—that enables men to launch out into every sort of chimerical and strange adventure, which is what makes our America. This idea came to me from one of the true stories my grandmother used to tell about the civil wars of the last century, which can be more or less equated with Colonel Aureliano Buendía's wars. She told me that a certain man went to the war and said to his wife, "You'll decide what to do with your children." And for a year or more the wife was the one who kept the family going. In terms of literature, I see that if it weren't for the women taking responsibility for the rearguard, the evil wars of the last century, which are so important in the history of our country, would never have taken place.

That shows that you're not antifeminist.

What I most definitely am is anti*machista. Machismo* is cowardly, a lack of manliness. (pp. 314-16)

What is the starting point of your novels?

A completely visual image. I suppose that some writers begin with a phrase, an idea, or a concept. I always begin with an image. The starting point of ***Leaf Storm*** is an old man taking his grandson to a funeral, in ***No One Writes to the Colonel*** it's an old man waiting, and in ***One Hundred Years,*** an old man taking his grandson to the fair to find out what ice is.

They all begin with an old man. . . .

The guardian angel of my infancy was an old man—my grandfather. My parents didn't bring me up, they left me in my grandparents' house. My grandmother used to tell me stories and my grandfather took me to see things. Those were the circumstances in which my world was constructed. And now I'm aware that I always see the image of my grandfather showing me things. (p. 323)

García Márquez and Rita Guibert, in an interview in Seven Latin American Writers Talk to Rita Guibert, *translated by Frances Partridge, Alfred A. Knopf, 1973, pp. 305-37.*

García Márquez [Interview with Gene H. Bell-Villada]

[*Bell-Villada*]: *How many languages has* **One Hundred Years of Solitude** *been translated into?*

[García Márquez]: Thirty-seven at my wife's latest count. (p. 26)

Outside of Spanish, which language has it sold best in?

It's hard to track down. The first Russian edition sold a million copies, in their foreign literature magazine. Apparently they're preparing translations into other Soviet languages too. The Italian version has done well, I believe. There are also pirated editions in Greek and Farsee—oh, and in Arabic. Arab readers seem to like the book. I hear those pirated translations aren't very good, though.

There's a very famous strike scene in **One Hundred Years.** *Was it much trouble for you to get it right?*

That sequence sticks closely to the facts of the United Fruit strike of 1928, which dates from my childhood; I was born that year. The only exaggeration is in the number of dead, though it does fit the proportions of the novel. So instead of hundreds dead, I upped it to thousands. But it's strange, a Colombian journalist the other day alluded in passing to "the thousands who died in the 1928 strike." As my Patriarch says: it doesn't matter if something isn't true, because eventually it will be!

You maintain a certain lightness of tone in that scene.

The Yankees are depicted the way the local people saw them, hence the caricature with Virginia hams and blue pills. You see, some of my relatives back then had defended the Americans and blamed the strikers for "sabotaging prosperity" and all that, so this was my reply. Of course, my own view of Americans is a lot more complex, and I attempted to convey those events without any hate.

Your **One Hundred Years of Solitude** *is required reading in many history and political science courses in the U.S. There's a sense that it's the best general introduction to Latin America. How have you felt about that?*

I wasn't aware of that fact in particular, but I've had some interesting experiences along those lines. René Dumont, the French economist, recently published a lengthy academic study of Latin America. Well, right there in his bibliography, listed amid all the scholarly monographs and statistical analyses, was ***One Hundred Years of Solitude***! On another occasion a sociologist from Austin, Texas came to see me because he'd grown dissatisfied with his methods, found them arid, insufficient. So he asked me what my own method was. I told him I didn't have a method. All I do is read a lot, think a lot, and rewrite constantly. It's not a scientific thing.

Some left-wing critics take you to task for not furnishing a more positive vision of Latin America. How do you answer them?

Yes, that happened to me in Cuba a while ago, where some critics gave ***One Hundred Years of Solitude*** high praise and then found fault with it for not offering a solution. I told them it's not the job of novels to furnish solutions. (pp. 26-7)

You've said on occasions that Bela Bartók is a prime influence on your work. Is it the way he combined folk with classical art?

That, and his sense of structure. Bartók is one of my favorite composers; I've learned a great deal from him. My novels are filled with symmetries of the kind Bartók has in his String Quartets. (People think I'm a spontaneous writer, but I plan very carefully.) Although I've no technical knowledge of music, I can appreciate Bartók's use of form, his architecture. Bartók also had a profound feeling for his people, and for their music. His iconography is amazing, too. There's a beautiful photograph of Bartók out in the field, turning the crank on a gramophone for a peasant woman to sing into it. He worked hard, you can see.

You're a writer with a very intimate knowledge of street life and plebeian ways. What do you owe it to?

(He reflects for a moment.) It's in my origins; it's a vocation, too. It's the life I know best and I've deliberately cultivated it.

With fame, is it hard, keeping in touch with your popular roots?

It's tough, but not as much as you'd think. I can go to a local café, and at worst one person will request an autograph. What's nice is that they treat me like one of their own, especially in hotels up in the States, where they'll feel good just meeting a fellow Latin American and sharing their gripes about the U.S. But I never lose sight of the fact that I owe all these experiences to the many readers of ***One Hundred Years of Solitude.***

Where it does get difficult is at public events—literary cocktails, government functions, the like. The minute I walk through the door, I find myself surrounded by people who want to talk with me. My biggest struggle is leading my private life, so I'm always with my old friends, who shield me from the crowds.

How has being a journalist influenced your writing?

Journalism keeps you in contact with reality. I write a weekly syndicated column for ten newspapers and a magazine. And it helps, it's like a pitcher keeping his arm warmed up. You know, literary people have a tendency to get off on all sorts of unreality. Besides, if you stick to writing only books, you're always starting from zero again. (p. 27)

García Márquez and Gene H. Bell-Villada, in an interview in Boston Review, *Vol. VIII, No. 2, April, 1983, pp. 25-7.*

THE BUENDÍA FAMILY TREE

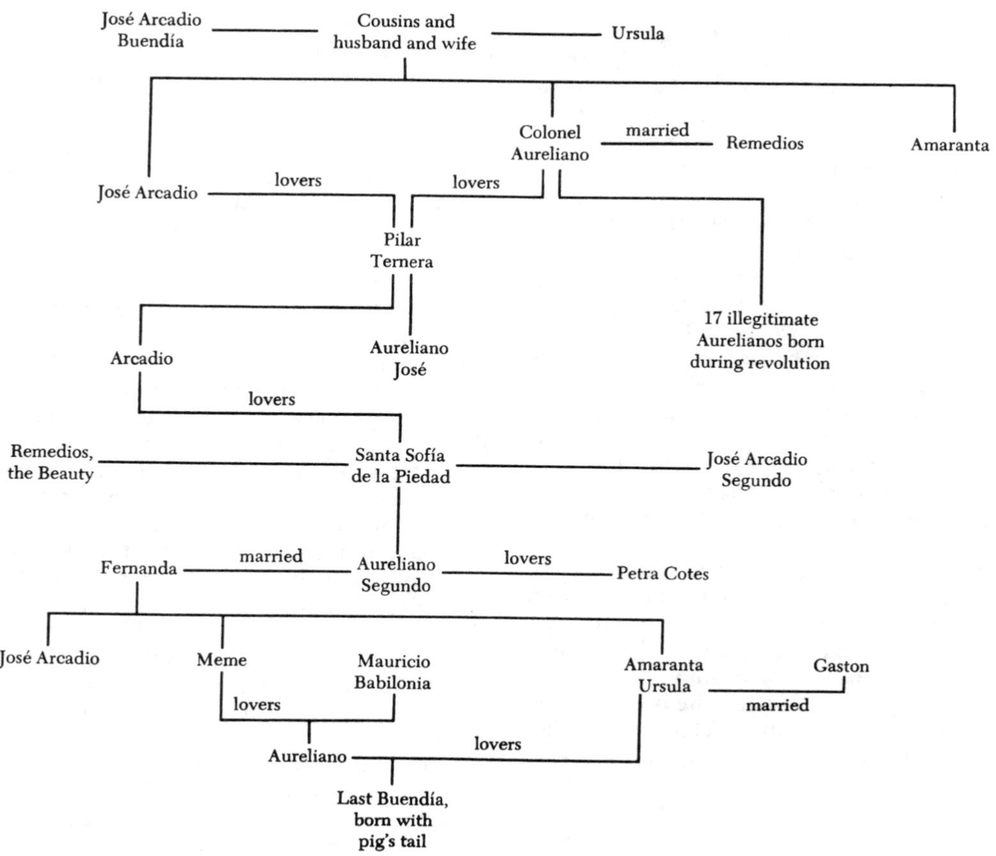

Genealogical chart of characters in One Hundred Years of Solitude.

III. SCHOLARLY ARTICLES

Ricardo Gullón

[*Gullón, a critic, essayist, and art historian who writes primarily in Spanish, is the author of* García Márquez; o, El olvidado arte de contar *(1970). In the following essay, he examines the use of such elements as space, tone, rhythm, theme, motif, and hyperbole in* One Hundred Years of Solitude.]

When speaking of the excellence of ***One Hundred Years of Solitude,*** it is not enough to say that Gabriel García Márquez has invented an original imaginary world; and yet it should not be forgotten that this is precisely what he has done. The invention is in itself a remarkable achievement, and in our day even unusual. It would not be idle to remind ourselves of something so well-known that it is usually forgotten, namely, that the creation of space in fiction is similar to that of sacred space insofar as it implies a transformation of chaos into cosmos and the imposition of order. The first impulse to accomplishing an act of creation is like the laying of a foundation, the tracing of boundaries, the making of a reservation (in the American sense of the word) where the fictional will develop.

That fictional space alternately communicates and does not communicate with the outside world, that is, with Life, is easy to understand when we consider the analogy that exists between fictional and sacred space. What has been introduced into, and assimilated by sacred and fictional space has form, whereas what remains outside does not and because of its lack of form continues to appear chaotic. For this and other reasons Gabriel García Márquez is correct in giving us the details of how the foundation is laid together with the foundation itself as indispensable parts of the novel. Macondo becomes and then *is* "the World." In that world the characters are born and from it they overflow. Everything is contained in that world and within its boundaries all the prodigious events occur. Things further removed are less dense, less consistent, almost misty, at times even formless.

One wonders how García Márquez came to create a world so similar to our everyday one and yet so totally different from it. Technically, he is a realist in the presentation of both the real and the unreal. He somehow skillfully handles a reality in which the limits of the real and the fantastic fade away quite naturally.

This feat requires analysis of his resources, beginning with the one which seems to me the most important—narrative tone. García Márquez intuitively grasped the vital relationship that exists between space and tone when he noticed that tone could serve as the main unifying force in the novel. Tone belongs by all rights to the narrator's voice, and the narrator is the Narrator: someone who is removed from his narrative; who knows all there is to know about the events; who reports them as a reporter would—calm and untouched, without comment, and without passing moral judgments on what has happened. He does not doubt or question events or facts. For him there is no difference between what is likely and what is not; he fulfills his mission—his duty—of telling all, speaking as naturally of the dead as he does of the living, associating with the greatest of ease the intangible with the tangible. His steadfastness reveals itself in his unchanging, constant tone. From the first page to the last he maintains the same tone levels, without fluctuation or variation.

Prodigious events and miracles mingle with references to village and household events. The narrator never allows it to become evident, by interjection or amazement, that there may be a substantial difference between the extraordinary and the commonplace. For example, there is a character who wakes up a ghost (whom he does not see) as he urinates on him. Phantoms may sleep and do other things that make one forget their state, just as the living may at any moment take flight without anyone's attaching the slightest importance to it. In García Márquez' novel, they all communicate easily. And why shouldn't they? They live side by side—immersed in an atmosphere which shelters them indiscriminately, making them equals. In the novel's space, proven and fabulous events are equally true, a fact which all great fiction should show.

In the *Odyssey* the Sirens are neither more nor less real than Ulysses. Understanding this fact, García Márquez breaks with the literary conventions of realism. Yet he does not stray from the tradition or from fictional reality. And his authentic presentation of events (that is to say, his tone) allows him to dispense with explanations and justifications. There is no need to justify the fact that a character dies, or appears to die, and later comes back to life, or appears to, twenty, a hundred, or five hundred years later; there is no reason to follow the clock's chronology, or the calendar's, when the only really important time is the novel's own time. One hundred years of solitude? Might it not be a hundred centuries? Might not the novel's own time be time in its totality, absolute, beginning with the awakening of humanity and ending with its expiration? Would it not be possible to calculate mathematically what the world is, put it in a nutshell and with it all of history, from Genesis to the Apocalypse?

The novel has the circular and dynamic structure of a gyrating wheel. The narrator has seen that wheel turn, and his way of relating the events which he came to see in the wheel's constant turning serves as a unifying force. Narrative authenticity becomes more readily perceptible when what is related oscillates between impossible and everyday occurrences.

As an example of this we have José Arcadio Buendía telling Prudencio Aguilar's obstinate ghost (it insists on appearing and reappearing) to go to hell, just as he would have told a bothersome neighbor.

The narration of events, we are told, was recorded twice. First, in a language unintelligible to the Macondo inhabitants (Sanscrit) by Melquíades, before they actually took place; as prophet-chronicler, he forsees what is to come (unless he has seen it in some other turn of the wheel) and anticipates it in his story. Second, by the narrator (in Spanish), after the events have occurred; he relates the past, recognizing it as such, and on the first page predicts the execution of Colonel Aureliano Buendía, which will not actually take place for years or centuries. Could the narrator be Melquíades' double, or in the terms of this novel, his reincarnation? In any case, we know that there is no discrepancy between his version and the immortal man's; one is a facsimile of the other, the result of a miracle similar to Pierre Ménard's when he unwittingly wrote a *Quixote* identical to Cervantes'. When we read on the last page that Aureliano IV deciphers Melquíades' parchments, we discover that the novel was contained in them—that they are in fact the novel—which is why they cannot be deciphered until the novel ends. The ancient papers do not allow their meaning to become clear until the prophecies are fulfilled, and the narrator describes that fulfillment step by step. He limits himself to the business of narrating: he neither predicts the future nor possesses the key to the past. Melquíades duplicates him and in some ways anticipates him; a mythical and legendary figure, he possesses special powers, and in the novel he plays multiple roles.

We do not know at the beginning what the difference consists of, even though we are aware of Melquíades' uprootedness, his readiness to be absent. We come to feel that he is only passing through Macondo. This gives him the special attribute of a being without a beginning or an end. He is not reincarnated in other people; he reappears after his spurious deaths, and when he withdraws from the novel, he does so because he has played out his role of prophet and scribe. Melquíades is successively and simultaneously alchemist, adventurer, experimenter, scientist, encyclopedic sage; he is mortal and immortal, a resurrected being. But most important, he is the wanderer who circulates freely through the space of the novel and beyond, crossing without effort the boundaries between one world and another. He serves as link and messenger between the living and the dead.

In the novel only the narrator's voice is heard; such is the demand of tonal unity. Through it the reader apprehends everything the characters say or think, their dialogues and monologues. The narrative voice is, as the tone suggests, friendly and familiar; it is a voice which instills confidence in the listener and succeeds in making itself heard and accepted without objections. The relationship between the narrative voice (that is, the narrator) and the reader is also one of familiarity, and therefore a close one. Events occur and characters parade before the reader in the most natural manner, nearby, and seemingly at the same spatial and psychological distance from him.

The narrator's speaking unfazedly, calmly (even when describing tragic events), does not prevent him from becoming a center of consciousness. Quite the contrary. The distance between the narrator and what he narrates reinforces his objectivity and allows him to speak without judging. What is said is ethically qualified because of the way it is said. The characters derive their consistency from the word and the consciousness from which that word springs; the imagery and a unique use of adjectives allow the reader to detect a value judgment which has not been formulated, but merely insinuated. When the army enters Macondo to end the great strike, the narrator says: "Its many-headed dragon-breathing impregnated the midday sunlight with pestilent vapors."

The extremely reduced distance between the reader and the characters, due to the intimacy of the narrative voice, practically disappears when a character, living his normal everyday life, performs the minute actions so familiar to the reader himself. Colonel Aureliano, without ceasing to be a kind of retired mythological figure, urinates at certain times during the day. The Colonel's regularity brings him closer to the reader, who thereby more readily identifies with him and tolerates everything else said about him in that and previous chapters.

The central character is Ursula Iguarán, wife of José Arcadio Buendía; together they make up the first couple. Ursula is both a mother and The Mother and is present throughout most of the novel. She articulates some of the key observations; her "normal" domestic activities, constructive and incessant, create a center where decisive events happen and others slowly germinate. That center is charged with the unique atmosphere which Ursula radiates. Ursula's function is to impregnate the fictional space with everyday realities so that the marvelous may enter it smoothly. Thus stabilized and "normalized," the novelistic space assimilates prodigious things and converts them into acceptable phenomena which the reader can easily admit.

García Márquez' success in creating such an atmosphere is more evident if we contrast that atmosphere to the backdrops of Gothic novels and other such narratives. Poe's castles, cemeteries, shadows, thunder, and phantasmagoria produce the opposite effects of those in ***One Hundred Years of Solitude;*** instead of fusing the extraordinary with the ordinary, such backdrops mark boundaries too sharply, thereby opposing the real to the unreal and preventing them from communicating; in Gothic tales "real" life is distinct from the fantastic episodes related.

There is still more to say about space in the novel. The Buendía house and the city of Macondo are representations of a vast universe where everything has its proper place, including time. Primordial space, which precedes creation, is not organized until the creator comes and gives objects names: "The world was so new that many things lacked names, and in order to refer to them one had to point them out." José Arcadio Buendía is the first to take space and conceptualize it, grasping it intellectually in all its fullness: "When he became expert in the use of his tools, he developed an idea of space which enabled him to sail unknown seas, visit uninhabited lands and engage in relationships with magnificent beings without ever having to leave the room." Together, José Arcadio's imagined space and Ursula's familiar space embrace everything that has ever existed or exists, from nothingness to infinity.

At least one critic, Emmanuel Carballo, has suggested the possibility that Macondo might be an equivalent of Spanish America. But it would be a mistake to narrow the scope of the novel to specific places. Though the novel may suggest parts of Colombia, it clearly transcends physical particularizing and offers instead a parable of creation, man's history and human nature.

The circular structure of the novel leads the reader from the chaos and void where creation occurs to the chaos and void where all ends and is resolved. The presence of a well-defined, concrete geographical space (Macondo) does not lessen its universality; it reinforces it. And the circularity is compatible with the plot, which moves forward in linear development, never retroceding, yet also searches constantly for its origins. The book contains no index and its chapters have no titles; it is a chain of reiterations; it is continuity itself. Names are constantly repeated. There is always a new beginning, a returning—I would almost say a reincarnation—of the characters, whose overwhelming personalities reappear continuously in accordance with the design-destiny of their names: the José Arcadios, the Aurelianos, the Remedios, the Amarantas and the Ursulas. Pilar Ternera, at once priestess and lust incarnate, knows that "the history of the Buendía family [is] a chain of irreparable repetitions, a gyrating wheel that would have continued turning forever had it not been for the gradual and inevitable wearing out of its axle." The gyrating wheel in the quotation is a suitable structural image for this novel. Because Melquíades is both magician and seer, the wheel is superfluous for him; he needs but look into the crystal ball, for in it he sees time in its totality—without duration, without past, without future. In a magical realm, events and worlds appear with a simultaneity and density that, we are told, may be captured only at the moment of death. It is no accident that Melquíades' documents guard their secrets, which may be deciphered only when the narrative concludes.

The wheel never stops; its constant motion, linking the beginning to the end, is visible in the case of Ursula. Her old age is and is not like that of others. As the years—centuries—pass, she becomes progressively smaller, "becoming mummified while alive to the point that, during her last months, she was a mere prune lost in the folds of her nightgown." That powerful image is anticipated when the narrator indicates that Ursula was becoming so "foetus-like" that she looked like "a newborn old lady." Nor is she the only one who ends up the way she started. The signs of repetition multiply in the course of the novel: at the end, the gypsies who had appeared at the beginning (years or centuries earlier) return to the village and bring once again the wonders that had earlier produced such widespread awe: the magnet, the gigantic magnifying glass, the false teeth. These objects are symbols of what is permanent in change or of what changes without ceasing to be identical to what it was. The Arab merchants are where they were before and where they will be again, "sitting in the same place and in the same posture as their parents, and grandparents, taciturn, fearless, invulnerable to time."

When Aureliano II returns to the house of his mistress, Petra Cotes, after the flood, he finds her worn out, aged, and sickly, but also beginning anew, preparing once again to engage in the activities that helped make their fortune. She was "writing numbers on scraps of paper for a raffle." Later, Ursula finds José Arcadio II in Melquíades' room and is surprised to find herself repeating something that Colonel Aureliano had said to her much earlier when she told him what José Arcadio had just told her. This is the moment of dreadful realization: "time did not pass . . . ; it went around in circles."

The contrast between tone and rhythm, which is characteristic of ***One Hundred Years of Solitude,*** is one more reason why this novel attracts, convinces and seduces the reader. If the familiar tone makes the suppression of limits between the real and the imaginary tolerable, the rhythm complements it by contrast: vertiginous beneath the apparent calm, the rhythm injects the narrative with a dynamic force that might seem incongruous with the tone. Yet this is not so: the narrator does not allow his pace to be affected by the accumulation of events. Rather, he concentrates, summarizes and equalizes them in his constant talespinning. The kaleidoscope turns, slowly shaping very different situations. So many things are compressed into the space of a few pages that one might say the narrator has overdone it. But no, he has merely reduced things to their essentials—condensed them without sacrificing vitality—and connected them through imperceptible transitions. Events accumulate naturally because of the natural tone. The transition from one delirious state to the next occurs as smoothly as the switch from the unreal to the real. Delirium is presented as trivial reality; in a state of hallucination, Amaranta is not surprised to see death sitting beside her, sewing in the hall. Reality, by logical contrast, is delirious. Wars succeed each other so rapidly that war eventually becomes a way of life. The gringos come, fleece and devour the country, destroying everything, like a plague, and then disappear. The killing of Colonel Aureliano's seventeen sons is a clear case of an event that occurs on the borderline of reality. The event lacks verisimilitude yet it *is* "real" and is told with the tonal objectivity and quick rhythm that García Márquez blends so well. In a single page the inhuman killing begins and ends.

This curious rhythm-tone symbiosis implies complete mastery of condensatory techniques, from the oxymoron to synesthesia. An example of the former: "The enchanted region" that José Arcadio Buendía explored when Macondo was founded and where banana plantations were to prosper later, "*was* a marsh of putrefied stumps." The verb "was" (which I have italicized) links the contradictory terms of the sentence. Synesthetic imagery ("delicate breeze of light") enlarges the frame of reference. Similarly, the use of paradox permits transitions to be made with verbal economy: "Ursula allowed decrepitude to drag her into the depths of darkness where only José Arcadio Buendía's ghost continued to be visible under the chestnut tree." Equally effective in the process of condensation is the systematic use of anachronisms, for they unite distant moments of time. By locating in one moment what happened in another, the author is able to stretch the temporal boundaries of his novel in a few lines: "Every time Ursula flew off the handle with rage because of her husband's follies, she skipped over three hundred years and cursed the day Francis Drake attacked Riohacha."

A sustained synthesis, ***One Hundred Years of Solitude*** covers centuries, perhaps millenia. On the first page alone we find prehistory and Arcadia (whence the "Adam" of the story—Arcadio—takes his name); then come Genesis and the journey to the "un"-promised land; the founding of the city; the plagues that devastate Macondo (insomnia and forgetfulness); the resurrection of Melquíades; and the Flood (which lasts four years, eleven months and two days), imposed as a punishment for man's sins, especially for the greed and pride of the directors of the Yankee banana company who spoil the regularity of the rainy seasons with their agricultural methods. The book contains all of History, synthesizing it in symbolic episodes such as the finding of the Spanish galleon or the arrival of the Magistrate, who brings with him the seeds of violence (of authority) that will later destroy José Arcadio's "Arcadia." Contemporary history is represented in the exemplary episodes of the corruption engendered by American banana interests; the capitalist exploitation; the poor people's strike and their execution by an Army that represents "the Law," that is, the violence which those in power (the uniformed executioners) use against the weak; the sinister black men who "legalize" the spoils; the falsification of the truth by a Government of assassins. And at the end, completing the circle, is the Apocalypse, announced from the pulpit by Father Antonio Isabel, who reads the omens as dead birds rain down, scouring the village (this episode is told in detail in the short story **"A Day After Saturday"** in ***Mamá Grande's Funeral***); a Biblical hurricane razes Macondo when the prophecies are fulfilled on the last page.

This feat of condensation takes place in 350 pages. They are taut, although somewhat slackened by the monochord tone; and they are dense, for individual and collective destinies are meshed. Each particular character's life and vital concerns are interrelated with the collective life of the town from the beginning: together they search for Arcadia; together they undertake expeditions and live the fleeting moments of paradise and the eternity of hell. Plague and war afflict them equally, just as the flood blinds them all and violence from without strikes them all. The structural curve is identical for the hero and the masses, and their fall is simultaneous, which is why these fabulous and mythified heroes never cease to be "representative."

Solitude, the novel's central theme, knits personal destinies closely. Whatever their essence, all the characters are born condemned to suffer it. It is a universal law and no one, not even Ursula, the Mother who lives for others, is spared it; her final blindness plunges her into "the impenetrable loneliness of decrepitude." The most obvious example, emphasized by the symbolism of the act, is Colonel Aureliano's order to have traced around him a chalk circle which no one may cross. His is the solitude of power, and in that solitude, as the narrator says, Colonel Aureliano is completely isolated. Later we read that "he locked himself in, as it were, and his family ended up thinking of him as if he had died." This line sums up the meaning of solitude by equating it with death.

Perhaps it is here that the novel—correctly read—yields its meaning and the reason why the living characters can co-exist and converse so naturally with the dead ones. Whoever lives his solitude as these people do, incapable of communication with the other alive-dead souls, is at the same distance from other people as he is from the dead-alive, or dead. Solitude is a common denominator that tinges them with a common sadness; it both unites and separates them as one may note in the relationship between Aureliano IV and José Arcadio IV: "That bond between the two loners of the same family was far from being a friendly one; it allowed them both to bear better that fathomless solitude which simultaneously brought them together and separated them." Aureliano IV is not at all interested in escaping from the confinement to which his grandmother has condemned him. He is content to live within himself, stubborn in his will to unravel the meaning of Melquíades' parchments: it is the duty of a loner.

Solitude is a vocation imposed by birth, in accordance with a law; it is an indelible mark. The successive Aurelianos and Arcadios have in common the family's "solitary look"; Aureliano IV has been "from the beginning of the world and forever branded by the pockmarks of solitude." The solitude of silence is a prison and a refuge. When Mauricio Babilonia is wounded, his lover Meme withdraws in "stony" silence and much later dies of old age without ever having uttered another word. In this case, solitude is a form of desperation, and in the case of Aureliano II, it is even more extreme; he surrenders to the "bitter solitude of drunken sprees." He loses himself in them in order to escape the solitude of Fernanda, the stern wife who, as an outsider and foreigner of Macondo, attempts to force the chains of isolation on their home and village. Fernanda wishes to live entombed, faithful "to the paternal decree to be buried alive," as her father had done and as she herself demands of her daughter and grandson. Rebeca does the same thing, but for different reasons: she shoots and kills the thief who attempted to force the door to her place of confinement. (The visit to Macondo by the dead boy's mother is told in **"The Tuesday Afternoon Siesta"** in ***Mamá Grande's Funeral.***)

In the case of José Arcadio Buendía, the solitude of madness is accompanied by the failure of language. He suddenly begins to speak in a strange language (which we later learn is Latin) incomprehensible to those around him. He will live for years or centuries tied to the trunk of a chestnut tree in the courtyard, and after his death he will continue to inhabit the same place with a ghostly life scarcely different from his former one. No less incomprehensible, although in a quite different way, is Remedios the Beautiful, impervious "to the language of man," always "wandering in the desert of solitude" and finally rising out of fictional time and space into oblivion.

Amaranta's solitude is that of rancor and death in life. She lives alone with her hate and solely for it. Her communication with Death is normal and no different from that which she has with people around her. Death is neither more nor less than "a woman dressed in blue, with long hair, of a somewhat antiquated appearance and bearing a certain resemblance to Pilar Trenera," who sews by her side and who one day asks her "to please thread a needle for her." Knowing the date of her own departure, she offers herself as messenger to the inhabitants of Macondo to carry news from the living to the dead, thus redeeming the wretched solitude of her hate. Her offer is accepted without objection: "The news that Amaranta Buendía was setting sail for the twilight zone carrying the mail of death spread through Macondo before noon, and by around three in the afternoon there was already a big box filled with letters in the room. Those who were not able to write spoke their messages, which Amaranta jotted down in her notebook with the name and date of death of the addressee." No one doubts that the requests will be carried out.

The Buendías are not the only ones who live as recluses. So do the veterans, whittling away their useless old age waiting for the promised government check that never comes. (In ***The Colonel Has No One to Write Him*** García Márquez has elaborated on this hopeless waiting.) There is only one way for mortal beings to transcend this common solitude: through love. But love during these hundred years (or centuries) is precarious and always in danger of ending in a catastrophe like the ones that undermine the lives of Amaranta, Rebeca, Mauricio, Meme. Amaranta, Ursula and Aureliano IV believe they have conquered solitude by forgetting themselves in frantic love, an erotic passion in which the family's last energies are consumed. Around them the world is destroyed and returned to dust. In Macondo, "forgotten even by the birds [. . .] it was difficult to breathe," but the lovers reconstruct for their passion the fatal solitude that consumes everything, withdrawing "through the solitude of love" into the house that is being devoured by ants—before they devour the last of the Aurelianos. They are the last living creatures in this fictional space: "in an empty universe where love [is] the only daily and eternal reality," in a world where they hear no voices other than those of their dead parents, grandparents, and great-grandparents, they achieve peace, persuaded that death itself will not be able to separate them. The birth of Aureliano V is the end of the novel; in him the prophecies of destruction are fulfilled, and Macondo, reduced to dust, disappears forever and with it the memory of those who made and inhabited it.

Among the unifying devices utilized by García Márquez, the reiteration of certain motifs is important. The motifs reappear at certain intervals and unite various parts of the novel, thus reinforcing the feeling of circularity (the sinister black men, charged with preparing and justifying the Government's pillage; the distant, invisible doctors with whom Fernanda communicates). One motif, of particular interest, accentuates the futility of human actions, and can be seen in the Buendía family's peculiar custom or vice of making things only to destroy them afterwards. Aureliano I falls into this characteristic mode of repetition, as the narrator observes, when instead of selling the little gold fish he makes, he melts them down to remake them and thus continues incessantly. Memories come back to them and thus continues incessantly. Memories come back to Ursula in a similar way. José Arcadio Buendía keeps busy reading and rereading Melquíades' parchments. Amaranta sews and unsews buttons, and alternately weaves and unweaves her shroud to retard the coming of death. These are solitary games, designed to regain lost time; they are also the novelist's technique of indirectly expressing small but significant details in order to press the creative process.

There is a kind of justifiable excess in the novel, a systematic distortion by means of hyperbole that fits the author's design: a design to create a world of fiction so perfect as to make it ideal. Events and figures contain dimensions, as they should. The novel's beginning is Genesis; its end is the Apocalypse; rain is equivalent to the Flood; wars are War. García Márquez' weakness for hyperbole is decisive when it comes to characterization. Being verbal inventions, the characters necessarily owe their substance to the way in which the author arranges his words; the traditional hypothesis that the novelist faithfully describes characters who exist previous to the narrative is a metaphor that suggests, at length, the autonomy of the character.

Hyperbole may produce a comic effect, as when Aureliano IV runs about the house "balancing a beer bottle on his inconceivable sex organ," or it may yield lyrical imagery: "His mistress was so close to him and so completely disarmed that Aureliano could perceive the deep murmur of her bones." Again, it may induce a fantastic vision: "The atmosphere was so humid that fish could have come in the doors and exited by the windows, swimming through the air in the rooms." Such hyperboles might be read as metaphors; but in context they should be accepted literally, because of the levelling off between reality and unreality which is characteristic of ***One Hundred Years of Solitude.***

A systematic study of the imagery (and the symbols, such as the plague of insomnia and forgetfulness or the indelible ash crosses that single out the Aurelianos for death) would show that it points towards that levelling and indeed contributes to it. The excesses of the Buendías are passed on from one generation to the next. Aureliano II is a Gargantuan, capable of devouring a whole calf; José Arcadio II, who went around the world sixty-five times and like Ray Bradbury's illustrated man had his whole body tattooed, became a cannibal when the moment demanded it. His overindulgence in bed or at the table knew no bounds. "His farts wilted the flowers," reads the expressive image.

War and the general strike are culminations of horror in the novel—nightmares that actually happen yet retain their delirious quality. There is no doubt about their function in the novel. The narrator, as he relates them, erases any differences that might have existed, indeed destroys the very idea of a possible barrier between the real and the imaginary. In the natural order of things, such nightmares fall within the realm of the possible—they are readily accepted as "historical" and natural events, and for the assassins they are even honorable—but in the novel they are more, rather than less, fantastic and incredible, in their naked brutality, than are specters and monsters. Whoever thinks they can be explained will easily accept the plague of insomnia or the rain of dead birds. There is no substantial difference between those horrors and these unnatural events, even though only the former are man-made. Narrative objectivity undergoes no change, not even when in the end the false version of the story must be told (a falsification occasioned by the criminal's desire to erase all traces of the crime and by man's refusal to recognize the monstrosity of the real).

As García Márquez completes his last fictional circles, he illuminates their and the novel's meaning. The difference between Márquez and other contemporary novelists lies in the fact that the latter may disperse themselves in a welter of techniques: he does not. His need to tell a story is so strong that it transcends the devices he uses to satisfy that need. Technique is not a mere game; it is something to be made use of. At its best, it serves only to relate the story. Should the novelist get lost in his own creation, it is so that he might find himself in it, in that imaginary world which is Macondo—the Macondo which has been compared to Faulkner's Yoknapatawpha county, if for no other reason than that both are relatively pure fictional regions, absolute inventions like Goriot's Paris or Fortunata's Madrid; inventions that are reserved for artists like Márquez who know how to revitalize the ancient and almost forgotten art of storytelling, reserved for those who practice it with the complex simplicity the genre demands. (pp. 27-32)

Ricardo Gullón, "Gabriel Garcia Marquez & the Lost Art of Storytelling," translated by José G. Sánchez, in Diacritics, *Vol. I, No. 1, Fall, 1971, pp. 27-32.*

García Márquez on the fantastic in Latin America:

Clearly, the Latin American environment is marvelous. Particularly the Caribbean. . . . To grow up in such an environment is to have fantastic resources for poetry. Also, in the Caribbean, we are capable of believing anything, because we have the influences of all those different cultures, mixed in with Catholicism and our own local beliefs. I think that gives us an open-mindedness to look beyond apparent reality.

Gabriel García Márquez in an interview with Claudia Dreifus in* Playboy, *February, 1983.

Gordon Brotherston

[An English critic, translator, and educator who specializes in Latin American studies, Brotherston is the author of Spanish American Modernista Poets: A Critical Anthology *(1968) and* The Emergence of the Latin American Novel *(1977). In the following essay from the latter work, Brotherston offers a practical overview of* One

Hundred Years of Solitude, *relating the book to García Márquez's previous works set in Macondo.*]

> Many years later, as he faced the firing squad, Colonel Aureliano Buendía was to remember that distant afternoon when his father took him to discover ice. At that time Macondo was a village of twenty adobe houses, built on the bank of a river of clear water that ran along a bed of polished stones, which were white and enormous, like prehistoric eggs. The world was so recent that many things lacked names, and in order to indicate them it was necessary to point. Every year during the month of March a family of ragged gypsies would set up their tents near the village, and with a great uproar of pipes and kettledrums they would display new inventions. First they brought the magnet. A heavy gypsy with an untamed beard and sparrow hands, who introduced himself as Melquíades, put on a bold public demonstration of what he himself called the eighth wonder of the learned alchemists of Macedonia. He went from house to house dragging two metal ingots and everybody was amazed to see pots, pans, tongs, and braziers tumble down from their places and beams creak with the desperation of nails and screws trying to emerge, and even objects that had been lost for a long time appeared from where they had been searched for most and went dragging along in turbulent confusion behind Melquíades's magical irons. 'Things have a life of their own,' the gypsy proclaimed with a harsh accent. 'It's simply a matter of waking up their souls.' José Arcadio Buendía, whose unbridled imagination always went beyond the genius of nature and even beyond miracles and magic, thought that it would be possible to make use of that useless invention to extract gold from the bowels of the earth. Melquíades, who was an honest man, warned him: 'It won't work for that.' But José Arcadio Buendía at that time did not believe in the honesty of gypsies, so he traded his mule and a pair of goats for the two magnetized ingots. Úrsula Iguarán, his wife, who relied on those animals to increase their poor domestic holdings, was unable to dissuade him. 'Very soon we'll have gold enough and more to pave the floors of the house,' her husband replied. For several months he worked hard to demonstrate the truth of his idea. He explored every inch of the region, even the riverbed, dragging the two iron ingots along and reciting Melquíades's incantation aloud. The only thing he succeeded in doing was to unearth a suit of fifteenth-century armour which had all of its pieces soldered together with rust and inside which there was the hollow resonance of an enormous stone-filled gourd. When José Arcadio Buendía and the four men of his expedition managed to take the armour apart, they found inside a calcified skeleton with a copper locket containing a woman's hair around its neck.

Earliest memories of García Márquez's imaginary Macondo are prehistoric, like the polished egg-like stones of its river. The town was founded, at an uncertain date, somewhere deep in the swamps of northern Colombia, by Colonel Aureliano's father, José Arcadio Buendía, after a long and arduous flight from the known world and his own past. He and Úrsula Iguarán, first cousins, were the first pair in this early world; they constructed the town and effectively arranged the lives of the people who came with them from the coast. The fortunes of the family they engendered, seven generations in all, give the book its thread and its title. Melquíades and his gypsies, ragged as they are, burst into the solitude of Macondo as men wiser and older than its founding family.

As the characters in ***One Hundred Years of Solitude*** themselves remark, events in Macondo seem often to repeat themselves, in apparent defiance of historical sequence. The very names of the characters, repeated from generation to generation (there are no fewer than four José Arcadios), reinforce this impression, which is created in the skilful vagueness of the opening sentences. Phrases like 'many years later', and 'that distant afternoon' lead back through the prehistoric stones to a timeless world where (in an allusion to Carpentier and his magic realism) we are told many things still needed to be named. Though a genealogical thread runs from the first José Arcadio and Úrsula to the ill-fated last scion of the family, the novel, divided into twenty sections of near-equal length, retains an episodic feeling. Many of the characters and events were familiar to García Márquez's readers before its appearance. Almost all his published work before ***One Hundred Years of Solitude*** is, or could be, set in Macondo and presents people from that town or who have to do with it. ***Leaf Storm*** (***La hojarasca,*** 1955) deals at length with the banana boom there, which surfaces again in the thirteenth and fourteenth chapters of ***One Hundred Years of Solitude.*** The lonely unrewarded hero of ***No One Writes to the Colonel*** (***El coronel no tiene quien le escriba,*** 1961) closely resembles Colonel Aureliano Buendía himself, whom, we are told, he served during the civil wars. In ***The Evil Hour*** (***La mala hora,*** 1961), Macondo suffers the deluge again described in the later novel, while his short stories, collected in part in ***Big Mama's Funeral*** (***Los funerales de la Mamá Grande,*** 1962), are vignettes of life in the town. In this sense the novel can be understood as a comprehensive gesture, the gathering into one context of moments hitherto existing separately. Macondo itself was the name of a plantation near the small town (Aracataca) on Colombia's Caribbean coast where García Márquez grew up. As the location of his various narratives he has shaped and populated it from the stories told to him by his grandparents, in whose house he lived as a child. In the novel, Úrsula, the mother and grandmother of all, is defined by her ability to recall and recount lives and situations otherwise threatened with oblivion or confusion.

The gypsies' visit was an experience Macondo could take, though José Arcadio is crazed with greed, wanting to tear gold like iron from Arcadia's breast. The gypsies' intrusion into the fairy-tale world of early Macondo is the first of many such intrusions, which present the question of the town's moral location. The gypsies are followed by the *corregidor* Moscote, sent by the central government, whose presence there is at first manifestly absurd but becomes normal, even necessary. There follows a series of secular and religious officials, vigilantes and surveyors carried in by ever-improved communications with the outside world. Even potent emblems of pre-temporal existence like those enormous polished stones in Macondo's river are pulverized, almost unnoticed, when José Arcadio II goes ahead with his scheme to build a canal connecting Macondo with the coast. Like the Sulaco of Conrad's *Nostromo* (which also lived through 'a hundred years' of isolation), the town Macondo itself thus acquires a special significance in the space and time of the novel, a significance García Márquez's beguiling prose neither highlights nor denies.

One Hundred Years of Solitude has been sold and read so widely in Latin America, and has been taken so very much to heart there, as to support the idea that Macondo might be exemplary of Latin America as a whole, a luminous chronicle of a special condition. And it is true that García Márquez contrives brilliantly to attribute to the town an experience both local and precise and more broadly characteristic. The hundred lonely years recounted in the novel would thus begin more or less with the (nominal) political independence won by the states of Latin America in the nineteenth century, and bring us up to modern times. To attempt to synthesize so much historical experience within a single novel is clearly an ambitious project, undertaken by few other Latin American novelists. Carpentier, in *The Lost Steps,* is one of them, and this must explain the frequent and not very flattering references to him.

Proceeding by categories, we may first note the imperial European presence symbolized in the fifteenth-century Spanish copper locket opened by José Arcadio, with the hair of a distant woman inside it, and (a few pages later in the same chapter) in the proud galleon stranded miles from the main (a virtuoso description of García Márquez's):

> When they woke up, with the sun already high in the sky, they were speechless with fascination. Before them, surrounded by ferns and palm trees, white and powdery in the silent morning light, was an enormous Spanish galleon. Tilted slightly to starboard, it had hanging from its intact masts the dirty rags of its sails in the midst of its rigging, which was adorned with orchids. The hull, covered with an armour of petrified barnacles and soft moss, was firmly fastened into a surface of stones. The whole structure seemed to occupy its own space, one of solitude and oblivion, protected from the vices of time and the habits of the birds. Inside, where the expeditionaries explored with careful intent, there was nothing but a thick forest of flowers.

Then comes a series of encounters with native Indian and imported black populations, variously resolved. After that the civil wars which ravaged Colombia and other Latin American countries in the post-Independent period are caught in the classic nineteenth-century struggles between liberals and conservatives which occupy the second quarter of the book and bring Colonel Aureliano close to death. Following a standard historical pattern, this strife is succeeded by the intrusion of Anglo-Saxon or *gringo* interests, epitomized in Macondo by Mr Brown and the banana growers, who exploit the local workers brutally. The whole condition of Macondo could initially be understood as that of a hinterland beyond rivers and ports, 'where the sun smiles and the seasons teem in vain, unseen and unenjoyed', its 'innocent' posture being that of a continent or subcontinent until recently at the mercy of purveyors of ideas and magnets from older parts of the planet.

This historical dimension undoubtedly exists in the novel, though things are more complicated, for Macondo and its inhabitants were never truly innocent. Moreover, García Márquez appears less interested in displaying it for its own sake or his reader's amusement than in having it there as something to play against. History is compromised from the very start, as we have seen, by the laying of those prehistoric eggs, and continues to be by subtle distortions of time which culminate in Aureliano's and our discovery that the wise Melquíades had foreseen what would happen in Macondo and had written it down, in Sanskrit (his mother tongue), on a sheaf of parchment. García Márquez also shows that he doesn't want merely to chronicle the past by his admirably constant disregard of precise ages and dates. Situations throughout the book are leavened with more or less direct allusions to Biblical and other 'timeless' myths. Colonel Aureliano's sons are mysteriously murdered as if by an order of Herod, while a later, illegitimate, Aureliano is found in the bullrushes like Moses. Other events are neutralized temporally by a series of 'plagues': insomnia, dead birds raining from the sky, and so on. The greater the danger that a given event may seem to be historical, the stronger is García Márquez's mythical antidote: the banana company's massacre of thousands of strikers, for example, is followed by endless rain and a portentous flood, subsequently referred to as the Deluge, which washes away precise memory. Down to the smallest detail, García Márquez's prose absorbs and loosens the possible intractability of a particular history. The words 'firing squad' in the opening sentence do not prompt us to wonder why or when Aureliano was facing it, any more than the 'gold' sought by José Arcadio specifically recalls the American substance which in history made his ancestors less amiably crazed with greed. Such potentially mythic terms sooner interact with each other, just below the surface of the narrative: 'father', 'ice', 'iron', 'bowels', 'earth'. On the other hand, the resonance they produce is never allowed to dehistoricize the narrative altogether. They are subject to the swift relating of events, and to an authorial superiority insinuated in phrases like 'useless invention', 'did not believe in the honesty of gypsies', 'the only thing he succeeded in doing'.

Our formal point of reference in this bemusing world of myth and history, even more than the place Macondo, is the Buendías' existence in it. From Aureliano's introductory memory of an afternoon spent with his father onwards, parochial genealogy acts as the guide to whatever larger message there is. The very founders of Macondo are José Arcadio's men, whose descendants exist only in so far as they have dealings with the Buendías. Later, García Márquez may convey brilliantly the sense of a moment in social and cultural history, in nineteenth-century bourgeois soirées round the pianola, for example, but in every case it is through the words, deeds and relationships of the family. We know about liberals of the period via the Colonel, and not as a party or group. Again, a mulatto like Nigromanta is introduced because the last Aureliano at one point needed a woman like her, not because the place had the remnants of a slave population. García Márquez even alerts us drily to his partiality. In the silly passions which involve the young Buendía girls Amaranta and Rebeca with Pietro Crespi, who is always in the family house as the pianola expert, there is a parody not just of their etiquette but of the bourgeois novel in the style of Isaac's *Maria* and of cameo description as a historiographical method. Similarly, Colonel Gerineldo Márquez's loyalty to the liberal cause is wrily equated with his personal devotion to Aureliano. Macondo exists only as long as the family tree flourishes there.

The family in turn owes its existence and its coherence to Úrsula, their guardian. Her insight alone can detect the 'real' motives behind her offsprings' actions; her memory alone can retain their history and she alone can condone or condemn their acts. Her concern to restrain José Arcadio in his failure to respect 'nature' with his magnet is the first of several interventions which, at first ineffective, finally fulfil their purpose. By far the most dramatic of these is her hounding of the triumphant and resplendent Colonel Aureliano at one point during the civil war; she assaults him directly in front of his men and stops him from carrying out his plan of reprisals. She decides who is legitimate and who is not among her progeny. And she keeps them afloat financially with a private enterprise worthy of Mother Courage herself. By paying for and designing the house she provides a physical focus, and the further anyone strays from it the more blurred and less substantial they become. Precisely on her death, at the age of one hundred, not long before the ill-fated last scion of the tree is born and dies, things begin to fall apart, and the family's inner meaning is seriously exposed to question. The solitude of the title derives, then, not just from Macondo's physical isolation but from 'the solitary destiny' of the family itself, which she embodies more fully than anyone else.

Freakish things do happen in the Buendía family, for all Úrsula's surveillance and authority. There is more than one case of incest; and the last child of the line is born with a tail. Colonel Aureliano insists on marrying a girl who is not yet adolescent, and so small that she has to be lifted up to greet the wedding guests. Some critics have made much of these and other oddities as examples of Macondo's fabulousness, and of its 'prelapsarian' inhabitants' way of living out Freudian fantasy, beyond taboo. Once again, this may be. But more to the point are the eminently normal Spanish-American ethics they otherwise adhere to. The men of the family may indulge their sexual urges ubiquitously, in scenes described with torrid zest by García Márquez. But the unmarried women either remain resolute virgins like Amaranta (Aureliano's sister), or get put into convents for indiscretion, leaving whores from outside the family, like Pilar Ternera, as social companions for the men. Ideals of man and womanhood are sharply distinguished; the men show unflinching courage in the face of violence and death, but are left to 'relieve their bellies' in the brothel run by Pilar Ternera, the Golden Boy, their only social centre. No untrammelled Eden, Macondo is strictly watched and influenced by Úrsula the matriarch, her ideal of the family being very like that traditionally revered in Colombia and other conservative Spanish-American countries.

Úrsula's injunctions are especially important in so far as they affect the family's racial and political attitudes. The early generations of the family could hardly help coming into contact with the Guijara Indians and went as far as allowing one or two Buendía children to speak their language. But Úrsula's tacit resistance to them is soon confirmed: and they and their language are forgotten by everybody in a plague of amnesia which the Indians themselves, conveniently enough, carry to the household. Again, the blacks, who appear 'out of nowhere', are assigned subservient roles as unquestioningly as they would have been anywhere in Colonial America. This subtle relegation of people there before Macondo's genesis or essential to its economy is always in favour of the Castilian blood flowing in José Arcadio's and Úrsula's veins. That suit of ancient Spanish armour dug up in the first chapter is a relic indeed, a palpable cult-object.

Translated from genealogy into history, the culture of Úrsula's family would no doubt appear oppressively reactionary and the obvious cause of their 'solitary destiny'. But this is a translation which García Márquez does not make as long as Úrsula exists as a living character in the novel. She may charm or disturb, but she is neither approved nor disapproved of. After her death it is another matter. Then she is held responsible for the 'pernicious vices' and the 'solitary calling' of the Buendías. And the last of the family line, Amaranta Úrsula and her nephew Aureliano earnestly hope that their child, the very last José Arcadio, can 'cleanse' them of this heritage since 'he was the only one in a century who had been engendered with love'. But this interpretation of Úrsula, as a kind of tropical Pedro Páramo, belongs only to the three final chapters of the novel. As long as Úrsula lives, we are prevented from thinking too long about her as a creature of political and social consequence, by the bemusing qualities of García Márquez's prose. To return to the example of the family's relationship with the native Indians of their region: after the plague of amnesia they bring to the household, the Buendías try valiantly to cope, by naming the objects of their environment, affixing labels to them with accompanying explanations where necessary, as if to make it lexically habitable. Now besides being an extremely witty parody of Carpentier's notion that Latin Americans, Adamic or Arcadian, should busy themselves naming the things of their world as if it really was an unpopulated Eden, this passage reminds us yet again of the backwardness, isolation and racial exclusiveness of Macondo. But we don't dwell for a moment on the implications, politically, of all this. The event simply happens, and passes, and so do tragedies like the incessant civil war around the town or the terrible massacre of the plantation workers.

One Hundred Years of Solitude benefits, in its episodic, serial narration of events, from García Márquez's talents as a journalist-reporter (who had 'used Hemingway as an antidote to early readings of Faulkner') and as a short story writer. The many luminous short stories about Macondo which preceded this novel, by virtue of their form and as a series of more or less marginal 'incidents', could avoid full confrontation with what García Márquez had made into the moral burden of his writing: the luxuriant and traumatic tropical world of Aracataca-Macondo. In his novels García Márquez could avoid this confrontation less easily, if only for formal reasons. The special achievements of ***One Hundred Years of Solitude,*** the best of these novels, may be gauged by reference to two previous ones: ***Leaf Storm,*** the first he published, and ***The Evil Hour,*** after which he remained silent for some time before producing ***One Hundred Years of Solitude.***

García Márquez's principal achievement in ***Leaf Storm*** was the invention of Macondo, which though 'like' his birthplace, enjoyed an existence of its own, as Yoknapatawpha did for Faulkner and Santa Maria did for Onetti. There, in his account of the activities of the United Fruit Company during the banana boom and their effects on the local population, he had room to develop his skill at perceiving 'the intimate relationship which exists between the political-social structure of a given country and the behaviour of its inhabitants', evident enough even in the separate and marginal incidents of his short stories. In the novel, however, this structure threatened to become too comprehensive and determinant, something which he himself, as another of its 'products', could not expect to escape from. As if to acknowledge this problem, the three Faulkneresque monologues which make up ***Leaf Storm*** (spoken by Isabel, her father the colonel, and her son) are brought to a close in the very year that the author was born (1928). Like the last José Arcadio in ***One Hundred Years of Solitude*** (born after Úrsula's death), he could thus at least intimate the notion of immunity from the historical and political processes observed in the novel. In ***The Evil Hour,*** his attempt to be 'equal' to, and to explain his heritage was more radical and overt. The intimate secrets of Macondo are exposed and analysed socially, by a device (the ubiquitous appearance in the town of *pasquinades*) which reveals the private thoughts of its inhabitants, about each other and themselves. This novel has been called a social and political 'x-ray' of the town, and in practice left García Márquez little opportunity to use his great story-telling talent. In their different ways, both novels attempted the same thing: to make sense of, in terms acceptable to a socially and politically conscious writer, and so to demystify, the amoral and overwhelming power of an inherited fable which holds him in thrall. In this respect the closing sentences of ***The Evil Hour*** are significant, with their reference to a 'new' possibility of liberation in Colombia and Latin America as a whole: 'The prison is full, but they say that the men are taking to the hills and that there are guerrilla groups everywhere.'

The main thing García Márquez went on to do in ***One Hundred Years of Solitude*** was apparently to forget this direct political concern and personality to come to terms with Úrsula. He releases her unconditionally as a narrative source, and no longer evaluates in the same way the world which he and she share. Remembrance of the massacre of strikers, so carefully analysed and assessed in ***Leaf Storm,*** is now washed away by the rain so that the story of the family can go on. The mesh of inner corruption in the town, so excruciatingly probed in ***The Evil Hour*** is now surveyed with bitter-sweet humour. It was this relaxation of focus which enabled him to attempt his grand synthesis of Latin American experience. By converting a family heritage into the narrative device of genealogy, chronicle and myth, he made Macondo's boundaries historically and geographically elastic. The evident success of this new approach prompted some critics to reproach García Márquez with loss of political faith, which they attributed specifically to the reverses suffered by revolutionary and guerrilla movements in Latin America in the 1960s, between the publication of ***The Evil Hour*** and ***One Hundred Years of Solitude.*** Whatever the truth of this may be, ***One Hundred Years of Solitude*** can hardly be considered a gesture of resignation. For García Márquez exorcises Úrsula not by absolving or annihilating her but by leaving her dead; he transfers the load to her living survivors.

The three chapters which come after Úrsula's death in the novel are devoted to Amaranta Úrsula and Aureliano, and their child José Arcadio. Now both parents, aunt and nephew, are distinguished not just by this narrative 'orphanhood' but by a moral independence from the family which few of their ancestors have had. More than once, Amaranta Úrsula is said to be a modern woman; she travels widely and on returning to Macondo with her Belgian husband she momentarily looks as though she can usurp her great-great-grandmother Úrsula as the woman of the house. For his part, Aureliano acquires friends in the town, on whom he comes to rely with an openness uncharacteristic of the family, and who offer him in addition an entry to the 'universal' world of literature and learning. The Catalan bookseller in the town shares with him knowledge said rightly to be 'encyclopaedic', since it can situate Latin America as historically it was first situated by the thinkers of the eighteenth century, and can provoke an emancipation begun historically with the Wars of Independence. The bookseller's own compositions become a modern and less enslaving equivalent of the parchments of Melquíades, Macondo's first Old World visitor (the handwriting of both is said to be startlingly similar). Melquíades had predicted the destiny of the place by drawing on the wisdom of the ancients, in a Sanskrit embellished with signs of Greek and Roman authority ('He had composed it in Sanskrit, which was his mother tongue, and had ciphered the even lines with the personal mark of the Emperor Augustus and the odd lines with military marks of the Lacedemonians'). Having been 'determined' to translate Melquíades's version of his family's and Macondo's fate, Aureliano awakens to a larger and more immediate environment, and makes the acquaintance of other modern writers, among them the Colombian novelist Alvaro Cepeda (whom García Márquez met in Baranquilla, having left Aracataca), and the author himself. This is not the first time, in this Latin American novel, that we find an allusion to other Latin American novels: a certain colonel Lorenzo Gavilán had earlier been transferred, from active service in Mexico in Carlos Fuentes's account of the Mexican Revolution in *The Death of Artemio Cruz,* to join forces with the male Buendías as champions of the liberal cause in Colombia. And we have already noted the adroit parodies of Carpentier, and his philosophy of 'naming the things' of America; later, fun is made of the axiom that 'style is affirmed through history' (by now tantamount to anathema), and at one point we glimpse the tempestuous Victor Hugues himself, 'at sea' on the Caribbean and sailing for Guadeloupe—in the wrong direction. By the stage of the novel, however, at which 'Gabriel Márquez' himself appears as a character, with old Úrsula gone, this kind of reflexive illusion acquires added force and appears more necessary to the survival of a lone, orphaned figure like Aureliano.

The final chapter of ***One Hundred Years of Solitude*** announces itself as a finale, and suggests that Amaranta Úrsula and Aureliano cannot save their tribe (*estirpe*). The town and the house collapse around them, and for all their great love for each other, they cannot prevent everything falling apart in the last corruption of the atmosphere. Pilar Ternera's The Golden Boy—like the brothels in Santa Maria, Vargas Llosa's Piura and Arguedas's Cuzco, a place of relative enlightenment—is ceremonially shut for ever on her death at the age of 144. Amaranta Úrsula's Belgian husband, who travels abroad and for whom, as a result of a post-office error, Macondo has become confused with the Congo, almost gratefully breaks his bond with her on learning about Aureliano. The Catalan bookseller leaves, and as he fades into the distance urges his friends to do the same; except for Aureliano they do. His letters from Barcelona, like those of the character García Márquez from Paris (where the author actually went), become the couple's only link 'with the world'. And then that link is gone. The Catalan dies, and Gabriel Márquez is last seen writing in the room in which Oliveira's adoptive child 'Rocamadour had died'. This is a reference to a moment in the Latin American novel to which Cortázar himself would later return in *Manuel's Book,* where the dead baby is resurrected, or at least for a time. García Márquez's elegant tribute to the integrity of the author of *Hopscotch* appeals to the reflexive power of literature, and serves as a redoubled presage.

For though the baby boy of Amaranta Úrsula and Aureliano is the first of the family to be engendered in love, the parents are too confined, genetically and otherwise, for the birth to 'cleanse' them of their heritage, as they had hoped it would. The mother dies in childbirth, and the last José Arcadio is born with the tail of a fabled creature, to be eaten alive by ants whose 'prehistoric' hunger reminds us of the implacable forces always latent in the stone eggs in Macondo's innocent-looking river. Thrown back entirely on himself, Aureliano can only think of going back to the parchments that will tell him his fate and from which the Catalan bookseller, and then love, had distracted him. With a tropical storm raging around him he reads ever more anxiously:

> Macondo was already a fearful whirlwind of dust and rubble being spun about by the wrath of the biblical hurricane when Aureliano skipped eleven pages so as not to lose time with facts he knew only too well, and he began to decipher the instant that he was living, deciphering it as he lived it, prophesying himself in the act of deciphering the last page of the parchments, as if he were looking into a speaking mirror. Then he skipped again to anticipate the predictions and ascertain the date and circumstances of his death. Before reaching the final line, however, he had already understood that he would never leave that room, for it was foreseen that the city of mirrors (or mirages) would be wiped out by the wind and exiled from the memory of men at the precise moment when Aureliano Babilonia would finish deciphering the parchments, and that everything written on them was unrepeatable since time immemorial and forever more, because races condemned to one hundred years of solitude did not have a second opportunity on earth.

Aureliano Babilonia puts his last faith in the authority of Melquíades's ancient script: he is immured (*encastillado*) in literature, as in the tower of Babylon his name. Only in the scattering storm he discovers, like a persona of Borges, that such faith alone cannot save him. But because of the way in which the narrative, in crescendo, includes the reader in the act that Aureliano is performing (reading the reading), this realization of Aureliano's sweeps to its limit García Márquez's exposé of the novel as a literary object in a larger situation. The tropical storm tears away not just the leaves of the trees, as it does in Asturias's *Strong Wind* or had done in García Márquez's ***Leaf Storm,*** but those of the very idea of the book. This could be just a sophisticated example of the ability to use literature to make fun of people (*burlarse de la gente*) which Aureliano had discovered on meeting García Márquez and other friends in The Golden Boy. But it still 'opens' the novel to include and involve the reader, as Umberto Eco has defined that process, in the way that Cortázar and José María Arguedas have done, each for his own reasons. Correspondingly, we move from the mode of exorcism of the past, with its secular load, to that of exhortation in the present. For, among the living, the last words can only be heard as a cry which demands its contradiction: 'they didn't have a second chance on earth'. (pp. 122-35)

Gordon Brotherston, "An End to Secular Solitude: Gabriel García Márquez," in his The Emergence of the Latin American Novel, *Cambridge University Press, 1977, pp. 122-35.*

Roberto González Echevarría

[*González Echevarría is a Cuban-born American critic and educator who has served as editor of such periodicals as* Latin American Literary Review *and* Review: Latin American Literature and Arts. *In the following excerpt, he examines García Márquez's mythologization of history as well as metafictional aspects in* One Hundred Years of Solitude.]

The importance of myth in ***Cien años de soledad*** was noticed by the first commentators of the novel and later studies have again taken up the topic. It seems clear that myth appears in the novel in the following guises: 1) there are stories that resemble classical or biblical myths, most notably the Flood, but also Paradise, the Seven Plagues, Apocalypse, and the proliferation of the family, with its complicated genealogy, has an Old Testament ring to it; 2) there are characters who are reminiscent of mythical heroes: José Arcadio Buendía, who is a sort of Moses, Rebeca, who is like a female Perseus, Remedios, who ascends in a flutter of white sheets in a scene that is suggestive not just of the Ascension of the Virgin, but more specifically of the popular renditions of the event in religious prints; 3) certain stories have a general mythic character in that they contain supernatural elements, as in the case just mentioned, and also when José Arcadio's blood returns to Ursula; 4) the beginning of the whole story, which is found, as in myth in a tale of violence and incest. All four, of course, commingle, and because ***Cien años de soledad*** tells a story of foundations or origins, the whole novel has a mythic air about it. No single myth or mythology prevails. Instead the various ways in which myth appears give the whole novel a mythical character without it being a distinct version of one given myth.

At the same time, there is lurking in the background of the story the overall pattern of Latin American history, both as a general design made up of various key events and eras, and in the presence of specific characters and incidents that seem to refer to real people and happenings. Thus we have a period of discovery and conquest, when José Arcadio Buendía and the original families settle Macondo. There is in this part of the book little sense that Macondo belongs to a larger political unit, but such isolation was in fact typical of Latin America's towns in the colonial period. Even the viceroyalties lived in virtual isolation from the metropolitan government. The appearance of Apolinar Moscote and his barefoot soldiers is the beginning of the republican era, which is immediately followed by the outbreak of the civil wars in which Colonel Aureliano Buendía distinguishes himself. Though Colombia is the most obvious model for this period, nearly the entire continent suffered from civil strife during the nineteenth century, a process that led to the emergence of dictators and *caudillos.* This period is followed by the era of neocolonial domination by the United States and the struggles against it in most Latin American countries. These culminate in the novel with the general strike and the massacre of the workers. There are, unfortunately, countless models for this last, clearly defined period in the novel. After the flood, there is a time of decay before the apocalyptic wind that razes the town at the end. The liberal priest and the various military types who surround Colonel Aureliano Buendía, are among the characters with counterparts in Latin American history. Lucila I. Mena [in a 1972 article in *Bulletin Hispanique*] has already demonstrated that some of the historical incidents in the novel can be documented, and a sedulous critic with time and the proper library can probably document many others. But to carry this sort of research much further than Mena has would be a rather gratuitous critical exercise. Set against the global, totalizing thrust of the novel are these historical details which, without being specific, are nonetheless true in a general sense. Each of the above mentioned epochs is evoked not only through major historical events, but also through allusion to specific minor incidents and characters. For instance, early Macondo is inhabited by a *de jure* aristocracy made up of the founding families, which is analogous to that of colonial Latin America, where conquistadores and their descendants enjoyed certain privileges and exemptions.

The blend of mythic elements and Latin American history in ***Cien años de soledad*** reveals a desire to found an American myth. Latin American history is set on the same level as mythic stories, therefore it too becomes a sort of myth. The lack of specificity of the various incidents, which appear to represent several related or similar events, points in this direction. The Latin American myth is this story of foundation, articulated through independence, civil war, struggle against U.S. colonialism, all cast within a genealogical line that weaves in and out, repeating names and characters. There is a Whitmanian thrust to the brash declaration of the existence of a literary language that underlies this mixture of historical fact with mythic story in ***Cien años de soledad.*** The novel is in fact intimately related to similar efforts in poetry, such as the ones by Neruda in his *Canto General* and Octavio Paz in his *Piedra de Sol. Canto General* in particular is one of the most important sources of García Márquez's novel. Framed by Genesis and Apocalypse, fraught with incest and violence, the story of the Buendía family thus stands as Latin American history cast in the language of myth, an unresolved mixture that both beckons and bewilders the reader.

This duality is present throughout ***Cien años de soledad*** separating the world of writing from the atemporal world of myth. But the play of contradictions issuing from this duality reaches a synthesis that is perhaps the most important feature of the novel. As we have seen, myth represents the origin. Latin America's history is narrated in the language of myth because it is the other, represented by incest, taboo, and the primitive act of naming. The novel's persistent preoccupation with genealogy and with supernatural acts performed by various characters belongs to this realm. History, on the other hand, is critical, temporal, and dwells in a special place: Melquíades' room in the Buendía house, which I have chosen to call the Archive. The room is full of books and manuscripts, and has a time of its own. It is here that a succession of characters attempt to decipher Melquíades' parchments, and the last Aureliano, in an epiphanic inspiration, orally translates the whole (or nearly the whole) manuscript and dies. What occurs here, the text of the novel suggests, is unrepeatable. In the fiction of the novel, on the other hand, there are many repetitions. Ursula, for instance, twice feels that time is going around in circles and that members of the family follow one or two patterns of behavior indicated by their names. Time is circular in the fiction, but not in Melquíades' room. The Archive appears to be linear and teleological, while the plot of the novel itself is repetitive and mythical. ***Cien años de soledad*** is made up of two main stories: one has to do with the family and culminates in the birth of the child with the pig's tail, while the other is concerned with the interpretation of Melquíades' manuscript, a linear suspense story that culminates in Aureliano's final discovery of the key to the translation of the parchments.

That there should be a special abode for documents and books in ***Cien años de soledad*** should come as no surprise to readers of modern Latin American fiction. In spite of its apparent novelty, there are such enclosures in *Aura, Yo el Supremo, El arpa y la sombra,* ***Crónica de una muerte anunciada*** and *Oppiano Licario,* to mention a few of the novels where it plays a prominent role. What is characteristic of the Archive is: 1) the presence not only of history, but of previous mediating elements through which it was narrated, be it the legal documents of colonial times or the scientific ones of the nineteenth century; 2) the existence of an inner historian who reads the texts, interprets and writes them; 3) and finally the presence of an unfinished manuscript that the inner historian is trying to complete. In ***Cien años de soledad*** the most tenuous presence is the legal texts, but one can infer it from the allusions to the chronicles that were in fact *relaciones,* and particularly in the founding of Macondo, for the founding of cities, primordial activity of conquistadores, was closely connected to the writing of history. The vagueness of this presence is only so in relation to the others, for at least two critics have convincingly argued in favor of the overwhelming influence of the chronicles in ***Cien años de soledad.*** The nineteenth-century travel-books are evident in the descriptions of the jungle and at a crucial moment when José Arcadio Segundo hears Melquíades mumble something in his room. José Arcadio leans over and hears the gypsy mention the name of none other than Alexander von Humboldt and the word *equinoccio,* which comes from the title of the latter's book, which in Spanish is *Viaje a las regiones equinocciales del Nuevo Mundo.* In Macondo's Archive, there are in addition two key words: the so-called English *Encyclopedia* and *The Thousand and One Nights.* These two books play an important role in Melquíades' writing, and the *Encyclopedia* is instrumental in the decoding of his manuscripts. The existence in Melquíades' fiction of precisely these two books adds a peculiar twist to the Archive, one that points to its own literary filiation.

I do not think that it would be too farfetched to say that *The Thousand and One Nights* and the so-called English *Encyclopedia* together are allusions to that master of fictions called Borges. In fact, Melquíades is a figure of the Argentine writer. Old beyond age, enigmatic, blind, entirely devoted to fiction, Melquíades stands for Borges, the librarian and keeper of the Archive. There is something whimsical in García Márquez's inclusion of such a figure in the novel, but there is a good deal more. It is not too difficult to fathom what this Borgesian figure means. Planted in the middle of the special abode of books and manuscripts, a reader of one of the oldest and most influential collections of stories in the history of literature, Melquíades and his Archive stand for literature; more specifically, for Borges' kind of literature: ironic, critical, a demolisher of all delusions, the sort of thing we encounter at the end of the novel, when Aureliano finishes translating Melquíades' manuscript. There are in that ending further allusions to several stories by Borges: to "Tlön, Ucqbar, Orbis Tertius," in that Macondo is a verbal construct; to "The Secret Miracle," in that Aureliano, like the condemned poet, perishes the moment he finishes his work; to "The Aleph," in that Aureliano Babilonia's glimpse of the history of Macondo is instantaneous and all-encompassing; and particularly to "Death and the Compass," for the moment of anagnorisis is linked to death. Like Lönnrot, Aureliano only understands the workings of his fate at the moment of his death.

The Archive, then, is Borges' study. It stands for writing, for literature, for an accumulation of texts that is no mere heap, but an *arché,* a relentless memory that disassembles the fictions of myth, literature and even history. The masterbooks in the Archive are, as we have seen, the *Encyclopedia* and *The Thousand and One Nights.* The *Encyclopedia,* which Aureliano has read according to the narrator from A to Z as if it were a novel, is in itself a figure of the totality of knowledge as conceived by the West. But how is it knowledge, and how has Aureliano read it? The moment we consider the order of knowledge in the *Encyclopedia* and the way in which Aureliano reads it, we realize the paradoxes inherent in the Archive as repository of history. The *Encyclopedia* is organized, of course, in alphabetical order, without the order of the entries being affected by any sort of chronological or evaluative consideration: Napoleon appears before Zeus and Charles V before God. The beginning is provided arbitrarily by the alphabet as well as by the sequence: apocalypse must appear in the first volume. *The Thousand and One Nights,* on the other hand, stands for a beginning in fiction, or beginning as fiction, as well as for a series of individual, disconnected stories, linked only by the narrator's fear of death. Aureliano is like Scheherazade, who tells her stories on the verge of death. Neither book seems to have priority over the other. Both have a prominent place within the Archive, providing their own forms of pastness, of documentary, textual material. The order that prevails in the Archive, then, is not that of mere chronology, but that of writing; the rigorous process of inscribing and decoding to which Melquíades and the last Aureliano give themselves over, a linear process of cancellations and substitutions, of gaps.

Writing and reading have an order of their own which is preserved within the Archive. It might be remembered that in Melquíades' room, it is always Monday and March for some characters, while for others his study is the room of the chamberpots, where decay and temporality have their own end embodied in the very essence of eschatology. The combination of feces and writing in the Archive is significant enough. Writing appears as an eschatological activity in that it deals with the end. Yet writing is also the beginning, insofar as nothing is in the text until it is written. Hence the prevalence of Monday and March in the secret abode of Melquíades, the beginning of the week and of spring respectively (March, not April, is the "cruellest month" in García Márquez). Melquíades is both young and old, depending, of course, on whether or not he wears his dentures; he presides over the beginning and the end. The Archive, then, is not so much an accumulation of texts as the process whereby texts are written; a process of repeated combinations, of shufflings and reshufflings ruled by heterogeneity and difference. It is not strictly linear as both continuity and discontinuity, held together in uneasy allegiance. This is the reason why the previous mediations through which Latin America was narrated are contained in the Archive as voided presences; they are both erased and a memory of their own demise, keys to filing systems now abandoned, but they retain their archival quality, their power to differentiate, to space. They are not archetypes, but an *arché* of types.

This process is evident in the way in which Melquíades' manuscript is written and translated. Throughout the

An Excerpt from García Márquez's Nobel Prize Acceptance Speech "The Solitude of Latin America"

Antonio Pigafetta, a Florentine navigator who went with Magellan on the first voyage around the world, wrote, upon his passage through our southern lands of America, a strictly accurate account that nonetheless resembles a venture into fantasy. In it he recorded that he had seen hogs with navels on their haunches, clawless birds whose hens laid eggs on the backs of their mates, and others still, resembling tongueless pelicans, with beaks like spoons. He wrote of having seen a misbegotten creature with the head and ears of a mule, a camel's body, the legs of a deer and the whinny of a horse. He described how the first native encountered in Patagonia was confronted with a mirror, whereupon that impassioned giant lost his senses to the terror of his own image.

This short and fascinating book, which even then contained the seeds of our present-day novels, is by no means the most staggering account of our reality in that age. The Chroniclers of the Indies left us countless others. Eldorado, our so avidly sought and illusory land, appeared on numerous maps for many a long year, shifting its place and form to suit the fantasy of cartographers. In his search for the fountain of eternal youth, the mythical Alvar Núñez Cabeza de Vaca explored the north of Mexico for eight years, in a deluded expedition whose members devoured each other and only five of whom returned, of the six hundred who had undertaken it. One of the many unfathomed mysteries of that age is that of the eleven thousand mules, each loaded with one hundred pounds of gold, that left Cuzco one day to pay the ransom of Atahualpa and never reached their destination. . . .

Our independence from Spanish domination did not put us beyond the reach of madness. General Antonio López de Santa Anna, three times dictator of Mexico, held a magnificent funeral for the right leg he had lost in the so-called Pastry War. General Gabriel García Moreno ruled Ecuador for sixteen years as an absolute monarch; at his wake, the corpse was seated on the presidential chair, decked out in full-dress uniform and a protective layer of medals. General Maximiliano Hernández Martínez, the theosophical despot of El Salvador who had thirty thousand peasants slaughtered in a savage massacre, invented a pendulum to detect poison in his food, and had street lamps draped in red paper to defeat an epidemic of scarlet fever. The statue to General Francisco Morazán erected in the main square of Tegucigalpa is actually one of Marshal Ney, purchased at a Paris warehouse of second-hand sculptures.

Eleven years ago, the Chilean Pablo Neruda, one of the outstanding poets of our time, enlightened this audience with his word. Since then, the Europeans of good will—and sometimes those of bad, as well—have been struck, with ever greater force, by the unearthly tidings of Latin America, that boundless realm of haunted men and historic women, whose unending obstinacy blurs into legend. We have not had a moment's rest. A promethean president, entrenched in his burning palace, died fighting an entire army, alone; and two suspicious airplane accidents, yet to be explained, cut short the life of another great-hearted president and that of a democratic soldier who had revived the dignity of his people. There have been five wars and seventeen military coups; there emerged a diabolic dictator who is carrying out, in God's name, the first Latin American ethnocide of our time. In the meantime, twenty million Latin American children died before the age of one—more than have been born in Europe since 1970. Those missing because of repression number nearly one hundred and twenty thousand, which is as if no one could account for all the inhabitants of Upsala. Numerous women arrested while pregnant have given birth in Argentine prisons, yet nobody knows the whereabouts and identity of their children, who were furtively adopted or sent to an orphanage by order of the military authorities. Because they tried to change this state of things, nearly two hundred thousand men and women have died throughout the continent, and over one hundred thousand have lost their lives in three small and ill-fated countries of Central America: Nicaragua, El Salvador, and Guatemala. If this had happened in the United States, the corresponding figure would be that of one million six hundred thousand violent deaths in four years. . . .

I dare to think that it is this outsized reality, and not just its literary expression, that has deserved the attention of the Swedish Academy of Letters. A reality not of paper, but one that lives within us and determines each instant of our countless daily deaths, and that nourishes a source of insatiable creativity, full of sorrow and beauty, of which this roving and nostalgic Colombian is but one cipher more, singled out by fortune. Poets and beggars, musicians and prophets, warriors and scoundrels, all creatures of that unbridled reality, we have had to ask but little of imagination, for our crucial problem has been a lack of conventional means to render our lives believable. This, my friends, is the crux of our solitude.

novel we are told that Melquíades writes undecipherable manuscripts, that his handwriting produces something that looks more like musical notation than script, that his writing resembles clothes on a line. Eventually José Arcadio Segundo discovers, with the aid of the *Encyclopedia,* that the writing is in Sanskrit. When Aureliano begins to translate from the Sanskrit, he comes up with coded Spanish verses. These verses have different codes, depending on whether they are even or odd numbered. Aureliano is finally illuminated when he sees the dead newborn being carried away by the ants and remembers the epigraph of the manuscript, which is supposed to read: *"The first of the line is tied to a tree and the last is being eaten by the ants"* (emphasis in the original). He realizes then that the manuscript contains the story of his family, and hurries on to translate it to discover his own fate and the date and circumstances of his death. We shall return to the significance of all this, but first let us complete our description of the manuscript and its translation, for it is very easy to leap to conclusions concerning Melquíades' writing. Aureliano begins to translate the text out loud, jumping ahead twice to get to the present faster. Once he reaches the present he has a second illumination: that he would die in the room where the manuscript is kept once he finished translating the last line of poetry ("el último verso"). Critics have been quick to say that what we have read is Melquíades's version of the history of Macondo, that is to say, ***Cien años de soledad.*** Even if in fact it is Aureliano's translation that we read, then some changes have been made. To begin with, the epigraph has been omitted, as we have seen. In addition, Aureliano's leaps to get to the present have either not been accounted for in this version, or the holes they left have been restored. But by whom? The only solution to this enigma is to say that our reading—that each reading—of the text is the text, that is to say, yet another version added or appended to the Archive. Each of these readings corrects the others and each is unrepeatable insofar as it is a distinct act caught in the reader's own temporality. In this sense, we, like Aureliano, read the instant we live, cognizant that it may very well be our last. This is the eschatological sense announced in various ways by the Archive.

The radical historicity to which the Archive condemns us belies its apparent atemporality and the bizarre order that the masterbooks within it have. It is a historicity that is very much like the one to which the narrator-protagonist of *Los pasos perdidos* is condemned at the end of that novel. In fact, Aureliano's reading of the manuscript in search of his origins and of an understanding of his being in the present is analogous to the reading performed by Carpentier's character in search of the origins of history and of his own beginnings. Such dearly achieved historicity in the face of the circularity and repetition of the family's history is somewhat ironic, given the sense of ahistoricalness with which many readers, intoxicated by the similarity of names and by Ursula's notion that time is going round and round, leave the novel. Such historicity, however, is needed to represent, within the anthropological mediation posited, the lucid consciousness of the West, able to understand itself by posturing as the other, but unable to abandon the sense of history to which writing sentences it. This is a sentence from which we can gain acquittal by means of a wilfull act of delusion, but one that ***Cien años de soledad,*** for all its fictive force does not allow the reader.

There is a curious fact that few readers of ***Cien años de soledad*** remark upon: even though the novel begins with Colonel Aureliano Buendía facing the firing squad, the one who dies at the end is not Aureliano the soldier, but Aureliano the reader. It seems to me that this displacement, plus the fact that Aureliano's moments of vision are flashes of insight parallel to those of the rebel, seem to suggest a most significant connection between the realms of history and myth, one that constitutes a common denominator between the repetitions of the family history and the disassembling mechanisms of the Archive. In the Archive, the presence of Melquíades and Aureliano (and in *Aura,* Felipe Montero, in *Yo el Supremo,* Patiño, etc.) is an insurance that the individual consciousness of a historian/writer will filter the ahistorical pretense of myth by subjecting events to the temporality of writing. But in ***Cien años de soledad*** the death of these figures is indicative of a mythic power that lurks within the realm of writing, a story that makes possible the Archive. In *Yo el Supremo* this is clearly indicated by Patiño's being a "swollen foot," that is, an Oedipus who pays a high price for his knowledge. In ***Cien años de soledad*** Aureliano suffers a similar fate. He commits incest with his aunt, engenders a monster with her and dies the moment he has a glimpse of his fate. Aureliano is the necessary victim for us to be able to read the text, for us to acquire the knowledge we need to decode it. He (we) is no Oedipus, but more likely a Minotaur, which would bring us back to Borges (and also Cortázar). The ritualistic death—which prefigures that of ***Crónica de una muerte anunciada***—is necessary because of the incest committed both at the genealogical and the textual level. In both cases, what has been gained is a forbidden knowledge of the other as oneself, or vice-versa.

As we have seen, the most salient characteristic of the text we read is its heterogeneity. However, this heterogeneity is made up of differences within similarity. The various versions of the story are all related, yet differ in each instance. Their difference as well as their relation is akin—*valga la palabra*—to the relationship between the incestuous characters and to the broader confrontation between writer and a primitive other who produces myth. Put differently, the self-reflexiveness of the novel is implicitly compared to incest, a self-knowledge that somehow lies beyond knowledge. A plausible argument can be made that the end results of both are similar, in the most tangible sense, or at least related. When the ants carry away the carcass of the monstrous child engendered by Amaranta Ursula and Aureliano, its skin is described in terms that are very reminiscent of Melquíades' parchments. (pp. 368-77)

The monster and the manuscript, the monster and the text, are the product of the turning onto onself implicit in incest and self-reflexivity. Both are heterogeneous within a given set of characteristics, the most conspicuous of which is their supplementarity: the pig's tail, which exceeds the normal contours of the human body, and the text, whose mode of being is each added reading. The novel is a monster, engendered by a self-knowledge of which we too are guilty, to which we add our own pig's tail of reading and interpretation. The plot line that narrates the decipherment of the manuscripts underscores our own falling into this trap. Like Aureliano, we follow along in search of the meaning of the manuscripts, constantly teased by scenes where Melquíades appears scratching his incomprehensible handwriting onto rough parchment, by scenes where José Arcadio Segundo or Aureliano make preliminary discoveries that eventually lead them to unravel the mystery. But like Lönnrot in "Death and the Compass," and like Aureliano himself, we do not discover, until the very end, what the manuscripts contain. Our own anagnorisis as readers is saved for the last page, when the novel concludes and we close the book to cease being as readers, to be, as it were, slain in that role. We are placed back at the beginning, a beginning that is also already the end, a discontinuous, independent instant where everything commingles without any possibility for extending the insight, an intimation of death. This independent instant is not the novel; it is the point to which the novel has led us. By means of an unreading, the text has reduced us, like Aureliano, to a ground zero, where death and birth are joined together as correlative moments of incommunicable plenitude. The text is that which is added to this moment. Archive and myth are conjoined as instances of discontinuity rather than continuity; knowledge and death are given equivalent value.

It is a commonplace, almost an uncritical fetish, to say that the novel always includes the story of how it is written, that it is a self-reflexive genre. The question is why and how it is so at specific moments. Clearly, ***Cien años de soledad*** is self-reflexive not merely to provoke laughter, or to declare itself literary and thus disconnected from reality or from history. In García Márquez, and I daresay in all major Latin American novelists, self-reflexivity is a way of disassembling the mediation through which Latin America is narrated, a mediation that constitutes the pretext of the novel itself. It is also a way of showing that the act of writing is caught up in a deeply rooted, mythic struggle that constantly denies it the authority to generate and contain knowledge about the other without at the same time generating a perilous sort of knowledge about one's mortality and capacity to know oneself.

What do we learn about Latin American history in ***Cien años de soledad***? We learn that while its writing may be mired in myth, it cannot be turned to myth, that its newness makes it impervious to timelessness, circularity, or any such delusion. New and therefore historical, what occurs in America is marked by change, it is change. García Márquez has expressed this by tantalizing the reader with various forms of myth, while at the same time subjecting him to the rigors of history as writing, of history as Archive. He has also achieved it by making Borges the keeper of the Archive, for the figure of the Argentine ensures that no delusions about literature be entertained. In a sense, what García Márquez has done is to punch through the anthropological mediation and substitute the anthropologist for an historian, and to turn the object of attention away from myth as an expression of so-called primitive societies to the myths of modern society: the book, writing, reading, instruments of a quest for self-knowledge that lie beyond the solace mythic interpretations of the world usually afford. We can always use ***Cien años de soledad*** to escape temporality, but only if we wilfully misread it to blind ourselves of its warnings against it. American history can only become myth enmeshed in this very modern problematic that so enriches its most enduring fictions.

For it is not toward a high-pitched rationality that ***Cien años de soledad*** moves, but toward a vision of its own creation dominated by the forces that generate myth. This is perhaps most evident if we consider that the Archive may very well be the most powerful of cultural retentions. The Archive is, first of all, a repository for the legal documents wherein the origins of Latin American history are contained, as well as a specifically Hispanic institution created at the same time as the New World was being settled. As is known, the great Archive at Simancas, begun by Charles V, but finished by the King Bureaucrat Philip II, is the first and possibly most voluminous such storehouse in Europe. The same Herrera who designed the Escorial had a hand in planning the Archive, that is to say, in turning a castle that was originally a prison into the Archive. America was discovered by Columbus, but really became a historical entity as a result of the development of the printing press. Latin America was created in the Archive. It may very well have been Carlos Fuentes in his *Terra Nostra* who most clearly saw the connection, making Cervantes the inner historian in that novel. In terms of the novel's ability to retain and pass on cultural values, the message contained in books such as Fuentes' and ***Cien años de soledad*** is indeed disturbing, for they tell us that it is impossible to create new myths, yet bring us back once and again to that moment where our desire for meaning can only be satisfied by myth. (pp. 377-80)

Roberto González Echevarría, " 'Cien años de soledad': The Novel as Myth and Archive," in MLN, *Vol. 99, No. 2, March, 1984, pp. 358-80.*

Gene H. Bell-Villada

[In the following excerpt, Bell-Villada accounts for the widely acknowledged success of the Banana Company episodes in One Hundred Years of Solitude *and explores the historical and factual basis on which these installments were founded.]*

The episode of the banana strike and military repression in ***One Hundred Years of Solitude*** constitutes the highest point in García Márquez's extensive chronicle of Macondo. It is a vivid and dramatic scene, packed with sociopolitical suspense, capped with sanguinary horror, and followed by uncanny official silence and a fantastical rain. Moreover it is the last occasion in which the Macondoites and their Buendía leaders will collectively resist the meddlings of a high-handed central government. With the army occupation and repression, the townspeople will lose once and for all the scant political autonomy still remaining them. With the five-year cloudburst, courtesy of the Banana Company, the decline of Macondo as historical subject and vital entity will be greatly accelerated. The biblical windstorm that sweeps everything off in the concluding paragraph only completes an inexorable cycle of physical and spiritual degradation.

In musical analysis it is often noted that the climax of a composition tends to occur at a point approximately five-sevenths (5/7) of the work's duration. Such happens to be the case with García Márquez's superbly constructed, now-classic novel. In the Avon paperback edition of the book, consisting of 372 printed pages, the strike and the massacre take place in what are pp. 270-80 of the actual text. The fraction 270 over 372 can be reduced to 54 over 74—or roughly, five-sevenths. What transpires in the remaining two-sevenths is a bittersweet and melancholy dénouement, involving (among other things) the successive deaths of Úrsula, Pilar Ternera, the Segundo twins, and the last of the José Arcadios and Aurelianos.

U.S. imperialism, a subject by no means new to Latin American letters, has attracted a good number of ranking Hispanic authors over the last hundred years. Among Pablo Neruda's most-anthologized single works is his 42-line attack on "La United Fruit Co.," first printed in his grand epic of the Americas, the *Canto general* (1950), where one also finds other equally impassioned protest poems about U.S. banking and mining firms and their local military puppets. In the field of narrative, an author of the genius of César Vallejo, the great Peruvian lyricist, published in 1931 his socialist-realist novel *El tungsteno* (*Tungsten*); and Miguel Ángel Asturias, the Guatemalan who was awarded the 1967 Nobel Prize, labored throughout the 1950s on his ambitious and lengthy United Fruit trilogy, comprising the novels subsequently Englished as

Strong Wind, The Green Pope, and *The Eyes of the Interred.*

The subject matter itself proved a stumbling block to these two authors. For want of a novelistic formula suitable both to their narrative raw material and their ideological world view, the resulting novels generally fail as art—notwithstanding Vallejo's and Asturias's formidable literary gifts. It was García Márquez's fortunate lot to hit upon a narrative approach that would definitively sidestep and transcend the notorious pitfalls of anti-Yankee protest fiction. Indeed, the magic and serenity of voice of the Colombian's Banana Company sequence are at the same high level as can be found anywhere in ***One Hundred Years of Solitude.*** I have taught this book in American college classrooms since 1971; to date I have encountered no student complaints regarding the Banana episode, which, on the contrary, affects them profoundly. It is also worth noting that the literary critics who look with disfavor upon García Márquez's sub-tale of exploitation, resistance, and slaughter, are very much in the minority.

My aim in this essay is twofold. First, I shall examine García Márquez's Banana Company episodes as formal narrative, with a view to elucidating their high artistry and possibly explaining why that section works so well. And second I shall be setting forth the historical facts which served García Márquez as basis for his Banana chapters. Strange as it seems, there has been minimal research done on the extent to which the great novelist built those episodes around a very real strike and repression which, in 1928, swept across the entirety of Colombia's Banana Zone, from the old Caribbean town of Santa Marta to García Márquez's inland village of Aracataca. What we see happening in the banana fields of Macondo is narrative, is novel, is fiction; but it is also basically a true story, a piece of history carefully reconstructed, and then artfully exaggerated.

What is paradoxical is that the strike and massacre, despite their centrality to ***One Hundred Years of Solitude,*** scarcely call attention to themselves. On the contrary, the walk-out and reprisals are presented simply as one more event in the string of occurrences starting out with the exodus from Riohacha (Colombia's northeasternmost town) and terminating with the apocalypse of the wind storm in imaginary Macondo. When we think of titles such as *Tungsten* or *The Green Pope,* we know from the outset what their narratives are about and deal with. By contrast, it could never be said of ***One Hundred Years of Solitude*** that it is a literary polemic against Yankee imperialism, though its plot does encompass that touchiest of topics. No doubt, social struggles are extremely important, are perhaps the most important thing—but they are not the only thing. The simple wisdom of García Márquez originates in his having acknowledged for Macondo the coexistence of such realities as love and sex, of eating and merrymaking, of aging and dying and other human processes and practices, which keep taking place, if not with total independence from the Banana Company, at least with rules and dynamics of their own. (We might say that García Márquez narrates in an intuitive way what Louis Althusser explains, presents, and theorizes in a scholastic way.)

And so in those very same Banana Company chapters one also finds scenes that depict the gourmandizing and dissipation of Aureliano Segundo, the torrid romance of Meme and Mauricio, and the languid evolution and abrupt ascension of young, virginal Remedios, the Beauty. No doubt, The Struggle Goes On, as a 1970s left-wing motto would say, but, Fruit Company or no Fruit Company, life and death go on too. Colonel Aureliano Buendía wastes away in bitter solitude and dies urinating before the chestnut tree; his sister Amaranta finishes weaving her shroud just before she perishes at nightfall; and an old nun shows up with a basket bearing infant Aureliano, bastard son of Meme and the last character to live in the book. Hence alongside the Banana Firm's time present there persists the elder Buendías' time past even as there appear the seeds of time future in Aureliano Babilonia, witness-to-be of the closing moments and privileged reader of/in Melquíades's text.

Not that these developments unfold in a space wholly free and separate from Banana Company control. On the contrary, there are links that, while casual on the face of it, are actually decisive. For instance, the hapless stranger who, from ogling femme fatale Remedios in the shower, slips and cracks his skull, is one of the countless out-of-towners who have converged upon Macondo in search of Company largesse. In the same way, Meme befriends some American teenagers, and it is through Patricia Brown, daughter of the manager of the firm, that she meets her lover-to-be Mauricio, himself a mechanic's apprentice for the Company.

García Márquez's narrator doesn't insist upon those connecting links. The Fruit Company may set the stage and create conditions for such escapades, but these in turn have sufficient existence and vitality, a narrative density and textured art all their own. This differs substantially from the Asturias trilogy, where virtually everything from sex to baseball occurs in the inescapable shadow of Tropical Banana Inc., fount and origin of the 1000-page work's actions and atmosphere. It is no accident that the best scenes in Vallejo's much briefer *Tungsten* are those that have the least to do with the mining firm and deal instead with intimate power relations between the sexes.

The relative autonomy of the non-Banana scenes in the same chapters of ***One Hundred Years of Solitude*** becomes most manifest in their comic quality. Few would disagree that the traits and conduct of, say, Aureliano Segundo or Remedios, the Beauty, are uncommonly funny. What we have here is not anything like Shakespearian comic relief, however, but the power of levity itself, a dynamic of plebeian drollery and physical humor (of the carnivalesque, if you will) that is equal in its force and validity to the harsh matter of embattled workers and repressive troops, with its dark dynamic of horror and tragedy.

García Márquez's own Yankees are pure caricature, but are drawn with such virtuoso precision and elaborate complexity that, both in aesthetic effect and narrative significance, the portraits are fully achieved. The scene in which the Buendías' guest Mr. Herbert tastes a banana, opens his toolbox, and then successively applies to the innocent fruit his optical instruments, special scalpel, pharmacist's scale, gunsmith's calipers, and thermometer and photometer, is a perfect satire of our notorious mercantile-technological fix, our mania for bringing to bear the latest and most sophisticated hardware onto the simplest of things. At some point in his career, García Márquez appears to have understood that too solemn a vision of U.S. imperialism contributes nothing to the art of fiction, and that on the other hand there exists a rich potential in exaggerating and ridiculing those technological obsessions of ours which, even in the years since his novel was first published, have become baroque and even grotesque.

García Márquez explained to me in an interview that his Yankees are depicted as the Macondoites perceive them—a key aspect of his novel. To us in our time, American global power—with its world-wide extractive and agricultural, manufacturing, marketing, and financial, military and media apparatus—is a fact we routinely take for granted as a given. For early twentieth-century Macondoites, however, the "gringos" are a novelty, and it is thus that García Márquez succeeds in defamiliarizing his Americans, "making strange" their wondrous technology and their "languid wives in muslin dresses and large veiled hats," and the almost fantastical milieu of their town across the tracks, with its "streets lined with palm trees, houses with screened windows, small white tables on the terraces, . . . and extensive blue lawns with peacocks and quails."

Such a description suggests Los Angeles in the 1910s (or in the movie *El Norte*'s 1980s). In the context of a tropical and less-developed Macondo, however, the entire ensemble is intrusive, virtually something from another planet. Neither the townspeople nor we readers can hope to penetrate that colonial enclave, save for Meme's consortings with the Browns, and even then all is seen through her tender adolescent eyes. The narrator of ***One Hundred Years of Solitude*** is of the omniscient kind, as critics often note, but the actual bounds of such omniscience lie precisely in the electrified fence surrounding and protecting the gringos' separate reality.

By so depicting his Americans, García Márquez adhered to the first and basic rule of every good writer—namely, "Write about what you know best." In contrast, a serious flaw of Asturias's banana trilogy is that the Guatemalan author made the mistake of inventing protagonists who are Yankees, even going so far as to portray them from within. The artistic result is terribly defective and false; from the outset readers are aware that Asturias lacks thorough knowledge of his materials, inasmuch as his Americans simply don't sound or feel like Americans. For example, we are informed that the Banana adventurer Lester Mead speaks English with an Oxford accent. And in an episode in *Strong Wind,* the Banana Company executives take to quoting, from memory, long passages from Shakespeare's *Othello*—all this without the slightest hint of parody (no post-Modernist harbingers of Barthelme here). Anyone minimally acquainted with the subculture of United States entrepreneurialism knows full well that Asturias's portraits are, to say the least, improbable. Similarly, the gringos of Asturias's trilogy, as well as those of Vallejo's *Tungsten,* speak a perfect unaccented Spanish, with no syntactic or phonetic peculiarities of their own.

García Márquez did read Asturias in the 1950s and early '60s, quite possibly in order to learn from the elder writer's mistakes. It's well worth noting that, in all the Banana Company-related episodes in ***One Hundred Years of Solitude,*** there is but a single occasion in which an American character is directly quoted, and that rare utterance is relayed to us second-hand, via an unreliable source. I am referring to the government's proclamation that, following their assurances that the strike had been peacefully settled, cites Mr. Brown as affirming that labor negotiations will resume "When the rain stops. As long as the rain lasts we're suspending all activities." The truth is that the rain will fall for almost a half decade and heap ruin on Macondo.

In his numerous interviews and journalistic writings García Márquez always demonstrates an excellent knowledge of United States history and culture. Moreover he lived in New York in 1960 and '61, and then en route to Mexico, he travelled through the Southern states (where, owing to Jim Crow laws, he and his family experienced some difficulty in finding hotel rooms). And yet he has never presumed to know the more intimately psychological, existential aspects of American life. Nevertheless the Colombian novelist was to make the most out of his small-town Caribbean point of view, transforming this perspective into a narrative strength and casting the mould for the satirical vision he at last articulates toward that most classic of U.S. agribusiness firms.

The Banana episodes themselves benefit from the author's formal and narrative genius—for example the humor in the reference to Virginia hams, and in the useless copper-colored pills that the children rip off for use as bingo markers. Moreover, in contrast to Asturias's amorphous and rambling prolixity, García Márquez's myriad symmetries and repetitions keep any loose ends carefully under control. The sudden arrival of Americans in Macondo is the second such intrusion by outsiders, the first having been that of the Conservatives; in the wake of the gringos we find once again the sextet of opportunistic lawyers dressed in black; and, in the same way that José Arcadio Buendía and Colonel Aureliano Buendía had been prime leaders in the anti-Conservative resistance, José Arcadio Segundo now becomes a prominent agitator in the struggle against the Banana Company. And finally, instead of allowing himself to be carried away by the sensationalism of the massacre, García Márquez goes well beyond it, steers our attention away from it with his wild fantasies of Orwellian oblivion and five-year rains, the work respectively of the Government and the Company. In all, it is a panoramic sociopolitical subplot constructed with utmost craftsmanship and imagination.

The Banana Company chapters in García Márquez's book adhere quite closely to the actual facts of the great strike of 1928 (the year also of the novelist's birth in Aracataca). The historical record of United Fruit Company's operations in Colombia furnishes a textbook case of overseas

An excerpt from *One Hundred Years of Solitude*

Around twelve o'clock, waiting for a train that was not arriving, more than three thousand people, workers, women, and children, had spilled out of the open space in front of the station and were pressing into the neighboring streets, which the army had closed off with rows of machine guns. At that time it all seemed more like a jubilant fair than a waiting crowd. They had brought over the fritter and drink stands from the Street of the Turks and the people were in good spirits as they bore the tedium of waiting and the scorching sun. A short time before three o'clock the rumor spread that the official train would not arrive until the following day. The crowd let out a sigh of disappointment. An army lieutenant then climbed up onto the roof of the station where there were four machine-gun emplacements aiming at the crowd and called for silence. Next to José Arcadio Segundo there was a barefooted woman, very fat, with two children between the ages of four and seven. She was carrying the smaller one and she asked José Arcadio Segundo, without knowing him, if he would lift up the other one so that he could hear better. José Arcadio Segundo put the child on his shoulders. Many years later that child would still tell, to the disbelief of all, that he had seen the lieutenant reading Decree No. 4 of the civil and military leader of the province through an old phonograph horn. It had been signed by General Carlos Cortes Vargas and his secretary, Major Enrique García Isaza, and in three articles of eighty words he declared the strikers to be a "bunch of hoodlums" and he authorized the army to shoot to kill.

After the decree was read, in the midst of a deafening hoot of protest, a captain took the place of the lieutenant on the roof of the station and with the horn he signaled that he wanted to speak. The crowd was quiet again.

"Ladies and gentlemen," the captain said in a low voice that was slow and a little tired, "you have five minutes to withdraw."

The redoubled hooting and shouting drowned out the bugle call that announced the start of the count. No one moved.

"Five minutes have passed" the captain said in the same tone. "One more minute and we'll open fire."

José Arcadio Segundo, sweating ice, lowered the child and gave him to the woman. "Those bastards might just shoot," she murmured. José Arcadio Segundo did not have time to speak because at that instant he recognized the hoarse voice of Colonel Gavilán echoing the words of the woman with a shout. Intoxicated by the tension, by the miraculous depth of the silence, and furthermore convinced that nothing could move that crowd held tight in a fascination with death, José Arcadio Segundo raised himself up over the heads in front of him and for the first time in his life he raised his voice.

"You bastards!" he shouted. "Take the extra minute and stick it up your ass!"

After his shout something happened that did not bring on fright but a kind of hallucination. The captain gave the order to fire and fourteen machine guns answered at once. But it all seemed like a farce. It was as if the machine guns had been loaded with caps, because their panting rattle could be heard and their incandescent spitting could be seen, but not the slightest reaction was perceived, not a cry, not even a sigh among the compact crowd that seemed petrified by an instantaneous invulnerability. Suddenly, on one side of the station, a cry of death tore open the enchantment: "Aaaagh, Mother." A seismic voice, a volcanic breath, the roar of a cataclysm broke out in the center of the crowd with a great potential of expansion. José Arcadio Segundo barely had time to pick up the child while the mother with the other one was swallowed up by the crowd that swirled about in panic.

imperialism and colonialism, a story vividly suggestive of a novel by Conrad, Forster, Graham Greene—or García Márquez. From what were comparatively modest holdings around 1900, United's dominions in the northern, coastal portions of Colombia expanded rapidly to become a state-within-a-state and the de facto power in that region. In addition to the best lands, United had its own railroads, general stores, and telegraph system; with its network of canals it monopolized irrigation; and its water practices violated Colombia's Civil Code. Its labor policies left much to be desired, and already in 1918 United Fruit had responded to protests over low wages with a promise to consult with Company headquarters in Boston. The promise came to nothing.

By 1925 a number of anarchist and communist labor unions were formulating strike plans and preparing organizers. On 6 October 1928, the strike leadership confronted management with their list of demands. The first and most basic of these was that the Company acknowledge the fact that it had employees, inasmuch as its labor recruitment method had been one of relying solely on subcontractors who rounded up workers for United, a tactic whereby the firm had successfully evaded national laws regarding employee safety and security. The strike organizers also demanded "hygienic dwelling places," "social hygiene," "a day of rest in seven," and "the establishment of hospitals in sufficient numbers." Last but not least, they wanted an end to the system of paying the worker in credit slips, with which he had been obligated to purchase his provisions, at high prices, in Company comissaries. With this practice, the firm had further reduced its labor costs, and also steered clientele away from local merchants, who, not surprisingly, felt no love for United Fruit.

Meanwhile tensions had been mounting, and Company manager Thomas Bradshaw feigned absence from Santa Marta. But, according to congressional testimony by union leader Alberto Castrillón, "the simple truth is that he was merely trying to evade any negotiations whatsoever with the workers and their demands. After several days' search . . . he was casually found . . . while arranging the purchase of an automobile, and he absolutely refused to deal with the workers, and in a rather surly voice he declared them legally incompetent for negotiations of any kind, *given that the Company had no workers.*"

With the talks at an impasse, the 32,000 workers went out on strike on 7 October. The response of the Conservative government in distant Bogotá was a military occupation of the Banana Zone. The soldiers themselves were eventually put to work cutting and shipping banana bunches as strikebreakers. In spite of repressive laws and constant intimidation the workers stood fast, and on 5 December the government declared a state of siege.

That night a few hundred workers and their families assembled in the central plaza at Ciénaga, a town located some thirty miles north of Aracataca. At 1 A.M., General Carlos Cortés Vargas sent an army detachment to make a show of strength at the plaza. The state of siege announcement was read out loud to the strikers, and they were given five minutes to disperse. The five minutes ticked by, and they were given just one more. And finally a massive barrage of gun fire broke out. The proprietor of a nearby hotel heard someone screaming "¡AY MI MADRE!" (a common Spanish exclamation, roughly equivalent to "Oh my God!"). Several witnesses reported having seen the bodies thrown into trucks which then headed toward the sea. A few months later it would be revealed that the Fruit Company had been directly paying off the military, lodging the officers in hotel rooms, and sending complimentary beer, food, and cigarettes to the grunts.

The massacre was followed by a reign of terror. Hundreds of labor leaders were arrested—a railroad foreman would recall having been on a fourteen-car train, filled with detained workers and headed towards Aracataca. Concerning casualties for the entire strike, General Cortés Vargas would cite a figure of 40 dead and 100 wounded, whereas Alberto Castrillón calculated 400 dead in the plaza alone, and for the strike a total of 1500 dead and 3000 wounded. Shortly thereafter, a young Liberal representative named Jorge Eliécer Gaitán would promote hearings about the affair and climax his now-celebrated congressional investigation with an eloquent Philippic denouncing the scale of the reprisals and also the inordinate power of United Fruit. (pp. 391-98)

In this recounting of the events of 1928 I have largely restricted myself to the material retained and elaborated upon by García Márquez in ***One Hundred Years of Solitude.*** Here are a few initial examples from the labor side. "The workers demanded that they not be obliged to cut and load bananas on Sundays." They protest against "the lack of sanitary facilities in their living quarters, the nonexistence of medical facilities," and their "not being paid in real money but in scrip, which was good only to buy Virginia hams in the company comissaries."

At first, management's tactic is—physical evasion.

> As soon as he found out about the agreement, Mr. Brown hitched his luxurious glassed-in coach to the train and disappeared from Macondo along with the more prominent representatives of his company. Nonetheless, some workers found one of them the following Saturday in a brothel and they made him sign a copy of the sheet with the demands while he was naked with the women who had helped to entrap him. The mournful lawyers showed in court that that man had nothing to do with the company and in order that no one doubt their arguments they had him jailed as an impostor. Later on, Mr. Brown was surprised traveling incognito in a third-class coach and they made him sign another copy of the demands. On the following day he appeared before the judges with his hair dyed black and speaking flawless Spanish. The lawyers showed that the man was not Mr. Jack Brown, the superintendent of the banana company, born in Prattville, Alabama, but a harmless vendor of medicinal plants, born in Macondo and baptized there with the name of Dagoberto Fonseca.

What García Márquez has done here is to take real-life manager Thomas Bradshaw's attempted escape (as we saw reported by Alberto Castrillón) and then 1) magically elaborate the episode with the passing reference to Mr. Brown's glassed-in coach, 2) alter the capture of Thomas Bradshaw during an automobile purchase, to the surprise entrapment of a supposed impostor by some pro-labor prostitutes, 3) invent the incident of Mr. Brown being nabbed in a third-class railroad car, and 4) further add the fantastical courtroom exorcisms concerning the identity of Mr. Brown.

In higher court, García Márquez's six lawyers skillfully argue that the workers' demands "lacked all validity for the simple reason that the company did not have, never had had, and never would have any workers in its service because they were all hired on a temporary and occasional basis." Agreeing with this position, the court solemnly decrees that "the workers did not exist."

In the wake of the martial law declaration there arrive three army regiments to cut and ship the bananas and thereby break the strike, and union leader José Arcadio Segundo is thrown in jail. The massacre order is signed by General Carlos Cortés Vargas (García Márquez thus retains the full name) and the protesters are given five minutes to disperse. At the outset of the slaughter, someone cries out, "Aaaay, mi madre!" (rendered as "Aaaaagh, Mother" in Rabassa's translation). García Márquez replaces the multiple trucks sighted by witnesses, with his mysterious two-hundred-car train seen only by José Arcadio Segundo. Of the figures being debated with regard to casualties, the novelist seems simply to have chosen the highest of them all, the three thousand wounded cited by strike organizer Alberto Castrillón.

To this combined historical-fictional account I wish to add an experience of my own. In August 1982 I visited García Márquez's original hometown of Aracataca. During my few hours' stay I saw certain basic realities from up close, for example the two-block trek leading from the local church to the town cemetery, strikingly similar to the street to be walked by the stouthearted woman at the end of García Márquez's powerful short story, **"Tuesday Siesta."** It was a sultry, noisy lunch hour when I strolled down that road, and as I entered the cemetery the first gravestones I noticed were for Mercedes and Ester Ternera, the family name of Pilar Ternera, the erotic and freewheeling madam in ***One Hundred Years of Solitude.***

But my "Macondian" experience would reach a kind of climax when the youthful General Secretary of the town introduced me to an elderly retiree, who for years had worked as a timekeeper (he used the English word) for

United Fruit. His brothers had also been Company employees, and he remembered with great wistfulness the glory days of Banana prosperity, when there was lots of money to spare and folks would dance the native *cumbia* with peso bills burning away in their upheld hands.

I asked him what he thought about the strikers. This is what he answered. "Look, those people only caused problems and ruined everything. And let me tell you, all that stuff about massacres or whatever, it's all just a story. Lies. It never happened. The most *I* heard of was two guys shot. Look, if there really were all those dead, then you tell me, where'd they dump the corpses?" Thus spoke the senior citizen, in those words more or less, and at that point I became especially aware of the extent to which García Márquez works from reality. Finally, as a capstone to these symbioses between history and fiction, I must make an observation regarding García Márquez's prophetic strain. In 1972, Senator Claiborne Pell (D-R.I.) revealed that, for twenty-five years, the Department of Defense had been pursuing weather modification research, and moreover that, since 1967, in order "to reduce trafficability along infiltration routes," the U.S. Armed Forces had been seeding clouds to cause rains along the so-called Ho Chi Minh trail in Laos.

To a certain degree, the Banana strike and military repression are to the history and literature of Colombia what the Napoleonic invasion and retreat were to the history and literature of Russia. In both cases one is faced with great events that bring to mind noble abstractions such as national sovereignty, but that also have to do with matters so basic as the lives, sufferings, and survival of entire peoples. In the aftermath of these events there arise new, liberalizing elements within each society (the Decembrists in Russia, Gaitán in Colombia), its consensus shaken by the harsh deeds of a more developed, more prosperous foreign invader. And, what for us matters most, those historic events play a key role in two panoramic novels, one by Tolstoy and another by García Márquez.

There is today in Ciénaga's central plaza an impressive memorial to the victims of the United Fruit massacre, a monumental fifty-foot statue of an Afro-Colombian field worker, machete in hand. For simple reasons of accessibility, few non-Colombians will ever set eyes on that commemorative sculpture. But millions world-wide have read and will read the chapter depicting the strike and repression in ***One Hundred Years of Solitude.*** Most readers of classic novels know that Napoleon Bonaparte invaded Russia. Perhaps some day they will also know that an American agribusiness firm invaded Colombia, and that the massacre in Macondo isn't "all just a story." (pp. 398-401)

Gene H. Bell-Villada, "Banana Strike and Military Massacre: 'One Hundred Years of Solitude' and What Happened in 1928," in From Dante to García Márquez: Studies in Romance Literatures and Linguistics, *Gene H. Bell-Villada, Antonio Giménez, George Pistorius, eds., Williams College, 1987, pp. 391-403.*

FURTHER READING

Amaral, José Vázquez. "Gabriel García Márquez: *One Hundred Years of Solitude.*" In his *The Contemporary Latin American Narrative,* pp. 135-56. New York: Las Americas Publishing Co., 1970.

Suggests reasons for the popularity of García Márquez's novel in Latin America, compares the character Aureliano Buendía to Miguel de Cervantes' Don Quixote, and examines García Márquez's portrayal of the white American capitalist influence in Macondo.

Bell-Villada, Gene H. "Names and Narrative Pattern in *One Hundred Years of Solitude.*" *Latin American Literary Review* IX, No. 18 (Spring-Summer 1981): 37-46.

Examines the recurrence of names in García Márquez's novel, particularly those of José Arcadio, Aureliano, and Remedios, and their importance to the book's circular structure.

Columbus, Claudette Kemper. "The Heir Must Die: *One Hundred Years of Solitude* as a Gothic Novel." *Modern Fiction Studies* 32, No. 3 (Autumn 1986): 397-416.

Assesses García Márquez's novel in accordance with the tradition exemplified by such works as Bram Stoker's *Dracula,* Mary Wollstonecraft Shelley's *Frankenstein,* and Emily Brontë's *Wuthering Heights.*

Deveny, John J., Jr., and Marcos, Juan Manuel. "Women and Society in *One Hundred Years of Solitude.*" *Journal of Popular Culture* 22, No. 1 (Summer 1988): 83-90.

Consists chiefly of "a critical inventory of the treatment of female characters in the Columbian author's novel, with the purpose of establishing the ideological coordinates which move them."

Janes, Regina. "At Home in Pope's Grotto: *One Hundred Years of Solitude.*" In her *Gabriel García Márquez: Revolutions in Wonderland,* pp. 48-69. Columbia: University of Missouri Press, 1981.

Structuralist analysis of *One Hundred Years of Solitude* in which Janes maintains that García Márquez's use of a biblical and historical framework endows the novel with more unity than his previous works.

Jelinski, Jack B. "Memory and the Remembered Structure of *Cien años de soledad.*" *Revista de Estudios Hispanicos* XVIII, No. 3 (October 1984): 323-33.

Focuses on "the theme of memory in the novel and the way in which the temporal disposition of the narrative sequences reflects the structural dynamics of the process of recall."

Kadir, Djelal. "The Architectonic Principle of *Cien años de soledad* and the Vichian Theory of History." *Kentucky Romance Quarterly* XXIV, No. 3 (1977): 251-61.

Delineates García Márquez's unintentional application of the historical model developed by eighteenth-century theorist Giambattista Vico to explain "the complete life-cycle, the ontogeny of nations in a way that can be commonly attributable to the history of all peoples."

Mac Adam, Alfred J. "Gabriel García Márquez: A Commodius Vicus of Recirculation." In his *Modern Latin American Narratives: The Dreams of Reason,* pp. 78-87. Chicago: The University of Chicago Press, 1977.

Interprets *One Hundred Years of Solitude* as a work

about eschatology and "a metaphor about ideas such as order, fictions, and endings."

McMurray, George R. "Myth and Reality: The Perfect Synthesis." In his *Gabriel García Márquez,* pp. 67-107. New York: Frederick Ungar Publishing Co., 1977.

Overview of *One Hundred Years of Solitude* in which McMurray analyzes the novel's temporal structure and combination of mythical and realistic elements.

———. " 'The Aleph' and *One Hundred Years of Solitude:* Two Microscopic Worlds." *Latin American Literary Review, Special Issue: Gabriel García Márquez* XIII, No. 25 (January-June 1985): 55-64.

Compares García Márquez's novel with Jorge Luis Borges' short story "The Aleph."

———. *Critical Essays on Gabriel García Márquez.* Boston: G. K. Hall & Co., 1987, 224 p.

Reprints reviews and critical articles on García Márquez's works by such critics as Michael Wood, Robert Kiely, and Birutė Ciplijauskaitė.

McNerney, Kathleen. *"One Hundred Years of Solitude."* In her *Understanding Gabriel García Márquez,* pp. 18-48. Columbia: University of South Carolina Press, 1989.

In response to García Márquez's assertion that *One Hundred Years of Solitude* is based on reality, McNerney examines major themes in the novel and compares this actuality to the subjective reality of "our senses, not leaving out the world as presented to us by the usual means of communication and the mass media."

Minta, Stephen. "Macondo—I, II." In his *Gabriel García Márquez: Writer of Columbia,* pp. 144-79. London: Jonathan Cape, 1987.

Reflects upon García Márquez's creation of the town of Macondo in *One Hundred Years of Solitude* and explores the Buendía legacy of solitude and extinction.

Penuel, Arnold M. "Death and the Maiden: Demythologization of Virginity in García Márquez's *Cien años de soledad.*" *Hispanica* 66, No. 4 (December 1983): 552-60.

Proposes that Amaranta and Remedios the Beauty function as destructive female characters who refute "the notion of the intrinsic merit of virginity."

Porter, Laurence M., and Porter, Laurel. "Relations with the Dead in *Cien años de soledad.*" *Mosaic* XV, No. 1 (Winter 1982): 119-27.

Equates death with the loss of memory experienced by characters during the insomnia plague in *One Hundred Years of Solitude* and interprets the deaths of the book's characters as "shocking harbingers of our own."

Saldívar, José David. "Ideology and Deconstruction in Macondo." *Latin American Literary Review, Special Issue: Gabriel García Márquez* XIII, No. 25 (January-June 1985): 29-43.

Endeavors "to relate García Márquez's ideological and aesthetic perspective in *One Hundred Years of Solitude* to a radical deconstructive reading of institutions in the text."

Scott, Nina M. "Vital Space in the House of Buendía." *Studies in Twentieth-Century Literature* 8, No. 2 (Spring 1984): 265-72.

Examines "narrative as well as fictional space" to demonstrate "the closely integrated nature of these two aspects of the novel, as well as [García] Márquez's ability to fuse them into an indivisible whole."

Taylor, Anna Marie. *"Cien años de soledad:* History and the Novel." *Latin American Perspectives* II, No. 3 (Fall 1975): 96-112.

Analyzes the social and political relevance of García Márquez's novel and "the role of historical consciousness in the evolution of a society."

Williams, Linda L. "Edenic Nostalgia and the Play of Mirrors in *Hopscotch* and *One Hundred Years of Solitude.*" *Latin American Literary Review* VI, No. 11 (Fall-Winter 1977): 53-67.

Explicates "what is self-consciously constructed rather than represented" in the novels of García Márquez and Julio Cortázar in hopes of demonstrating how these are not "tragedies of historical time" but rather "comedies of the first order."

Williams, Raymond L. *"One Hundred Years of Solitude."* In his *Gabriel García Márquez,* pp. 69-91. Boston: Twayne Publishers, 1984.

Provides an overview of the plot and critical trends of thought surrounding García Márquez's novel and examines the book's social and political implications, use of narrative technique, and universality.

Zamora, Lois P. "The Myth of Apocalypse and Human Temporality in García Márquez's *Cien años de soledad* and *El otoño del patriarca.*" *Symposium* XXXII, No. 4 (Winter 1978): 341-55.

Explores García Márquez's treatment of "the beginnings and ends of human beings and humanity" in *One Hundred Years of Solitude* and *The Autumn of the Patriarch.*

Edouard Glissant

1928-

Martinican novelist, essayist, poet, critic, playwright, and editor.

An important figure in Caribbean literature, Glissant writes of Martinique's geography, history, and diverse ancestry. In his work, Glissant rejects the common assumption that a Martinican identity must be based on either white supremacist values or on *négritude,* which Kenneth Ramchand defines as a "celebration of Africa as a cultural matrix; a favourable interpretation of the African past; a pride in Blackness: a contrast between a harmonious way of life and decadent White civilization lost in materialism." Instead, Glissant stresses that Martinicans can distinguish themselves by recognizing the "prophetic vision of the past" in terms of their present situation. Glissant's fiction is set in the Antilles, a group of islands in the West Indies, and often features nonchronological narration marked by occasional absences of capitalization and punctuation. Although such narrative strategies may confuse readers, they produce, according to Juris Silenieks, "evocations, referring to what might be images from Africa, the Middle Passage, *marronnage* [the state of runaway slaves], slavery, etc. . . . like brief flashes surging up from the collective unconscious, as it were, fading quickly into other images whose referential frame seems to be the present or myth and legend." In addition to praising Glissant for occasionally writing in *créole,* a combination of French and the rarely written local dialect, critics have recognized that his combination of varying narrative strategies and voices appropriately reflects a nation's evolving identity.

Glissant grew up in Sainte-Marie, Martinique, where his father was a plantation manager. After completing his studies at the Lycée Schoelcher in Fort-de-France and campaigning for the poet and political activist Aimé Césaire in 1945, Glissant went to France to study philosophy and ethnology at the Sorbonne and the Musée de l'Homme. There, he published several volumes of poetry, his first essay collection, *Soleil de la conscience,* the novels *La Lézarde* (*The Ripening*) and *Le quatrième siècle,* and the play *Monsieur Toussaint.* Because of Glissant's involvement in the Société Africaine de Culture, the Front Antillo-Guyanais pour l'Indépendance, and other West Indian political groups, the French government forbade him to travel outside of France. In 1965, however, Glissant was allowed to return to Martinique to teach philosophy courses at the Lycée des Jeunes Filles in Fort-de-France. He continued to write, publishing *Poèmes: Un champ d'îles, La terre inquiète, Les Indes,* the essay collection *L'intention poétique,* and the novel *Malemort.* In 1974, he established the Institut Martiniquais d'Etudes (IME), a school that stressed Antillean history, sponsored many cultural activities, and was heralded as an alternative to the French government's public schools. Glissant returned to France in 1980, worked as an editor at the United Nations Educational, Scientific, and Cultural Organization (UNESCO), and completed the poetry collection *Pays rêvé, pays réel,* the volume of essays *Le discours antillais* (*Caribbean Discourse: Selected Essays*), and the novels *La case du commandeur* and *Mahagony.*

Glissant's interest in historical events that have influenced Martinique is developed in the poems "Les Indes" and "La terre inquiète" and in his second novel, *Le quatrième siècle.* "Les Indes" and "La terre inquiète" relate how Columbus "found" the West Indies and how Africans were forcibly brought there as slaves. These poems focus on the sociocultural distance between Martinique, Africa, and Europe as well as the distinctions made between Martinicans of European descent, those whose African ancestors accepted their slave status, and those who were descended from *maroons,* nonassimilated fugitive slaves who lived in the jungle. Critics recognize that these poems end with hope for social growth. *Le quatrième siècle* continues the theme of historical influence by focusing upon the young Mathieu Béluse and Papa Longoué, whose predecessors came from Africa as slaves. While Mathieu's progenitor accepts his position, Papa Longoué's becomes Martinique's first *maroon.* Mathieu seeks out the aging Papa, the *quimboiseur,* or healer, who explains important events in Martinican history to him. Scholars have noted that Mathieu's attempt to know and transcend his past parallels Glissant's own objectives as a Martinican writer.

Glissant's first novel, *The Ripening,* is set after the events described in *Le quatrième siècle.* In the story, Mathieu explains how he and his compatriots, a group of young, idealistic political activists, planned the assassination of Thaël, a minor government official, to ensure themselves a victory in the election of 1945. The narrative, which is told from both an adolescent and an adult perspective by Mathieu, proved confusing for some readers. The novel, however, also drew praise for its descriptive passages and the characters' existential musings. The sagas of the Béluse and Longoué families continue in *La case du commandeur,* but the focus shifts to Marie Celat, known as Mycéa in *The Ripening. La case du commandeur* traces Marie's birth and childhood, her marriage to Mathieu, his departure to Europe, the death of her sons, and her ensuing insanity. As the descendant of both slaves and *maroons,* Marie is unable to fully accept either heritage; this ambivalence compromises her identity, results in her mental breakdown, and hints at the possible collapse of Martinican society. Juris Silenieks observed that despite *La case du commandeur*'s negativity, "attentive reading is likely to yield the novel's richness of meaning and poetic beauty and to extend its relevance beyond the regional context."

Glissant's third novel, *Malemort,* concerns three characters who search for escape from poverty and unemployment. Initially set in the post-World War II era, *Malemort* spans almost 140 years of island history by juxtaposing and interweaving the fates of these modern Martinicans, who are often treated and referred to as one individual, with those of their predecessors. Hédi Bouraoui notes that Glissant's later work, *Mahagony,* takes a similar approach to history so that a "date, though specific, is simply a trigger for spontaneous memories transcending past, present, and future, and creating an effect of simultaneity that intentionally blurs events and relationships." As in *Malemort,* time, space, and voice converge in the polyphonic *Mahagony,* for the histories of the *maroons* are linked to that of the mahogany tree and the entire island. The events that enfold around the tree, which proves a source of comfort and protection for many *maroons*—including Gani in 1831, Maho in 1943, and Mani in 1978—involve characters from Glissant's earlier works. Marie Celat and other prominent female characters reappear, and Maho is recognizable as Beautemps, one of Mathieu's allies in *The Ripening.* Because the principal narrator, Mathieu, continually speaks to and about Glissant, his biographer, *Mahagony* also examines the relationship between story and storyteller.

Glissant's most famous essay collections, *L'intention poétique* and *Caribbean Discourse,* provide additional insight into his works. Daniel Racine described *L'intention poétique* as a "248-page 'meditation on the essence of language and its relationship with poetry' in which [Glissant] tries to define a poetics of the Antillean people derived from his culture and identity and different from Western poetics." *Caribbean Discourse* was published concurrently with *La case du commandeur* and includes essays on Antillean literature, economics, sociology, history, anthropology, linguistics, and discourse patterns. Wilbert J. Roget has found both collections representative of Glissant's desire "to develop in the Antillais complete rootedness in his land and his history so that he may be equipped to interact on equal footing with peoples of different cultural proveniences."

(See also *CLC,* Vol. 10.)

PRINCIPAL WORKS

NOVELS

La Lézarde 1958
[*The Ripening,* 1959]
Le quatrième siècle 1964
Malemort 1975
La case du commandeur 1981
Mahagony 1987

ESSAY COLLECTIONS

Soleil de la conscience 1956
L'intention poétique 1969
Le discours antillais 1981
[*Caribbean Discourse: Selected Essays,* 1989]

POETRY

Le sel noir 1960
Le sang rive 1961
Poèmes: Un champ d'îles, La terre inquiète, Les Indes 1965
Pays rêvé, pays réel 1985

OTHER

Monsieur Toussaint (play) 1961

Selden Rodman

The action of this novel [***The Ripening***] of political violence in Martinique, which won the 1958 Prix Renaudot and received much acclaim in France, takes place in 1945. The young poet who wrote it (the book is a first novel) now lives in Paris: at the time of which he speaks, he was 15. Late in the book he introduces himself and explains how he came to undertake its composition:

> All this time I was running and yelling in the streets. I went everywhere, searching for the man who had come back alive, in so heroic a fashion. I wanted to know his friends, to tell them that I understood [understood what?], or at least that I was alive, that I was their comrade and friend. "Write a book," said Mathieu, "You're the youngest of us all, and you can remember. But don't put us into your story, not as we actually are, that wouldn't be interesting. Fill your book with something of this island heat, the monotony of our waning days and our endless nights." "Let people see the zigzag

> course we followed" [said Luc]. "And don't forget to say that our theories didn't really hold water."

It's a little hard to believe that political activists ever gave such advice, but if they did they are to be congratulated more for their honesty than for their literary acumen. The bitter truism still holds, even in avant-garde novels: a story about revolutionists who see through their every motive, and regard the very scene of their activities as a melancholy backwash of history, does not make for drama.

Thaël, "the man who had come back alive, in so heroic a fashion," is a young peasant from the hills who is selected by Mathieu, Luc and his other intellectual comrades in the town to track down and kill a petty official named Garin, who is believed to stand in the way of their consummating an imminent electoral victory. In the first part of the book, Thaël accepts this mission and falls in love with Valérie. In the second part he accompanies Garin on a long journey to the sea, takes him out in a boat, upsets it and swims to shore while his victim drowns. In the final chapters the election is won, Thael returns to his home in the hills, and stands by while Valérie is torn to pieces by his own dogs.

Unfortunately the author takes the advice of his friends (to "let the people see the zigzag course we followed") so literally that the tragedy is more existentialist than Greek. The first part is hopelessly bogged down in the ambiguous soul-searchings of a dozen friends and lovers. The second part, in which pursuer and pursued tell each other exactly what they're up to and become friends, is too wildly improbable to be believed. And the conclusion (which might have been fatefully ironic and even tragic were the reader persuaded of the reality of its protagonists) under the circumstances seems both melodramatic and pointless.

The novel sparkles throughout with subtle perceptions, descriptive magic, poetry. ("Her eyes filled with tears and through their sunlit prism the sand-bar looked like a splash of frightened stars.") But especially in the early chapters these qualities only serve to confuse the narrative. "In this country," the author writes, "where the mountains are everywhere subject to the temptation of the sea, a mountaineer must be able to say no." The reader, however much he may prefer poetry to prose, finally gives up following a narrative couched in such conundrums and reluctantly says no himself.

Selden Rodman, "One Returned Alive," in The New York Times Book Review, *October 4, 1959, p. 38.*

Wilbert J. Roget

In a relatively recent statement [Glissant] has repeated his well-known position, calling for the Antillais to recognize that while he should insist on asserting the importance of the long-neglected African part of his being, and that while he should not forget nor overlook the fact of his separation from his African womb, nevertheless, he should de-emphasize concern with an inaccessible Africa in his determination to achieve complete integration into his own world. . . .

This bi-focal image of Africa; this ambivalent movement of acceptance and rejection for the single purpose of developing heightened consciousness of the Antillais identity; in short, this dialectical perspective is the essential vision of Africa that one encounters in the writings of Glissant.

The basic images of Africa that are developed by Glissant may be summarized as follows. Africa is the loving mother from whose womb her children have been pulled away. Africa is seen as the locus of highly developed civilizations which were decimated by marauding traffickers in human flesh. On the other hand, he presents another Africa also: the abode of those forefathers who collaborated in the plunder of territory and in the ravishing of their own children during the era of the slave trade. Africa is seen again as the lost homeland from which the Antillais are cut off by the waters of the Atlantic. Corollaries to the latter view are also examined. The Atlantic is presented as a fluid link with Africa, as a repository of memories of The Voyage, and as the agent which participated in the commerce of Africans. The winds sweeping across the Atlantic serve as reminders of The Voyage and of the inaccessibility of the ancestral homeland. The seacoasts are vivid reminders of the definitive break with Africa. The most commonly used image, particularly frequent in Glissant's novels, is that of a certain segment of the original African settlers in the Antilles—the maroons—whom Glissant perceives as primordial negators. They are usually seen as embodiments of a defiant will to resist integration into the New World. The maroons are pictured as a breed destined to disappear in the unfolding of history and in the process of the development of Antillais consciousness. The forests and mountains, refuges of these primordial negators, are guardians of ancestral wisdom and hidden secrets which must be revealed and later transcended. The *quimboiseur* or healer, latter-day personification of the maroon, becomes then a living anachronism, destined too to disappear, but possessing knowledge that must be imparted to the emerging generations.

Seascape and landscape acquire special meaning when presented in the context of the Antillais past. In **"La terre inquiète"**, Glissant evokes the ocean as a repository of suffering. . . . The ocean is a physical reminder of the destruction of African civilizations during the era of the slave trade. It is also the agent of the definitive break with Africa. (pp. 394-95)

In **"Les Indes"**, the poet steps further back into history to evoke in broad sweeps of imagination the tragic encounter between Europe, Africa, and the indigenous peoples of the New World. He pictures civilized peoples whose tranquility and peace was brutally disturbed by European slave traders. . . . The agonizing crossing of the Atlantic is followed by the painful initiation to a new life on the soil of the New World plantations. This bitter experience, however, is evoked as the condition giving birth to a new people. . . . (pp. 395-96)

Cast into a new land, and molded by suffering, the New World man feels the necessity to free himself from the hold of Africa. In ***Le sel noir,*** Glissant recognizes and accepts his African provenience, its profound presence in his very being, and its inspiration in his creative efforts. . . .

But he is nevertheless determined to find his own way, to make his own original contribution as an Antillais. He has won this right to articulate his independence through his history of suffering. . . . (p. 396)

In this truly sacrificial poetry there is an absence of geographic detail and of specific human existence pertaining to Africa. Glissant is more concerned with sketching the grand view, with capturing the resonances of a tragic past as he follows the painful westward movement of his people in the crowded holds of the slave ships. Even though he expresses affinity with Africa, the original womb, he places greater emphasis on the separation. Africa is evoked as a starting point from which the Antillais must, by his own efforts, forge his identity. Africa and Africans as an ongoing everyday reality are outside the pale of Glissant's concerns.

In the novel, ***La Lézarde,*** the movement downstream of the principal river of Martinique is made to symbolize the movement from the African past, immobilized in the mountainous abode of the latter-day maroon, Papa Longoué, towards the revolutionary ferment of the plains and the sea. The mountains, the plain, and the sea represent in that order the African heritage (the past), the muted history of harsh plantation life (the present), and openness to new ideas and endless possibilities in concert with other islands of the Caribbean (the future). The river is a link between these three features of the Martinican landscape; but symbolically, as a recent commentator indicates, it also serves as a challenge to the island's inhabitants "to overcome despair that may arise from a contemplation of the Caribbean past." This challenge is worked out under the inspiration and guidance of the leader of the group of adolescents, Mathieu Béluse. They must confront and understand the past. . . . However, in full lucidity, they must transcend the past as they engage in constructive revolutionary action. . . . (pp. 396-97)

We see Mathieu again in ***Le quatrième siècle*** engaged in a confrontation with history. His ambition is to understand the Antillais past in a manner congruent with the very character of Antillais history. He attempts to achieve this by exposing himself to two modes of knowledge: the nonlinear, contorted revelations communicated by the old *quimboiseur* Papa Longoué, coupled with his own scientific investigation of the Antillais past. The African in the New World, Mathieu comes to realize, is a new man conditioned by a new sense of space and time. . . . Antillean man does not possess a sense of geographic expansiveness so familiar to the inhabitants of a continental land mass (the Africans). . . . Temporal and spatial relationships in the Antillais universe are different from those of the African universe. So, if he intends to integrate himself totally into his own world, the Antillais must transcend his African heritage. Africa then is that part of the Antillais identity which, paradoxically, must be vigorously questioned. . . . (pp. 397-98)

In conclusion, then, Africa is a constant source of reflection in Glissant's works. But what this writer presents is neither the "traditional" Antillais image of Africa—that negative stereotype as analyzed by Fanon—nor the nostalgic and pacifist (Senghorian), or else the strident and combative (Césairian) proclamations one encounters in the various voices of the *Négritude* movement. Glissant's evocation subordinates all African references, or rather, he utilizes these references in furtherance of a more urgent, though perhaps less immediately glamorous, project. This project is to develop in the Antillais complete rootedness in his land and his history so that he may be equipped to interact on equal footing with peoples of different cultural proveniences.

The African component of the Antillais make-up is consequently to be viewed as a contributing element, not the determining element. And given the historical precedence of an ideology which extolled the supremacy of the African features *(Négritude),* Glissant finds it necessary to resist such a tendency. He wishes to ascribe to Africa its just measure in the composite Antillais identity. . . .

Glissant is convinced that the Antillais' authenticity must be established on this side of the Atlantic; that it should emerge as the result of painful effort; and that it can be attained without the easy answer of nostalgia for an African past. (pp. 398-99)

Wilbert J. Roget, "The Image of Africa in the Writings of Edouard Glissant," in CLA Journal, *Vol. XXI, No. 3, March, 1978, pp. 390-99.*

Juris Silenieks

The Caribbean region is sometimes referred to as an archipelago adrift in search of its identity. In a way, the metaphor is appropriate. It characterizes not only the region's geo-physical and geopolitical situation, but also its sociocultural relations with the other continents. The geographical proximity to the Americas, especially the United States, is sometimes felt as a menacing presence, poised for attack, sometimes as a counterforce promising liberation from the strangulating cultural and economic paternalism of the Old Continent. The Caribbean ties with Africa are complex. For some, following negritude's rediscovery of Africa, the continent looms as a repository of nostalgic intimations of a lost past, as a metaphor for black beauty and vanished dignity. Others look to Africa as an instructive actuality, a paradigm of social co-operation, collectivism that can counter the imposition of European concepts of individuality, freewill, private property, and so on, upon the originally non-occidental, heterogeneous cultures of the Caribbean.

The trauma of the past is ever-present, reaching back to the genocide of the warring Indian tribes by the first European conquerors, the arrival of the African slaves, their brutalization, their violent uprisings and equally vindictive punitive countermeasures, the colonial exploitation that, persisting in the present, has brought about vehement strikes and fostered endemic unemployment and degradation of those who must accept social dole. The policies of cultural assimilation have encouraged the young and the gifted to shed their ethnic traits in exchange for education and job security. M. Jean Benoist concludes his study of the Caribbean region: 'To sum it up, . . . the original Caribbean societies and cultures, which have incurred both the good luck and the misfortune of having a past so murky that their future must be invented, first must know themselves more thoroughly.'

In a way, a vicious circle is implied: in order to know oneself, one must know one's past. But, as Césaire laments: 'I look into my mute past', the past is not immediately accessible. Fragments of old legends, chants and dances still echo the distant times of African freedom. Tales of defiant rebel slaves and brave maroons evoke the misery and the glory of the days of Caribbean slavery. Folklore, however, represents, as Glissant put it, the 'collective unconscious', and to raise the past to a higher level of conscious apprehension, the poet and the historian must co-operate in the effort. The white historians, with but few exceptions, have either distorted accounts of the past, or, even worse, deliberately neglected the history of the black race as essentially unworthy of the historian's interest. . . . Now it is a question of 'historical reinsertion', involving not only correction of factual inaccuracies and rectification of white bias, but also re-creation of the past concurrent with the vision of the future, 'a prophetic vision of the past'. Such is the attempt of Edouard Glissant whose life and work are dedicated to the elaboration of a viable concept of *Antillanité* from the inherited cultural *métissage* that is to be viewed not as a curse but as a unique potentiality for shaping a distinct regional destiny. (pp. 161-63)

[In ***L'intention poétique,*** Glissant asserts that the] function of the black writer is to commit himself to 'the decisive act, which, in the domain of literature, means to build a nation.' Nation-building exacts a vision that can 'perceive of the consciousness, the one and only operative, of our being.' It is also predicated on the recovery of the past. Glissant insists [in ***Monsieur Toussaint***] that 'for those whose allotted share of history is only darkness and despair, recovery of the near or distant past is imperative. To renew acquaintance with one's history is to relish fully the present.' A conscious collectivity is bound together by the apprehension of a common past. Thus, [he writes in ***L'intention poétique*** that]

> collective memory is our urgency: lack and need. Not the "historical" detail (not that alone), but the innermost is to resurge: the diastasis from the womb of Africa, the bifid man, the reshaped brain, the violent useless hand. An absurd manifestness—where poverty and exploitation are wedded to something ineffably ridiculous—and where, noticeable to us alone, a drama without apparent import is being enacted which it is incumbent upon us to transform soon into a fecund Tragedy.

Descriptive history, claiming objective criteria, seeking to reproduce *wie es eigentlich gewesen* according to Ranke's aspiration or from Jacob Burchardt's 'Armedian point outside events', is impossible here. The historian must be seconded by the poet, since the task is not only to record and to interpret events, but to re-create the past in a new image, to invest it with a new meaning.

In his epic poem ***Les Indes,*** Glissant recalls the discovery of the New World, replete with brutality, rapaciousness and idealism of the white adventurer, merchant and priest, who raped the land, massacred the Indians and enslaved the blacks. But the poem concludes with the hope that from this period of violence and mystique of white aggressiveness will emerge a new universal consciousness of humanity. Glissant comments [in ***L'intention poétique***], 'this history is not mine,' since the white individualist and adventurer reduced the black to a passive spectator of his own victimization. The black 'suffers a history I did not make and yet could not ignore.' Thus, for the black, 'history suffered' must become 'history to be made,' with the full realization of one's freedom from imposed and accepted ideologies and moralities: 'I can negate this History, if I am free to do it (if I am free to make it).' A new meaning is to be given to the passage of the chained black from Africa to the New World to replenish the void that came with the genocide of the Indians. The violent separation from Africa must serve as a kind of sacrificial consecration of a future communality. In the preface to Kateb Yacine's theatre, Glissant writes: 'Today more than ever, we cannot conceive of our lives or our art, independently of the tremendous efforts of those men who from various races and cultures seek to come together and to know each other. Today the circle is closed, we are all in the same place: it is the entire earth. From this arises the Tragedy of our times, which is that of Man facing the nations, that of the personal destiny confronted with a collective destiny.'

Consciousness of historical time becomes one of the major preoccupations of Glissant's novels. Glissant's first novel, ***La Lézarde,*** is set in Martinique during those hopeful postwar days when Martiniquans for the first time were allowed to elect their true representatives to go to the metropolis. The narrative focal point is the assassination of a turncoat, who epitomizes the success of French colonial policies, by a group of young conspirators to forestall his competing in the upcoming elections with the candidate of the progressive group. Much of the novel's action derives from the characters' consciousness of the past, 'juxtaposing the banality of the present and the splendor of remembrance'. In its physical features, the island, like the world itself, offers universal contrasts between the mountain and the plain, the land and the sea, the lush rainforest and the arid salt plain, the fertile field and the volcanic landscape, reminders of past disasters and proof of invincible regeneration, scarred and verdant, the immobile presence of the ocean and the unceasing flow of the Lézarde River. Martiniquan space has an immediate, interfacial relation with the past. The ocean is the repository of indelible, haunting visions of the crossing from Africa in the dark hulls of the slave ships and the severance of ties with the ancestral land. (pp. 163-65)

On his deathbed, Papa Longoué, the wise medicine-man, a direct descendant of the original maroons, the last link with Africa, once more recalls the Middle Passage: 'there was a smell of rotten sea, faint rolling tormented his body.' Isolated on his mountain slope, immobilized in the present, Papa Longoué lives in a preteritive state of consciousness of the turbulent past.

Papa Longoué becomes the antagonist in Glissant's second novel, ***Le quatrième siècle.*** As suggested by the title, black history in the Antilles enters its fourth century. But the subjective experience of time, the four temporal modal categories of present, past, future and conditional are to fuse into one consciousness of Martiniquan time. The subordination of chronology to the apprehension of the experience of time forms the novel's central dialectic confrontation between Papa Longoué and Mathieu, the young intellectual.

Mathieu visits Papa Longoué urging the old man to pursue his account of the past, from the crossing of the Atlantic to the present. The central motif of the narrative is the correlative destinies, disparate and fatally joined by hatred and mutual attraction, of two families, whose progenitors, Béluse and Longoué, upon arrival in the New World, fought a prodigious battle. Once on land, Longoué escapes to the hills where he leads the proud and precarious existence of a maroon. Béluse is sold to a plantation. The paths of their descendants, on the one side the savage mountain maroon, 'those who refused', and on the other side, the assimilable slave of the plain, 'those who accepted', constantly cross, resulting in vendetta murders and intermarriages. Papa Longoué, who lives alone high up on the mountainside in his solitary hut where he practises the magic arts of the past, is the last member of the maroon lineage. Mathieu, a Béluse descendant, the young intellectual, senses a kind of shallowness and weightlessness of his being in the presence of the old man. 'We try to use the light of the past, but we feel too fragile under the weight, and to fill our presence, we are too hollow in the absence, in this oblivion.' Mathieu must find answer to the burning question: 'What is the past? What is left us of the past?' Papa Longoué insists that we must not follow the facts logically, but guess, anticipate what has happened.' Mathieu, on the other hand, wants dates and motives. The voodoo sage and the educated young man symbiotically complement each other. 'We want to know by ourselves, you who know and yet would understand nothing, if I talked to you aloud, and I who know nothing and yet I can already understand you . . . yes, we want to uncover from the inside, restart from the moment when everything was not dark.' Papa Longoué cautions Mathieu: 'The past is not in what you know for sure.' If, however, Mathieu's quest for historical consciousness must go beyond mere acquisition and ordering of historical data, Papa Longoué's self-incarceration in the past is a gratuitous exercise of the will to refuse. The Antillean must recognize the irreversibility of history and the futility of the nostalgia for Africa. . . . Papa Longoué has reached an impasse, since he cannot "attach . . . the past to the future." But the past can derive meaning only from its relation to the future and the potential. The past is not the immobilized, congealed existential *being-in-oneself,* but rather its opposite, 'this absence, this oblivion,' whence, through a 'prophetic vision', will arise 'the dizziness of memory.'

The present, however, in this dialectic reciprocity between the past and the future, the actual and the potential, remains uncertain. The present 'is a yellowed leaf on the stem of the past growing on the far side where neither hand nor look can reach it. The present falls on the other side, it is dying endlessly. It dies.'

The agony of the present predominates Glissant's third novel, ***Malemort,*** where wry humour and poignant sense of helplessness admix. ***Malemort*** is a polymorphic work of a variety of narrative techniques with changing perspectives, contrasting stylistic devices, modulating rhythms and alliterative sound interplays, peculiar creole speech patterns, and so on.

Malemort has no chronologically sequential plot-line as the narrative focus scans back and forth between 1788 and 1974. Personages from ***La Lézarde*** and ***Le quatrième siècle*** reappear, sometimes unretouched, but most frequently with an added dimension as representatives of types formed and differmed by some historical-cultural determinants. These present-day Martiniquans, jobless, eking out a welfare subsistence, wander aimlessly like unwanted exiles in their own land.

They are contrasted with the primaeval maroon, the *négateur,* the archetype of the *enraciné* in banishment, who, nurtured by the land, lives in concordance with the forces of nature. This race of proud and uncompromising naysayers started with the newly enslaved black who escaped the very first night after his arrival in the New World. Hunted down, persecuted, banished and executed, they have always risen from the dust and death to continue the defiant nonacceptance of the colonizer's ideology and morality. These legendary figures are projected in a myth-like vision to apotheosize their eternal violent death, their pitiful and glorious destiny as 'fallen-risen'. The maroon is consubstantial with the totality of Martiniquan time and space. He emerges from the earth that has witnessed his suffering and soaked up his blood and sweat and, slain by the oppressor, returns to it, partaking of the Martiniquan spatio-temporal contiguity. [In ***Malemort***], Martinique is thus this 'uncertain land where the yesteryears disappear into the earth, but whence tomorrow never rises.'

Judging from ***Malemort,*** one would be tempted to conclude that today's geopolitical realities have dispersed Glissant's original poetic 'prophetic vision of the past'. In the glossary appendix of ***Malemort,*** while offering explanations of certain local creole terms to the outside readers, Glissant admits that the indigenous reader is yet to be born. From the *Realpolitiker*'s point of view, there may be something quixotic in his attempt to inspire in his people a vision of the future through a past sublimated. On the other hand, the historical sensibility that subtends his work accords resonances of high intensity and originality. (pp. 165-67)

Juris Silenieks, "Glissant's Prophetic Vision of the Past," in African Literature Today, *No. 11, 1980, pp. 161-68.*

Richard D. E. Burton

The publication, in 1981, of Edouard Glissant's ***La case du commandeur*** adds a further *palier*—and, with it, further densities, ironies, and complexities—to one of the most remarkable literary undertakings in French of the last twenty-five years: the series of novels, beginning with ***La Lézarde*** (1958) and continuing with ***Le quatrième siècle*** (1964) and ***Malemort*** (1975), in which Glissant has sought not merely to relive or reconstruct the history of the Martinican people from the beginnings of French colo-

Glissant on the concept of world community:

Today more than ever, we cannot conceive of our lives or our art, independently of the tremendous efforts of those men who from various races and cultures seek to come together and to know each other. Today the circle is closed, we are all in the same place: it is the entire earth. From this arises the Tragedy of our times, which is that of Man facing the nations, that of the personal destiny confronted with a collective destiny.

Edouard Glissant in a preface to Kateb Yacine's* Théâtre, *1969.

nization to the present day but, in a very real sense, to *create* that history, to deliver the island-department's past—and hence, perhaps, its present and its future—from the layers of repression and oblivion in which nearly three and a half centuries of metropolitan dominance have enshrouded it. The rewriting of colonial history 'from below' according to the viewpoint of the colonized has, of course, been a major preoccupation of West Indian and African writers in both English and French for many decades now and, to this extent, Glissant's project may be set beside the work of Edward Brathwaite, Wilson Harris, and C. L. R. James in the English-speaking Caribbean or, in the case of Francophone Africa, alongside that of Kateb Yacine, Mohammed Dib, or Yambo Ouologuem. But the history of Martinique differs significantly not only from that of France's former African possessions—uninterrupted French dominance since 1635, the quasi-genocidal destruction of the autochthonous Carib people, and their replacement by an entirely new enslaved, deracinated, and, to a large extent, culturally denuded population from Africa—but also from that of neighbouring British ex-colonies in the Caribbean. Whereas, to a greater or lesser degree, the histories of colonial Jamaica, Barbados, or Trinidad are distinct from that of the colonizing power in that British colonial policy consistently sought to maximize the cultural and political distance between *métropole* and colony, colonizer and colonized, the history of Martinique has, especially since 1789, been decisively bound up with that of the *métropole,* not merely in the obvious sense that it has been throughout that period politically and economically subordinate to France but, more profoundly, in that every significant change (and certainly every progressive or pseudo-progressive change) that has occurred in the island since the Revolution has been brought about not by the actions of individuals or groups *within* the colony (whether they be slave or free, colonial officials or colonized subjects, whites, blacks, browns, or whatever), but directly as a result or adventitious by-product of changes—most notably changes of régime—that have taken place in France itself. . . . As Glissant writes in ***Le discours antillais*** (a massive and remarkable collection of articles, conference papers, and other writings, also published in 1981, which forms an indispensable discursive counterpoint to his fictional, poetic, and dramatic works), the fundamental character of Martinican history lies precisely in its 'surdétermination'. The principal 'events' that mark its development—1794, 1848, 1946—are, in reality, pseudo-events, mimetic versions or refractions of events in *la mère patrie* that are given a particular twist or coloration by the interplay of local forces, but whose essential origin and meaning lie none the less *elsewhere*. . . . To the extent that, as Glissant argues, Martinique is a product of outside historical forces rather than a producer of its own history, that history, considered (if that is possible) from within, is quite simply a 'non-histoire'. There are no genuine historical periods, only different 'pans d'histoire' illusorily separated from each other by pseudo-events of metropolitan provenance whose sudden and apparently revolutionary irruption masks an underlying structural continuity based, externally, on the enduring subjection of island-colony or island-department to the needs and wishes of the *métropole* and, internally, on the seemingly unshakeable hegemony of the white creole élite (the five thousand or so Martinican-born whites known locally as *békés*) over the black majority, with an intermediary and predominantly mulatto middle class sandwiched uncomfortably in between. . . . But this structural invariant is itself deeply deceptive. Far from generating a body of inherited beliefs, skills, values, and customs that might be transmitted from generation to generation, the continuum of Martinican history is a continuum of oppression, uprooting, and alienation which in its turn conceals a multitude of discontinuities, cleavages, and ruptures on the cultural, psychological, and spiritual levels. . . . Above all, fissures open up in the minds of Martinicans themselves; the linkages between past, present, and future fray and are lost, either as a result of the imposition of an enervating allogeneous culture or, quite simply, because the past is too nightmarish ever to be confronted, accepted, and integrated into the present or assumed as a *tremplin* for future action and development. Like the St Lucian poet and dramatist Derek Walcott, Glissant sees his fellow West Indians as victims of a kind of collective historical amnesia. . . . History in the West Indies is everywhere and nowhere—everywhere in that the present is directly, decisively, and oppressively determined by the past; nowhere in that that past has yielded few if any lasting visible monuments in the external world and, still more seriously, no internal imprints in the minds of West Indians other than wounds, absences, and disjunctions that must at all costs be suppressed. How can a novelist come to terms with a history that is at once hopelessly continuous and hopelessly fragmented, shatteringly present and disconcertingly absent? Of one thing one may be certain: the vision of history he will produce, and the fictional form in which he will embody it, will in no way resemble the linear, teleological, progressive structures either of 'liberal' history or of the conventional historical novel as it evolved in nineteenth-century Europe. If ***La Lézarde, Le quatrième siècle, Malemort,*** and, now, ***La case du commandeur*** do, as I said earlier, constitute a fictional series, it is, assuredly, a series of a highly nonserial and nonsequential kind and, if we are to render intelligible Glissant's vision of the Martinican past and the place of ***La case du commandeur*** within that vision, we must provisionally suspend discussion of the first novel to be published, ***La Lézarde,*** in order to concentrate on its successor and 'prequel', ***Le quatrième siècle.***

The germ of ***Le quatrième siècle*** and the foundation of the principal narrative, structural, and metaphoric oppositions that underpin all four novels lie in the contrasted but intersecting histories of two families, the Longoués and the Béluses, whose African-born slave ancestors arrive in Martinique aboard the same slave-ship in 1788; their stories are told in the early 1940s (a crucial period in the development of Martinican political consciousness when the island, completely cut off from the outside world, was governed by Admiral Robert in the name of the Vichy régime) by Papa Longoué, a seventy-year-old direct descendant of the similarly-named founder of the Longoué dynasty, to Mathieu Béluse, the youngest member of the rival clan, born in 1926, and in certain respects, it would seem, an embodiment of Glissant himself. The key event that dominates—determines even—the whole of the subsequent history of the two families occurs on the very day of their forefathers' arrival in Martinique. As yet unnamed (or, more precisely, since the theme of names and naming is of vital significance for Glissant, bearing African names that are never revealed), the ancestors of what will become the Longoué and Béluse clans come to blows on the deck of the slave-ship as it lies at anchor off the Pointe des Nègres in Martinique (rivalry had, for reasons that again are not disclosed, arisen between them at the *comptoir* on the West African coast from which they had been shipped and had intensified during long months of agony in the hold of the *Rose-Marie*) and are sold off separately to two Martinican planters, themselves bitter rivals, the future Longoué to La Roche, the owner of a thriving estate known as L'Acajou, and the future Béluse to Senglis, the owner of a less prosperous adjacent plantation. Whereas Béluse accepts and becomes steadily reconciled to the condition of field-slave, on his first night at L'Acajou Longoué is released by a Martinican-born female slave (whom he himself will later return to liberate and who, in bearing his children, teaching him to speak Creole, and, not least, in giving him the name Papa Longoué, is both genitrix of the Longoué clan and its initiatrix into the long process of 'creolization') and flees to the uncultivated, untamed, unowned wooded highlands known in Martinique as the *mornes.* The polarity of lowland/plainsfolk/bondage and highland/hill-folk/freedom—one of the fundamental socio-topical structures of West Indian life—provides the essential binary opposition of Glissant's vision of Martinican history, one that will generate a whole series of further oppositions whose confrontation, combination, and interweaving, primarily in the form of kinship relations, constitute the intricate narrative web of the four novels. Longoué, Glissant writes in ***Malemort,*** represents 'le Négateur, le marron primordial', the *Ur*-Martinican who resists and of whom various avatars (not all of them necessarily members of the Longoué clan and none of them as uncompromising or 'pure' as his prototype) will appear throughout the decades and centuries to come; for his part, Béluse stands for the overwhelming majority of Martinicans who have, from the slave period onwards, accommodated themselves in one way or another to the Franco-*béké* diarchy and to the material, cultural, psychological, and other losses such accommodation entails. So to characterize the two patriarchs and their offspring might imply a straightforward Manichean struggle between 'noble savages' and 'collaborators', and so no doubt it would in a writer less exacting, less intelligent, and, above all, less intent upon grasping the full complexities of West Indian history than Glissant. The great strength of Glissant's historical vision (and here he diverges sharply from the *terribles simplificateurs* of the *négritude* epoch with their false oppositions of African 'base' and European 'superstructure', black unity-and-purity, white or white-inspired division-and-corruption) lies precisely in his determination to understand, espouse, and assume the Martinican reality in all its multi-faceted contradictoriness. In the creation of that complexity—that reality—four major groups, in Glissant's view, have been asymmetrically and antagonistically involved. The economic and social infrastructure of 'traditional' (that is, pre-1946) Martinican society is primarily the creation of the *békés* now in alliance, now in conflict, with metropolitan economic interests. On the other hand, the society's political and ideological superstructure has, at least since 1848, derived from the extension to Martinique of the principal institutions and ideas of French republicanism and, far from reflecting or sanctifying the socio-economic order, that superstructure in fact implicitly contradicts it at many significant points. Finally, the traditional Creole culture as it has emerged since the beginning of the slave epoch is a composite creation to which all participants in the island's history—Europeans, Africans, and (to a lesser extent) Caribs and Asian indentured labourers and their descendants—have contributed in their different ways. Heterogeneous in its origins and in the various patrimonies on which it draws, that culture none the less possesses—or possessed—a defining quiddity that makes (made) it something more than the sum of its parts, something neither 'African' nor 'European', nor yet a debased amalgam of both, but an original Creole creation, something quintessentially and uniquely Martinican. The underlying theme of ***Le quatrième siècle*** is the progressive formation of this cultural unity-in-diversity, a centuries-long process in which (and herein lies Glissant's great contribution to the understanding of Martinican history) both 'resisters' and 'collaborators', the Longoués and the Béluses, have actively participated, the former through their clinging onto an 'African' authenticity and their refusal of the plantation and its values, the latter through their flexibility, receptiveness, and ability to improvise, combine, and adapt creatively. This dialectical co-creation of the Creole culture is expressed in the novel through the constant [coming and going] between highlands and lowlands, *mornes* and plantation. Just as the Longoués cannot survive in isolation in their highland fastness but must enter into economic, sexual, and other transactions with the people of the plain, so generations of Béluses, from the paradoxically named Anne, son of the original Béluse, in the 1820s, down to Mathieu in the 1940s, are drawn to the uplands in search of the medical and magical lore of the 'pays d'avant' that, together with a knowledge of the two clans' history since 1788, the Longoués have preserved. But though a common, if internally divided, culture emerges from this interaction, at no point is there a synthesis between highlands and lowlands, Longoués and Béluses. . . . Significantly, those members of the two clans, or others related to them, who attempt to establish themselves in the intermediary zone between plantation and *mornes,* hoping there to combine the material and psychological advantages of both, invariably come to grief. Survival is possible, Glissant appears to be saying, either on the plantation or in the almost entirely marginal world of the *mornes,* provided that a mutually fecundating intercourse continues between them, but impossible in the interstitial realm that lies between; the tragedy is, of course, as the later novels will amply reveal, that it is precisely in this no-man's-land between *hauteurs* and *habitation,* especially in towns, that the vast majority of Martinicans today live, move, and have whatever being is vouchsafed them and from that same in-between world that the characters of ***Malemort*** and ***La case du commandeur*** will principally be drawn.

The final pages of ***Le quatrième siècle*** deal briefly with the period to which the first novel of the sequence, ***La Lézarde,*** is exclusively devoted, namely, the immediate aftermath of Martinique's 'Vichy interlude' and, in particular, the elections of 1945 that led directly to the island's incorporation into the *métropole* the following year. Through the thoughts, feelings, and actions of a group of young Martinicans, including Mathieu Béluse and his distant cousin Marie Celat, herself distantly related to the Longoué clan and destined to be the tragic pivotal figure of ***La case du commandeur,*** Glissant captures superbly the mood of expectation, tinged with an undercurrent of anxiety, that was, by all accounts, prevalent in the island at the time of departmentalization. . . . Taken together, ***La Lézarde*** and ***Le quatrième siècle*** are themselves products and reflections of the enormous optimism generated by departmentalization. Despite their troubled shadow-side, both novels are animated by an unmistakable propulsive movement forwards and outwards. Basically chronological in their structure, the vision of history they embody is essentially progressive, cumulative, and purposeful as, beneath the negative continuum of oppression and the psychological and other discontinuities born of that oppression, a hitherto-suppressed positive continuity of resistance and cultural creation is steadily revealed. But no sooner are the subterranean rehumanizing, repersonalizing powers of the Creole counter-culture made known than further ruptures break forth: on the very day of the election Papa Longoué dies heirless and, shortly afterwards, Mathieu, the one person to whom he has imparted his knowledge and sense of historical continuity, leaves the island for France, as Glissant did at much the same time. With the loss of these two contrasting links between past, present, and future, the newly-departmentalized island is abandoned to the corrosive mechanisms of material, cultural, and psychological *decreation* that will be described in ***Malemort*** and ***La case du commandeur.*** (pp. 301-06)

Assimilation having led to an intensification of the very imbalances it was supposedly to rectify and the hyper-assimilation of the 1960s and 1970s to a condition of hyper-alienation prevalent, Glissant claims, amongst all sections of the Martinican people, black, brown, *and* white, it is hardly surprising if first ***Malemort*** and now ***La case du commandeur*** embody a vision of history which, though it develops logically out of that of the first two novels, is none the less essentially negative, even despairing, in its purport. Gone is the future-directed chronological progression of ***La Lézarde*** and ***Le quatrième siècle;*** it is replaced by a fragmented, disjunctive structure in which distant 'pans d'histoire' are juxtaposed in order to reveal both the relentless sameness of the Martinican condition in time and the deep mental cleavages that prevent Martinicans from linking their present to their past and hence from transcending both in purposive, forward-looking activity. In ***Malemort*** attention shifts from the Longoué and Béluse families to focus instead on three unrelated agricultural workers named Dlan, Médellus, and Silacier and their various attempts, between the late 1930s and the early 1970s, to come to terms with the condition of unemployment or half-employment that, as both plantation and peasant agricultures collapse, appears to be their permanent lot. So closely associated with each other at the outset that they are referred to monolithically as 'Dlan Médellus Silacier', the three men are steadily split asunder to form separate selves, as each retreats into one or another phantasmal or violent pseudo-solution to an intractable reality, Dlan into chiliastic religion, Silacier into bewildered bloody-mindedness, and Médellus into founding a utopian agricultural commune that is eventually bulldozed down to make way for flats by one of the countless 'SO MI DO VAG DE RAG ME SI DAM CA MAG REM NO PAM' construction companies that proliferate in contemporary Martinique. Resistance is still possible—one of the most memorable passages in the novel chronicles in brilliantly foreshortened form the history of contestation in Martinique from the slave revolts of 1788 and 1848 to the riots in Fort-de-France in 1959 and 1971 and the banana-workers' strike in the north of the island in 1974. . . . Yet resistance in ***Malemort*** appears more and more to derive rather from a sense of inner emptiness and despair than from one of cultural and human strength. . . . [La] Lézarde, the river which, in the novel of that name, linked *mornes* and plains, past and present, and flowed out to sea, the wider world, and the future, has by 1960 almost completely dried up while the *mornes* themselves are now being colonized. . . . The material and cultural *arrière-pays* that still existed at the time of departmentalization is now visibly disintegrating and, as it does so, the psychological and spiritual infrastructure of men like Dlan, Silacier, and Médellus itself collapses, leaving them only delirium, delusion, or undirected destructiveness as ways out of their desperation.

La case du commandeur takes as its starting and finishing points the story of Marie Celat (also known as Mycéa), perhaps the most fervent of the young radicals of ***La Lézarde*** . . . whose progressive psychic disintegration since 1945 both symbolizes and is produced by the multiple imbalances that have disrupted Martinican life since departmentalization. The whole orientation of ***La case du commandeur,*** in marked contrast to that of the early novels, is backward-looking as, starting with Mycéa, Glissant traces back generation by generation the history of the Celat family, which does not possess a historically identifiable progenitor like the original Papa Longoué and Béluse but only an indeterminate slave-ancestor who may have arrived in Martinique around 1715 and whose name, Odono, has somehow been handed down the generations to haunt Mycéa and her father, Pythagore, with its forlorn but infinitely suggestive resonance. Unlike the Longoués and the Béluses, the Celat clan belongs neither wholly to the *mornes* nor wholly to the plains. Around 1870 Augustus Celat, the son of Anatolie Celat and Liberté Longoué, the grand-daughter of the original Papa Longoué, had taken as his common-law wife Adoline Alfonsine, the daughter of Euloge Alfonsine who, though black, works . . . as *commandeur* or foreman on the plantation. This socially, culturally, and geographically mixed union between 'la descendante du commandeur' (Adoline) and 'le petit fils du quimboiseur' (Augustus) produces a dynasty which, in one way or another, is always divided between the contradictory, if complementary, worlds of *mornes* and plantations; Mycéa's parents, for example, live in the *mornes,* but . . . her mother (like Adoline before her) eventually goes down to live and work in the *bourg.* Other genealogical uncertainties add to the confused identity of the Celat clan. The identity of Adoline's mother is never disclosed, and Mycéa's own mother, Cinna Chimène, is a foundling of indeterminate ancestry; Mycéa herself has a daughter by Mathieu Béluse (who promptly abandons her and departs for France) and later two sons by an unidentified father. Whereas the world of ***Le quatrième siècle*** is patrifocal, patrilinear, even patriarchal, in structure, that of ***La case du commandeur*** is notable for the number of absent, unknown, or suspect parents and forebears that it contains. Initially experienced as an absence of void, the Martinican past had, in the course of ***La Lézarde*** and ***Le quatrième siècle,*** been gradually endowed with a content, a presence; in ***La case du commandeur,*** that carefully contrived plenum becomes once more a vacuum, 'un trou' which none of the modern characters in the novel—and, Glissant would claim, no modern Martinican—can contemplate without terror and vertigo. It is indeed literally in 'un trou du passé'—a former punishment cell for slaves in a ruined fortress in the *mornes* where Liberté Longoué and Anatolie Celat first make love—that the Celat clan has its only identifiable origins and this constitutes its one wholly ambiguous historical inheritance. . . . Above all, there is the mystery concerning Odono himself. Did he really exist and, if he did, was he treacherously sold into slavery in the 'pays d'avant' by his own brother, also named Odono? And who is Aa, who, earlier even than Papa Longoué, flees to the *mornes,* makes contact with what remains of the island's original Carib population (whose final collective cliff-top suicide is memorably evoked), and is then himself betrayed and burnt to death in another horrendous 'trou du passé'? None of these questions receives an adequate answer, so that history confronts the Celat clan, and particularly the ultimate product of that history, Marie Celat herself, as an inscrutable, faceless that-ness. . . . Lacking any anchorage in the past and in the landscape that surrounds them, the characters of ***La case du commandeur,*** like those of ***Malemort*** before it, are devoid of real personal substance and, as such, are locked in themselves, unable to establish sustaining relationships with each other. . . . [Glissant writes in ***La case du commandeur*** that the problem of origins]—that problem to which, by identifying the forefathers of the Longoué and Béluse clans, ***Le quatrième siécle*** had apparently given a solution—is reopened in ***La case du commandeur*** with traumatic consequences for individuals and community alike. (pp. 308-10)

Mycéa simply has no psychic, cultural or other resources on which to fall back in the face of the numerous crises, both private and public, that befall her. To this extent, her condition is, in its nonproductiveness, instability and essential evanescence, but an intensified version of the Martinican people as a whole, as described in ***Le discours antillais.*** . . . The situation of Mycéa's two sons is even more precarious. Patrice, born in 1958 and named after Lumumba, grows up [with a predilection for violence] . . . and apparently devoid of any kind of cultural or historical heritage whatsoever. . . . A demon that is no less historical than personal drives him to death in a motor-cycle accident at the age of nineteen. His brother, born in 1959 and given the name Odono, is no less shadowy and indeterminate than his putative ancestor; he too is killed at the age of nineteen, drowned whilst scuba-diving in the ocean which bore the original Odono (if he existed) from the 'pays d'avant' to the 'pays d'ici'. . . . Eventually Mycéa is taken along 'la Trace du Temps d'Avant' to the island's French-style, French-equipped, French-manned mental hospital from which, like Papa Longoué and, perhaps, the original Odono from the slave plantation, she escapes into the *mornes.* Pursued and recaptured by French *gendarmes* in their French-made jeep, she briefly returns to 'normal' life and is visited at home every day by her father who, in a final bitter irony, spends his time with her watching French or French-inspired programmes on a French-made colour television bought on credit, no doubt with the help of French social security payments! Mycéa suffers a further breakdown, and the novel concludes with an article in *Le Quotidien des Antilles* dated 13 September 1978 blandly extolling the provisions for the treatment of mental illness . . . in the department, provisions which are, needless to say, based on those available in the *métropole,* though, as *Le Quotidien* is the first to concede, [insufficient]. (pp. 310-11)

Richard D. E. Burton, "Comment Peut-on Etre Martiniquais?: The Recent Work of Edouard Glissant," in The Modern Language Review, *Vol. 79, Part 2, April, 1984, pp. 301-12.*

Juris Silenieks

Mahagony, Glissant's fifth novel, invokes the chronotopes, to borrow the Bakhtin term for the joining of time and space, that have always informed his entire œuvre: Martinique and its people at critical disjunctures of their history. The novel harks back to characters, episodes, motifs already treated in Glissant's previous novels, particularly ***La Lézarde,*** his first novel. The anecdotal framework is a kind of triptych consisting of the "marronnages" of three fugitives: a precocious youth, Gani, in 1831; Maho, who previously has appeared as the "géreur" Beautemps, in 1943; and a young delinquent, Mani, in 1978. The maroon figure looms large throughout Glissant's work. For Glissant, the maroon transcends history to become a mythopoeic construct, the prototype of those who, in their relentless struggle for dignity and justice, have defied the order of the slave owner, the colonizer, the present-day exploiter. . . . The maroons themselves are almost voiceless presences, both admired and feared, much celebrated in legends and tales. Hence, this is a "récit aux voix mêlées" by those who witnessed, remembered, or imagined the events. Particularly important among them are the women who provided the maroons with food as well as love, creating "grande circulation dans les bois." To organize the raw material, Mathieu has to grapple with the problem of reconciling orality with literacy, of transcribing what is oral into a written record. . . . The Martinican past [which he records] is a series of disjunctures, hardly amenable to chronology and causality. [However, the mahogany] tree, from which the three names, Gani, Maho, Mani, are derived, becomes the unifying metaphor of the narrative.

Besides the difficulties with the chronotopes, Mathieu has a personal grudge against the "author." In a game of intertextuality, very much à la Pirandello, Mathieu tries to disassociate himself from the fictional reality imposed upon him by the author, whom he variously calls "ce chroniqueur," "cet hagiographe des sites," "mon portraitiste." . . . At the end, however, having vented his anger, Mathieu dedicates his work "à mon auteur et biographe." Glissant should feel content, also for the fact that his name appears on a book that is so rich and complex, but also so rewarding to the reader. (pp. 362-63)

Juris Silenieks, in a review of "Mahagony," in The French Review, *Vol. LXII, No. 2, December, 1988, pp. 362-63.*

Alain Baudot

Edouard Glissant, or Epiphany of History, or Time Regained. Or rather, another life, another Time. "Breaker of the stones of Time," stubborn roadmender of a hidden History. He is all these, of course, but it is also necessary to see that this search for lost time—this "frenzied" search ("un temps éperdu")—mocks the traditional linear view of history, is in fact made in opposition to this one-dimensional view, and is registered in a space which it energizes while at the same time taking on the properties of that space.

Glissant, historian, juggler of Time and History as well as of rhythm and narrative form. He is all these too. But Glissant is just as much geographer, in search of a space which will fit his poetic design. For him, history as a vertical or univocal expression can only lead to the triumph of the One at the expense of the Diverse. What is necessary therefore is not a horizontal History, but a History in layers. [He writes in ***Malemort***]:

> Papa Longoué knows how to talk on space, he said. To talk on space, you have to divide yourself into several parts, he said. Silacier stretched himself out like a row of rocks spread out over a bed of seaweed. He experienced it. He forgot his surroundings. He forgot about the future. He was falling into the world like the big wheel at the fair.

There is an esthetic quality of layering in his writing, like geological strata, a diaspora which is not disparate but "composite," harmony and not melody. One of the pieces that he recommends in *Lettres Nouvelles*—when he was on the editorial board of this journal—is by Inca Garcilaso de la Vega, which promotes the use of synchrony or, more precisely, the use of spatial representation to tell a story which the West changed to its own advantage, by multiplying the comings and goings within another cultural space. (p. 583)

The consistency [of historical layering in Glissant's works] is remarkable in any case: ***Un champ d'îles*** (An Island Field), ***La terre inquiète*** (The Unquiet Land), ***Les Indes*** (The Indies), ***Le sang rive,*** (blood riveted to which bank?)—this last volume significantly dedicated "to tortured geography everywhere"—***L'intention poétique*** (Poetic Design), for which Glissant had planned the subtitle "Notes for a Landscape" and whose various sections trace a meaningful topology ("From the Desire for the Whole to the Sites of the One," "Pure Landscapes," "Open Lands," "The Voice of the Earth"): headings or instructions which are like milestones and landmarks on an eminently coherent course. It is fascinating to see what he invests places with, from the highest, from the most exalted, ***Les Indes,*** dream country of the West, real country to be built, to the most humble, as in ***La case du commandeur,*** which is both the smallest unit of space—just a little square on one of those beautiful Swiss maps offering safe adventure—and a complex place where an entire "people, composite, scattered, but inevitable" anxiously await their turn to speak ***(L'intention poétique).*** Just as the forest is the primordial place, so the river is the baptismal place and the sea the abyssal place. In an earlier chapter of ***The Ripening,*** which is like a geography lesson, he takes us over all the cardinal points with the effectiveness of a schoolteacher using the gentle approach to learning.

> This is the place: a stretch of galvanized iron roofs, among which the red earth familiarly surfaced. Between the town and the mountains runs the road, guarded by the terrible silk-cotton tree [*le fromager,* which reappears in ***Mahagony***]. In the opposite direction, the immutable plain stretching down to the whiteness of the south. On the west, the tortuous curve of the Lézarde tries to surround the town, then suddenly stops short, refuses such a role and, turning back to the east, runs past the sinister cane fields and gets lost in its delta. . . . And yet it is beautiful enough when it comes rushing down from the highlands in the north.

Physical geography, and what geography! The river, the Lézarde, which retains something of its animal name but less its sleepiness than its sinuous thirst for the sun—the Lézarde is also the crack (the French word for "lizard" is the same word as for "crack"), which Glissant calls the *cassure* or "break" [in ***Le discours antillais***]: "the break of the Africans with their continent on the other side of the ocean; break with their new and real country in 1848, when they would lose the opportunity to claim 'property' in Martinique; break of 1946, when Assimilation made the possibility of repossession even more remote." The crack from which the country is running dry (the specter of drying up haunts ***Malemort***) or from which meaning is insinuated. . . . Is this a history, or is it a geology lesson? Both: "We jump from rock to rock in time." (pp. 583-84)

However, this is also human geography. ***Monsieur Toussaint*** is no longer a historical character, but a person, just as ***Les Indes*** was peopled with the humble witnesses of daily existence. (In this, Glissant is not only anti-*Anabase,* as Bernadette Cailler rightly postulates, but anti-Césaire, if Lilyan Kesteloot was correct in seeing in Césaire's work an effort to give Negritude larger-than-life heroes.) This is ethnology, in fact—[Glissant writes in ***Soleil de la conscience***] "I am thus my own ethnologist"—and an ethnology which is marked by great attention to everyday detail. . . .

As for the fauna and flora, here we have a real natural history to be superimposed on a history which has been sugarcoated and disfigured by Western artifice. The subtitle for the first edition of ***Boises*** (1979) was "Natural History of a Barren Land." In the glossary for ***Malemort*** Glissant has fun drawing up the partial list: "*Fauna:* the long beast or the Enemy (the snake), mongoose, etc." . . . Then another glossary, this time in ***Mahagony,*** groups together flora, fauna, and everyday speech (the language of food again).

And the trees, all of them. In the middle, the "acoma," [discussed in ***Le discours antillais***] which will remain memorable: "One of the trees which has disappeared from the Martinican forest. Let's not become too attached to the tree, it will make us forget the forest. But let's remember it." . . . Indeed, this was the name of Glissant's journal, and on its cover was the following observation by Father Du Tertre: "A very long time after being cut, the heart is as healthy, moist, and full of sap as if it had just been felled." The most recent, the mahogany—a tree which is almost eponymous, except for the vibration, or rather the stammer, produced by the inversion of its syllables (a healthy regression?)—the mahogany of the novel ***Mahagony*** shows how in Glissant the milieu is inseparable from the human being, and how the human being is a tributary of the environment. (p. 584)

It is at the foot of this tree of America that the three fugitives of ***Mahagony*** (one from 1831, another from 1936, the third from 1978) take refuge: three dates, three lives, but one and the same place-mark keeping the indelible evidence. . . . And it is the tree itself which reveals the secret of their names: Gani, Maho, Mani, "three plays on syllables demonstrating the relationship of the characters and the landscape." [In ***Mahagony***], in fact, the trees do not hide the forest: "A tree is a whole country, and if we ask what is this country, we immediately plunge into the obscure root-tangle of time. We labor to clear the brushwood, we are wounded by the branches, our legs and arms are left permanently scarred." In fact, the tree is by its very nature a landmark, the emblem of a space recorded in time, at once witness and guarantor of successive generations. The tree is an essential element of Glissant's imagery—the tree felt, touched, breathed—as in this description of the silk-cotton tree in the Lamentin (the one that geography teacher showed us a moment ago): "This giant pushes its roots out of the earth in a spiral with such power that they are like a dizzying circle. Its upheaval is as frenzied as our restive memories. There is a musty smell of thorns and of unripened breadfruit, which reminds me of the smells, mingled together, of acacia and mahogany."

Perhaps the thing that stands out the most is that in all these texts the tree is never associated with the vertical dimension, unless from a moral standpoint: it is the "Don't ask me why we are still standing" of the Acadian song. Rather, and much more, it goes down into the depths of the earth, not to rape her but to return to her, entwined in her bosom. When it is evoked, as we just saw in its upheaval—and on its underside, its roots, and not the shaft of its trunk, nor the splayed claws of its branches—the tree remains all-embracing, seldom rigid, matrix more than mast. The words used here have the value of a *mise en demeure* (a demand for settlement): "circle," "spiral," "dizzyness," in which one becomes absorbed, as in the womb.

This leaves ***Le quatrième siècle*** (1964) and its apparently diachronic narrative, but first of all it must be seen that this narrative is the fruit of a geometric translation, of a radical change of epicenter, of a leap over the meridians, of a gesture—a *geste*—which displaces History in order to give it back another meaning. Then there is Glissant's technique as a novelist, sending the nearly four centuries of West Indian presence off in all directions, which precludes a simple sequence of events. Likewise his habit of multiplying chronologies (in ***Malemort*** he calls this "datation"), and of course the chronology at the end of ***Mahagony*** (What a chronology! Three destinies, Gani, Maho, Mani, as well as dates which do not "correspond" to what one expects them to be but which proclaim themselves and force us to take a stand), and also the genealogical table on which ***La case du commandeur*** ends. Moreover, is it not curious to place a genealogy at the end, as if to mock chronological sequence? The mockery is explained in ***Le discours antillais:*** "The chronological trap. It is possible to reduce our chronology to a skeleton of "facts," no matter what. [A list of well-known dates follows, which could have been taken out of French high-school textbooks.] Once this chronological table has been drawn up, completed, everything remains to be untangled about the history of Martinique."

Indeed, let us not fall into this trap. It matters little that [in ***Mahagony***] Mathieu or the narrator or the author made "a mistake in the long-distant past about his dates. . . . 'Dates die quickly,' Raphaël had told me. 'Let's not worry about their passing logic. We can play in between dates as between hopscotch lines.' " They have much more to do with moorings, with signs of the time, with "landmarks" (a frequently occurring term) which the traveler strews all along his meandering journey. It seems to me, moreover, that the "ordering" (another favorite word) here is much more a painter's than a musician's: it is a map of time which Glissant draws, to be read in all directions, "forward and backward," says the Mathieu of ***Le quatrième siècle.*** The directions for use are given several times, never more clearly perhaps than in ***Le discours antillais,*** however "shattered" *(éclaté)* Glissant proclaims it to be.

There remains much to be said about Glissant the musician, the ear which catches all the intonations, the rhythm especially. One should read aloud the thundering overture to ***Malemort,*** the ritual of carrying around the dead body, which is really the key in which the entire novel is written, giving it its tonality, *carrying* it completely, a dance which is born of the trance. In fact, Glissant's care with correcting his manuscripts seems to me due to his attention to the music of words (without using metaphors). Listen to his play on the sound of words, for example: *facture* (construction) and *fracture* (destruction), *perdu* (lost) and *éperdu* (confounded). His changes often tend toward purifying the word, or rather finding the right "note" (cf. the first version of **"Billons"** [which appeared in *Acoma*] and the definitive text refined for ***Malemort***). And ***Un champ d'îles*** goes from the original Instance edition of 1953—"Is it the street or his heart?"—to the Seuil edition of 1965: "Is it the street or rather his heart?"—one word, one beat, which is rhythmically the right one.

Another example of the importance of space is ***Monsieur Toussaint,*** in both the original version (Paris, 1961) and the abridged stage version (Fort-de-France, 1978). It has sometimes been called a static drama, and indeed Toussaint only defines himself by his relationship to the soil and to the inhabitants of his country. Because times and places are superimposed on each other, he is at the same time both on the island, participating in the battles of his people, and in prison at Le Fort de Joux (in the Jura), living each moment of those battles, "for there is no definite frontier between the universe of the prison and the lands of the Caribbean island" (according to the stage directions of the original version). Toussaint is here and there, today and yesterday, and much less perhaps than tomorrow: in the play, simultaneity and becoming are captured by dramatic space.

Detours, returns, repeats, variations, even variants: insufficient attention is paid to Glissant's rewriting, to his continual reworking of the text, even if it is just to take out one word and put in another, the pruning and grafting which show his concern about finding the right language, appropriate language. His concern for the vibration of the word, his lack of fixations, which is the fullness of his writing, and at the same time his refusal to be subjected to tyranny. He scales his writing to island space (in the rhythmic and dimensional sense). Glissant chooses layering over the straight line, over measuring in straight lines, polyphony over plainsong, perhaps because linear thinking or one of its incarnations, the idea of progress, has been imposed on him like the metaphor of the Other. The novels of Glissant should be deciphered to the letter, like a several-part invention (of the land), with basso continuo (Papa Longoué) and obligatory repeats (the endless recurrences of History and the stories in the narrative). This course, leading in many directions, often backward, appears to make no progress or to wander only to those who are accustomed to reading horizontally, from left to right. For the young Mathieu digging into his past through the visions of Papa Longoué, the healer *(quimboiseur),* this is how one learns about the island in all its convolutions and layers. Moreover, topology of this sort is neither closed nor static: it integrates the temporal dimension without which the country would not be able to find its right "mind." (pp. 584-85)

It is of course the recourse to landscape—a notion eminently rooted in History, if we recall that the historian Herodotus was also an explorer—that is the most obvious way to arrive at the recognition and reconstruction of a country. Again, in ***Le quatrième siècle,*** "All history is explained in this land according to the changing appearance of the land through time." (p. 586)

[In ***L'intention poétique,*** Glissant writes that the landscape] is the meeting of one time and one sensibility, is connected to one land: "A landscape. What is it for man? A deliberate series of fleeting relationships." Dreamed landscape, real landscape. Not the projection of a desire or an anxiety as in romanticism, but rather the adventures of a being-in-the-world, the cycle of exchanges between man, and woman, and their successive milieus. Glissant's literary space is of course at the opposite extreme from exoticism, which always presupposes a distance—conscious or not—between the writer and what he observes (as in colonial literature). Wherever his travels have taken him, his odyssey unquestionably finishes on his native soil. The virtue of ***The Ripening*** is precisely "to have allowed [him] to renew contact with the Caribbean landscape." His first stay in Paris had marked the meeting of other lands, as ***Soleil de la conscience*** evokes.

> The interminable plain: Europe. Practice recognizing the changes of landscape, where at first the eye could only formulate an exhausting flat surface. . . . I like the fields, their order, their patience, but I have no part in them. Never having had my own land at my disposal, I don't have this thing in my genes about saving the soil, about organization. My country's landscape is my passion; the symmetry of planted plots bothers me.
>
> (pp. 586-87)

Whence Glissant's writing, which is neither definitive nor decisive, for, far from being possessed (as it has been called at times), Glissant's poetic discourse is a repossession (without violence). It is faithful, certainly, and entirely coherent, but never tyrannical. As a writer and thinker who spends a long time meditating and never hesitates to reread what he has written, to correct himself, to make detours and to come back to himself, the forms he carries within him are in perpetual gestation. To return, for example, in ***Le sang rive,*** to texts which had been conceived several years previously, he emphasizes [in ***Soleil de la conscience***] what he calls the "never-ending process" of recasting in his creative work: "The important differences between the first versions and the actual text were not decided at the time of the present edition. They came about, nagging, over the years." (p. 587)

One cannot emphasize too much this "extreme attention to language—oh, not to its formal perfections, but extreme attention to the sonorities, to the sounds, to the rhythms of writing, to the choice of words which must each have meaning and not be used at random." They are also a guarantee of the impossibility of being locked in—an obsessive image, from these lines [in ***Poèmes***]: "The whole island is a pity / Which is committing suicide on itself," to the retreat from the slave warden's sea, the island prison of Toussaint, the ambulance walling in Marie Celat. Here is the character Mathieu who, in ***Mahagony,*** becomes the narrator and who complains (ironically) of having to be plunged into the obscurity "of the chaotic piles and obsessions of his chronicler's writing." But the interlacing, the opaqueness, are necessary, because the recurrences, the referral from one piece of writing to another, the echoes, the constant themes are simply the most effective way of reining in a landscape which is always on the point of fleeing and which one always submerges. In the same way the basic themes, or rather the root words, which tie down the landscape like the trees that my father planted to combat the erosion of his dunes, appear right from the beginning of Glissant's work. . . . [Glissant writes in ***Poèmes*** that it] is indeed the entire text which claims to be the landscape: "Every word is a land / You have to dig down underneath / Where a soft space is kept / Hot, for what the tree tells." In fact the whole work, in its entirety, *is* landscape: not the sum total, not the accumulation (unless cumulus clouds in a windy sky), not the Caribbean comedy à la Balzac—nor even à la Zola, in whom the hierarchical structures of time, place, and sensibility are striking—but a constellation, "a multiple and radiant body, from an example lived" (what he writes about the Caribbean in ***L'intention poétique***), where the texts respond to each other, without preeminence, without order, *senza ordine,* as Mozart-Da Ponte's Don Giovanni says, to create, for the time it takes to play a chord, a real Utopia. They have no meaning, or rather, it is all together, upside down, backward and forward, that they make sense.

The analogy land(world)/word, landscape/text is taken to the extent of perfect identity in the project itself. Since it is about being Caribbean *(l'antillanité)*—the reunion of a people with their landscape—it is never considered by Glissant as an asset or as a slogan: it is still to come, just as the readers [of ***Malemort***] are "future readers." What finer solidarity between mental universe and sensory construction, between vision and form (Rousset)? For such are the fruits of labor: a "flash" *(un éclat)* but also a prolonged "dawn" (to use other favorite terms), writing that gleams, as befits its design, and its landscape, which continues to develop in what Segalen called the "*éjouissement* [profound enjoyment] of the diverse." And how better to conclude than by these not disillusioned thoughts of the hero-narrator [of ***Mahagony***], Mathieu Béluse: "We are meditating together this mahogany, multiplied in so many trees in so many countries in the world." (pp. 587-88)

Alain Baudot, "Edouard Glissant: A Poet in Search of His Landscape ('For What the Tree Tells')," translated by Marianne R. Holder, in World Literature Today, *Vol. 63, No. 4, Autumn, 1989, pp. 583-88.*

"It is a significant fact that in the works of Glissant and in the literary production of several Martinican and Guadeloupean writers there is a consistent emphasis on the interdependence of the peoples of the Caribbean. There is a desire to reach beyond the insularity of an untenable social and psychic situation and to give meaning and significance through a pan-Caribbean vision that is often expanded to a measure of solidarity with oppressed peoples wherever they may be found; but this is the vision of the writer who has recognized the responsibility that she or he has to educate."

—Frederick Ivor Case, 1989

Bernadette Cailler

In my opinion, a careful analysis of Glissant's creative texts will bring out a constant and perhaps growing tension between the exaltation of a primordial, quasi-allegorical Maroon and the attention paid to the daily life and sufferings of the common people. On the one hand, the figure of the Negator, in its most allegorical dimension, can certainly be regarded as a reference to a particular segment of the population as well as to an "aristocratic" heroic order. On the other hand, as noticed by a number of critics, from Glissant's early pages on, the figure of the Negator (Black Maroon, Indian Rebel, Militant, Storyteller) does not function merely, or even essentially, in opposition to that of the Conqueror (Colonizer, Plantation Owner, Administrator, *Béké*), but, more essentially, it functions in relation to the "nonheroic" characters of the Antillean population, the plantation slaves, and later on, the peasants, townsfolk, workers, soldiers, police, and even *bourgeoìsie de couleur.* Moreover, at the heart of the narrative structure, where the common people are born, live, and die, the role played by women appears to be not so much increasingly important as it becomes embodied in an increasing number of female characters. It is also noteworthy that, as early as in ***La Lézarde,*** political success is envisaged as dependent upon grass-roots activities and efforts.

Though here it may be worth mentioning that the reference to a largely male Maroon society—or at least group—is not inconsistent with historical "truth," the extent to which the dream of a heroic male order includes an unconscious nostalgia in the author's psyche is of no interest for the present investigation. However, at the textual level, the tension existing between the heroic male order and a popular, life-sharing, and often life-giving "disorder" is patent, and, I believe, increasingly so in the later texts. Of course, the progressive disappearance of the figure of the Negator from people's memory—manifest in particular in ***Malemort***—may represent a turning point in the dialectic which I am trying to evoke here. On the other hand the reader is thus strongly reminded that the memory of the Negator had never been organically integrated into popular consciousness: not to be forgotten, Papa Longoué, the storyteller of ***Le quatrième siècle,*** stands as one of the few descendants who have religiously preserved some elements of the lives and deaths of the Longoué Maroons. On the other hand the ghostlike epiphanies of the Negator in the later texts, or his frequently derisory, or even frankly shameful, banditlike reincarnations, seem to embody the alienated, often cacophonic aspects of a colonized or marginal society. Indeed, Glissant's ability to make his reader understand that, from the glorious Maroon to the pathetic misfit or even the despicable bandit and sometimes collaborator, there exists the logic of a historical chain of situations, events, and relationships is not one of his smallest merits.

In Glissant's work the legend of the Negator is never divorced from an awareness and analysis of the dehumanizing conditions brought about by colonization, is never divorced from an awareness and analysis of the economic exploitation and "deculturation" process to which the island people have been subjected since the sordid "epic" of the Conqueror began. . . . Moreover, as I see it, such modulations on the Negator theme symbolize an ironic, critical distanciation with regard to the dream of a "new" epic as heroic order, rediscovered History, national literature. At the positive end of the interpretive spectrum, however, I believe that the weakening or even disintegration of the grandiose, simple, allegorical figure of the Negator emphasizes the need for new visions, new tactics, new stories, new styles, and new "heroes"—new heroes not so much perhaps because such heroes did not exist in the past, as new heroes in the perception which their fellow Antilleans might have of them. Good examples, for instance, would be Médellus, stubbornly riveted to his dream of land reform, and, no doubt, the endless "procession of women" [found in ***Mahagony***], whose chorus invades and ironically weakens the voices of the "old" or "new" male storytellers, scribes, writers: Lanoué, Longoué, Hégésippe, Mathieu, and He-whose-name-is-the-reverse-of-Senglis.

Omnipresent in Glissant's work, women's vision sometimes strengthens and supports the vision of their male partners, sometimes threatens to destabilize the order of the many male triangles which sustain the legend of the Negator. Of course, the reader of ***Mahagony*** will observe that, to the trios which had already appeared in Glissant's previous texts, more are added in the fifth novel around a "new" archetypal model: Maho, *nom de voisinage* for the former Beautemps; Gani, the young Maroon who died in 1831; and Mani, the young rebel who died in 1978 and whose name appears at the beginning and at the end of the mahogany—***Mahagony*** (my agony)—story. (p. 590)

A study of the role played by the female characters in Glissant's novels should help bridge the gap which unwary readers might be tempted to imagine between the heroic figures in the work and ordinary folk. Clearly enough, female Maroons and militants are never fooled by grand ideas; they may have more in common with the women at large than with the male "heroes." As Eudoxie, one of the narrators in ***Mahagony,*** keeps repeating: "Toutes femmes, c'est femme." The weight carried by a growing number of women figures in the later texts, especially in ***Mahagony,*** is striking: Eudoxie, Tani, Adoline, Emerante, Trémise, Adonie, Artémise, Adélaïde, Jézabel, Anne-Marie, Mani's grandmother Ida, and, more present than ever, Mycéa. In Glissant's work, female characters most often embody seasoned wisdom, pragmatism, fidelity to the past, to the land, and to the story of the people . . . and what they, the women, know may be the whole story. (p. 591)

Side by side with the (hi)story which the male narrators have tried to unearth from oblivion in their efforts to write a "new" book, this time never to be forgotten, another text continues to unfold, unwritten, inscribed in the deep, undomesticated paths of the heart: a text preserved in women's "night." The true story remains largely clandestine, uncanny, pregnant with feeling, and spoken in Creole. It is remarkable that Mycéa, who from the start partakes of the political and cultural vision of her male companions, is also the character who carries the common dream to its most logical (and, for herself, dangerous) limits. Through daily experiences, but also through patient and often agonizing mental exploration, Mycéa allows herself to reach a point of perhaps no return. For having understood (or intuited) the greatness but also the misery of the past, for having suffered the multiple and painful details of what relating to oneself and to others really means, Mycéa, as "they" say, has lost her mind; but Mycéa may save the dream. As a contemporary Maroon, Mycéa makes more sense than any of her male fellow characters (and, in ***Mahagony,*** male fellow narrators): so that the future may have a chance to be, Mycéa is ready to put behind her what she has learned and suffered, a long story of agony. As a creative critic, Mycéa is best of all. In ***Mahagony,*** at the very moment when she lets herself fall into poetic "cadence" and creativity, she ironically—and very sanely—announces that she no longer has any use for great rhythms, great words, great styles, great subjects, great trees. . . . Mycéa will go so far as to mischievously uproot the mahogany stem, the sacrosanct symbol of all the heroic commitments of younger days. However, . . . the reader cannot fail to see an act of faith on her part in the creative strength of the people and in the fecundity of the land. The reader will also notice that, in the concluding chapter of ***Mahagony,*** entitled "Passion, selon Mathieu," the polysemous dimension of the term *passion* is at full play. Passion is suffering, love, and endurance; it is the story of suffering, love, and endurance as told by the people through the mediation of Mathieu's narrative scheme; it is also the collective name given by Mathieu to the numerous sisters of whom he is dreaming and whose stories, in the future, should be—will be?—heard. Ultimately, the best name (*nom de voisinage*) which Mathieu declares to have found for Mycéa is Passion: could the Antillean discourse in its variety and multiplicity make sense irrespective of Passion's story?

Indeed, in his new posture as narrator and stage manager of the polyphonic theater set up in ***Mahagony,*** Mathieu is in a most critical position: not only as a critic of the "former" authorial voice, but also because his new status is bound to be precarious. Since his ambition is to let numerous voices and points of view fill up the Antillean space, Mathieu's own voice may never acquire sufficient authority to be either credible or capable of spinning the yarn of a counternarrative. Following the critical itinerary mapped out by the "real" author, the reader of ***Mahagony*** will be led to wonder whether anyone could be a "better" author than the unnamed narrator of the first four novels, whether any piece of writing could avoid being a distortion, simplification, or invention of History. Will Mathieu continue to preserve and cultivate a critical stance vis-à-vis his own research, vision, style, choice of characters, plots, and events, as he seems to be willing (forced?) to do in ***Mahagony?*** How is it possible for Mathieu to uphold the challenge of being at the same time the narrator of *a* new story, the conarrator of multiple stories, and the character manipulated by narrators/characters who, in the "former" author's story, are Mathieu's fellow characters (Mycéa)?

Throughout Glissant's creative discourse, the search for a collective plural subject as narrator and narratee and also the careful construction of a complex network of characters whose destinies, in the reader's mind, appear to be more and more closely connected, related willy-nilly, consciously, unconsciously to one another, run parallel to the transformation undergone by the primordial figure of the Negator: from being a master figure, the Negator progressively yields his leadership position to the many unstable, impure, "poetic" figures of resistance or endurance, sometimes even figures of betrayal and often of mere survival. In ***Mahagony,*** as I have briefly indicated, both the authoritative "I" of the inherited "written" tradition and the communal "we" of the imagined "oral" popular discourse are loudly challenged through a dissident narrative structure in which each narrator, in his or her own time and turn, offers one section, or one version, of one story. (pp. 591-92)

In my opinion, ***Mahagony*** stands out as the logical outcome of a lifelong narrative scheme which was to reach its apex in ***La case du commandeur;*** but it also represents its subversion. Surely enough, bringing together the many words (languages), the many voices, the many *times* which emerge, and, one hopes, at some level interconnect in ***Mahagony*** should ideally produce *a* book of the people and bond many past and present pages to one another. Once they have completed their study of this admirable poetic patchwork, however, readers will perhaps wonder what may have become of the "text" of national (Antillean) history and culture. The extent of Glissant's critical audacity cannot be overemphasized here. Instead of asking the question which, routinely, would come to mind—can the center still hold when the fabric is stretched to the extreme limits of its resistance?—one should perhaps not lose sight of the fact that, within the Antillean predicament, the center is still ahead of, not behind, the act of speaking. If it is true that ***Mahagony*** completes the saga initiated in ***La Lézarde,*** reading this text as a formidable challenge posed to whatever may come next in Antillean literature may be even more meaningful. Nowhere else in Glissant's oeuvre is, I believe, the "poetics of relation" explored more productively but also more recklessly than in this work. Nowhere else is the critically creative approach to many enduring if somewhat questionable binary oppositions more convincingly proposed to the reader's own critical eye: Maroon/slave, hero/people, past/present, history/story, conqueror/conquered, teller/told, written/spoken, French/Creole, and, last but not least, author/commentator, artist/critic. For such reasons, and for some correlated other reasons which I have examined elsewhere—namely, the rather rigorous conceptual framework within which Glissant places his creative activities, as well as the constant interaction in his work between theory, criticism, and "poetry"—for all these reasons, I believe that Glissant's Antillean discourse is one step ahead of Negritude. As such, it has opened a tear in the epistemological territory of dominant discourses. The next step will no doubt have much to do with Antillean politics. Today I see in Glissant's work, and in the work of some kindred spirits, a strong deterrent to poetic aphasia and cultural sterility, a viable discourse on and by the Antillean subject—a subject which, to this day, has not chosen to disappear. (p. 592)

Bernadette Cailler, "Edouard Glissant: A Creative Critic," in World Literature Today, *Vol. 63, No. 4, Autumn, 1989, pp. 589-92.*

Diva Barbaro Damato

In a discussion on the Antillean intellectual—"l'antillectuel"—Jacques André, commenting on ***Le discours antillais*** by Edouard Glissant, once remarked that "it is difficult to find a text, in the last twenty or thirty years, as important as this one, and yet it provokes no real discussion, beyond a few mediocre debates." In fact, ***Le discours*** frightens as much as it fascinates. Western intellectuals, especially the French, have a need to organize, classify, and order the world. Glissant's multiplicity of themes, at times dealt with in a systematic fashion, at other times in a fragmentary fashion, his series of blank spaces, his theoretical texts, his poetic texts, his accounts of experiences, and his other texts, give the reader the sensation of being dragged over a precipice.

Le discours reveals another facet of this poet, critic, novelist, and playwright: an unflagging researcher with an admirable production of theoretical writings, engaged in blazing new trails (or in following old ones from a new perspective) in search of clues that may better explain the reality of his country. The importance of ***Le discours*** (and the difficulty in its reading) lies also in its great diversity. By discussing a whole variety of topics in the most diverse manners in a sequence not always clear to the reader, Glissant demonstrates that the study of a situation as original and complex as that of Martinique demands an entirely new approach. He is aware of the fact that "no method is ever innocent," and one of his main concerns is to escape the pitfalls of Cartesian logic and academic formalism, the great danger for Antillean intellectuals. . . . Notwithstanding Glissant's complexity, I believe it relevant to point out one particular concept from his work, and by organizing some of his considerations around this concept, I hope to make clear the relation between poetics and politics in those countries which emerged out of the colonial system.

It seems to me that one of the key concepts of Glissant's analyses is that of *dispossession* (the subtitle to book 1 of ***Le discours***). This concept also appears under the names of "lack," "absence," and "privation" and forms part of an economic and political but also philosophical consideration. On the other hand, considering that Glissant's literary project is fundamentally concerned with the land, the history, and the language of his people, as became apparent in 1969 with ***L'intention poétique*** . . . one may say that Martinique, according to Glissant's criteria, is the locus of threefold dispossession: of place, of history, of language.

With the extermination of the indigenous inhabitants, the present-day population of the French Antilles (and of other American countries) descends from a handful of European colonizers and a great number of African slaves, added to later by Asian, European, and African immigrants. All these people, slaves or masters, have something in common, however: they all came from another country, another continent. Thus, for these people, the New World is not an ancestral land, already identified, familiar, relished, venerated, the backdrop of various struggles, myths, of a whole culture. This land—for some the source of suffering, for others the source of wealth, and for all the source of challenge—is alien territory, a foreign land.

As this land is not ancestral land, there is no sense of ownership either. In spite of the high economic standard, the land does not belong to those who work and live there. Man's relationship with his own land is determined elsewhere, outside this land. Since the land is a dependent economy, man here has no power to decide what, where, and how to plant, to produce—to be. The locus of power, the locus of decisions, the economic and cultural nerve center, is external to the land lived in. These people all live in a land which does not belong to them, surrounded by objects that are not products of their own culture.

If we depart from the assumption that behind all of Glissant's reflections lies a proposal for an Antillean poetics (or dare I say "American" poetics), the question of the dispossession of place and this new poetics may be linked on the basis of a redefinition of the landscape (and a consequent redefinition of its description). . . . Philippe Hamon and Ernst Curtius have analyzed how the landscape in European literature has undergone a process whereby it has become technicized and intellectualized. As a consequence, the resulting literary conventions focus on detail, on consecutive exposition, on harmony. A dominated, familiar place requires a poetics that assumes a highly technicizing posture; any exceptions would be *reactions* to this posture. Description presupposes organization and a preexisting system. (p. 606)

In Glissant's landscapes there is no significant detail: insofar as the land has not yet been culturally appropriated, no element can represent it significantly. This refusal to privilege certain traits may give the reader familiar with Western literature a sense of incompleteness, of chaos. Hence the predicament of the critics: how to analyze a "corpus" without privileged or clarifying moments, where traits are simply *accumulated.*

The concept of accumulation, one of the most recurrent in Glissantian analyses, is also one of the most productive for the development of a poetics of the dispossessed. Accumulation is the appropriation of reality by means of repetition, of probing. It is an appropriate process for dealing with the discontinuous. In the face of an evanescent reality, it is a form of unceasing approximation. When the relationship between a people and its surroundings is obliterated by the intervention of another culture, whose greater power comes from its far-reaching dominance (both economic and political), this people's process of conquest of its own space must necessarily occur by means of accumulation. Choice, selection, leads to the elimination of all that cannot be apprehended by the dominant model. The appropriation into a system or the adoption of a model is reassuring but castrating, like the bed of Procrustes. In order that nothing gets lost, since everything is important, one must necessarily *begin* by accumulating.

In this perspective, accumulation (repetition, redundancy) would be the mimesis of a nonintellectual process of apprehension of the unknown or the strange, a process one may call "popular" as opposed to "scientific" or technological, which are exclusive to an "elite" and often linked to the dominant ideology. The Antillean writer *patiently* constructs his landscape.

One of the most recurrent issues among Antillean intellectuals—including Martinicans—is the concern with what Glissant calls "nonhistory." The history of the French Antilles (and of the Americas) has been recounted in such a way as to be necessarily consistent with versions that the dominant groups have imposed on their own history. The apparent "continuum" present in official handbooks of Antillean history—the succession of periods, lists of governors, the "compatibility between local and metropolitan movements"—is partly the result of the concealment (or exclusion) of certain facts, of certain gestures that could question the established order. History has thus proved to be a powerful instrument of domination, permitting the West to impose on the world, in the form of universals, its own particular values. History as a whole has excluded any histories incompatible with the history of the West and has established a hierarchical relationship between European and concurrent histories.

The dispossession suffered by a people of its own history prevents this people from seeing itself inserted within a continuity, within a certain chronology. Literature has a particularly significant role to play so that this repressed history may emerge and this lost time may be conquered. The task of literature is to reveal apparently insignificant elements which may be evidence of an unconfessed privation, of a historically denied gesture. Here, once more, one may appreciate the importance of *accumulation* as a means of revealing reality. It is only through repetition that these imprecise elements may be perceived by an ever greater number and thus become part of the collective consciousness of a whole people.

The writer must identify the weaknesses that may exist in

the ideological armor of the dominant groups and thus be able to activate remaining focuses of resistance. On the other hand, fiction becomes an effective instrument in the construction of the past, of which only apparently unconnected fragments remain. The crucial point here is that at the same time that the writer reveals this resistance, he also becomes part of it, for his work forms part of the process whereby a continuity is established between cultural production and the environment giving rise to it.

The writer, in the face of the collective impossibility of articulating one's own history, must attempt to set up a chronology: that is, he must attempt to *create* (not uncover) a continuity in events, if his people is to be able to locate itself in the present. This is what Glissant calls "vision prophétique du passé." Glissant's definition of the poet matches closely Paul Veyne's definition of the historian: "Historians are merely inverse prophets, who pad and reanimate, by dint of imagination, their *post eventum* predictions . . . and this imaginative faculty is the author of three-quarters of every page in history, the remaining quarter coming from documents. . . . History is also a novel." . . . Literature in emergent nations has a remarkably significant political role. To allow dispossessed peoples to establish their own histories and gain citizenship, to enable them to establish relationships with other cultures, to be the point of articulation for the voice of a people—all this means to engage in a struggle against the predatory actions of a civilization that lays claim to universality. (p. 607)

In the French Antilles, with the total suppression of the native population, and given the African slaves' impossibility of communicating with one another in a common language (due to the policy of not putting together slaves from the same ethnic group), the imposition of the French language came about "naturally," as if it were a "necessity." However, two distinct languages soon began to appear: French, the language of decrees, reports, books, and of eminent visitors, the official language, the language of culture, of the metropole; and Creole, the language forged by the local populace (whites, blacks, and mulattoes), which molded it according to its environment and its way of life within this environment, the language of orality.

From the very beginning a hierarchical relationship had been established between these two languages: the opposition between French and Creole was that between "civilization" and "barbary." This relationship continues practically unchanged today. It is not a question of two languages vying with each other on the same plane, but of a written language possessing a literary tradition which enjoys remarkable prestige in Western civilization vying with an oral language whose origin is intimately related to the colonial situation itself and to slavery. The role of the Antillean writer, working on such unstable and polemic territory, at the confluence of the written and the oral, will be to ennoble the latter. . . . (pp. 607-08)

In the European countries literature emerged from the oral tradition almost naturally, smoothly. Only the long and gradual work of generations gave rise to the relative autonomy of literature in relation to the oral tradition. In the case of textual production in Martinique, the relation of continuity is not established with the tradition of the local people but with that of French literature. A French writer's relationship with his language is one of internal crisis; it does not question the existence of France. The French writer's poetics is what Glissant calls "a natural poetics": it presupposes a language common to the whole community—that is, a common practice of confidence in the language or languages of this community. This can only occur in a culturally cohesive social unit. It does not impede the emergence of contestations of great virulence; on the contrary, it guarantees the continuity between the established social order and the criticism of itself. This natural poetics can question language by means of the most radical of experiments, yet this language will continue to be a possible language.

A Martinican poet's choice to write represents an opportunity for his people to come before the world, to participate in the relations between peoples. His poetics, according to Glissant, can only be "a strained poetics": that is, an attempt to construct a form of language through a language (or languages) which does not of itself permit such a thing. . . . This strained poetics or counterpoetics is concerned with bringing together disparate, at times antagonistic elements. It also permits the community to perceive the presence of these elements. This is the reason why a strained poetics tends to be natural. A community which does not succeed in perceiving this, which itself presupposes the commitment of a whole people collectively responsible for its creative practices, is doomed to disappear. This counterpoetics should be regarded as the task of writers, of "investigators" aiming at raising to the level of the collective consciousness the forms of resistance that this same community employs in a spontaneous and naïve manner. The creation of a rhetoric in French using originally Creole discursive practices forms part of a larger project of the Antillean people toward the conquest of citizenship.

In my reading of ***Le discours antillais*** I have attempted to throw light on the political implications of Glissant's literary project. Departing from a study of the situation in his own country, the writer reflects on the consequences of the process of dispossession—or plundering—a process suffered by all peoples subjected to the colonial system established by Europeans on all continents, particularly in the Americas. The work of the poet . . . not only helps the community become aware of aspects of the past hidden in its landscape, but also permits this restored memory (uncovering historic bonds which unite those who live there) to contribute toward the constitution of a cohesive and solidary *people.* (p. 608)

Diva Barbaro Damato, "The Poetics of the Dispossessed," translated by Leila Cristina Darin and Leonina C. Menezes de Souza, in World Literature Today, *Vol. 63, No. 4, Autumn, 1989, pp. 606-08.*

Daniel Racine

It seems fitting to discuss the Antilleanity of Edouard Glissant, as this appears to be the most obvious aspect of his personality and his entire work. Born and raised in Martinique, the French Antilles, Glissant has devoted all his life and creative activity to the quest for the Antillean identity. In his major essay entitled ***Le discours antillais*** (Eng. ***Caribbean Discourse***) he gives the following definition of Antilleanity:

> More than a theory, a vision. The force of it is such that it is applied to everything. I have heard *antillanité* proposed on a few occasions (without any further details) as a general solution to real or imagined problems. When a word acquires this kind of general acceptance, one presupposes that it has found its reality.

As far as he is concerned, Glissant thinks that Antilleanity has not yet been achieved and that there is something unhealthy in the Antillean community which writers should try to help heal. In order to find out what may be wrong and to offer some appropriate solution, Glissant attempts to analyze in his works the Antillean community and its world. In so doing he takes into account their origins, geography and history, their culture and socioeconomic realities, their political context, their language, their complexity along with their specificity, and, above all, their aspirations.

According to Glissant, Antilleanity—which may eventually refer to some Caribbean federation—is above all engraved in geography. The geography of the Antilles is unique in its one-season climate. . . . The presence of the sun, which is a permanent reality in the Antilles, is responsible for this one-season world and prevails in most of the writings of Glissant, who entitled one of his volumes of essays ***Soleil de la conscience.*** The sun stands as an element of energy, hence vitality, which generates beauty and hope. Above all, the sun has contributed to the protection and survival of the Antilleans under the worst circumstances. . . .

No less significant is the surrounding sea, which inspired Glissant's verse collection ***Le sel noir*** and has been analyzed as the black counterpart of Saint-John Perse's *Amers*. . . . Old Papa Longoué counts the sea as the first century in ***Le quatrième siècle*** because it was the means of his initial contact with the New World and with slavery. Conversely, in ***La Lézarde*** the journey leads the young Maroon's descendant back to the sea, where the symbol of the old oppressive system is destroyed. Glissant recognizes the part of man's responsibility as far as the victims of the sea are concerned, and he would rather turn to its positive aspects, since the salt of the sea can also preserve and give taste to life. Moreover, the sea is a reservoir of food and a link between the islands. . . . Symbolically, it also links the past to the present and the future and may be seen as an element of hope. . . . (p. 620)

Glissant's impassioned attachment to the Antillean land could only lead him to use his talent as a writer to describe its landscape, which is always related to the people. . . . This means that different parts of the island of Martinique correspond to different historical events or activities of the people, as illustrated in ***La Lézarde*** or ***Le discours antillais.*** In both cases Glissant gives the reader a guided tour from the top of the mountain—which happens to be in the North—to the sea, which is in the South, and along the way he comments upon every pertinent face of the landscape. The mountain, with its thick forest and intricate fern trees that stop sunlight, was the privileged refuge of the Maroons. It is the symbol of the past, of faithfulness to Africa and refusal of servitude. The center, called the *plaine,* with its sugarcane fields, its decaying sugar and rum factories, was once entirely occupied by the plantations and the slaves, who would first land at the Dubuc mansion, now in ruin, before distribution to their masters. The junction of the mountain and the *plaine* is made by the Lézarde River, whose winding brings us next to the city and the people who use it for their laundry and their bath. In recent years its delta has been used for airport traffic and various enterprises, which has caused the crabs to disappear. Finally, comes the southern part bordering the coast, with its coconut trees, whose trunks were used to cross the sea by those slaves who unsuccessfully tried to join Toussaint Louverture in his revolt. The beaches and other parts of the island are now put at the disposal of tourist companies and their customers, a modern substitute for the plantations. In ***Mahagony*** Glissant parabolically compares Martinique to a colonial museum, a showcase not only for the everyday visitors but also for researchers such as sociologists and psychiatrists, who may be inquisitive about the possibility of such a human phenomenon.

In his presentation of the island Glissant does not forget to acquaint us with its flora, one of the richest in the Antilles. Martinique, whose original Caribbean name was *Madinina,* meaning "the island with beautiful flowers," is indeed famous for its tropical rain forest. Glissant seems to love trees, among other elements of the flora. He may name a good score of them in a single novel. The most popular ones are those which have some symbolic, nutritive, or sheltering significance. Among the former is the acoma, described as one of the biggest and tallest on the island; long after it has been cut down its heart remains moist with sap as a sign of survival, and it may symbolize the endurance of the Martinican people. The *fromager* or silk-cotton tree is described as a "big tree with a magic reputation. It is said that it screams when it is being cut. It has often screamed." Another symbolic tree is the flamboyant or flame tree, which is also large and turns completely red when it blossoms. . . . This image may refer to people who have been killed by government police at some political protests. (p. 621)

No less important is the place which the local fauna occupies in Glissant's works. A list of some of its components is to be found at the end of ***Malemort,*** in the section entitled "Parlers." It is interesting to note that the animal most frequently referred to in the whole bestiary is the snake, often called "la bête longue" or "l'Ennemi." Frequently found in some regions of Martinique, it is considered a taboo animal which strikes one with awe due to its venom and its symbolic significance. This goes back to Papa Longoué, who came from Africa with a barrel containing a snake which embodied a power he could use every time he drew the form of this animal in the air. Ironically enough, in ***Le quatrième siècle*** this gesture is compared to the one made by a Catholic priest when bestowing a blessing. We are told that the snake and the mongoose can engage in very ferocious fights, which serve as a great attraction for some people, just like cockfighting. Among other animals of great interest in the everyday life of the Antilleans is the pig, whose meat is very popular, particularly at Christmas time, and was most valuable during World War II, when import of any food proved to be difficult. Glissant's list contains other consumable animals, including a great variety of typical Antillean fishes such as "balarou, chatrou, coulirou, lambi, titiri," et cetera. (pp. 621-22)

Deeply attached to his native land, Glissant remains at the same time faithful to its tradition and culture, which, he believes, can only be appraised and respected if one is aware of the human background. In devoting his writings to the Antilles in general and Martinique in particular, he refers a great deal to the history of Caribbean man. . . . He thinks that in order to prepare the path to the future, one must have some knowledge of where one comes from. As early as 1956, we find in one of his first volumes of verse, ***Les Indes*** (The Indies), a six-part epic presentation of the discovery of the New World and its subsequent involvement in the slave trade. Significantly, the different sections are "The Call," "The Voyage," "The Conquest," "The Trade," "The Heroes," and "The Relationships." Emphasis is naturally placed on the colonization of the Antilles, but rather than praising Europeans for their victories over native Americans and their conquest and exploitation of the land, Glissant gives their fair share to those black men and women brought from Africa who also contributed to the history and the development of the Antillean community built up with their labor. This was done the hard way, however, as we can read in Glissant's description of the horror of the slave trade, the infernal experience endured by his race in the sea voyage, the inhuman condition of slavery itself, the ordeal of three centuries of torture. Still, the main message in this work is the ultimate reconciliation between antagonistic human groups. (p. 622)

In a systematic and didactic way, Glissant will undertake to rewrite the history of the Antilles in his autobiographical novel ***Le quatrième siècle*** (The Fourth Century), published in 1964 and honored with the Charles Veillon International Award. Under the pretext of writing the first official history of his island, Mathieu, a young archivist who may represent Glissant himself, asks an elderly *quimboiseur*—a witch-soothsayer and griot—to tell him what he knows about the topic. He expects that the old man, Papa Longoué, who can encompass the past, the present, and the future, will also provide information for his own political activities and will help him at the same time discover his own identity along with public truth. This historical novel turns out to be the chronicle of several families, including two black, two white, and one mulatto. The two black families stand for Africans like the Longoués, who refused slavery and started a community of Maroons, and others like the Beluses, who were assigned to plantations by their acceptance of enslavement. Eventually these two lines will converge as components making up the Caribbean people. Similarly, the white families, the La Roches and the Senglises, will serve as types. In between, the development of the Targin family illustrates the mulatto class that usually derives from miscegenation between white masters or overseers and female slaves. It is recorded that this new group grew away from the others and remained a floating element within society. This explains the development of the divisions of class and color which were to persist within the Antillean population even after emancipation.

"[Glissant's objective] was to initiate among Martinican readers an authentic awareness of their true nature, their interests, and their hidden aspirations: namely, taking their destiny into their own hands, becoming their own masters, without any hatred but in a spirit of comprehension, esteem, and fidelity vis-à-vis their traditional ruler."

—Daniel Racine

The eventual merging in ***La Lézarde*** of two strains of ex-Maroons and slaves will initiate the expected unity, although the differences may be revealed by their names. Whereas the former had the privilege of preserving or choosing their own names such as Longoué, Liberté, or Apostrophe, the latter were given names depending on the fantasy, the background, or even the ignorance of their masters. In his *Grammaire Créole* Robert Germain devotes an entire section to the origin and formation of Antillean anthroponyms. . . . In ***Le quatrième siècle*** we are told, for instance, that Beluse's name comes from "bel usage" as given by a *gérеur* or plantation overseer who put him at the disposal of Senglis's wife, who would use him as a stud to increase the manpower of the plantation. Other sample names are Alizées, Sapins, Plaisance, Capottes. Many are borrowed from Latin patronymics—Cicero, Cato, Scipio, Horace, Manlius, Cornélius, Romulus, Mandelus—or Greek mythology: Anaïse, Zéphyr, et cetera. Another source of names is the Bible, which gives Melchior, Balthazar, and even Apocal, short for "apocalypse"; the calendar furnishes Saint-Yves, Epiphane, and Annonciation, depending on the birthday. Some people are given the names of African localities such as Lomé, Oubangui, or Congo, probably based on their birthplaces. Quite frequently nicknames become permanent, as in the cases of Malpain, Ti-Jojo, Tigamba, Coco, and Mycéa, which is a contraction of Marie and Celat, the latter part deriving from "ceci cela." Most of these names found in Glissant's novels still exist in the Antilles according to the nomenclature made by Germain. They are taken from several generations of the family chronicle recorded in ***Le quatrième siècle,*** a sequence of events which include slavery, emancipation, the eruption of a volcano, the great devastation wrought by a hurricane, and the arrival and departure of troop ships taking men to fight in Europe—a recurrent tribute that Antilleans must pay for their allegiance to France, assimilation. There might also be a disguised account of the postwar political campaign in Martinique, when Glissant and Fanon supported Césaire. The chronicle ends with the death of Papa Longoué during this period, which means that the past is being replaced by the present.

Paradoxically enough, in his attempt to represent a chronicle of the island, Glissant chooses 1788 as a starting date—that is, two centuries after the beginning of slavery. This reduction in time does not affect his narrative, as the essentials are said for him to make his point. In fact, in talking of the "fourth century [in ***Le quatrième siècle***]," he also makes another reduction in confounding space and time to explain that the first century is the sea you cross, the second, "the coast where you land, blinded, without soul or voice. And the forest, kept in its strength until the days when you were a Maroon . . . is another century. And the earth, slowly flattened, stripped where those who came down from the hills and those who waited patiently in the plain met to begin weeding together is the fourth century." Through the perspective of Papa Longoué, the narrator, whose story is so rich in detail and drenched in the painful experience of the blacks, there is no doubt that the ordeal of Antillean man does not fill over three centuries. Here again we have a moving description of the cruelties, horrors, and shocks of the slave crossing on the *Rose Marie.* The arrival of the ship after the Middle Passage is followed by the bargaining procedures and the blessing by a priest. Such details are presented without irony as simple historical facts.

Written six years before ***Le quatrième siècle, La Lézarde,*** which won the coveted Renaudot Prize, is constructed using a similar pattern of time—past, present, and future—except that it deals with a more contemporary period. Here Glissant brings together two different social classes, the one from the high country, the other from the plain, through the means of a group of Martinican students. Thaël descends from the Maroon tradition far from the main town of Lambrianne. He journeys to the south, where he meets with his comrades, who are planning to assassinate the renegade Garin, an agent sent by the central government to put down the movement of the younger generation. The Lézarde River serves as a temporal and spatial symbol of the link between past and present. The fatal journey by Garin down the river with his intended executioner Thaël complements the one made in time by Mathieu through the archives of the town in the company of Longoué. The real protagonist in this novel is, as the title indicates, the Lézarde River, the vital nerve of the island as a fertilizing element and a link between the people of the mountains and those of the plain, the past and the present. This may explain why Garin, the reactionary traitor, wants to take over its control in trying to buy up the property at its very spring and speculates on the land along its course. Similarly, when Thaël plans Garin's death, he retires to the spring to draw from it the strength necessary for his act. Still more, the Lézarde becomes an accomplice in Garin's assassination by casting him beyond its barrier reef and out to sea.

The objective of this autobiographical novel was to initiate among Martinican readers an authentic awareness of their true nature, their interests, and their hidden aspirations: namely, taking their destiny into their own hands, becoming their own masters, without any hatred but in a spirit of comprehension, esteem, and fidelity vis-à-vis their traditional ruler.

> Tell them that we love the outside world. That we love it for the best it can produce. That we know its great works, that we are learning. But that this world is poorly represented here. Tell them that by 'the metropolis' we mean France. But that we want first of all to be at peace with ourselves. That our metropolis is right here and that is where we looked for it.

This nationalistic message came precisely at a moment of political stagnation in Martinique, in the midfifties, when most colonized countries were moving toward independence. While Frantz Fanon was in North Africa helping the Algerians start the war of liberation, Glissant found that the best solution for Martinique was also independence. His call was not followed by Martinicans, who did not feel quite ready for a decisive separation, or by their representative, who could not make up his mind.

Another politically geared work is ***Malemort*** (1975), which has been termed Glissant's "most Antillean novel." It deals with life among lower classes of the island and centers on a murder committed at election time. The irregular way of conducting political campaigns to the advantage of progovernment candidates is one of the satiric objects here, and we are also introduced to the famous *vidé,* "a parade with torches, songs, and slogans to celebrate an electoral victory." The *vidé* is also used during carnival and gives people an opportunity to parade, dance, and externalize their feelings as much as they can. Here again Glissant ferrets out the roots of his people, buried under four centuries of slavery, foreign culture, and language. These roots are only to be found in legends, the recollections of Maroons, whose revolt is like "book words." ***Malemort*** is a prolongation of ***Le quatrième siècle*** with an amplification of the effects of the story of old Papa Longoué. What seems to be a major innovation here in favor of Antilleanity is the frequent use of the Creole language in the narrative or the dialogues as a natural means of communication among the people. This makes it necessary for Glissant to provide the novel with a glossary for the European reader, or for anyone not familiar with this language. Henceforth he will continue this practice, as Creole will be used more and more in his subsequent works.

The question of communication in one's natural language will become so important in Glissant's quest for the Antillean soul that he will devote two voluminous essays to the matter. The first is ***L'intention poétique,*** a 248-page "meditation on the essence of language and its relationship with poetry" in which he tries to define a poetics of the Antillean people derived from his culture and identity and different from Western poetics, which imposes on the world basic metaphysical notions opposed to the cultural diversity of non-Western people. The second essay devoted to language is ***Le discours antillais*** (1981), a 500-page volume wherein, among other topics, Glissant deplores the fact that the Antillean is more and more in danger of losing his culture and his identity. Because of his alienation through French assimilation, his language—Creole—is becoming more and more "Frenchified": self-denial and imitation of the metropolitan model are prevailing, which means more servitude. Only the reinforcement of the concept of "Antilleanity" will preserve an Antillean specificity. This reinforcement, in Glissant's view, will occur through the rehabilitation and enrichment of the Creole language. However, the Antillean writer, a "pusher of language," cannot yet immediately produce in Creole without reservation, though he can participate in its development. It is necessary first that Creole have a variety of texts available, whether they are literary or not: teachers, political militants, and sociologists must play an important role in the defense and practical application of Creole, which is losing ground; emphasis must be placed on its function and productivity as well as on its integration to formal education. The matter involves the works of sociolinguists as well as educators and the intervention of the community as a whole. In order to counter the constrained neutrality of Antilleans, the writer's function [as related in ***Le discours antillais***] is

> . . . perhaps to propose language as shock, language as antidote, a nonneutral one, through which the problems of the community can be restated. This function could require the writer to "deconstruct" the French language that he uses (and that is one of the fundamental aspects of the situation); first as a means of demystification in relation to any automatic reverence for this language, then as a tool for locating major themes, cultural projections that from within the French language will be able to facilitate (by clarification) the future use of a written or revitalized Creole.

In this sense, Glissant continues, the works of the Antillean writer would be a "preface to a future literature." To the objection of one Martinican teacher who thinks that such works would be "archeological"—i.e., out of fashion or dead—he replies that this only proves a great analytical pretension which ignores the necessary dynamic links between our present constrained poetics and the freedom of the Antilles of tomorrow. No one, he explains, can decide today what this poetics will be—for instance, whether mono- or multilingual—or consequently draw the line between the illegible ruin and the decipherable monument. Moreover, Glissant points out that the objective is not the Creolization of the French language but the exploration of responsible usage—creative practice—that Martinicans may make of it. He concludes that, in such a context, the writer's function, which is comparable to that of the researcher and explorer, will often isolate him from the "current language" and therefore from the "daily" reader. Glissant considers this a regrettable but necessary condition to which the writer must adjust, if he wishes to produce a technically adept work without believing himself to be some kind of messianic spokesman.

This appears to be the crucial strategy advocated by Glissant for the promotion of the Antillean language and the preservation of its authenticity. Linguistic concerns had also been discussed by writers of the Negritude movement. Although Glissant does not belong to that movement, he seems to share its adherents' view of the French language. As Jean-Paul Sartre pointed out, the works of the Negritude writers show a deliberate "deconstruction" or "destructuring" of the Cartesian, rational French language, adjustments made with a view toward communicating their own messages. However, none of them chose to use Creole as a means of expression, for they wished to address their concerns to the French-speaking world at large. On the contrary, Glissant's works are marked by an ever greater intrusion of Creole into the traditional French language. As he tries to "explore" the latter, he will not only borrow from the vocabulary of the former but will also use entire sentences (with or without translation), syntactic structures, and proverbs and sayings familiar only to Antilleans. Similarly, most of his imagery will be drawn from Creole, which is reputed to be a colorful language. Such literary behavior is thus an attempt to resist the menace imperiling the integrity of Creole, which is part and parcel of the Antillean cultural heritage. (pp. 622-25)

Edouard Glissant is well aware of the complexity of the Antillean universe, which is "exploded" and "tormented" from the geographic standpoint and which consists of a people made up of Africans, French, Hindus, Chinese, Lebanese, and others who share some four centuries of history. His message is to invite this people to take pride in and preserve the beauty of their country against any kind of mutilation, to enjoy the richness of their culture, to communicate in the language they have built up together, to claim their right to difference based on their specificities, and to think in terms of unity and independence. According to the Guadeloupean novelist Maryse Condé, "Glissant subordinates his birth and personal interest to the healing of the Antillean community. For this healing will enable it to be responsible for its destiny. Antilleanity will start only after the liberation of the Antilles or, if one prefers, at the end of its cultural and political dependence." (p. 625)

Daniel Racine, "The Antilleanity of Edouard Glissant," in World Literature Today, *Vol. 63, No. 4, Autumn, 1989, pp. 620-25.*

Wilbert J. Roget

[The use of myth in creative literature] poses a fundamental difficulty, particularly in the case of Glissant, who has chosen a mode of expression that is intended to reflect the ravages which History has left on his community; for if individuality is characteristic of the modern tradition and collectivity or the community is paramount in the mythic mode, the author intends to bridge these polarities. In a recent study titled *Myth, Realism, and the West African Writer* Richard Priebe uses the concepts "mythic consciousness" and "ethical consciousness" as the critical devices for examining writers who fall within these two traditions. He defines his concepts as follows:

> The style of [ethical consciousness] tends to be realistic with little being left unexplained by the action or the description, historical in its specificity of time and place, didactic in its rendering of the human condition, and continuous in its

> rhythm as we are led from a clear beginning through a definite end. In contrast, the mythic style is expressionistic with much that is seemingly obscure or incomplete, ahistorical in that we find a move towards time *ab origine*, problematic with regard to the human condition, and cyclical in its rhythm, symbolic or real death being followed by resurrection.

By Priebe's critical yardstick, Glissant's novels tend to fit into the mythical mold, although his repeated insistence on specificity of time and place anchors him also in the realistic tradition.

An extensive study of myth in all of Glissant's novels will not be attempted here; such an undertaking goes well beyond the limits of the present article and merits book-length treatment. Indeed, it has become apparent to me that a deeper analysis of Glissant's entire oeuvre will reveal hitherto unmentioned affinities, parallels, and influences from mythical traditions in Europe, Africa, and the New World. I would instead consider primarily ***La Lézarde,*** guided by the pertinent observations as they appear in Beverley Ormerod's recent study of Glissant.

La Lézarde is structured around the dual initiation of Thaël and Mathieu and contains many conventional mythical themes: the mythical quest of the protagonist, the interplay of light and darkness, good and evil, the presence of spirits, sacrificial death. At every moment, however, there is conscious political and social awareness, thus evidencing the author's anchoring of his work in the real history of his people. ***Le quatrième siècle,*** on the other hand, shows the adolescent Mathieu eager to penetrate the mystery surrounding the two antagonistic groups of Martinicans, whose enmity dates from their very first landing on the island in the eighteenth century. It is a confrontation of two different epistemologies, what Ernst Cassirer would designate as the rational-empiric thought in opposition to mythical consciousness. Mathieu, in his effort to understand what happened in the past, is engaged in an attempt to defeat the mythical mode as represented by Papa Longoué.

The early parts of ***La Lézarde*** present the themes of genesis and exploration, as we see the protagonist Thaël moving downstream, from the locus of trees and other elements of the natural environment imbued with spiritual force, toward the plains, and ultimately to the sea. It is a journey that effectuates an inner change in the protagonist, as he is impelled from his world of myths toward the historical world of rational analysis. At the end of this journey he is confronted with the reality of political life in the company of a group of youthful radicals, who persuade him to participate in their project: the assassination of their political foe, who has established his abode near the source of the life-giving river.

Thaël returns upstream—the hero on his quest to confront the source of evil. He accomplishes his mission at the end of his second journey downstream. More significantly, the act of slaying is accompanied by the conquest of the symbol of limitation: he crosses the sandbar, thus entering a new life and opening a new perspective in his quest, for we see him next in his second journey upstream, where he must engage in a further confrontation with the power of myth. This dramatic encounter encompasses the ironic, violent death of his intended wife, ferociously torn apart by the hero's monstrous dogs, which in turn the protagonist destroys with calculated ferocity.

There is, however, another important symbolic presence in the novel in the person of Papa Longoué, the very embodiment of the ancient ways, whose abode is the forest. He is the last representative of the Maroons, who through mythical representation have been transformed into ancestral heroes. Longoué's consciousness is distinguished from what Cassirer would call empirical consciousness: "Instead of the dialectical movement of thought, in which every given particular is linked with other particulars in a series and thus ultimately subordinated to a general law and process, we have here a mere subjection to the impression itself and its momentary presence.

What Glissant is showing in ***La Lézarde*** through the internal transformation of Thaël, and his meetings with Mathieu and Longoué, is the necessity for an understanding of the mythic mode as a more complete assessment of the true nature of his people. The claims of the past should not be overlooked in the attempt to transform society. At the same time, however, fixation with the past is also unacceptable: Thaël's decision to return to the forest merely reinforces the utter unregenerative marginality of the traditionalist Longoué.

One can readily discern in Glissant and the deconstructionist theoreticians a similarity of preoccupation with the limits of logocentrism and hierarchy, which they associate with the exercise of dominance in the relations between peoples and cultures in our time. However, this convergence of interest should not mask a real difference here: Glissant's notion of relatedness/relating (telling)/ relationship, all subsumed under the concept *relation,* emerges, not from mere disenchantment and a sense of unease with a dominant or dominating force. Rather, beginning from a tragic sense of loss, he regards the persistent limitation of authentic expression in all its dimensions—artistic, economic, political, and social—as a condition of a *real* community, in a *real* place, at a *specific* time. This condition, he affirms, must be changed, but the mode of change must be effectuated in a manner that would be meaningful to all segments of that community, and especially those that heretofore have been denied their expression by external and internal (that is, internalized) forces. Such a project imposes an extremely difficult challenge to the writer, who, in a sense, must project himself, at various levels, into the very consciousness of the community so as to become fully capable of articulating their expressive needs and limitations without seeming to be an alien presence. (pp. 629-30)

This challenge is further exacerbated by a fundamental absence, or what I call an *unhinging* in that community. In a settled national community—a *hinged* community, if you may—land and myth, territory and a long-recognized and accepted account by the community of its origins and identity, are always in evidence and are continually reinforced by rituals and other social practices. There is an intimate relationship between occupied territory and the very accounts of the legitimation for such occupation based upon a primordial claim articulated by the founding fathers or patriarchs. The ancient Hebrews, for example, had their myths of origin and myths of future national identity to sustain them during their sojourn in hostile lands. Their experience of the diaspora, then, could be seen as a passing phenomenon, insignificant in terms of the overall movement toward fulfillment. In her discussion of the mythology of writing in the Afro-American poet Jay Wright, Vera Kutzinski cites his references to the historico-mythical thought of the Aztecs, whose myths, for example, provided explanations for the cycles of creation, destruction, and reconstruction, thus assuring community stability.

In an *unhinged* community like the Antilles of Glissant, there are no myths of origins to which the writer can appeal; there are no myths of a preordained destiny of his people around which he may exercise his creative talent; and there is no ready, harmonious response of the community to the land, to the territory which it occupies. Indeed, it is this very absence of myths of origins and continuity which drives our author to create myths appropriate to the condition of the community, and to anchor these myths in the *real experience* of the community. Hence the myth of the Maroon as hero of the community; the myth of a "submarine unity" of the transported peoples; the reverence for the land and especially the mythic nature of the *fromager* (silk-cotton tree) and the mahogany—the one a repository of certain spiritual presences, the other the silent witness to the troubled history of the community.

In Glissant, then, we find a unique convergence of mythic consciousness—the denial of history—with historical consciousness: the affirmation of movement in time, with specifics on what Auerbach sees as "the confused, contradictory multiplicity of events, the psychological and factual cross-purposes" in the revelations of "true history"; for if myths may be considered as the "storehouses of cultural values and beliefs," societies (like the Antilles of Glissant) in the process of defining themselves afford us a privileged perspective on the very formation of the human spirit. The convergence of the mythic and the historical, then, I aver, is the manifestation of a new humanism marked by the rejection of claims of exclusivity and hierarchy, the eschewing of the search for essence, and the determination to approach the Other in full cognizance of one's own and the Other's difference and ineradicable presence. Finally, by his unique and innovative exploration of the significance of land and myth in Antillean culture, Glissant's literary creativity is in consonance with—to adapt Vera Kutzinski's terminology—the growing corpus of "New World" writings from plantation America. (p. 630)

Wilbert J. Roget, "Land and Myth in the Writings of Edouard Glissant," in World Literature Today, *Vol. 63, No. 4, Autumn, 1989, pp. 626-31.*

FURTHER READING

Baudot, Alain. "Edouard Glissant: A Selected Bibliography." *World Literature Today* 63, No. 4 (Autumn 1989): 568-77.

Lists works by and about Glissant.

Case, Frederick Ivor. "Edouard Glissant and the Poetics of Cultural Marginalization." *World Literature Today* 63, No. 4 (Autumn 1989): 593-98.

Assesses the theory of marginalization within Glissant's poetry and essays.

Clark, Beatrice Stith. "IME Revisited: Lectures by Edouard Glissant on Sociocultural Realities in the Francophone Antilles." *World Literature Today* 63, No. 4 (Autumn 1989): 599-605.

Summarizes Glissant's opening remarks at the Institut Martiniquais d'Etudes lecture series of 1974.

Dash, J. Michael. "Writing the Body: Edouard Glissant's Poetics of Remembering." *World Literature Today* 63, No. 4 (Autumn 1989): 609-12.

Discusses the concept of the "liberated body" and its relationship to consciousness, culture, history, and surroundings within Glissant's fiction.

Degras, Priska. "Name of the Fathers, History of the Name: Odono as Memory." *World Literature Today* 63, No. 4 (Autumn 1989): 613-19.

Links Glissant's naming of individuals and objects with the Antillean search for identity.

Glissant, Edouard. "Beyond Babel." *World Literature Today* 63, No. 4 (Autumn 1989): 561-63.

Examines diversities and difficulties of oral and written languages within national and regional contexts.

Miller, Elinor S. "The Identity of the Narrator in Edouard Glissant's *La Lézarde.*" *South Atlantic Bulletin* XLIII, No. 2 (May 1978): 17-26.

Studies multiple dimensions of the narrator in *La Lézarde.*

———. "Narrative Techniques in Edouard Glissant's *Malemort.*" *The French Review* LIII, No. 2 (December 1979): 224-31.

Delineates among narrative voices to prove *Malemort*'s difficulties do not result from "cultural differences, but rather from Glissant's unique artistic interpretation of the best means to achieve his ends."

Silenieks, Juris. "Pays rêvé, pays réel: The Martinican Chronotope in Edouard Glissant's Oeuvre." *World Literature Today* 63, No. 4 (Autumn 1989): 632-36.

Examines Glissant's perceptions of Martinican history, time, and space within Russian literary critic Mikhail Bakhtin's theory of the chronotope—"the intrinsic connectedness of temporal and spatial relationships that are artistically expressed in literature."

John Howard Griffin

1920-1980

American novelist, essayist, journalist, critic, and biographer.

Griffin's work is predominantly concerned with humanity's spiritual well-being as determined by social and personal growth. For example, his first novel, *The Devil Rides Outside,* examines both monastic and secular lifestyles as encountered by a young man obsessed with physical pleasure, divine grace, and spiritual salvation. His next novel, *Nuni,* is an anthropological account of a Westerner stranded on a South Pacific island whose inhabitants consider Western expressions of love and affection *zagata,* or "no good." Griffin's belief in humanity's potential for reform led to his active participation in the American civil rights movement during the 1960s. His most famous book, *Black Like Me,* chronicles the racism he encountered in the South when he disguised himself as a black man. The controversial subject matter of his works catapulted Griffin into the role of social commentator, combating what he called the "very worst development of recent years . . . that people no longer feel a sense of horror (or even *uneasiness*) in the face of injustice that simply wrecks human lives."

Griffin was born in Dallas, Texas. While in his teens, he attended the Lycee Déscartes in Tours, France, where he studied science, music, and philosophy. After graduation, Griffin studied psychiatry at the Ecole de Médecine de Tours. Despite his decision to pursue a career in medicine, Griffin continued his musical studies. He collaborated on a book about the early modern music of the Roman Catholic church and combined his love for music and medical science by prescribing music therapy for his patients. When World War II broke out, Griffin was placed in a supervisory position at the Asylum of Tours, became active in the French Resistance, and helped many Jews escape Nazi persecution by loading them on ambulances under the pretense that they were patients being transferred to other facilities. When France fell to Germany in 1940, Griffin returned to the United States and enlisted in the Air Force, serving in the Pacific, first on the island of Nuni and then on Morotai as a liaison between the islanders and American forces. During an air raid on Morotai, he sustained head injuries that left him legally blind and received a medical discharge. After the war ended, Griffin returned to France to study music with Nadia Boulanger—an acclaimed conductor, lecturer, and teacher of music composition. While researching the origins of the Gregorian chant, a melody used in Roman Catholic liturgies, he visited the Couvent St. Jacques as well as the Benedictine Abbey of Solesmes, where he became familiar with the teachings of Roman Catholicism. These experiences led to Griffin's conversion and provided the basis for *The Devil Rides Outside.*

After Griffin completely lost his sight in 1947, he returned to the United States to attend schools for the blind and to study philosophy with Jacques Maritain, of whom he later wrote a biography. He eventually settled on his parents' farm in Mansfield, Texas, and took up cattle-breeding, teaching piano, and creative writing. By dictating his work into a wire recorder, Griffin was able to compose *The Devil Rides Outside* and *Nuni.* During this time, Griffin also began taking strychnine to treat a case of malaria which had left him partially paralyzed. An unexpected side effect of the drug restored circulation to blood vessels in Griffin's eyes and allowed him to regain his vision. In 1959 he suggested to the editors of *Sepia,* a magazine directed at a black audience, that he research a story on the treatment of the black person in the American south. In order to experience the hardships suffered by his subjects, Griffin affected the appearance of a black man using sun lamps, vegetable dyes, and pigment-enhancing drugs. His experiences were reported in *Sepia*'s "Journey into Shame" series and were later published as *Black Like Me.* Griffin's reproach of southern white society prompted hostility in his community, and, in order to escape harassment, he and his family fled to Mexico. Upon his return to Texas in 1961, Griffin abandoned writing projects that were near completion and began lecturing on civil rights. Prior to the

1969 publication of *The Church and the Black Man*, which called for the Catholic church to become more actively involved in the civil rights movement, he befriended and worked with Trappist monk and author Thomas Merton. Between 1968 and 1971, Griffin made frequent trips to Gethsemani Abbey in Kentucky, where he visited Merton and made numerous spiritual retreats, eventually earning a commission from the Merton Legacy to write Merton's biography. Poor health prevented Griffin from meeting deadlines for the book, however, and permission was revoked in 1978. Griffin died in 1980, but the journals he kept while working on the biography were published a year later as *The Hermitage Journals.*

Griffin's first novel, *The Devil Rides Outside*, chronicles a young man's struggle for spiritual salvation. While studying at a monastery, the narrator longs for the mystical spirituality and inner peace that the monks have achieved, and strives to imitate their lifestyle by curbing his own carnal desires. While the work was praised for its accurate descriptions of monastic life and its confessional honesty, critics thought the novel overlong, unorganized, and marred by extended philosophical digressions which were often disguised as speeches. Griffin also faced opposition from the Legion for Decent Literature, which took offense at graphic descriptions of the characters' sexual urges and encounters; these passages became the basis for lawsuits that the state of Michigan brought against the book's distributors. Eventually the case was brought before the United States Supreme Court, which ruled in the distributors' favor.

Like *The Devil Rides Outside, Nuni* is largely autobiographical. This novel stems from Griffin's experiences in the South Pacific during World War II and his observations of the islanders' culture. In *Nuni*, the protagonist learns the language, legends, rites, and norms of the natives and attempts to instill Western values in them. While critics found Griffin's stream-of-consciousness technique and use of the present tense confusing, they also recognized the novel's importance as a sociological account of life among the Pacific aborigines. Some commentators also argued that *Nuni* might have been more effective if presented as an anthropological study rather than as a piece of fiction.

Black Like Me is Griffin's most famous and controversial book. In this work, Griffin described his travels in New Orleans, Mississippi, Alabama, and Georgia, during which the simplest tasks of obtaining food and lodging became obstacles. Under the Jim Crow laws, blacks were treated as second-class citizens who were often legally prevented from voting; restricted to the "colored" sections of towns, restaurants, trains, and buses; and denied employment and entrance to social institutions and educational facilities. More devastating and humiliating, however, was the way in which Griffin was treated by the white people he encountered. Frank London Brown notes that Griffin now "met the 'hate stare' ['I walked up to the ticket counter. When the lady ticket seller saw me, her otherwise attractive face turned sour, violently so.']; he met neurosis in depth ['I understand you make more of an art—or maybe *hobby*—out of your sex than we do.']; he met despair ['Suddenly I had had enough. Suddenly I could stomach no more of this degradation—not of myself but of all men who were black like me.']" The descriptions of life in a racist society struck a nerve in many Americans, and most negative criticism came from the reading public. As a result, Griffin was hanged in effigy, denounced, and often banned from speaking in public. Literary critics praised the book as an example of the New Journalism movement, citing the author's participation in the story; yet others found the work unbalanced and wanted either more emphasis placed on everyday experiences faced by black men and women, or more examples of Griffin's own experiences and fewer philosophical digressions. Despite claims that the book belittled both black and white cultures, *Black Like Me* received praise for its honesty and emotional impact, and became the basis for a motion picture in 1964.

(See also *Contemporary Authors*, Vols. 1-4, rev. ed., Vol. 101 [obituary] and *Contemporary Authors New Revision Series*, Vol. 2.)

PRINCIPAL WORKS

NONFICTION

Mansfield, Texas 1957 [with Theodore Freedman]
Black Like Me 1961
Black, White and Gray 1964 [with others]
The Church and the Black Man 1969
A Time to Be Human 1977

NOVELS

The Devil Rides Outside 1952
Nuni 1956

BIOGRAPHIES

Thirteen for Christ 1963 [with others]
Jacques Maritain: Homage in Words and Pictures 1974 [with Yves R. Simon]

OTHER

Scattered Shadows (autobiography) 1963
The John Howard Griffin Reader (prose collection) 1968
The Hermitage Journals (memoir) 1981

Thomas Sugrue

John H. Griffin has written a long, intimate novel [***The Devil Rides Outside***] about a man who is obviously himself, but who is also every other male; a man who is young and interested in music, who goes to a Benedictine monastery somewhere in France to examine manuscripts of Gregorian chants, and who becomes enchanted with the idea of turning himself into a saint. The story is told in the first person singular, and in the course of its nearly 600 pages the name of the narrator is never revealed. After a while the reader—and this is Mr. Griffin's triumph—realizes that naming the narrator is unnecessary, since the reader is himself the teller of the tale.

Against this triumph—and it is a large one—are lined up a series of heavy faults. Passage after passage is overlong; the prose is overblown and trails endlessly, like a thin mist on a Scottish moor. The man who is telling the story is confused in his thinking, but so is the man who is writing it, and this becomes intolerable for the reader. The scenes of action and conversation are excellent, but the moving picture of the narrator's mind is a continuous blur.

He comes to the monastery, this young man without a name, from the bed of a mistress in Paris. He resents the harsh life of the monks until he glimpses in them the serenity of those who immerse themselves in the assault on heaven. He attaches himself to a mystic and sets out with a child's notion of morality to attain a child's idea of saintliness. If only once he can resist the temptation of a woman, he will be, he thinks, on the road to Assisi.

He goes to live in a villa in the town near the monastery. There, after failing signally to achieve his ambition whenever hunger of the flesh originates in himself, he finally resists, when she attacks him, a woman he loathes. The woman he rejects, is the character for which the book is memorable. She is a nasty, selfish, cunning, unscrupulous female who recognizes everyone's sinfulness but her own. She rules the town by impersonating a good and magnanimous woman; she ruins the life of her son and fastens like a leech on the narrator. In her he sees all that disgusts him, and, since she is a mirror for his ego, when he is able to reject her he is able for the first time to resist himself.

This is the heart of the book, and it is well done; it reveals a genuine talent in Mr. Griffin, and one he will no doubt practice with more skill as time proceeds. By violence and by honesty he has in this work achieved what later he will attain by craftsmanship and perception. This is a spate of self-revelation, of memory, of confession; its notions of sex and mysticism are adolescent; but scattered through it there is a good novel about a selfish young man and a possessive older woman.

Thomas Sugrue, "Everyman's Triumph," in The New York Times Book Review, *October 26, 1952, p. 5.*

Ben Ray Redman

Into the monastery, along with his studious intentions, the young musicologist [of ***The Devil Rides Outside***] brings a lusty body with imperious desires, fond memories of much sexual pleasure, and hopes of similar pleasures to come. He finds himself among men who have vowed themselves to chastity, poverty, humility, and obedience; men who have mastered but not abolished temptation. He finds himself in a house that has shut its doors against all wordly values and all worldly thoughts; and in this house, among these men, he senses spiritual peace of a kind that he has never known, of which he has never dreamed.

His first reaction is rather like that of a small boy who is envious at sight of what seems to be a prized possession in the hands of another child. ***The Devil Rides Outside*** tells how his desire for this peace matures and purifies itself, how his understanding of the nature of this peace grows and deepens. It records, too, with naked physiological detail, and in panting, sweating rhetoric, the ferocious, finally successful battle which he wages against "the devil who prowls outside monastery walls," the devil who with unerring accuracy exploits his greatest weakness—the concupiscent flesh.

Mr. Griffin spares his hero and his readers nothing. He stops at no frontier of good taste—and, indeed, some saints have not—in his fusion of the sacred and the profane. But it seems that he must deliberately intend to shock his readers when he describes a momentary, mystical union with the Virgin in exactly the words that he has used previously to describe the physical consummation of an afternoon's casual encounter between a man and a woman. And surely he errs when he has Father Clément violate the secrecy of the confessional in his talks with the narrator.

He errs in another way, and more importantly, when he asks us to believe in the absurd, unendurable, daily relationship of the hero and Madame Renée; and again when, for a time, he makes Madame Renée and her son the center of interest. But, despite its many faults of various kinds, this first novel has in it the power of life itself, for which faultlessness can never be a substitute in literature. Mr. Griffin's reach may have exceeded his grasp, but he has reached boldly and strongly, with conspicuously original talent.

Ben Ray Redman, "The Two Faces of God," in The Saturday Review, *New York, Vol. 35, No. 44, November 1, 1952, p. 16.*

Frederic Morton

[The most striking thing about ***The Devil Rides Outside***] is its medieval fascination with the ordeal and triumph of the spirit. The nameless hero of Mr. Griffin's story, a young American musicologist, obtains permission to live in a French monastery in order to do research on manuscripts of the Gregorian chant. At first his consciousness of the new environment is for the most part worldly, limited to esthetic and scientific interests. Before long, however, the rhythm of the litanies, the murmurings of Matins, the ancient prayer-steeped isolation of the cloister, the calm day-long absorptions of the Benedictines reveal to him glimpses of immense meaning. Somewhere within him develops an almost helpless susceptibility to God.

Yet along with his discovery of the soul's possibilities, he suffers the delicious assault of the senses. In fact, the more he strives toward the religious, the stronger and more ingenious the invitations of the flesh. Inside the monastery Father Clement, Father Marie-Ornoux and others try to steady him in his search, but outside—not bound by the monks' routine, he may come and go as he pleases—outside rides the devil. There the women and the taverns of the village wait for him. Madame Reneé, apparently anxious to facilitate his studies, involves and implicates him in her snobbery and pride. Madame Vincent arrives to celebrate the Feast of St. Hilaire, but stays to take him into her bed. Leering taxi drivers, willing servant girls never let him rest. Mr. Griffin's story mounts into a tortured dialectic between temptation and purgation, indulgence and atonement, resolution and relapse. The energies of sin and salvation duel explosively on every page.

Mr. Griffin faced a gargantuan problem in translating into a novel so raw a confessional and so literal a conversion. His story relates a sojourn in a place of painful but luminous seclusion. And when Mr. Griffin describes his young man's efforts to distill the light of the spirit from the heat of the flesh he touches on the timeless motifs of St. Anthony and St. Augustine. Sometimes he does full justice to his great theme. He can project with a lacerating vividness the mesalliance between body and soul. He is at home in the subtleties of asceticism:

> To be obsessed with chastity is also to be obsessed with the flesh: to be obsessed with humility is to be obsessed with self-righteous pride: to be obsessed with food is to be obsessed with hunger. . . .

Mr. Griffin can also paint fine verbal frescoes of monastic life: white vested celebrants at Solemn High Mass; moonlit habits rustling toward Compline; the foot-washing ceremonies of the Father Abbot; the cool arches of the chapel; the crystal Latin of the hymns. Outside the monastery walls the author's brushwork can be efficient too: Madame Reneé is a repulsively real portrait of a woman full of profane appetites and hypocritical sentiments.

On the whole, though, Mr. Griffin has not successfully organized his huge material into the form of fiction. He himself spent considerable time in French monasteries on a mission similar to the protagonist's. He enjoys an obviously first-hand acquaintance with the subject matter but approaches it with the headlong intensity of a manifesto-writer. Entirely too many pages are given over to extended homilies on the spirit and these disquisitions are not integrated into the narrative; after a while they seem to degenerate into a vague moralistic din. The hero's prolonged sexual ecstasies suffer from apoplectic imagery. And the diary form, using the first person, present tense, only accents such excesses.

Yet ***The Devil Rides Outside*** is a novel of rare though purely spasmodic power. If its drive had been better organized, its ardors less ever-incandescent, I would look ahead with even greater interest to those six other books Mr. Griffin has on tap.

Frederic Morton, "The Ancient War of Body and Spirit," in New York Herald Tribune Book Review, *November 2, 1952, p. 16.*

Charles J. Rolo

To produce a novel that is genuinely big takes a big talent, which is necessarily rare. Even the better-than-average big novels that come my way often owe a sizable part of their girth to artistic indiscipline—to nonremoval of "surplusage." A case in point is a first novel with some remarkable qualities, ***The Devil Rides Outside*** by John H. Griffin. (p. 82)

The novel's basic weakness is that the hero, though a man in years, is a juvenile figure who has not outgrown the sex-turmoil of an adolescent, and whose spiritual conflict sounds more like a crisis of puberty than an adult drama of the soul. For his conflict hinges on the naïve idea that if he can once resist fleshly temptation—and the woman he finally resists is peculiarly untempting—he will be all set to become a saint. Most of the novel's sound and fury is bound up with the medieval notion that sex is the domain of Satan; and the hero's morality is of roughly the same order as that of an alcoholic in whose eyes all evil is lodged in a bottle of booze. From the purely literary standpoint, the novel is marred by excess—it is full of redundancies and of passages overblown with emotionalism.

But when all this has been said on the negative side, there remain very considerable literary merits—the convincing description of life in the monastery; individual scenes that have a powerful impact; a superb portrait of a vain, nasty, insanely possessive woman; above all, energy and a sense of life intensely felt. (pp. 82, 84)

Charles J. Rolo, in a review of "The Devil Rides Outside," in The Atlantic Monthly, *Vol. 191, No. 1, January, 1953, pp. 82, 84.*

Paul Engle

[***Nuni***] is an extraordinarily interesting account of a white man's life in a savage island village of the Pacific. Preceding and following the story of his experiences among the natives are passages of rhetorical meditation. These slow down the pace of the book, and try to do by generalization what ought to be done by event and narrative and dialog.

But the greater part of the novel is concerned with the growth in the white man, Prof. Harper (who has survived a plane crash on the island), of a knowledge of as well as affection for the curiously innocent people, along with a need in his own life for the companionship of a native child to replace his own children back in America.

He finds the people, after he has learned their language, brutal and yet not really cruel, trapped in a great web of superstition and fear. By sitting with the men and chewing betel nuts, which act on him like a dizzying drug, he learns a great deal about their rigid states of mind, the terrible drive toward conformity, the pathetic struggle in them between an occasional generous impulse and the push toward utter selfishness.

Although the language becomes occasionally trite, and at times is pretentious, the book is attractive. The author might have done a better job by sticking more closely to the fictional structure. Yet the speculative chapter at the end is no doubt a crucial part of his conception of the story. Trite as it sounds to say so, I feel rewarded for having read it.

Paul Engle, "Able Novel of White Man on Pacific Isle," in Chicago Tribune, *part 4, May 20, 1956, p. 3.*

Maxwell Geismar

The real question for the novelist of this period is how to escape from the balm of moderation and the bane of normalcy. Perched as we are on the edge of the crater, it is only natural for the rest of us to close our eyes and pray—or to cling to whatever is banal and trite, customary and reassuring. Popular novelists, as well as politicians, have sensed this mood, and catered to the euphoria that masks our anxiety. [Nelson Algren, John Hersey, and John Howard Griffin] have chosen another way to handle this situation, and they have turned out three good novels. . . .

[Griffin] has avoided all the pressures of conformity by simply not noticing them. Like Algren and Hersey, he has by-passed all the deadening restraints in the present phase of our "free society." His first novel, ***The Devil Rides Outside*** . . . is probably the most original novel by a new writer in the last four or five years; it is still very much worth reading. The present tale, ***Nuni,*** is closer to a novelette—or a brilliant kind of nightmare that is horrifying, absorbing and ironic.

The hero, a respectable academic figure, is dropped by an air crash into the midst of a primitive Pacific tribe whose mode of life outdoes the worst of Jack London's south-sea savages. The problem is how a man can retain his humanity in the lowest human circumstances; which are described with humor and even with a kind of lingering tenderness. Technically the story is superb, since Griffin also discards other conventional props of the novel, such as women, sex, love, and yet maintains an immense narrative interest. The climax is a little heavy, but the story as a whole makes us uneasy and alert.

Maxwell Geismar, "Against the Tide of Euphoria," in The Nation, *New York, Vol. 182, No. 22, June 2, 1956, p. 473.*

The Christian Science Monitor

Nuni asks the promising question; What would happen to a civilized man on a desert island?

Robinson Crusoe gave one answer on the level of physical survival. ***Nuni*** 's challenge is subtler and more demanding—the twentieth century's challenge, the challenge to spiritual survival. For John Harper's body is cared for all too well by friendly savages. It is his doubt-filled disoriented mind which falls into profound peril.

Mr. Griffin's second novel, judged by its own large intentions, is a failure, but an interesting one. It fails first to establish the world of which Professor Harper is a product—a world of good books not too intensely studied, of congenial wives not too intensely loved; a world of well-fed children, starched curtains, waxed floors.

In a prologue leading up to the plane crash which deposits his hero on his island Mr. Griffin makes us see this world, but he does not quite get us within it. Nor does he individualize Professor Harper so as to engage the reader's concern for him.

This weakness plagues the story sorely when Harper, finally divested of all the accouterments of civilization except for a few rags and a paperbound volume of *Great Essays,* slips into the betel-nut habit and primitive degradation.

A second, and obviously related failure, is the novel's inability to dramatize the native society in which Harper is forced to live. . . .

The flat quality to ***Nuni*** 's two environments is almost fatal, for the novel's meanings derive chiefly from their contrast. One brilliant trick could have compensated perhaps: if Harper's introspective crises had been made so vivid and circumstantial that the hero's mind might have become the true setting for the book.

As his story grows ever more abstract, the author attempts to salvage it as at least a thesis. "Here [on the island]," he writes of Harper, and man in general,

> the primitive is so completely absorbed in Elemental Nature that it has contrived to make him forget the forever hungering goals of his spiritual being. In civilization . . . man has become so completely absorbed in Mechanized Nature that it has equally contrived to make him forget . . .

This is a provocative if oversimplified theory, but it is a little tacked on, and that too late.

M. M., "Novel with a Challenge," in The Christian Science Monitor, *July 12, 1956, p. 91.*

"No one can deny that Griffin's life, despite a tendency to despise his own ethnic origins and to dwell on the state of his health, was fine art. Neither can one deny that his books, all autobiographical, are masterpieces of prose. But how free are they of artifice, how far short of true artistic accuracy they fall—these questions continue to disturb me. . . .

[The problem] with Griffin's role-playing is that he began to believe and to convince his readers that he had really become, and therefore really understood the life of, a south sea islander, a black man, a Trappist monk. He made the common mistake of confusing imitation with incarnation. Imitation can, of course, be a valid act of Christian dedication, as in the social and ethical imitation of Christ; but it should not be confused with or substituted for incarnation. To do so is to give false impressions and, inevitably, false information. It is artifice."

—James T. Baker, 1982

P. J. Searles

The major part of [***Nuni***] is concerned with the struggle between Harper and a vicious, bestial "rauka," a female shaman, for possession of a small child whom the "rauka" sought to disfigure and perhaps kill. It is the age-old struggle between modern man bringing love and friendliness and the savage with his dread of the unseen. The denouement is a powerful passage of life and death.

The story both interests and irritates. The interest lies in the portrayal of savage existence, of its fears and hates and indifference to cruelty, its interminable legends and pointless taboos. As an anthropological document the novel is excellent. But the irritation comes in the manner of telling. The entire tale is told in the present tense, probably symbolical of the native ignorance of time, but annoying to the reader who attempts to disentangle past and present. There are cut-backs to Harper's pre-Pacific days which confuse because the cut-backs are to various times, yet all told in the present tense. Then, too, the author grows philosophical, even metaphysical, to an extent that is confusing and at times so involved as to be beyond comprehension. The stream of consciousness appears now and then to add to complication. It seems as if the author is deliberately becoming more and more cloudily involved. One could wish that Mr. Griffin had written a straightforward anthropological study and not a novel.

P. J. Searles, "Modern Man, Savage World," in New York Herald Tribune Book Review, *July 22, 1956, p. 7.*

Maxwell Geismar

For sheer talent, power, and virtuosity of craft, Griffin ranks very high among the new writers; but he has deeper powers still than these, and more interesting facets in his temperament and work. It is another ironic commentary on the literary quarterlies and popular press of the present day that he is virtually unknown to many readers. . . .

[***The Devil Rides Outside***] is odd enough in its own right to perplex the audience which might ordinarily welcome another story of Christian redemption. This is, to be frank, a category of books to which I am ordinarily averse. What we need now, in an epoch of underlying fear and hostility, is perhaps a few less Christian converts and a little more Christian morality. Part of the ***Devil***'s distinction is that it embodies a true Christian ethic, set against a background of pagan human nature—and it is hard to say which element in the novel is more disturbing. (p. 251)

But it *is* a work of art just because it is perplexing, disturbing, eloquent, and entertaining. The hero-narrator is a young American, educated in France, who arrives at a Benedictine monastery in order to study the Gregorian chants. It is autumn, and he is appalled by the damp, the coldness, the dirt, the poverty, and what he feels to be the asceticism of a vestigal medieval order. There is the daily routine of the monastery which is intolerable, and wonderfully well described. The hero is filled with anger, disgust, and loneliness. He misses his girl in Paris, all the comforts and luxuries of city life—of modern life. He feels shut off, isolated, "out of all time." (pp. 251-52)

There is the "malevolent crucifix" over his cot while he reads and studies to avoid the "nightmares of carnality." And then, slowly revealing itself in the narrative, there is the childlike manner, the great learning, and the great humanity of the individual Benedictine brothers. "Here you must develop a new standard of facial judgment, for these are men of great intelligence without appearing in any way intelligent, according to outside standards." This human understanding and companionship is the hero's only consolation for all his misery—it is indeed the spiritual state of mind which this misery is designed to create. "God makes suffer only those whom he loves." And still the hero yearns for Paris, life, and his girl—"to be happy and shallow!"—amidst the silence of Compline, the adoration of Vespers. (p. 252)

The raggedness and turbulence of the outside world are contrasted with the inner peace of the monastery, the devotion to spiritual works, the consuming fire of total purity. The sexual act is described recurrently as "hasty," "peremptory," "fumbling." And yet it is so necessary, so desirable, so inevitable; chastity is impossible! The novel's action swings out from the divine purity of the monastic world, which the hero so yearns for and cannot achieve, to the little French village nearby—and to the nether regions of the flesh and the ego. . . .

This provincial French village life, whose atmosphere is rendered quite as brilliantly and vividly in ***The Devil Rides Outside*** as is that of the Benedictine monastery, may remind us in turn of a Kafka nightmare with some Rabelaisian touches. In this close, narrow, stifling little scene of scandal, intrigue, malice, of petty power, jealousy, fear, and suspicion, Madame Renée is the devil who rides outside of the monastery walls. She persecutes the Paris visitor, Madame Vincent, for yielding to the hero. She wants to drive out of the valley Salesky's mistress and the two illegitimate children. She tries to destroy the impending marriage of her unfortunate son, Michel, who is struggling to escape from her imperious and avaricious dominion. She wants complete control of the hero himself, through feeding, nursing, and "protecting" him, and then by gradually offering her body to him under the most "respectable," moralistic, and lascivious auspices. With her devouring ego and vanity, her wiles, and then with her aging and helpless passion for the young American stranger, she is a remarkable literary portrait. (p. 254)

The Devil Rides Outside really moves on three levels of human or historical development: the primitive level of the senses, the medieval Christian level of spiritual renunciation, the "modern" level of worldly society.

There is also the obvious fact that in this novel by a young Texas writer there is hardly a reference to twentieth-century American life. And the provincial French life of the narrative is still essentially feudal and peasant. When the dark-hued Doctor Castelar reproaches the hero for being, with all his wild outcries of lust, an essentially pale and weak young man, restrained, inhibited, "good in a small little mean way," the Griffin narrator agrees.

"I think you're right, Doctor. . . . I'm the type who'd make. An impeccable clerk. Or a good politician. I write a nice neat hand. I can speak several languages. I'm soft. Where I should be hard. I know this. And I loathe it. I'm the sort of person. I can't tolerate. What do I do but take up space? Fill the sewers? Vote like everyone else? Some day produce my share of children? Who'll be like me? Without understanding. Without ever understanding."

This is hardly a flattering view of either modern life or the modern protagonist. And does this haunting self-image account in some part for this hero's aversion to the narrow mediocrity—the "sordid affairs"—of even his little foreign village? Is this the impelling force behind his hatred of conformity and social compulsion in any form—legitimate and sharp as the satire is? Is it perhaps behind his wild carnal urges, and his recurrent and repentent moods of ego-renunciation, total purification of the flesh, and a purely ascetic exaltation? In the same remarkable scene with the demonic Doctor, where both protagonists become drunker and drunker as their discussion ranges more widely, Castelar finally admits that the search for God is the best of all the many narcotics. (Like his generation, the Griffin hero also believes that self-expression is no longer possible in the movements of social reform or social revolution.)

What is certain, at least, is that the cards are stacked here, as to both modern society and the values of common ordinary life.

The central dichotomy of utter purity (goodness) in the monastery and prevailing evil, or mediocrity, in the village surely represents an author's yearning rather than an established fact. (Yet Griffin's talent as a novelist can make both sides of this chasm equally interesting.) Even the village priest, Father Sauvac, is presented in a not altogether flattering light. In the battle with Madame Renée—"a woman literally eaten up with pride; a woman in love with herself"—the priest operates with worldly wisdom, rather than Christian humility. Outside the monastery, too, in the sway of Catholicism's temporal authority, we see the evidences of clerical superstition operating on the village people in terms that the Benedictines would hardly tolerate. ("Surely one little heathen smuggled into heaven can do no harm," the hero thinks in the struggle over the church burial of the Petite Chevissier.) Beneath the great abstractions of God and Art, all purely human motives and actions are bound to be imperfect. So, too, in the central thinking of the hero (and the author?), human morality is viewed as another absolute.

When a man can act "without the risk of another's judgment," we are told, then only is he real; and this is a commendable if a difficult standard of behavior. On the other hand, the tolerant and highly flexible moral judgments of the Benedictines proceed from the fact that in their orbit "there are no illusions to be destroyed—nothing that is forbidden." These saintly monks have indeed become brothers in "the search for the infinite"—but is there no brotherhood possible within the ordeals of the finite? It is the same Doctor Castelar (whose name suggests social caste as well as moral heights) who declares that "Man is basically an entity, complete unto himself, who has become dependent on society." And this striking statement may represent either the climax of spiritual aspiration or the deepest and darkest depths of man's primitive fear. The central psychological concept in ***The Devil Rides Outside*** is indeed that of the stranger, the exile, the solitary hero who struggles against not merely an imperfect but a hostile society. Beneath this chronicle of divine love, there are echoes of that somber and savage Darwinian cosmos of dog eat dog which for a while, earlier in the century, dominated American thought and art.

Yes, and maybe within the psyche of this estranged and gifted young American artist himself—conversant as he also is with Cocteau and Apollinaire, Huysmans and Mallarmé—there are still other ambiguous strains. The great charm of many of the sexual scenes in the novel is due to their direct infantile fantasy quality. The element of voyeurism is strong here, and how much washing and bathing, dressing and undressing, the forbidden (and delightful) fondling of child and nurse, and the incestuous physical contact of what is also, in effect, mother and son. This is beautifully done in the story, and is true at least to some of the deepest levels of the male psyche. But what is curious is the mixed tone of all the later, or more mature, sexual episodes. There is the enormous power of the sexual drive, and the immense revulsion either during or after the sexual act. (pp. 255-57)

And what one notices also is that these powerful sexual drives, and equally powerful repulsions, are concerned always with lust and carnality, for good or for evil, rather than with mature sexual love. The hero's "passion" for Madame Vincent has only one direct sexual encounter in it, and then, burdened with guilt, relapses into a "pure" and a doomed friendship. The true sexual currents of the novel are divided between the phallic worship of the peasant women and the repressed, sinful, provocative puritanism of the aging Madame Renée. (p. 258)

In a curious way, incidentally, this mystic and religious writer, so remote from his own time and place, is directly linked to the other leading talents of his day. If Griffin's touch is less subtle and tender than William Styron's, if it deals with bolder themes in broad and heavy colors, he is surely aware of that lost world of infantile sexuality which is here described in terms of both pagan laughter and Christian horror. . . . And Griffin's second novel, ***Nuni,*** in 1956, was both completely different from his first one, and yet, psychologically and aesthetically, a revealing supplement to it. (pp. 258-59)

But this tantalizing glimpse into the origins of ***The Devil Rides Outside*** is all that we get in ***Nuni.*** Amidst the dazzling coral, the overpowering sun, the hallucinations of nourishment and water, the dreams and nightmares of tulips and giant purple grapes, Professor Harper is rescued by a curious and merry black child, and by an old black patriarch with a club. The tone of the narrative is reminiscent of Jack London's tales of the south-sea savages, along with something else. When the hero starts learning the primitive and guttural tribal language: "Ta-eega. . . . Angua Kulangu . . . Kmai Kakosekani. . . . Au-gooah!"—these phrases which he repeats to himself in fear and panic are close to a sort of black Swiftian baby talk. And what Harper notices immediately is the contrast between the blank, inhuman eyes of the patriarch Tombani and the expressive young eyes of the child. "What has happened between childhood and age to glaze those of the old man?"

This is the real point of ***Nuni*** on its first level of import. The novel is a brilliant satire of a tribal culture whose whole aim is to suppress every human emotion. Tombani is a hostile old man whose eyes are indeed dead to affection, "eyes that speak only in degrees of contempt." Enforcing the tribal mores with his heavy club, this "black ball of whimsy and caprice" is without a trace of interest in his fellow human beings. And what mores! As the hero gradually learns the tribal language, he discovers the names for all parts of the body except the intimate parts, which are completely taboo. The normal functions of the body must never be witnessed under pain of death—though everybody is completely naked and completely sexless. Mating is "zagata"—no good—though it is necessary for the bearing of children. Sex is considered painful and unpleasant, to be consummated as a duty to society. Indeed, the sexual act means the loss of virility for the man who performs it. (p. 260)

Griffin in New Orleans after his transformation.

The faces of the people are "tattooed black masks, not human faces, masks with yaw sores around their eyes, stoic masks, cold and feelingless." The women, who are perhaps the saving element in all societies, are here "untouchable . . . disinterested, dulled by dusts of resignation." And Harper feels his own stability of character beginning to disintegrate under the tribal pressures. "We leave you in sunlight," says the witch Rauka to the corpse of Maigna, "and we go back and wait in shadows"—while the tribe howls in savage derision at a sudden mishap to one of the body-carriers. Nightmare imagery and a nightmare tale: at the mid point of the narrative ***Nuni*** is a novel which rouses all kinds of dark shadows in our mind. While Harper, giving up hope and pleasure, is lying in a desolate stupor, the little Ririkinger nestles into his chest and gives him the only affection he has met with in the tribe. He looks up to see the swinging genitals of Tombani over his face and the patriarchal club descending upon his head. It is taboo to touch a girl-child. (p. 261)

[In the village of] Vanua "all that is right, all that is human, is taboo," the hero thinks. "If I move to counter it, I am clubbed." And there is the description of Tombani's "benign face" as he carries out the tribal "law"—making people into animals. On the surface ***Nuni*** is a grand vision of human evil which must be placed against the vision of divine good in ***The Devil Rides Outside.*** (And part of the attraction of this writer's talent lies just in its movement between these polar extremes.) In part, too, the angry satire of Griffin's second novel, the Swiftian tones of repudiation and disgust as well as the language, is certainly directed against the American social values and institutions which are carried to their ultimate point in Vanua. In the portrait of this hostile, angry, taboo-ridden, sexless, and loveless black tribe there are obvious references to the darker side of the national spirit. (p. 262)

In a larger sense, of course, ***Nuni*** is dealing with the tyranny of all societies: of Society. These are the constraints, repressions and taboos which are always put upon the innocent effusions of the human spirit that wishes to soar and to flower. Here Griffin is joining in a common chorus of the literary voices during the 1950's which beholds the warm and innocent life of childhood constrained into the mold of a civilization which is always repressive and banal. (Ernst Schactel's thesis of "Childhood Amnesia"—the loss between the original vision of childhood, the modes of adult perception—is a key source for all these novels.) How almost compulsively Griffin's novel describes these free, happy, and nameless children, who are then trained in stoic renunciation, who are crucified and cut in accordance with tribal mores, until only the hardiest, most brutal survivors become the tribal "individuals"! There is the vivid image of the professorial hero himself, so much like an indignant, outraged, ostracized child-man, who stands apart from the odious mass of tribal humanity, clutching his yellow buttercup as the single token of natural harmony and grace. Not only in the more or less superficial view of "social adjustment," but in the deeper, more personal psycho-biological currents of ***Nuni*** there is a fundamental sense of estrangement and alienation. Is the symbol of paternal authority really that of the ignorant old savage with his heavy club—a paternal authority, I mean, which is not that of the Lord himself? On the distaff side, the witch-hag Rauka, though an "adversary of stature," and in effect a more extreme version of Madame Renée in ***The Devil Rides Outside,*** is hardly much better. And are all the "children," for whom the professorial hero risks his life in defiance of the tribal taboos, really so defenseless, crucified, and cut?

Here indeed the earlier theme of the isolated stranger and the hostile universe becomes dominant—a black, savage, and threatening world. All the submerged fears, hatreds, aggressions of the first novel are channeled into a central hostility and alienation. But this is a familiar phenomenon in literature. The major figures of this "school" include such varied writers as Byron, Poe, or Melville, as well as the archetypal Dean Swift himself, or the nineteenth-century French decadents whom Griffin knows so well. One notices the strain of incestuous affection in the present writer's work too, as well as elements of both the superman and the demonic spirit. Not all of this anger, rage, and cruelty must be attributed to the hostile outer world. Some—how much?—must reside in the hidden, fuming, sulphurous psyche of the artist himself. If he seems to be a born, or indeed a hereditary outcast, so was Lucifer, so was Satan. From another angle, the nightmare visions of ***Nuni*** also project backward into the primitive childhood of the race. (Are children, after all, so pure, innocent, and blameless?) And with this horrid dream of a "black birth" Griffin has allied himself, even more than in the earlier conflict of good and evil, with the "dark writers" of literature. The Devil also rides in Texas.

Perhaps, indeed, the intense struggle to reach God and the orbit of divine love—through the sanctity of monastic renunciation—derives its intensity just from its "diabolical" sources. (The possessed and "puritanical" Hawthorne, who was also conversant with witches, might see the attraction of this theme.) The voodoo world of Vanua is too well described, too vivid and intimately known, *too* familiar! But indeed, how many tantalizing levels of meaning are half revealed in the flickering midnight symbolism of ***Nuni*** which continually shifts between the personal, the social, the racial. If the primitive tribe of Vanua is meant to describe the worst aspects of white civilization, there may also be a latent content of the South's own deep and abiding fear of and guilt about the Negro race itself. How many other young artists from the nether world of Faulkner and Faubus have described so vividly their own terror and isolation among these savage black people?

Yet we must add that it is also the Griffin protagonist who sacrifices symbolically his own daughter in the hope of saving his adopted black child, Ririkinger. This is the final "message" of the tale, and the method through which the outsider regains his own sense of identity, of belonging and of love. In the end the professor tries to humanize both the tribe and himself through the black child who is indeed the missing "key" of the South's drama, as well as the novel's. On the rational and moral level, nothing could be better than this last gesture on the part of the outcast hero; and at the story's close, as in the Easter music of ***The Devil Rides Outside,*** there is the scent of flowers and "peace drifts to me on the lively twitterings of birds." (pp. 262-64)

This writer is fertile and prolific, as well as bold and sweeping in emotional range, almost to the point of melodrama and farce. Still another novel is awaiting publication, and these works will doubtless sustain our interest in this original and, as I think, large-sized artist, who should be classified meanwhile in the upper bracket of contemporary writing. (pp. 264-65)

Maxwell Geismar, "John Howard Griffin: The Devil in Texas," in his American Moderns: From Rebellion to Conformity, *Hill and Wang, 1958, pp. 251-65.*

Stuart H. Loory

On October 28, 1959, John Howard Griffin—family man, author, Texan, Roman Catholic, and "specialist in race issues"—decided he must transform himself into a Negro. "How else, except by becoming a Negro could a white man hope to learn the truth? . . . The only way I could see to bridge the gap between us was to become a Negro. I decided I would do this," he wrote. . . .

Mr. Griffin's [***Black Like Me***], in diary form, is uneven, at times ungrammatical, and based on a doubtful premise. The idea that a white man must live a Negro's life to understand his problems disregards the capacity of the white man (or any member of any majority group) to see through the evils of oppression and discrimination. It also does a disservice to the growing number of Negroes from all walks of life who are able to articulate the nature of the life the white man has forced upon them in this country.

Mr. Griffin is at his best when he describes a bus-ride from New Orleans to Hattiesburg shortly after the Mack Parker lynching, a hitch-hiking tour from Biloxi, Miss., to Selma, Ala., and various accounts of his fleeting contacts with whites cruelly intent on "keeping Negroes in their place," never realizing that by their antics they were degrading themselves and exposing the barbarian instincts in humanity. These descriptions include glimpses of such people as:

A scowling woman ticket agent who first refused to change a $10 bill and then flung the change and a bus ticket off the counter and onto the floor in front of Mr. Griffin; a bus driver in Mississippi who refused to let Negroes off his vehicle at a rest stop; a New Orleans bus driver who carried the author eight blocks past his stop before letting him off, and a number of white motorists who endlessly and lasciviously questioned Mr. Griffin on what they presumed to be the sexual desires and aberrations of all Negroes.

Unfortunately, there is too little of such accounts of personal experience in Mr. Griffin's report and too much unoriginal philosophizing about "The Negro Problem." The last nineteen pages of the book are devoted to the aftermath of his adventure—such extraneous topics as how *Time* magazine reported his story and how Dave Garraway, Mike Wallace, and Long John interviewed him. The best that can be said is that Mr. Griffin's book represents an interesting journalistic experiment that does not yield its full promise.

Stuart H. Loory, "He Crossed the South's Racial Boundary," in Books, *New York, October 15, 1961, p. 13.*

Bruce A. Cook

It is difficult to know exactly how to feel about this book, and the difficulty springs, I think, from its very nature. ***Black Like Me*** is novelist John Howard Griffin's report on six weeks in his life (November 7th to December 14th, 1959) which he spent traveling through the Deep South disguised as a Negro.

For years, he tells us, he had been haunted by the question of what the Negro in the Deep South feels. "What is it like to experience discrimination based on skin color, something over which one has no control?"

Griffin went to New Orleans where he consulted with a dermatologist who reluctantly agreed to change the color of his skin through a series of drug treatments. He then passed successfully into the Negro world, but his experience "as a Negro" cannot easily be summarized. They range from the terrifying (being hounded down a New Orleans street by a white tough who threatened to beat up Griffin simply because he thought him a Negro) to the deeply irritating (having to walk miles across a city just to find a Negro water fountain or toilet) to the heart-warming (enjoying the limitless hospitality of a dirt-poor Mississippi Negro farm family—"If you gave us a penny," said the wife, "we'd owe you change."). His narrative, cast in the form of a diary, is spare, clear and concise—quite free of the redundancy which has sometimes marred his novels. He never succumbs to the temptation to inflate his report with generalization and hearsay, but limits himself strictly to what he saw, heard and felt as he traveled through Louisiana, Mississippi, Alabama and Georgia in his Negro guise.

Telling, as he does so well, what he *felt* during these six weeks, Griffin, the novelist, adds a dimension to his book that no mere reporter could hope to achieve with even the most impressive array of facts and figures. The whole thing was a shattering experience for him, an ordeal that almost destroyed him emotionally before it was ended. He is quite frank about this. And indeed it is the frankness and personal honesty of the author which raises the book high above the sensational aspect of its conception.

It does, after all, smack of sensation and scandal when a white man uses such dramatic and final means of achieving empathy with the Negro. In a sense, it seems almost perverse to tamper with one's identity in this way, no matter what the motive. This is the kind of thing that George Orwell did in that curious first book of his, *Down and Out in Paris and London,* in which he sought to show the world once and for all what it is like to be poor. But Orwell was not *really* poor in his "down and out" period just as Griffin was not *really* a Negro when he made his journey through the South. In each case, the simple fact somehow dulls the point of the book, reducing the effort essentially to a kind of well-intentioned voyeurism.

John Howard Griffin himself seems aware of these difficulties. In his Preface, he says, "Some whites will say this is not really it. They will say this is the white man's experience as a Negro in the South, not the Negro's." Then, rather than answer it, he brushes it aside: "But this is picayunish and we no longer have time for that." (pp. 128-29)

Mr. Griffin has . . . earned the right to be heard—to be read. That much at least he has earned for this strange, pain-filled book. (p. 129)

Bruce A. Cook, "What Is It Like to Be a Negro?" in The Commonweal, *Vol. LXXV, No. 5, October 27, 1961, pp. 128-29.*

Ernest Sharpe, Jr.

Nearly three decades have gone by since Griffin made his journey through the South, but ***Black Like Me***'s power to move and outrage remains undiminished. Still in print, it has sold more than twelve million copies and been translated into fourteen languages. Most recently it was published in South Africa. Part of its enduring appeal comes from what seems the very transparency of the author's imposture.

It is hard to imagine a person worse suited than Griffin to pass for black. A cultural epicure who had spent his adolescence in France and lived a blind, sheltered existence for the previous decade, Griffin had remarkably little in common with most Southern whites, let alone with blacks. In the book his relations with blacks are cordial but never intimate. He practically shudders every time his ears are assaulted by jazz or the blues. Griffin was able to change his color, but not his heritage.

Which makes it all the harder to see how he pulled it off. Naturally he fooled whites; whites didn't look at blacks. But how did he dupe blacks? Surely somebody should have seen through such a thin disguise. No one did. His transformation was skin-deep, but neither whites nor blacks ever looked deeper. As readers we are in on the secret. Griffin's voice—courtly, refined, educated—is so evident throughout the book that we are amazed at the blindness of bus drivers and shopkeepers and all the others. We hear him secretly wail, "I'm just like you," at each new indignity or abuse, and we cannot believe that no one else hears him.

It is on this level of moral protest that ***Black Like Me*** is best known and most celebrated, as a work of civil rights advocacy and a tract on man's inhumanity to man. But also it was one of the first works of a new kind of journalism—what was called in the sixties the New Journalism—with its personal, participatory, novelistic approach. In fact, the book is arguably the genre's first masterpiece, even though Griffin was really less a journalist than a personal essayist. Judged as reporting, ***Black Like Me*** is an imperfect work. There is too much of the author, too little of others; too much earnest discussion of issues and too little personal observation and encounter. Assuming they had Griffin's bullheaded courage, one can imagine other writers—Norman Mailer, Tom Wolfe—rendering the experience with more nuanced insight and elegance of style.

What one cannot imagine is these masters of irony abandoning their strategic distance for the raw, racked emotion that powers Griffin's prose. ***Black Like Me*** is not simply a record of oppression and injustice; it is an account of painful personal discovery. Griffin began his experiment as an adventure. He assumed he would find racism, but he did not expect to find it everywhere, least of all in himself. By the end of his four weeks, he ached with hurt and humiliation. The adventure had turned into an ordeal. In discovering the brutal reality of racism, however, he also discovered compassion for the fierce stranger he had first seen three weeks before [in the mirror], the one with whom he had felt no kinship.

> I switched on the light and looked into a cracked piece of mirror bradded with bent nails to the wall. The bald Negro stared back at me from its mottled sheen. I knew I was in hell. Hell could be no more lonely or helpless. . . .
>
> I heard my voice, as though it belonged to someone else, hollow in the empty room, detached, say: 'Nigger, what you standing up there crying for?'
>
> I saw tears slick on his cheeks in the yellow light.

(pp. 52-4)

Ernest Sharpe, Jr., "The Man Who Changed His Skin," in American Heritage, *Vol. 40, No. 1, February, 1989, pp. 44-55.*

Jamaica Kincaid

1949-

(Born Elaine Potter Richardson) West Indian-born American novelist, short story writer, essayist, and journalist.

Kincaid's work is largely autobiographical and often draws upon her childhood experiences on the Caribbean island of Antigua. In her fiction, for which she is best known, Kincaid examines the intense emotional bonds between parents and children and the psychological effects of the maturation process on both generations. Because her writing extracts elements from West Indian language, folklore, and voodoo, Kincaid is often viewed as a participant in the West Indian literary movement, in which white colonialist values are rejected in favor of African or native West Indian modes of expression. Similarly, her emphasis on female characters and what Susan Sontag called the "emotional truthfulness" with which she examines their lives, prompted critics to examine Kincaid's works from a feminist perspective. While acknowledging the validity and importance of these movements, Kincaid claims: "I don't really see myself in any school. I mean, there has turned out to be a rise in West Indian literature, but I wouldn't know how I fit in it. I am very glad that there is such a thing, but on the other hand, belonging to a group of anything, an 'army' of anything, is deeply disturbing to me. I think I owe a lot of my success, or whatever, to this idea of feminism, but I don't really want to be placed in that category. I don't mind if people put me in it, but I don't claim to be in it. But that's just me as an individual. I mean, I always see myself as alone."

Kincaid began her writing career as a magazine journalist. Editors of the *New Yorker* found that Kincaid, an immigrant to the United States, could effectively distance herself from and relay playful insights on American culture. They often quoted her in their articles and eventually encouraged her to write for the magazine's "Talk of the Town" column. When Kincaid began to write fiction and proved a perceptive observer of her native Antigua, her editors supported her by publishing her novels in installments in the *New Yorker.* Kincaid attained critical success with her first book, *At the Bottom of the River,* a collection of sketches depicting life in the Caribbean. Kincaid's elliptical narratives reflect the mysticism with which her characters view life and blur the distinction between the physical world and the subconscious realm of dreams and desires. Suzanne Freeman described each piece as marked by "images that are as sweet and mysterious as the secrets children whisper in your ear."

Annie John, a tale of maturation, followed *At the Bottom of the River.* Critics debated whether this autobiographical work was a novel or another collection of stories but generally agreed that it functions thematically as a companion piece to *At the Bottom of the River.* With *Annie John,* which focuses on a mother and daughter who share the same name, Kincaid acquired a reputation for portraying parent-child relationships marked by defiance, ambivalence, dependence, love, and hate. At first the two characters are inseparable; young Annie John follows her mother everywhere, helps her with the housework, and dresses like her. However, when Annie John enters puberty, her mother's behavior changes; conflicts arise as the mother emotionally distances herself from her child. Annie John begins to resent her mother's change in attitude, and the two women are soon competing within the flux of cultural, racial, and, ultimately, patriarchal norms. Although reviews often focused on the narrator, recent scholarship has emphasized the predicament of the loving yet dominating character of the mother. Several commentators have examined the characters' relationship within the framework of psychoanalytic theory.

Kincaid introduces new characters in her next novel, *Lucy,* which picks up where *Annie John* ends. The eponymous protagonist, an *au pair* for an affluent white family on the East Coast of the United States, has left her Caribbean homeland to escape her mother, whom she considers her "only true love," and to create a life of her own. While adjusting to American culture, her mother's rejection, and her fall from childhood innocence, Lucy is unable to resolve conflicts in her life. She fails to attend the nursing school in which she has enrolled, refuses to open letters from her mother, and watches her employers' marriage unravel. Although Lucy's anger and flippancy alienated some readers, most critics praised *Lucy* for its fresh metaphors, rhythms, and insights, acknowledging that the protagonist's anger stemmed from her realistic fears and sorrows. According to Emily Listfield, this "tale of growing enlightenment is as intimate as a diary; Kincaid inspects each emotion under a microscope until she finds precisely the right words. Yet her gaze is remarkably clear and unsentimental."

Kincaid's essay, *A Small Place,* which she called a "prolonged visit to the bile duct," is directed largely toward white tourists in Antigua and records the misfortunes inflicted upon the island and its native residents by colonial powers. Critics complained that Kincaid was too close to her subject to be objective and questioned the validity of some arguments, but enjoyed her cutting descriptions of class-conscious tourists and corrupt English officials. Others saw the necessity for this personal essay and agreed with Salman Rushdie, who proclaimed it "a jeremiad of great clarity and a force that one might have called torrential were the language not so finely controlled."

(See also *CLC,* Vol. 43; *Contemporary Authors,* Vol. 125; and *Black Writers.*)

PRINCIPAL WORKS

NOVELS

Annie John 1985
Lucy 1990

OTHER

At the Bottom of the River (short fiction collection) 1983
A Small Place (essay) 1988

Evelyn C. White

[Kincaid] crafts equally fetching moments of joy and sorrow for her seemingly autobiographical protagonist, Annie John. The quick prose and distinctive detail that are the hallmarks of successful short stories are often difficult to achieve in longer works. Characters and images that breathed fully on twelve pages can be found huffing and puffing at a hundred. Sometimes the only recourse is to perform a type of literary euthanasia. That Kincaid, in her first novel, does not produce one clause that tempts one to "pull the plug," is a testament both to the rich texture of her West Indian childhood and her extraordinary skill as a writer.

Banana fritters, ripe guavas and pumpkin soup color Annie's world on the lush island of Antigua. Like the blue-green tropical landscapes of Gauguin, Kincaid's pages are brushed with images that glisten like swaying palmtrees in the sunlight.

> Her face was big and round and red, like a moon—a red moon. She had big, broad, flat feet, and they were naked to the bare ground; her dress was dirty, the skirt and blouse tearing away from each other at one side; the red hair that I had first seen standing up on her head was matted and tangled; her hands were big and fat, and her fingernails held at least ten anthills of dirt under them. And on top of that, she had such an unbelievable, wonderful smell, as if she had never taken a bath in her whole life.

Although characters like the Red Girl and Gwen, a beloved classmate, earn Annie's adoration, the singular force in her life is her mother. Their relationship is a bittersweet one that Kincaid depicts in a way that any daughter who has ever felt at odds with her mother can understand.

For example: blissful days spent in the protection of a mother graced with "such a beautiful mouth I could have looked at it forever if I had to and not mind" come to an abrupt and cataclysmic end for Annie John at age twelve, when on a shopping trip her mother tells her that they can no longer wear dresses made from the same cloth. "To say I felt the earth swept away from under me would not be going too far." This sudden and, in Annie's eyes, drastic change in the intimate bond with her mother is an episode Kincaid uses to symbolize the painful words and actions that can separate mother and daughter during the turbulent pubescent years. Annie stands among the bright bolts of cloth that had for years adorned the two of them as her mother says, "You just cannot go around the rest of your life looking like a little me." The sense of loss and abandonment is profound. From that moment on, Annie's feelings about her mother and her own identity are fraught with the confusion and rebellion that make adolescence a time few wish to relive.

The day she begins to menstruate, Annie expresses a sentiment whose accuracy makes one revel—and then despair.

> I walked to school with Gwen feeling as I supposed a dog must feel when it has done something wrong and is ashamed of itself and trying to get somewhere quick, where it can lie low. The cloth between my legs grew heavier and heavier with every step I took . . . For the first time in my life, I fainted . . . Nurse said it was the fright of all the unexpected pain . . . but I knew that I'd fainted after I brought to my mind a clear picture of myself sitting at my desk in my own blood.

The "my mother/myself" currents of Annie's life reach full force when she turns fifteen. Feeling "more unhappy than I had ever imagined anyone could be," she must nonetheless go to school, go to church, and worst of all, continue to live with a mother who has "suddenly turned into a crocodile." Instead of raised voices or angrily slammed doors, Kincaid uses simple whispers to create the emotional strain of the parental relationship all adolescents (and adults too) struggle with. "When I started to walk down the road, my steps were quick and light, and as I walked these words would go around in my head: 'My mother would kill me if she got the chance. I would kill my mother if I had the courage.' "

The courage of the youthful spirit, even when it is broken or tormented, bursts like a ripe mango in ***Annie John.*** Although Kincaid touches upon the inharmonious consequences of colonization in the West Indies (Annie is punished for "defacing" a picture of Christopher Columbus), political polemics are an aside to the personal passage of a young girl.

Perhaps Kincaid's writing has less of the charged racial intensity that is often found in the works by blacks born in America because she grew up on an island filled with the culture and traditions of her ancestors. The British may well have ruled the physical earth of Antigua, but they were not masters of the heart or spirit of a people who knew that the country pulsed with their lives, deaths, history and dreams.

Evelyn C. White, "Growing Up Black," in The Women's Review of Books, *Vol. III, No. 2, November, 1985, p. 11.*

Alison Friesinger Hill

Readers familiar with the dazzling lyricism of Jamaica Kincaid's short stories or the gentle grace of her novel, ***Annie John,*** may find this slim nonfiction work [***A Small Place***] jarring. The loosely organized essay describing the small West Indian island of Antigua, Ms. Kincaid's homeland, is really about her bitterness and sorrow over its fate. Antigua became self-governing in 1967 and gained its independence from England in 1981, but is still fettered by imperialist attitudes and corruption. The book is roughly divided into three sections: a sketch of the island, with a roundabout history; a brief and rather impersonal taste of the Antigua of Ms. Kincaid's childhood; and tales of graft and nepotism in the Government. ***A Small Place*** is strongest when Ms. Kincaid is concrete in her grievances, or when she indulges in her wily, wonderful descriptions. Often, however, the writing is distorted by her anger, which backs the reader into a corner: "An ugly thing, that is what you are when you become a tourist, an ugly, empty thing, a stupid thing, a piece of rubbish pausing here and there to gaze at this and taste that, and it will never occur to you that the people who inhabit the place in which you have just paused cannot stand you." Ms. Kincaid, her beautiful voice turning raspy at times, well conveys Antigua's poignant fate; yet, as she admits, "nothing can erase my rage—not an apology, not a large sum of money, not the death of the criminal—for this wrong can never be made right, and only the impossible can make me still." Consequently, both writer and reader are left unsatisfied.

Alison Friesinger Hill, in a review of "A Small Place," in The New York Times Book Review, *July 10, 1988, p. 19.*

Michiko Kakutani

[In] ***A Small Place,*** Ms. Kincaid, who left Antigua herself at the age of 17, gives us a nonfiction portrait of that damaged paradise, a portrait that is fueled in equal parts by love and nostalgia and Swiftean indignation. "The Antigua that I knew, the Antigua in which I grew up, is not the Antigua you, a tourist, would see now," she writes, echoing Joan Didion's memories of California. "That Antigua no longer exists. That Antigua no longer exists partly for the usual reason, the passing of time, and partly because the bad-minded people who used to rule over it, the English, no longer do so."

In speaking of Antigua's colonial past, Ms. Kincaid never hesitates to voice her anger and her pride. Of the Europeans and North Americans who routinely patronized and humiliated the Antiguans, she writes: "We thought they were un-Christian-like; we thought they were small-minded; we thought they were like animals, a bit below human standards as we understood those standards to be. We felt superior to all these people."

Of the British empire builders who annexed Antigua and tried to remake it in the image of England, she writes, "They should never have left their home, their precious England, a place they loved so much, a place they had to leave but could never forget."

And of those Anglophiles who speak of their love for England and its traditions, she writes:

> All they see is some frumpy, wrinkled-up person passing by in a carriage waving at a crowd. But what I see is the millions of people, of whom I am just one, made orphans: no motherland, no fatherland, no gods, no mounds of earth for holy ground, no excess of love which might lead to the things that an excess of love sometimes brings, and worst and most painful of all, no tongue.

Ms. Kincaid points out that the only language she has "in which to speak of this crime is the language of the criminal who committed the crime," and similar ironies proliferate throughout this volume like delicate, poisonous blossoms. As seen through Ms. Kincaid's eyes, Antigua is a vacation spot where the sewers empty into the pretty blue sea; a place where the streets are named after English maritime criminals; a place where the British built schools in celebration of their love of knowledge and ended up erasing another people's history. It's a place that exports food to Miami, then imports it back, at inflated prices, to feed the tourists; a place where people remain obsessed with their history of slavery but celebrate the graduation ceremonies of the local Hotel Training School, "a school that teaches Antiguans how to be good servants, how to be a good nobody, which is what a servant is."

In fact, Ms. Kincaid's observations concerning contemporary, self-ruled Antigua (the country became self-governing in internal affairs in 1967, fully independent in 1981) tend to be just as unsparing as her assessments of its colonial condition. Though she sides firmly with the Antiguans, she, like V. S. Naipaul, can see the brutalities of history that both accompany colonization and follow its demise. She observes that "in Antigua today, most young people seem almost illiterate. On the airwaves, where they work as news personalities, they speak English as if it were their sixth language." She says that sooner or later everybody in Antigua comes to the same conclusion: that "the government is for sale; anybody from anywhere can come to Antigua and for a sum of money can get what he wants."

And she goes on to list some accusations against the Government: that it allowed special ammunition, headed for the Government of South Africa, to be tested on the island; that it allowed meat known to be contaminated by radiation to be distributed to Antiguans; that one of its Cabinet members is involved in drug trafficking, another in a dubious offshore bank. Given such conditions, she adds, many Antiguans see their country as poised between two fates—that of Haiti under the Duvaliers on one hand, and that of Grenada under Maurice Bishop on the other.

There are moments in ***A Small Place*** when Ms. Kincaid's rage leads to somewhat clichéd generalizations—for instance, she mocks the escapist fantasies of the tourist who has left behind a nice bourgeois house ("and all its nice house things") to take a vacation in the sun. Such moments, however, are rare. Ms. Kincaid writes with passion and conviction, and she also writes with a musical sense of language, a poet's understanding of how politics and history, private and public events, overlap and blur.

"I look at this place (Antigua)," she writes

> I look at these people (Antiguans), and I cannot tell whether I was brought up by, and so come from, children, eternal innocents, or artists who have not yet found eminence in a world too stupid to understand, or lunatics who have made their own lunatic asylum, or an exquisite combination of all three.

Michiko Kakutani, "Portrait of Antigua, Warts and All," in The New York Times, *July 16, 1988, p. 16.*

Caryl Phillips

In her two autobiographical novels, ***At the Bottom of the River*** and ***Annie John,*** Jamaica Kincaid succeeded where few Caribbean novelists, and certainly no women from that part of the world, have succeeded in capturing the languid rhythms of tropical life in a rich and evocative prose that is also both urgent and poetic.

A Small Place is a departure, not so much of style but of content. Kincaid has chosen to write a powerful nonfiction essay which, like her novels, centers on her native Antigua, but unlike her novels spills over into an assault of great *saeva indignatio* toward not only the English who colonized Antigua, but also toward the local natives who "liberated" and now rule this small independent country.

The essay begins with an account of how it feels to arrive as a tourist in a country such as Antigua. (p. 1)

It is only when the author steps beyond her preoccupation with the "tourist" that the essay begins to develop a flavor that marks it out as not only original in tone but historically important as a document that throws light on Caribbean history past and present. (pp. 1, 12)

As she castigates the English for their behavior and attitudes in the "old" Antigua, we are led to assume that the newly independent Antigua will be for her a place of spiritual rebirth. But when she returns to her island, she finds the place darker. Her disappointment fuels the essay, and it soars with the passion of Baldwin's *The Fire Next Time* as she exposes the corruption and double-dealing that exists in all areas of modern Antiguan life. The St. Lucian Derek Walcott and the Trinidadian V. S. Naipaul have launched similar attacks against the parochialism of their home countries, and it is into this tradition of West Indian literary exiles looking back with a sense of loss compounded by disappointment that this book falls.

The essay begs one question. Why does somebody who lives so comfortably outside think she has the right to criticize those who have to live inside? After all, it is easy to arrive with a return air ticket, make sweeping judgments, and depart. Baldwin, a longtime French resident, was often accused by his peers of a lack of "commitment" to America, but his answer is to be found in the same place that we find Kincaid's riposte to those who might castigate; in the passion of the writing. Kincaid may reside in America but only somebody with her heart in Antigua could have written with such ferocity of purpose and self-revelatory hurt. Quite simply, she has a right to criticize because, irrespective of residence or nationality, she belongs. (p. 12)

Caryl Phillips, "Island in the Dark," in Los Angeles Times Book Review, *July 17, 1988, pp. 1, 12.*

Patricia Ismond

Kincaid gives testimony of the powerful ties between mother and child in what must rank among the most penetrating studies on the subject so far. ***Annie John*** traces the various stages of her progress from childhood to adolescence in terms of this relationship with her mother. It began with the fullness of maternal love, care and nurturing in infancy. The experience of being "weaned," a sundering between herself and her mother, marked the passage to girlhood. So that growing up and beginning to fend for herself meant an experience of increasing disfavour with her mother, presaging a silent opposition and undeclared war between them.

Her mother, in effect, was the medium through which she entered her first world. She provided her with her earliest glimpses of the bigger world; she was the one most responsible for initiating her into the inner areas of self by arousing those complex emotions and sensitivities associated with the experience of growing up. The deeply embedded sense of her mother was to follow her down the years, retaining the painful doubleness of the early period. Kincaid-Annie John recalls her early prescience of this in the novel: "For I could not be sure when it was really my mother, and when it was really her shadow standing between me and the rest of the world."

"My Mother," an outstanding sequence in ***At the Bottom of the River,*** is the mythologized burden of ***Annie John.*** It plots her progress through life in terms of this sense of her mother, to take the form of a journey extending from childhood right into the present struggle for survival. The first piece tells of the painful necessity of being weaned from total dependence on her mother, and the submerged tensions and hostilities that entered their relationship from that time:

> Placing her arms around me, she drew my head closer and closer to her bosom, until finally I suffocated. I lay on her bosom, breathless, for a time uncountable, until one day, for a reason she has kept to herself, she shook me out and stood me under a tree and I started to breathe again. I cast a sharp glance at her and said to myself, "So." Instantly I grew my own bosoms, small mounds at first, leaving a small soft place between them, where if ever necessary, I could rest my own head. Between my mother and me now were the tears I had cried, and I gathered up some stones and banked them in so that they formed a small pond. The water in the pond was thick and black and poisonous, so that only unnameable invertebrates could live in it. My mother and I now watched each other carefully, always making sure to shower the other with words and deeds of love and affection.

The strange movement of imagery here is remarkably direct and literal in its impact: it is almost as if the feelings and incidents she recalls actually registered in that way. This particular piece . . . gives a clear insight into the underlying sources and dynamic of Kincaid's style, especially in ***At the Bottom of the River.*** We are taken with child-like simplicity and spontaneous fantasy into what emerges as the dream-scape of the subconscious. Images and fragments from favourite children's stories, and strong personal symbols from Kincaid's childhood surface in the memory of that experience. Thus, the "pond of tears" separating her from her mother is reminiscent of Alice's "pool of tears" in *Alice in Wonderland;* while the image of being "shook out and stood under a tree" survives from the memory of being sent out to eat her dinner under the breadfruit trees whenever she was being punished. These images hark back to the child's original acceptance of the world of fantasy and symbol. One factor is of special significance here. The climate of local superstition and obeah practices in which Kincaid grew up had a lasting influence in deepening these impulses towards the fantastical. These extend, increasingly as the sequence unfolds, into the surreal accesses of dream.

Following on this initial crisis of estrangement, the relationship with her mother becomes one in which she must struggle for her very survival. Subsequent stages of the journey see her engaged in a trickster-like effort to outstrip and leave her mother's influence safely behind her ("I had hoped to see my mother permanently cemented to the seabed"). She later succumbs to the inescapable destiny of their journey "down the valley" together—an unhappy compromise whose bitter traces leave "in [their] trail, small colonies of worms." It is a process of increasing strife and trial, until she finds her way to an envisioned reconciliation with her mother, evoked in this paradisal movement:

> My mother and I live in a bower made from flowers whose petals are imperishable. There is the silvery blue of the sea, crisscrossed with sharp darts of light, there is the warm rain falling on the clumps of castor bush, there is the small lamb bounding across the pasture . . . It is in this way my mother and I have lived for a long time now.

The child-mother relationship thus deepens into an ultimate significance in Kincaid's imagination. It is a paradigm of the struggle between the self and the other, the tug between the yearning for completion and all outside us that seem to resist it, provoking, as Kincaid tells us, the will to master or be mastered. Beneath this struggle lies the final need for union. Kincaid's journey thus recovers an authentic mythic level in **"My Mother":** the loss of innocence and security, initiation into experience, and the struggle to regain that innocence.

Kincaid remains close to the child's modes of perception and language in these renderings. The roots of her style, as earlier noted, lie in the child's instinct for fantasy; the free play between its imaginings and the world of fact; its spontaneous connections between widely different spheres and categories; and the natural simplicity with which it does all this. We are almost in the presence of the writer-child, as [Cynthia Ozick] puts it. Kincaid seems to have retained the child-faculty intact. Repossessing it in her adult years, she authenticates and affirms the power of the imagination of childhood. What has crystallized in this child-language extends into a number of powerful visionary modes in Kincaid's hands. There are accesses of clairvoyance and divination, of the prophetic and apocalyptic in her work. In a piece entitled **"At Last"** from ***At the Bottom of the River*** she reflects on the irreducible essence of things, despite the world according to science and technology. The passage in question attains prophetic, biblical force, while we still hear the voice of the child: "Will the hen, stripped of its flesh, its feathers scattered perhaps to the four corners of the earth, its bones molten and sterilized, one day speak? And what will it say? I was a hen? I had twelve chicks? One of my chicks, named Beryl, took a fall?"

The preoccupation with childhood lies at the core of Kincaid's work and represents a very special achievement. In exploring it, she renews our understanding of the meaning of innocence and the value and possibilities of our first world. . . . It is not a state free from stain and imperfection. Growing up in ***Annie John*** involves an openness and receptivity to all manner of emotions and impulses, creative and destructive—love, dawning cruelty, generosity, possessiveness, instincts of hubris. In other words, the child is fully in touch with the complex motions of her own nature and being. It is also the freedom of the child's natural curiosity, the intentness with which it relates to the world around it, animate and inanimate forms alike. In Kincaid's testimony, the mother comes to contain and embody the world because of the totality with which the child lived that first relationship with her; and the struggle to be reconciled with her mother contained in embryo the struggle to be reconciled with life itself. In another piece entitled **"Blackness,"** Kincaid intimates the possibilities and depths of remaining in touch with these sources as she, now a mother, looks through the prism of her own child. The image is, as it were, twice reflected:

> [My child] traces each thing from its meagre happenstance beginnings in cool and slimy marsh, to its great glory and dominance of air or land or sea, to its odd remains entombed in mysterious alluviums . . . She feels the specter, first cold, then briefly warm, then cold again as it passes from atmosphere to atmosphere. Having observed the many differing physical existences feed on each other, she is beyond despair or the spiritual vacuum.

(pp. 338-40)

Patricia Ismond, "Jamaica Kincaid: 'First They Must Be Children'," in World Literature Written in English, *Vol. 28, No. 2, Autumn, 1988, pp. 336-41.*

"I'm someone who writes to save her life. I mean, I can't imagine what I would do if I didn't write. I would be dead or I would be in jail because—what else could I do? I can't really do anything but write. All the things that were available to someone in my position involved being a subject person. And I'm very bad at being a subject person."

—Jamaica Kincaid, 1990

Isabel Fonseca

In a short book [***A Small Place***] whose style owes more to the manifesto than the essay, Jamaica Kincaid condemns her native Antigua's tragic development, from its colonial past to the new tourism which has replaced it and which she sees, alarmingly, as identical. . . .

Kincaid's (laudable) purpose is to make the readers of this grisly tale as uncomfortable as possible. Her shrill, radically subjective method, however, serves only to alienate. She buries Antigua's sad and familiar story in a graveyard of clichés (for "only a cliché can explain you") and the result is a deadened and dogmatic prose which tells all but reveals little. Antigua is presented as a generic outpost of colonial memory. It is true that Antigua, like all of the Caribbean islands, has for centuries always been fought over and owned by foreign powers. What Kincaid does not say is that for more than twenty-five years Antigua, along with its own dependencies, Redonda and Barbuda, has had full internal self-government and the right to opt for full independence at any time without reference to—permission from—the British Government. . . .

No one would question the gist of the story as Kincaid tells it. . . . More dubious, perhaps, is her characterization of all visitors to Antigua as stingy, incurious and contemptuous (not to mention "incredibly unattractive, fat and pastry-like fleshed"). Her idea of contemporary Britain is of a nation of retired officers, lamenting the lost empire . . . The force of her argument is further undercut by a curiously wilful scrappiness about such things as, for example, the food an overfed tourist might eat, which is supposed to convey the pervasive corruption of the island in a single bite: "A good guess is that it came from a place like Antigua first, where it was grown dirt cheap, went to Miami, and came back. There is a world of something in this, but I can't go into it right now." Her savage tone is also diffused by the shapelessness of the essay: she shifts from an attack on the Swiss (which they earn partly for being so clean and partly for harbouring blood-money), to rambling reminiscences of her childhood, notably of happy days spent stealing from the now destroyed public library ("once I had read a book I couldn't bear to part with it"). The book is full of inconsequential anecdote and *non sequitur.* It is hard, for example, to grasp why the library, which she remembers as the place where "you distorted and erased my history and glorified your own", should, more than any other place, come to symbolize her beloved "old Antigua".

Kincaid's disregard for both her reader and her subjects suggest that her central purpose in ***A Small Place*** is not illumination, but something more personal. She is trying, from her adopted home in the place most unlike Antigua except in size (the cold New England state of Vermont), to "work through her rage". However satisfying it may be for the writer, rage seems an ill-chosen idiom for the expression of anything one really wants to make understood—like the letters that one writes but should never send.

Isabel Fonseca, "Their Island Story," in The Times Literary Supplement, *No. 4446, January 13-19, 1989, p. 30.*

Wendy Dutton

The magic of ***At the Bottom of the River*** comes from its language. It is as rhythmic and riddlesome as poetry. Lovely though the words are, they often read like a coded message or a foreign language. Throughout ***At the Bottom of the River*** the reader is left wondering how to decipher this writing. The decoder comes in the form of Jamaica Kincaid's novel ***Annie John***. . . . [***Annie John***] tells the same story as ***At the Bottom of the River,*** that of a girl coming of age in Antigua, but uses straightforward novel talk and presents few comprehension barriers to the reader. ***Annie John*** is a kind of personification of ***At the Bottom of the River.*** It fleshes out the fantasy and the philosophy of ***At the Bottom of the River***'s poetry, and between the two books there exists a dialogue of questions and answers. They ultimately read as companion pieces or sister texts. (p. 406)

Since ***Annie John*** tells the same story as ***At the Bottom of the River,*** it is instrumental in illuminating the difficult text of the latter. It fills in the spaces. It replaces the fuzziness of ***At the Bottom of the River*** with facts. For example, Annie is an exceptional student and at fifteen is accelerated to a class with girls who are two or three years older than herself. Once this specialness is clearly defined in ***Annie John,*** the intense imagination and inventiveness of ***At the Bottom of the River*** is easier to understand. Then a strange thing happens, however. Annie, at fifteen, has a nervous breakdown. The same breakdown occurs in ***At the Bottom of the River*** in the story **"Blackness,"** but the language in **"Blackness"** is so clouded and intentionally sparse that the point is almost completely missed. The story reads as a mere mood piece, with passages like, "In the blackness, then, I have been erased. I can no longer say my own name. I can no longer point to myself and say 'I'."

The moody, evocative world in ***At the Bottom of the River,*** with its fine line between truth and images, helps justify the hypersensitive emotion that must have fed into the breakdown. Nonetheless, the reader is not well prepared for that occurrence. Annie is shown as different and exceptional, but these traits are not stressed enough to necessitate a breakdown. Moreover, Annie's childhood has not been rough; rather, it was a childhood filled with passion, adoration, and adventure. (pp. 406-07)

Compared to ***At the Bottom of the River, Annie John*** reads like a photo album. . . . [The latter] looks at the surface of things and lacks rationale, explanation, motivation. ***At the Bottom of the River*** acts as the cerebral text for the pictures in ***Annie John.*** Together the two books allow the reader to develop one cohesive story.

At the Bottom of the River has been billed as "Caribbean fiction" portraying "a childhood in the Caribbean" that is "partly remembered, partly divined," but the most obvious alternative reading of Kincaid's collection of stories interprets it as being not so much about growing up on the islands as about growing up female. Every sentence of Kincaid's writing breathes this feminine sensibility. . . .

Growing up is not seen as something that is inevitable, something that will happen anyway. For the girl, the process is intrinsically connected to her mother. Both books revolve around the mother and are indeed mother-obsessed, much as the girl character herself is. . . .

The all-consuming mother-daughter relationship is more metaphorical in ***At the Bottom of the River.*** The intensity of it is difficult to reckon with. As with the breakdown in ***Annie John,*** the reader is not given enough groundwork to comprehend fully the relationship in ***At the Bottom of the River. Annie John,*** however, makes the maternal conflict a universal one, the natural rebellion of a fifteen-year-old girl against her mother. Therefore ***Annie John*** fills in some of the missing pieces in the groundwork for this conflict. For example, Annie speaks of her mother's "betrayal": "Why, I wonder, didn't I see the hypocrite in my mother when, over the years, she said that she loved me and could hardly live without me, while at the same time proposing and arranging separation after separation." (p. 407)

The father's absence is keenly felt in ***At the Bottom of the River.*** He mainly appears in a five-page male perspective in **"At the Bottom of the River"** that offsets the mother's perspective in **"Blackness."** The father in **"At the Bottom of the River"** "cannot conceive of the union of opposites, or, for that matter, their very existence." He cannot conceive of anything, because he is a man outside the woman's world. The reader is left wondering where the father is, and indeed who the father is.

The father's perspective comes after the breakdown. **"At the Bottom of the River"** is a story of recovery, of the girl's coming to terms with her place in the universe. To do this, she too needs to reconcile with "the union of opposites," the father part of her as well as the mother part. In ***Annie John*** the father is as much a part of her growing-up anxiety as the mother. She says: "For most of my life, when the three of us went anywhere together I stood between the two of them or sat between the two of them. But then I got too big, and there I was, shoulder to shoulder with them more or less, and it became not very comfortable to walk down the street together."

Annie's father is thirty-five years older than her mother. This adds to the sense of Annie and her mother living in a separate world, since they are both children compared to the father. On one occasion Annie and her mother were walking down the street when they were attacked by another woman. Annie concludes: "I knew that it was one of the women that my father had loved and with whom he had had a child or children, and who never forgave him for marrying my mother and having me." Annie and her mother are the chosen ones, the adored ones. This shines light on Annie's specialness. She is an only child, doted upon; but are special dynamics with her parents enough to bring on an adolescent nervous breakdown? Illuminating though ***Annie John*** is in bringing out these dynamics, the breakdown still remains a mystery.

Annie John offers another explanation for the breakdown, which plays a potent but undeveloped part in both books: voodoo, or "obeah" in patois. In ***At the Bottom of the River*** the mother mentions a "jablesse," explaining, "It's a person who can turn into anything. . . . Take good care when you see a beautiful woman. A jablesse always tries to look like a beautiful woman." . . . ***At the Bottom of the River*** is rife with conjure references such as this, though the world of conjure is treated more literally in ***Annie John.***

The mother believes Annie's breakdown has been brought on by a hex and that one of her husband's former mistresses administered the hex. In addition to the British physician Dr. Stephens, she also consults an obeah woman named Ma Jolie. Annie describes the encounter:

> When my father came in to see me, he looked at all my medicines—Dr. Stephens's and Ma Jolie's—lined up side by side and screwed up his face, the way he did when he didn't like what he saw. He must have said something to my mother, for she arranged the shelf in a new way, with Dr. Stephens's prescriptions in the front and Ma Jolie's prescriptions in the back.

(pp. 407-08)

When Annie continues to be sick despite Ma Jolie's and Dr. Stephens's efforts, Annie's grandmother Ma Chess appears, herself a formidable obeah woman. The reader learns that conjure is like a family trade: "Whatever Ma Jolie knew, my grandmother knew at least ten times more. How she regretted that my mother did not show more of an interest in obeah things." Though her mother rejected voodoo, Annie's exceptionalness suggests she is clicking into her power. Then Ma Chess disappears as mysteriously as she appeared, and Annie is cured after three-and-a-half months. Ma Chess is never given credit for Annie's cure, however. It is Annie who cures herself. Through the long internal and spiritual rigmarole outlined best in **"At the Bottom of the River,"** she reasons her way back to sanity and finds a place for herself in civilization. (pp. 408)

This takes the reader one step closer to reckoning with the curious nature of an adolescent breakdown. It also suggests an alternative reading for both ***At the Bottom of the River*** and ***Annie John.*** The standard reading asks the reader to believe the breakdown was caused by severe growing pains, a theory that is difficult to accept despite the fact that Kincaid takes great care to set Annie apart from regular girls. It is easier to believe that Annie has inherited her grandmother's mystic powers. . . . Annie (and the girl in ***At the Bottom of the River***) demonstrates considerable storytelling powers. This kind of creative power is greatly akin to conjure. Creative women have long been called conjurers. The sheer act of creation classified women writers as witches of sorts. By taking up the previously male task of writing, they were seen not purely as creators but as warped creators, "as if the very process of writing had itself liberated a madwoman, a crazy woman and an angry woman." This madwoman is not only the author, but often the female character which she creates.

The idea of voodoo running in her family sets Annie up for a unique kind of matrilineage. As just mentioned, however, this matrilineage is not for the protagonist alone; the author shares in it as well. The history of women's writing moves in fits and starts and often centers on the quest for literary foremothers. Foremothers act as a sort of launching pad for contemporary women writers, and they also give the woman writer a history of her own, a tradition. Until recently, literary foremothers were difficult to find. Often the creative precursors of women writers had to be found in the traditional domestic world. They were the quiltmakers, the fine cooks, the women with "green thumbs." Similarly, the conjure woman serves as a creative foremother, especially for the black woman writer. . . .

Annie's breakdown can also be read as a breakdown with the past, with tradition, with our mothers. Both ***Annie John*** and ***At the Bottom of the River*** portray a longing for connection with the past. This does not encompass just the immediate past or even a past that includes literary foremothers. Instead, Kincaid reaches back through the history of humankind. Prehistoric allusions run like an undercurrent or a subtheme through the book. [In ***At the Bottom of the River,*** the] girl declares, "I am primitive and wingless." She watches her mother turn into a reptile, then does the same: "Silently, she had instructed me to follow her example, and now I too travelled along on my white underbelly, my tongue darting and flickering in the hot air." Before long, mother and daughter "merge and separate; merge and separate; soon we shall enter the final stage of our evolution." In this passage the girl aligns herself with the universe, not just with her personal world. This is a crucial connection that aids in her recovery. (p. 409)

It is also a journey that Annie makes to bring herself back from sickness. She must revise and recreate herself. Her problem as proposed in **"Blackness"** is not only one of being erased, but one of silence, long the enemy of women. She is "living in the silent voice." The problem is solved in the apocalyptic **"At the Bottom of the River"** when, in the last paragraph, she gets her voice back. The first thing she then says is her name.

> And so, emerging from my pit, . . . I see things in the light of the lamp, all perishable and transient, how bound up I know I am to all that is human endeavor, to all that is past and all that shall be, to all that shall be lost and leave no trace. I claim these things then—mine—and now feel myself grow solid and complete, my name filling up my mouth.

This is echoed in the last chapter of ***Annie John,*** which begins, " 'My name is Annie John.' These were the first words that came into my mind as I woke up on the morning of the last day I spent in Antigua." . . .

In fact, ***At the Bottom of the River*** is so strange and new that it often reads like not only a foreign language, but an entirely new kind of writing that could specifically be called a woman's writing. The name filling up her mouth is not only "Annie John" and not only "Jamaica Kincaid." The name is also "woman." (p. 410)

Wendy Dutton, "Merge and Separate: Jamaica Kincaid's Fiction," in World Literature Today, *Vol. 63, No. 3, Summer, 1989, pp. 406-10.*

H. Adlai Murdoch

One of the most intricate questions dealt with by the Caribbean writer in recent years has been that of identity. The issue of subjectivity, beset with problems such as recognition of self and other and oedipal conflict under the most conventional circumstances, is complicated further here given the additional factors of colonialism and pluralism which continue to mark Caribbean society and culture. One recent work which tackles such questions is Jamaica Kincaid's ***Annie John.*** Set in the Antigua of the 1950s, this autobiographical novel recounts a succession of experiences which culminate in the protagonist's almost palpable hatred for her mother. Underlying its apparent linearity, however, are various tropes and figures which trace Annie's desire to establish an individual identity within the complexities of Caribbean social structure. The specific psychoanalytical concepts which bear upon and explicate her wish for separation will be shown at several points to be impacted not only by the exigencies of Caribbean history, but by its racial pluralities as well. (p. 325)

In terms of genre, ***Annie John*** must be classified as a *Bildungsroman,* or novel of coming of age, of discovery of self, which recounts the process of growing up and coming to terms with the world. Conventions of reading lead us to posit the treatment of the protagonist's physical and spiritual development within this genre, leading to the destruction of illusion and the acquisition of maturity. It is in these terms that the literary world has recognized and codified masterworks by such European authors as Joyce, Proust, and Flaubert. We may say, at the outset, that the treatment of content and theme makes ***Annie John*** a part of this tradition, although in a rather specialized way: the concatenation of sex and race, geography and culture, tends to cause the novel to diverge somewhat from the white, male, European tradition of the *Bildungsroman.* Not only is the novel the product of an author who differs from this tradition in terms of sex, race, and culture, but the ontological basis of the protagonist's struggle is itself couched in terms of the establishment of a self which will draw its validity and its motivation for being from a vision of difference based, at least in part, on perceptions of gender, race, and culture. As such, the very discourse of the novel—specifically, the genesis of identity as it is addressed here—derives from and speaks to a particular cultural milieu whose conditions of existence determine, in their turn, the way in which signification is constructed in the novel. This particularity of culture also serves to differentiate the novel from the canon of Afro-American women's fiction, for considerations of history, social structure, geography, and culture suggest that such canonization represents a misreading of crucial elements of the text. As was indicated above, the exigencies of Caribbean culture are of a very specific nature, and it is to this cultural milieu that we must now turn. (p. 326)

People from separate islands, in fact, tend to see each other as being "different," and this seems an unalterable feature of West Indian culture. Indeed, the very racial structure of the territories varies as well, with those of French background demonstrating the results of a more thorough-going racial admixture. By putting Annie's Dominican mother into place as a creole "metis," or mixed, woman, then, one who incorporates a certain "difference" in terms of appearance and language, these secondary characteristics become the ones which are jolted to the forefront of Annie's perception as part of the recognition process in the primal scene. Her mother, as we shall see, becomes "foreign" to her on a plural level, one which joins the issues of race and culture to the creation of identity. But before exploring this question, let us turn, briefly, to another context signified by and necessary to this text; that of the feminine oedipal paradigm.

On the face of it, the narrative of ***Annie John*** and the mother/daughter relationship do not demand analysis exclusively through the prism of the feminine oedipus. There are, however, certain elements of the narrative structure which suggest the possible efficacy of a reading of this kind. First among these are the character relationships, especially among the three primary participants, Annie and her parents. An explanation of the Freudian oedipal paradigm may provide some grounds for reading from such a perspective.

The Freudian paradigm of the feminine oedipus is derived essentially from Freud's general oedipal theory. In both cases, emphasis is laid on the function of the castration complex. The well-known formula of the male oedipus has the boy wanting to kill off his father and sleep with his mother, a desire to which the father puts an end by asserting his power over and possession of the mother, effectively castrating the boy. In the feminine paradigm, the girl blames her mother for the state of castration that she perceives in them both during her phallic phase, and denigrates her mother at the same time for having succumbed to a phallic power greater than that of the clitoris. It is at this point that the father, the repository of greater phallic power, becomes the focal point of the girl's predilections, the mother's submission being seen as a sort of betrayal.

There is another explanation for the girl's turn to the father, one favored by object-relations theorists, and elaborated by Nancy Chodorow in *The Reproduction of Mothering.* Here, an all-powerful mother fulfills the role of castrator, and the turning to the father is seen as a means of liberation from the all-subsuming female, a way for the girl to establish a separate feminine self. We will argue that it is the attempt at separation and differentiation from the mother, as well as the perception of maternal castration as viewed in and stemming from the primal scene, that initiate Annie John's rebellion against her mother. But to do this, we must first look more closely at the nature of the West Indian family, whose paradoxical form has implications not only for Annie's recognition of and identification with a maternal power structure, but for the particular operation here of the feminine oedipal paradigm as well. (pp. 327-28)

West Indian men enjoy much greater social and sexual freedom than do West Indian women. They are the focus of society's power relationships and occupy, in general, positions within it which inculcate concomitant attitudes of social and psychological authority. They maintain sometimes numerous and contemporaneous extra-familial sexual relationships, a luxury that women certainly are not afforded by them. Theirs is also the major share of responsibility in financial maintenance of the household, and upkeep of the children in or out of wedlock, although this may be the ideal rather than the reality. West Indian men, in other words, are allowed by society to indulge in libidinal pleasures; tacit recognition is given to their overwhelmingly dominant role in all social relationships.

However, this paradigm of male dominance overlooks a paradox crucial not only to filial relationships within the society at large, but to Annie's relationship to her mother in particular. Here is Edith Clarke . . . : "mother and children co-operate in the small daily duties in the home. They are continually together. . . . Whatever she may be doing in the yard, the children are never very far away. There is constant companionship, and *a constant interdependence. The girl child identifies herself with the mother.*" This matriarchal structure is the locus of the power with which Annie identifies, and which sets up the groundwork for the oedipal paradigm to function as a means of maternal separation within the Caribbean cultural context. In other words, the tendency of the girl to seek identity through the (m)other, valorizing this relationship as it occurs within the cultural and domestic domains, will elicit rebellion when such a symbiosis is perceived as being betrayed. This will be the ultimate result of Annie's incursion into the primal scene; the repudiation of the mother and the turn toward the father both are determined culturally, as well as psychologically. (pp. 328-29)

The closeness of Annie to her mother, the extent to which she identifies with the maternal image, is valorized in fact through their mutual participation in things like the ritualized baths, where the description of *obeah* practices—*obeah* being the Antiguan term for a local form of "voudoun"—provides an element of added realism beyond the purely geographical. This closeness is elaborated upon further by Annie's description of her initiation into the domestic world of the period: "I spent the day following my mother around and observing the way she did everything." She states how important she felt to be with her mother and, beyond the culinary realism of describing local dishes and ingredients, indicates that her mother simply wanted to "include [her] in everything." Finally, here, Annie's description of her mother begins by equating her beauty and her daughter's feelings for her with those of a queen, whose head would in fact have been on the sixpence to which she refers. . . . Now, what is most striking about this comparison is that it has the effect of creating an emphatic reinforcement of Annie's attachment to and identification with her mother in the mind of the reader. It also demonstrates the narrative value of the mother as well as the secondary value which both narrative and protagonist attach to the father, a hierarchy which also will progressively change. In other words, Annie's tendency to seek her identity through the image of the (m)other, as well as possibilities for eventual racial and oedipal differentiation, are already in place at this juncture. There can be no doubt, then, of the extent to which Annie John identifies with and valorizes the maternal image at this stage: no overt hint of the approaching struggle to achieve a separate identity. (pp. 329-30)

The significance of Annie's mother's trunk cannot be overstated. It eventually will assume primary importance in the text as an indicator of repression and discontent. Here are stored garments and other markers of Annie's infancy, as well as certificates of merit and other objects associated with, tracing, and representing Annie's life. The trunk and its contents will assume their function later in the text, in an excellent use of narrative deferral, as representations of Annie's fragmented self and her need for self-identity and self-expression; they are put into place here as a symbolic depiction of Annie herself, and thus of the mother's enclosure, containment, limitation, possession and direction of her daughter's life and identity. This *topos* of unnaming, of reification and reduction of the protagonist, is given further import by the mother's practice of recounting to Annie stories of her life which seem themselves to be buried in the trunk along with these objects, and gives additional credence to a certain superiority and control on the part of the mother, based on knowledge which she alone, of the two, possesses.

Further complicating this situation is the fact that both mother and daughter have identical names: Annie John bears exactly the same name as her mother, Annie John. By and large, there is nothing intrinsically wrong with such an arrangement. But when it is combined with the behaviorial and psychological factors which have been delineated above, one must conclude that we are being presented with a vision of an omnipotent, all-subsuming mother—a phallic mother, if you will, a figure generated by this particular Caribbean family structure—who holds ultimate power both in the family hierarchy in general and over her daughter in particular. . . . In this context, the placement of the objects in the mother's trunk, in conjunction with that prized filial bond and the coincidence of names, point to an almost total assimilation of one Annie by the other—the enclosure and erasure on the part of the mother of any attempt by her daughter to lead an independent existence in whatever form. In other words, Annie's ability to recognize herself as a subject is circumscribed severely; in seeking the truth of herself through the image of the (m)other, with whom she identifies, she is alienated both from herself and from the world around her. Her inability to perceive this alienation will render the break between them that much more inevitable and agonizing.

Annie therefore is left with a structured self whose particular elements—especially the tendency to recognize the self in and through images of the other—may be defined as being characteristic of the mirror stage of the Lacanian Imaginary [according to Kaja Silverman in *The Subject of Semiotics,* 1983]:

> This self-recognition is . . . a mis-recognition; the subject apprehends itself only by means of a fictional construct whose defining characteristics—focus, coordination—it does not share. It must also be stressed that the mirror stage is one of those crises of alienation around which the Lacanian subject is organized, *since to know oneself through an external image is to be defined through self-alienation.* (emphasis added)

It is by exposing the false nature of this external image that Annie eventually will recognize the need for separation and individual identity. Her involvement in the primal scene will illuminate a clash of race and culture between herself and her mother, elements heretofore perceived in terms of indivisibility and homogeneity. (pp. 330-31)

One Sunday afternoon, Annie returns home unannounced and, unknown to them, witnesses her parents making love. This is a vision that signifies a major turning point, both psychologically and narratologically, in the chain of events. First, this event constitutes what is known in psychological terms as the "primal scene," a term defined in *The Language of Psychoanalysis* as the "scene of sexual intercourse between the parents which the child observes. . . . It is generally interpreted by the child as an act of violence on the part of the father." Now, already having made the point that West Indian society is a matriarchal one, it is important to emphasize here that the mother is thus usually the wielder of ultimate authority within the structure of the family. (p. 332)

The attribution of violence, itself a recognition of a capacity for power, may be linked to sexual position; the male-superior position, which is the case here—or in fact any position which allows a physically superior participant—may be made to bear the imputation of prepotence, activity, and power, while the person beneath will be seen as passive, powerless, and inferior. Thus what Annie perceives is a massive, unconscionable, and inexplicable loss of power on the part of her mother—one amounting to a betrayal—as the sole means of accounting for her succumbing to the greater physical and phallic power of the father. Such a perceived abandonment of power will engender revision of the appropriateness of fusion with the image of the (m)other, causing Annie to rebel in revenge for having been deserted. More importantly, perhaps, the scene also conveys the recognition of the mother's racial difference, linking race, culture, oedipus, and identity in a single, specific, polyvalent signifier. . . .

Her mother is now doubly different to her, the creole element in her appearance and language, previously unimportant and unobtrusive, now taking on a negative significance. The idea of racial difference, in the specific form that it assumes in these islands as the result of colonial history and a historically-imposed separation of peoples, is uppermost in the perception of difference that accompanies Annie's sense of betrayal. . . . The "beautiful long neck" and the "long plaited hair . . . pinned up around the crown of her head," signs of beauty at an earlier point in the narrative, now reflect a heritage and culture which are "foreign" to Annie's Antigua-based experience. There would have to be a point in her development where Annie would perceive her mis-recognition for what it was and realise what it had cost her. The fact that her perception takes this form may be explained by the Caribbean subject's subordination to historical and cultural forces beyond her control and, usually, her awareness. Yet, paradoxically, difference is at the service of identity here. For the mother's difference must be recognised and rebelled against if Annie is to have an *Antiguan* identity of her own. When, in its turn, this identity becomes insufficient, Annie will leave Antigua for England, replacing the mother with the colonial "mother country." The duality of her alienation at this point is crucial to both her own development and to that of the narrative itself. (p. 333)

[Annie] now sees herself as betrayed, and assumes, in turn, a position of power within the mother/daughter hierarchy, signified by the act of talking back to her mother for the first time: "I had never talked back to her before. . . . From the back, she looked small and funny. . . . I was sure I could never let those hands touch me again; I was sure I could never let her kiss me again. All that was finished." Subsequent efforts on Annie's part will be aimed at distance and divorce from that mother who betrayed them both, revealed the hitherto unseen creole side of herself, and is seen now as unworthy. . . .

Annie's growing love for Gwen, which is recounted in the latter half of Chapter Three, accomplishes two things—it replaces one female object of adoration, the mother, with another, Gwen herself; and it parallels in its growth Annie's increasing hatred of and distance from her mother. (p. 335)

Annie's paradoxical love for the Red Girl embodies her new-found delight in evil and rebellion, for she befriends her precisely because her appearance and personal hygiene belie everything that Annie's mother had ever taught her: "her dress was dirty . . . the red hair . . . was matted and tangled . . . her fingernails held at least ten anthills of dirt under them . . . She had such an unbelievable, wonderful smell, as if she had never taken a bath in her whole life." She personifies all the personal and practical negatives which would spur on Annie's revolt against maternal repression, and Annie associates with her to further this end. The reference to the Red Girl playing marbles against Skerritt boys—this being a term referring to boys of the local juvenile reform school, located on Skerritt's estate—associates Annie, in effect, through a double metonymy mediated by the Red Girl, with the principles and practices of evil and criminality, and crowns her efforts at self-identity to this point. For Annie's activities are directed toward nothing else but the achievement and attainment of a valid self-identity and self-image. Her energies, as they are represented here, are signs of actions aimed at the accomplishment of this goal. Once again we see the return of the repressed, wish-fulfillment translated into both deed and word: Gwen remained her friend "in spite of" her mother's approval, and because of her "shyness," which went along with Annie's practice of "betrayals," through which reference she tropes and repeats her perception of her mother's actions. But signs of repression manifested through word and deed also take different forms; the sadomasochistic activities practised by Annie with the Red Girl may be interpreted as a dual sign pointing to an attempt at individualism and self-assertion, as well as the purchase of pleasure, two things which the metamorphosis in the maternal relationships were denying her. (pp. 335-36)

Her new-found sense of equality and individuality [resulting from various run-ins with her parents] are the culmination of this protracted oedipal struggle, permitting her to repudiate the maternal envelopment to which she had been subjected and finally to assume a subject position. And this change in status means, also, that she must act. Now her existential awareness of the furniture in her room leads to what is undoubtedly the major psychological event of the novel: her demand that her father make her her own trunk. This demand is the overwhelming, preponderant sign of Annie's desire finally to escape and overcome the containment, possession and control that her mother's trunk signifies. Establishing her own life and identity will constitute a sort of rebirth, phoenix-like, from the deathly images and fears of dissolution which had haunted her for so long.

Chapter Seven charts the progress of this rebirth, the pupal stage which is necessary before the formation of the chrysalis and the emergence of the butterfly. Several striking figures mediate this process. First among these is Annie's vision, in her delirium, of the death of her parents' word: "I could see the words leave their mouths. The words traveled through the air towards me, but just as they reached my ears they would fall to the floor, suddenly dead." Now, if the parental word signifies the Law of the Father, the ultimate sign of authority and power, then Annie has effectively removed herself as subject to this law: not only does the word not reach her, it dies of its own accord. Both parental and paternal authority—the latter exercised here by the mother—are laid to rest finally and permanently. The erasure of the photographs on her night-table derives its significance from the areas removed from the bodies. By erasing her mother and father "from the waist down," she takes revenge on the primal scene, immobilizing them and negating their physical and sexual power. . . . (p. 338)

The process of rebirth reaches its conclusion at the rain's end, where all is regenerated, fresh and new—including herself, for she has grown, physically as well as psychologically. She now has succeeded in repudiating every aspect of her former life; both Antigua, the locus of repression, and her mother, the cause of it, must be rejected in order that this newly created self might flourish in fresh surroundings. Remaining would have nullified any attempt at renewal. Every element of that existence is linked to the stifled, enclosed nonentity she had been before: "I was feeling . . . how much I never wanted to see my mother . . . how much I never wanted to hear her voice again." With rebirth, repression has disappeared and desire, formerly sublimated, is untrammelled now, marked by a new wish to be other, for the security of complete anonymity: "I longed to be in a place where nobody knew a thing about me and liked me for just that reason." Only the freedom of being unknown can assure the avoidance of past errors.

Annie's complete alienation—even from her close friend, Gwen—on the day of her departure is the final sign of her rejection of the old and accession to the new. Even such friendships, formerly valorized as signs of repression and rebellion, now can find no place in the new order. Significantly, her new trunk, a metonym of her new identity and the existence she is about to begin, precedes her to the jetty. Her walk there becomes a sort of triumphal parade, a recounting and dismissal of the life she is leaving behind, as well as a troping of her mother's departure from Dominica at a similar age years before. Such repetition is necessary for the wheel to come full circle, for Annie to establish her own separation from the non-differentiated structure of which she previously had been a part. There is a final ambiguity in her double reading of the realization that "I shall never see this again," one which is extended into the text's final metaphor. The figure of the "vessel filled with liquid [which] had been placed on its side and now was slowly emptying out" embodies ambivalence, writing itself as sorrow, relief, release, joy, or any combination or permutation of the above. Oedipal repression and racial difference as a subset of "foreignness," the overriding tropological constructs of the novel, finally allow self-assertion pride of place.

How then can one summarize the resonances of this remarkable text? The linking of the repression and recognition inherent in the feminine oedipal paradigm to the problematics of race and culture particular to the Caribbean region figures the text in two fundamental ways, it seems to me. First, the psychological grounding of the text in the feminine oedipus provides a springboard from which to broach problems of some significance. The question of the oedipal nature of mother/daughter relationships is one which figures strongly in women authors of several bicultural contexts, and is an almost constant signifier of the struggle to establish an identity which is independent of the mother, and of the clash of cultures. With her mother fulfilling what was in essence a phallic role, enveloping Annie's budding personality and giving it no chance to flower, turning Annie into a simple extension of herself, Annie had no opportunity for identity, no possibility of establishing a valid, functioning persona. Once the primal scene had brought her situation to the forefront of her consciousness, placing her mother under the rubric of betrayal, difference, and loss of power, her need to establish her own identity was inevitable. Death and separation, repeated tropological representations of the repressed nature of Annie's desire to replace identification with the (m)other with full subjectivity, persistently would figure crucial points on her road to selfhood.

Yet to be contextualized finally is the question of the function of geographical location and cultural setting within the narrative matrix. The heterogeneous structure of Caribbean society and culture, historically linked to the perpetuation of artificial boundaries and divisions among the islands, particularly within a colonial context, would make issues of identity and perceptions of difference dependent each upon the other for their resolution. In this case, the repressive mother was the other in whom the daughter sought images of herself. Given her perceived otherness, "foreignness," and racial difference, and with the primal scene as the locus of this perception, the mother's loss of power and authority would be mirrored by the daughter's concomitant assumption of identity and selfhood. This entire oedipal process is tied inextricably to the cultural matrix, which is itself mediated by perceptions of difference in myriad forms. Indeed, one might observe that the polyvalence which is germane to the Caribbean region is reflected in the structure of the narrative. The West Indian setting, with its own distinct cultural constructs, particularizes both story and discourse as it problematizes its own mode of being.

So it is Kincaid's own Caribbean self-reflexive perception which provides the narrative motor for this story for all seasons. The maternal/filial conflict, the attempt to name and to be oneself, the struggle with difference and biculturality, and the repeated use of key tropes, generating the binary oppositions which figure the entire work, all herald a skillful, conscious and controlled narrator, as well as a marvelous addition to the canon of Caribbean literature, which is itself concerned with the crucial questions of naming and being given the polyvalence of its own cultural particularity. (pp. 338-40)

H. Adlai Murdoch, "Severing the (M)other Connection: The Representation of Cultural Identity in Jamaica Kincaid's 'Annie John'," in Callaloo, *Vol. 13, No. 2, Spring, 1990, pp. 325-40.*

Jane Mendelsohn

"For ten of my twenty years," says Lucy, the heroine of Jamaica Kincaid's new book [***Lucy***], "I had been mourning the end of a love affair, perhaps the only true love in my whole life I would ever know." In this straightforward, self-consciously assured voice, ***Lucy*** tells the story of a girl from the West Indies who comes to an unnamed American city to work as an au pair for a married couple and their children. Lucy's "only true love" is her mother, back in Antigua, and the death she has been mourning is the death of childhood—that exquisitely painful turning point captured in Kincaid's previous novel, ***Annie John.*** Although not a sequel to ***Annie John, Lucy*** picks up, in a sense, where the earlier book left off: at the bitter end of the mourning process, in limbo between adolescence and adulthood. An angry heroine in the tradition of Virginia Woolf's Lily Briscoe, Lucy experiences life as a long rainy weekend, clouded by ambivalence and streaked with threatening glimmers of future happiness. Her story, told in the calm, repetitive manner of a fairy tale, yet taut with the tensions of controlled anxiety, describes, like *To the Lighthouse,* the process of one woman's dissolution and another's self-invention. A mournful book filled with betrayals and death, it follows the progress of longing, not of love. . . .

[***Lucy***] is a book about salvation. Coming to work for Lewis and Mariah and their four fair-haired little girls, Lucy leaves the unhappy location of her past only to find herself in purgatory. But the book doesn't deal with damnation in any religious sense; it's concerned with guilt and its relation to life as well as to art: "Mariah said that I was feeling guilty. Guilty! I had always thought that was a judgment passed on you by others, and so it was new to me that it could be a judgment you pass on yourself. But I did not feel like a murderer; I felt like Lucifer, doomed to build wrong upon wrong." Named for Lucifer, as her mother only somewhat jokingly chides her, Lucy shares with Milton's demonic hero a gift for creative destruction.

This gift finds its most potent expression in Lucy's struggles with Mariah, her surrogate mother. While the book follows several narratives from Lucy's point of view—the story of the dissolution of Lewis and Mariah's marriage, the story of Peggy, Lucy's unfriendly friend, the story of Lucy's sexual awakening—the central relationship in the book, the one that most touches and changes Lucy, is between Lucy and Mariah. Like Lily Briscoe struggling to maintain and ignore Mrs. Ramsey's overbearing, irresistible love, Lucy measures herself against Mariah in a way that would be impossible if she were really her mother. Their difficult friendship provides her with an object to adore and destroy:

> Mariah, with her pale yellow skin and yellow hair, stood still in this almost celestial light, and she looked blessed, no blemish or mark of any kind on her cheek or anywhere else, as if she . . . had never done anything wrong and had never been to jail, had never had to leave anywhere for any reason other than a feeling that had come over her. She had washed her hair that morning and from where I stood I could smell the residue of the perfume from the shampoo in her hair. Then underneath that I could smell Mariah herself. The smell of Mariah was pleasant. Just that—pleasant. And I thought, But that's the trouble with Mariah—she smells pleasant. By then I already knew that I wanted to have a powerful odor and would not care if it gave offense.

The language in ***Lucy*** sustains this cadenced, perfectly balanced pitch. It's a short book made up of chapters that begin and end abruptly, like summer rain. Kincaid connects the episodes with anecdotes from Lucy's childhood, memories of which are sparked by tiny details: a walk through the woods, the tastelessness of a tongue, pale hands moving about in a fish tank. The resulting portrait is of a young woman determined to establish her independence from the past, less spunky than the little girl Annie John, more probing, observant, and cold. Trying to put on a tough front in her new home—"I had to smile with my mouth turned down at the corners"—Lucy speaks in a strangely detached voice, and her dark sense of humor reveals her loneliness. As she positions herself within various triangular relationships, she slowly begins to understand not who she is—that seems too much to ask for—but how to find out. "I understood that I was inventing myself, and that I was doing this more in the way of a painter than in the way of a scientist. . . . I did not have anything exactly in mind, but when the picture was complete I would know." What Lucy discovers, almost without realizing it (and like Lily Briscoe, only after her surrogate mother is gone), is herself as an artist. With its subtle evocation of shifting patterns, ***Lucy*** reveals more gradations in the quality of possible experience than any of Kincaid's previous books.

Jane Mendelsohn, "Leaving Home: Jamaica Kincaid's Voyage Round Her Mother," in VLS, *No. 89, October, 1990, p. 21.*

Michiko Kakutani

[In ***Lucy,*** the narrator, Lucy, describes the past as] "a line; you can draw it yourself, or sometimes it gets drawn for you; either way, there it is, your past, a collection of people you used to be and things you used to do. Your past is the person you no longer are, the situations you are no longer in."

In Lucy's case, the past she's left behind is a small place in the sun—an unnamed island in the Caribbean, 12 miles long and 8 miles wide. She has also left behind her younger self: the girl who was raised by her parents to be dutiful and obedient, the girl who was supposed to grow up and become a nurse, the girl who was "so beyond reproach in every way that if you asked her a question she would reply in her mother's 40-year-old voice."

Indeed, Lucy's story (like that of Annie John, an earlier Kincaid heroine) is a story of goodbyes—the goodbyes of exile, adolescence and disillusionment. It is the sort of coming-of-age story that many people tell with a mixture of nostalgia, sadness and affection. Lucy, in contrast, tells her tale with unvarnished anger and despair. . . .

When Mariah takes her to the park to see the daffodils in bloom, Lucy tells her about the resentment she felt, as a schoolgirl, at having to memorize Wordsworth's famous poem "Daffodils" in class: the resentment someone living in a colonial country feels toward the cultural imperialism of a faraway land. Though Lucy says she knows that Mariah was only trying to share something she loved, "nothing could change the fact that where she saw beautiful flowers I saw sorrow and bitterness."

A similar hardheartedness informs the rest of Lucy's observations and reminiscences. She does not allow herself to love the men she sleeps with. She proudly distances herself from Mariah's offers of friendship. And she resists her mother's efforts to remain in touch, refusing to open any of her letters.

When she learns that her father has died and left her mother penniless, Lucy sends some money home, along with a note.

> In the letter I asked my mother how she could have married a man who would die and leave her in debt even for his own burial. I pointed out the ways she had betrayed herself. I said I believed she had betrayed me also, and that I knew it to be true even if I couldn't find a concrete example right then. I said that she had acted like a saint, but that since I was living in this real world I had really wanted just a mother.

It's hard for the reader to come to terms with such brutal expressions of anger, and Ms. Kincaid does nothing to soften or sentimentalize her heroine's state of mind. She does not ask the reader to sympathize with Lucy, and she does not try to explain the events that shaped Lucy's hostility and hurt. Instead, writing in beautifully precise prose, she allows Lucy to present herself to the reader, as she might present herself to a new acquaintance: through a series of impressionistic reminiscences, assertions and vignettes, we glimpse Lucy's tortured relationship with her mother, her fumbling initiations into sex, her unhappy efforts to come to terms with her parents' expectations and her own confusions.

The portrait that emerges is one of a woman who experiences life as a succession of losses: sex means the loss of innocence; exile, the loss of roots; growing up, the loss of family and friends. Somewhere along the line, Lucy has accepted, even embraced, such losses as an inevitable part of life; for her, moving on has become second nature. The book ends with her leaving Mariah and Lewis to begin a new life on her own, and it leaves the reader with the unforgettable experience of having met a ferociously honest woman on her own uncompromising terms.

Michiko Kakutani, "From the Caribbean," in The New York Times, *October 12, 1990, p. C31.*

Richard Locke

In 1916, for the centenary of Charlotte Bronte's birth, Virginia Woolf wrote a tribute that still rings true today when so many are thinking with new urgency about women writers—especially Bronte and Woolf—and about writers born outside the centers of power, especially black, colonial and Third World writers:

> All her force, and it is the more tremendous for being constricted, goes into the assertion, 'I love,' 'I hate,' 'I suffer.' For the self-centered and self-limited writers have a power denied the more catholic and broad-minded. Their impressions are close packed and strongly stamped between their narrow walls. Nothing issues from their minds which has not been marked with their own impress.

This heroic effort has enabled Bronte to "forge" for herself "a prose which takes the mould of [her] mind entire; which has . . . a beauty, a power, a swiftness of its own. . . . There is in [her] some untamed ferocity perpetually at war with the accepted order of things . . . " Like Milton's Lucifer or Blake's. Or Jamaica Kincaid's heroine in her new novel, ***Lucy.***

Among the many who have felt the power of *Jane Eyre* was Elaine Potter Richardson, the only daughter of a black West Indian carpenter living without electricity or running water in St. John's, Antigua, still a British colony peopled by the descendants of slaves when she was born in 1949. Today his native daughter has become "Jamaica Kincaid," a resident of Vermont, a writer published in the *New Yorker,* the author of a collection of stories, ***At the Bottom of the River*** (1983); a novel,***Annie John*** (1985); and a ferocious essay on Antigua,***A Small Place*** (1988), which Salman Rushdie wisely described as "a jeremiad of great clarity and a force that one might have called torrential were the language not so finely controlled."

Lucy confirms Ms. Kincaid as both a daughter of Bronte and Woolf and her own inimitable self, "forging" a prose that has changed in remarkable ways, even though her subject might well have tempted a lesser writer to repeat herself or exploit the glamour of its impoverished tropical setting.

Ms. Kincaid's fiction is always narrated by a black Antiguan girl of no more than 20, and her tale is always one of passionate self-definition: a paradisiacal early childhood with an adored, abundantly generous mother, the slow growth of independence through school years (academic success, powerful friendships, growing hypocrisy, "back-chat," "impertinence"), and then the crisis of puberty that plunges mother and daughter into a war to the death—of that symbiotic early childhood. The universal tragedy and triumph of maternal separation, with all the anger and horror of being abandoned or of being smothered or devoured by a feared, beloved and despised mother, is the great obsessive subject of Ms. Kincaid's work. She is a brilliant portraitist of adolescent ambivalence.

But what enlarges and particularizes her work is its fidelity to West Indian landscape and culture: not in any facile or external political sense (though what she writes is profoundly political), but with full novelistic intelligence. Her imagery is naturally enriched by the color (in all senses) of her characters and their world, but she never exploits it. She is not grandiloquent, but precise; there is no self-dramatizing melodrama in her narratives or her prose; she never stoops to exotic effects, tropical cocktails, slogans or cliches.

Not that she's ever timid or merely well-behaved. Her first book [***At the Bottom of the River***] was astonishingly bold, difficult, un-narrative, a collection of memories, visions, incantations and dreams. The change in Ms. Kincaid's second book, ***Annie John,*** was startling: Instead of surreal flashes of St. Elmo's fire there was a clear portrait of the artist as a young woman, wrestling for her life with her mother, her school and the paired temptations of turning into a "slut" or nothing more than an "echo" of her mother for the rest of her days. If ***At the Bottom of the River*** portrayed a tropical young Jane Eyre's fantasy life, ***Annie John*** was its complement: a realistic narrative of her daily life until she left home at 17, a book less startling in its form but uncommonly moving.

Lucy now continues to explore the themes of separation and self-creation in an even more linear narrative and an even more chaste and controlled style. (One comes to understand how much Lucy's clear, even voice represents an act of courage, of will.) The setting is no longer only Antigua. Lucy has come to America at 19 in 1968 to work as "the girl who takes care of the children" for a rich, handsome lawyer and his naive blond wife in their Manhattan apartment and their summer house on the Great Lakes. Profoundly alone, fleeing her past and its restrictive demands, discovering America and her new self, Lucy observes the liberal sentimentalities and delusions of her employers as their marriage dissolves.

After a year she quits and goes out on her own. She is no longer an au pair girl; she has friends, lovers, colleagues; she admires Gauguin; she thinks of becoming a photographer like Henri Cartier-Bresson. She is even further from home. She has proclaimed her independence anew and must now contend with the singularity she fought so hard to win. And there's the rub. For it is Ms. Kincaid's gift to be able to present her heroine's experience of self-liberation as not simply a triumph but also perhaps as a Pyrrhic victory or a version of Lucifer's fall from grace. To embody and to animate such a passionate paradox is to fashion a secure literary success.

Richard Locke, "An Antiguan Girl in America," in The Wall Street Journal, *October 16, 1990, p. A24.*

"There is a self-contained world which [Jamaica Kincaid explores] with great detail. Not to chart the existence of that world, but to show that human emotions manifest themselves everywhere. She never feels the necessity of claiming the existence of a black world or a female sensibility. She assumes them both. I think it's a distinct departure that she's making, and I think that more and more black American writers will assume their world the way that she does. So that we can get beyond the large theme of racism and get to the deeper themes of how black people love and cry and live and die. Which, after all, is what art is all about."

—Henry Louis Gates, Jr., 1990

Richard Eder

Lucy is transparent, like one of those models of the human body where everything is visible: bones, muscles, veins, lymph and digestive systems, and the organs. Everything except the soul, of course. But in ***Lucy,*** transparency *is* the soul. That, and anger.

The anger of Lucy, a 19-year-old who comes to New York from Antigua to work as an *au pair,* is an instrument of discovery, not destruction. It is lucid and cold, but by no means unsparing. In the book's transparency we see it in delicate and painful dialogue with longing. It is the energy that propels her journey between distant places: between the Caribbean and the United States, childhood and growing up, the hunger for love and the hunger for autonomy.

Jamaica Kincaid, whose life is closely reflected in Lucy's, has gone far beyond autobiography. At best, a biographical or autobiographical protagonist will be vivid and true. Lucy has ascended into fiction: She is vivid, true and necessary. Her voice in this harsh and graceful book tells us in the only possible way—at least while we are reading it—what it is to be a colonized subject, a Third World sensibility in the United States, a child battling with her past and a woman battling with her identity.

Lucy arrives in wintertime New York—cold is hostile—wearing new underwear that chafes—change is hostile—and stretched by contradiction. She is desperate to escape the poverty and oppressiveness of a tiny island and an overwhelming mother; she must struggle to be herself in an overwhelming new country.

From her bookish, argumentative childhood in Antigua, she imagines herself as Gauguin escaping bourgeois constrictions and turning hero in the South Seas. And in the tiny Upper East Side maid's room that reminds her of a packing crate—"But I am not cargo," she reminds herself—she realizes how far she is from her model: "I was not a man; I was a young woman from the fringes of the world, and when I left home I had wrapped around my shoulders the mantle of a servant."

Lucy's voice—detached, furious, shrewd and desolate by turns—tells us of no settled state but of a 19-year-old's explosion into connections being made. She is lonely and homesick but consumed by the painful need to explore herself and the two worlds she is bridging.

It has taken some discerning foreign eyes—De Tocqueville's, Bryce's—to tell us things about ourselves that we did not know, Lucy, at work puzzling out the kindly, privileged and obtuse family she works for—Lewis, Mariah and their four blond daughters—has such an eye. The family is socially conscious by American standards. From the Third World, things look a little different. Mariah, the young wife and mother, is a romantic environmentalist, concerned about preserving nature against despoilment, Lucy thinks:

> I couldn't bring myself to point out to her that if all the things she wanted to save in the world

> were saved, she might find herself in reduced circumstances.

Mariah is a child of show-and-tell. She wants Lucy to love and admire the life she takes pleasure in. Lucy is a child of hide-and-consider. Her island was colonized, her ancestors slaves, and she is an *au pair*. . . .

Lucy, the glowering Third World making sandwiches in Mariah and Lewis' smiling American kitchen, is much more than that. She is a child-woman with an unhealed wound of love. Her father ran around with other women; her mother was too crushing a presence to let her grow. Now she leaves her mother's letters unopened and cannot stop thinking of her. "Half my life I'd been mourning the end of a love affair."

The history of women's pain, and the bond among those who suffer it, is something she cannot throw off. Bit by bit, she notices a hint of "ruins" in the blithe New York household; beneath her mockery of Mariah, the bond of pain is forming. Mariah's hands arranging flowers reminds her of her mother's. "I almost started to cry, I loved her so."

Lewis, she discovers, is having an affair. For all his grace and kindness, he is no different from the men back in Antigua. "Everyone knew that men have no morals, that they do not know how to behave, that they do not know how to treat other people. It was why men like laws so much; it was why they had to invent such things—they need a guide."

Lucy has her own succession of boys and young men; Kincaid writes of the affairs with comic insouciance. Sex is an untroubled hunger for her and none of her lovers touch her in any real way. But she carries with her a deeply troubling fantasy about a fisherman who groped one of her friends back in Antigua when she was a child.

She will leave her *au pair* job, remain friends with Mariah, find work as a receptionist, share an apartment with a New York roommate. She will continue to look at things and learn, coolly and voraciously; suspended between first and third worlds, between hunger and self-sufficiency, yearning and detached judgment. At the end, she has started a journal and has wept over the very first line: "I wish I could love someone so much that I would die from it." She will turn the page and go on writing.

Richard Eder, "Third-World Person Singular," in Los Angeles Times Book Review, *October 21, 1990, p. 3.*

Carol Anshaw

Literature has a long tradition featuring the servant as observer, reporter on the lives lived in the "upstairs" of the house. In much the same way, the foreigner is often fictively employed to comment on the culture in which he or she is a stranger. Lucy, the narrator of [***Lucy***], is both servant and stranger, and from these vantage points views the fragile constructs of happiness designed by the family she works for, upper-middle-class Americans of the late 1960s.

Jamaica Kincaid's brilliant stroke in this book, though, is to make its narrator-observer also its most interesting character. Behind the unblinking stare and opaque surface she presents to her employers, Lucy is terribly tangled in the crossed wires of old and new, of the life she came from and the one she has escaped to.

She is 19 when she is brought up from the West Indies to serve as *au pair* for Lewis, a lawyer, and his wife, Mariah.

> The husband and wife looked alike and their four children looked just like them. In photographs of themselves, which they placed all over the house, their six yellow-haired heads of various sizes were bunched as if they were a bouquet of flowers tied together by an unseen string. In the pictures, they smiled out at the world, giving the impression that they found everything in it unbearably wonderful.

The family, in turn, sees Lucy as curiously cool. They begin to call her "the Visitor." In reality Lucy is fascinated with them, particularly with Mariah, who is to Lucy a nearly unimaginable kind of person.

"Mariah was beyond doubt or confidence. I thought, Things must have always gone her way and not just for her but for everybody she has ever known from eternity; she has never had to doubt and so she has never had to grow confident; the right thing always happens to her; the thing she wants to happen happens."

Over the year or so Lucy lives with Mariah and her family, she comes to see this isn't true. The things Mariah wants to happen stop happening. Lucy sees this when she comes upon Lewis with his mouth on the neck of Mariah's best friend.

Although she frames her feelings for Mariah as love, they really are much more complicated. She is also disdainful of Mariah's uninvestigated worldview and makes sharp separations of herself from this object of attraction. (p. 6)

This ambivalence is really a paler, third carbon of the love/hate she has for her mother whom she has left—with a vengeance—back on the island of her birth. But within Lucy's hardened heart is soft tissue, behind this rejection is the sadder truth about her connection to her mother: ". . . for ten of my twenty years, half of my life, I had been mourning the end of a love affair, perhaps the only true love in my whole life I would ever know."

Love confounds Lucy. Sex she can find with men she doesn't love. Friendship she can have without much investment. She can stay at a comfortable remove from Lewis and Mariah and their civilized troubles, leave without feeling a tug. But love and the fear of it set her reeling. Near the beginning of the book she says, ". . . I didn't want to love one more thing in my life, didn't want one more thing that could make my heart break into a million little pieces at my feet." At its end, she writes in the journal Mariah has given her, "I wish I could love someone so much that I would die from it.' And then as I looked at this sentence a great wave of shame came over me and I wept and wept so much that the tears fell on the page and caused all the words to become one great big blur." . . .

With ***Lucy,*** [Kincaid] assembles a graceful, complex narrative that is at the same time about sexual awakening, the construction of identity out of the scraps at hand, the elaborate misunderstandings that can arise from different cultural assumptions and the essentially harrowing nature of love. (p. 7)

Carol Anshaw, "More Than a Servant: Jamaica Kincaid's West Indian Au Pair Girl," in Chicago Tribune—Books, *October 28, 1990, pp. 6-7.*

Thulani Davis

Jamaica Kincaid's new novel, ***Lucy,*** the first-person narrative of a young woman coming to America, runs like a quiet brook, rising and falling over rocks and gullies, brushing past places it has run before but never resting, never latching onto anything in its path. Lucy herself is like this, absorbing only small details of her new home (where she will work as an *au pair*), never trying to take in the place as a whole, not looking beyond what is at hand. On her first day in America she reacts only to a few new experiences: the lights of the unnamed city, the dingy ordinariness of the landscape, her first elevator ride, food from a refrigerator. "I slept soundly that night, but it wasn't because I was happy and comfortable—quite the opposite; it was because I didn't want to take in anything else."

Lucy has come to get away from her home in Antigua and all its familiarity. Her story is not about the shock of emigrating from one culture to another; it dwells in the psychological space between leaving and arriving. In sparse prose punctuated with the most economical yet precise description, Ms. Kincaid's Lucy makes an accounting of her first year abroad—a year in which she never quite arrives where she expected to be, or even unpacks her trunk of documents that purport to show who she is and what she will be doing. By some arrangement she has come directly to the maid's room of a spacious apartment, to take care of the four children of Mariah and Lewis and to become ensconced in the couple's cozy but eroding family life.

She seems to have used her nursing studies as an excuse to get away from home, but she never mentions time spent at school and soon gives it up. After her first winter Lucy reflects: "It was my past, so to speak, my first real past—a past that was my own and over which I had the final word. I had just lived through a bleak and cold time, and it is not to the weather outside that I refer." Lucy's real preoccupation is her own unhappy state of mind and the sad discovery that, as the old folks used to say, every goodbye ain't gone.

Lucy finds no home in her warm but distant relationship with the unfaithful Lewis, tolerant Mariah and their children; in her casual, unremarkable liaisons with men; or in her friendship with Peggy, an Irish working woman who offers easy company if not genuine compatibility. It is as if in choosing to leave home to loosen her connection to people, the young woman finds she can no longer make any connections at all.

And there is the problem of those memories Lucy confronts at odd moments. Seeing a man's tongue lick a woman's ear, Lucy recalls a boy back home. She remembers her father the philanderer trying to count up how many children he had—perhaps 30—without ever being sure. And more and more she stumbles upon reminders of the advice and habits of her mother, whose letters she refuses to open.

Ms. Kincaid is a marvelous writer whose descriptions are richly detailed; her sentences turn and surprise even in the bare context she has created, in which there are few colors, sights or smells and the moments of intimacy and confrontation take place in the wings, or just after the door closes. Lucy moves affectlessly through the unnamed places, among the new people, reacting with almost insensitive frankness to their desires and disappointments. Lucy is a delicate, careful observer, but her rage prevents her from reveling in the deliciousness of a moment. At her happiest, she simply says, "Life isn't so bad after all." Lucy in America is a much-disappointed girl, despairing over unfulfilled expectations. Of course one knows what demons expectations always are, but it is never clear what Lucy's particular expectations have been. Lucy in Antigua was a fiery girl who had bitter fights with her idol-mother and felt driven to leave home forever once she sensed she could no longer worship this perfect, self-sacrificing woman; Lucy in America is lost without an object for such passion.

But I am very puzzled by ***Lucy.*** If I had not read Jamaica Kincaid's other fiction, I might have been left with the feeling of wanting to know more about this young woman, who is not at home in her skin, and about the unresolved relationships left behind in Antigua. One gets only small tastes of those parts of life that filled and consumed Lucy earlier. While the book would seem to tell a story of the floating life of one of the nameless brown faces we see strolling with blond-haired tots along city streets, it also provides a new rendering of material explored in Ms. Kincaid's two very different, previous works of fiction. The manner of telling varies, but the seminal events and the narrow, internal focus are the same in all three books. . . . Whereas the images in [***At the Bottom of the River***] are luminous and disjointed, as if refracted through a pool of water, they return as singular, sparkling pictures in the more orderly, representational narrative of ***Annie John.*** In ***Lucy,*** they recur as slightly misshapen by memory and distance.

At the Bottom of the River opens with a mother's voice reciting years' worth of warnings, how-tos and little gems like "This is how to behave in the presence of men who don't know you very well, and this way they won't recognize immediately the slut I have warned you against becoming." This mother in ***Annie John*** is a never-sits-still kind of woman—washing the clothes and drying them on rocks, fetching fish from the two fishermen who share their catch with her. And it is this same woman, with her wash, advice and all, from whom Lucy has run so hard. She is the loving, frightening mother-goddess looming in all three books, creating a blissful, verdant paradise in ***At the Bottom of the River*** that some might call an idealized "woman-space," a place of unending nurture, where a voice always closes the night with a story that begins, "Before you were born."

Lucy could be construed as a kind of sequel to ***Annie John,*** but I am not convinced there was any such intent. The two books are like night and day in style and structure: one lush and descriptive, moving chronologically and underscoring its major themes with imagery and metaphor; the other narrative sparse and seemingly scattered, meandering in and out of situations rather than resolving or coming to conclusions, perhaps more like life. And I found it difficult to recognize the lively, curious and engaged child Annie in the angry but disengaged Lucy. Unfairly, perhaps, I found myself drawing from the other books to complete the picture—assuming, for instance, that this young Lucy (also called Little Miss in all the books), who hates Wordsworth, loves the Brontës and has no plans to continue her education, *could* be the gifted scholar and irreverent class prefect Annie. When Lucy berates her mother for ignoring her intelligence, it comes late and as a surprise that this is a matter of rage for her. When Lucy wonders—rather oddly, it would seem—who made her father's coffin, I knew she might be asking that question because Annie John's father made everyone's coffin at home. I remain puzzled, wondering still who exactly is telling this story, who is accounting for herself here and there by saying, "It must have been my age." Surely it was more than that.

Thulani Davis, "Girl-Child in a Foreign Land," in The New York Times Book Review, *October 28, 1990, p. 11.*

Mary Warner Marien

[The narrator in] ***Lucy*** is neither a sad statistic nor a vacant-eyed hostage to circumstances. The opening paragraph of this first-person novel testifies to the vigor of her mind and to the fact that her psychic bruises and impetuous anger have little to do with the immediate experience of cultural clash. On the contrary, she writes that the buildings, parks, streets, and bridges of her new locale once "were lifeboats to my drowning soul, for I would imagine myself entering and leaving them, and just that . . . would see me through a bad feeling I did not have a name for."

How the physical landscape of the developed countries came to signify both solace and intellectual accomplishment to the young West Indian and how she comes to terms with the inevitable disenchantment are the substance of Kincaid's simple, yet spellbinding story. In prose that moves as gracefully as sea grass in a tidal pool, Lucy's consciousness fluently undulates between her present and her past. In the course of a year the gleam of both the storybook island of her birth and the storybook family with whom she now resides will darken. Such is the cost of being able to see more clearly and to partially resolve what lies beneath the surface.

In a moment of twinned pain and liberation, Lucy comes to terms with having been named for Lucifer. Her mother confesses to having dubbed her Lucy because she was "a botheration" from the time she was conceived. Relatedly, she will give voice to an abiding resentment of her family's confident aspirations for their male children, from which she was alienated both by gender and by temperament.

Similarly, the snug and provident world of Mariah, the mother of the four little girls in Lucy's charge (and not, coincidentally, a delicious concoction of bourgeois liberal platitudes) must confront the reality that her husband is having an affair with her closest friend.

By going back to the past, either physically, as Mariah does by spending the summer at her ancestral home near one of the Great Lakes, or in the imagination, as Lucy so frequently does, each of these women forges a new compact with the past, one freer (but not free) of its inhibiting burdens.

Like the schoolmate of her youth, whom island lore claimed was possessed, Lucy has "had to cross the sea where the Devil couldn't follow her" in order to make a fresh start. The novel ends at the beginning of her new life and at the beginning of the journal that will become the novel. Thus the finale becomes the fountainhead and life becomes art.

For many readers of this story, recently published in *The New Yorker,* the magazine for which Jamaica Kincaid has written, art and life are too cozily connected in ***Lucy.*** Lucy Josephine Potter has been mistaken for Elaine Potter Richardson, the name and the life Jamaica Kincaid put behind her as she became a writer. . . .

But ***Lucy*** can no more be discounted as autobiographical transcription than *Moby Dick* can be reduced to a fish story.

In a second reading, which this outstandingly well-crafted tale deserves, one can move beyond the details of plot to a view of the novel's subtle, yet strong structure. It is that structure, packed with fresh metaphor, that transforms the elements of life into art.

In a bold appropriation, Jamaica Kincaid has adapted the double theme of falling from grace and the possibility of repentance from the Book of Genesis and from John Milton's *Paradise Lost,* a poem both Lucy and Elaine Potter Richardson were forced to memorize. Lucy admits that "the stories of the fallen were well known to me, but I had not known that my own situation could even distantly be related to them."

The great motifs of Western literature, like goodness and evil, innocence and experience, resonate in Kincaid's novel in a completely updated and unselfconscious way. In other hands, this story of a West Indian *au pair* would just be sociology. In Kincaid's recasting, it is both art and argument. ***Lucy*** should be required reading for those who find the so-called canon of works by Dead White European Males (the DWEMs, in current parlance) ill-adapted to the intellectual needs of multicultural America.

Mary Warner Marien, "Life Becomes Art," in The Christian Science Monitor, *November 26, 1990, p. 13.*

Roni Natov

In 1976 Adrienne Rich wrote that the bond between mother and daughter—"essential, distorted, misused—is the great unwritten story. Probably there is nothing in human nature," she asserted, "more resonant with charges than the flow of energy between two biologically alike bodies, one of which has lain in amniotic bliss inside the other, one of which has labored to give birth to the other. The materials are here for the deepest mutuality and the most painful estrangement." Rich claimed that there was "no presently enduring recognition of mother-daughter passion and rapture," that the "story" of the mother-daughter bond, in language evocative of that intimacy, had not yet been written. Jamaica Kincaid's penetrating novel ***Annie John*** is just such a story. Focusing on the painful struggle to separate from the mother that characterizes early adolescence for many girls, Kincaid evokes with intensity the wrenching many of us shudder to remember.

The simple yet richly sensuous language, the emphasis on an adolescent's point of view, and the immediacy of the subject matter make ***Annie John*** an appealing book for adolescents. Perhaps because ***Annie John*** was not written specifically with a young adult audience in mind, it lacks the preciousness and the superficiality of many novels aimed at the young adult market. Often in the adolescent "problem novel," issues are raised and then hurriedly resolved. Characters and plot tend to be secondary, the narrative forced, and the characters one-dimensional. By contrast, ***Annie John*** is a fully developed psychological study. And perhaps because the work draws so heavily on autobiographical material, ***Annie John*** feels authentic. Annie, the young heroine, is honest and engaging; the portraits of her parents, based on Kincaid's own mother and father, are complex and convincing. They love their daughter, but they ultimately fail her, as we all were failed by the imperfections of our parents. (pp. 1-2)

As a pre-oedipal narrative, a story in which the mother is the central source of all conflict and movement, [***Annie John***'s] language powerfully suggests merging with the mother's body. It is metaphoric and metonymic, essentially organized and defined by shifting constellations that suggest shading and nuance, rather than unilateral meaning. This is not to say that it is vague, but rather resonant. The narrative unfolds through natural, organic images that cluster around the mother's body—her hands, her neck, her mouth and hair.

In the first two sections of the novel, the dominant image is of the mother's hand, which metonymically evokes the infant's primary sensation of the mother. The first section, "Figures in the Distance," begins with a loss of innocence: the dead people Annie has heard about come closer and more sharply into focus when, at the age of ten, she learns that a girl younger than she has died in her mother's arms. "Until then," she says, "I had not known that children died." Death is associated with her mother, particularly with her mother's hands, which she avoids once she discovers they have helped prepare the dead girl for burial. In fact, the death of her own child self is prefigured here. For her, the separation to come is like a death in its severity.

Annie John begins with a death and ends with the promise of rebirth. From the initial image of a child dying in a mother's arms to the final image of a "vessel filled with liquid . . . placed on its side . . . slowly emptying out," ***Annie John*** chronicles the child's psychological journey away from the mother toward adulthood. In her close attention to the severing of this most primal bond between mother and daughter, Kincaid offers a kind of anatomy.

The novel builds like a poem as the images gather and intensify. The first images of the mother's and child's bodies together, bathing in the rich scents of various barks, flowers, and oils, suggest the amniotic waters that once connected mother and child. Bathing—the ritualistic washing of body parts—forms part of the mysteries associated with the obeah women, who in the Antiguan culture of Annie's home embody the feminine principle. This act of spiritual bonding represents Annie's entry into an exclusive, female world and affirms her primal intimacy with her mother.

Annie is completely immersed in her mother's world as she follows her through her day, observing the way she shops and cooks, eats and laughs. Her sense of self is created through the reminiscences her mother stores away for her along with her childhood belongings. Annie remembers looking through her mother's trunk of keepsakes with her, and "as she held each thing in her hand she would tell me a story about myself." So closely does she identify with her mother that the necessary separation, when it comes, feels like a fall from grace. Although there are hints of imperfection in their relationship during Annie's earlier years, whenever there was a rift between them there was always a way back, a reunification that felt like a return to paradise. The garden where her mother grew the herbs that Annie picked is her Eden. Annie says, "Sometimes when I gave her the herbs, she might stoop down and kiss me on my lips and then on my neck. It was in such a paradise that I lived." (pp. 3-4)

Annie's love for her mother, charged with the narcissism of childhood and early infatuation, is the erotic adoration associated with first love. In her intimacy with her mother, Annie submerges her sense of self. Like the infant, she experiences no boundaries between her body and her mother's. They are like animals, instinctually and mutually responsive and, from Annie's perspective, self-enclosed. This pre-oedipal world, of course, excludes the father, whom Annie experiences peripherally.

> When my eyes rested on my father, I didn't think very much of the way he looked. But when my eyes rested on my mother, I found her beautiful. Her head looked as if it should be on a sixpence. What a beautiful long neck, and long plaited hair, which she pinned up around the crown of her head because when her hair hung down it made her too hot. Her nose was the shape of a flower on the brink of opening. Her mouth, moving up and down as she ate and talked at the same time, was such a beautiful mouth I could have looked at it forever. . . . Her lips were wide and almost thin, and when she said certain words I could see small parts of

> big white teeth—so big, and pearly, like some nice buttons on one of my dresses. I didn't much care about what she said when she was in this mood with my father. She made him laugh so. She could hardly say a word before he would burst out laughing. We ate our food, I cleared the table, we said goodbye to my father as he went back to work, I helped my mother with the dishes, and then we settled into the afternoon.

This story is told exclusively from Annie's point of view, though we never lose sight of her mother. Our sympathies go out to her as well as to Annie, even if she can appear cruel and rejecting through Annie's eyes. With the onset of puberty Annie is forbidden to dress like her mother, and when she asks to engage in their special play with the objects in the trunk, "a person I did not recognize answered in a voice I did not recognize, 'Absolutely not! You and I don't have time for that anymore.' " The sense of betrayal grows, and with it a deep rage festers. The brutality with which such strong bonds are severed seems almost inevitable here. The anguish of being cast out of her mother's world precipitates the shift from her mother to her school friends as the primary objects of her affection.

What speeds up this process, what transforms her mother-love into erotic bonding with her peers, is something Annie perceives as the ultimate betrayal, portrayed again through the image of her mother's hands. When Annie comes home one afternoon to find her parents in bed together, she sees only her mother's hand circling on her father's back. The hand that fed and bathed her, that symbolized comfort and utter security, now seems unfamiliar and beyond her reach. . . . The hand that "had to prepare the little girl to be buried" now prepares her for witnessing the exclusive circle in which her mother and father are enclosed and from which she is shut out, and for the bitter knowledge that her father, her rival, has replaced her in her mother's affections.

Longing to recapture her closeness to her mother, at school she writes about a childhood memory of swimming on her mother's back, united with her as if they were one creature: "When we swam around in this way, I would think how much we were like the pictures of sea mammals I had seen, my mother and I, naked in the sea water. . . . I would place my ear against her neck, and it was as if I were listening to a giant shell, for all the sounds around me—the sea, the wind, the birds screeching—would seem as if they came from inside her, the way the sounds of the sea are in a seashell." Annie is the listener, her mother the interpreter of the world and the source of entry into it. The image of bathing recurs here, though the waters are less enclosed, oceanic rather than amniotic. Annie is older now and the separation from her mother imminent. The boundaries here are still porous and the sea element connects the mother and child, yet Annie tells a story of separation. Unable to swim alone, she recounts watching her mother from an island as she swims. A ship comes between them, cutting off her mother from her view, and she panics, like an infant who experiences the loss of the mother if she is not within sight. When the ship has passed, Annie is devastated to discover that her mother had not been paying any attention to her. (pp. 4-6)

As her mother shares less and less of her vision, Annie is forced to create a secret world with her friends. The second section, "The Circling Hand," leads to the third and fourth, entitled "Gwen" and "The Red Girl," the names of the two girls who function as transitional objects in her journey toward separateness and individuation. Gwen and the Red Girl are her light and dark sides. Gwen is neat, clean, serious—all that is acceptable and familiar to her mother. Like her mother, she smells of lavender. . . . While her mother recedes into the distance, Annie finds a new paradise with her friends in a world they "hoped forever to occupy [where] boys were banished." But she never really forgets her original loss as she sits on the tombstones at the back of the churchyard, listening to the tolling of the school bell. School becomes tainted for her—restrictive and punitive, associated as it is with her mother's wishes and with her former childhood innocence. Annie rebels against all that is considered respectable, as she leads the other girls in singing "bad songs," using "forbidden words, and, of course, show[ing] each other various parts of our bodies . . . walk[ing] up and down on the large tombstones."

Annie, who is essentially spirited, becomes increasingly irreverent and iconoclastic. But transferring her love from Gwen to the Red Girl is her most rebellious act. The Red Girl embodies Annie's notions of impropriety. She never bathes, never attends Sunday school, and represents all that is untamed and free. She is associated with Annie's sexuality—with the menstrual blood that precipitated the distance between her and her mother. With the Red Girl Annie enacts the dark and forbidden sides of erotic love, love mingled with guilt and rage, redirected in the fusion of pain and pleasure:

> Then, still without saying a word, the Red Girl began to pinch me. She pinched hard, picking up pieces of my almost nonexistent flesh and twisting it around. At first, I vowed not to cry, but it went on for so long that tears I could not control streamed down my face. I cried so much that my chest began to heave, and then, as if my heaving chest caused her to have some pity on me, she stopped pinching and began to kiss me on the same spots where shortly before I had felt the pain of her pinch. Oh, the sensation was delicious—the combination of pinches and kisses. And so wonderful we found it that, almost every time we met, pinching by her, followed by tears from me, followed by kisses from her were the order of the day.

For Annie, everything becomes tinged with ambivalence, with the arousal of both longing for and aversion to her mother. The most frequent pastime of this period of her life, playing marbles with the Red Girl, becomes the focus of contention between Annie and her mother. In the marbles, first introduced but now forbidden to her by her mother, Annie sees a reflection of the whole world, land masses and sea. But now her world must be hidden from her mother and the marbles stored under the house. Here she moves about in darkness, the underground girl, secretive and deceptive, stealing from her mother to buy gifts for the Red Girl. Whereas the early sections of the book focus on the upper part of the mother's body—her hands, arms, neck—in this section Annie experiences her mother as two enormous feet which she views from her hiding place. Once Annie saw her mother's feet, which are identical to her own and to her grandmother's, as "beautifully arched, pink-soled"; now they loom large and threatening before her. Once she gazed up at her mother in worship and trust; now her lowered perspective suggests her own descent, the fallen state in which she feels trapped with her mother.

Annie discovers how to be treacherous. She does not yield to her mother's attempts to disarm her into confessing that she indeed stores the forbidden marbles under the house. In order to separate, she learns to be two-faced. Although her mother forces her to give up the Red Girl, in her dreams she creates a tale of heroism and revenge in which she rescues the Red Girl from shipwreck, and, secluded together on the island, they cause ships to crash by sending them confusing signals.

Annie's impulse toward destruction pervades the second half of the novel. If the first half is dominated by oceanic imagery, expansive and lush, in the second half the imagery becomes increasingly constricted. The governing metaphor is "a black ball . . . no bigger than a thimble, even though it weighed worlds," lodged inside her and associated with her secretive self and with her self-doubt. The "thimble that weighed worlds" is her defense against her mother's barbs; what weighs so heavily on her is her anger and repressed love. Her world becomes increasingly airless, a "dark cloud that was like an envelope in which my mother and I were sealed." In her dreams she walks down a sunless road where the leaves of the trees are so thickly enmeshed that they block out the sky entirely. This is the psychic space in which she and her mother live. They are enemies; so intense is the rage that connects them that their world cannot contain it. . . . Each is reduced to the "frightening black thing" that lives within them both.

The split between mothers and daughters often grows with the recognition of the sexuality of both women; they become rivals. The sexual attention shifts to the father, and with this movement, the younger woman seeks relief outside the home. What retards this expansion in ***Annie John*** and intensifies the connection between the two females is the association of male sexuality with danger and fear. Although Annie's father is kind, nurturing, and nonthreatening, the obeah women have warned Annie's mother about the harmful spells cast on them by her father's previous lovers, several of whom have borne his children. Annie remembers as a child being swept into the protection of her mother's skirts when they passed one of these women on the streets. In addition, Annie has little contact with boys of her own age. One childhood memory is of a boy laughing sadistically when he tricked her into sitting in a nest of stinging ants. As an adolescent, when she meets this same boy and again he humiliates her, her mother turns on Annie by telling her she has acted like a slut. This final assault on her sexuality increases the gulf between them, until her mother becomes a shadow on a wall that stands between her and the rest of the world.

Annie finally retreats into illness, into a world of silence and darkness. This regression into the pre-verbal semiotic world of pulsations, where sounds "rocked back and forth," is paradoxically a movement toward healing. She goes back to the pre-oedipal world that predated her fall from grace to restore herself. She does not speak. Since words, substitutes for the desired object, are part of the Symbolic Order of the Father, she needs to return to an earlier stage of life where words appear dissociated from their meanings. She recounts that during her illness, "my mother and father . . . stood at the foot of my bed and looked down at me. They spoke to each other. I couldn't hear what it was that they said, but I could see the words leave their mouths. The words traveled through the air toward me, but just as they reached my ears they would fall to the floor, suddenly dead." (pp. 7-10)

As Annie remains removed from her mother, the waters associated with the maternal come in the form of rain pounding outside on her roof at a distance, while inside, in her head, she sees the "black thing . . . lying down." She tries to cleanse herself of all impure feelings by literally washing some family photographs she finds during her illness. In a photograph of her aunt's wedding, she tries to wash away the creases from her aunt's wedding veil, the dirt from her father's trousers, all the faces of her family. In another, she washes away every part of herself except for her confirmation shoes, the symbol of her rebellion against her mother, who thought them unladylike. Most telling of all, she washes away her parents from the waist down in an attempt to restore the imaginary presexual world of her girlhood innocence. She sees herself as a distorted remnant of her childhood, small and mechanical, a "toy Brownie," dissociated from the world of adults. "Settling back in my bed," she reports, "I looked up at the beams in the ceiling. I then sat on one of them and looked down at my mother and me."

In her dreams she takes in the maternal waters of the sea, but in her desperate longing she drinks the sea dry and cannot contain it. She cracks and splits open, and wakes to find that she has wet her bed. For Annie, as for most adolescents, the world is polarized: either you are an adult or you are a child. And in identifying with either position there is danger and loss. As she snuggles against her father, she is a child who has wet her bed, but on his lap she feels the stirrings of sexuality, the surfacing of oedipal feelings. "Through the folds of my nightie, I could feel the hair on his legs, and as I moved my own legs back and forth against his the hair on his legs made a swoosh, swoosh sound, like a brush being rubbed against wood. A funny feeling went through me that I liked and was frightened of at the same time, and I shuddered." She retreats from these feelings, from sexuality altogether, as she returns to her original source of sustenance, her mother—but only by indirection. Through the maternal world of the obeah women and of her grandmother, who is steeped in their spiritualism and magic, she re-enters the prerational world associated with the pre-oedipal. She experiences her grandmother semiotically through her smells and the "sound of her breath as it went in and out of her body," and at night "I would lie on my side, curled up like a little comma, and Ma Chess would lie next to me, curled up like a bigger comma, into which I fit. In the daytime, while my mother attended my father, keeping him company as he ate, Ma Chess fed me my food, coaxing me to take mouthful after mouthful. She bathed me and changed my clothes and sheets and did all the other things that my mother used to do."

Interestingly, Kincaid says that of all the sections in this essentially autobiographical piece, only the long rain and the illness are fictional. Periods of rain are rare in Antigua; the deluge here is clearly metaphorical and her breakdown, an emblem for the dark night of the soul through which she must pass. When she emerges, however, it is not with a sense of wholeness, as is often suggested in novels for young adults, but rather with a fragmented vision and a deep sense of loss. For her that loss echoes everywhere; everything around her is charged with associations of her father and mother. Her house, bed, chair, and porridge spoon were all carved by her father's hands; the sheets on her bed, the curtains on the windows of her room, and the nightgown she wears through her illness were all made by her mother's hands. She concludes, "I suppose I should say that the two of them made me with their own hands." She experiences a claustrophobic need to escape from everything familiar, from both her parents and her school friends. What was founded in light for her now, through her young and bitter vision, appears tainted. Her own integrity is suspect, inextricably linked as it is with her family, and particularly with that paradigm of betrayal—her mother's body. She says, "So now I, too, have hypocrisy, and breasts (small ones), and hair growing in the appropriate places, and sharp eyes, and I have made a vow never to be fooled again." (pp. 10-12)

Although there is a promise of new life as Annie sails for England, the last image of the amniotic waters "emptying out" recalls the broken membrane—the first separation of the infant from the mother—and foreshadows the new independent self Annie will birth. But the tone is somber and suggests weariness, depletion. For Annie the old world is dying, but the new one has yet to be born. With great acuity, Kincaid portrays this terror of stasis, of being frozen between childhood and adulthood, from the perspective of the adolescent Annie.

Although Kincaid emphasizes the pain of the connection between mother and daughter in ***Annie John,*** a framework for resolution beyond the end of the novel is provided by her mother's parting words, which assert the continuous and primary nature of the pre-oedipal bond: "I'll always be your mother and this will always be your home." The potential reunification of mother and daughter, foreshadowed in ***Annie John,*** is explored in her other published book of fiction, ***At the Bottom of the River,*** which invites a more exclusively adult viewpoint:

> My mother and I walk through the rooms of her house. . . . The rooms are large and empty, opening on to each other, waiting for people and things to fill them up. Our white muslin skirts billow up around our ankles, our hair hangs straight down our backs as our arms hang straight at our sides. I fit perfectly in the crook of my mother's arm, on the curve of her back, in the hollow of her stomach. We eat from the same bowl, drink from the same cup; when we sleep, our heads rest on the same pillow. As we walk through the rooms, we merge and separate, merge and separate; soon we shall enter the final stage of our evolution.

Kincaid suggests here the fluidity of this most primal bond; complete separation is never fully achieved (and is perhaps not even desirable). (pp. 13-14)

Like the writings of other contemporary black women, particularly the work of Paule Marshall and Alice Walker, Jamaica Kincaid's fiction focuses on the importance of continuity and community as they are preserved and kept alive by mothers, through their stories and through their connection with their daughters. Even though the intimacy between mother and daughter threatens at times to devour the newly developing spirit of the adolescent girl, it is an essential and integral source of nourishment, based as it is on connection, fluidity, and mutuality. ***Annie John*** is the story of the passion and power of that bond. (p. 14)

Roni Natov, "Mothers and Daughters: Jamaica Kincaid's Pre-Oedipal Narrative," in Children's Literature: Annual of the Modern Language Association Seminar on Children's Literature and The Children's Literature Association, *Vol. 18, 1990, pp. 1-16.*

Helen Pyne Timothy

Both ***At the Bottom of the River*** and ***Annie John*** are primarily concerned with intense mother/daughter relationships, the psychic development of the girl child, the teaching and learning of appropriate gender roles, and the breaking of the strongly imposed image of the mother for the development of individuation in adulthood. (p. 234)

The stages of Annie's psychosocial development are all amplified within the context of Caribbean cultural practices and beliefs. In the early stage of intense primary love and involvement with the mother, the first hint of separation comes with the child's awareness of death and her understanding that the perceived integrated personality of the two might be split by the loss of one individual. Annie's perception of her mother begins to change when she realizes that her mother has links with a community outside of her own perception:

> One day, a girl smaller than I, a girl whose mother was a friend of my mother's, died in my mother's arms. I did not know this girl at all . . . I heard my mother describe to my father just how Nalda had died . . . My mother asked my father to make the coffin for Nalda, and he did, carving bunches of tiny flowers on the sides. Nalda's mother wept so much that my mother had to take care of everything and since children were never prepared by undertakers, my mother had to prepare the little girl to be buried. I then began to look at my mother's hands differently. They had stroked the dead girl's forehead, they had bathed and dressed her and laid her in the coffin my father had made. My mother would come back from the dead girl's house smelling of bay rum—a scent that for a long time afterward would make me feel ill. For a while, though not for very long, I could not bear to

> have my mother caress me or touch my food or help me with my bath. I especially couldn't bear the sight of her hands lying in her lap.

Here Annie's mother is closely involved in a momentous happening in which she was not the center. She could clearly envisage the possibility of her dying and leaving her mother as well as the possibility of her mother betraying the primary love tie and dying herself and leaving Annie, like her classmate, "such a shameful thing, a girl whose mother had died and left her alone in the world."

Furthermore, the details of the death rituals as delineated are strongly indicative of Caribbean cultural habits. Annie's mother must of necessity be available to her neighbor in times of sickness and death; she must assist in transporting the child to the doctor, must help with the laying out of the body, must support and nurture the mother through the time of grieving. The father assists by carving the handmade coffin. This act is his personal involvement, but the male figure is not central to the emotional ritual. Thus the death is reported to him by the mother; but it is she who is central to all its demands, and her involvement is personal. Of course, Annie's feelings toward death are ambivalent: she is deeply aware of the understanding that death could rob her of the most intensely loved person, her mother. Yet in her attempts at role-modeling she wishes to become schooled and to penetrate the secrets of the ritual so she can be like her mother, an important person in a gender-binding ritual.

The burgeoning perception of subject/self, object/mother reaches the moment of separation, as expected, at puberty. Annie begins to see everything about her mother in a negative light and, typically, transfers the intensity of her emotion to a friend, Gwen. Her sexual urges are beginning to develop, as is the awareness of her physical presence and that of others. What is interesting about the presentation here is the way the mother is portrayed as relating to her daughter's developments:

> The summer of the year I turned twelve, I could see that I had grown taller; most of my clothes no longer fit. . . . My legs had become spindle-like, the hair on my head even more unruly than usual, small tufts of hair had appeared under my arms and when I perspired the smell was strange, as if I had turned into a strange animal. I didn't say anything about it, and my mother and father didn't seem to notice, for they didn't say anything either.

But in fact the parents had noticed, and the change in behavior manifested itself most violently in the mother, not the father. Kincaid seems to be making the statement here that in the Caribbean context, the mother is unable to continue successful role-modeling after the child reaches puberty. Up to this point, Annie's mother has been a strongly loving, caring, nurturing mother figure. Annie receives no beatings, only minor punishment. "I ate my supper outside, alone, under the breadfruit tree, and my mother said that she would not be kissing me goodnight later; but when I climbed into bed she came and kissed me anyway."

Moreover, Annie had been encouraged to model herself in every detail on her mother's conduct and behavior so as to become a perfect woman. Kincaid is at pains to show the mother's involvement with every detail of the child's development. The mementos of important stages in her prepubescent development are locked in a trunk to be taken out and lovingly recalled from time to time. But this Caribbean mother is unable to speak about the later stage of the child's development; she "didn't seem to notice." Kincaid's message seems to indict the Caribbean mother: she does not know how to communicate openly about the girl's development into a sexual being.

The contrast between the mother's attitudes in the girl's pre- and post-pubescent periods is almost shocking. In her relationship with Annie there had previously been a highly pleasurable integration of the child's body and the mother's as part of the relationship of loving and caring; and the child displayed an acutely sensitive response to her mother's body shape, touch, and smell. In this Caribbean family there is a lot of touching, hugging, and caressing between mother and daughter. . . . (pp. 234-36)

Up to puberty, then, the mother's role-modeling signals affirmatives about the body, sensation, and sensuality. These affirmatives are further reinforced in Annie's school life. Her friends in a girls' school, cut off from boys, are almost hysterical in their desire to "prove" their womanhood by growing breasts and menstruating. Annie's description of her first period is full of drama and emphasizes the emotions of awe and reverence, beauty even, in this event, and in the response of the other girls to whom it is revealed:

> At recess, among the tombstones, I of course had to exhibit and demonstrate. None of the others were menstruating yet. I showed everything without the least bit of flourish since my heart wasn't in it. I wished instead that one of the other girls were in my place and that I were just sitting there in amazement. How nice they all were, though, rallying to my side, offering shoulders on which to lean, laps in which to rest my weary, aching head, and kisses that really did soothe.

Annie's personal response betrays the uncertainty of the moment engendered by the fear of the future which this watershed must of necessity entail. But the fear is devoid of any suggestion of shame or secrecy; rather, it is a fear of adulthood, of uncontrollable changes in her life. (pp. 236-37)

This child is an extraordinarily sensitive participant/observer of her mother's life; and at this stage her acuity is trained toward the asymmetrical aspects of her behavior which can now be negatively assessed. The most obvious and, for the child, the most confusing and searing are concerned with questions of sexuality between mother and father.

In ***Annie John*** the figure of the father is peripheral to the intense absorption that links the daughter to the mother. Nevertheless, to the preadolescent, he is an important love object. Interestingly enough, however, when Annie begins to assess her mother negatively, she also transfers her negative viewpoint to her father, who is then seen as being more a part of her mother's universe than of her own:

"They were eating away as they talked, my father's false teeth making that clop-clop sound like a horse on a walk as he talked, my mother's mouth going up and down like a donkey's as she chewed each mouthful thirty-two times . . . I was looking at them with a smile on my face but disgust in my heart." Even if there are adjustments for Annie's tendency to an overwrought sensibility in her emotional assessment of her parents, there is a suggestion of sexual jealousy in her perception of the mother's physical closeness to the father. Alexander's relations with other women, although they occurred before his marriage, also appear to have had some impact on Annie. Although this description that the father has had affairs and "outside children" which he does not acknowledge represents a social truth of Caribbean society, the fact that he has been intimate with women whom he now passes by without speaking in the street invests sensitive young Annie with a subliminal sense that there is something shameful in a sexual relationship. Kincaid seems to be indicating here that male sexuality has no consequences, whereas for females the consequences are severe.

But more important is the mother's ambivalence about her own sexuality; she has suppressed this aspect of herself in her role-modeling although she does at one point recommend marriage and motherhood to Annie. But these concepts seem divorced from any sexual involvement. Heterosexual involvement is seen by the child as sin and shame, not joy or pleasure.

It is therefore totally understandable that when Annie unexpectedly sees her mother joyfully engaged in a sexual act with her father she is thrown into an emotional turmoil that causes the split and antagonism of daughter and mother with its consequent consuming negative assessments of the mother's role and behavior. These negative assessments begin strongly with the inability of the mother to negotiate the meaning of the girl's burgeoning sexuality.

Indeed, the ambivalence of the Caribbean mother is reinforced by Annie's mother's extreme reaction to a most innocent meeting and greeting of three boys which Annie engages in on her way home from school. Kincaid describes:

> On looking up, she observed me making a spectacle of myself in front of three boys. She went on to say that after all the years she had spent drumming into me the proper way to conduct myself when speaking to young men it had pained her to see me behave in the manner of a slut . . . in the street and that just to see me had caused her to feel shame. The word "slut" (in patois) was repeated over and over, until suddenly I felt as if I were drowning in a well but instead of the well being filled with water it was filled with the word "slut," and it was pouring in through my eyes, my ears, my nostrils, my mouth. As if to save myself I turned to her and said, "Well, like father like son, like mother like daughter."

Of course, behind Annie's impudence lies the understanding that she has discovered a serious weakness in her erstwhile strong, dominant, and correct mother. Moreover, this weakness points to a deep-rooted ambivalence, an insecurity that brings into question the very basis of the mother's existence and can be read further as the mother's inability to transmit to her daughter a coherent value system that embraces the various aspects of her role as woman in a Caribbean society. (pp. 237-39)

Sexuality is almost instantly related to sluttishness, possibly because of the mother's fear that her daughter will become the exploited female of "wharf-rat boys" or even of the father's former lovers, who view her with hate, in other words, will lose her chance to rise in class, in the world. There is also the possibility that, with the male who is acceptable in class, sexuality is possible, even desirable: "this is how to love a man, and if this doesn't work there are other ways." The girl is being urged to use her womanly wiles to accomplish results from an act she is simultaneously being taught is shameful. Included here is also a recognition that a woman's sexuality must be used to accomplish a rise in social status—possibly an unconscious explanation for the beautiful, strong, young mother's marriage to a much older, weaker, far less beautiful husband, who offered her marriage and a comfortable home.

Moreover, the Caribbean mother who is bent on seeing her daughter rise from the lower classes to the middle ranks must not only teach her useful housekeeping tasks, cleanliness, good manners, and practical knowledge of her environment but also European norms and the need to desist in the practice of African ones. The girl perceives these paradoxes inherent in the mother's relationship to her own Caribbean culture, and they become part of the negative features that help reinforce the split between the egos of mother and daughter and the daughter's subsequent rebellion. Thus in the mother's perception, Christianity, Sunday school, good manners (the ability to curtsy), and piano lessons are all essential to her daughter's acceptability and respectability. Consequently she must not sing benna songs (folk/African songs) in Sunday school; but Christian training becomes far less important when dealing with the real problems of life. Here the mother falls back on the belief in folk wisdom, myth, African systems of healing and bush medicine, the mysteries of good and evil spirits inhabiting the perceived world of nature. "Don't pick people's flowers—you might catch something; don't throw stones at blackbirds, because it might not be a blackbird at all. . . . This is how to make a good medicine for a cold; this is how to throw away a child before it even becomes a child."

It is therefore significant that Kincaid juxtaposes the event that causes Annie's awakening to this dimension of her mother's life with her return from Sunday school. For the child there is a complicated clash of eschatological systems which she cannot articulate. She can only feel that some important principle has been violated which she attributes to her mother's hypocrisy.

Annie's rebellions are directed primarily against her mother's notions of respectability—being "a lady" in her sense of what would be required for the socially ambitious in a European context: the battle of wills takes place over Annie's lessons in good manners ("how to meet and greet important people in the world"), piano lessons, Christianity, and a good European-style secondary education. The emotional split leads to a clash and finally an isolation of Annie that becomes so burdensome it leads to a mental breakdown.

The signals given during this period of mental and emotional collapse confirm the insecurity of the search for a coherent cosmology in which the child's social ambition, her intellectual and romantic yearnings, gleaned from European books (Blyton, the Brontës) and a European education, her moral, spiritual, and cultural landscape, and her sexual urges can all be accommodated. (pp. 239-41)

[The] most important influence on Annie at this time is the formidable figure of Ma Chess, the grandmother. Kincaid has cast her in a fully African world. She inhabits the world of the African spirits and, as long as she remains true to that vision, is able to control life and death. Her beloved son dies when she defers to the unbelief of Pa Chess and gets a doctor about an illness which "the doctor knew nothing about, and the obeah woman knew everything about." After that irretrievable and distressing error her commitment to the African-Caribbean spiritual universe is total and unwavering. In her Kincaid has provided a portmanteau figure of African myth and reality: Ma Chess is African healer, bush medicine specialist, and Caribbean obeah woman, extremely conscious of the presence of good and evil in life and able to ward off evil. She is also the mythological "flying African" able to cross the seas without a boat, and the flying "soucouyant" (female witch) who lives in a hole in the ground. Her world, however, is not threatening to the child but comforting and healing because of its coherency, its validity, and its verity. (p. 241)

This tension-free relationship is typical of a grandmother/granddaughter link, but it also records the sense of security the conforming world of Ma Chess exudes. A valid sociological point emerges here: for some of the older generation of Caribbean women, the penetration of European cultural values into the African cosmology was not so intense or so desirable. Most of these systems of belief, syncretism, are beginning to appear in Annie's mother's universe. Annie herself is going to "somewhere; Belgium," the heart of Europe, far away and in rejection of "obeah women" (African systems of belief). But there is a recognition that like her grandmother and mother before her, she must carry a trunk, that is, the cultural baggage of a race, a country, and a class, although for each generation, the trunks are packed with different contents. (p. 242)

Helen Pyne Timothy, "Adolescent Rebellion and Gender Relations in 'At the Bottom of the River' and 'Annie John'," in Caribbean Women Writers: Essays from the First International Conference, *edited by Selwyn R. Cudjoe, Calaloux Publications, 1990, pp. 233-42.*

FURTHER READING

Perry, Donna. "Initiation in Jamaica Kincaid's *Annie John.*" In *Caribbean Women Writers: Essays from the First International Conference,* edited by Selwyn R. Cudjoe, pp. 245-53. Wellesley, MA: Calaloux Publications, 1990.

Discusses storytelling, the *obeah* woman, and "matrilinear bonding" in *Annie John* as prerequisites for female initiation into Caribbean adulthood.

Milan Kundera

1929-

Czechoslovakian novelist, short story writer, essayist, playwright, and poet.

Kundera is considered one of Europe's most outstanding contemporary novelists. Forced to leave Czechoslovakia in 1975 after his books were deemed counterrevolutionary and banned by the Communist government, Kundera is frequently labeled an Eastern European "dissident" writer despite his insistence that his works are not inherently political or propagandistic. Rather than serving as ideological representatives, Kundera's characters are usually vulnerable individuals whose views and lifestyles are challenged through events and dilemmas in their personal lives and in society. These conflicts gain broader implications through Kundera's use of various narrative devices. For example, he often infuses authorial commentary into his texts, presents events in disjointed time frames and from multiple viewpoints, and patterns his novels in a manner similar to musical compositions. These narrative techniques, while sometimes castigated as disorienting, are integral to what Kundera terms his aesthetic of the novel. Highly influenced by the works of such writers as Miguel de Cervantes, Denis Diderot, and Franz Kafka, Kundera dismisses traditional novelistic structures, emphasizing instead parallel explorations of related themes, active philosophical contemplation, and the integration of dreams and fantasy with realistic analysis. Kundera explains: "A novel does not assert anything; a novel searches and poses questions. I don't know which of my characters is right. I invent stories, confront one with the other, and by this means I ask questions."

Kundera was born and raised in Brno, Czechoslovakia. His father, Ludvik, was a well-known pianist who collaborated with the celebrated Czechoslovakian composer Leoš Jǎnaček. Although he once studied piano and stated that "Jǎnaček's music [was] for me the first revelation of art," Kundera decided at age nineteen that music was not his true vocation. He left Brno in 1948 to study scriptwriting and directing at the Film Faculty of the Prague Academy of Music and Dramatic Arts. At this time Kundera, like many other idealistic and progressive students who had experienced the horrors of World War II, joined the Czechoslovakian Communist party. He began teaching cinematography at the Prague Academy in 1952 and published his first poetry collection, *Člověk, zahrada širá,* a year later. While Kundera's Communist convictions are reflected in this volume, his use of surrealistic elements caused the Communist party to condemn the book for lacking universality. Kundera published two other volumes of poetry, *Poslední máj* and *Monology,* while teaching at the academy. The first collection recounts the life of Julius Fucik, a Communist hero who resisted the Nazi occupation of Czechoslovakia; the second is a collection of "confessions" by romantically frustrated women. Kundera wrote in 1980 that "my earliest writings were several collections of poetry. I don't have very high regard for them." He later renounced these works as adolescent and insignificant.

During the early 1960s Kundera was recognized as an important literary figure in his homeland. He served on the Central Committee of the Writer's Union and the editorial boards of the journals *Literarni noviny* and *Listy.* He also wrote a play, *Majitelé klíčů* (*The Owners of the Keys*); a critical work about Czechoslovakian novelist Vladislava Vančury, *Unemí románu: cesta Vladislava Vančury za velkou epikou;* and a short story collection, *Směšné lásky* (*Laughable Loves*). In *The Owners of the Keys,* Kundera began to exhibit disenchantment with the Communist party's increasing use of force and what he perceived as the corruption of high-ranking officials. Set during World War II, this play concerns an idealistic student who attempts to dissociate himself from the violence of the Czechoslovakian resistance to Nazism. Despite his good intentions, he is ultimately forced to forgo pacifism and join the bloody struggle against the Nazi invaders. *Směšné lásky,* which became the first book in a trilogy of short story collections that includes *Druhý sešit směšných lásek* and *Třetí sešit směšných lásek,* addresses the illusory nature of love and the consequences of using sexuality to gain power and influence. In "The Hitchhiking Game," one of the best known stories, a young couple engage in role-playing while on vacation. The woman, usually very inhibited and conservative, pretends she is a prostitute and at the man's urging performs a striptease on a table in a disreputable hotel. While the game begins innocently, the implications of their respective behavior become painfully revealing when the woman pleads at the end of the story, "I am me, I am me, I am me. . . . "

Despite his reputation as one of Czechoslovakia's most notable writers, Kundera encountered resistance after submitting the manuscript of his first novel, *Žert* (*The Joke*), to a Prague publisher in 1965. This work focuses on Ludvik, a university student who firmly embraces Communist ideology. Ludvik sends a postcard in which he playfully parodies Marxist slogans to his zealously political girlfriend. Alarmed, the girlfriend shows the postcard to Zamenek, a fervent and humorless Communist student-leader, who gets Ludvik expelled from both the Communist party and the university. Ludvik is soon drafted into the army and forced to work in a coal mine. Years later, he seeks revenge by seducing Zamenek's wife who, unknown to Ludvik, has been separated from her husband for two years. Due to the perceived negative political implications of the book, Kundera spent two years battling the censorship board before *The Joke* was published in its original form in 1967. During the Prague Spring of 1968, when the push for cultural freedom reached its zenith and writers and intellectuals enjoyed fewer restrictions, Kundera's novel was enormously popular. Francois Ricard explains: "The 'fall' of Ludvik Jahn in a sense really does represent the disillusion of an entire generation, of an entire people who, having believed in the 1948 Prague coup, then waited twenty years to laugh about it."

Prior to the Prague Spring many writers and artists were attempting to speed reform and liberalize cultural policy by creating ideologically challenging works. In his opening address to the Fourth Czechoslovak Writers Congress in 1967, Kundera candidly admonished censorship and other repressive tactics used against Czechoslovakian writers: "We all remember so well those congresses and, in particular, those conferences where one book after another was lined up as if for Judgment Day. . . . Obviously the criteria we used in those days were wrong ones. . . . The very principal of authoritative institutional evaluation is, I feel, basically unsound." While Kundera's speech had been approved in advance by the Czechoslovak Communist Party Central Committee, it was considered very controversial by governmental bureaucrats and some writers. Kundera's status as a major literary figure changed radically when Czechoslovakia was invaded by Russian forces in 1968. He was expelled from the Communist party, released from his teaching position at the Prague Academy, and his works were removed from libraries and bookstores. Kundera eventually lost all rights to publish in Czechoslovakia. He finally fled his native country in 1975 after being offered a teaching position at the University of Rennes in France. In 1979 the Czechoslovakian government, in order to ensure that Kundera could never return, revoked his Czechoslovakian citizenship.

Although Kundera's second novel, *La vie est ailleurs* (*Life Is Elsewhere*), was written in Czechoslovakia, the book was first published in France in 1974. *Life Is Elsewhere* is a satirical portrait of Jaromil, a young poet. After being bullied by his doting mother to develop an artistic temperament, Jaromil runs off to become a writer. Paralleling the life of the young French poet Arthur Rimbaud, who passionately declared he would alter the course of modern poetry and then, at age twenty, ceased to write, *Life Is Elsewhere* is an exposé on how poetry can contribute to the hysteria of revolution. In this work, Kundera presents his belief that youth is a "lyrical age" laced with neurosis, romantic illusions, and endless self-contemplation. Kundera's next work, *La valse aux adieux* (*The Farewell Party*), also originally published in France, focuses on the destructive nature of sexual politics and self-deception. Set in a Czechoslovakian resort town renowned for the treatment of infertility, *The Farewell Party* chronicles the aftermath of a one-night stand that results in pregnancy and addresses such ethical issues as abortion, sperm-banking, and suicide.

In his next novel, *Le livre du rire et de l'oubli* (*The Book of Laughter and Forgetting*), Kundera focuses on numerous characters who are thematically linked, although they never interact. Mirek is a Czechoslovakian writer who was removed from his job and surrounded by undercover agents after the Russian invasion; Tamina is a woman in exile who remains obsessed with her husband after he dies while fleeing Prague. *The Book of Laughter and Forgetting* also contains references to the French poet Paul Éluard, who, after becoming transfixed with the revolutionary zeal of communism, refuses to save his friend, surrealist writer Zalvis Kalandra, from hanging. Focusing on the repercussions of forgetting personal and cultural histories, the metaphysical implications of laughter, and how ideological doctrines often lead to deluded notions of good and evil, Kundera presents memory as a form of self-preservation in a world where history is often distorted by cultural forces. In his next novel, *L'insourenable l'égèreté de l'être* (*The Unbearable Lightness of Being*), Kundera addresses similar themes by centering on the connected lives of two couples—Tomas and Tereza, and Franz and Sabina. Set in Czechoslovakia around the time of the Russian invasion, *The Unbearable Lightness of Being* is often considered an examination of the hardships and limitations that can result from commitment and the meaninglessness of life without such responsibility. In this work each of Kundera's characters represents a particular motif that is explored throughout the novel in varying contexts. Kundera explains: "As I was writing *The Unbearable Lightness of Being* I realized that the code of this or that character is made up of certain key words. For Tereza: body, soul, vertigo, weakness, idyll, Paradise. For Tomas: lightness, weight. In the part called 'Words Misunderstood,' I examine the existential codes of Franz and Sabina by analyzing a number of words: woman, fidelity, betrayal, music, darkness, light, parades, beauty, country, cemetery, strength."

After garnering international praise for *The Unbearable Lightness of Being,* which was later adapted to film, Kundera wrote *L'art du roman* (*The Art of the Novel*). This volume comprises three essays, two interviews, an acceptance speech for the Jerusalem Prize, and the definitions of sixty-three words the author believes are frequently mistranslated. In the essays—"The Depreciated Legacy of Cervantes," "Notes Inspired by *The Sleepwalkers,*" and "Somewhere Behind"—Kundera traces the development of the European novel. Although most critics praised Kundera's belief that the novel is a "sequence of discoveries," they also accused him of being arrogant and ethnocentric for his failure to consider any works by non-European or women writers. Kundera states: "Need I stress that I intend no theoretical statement at all, and that the entire book is simply a *practitioner's confession?* Every novelist's work contains an implicit vision of the history of the novel, and an idea of what the novel is: I have tried to express here the idea of the novel that is inherent in my own novels."

Kundera's novel *L'immortalité* (*Immortality*) is his first to be set in France. In this work, Kundera examines how media manipulation, popular culture, and capitalist technocracy have developed into instruments of propaganda that distort humankind's perception of reality. Throughout *Immortality,* Kundera pervades his fictitious text with information about how he came to create the various characters. The protagonist, Agnes, for example, "sprang from the gesture of [a] sixty-year-old woman at the pool who waved at the lifeguard," and Bernard from the voice of a radio broadcaster. In addition to discussing the love triangle between Agnes, her husband Paul, and Agnes's sister, Laura, *Immortality* contains episodes from the lives of such literary figures as Johann Wolfgang von Goethe and Ernest Hemingway. While Kundera has consistently won praise throughout his career for juxtaposing fictitious and biographical elements and simultaneously exploring recurring themes, many critics faulted *Immortality* for its disjointed plot and episodic characterizations. Frequently entering his texts to explain his characters and motivations, Kundera addresses directly in *Immortality* his theory of the novel: "I regret that almost all novels ever written are much too obedient to the rules of unity of action. What I mean to say is that at their core is one single chain of causally related act and events. These novels are like a narrow street along which someone drives his characters with a whip. Dramatic tension is the real curse of the novel, because it transforms everything, even the most beautiful pages, even the most surprising scenes and observations merely into steps leading to the final resolution. . . . A novel shouldn't be a bicycle race but a feast of many courses."

(See also *CLC,* Vols. 4, 9, 19, 32; *Contemporary Authors,* Vols. 85-88, rev. ed.; and *Contemporary Authors New Revision Series,* Vol. 19.)

PRINCIPAL WORKS

NOVELS

Žert 1967
 [*The Joke,* 1969]
**La vie est ailleurs* 1973
 [*Life Is Elsewhere,* 1974]
**La valse aux adieux* 1976
 [*The Farewell Party,* 1976]
**Le livre du rire et de l'oubli* 1979
 [*The Book of Laughter and Forgetting,* 1980]
**L'insourenable l'égèreté de l'être* 1984
 [*The Unbearable Lightness of Being,* 1984]
L'immortalité 1990
 [*Immortality,* 1991]

SHORT STORY COLLECTIONS

Směšné lásky 1963
 [*Laughable Loves,* 1974]
Druhý sešit směšných lásek 1965
Třetí sešit směšných lásek 1968

CRITICISM

Unemí románu: cesta Vladislava Vančury za velkou epikou 1961
L'art du roman 1986
 [*The Art of the Novel,* 1988]

POETRY

Člověk, zahrada širá 1953
Poslední máj 1955
Monology 1957

PLAYS

Majitelé klíčů 1962
 [*The Owners of the Keys,* 1962]
Dvě uši dvě svatby 1968
Ptákovina 1968
Jacques et som maitre: Hommage a Denis Diderot 1981
 [*Jacques and His Master,* 1985]

SCREENPLAY

The Joke [with Jaromil Jires] 1968

*These novels were published in the original Czech under the following titles after the publication of the French and English translations: *Život je jinde* (1979), *Valčík na rozloučenou* (1979), *Kniha smíchu a zapomnění* (1981), and *Nesnesitelná lehkost bytí* (1985).

Roger Kimball

The Czech novelist Milan Kundera was in his late thirties when he published his first novel, ***The Joke,*** in Prague in 1967. The book traces the fortunes and amours of a young student, Ludvik, after his exasperatingly patriotic girlfriend decides to show the authorities a postcard he had written her as a joke: "Optimism is the opium of the people! A healthy atmosphere stinks of stupidity! Long live Trotsky! Ludvik." As a result of this whimsy, Ludvik finds himself expelled from the Communist Party and the university, and is eventually conscripted to work in the mines for several years.

The appearance of Kundera's acerbically political novel

coincided with—indeed, it was only possible in—the short-lived liberalization of Czech society that has come to be known as the Prague Spring. ***The Joke*** went through three large printings in quick succession and instantly won Kundera a wide and enthusiastic readership in his homeland. It also won him the somewhat less enthusiastic attention of the Communist Party. At the end of August, 1968, Russian troops abruptly occupied Czechoslovakia, putting an end to the Prague Spring and the reformist government of Alexander Dubček. In a bitterly ironic variation on the fate of his character Ludvik, Kundera was relieved of his teaching position at the Prague Film School and deprived of the right to work. ***The Joke*** was banned and removed from public libraries—"erased," as Kundera put it, "from the history of Czech literature." Finally, in 1975, Kundera emigrated to France, where he has since resided.

Kundera first came to the notice of American readers in the mid-Seventies with a collection of short stories, ***Laughable Loves*** (1974), and ***The Farewell Party*** (1976), a novel. Together they earned him a small but devoted following among aficionados of contemporary fiction. But it was not until the publication of ***The Book of Laughter and Forgetting*** in 1980 that Kundera really established himself among the American literary intelligentsia—though, in fact, ***The Book of Laughter and Forgetting*** did not so much *establish* Kundera's reputation here as *enshrine* it; it elevated him to that pantheon of writers whose productions exist more as untouchable objects of admiration than as works susceptible to critical commentary. And Kundera's latest novel, ***The Unbearable Lightness of Being*** (1984), only confirmed his apotheosis. Most reviewers dispensed with criticism altogether and instead vied with one another to concoct suitably handsome words of praise. Not merely "brilliant," "daring," or "provocative," ***The Unbearable Lightness of Being*** was widely held to constitute Kundera's patent of literary immortality, establishing him, in the words of one reviewer, "as the world's greatest living writer."

Now, Kundera is indisputably a writer of enormous talent. Especially at a time when fiction in this country seems caught somewhere between the dreary banalities of Ann Beattie, the quasi-pornographic imaginings of John Hawkes, and the narcissistic obscurities of Donald Barthelme, he appears as a novelist of almost preternatural force and inventiveness. But precisely because Kundera has assumed such eminence, his work deserves more than indiscriminate celebration. Though he has developed a voice that is unmistakably his own, his best work exercises an appeal that can be said to epitomize the *ethos* of contemporary "dissident" fiction: fiercely intellectual, it is charged with a cool, at times almost brutal eroticism and ironic humor, and it is everywhere at pains to declare its fictionality, to call attention to its novelistic status. Thus in coming to appreciate the distinctive appeal of Kundera's fiction—its substance, its vitality, its challenging idiosyncrasies—we may also come to understand one of the most important (if also perhaps one of the most problematic) aspects of contemporary fiction generally.

At the same time, we may discover something about the sensibility of the *audience* for this species of contemporary fiction. For despite its obvious literary sophistication, Kundera's work is also deeply political, drawing heavily on his experience of totalitarianism in an effort to explore the difficult spiritual landscape that his characters populate. Kundera has by no means always affirmed his status as a dissident writer; on the contrary, especially in recent years, he has striven to qualify, even deny, that status at every turn. But it is, I believe, in the political dimension of his work—or, more accurately, in the ambiguous attitude Kundera adopts *toward* the political dimension of his work—that we will find an important source of his tremendous appeal both in this country and in Western Europe.

"The identity of a people or civilization," Kundera wrote in an essay that appeared in the English quarterly *Granta,* "is always reflected and concentrated in what has been created by the mind—in what is known as 'culture.'" Many, perhaps most, of us tend to equate the culture of Czechoslovakia and its Austro-Hungarian neighbors with the culture of Eastern Europe. That we should so blithely cede the cultural as well as the political heritage of these countries no doubt tells us much about the nature and success of the Soviet Union's custodianship there. According to Kundera, though, the defining cultural impulse of that area has its source not in the patrimony of the East but in the spiritual legacy of the West. "What does Europe mean to a Hungarian, a Czech, a Pole?" he asks. "Their nations have always belonged to the part of Europe rooted in Roman Christianity. They have participated in every period of its history. For them, the word 'Europe' does not represent a phenomenon of geography but a spiritual notion synonymous with the word 'West.'"

In proclaiming this cultural affiliation with Western Europe, Kundera underscores his allegiance to the fundamental Enlightenment values of skeptical rationality and individualism—traditional liberal values that he summarized in another essay as "respect for the individual, for his original thought, and for his inviolable private life." It is no secret that these values have come increasingly under siege in modern society, most brutally and systematically in totalitarian regimes, but also, Kundera would insist, in democratic regimes, where the imperatives of mass culture compromise private life and discount genuine individuality. It is of course this latter insistence—that freedom and man's privacy are threatened as much in Western democracies as under Communism—that has won Kundera so many friends on the Left, for whom the defiant, anti-Communist stance of the dissident writer is perfectly acceptable provided that his defiance extends to all expressions of authority, notably to those that provide a haven for his dissidence. But taken in conjunction with his attempt to downplay the frankly political message of his work, Kundera's criticisms of the West highlight ambiguities at the heart of his position—ambiguities that force us to question the good faith and ideological motives of this troubling writer.

Time and again, Kundera has praised the "wisdom of the novel" as a counter to the leveling influence of modern society. In the midst of an environment hostile to private life and the integrity of the individual, the novel appears as a sanctuary where the "precious essence of European individualism is held safe as in a treasure chest." It is thus not surprising that the major thematic concern of Kundera's fiction, from ***The Joke*** through ***The Unbearable Lightness of Being,*** is with the fate of the individual in modern society, especially in modern Communist society.

Of course "the fate of the individual in modern society" is hardly uncharted territory for novelists. But this venerable theme breathes with new life in Kundera's work, in large part because of the adroit way in which he manages to interweave fact and fiction. His characters occupy a stage that is defined half by Kundera's imagination, half by the historical reality of recent Czech history. He tends to work with extremely short chapters and a shifting, episodic narrative that together create a montage of images, story lines, and characterizations. To this end, he has developed a terse, sinewy style, sharply ironical yet urgently engaged. The narrative is constantly interrupted as Kundera steps back to impart a bit of philosophy, autobiography, or psychological conjecture. ***The Unbearable Lightness of Being,*** for example, begins with a reflection on Nietzsche's doctrine of the eternal return—a reflection that itself returns to become one of the book's leitmotifs—and ***The Book of Laughter and Forgetting*** is studded with straightforward factual accounts of historical incidents.

In many ways, ***The Book of Laughter and Forgetting*** is Kundera's most accomplished work to date. With it he perfected his digressive narrative technique, in which themes are stated, developed, transformed, and interwoven more or less on the model of a musical variation—an analogy that Kundera has been fond of invoking when describing his writing. Yet in ***The Book of Laughter and Forgetting,*** Kundera's "variations"—his excursions into philosophy, say, or intellectual history—never strike one as being mere intellectual decorations, inessential to its life as a novel, as they do, at times, in ***The Unbearable Lightness of Being.*** The book follows the melancholy, often overlapping careers and erotic entanglements of several sets of characters as they struggle to salvage some sense of joy and vitality, some sense of themselves as individuals, against the bleak backdrop of present-day Czechoslovakia. Kundera pauses throughout to descant on subjects as diverse as mass psychology, the nature of the novel, and the fate of various heroes of the Czech resistance. In one of two key chapters entitled "The Angels," for example, Kundera suddenly interrupts his story, recalling that

> [Soon] after the Russians occupied my country in 1968, I (like thousands and thousands of other Czechs) lost the privilege of working. No one was allowed to hire me. At about that time some young friends started paying me regular visits. They were so young that the Russians did not have them on their lists yet and they could remain in editorial offices, schools, and film studios. These fine young friends, whom I will never betray, suggested I use their names as a cover for writing radio and television scripts, plays, articles, columns, film treatments—anything to earn a living. I accepted a few of their offers, but most I turned down. I couldn't have gotten to them all, for one thing, and then too it was dangerous. Not for me, for them. The secret police wanted to starve us out, cut off all means of support, force us to capitulate and make public confessions. They kept their eyes out for all the pitiful little escape routes we used to avoid encirclement, and they meted out severe punishments to the friends who gave me their names.

Characteristically, this sober report is sandwiched between two very different and seemingly unrelated narratives, the first installment of a tale about two naïve American schoolgirls at summer school abroad preparing a presentation on Ionesco's *Rhinoceros,* and Kundera's essayistic elaboration of a metaphysics of laughter. His commitment to irony naturally leads him to extol laughter, but he is careful to distinguish two kinds of laughter: "demonic" laughter, which is fundamentally dissenting, lonely, even nihilistic, and "angelic" laughter, which sentimentally rationalizes a world whose contradictions and sufferings it deliberately blinds itself to. It follows that, in Kundera's bestiary, "Devils," though essentially a negative, admonitory force, manifest an heroic skepticism that immunizes them to the hypocrisy of sentimentality; "Angels," on the other hand, acquiesce in illusion and refuse to acknowledge the lie at the heart of the utopia they crave.

What Kundera calls demonic laughter plays an enormously important role in his work. Though his fiction can be as freighted with existential pathos as anything by Sartre or Camus or Kafka, it is nevertheless possessed of a levity and insouciance that make it as entertaining as it is thoughtful. His depiction of the American schoolgirls' report on *Rhinoceros,* for example, crystallizes the book's central themes in a moment of surreal, "demonic" hilarity.

Given the self-consciously playful character of Kundera's novels, it is hardly surprising that he cites Sterne's *Tristram Shandy* and Diderot's *Jacques le fataliste* as crucial inspirations. And while the tone and "feel" of Kundera's fiction is distinctly more modulated—more "linear," one might say—than those rambunctious early novels, their influence can be felt throughout his work, both in its self-consciously digressive narratives and in the ironic humor that Kundera insinuates into even his most stringent philosophical meditations.

Closer to hand, Kundera's humor reminds one even more of the great Austrian novelist Robert Musil, whose sprawling, unfinished masterpiece, *The Man without Qualities,* is perhaps the most profound and certainly the funniest portrait of decaying *fin-de-siècle* Austrian culture we possess. Kundera has not created any character as memorable as Musil's Ulrich—the protagonist of *The Man without Qualities*—nor has he rivaled Musil's scope or incisive social satire; but his fiction bristles with a kindred ironic, highly intellectualized wit.

Kundera also specializes in that brand of emotionally distanced, often farcical, eroticism that has become a hallmark of so much modernist and "postmodernist" fiction. Here again, we can see the influence of the ribald tradition of Sterne and Diderot. Diderot's novel especially is celebrated by Kundera for its "explosion of impertinent freedom without self-censorship, of eroticism without sentimental alibis."

In fact, though, Kundera's depictions of sex are edged with a loneliness and even desperation quite absent from the more playful work of his acknowledged precursors. His fiction abounds in explorations of what we might call intimacy in distress. The erotic lives of his characters become a theater in which a wounded individuality, half capitulating to forces inimical to it, struggles to preserve itself. As Kundera put it in the interview with Philip Roth that appears as the afterword to ***The Book of Laughter and Forgetting,*** "with me everything ends in great erotic scenes. I have the feeling that a scene of physical love generates an extremely sharp light which suddenly reveals the essence of characters and sums up their life situation."

There are dramatic and usually unhappy sexual liaisons throughout Kundera's work, generally centering on his characters' inability to combine love with sexual passion. "Physical love only rarely merges with spiritual love," he concludes sadly in ***The Joke.*** Particularly revealing, I think, are Tomas's reflections on "erotic friendship" in ***The Unbearable Lightness of Being.*** They exhibit a thoroughgoing aestheticism that not only typifies Kundera's treatment of erotic matters but also says a good deal about the underlying sensibility of his work *tout court.*

Like Kierkegaard's aesthete in *Either/Or,* who attempts to defeat boredom by cultivating a systematically arbitrary approach to life, Tomas attempts to establish "a compromise between fear and desire" by steadfastly avoiding any genuine emotional involvement in his relationships with women. He has become a connoisseur of what Kierkegaard called "the rotation method." "To insure that erotic friendship never grew into the aggression of love," Kundera explains, Tomas

> would meet each of his long-term mistresses only at intervals. He considered this method flawless and propagated it among his friends: "The important thing is to abide by the rule of threes. Either you see a woman three times in quick succession and then never again, or you maintain relations over the years but make sure that the rendezvous are at least three weeks apart."
>
> The rule of threes enabled Tomas to keep intact his liaisons with some women while continuing to engage in short-term affairs with many others. He was not always understood.

The problem for Tomas, as again for Kierkegaard's aesthete, is the intractable *reality* of his lovers; once they are gone they assume a pleasing poetic existence that can be enjoyed at will without the endless accommodations that any real relationship involves. "His love for Tereza was beautiful, but it was also tiring: he constantly had to hide things from her, sham, dissemble, make amends, buck her up, calm her down. . . . Now [that she had left him] what was tiring had disappeared and only the beauty remained."

There is of course a large element of satire in Kundera's depiction of Tomas, as there is in most of his depictions of intimate feelings. But satire has authority only to the extent that one can discern a credible alternative to the reality being satirized; otherwise it becomes indistinguishable from what it satirizes. And the truth is that Kundera's own aestheticism, his own rebellion against the reality of what he describes, robs his work of any such alternative.

Kundera suggests that erotic intimacy promises a real, if already threatened, refuge for individuality in the modern world; hence he often insists that his books are essentially "love stories." Yet it must be said that in Kundera's novels sex is generally a rather chilly, dehumanizing event, an exercise that offers precious little refuge. Not to put too fine a point on it, there is something distinctly creepy about his portrayals of intimate relationships. One thinks, for example, of Ludvik's aborted seductions in ***The Joke,*** of the amusing but strikingly passionless orgies in ***The Book of Laughter and Forgetting,*** or of the dismal erotic adventures featured in ***Laughable Loves;*** in every case what we see is sex in the service of power, betrayal, diversion, or despair, only very rarely in the service of affection or genuine intimacy. Not surprisingly, this aspect of Kundera's work has added greatly to its appeal, especially in the academy, where there is an abiding appetite for this sort of lugubrious depiction of sex.

The cumulative—and carefully calculated—effect of Kundera's style is fiction endowed with a sense of great immediacy and directness, with a nimbus, so to speak, of reality. Though we are everywhere reminded that we are reading fiction, in the end such reminders tend to increase rather than diminish our confidence in the authority and truthfulness of the narrator. "It would be senseless for the author to try to convince the reader that his characters once actually lived," Kundera writes of his main characters in ***The Unbearable Lightness of Being.*** "They were not born of a mother's womb; they were born of a stimulating phrase or two or from a basic situation. Tomas was born of the saying *'Einmal ist keinmal'* ('Once is never'). Tereza was born of the rumbling of a stomach." It is all merely fiction, yes, but we somehow feel that in admitting this the author is taking us into a deeper confidence, preparing us for some important truth.

By self-consciously warping the border between fact and fiction, Kundera's work manifests a characteristically modernist preoccupation with the relation between art and truth, between art and reality. (pp. 5-10)

[Kundera] would seem to ask whether the beautiful illusions that art produces are to be taken seriously; certainly, his fiction adopts a posture of questioning their apparent self-sufficiency. He continually intrudes images of all that is problematic, insecure, unharmonious about daily life into the untroubled kingdom within which art reigns supreme. But unlike Mann, Kundera does not use the conventions of art to question our faith in art's illusions; rather, he skillfully imports *gestures* of reality in order to give his fiction an aura of truth and critical weightiness.

Probably the central critical element in Kundera's work is his attack on sentimentality. This takes various forms, and is evident throughout his writing, in his essays as well

"By self-consciously warping the border between fact and fiction, Kundera's work manifests a characteristically modernist preoccupation with the relation between art and truth, between art and reality."

as his novels. Everywhere there is a deep suspicion of sentimentality, of feeling unscrutinized by doubt. Thus he pokes fun at "the obscure depths," the "noisy and empty sentimentality of the 'Slavic Soul.' " And in his introduction to ***Jacques and His Master,*** he criticizes Dostoevsky's novels for creating a "*climate* . . . where feelings are promoted to the rank of value and of truth."

For Kundera, the battle against sentimentality is at the same time a battle against forgetting. "The struggle of man against power," we read at the beginning of ***The Book of Laughter and Forgetting,*** "is the struggle of memory against forgetting." In Kundera's terms, the struggle of memory against forgetting is man's struggle against whatever social or psychological forces would deny the continuity and individuality of his personal history. Hence the attack on sentimentality is only the other side of his defense of individualism. For it is just this—the lonely and irreducible *privateness* of experience—that sentimentality promises to dissolve. The essential appeal of the sentimental is precisely that it relieves one of the burden of individuality and the responsibilities of adult experience. As the literary critic Northrop Frye observed, sentimentality "resists, as a child would do, the inexorable advance of all experience in time, which it tries to arrest by nostalgia. . . . Sentimentality is the subjective equivalent of the mob's stock response to mood."

It is a version of sentimentality that Kundera explores in ***The Book of Laughter and Forgetting*** under the name of circle dancing. "Circle dancing" is his metaphor for the intoxicating lure of the group, the mob, what Frye calls the stock response. Kundera pictures his characters joining together to make a circle. They "take two steps in place, one step forward, lift first one leg and then the other. . . . I think I understand them. They feel that the circle they describe on the ground is a magic circle binding them into a ring. Their hearts are overflowing with an intense feeling of innocence. . . . Circle dancing is magic." This magic is the spell cast by the dream of a paradise where distinctions vanish and all men are brothers. In this sense "paradise" tokens not the fulfillment but the denial of the human condition. "The longing for Paradise," as Kundera put it, "is man's longing not to be man."

Underscoring the political dimension of circle dancing, Kundera confesses that in 1948, after the Communists had taken power in Czechoslovakia, he also "danced in a ring," until he was expelled from the Party and "had to leave the circle." It was then, he tells us, that he became aware of the "magic" qualities of the circle, a magic that gives weight to his claim that "totalitarianism is not only hell, but also the dream of paradise." (pp. 10-11)

What Kundera dramatizes as circle dancing in ***The Book of Laughter and Forgetting*** he analyzes as "kitsch" in ***The Unbearable Lightness of Being*** and in several occasional essays. While he points out that the term has its origin in Munich art circles in the nineteenth century, for Kundera "kitsch" refers not simply to a species of bad art but to the deliberate sentimentalization of reality. As Kundera notes, his discussion of kitsch is deeply indebted to the writings of the German novelist and essayist Hermann Broch. Following Broch, he views kitsch not so much as an aesthetic as an ethical or metaphysical category. What we generally think of as kitsch art is for Kundera merely one, rather minor, product of kitsch. Like circle dancing, kitsch is an instrument of forgetting. It offers man an escape from the burden of individuality. "Kitsch," he wrote in one essay, "is the translation of the stupidity of received ideas into the language of beauty and feeling." In ***The Unbearable Lightness of Being,*** he remarks that kitsch has its source in the "*categorical agreement with being,*" meaning that kitsch involves what he would call an "angelic" blindness to everything problematic and unaccommodating about experience. Ultimately, the ambition of kitsch is to set up "a folding screen to curtain off death."

For Kundera, as for Broch before him, kitsch appears as a universal human temptation. "No matter how we scorn it," he writes, "kitsch is an integral part of the human condition." In this sense, kitsch bears witness to man's desire to secure himself against the incursions of a reality that can never be adequately mastered. The problem with Kundera's analysis, however, is that by so expanding the meaning of kitsch, he threatens to empty it of critical content. It may be that kitsch cannot be understood as a *purely* aesthetic category; the aura of moral disapproval that it carries with it suggests that this is the case. But what does it mean, for example, when Kundera asserts that "we can regard the gulag as a septic tank used by totalitarian kitsch to dispose of its refuse"? There is no doubt that totalitarianism can make effective use of kitsch; but to speak of "totalitarian kitsch" is to trivialize totalitarianism by assimilating it to a category that has its home in aesthetics; it is in effect to poeticize totalitarianism. To say, with Kundera, that "kitsch is the aesthetic ideal of all politicians and all political parties and movements" is to elide just those differences among political parties and movements that really matter. Similarly, when he has a character in ***The Unbearable Lightness of Being*** compare the sentimental response of an American senator watching children playing on the grass to "the smile Communist statesmen beamed from the height of their reviewing stand to the identically smiling citizens in the parade below," he ignores the fact that what matters here is not so much the kitschy sentiment as the uses to which it is put.

The great appeal—and great danger—of concepts like kitsch is that they invite one to discount the real differences among things in the name of a putatively deeper, more essential unity—a unity, however, that enjoys merely a conceptual existence. They thus allow one to maintain a pose of critical distance without the inconvenience of having to make the hard choices that genuine criticism involves. And while there is no doubt that Kundera brings considerable insight—not to mention cleverness—to his explorations of sentimentality, circle dancing, and kitsch, he also indulges in a lamentable tendency to aestheticize these concepts, to use them to disarm the very distinctions they were meant to illuminate.

Kundera's response to this objection would be simply that, as a novelist, he is not in the business of taking positions. "Now, not only is the novelist nobody's spokesman," as he put it in one essay, "but I would go so far as to say he is not even the spokesman for his own ideas." He goes so far, in fact, as to insist that we view his work as little more than an ironic game, as writing "on the level of hypothesis." This is evident, for example, in his objection to being regarded as a political writer. Admitting that he detests Communist regimes, he hastens to add that "I detest them as a citizen: as a writer I don't say what I say in order to denounce a regime." A political reading of his work, he suggested in one interview, is "a bad reading." Even the label "dissident writer" annoys him because it imports a political terminology that he claims to be "allergic" to. Again, in the 1982 preface that he contributed to ***The Joke,*** Kundera recalled that "When in 1980, during a television panel discussion devoted to my works, someone called ***The Joke*** 'a major indictment of Stalinism,' I was quick to interject, 'Spare me your Stalinism, please. ***The Joke*** is a love story' "—this in a book whose entire psychology is unintelligible without the assumption of such an indictment.

Of course, there is an important sense in which Kundera is right: fiction does exist "on the level of hypothesis," not on the level of fact; novels are not position papers. But there is something deeply disingenuous about appeals to the hypothetical or gamelike character of fiction when those appeals are meant to mask or deny the very real political content of one's work. And this, unfortunately, is the effect of Kundera's rhetoric. For like so many dissident writers, Kundera, though he embraces Western culture and Western freedom, maintains a fundamentally equivocal attitude toward the West. True, as he would be the first to point out, there is much to bemoan about the aggressive superficiality of Western mass culture and the tasteless intrusions of the media into our private lives. But it is one thing to criticize these cultural failings, quite another to pretend that they are in any relevant sense cognate with the evil of totalitarianism—to pretend, that is, that they are somehow merely different versions of the same spiritual malaise.

In fact, though, in statement after statement this is precisely the posture that Kundera has adopted. In an interview with Philip Roth that appeared in *The Village Voice,* for example, Kundera was asked if he thought private or intimate life were less threatened in the West than under Communism. "The evolution of the modern world is hostile to intimate life everywhere," he replied. Indeed,

> [in] countries with Communist regimes there's an advantage: we can see clearly what's bad and what's good—if the police tape your private talks, everybody knows that's bad. But in Italy when a photographer lurks around to photograph the face of the mother of a murdered child or the agony of a drowning man, we don't call this a violation of intimacy but freedom of the press.

The implication is clearly that one's privacy and intimate life are just as much in jeopardy in a Western democracy as they are under Communism—perhaps more insidiously in jeopardy in a democracy, for in a Communist society one at least knows where one stands and there is no attempt to glorify shallow curiosity in the name of freedom of the press. No matter that one's writing, one's livelihood, one's very life are at stake in one society where in another one is coddled and showered with acclaim—"essentially" the societies must be made to seem two sides of the same coin. Such a pretense is possible only if one substitutes a thoroughly intellectualized—perhaps one should say "kitschified"—view of the world for the sharper, if less Romantic, discriminations of lived experience. The habits of the media in the West often border on obscenity; but to suggest that the intrusiveness of an Italian news photographer is somehow comparable with the brutality of totalitarianism is absurd. The former may consign one to the front page of a noxious tabloid; the latter abandons one to the cellars of the secret police.

In effect, Kundera wants to have it both ways: he wants both the freedom of fiction and the authority of historical fact; he wants, that is, the cachet of being a dissident writer without the uncomfortably definite political commitments that that status brings with it. Instead, he strives to maintain a completely ironical view of the world, a view that would exempt him from any definite commitment—a view that Friedrich Schlegel, the great theorist of Romantic irony, aptly dubbed "transcendental buffoonery." Thus Kundera describes the "basic event" of ***The Book of Laughter and Forgetting*** as "the story of totalitarianism, which deprives people of memory and thus retools them into a nation of children," and yet still insists that "no novel worthy of the name takes the world seriously." But how can a novel recount "the story of totalitarianism" and *not* take the world seriously? No one would suggest that Kundera's writing should be reduced to its political content; but to dismiss that content as part of a "game," as incidental embellishment or atmosphere to what is really a "love story," "*merely* a novel," is to ignore the element that, more than any other, grants it its authority and weight.

Near the end of his essay "Writing," W. H. Auden remarked that "In so far as poetry, or any other of the arts, can be said to have an ulterior purpose, it is, by telling the truth, to disenchant and disintoxicate." In a way, Kundera would seem to agree with Auden's deeply anti-Romantic sentiment. Thus he extols the novel as an ally of individuality—this is its point, its "ulterior purpose": to salvage some remnant of individuality in an age when it is threatened by the equalizing pressures of mass media, sentimentality, and totalitarianism. Like Auden, Kundera champions art as a refuge of the critical, ironic, questioning spirit, as a bulwark against the illusions and intoxicating certainties of kitsch, the forgetfulness of "circle dancing."

Yet in the end the ambiguities of Kundera's position tend to cut the other way. For by insisting on the purely novelistic status of his work—by denying that a large measure of its authority comes precisely from its "seriousness" and accurate reflection of social and psychological realities—Kundera brews an intoxicating potion of his own. Indeed, it is all the more powerful for the whiff, the *suggestion* of truth and reality that it purveys. In this context, we should remind ourselves that criticisms of kitsch, too, can have their kitschy appeal. And it is here, perhaps, that we can witness most clearly the essential ambiguities of Milan Kundera—ambiguities that are not, alas, the inexhaustible ambiguities of human nature but the meaner, more predictable ambiguities of a writer struggling to maintain a predefined image of himself as ideologically correct. (pp. 11-13)

Roger Kimball, "The Ambiguities of Milan Kundera," in The New Criterion, *Vol. IV, No. 5, January, 1986, pp. 5-13.*

Anthony Lane

When I opened [***Life Is Elsewhere***] and read the words 'Part Three: The Poet Masturbates', I thought that a copy of *Low Life* had been sent by mistake. Would that it were so; for whereas Jeffrey Bernard can review the progress of his adult experience with a calm and alcoholic mind, Mr Kundera (or rather M. Kundera, for he is now a French citizen) presents us brightly with one of his early works, and begs no forgiveness. It was his second novel, and the translation is being published [in Great Britain] for the first time; depending on your point of view, it displays either the youthful exercisings of genius or the first, ominous stirring of all the excesses to come. Whatever the case, Kundera the young stylist was plainly up to the same sort of thing as the poet knuckles down to in Part Three.

The poet in question is Jaromil, a proud, unpleasant lad with an adoring mother and an ability to rhyme. He grows up with an increasing devotion both to his art and to the communist Czech state in which he lives, hoping to connect the two. He discovers girls and, despite maternal disapproval, manages to arrange the odd session of rumpy-pumpy. In a grand gesture to the state, and as a paradigm of aesthetic control, he informs on his girlfriend to the police; they get the girl, he gets pneumonia, and that's enough of him. M. Kundera stretches this out to 300 pages by adding various ruminative chunks, blocks of sample bad verse and an overloaded dream-passage. It is as pointless as most modern dream-prose (sunsets, 'as beautiful as the death of a policeman'), and reads like Herman Hesse choreographed by Ben Travers. The intention is to provide a model of the creative mind, 'crossing from one dream into another' as poets are supposed to do. It must be tough, being a poet.

M. Kundera's intentions, here as elsewhere, are not that hard to spot, for he is not the kind to hold them close to his chest; indeed, his novels are not so much like card-tricks as like the patient explanation of card-tricks, with all the ostentation and none of the surprise. When writers like Salman Rushdie and Philip Roth praise his cleverness, they risk playing straight into his self-congratulation; Rushdie relies on much the same formula of studied absurdities, and of a continual resort to the 'magical' properties of the text. Nabokov, to whom Kundera bears obvious affiliations, had no such desire to play the critic to himself; his attention was on the delivery of good prose in the service of accurate perception, and the pitch of his phrasing was more finely judged than anything Kundera (or Rushdie) is likely to achieve. Moreover, he either wrote in English or made his own translations; Kundera relies on someone else, whom he praises as 'a true artist among translators', as if he were Dryden or Marlowe, but who in fact produces little more than a flat surface of English prose, with odd moments of infelicity sticking through: 'Mother love stamps the forehead of boys with a stigma that repels the friendship of buddies . . . I hate your lukewarmness . . . how do you judge a derriere?' How indeed?

With so little good writing to get in their way, novels in translation, as Martin Amis has noted, are free to hand out 'tips on living' to the reader. ***Life Is Elsewhere*** is full of such tips, not merely on how to give poetry readings (thus yielding the best scene in the book), or to spy on maids in the bath, but on the risks and charms of 'the lyric attitude', which Kundera's own postscript names as 'one of the basic categories of human existence'. But an attitude is not a category, and for all the chops and changes in the book's technique, which I suspect would in other authors turn out more subtly as simple matters of viewpoint, it is beset by a love of the categorical, untempered by passing wit: 'Tenderness is fear of maturity . . . the shimmering essence of flame is an image of thought.' Such loudmouth prose is not sufficiently relieved by the alleged satirical purposes in hand; in attempting to deflate poetic pride, to trace its political likeness and expose its consequences, M. Kundera falls foul of exactly that intense solemnity which first inflates it.

This is a temptation, I think, particularly infectious to those who have suffered artistic oppression; they feel obliged to react in kind, and their work, as a result, grows too intent on cultural significance, and tends to show the strain. A way with words, for them, is forced to become a way of life. Such threatened literature is often brave, and entirely honourable, but it is not necessarily good literature; 'a novel has more freedom' than a man, according to Kundera, but his natural envy of its powers should not lead him to abuse that freedom in quite the way he does. If, as he has said, Czechoslovakia is 'sinking under the weight of history', then his novels, too (not only this early one), seem to sink under the weight of their assumed responsibility towards history, never daring to think that one might, even for a moment or for the sake of art, turn from it without shame. (pp. 38-9)

Anthony Lane, "Weighed Down by History," in The Spectator, *Vol. 257, No. 8263, November 22, 1986, pp. 38-9.*

Karl Miller

Kundera has become a common name in the conversation of Western readers. . . . The free world may like him both for having been, and for having ceased to be, a communist of a sort, and for the freedoms he seeks in matters of literary form, for the modern inventiveness and manipulation of the literary games he plays, games that nonetheless commemorate, as he acknowledges, Cervantes, Sterne and Diderot, and for the sexual games which he plays in an age when, as he once put it, sexuality has ceased to be taboo. We like him for being into free speech and free love, and for what he has to say about convergences of the two, and about the enmity which revolution and its regimes may bear to both. The West has been grateful to Kundera, extravagantly so at times: there's been an impulse to beat itself with his buoyant fictions. Heads have been turned, and have begun to swim, amid the flow of invention, delivered in works which have been Englished in rapid succession and which are not always easy to tell apart. Which is the one that has *litost*—a form of self-pity—and which is the one that has 'unbearable lightness of being'? Which of these two conceptions, for that matter, we may even sometimes wonder, is which? His fertility, narrative gift, gift for experiments and impromptus, are such as to bewilder the attempt to form a judgment of any particular work. Not that he can mind that.

What he does mind—and what even the most arbitrary-seeming, the most ludic, of his ironic and erotic diversions and excursions show that he minds—is the regime that came to power in his native country after the revolution of 1948. Many of his most memorable literary effects attest to this. In ***The Unbearable Lightness of Being*** the Czech exile Sabina disturbs her French friends by being unable to last out a parade held to protest against the Soviet invasion of Czechoslovakia in 1968: 'She would have liked to tell them that behind Communism, Fascism, behind all occupations and invasions lurks a more basic, pervasive evil and that the image of that evil was a parade of people marching by with raised fists and shouting identical syllables in unison.' The British reader, who has been spared the degree of suffering which enters the books of Kundera . . . , where a joke, or no joke, or nothing whatever, can sequester you for years from the people you grew up with, is in a position, for all that, to know what Sabina means here. The British reader has only to listen to the sounds that protest makes in his own streets, to the cruel, brutal voices that bellow over loudhailers about injustice and the disadvantaged.

In thinking about what Stalinism brought to his country, Kundera thinks of the support which this despotism has received from the writers of his country, and of other countries. Literature, with its store of memories, is suspected by the state: and yet the state is served by certain writers. In books and interviews he has reminded the world that the French Surrealist poet Aragon, having praised Kundera's wonderful novel ***The Joke*** in 1968, and having fulminated against the Soviet invasion of Czechoslovakia—his legs would 'refuse' to take him to Russia any more—made it to Moscow four years later; and that another French poet, Eluard, abandoned his Prague friend, the Surrealist Kalandra, to the executioner.

> Nowadays, people all over the world unequivocally reject the idea of gulags, yet they are still willing to let themselves be hypnotised by totalitarian poesy and to march to new gulags to the tune of the same lyrical song piped by Eluard when he soared over Prague like the great archangel of the lyre, while the smoke of Kalandra's body rose to the sky from the crematory chimney.

Tyranny is a force which locks writers up and which lyrical writers may assist.

Eluard's soaring 'lyricism' helped to perpetuate a tyranny, and is the kind of thing which led Kundera to entitle this early novel of his *The Lyric Age:* but then his publishers got him to change the name [to ***Life Is Elsewhere***]. The novel was finished in 1969 and was published in America in 1974, translated by Peter Kussi, who has now revised his translation. The provisional title referred to the life-span of Jaromil, who dies young, as lyric poets will, but also to the enforced, mass-produced, writer-proclaimed revolutionary ardours which ensued in 1948. At the outset, Jaromil's lyricism is a Modern affair in which biological compulsion and biographical reference—peeps at the maid Magda in her bath, for instance—are enveloped and disguised in a poetry which his doting and self-pitying mother finds inscrutable. His first loves . . . prove to be his last, but prove as engrossing to him as the lyrics in which his emotional development is encoded.

Jaromil is not so much a character as a type, and is not unlike the Shelleyan poet in Shaw's *Candida,* Eugene Marchbanks. Aerial creatures, these, ineffectual angels. Eugene, 'so uncommon as to be almost unearthly', wants to go 'up into the sky'. His brow is 'lined with pity'. He speaks with 'lyric rapture'. But he is all right when you get to know him. 'Don't say that Jaromil is a bad poet!' Kundera's Postscript implores. He is a 'sensitive young man'—a monster too, but the same monster is in you and me. And in Shelley, and Rimbaud, and Hugo. Jaromil and his mother are portrayed, we learn from the Postscript, quite without any satirical intention. In that respect, Kundera could have fooled the present reviewer: but I do see that it belongs to the point of it all that the uncommon Jaromil should be thought humanly representative.

By a painter who befriends him, and who sleeps for a while with his mother, Jaromil, already self-perceived as exceptional, original, is introduced to modern art, which 'had not yet become the shopworn property of the bourgeois masses and retained the fascinating aura of a sect, a magical exclusivity fascinating to childhood—an age always daydreaming about the romanticism of secret societies, fraternities and tribes'. Soon he is writing modern poems. 'This verse described a boy who had been trembling in front of the bathroom door, but at the same time this boy was swallowed up by the verse; it surmounted and survived him. *Alas, my aquatic love,* said another line, and Jaromil knew that the aquatic love was Magda; but he also knew that nobody else could find her in that line . . . ' These lines are short and do not rhyme. They are free. Magda was lost in a poem which was 'as independent and unintelligible as reality itself. Reality does not discuss, it simply *is.* The independence of the poem provided Jaromil with a marvellous world of concealment, the possibility of a *second* existence.'

Much later we read: Everything seemed to indicate that

Jaromil's enormous yearning for newness (the religion of the New) was only the disguised longing of a virginal youth for the unimaginable experience of the sex act. When he first reached the blissful shore of the redhead's body, a peculiar idea occurred to him: he now knew at last what it meant to be absolutely modern; it meant to lie on the shore of the redhead's body. By now he has also reached 'the realm of real life'—by which he 'understood a whirling world of parading throngs, physical love and revolutionary slogans'. It turns out that real life rhymes, that the revolution wishes its poetry to do so. There is a magical power in rhyme and rhythm. 'Can a revolution dispense with repeated affirmation of the new order? Can a revolution dispense with rhyme?' By now free verse has been exposed as decadent, and modern art as the shop-worn property of the bourgeois masses.

Lyricism, then, is the poetry which sings along with the triumph of the proletariat, and with the repressions which accompany its triumph. What is required is a poetry which does not analyse or criticise, and is suitable for throngs and parades, where the self-portraits of the lyric author can thus be displayed like placards. Lyricism is inexperience, and it is the desire for glory. Such poems 'need not be stimulated by real-life events' such as the plight of the Marseilles dockworkers, which has effaced the sight—darkly limned in Jaromil's juvenilia—of Magda in her bath. Meanwhile the poet who displays his ignorant, indifferent self-portrait is hoping for applause, and this is more than ever the case in the new world of revolution, which rings with applause, and with blame.

By the end of the novel Jaromil has forsworn his artist friend, who is under the ban of the regime and compelled to paint by candlelight: 'The whole world of his pictures has been dead for years. Real life is elsewhere!' We are told that these last four words are Rimbaud's and the Surrealist André Breton's and that in 1968 they were a slogan of the protesting Sorbonne students. They are words that can be made to mean different things, and perhaps they are applicable as such to the story of Jaromil's poetic progress from private to public, which can also be recognised as a simultaneity of the two, based on an enduring self-engrossment. Kundera asks us to join together two things that are often kept apart: lyrical effusions and public poetry. The quoted words point back to the privileged second existence which poetry had once promised Jaromil—a meaning that can now appear to have been reversed, with the claim that real life resides in a revolutionary solidarity. Just before this snarl of his about real life, Jaromil has betrayed his redhead to the police, by swallowing a lying excuse of hers concerning a subversive brother.

The poets Czeslaw Milosz and Donald Davie are bothered by the insufficiency and irresponsibility of the lyric genre. . . . It could be felt that Kundera goes further, in denouncing the lyric, and fares worse. The lyricism that sells out to a state-ordained reality and solidarity is not the only lyricism we know, and it is the opposite of much of what we know by that name. Youthful as some of them are, the lyrics of Heaney do not embody the genius of inexperience, whatever some of Shelley's may do. In other words, Kundera's novel isolates certain tendencies in the behaviour of poets (and others) in order to prosecute an attack on Stalinist Czechoslovakia. It will be clear to most people here that the attack is deserved, and that writers sold out. Jaromil's adventures, moreover, are shrewdly observed. Lyricism is indeed very like this description of it. Poetry has often been a form of self-pity and a means of self-advancement, and it has often pretended otherwise: Kundera's book rumbles such pretence, as in the comedy he stages of an embassy of poets to a college of policemen and a debate there over the aesthetic of the socialist love-poem. But he does all this at the cost of suspending a due sense of the tendency there has also been for poets to see further than their noses, and to speak out, and to go to the wall for it. His Postcript evokes the aim of a white-coated Doctor Kundera 'to solve an aesthetic problem: how to write a novel which would be a "critique of poetry" and yet at the same time would itself be poetry'. (p.10)

Karl Miller, "Ariel Goes to the Police," in London Review of Books, *Vol. 8, No. 21, December 4, 1986, pp. 10, 12.*

Francois Ricard

Despite its innocent appearance, Milan Kundera's work is one of the most *demanding* we have been given to read today, and I use the word *demanding* in its most radical sense, to mean that this work presents a challenge to the mind and the heart that is extremely difficult to take up. To accept it, to consent truly to it is to risk being swept much further away than one had at first believed, to the very limit of consciousness, to that "ravaged galaxy" where the hero of ***The Joke*** finds himself at the end of the novel.

This is why critics don't know how right they are when they use the word "subversive" to describe Kundera's novels. But they rarely say just how total that subversion is, and for good reason. Kundera's work, unlike that of other, clearly identified "subversives" (like Artaud, Bataille or Duvert), never states that it is subversive, does not propose a theory of subversion or make a lot of noise. Subversive it is, but simply, softly, insidiously one might say, yet deeply and without remission.

Outwardly, Kundera's novels and stories are relatively inoffensive: they most often display a rather traditional form, with easily located settings, well-identified characters, realistic time frame and plot, and, especially, simple writing, much like the spare and rigorous writing of the eighteenth century; in any case, they are far from those "textual explosions" (often purely textual, in fact) to which the new academicism of the novel has *accustomed* us in the last fifteen or twenty years. Theoretically, at least, it would be possible to read ***The Joke, Life Is Elsewhere, The Farewell Party,*** or the novellas that make up ***Laughable Loves*** simply as good stories—well constructed, captivating, interesting and amusing, but no more. But such a "superficiality" did not come over us as we were reading, or if, while reading, the awareness that we found ourselves confronted with a deceptive, trumped-up tale suddenly left us. But the reader can not escape this awareness and perplexity. Early on his innocence becomes untenable and he must begin to read differently, authentically, that is, with suspicion and deep uncertainty. What he has "before his eyes" is soon no longer a story, but the simulacrum of a story; characters are characters no more, but shadows; the resort town is no longer a watering hole, but a kind of cardboard stage, lighted by a paper moon, and crossed by costumed extras who no longer know in which play they are acting; and finally, I, the reader, am no longer someone reading, but one *pretending* to read, for suspicion has reached my identity, and undermines me completely. The masks do not fall: they simply allow themselves to be seen for masks, which may be worse, as Jaroslav realizes in ***The Joke*** when he begins to see not the King's face, but the veil that hides it from his view.

This subversion in a "minor key," one might say, is far more effective than straight forward assault. Kundera does not bring the world crashing down, he undoes it piece by piece, methodically and noiselessly, like an undercover agent. In the end nothing collapses, no ruins strew the soil, no explosion is heard, things seem in no way changed; rather, they seem emptied, false, fragile, struck by a definitive unreality. But this subtlety and lightness, though they increase the subversion's effectiveness, are what make the subversion at times nearly imperceptible to the reader in a hurry, even if, despite himself, he can not help but be secretly shaken.

But even more than an anodine appearance, what characterizes Kundera's subversive spirit, what makes it so demanding, even as it explains why that spirit has been so poorly understood, is its *radicalism,* the negativity it rests upon and towards which it draws the reader being to some extent nearly intolerable: so much so that recuperation takes over, which ultimately is nothing more than the refusal to follow truly and to the very limit the call of a work.

This is what happens, for example, in political "recuperation." In its good conscience, the West has recently created *dissidence:* a comfortable category in which to place writers from the socialist block. Its manifestations are by now well-known: political persecution, the inability to publish (except in "samizdat"), exile, and especially the fact, for a writer, of holding political positions other than those of the regime in place in his country. Now it happens that most of these characteristics apply to Kundera. So he too has been placed in the dissident category, to wit, writers who denounce Soviet Terror and take up the defense of their people against the military and ideological invasion of Czechoslovakia. This is obviously true. But only at one level, the level where those who give Kundera's novels only a historico-politico-ideological reading are stuck. This in fact is what I call "recuperation." Let me explain.

It is correct to see, as most do, a complete and striking picture—all the more striking for being presented in what I would call the private epic mode—of Czech political history from the thirties to the end of the Prague Spring, not only in ***The Joke,*** but also in ***Life Is Elsewhere, The Farewell Party,*** and even in parts of ***Laughable Loves.*** The "fall" of Ludvik Jahn in a sense really does represent the disillusion of an entire generation, of an entire people who, having believed in the 1948 Prague coup, then waited twenty years to be able to laugh about it for a moment only to have to fall instantly silent again. And in that sense, it is absolutely true that Kundera's writing constitutes one of the most virulent denunciations of Stalinism, whose mechanism it pitilessly undoes, and whose immense trickery it reveals.

But why stop at that? One must go on, one must dare go further to see that if Kundera is able to cast on the politics and history of his country his penetrating gaze, it is of course because he lived through it all, and was himself involved as both victim and opponent; but also, perhaps more significantly, because at some time, or at some point of thought, he made a radical move away from it, he became absolutely detached, a bit like Ludvik, the hero of ***The Joke,*** who only truly knows his own life from the moment he literally ceases to believe in it. Kundera is often seen as a political writer (the common fate of "dissidents"), and his novels read as pro-Dubcek, anti-Soviet, anti-C.C.P. [Czech Communist Party] manifestos, when in fact they are something else entirely. For it is all politics, not just left or right regimes, it is political reality itself that Kundera's work impugns. "Political subversion" is global; it does not only attack one or another incarnation but the idea itself, the *idol* of politics, as Valery, whom Kundera resembles in more ways than one, might have said. Kundera's scrutiny of history and politics is what it is only because he does not treat either *seriously,* but with a *distance* that has nothing to do with scientific or historical "objectivity," nor with the analysis of an opposition militant (these comprise a purely tactical distance). It is an absolute, unconditional distance, that of *unbelief,* from which, unlike the others, there is no return. "What if history were joking?" wonders Ludvik. This question, which neither historian nor politician—even opposition politician—can ask, for it would void them, contains its own answer. It is with this question that inspires it and establishes its lucidity that Kundera's writing is quite the equivalent and the continuation of Jaroslav Hasek's work, as yet so poorly known to us. Written forty years earlier, it is the most *authentic* picture of Austro-Hungarian Czechoslovakia, quite as Kundera's work provides an authentic picture of Czechoslovakia today. But again, *picture* does not go far enough: what Kundera provides is a radical demystification, an immense burst of laughter, such as only literature can aim at politics or history in order to strip them pitilessly naked, to reduce them to *nothing,* which is not at all an attempt to escape them, but rather to penetrate them, to profoundly defuse them, and to denounce their horrors, all the more scandalous for no longer having *any* justification beyond the aberrant discourse in which they clothe themselves. In other words, if Kundera's novels are to a great extent a faithful portrait of contemporary political history, it is because they view this history, any history, as nothing more than an unconscious fiction, a monumental, derisory tragicomedy, a bubble that perhaps only literature can *burst.*

Not to go that far, to consider Kundera's novels simply as works of political polemic is thus, in fact, to recuperate them. Just as, to change contexts without really changing, to see only a satire of "bad poetry" in ***Life Is Elsewhere*** is to recuperate the novel. Once again, this is a kind of stopping midway, of not following the novel's aim to the very end, perhaps because, as I have suggested, there is something too demanding and almost unbearable in that end. For the object of criticism (of "subversion"), in this case, is not "bad" poetry, but indeed, it must be said, all poetry, lyricism of any kind.

But the reader does not reach this conclusion painlessly, that is, without having to surmount extremely stubborn resistance that, deep within, keeps him from confronting it. At first everything is well, and the novel provokes good-hearted laughter. Jaromil seems ridiculous to me right away; I see in him, in the overprotected child, then in the pimply adolescent, the caricature of the poet, nothing else, and I am aware only of the deformation, of the *perversion* of poetry through him. I laugh at this bad poet who thinks himself a genius, I laugh *serenely,* because I can tell myself that Jaromil is not me, and that I am not him, that "true" poetry escapes him, and thus that my *confidence* is safe. But then, quickly, if I continue to read (to *really* read), my laughter begins to sound hollow, and Jaromil begins to seem dangerously like me, especially in the sincere faith he places in Rimbaud, Lermontov, Lautreamont, Mayakovski, Rilke, in all those in whom I too, as they say, have found accommodation, and about whom I can consequently no longer laugh in the same way, with the same serenity. The fool who moments ago played on stage before me has now come down into the audience to sit beside me, to enter me so that soon I can no longer keep my distance from Jaromil; and if I want to or am able to continue laughing, little by little I must turn the laughter against myself. I am drawn from Jaromil's otherworldliness to my own, towards my own lyrical side, towards the part of me that revels in poetry: I am essentially drawn to my own innocence. Caricature has become a mirror.

So I try to cling to a final straw: at least, I tell myself, Jaromil's poetry is pretentious; in thinking himself a poet he is "objectively" wrong. But is this really the case? Let us "honestly" reread Jaromil's poetry, or detach it from the novel. Is it really poor poetry? Am I not the one who is wrong, who latches on to the supposed poverty of his verse to protect myself and my conscience from the irony aimed at them? In fact, Jaromil's poetry has as much *worth* as any other, his talent is *authentic*—and if I deny him that authenticity, if I refuse to acknowledge his poetry its worth, isn't it so as to preserve intact my own faith in the "authenticity" and the "worth" of poetry? Isn't it only because I refuse to make this terrible yet simple acknowledgment: that poetry, all poetry, all poetic thought is a hoax? Or rather a *trap,* and one of the most fearful of all?

Let's say this is so. It is extremely difficult to follow the novel's course to this point (to this scandal), and many havens on the way can make me turn away or *warn me off.* But if I avoid the safe havens, the "subversion" to which I am led is of the most radical kind, for it forces me to question the very means by which I thought myself able to be free of the political comedies and jokes of the world; to question the very thing that, once all the rest was deemed unreal, and all the masks revealed, seemed to be the naked face of reality. Now that mooring itself slips away, and I am irremediably sent back to a rondo of masks that will not be undone.

Thus, with *Don Quixote* and *Madame Bovary,* ***Life Is Elsewhere*** is perhaps the harshest work ever written against poetry: Poetry as the privileged space of affirmation, intoxication and "authenticity." Poetry as God's last lair. Let people read this novel as a satire on bad verse if they wish; it is an excellent defense against what is a far more radical undertaking: the destruction of the last ramparts of innocence.

But what is there beyond innocence? What is there beyond poetry? Nothing. Or rather, this beyond is no more than a below. Beyond poetry, as below it, prose reigns, that is, uncertainty, approximation, disparity, play, parody, the incongruity between the body and soul or between words and things, masquerade, error—in a word: Satan, God's double; but, as in a mirror, a reverse double, degraded, false, ironic, absurd; a double trying to pass for the model, who succeeds more often than not, and for that reason never stops his mocking. In which case the only way for me to avoid being had is to do the mocking myself.

To read Kundera is then to adopt Satan's point of view on politics and history, on poetry and love, and in a general way on all knowledge. And it is really for this reason that Kundera's work is not only pure subversion, but also pure literature. For it offers no knowledge except that of the relativity, and I would almost say the theatricality, of all knowledge, even the knowledge of poetry and dreams. It affirms nothing unless it is the inadequacy and therefore the impertinence of all affirmation. It demonstrates nothing except the eternal and derisory empire of accident and error. In short, it brings me back to my first *awareness,* which no ideology, no science can tolerate nor ever recover, the awareness that all reality is mixed up with unreality, that in all order a still deeper disorder subsists, and that I am myself other and less than myself. Which, in the last analysis, deserves no more than a burst of laughter, but deserves it fully.

All Kundera's heroes, whether Ludvik or Jaroslav (***The Joke***), or Jakub (***The Farewell Party***), the "forty year older" (***Life Is Elsewhere***), the assistant (**"No One Will Laugh"**) or Edward (**"Edward and God"**), have lived, suffered, loved, and aged only to arrive inevitably at the conclusion that in living, suffering, loving they have never in truth (in truth?) done anything but take themselves for somebody else, and especially take the world for what it should perhaps have been, but isn't: God's creation. In all its simplicity, this conclusion is the ultimate subversion, the one that in the reader meets with the greatest resistance, for it is this resistance that makes him what he is: an executioner disguised as a victim, an object dressed as a subject, a shadow that believes itself endowed with reality. But, as Shweik says, "it is the nature of men; as long as one lives, one is mistaken." And one has to live . . . (pp. 58-64)

Francois Ricard, "Satan's Point of View: Towards a Reading of 'Life Is Elsewhere'," translated by John Anzalone, in Salmagundi, *No. 73, Winter, 1987, pp. 58-64.*

"If I write a love story, and there are three lines about Stalin in that story, people will talk about the three lines and forget the rest, or read the rest for its political implications or as a metaphor for politics."

—Milan Kundera, 1984.

George Szirtes

When Keats referred to the "Wordsworthian or egotistical sublime", he was defining one aspect of the poet as romantic. He went on mercilessly to pin down the specimen in all its chameleon-like splendour: the poetic character had "no self", was "everything and nothing" and was continually "filling some other body".

Jaromil, the poet in Milan Kundera's ***Life Is Elsewhere,*** written in 1969, certainly conforms to this pattern. The narrative is interspersed with instances from the lives of various poets: like Rimbaud he is a mother's boy turned revolutionary, like Hugo he longs to be loved by the whole world, like Lermontov he is terrified of ridicule, and like Shelley he dreams of a fiery death which he achieves only by proxy. He is described as living in a world of mirrors, a world prepared by his manically possessive mother, who remains both his closest friend and most intimate enemy. Jaromil is a failure with other women; the only one who loves him selflessly is a plain redhead whom he picks up by mistake and whose brother he betrays to the security police. (His greatest admirer as a poet is an old classmate who has joined the force.) But Jaromil betrays everyone in the process of fulfilling his poetic destiny: he even manages to corrupt that when he deserts his lyrical instincts and turns to public exhortatory verse in service of the Party. Whatever he does, though, he believes in and justifies to himself at the time. All weakness and treachery are thereby the shadow of some virtue. He is, in short, a monster—a nonentity dominated by his mother, whose one gift is to transform outside events into an interior drama of language and symbol.

This picture of the lyrical imagination would not in itself be particularly original: the species has often been observed. Ortega y Gasset spoke of poetry as "adolescence fermented and thus preserved", and Kundera's book is steeped in the colours of adolescence. What gives this study its peculiar poignancy is the setting, that turning-point in Czech history when the Communists took over after the War. Why is it, asks Kundera, that poets of real talent could devote themselves to movements that behaved abominably, and write perfectly genuine poems in their praise? Is there something inherently corruptible in the nature of poetry? The tag from Rimbaud, which gives the book its title, provides him with the answer. For the poetic imagination, life is always elsewhere: the self is insulated from it with its own passions and dramas.

Like many Central Europeans, Kundera is a natural fabulist who observes the follies and hypocrisies of human behaviour and keeps his characters at a distance. But, like other Kundera books, ***Life Is Elsewhere*** also contains a dream sequence of great clarity and power, an excursion into the element of poetry. As usual it serves to concentrate the reader on the real wishes and fears of the central character. The distancing of his prose is equally dreamlike in effect: its eroticism is a function of the distance.

The plot of this early book is very much like a case study: small humiliations and flattery alternate throughout the poet's childhood. The characters think in a complex, yet often mechanical, way and we are not really aware of them as individuals—it is through their dreams and their fates that we know them. We see them rather like voyeurs. Indeed, at one point we switch focus to the red-haired girl, and know of Jaromil's death before the narrative proper has revealed it to us. The natural transition from narrative to dream might be said to be conditioned by a society where dream and nightmare are inextricably bound up with the quality of life. What we see is precisely what the narrator-god wishes us to see: we know he is presenting us with loaded evidence, but are arrested by the technique and by the humane vision. ***Life Is Elsewhere*** is a little too much like a thesis to be counted among Kundera's very best books, but it remains essential reading.

George Szirtes, "Monster-poet," in The Times Literary Supplement, *No. 4372, January 16, 1987, p. 55.*

Ian Watt

One of Max Beerbohm's cartoons shows Mrs. Humphry Ward as a very little girl, saying to a sardonically smiling Matthew Arnold: "Uncle Matthew, oh why will you not be always wholly serious?" The question arises unbidden in the novels of Milan Kundera. The mind behind the novels is essentially serious, and yet they are very funny, sometimes farcical. Our puzzlement is not wholly laid to rest in Kundera's new book, ***The Art of the Novel.*** The title evokes the methodological solemnity of Henry James; but the book is in fact a rather short collection of essays which have already been published separately. It is true that Kundera affirms that he "conceived" this "seven-part essay" with the idea that they would someday be linked together in "one book-essay setting out my thoughts on the art of the novel." But this sounds rather like a publisher's ploy to turn a miscellany into a unity; the contents were conceived of as a "unified whole" and must therefore compose one. In form, they do not make that impression—three essays, two interviews, a public address, and a dictionary of 62 words. Yet the mind in the book is certainly consistent.

The first essay is entitled **"The Depreciated Legacy of Cervantes,"** earlier published as **"The Novel and Europe."** Both titles are apt. Kundera begins with the lecture, given in Vienna and Prague, on the crisis in the humanities, by Edmund Husserl. By "European," Husserl meant that "passion to know" which began in Greece, and which has since characterized the Western philosophic tradition. It began its modern secular trajectory when Galileo and Descartes narrowed the emphasis of thought to what could be demonstrated scientifically; they wholly neglected the *Lebenswelt,* Heidegger's "beautiful and almost magical phrase," for the concrete experience of living in the world. Cervantes founded another vital modern tradition: the novel with its chosen concentration on being. Cervantes took up the problem of adventure; and there followed him other writers who "discovered other dimensions of existence one by one." There was Samuel Richardson with "what happened inside," the "secret life of the feelings"; Balzac, with man's rootedness in history; Flaubert, and the quotidian dimension of life; and later Tolstoy, Proust, Joyce and Mann all devoted themselves to exploring new areas; for, as Kundera, quoting his Austrian master, Hermann Broch, wrote: "the sole *raison d'etre* of a novel is to discover what can only be discovered by a novel."

Descartes faced the world as a "thinking self"; Cervantes in a world apparently devoid of any divine order, faced it as a "welter of contradictory truths," where the only "certainty" was the "wisdom of uncertainty." The open adventurous spaces of Cervantes' world were gradually foreclosed in the 19th Century. There is some possibility of adventure still left in Balzac, but there is no such possibility for Emma Bovary; the lost infinity of the world can only be replaced by the "irreplaceable uniqueness of the individual." This process goes much further in Kafka, where the "suprahuman force of an omnipotent society" takes over, and adventure is reduced to "a petty squabble with the administration over a mistake in the file of Kafka's K."

Is the novel, then, now over? Kundera asks. He answers no, but, gravely threatened by the "whirlpool of reduction" of the media, it can continue "only against the progress" of the "spirit of our time." Kundera ends the Cervantes essay by asking himself what he is personally attached to? "My answer is as ridiculous as it is sincere; I am attached to nothing but the depreciated legacy of Cervantes." Such is Kundera's wry assertion of his devotion to the diminishing inheritance of the novel.

The essay as a whole is very serious, which is not surprising. Kundera's first prose work was a critical study of a Czech writer: ***The Art of the Novel: Vladislav Vancura's Search for the Great Epic*** in 1961; Kundera has also been a university teacher most of his life, in Prague and now in Paris. Kundera does not mention Cervantes' humor or comedy in his essay; but there are other parts of ***The Art of the Novel*** where he tackles this topic.

His main treatment comes in the last essay, which is Kundera's thank-you speech for the award of the Jerusalem Prize in 1985. There he cites the Jewish proverb, "Man thinks, God laughs," and says that it pleases him to think that "the novel's wisdom . . . different from that of philosophy . . . is born not of the theoretical spirit but of the spirit of humor." The novel was born "as the echo of God's laughter"; and Kundera concludes his address by saying that "it is time for me to stop. I was forgetting that God laughs when he sees me thinking."

Kundera was born on April Fools Day in 1929, and his first novel was called ***The Joke*** (1967). There, as in the later novels, the reader is aware of the omnipresent comic spirit; but still, the comedy is in the manner, not the matter. We must then accept that Kundera's comic sense is very bitter; true to the spirit of his compatriots Kafka and Jaroslav Hasek's *The Good Soldier Schweik,* Kundera's comedy is a chillingly sardonic resistance to the seriousness of his thought. (pp. 3, 7)

Ian Watt, "The Craft of Kundera," in Los Angeles Times Book Review, *March 6, 1988, pp. 3, 7.*

"Only a literary work that reveals an unknown fragment of human existence has a reason for being. To be a writer does not mean to preach a truth, it means to *discover* a truth."

—Milan Kundera, 1985.

Terrence Rafferty

[Kundera's ***The Art of the Novel***] is predictably lucid, detached, and epigrammatic. It's composed, as are all of his books except ***The Farewell Party,*** of seven parts, with deliberate variations in tone and technique. Only two of its parts could really be called essays; two more are taken from an interview ("which is not," Kundera tells us, "a transcript of an actual conversation but an edited dialogue"); one is presented as a set of notes (on Hermann Broch's novel *The Sleepwalkers*); another is simply a glossary of "key words," like "novel," "being," "Czechoslovakia," "modern," "Europe," and "forgetting;" and the concluding section is the transcript of a speech. The book has its author's familiar swiftness and variety of attack and his elegant, provocative irony. (p. 110)

In a brief preface [Kundera] says, "Every novelist's work contains an implicit vision of the history of the novel, an idea of what the novel is; I have tried to express here the idea of the novel that is inherent in my own novels." Later on he writes, "The novel's spirit is the spirit of continuity: each work is an answer to preceding ones, each work contains all the previous experience of the novel." For him, these nearly equivalent statements are articles of faith—or, in more scientific terms, axioms. What Kundera says may be true, but it's not difficult to imagine a novelist—even one of Kundera's stature—whose sense of his own work's relation to the history of the novel is considerably more anguished: for whom the novel's "spirit of continuity" is a demon, not an angel. The bracing clarity of Kundera's discourse in ***The Art of the Novel***—and, for that matter, in his fiction—reflects a hard-earned sense of security, of belonging to a tradition. "The novel is Europe's creation," he says bluntly, and, perhaps more arguably, "The only context for grasping a novel's worth is the history of the European novel." His personal "idea of the novel" is so profoundly Eurocentric that it's likely to seem exotic, even perverse, to American readers: the heroes of his history of the genre are Rabelais, Cervantes, Diderot, Kafka, Broch, and Robert Musil (*The Man without Qualities*)—with Flaubert, Tolstoy, and the Polish novelist Witold Gombrowicz (*Ferdydurke*) mentioned admiringly but less frequently. The only English-language writers admitted to Kundera's pantheon are Sterne and Joyce; the only American whose name appears at all is Faulkner (as part of a list); the only non-European novel cited in the entire text is *Terra Nostra,* by Carlos Fuentes. Kundera has been in exile from Czechoslovakia since 1975 (he lives in Paris), but he clearly doesn't feel exiled from his art—or, at least, his idea of it. He's still very much a part of the tradition that shaped him: the literature and philosophy and music of Europe. In terms of the novel, he may even be the Continental culture's greatest current exemplar, its reigning king. In his pronouncements on the novel he seems to have as little anxiety about his sources as a monarch has about his genes.

This is not to say that we'd wish more anguish on Kundera, who has, in other respects, certainly had his fair share; or that the perspective on the novel he presents isn't a valuable one. (It is, at the very least, a refreshing change from the standard English Department version of literary history.) Still, ***The Art of the Novel*** gives off the occasional (but pungent) whiff of cultural arrogance, and we may feel that Kundera's discourse, unmediated by narrative invention, reveals an aspect of his character that we'd rather not have known about. It's an index of the perils of this kind of book that as we read it we keep having to remind ourselves of Kundera's real virtues. The style of his writing here is close enough to that of the discursive passages in ***Life Is Elsewhere, The Book of Laughter and Forgetting,*** and ***The Unbearable Lightness of Being*** so that we're nearly seduced into thinking that the two modes—statements made in his own voice and statements inserted in a fictional structure—are equivalent, and they're not. Kundera himself, in discussing *The Sleepwalkers,* helps explain why:

> The moment it becomes part of a novel, reflection changes its essence. Outside the novel, we're in the realm of affirmation: everyone is sure of his statements: the politician, the philosopher, the concierge. Within the universe of the novel, however, no one affirms: it is the realm of play and of hypotheses. . . . There is a fundamental difference between the ways philosophers and novelists think. . . . [Dostoyevski] is a great thinker only as a novelist. Which is to say that in his characters he is able to create intellectual universes that are extraordinarily rich and original.

Kundera's own best novels create that sort of intellectual universe, and his literary criticism doesn't, although they're informed by the same qualities. In his novels, his command of European literary and philosophical traditions is so sure, so apparently easy, that it transcends virtuosity. We experience it as a kind of grace, a gift that makes his characters and their culture appear to reflect each other with uncanny precision—that makes writing itself seem a dance on a mirrored floor. In ***The Art of the Novel,*** this sublime confidence frequently shades into smugness. Milan Kundera knows exactly who he is, which is why it's dangerous for him to speak directly about himself and his art—and why we shouldn't draw too many conclusions from the off-putting tone of this book. Anybody this secure who's drawn into "the realm of affirmation" is likely to sound a little pompous.

What's fascinating is that the persona Kundera assumes in this book—that of an obstinate French academician, the concierge of fiction—is available to him at all. His life as an artist seems to have turned on the horrible moment in 1968 when the Russians invaded his country. At that point, Kundera was the author of one superb novel, ***The Joke,*** and the collection of stories called ***Laughable Loves,*** but from then on he could no longer be a *Czech* novelist in any significant sense—there was no vital national culture left for him to contribute to. But the great tradition of the *European* novel hovered like an angelic host in the sky above him, offering a new identity, a new perspective, if he could rise to it. And he did: it was, in a way, everything his reading had prepared him for. His first post-1968 novel, ***Life Is Elsewhere,*** which was published first in France but written while the author was still living in Czechoslovakia, shows signs of some uncertainty, of the inevitable difficulties of transition: it's a rather schematic novel, the only one of Kundera's books in which the author never comes out from behind his mask of irony. His portrait of a young Communist poet has an almost inhuman detachment—it's like Broch's disdainful anatomy of the military officer Pasenow in *The Romantic,* the first volume of *The Sleepwalkers*—and we feel that the author's control over his rage and sorrow at history's indignities is too absolute. ***The Farewell Party,*** his next novel, published in France the year after he moved there for good, is more assured, less anxious to proclaim itself a "novel of ideas": it's a beautiful dark farce, a Central European *Rules of the Game,* in which the complex spirit of ***The Joke*** seems to have been reincarnated in a more elegant, classical form. Kundera tells his interviewer in ***The Art of the Novel*** that ***The Farewell Party*** is "the novel dearest to me, in a certain sense. . . . I had more fun, more pleasure writing it than the others. In a different state of mind." Although it's a bit of an anomaly among the author's works—it lacks both the seven-part structure and the "polyphonic composition" of the rest—this novel marks Kundera's entry into the lofty reaches of the European-novel tradition. We feel in it his discovery of the principles that connect his experience as a Czech with his experience as a reader of French and German and Russian fiction—the principles that will allow him to *place* himself again, this time in the history of the novel.

That discovery accounts, perhaps, for the giddy virtuosity of the works that followed, ***The Book of Laughter and Forgetting*** and ***The Unbearable Lightness of Being,*** in which Kundera seems at times to be trying to orchestrate the most disparate modes of discourse, the highest and the lowest realms of human experience, the narrative means of both realism and the fantastic, the rigorous disciplines of music and philosophy, the voice of the individual and that of the broader culture, the mundane and the angelic—to bring everything he knows together in a kind of chorus, a full-throated Requiem that commemorates the end of European humanism while offering the most convincing evidence of its survival. We hear in the often irritating, priestly tone of ***The Art of the Novel*** a note of genuine reverence on Kundera's part for something beyond him, a legacy conferred on him by his sentimental education. This book is a defense of the values that saved him from being merely an exile.

In order to become the artist he now is, the Czech novelist had to discover himself a second time, as a European. But what if that second, grander possibility hadn't been there to be discovered? What if Broch, Kafka, Musil—all that reading—had never been a part of his education, or had entered it only as exotic, alien presences? Kundera's polemical fervor in ***The Art of the Novel*** annoys us, as American readers, because we feel defensive, excluded from the transcendent "idea of the novel" that for him seems simply to have been there for the taking. (If only he had cited, in his redeeming version of the novel's history, a few more heroes from the New World's culture.) Our novelists don't discover cultural values within themselves; they invent them. (pp. 110, 113-14)

Terrence Rafferty, "Articles of Faith," in The New Yorker, *Vol. LXIV, No. 13, May 16, 1988, pp. 110, 113-18.*

Gabriel Josipovici

Milan Kundera makes it quite clear at the start of [***The Art of the Novel***] that it is not intended to be either a treatise or a theoretical statement. It is made up of pieces written at different times and in response to specific requests: an interview for the *Paris Review,* the acceptance speech for the Jerusalem Prize, and so on. Nevertheless, says Kundera, "I conceived them all with the idea that they would someday be linked together in one book-essay setting out my thoughts on the art of the novel." We must not expect too much, however: it is merely "a practitioner's confession": "Every novelist's work contains an implicit vision of the history of the novel, an idea of what the novel is; I have tried to express here the idea of the novel that is inherent in my own novels."

He has done more than that, though. As we learn in the fourth piece, practically all his works have tended to fall into seven sections. Even when, as in ***The Unbearable Lightness of Being,*** he began with the determination to break the pattern, he found, in the end, that the book only felt right if he took away something here, added something there, divided a section in two—and lo and behold, there were the seven sections again. It is no surprise then to discover that he has turned ***The Art of the Novel*** into a seven-part essay by splitting the single interview into two. Not only does it work better that way, but it also signals to us his concern that we see this book as on a par with his novels, to be treated with the same respect and consideration.

Perhaps every significant artist has only one theme, on which he performs endless variations. All Dostoevsky's novels, Proust said, could be called *Crime and Punishment,* all Flaubert's *L'Éducation sentimentale.* All Kundera's novels could be called ***Life Is Elsewhere.*** In the first essay of the present book he starts from the famous series of lectures given by Husserl in Vienna and Prague in 1935, three years before his death, on the crisis of European humanity. The root of the crisis, for Husserl, lay at the beginning of the Modern Era, when Galileo and Descartes set modern science and philosophy on their way, but at the cost of what Husserl's pupil, Heidegger, called "the forgetting of being". And yet, says Kundera, this was the very moment when the novel was emerging, and the novel, in the hands of Cervantes and his successors, would take as its task precisely the function of reminding man of his "being". The crisis of European culture, then, so starkly analysed by modern philosophers, may only have been the result of philosophy's refusal to recognize the place of the novel in that culture. Kundera seems to waver between holding that it is therefore a purely philosophical crisis, and holding that it was a crisis which affected the whole of society but to which philosophy has, for most of its history, been blind. He is in no doubt though about the role of the novel:

> The novel has accompanied man uninterruptedly and faithfully since the beginning of the Modern Era. It was then that the "passion to know", which Husserl considered the essence of European spirituality, seized the novel and led it to scrutinize man's concrete life and protect it against "the forgetting of being"; to hold "the world of life" under a permanent light. That is the sense in which I understand and share Hermann Broch's insistence in repeating: the sole *raison d'être* of a novel is to discover what only the novel can discover.

What does it mean, to discover what only the novel can discover? Most readers, Kundera suggests, like most philosophers, want to "sort things out". They want to know if Anna Karenina is "the victim of a narrow-minded tyrant", or if, on the contrary, Karenin is "the victim of an immoral woman"; if Joseph K is "an innocent man crushed by an injust court" or if on the contrary, the Court is right and Joseph K is guilty. But, says Kundera,

> This "either-or" encapsulates an inability to tolerate the essential relativity of things human, an inability to look squarely at the absence of the Supreme Judge. This inability makes the novel's wisdom (the wisdom of uncertainty) hard to accept and understand.

The novel, he says elsewhere, "is the imaginary paradise of individuals". It is "the territory where no one possesses the truth, neither Anna nor Karenin, but where everyone has the right to be understood, both Anna and Karenin". But that of course is why the novel is so hated by totalitarian regimes, and why it seems to have less and less of a place in a consumer culture which is growing daily more monolithic and more devoted to what can be assimilated without effort:

> The novel's spirit is the spirit of complexity. Every novel says to the reader: "Things are not as simple as you think." That is the novel's eternal truth, but it grows steadily harder to hear amid the din of easy, quick answers that come faster than the question and block it off.

That is why, he says in conclusion, when he is asked to what he is attached, to God, to Country, to the people, to the individual, he can only answer: "I am attached to nothing but the depreciated legacy of Cervantes."

This is a moving statement, to be taken all the more seriously since its author has himself been the victim of totalitarianism and demonstrated in practical ways his commitment to the legacy of Cervantes.

But how does Kundera see the history of the novel from Cervantes to the present? He stresses different aspects of it in different essays, but in essence the story goes like this. The novel, as we find it in Cervantes, Diderot and Sterne, is a free and easy form: many different adventures can be undertaken, and the author himself feels free to digress when he wants, or to pile up coincidences in an arbitrary manner. By the time of Balzac, though, "the distant horizon has disappeared like a landscape behind those modern structures, the social institutions. . . . In Balzac's world time no longer idles happily by as it does for Cervantes and Diderot. It has set forth on the train called History."

This train is easy to board and it is full of promise, at least for those with enough money and spirit. But by the time of Emma Bovary the horizon has shrunk; it now appears as a barrier. We are hemmed in by social institutions, and as a result all adventures can only take place in our heads. In this way "the lost infinity of the outside world is replaced by the infinity of the soul. The great illusion of the irreplaceable uniqueness of the individual—one of Europe's finest illusions—blossoms forth."

But History is relentless. By the time we get to Kafka, daydreaming can no longer replace reality. For daydreaming has itself become unreal, and we with it. It becomes necessary to force reality to acknowledge us, for without that acknowledgement we have no sense of even being alive. It becomes better to die for a reason than to live with none.

Kundera devotes two of the seven sections of this book to individual authors, Broch and Kafka. And if so far his story of the development of the European novel is more or less the standard one, as it has been told by, for example, Marthe Robert and Jay Bernstein, these two pieces allow him to develop a distinctive view of its recent history. With what he calls the pleiad of Central European authors, Kafka, Musil and Broch, to whom he adds from time to time Hasek and Gombrowicz, we have moved into a new dimension, he suggests. There is no longer any attempt to enter character or to develop a linear plot. The author is happy to interrupt the action with meditations on culture and metaphysics. Even the notion of plot no longer holds. The work develops polyphonically, by means of play, of dream, of thought, and of a perspective which encompasses a much larger view of history than that of single individuals. The novelist is now no longer a teller of tales or a recorder of truth, but an experimenter with character, situation and tone.

Kundera, though, has no desire to set these writers up as models. "All great works", he wisely says, "(precisely because they are great) contain something unachieved. Broch is an inspiration to us not only because of what he brought off but also because of what he aimed for and missed." *The Sleepwalkers,* great as it is, only stimulates us to go beyond it. We need, he argues, first "a new art of *radical divestment* (which can encompass the complexity of existence in the modern world without losing architectonic clarity)"; second, "a new art of *novelistic counterpoint* (which can blend philosophy, narrative, and dream into one music)"; and, third, "a new art of the *specifically novelistic essay* (which does not claim to bear an apodictic message but remains hypothetical, playful, or ironic.)"

Kundera is now clearly talking about himself and his aims. And when he ends the "Notes Inspired by *The Sleepwalkers*" by insisting that the modern novel continues the quest that has preoccupied all the great novelists since Cervantes, and that to talk of the death of the novel is really to acquiesce in the death of man, he is throwing down the gauntlet not only to academic historians of "modernism" and the novel, but also to the prevailing spirit of the times. In his chilling vision, poetry (implying also the novel) begins to disappear when we no longer feel the need for it, so that its actual disappearance will pass unnoticed. But not, he implies, without a struggle on his part.

And so we move into the fourth and most fascinating of the sections, that **"Dialogue on the Art of Composition"** in which Kundera discusses the composition of his own novels and demonstrates a thrilling familiarity with the art of musical composition. (Like Anthony Burgess, it seems, he first planned to become a composer, but he has a far greater ability than Burgess to express what the novelist can learn from the musician.) In reply to Christian Salmon's questions, then, he runs through a number of elements which seem to him fundamental to the art of fictional composition, elaborating, as he does so, on the credo he had enunciated in the Broch essay. First there is ellipsis. This is essential because only in a compact work can the architectonic element be clearly seen. It may be there in Broch or Musil, but it gets lost in the sprawling mass of their books. Then there is polyphony. Already in Dostoevsky's *The Devils* we find three quite distinct plots, cleverly intertwined, and the meaning of the whole becomes far more than the sum of these three strands. But why just three? And why only different plots? Why not intertwine essays, dreams, stories which have nothing to do with the "main" plot but which only open a window on one of its walls, so to speak, or are only thematically linked to it? Since "the novel is a meditation on existence as seen through the medium of imaginary characters", surely we ought to use every means at our disposal to bring that meditation to fruition?

The nineteenth-century novel was held together by plot and character and by certain conventions which, taken together, we call Realism. If we are to develop the many other possibilities inherent in the novel form then we have to be aware of how the different elements relate to each other. We need to understand how a work is articulated, and for this a grasp of tempo becomes crucial. In a fascinating table Kundera lays out the seven parts of ***Life Is Elsewhere*** as if they were seven movements in a piece of music, each with its own tempo. Commenting on the table he points out that "Part Five has 81 pages and only 11 chapters; a slow, tranquil pace: *moderato.* Part Four has 25 chapters in 20 pages! Which gives a feeling of great speed: *prestissimo*". When Salmon points out that Part Six has seventeen chapters and only seventeen pages, yet is labelled *adagio,* Kundera replies that this is

> because the tempo is further determined by something else: the relation between the length of a part and the "real" time of the event it describes. Part Five . . . represents a whole year of life, whereas Part Six . . . deals with only a few hours. Here the brevity of the chapters functions to slow time down, to fix a single great moment.

This is excellent because it shows Kundera's awareness of the fact that though narrative art and music both exist in time, and are therefore both subject to some of the same laws, they also consist of different kinds of elements, each of which affects all the others. Writers who are fond of talking about their work in musical terms are so often unconvincing precisely because they seem to imagine that precisely the same rules hold for both.

It is because Kundera has such a clear grasp of the nature of music that he can see the differences from, as well as the similarities with, narrative. **"Dialogue on the Art of Composition"** contains analyses of works by Bach, Beethoven and Chopin that are both completely comprehensible to the layman and musically acute. They are this because, we sense, he has himself spent long hours weighing and balancing temporal sequences against each other, without theoretical preconceptions, but solely in order to achieve his own ends. Nevertheless, it is at this point that the reader who is less than enthusiastic about Kundera's fiction may begin to see what it is that bothers him.

Kundera's admirable clarity about the formal possibilities of the novel stems at least in part from his awareness of the fact that the nineteenth-century novel, far from being a natural phenomenon, consists of man-made objects; objects, moreover, which are made according to a very limited set of possibilities. Cervantes, for example, could allow dozens of characters to meet at an inn, quite against the laws of probability, simply because he needed them there for his own purposes. Kundera is aware that we cannot simply go back to Cervantes, but he asks why we should not make use of the fact that novels are not life but compositions, in order so to compose them as to throw as much light as possible on life.

But this is not merely a writer's awareness of a literary problem. The notion of a work as being filled with "life" has cultural and existential, as well as aesthetic dimensions. Kundera had originally been going to call ***Life Is Elsewhere*** "The Lyrical Age", but changed it—wrongly in his opinion—at the urging of friends. The lyrical age, he explains, is the age of youth, but it is also the nineteenth century, the age of Keats, Shelley, Pushkin and Rimbaud. In his 1986 postscript to the novel he explains:

> Don't say that Jaromil is a bad poet! That would be too cheap an explanation of his life's story! Jaromil is a talented poet, with great imagination and feeling. And he is a sensitive young man. Of course, he is also a monster. But his monstrosity is potentially contained in us all. It is in me. It is in you. It is in Rimbaud [the title is a phrase of Rimbaud's]. It is in Shelley, in Hugo.

But the full monstrousness of the lyric poet only perhaps appears in our century:

> I heard my admired French poet Paul Éluard publicly and ceremonially renounce his Prague friend whom Stalinist justice was sending to the gallows. This episode (I wrote about it in ***The Book of Laughter and Forgetting***) hit me like a trauma: when an executioner kills, that is after all normal; but when a poet (and a great poet) sings in accompaniment, the whole system of values we considered sacrosanct has suddenly been shaken apart.

At such moments it becomes the duty of the writer—the non-lyric writer—to try to reveal the psychological and social roots of lyric poetry, and of the kitsch that lies at the heart of so much nineteenth-century culture.

Here Kundera is only following in the wake of Flaubert, Musil and Broch. For it was Flaubert who showed that stupidity is never simply the absence of knowledge, but "an inseparable dimension of human experience"—"the non-thought of received ideas", as Kundera puts it. And kitsch, about which Kundera writes at length in ***The Unbearable Lightness of Being,*** is only the translation of the stupidity of received ideas into the language of beauty and feeling: "It moves us to tears of compassion for ourselves, for the banality of what we think and feel."

Lyricism, stupidity and kitsch are an inseparable part of our era, and they are so dangerous because they are all ways in which we try to remove the unbearable lightness of being, to free ourselves from the sensation that life is elsewhere. But of course, instead of giving us back our true weight, our deserved life, they only lead to the denial of ambiguity and uncertainty, and so to totalitarianism in its many guises.

But is there not something awkwardly defensive about this? When I compare Kundera's work with that of Nabokov (who was also appalled by kitsch, or *poshlust,* in his Russian designation), or with that of Leonardo Sciascia and Aharon Appelfeld, who have also witnessed, and borne witness to, the horrors and evasions of the age, I am struck by his coldness, his lack of sympathy for any of his characters. It is as if for Kundera, sympathy is so tainted with kitsch that it must be avoided at all costs. But what we find in the great lyric poets of the nineteenth century, as well as in the three novelists I have just referred to, is a much more complex sense of the intermingling of the value of sympathy with its possible distortion. It will not do to say that Jaromil is not a bad poet. We have only to compare him with Mann's Adrian Leverkühn (Kundera refers with admiration to *Doktor Faustus*) to see the difference. Mann's novel is profoundly disturbing precisely because Leverkühn is such a remarkable figure, to whom our hearts go out. *Lolita* is disturbing precisely because we cannot stand above Humbert and dissect his weaknesses. *Badenheim 1939* is disturbing precisely because we sense Appelfeld's compassion for these Jews in all their tragic blindness.

I am suggesting that Kundera's sense of the novel and its possibilities, his desire to get away from a nineteenth-century "lyrical" realism, is bought at too high a price. His attitude to Don Quixote is symptomatic. No one imagines, least of all Cervantes, that the Don is a real character. He is an experiment. But is this quite right? Cervantes may be fully aware of the fact that he has himself created the Don, but he nevertheless is fascinated by his creature. Kundera will never allow himself to become fascinated; he has always to maintain his ironic superiority. And though he invokes Rabelais in his Jerusalem Prize address, and quotes the Jewish proverb, "Man thinks, God laughs", and though he constantly reverts to the fact that laughter is the best defence against the totalitarian imagination, there is no real laughter in his books. Nor, despite his comments about the novel being a wise and generous form, do I find any generosity in his own novels. He is too busy showing up the self-deceptions in which his characters are caught, and too concerned never himself to be caught in this way.

As a result his novels seem far less open than most nineteenth-century novels. We are constantly being brought up against Kundera himself and his views. For example, he rejects Proust's "psychologoical time" (whatever that means) and asks that we move on to the point where the novelist can deal with large sweeps of history. But what does it tell us about history or about human character to link Shelley and Rimbaud and Paris in 1968 and Prague in 1949, as he does in ***Life Is Elsewhere?*** There is a sort of insight there, but its value is quickly exhausted. Kundera would no doubt say that these comparisons are partly ironic, and that the narrators of his novels must not be confused with himself, even if they do often say the same things as he does in interviews. (pp. 695-96)

Moreover, despite his criticism of philosophers for abstracting man out of existence, Kundera's whole approach to fiction is relentlessly abstract. When I read "the lyric attitude . . . is one of the basic categories of human existence", or "Does man deserve to live on earth . . . ?" I simply do not know what he is talking about. What is "a basic category of human existence"? Does existence have categories? And what does it mean, to deserve to live? How can questions about human beings be posed in these terms?

In the end, it seems to me, Kundera's stance of ironic aloofness, that mixture of eroticism, cynicism and playfulness, is really only a variant on, and not a rejection of, Romantic lyricism. That, I suspect, is why it has struck such a chord in Western readers (and become almost the hallmark of so-called "post-modernist" novels). It would indeed be ironic if his work were itself the symptom of the decline he warns us against, if the esteem in which his novels are everywhere held were precisely the result of that decline in any genuine interest in art against which he has constantly warned us.

But one could take a less apocalyptic view. My response to his fiction may simply reflect my own lack of enthusiasm for the tradition he cherishes, the tradition of Flaubert, Musil and Broch. But at least one of the things the writers in that tradition do, and which Kundera too does so splendidly in this volume, is to make us rethink the possibilities of the novel. Kundera's is not the only story of the development of the novel (one could argue that Biblical narratives and Chaucer's *Canterbury Tales* have all the characteristics he ascribes to the European novel since Cervantes), nor are his novels the only actualizations of its possibilities. One does not have to adhere to the norms of the nineteenth-century novel to feel that there are many other, as yet unrealized, possibilities in the form, and that quite a few are realized in ways very different from Kundera's. . . . (p. 696)

Gabriel Josipovici, "The Ironist Aloof," in The Times Literary Supplement, *No. 4447, June 24-30, 1988, pp. 695-96.*

Milan Kundera (Interview with Lois Oppenheim)

[*Oppenheim*]: *I would like to take advantage of* [*this meeting*] *with you to clarify a number of more or less concrete points. To begin, in* ***The Art of the Novel*** *you very explicitly condemn the interview as it is traditionally practiced and, in a rather forceful manner, you reiterate your decision to not grant any more interviews unless they are accompanied by your copyright. I understand your frustration with journalists who, in utter disregard of the possible ramifications, deprive the interviewee of any opportunity to review his remarks prior to their publication. And I appreciate your distinction between dialogue, where there is a real give and take, a sincere sharing of thoughts on issues of mutual interest, and interview, where only those questions of interest to the interviewer are posed and only those answers that serve his purpose are reproduced—and all too often in a context different from that which inspired them in the first place. Nevertheless, I wonder if you are not somehow depriving your public in restricting the interviews you grant to those that you will co-edit?*

[Kundera]: Interviews, such as they appear in the press, are merely approximate transcriptions of what the interviewee said. This wouldn't be quite so serious if your words weren't quoted by everyone, even by academics and critics, as though it were really a matter of your formulations, your wording. All exactitude is lost in approximation. Once, I was made to relate not only inaccuracies in an interview, but ideas that were not at all mine. I protested. The answer: The journalist is retaining the quote. I understood one very simple thing: An author, once quoted by a journalist, is no longer master of his word; he loses the author's rights to what he says. And this, of course, is unacceptable. The solution, however, is easy and, I hope, agreeable to you: We have met, you and I; we have spoken at length; we have agreed to the subjects that interest us; you have composed the questions; I have composed the answers and we are adding at the end a copyright. This way, everything is okay, everything is fair play.

This seems entirely reasonable to me. In fact, I can't see what more could be wanted than the guarantee of authenticity that the copyright provides. You have provoked many discussions about Central Europe. All of your fiction takes place in Czechoslovakia and even in your theoretical work, ***The Art of the Novel,*** *Central Europe is very important.*

Would you mind clarifying just what this notion of Central Europe represents for you, just what its real perimeters are?

Let's simplify the problem, an enormous one, and limit ourselves to the novel. There are four great novelists: Kafka, Broch, Musil, Gombrowicz. I call them the "pleiad" of Central Europe's great novelists. Since Proust, I can't see anyone of greater importance in the history of the novel. Without knowing them, not much of the modern novel can be understood. Briefly, these authors are modernists, which is to say that they are impassioned by a search for new forms. At the same time, however, they are completely devoid of any avant-garde ideology (faith in progress, in revolution, and so on), whence another vision of the history of art and of the novel: They never speak of the necessity of a radical break; they don't consider the formal possibilities of the novel to be exhausted; they only want to radically enlarge them.

From this as well there derives another rapport with the novel's past. There is no disdain in these writers for "tradition," but another *choice* of tradition: they are all fascinated by the novel preceding the nineteenth century. I call this era the first "half-time" of the history of the novel. This era and its aesthetic were almost forgotten, obscured, during the nineteenth century. The "betrayal" of this first half-time deprived the novel of its play essence (so striking in Rabelais, Cervantes, Sterne, Diderot) and diminished the role of what I call "novelistic meditation." Novelistic meditation—let's avoid any misunderstanding here: I'm not thinking of the so-called "philosophical novel" that really means a subordination of the novel to philosophy, the novelistic illustration of ideas. This is Sartre. And even more so Camus. *La Peste.* This moralizing novel is almost the model of what I don't like. The intent of a Musil or a Broch is entirely different: it is not to serve philosophy but, on the contrary, to get hold of a domain that, until then, philosophy had kept for itself. There are metaphysical problems, problems of human existence, that philosophy has never known how to grasp in all their concreteness and that only the novel can seize. This said, these novelists (particularly Broch and Musil) made of the novel a supreme poetic and intellectual synthesis and accorded it a preeminent place in the cultural totality.

These authors are relatively little known in America, which I have always considered an intellectual scandal. But really it is a matter of an aesthetic misunderstanding that is quite comprehensible when one considers the particular tradition of the American novel. In the first place, America didn't live through the first half-time of the history of the novel. In the second, at the same time that the great Central Europeans were writing their masterpieces, America herself had her own great "pleiad," one which would influence the entire world and which was that of Hemingway, Faulkner and Dos Passos. But its aesthetic was entirely opposed to that of a Musil! For example: a meditative intervention of the author into the narrative thread of his novel appears in this aesthetic as a displaced intellectualism, as something foreign to the very essence of the novel. A personal recollection: The *New Yorker* published the first three parts of ***The Unbearable Lightness of Being***—but they eliminated the passages on Nietzsche's eternal return! Yet, in my eyes, what I say about Nietzsche's eternal return has nothing to do with a *philosophic* discourse; it is a continuity of paradoxes that are no less *novelistic* (that is to say, they answer no less to the essence of what the novel is) than a description of the action or a dialogue.

Would you say that these writers have influenced you in any concrete way?

Influenced me? No. It's something else: I exist under the same aesthetic roof that they do. Not under the roof of a Proust or a Joyce. Not under the roof of a Hemingway (despite all my admiration for him). The writers I'm speaking about weren't influenced by each other either. They didn't even like each other. Broch was very critical of Musil, Musil nasty about Broch, Gombrowicz didn't like Kafka and he never spoke of either Broch or Musil and was himself probably unknown by the three others. Perhaps if they knew that I grouped them together they would be furious with me. And perhaps rightly so. Perhaps I've invented this pleiad to be able to see a roof over my head.

How does your concept of Central Europe relate to that of the "Slavic world," of "Slavic culture"?

There is, of course, a linguistic unity of the Slavic languages. But there doesn't exist any Slavic cultural unity. "Slavic literature" doesn't exist. If my books were situated in a "Slavic" context, I wouldn't recognize myself. This is an artificial and false context. The Central European context (which, linguistically, is Germano-Slavo-Hungarian) is, for my books, a more accurate context. But even this context will not amount to much if we want to grasp the meaning and value of a novel. I'll never stop repeating that the only context that can reveal the meaning and value of a novelistic work is the context of the history of the European novel.

You refer constantly to the European novel. Is this to say that for you the American novel is generally less significant?

You are right to mention this. It really bothers me to not be able to find the right term. If I say "Western novel," it will be said that I am forgetting the Russian novel. If I say "world novel," I am concealing the fact that the novel I am speaking of is the one historically linked to Europe. That is why I say "European novel"; but I understand this adjective in the Husserlian sense: not as a geographical term, but a "spiritual" one which takes in both America and, for example, Israel. What I call the "European novel" is the history that goes from Cervantes to Faulkner.

It occurs to me that among the writers you are citing as being of greatest importance to the history of the novel, and among those that you cite elsewhere in connection with the development of the novel and its relation to any given cultural history, there are no women. Correct me if I am wrong, but there is never any mention of women writers either in your essays or interviews. Can you explain this?

It is the sex of the novels and not that of their authors that must interest us. All great novels, all true novels are bisexual. This is to say that they express both a feminine and a masculine vision of the world. The sex of the authors as physical people is their private affair.

All of your novels vividly document the Czech experience. I wonder if you feel able at this point to create a fiction within another socio-historical context, like that of the French, for example, given that you are so at home in Paris.

We'll see. For the moment, I will say only this: I lived in Czechoslovakia until I was forty-five. Given that my real career as a writer began when I was thirty, I can say that the larger part of my creative life is taking place and will take place in France. I am much more tied to France than is thought.

Your ***Art of the Novel*** *is certainly a fascinating personal testimony. I think that, to a great extent, its appeal is due precisely to the fact that, over and above the insight it offers into the universal dimensions of aesthetic experience, and this is considerable, it offers a very personal theory of the novel.*

It's not even a theory. It's a confession of a practitioner. Personally, I very much like listening to practitioners of art. Olivier Messiaen's *Technique de mon language musical* interests me a thousand times more than Adorno's *Philosophy of Modern Music.* Perhaps I've erred in choosing a title that could, by its generality, evoke a treatise on theoretical ambitions. Aaron Asher, my American editor, proposed a title taken from the last part of the book: *Man Thinks, God Laughs.* Today I see that that would have been better. But I retained the title ***The Art of the Novel*** for a personal, almost sentimental reason: When I was twenty-seven or twenty-eight years old, I wrote a book on a Czech novelist that I deeply cared for, Vladislav Vancura. The book was entitled ***The Art of the Novel.*** This book, at once likable (thanks to Vancura) and immature, will never again be reissued and I wanted to at least keep the title as a memory of years past.

Finally, do you see any major turning points in the evolution of your thinking on literature, on its relation to the world, to culture, to the individual? Do you see the evolution of your thinking in terms of a strictly linear progression or can you pinpoint any moments of significant change in the development of your aesthetic?

Until I was thirty I wrote many things: music, above all, but also poetry and even a play. I was working in many different directions—looking for my voice, my style and myself. With the first story of ***Laughable Loves*** (I wrote it in 1959), I was certain of having "found myself." I became a prose writer, a novelist, and I am nothing else. Since then, my aesthetic has known no transformations; it evolves, to use your word, linearly. (pp. 7-11)

Lois Oppenheim, in an interview with Milan Kundera, in The Review of Contemporary Fiction, *Vol. IX, No. 2, Summer, 1989, pp. 7-11.*

D. M. Thomas

In the course of his latest novel, ***Immortality,*** Milan Kundera talks enthusiastically to a professorial friend about the novel he is writing. It does not consist of a chain of causes and effects, he says; rather, it is like a feast of many courses. In Part Six, to which he is looking forward, he will introduce an entirely new character, who will disappear at the end, leaving no trace and causing nothing to happen. In answer to a query, he says the novel will be called ***The Unbearable Lightness of Being.*** The professor says he thinks somebody has already written that book, and Mr. Kundera confesses: "I did! But I was wrong about the title then. That title was supposed to belong to the novel I'm writing right now."

I'm not sure what Mr. Kundera meant, but his new novel does have a weightless, unearthly quality. Smells, for instance—they do not exist in ***Immortality.*** I noticed a reference to the "smell" and "stench" of a tramp's alcoholic breath and his clothes; and I may have missed one or two others. But this is essentially a novel without smells. It is also, apart from conversation, almost soundless. There are the occasional sounds of music, and of cries in sexual activity, but sound does not permeate the text in a normal way. We are missing, of course, the novel's native sound, Czech; but certainly in Peter Kussi's graceful English the style seems muted—almost a book of the deaf. Mr. Kundera gives us reflection and discourse, mixed up with narratives that develop almost entirely through images and gestures, often interpreted and reflected upon by the author.

The novel grows out of a gesture. Mr. Kundera describes himself as lazing on the top floor of a high-rise health club in Paris; he is idly watching a woman in her 60's, standing waist-deep in the swimming pool. Her lesson concluding, she turns and waves to her instructor in the manner of a coquettish 20-year-old; and Mr. Kundera is entranced by the gesture of a woman briefly forgetting that she is no longer beautiful.

A name comes to him: Agnes. "I had never known a woman by that name." She fills him with immense, inexplicable nostalgia. When he wakes the next morning, to the banalities of the radio, he imagines Agnes waking in her wide bed. Where can her husband be? He must be someone who leaves home early on Saturday mornings. And so the fiction begins, with a magical lightness and sureness of touch. In the hands of a less gifted novelist, the process of turning a daydream into a heroine might well seem pretentious and unconvincing; yet Agnes is real from the moment she wakes alone in the double bed. She is real largely because the author immediately turns his attention to the absent husband—to Mr. Kundera, Agnes is already sufficiently alive to be taken for granted.

She is a woman who feels cut off from other people, who craves solitude. Though her marriage is satisfactory enough, she decides that if she had to choose an eternity with her husband, Paul, or without him, she would choose the latter. And would even have the courage to say so if the question were asked in his presence. She has a younger sister, Laura. They differ erotically—which for Mr. Kundera, I suspect, means essentially. Agnes's body only becomes sexual at rare moments of ecstasy whereas Laura's is never unerotic. Agnes realizes this when she sees her sister caress a brassiere in a lingerie store.

We are never allowed, however, to forget entirely that these interesting, hugely self-conscious Parisian characters exist by Mr. Kundera's will and permission. In Part Two, he forgets them, turning instead to the relationship of Goethe with his amorous admirer, Bettina von Arnim. The fictional story and the literary-biographical one are related, to all appearances, only through incidental gestures common to both (a virginal breast briefly touched; spectacles falling to the floor during jealous confrontations) and in the common pattern of a married couple, with a second woman lurking in the wings. Beyond these, it is probably no more relevant to look for connections than it is to connect Duck à l'Orange and Black Forest Gateau, successive courses in a feast.

Just as, in the opening scene by the high-rise pool, the whole of Paris is visible to Mr. Kundera, so the Goethe scenes open up a rich panorama of European culture. From the Romantic cult of love and sentiment, we move through ideology to "imagology," embracing "advertising agencies; political campaign managers; designers who devise the shape of everything from cars to gym equipment; fashion stylists; barbers; show-business stars dictating the norms of physical beauty that all branches of imagology obey." Alongside the cult of images, Mr. Kundera appears to suggest, is an excessive individualism parading a plethora of "rights": the right of Parisian drivers to drive too fast; the right of a suicidal woman to sit down in a road, an act that causes a fatal pileup. The would-be suicide alone is untouched; she gets up and walks away.

Any impression we may gather from the opening pages that this is an improvisation is firmly denied in a late episode in which the author talks with Agnes's husband—rather, by this stage, her surviving widower and brother-in-law. Paul, discussing Mahler's Seventh Symphony, asserts that it owed nothing to chance, that everything was worked through, but such perfection overwhelms us, surpassing our capacity for attention. "His idea," Mr. Kundera reflects, "cheered him up, whereas I was becoming sadder and sadder: if a reader skips a single sentence of my novel he won't be able to understand it, and yet where in the world will you find a reader who never skips a line? Am I not myself the greatest skipper of lines and pages?"

Unless Mr. Kundera the narrator differs from Mr. Kundera the author—and I see no sign of distance or self-mocking irony—this is an extraordinarily daunting comment; indeed, an extraordinarily arrogant one. Would even Dante have claimed that if you skipped a single line of "The Divine Comedy" you would fail to understand it?

Immortality is certainly a daunting novel: almost devoid of the good-natured or ill-tempered bustle of ordinary humanity and overstuffed, to my taste, with a very Gallic cerebration. The explanatory intrusions are sometimes irritating: "Agnes did not want Paul to suffer from a sense of guilt. Not out of compassion for him, but rather out of jealousy: she didn't want him to feel so responsible for Laura, to be so tied to her in his thoughts. That's why she said, 'How can you be so sure that she actually found a gun?' " This strikes me as working very hard to make a point.

And yet the novel fascinates. There is some stylistic or narrative felicity on every page that demonstrates Mr. Kundera's mastery. I sense, though, a writer struggling with desolation; and I wonder to what extent this novel has been shaped by his exile to the West—an exile that is presumably no longer necessary for any ideological reason, now that political conditions have changed so greatly in Mr. Kundera's native Czechoslovakia. The Paris he inhabits and describes is bleak. Even its women seem ugly: "That woman could have found a dozen outfits that would have . . . made her behind less monstrous. Why hadn't she done so? Not only have people stopped trying to be attractive when they are out among other people, but they are no longer even trying not to look ugly!" It is Agnes observing the woman in baggy knee-length trousers, but Agnes is a projection of Mr. Kundera.

In another section of the novel, a young Australian woman comes to make love to a painter nicknamed Rubens, and she is dressed unromantically. She takes off her clothes, "leaving her linen trousers on the chair and under the chair the huge tennis shoes with the thick socks, which she had stuck into them, tennis shoes that paused for a while in Rubens's apartment on their long pilgrimage through Australian universities and European cities." The lovemaking is "unbelievably calm and silent." Rubens will not see her again, and she will feel hurt, not knowing why. If he is to find new excitement, Rubens reflects, he must look to the past.

It is for the stylistic deliciousness and the mordant humor of that sentence about the journeying tennis shoes, and a thousand others like it, that I shall remember ***Immortality*** with pleasure. The tennis shoes will squeak on in my imagination when the paradoxical reflections on love and culture have faded. It's a cordon bleu, nouvelle cuisine novel, though the chef has cooked more mouthwatering feasts.

D. M. Thomas, "The Woman of His Dreams," in The New York Times Book Review, *April 28, 1991, p. 7.*

James Wolcott

Czech author Milan Kundera is harem master of his own mind. An idea man with the soul of a sensualist, he makes servants of all he surveys. Dolling up even his darkest ideas in diaphanous gauze, he puts on a floor show for the reader—a fleshy symposium. Jeweled navels jiggle in a bazaar hubbub of bittersweet contentions. Salman Rushdie called Kundera's novel ***The Book of Laughter and Forgetting*** "a whirling dance of a book."

It was ***The Unbearable Lightness of Being*** that gave him international stature. Coldly summarized, ***Unbearable Lightness*** was a drizzly story of doomed love set beneath a clotted sky of intellectual congestion. Yet it too had its ripply effects. For all its lecture notes from Alienation 101 ("The daily defecation session is daily proof of the unacceptability of Creation"), its love story traced a long curve of hope and hurt. When the director Philip Kaufman adapted ***Unbearable Lightness*** to the screen, most of Kundera's mental gymnastics had to be junked to make room for the cast's impressive flesh, which seems to have miffed Kundera. He's devised his new novel, ***Immortality*** . . . , to be tamperproof. Making a cameo appearance in his own pages, Kundera declares, "If a person is still crazy enough to write novels nowadays and wants to protect them, he has to write them in such a way that they cannot be adapted." He adds that this novel will be the true ***Unbearable Lightness.*** Sole impresario, he has big plans for this production, gobs of ideas. Get out there, girls, and roll your jelly.

Like ***Unbearable Lightness, Immortality*** concerns a triangle dented by tragedy. There's Agnes, her husband, Paul, and her sister, Laura, whom Paul marries after Agnes dies. There's also a fourth partner, Rubens, whom Kundera gleefully foists on us near the end, flouting an unwritten law in fiction about not introducing a major player so late in the game. That's the advantage of metafiction—you can fiddle around with the stale formulas. As Kundera argues, "A novel shouldn't be like a bicycle race," focused on a single goal, "but a feast of many courses." That Kundera insists on showing his hand doesn't mean that he can't achieve convincing effects, however. As the critic John Bayley said of ***Unbearable Lightness,*** "When the novel begins to insist that it is all made up, it tends to strike the reader as not made up at all." Like Ford Madox Ford's anecdotal *The Good Soldier,* it's a ball of yarn that achieves the bigness of fate. ***Immortality*** hasn't the same air of consequence. Chalk that up partly to the change in political climate. ***Unbearable Lightness,*** like Kundera's earlier Czech novels, played secret games beneath the sluggish gaze of Communist rule. ***Immortality*** is set in Paris, Kundera's adopted home. The authoritarian dome of Eastern-bloc oppression has been cracked by a mind-zap collage of media images. Capitalism is a photostat machine run amok, purveying a false individualism by inundating us with faces. Magazines are thick with them, movies, TV. But they fail to signify. "The face is only the serial number of a specimen," he states. Bourgeois baggage, the blank characters in ***Immortality*** receive little breathing space in their specimen jars. They're subordinated to the play of Kundera's mind.

Much of it is idle play. Kundera sits high on the culture bus as it takes its magical mystery tour toward a possible Nobel Prize. There are extended flashbacks to Goethe's tortured relationship with a groupie named Bettina. There are extended sneak previews of the afterlife, with Goethe and Hemingway doing a vaudeville act. There's a puzzling reference to Heidegger. "If at the time I was writing these pages everyone decided that Martin Heidegger was to be considered a bungler and a black sheep, it was not because his thought had been surpassed by other philosophers, but because on the roulette wheel of imagology, this time he had landed on an unlucky number, an anti-ideal." Puzzling, because the reason Heidegger has fallen into ill repute is rooted in enlarged revelations about his Nazi affiliations, which certainly amount to more than bad luck.

Kundera plays kissy-face with a number of sketchy concepts in ***Immortality.*** One chapter is devoted to the rise of Sentimental Man. "Homo sentimentalis cannot be defined as a man with feelings (for we all have feelings), but as a man who has raised feelings to a category of value." Sentimental man is kitsch incarnate, wearing his heart on his forehead. There's nothing intrinsically wrong with Kundera's fable except that it lacks a moral. Nabokov said it better and stronger when he stressed that one should be sensitive rather than sentimental. A sensitive person is never purposely cruel. A sentimentalist is often a closet brute. "Stalin loved babies. Lenin sobbed at the opera." Kundera knows official bullying firsthand. The Czech government revoked his citizenship upon the publication of ***The Book of Laughter and Forgetting.*** But his worldly stance and émigré status seem to have rendered him rather angelically aloof. He's dealing in highbrow infotainment.

It's hard for a novelist and an intellectual to share the same skin. There's an ingrained rub. Crudely put, novelists specify, intellectuals generalize. Novelists nurture, intellectuals construct. In Kundera, the intellectual has routed the novelist. He seldom dramatizes now. Cut off from natural feedback, he universalizes about human behavior from some abstract plane. "Rubens tells himself: Laughter is the most democratic of all the facial aspects: we differ from one another by our immovable features, but in convulsion we are all the same." Sounds impressive, but isn't weeping equally convulsive, equally democratic? And try this on for size:

> Imagine that you have a friend who loves Schumann and hates Schubert, while you madly love Schubert and Schumann bores you to tears. What kind of record would you give your friend as a birthday gift? The Schumann he loves, or the Schubert you adore? Schubert, of course. If you gave him a record of Schumann you'd have the unpleasant feeling that such a gift would not be sincere and would be more like a bribe calculated to flatter your friend. After all, when you give someone a present, you want to do so out of love, you want to give your friend a piece of yourself, a piece of your heart!

Totally bonkers. We purchase what will please the other person, not ourselves. (Unless of course we want to bug him.) It's what's known as consideration.

Ah, but I've neglected to mention a relevant detail regarding the above passage, one that shines *considerable light* on the subject, my dear Watson. The gift giver was a woman. And we know how women are—bossy, pushy, and out to lunch. They drink your blood, drain your bankbook, and hang around after sex. (Can't they take a hint?) They're incapable of basic ploys. They make everything a package deal. "You can have me, but the way I really am, and that includes my cat" is how Kundera sums up the gift woman's stance. "The cat became the image of her soul, and a lover had to accept her soul if he wished to have her body." Odd that Kundera's aversion to women *and their insane demands* hasn't received more notice. It's not as if he's kept it under his helmet.

In ***The Art of the Novel,*** Kundera distinguishes between machismo and misogyny. A macho man, he says, aspires to preside over a family. A misogynist wishes to surround himself with mistresses, or, failing that, a childless woman. Kundera's men fall into the latter camp. Ideally, they want their women wall-to-wall. In ***Unbearable Lightness,*** the doctor Tomas was more ringmaster than harem master, ordering women to undress with a whiplash of his tongue. The painter Rubens in ***Immortality*** is Tomas minus temperament. He's such a benumbed misogynist that his mistresses don't even have names, only irritating traits. "The one he saw most often was G, a young woman whose main characteristic was a propensity to use coarse words in conversation." The two of them are out of sync. "When he was capable of tenderness, she talked coarsely; and when he longed to talk coarsely, she kept stubbornly silent." Men and women *do* get on each other's cases—it isn't sexist to make that a source of comedy. (Montherlant's *The Girls* is a masterpiece of piqued male pride, and Kingsley Amis's *Stanley and the Women* rises to paranoid delirium.) But Kundera isn't interested in bad manners or behavioral conflict. He disdains women not for what they occasionally *do,* but for what he thinks they unchangeably *are.*

Women to Kundera are walking messes. "It starts with the shock of the first bleeding; the body is suddenly present and she stands facing it like a poor mechanic ordered to keep a small factory running: to change tampons every month, to swallow pills, snap the brassiere in place, get ready for production." Even when the blood flow is contained, it can't be trusted. "She blushed. It is a beautiful thing when a woman blushes; at that instant her body no longer belongs to her; she doesn't control it; she is at its mercy; oh, can there be anything more beautiful than the sight of a woman violated by her own body!" That "violated" speaks volumes.

Perhaps the prime breakdown moment in basic human sympathy in ***Immortality*** comes when Agnes notices that her sister, Laura, who has been courting suicide following a drastic love affair, has lost weight. "Agnes watched the thin body with uncontrolled distaste, and this idea occurred to her: What happened to those fifteen pounds that Laura lost? Did they disperse into the blue like used-up energy? Or did they follow her excrement into the sewer?" Most of us can grasp that men and women alike lose weight during downfalls of grief without sticking our heads down the toilet. That "uncontrolled distaste," I submit, is Kundera's own. That weight loss, like the monthly blood, is simply more female mess.

Being a harem master isn't all it's cracked up to be, warns ***Immortality.*** The company of women shrivels a man. At the end of the novel Paul exclaims his happiness at having a wife, a daughter, and a granddaughter—a mini-harem! But as he speaks he becomes effeminized. "His mighty gray shock of hair had suddenly turned into the coiffure of an old lady." Plus, he's revealed to be a future cuckold.

Eternity, laments ***Immortality,*** is a ceaseless babble of women's voices, a steam bath with locked doors. In Kundera's heaven, women would be mute, modeling their enigmatic smiles before endless mirrors. That's how he divides sexual roles: intellectual exhibitionism for men, physical exhibitionism for women. The advantage goes to men, since their minds outlast women's bodies. Amazing, the kind of exhausted crap you can sneak by under the guise of Culture. (pp. 54, 58)

James Wolcott, "The Unbearable Lightness of Reason," in Vanity Fair, *Vol. 54, No. 5, May, 1991, pp. 54, 58.*

Joseph Coates

[***Immortality***] is the sixth funny and subversive novel the emigre Czech novelist Milan Kundera has published in this country about the "terminal paradoxes of the modern era," by which Kundera means, roughly, this century's drift toward totalitarian control over the minds as well as the bodies of individual citizens.

As he puts it in ***The Art of the Novel*** (1986): "In the course of the Modern Era, Cartesian rationality has corroded . . . all the values inherited from the Middle Ages. But just when reason wins a total victory, pure irrationality (force willing only its will) seizes the world stage, because there is no longer any generally accepted value system to block its path."

Beginning about 20 years ago, Kundera's works—including ***The Art of the Novel*** as well as a book of hilarious short stories, ***Laughable Loves,*** and the five previous novels—have been respectfully and sometimes enthusiastically received in the United States and Western Europe. They have sold especially well since a highly erotic movie was made from his ***The Unbearable Lightness of Being.***

All of Kundera's works, at least by implication, have had the same relevance to the cultures of Western and Eastern Europe when the latter was still under Soviet domination. But ***Immortality*** is the first to be set in the West (Paris, where Kundera has lived since 1975), and the first to state that communism has been replaced by capitalist technocracy and media manipulation—what Kundera calls "imagology."

"All ideologies have been defeated," says the novelistic voice named Kundera who weaves together stories of desperate imagemongering going back to the celebrity of Goethe and the Romanticism he both helped invent and despised.

> Communists used to believe that in the course of capitalist development the proletariat would gradually grow poorer and poorer, but when it finally became clear that all over Europe workers were driving to work in their own cars, they felt like shouting that reality was deceiving them. Reality was stronger than ideology.

Now, however, "imagology is stronger than reality," and lifestyles are dictated by advertising and opinion polls, which "enable imagology to live in absolute harmony with the people. . . . Since for contemporary man reality is a continent visited less and less often and is, besides, justifiably disliked, the findings of polls . . . have become the truth."

Kundera's method is to make the novel give us something only the novel can provide, "a meditation on the great themes of existence." It has been said that in ***Unbearable Lightness*** especially there was too much essayistic meditation and too little existence. But in ***Immortality,*** Kundera gives us an abundance of life (even a playfully hypothesized afterlife), felt and experienced by real people in the grip of modernity's terminal paradoxes.

The main present-time story is a love triangle involving a woman named Agnes who lives in Paris with her husband Paul, who is pursued by Agnes rapacious sister Laura. Agnes and Laura are psychological opposites. Agnes, the novelist's main viewpoint character, is beautiful, ascetic and distrustful of her body. Laura is a sensualist who seemingly imitates everything Laura does and deliberately fails at it in order to reproach Agnes for not doing something more with your life."

Both are talented, but while Agnes is content with simple existence, Laura adds attributes to herself like layers of skin or clothing. Agnes finds the modern world unbearably ugly as she walks down a Paris street feeling less and less in common with the rest of humanity. She is assaulted by the racket of a girl driving a motorcycle without a muffler, but it

> wasn't the machine that made the noise, it was the self of the black-haired girl: in order . . . to penetrate into the consciousness of others, she attached the noisy exhaust of the engine to her soul. Agnes watched the flowing hair of that blaring soul and she realized that she yearned intensely for the girl's death.

Agnes is soon punished for this. Into the street racket comes the sound of a fugue played at full volume from a top-floor apartment "so that Bach's severe beauty sounded a warning to a world that had gone awry." But "cars and drills appropriated Bach as part of their own fugue, so that Agnes had to cover her ears with her hands" and a passerby "gave her an angry glance and tapped his forehead. . . . It was equality itself that reprimanded her in the guise of this man, not allowing that an individual refuse to undergo something that everyone must experience."

Thus another of Kundera's terminal paradoxes: The "long-desired unity of mankind . . . means: No escape for anyone anywhere." The world went awry when the average educated man stopped understanding his natural habitat and the sciences that explained it and retreated into "his self, into his nostalgia . . . into his revolt." The ultimate assertion of self becomes the immortality all of us spend our lives trying to manufacture in advance.

Kundera has great fun showing how such attempts always fail, primarily in an extended historical sequence detailing Goethe's 20-year dalliance, beginning at age 60, with a silly young married groupie named Bettina, who was determined to ride into immortality on his coattails.

This triangle involving Goethe, his peasant wife Christiane and the ambitious Bettina parallels the modern erotic intrigues among Agnes and an anonymous lover, as well as her husband Paul and her sister Laura; and Laura and a young broadcast journalist named Bernard. Just as Bettina realizes that "she was a pistol aimed at the heart of [Goethe's] immortality," Laura knows that the path to her immortality is Bernard, who dropped his legal studies for a profession where there was real power: journalism, whose might is based on "the right to demand an answer."

"The inequality between one who gives orders and one who must obey," Kundera notes, "is not as radical as that between one who has a right to demand an answer and one who has the duty to answer." It's an observation that has weight, although this aspect of the book may seem naive in tone to anyone drenched in the slickness of American image-mongering.

On the other hand, the charge that Kundera's characters exist only to mouth ideas certainly doesn't stick this time. We care deeply about Agnes, and her deeply etched individuality doesn't prevent her from representing the last and best of Europe's humane tradition—someone who wants simply to be and is not allowed to by the insistently ambitious souls that surround her. She is Christiane to her sister's Bettina, and they exist in a sense far more palpable than as occasions for Kundera's ideas.

Even among the immortals, Hemingway sounds like Hemingway when he complains to Goethe about the Kenneth Lynn biography in the alternate universe of the hereafter. And Goethe has his own problems with Bettina's revision of their correspondence, an artful fiction published as *Conversations with a Child* in 1835.

Kundera has Goethe realize eventually "that when a person ceases to minister to his immortality and no longer considers it a serious matter. . . . there, and only there, can true freedom be found." As he tells Hemingway in the hereafter: "That obsession with one's own image, that's man's fatal immaturity."

In any case, Kundera's people are recognizably ourselves, his world ours and his authorial presence more invigorating than intrusive. He has miraculously managed to temper his bleak view of the immediate future with a lightness of erotic wit that restores to the modern novel the ontological gusto of Rabelais and the philosophical cutting edge of Cervantes.

In doing so, Kundera opens to the West the possibility "that human beings can be helped to understand their situation through literature and thereby save themselves," as critic Andrei Codrescu put it in speaking of him. And, like it or not, we may need to be saved. As Agnes says to herself:

> The world is at some sort of border; if it is crossed, everything will turn to madness; people will walk the streets holding forget-me-nots or kill one another on sight. And it will take very little for the glass to overflow, perhaps just one drop: perhaps just one car too many, or one person, or one decibel.

(pp. 1, 4)

Joseph Coates,, "Amid the Din of Images," in Chicago Tribune, *May 12, 1991, pp. 1, 4.*

Jonathan Yardley

Like Milan Kundera's previous novels, ***Immortality*** is ingenious, witty, provocative and formidably intelligent, both a pleasure and a challenge to the reader. But unlike the best of those earlier novels, which weave their intellectual arguments into larger tapestries of character and plot,

Immortality is all talk and no story; this is fine so long as the talk is interesting, but whenever it palls—as too often it does—the novel's energy wanes and the reader finds himself restlessly turning the page in hopes of relief.

"I regret that almost all novels ever written are much too obedient to the rules of unity of action." Thus speaks a character named Milan Kundera, who continues: "Dramatic tension is the real curse of the novel, because it transforms everything, even the most beautiful pages, even the most surprising scenes and observations, merely into steps leading to the final resolution, in which the meaning of everything that preceded is concentrated . . . A novel shouldn't be like a bicycle race but a feast of many courses."

Such a feast is what Kundera has attempted to concoct in ***Immortality.*** The novel begins with a mere gesture, observed by the novelist as he lounges at poolside in Paris: a handsome woman in her early 60s turns her head, smiles, waves at the lifeguard, and "the essence of her charm, independent of time, revealed itself for a second in that gesture and dazzled me." The scene "aroused in me immense, inexplicable nostalgia, and this nostalgia gave birth to the woman I call Agnes."

She becomes the central character of ***Immortality,*** although her centrality is clouded by her elusiveness; however much he may be captivated by her, Kundera never manages to give Agnes an identity over and above the symbolic. She represents the deep longing to transcend time, to "remain in the memory of posterity," just as her marriage to Paul represents "the illusion of love, an illusion which both of them have been anxiously guarding and nurturing," but she never emerges as a believable or interesting character.

That is true of virtually all the people in ***Immortality*** except, oddly enough, those who are drawn from historical fact. Most notable among these is Johann Wolfgang von Goethe, the great German writer, whose unconsummated romance with the far younger Bettina becomes, in Kundera's imagination, a metaphor for the longing for immortality and the odd tricks that can be played on those who seek it. "What was at stake between them was not love," Kundera writes. "It was immortality"—the aging writer trying to shape and control his image for the ages, the young and ambitious woman trying to exercise her own influence, yet in the process coming up against the hard truth that "man reckons with immortality, and forgets to reckon with death."

By contrast with this yearning to win immortality because of one's deeds or artistic creations, Kundera posits "imagology," a word that "finally lets us put under one roof something that goes by so many names: advertising agencies; political campaign managers; designers who devise the shape of everything from cars to gym equipment; fashion stylists; barbers; show-business stars dictating the norms of physical beauty that all branches of imagology obey." Ours is an age in which we live "for appearance and not for reality." An age in which "reality no longer means anything to anyone."

The pages of ***Immortality*** are riddled—some might say littered—with epigrams, bon mots and *aperçus* such as these. Kundera is no Montaigne, but he cannot resist the well-turned and deftly incisive phrase. At times he is as irreverent as he is penetrating:

> Because people in the West are not threatened by concentration camps and are free to say and write what they want, the more the fight for human rights gains in popularity the more it loses any concrete content, becoming a kind of universal stance of everyone toward everything, a kind of energy that turns all human desires into rights. The world has become man's right and everything in it has become a right: the desire for love the right to love, the desire for rest the right to rest, the desire for friendship the right to friendship, the desire to exceed the speed limit the right to exceed the speed limit, the desire for happiness the right to happiness, the desire to publish a book the right to publish a book, the desire to shout in the street in the middle of the night the right to shout in the street. The unemployed have the right to occupy an expensive food store, the women in fur coats have the right to buy caviar, Brigitte has the right to park on the sidewalk, and everybody, the unemployed, the women in fur coats, as well as Brigitte, belongs to the same army of fighters for human rights.

That paragraph is absolutely right on, a devastatingly accurate summary of all the ways in which we've managed to turn self-indulgence into entitlement; perhaps only a writer with Kundera's Eastern European slant, part bitter and part wry, could see us so clearly. But perhaps you are asking, Who is Brigitte and how did she get mixed up in this? Well, she is the grown daughter of Agnes and Paul and, more to the point, she is one of the many characters who get lost in the funhouse of Kundera's social, cultural and artistic commentary. ***Immortality*** is at its best a splendid essay, but as a novel it leaves a lot to be desired; Kundera's elaborate apologia to the contrary notwithstanding, "dramatic tension"—character, setting, plot, structure, narrative—is a desirable and necessary element in fiction, and its absence in ***Immortality*** is debilitating.

The novel of ideas has a long and honorable tradition, to which in fact Kundera has contributed, most notably in ***The Book of Laughter and Forgetting*** and ***The Unbearable Lightness of Being.*** But the very phrase "novel of ideas" implies the coexistence of the two in mutually revealing and supportive ways; inasmuch as ***Immortality*** is all ideas and no novel, its failure as the latter ultimately diminishes the interest of the former.

Jonathan Yardley, "Talking About the Big Questions," in Book World—The Washington Post, *May 5, 1991, p. 3.*

Adam Mars-Jones

[In ***Immortality***], this novel full of definitions, nice distinctions and dialectical character-drawing, one particular opposition hangs around like a guilty conscience, the opposition between loving music for its notes or for its associations. Transposed to the realm of fiction, the question be-

"[Great] novels are always a little more intelligent than their authors. Novelists who are more intelligent than their books should go into another line of work."

—Kundera, from his acceptance speech for the Jerusalem Prize in 1985.

comes: do we love novels, or the things they make us think of? ***Immortality*** is either a novel of ideas or an inventory of more or less stimulating opinions.

Kundera appears in person in the book, inspired to create his heroine, Agnes, by seeing an old woman at his health club in Paris wave at her swimming instructor with sudden youthfulness. He speculates that gestures are in some sense immortal, only fleetingly incarnated in individuals, and he sets out to trace the gesture's history in an imaginary life.

Having set the scene for Agnes, however, Kundera remains on stage, interspersing her story with his own reflections on immortality. He concentrates on immortality as Goethe imagined it and prepared for it, and as Bettina von Arnim sought to commandeer it—first by maintaining a relentless correspondence with the great man, and then by publishing it after his death, much improved.

Kundera gives Agnes a past, but a rather desultory present. She walks through Paris after visiting her health club (which she shares with her author), registering impressions—the borderline tolerability of life in modern cities, the privileged position of the camera in modern life—that it is easy to imagine appearing in Kundera's journal. It begins to look as if Kundera's fiction is itself a matter of characteristic gestures, imprinted on material rather than arising from it.

In due course, Agnes acquires a sister, Laura, and a husband, Paul; Laura acquires a lover, Bernard. Kundera gives their interrelationships a certain amount of fictional texture, but he also denies his characters their expected primacy in his book. Readers of ***Immortality*** may find themselves in the position of concert-goers expecting a string quartet, disconcerted to find a podium set up among the music stands, and a lecturer interrupting the performance every few bars. It's a stimulating lecture but an unsatisfying concert.

It isn't altogether clear, however, who is interrupting whom. Some chapters begin with the Goethe material, and then drop in a reference to the fictional characters, as if Agnes's story was in some way illustrative, and of only secondary importance. There is a small and not very helpful overlap between the different registers of the book, in that Agnes remembers being taught a Goethe poem by her father. The uncertain relationship of subject and counter-subject has the same disorienting effect as the hanging of an abstract painting upside down, all the more troubling if the inversion isn't immediately obvious.

Kundera's fictional workings are naturally dialectical. If one of the sisters wears dark glasses then the other, if she shares the affectation, will have an antithetical reason for it. If one thinks of suicide as a *vanishing,* the other must see it as a definitive *inflicting* of a body and a memory on the survivors (the italics are not Kundera's but in his manner).

Up above the world of his book, Kundera nevertheless feels in need of a conversational partner, and invents for the purpose a Dr Avenarius. Avenarius is announced as having a peculiar penis, "not only enormous but [differing] from other members by the horned devil's head at its tip", which is rather confusing since his life's work is combatting "Diabolum", his word for the inexhaustible stupidity of the world.

One of the topics discussed by Kundera and Avenarius is, inevitably, the novel: "I regret", says Kundera, "that almost all novels ever written are much too obedient to the rules of unity of action. . . . These novels are like a narrow street along which someone drives his characters with a whip." How much is gained, though, by dropping the whip?

The narrative of ***Immortality*** has an air of improvisation which is almost certainly deceptive. One early page, for instance, describing Kundera's early morning reveries while listening to the radio, acts as a sort of overture. There is a fur shop, for instance, and a women's choir, respectively Laura's job and her hobby. There is a Bernard speaking on the radio, as Laura's lover does later in the novel. There is mention of a biography of Hemingway, who features in posthumous conversations with Goethe, and so on.

If Kundera's various strategies in ***Immortality*** have anything in common, it is being somehow high-risk and low-yield. The repudiation of conventional form doesn't bring an increase in intensity; rather the reverse. The book is perfectly readable—it isn't difficult in any obvious way—but far from reader-friendly. The author's underlying attitude towards his readers, in fact, seems to be a sort of suave hostility.

Take the matter of his self-presentation, for instance. In the opening pages, the narrator is simply a novelist. On page 89, he is revealed as a Czech. On page 137, he is the author of a novel whose hero is called Jaromil. Finally on page 152 he is referred to as "Mr Kundera", and the novel with Jaromil in it identified as ***Life Is Elsewhere.*** (Later, Kundera confides that ***Immortality*** should really be called ***The Unbearable Lightness of Being,*** a title unfortunately pre-empted by a novel less deserving of it.) Experienced readers of modern fiction (and it is hard to imagine Kundera wanting any other audience) will have been saying to themselves, "Ha! You don't catch me out identifying character with author on the basis of vocation or nationality or . . . er, name or book-title." The distinction between Kundera and his persona is whittled away, without of course ever disappearing, yet the equivocation doesn't become a crucial issue as it would, say, in a Philip Roth novel.

Other important pieces of information are perversely delayed. Agnes is off-handedly referred to as a cybernetics expert on page 75, which in retrospect would seem to make a childhood conversation with her father—in which he said he believed not in God but in the Creator's computer—a turning-point in her life. Nothing is made of this. Kundera seems to be flaunting the capriciousness of his choice of a career for his heroine, and hardly refers to it again.

Another off-hand moment comes on page 202, with the sentence: "About a week after the terrible death of Agnes, Laura visited a despondent Paul." This is the first reference to Agnes's death, terrible or otherwise, but we don't learn what happens to her for another sixty pages. In most novels, such a device would be a way of sharpening the appetite. In ***Immortality*** it seems to be a way of punishing the reader for being interested in the heroine rather than the author's unmediated opinions. When Kundera gets round to describing the death, he gives as much prominence to the point of view of the unnamed woman who causes the accident (by walking into the path of Agnes's car) as he does to the victim, his heroine. No one could accuse Kundera of foisting an artificial coherence on the reader, but the foisting of an artificial incoherence is not self-evidently a higher aim.

This stricture does not apply to Part Six of the book, which almost lives up to Kundera's cheeky announcement of it to Avenarius: "I am really looking forward to Part Six. A completely new character will enter the novel. And at the end of that part he will disappear without a trace. He causes nothing and leaves no effects. That is precisely what I like about him. Part Six will be a novel within a novel, as well as the saddest erotic story I have ever written."

In Part Six Kundera returns to an earlier set of themes, and becomes again the philosopher of carnality. He tells the story of a Swiss man nicknamed Rubens, and the various phases of his sexual life. Elsewhere in ***Immortality*** Kundera displays a chauvinism that is either unselfconscious or defiant, but in either case largely a matter of manners. It's hard to imagine an experienced writer rereading his own work and not detecting the false note in this sentence, for instance: "Nothing is so pleasant as meeting a woman we once feared and who, disarmed, is no longer threatening." At the same time, it is not a hard sentence to rewrite.

The sexism of Part Six is deeper—Rubens's sexual partners are referred to by successive letters of the alphabet—but paradoxically less offensive. Kundera is one of the few male writers to care about what sex means, about how the flesh at its fleshiest continues to play symbolic roles. It is true that women are regarded as steps on Rubens's path to self-knowledge, but at a late stage he realizes that they too can be learners, even teachers, rather than lessons.

Part Six intersects with the rest of the book at precisely one point, the word "Agnes" in its penultimate section. An incident described in passing 200 pages before turns out to have had a decisive effect on Rubens. But when the reader issues the mental command to file Part Six under the heading *Agnes,* nothing happens. Kundera's "heroine" remains a footnote to the story within her story. It is his last strange act of aggression against his character, or against the reader's preference for dealing with her rather than with the writer direct.

For much of ***Immortality,*** it is as if the Greeks in making their Horse had chosen to use perspex. The Trojans from their battlements would have been fascinated by this object, with its warriors visibly crouched inside. They would perhaps have puzzled over the fact that something so clearly not a horse had four legs and a tail. But they wouldn't have taken it inside their gates.

Adam Mars-Jones, "A Lecture from the Philosopher of Carnality," in The Times Literary Supplement, *No. 4598, May 17, 1991, p. 17.*

Gabriele Annan

Milan Kundera's new novel ***Immortality*** is a tragicomic *jeu d'esprit* stuffed with references and meanings, and even, you might say, ready-annotated. The story is set in Paris and very simple: Paul is a lawyer with a wife, Agnes, who works for a computer company. They have a grown-up daughter, Brigitte. Brigitte is closer to her father than Agnes is. Agnes has a lover, Rubens, whom she has known since she was seventeen and whom she sees only once every few years. Agnes's younger sister Laura is having an affair with Paul's friend Bernard, a radio commentator. When Bernard deserts her, she decides to love Paul. Agnes is killed in a motor accident, and Paul marries Laura. Laura starts an affair with Professor Avenarius, who is the friend of the narrator, who is Kundera, and who, in Chapter 1, invents first Agnes and then the rest of the story.

Immortality is like the Pompidou building in Paris. All the things that keep it going are in separate chapters or ducts. The ducts make a lively pattern over the outside of the narrative, which corresponds to the body of the museum. The stuff inside the ducts is philosophy, history, cultural history, *Ideengeschichte,* literature, aesthetics, politics, semiotics, theories about time and chance, and many enthusiastically illustrated reflections about the nature and role of the erotic. The ducts are gaily colored, definitely part of the entertainment; they are also explanatory notes to help you with the story.

A huge amount is packed into 345 pages, but there is no sense of rush on the one hand or overcondensation—heaviness—on the other. The novel dances along on its toes—on its lightness of being, perhaps. The narrator's tone is debonair. But his view of the world is pitch black. Professor Avenarius shares it. He goes around at night slashing tires in an apparently idiotic protest against pollution. Though he doesn't come into the story much, he must be intended to be the hero of it. He deals with the horror of life by turning everything into a joke—a familiar East European strategy, only in this case the enemy is not totalitarian repression, but the Western world with its dreadful new delusion, which Kundera calls Imagology. We will come to Imagology later.

At the end of the novel Kundera celebrates its completion by ordering a bottle of wine to share with Professor Avenarius:

> At that moment I understood him at last. If we cannot accept the importance of the world, which considers itself important, if in the midst of that world our laughter finds no echo, we have but one choice: to take the world as a whole and make it the object of our game; to turn it into a toy. Avenarius is playing a game, and for him the game is the only thing of importance in a world without importance. But he knows that his game will not make anyone laugh. When he outlined his proposal to the ecologists, he had no intention of amusing anyone. He only wished to amuse himself.
>
> I said, "You play with the world like a melancholy child who has no little brother. . . . "
>
> Avenarius smiled like a melancholy child. Then he said, "I don't have a little brother, but I have you."

Their conversation takes place in the most mundane and modern environment imaginable: by the pool in a glitzy health club at the top of a Paris high-rise, with Muzak blaring from the amplifiers. It is the kind of place Kundera and Agnes hate. But it was where she popped into his head two years earlier when he was waiting, as usual, for Avenarius. He knew that her name must be Agnes—a gentle, old-fashioned name. There is no doubt that she is the novel's heroine. She is born of a gesture, a peculiarly charming wave of the arm which Kundera observes in an old woman bidding good-bye to her swimming instructor. Kundera invests Agnes with this gesture, but she in turn has copied it from another character in the novel's past: from her father's old secretary, who loved him. One day, Agnes sees Laura using it and realizes that "the gesture was available to all and this did not really belong to her."

This is one of Kundera's favorite notions: there are words and gestures hanging around in the universe waiting to be used, and with a longer lineage than the people who will use them. They give sex its special value because the words and gestures we use in the act have all been used before; they belong to the primordial stream of being. Sex is older and more precious than what we call love—which is only a latter-day European invention of doubtful worth. Agnes and her lover Rubens understand this, but so did Maupassant. The antique collector in his story "Le Chevelure" is driven mad by the pathos of an old watch as he thinks of the woman who wore it. . . .

Agnes is also *de jadis.* She does not fit into the modern world and suffers from it: the noise, the bustle, the lack of privacy, the people bearing down on her from all sides, even her husband, Paul, and her grown-up daughter, Brigitte, whom she loves. She is aloof, a princess, "a real princess of episode," her lover thinks, "elegant yet not ostentatious, beautiful without being dazzling, ready for physical love and yet shy; she never bothered [him] with confessions about her private life, and yet she never dramatized her discreet silence or tried to convert it into disquieting mystery." Agnes tries to drop out of the world as much as she can. Sex with her lover is one way of doing it, a sort of nirvana. Eventually she drops right out by being killed in an accident. It is the alternative strategy to Avenarius's jokes. Agnes distinguishes between living, which is busy and full of pretension, and being, which is quiet. She longs for quiet. A few pages into the novel Kundera pays tribute to the ineffable beauty of quietness by quoting "the most famous German poem ever written," Goethe's "Uber allen Gipfeln ist Ruh."

Goethe inhabits the novel's conceptual/anecdotal ducts along with Hemingway (they meet in the Beyond. . . . and have a very funny conversation about immortality), Rimbaud, Cervantes, Romain Rolland, Mitterrand, Giscard, Jimmy Carter, Tycho Brahe, Napoleon, Dali and Gala, Woodward and Bernstein, and his own passionate admirer, Bettina von Arnim. Bettina has been the Shirley Temple of German literature for a century and a half, ever since she published her correspondence with Goethe (heavily edited by her, Kundera reminds us) under the title *Goethe's Correspondence With A Child.* She was no child, but a married bluestocking given to sitting on famous men's knees in a childlike manner. Generations of upper-middle-class German girls have borne her name which no one in Germany had ever heard until she made it famous.

Rilke put her among the great women lovers of all time and Kundera mocks him for it. He really has it in for Bettina and sends her up with gusto: she is his pill of pills, typical of what is wrong with modern sensibility, and responsible for some of it, too. Kundera may not care for modern sensibility, but he understands it in a way that makes the characters in many modern novels seem premodern, however modern or postmodern those novels may be in form. Since ***The Unbearable Lightness of Being,*** Kundera's characters have had at their disposal a whole new repertoire of feelings, reactions, and motives, including, of course, the counter-feelings, counter-reactions, and counter-motives of the good, or unspoiled, characters like Agnes.

According to Kundera, Bettina von Arnim wasn't in love with Goethe (or Beethoven, or any of the other famous men she tried to attach herself to) but with immortality, and that is why he calls his book ***Immortality.*** She thought she could attain it by being the lover of the great. She was a groupie, and the incarnation of Romanticism, for which Kundera has no time at all. Romanticism is founded on self-regard, self-absorption, solipsism. . . . (p. 3)

Kundera has coined the name Imagology for people's obsession with their image, the habit of seeing themselves as a lover or a revolutionary—or perhaps a pop star or a tycoon or a gangster. You could say that Imagology is a modern variant of the second half of the old firm *Sein* and *Schein,* and even—though Kundera doesn't—that worrying about it is a kind of structuralism; everything is invented by you yourself, depends on you, refers to you; so it can't have any intrinsic value. What Kundera does say is that Imagology is dire, not only because it leads to ideology and war and revolution, but because it has killed off proper sexual relations. Everyone would like to be seen as a hedonist, says Professor Avenarius, but "nowadays hedonists no longer exist. . . . Except for me . . . all of them are eager for admiration and not for pleasure. For appearance and not for reality. Reality no longer means anything to anyone." Combined with the noise and squalor of the modern world, this is a reason for wanting to stop it and get off: Agnes's position.

Agnes is noble, sensitive, and alluring, but she has no sense of humor. And so she has to die. Professor Avenarius's sense of humor enables him to go on living: he also has an expensive Mercedes and a mistress. True, Laura has many of Bettina's drawbacks including *her* habitual gesture which is a sort of yearning movement of the arms. But Professor Avenarius makes do with what is available and jokes about it. That, or death, as in Agnes's case, are the two choices available now. Nothing has changed since ***The Unbearable Lightness of Being,*** in which Sabina was first dealt a life of lightness and Tomas and Tereza got the automobile accident. It was naive to read Kundera's penultimate novel as an indictment of Communism. He indicts the whole modern world. (pp. 3-4)

Gabriele Annan, "Selective Affinities," in The New York Review of Books, *Vol. XXXVIII, No. 10, May 30, 1991, pp. 3-4.*

John Leonard

We are at the end of Europe, the end of history, the end of culture and the end of this novel, in deck chairs at a health club with a swimming pool. We can look at ourselves in twenty-seven mirrors on three sides of the rooftop club, or we can look through the fourth wall at a panoramic view of Paris. Milan Kundera is talking to one of his characters in ***Immortality,*** the accused rapist and guerrilla tire-slasher Professor Avenarius. He seeks a metaphor. To Avenarius, he says, "You play with the world . . . a melancholy child who has no little brother." Avenarius smiles, very much like a melancholy child, and then remarks. "I don't have a little brother, but I have you."

And we have Kundera, a 62-year-old melancholy child, a little brother of the bloody borders and the lost faith. He has written this novel in front of our eyes, out of chance encounters with enigmatic strangers, and radio news reports of anomalous events, and imaginary conversations among the lofty likes of Goethe and Hemingway, and snippets of books, and shards of memory. He has interpolated little essays—on journalism, sentimentality, coincidence, astrology and the phases of the erotic moon—that turn out, of course, not to have been digressions at all. Everything fits inside with a satisfying snap, like the hasp on a jewel box or the folding of a fan. Left in the air, like smoke, are ghosts and grace notes.

I'm sure there's a musical analogue; there usually is, in Kundera's fiction: Mozart's *Don Giovanni* or Beethoven's last quartet or any one of sixteen fugues by Bach. Our lives "are composed like music," Kundera told us in ***The Unbearable Lightness of Being.*** "Guided by his sense of beauty, an individual transforms a fortuitous occurrence . . . into a motif, which then assumes a permanent place in the composition of the individual's life."

Certainly, in ***Immortality,*** there's a lot of Mahler.

But along with linear time, Romantic poetry, modern art, the idea of progress, the ardor of revolution and the consolations of nostalgia, he has also given up on music. "Romantic music," we're told,

> can be heard every time some statesman is murdered or war is declared, every time it is necessary to stuff people's heads with glory to make them die more willingly. Nations that tried to annihilate each other were filled with the identical fraternal emotion when they heard the thunder of Chopin's Funeral March or Beethoven's *Eroica.*

Kundera himself explains that "music taught the European not only a richness of feeling but also the worship of his feelings and his feeling self. . . . Music: a pump for inflating the soul. Hypertrophic souls turned into huge balloons rise to the ceiling of the concert hall and jostle each other in unbelievable congestion."

Whether this constitutes a symbolic patricide—Kundera's father, mourned so lovingly in ***The Book of Laughter and Forgetting,*** was a musicologist—I can't say. But it leaves us lonelier in Paris than we were before we ever met Agnes (a computer expert and "the clear-minded observer of ambiguity") or her sister, Laura (a *haute couture* shopkeeper and "the addict of ambiguity"), or Agnes's husband, Paul (a clever lawyer and "the simpleton of ambiguity").

Laura, because she thinks she loves Paul, plays Mahler on a white piano and collects money for African lepers in the Paris Metro system. Agnes, because she decides she doesn't love Paul anymore or not enough, leaves Paris for Switzerland, where her father and her money are both stashed. Paul, who's come to deplore Mahler as much as rock and roll, and to despair of Western civilization, drinks too much. Professor Avenarius meets Laura in the Metro when she's humiliated by *clochards,* seems never to have heard of Agnes and hires Paul to defend him against the charge of rape. (Though there's always a lot of rape in Kundera novels, this one didn't happen.)

I neglect Rubens, who renounced art in favor of erotomania, because he is one of Kundera's several wicked surprises. So I won't tell you about his affair with the lute player, also known as the Gothic Maiden, and their stroll among "the severed heads of the famous dead." Besides, you've met him before. Like Zemanek in ***The Joke,*** Jaromil in ***Life Is Elsewhere,*** Klima in ***The Farewell Party*** and Tomas in ***The Unbearable Lightness of Being,*** he's a compulsive womanizer. There are signs here that Kundera is at last as weary of Don Juan and his roundelay of one-night stands as he wearied earlier of Don Quixote. But there are signs here that Kundera has wearied of everything else too, even laughter: "Humor," says Avenarius, "can only exist when people are still capable of recognizing some borders between the important and the unimportant."

These people are unhappy because God is dead, and neither sex nor politics will guarantee them a life everafter. They're short on meaning and being. In all of European culture there are only fifty or so geniuses (fifty-one, counting Kundera) who deserve remembering after they have gone. Laura, Agnes, Paul, Rubens and Avenarius are not among these happy few. ("Class inequality is but an insignificant shortcoming compared to this insulting metaphysical inequality.") Kundera plays them on his fiddle. Or, to stick to his own quite wonderful conceit of the clock in Old Town Square in Prague, with the twelve apostles and the bell-ringing skeleton, he pops them in and out of his narrative like marionettes. In a world of "many people, few ideas," not even their unhappiness is original. They've borrowed it, like their gestures, from Goethe, Beethoven and Napoleon; from Tycho Brahe and Robert Musil; from Marx and Rimbaud. In one thirty-page section midway through ***Immortality*** Kundera mentions Lacan, Apollinaire, Rilke, Romain Rolland, Paul Eluard, Knut Hamsun, Cervantes, Shakespeare and Dostoyevsky. In spite of all this culture, Europe got Auschwitz and the Gulag. Somebody must be doing something wrong, so everybody will be punished.

According to Paul, who is about to be fired from a radio station where he has a commentary program, "High culture is nothing but a child of that European perversion called history,"

> the obsession we have with going forward, with considering the sequence of generations as a relay race in which everyone surpasses his predecessor, only to be surpassed by his successor. Without this relay race called history there would be no European art and what characterizes it: a longing for originality, a longing for change. Robespierre, Napoleon, Beethoven, Stalin, Picasso, they're all runners in the relay race, they all belong in the same stadium.

To which the man who will fire him replies:

> If high culture is coming to an end, it is also the end of you and your paradoxical ideas, because paradox as such belongs to high culture and not to childish prattle. You remind me of the young men who supported the Nazis or communists not out of cowardice or out of opportunism but out of an excess of intelligence. For nothing requires a greater effort of thought than arguments to justify the rule of nonthought. I experienced it with my own eyes and ears after the war, when intellectuals and artists rushed like a herd of cattle into the Communist Party, which soon proceeded to liquidate them systematically and with great pleasure. You are doing the same. You are the brilliant ally of your own gravediggers.

This, of course, is Kundera's right brain talking to his left. Indeed, the novelist, eavesdropping on this exchange as if he hadn't made the whole thing up himself, is reminded of another of his characters in another of his novels, Jaromil in ***Life Is Elsewhere.*** Like Paul (and Rimbaud), Jaromil felt it necessary "to be absolutely modern." He, too, was the "ally of his gravediggers." Kundera counts on us to remember on our own that Jaromil—an amalgam of Rimbaud, Lermontov and the Czech "proletarian" poet Jiri Wolker—was everything the novelist despises about modernism: its confusion of youth, poetry and revolution; its muddling of the vanguard and the avant-garde. Since Jaromil, in the storied Czech tradition of the Bohemian Catholic governors in 1618 and of Masaryk in 1948, was defenestrated, I'm somewhat surprised Paul doesn't take a header out of the panoramic window of the Paris penthouse. But the surprise death in ***Immortality*** is reserved for someone else. Paul, instead, declares it is time "at last to end the terror of the immortals. To overthrow the arrogant power of the Ninth Symphonies and the *Fausts!*"

Clever, yes? Yes. And so are Kundera's "existential mathematics," his listing of the varieties of coincidence—mute, poetic, contrapuntal, story producing, and maybe even morbid—he has employed to keep us turning his pages. Equally clever is Goethe's reminding Hemingway, in the middle of a chat in the afterlife, that they are both "the frivolous fantasy of a novelist who lets us say things we would probably never say on our own."

The trouble with this cleverness is that it also reminds us we've been here before, with the sendup of Pavel Kohout in ***The Joke;*** with the sendup of Dostoyevsky and Gide in ***The Farewell Party;*** with the sendup of Nietzsche, Tolstoy and Sophocles in ***Unbearable;*** with the sendup of Milan himself as the misogynist Boccaccio in ***Forgetting.*** The essay in ***Immortality*** on imagology (ad agencies, public opinion polls) is inferior to the essay in ***Unbearable*** on kitsch ("kitsch excludes everything from its purview which is essentially unacceptable in human nature"; "a folding screen set up to curtain off death," to "deny shit"), just as the meditation on *Grund* (a German word for reason in the sense of a cause, "a code determining the essence of our fate") is inferior to the meditations in ***Forgetting*** on *lítost* (a Czech word meaning "upsurge of feeling") and in ***Unbearable*** on *soucit* (a Czech word meaning "human co-feeling").

It's not as though he hadn't already told us in ***Laughable Loves*** that sex is powerless against socialism; or in ***Elsewhere*** that poets will always sacrifice shopgirls for the good opinion of the revolution; or in ***Farewell*** that "Western culture such as it was conceived at the dawn of the modern age, based on the individual and his reason, on pluralism of thought, and on tolerance," has come to a violent end; or in ***Forgetting*** that cultural progress is no longer possible; or in ***Unbearable*** that *Einmal ist keinmal:* The horror of history signifies nothing.

We've even been with him into swimming pools before, maybe for lightness of being.

Nor, really, do we need Laura's skirt flying over her head in the Paris Metro, among rioting *clochards,* to remind us of the humiliation of other women in other Kundera novels: Helena and laxatives; sex-starved Alzhbeta and sleeping pills; pregnant Ruzena and the poison capsules; the spinster, in **"Edward and God,"** on her knees; and Tereza, in shame, on the toilet. Avenarius may be innocent of rape, but Lucie in ***The Joke*** was a victim of its viciousness, and we were encouraged to believe that Sabina, with her bowler hat, dreamt about it, and we can be pretty sure that Kundera does. About all his eros, there is a sadistic and masochistic edge—the whistle of the whip. Even mothers tend to be monsters. Jakub in ***Farewell*** pictures his own birth: "He imagined his tiny body sliding through a narrow, damp tunnel, his nose and mouth full of slime."

Even women with whom we are expected to identify, like Tamina in ***Forgetting,*** like Agnes in ***Immortality,*** belong to men in the molecules of their memory: Tamina to her dead husband, Agnes to her dead father—although there's an indication here that Kundera may have briefly entertained another role for his women to play besides the pathetic, one that's not so metaphysically insulting. I'll make fun of that in a minute.

If there is much that's familiar in ***Immortality*** from the other novels, there is also a great absence. That absence, except for the clock in Old Town Square, is Czechoslovakia, particularly Prague, the capital of Kafka and forgetting. We're in Paris, to which Kundera fled in the mid-seventies, but we might as well be anywhere. Paris is irrelevant to ***Immortality,*** a deracinated novel, a sacred monster-ego, one of those severed heads of the famous dead by which Rubens and his Gothic Maiden stroll. This head makes witty remarks ("Napoleon was a true Frenchman in that he was not satisfied with sending hundreds of thousands to their death, but wanted in addition to be admired by writers"), but it floats, on the water, in the air, trailing its nerve-strings like cut cables.

There's no hint here of the intersection of the personal and political that made ***Forgetting*** a masterwork: the magic circle of Young Communists, levitating angels in "a giant wreath," from which Kundera fell; the slit throats of six ostriches and six poets; the passage of the totalitarian state from a Bach fugue to a twelve-tone "single empire" to the abolition of notes and keys; the statues of Lenin growing "like weeds on the ruins, the melancholy flowers of forgetting." This same intersection was also the key to ***Unbearable.*** Not all the violence belonged to the Russians; there was a lot of it in Tomas before the tanks came to Prague in 1968.

(Oddly, it was this personal violence that was omitted from the overpraised movie version of the novel. Yes, Lena Olin, as Sabina, did for bowler hats what Pythagoras did for triangles and Melville did for whales: She gave them a whole new meaning. But the old meanings got lost. In the novel, the bowler is a sex-games prop, a memento of her father, "a sign of her originality" and something else. When Tomas and Sabina look at each other in the mirror, at first it's comic. But, suddenly,

> the bowler hat no longer signified a joke; it signified violence; violence against Sabina, against her dignity as a woman. . . . The fact that Tomas stood beside her fully dressed meant that the essence of what they both saw was far from good clean fun . . . it was humiliation. But instead of spurning it, she proudly, provocatively played it for all it was worth, as if submitting of her own will to public rape.

Likewise, the movie lets Tereza swim in one of Milan's pools with other naked women, but leaves out her dreams about it, in which "Tomas stood over them in a basket hanging from the pool's arched roof, shouting at them, making them sing and do kneebends. The moment one of them did a faulty kneebend, he would shoot her.")

Last summer in Prague, Czech writers complained to American visitors that not only had Kundera deserted them but he was so busy designing himself a Nobel Prize, he hadn't managed to say a word on the Velvet Revolution, when history resumed, not having come to the end he predicted; and so did European culture, but strangely without him. I don't know when he finished ***Immortality***—the copyright is 1990—and therefore can't tell you whether he chose deliberately to ignore this astonishing and essentially nonviolent sea change, or it arrived too late to be thought about this time around, or he no longer cares at all anymore. Besides, what writers do best is gripe.

But history doesn't end; it *can't;* it's internalized, in nations and cultures and families and lovers. There's no reason to believe that we don't evolve, for better or worse, in the history of our cultures like the species in its Darwinian messiness, as much a consequence of chance, contingency, compromise and quirk as of necessity and design; with some adaptations that are nifty, and some inefficient, and some full of surprising surplus value. Surely cultures are their own feedback loop, susceptible to Chaos and Catastrophe Theory, and capable of rearranging themselves in a hot flash after an idea or a bomb, like Islam or the Mafia or the Party line. And surely individual citizens tend to recapitulate the culture, as ontogeny recapitulates phylogeny. The Khmer Rouge was implicit in the brutal kings and the tenth-century Cambodian command economy of slaves that created, in the jungle, a sandstone cosmology and a vision of thirty-two hells, those golden lions and golden Buddhas and dancing girls and corncob towers and sea-serpent cults—which is probably why Pol Pot let stand so undisturbed those temples and tombs, the bare ruined choirs of Angkor Wat. Maybe despair, like so much else, is cyclic, millennial.

I can be lofty too. For that matter, it doesn't seem to me that kitsch is anything new. What else are folk songs and fairy tales, lullabies and festivals, the shinbones of saints for sale on the roads to cathedrals, or the comfort stations of the miraculous, in the Middle Ages? Wasn't "imagology" invented by the great religions? Didn't the media, by sympathetic magic, help make possible what happened, another *Eroica,* in Eastern Europe in 1989? And yet in his very own bare ruined choirs, Milan Kundera feels himself beached; and this vastation he patrols in a canary-yellow Spenglerian doom-buggy.

What we get in ***Immortality,*** instead of any Czechoslovakia, is a lot of Goethe. Why, you may wonder, so much Goethe? For two reasons. First, he was "the great center,"

> a firm center that holds both extremes in a remarkable balance that Europe will never know again. As a young man, Goethe studied alchemy, and later became one of the first modern scientists. Goethe was the greatest German of all, and at the same time an antipatriotic and a European. Goethe was a cosmopolitan, and yet throughout his life he hardly ever stirred out of his province, his little Weimar. Goethe was a man of nature, yet also a man of history. In love, he was a libertine as well as a romantic. And something else . . . Goethe knew how and with what materials his house had been constructed, he knew why his oil lamp gave off light, he knew the principle of the telescope with which he and Bettina looked at Jupiter. . . . The world of technical objects was completely open and intelligible to him.

Not since Mann has another writer wanted so much to re-incarnate Weimar's wiseguy, trashed by modernism. (Never mind that Kundera belongs more to Vienna at the turn of the twentieth century than to Weimar on the straddle of the eighteenth and nineteenth; to Ludwig Wittgenstein and the Secessionists. His novels are peopled with Schieles and the wild-haired women of Klimt.)

The second reason for so much Goethe is that Kundera has borrowed, with credit, his brand-new role for women right out of Part II of *Faust.* According to Paul at the swimming pool on top of Paris, "Woman is the future of man." (Without knowing it, though Kundera does, Paul quotes Aragon.) Paul has been drinking and thinking about his daughter and his granddaughter: "Either woman will become man's future or mankind will perish,"

> because only woman is capable of nourishing within her an unsubstantiated hope and inviting us to a doubtful future, which we would have long ceased to believe in were it not for women. All my life I've been willing to follow their voice, even though that voice is mad, and whatever else I may be I am not a madman. But nothing is more beautiful than when someone who isn't mad goes into the unknown, led by a mad voice . . . *Das Ewigweibliche zieht uns hinan!* The eternal feminine draws us on!

How seriously are we supposed to take this? Not very. Paul, after all, "the simpleton of ambiguity," is the one who says it. Kundera can't help adding that "Goethe's verse, like a proud white goose, flapped its wings beneath the vault of the swimming pool." I can no more imagine this novelist buying into the eternal feminine than I can see him abandoning the (dead) cultures of the great cities for some woodsy totem worship under the sign of Gaia, the Mother of Titans. And the last thing women need done to them, anyway, is another abstraction, another metaphor.

But where does that leave the severed head? Being melancholy, being brilliant, dreaming of gestures. As much as Thomas Mann at the end, Kundera reminds me of Vladimir Nabokov—another exile, another Bolshie-basher, another father-phile, another disdainer of the determinisms of Marx and Freud, another sacred monster of immortal art, opposed to the very idea of a "future," inventor of Zemblas. Nabokov's magic kits were also full of masks and mirrors, artist-madmen and artist-criminals, insanity and suicide, strangled wives and slaughtered sons and debauched nymphets. (pp. 770-74)

I think ***Immortality*** is Kundera's game against death. I think he'd feel bad anywhere. . . . Kundera jumped ship before it suddenly set sail into new meanings and new beings. All his borders are scheduled to disappear next year. Somewhere Marx says that when the train of history turns a corner, all the thinkers fall off. This included Marx. And Kundera. And many other lonely severed heads. (pp. 774-75)

John Leonard, "Morte d'Auteur," in The Nation, *New York, Vol. 252, No. 22, June 10, 1991, pp. 770-75.*

An excerpt from *Immortality*

Naturally, when it comes to immortality people are not equal. We have to distinguish between so-called *minor immortality,* the memory of a person in the minds of those who knew him (the kind of immortality the village mayor longed for), and *great immortality,* which means the memory of a person in the minds of people who never knew him personally. There are certain paths in life that from the very beginning place a person face to face with such great immortality, uncertain, it is true, even improbable, yet undeniably possible: they are the paths of artists and statesmen.

Of all the European statesmen of our time, the one who has most occupied himself with the thought of immortality has probably been François Mitterrand. I remember the unforgettable ceremony that followed his election as President in 1981. The square in front of the Panthéon was filled with an enthusiastic crowd, and he was withdrawing from it: he was walking alone up the broad stairway (exactly as Shakespeare walked to the Temple of Fame on the curtain described by Goethe), holding the stems of three roses. Then he disappeared from the people's sight and remained alone among the tombs of sixty-four illustrious corpses, followed in his thoughtful solitude only by the eyes of the camera, the film crew, and several million Frenchmen, watching their television screens from which thundered Beethoven's Ninth. He placed the roses one by one on three chosen tombs. He was like a surveyor planting the three roses like three markers into the immense building site of eternity, to stake out a triangle in the center of which was to be erected the palace of his immortality.

I was always fond of the American president Jimmy Carter, but I felt something approaching real love when I saw him on the television screen, jogging with a group of fellow workers, trainers, and bodyguards; his forehead suddenly began to sweat, his face became distorted with pain, fellow joggers rushed to his side clutching and supporting him: it was a minor heart attack. Jogging was supposed to be an occasion for showing the nation the President's eternal youth. That's why cameramen had been invited, and it was not their fault that instead of an athlete bursting with health they had to show an ageing man with bad luck.

A man longs to be immortal, and one day the camera will show us a mouth contorted into a pathetic grimace—the only thing we will remember about him, the only thing that will remain as a parabola of his entire life. He will enter a kind of immortality that we may call *ridiculous.* Tycho Brahe was a great astronomer, but all we remember about him today is that in the course of a festive dinner at the emperor's court he was ashamed to go to the lavatory, so his bladder burst and he departed among the ridiculous immortals as a martyr to shame and urine. He departed among them just like Christiane Goethe, turned forever into a crazy sausage that bites. No novelist is dearer to me than Robert Musil. He died one morning while lifting weights. When I lift them myself, I keep anxiously checking my pulse and I am afraid of dropping dead, for to die with a weight in my hand like my revered author would make me an epigone so unbelievable, frenetic, and fanatical as immediately to assure me of ridiculous immortality.

Michael Wood

Milan Kundera writes novels, but are they philosophy or fiction? Kundera himself (in an interview collected in ***The Art of the Novel***) finds the comparison with philosophy 'inappropriate': 'Philosophy develops its thought in an abstract realm, without characters, without situations.' That is what a certain tradition of philosophy does. But when Richard Rorty describes philosophy as turning to narrative and the imagination, pointing us towards solidarity through 'the imaginative ability to see strange people as fellow sufferers', we seem close to Kundera's work, and to much traditional thinking about what fiction will do for us.

Conversely (and like many modern philosophers), Kundera examines particular words ('tenderness', 'vertigo'), turns them over, defines them in relation to his characters. Tenderness is 'the fear instilled by adulthood', the creation of 'a tiny artificial space in which it is mutually agreed that we would treat others as children'; vertigo is 'the intoxication of the weak'. He calls this business of investigating words (and characters and situations) 'meditative interrogation' or 'interrogative meditation', which sounds more like Descartes than Dickens. Kundera goes on to say his narrative/verbal 'definitions' are 'neither sociological nor aesthetic nor psychological'. His interviewer proposes 'phenomenological' as a possibility, which Kundera courteously says is not bad, but refuses.

We are left, I think, with fiction which must be philosophical in some sense, but won't call itself that. Kundera attributes to Hermann Broch 'a new art of the *specifically novelistic essay* . . . hypothetical, playful or ironic' (Kundera's italics). Tone is very important in this context—Kundera calls his own tone playful and ironic, like Broch's, and adds 'provocative, experimental, or inquiring'. His essay on Kitsch in the sixth section of ***The Unbearable Lightness of Being*** is, he says, not only part of the novel but 'unthinkable' outside of a novel: 'there is a great deal of reflection, experience, study, even passion behind it, but the tone is never serious.' What is seriousness? It is, Kundera suggests in his introduction to his play ***Jacques and his Master,*** what literary critics can't do without, the ingredient whose absence drives them to panic. 'Serious is what someone is who believes what he makes others believe.' A novelist who was serious in this sense would be in bad shape. The appeal and the challenge, as Kundera says, thinking of Broch and Musil, is 'not to transform the novel into philosophy' but to bring to the novel 'a sovereign and radiant intelligence'.

Immortality is rather too winsome at times and dips too often into pop sociology, but it is also an extraordinarily rich and elegant and engaging work, a proof that novelists can afford (even analytic) intelligence, that they don't need to keep secrets from themselves. Or that self-consciousness doesn't have to be crippling, opposed to an awareness of the world.

Characters in Kundera acquire psychologies and histories, but they start out and continue to function chiefly as images, provocations: a man staring at a wall, or repeating a phrase; a woman arguing, putting on her glasses, shaking her head; a girl sitting in the middle of a major road amidst rushing traffic. These images are not illustrations of pre-formed thoughts, but they are not simply pieces of novelistic behaviour either. They are meetings between persons and notions, or more precisely, written, re-created, invented records of such meetings. 'I have been thinking about Tomas for many years. But only in the light of these reflections did I see him clearly. I saw him standing at the window of his flat . . . ' An elderly woman leaving a swimming-pool makes a young woman's gesture of goodbye:

> Her arm rose with bewitching ease. It was as if she were playfully tossing a brightly coloured ball to her lover . . . The instant she turned, smiled and waved . . . she was unaware of her age. The essence of her charm, independent of time, revealed itself for a second in that gesture and dazzled me. I was strangely moved. And then the word Agnes entered my mind. Agnes, I had never known a woman by that name.

Who are Agnes and Tomas? Who is 'I'? Agnes and Tomas are independent (albeit imaginary) persons, not mere projections of Kundera, in spite of his saying that the characters in his novels are his own 'unrealised possiblities'. They are sympathetic guesses at other minds and lives, combinations of wish, observation, extrapolation. They resemble people we have met, and better still, people we have yet to meet. 'I' is a textual version of Milan Kundera, author of the novel we are reading, and (in ***Immortality***) of other, mentioned novels, ***Life Is Elsewhere,*** for example. He is not of course writing before our very eyes, and he is not exactly reporting on the way he writes. He is *miming* the art of the novel, producing a picture of the sort of interest a character has for him; not unravelling fictions but showing us how they get ravelled.

Kundera, or 'Kundera', expounds a theory about character in ***Immortality,*** suitably wrapped in irony and questionable context, but powerful all the same. He distinguishes between the Latin notion of reason *(ration, raison, ragione)* as inescapable rationality and the German *Grund* (ground, basis). We have reasons for our actions, Kundera is suggesting, we inspect motives and causes, but we also have grounds, deeper, irrational inscriptions governing much of our behaviour. A Freudian would wonder why Kundera was avoiding the notion of the unconscious, and various jokes about Jacques Lacan in this novel suggest the evasion is deliberate. The answer, I think, is that a ground could be intuitively understood—in a fiction, for example—while analysis might never take us beyond reasons, however buried they initially seemed. 'I am trying,' Kundera the novelist says in this novel, 'to grasp the *Grund* hidden at the bottom of each of my characters and I am convinced more and more that it has the nature of a metaphor.' His companion, the portly and eccentric Professor Avenarius, says, 'Your idea escapes me,' and Kundera replies: 'Too bad. It is the most important thought that ever occurred to me.'

The tactic here is the double bluff, with complications. This is not the most important thought that has ever occurred to Kundera, or even to 'Kundera', and it is in any case absurd to speak of your own thought as important, especially when it doesn't look better than a bright idea, isn't even sketchily worked out. The dramatised implication, though, is not that the idea *isn't* important but that Kundera, quite properly, doesn't know how important it is. Metaphors, in this argument, are means of comprehension rather than decoration or escape—perhaps the only means we have. This is a self-interested claim for a novelist to make, a defence of the trade, but it is not a self-absorbed claim. It states, I think rightly, that if we can't imagine others, if we are not in some modest way novelists in our daily lives (historical novelists perhaps), we shall not understand much of anything.

Kundera pictures the girl sitting in the middle of the road, for example, as having felt herself unheard by others, become anxious to assert her presence in a world which has refused to acknowledge her.

> Or another image: she is at the dentist's, sitting in a crowded waiting-room; a new patient enters, walks to the couch where she is seated and sits down on her lap; he didn't do it intentionally, he simply saw an empty seat on the couch; she protests and tries to push him away, shouting: 'Sir! Can't you see? This seat is taken! I am sitting here!' but the old man doesn't hear her, he sits comfortably on top of her and cheerfully chats with another waiting patient.

Such a project of imaginative understanding is a generous, even an 'important' one. But we have to see, as Kundera so clearly sees, how flimsy it is. Better to guess at the girl's feelings than to have no feeling for her. But what if we learn that she felt nothing of the kind? Some writers of fiction will say it doesn't matter, but most will try another metaphor.

Tomas is a character in ***The Unbearable Lightness of Being,*** Agnes in ***Immortality.*** There is a strong connection between the two novels, spoofed in the new work in a brilliant, multi-storeyed joke. Kundera tells Avenarius he is writing a new novel (this novel), and announces what will happen (what does happen) in the next section. Avenarius thinks the promised novel sounds pretty boring, but he wants to be polite, and asks 'in a kindly voice' what it is called. Kundera doesn't hesitate.

> 'The Unbearable Lightness of Being.'
>
> 'I think someone has already written that.'
>
> 'I did! But I was wrong about the title then. That title was supposed to belong to the novel I'm writing right now.'

In the earlier novel Kundera invited us to wonder, with Nietzsche, how we would behave if everything we did were to be repeated, were loaded with the weight of return. Here we are to think of gestures prolonged into immortality. Would we do it all again? What wouldn't we do again? Would we—here is the hard question—wish to stay even with the people we love? Could we admit that we might not wish to? Agnes loves her husband Paul and her daughter Brigitte but not as much as she loves the memory of her dead father and the peace she finds in certain places away from her job and family and ordinary life. She is not unhappy with marriage, or France in the 1980s, but she wouldn't want them for eternity.

One of the most poignant and ambiguously beautiful moments in the novel records Agnes' death, a compound of horror, waste and a kind of grace. Agnes has been fatally injured in a car crash (caused by the girl sitting in the middle of the road, who herself walked away uninjured). Her husband, desperate to be at her bedside, has been delayed by an absurdist twist in the apparently absent plot: Avenarius, given to randomly slashing tyres at night as a gesture against the drift of the world towards order and repression, has disabled Paul's car. Paul arrives too late, finds his grief baffled by an 'unknown smile' on Agnes' dead face: 'it was meant for someone he did not know and it said something he did not understand.' It was meant for no one. Agnes had not wanted anyone to see her dying, or to die into anyone's world. She had longed for a realm without faces, and believes she has found such a realm as she dies. Her smile reflects her gratitude or her illusion; a happy end, unhappy only for the excluded Paul.

Others who worry about immortality in this novel are Goethe and Bettina von Arnim, whose relationship is fancifully re-created and analysed; Napoleon, posing for posterity as if our cameramen were already there; Beethoven, refusing to doff his hat for an empress; and above all a series of fictional characters in contemporary Paris, Agnes and Paul, Agnes's sister Laura and her lover Bernard, a fashionable and insecure radio interviewer, Agnes's lover Rubens, whose nickname mocks his abandoned artistic ambitions. The central and most interesting figures are Agnes and Laura, affectionate, intelligent, often distraught women who are alike and unalike, and both born of the old lady's young gesture as she leaves the swimming-pool.

Kundera himself must be anxious about the test of eternity—would he want to spend it writing novels, or writing *these* novels?—and amusingly gets his characters to bite back at him. He invents Agnes and Paul and then, much later, *meets* Paul, drunk and mildly abusive, a disappointment but not now dismissible. Professor Avenarius circulates freely between worlds, has lunch with Kundera but also (probably) sleeps with Laura. The girl who sits down in the roadway has a similar double life: she appears as a news item on Kundera's radio (and possibly on ours) and is then incorporated into the novel he is writing and we are reading. She is in a sense the most important figure in the book: the one we understand least and who causes the most havoc, an image for the limits of reason. She is coincidence itself, a figure whose loneliness and distress cause the deaths of three sets of people quite unrelated to her. This is exactly what we mean by an accident. Taken up into a novel, though, such an accident becomes a metaphor: a *Grund* not for character but for the way we experience the order and disorder of our lives, the instrument of a crazed disreputable, modern form of fate.

Some of Kundera's best pages, here and in earlier work, are dedicated to the dry, grimly comic deconstruction of what he calls *homo sentimentalis: 'Homo sentimentalis* cannot be defined as a man with feelings (for we all have feelings), but as a man who has raised feelings to a category of value.' This is the world of Kitsch, the world where we worship emotion, and then worship our worship of it, charmed by the delicacy of our own tears. Dostoyevsky is Kundera's touchstone in this respect, the great, perilous teacher of the authority of suffering; and Mahler is the last great European composer who 'naively and directly' wanted to move us.

> *I think therefore I am* is the statement of an intellectual who underrates toothaches. *I feel therefore I am* is a truth much more universally valid . . . Suffering is the university of egocentrism.

This austere joke is quite complicated. Kundera is asking us to think not about the dignity or reality of suffering but about the way we abase ourselves before it. Descartes, in ***The Unbearable Lightness of Being,*** is attacked for denying that animals have souls, and Nietzsche, embracing a whipped horse in Turin before his last madness descended on him, is memorably said to be 'trying to apologise to the horse for Descartes'. In ***Immortality*** Descartes's presumed ignoring of toothaches seems not only cerebral but stylish, a moment of light before Europe plunged itself into an orgy of boastful suffering. The shift nicely illustrates Kundera's claim that philosophy is necessarily playful in novels, that dogma must become hypothesis. Philosophers themselves become characters with changing roles: 'Descartes' here is not René Descartes the person, and not the corpus or reach of Descartes's philosophical work; not even Descartes's general reputation. He is a pair of famous remarks, and the images they evoke; a miniature colleague of Agnes and Tomas.

Kundera's humour in ***Immortality*** is often so ascetic as to be scarcely visible. As with Borges, it wouldn't be hard to mistake his games with philosophy for an unreconstructed philosophy itself, and we can already imagine the scholarly works which will re-literalise his speculations, smudge their contexts and mislay their irony. At other times, as if to compensate for the austerity and slyness of the jokes, Kundera becomes both coy and lumbering. (pp. 13-14)

Michael Wood, "Kundera's Man of Feeling," in London Review of Books, *Vol. 13, No. 11, June 13, 1991, pp. 13-14.*

David Woolf

Taken together, [Kundera's] novels and short stories suggest nothing less than a close, unflinching scrutiny of the human condition. But Kundera has no systematic philosophy to expound. He is more concerned with posing interesting questions, with replacing certainties with ambiguities, than with furnishing lazy readers with short, snappy solutions to difficult puzzles.

Just as it is misleading to associate Kundera with political fiction, so it is misleading to view him as representative of contemporary Czech writing. His irony, and his surreal humour, do indeed suggest an indebtedness to Czech writers such as Hasek, Capek and Vancura, but it also needs to be remembered that Kundera's own career as a writer did not really begin until he was 30, when, in 1959, he wrote the first story of ***Laughable Loves.*** In fact the larger part of his life as a writer has taken place in France, and his new novel, ***Immortality,*** is set in Paris in the 1980s, a lurid, noisy city, and a far-cry from the Prague of the 1960s.

If ***Immortality*** reminds us of how truly European Kundera the novelist has become, it also reminds us of how narrow and impoverished our understanding of the art of the novel has grown. ***Immortality*** is Kundera's most ambitious novel to date, and the result even eclipses the achievement of ***The Unbearable Lightness of Being.*** Towards the end of ***Immortality,*** we listen to Kundera himself, in conversation with a friend called Professor Avenarius, a curious character who vents his anger at the congested state of Paris streets by venturing out at night to slash car tyres.

Most novels, Kundera suggests, convey the reader from beginning to end with ever-increasing speed, driven on by acts and events. ***Immortality,*** however, is a radically different sort of novel. Not only are there stories being told and points being made, but we are invited to watch the fictional process at work. ***Immortality*** is a novel without walls, or if the walls are there, they are made of glass. Like the 18th Century novels of Laclos, Sterne and Diderot, ***Immortality*** erodes the boundaries between storytelling and philosophical meditation. Kundera's vision of the art of the novel is not new, just old and largely forgotten. While some critics declare the death of the novel, Kundera lends the form a new lease of life by viewing the novel, in the manner of writers of the 18th Century Enlightenment, as a way of discovering truths about the world.

The result is far from dry and abstract. But ***Immortality*** is so much more than the sum of its parts, and those parts are so cleverly joined together, that the novel as a whole proves summary-resistant. At the beginning we meet Agnes, who springs from a gesture, just as Eve was fashioned from Adam's rib, and Venus emerged from the sea. Agnes has a sister called Laura, and a husband called Paul. One narrative thread of ***Immortality*** recounts the story of their relationships with one another, and-listens-in on the conversations they have with themselves.

This main narrative, and its related interior monologues, is interspersed with short philosophical essays on subjects as diverse as the iniquities of photographic journalism, the connections between gestures and personalities, and between faces and personalities (is character revealed in a face?), romantic love and the mortal longing for immortality. In short, we are told a story, and invited to witness how such a story takes shape. We are then asked to consider questions posed by the story. And we discover some of the things that only a novel can do, such as have Goethe and Ernest Hemingway take a walk together, while they compare notes on the burdens and benefits of immortality. This is pure invention, and a timely reminder that perhaps the history of the novel is only just beginning.

David Woolf, "A Radically Different Sort of Novel," in Books, *London, No. 3, July-August, 1991, p. 6.*

FURTHER READING

Baranczak, Stanislaw. "Life Is Elsewhere." *The New Republic* 205, No. 5 (29 July 1991): 36-9.

Comparative review of *Immortality* and Ivan Klima's *Love and Garbage.*

Bemrose, John. "Bawdy Tales of Betrayal." *MacLean's* 99, No. 21 (26 May 1986): 58.

Negative review of *Jacques and His Master.* Bemrose states that this play "does not always show Kundera at his best: it is a frothy, modernized piece of Restoration-style bedroom farce weighed down by some pretentious philosophizing."

Carlisle, Olga. "A Talk with Milan Kundera." *The New York Times Magazine* (19 May 1985): 72, 74, 80, 82, 85.

Interview in which Kundera discusses his Czechoslovakian heritage, his literary influences, and his distaste for political rhetoric.

Coates, Joseph. "The Humane Conscience of the Novel." *Chicago Tribune* (3 April 1988): 4.

Review of *The Art of the Novel* in which the critic examines Kundera's theory of the development of the modern European novel.

Donatich, John. "Kitsch and Tell." *The Village Voice* XXXIII, No. 13 (29 March 1988): 70.

Asserts that while Kundera "seems aggressively self-righteous" in *The Art of the Novel,* he also "defines his position defending the nobility of human emotion."

du Plessix Gray, Francine. "Journey into the Maze." *Vogue* 172, No. 2 (February 1982): 302, 356-58.

Indepth interview in which Kundera discusses the major motifs of *The Book of Laughter and Forgetting,* the political and sexual implications of his works in general, and the relationship between writer and reader.

Medwich, Cathleen. "People are Talking about . . . Milan Kundera." *Vogue* 171, No. 2 (February 1981): 260-61, 330-31.

Examines the motifs of survival, memory, and political exile in *The Book of Laughter and Forgetting.*

Meisel, Perry. "Beautifying Lies and Polyphonic Wisdom." *The New York Times Book Review* (10 April 1988): 13.

Review of *The Art of the Novel* in which Meisel discusses Kundera's "overt disavowal of any political agenda" in his works.

Restuccia, Frances L. "*Homo Homini Lupus:* Milan Kundera's *The Joke.*" *Contemporary Literature* 31, No. 3 (Fall 1990): 281-99.

Freudian analysis of the sadomasochistic elements of *The Joke.* Restuccia attempts to determine if Kundera believes "human ruthlessness is instinctive" or if he is "merely posing questions . . . , exploring human possibilities."

The Review of Contemporary Fiction IX, No. 2 (Summer 1989).

Special issue devoted to Kundera and his works. Includes essays by Ann Stewart Caldwell and novelist Italo Calvino, an interview by Lois Oppenheim, and a selective annotated bibliography of Kundera criticism.

Salmagundi, No. 73 (Winter 1987).

Special issue which contains articles by critics John Bayley, Terry Eagleton, and Calvin Bedient, and an excerpted interview from *The Art of the Novel.*

Vejvoda, Serge. "Kundera's *Immortality:* The Sneak Foretaste." *San Francisco Review* XV, No. 4 (Spring 1991): 6, 12.

Review of the French edition of *Immortality.* Vejvoda states that while *Immortality* is complex, it is an experimental work with which Kundera is "pushing ahead into unexplored territory."

Weightman, John. "Having Fun with Fatalism." *The Observer,* No. 10168 (24 August 1986): 20.

Comparative review of *Jacques and his Master* and the book that inspired it, Denis Diderot's *Jacques the Fatalist.*

Weiss, Jason. "An Interview with Milan Kundera." *New England Review and Bread Loaf Quarterly* 8, No. 3 (Spring 1986): 405-10.

Interview in which Kundera discusses *The Unbearable Lightness of Being,* the themes inherent in all of his works, and how Franz Kafka influenced his theory of the novel.

Williams, Nigel. "Men of the World." *The Listener* 119, No. 3067 (16 June 1988): 30-31.

Comparative analysis of *The Art of the Novel* and Carlos Fuente's *Myself with Others.*

Archibald MacLeish

1892-1982

American poet, playwright, critic, essayist, scriptwriter, educator, and statesman.

One of the best-known American poets of the twentieth century, MacLeish is noted for poems and verse plays that examine the public and private responsibilities of individual citizens in an increasingly complex world. MacLeish addressed these themes in a wide variety of poetic styles, including sonnets, blank verse, and epics, and he experimented with varied line lengths and speech rhythms in an attempt to create a distinctly modern American voice. MacLeish's poetry of the 1920s—a period marked by his expatriation to Paris with other "Lost Generation" writers, including Ernest Hemingway, F. Scott Fitzgerald, and E. E. Cummings—is noted for its similarities to T. S. Eliot's *The Waste Land* and Ezra Pound's early *Cantos* and *Hugh Selwyn Mauberly.* Like the works of Eliot and Pound, MacLeish's poetry of this era is an attempt to revive broken cultural traditions through the use of literary allusions and references to works such as Sir James G. Frazer's *The Golden Bough.* MacLeish's later thematic explorations of the process of aging and the spiritual and physical exile of modern humanity drew critical comparisons to, respectively, Irish poet William Butler Yeats and French poet St.–John Perse.

MacLeish was born in Glencoe, Illinois, a wealthy suburb of Chicago. He attended Yale University, where he was a successful football player, swimmer, and scholar, and was elected to Phi Beta Kappa during his junior year. After graduation in 1915, MacLeish entered Harvard Law School, but temporarily suspended his studies to serve as an ambulance driver in France during World War I. He transferred to active duty shortly thereafter and rose to the rank of field artillery captain. Following the war, MacLeish returned to Yale and completed his law degree as class valedictorian. After teaching constitutional and international law at Harvard for a year, MacLeish worked with a New England law firm until 1923, when he decided to pursue a full-time career as a poet. Moving to Paris with his wife and sons, he associated with many of the writers who were to revolutionize twentieth-century literature, including Pound, Hemingway, and James Joyce. MacLeish also devoted himself to perfecting his writing and learning to read Dante's *Inferno* in its original Italian dialect. When he and his family returned to the United States in 1928, they briefly attempted turkey farming in Conway, Massachusetts. When that venture failed, MacLeish accepted an editorial position with Henry R. Luce's *Fortune* magazine, where he wrote essays on a wide variety of topics. During the 1930s, he also chaired the League of American Writers, an antifascist organization that also included Hemingway and John Dos Passos. In 1939, President Franklin Roosevelt appointed MacLeish Librarian of Congress. As Assistant Secretary of State, MacLeish was a member of the committee that drafted the constitution for the United Nations Educational, Scientific, and Cultural Organization (UNESCO). After retiring from public life in 1945, he taught literature and creative writing at Harvard from 1949 to 1962 and then returned to his farm in Conway, where he continued to write poetry, essays, and verse plays until his death in 1982.

One of MacLeish's early poems was published in the *Yale Literary Review* during his freshman year, and a small collection of verse entitled *Songs for a Summer Day* won the Yale University Prize for Poetry in 1915. Another early volume, *The Tower of Ivory,* was published in 1917 by a friend while MacLeish was fighting in France. After moving to Paris in 1923, MacLeish published several volumes that were to distinguish him as one of his generation's most promising poets. In *The Pot of Earth, Streets in the Moon, Einstein, The Hamlet of A. MacLeish,* and the verse play *Nobodaddy,* the influence of Eliot and Pound was immediately recognized by critics. *The Pot of Earth,* for instance, prompted comparisons to *The Waste Land* for its inclusion of the Adonis myth from *The Golden Bough* to examine "Birth, copulation, and death / that's all, that's all, that's all." Similarly, such pieces from *Streets in the Moon* as "The Silent Slain" and "Memorial Rain"—the latter an embittered elegy to MacLeish's brother killed in World War I—reflect the themes of alienation, despair, and World War I's destruction of cultural traditions addressed in *The Waste Land* and *Hugh Selwyn Mauberly. Streets in the Moon* also contains MacLeish's frequently anthologized modernist manifesto "Ars Poetica," which contains the line "a poem should not mean but be," and "L'an Trentiesme de Mon Eage," which takes its title from the first line in Francois Villon's "Grand Testament" and recalls Pound's similar adaptation in *Hugh Selwyn Mauberly. The Hamlet of A. MacLeish* presents action from Shakespeare's play about the Prince of Denmark as a background for MacLeish's examinations of many topics, including the deaths of his son and brother and humanity's penchant for self-destruction.

After returning to the United States, MacLeish published *New Found Land: Fourteen Poems,* which further displays the influence of Eliot and Pound. This volume also evidences MacLeish's growing affinity for the works of St.–John Perse, whose *Anabasis* served as the model for many of MacLeish's poems, particularly "Land's End," "Cinema of Man," and "You, Andrew Marvell." Like Perse, MacLeish was increasingly interested in depicting the temporal nature of life through sensual imagery and allusions to the rise and fall of ancient civilizations. For example, "You, Andrew Marvell," considered by many critics to be MacLeish's finest poem, expands on the lines from the seventeenth-century English poet Marvell, "But at my back I always hear / Time's winged chariot hurrying near," to document the passing of such cultural meccas as ancient Persia, Sicily, and Spain. In the Pulitzer Prize–winning epic *Conquistador,* MacLeish updated the Tuscan verse form of *terza rima,* popularized by Dante in his *Inferno,* for a retelling of Cortez's expeditions in Mexico. Related from the point of view of Bernal Diaz del Castillo, a foot soldier in Cortez's army, *Conquistador* objectively chronicles the destruction of native Mexican cultures by Spanish explorers.

MacLeish developed a more public voice during the late 1930s and 1940s, a period characterized by poetry and prose that are didactic and rhetorical. In *Frescoes for Mr. Rockefeller's City,* for example, he castigates both Marxists and capitalists who wish to manipulate culture for their own ends. MacLeish was inspired by an incident at New York City's Radio City Music Hall involving Marxist artist Diego Rivera and billionaire John D. Rockefeller, Sr. Although Rockefeller had commissioned a work by Rivera to replace what he considered offensive nude statuary, Rockefeller ordered Rivera's fresco destroyed and the nude statuary returned when he found that Rivera had included a portrait of communist hero Vladimir Lenin. In the six poems comprising *Frescoes for Mr. Rockefeller's City,* MacLeish emerges as a champion of democracy who opposes both capitalist empire builders and communism. MacLeish's increasingly didactic public voice was further evident in his verse collection *Public Speech,* his radio plays *Panic, The Fall of the City,* and *Air Raid,* and in his essays of the period, including "Public Speech and Private Speech in Poetry," "Poetry and the Public World," and "The Irresponsibles." The latter essay generated controversy due to its indictment of other writers for either their individual inaction or for engendering passive attitudes among the public during a time of great crisis. MacLeish felt the writers of his generation had objectified the horrors of war without consideration of war's moral justification. MacLeish's continued writing polemical poems in *America Was Promises* and *Actfive and Other Poems.* Signi Lenea Falk commented on this period of MacLeish's career: "MacLeish reacted to the depression which impoverished one-third of the nation, and he reacted to the alarming increase of Nazi power in Germany. He identified himself with economic, social, and political problems; he spoke directly about the issues. These poems were written to reach a large public, carrying an overtone of urgency."

The publication of MacLeish's *Collected Poems, 1917-1952* earned him a Pulitzer Prize, National Book Award, and Bollingen Prize for Poetry in 1952. For the remainder of his career, MacLeish concentrated on verse plays and occasionally published slight volumes containing elegies and tributes to other poets. His final collection of original verse, *The Wild Old Wicked Man and Other Poems,* is noted for its similarities to the later work of William Butler Yeats and for its sensitive and moving treatment of an elderly couple's love. The verse play *J.B.,* a retelling of the biblical story of Job, won MacLeish his third Pulitzer Prize as well as a Tony Award in 1958. He also received an Academy Award for his screenplay for the film *The Eleanor Roosevelt Story.*

(See also *CLC,* Vols. 3, 8, 14; *Contemporary Authors,* Vols. 9-12, rev. ed.; *Contemporary Authors,* Vol. 106 [obituary]; *Contemporary Authors New Revision Series,* Vol. 33; *Dictionary of Literary Biography,* Vols. 4, 7, 45; and *Dictionary of Literary Biography Yearbook: 1982.*)

PRINCIPAL WORKS

POETRY

Tower of Ivory 1917
The Happy Marriage and Other Poems 1924
The Pot of Earth 1925
Streets in the Moon 1926
The Hamlet of A. MacLeish 1928
New Found Land: Fourteen Poems 1930
Conquistador 1932
Poems, 1924-1933 1933
Public Speech: Poems by Archibald MacLeish 1936
America Was Promises 1939
Actfive and Other Poems 1948
Collected Poems, 1917-1952 1952
Songs for Eve 1954
The Collected Poems of Archibald MacLeish 1963
The Wild Old Wicked Man and Other Poems 1968
The Human Season: Selected Poems 1926-1972 1972
New and Collected Poems 1917-1976 1976

PLAYS

Nobodaddy 1926
Panic: A Play in Verse 1935
J. B: A Play in Verse 1958
Herakles: A Play in Verse 1965
Scratch 1971

Six Plays 1980

RADIO PLAYS

The Fall of the City 1937
Air Raid 1938
The Trojan Horse: A Play 1952
This Music Crept by Me Upon the Waters 1953
The Great American Fourth of July Parade: A Verse Play for Radio 1975

OTHER

Union Pacific: A Ballet (libretto) 1934
The Irresponsibles: A Declaration (essay) 1940
The American Cause (essays) 1941
American Opinion and the War: The Rede Lecture 1942
A Time to Act: Selected Addresses 1943
The Eleanor Roosevelt Story (screenplay) 1965
Riders on the Earth: Essays and Recollections 1978

Harriet Monroe

[*As the founder and editor of* Poetry, *Monroe was a key figure in the American "poetry renaissance" that took place in the early twentieth century.*]

[***The Happy Marriage and Other Poems*** and ***The Pot of Earth***] are "tone-poems" played with muted strings; played in the half-light or the half-dark when rapture and anguish, however real, become suspect of dreams. What we all fear, the poet sees come to pass—life blurs and dissolves before his eyes; lovely concords are hushed; beauty that is too beautiful perishes of its own fragility, like a soap-bubble vanishing with its flicker of iridescence.

All this is not expressly said, any more than in music. In the earlier book we have indeed the delicate raptures of a happy marriage—love as fleet as a fawn to tempt and elude, as warm as a bird in the nest to cherish and guard; but the poet, singing the changes of joy, feels always how perishable is joy in this vibrating, swinging, dissolving world. And he knows that the soul can not be bound, but must beat away from the closest contacts. (p. 44)

This first book by Mr. MacLeish shows an unusual instinct for rhythms and tone-values, and in ***The Pot of Earth,*** published a year later, we find this instinct developing almost to virtuosity. A few critics have commented on this poem's indebtedness to *The Waste Land,* and indeed a certain relation is obvious. Mr. MacLeish, either consciously or unconsciously, has set himself to study Mr. Eliot's wavering variable rhythms, his way of neither beginning nor ending, of leaping backward and forward, and somehow reaching his goal by wayward paths no other poet could travel. But if the young poet has taken a few hints from the elder one, he has shown extraordinary intelligence in recognizing their adaptability to his theme, and in heeding them just so far as they suited his purpose.

In other words, ***The Pot of Earth*** is beautifully done. Celebrating the springtime awakening, it washes its waves of sound over the blooming earth and its harvests, and over the young bride who carries the seed of life and brings it to birth at the cost of her own. Often one meets lovely lines, of a fragile beauty like old Venetian glass. . . . (p. 46)

Enough has been said to show that we have in Mr. MacLeish a young poet of rare promise and already fine achievement, whose delicate musical instinct is set to the expression of a brooding imagination and a deep feeling of the wonder and mystery of life. (p. 47)

Harriet Monroe, in a review of " 'The Happy Marriage and Other Poems' and 'The Pot of Earth'," in Poetry, *Vol. XXVIII, No. 1, April, 1926, pp. 44-7.*

Yvor Winters

[*Winters was a prominent American poet and critic whose works support his lifelong conviction that all good literature serves a conscious moral purpose.*]

It is with certain ineradicable prejudices that I approach [***Streets in the Moon***], and yet I find myself won over. Those writers of my own generation, or of what I take to be roughly such, whose ideals seem to me most definitely related to my own—McAlmon, Carnevali, Cummings—repel me in their verse (despite my tremendous admiration for their prose) by various species of hit-or-miss awkwardness, cuteness, or sweetness. Their attempts to leap clear of literature, to see nakedly, are too seriously modified by these vices to satisfy me. MacLeish, on the other hand, is frankly literary; but his work has at its best a seriousness, a smoothly rolling power, that cannot be denied. And embedded in all his literary loam are living grubs, fat and squirming. I have read two other books of verse that he has published—***The Happy Marriage*** and ***The Pot of Earth***— that seemed to me not overly happy dilutions of Eliot, Swinburne, and anything else that came handy. The present book contains a few rather tawdry imitations of Eliot—such as **"Le Secret Humain,"** for example—which rely on the rhymed plop of something damp and ill-smelling but otherwise obvious and uninteresting, a trick in part responsible for the tragic collapse of *The Waste Land.* But for the rest—and the rest is most—the Eliot becomes a vague background, largely and very vaguely technical: the matter is more richly and immediately perceived than is usual with Eliot, and is all over the book. There is a remarkably high percentage of completely and beautifully achieved poems.

One finds poems with a certain heavy smoky grandeur, that are comparable only to that magnificent and unread master Henry Vaughan. . . . (pp. 278-79)

As in **"Signature for Tempo II,"** one finds a projection into Time and Space of common things, that, seen anew, suspended, acquire a tremendous and curiously abstract identity. And last, and possibly least, though not insignificant, is the breath-taking accumulation of the ponderous vocables of commerce, law, and professional publicity, to be found in such poems as **"Man!"** and **"Corporate Entity,"** an accumulation that has no equal in all the archives of Dada.

Metrically, MacLeish is at his best in rhymed—and short—poems. His blank verse, using the same heavy movement that is so impressive in his shorter pieces, becomes monotonous: one thinks with longing of the more elusive and athletic poems of Hart Crane. But MacLeish, where he succeeds, succeeds like a master.

These poems, written, printed, bound, with a lunar clarity, mark for me the advent of one of the very few poets, who, alone of all the set that have appeared since the Others-Imagist-Vorticist upheaval of twelve or fourteen years ago, can rightly take a place beside the most distinguished poets of the preceding generation. (pp. 280-81)

Yvor Winters, in a review of "Streets in the Moon," in Poetry, *Vol. XXIX, No. 5, February, 1927, pp. 278-81.*

Conrad Aiken

[*Aiken was an American man of letters best known for his poetry. In the excerpt below, Aiken writes that* Streets of the Moon *is the fulfillment of MacLeish's early promise.*]

These are lean days for the poetry-lover—it is now a decade since that exciting time when every week or so brought us another new and brilliantly promising poet, of whose future one might dare to predict in terms both hopeful and spacious. Those hopeful futures have now, for the most part, become disappointing pasts or hopeless presents; since Mr. Eliot gave us *The Waste Land,* there has been little to inspire in us the sacred terror, unless we except an occasional poem by Mr. Stevens or Mr. Cummings or Mr. Sacheverell Sitwell, and perhaps also Mr. Ransom. Even with these, however, we are in a sense already familiar—we feel that we know what sort of thing they are likely to do. What we really desire—for we are all of us lovers of the new—is a young poet whose brilliance has progressed beyond that point at which both he and ourselves might be deceived by a mere youthful flash, and in whose promise one can begin to see the outlines of something large.

Mr. Archibald MacLeish, who entitles his latest book (for no discoverable reason) ***Streets of the Moon,*** qualifies admirably for this rôle. One has felt of him from the beginning that he had a very exceptional talent, and that, if he might once escape from the several "influences" which have in succession so deeply stained him, and succeed in discovering his own identity (most difficult of the poet's tasks), he might easily become one of the most exciting of contemporary American poets. ***The Pot of Earth,*** despite its "monstrous debt" to *The Waste Land,* was a very impressive piece of work: if one failed to do it justice, it was because it posed for the critic the subtlest of problems, that of assaying, in the midst of so much that was obviously derived (whether in texture of thought or texture of rhythm) the precise weight and value of the individual contribution. Might the thing have been merely wrung out of Mr. MacLeish by his reading of *The Waste Land*—or was there more to follow? And Mr. MacLeish's next book, ***Nobodaddy,*** a play in blank verse, helped one very little, for it was written earlier than ***The Pot of Earth,*** and clearly belonged to a more formative and more academic period in his growth. It was good, but it was not, in the same way, exciting.

Streets of the Moon, however, sets one's doubts at rest. Influences there still are—one could enumerate three or four; but in these three groups of poems Mr. MacLeish makes it perfectly clear at last that he is very much himself, and that he has found a murex of his own. One regrets a little that in some of the shorter things he should have yielded to the contemporary taste for typographical and punctuational oddity—devices which, as he shows us himself, he can better dispense with; one regrets also a slight leaning, now and then, to the sentimental-interrogatory and sentimental-exclamatory; and one wishes that he would oftener eschew the fragmentary and asymmetrical, though he occasionally makes delightful things of them. His ability really runs the other way—it is in the full and rounded, in the richly organized, that he finds his natural expression; he writes, when he wants, magnificent blank verse; he is an Elizabethan in his love of fine phrases and in his power to grasp the metaphysical in sensuous terms; and he knows how to build toward a climax, both conceptual and prosodic, in a large and complex fashion of which most of his contemporaries seem to be sentimentally afraid. Certainly Mr. MacLeish need not be afraid, as his **"Einstein,"** in the present volume, superbly proves—a long poem which any living poet might envy, as rich in thought as it is in color and movement. If he can do this, and such exquisite smaller things as **"Selene Afterwards,"** not to mention a dozen others, what mightn't he do next? One simply abdicates as critic, and flings one's hat in the air.

Conrad Aiken, "Another Murex," in The New Republic, *Vol. XLIX, No. 636, February 9, 1927, p. 337.*

Babette Deutsch

The title of [***The Hamlet of A. MacLeish***] is misleading. Aside from the marginal notes referring to scenes from the tragedy, and the occasional interpolation of phrases and songs from the play, there is little to suggest Hamlet here. Or, if this be Hamlet, it is a Hamlet whose inner conflict centers not about his inability to act when confronted with the need for action, but about the question of consent to this mortal life on any terms. It is an embroidery on the particular theme of the famous soliloquy. It is the gravediggers' scene set to different music. It is, indeed, not so much a variant on a single drama as a plunge backward into the dark chambers of Elizabethan thought, forever harping on death and death and death.

What is it Virginia Woolf tells us of the Elizabethan era in her recent biography?

"The sun blazed," says Mrs. Woolf, "or there was darkness."

If this is the case, is not Mr. MacLeish's latest venture a piece of pure pastiche? Scarcely. For while it is reminiscent, it recalls not merely the vehemence, the extravagance, the terror that fill the tragedies of Shakespeare and

Webster, but also the more familiar depressions and despairs of Mr. T. S. Eliot. True, Mr. MacLeish refrains for the most part from the abrupt transitions to vulgar parlance that lend such queer spices to the lyricism of *The Waste Land.* But there is some evidence that if his desperate mood is rooted in the horror of death that the Elizabethans felt, it has been manured by the waste and ugliness of life in this twentieth century.

Oddly enough, while it is the poet's indebtedness that strikes one first, and sharply, one is left with a deep sense of the truth of his emotion and the excellence of his poetic gift. He may share the mood and even, to a degree, the manner of other men, but his work is fed on his own feeling, not on mere literature, and his vigor of utterance is too great to be purely derivative. . . . His difficulty seems to be that he moves like a bareback rider astride two horses at once: one, that Pegasus who remembers other hands on the bit; the other, his own private mount. If he can curb the immortal horse, or give freer rein to his own steed, there is no saying to what far country he may not yet go galloping.

Babette Deutsch, "Two Horses," in New York Herald Tribune Books, *December 16, 1928, p. 23.*

Theodore Spencer

Mr. MacLeish's poetry puts the reviewer in a quandary. Almost more than any contemporary American poet, with the exception of Conrad Aiken, he has the authentic gift of words. His lines gleam and flow; they have a character of their own; at his best, in **"The Too Late Born"** and **"You, Andrew Marvell,"** Mr. MacLeish's poems are like the pouring of a rich, honey-colored liquid from a vase. And yet there is something the matter. Mr. MacLeish is still curiously adolescent; he is only at intervals himself. One reads his long poems, and at once one is haunted by the ghosts of various contemporary poets, English, French and American, so that the result is hardly personal at all; the liquid is diluted from a dozen alien streams.

[***The Hamlet of A. MacLeish***] is like that. Again and again there are beautiful and passionate lines; the part that corresponds to Hamlet's outbreak in Ophelia's grave shakes the reader with its vivid emotional description, its admirable communication of strong feeling. Yet the subject of the poem as a whole (the spirit of man futilely questioning and struggling with the material world) is largely considered in borrowed terms, and consequently there are long passages, like the Grail story, which are merely good writing. The emotion is second-hand, and comes, one imagines, from reading Miss Jessie L. Weston with spectacles belonging to T. S. Eliot.

It is this lack of fusion between style and content (as if the paint and the table it was supposed to cover had a space between them), this lack of a mental Bessemer process, that bothers the critic. For, granted that a poet may share the feeling of futility which is at the bottom of so much contemporary writing, and granted that, to express such a feeling, it may be a good thing to have a symbolism which is shared by several poets, nevertheless that symbolism is useless for satisfactory communication unless the poet makes it emotionally his own. Jacopone da Todi and Dante both wrote about the Virgin, using similar symbols, and both wrote fine poetry, because those symbols were in each case shaken to life by a strong current of personal feeling. But Mr. MacLeish does not make his symbols live; perhaps it is because the emotion implied by futility is more individualizing than the emotion implied by worship, and therefore does not authorize the use of communal symbols. Whatever it may be, the fact remains that one does not feel that Mr. MacLeish is relying on his own emotion, and as a result, the advance made in this poem over his previous work is merely technical. This is unfortunate, for Mr. MacLeish has the potentialities of an important poet, and his continued dependence on other experience than his own makes one wonder when he is going to fulfill them.

Theodore Spencer, in a review of "The Hamlet of A. MacLeish," in The New Republic, *Vol. LVII, No. 736, January 9, 1929, p. 226.*

Morton Dauwen Zabel

[*Zabel was an American poet, critic, and prominent scholar. From 1928 to 1937 he was associate editor, then editor, of Harriet Monroe's magazine* Poetry.]

Mr. MacLeish's [***New Found Land***] is made up of fourteen poems, beginning with the familiar **"You, Andrew Marvell"** of five or six years ago, and ending with several poems in a somewhat later manner which have appeared in periodicals during the last year. The collection is distinguished, however, by a style which, for all its slack and discursive rhetoric, carries a definitive accent, unmistakably Mr. MacLeish's own. Even where certain external effects carry one back from these lines to the Swinburnian distension in the meters of ***The Happy Marriage*** or ***The Pot of Earth,*** there is no confusing the early uncertainty with the later stylistic sobriety and deliberation. MacLeish still handles his line with a kind of amateurish laxity from which the experimental note is not likely to disappear. More than any other poet of his standing, he has retained his affection for Eliot's early idiom. But this leaning, as it now reasserts itself after the discipline of ***The Hamlet,*** is less a matter of expression than of temperament; less, that is, to be seen in his phrases than in his themes. Apparently MacLeish intends to remain an elegiast, commemorating in his sombre and muffled oratory the historical melancholy of mankind, deliberating on the flight of illusion and the death of heroes.

If any doubt remains that Eliot's influence is still an open secret in the poems of ***New Found Land,*** one may pass from their colloquial-heroic intonation to an inspection of their anthropology. Here Frazer and his colleagues still furnish the properties and symbols. Here, as in ***The Hamlet,*** the sun supplants the water allegory of *The Waste Land,* and the cosmography is expanded to include a wide scattering of terrestrial and stellar geography, the historical background meanwhile becoming a sort of panorama of man's physical progress on earth. MacLeish has inherited Eliot's predicament without approaching Eliot's conformity to a newly discovered doctrine of being and destiny. He stops short at a compromise which may be considerably more rational and persuasive than Eliot's latterday submissions, but which, fundamentally, involves no greater assurance of esthetic and spiritual integrity. He stands on a star revolving among planets, still cloaked in the polite bewilderment of Senlin facing the dawn or Prufrock walking by the sea. In the present volume he offers, from the midst of his perplexity, no solution beyond embracing the sun-warmed earth, cleaving to his faith in the common heroism of men, and waiting passively for such gleams of higher intelligence as may be communicated to him through the ministries of friendship, art, and love.

In his last two books MacLeish has shown, in a score of poems openly and in most of the others implicitly, his desire to lose personal identity in the common body of humanity. Apparently he reached a climax, emotionally and conceptually, in his poem called **"L'An Trentiesme de Mon Eage"** where his earlier irony began to soften into a querulous and wandering nostalgia, expressed with remarkable beauty:

And I have come upon this place
By lost ways, by a nod, by words,
By faces, by an old man's face
At Morlaix lifted to the birds.

. . . .

By words, by voices, a lost way—
And here above the chimney stack
The unknown constellations sway.
And by what way shall I go back?

This poem remains the pivot of his subsequent thought. It has been his patient attempt to answer its last question. ***The Hamlet*** has been the most ambitious part of the program—a minor epic-allegory wherein men, devising their common destiny under the sun, find ultimately their only brotherhood and heroism in sorrow, and their hope in the creative fruition of natural processes. The serio-fantastic analysis of the **"Einstein"** (elsewhere carried to the point of travesty in the humorous pieces, or again expressed with sharp refinement in **"Ars Poetica"** has yielded to a style expressive of this theme of mute inglorious heroism. It is this style whose character is fully developed in ***New Found Land.*** The tone is persistently autumnal, the cry nostalgic, the content excessively miscellaneous. Unquestionably the lines have a flowing searching order—the curious and unflagging impulse which means style. It is, on the whole, the most successful attempt thus far to convert Eliot's nervous lucidity, Aiken's tinkling languor, and Robinson's clipped aphorisms into an amalgam which will constitute a genuine rhetoric of elegy.

The fact remains, however, that one of the first sources of stylistic durability in a poet is the "rebellious labor" which is motivated by some unequivocal form of private moral resolution. If MacLeish's style never gains the firm edge of individuality, and if his slow sentences with their too casual and unpunctuated phrases are unquickened by decisive impulse, it is because he has been too willing to lose himself in the crowd of men whose greatness lies only in unconscious union, or to surrender to the vast historical memory, inchoate and unanalyzed, which he has made his principal theme. ***Streets in the Moon*** is likely to remain his best volume (barring the unpredictable), because in its finest poems he exhibited a sensitive formal mastery, and a genius in understatement which the present **"American Letter"** and **"Cinema of a Man"** have probably disabled permanently. Today only the fragments of this unusual style remain; its beauties have been lost in catalogues and inventories.

The temptation to sound a warning against the complete dissolution of a fine poetic talent into verbosity and tedious repetition is irresistible, even when Mr. MacLeish's errors exasperate rather than dismay. His creative processes are synthetic, and his poems are mostly documentary in substance. Like Hemingway in prose, he urges the immediacy of his sensations by presenting them on a level of detached observation, connected by coordinating conjunctions and the simplest prepositions, but no longer by conventional periods and commas. If this method involves grave doubts in a novel, there can be no question of its dangers in a poem. The flat monotony of this style is capable of the finer moments in **"Return"**, **"Memory Green"**, and **"Immortal Autumn"**:

I praise the fall it is the human season now
No more the foreign sun does meddle at our earth
Enforce the green and bring the fallow land to birth
Nor winter yet weigh all with silence the pine bough

But too often it achieves only the open banality of **"You, Andrew Marvell"** (where the mechanism and the moral alike revolve with the naïve inconsequence of Mr. Wilder's recent fable); or the limp humility of **"American Letter"** whose theme, tiresomely reiterated, is "It is a strange thing to be an American"; or the sheer parody of **"Men"**:

We believed in the feel of the earth under us
We planted corn grapes apple-trees rhubarb
Nevertheless we knew others had died
Everything we have done has been faithful and dangerous

Few sensibilities can survive such monotony. This fluid ambiguity is charming only until it obliterates the design of a thought. That design, often brilliantly achieved in ***Streets in the Moon,*** reappears in **"& Forty second Street"** and in the **"Poem Dedicatory,"** the latter a kind of ejaculatory apostrophe which threatens to break heartlessly and insignificantly at the end of every exclamation, but which achieves succinctness. There remain **"Reproach to Dead Poets,"** some lines in "Part I" of **"Land's End,"** the grave beauty of **"Immortal Autumn"** and six fine line-couples in **"Anonymous Signature"** to assure us that Mr. MacLeish is not closing his accounts in this book. He has a serious task ahead if his future work is to rise above the threat of anonymity and indecision which at present overshadows it. From the first there has appeared in his work a strain of genuine nobility; to lose that quality, particularly in that full stature which Mr. MacLeish once promised to give us, would be to lose one of the finest personalities in recent American verse. Not with complete confidence yet with a considerable reliance on his creative responsibility, we await the larger projects upon which Mr. Mac-

Leish has been engaged for some months past. (pp. 270-75)

Morton Dauwen Zabel, "The Compromise of A. MacLeish," in Poetry, *Vol. XXXVI, No. 5, August, 1930, pp. 270-75.*

George Dangerfield

[*Dangerfield is an Anglo-American historian and critic. In the excerpt below, Dangerfield predicts that MacLeish will be one of the few writers of his generation to become a major poet.*]

The publication of ***New Found Land*** early in 1930 was an event of the first importance, both as regards a certain aspect in the development of modern American poetry which one might call the revival of the Anglo-Saxon tradition, and as marking a half-way stage in MacLeish's progress towards the articulation of a major poetry. . . . [We] cannot consider MacLeish's position in the development of modern American poetry without insisting upon this "Anglo-Saxon" element. It is at the very heart of such a typical phrase as

deeper than clouds are
Down or the underneath wings of the gulls go:

and for the purposes of a more exact comparison there is a single line from **"Immortal Autumn"**—

Or winter yet weigh all with silence the pine bough.

Consider the unity of sound and sense: the weight and distribution of the words: and how each separate word has been given a full value. And then compare it with this single line from that great and anonymous fourteenth-century poem *Gawayne And The Greene Knight*—

"Now iwysse," quod Wowayn, "wysty is here."

"It is desolate here". . . . We may have to go to a glossary for the sense, but the sound is inevitable; and again there is the proper distribution of words, the full meaning given to the word, the careful balance of vowel and consonant. The line is beautiful poetry because it is right . . . it *is* the desolation of the valley of the Green Chapel, where Gawayne expected to meet his death. In vocabulary and technique the poet of the twentieth century has a six-hundred year advantage: the fourteenth-century poet needs a careful and devoted reading. But the *likeness* in the use of words, in the *feeling* for words, is exact and unmistakable; it is of the utmost importance in this stage of the history of American poetry; and MacLeish, though not the only exponent of it, is certainly the clearest. (pp. 493-94)

MacLeish in this century can be said to carry on the Middle English tradition; he is not creating a new poetic language but re-creating an old one—which is one of the ways in which poetry is constantly keeping itself alive. He is always approaching nearer to the full *being* of the word, penetrating the word; and he, far more than almost any other poet today, appears at times to be fully conscious of the word as an ancient, mysterious, and living entity.

"To put it as baldly and as briefly as possible: no poet alive can give to the word, as a separate entity, such a full, single, lucid, and profound being; and no poet can write of the earth, the air, and the light in more startling or clearer imagery."

—George Dangerfield

It is my certain belief that Archibald MacLeish is one of the few contemporary poets, whether in America or England, who seem to be capable of achieving a major poetry. For not only are there at least the *intimations* of major poetry, in a great deal of his work, but he has written in **"Immortal Autumn"** the most beautiful single poem of his generation. It is a completely relevant poem, in the sense that from the first word to the last not one is out of place, or unnecessary, or weak. To quote from it would be to do it violence: but certainly both for its formal relevance, and for the imagination which fills it with a sharp, spacious, and insistent meaning, it is a great poem. There is evidence of a less sustained, more occasional, but at the same time more detached and objective imagination, which is embodied in a whole imagery, but not as yet in a complete poem.—

And here face down beneath the sun
And here upon earth's noonward height
To feel the always coming on
The always rising of the night

To feel creep up the curving east
The earthly chill of dusk and slow
Upon those under lands the vast
And ever climbing shadow grow.

These verses have a certain deceptive ease, which is not facility, and which, once you have read them two or three times, comes clearly beyond the scope of minor poetry—and yet what follows the magnificent conception contained in them is comparatively facile, clever, ingenious, over-elaborate. We have had merely the intimation of major poetry. But to turn from these general considerations to more particular cases, there is something which MacLeish has to say, which it is especially his property to say, which he is too often blamed for saying, and in which the whole direction of his future lies. It is first clearly, though not completely, set forth in **"Einstein".** It is the lack of communication between man and the earth, the soil; it is the sense of earth's withdrawal, of earth's denial of itself to man; it is a perpetually unsatisfied desire to understand, to put into words, to re-discover the earth, the air, and the light:

Now there are no words
Nor names to name them and they will not speak

—a statement which is in the later poetry to become an insistent complaint, an unanswerable question.

But is we turn back some five years to the facile imagery, and the somewhat toneless verse of ***The Pot of Earth,*** which seems to have its origin in all that is pleasant and beautiful in *The Golden Bough,* all that has given so many poets an easy impetus to write, supplied the imagery, and furnished the content, all that has not revealed the fearful and terrible meaning behind its beauty, the cruel and eventually false and shameful communication between man and the earth; and if we then move onward to . . . ***The Hamlet of A. MacLeish*** . . . we find a complete revolution, of which the **"Einstein"** was only the half-way stage; we find an insistent desire to return to the innocent world, to establish an innocent communication between man and the natural world, to return to the world as it was before the "irremediable woe, long done, lost in the times before memory"—a world without shame or superstition, no longer hostile, and no longer alien. This desire is linked up with a sense of great loneliness, great terror, and great frustration. And the frustration is embodied in a perpetual question, a question which the poet seems unable to answer and to which, because it is at the very heart of his later work, he must find an answer before he can achieve a major poetry. (pp. 494-95)

[There] is in MacLeish's poetry an intentional obscurity, the sources of which we can only guess at, and an unintentional obscurity, the obscurity of a poetry that is still at odds with itself; and both of these make one's task of elucidation a difficult and an unsatisfactory one. But we are always in danger of trying to read into his work the meanings we want to find there, and so of missing the fact that in his best work we *feel* that some answer has been provided to the question which is at the heart of it. For every poem of any value is itself a living and a positive thing, with a life separate from and independent of the life of its author; and when we find at the root of MacLeish's poetry the question "Where are the words?" the poem itself supplies an answer. To put it as baldly and as briefly as possible: no poet alive can give to the word, as a separate entity, such a full, single, lucid, and profound being; and no poet can write of the earth, the air, and the light in more startling or clearer imagery. Because these words and this imagery are used to give full meaning to the poet's question, to bring the poet face to face with himself, as it were, they only provide half the answer. But if we go on to consider the inequalities of ***The Hamlet,*** the poem in which MacLeish fully confessed himself, his frustration, his terror, and his despair, and in which flung a sort of hopeless challenge to himself, and compare them with the relevance of certain poems in ***New Found Land,*** where all his sense of inability has been clarified and confronted in poetry of a positive and ponderable value, we have a fair idea of the progress he has made. There is no other poet alive who could do the same thing, who could state a case against himself so clearly, and with such courage. An immediate and highly significant comparison is provided by T. S. Eliot's work, which is marked more clearly year by year with Eliot's refusal to commit himself, almost with his fear of being found out. Between Eliot's refusal and MacLeish's inability there is this difference in chief: that MacLeish is not afraid of laying himself wide open to attack and to criticism; he is not afraid to commit himself. He has still the opportunity of becoming a great poet; for not only has he reached a point in ***New Found Land*** where he has given a full and whole articulation to his frustration, his ignorance, his fear, and his desire, but in doing so he has already begun to escape from himself, to turn outward, and to set his face resolutely towards his destination—the discovery of an innocent world and of the words in which to tell it.

MacLeish is now midway in his Anabasis, with no straight or easy path ahead of him; but for my part I am sure that he will arrive within sight of "Thalassa, the sea, the Sea": which is perhaps a vague and sentimental way of saying that considering his past achievement, and considering his present position, he is almost certain to become one of the major poets of our time. But even if he were never to write another word, he would still be a poet of definite importance: for he has already created a poetry of a lucid and visible beauty in words that are "solid and real, live things". (p. 496)

George Dangerfield, "Archibald MacLeish: An Appreciation," in The Bookman, *New York, Vol. LXXII, No. 5, January, 1931, pp. 493-96.*

Lincoln Kirstein

Conquistador [is] a poem which is the finest consecutive narrative since *The Ring and the Book,* the single narrative worthy of the inheritance by an American, and what is far more important, a poem which is a rehabilitation of a language, raising new standards in symbols and reasserting the idea of heroism. Incidentally ***Conquistador*** is a monument of metric, a treasure house for quotation and indestructible testimony to the fact that whoever are the half dozen living poets, MacLeish must be considered one.

In his six published volumes he has emerged from the echoes of his education, through the scholarship of preceding and contemporary practitioners of his craft to an intensified personal quality, increasingly free from private association, towards the anonymous artistry of action. Up to the present his subjects have been that of much verse;—the praise of seasons, one's lovers, one's selves—a romantic lyricism of peoples and places. Keats never exhausted this subject matter, fortuitously or not, nor have any of the minor lyrists in English. Shakespeare and Donne have surely penetrated into it to the essence of human heat and cold; but it is exhaustible. After a young man is sick of himself, his loves, his hates, there are two or three aspects of experience left for him to correspond and describe,—geography, the praise of nature, and the histories of men in the earth. They are, by record, the subject matter of great poetry.

If one once considered the essential personal quality of MacLeish as nostalgia, a regret for times lost, places missed, the difficulty of a poet, as a poet, in a new land in a hard time, or the frustration of human relations, one can no longer so judge him. For ***Conquistador*** proves him not a poet as a man of letters, but a poet as a man of action occupied in the praise of arms and men.

The story of ***Conquistador,*** roughly, is the story of the first conquest of Mexico by the Spanish under Cortés. It is not a complete history. It glorifies no one person. By a device of great ingenuity this progress of men is conceived with consummate selectivity. In fragments, in shifting facets one constructs for oneself the multiple whole, which no complete documentation full of all incidental detail could ever have combined to do.

For, years after the Conquest, back in his own country and an old veteran, Bernál Díaz del Castillo, one of the conquerors, sick of the official volumes, writes his "True History of the Conquest of New Spain." ***Conquistador*** is what the old man remembers. He presupposes the well-known part of the history. His contribution is his own experience, the actual soul of the conquest, which can never be fused into a mere historian's synthesis. (pp. 484-85)

One can have only the utmost admiration for Bernál as MacLeish has erected him. The old man drones on, almost in a monotony of remembrance until an event will overwhelm him, . . . a fragment, a shattered image, a forgotten word, a mumbled line and then the sharp, tacit quirt of memory. Not riches, not the rewards of honor impressed the old soldier. Indeed he slurs over many events which might have called forth resplendent descriptions;—the meeting with Montezuma or the final triumph. Bernál has the professional soldier's cold-blooded interest in the technique and conduct of warfare. He recalls the harshest of the fighting, the worst of the pain, the real panic of retreat and more vaguely, the alien paradise he enjoyed for a moment and never knew why he lost. The Aztec sacrifices, the ceremonials made little dent in his mind. After all, he had the mythology of Catholicism to support him and the heathen belief was as incomprehensible as the infidel religion of the Moors. Bernál uses a technical or particular expression in its proper sense, his talk has that quality of intrinsic fascination that the shop-talk of aviators, or engineers or sailors have, when they assume your equal interest in their affairs.

Indeed the whole language of ***Conquistador*** is remarkable. MacLeish never for a second forgets who his narrator is, though he never directly describes him, and the soldier's diction is a smelting together of that tongue which we have come to know as the traditional poets' with a middle tongue of the common man's, a slight suggestion that the original of his history is in a foreign speech, that the Spanish is an antique Spanish, and that the old soldier is a humble ignorant fellow who sometimes feels the necessity of aping the scholars', the historians' flourish which had "the school taught skip to their writing."

And among many other extraordinary things MacLeish has done with words, perhaps his most immediate innovation is a rehabilitation of certain adjectives which with inert use have had their edges worn away;—"*famous* city," "*fortunate* wars," "*solemn* hands," "and they had no *ease* at all in that war and no *joy* of it," "gallows of wood and a *good* jail," "the whole thing was a very *beautiful* victory." He invests them with a new-to-us virtue, and restores their original usefulness.

Conquistador has a supple unity in its flexible linear design. Bernál tells his story by what MacLeish chooses to make him remember and the form of his line fits the mood of the memory. He can start the poem with an invocation to his muse, he can shift the cadence to an evocation, the actual summoning up of ghosts with his own breath, and by shortening the metre shift to a declamatory, vocative address, fused in between the various stages of the march of history. He can suggest prose in the verse not ever by being prosaic but by a change from the stricter rhythm to an almost legal cadence of formal writ, a lean piling up of facts, facts necessary but unadorned. For example, the poem ends with a movement like the coda of a symphony. That word of metal, "*Conquistador,*" is sounded or struck and left to vibrate in the silence of its broken line. Then follows the dignity of the downward turn, the narration not quite over but its end in sight, a recapitulation, a short development in reconsideration of the whole work, and then the three consecutive phrases as the final emphatic chords that swiftly terminate, define and inscribe forever the past resounding tale—

> That well swept town that island and those
> towers . . .

MacLeish's diction is his own gift and forging. He has, through many years of creation, submitted himself to a discipline. The greater variety of line length and freedom of metre in his earlier works have been smouldered down to a damascened length of variety, color, flexibility but essential and indestructible unity. First and foremost the line of ***Conquistador*** recalls not an English but an Italian poet. . . . ***Conquistador*** is written in a form of terza-rima, though often there is no rhyme. Occasionally the last syllables rhyme, often the penultimates reëcho and there is unremitting use of strict nets of dissonance and assonance with a skill and subtlety hardly ever before so consciously or successfully risked in the history of modern English prosody. (pp. 486-89)

MacLeish is, of course, drenched in the documentation of the period and yet he is never seduced by the temptations of decorative detail. He only records the exact image that has a direct bearing on the people of the sixteenth century in relation to the weather of their locale. The images are not necessarily referable or comprehensible to us at first glance. But there is no concession in attempting to "modernize" the Spaniards or the Aztecs for our easier consumption. They exist in this poem as much as the Chinese of Pound's *Cathay,* waiting for us to release them into the activity of our imagination by the slight flattery of an undivided attention.

In addition to the talents of his narrative sweep, and his powers as a technician MacLeish has the added gift of a penetrating, persistent attention to the quintessential activities of a natural event, the quality as it were, of individuation. He can express the essence of a particular kind of air; for example, the very weather for sailing. . . . These images are hardly ever merely visual but almost always audibly relevant. They spell the sounds they mean. And combined with his exhaustion of the descriptive possibilities in nature, MacLeish can isolate the core of physicality, the interior essential fluid of men in violent action, which is the spring of action, stronger than almost any poet save the great Greeks, Dante and Shakespeare. He can expose the raw nerve to the air, he can exhaust the mind's concept of fatigue into actual lassitude by wrenching an image from a pierced or anguished body so that the divisions of the poem come as a relief, and a blank page is a real rest. . . . It is a fable of the necessity for action in adventures of adversity, in the maintenance of an interest after all satisfaction in it had ceased and only a greater consciousness can be gained by further perseverence. It is the tragedy of the self-betrayal of the human will, the failure of the human organism itself, by its own mortality, of the pioneer's dignity in tragedy when he is aware enough to know that the pattern of his destiny is larger than his capacity to conquer it, but who always behaves even in the ultimate fatality with the gallantry of a conqueror. "Our lives are brief, noble and tragic," this poet has written in another poem.

MacLeish, not only by his gifts and talents but also by the implicit attitude of an undefined philosophy, deserves comparison with the two others of our chief contemporary poet-philosophers. In Pound's *Cantos* there is a consistent attitude towards a lyric correspondence. In Eliot's *Ash Wednesday* and in ***Conquistador*** there are consistent examples towards a method of behavior.

Pound is a lyric, rather than a philosophic poet and the philosophy implicit in his sense of the fusion of time and times is a lyric attitude, a personal frame, a frame which too often comes first before the reader. It has more to do with the tradition of poetry than with the poetry of life. To Eliot and Pound the suggestions for their attitudes have come from the nurture of abstract thought or the activity of their intelligences in cerebration. The battles of the mind are no less muscular or tiring or even rewarding than the battles of physical imagery in action, only perhaps to us of a younger generation they have become enervating.

In short, MacLeish's religion is the hero's belief in the possibility of a hero. "I am well aware that in these days hero-worship, the thing I call hero-worship, professes to have gone out and finally ceased. . . . But I liken common languid times, with their unbelief, distress, perplexity, with their languid doubting characters and embarrassed circumstances, impotently crumbling down into ever worse distress towards final ruin;—all this I liken to dry dead fuel, waiting for the lightning out of Heaven that shall kindle it. . . . For myself in these days, I seem to see in this indestructibility of hero-worship the everlasting adamant lower than which the confused wreck of revolutionary things cannot fall." Whether or not we can tolerate this ninety-two year old optimism of Carlyle, whether we believe a hero is a divinity, a prophet, a poet, priest or king, a belief in the existence of the hero at all is still more valuable than the opposite.

To have written ***Conquistador*** is to have erected a monument to the possibility of heroism. It is an act of faith in the belief of poetry and human action, on a grand scale, again. (pp. 489-92)

Lincoln Kirstein, "Arms and Men," in The Hound & Horn, *Vol. V, No. 3, April-June, 1932, pp. 484-92.*

Harriet Monroe

[*In the excerpt below, Monroe praises* Conquistador *as a major literary work.*]

There are obvious things one may say of ***Conquistador:*** that its subject is a great story, a tragic romance of conquest, the truth that is stranger than fiction, ready-made to the poet's hand; that it goes swinging along through incredible adventures in the wild unknown of early sixteenth-century Mexico, where each step strides off into myth and leaves the imagination free; that by basing his poem on the hot-tempered narrative of the Conquest written in old age by Bernal Diaz del Costello, the common soldier who fought with Cortez from Cuba to Montezuma's capital, the poet gives us the very feeling and atmosphere of a more spacious primitive world, and makes his work an epic of races rather than heroes; through his imaginative intensification of the aggrieved old soldier's tale revealing the fierce courage of the lawless adventure: the dash into unknown seas and lands; the battles with formidable tribes—horde after horde pouring upon the invaders, and their killings avenged by massacres; the ruin of cities and confiscation of treasure; the obliteration of a whole civilization and its literature and arts—

> And the town gone—no stone to a stone of it—
> And the whole thing was a very beautiful victo-
> ry—

and finally the building of Spanish cities and the settlement of that "good land" by its conquerors. One may even admire the skilful technique, show how the poet shapes a very irregular pentameter line to his purpose, and works it into an adroit *terza rima* of assonances—assonances so diabolically subtle that they hide in ambush and conquer you unseen with their music of half-tones and strangely varied harmonies. I say one may grant all these excellences without in the least accounting for the beauty, the varied and distinguished artistry, and the epic size of the poem. Its quality lies in something beyond details of subject or technique; it springs from a mind capable of fusing these into a grandly molded work of art, wherein each unobtrusive detail counts toward the symmetry of the whole. (pp. 216-18)

Here there are neither the closely syllabled iambics of blank verse as in Milton and the Elizabethan dramatists, nor the exact rhyming structure of the heroic couplet; the measure is freer, as becomes a modern poet, both in its counting of syllables and stresses, and in its hidden half-smothered assonantal rhymes. The poet's mastery of such details of his technique show how far he has traveled since the days of ***Happy Marriage,*** which announced the début of a promising new poet. He has perfected his command of a richly tuned instrument, and has proved his ability, moreover, to sustain its quality and test its resources through the exacting changes of mood in a long narrative poem. (pp. 219-20)

Harriet Monroe, "The Conqueror," in Poetry, *Vol. XL, No. 4, July, 1932, pp. 216-22.*

Allen Tate

[*Tate, along with Robert Penn Warren, John Crowe Ransom, and Cleanth Brooks, was a proponent of New Criticism, which emphasized the evaluation of literary works based on image, symbol, and meaning. The essay below was originally published in 1932.*]

Mr. MacLeish has been up to this time a poet like most of his contemporaries, limited to the short flight. There is, in his earlier work, no premonitory sounding of the finely sustained tone of ***Conquistador.*** For modern poetry the poem is long. It is an epic in miniature of about two thousand lines. In versification and style, and with respect to the narrational "point of view," there is no other poem in English with which as a whole it may be compared. It is evident, of course, that MacLeish has studied Ezra Pound; but this is no disparagement of Pound's pupil. The *Cantos* are full of technical instruction for the poet who knows what he needs to learn. The followers of Eliot take his "philosophy" as well as his style, and give us work of "lower intensity" than the original. Pound's disciples are either less plausible or more independent. They exercise thinly with Mr. Dudley Fitts or practice the admirable craft of ***Conquistador.***

The background of the poem is the conquest of Mexico. For a complete history of the conquest one will have to go to the historians. The poem is a reconstruction of the part played by one of the lesser heroes, Bernal Diaz del Castillo, who as an old man wrote his own story in resentment against the official histories by Gomara and others—

> The quilled professors: the taught tongues of fame:
> What have they written of us: the poor soldiers . . .
> They call the towns for the kings that bear no scars:
> They keep the names of the great for time to stare at—
> The bishops rich men generals cocks-at-arms . . .

Bernal tells the story in flashes of recollection that have just enough narrative progression to give to the narrator a constantly new field of imagery. But the historical pattern of the conquest is never explicit, never obtrusive enough to take the reader's attention from the personality of Bernal and the quality of his character. For the personality of Bernal is the subject of the poem.

Thus narrowing the action down to the focus of a single mind and what it saw, MacLeish disposes of two enormous difficulties of epic poetry: he eliminates the objective detail of the total scene, at once the conventional privilege and the burden of the classical poet; and he dispenses with the need of cosmic machinery. There is no external "idea"; there is no theme; there is no "typical action."

We get the peculiarly modern situation: the personality of one man is dramatized against an historical setting. "What have they written of us: the poor soldiers"—what can the private sensibility get out of history to sustain it? What can Bernal get out of his past? Nothing appears in the story that Bernal did not see; it is all enriched by memory. Although Bernal announces his subject as "That which I have myself seen and the fighting," there is little fighting; there is little action; for the dramatic tension of the poem grows out of the narrator-hero's fear of death upon the gradual disappearance of sensation. The dramatic quality of the poem—a quality that has little to do with the story as such—lies thus in the hero's anxiety to recover his sensuous early years, upon which his identity as a person, and hence his life, depends.

This is the subject of the poem. The "meaning" of the poem is an implicit quality of Bernal's mind, but only a little logical violence will isolate it. It is the futility of individual action. For unless the hero, in his old age, can recapture the sensation of action, the action itself must fade into the obscure shuffle of abstract history. We have seen that Bernal cannot accept the public versions of the conquest. (Is Bernal, then, a soldier of the sixteenth century or of the first World War?) He cannot identify the moment of action with the ostensible common purpose for which the whole series of events took place. He is confined to memories, to the mechanism of sensation.

I dwell upon this "meaning" of ***Conquistador*** for two reasons. It obviously, in the first place, explains the form in which MacLeish found it necessary to cast his narrative, a form that I have briefly described; the necessity of this form explains the presence, I believe, of those features of the style that MacLeish borrowed from Pound and perfected. And, secondly, the meaning of this distinguished poem, as I apprehend it, may lead some of the younger critics to reconsider, not their enthusiasm for the workmanship, which it richly deserves, but their hasty acceptance of its "philosophy." It is a mistake to suppose that MacLeish has offered a "way out" of the introspective indecision of the school of T. S. Eliot, affirming a faith in heroic action against the moral paralysis presumably suffered by the best minds of that older generation. Not only is there, in the poem, a lack of belief in any kind of action that we might imitate; the poet does not feel much interest in the action implied by the reminiscences that support the narrative.

There is not one moment of action rendered objectively in the entire poem. There is constantly and solely the pattern of sensation that surrounded the moment of action—the fringe of the physical shock and awareness that survive in memory. The technique of rendering this special quality of memory is MacLeish's contribution to poetic style. . . . This clarity of sensuous reminiscence that suffuses the poem is a new quality in American verse. The images are not imbedded in metaphor; they exist spatially in the round. . . . The images are impersonal, objective, and timeless, detached from Pound's moral position. The focus of MacLeish's imagery is personal: the image exists in terms of Bernal's recovery of memory, of his struggle for personal identity. Its precision has been disciplined in the workshop of Ezra Pound, whose quality of floating clarity is localized by MacLeish in a Browningesque monologue, where the casuistry gives way to a sophisticated version of the *chanson de geste.*

Poets in this age cannot set forth with security a conscious philosophical system. Reasons for this I have mentioned in another place. When there is no systematic philosophy at hand, the poet is likely to slip into an unsystematic one of his own: this, perhaps, is better than an elaborate system that he cannot assimilate and understand. MacLeish's philosophy is personal and unarticulated. It may be stated in moral terms. We cannot linger over even the finest passages of ***Conquistador*** without becoming aware that we are in the presence of a sentimental view of experience. I have said that there is no objective design to uphold the sensibility of the narrator-hero. Perhaps, in this poem, MacLeish is no less able a poet than the young Milton of "Lycidas"; but Milton had an objective convention that absorbed every implication of his personal feeling. I use the term sentimental, then, in a strict, not a pejorative, sense. The melancholy of the hero's disgust with the "taught tongues of fame" is personal, sentimental; it is necessarily meaningless and obscure.

The disgust of Bernal does not rise to the level of rational criticism. It would serve as a rational evaluation of the "conquest" if there were a full stream of objective action in the light of which it could acquire significance. To have set off the private experience of the soldier against the grandiose avowals of purpose by the conquerors, might possibly have provided the poet with the situation of tragic irony. But there is no conflict of this order in the poem. The emotion is pathos. We get Bernal's sentimental regret; his anger rises at the failure of the official historians to recreate the sensuous correspondence to his own part in the campaign. He says in effect not *quorum pars magna fui* but rather *solus quorum omnis fui*—alone in his perceptions. The poem recovers the perceptions but it does not place them against a coherent stream of events. The hero is concerned with his personal survival. He is modern and sentimental; not tragic and ironic. The motivation of his story is the fear of death.

I am ungrateful to MacLeish; I have dwelt upon a philosophical limitation that is not peculiar to this poet, but is deeply rooted in the age. The technical perfection of ***Conquistador*** is, of course, not merely a technical feat. The poem is one of the examples of our modern sensibility at its best; it has the defect of its qualities.

The verse is *terza rima,* a metrical form enormously difficult in English. The paucity of English rhymes leaves it clumsy and monotonous in all but the hands of a master. Shelley tried it once with moderate success; Wyat adapted it to an epistolary style that doubtless should have been but never was a model for later poets. But MacLeish, foreseeing in a long poem the monotony of conventionally rhymed *terza rima,* varies rhyme with terminal assonance that is usually hidden and always cunningly placed. He achieves something of the fluent ease of the Italian, which is rich in rhyme words, and gives us the first successful example of *terza rima* in a long English poem.

It is the only considerable metrical achievement by a poet of this generation. Yet the perfection of the experiment will make future use of *terza rima* dangerous. The technique of the verse is a quality of MacLeish's mind, and is inimitable. "Waller refined our numbers"—but this time Waller is a hard-pressed modern whose brilliance, once flashed, burns out before it can be passed to other hands. It is the present fate of poetry to be always beginning over again. The kind of "culture" in ***Conquistador*** is purely literary; the kind of experience in it is the sentimentality of moral isolation. The refinement of the craftsmanship hovers over a void. (pp. 358-63)

Allen Tate, "MacLeish's 'Conquistador'," in his Essays of Four Decades, *The Swallow Press, Inc., 1968, pp. 358-63.*

Michael Gold

[*The following essay is credited by many critics with expediting MacLeish's public voice. In it, Gold, an American Jewish Marxist, finds traces of fascism and anti-Semitism in MacLeish's* Frescoes for Mr. Rockefeller's City.]

It has been piously said, there can be no fascism in America. But signs appear in the political sky, and Hitler's program, somewhat veiled in cauls and mysteries of the poetic womb, may also be discerned in these latest verses of Archibald MacLeish [***Frescoes for Mr. Rockefeller's City***].

Here is mystic nationalism, first stage of the true fascist mind. Hitler and Mussolini exploit race loyalty for their demagogy, but in America there are too many powerful races. So we may expect the fascist-nationalists to fall back on a mystic geography, and to say with MacLeish:

> She's a tough land under the oaktrees, mister:
> It may be she can change the word in the book
> As she changes the bone of a man's head in his children:
> It may be the earth and the men remain. . . .

(meaning, of course, America is too tall, wide and different to be subject to the secular economic laws that govern prosy little Asia and Europe . . .).

And another sign of his fascist mission is Mr. MacLeish's contempt for Marxists, Jews and those disturbed intellectuals who recently have taken the road to the political left:

> Also Comrade Edward Remington Ridge
> Who has prayed God since the April of Seventeen
> To replace in life his lost (M.E.) religion . . .
>
> Even Comrade Grenadine Grilt who has tried since
> August Tenth for something to feel strongly in
> Verses—his personal passions having tired . . .
>
> *I can tell my land by the jays in the apple trees*
> *Tell my land by the jays in the apple 'rees*
> *I can tell my people by the blue-jays in the apple trees*
>
> Aindt you read in d'books you are all brudders?
> D'glassic historic objective broves you are all brudders?
> You and d'Wops and d'Chinks you are all brudders?
> Havend't you got it d'same ideology? Havend't you?

Fascism is the revolt of the lower middle class, a cruel and futile rage of little traders who have been wiped out by

MacLeish wrote several successful verse plays for radio. He is flanked in the photograph above by Orson Welles (left) and William Robson.

chain stores, bankers and big business. Mr. MacLeish therefore hates the Harrimans, Vanderbilts and Morgans who "screwed America gaunt and scrawny with their seven year panics." He cartoons them savagely in one of his frescoes, but no more than Hitler does he demand that the wealth of the nation be restored to the nation, the stock market plowed under for a truck farm. No, all that Mr. MacLeish seems to ask is that the bankers "look at the land, they never looked at it, it was all prices to them." He wants J. P. Morgan and Otto Kahn to be heroes, pioneers and poetic explorers, like that Captain Lewis who penetrated the Northwest, and whose letter to Thomas Jefferson is paraphrased in the only touching passage in these six poems. This is confusing, of course, but then all fascism is generally a welter of confusions, grandiose phrases and murder.

Mr. MacLeish may be an unconscious fascist, but it is curious that he has lyricized the major attitudes of German and Italian fascists. How could he have stumbled so accurately upon the fascist attitude toward the proletariat? In his fifth verse he describes those hordes of immigrant workers who built the railroads of the nation. They died in holocausts, and were buried in nameless graves under the ties, for the triumphant engines to pass over their bones.

The fascist author is permitted, like Mr. MacLeish, to chant the pathos and heroism of Labor, even to fight against those who would degrade it. Only against those workers who become class conscious, and themselves revolt against their slavery, are torture-squads to be directed. Yes, labor is heroic, pathetic, and has its place in the hierarchy of values; it has been created eternally to serve, and is to be offered mystic compensations, nothing sordid and real like bread or freedom, but the glory of the fascist Integral State:

> Do not pity us much for the strange grass over us:
> We laid the steel to the stone stock of these mountains:
> The place of our graves is marked by the telegraph poles.

The device of contrasting images is much favored by Mr. MacLeish. This technique in poetry was originated by Ezra Pound; T. S. Eliot made it popular; now it is the property of every college literary snobling. It is also the favorite device of political reactionaries. A mythical golden past is always pitted against the sordid commercial present. Hitler invokes the blonde Aryans; Mussolini restores the eagles of Caesar; the awakened Magyars remember their forebear, Attila; and here is Archibald Mac-

Leish using all the epic splendor of the American past, the red Indians, the pioneers, the railroad hunkies, and even the Rocky Mountains and the strong savage American landscape as a political argument against sordid Marxists, Jews and intellectuals!

But this is neither poetry nor logic. The Rocky Mountains should be left to their snow and eternal stars. They are no answer to make to the demands of 16 million unemployed men and women Americans. Mr. MacLeish has no political rights to the Rockies or the landscape. This great magnetic continent belongs to the masses, to the workers. White-collar fascists out of Harvard and Wall Street have less spiritual claim on America than the share-croppers, miners, sailors and gandy dancers. Walt Whitman said it once, but it needs to be said again and again; every land belongs to those who fertilize it with their blood and sweat.

Who is there in America today to carry on the revolutionary democracy of the pioneers? Certainly not the decadent Black or Brown Shirts, the Huey Longs and Smedley Butlers. Mr. MacLeish sneers at the men of the left. He has heard some speak with a Yiddish or Negro accent. It is a pity he is so fastidious about trifles, for he has missed the true home of the American tradition. This land is great because it was founded on a democratic revolution. That revolution continues in the hearts of hundreds of thousands of Kentucky miners, Chicago stockyard butchers and Tampa cigarmakers, Oregon lumberjacks and New England weavers. It burns in the Rockies and Alleghenies. It goes to sea on every American keel. New York poets feel it, Back Bay blue-noses, too, the intellectuals of San Francisco and New Orleans stir with the tradition of Thoreau and Emerson.

As for us unfortunate Jews who happen to be Communists and annoy Mr. MacLeish so much, we shall go on repeating in our vulgar dialect, despite Hitler and MacLeish, "Aindt you read in d'books you are all brudders? Aindt you read in d'books you are all brudders? Aindt you read in d'books you are all brudders?" (pp. 295-96)

Michael Gold, "Out of the Fascist Unconscious," in The New Republic, *Vol. LXXV, No. 973, July 26, 1933, pp. 295-96.*

William Rose Benét

[*In the essay excerpted below, Benét refutes Michael Gold's claims in the preceding essay.*]

Since Archibald MacLeish won the Pulitzer Prize this year for poetry, ***Frescoes for Mr. Rockefeller's City*** is the first group of poems he has published. His best single poem since then is **"1933"** which appeared in the Summer issue of *The Yale Review.* That poem concerned the Elpenor whom both Homer and Ezra Pound have celebrated. MacLeish's Elpenor is nothing if not symbolic, and I am privy to an anecdote concerning the reading of this poem as the Phi Beta Kappa poem at Harvard this year. After the event, it seems—at lunch, I believe it was—Mr. MacLeish encountered the cold and extortionate eye of a certain dignified elder gentleman, a mentor of no inconsiderable classical repute. "Mr. MacLeish," quotha, "there is just one thing about your poem I did not understand." Feeling a slight chill at the pit of his stomach in the presence of so much scholarship, the poet embarked upon an explanation of his Elpenor. That prophetic shade incidentally counsels Ulysses eloquently to seek a new land whose spartan characteristics he describes. "Oh yes," interrupted the Cambridge sage, "I know the story. But what I wished to ask you was—just what is this country to which we are all going?" The poet found much relish in the episode.

This anecdote seems pertinent in view of a discussion of Mr. MacLeish's ***Frescoes,*** in *The New Republic* for July 26th. The review is written by that lively Communist, Michael Gold. It is headed "Out of The Fascist Unconscious," and Mr. Gold finds Mr. MacLeish espousing a mystic nationalism that is, according to Mr. Gold, the "first stage of the true fascist mind." I, on the other hand, find the poet merely trying to understand his own country and his own time. In his sixth and last poem in the ***Frescoes,*** entitled **"Background with Revolutionaries,"** he has bitterly offended Mr. Gold by his casual references to certain kinds of "Comrades." This extreme sensitivity bespeaks a soft-mindedness in Mr. Gold that I should not have expected. While excoriating Mr. MacLeish for being trivial, his exasperation is chiefly aroused by one particular vaudeville stanza (of four lines) in dialect. Therefrom he deduces that the poet is a pronounced anti-Semite, a large deduction to draw from a few teasing words! As I read the poet he has become a little tired of the slight amount some insurrectionaries actually know of the vast country they would like to transform into the measure of their own dream. Mr. MacLeish's

> She's a tough land under the corn mister

seems to me merely a rather sage statement of fact, if one has been round and about the United States a good deal. The italicized ending of ***Frescoes,*** needs, I think, only to be quoted to show it for a shrewd poetic comment that has nothing to do with the excited Fascist state of mind. I have no space to quote its words here and must ask you to buy the pamphlet for twenty-five cents from the John Day Company and read at least the last page.

I do not wholly disagree with Mr. Gold in his contention that poetry and the arts have political significance. I merely believe that they have a much larger significance than that. If this is to be a mystic, I am one, and so must all pondering poets be. I feel that the recent manifestations in Germany have set back the clock. It has been a fearful spectacle. Just that. But Mr. MacLeish's Elpenor, in his **"1933"** is looking forward to a hope, and I do not believe that in ***Frescoes for Mr. Rockefeller's City*** the poet is in the least "an unconscious fascist," as Mr. Gold would have him. . . .

Now on the face of it no intelligent man, much less a poet, believes a Marxist, a Jew, or an intellectual (that is, I gather, one who tries to use his reason more than does the average person) to be "ignoble," which is one of the meanings of "sordid." All dreams that have to do with the rehabilitation of the human race are noble dreams. And it should be sufficiently obvious—except to Mr. Hitler—that the

Jewish race has contributed some of the most courageous reasoning, civic virtue, and artistic achievement in the history of mankind. Hastily to draw the conclusion that a poet, who has demonstrated the breadth of vision and sensitivity to the sufferings of the human race which are everywhere apparent in Mr. MacLeish's poetry, is using that poetry for a paltry and ignoble purpose is, to say the least, most short-sighted. A poet, like anyone else, may question the efficacy of a certain definite political scheme. He may be right, he may be wrong, I do not believe that even greater mystical poets than Mr. MacLeish have been infallible, or omniscient. But it seems to me that Mr. Gold is claiming for the communistic view of things an omniscience that it has not justified. Nor do I believe that he helps his cause by an essentially superficial attack upon the musings of one of the most cogently ironic poets of our time in America. Of the Empire-Builders, of the great financiers, Mr. MacLeish says, through his red-skinned American speaking, that this country "was all prices to them: they never looked at it . . . it was all in the bid and the asked and the ink on their books . . . " a fact that we have, perhaps, bitterly learned. But that does not seem to me to be invoking the Rocky Mountains as a political argument against those of us today who are trying to do a little thinking!

For a brief pamphlet, which it is, Mr. MacLeish's ***Frescoes*** contains quite a range of thought concerning America. His poems are not material for the hustlings. The trouble with Mr. Gold, flatly, is that he would have the poets turn propagandists for a particular political and economic thesis. If they refuse to do that, they are simply speaking out of turn and wasting his time. This ground has been gone over already by Mr. MacLeish himself, in prose, in his **"Invocation to the Social Muse"** which caused much controversy in the pages of *The New Republic.* So I shall not labor the point that if you reduce poets to propagandists you kill poetry deader than a door-nail. The poet is an independent and must remain so. The private religious, political, and economic views of poets as human beings are in most cases as fallible as those of other average people. Nor do I mean that poetry is some sort of mystic incantation, though at its best it may be—drawing on sources that no one has ever been able completely to define. But you should not desire to label a poet Fascist, Communist, or any other kind of *ist.* Whitman has been used so much, now, as propaganda that we have almost forgotten that he was, first and foremost, a poet. Mr. Gold drags out the old radical stereotype when he cries, "White-collar fascists out of Harvard and Wall Street." He is ready with catchwords. His ideas of class-struggle seem to me to partake of antiquated caricature. Today's is a bitter and complicated dilemma, and it will not get us anywhere in particular to call names. Mr. Gold accuses Mr. MacLeish of sneering and indulges himself in an equal sneer. All of which is childish.

One compliment Mr. Gold has paid to Mr. MacLeish's most recent poems. He has taken them seriously; and they are serious. But he has taken them so seriously that one would think Mr. MacLeish in them had outlined, at the very least, a complete American attitude; whereas, he has actually touched upon but a few aspects of America as seen with his own particular vision. That vision is valuable. And Mr. MacLeish is one of the very few American poets who are trying to get any perspective at all upon their own country. I should like to see many more American poets address themselves to this task. I believe there will be more and more of them as time goes on. But the poets must observe detachment from propaganda to do it. They must work each in his own way, preserving the most strict individual honesty.

William Rose Benét, "Round About Parnassus," in The Saturday Review of Literature, *Vol. X, No. 2, July 29, 1933, p. 21.*

Edmund Wilson

[*Wilson, considered America's foremost man of letters in the twentieth century, wrote widely on cultural, historical, and literary matters. The poem below is Wilson's parody of MacLeish's* The Hamlet of A. MacLeish. *The italicized sections are the critic's comments.*]

And the mist: and the rain in the west: and the wind steady:
There were elms in that place: and graven inflexible laws:
Men of Yale: and the shudder of Tap Day: the need for a man to make headway

Winning a way through the door in the windowless walls:
And the poems that came easy and sweet with a blurring of Masefield
(The same that I later denied): a young man smooth but raw
(*MacLeish breaks an egg for his omelet*)

Eliot alarmed me at first: but my later abasement:
And the clean sun of France: and the freakish but beautiful fashion:
Striped bathhouses bright on the sand: Anabase and The Waste Land:

These and the Cantos of Pound: O how they came pat!
Nimble at other men's arts how I picked up the trick of it:
Rode it reposed on it drifted away on it: passing

Shores that lay dim in clear air: and the cries of affliction
Suave in somniferous rhythms: there was rain there and moons:
Leaves falling: and all of a flawless and hollow felicity:
(*He puts plovers' eggs and truffles into his omelet*)

In that land there were summer and autumn and nighttime and noon
But all seemed alike: and the new polished planets by Einstein:
And a wind out of Valéry's graveyard but it never blew anything loose:
(*He slips in a few prizes for philosophers*)

And the questions and questions
questioning
What am I? O

What shall I remember?
O my people
a pensive dismay

What have I left unsaid?
Till the hearer cried:

"If only MacLeish could remember if only could say it!" . . .
And young girls came out: they were innocent strong in the tendons
Hungry for all that was new: and hearing their eyelids were hazy with

Tears and delight: and the campuses brown in November:
Hey but white shirt fronts pink faces: the prizes won:
The celluloid tower with bold intonations defended:
(*The omelet becomes a national institution and gets into Fanny Farmer*)

And the mean tang of Cummings turned saltless and sleek on the tongue:
And a Dante gone limp: and a shimmer and musical sound
That gleamed in the void and evoked approbation and wonder

That the poet need not be a madman or even a bounder.
(*He experiments with a new kind of peppercorn*)

And at last I drew close to a land dark with fortifications:
Men shrieking outlandish reproaches till all my blood tingled:
It was ragged and harsh there: they hated: heart horribly quaked in me:

Then I thought "I have staved off the pricking of many a sting:
These perchance I may placate too": I put in at that place:
I met them with scorn and good-natured agreement mingled:
(*He seems likely to lose his investment in his omelet*)

Their fierce cries of "Aesthete!" and "Fascist!": and like them I railed at the
Bankers and builders of railroads: I said "Social Credit":
(He's a tough lad under the verse mister all the same!):

And the Polacks and Dagoes and Hunkies undoubtedly dead:
And behold these savage and sybarite-baiting strangers
Had many among them like me well-mannered well-fed
(*He is obliged to reopen his omelet and put a little garlic in*)

Bubbling over with schoolboy heroics: their line had been changing:
And long in that plentiful land I dwelt honored in peace:
And then schoolboys from Britain came over us flying like angels:

Them too I courted: and labored to roughen the sweet
To stiffen the wilt of a style that seemed lax in that land:
A starch of Greek tragedy: stark Anglo-Saxon the beat of it:

Stock-market talk: still my numbers as mawkishly ran:
(Señora, I could go on like this forever:
It is a strange thing to be an American):

I was wired for sound as I started again down the river:
And my colons went out on the air to the clang of a gong:
O when shall I ring with the perilous pain and the fever?

A clean and clever lad
who is doing
his best
to get on. . . .

(*He is doomed to go on doctoring his omelet*) (pp. 23-4)

Edmund Wilson, "The Omelet of A. MacLeish," in The New Yorker, *Vol. XIV, No. 48, January 14, 1939, pp. 23-4.*

Cleanth Brooks

[Brooks's criticism strongly influenced critical writing and the teaching of literature in the United States during the 1940s and 1950s. In the following essay, Brooks praises MacLeish's "remarkable talents and his rich sensibility."]

MacLeish, like Sandburg, deals in a detemporized past. His longer poems are rather consistently "histories" and the world which they reveal is timeless—with the emphasis, not like Sandburg's on a timeless present, but on a timeless past. Sandburg tends to be brash and topical, and he is obsessed with the immediacy of his point, namely, that the real past was the world of ourselves—the trivial, tawdry, and yet somehow glorious world that we know in common experience. MacLeish has more delicacy and restraint. His imagery is richer, his canvas broader, his control of rhythms far more profound. Compare with "Four Preludes on Playthings of the Wind" MacLeish's **"Men":**

> Our history is grave noble and tragic
> We trusted the look of the sun on the green leaves
> We built our towns of stone with enduring ornaments
> We worked the hard flint for basins of water. . . .

The poem continues with a recitation of a miscellany of items typical of the life of men:

> We planted corn grapes apple-trees rhubarb . . .
> We believed in the promises made by the brows of women . . .
> We fought at the dikes in the bright sun for the pride of it . . .

to conclude with the lines,

> Many cities are gone and their channels broken
> We have lived a long time in this land and with honor.

The poem is typical of all men everywhere. It might be spoken by Assyrians or Greeks or modern Americans. It is a tribute to MacLeish's skill in the use of imagery that the items, though sharp and distinct, give no clue—do not date or locate (and therefore, in this case, limit) the poem.

The images, of course, do a great deal more than this. They establish and sustain a certain tone. The history has its dignity and its simple seriousness. Man's foolishness and knavery are an integral part of that history—

> We were drunk and lay with our fine dreams in the straw . . .

They need not be, and are not, glossed over. In turn, the frank and even casual mention of such items removes any tinge of vaingloriousness from the recital. The poem is thoroughly successful; but the technique of the poem (and it is typical of MacLeish) is stringently limited.

Consider the way in which the poem is built. The poem is made up of a series of parallel statements, apparently stacked together with no effort at subordination or order of any sort. The naïve parallelism is, of course, part of the artistic method: it sorts with the character of the men who speak, men who see no pattern in their history and who have no point to make but merely set forward, simply and seriously, the memorable items of that history.

Thoroughly parallel to this method of organization is the piling up of nouns and noun phrases in ***Conquistador*** . . . It is the kind of imagery that dominates long sections of the ***Hamlet*** and ***The Pot of Earth,*** and is the staple of the **"Land's End"** poems.

This piling up of separate items of detail is often, on the level of direct evocation, extremely successful, and in many of the poems it is dramatically justified. An index of its potentialities is one means of arriving at the scope and limitations of the poet himself. For MacLeish is in one sense an Imagist—though he surpasses the poets conventionally known as Imagists at every point. (pp. 116-19)

[***Conquistador***] makes the Imagists seem very thin indeed. Moreover, in ***Conquistador*** the structure of detail set upon detail, loosely held together with and's and then's, admirably suits the conditions of narration. The succession of images, each momentarily held and illuminated for an instant by the mind, represents very well the process of memory as the old soldier lives back over his campaign.

But the poem is essentially reverie, not drama; the final effect pathos, not tragedy.

The point of this observation is not to censure ***Conquistador*** for failing to be something which the poet did not attempt. The poem is what it is, and surely must be judged one of the finer accomplishments of modern American poetry. The point of the remark is to define more narrowly the terms in which the poem achieves its success.

MacLeish's poetry, in this poem and elsewhere, is essentially a poetry of the noun, not of the verb. His images, far more than those of the Imagists, do tend to become symbols; but the symbols are relatively static, lack dynamic quality. MacLeish's sensibility is rich but lacks principles. His poetry does not have the intricacy of idea necessary to the poetry of a poet like Yeats. One may sum up by saying that his poetry lacks dramatic tension.

This fact may explain why his successful poems so often deal with a primitive people going about the essential concerns of human life, and why the imagery stresses only those things which are the common denominator of all peoples. In such "histories," there are no meanings, no interpretations, apart from the fact that the histories are "grave noble and tragic." Or to make the application to ***Conquistador,*** there can be no meaning to the history of the conquest of Mexico apart from the meaning of the campaign to Bernal Diaz as a man.

The poet asks in the prologue to this poem:

> What are the dead to us in the world's wonder?
> Why (and again now) on their shadowy beaches
> Pouring before them the slow painful blood
>
> Do we return to force the truthful speech of them
> Shrieking like snipe along their gusty sand . . .

The lines are noble, but no truth is forced from the dead. The parallel to Odysseus is superficial: what Bernal brings back from Hades is a personal possession—not wisdom but memory. The poem in essence is lyric, and a very fine one it is, but it is not an epic of the conquest of Mexico. (pp. 119-20)

Romantic irony and a fairly obvious external and satiric irony—see **"Memorial Rain"** and the ***Frescoes***—these are the kinds of irony which MacLeish is capable of. Irony . . . , which maintains an equilibrium between opposed attitudes, irony which acts as a stabilizing force, is hardly to be found in MacLeish's poetry at all. His best poetry is of a kind to which such irony is irrelevant.

Examination of MacLeish's most successful poems will bear out this generalization. His best poems are "palpable and mute . . . motionless in time." They are remarkably solid, but they are as static as statuary. They do not involve shifts in tone; there is little or no development in the poet's attitude. This static quality holds true, even when, as in the celebrated **"You, Andrew Marvell,"** the specific theme is the poet's sense of the passage of time.

The poem is a brilliant example of the philosophy of **"Ars Poetica."** The images are more than instances of the fall of the night; they suggest the tempo of the movement of the creeping shadow—

> . . . the always coming on
> The always rising of the night.

Moreover, through their organic relationship they bring together all sorts of enriching suggestions. The undertone of suggestion that the "rising of the night" is a flood is a simile which, though never explicitly declared, is sustained throughout the poem:

> And strange at Ecbatan the trees
> . . . .
> The flooding dark about their knees
>
> . . . and the bridge
> Across the silent river gone . . .
>
> And Spain go under and the shore
> Of Africa. . . .

But rich and full-bodied as the poem is, the suggestions are overtones, brilliantly controlled, of one rather simple theme. And it is significant that the poem uses MacLeish's typical structure: detail piled on detail. (pp. 121-22)

Outside of the lyrics of the sort just discussed, probably the most successful of MacLeish's poems is the ***Frescoes for Mr. Rockefeller's City.*** It will not be difficult to show why. Whether or not MacLeish's sense of history is defective, there can be no censure of his sense of the individuality of place. America has its own quality—

She's a tough land under the corn mister:
She has changed the bone in the cheeks of many
races—

and the realization of the incommensurable character of the country, in the light of which all mere abstractions break down, is powerful enough to generate a theme which holds together the various parts of the poem. It is powerful enough to furnish MacLeish with an interpretation of history.

It is this theme which gives direction to the masses of rich detail which he is always able to assemble. For example, the legend of Crazy Horse is given in the sort of detail used in ***Conquistador;*** but there is an added meaning. Crazy Horse was fighting for something—

My God should he not fight? It was his.

In the same way the journey of exploration carried out by Meriwether Lewis meant something to him over and above recovered memories of the "winter rattling in the brittle haws," and "the buffalo numberless," and "the quail calling."

In one sense, the poem is a pastiche of the various effects MacLeish deals in. But here, because the various sections bear an organic relation to a larger theme, the poem is literally greater than the sum of its parts. The satirical sections, for instance, because of their relation to the positive core of the poem, go deeper than merely cheap jesting, and take on, in the light of the earlier passages of the poem, the effect of bitter taunting. For the types satirized are defined, even as Crazy Horse and Lewis are defined, by their relation to the land—the empire builders to whom the land was merely an abstraction. It was all prices to them: they never looked at it—it was also merely an abstraction to the expatriate artist and the abstract revolutionaries who have never looked at it either.

There are doubtless finer passages in some of MacLeish's other poems, but the ***Frescoes*** probably remains the most ambitious successful poem which MacLeish has written. And it represents a direction which one could wish he might follow up if his remarkable technical talents and his rich sensibility are to yield their best poetry.

The point is worth raising in view of the fact that MacLeish seems to have sensed a defect in his poetry, and seems to be searching for a theme, a controlling principle. The fruitful direction for him, in view of what has been said above, does not seem to lie in the direction of Sandburg; and his recent flourishing of the phrase, "—the people, yes," makes one apprehensive for his future career. For "the people" is too vague. (pp. 124-25)

Cleanth Brooks, "Frost, MacLeish, and Auden," in his Modern Poetry and the Tradition, *The University of North Carolina, 1939, pp. 110-35.*

James G. Southworth

Mr. Archibald MacLeish is an important poet of the middle generation of modern American poets. His first volume meriting attention appeared in 1925. He had, it is true, published two volumes before this—***Songs For a Summer's Day*** (1915) and ***Tower of Ivory*** (1917)—but these are juvenile verses and devoid of the intellectual content which an early mentor felt to animate them. We can dismiss them as Mr. MacLeish has done.

Many persons are inclined to look upon Mr. MacLeish as the Joseph Addison of the New Deal. Such an attitude focuses attention on one small phase of his work, and that the least important from the point of view of his stature as a poet.

It is true that his most insistent subject is political, but he is not political in the party sense of the word, but in its larger connotation of the problem of man's relation to society. Other subjects, however, are equally important from the point of view of his survival as a poet. These are the subjects that concern every poet at some stage of his poetic life: autobiographic reminiscences, love, nature, the consciousness of and attempted solution of his aesthetic problems, and miscellaneous subjects. A better insight into his treatment of his materials would be their grouping as nostalgic, contemplative, and active; or into poems of feeling and poems of the intellect. But to divide into compartments is to abstract and deprive.

The autobiographic poems—and I exclude those on love—deal with childhood and gradually maturing reminiscences; those of a sensitive boy, as in **"Eleven,"** a poem difficult to discuss because its significance is in its feeling; of a developing youth, as in **"Cook County,"** the place where he grew up; of a young man, as in **"L'an Trentiesme de mon Eage,"** which records the gradual maturing of the poet; in **"Le Secret Humain,"** in which he realizes that he will understand the secret of man's being after death; and in **"Memorial Rain"** and its later complement of disillusion, **"Lines for an Interment."** Of all these **"Memorial Rain"** is the most successful. By the juxtaposition of the memorial words of the ambassador dedicating an American cemetery in Brussels, with the description of the gathering storm, and then the rain on the grave of the person dear to him, Mr. MacLeish communicates a deep sense of personal bereavement. Particularly interesting is the heightened emotion contributed by the final eight lines.

"Mr. MacLeish is most original as a poet in his stanzaic innovations. Here one finds his greatest sensitivity, the finest expression of a subtle and delicate ear, the deepest insight into the poet's innermost soul."

—James G. Southworth

Less assignable to specific experiences, yet far removed from the abstract, are the poems on nature. **"Immortal Autumn,"** more rhetorical than Keats' ode on the same subject, shows, however, as great a love for that golden season. But it would give an incomplete picture of the poet's love for nature to overlook its influence on his images and its background value in numerous poems. **"Memory Green"** has almost the Frostian quality of "The Tuft of Flowers" without in any specific way resembling it. It communicates the feeling common to sensitive persons of having previously shared the beauty of the moment, whether it be a view of the hills or of the moon, and deriving therefrom a modicum of immortality or of an intensified aesthetic experience (**"Pony Rock," "Nocturne," "Selene Afterwards," "The Farm"**).

Mr. MacLeish, like Hardy, seems to be more interested in the reverse side of love than in its positive qualities. But at no time does he approach Hardy's subtlety of analysis. In one of his better poems on the subject (**"Against Illuminations"**) he recognizes that what we love is not the girl herself, but the projection of our love on her. When he does praise the beloved, however, he does it in a modern key and in the spirit of revolt from the traditional sonneteers (**"Not Marble in the Gilded Monuments).** He recognizes, too, like Arnold with a difference, that when liberty, pride, and hope vanish—heretofore men's guides—love alone remains (**"Pole Star for this Year"**). The poems dealing with the less happy aspects of love are in general more effective than those of a more favourable tone, and probably because the inherent drama in them is greater. Even these, however, fail to communicate a sense of appreciable depth (**"Broken Promise," "Before March," "De Votre Bonheur etc."**). Some of the finest poems in this genre are in the sequence **"The Woman on the Stair,"** strongly reminiscent in plot of Meredith's "Modern Love." Since their distinction lies in their technical qualities, their discussion is delayed to Part II.

Except for **"You, Andrew Marwell," "The Pot of Earth,"** ***Conquistador,*** and perhaps one or two others, the poems in ***Poems: 1924-1933*** are the weakest because of their too frequent stress on the obvious. **"Verses for a Centennial," "March,"** and **"Men of My Century Loved Mozart,"** among others, detract rather than add to Mr. MacLeish's stature. From **"The Pot of Earth,"** originally published in 1925, Mr. MacLeish has deleted several passages in the version found in ***Poems: 1924-1933.*** The general effect of the deletions is a tightening of the poetry at the expense of clarity. As it stands, however, it is a good poem and illustrates a fact, elsewhere negatively supported, that when confronted with a muscular idea, the poet can handle it. He has made a happy fusion of a modern American setting with the old ritual of the Gardens of Adonis, which had as its purpose the insuring of fertility of women as well as of grain. The poem, impressionistic in the manner of *The Waste Land,* details the maturing of the young girl, her ripening, marriage, childbirth, death, and the assurance of the continuity of life through her children. The poet moves deftly from the symbolism of the Adonis cult to its present manifestation in the mystery of life.

Conquistador is, to me, an overpraised poem. It is needlessly obscure and remains so even with subsequent readings. If the reader turns from the poem itself to Bernal de Diaz' *The True History of the Conquest of Mexico,* he immediately realizes that the obscurities are the poet's and not those of his source. Often the telescoping of events, the too abrupt breaks between books, the paucity of materials make any strong unified aesthetic import impossible. Then, also, the too frequent occurrence of broken lines, partial thoughts, and the overuse of dots distract and annoy the reader. At times, fortunately, the story grips the poet so strongly that he stirs the reader profoundly. Books six and seven are good, and eight to ten are excellent. In this latter section the poem sweeps and rises steadily to the end, holding the reader in its grasp with its speed, forward movement, and imperceptible concentrating force.

It is as a political poet, however, that Mr. MacLeish is at his best. I do not include in this category his verse plays designed for radio production such as ***Panic, The Fall of the City, America Was Promises,*** and ***Air Raid,*** or his verse complement to the photographic commentary of America, ***Land of the Free.*** These belong in a separate category and cannot be judged by the same standards as the poems with less obvious propagandist intentions. Strict chronology is unimportant. An attempt at an orderly discussion of his thought, however, soon discovers that the poet is not static and that the farthest reaches of his political thought coincide with his latest periods of composition.

Although inclined to believe that nothing is at the end of the world, the poet realizes the impossibility of running away from life. But does he find some meaning to life in this complex world? He is aware of the waste land, he is unable to accept traditional religion, and he senses that we can never know ourselves. We must learn, then, to accept life without understanding it. The resolution of the conflicting elements one constantly encounters not only presents a problem to the poet, but is a resolution not often solved. Mr. MacLeish attempts it in ***The Hamlet of A. MacLeish,*** inspired, I believe, by his awareness of Shakespeare's solution of a similar contemporary problem in his *Hamlet.* Shakespeare has, for example, he says,

> reduced to poetic order and made recognizable the common experience of his age. He has shown how the conflict of appearance and reality which give *Hamlet* its dramatic tension relates to the conflict of appearance and reality characteristic of the thinking of his time. . . . Shakespeare's play is such an organization of the moral confusion and intellectual anxiety of his contemporaries as a great poet can accomplish; and Hamlet remains to our day the one figure in which we recognize the experience of intellectual doubt at that extremest point where doubt is no longer possible and only belief can be supported. . . . What is really remarkable about the experience of our generation is the fact that no comparable organization of the public yet private life of our time has been attempted by contemporary poetry.

In Shakespeare's day it was the struggle between the Ptolemaic and the Copernican systems of the universe. To-day it is between the traditional and the Einsteinian, and the problem of what we are remains a riddle even though we can split atoms (**"Einstein"**). Because the poet's experiences with these riddles stir him to intense and personal emotions the expression resolves itself into excellent poetry.

Mr. MacLeish makes his public avowal of a change from aesthetic to political interests in a series of poems more rhetorical than basically poetic (**"Sentiments for a Dedication"** and **"Yacht for Sale").** Using the image of a yacht as a symbol for his youth, he acknowledges that it was 'frail at the keel And too sharp in the bow.' He reproves the poets of the past for having concerned themselves with kings and aristocratic matters rather than with the democratic—the life and ways of the common man—because he sees that man's constant hope and upward struggle is 'grave, noble and tragic' (**"Reproach to Dead Poets," "Men").** He is at his best in such poems as the patriotic **"American Letter."** Aware of the homogeneity of the people of France or Italy, he regrets this lack in America—'dressed as one—no brothers among them'—because it gives us the sense of being anchorless. In spite of that, however, we must face the fact that it is only in America that we can have any real being. Granted that America has been exploited by men like Morgan, Mellon, and other so-called 'Makers' of America; despoilers rather—

> They screwed her scrawny and gaunt with their seven-year panics:
> They bought her back on their mortgages old-whore-cheap:
> They fattened their bonds at her breasts till the thin blood ran from them:
>
> Men have forgotten how full clear and deep
> The Yellowstone moved on the gravel and grass grew
> When the land lay waiting for her westward people!

There remains, however, her deep-seated vitality that has exerted such a profound influence on the different nationalities in the melting-pot.

We must recognize, he continues, that it is useless to take a nostalgic backward look at the seeming security and solidity of our ancestors when political changes were imperceptible. We can only look forward, even though life is too fluid for our desires (**"Land's End," "1933").** Class distinctions must not narrow our vision. We should love excellence wherever found, because otherwise 'we cheat ourselves in cheating worth of wonder.' Man must realize that it takes courage to force the world to give us what we are justified in demanding of it. Too many, unfortunately, cannot face such facts. They are optimists only so long as they are the 'haves' in an unchanging society, but they become strangely silent when confronted with the necessity for a change of political thinking; they emulate the flies who freeze and numbly accept the coming on of winter rather than attempting to emulate the hawks who, unperturbed, dominate the situation, however sharp the struggle (**"Speech to the Detractors," "Speech to a Crowd," "The Lost Speakers," "Poem for a Time of Change").** (pp. 122-28)

In his **"Ars Poetica"** Mr. MacLeish mentions that 'a poem should be equal to: not true' and that it 'should not mean, but be.' Since his lasting quality as well as present stature depends upon his ability to make a poem 'be,' let us review some of the methods used for creating this state of being. His earliest poems are in every respect traditional in the manner of the Georgians, particularly Rupert Brooke, of whom there are innumerable echoes. This is to be expected since Brooke was at the height of his popularity in 1915 and 1916, particularly at Yale. The diction, imagery, and verse-patterns of this early work have little originality; at best they reveal a sensitive ear. In the work of the immediate post-war years and, in fact, until fairly recently, Mr. MacLeish attempted to give greater strength to his verse in the same way as the novelists like Hemingway and Dos Passos—by the use of strong Anglo-Saxon four- or five-letter words. He uses these words, however, with a self-conscious air and calls attention to them in a manner that one would not do in whose vocabulary they are at home. Instead, therefore, of these words investing the poem with greater masculinity, they have the opposite effect. On the whole, however, his vocabulary is simple and direct and becomes increasingly so in his later work, in spite of such aberrations as 'cooked dough' when he obviously means bread.

Alliteration is a stylistic device which, instead of subtly controlling his communication, frequently draws attention to itself. This I found to be particularly true in ***Conquistador.*** Generally, however, it is integrated in the poem, and, at times, happily combined with repetition, as on 's' in 'They think how the sound of the surf is the sound of forever.' He rather likes this trick and we find it not only in such lines as 'In love not live there never are two lovers' (**"The Woman on the Stair,"** vi), but on a larger scale faintly echoing Eliot's "Ash Wednesday":

> I have forgotten you. There is a grey light on my
> Hands and I have forgotten you. There is light enough.
> There is light enough left to forget your face by—
> Voice by: to forget you. As long as the
> Light lasts on my hands I forget you.
> There needs be some light; a little.

Unfortunately, however, such lines, devoid of inner tension, have little survival value.

Repetition not only serves to give form to the parts of a poem, but to a whole poem. Frequently, he will begin and end the poem with the same words. In **"The Farm,"** for example, a poem that reveals his mastery of prosody, he begins and ends with the question, 'Why do you listen trees?' Repetition can be, however, too self-conscious as in 'and he ate simnel And sweet cakes he ate and a kind of partridges.'

Mr. MacLeish makes an abundant use of similes, many of which are not readily grasped in a first reading. This, of course, is not a fault. The fault lies in his too easy ones; those that are too much on the surface, that come too readily to hand. His metaphors are apt to be tighter. Birds, particularly the strong-winged hawks, and gulls, ships, and the sea fascinate him and furnish his best figures. In this he resembles Robinson Jeffers. **"The Sunset Piece"** is a sustained metaphor in which the ship is the earth and the present 'the squall of time.' He captures the quality of a snow-storm in such lines as 'the white unable wandering of the air Whirled everywhere' (**"The Woman on the Stair,").** 'Unable' is a happy choice. More effective than any set of figures for capturing the mood is his selection of telling details. . . . (pp. 128-30)

Mr. MacLeish is most original as a poet in his stanzaic innovations. Here one finds his greatest sensitivity, the finest expression of a subtle and delicate ear, the deepest insight into the poet's innermost soul. His first major contribution derives from the *terza rima* of Dante. Instead of rhyme, he substitutes assonance. For convenience's sake let us dub this *terza assonanza.* His most sustained use of the form (although he is not here slavishly tied to it) is in ***Conquistador.*** It is admirably suited to narrative and is capable of speed, forward movement, and possesses an imperceptible concentrating force. At other times it takes on the quality of ritual, or the reader unconsciously thinks of the movement of Eliot's "The Journey of the Magi." It is one of his most recurring prosodic patterns and often his most successful. He also uses assonance in couplets (**"Frescoes for Mr. Rockefeller's City," "American Letter,"** and others) and in quatrains **("Frescoes")**. In **"The Sunset Piece"** he goes one step farther, having lines one and three in assonance and two and four in rhyme. Half-rhymes (consonance)—lake-like, far-for, vine-vane, altogether-to gather, west-waste—are largely responsible for the effect in **"Cook County."** Or, he may eschew rhyme or assonance in his stanza-patterns, depending on his purpose **("Men")**.

I think he has been primarily concerned in his experiments in finding that prosodic pattern which best reflects the temper of our contemporary life. It may be the rhythm of a popular song, as in **"Frescoes,"** or a somewhat syncopated jazz rhythm as in those instances when the accent falls unexpectedly. . . . Or it may be a different rhythmical effect, as in **"The Lost Speakers"** and **"Dover Beach"—a note to that poem."** By placing unaccented articles and prepositions—'the,' 'a,' and 'of'—at the end of a line he subtly produces in the mind of the reader, almost without his awareness, the effect of the pause just before a wave breaks on the shore, followed by the water's retreat over the shingle:

> After forty a man's a fool to wait in the
> sea's face for the full force and the roaring of
> surf to come over him: droves of careening
> water.

As important as any of these more obvious prosodic devices is the poet's use of falling rhythms, prominent in many of the already cited poems. He attempts to achieve the quality of American speech which he feels *descends from* stressed syllables, rather than *rising toward* them. This is not a discovery of Mr. MacLeish, however, as any student of metric is aware. It has long been recognized that to avoid complicated terminology in the discussion of modern prosody it has been almost necessary to employ the amphilbrach (υ/υ) and the paeon, the third paeon (υυ/υ) being the most frequently used. Hardy used both extensively. Actually, I think, Hardy achieves what would be a closer approximation to American speech, and without meaning to do so, than does MacLeish, and he does so by a judicious mixture of iambs and anapests with frequent third paeons. I do not think the differences between American and English speech-rhythms as basic as MacLeish thinks them to be. (pp. 130-33)

I mentioned in connection with ***Conquistador*** that Mr. MacLeish is apt to obscure his communication by broken sentences and the over-use of dots. He provides the springboard, but the reader must judge the depth of the water from the dots. It is the same as blind-diving, never a comfortable pastime. He makes this same over-use in many of the shorter poems. He further needlessly confuses the reader by the absence of punctuation. **"Immortal Autumn"** is a case in point. What does he gain by the omission of semicolons and periods at the fourteen strong stops besides the omission of commas at the lesser stops? I cannot believe that he is like the young English poet (was it Auden, Spender, or MacNeice?) who omitted them because he didn't know where to put them in.

Many influences are evident in his work. That of Mr. T. S. Eliot is too evident. Not only one or two, but almost every well-known poem of his is definitely echoed in some poem or other of Mr. MacLeish. This is natural but unfortunate. Mr. MacLeish has shown himself capable of writing poetry that is so complete a fusion of his influences that we have a new voice. It is in such work that we must expect to find the qualities of permanence. In many ways he is at a crucial point in his career—that point when the domination of the sensuous yields to the domination of the intellect. Will he, as Yeats and Mr. Frost have done, so blend and fuse these elements that his later poetry will be the natural outgrowth of his earlier; or will he make a sharp dichotomy? His more recent works would indicate that perhaps he is confused in his own mind as to the true function of a poet, or, if not that, as to what sort of audience he wishes for himself. He cannot serve two masters. True enough, several of his prose utterances (**"In Challenge, not Defence," "Public Speech and Private Speech in Poetry," "Poetry and the Public World"**) reveal his attempt to solve the dichotomy in his own mind. He should remember, however, that time has already given us the best answer in the poems that have survived, and he knows the answer—'a poem should not mean, but be.' (pp. 133-34)

James G. Southworth, "Archibald MacLeish," in his Some Modern American Poets, *Basil Blackwell, 1950, pp. 122-34.*

Richard Eberhart

[Eberhart is a prominent American poet, educator, and critic.]

The best of Archibald MacLeish's work takes poetry out of the library and, while it does not hand it to the man in the street, it offers a highly intelligible style to the many rather than the few, and is best when it is nonpolitical.

This volume, [***Collected Poems: 1917-1952***], covering the work of thirty-five years, shows the direct, wiry and forceful nature of MacLeish's talent and will be indispensable to the full understanding of his life. He has an Elizabethan sort of exuberance which has been exercised on nonliterary fields as well as on poetry and prose.

He early imitated Eliot, Pound, and certain French poets, at the same time sounding like his Midwestern friend

Sandburg. It was sometimes difficult to find and assess the real MacLeish. This welcome collection demonstrates that the real MacLeish has a total impact of strong intellectual poise, widespread ability with verse forms, and great lyrical charm.

He had many followers twenty-five years ago. Something happened to him during the depression. He lost followers, paradoxically because he became the more a leader, in one sense, but in the wrong sense, as some felt. He became a political leader; that is to say, as a literary man he became a polemicist, an advocate. He raised throughout the Thirties the raging problems of the wars and the relationship of art to society, of the artist to democracy.

He considered scholars and artists irresponsible when they kept disinterestedly to their crafts, since, he argued, if they did not fight for our democratic freedom and democratic freedom everywhere, the very possibility of their lives as scholars and artists might not exist.

America Was Promises was the culmination of this period in 1939. For me it represented an abuse of art, to which I reacted strongly. It became a political poem. However, in the perspective of time this poem reads better than it did when it appeared, as do some others of the type. There is a divorced poetical residuum left after the current event.

Sentimentality still accrues to **"The Spanish Lie,"** which bravely asserted that "This will be answered" of "The blood of Guernica, Badajos, Almeria." The answer never came. But would it occur to MacLeish to call for an "answer" to the deaths of American Indians murdered on our Western plains of which he writes so glowingly? Dylan Thomas had a deeper perception in "A Refusal to Mourn the Death, By Fire, of a Child in London": "After the first death, there is no other." MacLeish had confused art and politics.

I feel that MacLeish is best, that the nature of his talent shows best, in his short lyrics. Of these there is a copious number of indestructible pieces. It is gratifying to discover among his most recent poems lyrics as pure and effective as the best of his earlier ones, as for instance, the charming poem entitled **"Where the Hayfields Were."**

The book contains a new verse play, ***The Trojan Horse,*** intended "for a presentation in which the scene is created by the imagination." It is a somewhat austere and stripped vocal telling of the story, but should be effective on the radio or other vocal presentation.

His ***Hamlet*** stands up well,—dense, honest, and final. His **"Einstein"** I admire also; somehow it gets Einstein on the page. ***Conquistador*** is still readable, its litheness and small-epic force enjoyable (lessons are learned there from Old English and from Pound), although monotony invades it and the whole somehow ends in wordy vapors.

The ***Frescoes*** seem to give now a sense of what America is like, or was like, in part. Some readers, at least, may think so in 2000. The word remains.

At this point let us consider what is the essential style of the man. There is a plain line, from which one seizes the meaning as it flies. The pleasure is direct, simple, and may be forceful. Hundreds of these lines blow over one with a windy, gallant tone, a fine swing, carrying one along. This is MacLeish's line. It deals with what it touches resiliently and intelligently, always sensitively. It states more than it evokes.

There is the line of the deep evocation, the rock-spring. To these mysterious lines, these strange pervasive images, one returns again and again. They have always new meanings, subtle shifts of significance as the years change the body and the mind. This is not MacLeish's line. He has some such lines, of course, but he is not a mysterious poet, not seminal in that sense. He lacks some qualities of suffering, and must pay for an objective ability with some lack of subjective depth. He often says what he means rather than meaning what he suggests. Yet how lithely often his lines leap tonic to the turgic!

Archibald MacLeish's ***Collected Poems*** is a major achievement in American letters. The author shows better in this full, massive appearance, where each work may be assigned to the place one gives it, than in single volumes. There is something basically lithe, wiry, direct and clear-seeing about his talent. We feel him as distinctly American. (pp. 5, 48)

This book will benefit MacLeish, I should think, for many readers may have had the experience that I have had. Where he has impinged on the consciousness heretofore sporadically and partially, it is now possible to feel the scope and brunt of the whole man. This sense of scope, of excellence, of sanity and of balance is good. And perhaps we can look forward to a new period, a new flowering in the perspective of added years. The indication is there in the zest of the latest work. (p. 48)

Richard Eberhart, "The Pattern of MacLeish's Poetry," in The New York Times Book Review, *November 23, 1952, pp. 5, 48.*

Howard Nemerov

[*Nemerov was a respected American poet and former Consultant in Poetry to the Library of Congress. The essay essay excerpted below was originally published in the January-February 1953 issue of Partisan Review.*]

The poet's responsibility to society—a matter much debated. In the phrase itself there is implicit some prospective metaphor of the poet as criminal, vainly trying to *discharge his debt* by means of his poems while all the time, really, it is something else that "society" wants. What? This has not been made clear, but seems to have confusedly to do with, on the one hand, messages of life and hope; with, on the other, moral earnestness and a severe, traditional look at current events. Archibald MacLeish takes in many places a severe view—with virtue, with this Republic, with poetry itself, things were formerly different, are now much degenerated, but the poet by his images may redeem the time, "Turn round into the actual air" and "Invent the age! Invent the metaphor!" (p. 118)

Archibald MacLeish, for a very few poems [in ***Collected Poems 1917-1952***], is one of the finest lyric poets now writing. That after these few poems, a long way after, there follow many which strike one as forced, incomplete, not thoroughly considered, and some which seem to betray an impatience, an exasperation with the mere idea of poetry as an art, is something that does not affect the position. We do not much like to speak of "immortality" in this connection any more, nor even of future times (for who knows what altogether dreadful nonsense people will admire day after tomorrow?), but if I may pretend the old usage still to apply, as though we looked forward to an Oxford Book compiled by archangels, it is to say that the author of the simple and noble **"You, Andrew Marvell"** will have a place there, where room will be denied to many whose flabby complexities now pass for muscle. This poem reads, surely, as though it were imperishable; it has no false note, and neither hesitation nor haste in its grave, steady rhythms, the exact timing of its rimes. Though in my opinion Mr. MacLeish nowhere fully equals it in any other poem, this one is yet characteristic of his design, its intention of remote voyages is uniquely his intention (and responsible elsewhere for his bad poems as well as for his good ones); its subject is such that his distantly seen and, so to say, *generalized* details give the greatest intensity with the greatest controlling calm. I am reminded, reading it, of a passage of Dante with a similar subject: the great lyric at the close of Paradiso XXII where the poet at Beatrice's hest turns to look back through the seven spheres at the earth which he has left behind, below; looking through the orbits of the planets, seeing them vary their relations one with another, he sees "from ridge to river mouth" "the little threshing-floor which makes us so fierce" ("L'aiuola che ci fa tanto feroci"). I think the MacLeish poem is of that kind, and of that quality so far as the complete lyric can be compared with the fragment of a greater design.

Of the poems published through 1933 a number of others keep their tension and their strength: **"The Silent Slain," "Yacht for Sale," "Grazing Locomotives," "Pony Rock," "The Night Dream"**; of the satirical pieces, **"Corporate Entity"** and, perhaps, the Museum Attendant's speech from **"Empire Builders."** Two poems, **"Nat Bacon's Bones"** and **"Galán,"** seem to me to approach, in a different way, the excellence and finish of **"You, Andrew Marvell."** . . . (pp. 119-20)

Of the hortatory and political poems, the **"Speeches"** reprinted from ***Public Speech*** and ***Actfive,*** not much remains to be said; they do not seem to be good poems, and if they were ever good speeches that does not now appear about them either. The poet as poet knew what the poet sacrificed as citizen, he had spoken about it boldly enough in **"Invocation to the Social Muse."** . . . (p. 120)

In the long poems the poet's characteristic figure becomes his obsession; these works are voyages, their protagonists sailors, explorers over the sea, into the mind, among the dead. In ***The Pot of Earth*** the dying god sails out on his journey; in ***The Hamlet of A. MacLeish*** the hero, after passing the night of terror in the Perilous Chapel, goes forth and fails to found his city; **"Einstein"** explores the universe in the mind and at last invades the earth in search of "reality." There is Bernal Díaz, there is Elpenor, **"America Was Promises"** has the figure of the voyage west. The cadences of this poetry are in general long, often formed in double-harness or placed in parallel series cataloguing details which are themselves characteristic, a generalized nature, a generalized mythology, with a consequent remoteness of tone even at moments that should be dramatically urgent, a tone that seems distantly to reflect and echo a long swell of the sea—

> Here where the walls end and the ruinous tower
> Leans with its uninhabitable black
> Long builded stones above the ultimate sea . . .

and

> We were the first that found that famous country:
> We marched by a king's name: we crossed the sierras:
> Unknown hardships we suffered: hunger:
>
> Death by the stone knife: thirst: we fared by the
> Bitter streams: we came at last to that water:
> Towers were steep upon the fluttering air . . .

The first of these passages comes from ***The Hamlet,*** the second from ***Conquistador.*** Both these poems are ambitious, well-conceived and in places very moving, yet at last the singleness of tone (in ***The Hamlet*** there is also some imitation Shakespeare, though) fails in or even defeats its purpose; all becomes too distant, dreamy, too much abstracted and generalized.

I have not yet spoken of the recent poems, first collected here, nor of the new play, ***The Trojan Horse.*** Of the play I cannot say much: its language is more spare and active than much that precedes it; as poetry it reads not very well, perhaps, but one has learned that such language may be extremely well suited to declamation, and that given a competent performance it is likely to surprise by a vigor and tension not always easily seen on the printed page.

Nor will I say more than a few words of the latest poetry. There is an implicit assumption, when poems are "Collected," that the returns are now in, that all is over and the vote may safely be counted. In this instance I doubt it is so. The new poems seem to return to the privacy and seriousness of the earlier ones, but with a more energetic rhythm, a stripped ferocity reminiscent in places of late poems by Yeats. Some brief poems here are fine, though not always fully so—in **"Out of Sleep Awakened,"** for example, the moralizing last couplet seems to spoil—and those pages in this book suggest the hope that this poet has turned from empty and angry public declamation to reach again "The real encounter kept at night / Alone where none will praise our art." (pp. 121-22)

Howard Nemerov, "MacLeish and Viereck," in his Poetry and Fiction: Essays, *Rutgers University Press, 1963, pp. 118-24.*

Dan Jaffe

Archibald MacLeish's **"Ars Poetica"** has probably been more often anthologized than any of his other poems. Almost all anthologies that include MacLeish's work, and that means most anthologies of American poetry published during the last 30-35 years, reprint it. Its lines have been mimicked, parodied, and widely misunderstood. Perhaps no contemporary poem has created such aesthetic rage in some quarters. Few poems have been treated so shabbily, for reasons that have little to do with the poem itself.

Most of the furor caused by the poem concerns MacLeish's final statement, one that has become so familiar that it may soon offend to quote it at all:

> A poem should not mean
> But be.

Those enemies of "modern" poetry who read only enough of it to furnish themselves with ammunition for the onslaught have for years used these lines to prove the effeteness of verse that is not "traditional." One can see them rubbing their fingertips together gleefully as they quote the lines. They remind one of William Buckley appraising a speech of Eleanor Roosevelt. And they were often joined by the Marxian critics who never forgave MacLeish for his refusal to leap to the communist barricades in the 30s.

The standard interpretation runs something like this. In **"Ars Poetica"** MacLeish advocates a poetry that is self-sufficient, in which texture is more important than idea, a poetry removed from the relevancies of life, a poetry that exists for its own sake and for the sake of an aesthetic elite.

Such an interpretation fails to take into consideration either the context in which the lines appear or the context in which the poem appears, the imposing body of MacLeish's work.

Those who have insisted on the "art for art's sake" interpretation disregard the curious contradiction such an interpretation requires. They maintain that MacLeish is denying the importance of ideas, but at the same time they stress the ideological content of the poem. They maintain that MacLeish denies meaning, but they nevertheless attack his literal meaning. And if one points out this curious paradox they more than likely will reply that it reveals the failure of "modern" poetry to accomplish even the little it tries.

But **"Ars Poetica"** is a performance of the principle MacLeish states in the final lines. The poem gives the statement what significance it has by dramatizing what MacLeish means by "be"ing. It is essentially a catalogue of images related in tone and linked by declarations. And the declarations serve as a regular reminder that MacLeish is not denying the importance of idea, of theory, of intellectual position. Three times the poem asserts "A poem should be" and goes on to talk imagistically. Then the last stanza opens:

> A poem should be equal to:
> Not true.

These repetitions make the poem in effect didactic. But is MacLeish insisting on dumping ideas? If so his very didacticism would make that position untenable.

Throughout the poem MacLeish says that poetry should be as real as the images of the world. The images he provides are enormously evocative, full of symbolic potential. They are images chosen not only for their sensory impact but because of the intellectual and mythical ripples they set in motion. "Be"ing then is a larger category than "mean"ing. In the last lines of the poem MacLeish is not shying away from idea, from what is usually meant by "meaning." Instead he indicates that that kind of "meaning" alone is not enough. Message does not make poetry. The poem is first of all an experience; it must have the reality of a happening, not of a statement. But of course, like any occurrence, it may have and probably should have intellectual consequence.

The notion that MacLeish believed poems should have no substantial relevance to intellectual or social written matters seems ludicrous if one looks at the other poems in ***Streets in the Moon*** (1926), the book in which **"Ars Poetica"** appeared; for one soon becomes aware that MacLeish even in his early work revealed his concern with the outer world, the world of trade and technology. He was to consider it, to try and capture its meanings. And so in **"Man!"** he satirizes the social animal of the twenties:

> LIFE in the vial with Safety Catch,
> LIFE in the Perpendicular Decanter,

In his early books MacLeish experimented with styles, often, sounded like other poets. But he was more than a literary laundryman taking in other writers' washing. We cannot even insist that all his best early poems were introspective, personal lyrics rather than social considerations. Some of them certainly were, poems like **"L'an Trentiesme De Mon Eage"** and **"You, Andrew Marvell."** But others like **"The End of the World"** are hardly just interior poems. Very early MacLeish began judging the world about him, and those judgments make their way into poems written even before the startling occurrences of the 30s, occurrences that were to make even the most introspectively inclined aware of the events going on around them. The first stanza of **"The End of the World"** makes MacLeish's view of his society clear:

> Quite unexpectedly as Vasserot
> The armless ambidextrian was lighting
> A match between his great and second toe
> And Ralph the lion was engaged in biting
> The neck of Madame Sossman while the drum
> Pointed, and Teeny was about to cough
> In waltz-time swinging Jocko by the thumb—
> Quite unexpectedly the top blew off:

Although MacLeish develops the circus metaphor without comment, it is a judgment of the world. And the judgment makes the whole poem seem strangely prophetic of the way in which the illusions of the wild 20s shattered on the rocks of depression.

It now seems especially ironic that after the publication of **"Invocation to the Social Muse"** in 1932, letters reminded MacLeish that historically many poets had been men of affairs. The letters must have been from readers who read the poem's last line, "Is it just to demand of us also to bear arms?" as the poet's weaseling out of public responsibility. But **"Invocation"** could only have been written by a man ready to speak publicly. He refers early in the poem to tractors, Marx, and "wars more antiseptic and murderous." He rejects Hoover and "Mister Morgan." In a taunting tone he identifies poets as

> persons of
> Known vocation following troops: they must
> sleep with
> Stragglers from either prince and of both views.

Whatever his conscious intent at the time, his tone and metaphor suggest disdain for those who take the position he later attacks so furiously in his essay **"The Irresponsibles."** Further on in **"Invocation,"** MacLeish notes that the poet must speak individually to the individual. He asks rhetorically,

> How to take to one's chamber a million souls?
> How to conceive in the name of a column of
> marchers?

It seems unlikely that he is recommending a skittish turning away from all causes. Rather he insists on speaking for the single self to the single man, instead of becoming an instrument of the collective. The last line of the poem follows immediately after MacLeish says that the poet is more than a member of a class or a trade. His question about bearing arms is addressed to the Communists. It is a rejection of Marxian doctrine and as such it is the public act of an individual who symbolically bears arms but only as an individual.

In later poems MacLeish pointedly attacked the Morgans, Harrimans, and Vanderbilts. He sounded in Whitmanian fashion the romantic yawp of democracy. He was not standoffish, not the pimple-faced boy at the mixer. He was, in fact, in 1940 to call to task the intellectuals of his time for not speaking out against those who would replace law with force, beauty with cruelty, singleness with numbers. He called those who practice their arts in insulated cells, **"The Irresponsibles."** Of the men who practiced "academic narcissism," he said, "They emerged free, pure, and single into the antiseptic air of objectivity. And by that sublimation of the mind they prepared the mind's disaster." Nor was such a statement from MacLeish surprising. He had after all during the 30s written a whole series of rather transparent radio plays dealing with the immediate problems of the times. He had gone so far as to write a long poem, ***Land of the Free,*** which he himself said in a note was the "opposite of a book of poems illustrated by photographs,"—"a book of photographs illustrated by a poem." The photographs were taken for the Resettlement Administration. The poem does little more than summarize the realizations of a generation that had seen breadlines form after the stock market crash and the breakdown of the banking system, who had felt the muscles of industry cramp, seen top soil wash farms into flood waters and literally millions of men ride the rails to mealless tomorrows. MacLeish during those years became the poetic reporter of American deterioration.

MacLeish has never stopped writing those melodic, melancholy lyrics that first brought him to fame. But as the decades passed he became more and more the polemicist, more and more interested in making meaning in the old fashioned sense of that word. All too often it seemed that he had turned his back on the principle he had so superbly dramatized in **"Ars Poetica."**

During the 30s MacLeish set out to do as man and poet what no other twentieth century American poet has dared. Stirred by devastating effects of the economic breakdown at home and startled by the hints of a dangerous anti-humanistic and anti-intellectual revolution abroad, he set out to make the entire social scene his domain. He was to try to do Shelley one better, to make the poet the *acknowledged* legislator of his time. (pp. 141-45).

MacLeish did not discard the laurel to put on the Homburg [in the 1930s]. He was never a literary man graduated into the political spotlight. Nor was he privately a poet and publicly a civil servant. He was both at once. The concerns that he felt as public man revealed themselves in his writing; those that had been revealed in his writing dictated the course of his life.

He returned from Europe in 1929 after five years as an expatriate. ***New Found Land*** (1930) pointed the direction his work was to take. Like so many novelists and poets he was to seek a definition of America through his work. In **"American Letter"** he wrote, "It is a strange thing to be an American." He found America strange because of its youth and diversity, because of its challenge and seeming lack of tradition. But in **"American Letter"** his commitment is clear, "Here we must live or live only as shadows." And yet he feels the old nostalgia for Europe.

It is a nostalgia that will not last. He seeks to replace it by mapping out a tradition. He returns to materials he had almost forgotten were his to work with. It was as if he were returning to old haunts. Five years earlier in **"The Farm"** he had shown Ephraim Cross driving up the trail from Massachusetts in 1750. Now he was to take to the trial himself, on foot and muleback to follow the route of Cortes from the seacoast to the Valley of Mexico. That trip (1928) and his study of the account of Bernal Diaz del Castillo, *True History of the Conquest of New Spain,* resulted in ***Conquistador*** (1932) and the Pulitzer Prize.

After exploring at the periphery, he zeroed in. In ***Frescoes for Mr. Rockefeller's City*** (1933) he pictured America as a fertile nude, "belly . . . flecked with the flickering light of the corn." He contrasted Crazy Horse's love of the land with Mister Morgan's concern with real estate values. He scored the Communists who would replace the experience of the land with the abstractions of Dialectical Materialism.

America's tradition, he came to see, was a tradition of possibility, of promises inherent in the land itself. But, he was to ask himself, have the leaves of that tradition withered? Is the American present a shoot of the original plant? In ***Land of the Free*** (1938) he notes the disillusionment of the people, their children "canning . . . crawfish in . . . ten cent cans," their voices stilled by company cops, their land blowing out from under their hoes, their independence destroyed by poverty. The poem is an indictment of those who have for their own profit poisoned the tradition. "We wonder whether the great American dream . . . is behind us now." ***Land of the Free*** ends despairingly; hopes are muted, disappointments emphasized.

In ***America Was Promises*** (1939) MacLeish assumes a more militant attitude. He also, in a way, reassesses responsibility. He provides not a question but an answer:

America is promises to
Take!
America is promises to
Us
To take them
Brutally
With love but
Take them.
Oh believe this!

MacLeish engaged himself as a public man to fertilize and protect the tradition. As a poet he tried to embody it in his work. Like Robert Frost and William Carlos Williams he sought a technical means of capturing the American voicebox. In the introduction to ***Panic*** (1935) he discusses the difference between the genius of the American language and that of the English language. He maintains that American is a language of accents, that its rhythms tend to fall rather than rise, are more generally trochaic than iambic. But despite his concern with such problems and despite the fact that he unashamedly introduces idiomatic expressions into his poetry, MacLeish's poems and plays sound more often theatrically American than authentically so. The roll of rhetoric he so often depends on is as far from the voice of the people as the podium is from the street. Let this be read as a general judgment rather than as an absolute one, for there is no doubt that at moments MacLeish accomplishes what he sets out to do. But the task he set for himself was enormous and he succeeds only on occasion in making the kind of poems he called for in **"Ars Poetica."** As a poet of social consciousness he satirizes more effectively than he dramatizes. And though he seeks to put America into his poems, over and over again the same images appear, the images we find in his early work. Too often he is over-insistent, a shouter and convincer rather than a seducer.

To talk about a writer's failings is not to underestimate his contributions. Archibald MacLeish took the major risk and for that he will be remembered. He is, no doubt, one of the great American lyricists. Even in poems marred by excess he can jolt the reader unexpectedly. In desperate times he sought to revitalize American democracy. What progress we make in part may well be the result of the images he projected. (pp. 146-48)

Dan Jaffe, "Archibald MacLeish: Mapping the Tradition," in The Thirties: Fiction, Poetry, Drama, *edited by Warren French, Everett Edwards, Inc., 1967, pp. 141-48.*

Ralph J. Mills, Jr.

At eighty, Archibald MacLeish has made his own selection from his prolific work as a poet in an effort to correct the misleading impressions created by anthologies, which, he notes, tend to reprint the same small handful of poems. He seeks in this volume "not a choice *from* but a representation *of*" his writing over the years, including pieces which seldom, if ever, find their way into the innumerable anthologies of modern verse.

The choice is a felicitous one. While a full-scale assessment of his work—and I shall not attempt anything of that size here—would lead the reader to individual titles or at least the ***Collected Poems*** of 1952, a reader coming to MacLeish's poetry for the first time or one who simply wishes to reconsider its qualities, will find ***The Human Season*** admirably fulfills such purposes.

Because MacLeish has been a "poetic weathercock," to borrow Hyatt Waggoner's term, an indicator of intellectual and stylistic trends during the past five decades, we might dismiss him. Yet Waggoner certainly does not—nor do a number of other considerable critics—rightly viewing him as an assimilator of attitudes and ideas, though never extreme ones, changing and formulating in poetry an expression of the liberal, rational, humane, scientifically aware modern mind. It is likewise true that MacLeish, with apparent ease, has appropriated stylistic innovations from the Imagists, Eliot, Pound, Stevens, St.-John Perse and other masters of the century, leaving the traces of his borrowings in full display.

Three years after *The Waste Land,* for example, MacLeish published ***The Pot of Earth,*** with its epigraph from Frazer and its plain indebtedness to Eliot; yet there is still a talent and sensibility on which these influences operate yielding their effect in the rich accumulations of imagery, in both visual and auditory sensitivity to the world of particulars and in the grace and fluidity of language. The result is an elegance without ornateness and, at best, a fine, lingering evocativeness. In **"Memorial Rain,"** MacLeish writes a moving elegy to his brother, killed in World War I, by shifting between the empty rhetoric of an Ambassador speaking of the sacrifices of the war dead and the thoughts of the poet, who observes the details of weather, mingling the impression they make upon him with his sense of this death. (pp. 211, 213)

[A] kind of lyricism pervades MacLeish's responsiveness to nature's particularity, and his feeling for human history "grave noble and tragic," as he says in **"Men."** If he is cognizant of time's flux and change, as is evident enough in the numerous poems on historical themes, he is also adept at building up in parallel lines dense with concreteness, vivid in their notation of *things,* a vision of men's lives and activities as essentially universal and timeless. . . . (p. 213)

[There is] a recurrence of the archetypal in MacLeish's poetry, a background of eternal quest, discovery, human enterprise which is forever threatened by failure, death, metaphysical and religious uncertainty and against which the specifics of history in various other poems may be read. Along with the strongly felt rendering of the imagery of nature and season, they confer a certain unity on the writing which frequently declares itself a descendent of Whitman and of similar intentions—though not achievement—with Perse's and Neruda's poetry of the epical gesture, and thus he makes frequent use of the catalogue, the long, hortatory line, the universalization of men's endeavors. Of course, a great many poems do not share in those interests: satirical and ironical pieces; portraits and socio-historical poems; some beautiful poems of place and love lyrics. Then again, the anthology pieces most readers know—**"Ars Poetica," "You, Andrew Marvell," "Epistle To Be Left in the Earth," "The End of the World"**—works to which the poet does not want to be limited, are undeniable, haunting accomplishments.

MacLeish has, finally, fashioned an eminently readable poetry in a considerable number of his poems, endowed as he is with linguistic and musical facility and a gift for the suggestive image. But he lacks an innovative poetic imagination. If we place his poetry next to that of Eliot, Pound, Williams and Stevens—to all of whom he appears indebted—we will perceive that it takes over features and practices from theirs to make a pleasing work that yet neither sustains nor engages the intelligence and sensibilities of the reader in the manner of those pioneers. We may delight in MacLeish's lyrical gifts, be drawn into the celebratory or elegiac moods he casts, but where in his writing can we locate—except at second hand—anything like the dynamic, individual, complex wrestling with language and form, with history, myth, personality, mystical experience and the modern environment so prominent, so much a shaping force (though differing in disposition and degree) of artistic practice for such poets as Yeats, Eliot, Pound, Stevens, or Williams? Theirs was the deep, desperate, wholly engaging struggle which brought about innovation, often from an eccentric, unpopular, isolated, or even wrongheaded perspective. MacLeish has lived and written from a more commonsense center, as befits a man of long and distinguished public service. His enterprise as a poet, it would seem, especially in view of his longer poems, was a major one, but the achievement is not. The stylistic means were perhaps there, yet an infusion possibly of less conventional thought, a darker, more terrible grappling with the inward life were required. These are pointless guesses, all too easy for the reviewer or critic to sit back and make. Let us say, more affirmatively, that MacLeish has given readers some very fine, durable poems; the present selection offers an appealing access to them. (pp. 214-15)

Ralph J. Mills, Jr., "In the Fields of Imagination," in Parnassus: Poetry in Review, *Vol. 1, No. 2, 1973, pp. 211-24.*

FURTHER READING

Drabeck, Bernard A., and Ellis, Helen E. *Archibald MacLeish: Reflections.* Amherst: University of Massachusetts Press, 1986, 291 p.

Contains several insightful interviews with MacLeish, a foreword by Richard Wilbur, and a bibliography and index.

Falk, Signi Lenea. *Archibald MacLeish.* New York: Twayne Publishers, Inc., 1965, 189 p.

First full-length study of MacLeish's career. Includes book-by-book discussion with special attention to MacLeish's public career.

Lorrie Moore

1957-

(Born Marie Lorena Moore) American short story writer, novelist, essayist, and critic.

Moore has earned critical respect for fiction that faithfully represents emotional and psychological reactions to one's surroundings, perceptions of self and others, and the relationship between these perceptions. Her characters are typically intelligent people at turning points in their lives who are self-consciously aware of their present conflicts and dilemmas. This self-knowledge, however, contributes to heightened turmoil, and Moore's characters react by turning inward and attempting to alleviate or distance themselves from their pain and confusion through wit and humor. All of her protagonists are in some way isolated, trapped, and in search of redemptive self-actualization.

Most of the stories in Moore's first collection, *Self-Help,* lampoon popular personal improvement manuals by using imperatives as a primary means of narration. As a result, most of these sketches evolve into straightforward accounts placing readers in the roles of both observer and participant as they learn "How to Be an Other Woman," "How to Talk to Your Mother (Notes)," "How to Become a Writer," and just "How." *Like Life,* Moore's second collection of short stories, is, according to Ralph Sassone, "impressive not only for its precise sketches, of, say, limousine liberals, oily Hollywood film types, and men as lovelorn and neurotic as women, but for its respectful reportage about lives that aren't overtly extremis." Like the characters in Moore's earlier works, those in *Like Life* are witty, perceptive, and introspective as they confront loneliness, frustrations, disappointments, and obstacles. These qualities are evinced in the title story; when a woman is informed by her doctor that a growth on her throat is precancerous, she asks her doctor if it is "like life," and, by extension, questions whether it is similar to the life she planned or the life she has lived. Anna Vaux praised *Like Life* for the "laid back sense of humor and the note of alarm" which it exhibits and which make Moore's stories touching (often in spite of the humor) and accurately "lifelike."

Moore's first novel, *Anagrams,* comprises five distinct sections; in each, the characters find themselves in the same town but in a different situation. In one portion of the text, Benna is a poetry teacher and in another a lounge singer; in one section she and Gerard are lovers, while elsewhere they are strictly friends. Consequently, the lives and attitudes of each character are subject to change; like the letters in an anagram they are interchangeable, evolving, and capable of producing a new word or story. Ultimately, the reader discovers that the first four sections of the novel are merely versions of Benna's life that she has constructed and revised in an attempt to forget about the unpleasantness of her past and present. *Anagrams* received mixed criticism. Critics noted that Moore again employs witticisms, intelligent characters, clear and crisp prose, and insightful commentaries on the frailties of human nature found in *Self-Help.* They disagreed, however, as to whether *Anagrams* is a novel or a volume of short stories. Some also charged that the incessant one-liners lessen the emotional connections between text and reader. Merle Rubin remarked that *Anagrams* is marked by "freshness, wit, and vitality, but her characters (in any and all of their various incarnations) are finally less than the sum of their clever conversations."

(See also *CLC,* Vols. 39, 45 and *Contemporary Authors,* Vol. 116.)

PRINCIPAL WORKS

Self-Help (short fiction collection) 1985
Anagrams (novel) 1986
Like Life (short fiction collection) 1990

Carol Iannone

[In ***Self-Help***] Miss Moore seems to be saying with some sarcasm that modern life has grown so complex, its possibilities so multifarious, we are continuously in urgent need of fresh guidance. But the self-help form also mocks the old American idea that we can be steered smoothly through any situation, no matter how trying, painful, or even bizarre (one of the book's epigraphs is a quotation from Amy Vanderbilt on how to shake hands with a man who has lost both arms), as well as the more contemporary notion that we should be able to manage life's vicissitudes, including death, divorce, and all-purpose unhappiness, with the utmost equanimity. . . .

In fact, the forms she has chosen precisely serve her purpose in creating women who are "stylish about their victimization" (as she has put it). Thus, in **"How to Be an Other Woman"** a bright young college graduate stuck in a secretarial job becomes involved with a more established and professionally successful older man who turns out to be otherwise engaged. . . . The character tries to cope with the situation by making lists—lists of her former lovers, of things to do when she becomes angry with the man, of items in his medicine chest that clearly belong to a woman. She even assesses the relationship itself by means of a list:

> 1. The affair is demeaning.
> 2. Violates decency. Am I just some scampish tart, some tartish scamp?
> 3. No emotional support here.
> 4. Why do you never say "I love you" or "Stay in my arms forever my little tadpole" or "Your eyes set me on fire my sweet nubkin"?
>
> (p. 60)

As a narrative device, the self-help "rap" is slyly, unfeelingly agnostic. Miss Moore follows her heroines into messy relationships and out of them again, gaining and offering no particular insight in the process. A woman feels she should not abandon a sick man but then leaves anyway, and yet can give no shape to the event:

> A week, a month, a year. The sadness will die like an old dog. You will feel nothing but indifference. The logy whine of a cowboy harmonica, plaintive, weary, it will fade into the hills slow as slow Hank Williams. One of those endings.

Miss Moore's presiding deficiency in ***Self-Help*** is this willingness to settle for an utter lack of consequence, and it besets her second book, ***Anagrams,*** as well. The heroine of this novel, Benna Carpenter, is living through "that awful stage of life from the age of twenty-six to thirty-seven known as *stupidity.* It's when you don't know anything." Appropriately enough, this may be all *we* know for sure in this looking-glass novel. In five separate sections, Miss Moore creates five different lives for Benna, using the same basic set of characters. ("I was inspired by the idea of an anagram," she has explained, "which is the rearrangement of characters to make a new word. What I did was rearrange characters to make new worlds.")

Thus, in her different avatars, Benna is a cocktail-lounge singer, an aerobics instructor, a creative-writing teacher, a suburban housewife, and a mother, sometimes more than one at the same time. A character named Gerard also plays different roles in each section—sometimes a lover, more often a friend—and he too has different occupations. In most of the sections Benna has a delightful six-year-old daughter—but, we are told, she has imagined her—and a friend, Eleanor, smart, tough, witty, over thirty, and overweight. (pp. 60-1)

At the novel's end Benna has nothing left but the imagination that has apparently fashioned her different lives and even the daughter who is now her only friend.

The narrative switches back and forth between first and third persons, heightening the dizzy sense of displacement, as does the steady stream of sardonic, sometimes mordant jokes, ranking from standup comedy ("Our sex life is disappearing . . . Gerard goes to the bathroom and I call it 'Shaking Hands with the Unemployed' ") to linguistic wordplay ("Anguish as a Second Language") to Woody Allen mock-philosophy ("What does poetry owe the world? Are we all vagabonds at a cosmic dump or are we just not paying attention?"). As usual in Miss Moore's universe, Benna seems to understand her own defenses—both her self-absorption and her imaginary escapism—but, typically, such knowledge brings no consequence. Near the end of the novel, Benna is "stupid with loneliness, bereft of any truth or wisdom or flicker of poetry, possessed only of the wild glaze of a person who spends entire days making things up."

In a different era this statement might have marked the beginning of a character's true self-confrontation, or at least of an author's confrontation with her material, but in ours it is just the lull before the next imaginary escape. (p. 61)

Carol Iannone, "Post-Counterculture Tristesse," in Commentary, *Vol. 83, No. 2, February, 1987, pp. 57-61.*

Anna Vaux

The narrators of the stories in Lorrie Moore's first book, ***Self-Help,*** may have found ways of dealing with their inertia, but they never quite shook off the "virus of discontent" they suffered from. Moore's endings there were notable for their casual indifference, coming with a shrug of the shoulders as her heroines gritted their teeth in a small-town America where men came and men left. Such endings persist in—are the stuff of—this novel, which doesn't so much start as begin with a dying cadence. There is little that might be called a plot. Fragments of ennui neither cohere nor acquire momentum, and at times ***Anagrams*** reads more like a loose assembly of short stories (and this may be the point) than a sustained piece of fiction. . . .

Benna presents each of the book's five sections as a new possibility, each one a way out of the inertia and emptiness of the one before. Indeed, the book's primary paradox is that the narrator's bleak vision that "Life will disappoint you" gives way to a sustained imaginative game in trying to overcome it. . . . The connections between parts are fragile and depend on Benna never quite letting us know what is real and what is not: just as she has a pretend daughter, Georgianne, whose imagined life must be seen as neither tenuous nor sad, but a "lozenge" of "comfort" and "possibility".

Moore's variations on life's "humiliations, occasionally relieved by the humiliations of others" is in the end a series of jokes which she allows Benna to make while placing her at the centre of them. . . . But Moore makes sure emotion is restored as well as stripped, and though the book's central relationship between Benna and Gerard is dogged by misunderstanding, their devotion is replenished with each small failure.

Moore's method has its disadvantages. Her preoccupation with puzzles whose answers can be reorganized and newly resolved—as the title implies—results in some disastrous linguistic quips and threatens the narrative with constant dissolution. Moore may make a virtue out of being in the dark, but the pleasures of her book lie less in its obliqueness than in the odd twists of tone that set its fastidiously flat narration somewhere between despair and promise:

> I look at the paper again. The human race is dying. We are all dying and we are sitting up in our beds smoking cigars and making dying jokes, an impressively, compulsively vaudevillian species. Monkeys with spiff.

Anna Vaux, "Tricky Connections," in The Times Literary Supplement, *No. 4405, September 4, 1987, p. 949.*

John Casey

Fans of [Lorrie Moore's] first book of stories, ***Self-Help*** won't be disappointed by ***Like Life***—far from it, they'll be thrilled—but the new stories are distinct from the earlier ones. They claim more, they play faster and they display more deliberate, stylized devices. Here is a passage from **"Two Boys."**

> 'I love you,' Mary said to Number One . . .
> 'You're very special,' he replied.
> 'You're very special, too,' said Mary. 'Though I suppose you'd be even more special if you were single.'
> 'That would make me more than special,' said Number One. 'That would make me rare. We're talking unicorn.'
> 'I love you,' she said to Number Two. She was romantic that way. Her heart was big and bursting. Though her brain was drying and dividing like a cauliflower. She called both boys 'honey' and it shocked her a little. How many honeys could you have? Perhaps you could open your arms and have so many honeys you achieved a higher spiritual plane, like a shelf in a health food store, or a pine tree, mystically inert, life barking at the bottom like a dog.
> 'I love you, too,' said Two, the hot lunch of him lifting off his skin in a steam . . .

In these stories you don't have to spend a lot of time waiting around to find out what's going on. The slick married lover, the wholesome, thicker other love, the woman in a state—they're familiar characters in a modern *commedia dell'arte* troupe. In this particular story their job is playing the set piece with style. Moore has them prancing nimbly, kept to the pace with a flick of a simile. . . .

The rhythm and precision of the witty (and sometimes wisecracking) narration is wonderfully theatrical, and the reader is immediately alert to it. When the curtain goes up, there is the assurance of thrill—the set is clever, the lighting is right, it's opening night and the cast is all pro. But in the first story, **"Two Boys,"** and in almost all those that follow, something else is going on.

Yes, it is artifice, it does have the feel of being played by voices that are more polished, cadenced and projected than the usual slack, close-miked realism of movies, of life. These figures are moving crisply in the bright light of comedy; the glamor of performance is there under the blue and amber gels . . . and yet there is a part of the reader's mind that is drawn out into the dark air, into a dream alertness in which the shadows of the story are the shadows of true wishes, true seizures of sorrow.

Sometimes this re-direction of the reader's attention is done directly and explicitly. In the title story **["Like Life"]**, the heroine thinks of her husband: "Rudy always walked home alone, slow across the bridge, his life the same as it was. His heart, she knew, was full of that ghetto desire to leap from poor to rich with a single, simple act, that yearning that exhausted the poor. . . ." . . .

All these stories are related to each other, even the one short skimpy sketch I wasn't crazy about. They are about solitude. For all her heroines (and one hero), an independent solitude seems to be the only fit state from which to contemplate the disintegrations of the world, the only source of reliable strength and pure action. There is solace in love, but it makes a mess. All the characters in these stories want both solitude and love.

This is, of course, not a newly discovered quandary, but Lorrie Moore brings her own variations to it, her own comic talent and her own eloquence. It's hard to think of writers with whom to compare her. In her wry, precise remarks, she sometimes seems like a witty foreigner describing American life—like English novelist David Lodge, for example, though Moore has more pointedly lyric areas in her work. And in the way she mixes comedy and sadness, wisecracks and poignancy, there's a resemblance to the Woody Allen of *Annie Hall* and *Manhattan.*

But these comparisons can only indicate an approximate zone of style, intricacy and flavor. Lorrie Moore makes her own vintage. It has an immediate clear tang to it, followed by longer and subtler satisfactions.

John Casey, "Eloquent Solitudes," in Chicago Tribune—Books, *May 20, 1990, p. 3.*

Stephen McCauley

A character in the title story of ***Like Life,*** Lorrie Moore's second collection of short fiction, compares her faltering marriage to "a saint, guillotined and still walking for miles through the city, carrying its head." That, as it turns out, is also an apt description of many of the characters in these insightful and moving stories; they are not, overall, a happy lot. They're women and men struggling with displacement, disappointment, the breakdown of both the earth's environment and their own sense of emotional stability.

Almost all of the people in ***Like Life*** seem isolated, as if some essential connection between head and body has been severed, leaving them lost, a little aimless, besieged by doubts about the courses their lives have taken. "How did one get here?" a character with two boyfriends but no single real relationship wonders. "How did one's . . . life lead one along so cruelly, like a trick, to the middle of the sea?" In another story, a bewildered clerk in a cheese shop observes, "You could look out at your life and no longer recognize it." A woman attending a Halloween party in Manhattan scans the city from the apartment's balcony and feels, momentarily, "like someone lifted into heaven by mistake and then spurned." . . .

Few [characters] are settled in their homes or their lives. Like the headless saint, they do a lot of wandering. The woman living above the meat company escapes daily to a nearby park where she can be "unsullied" and, upon returning, approaches her building "in a halting tiptoe." The playwright walks the streets of Manhattan all night to be free of the real and imagined toxins that are seeping into his life. The wife in the converted Brooklyn beauty salon dreams of a different existence in a real house, a house in which "the lovely brow of its mansard roof" is "thoughtful with rooms." Even the pleasant small cities have to be fled from time to time. "Illinois. It makes me sarcastic to be here," an uneasy professor explains to her sister in **"You're Ugly, Too."**

So how did they get here, these bright, articulate people, spurned in midair, adrift in the middle of the sea? The short answer is: love. The belief in it, the hope and longing for it, the desperate fear of it, the mad dash toward it and the frantic flight away from it. Love. The whole damned, disappointing mess of it.

For the most fortunate characters in these wonderful stories, love has been elusive. ("I don't have a love life," one woman tells another. "I have a *like* life." In response, "Mamie smiled. She thought how nice that might be, to be peacefully free from love—love and its desire for itself.") For those who are not so lucky, love has turned to tears, sarcasm and bitterness; it has sickened or died. In the most touching story in the collection, **"The Jewish Hunter,"** a poet finds love with a kind, steadfast man, despite her protestations. But she flees from it, reasoning that to preserve the feeling of having her life unfold before her "still unspent," all love will have to be as "a truck on the interstate roaring up from the left, a thing she must let pass." . . .

Like Life heads in a new direction [for Moore.] The stories are traditionally told, less capricious and far more capacious [than her earlier work.] There's a stronger sense of place, a unity of time and a new richness and variety of characters. The direct, matter-of-fact storytelling seems here to be born of deserved self-confidence.

It is the strength of Ms. Moore's writing—the accuracy of her observations, the lyricism of many of her descriptions and the wry view of behavior wryly expressed—that prevents these stories about mostly unhappy people from ever being grim or maudlin. In **"Places to Look for Your Mind,"** a man who seems to be incapable of communicating with anyone studies his wife beside him in bed: "She had the round, drying face of someone who once and briefly—a long ago fall, a weekend perhaps—had been very pretty without ever even knowing it. 'You are my only friend,' he said." Elsewhere, hands "move around nervously, independently, like small rodents kept as pets." . . .

Although love in these stories leaves one stranded and adrift, offers anything *but* hope and salvation, it does have its splendid moments:

> He closed his eyes and kissed her, long and slow, and she left her sunglasses on so she could keep her eyes open and watch, see how his lashes closed on one another like petals . . . how his lips pushed sleepily against her own to find a nest in hers and to stay there, moving, as if in words . . . his hands going round her in a soft rustle . . . blooming large and holding her just briefly.

All right, so that relationship doesn't work out in the end. Still, the tenderness of the scene lingers. And even the least optimistic insights are written with such truthfulness and wit that they make ***Like Life*** a rewarding, even exhilarating book.

Stephen McCauley, "Love Is Like a Truck on the Interstate," in The New York Times Book Review, *May 20, 1990, p. 7.*

Ralph Sassone

[In the hilarious and affecting ***Self-Help,*** Lorrie Moore showed she] was a brittle, comic writer who structured her stories in fragments or in reverse chronology, reveled in an excess of wonderfully odd metaphors, and played with genre. Moore's protagonists were people attracted to wordplay nearly as often as they were drawn to unsuitable love objects. Puns, malapropisms, and quirky turns of phrase galvanized her narratives. . . . Moore invested prodigious verve and intelligence in every story (including those few that broke from the imperative mold), and not one was lacking in moments of compassion for the seriously aggrieved women who populated her work. The collection's only shortcoming was that Moore's repetitive approach allowed for fewer tonal variations than one would have liked from a writer so clearly capable of letting it rip.

This was less of a problem in Moore's next book, the cubistic and emotionally overwhelming ***Anagrams*** (1986). The urgency with which the characters in ***Self-Help*** hotflashed through her fictions was sustained, as were many of Moore's initial preoccupations. The novel featured men who weren't quite worthy, intellectually or ethically, of the jangle-nerved and at times aggressively clever heroine. And it was all variation—the equivalent of a word scramble in which certain basic components persist despite

Moore's reshufflings of circumstance and event. . . . [***Anagrams*** follows] a multi-faceted woman whose best defense against a life of mounting solitude is her fierce imagination and humor.

Moore's own use of humor is as complicated as her protagonists'. Although a cursory reading of her work might make it seem coolly satirical, its aftereffect is the memory of palpable pain. Moore's comic sensibility is closer to Dorothy Parker than to Fran Lebowitz. Like Parker, she shows the wounds that wisecracks are meant to cauterize, and the desperate loneliness that gives rise to humor. Funniness is simultaneously a leavening agent for her wrenching narratives, a temporary paregoric for her characters, and a distancing device that perpetuates their alienation. When someone in ***Like Life,*** Moore's most recent collection, is told, "Everything's a joke with you," her response is, "Nothing's a joke with me. It just all comes out like one."

Like Life has its share of witticisms. There's hardly a page that doesn't have several quote-worthy lines or aperçus that make you stop short in admiration. . . . But the most inspired writing in ***Like Life*** is, as always with Moore, about love: love with its lures; love with its vagaries and dangers. . . . In one of Moore's many compound similes, she writes that "You chose love like a belief, a faith, a place, a box for one's heart to knock against like a spook in the house."

Most of the characters in ***Like Life*** are as haunted by love as their predecessors in Moore's earlier work. They long for attachment yet shun it. . . .

Like Life is remarkable for delivering both the quick verbal zings of ***Self-Help*** and the depths of ***Anagrams,*** which apparently liberated Moore to try for tones other than antic despair. Moore has learned to slow down her short fiction and register the subtler notes. The new collection is her most conventionally structured book, but it may also be her boldest. . . .

Like Life is impressive not only for its precise sketches of, say, limousine liberals, oily Hollywood film types, and men as lovelorn and neurotic as the women, but for its respectful reportage about lives that aren't overtly in extremis. **"Places To Look for Your Mind"** and **"Joy"** focus on ordinary people who express their anxieties quietly. The first is a subdued yet heartbreaking piece about Millie, a timid housewife who re-experiences the loss of her son when a young British tourist comes to stay with her. **"Joy"** tells the story of Jane, a withdrawn romantic burnout who operates under the corseted assumption that the adage "You only live once" is "all the more reason to be careful, to take it easy, to have an ordinary life." She believes that "there were only small joys in life—the big ones were too complicated to be joys when you got all through—and once you realized that, it took a lot of the pressure off." In the end Jane is left with only her freshly groomed cat, and Millie with little but disappointment. Yet in Moore's hands they both become objects of contemplation rather than witty disdain. She proves that although her natural gift is for kinetic prose about the bright and wired, she can also write understated stories in which the mood is closer to a hush.

Which hardly means that she's gone soft. If anything, ***Like Life*** is Moore's toughest work: It shows human vulnerability in various contours, and with heightened sympathy, while never dropping its cynicism. Moore's world remains a place where nearly everybody ends up isolated or alone. Self-help manuals don't help; strangers don't become any less strange; lovers and family members aren't enough to protect you from impending loss or disaster. It's no wonder that when a doctor tells the protagonist of the title story that her throat condition is precancerous, she says, "*Pre*cancer? Isn't that . . . like *life?*" Such a question—part joke, part horrified insight—is emblematic of Moore's resonant ambivalence. Her answer would appear to be *yes,* but her brilliant and ever-expanding body of work suggests there are a few enduring pleasures left to us anyway—not least of which are laughing, weeping, and marveling at the countless ways we stumble through.

Ralph Sassone, "This Side of Parody," in VLS, *No. 86, June, 1990, p. 15.*

"[Moore] relishes the differences between the sexes and our terminal incompatibility. Her women are high-spirited in their disappointments and alarming in their insights; her men are rarely so accomplished in the matter of perception. Their failure to grasp what is going on makes for some of the funnier moments [in *Like Life*] as well as some of the most surreal."

—Anna Vaux, 1990

Merle Rubin

[***Like Life***] confirms my impression of Lorrie Moore as a writer with a wry, skittish sense of humor and enough verbal glibness to provide material for all the stand-up comics in Los Angeles, but with very little ability to create convincing characters or tell stories that invite us to suspend our disbelief as we read them or to brood upon them after they've been read. . . .

Like Life is . . . Moore's third story collection, its title perhaps an ironic acknowledgement of potential criticism from those who may complain that her work lacks the fleshed-out verisimilitude of old-fashioned realism.

Moore, who is nothing if not coolly self-aware, would seem to be tacitly responding that all fiction—from the most painstaking realism to the most playful allegory—can only be like life and cannot, should not, be life. And, indeed, when the phrase *like life* occurs in the context of the story bearing this title, Moore is actually suggesting that life itself, as we experience it, is only "like life": not quite the real thing we expected, but only a close approximation of it. Self-consciousness and self-estrangement—the suspicion that everything they do is only a pose—are attitudes that distance Moore's characters from their lives and provide the mordant twist that distinguishes their author's style and stance.

Moore's stories have appeared in *The New Yorker* and other magazines. Although most critics would never dream of labeling this kind of self-consciously "literary" writing "commercial," it does, in fact, have characteristics that render it surprisingly marketable: a kind of Lean Cuisine for street-smart urban sophisticates who like to read and run.

The eight stories in this collection are crisply packaged, skillfully produced and light-yet-piquant enough to appeal to the weariest palate. **"Two Boys"** presents Mary, who is juggling two love affairs at the same time. She recommends the practice in postcards to her friends. Mary's breezy insouciance soon yields to a "subtle" kind of "nervous collapse," which Moore renders in the same breezily insouciant style.

"Vissi d'Arte" is a mocking thumbnail sketch of a self-important playwright living in squalor near Times Square. It is a slick, yet unconvincing blend of irony and pathos. The same goes for **"Joy,"** a day-in-the-life of a woman who works in a cheese store in "the deep Midwest," where there is "no real seafood for miles" and "meat sections in the grocery stores read: BEEF, PORK and FISH STICKS."

The Midwest is viewed even more ironically in **"You're Ugly, Too,"** where it is seen through the eyes of expatriate Easterner Zoë Hendricks, whose uniformly blond students assume that brunettes come from foreign countries. "Just because Prof. Hendricks is from Spain doesn't give her the right to be so negative about our country," runs one comment. Moore's sense of comedy can be priceless.

It's when she tries for greater depth of emotion that she seems to lose her touch. Three more stories—**"The Jewish Hunter," "Places to Look for Your Mind"** and **"Like Life"**—reveal this limitation.

"Starving Again," the shortest, least substantial story in the book, shows Moore doing what she does best. In essence, this story is nothing more than a conversation between Dennis, recently divorced, and his friend Mave, who is currently dating a womanizer. It contains some of Moore's funnier lines:

"I've got my own means of revenge," says Dennis, who's upset by his ex-wife's new romance. "If she wants to go out with other men, I'm going to sit here and just let her." Replies Mave: "That's an incredibly powerful form of revenge." Later, Dennis gets his own back by accusing Mave of getting all her boyfriends "on sale. It's called Bargain Debasement."

One must credit Moore for her flair at doing what she does, but having praised her for her polish, one must also question the value of her enterprise. It is perfectly defensible for a writer to concoct ingenious, flimsy, self-referential card houses built of attitude and verbal sallies; it may even be the height of literary fashion. But when style becomes this stylized, it is likely to prove a fad.

Merle Rubin, "Lean Cuisine for Picky Palates," in Los Angeles Times Book Review, *June 3, 1990, p. 11.*

Michiko Kakutani

The characters in Lorrie Moore's impressive new collection of stories [***Like Life***] are all at turning points in their lives, negotiating the slender walkway between stoicism and despair, disappointment and rage. Their vulnerability has a way of manifesting itself in peculiar ways. . . .

A teacher who has been unable to settle down with the right man keeps returning her new furniture to the store—the plain pine chest that was supposed to serve as a love seat looks like a child's coffin; the symbols on the Chinese rug, she is now convinced, say Bruce Springsteen in Chinese. A man who has been dumped by his girlfriend fixates on the unwholesomeness of his apartment: he imagines that he is being poisoned at night by deadly fumes, that miso soup has come bubbling out of his bathtub drain.

These obsessions, of course, are all means these characters have contrived for avoiding the real dilemmas in their lives: they are distractions, diversions, disguises for more permanent and intractable sorrows. Other characters seek refuge in the defensive pleasures of humor. They crack jokes, volley wisecracks, trade sarcastic remarks. These are ways for them to avoid conversations, deflect emotions, mock their own dilemmas. . . .

Although the stories in ***Like Life*** are as funny and archly observant as those in Ms. Moore's earlier collection (***Self-Help***), they are also softer, wiser, more minor-key. In between the jokes and the banter, Ms. Moore allows herself to slip into passages of lyrical meditation, and she permits her characters to examine—however gingerly—their hurts and missed connections. The results are richer, more ambitious stories—stories that work not as quick comedy sketches, but as moving examinations of lives in transition.

Like their counterparts in Ms. Moore's earlier stories, the women in this volume tend to be alone or in unfulfilling relationships; they long for the sort of romance found in the movies, but find that the real-life alternatives fall disappointingly short of their ideals. . . .

Love, for these characters, is something that other people are good at, something that inevitably ends—for them, anyway—in apology, tears or sarcasm. In a sense, their failures in passion and intimacy are simply symptoms of a larger sense of dislocation—their sense that they will always be outsiders, that they will never look in the mirror and recognize their own reflection.

Whether her characters live in Manhattan tenements or Midwestern bungalows, whether they are timid girls working in small-town boutiques or street-smart artists trying to hustle a career in New York City, Ms. Moore demonstrates an unerring ability to delineate the shape of their daily lives. She has an eye for the telling detail (the aspirins kept in a Baggie; the quotation marks shaped as careful sixes and nines), as well as a sure sense of her people's emotions. Together these gifts make for stories that are, at once, sad and funny, entertaining and affecting.

Michiko Kakutani, "Observations on Failures in Passion and Intimacy," in The New York Times, *June 8, 1990, p. C28.*

Mary Warner Marien

Lorrie Moore's taut, subversive tales [in ***Like Life***] should have come with a warning label: These stories may cause permanent February in the soul. . . .

In her previous work, Moore treated readers to wry observations of the way we live now. There are still some laugh-out-loud moments in this anthology. Thankfully, her eye for faddishness has not dimmed. Coming upon a beauty salon called Dorian Gray's, for example, a character remarks that beauty salons these days bear names "hostile with wit, cutesy with warning."

However entertaining they may be, one-liners are distracting. Sensing this, perhaps, Moore has included fewer droll moments here than in her previous novel and stories, giving full throttle to the formidable engine of her plot skills. Most short stories move with the languor of pond grass. Moore's tales, fueled by a sensibility as dark as Margaret Atwood's but without the pensive dawdling, race through events like the summer's hottest roller coaster. It will take you longer to tell your friends what happens in a Moore short story than it will take to read one.

For reasons that are never very clear, Moore's characters are poised to pitch through the thin veneer of self-control into chilly psychic spaces. Their becoming fragile is never part of the plot. They are fragile when we meet them.

Nerves are frayed, not so much as a result of what has happened, as from what is not likely to happen. Moore's people are persistently lightheaded with disappointment—the kind that follows on the realization that the only people they can get to love them are as dull as they are doggedly devoted.

As if to compensate, these characters develop an intense inner monologue. They don't have real lives, they have "like lives," and they don't really like life anymore, either.

Odette, a peripatetic poet, finds love and discontent with a Jewish farm lawyer who considers most verse "a little too literaturey." When his no-nonsense doctor-lover, Brecky, moves uptown, things get shaky for Harry, a playwright so shy he flushes with sweat at the thought of someone reading his masterwork. Millie, a middle-aged mom from New Jersey, shatters when her punkish English house guest leaves unexpectedly.

And so it goes. "Emergency. Love. Emergency," as one character comments. Most often Moore's people-characters spin in a stable disequilibrium. But when "Love" is eventually left out of life's sandwich, it's all "Emergency. Emergency. Emergency." . . .

Reviewing Lorrie Moore's short stories is like retelling a roller coaster ride. Some things you just have to experience. Sure, an encounter with Moore's original gifts at this juncture in her career may leave you a little woozy. But when's the last time a writer was able to do that?

Mary Warner Marien, "Lives on a Short-Story Roller Coaster," in The Christian Science Monitor, *August 2, 1990, p. 12.*

Nick Hornby

The bad news is that in two or three of the stories [in ***Like Life***], Moore writes as if she has been listening to advice from grown-ups: 'Rein yourself in more! Forget those stories narrated in imperatives! Don't feel you have to be witty all the time! Read more Alice Munro!' Consequently, **"Joy"** and **"Places To Look For Your Mind"** are beautifully-written, credible, well-observed and somehow anonymous, the product of the best computer in the best American creative writing class. The good news is that in the remaining half-dozen tales, she sticks her tongue out at the grown-ups and concentrates on what she does best.

The characters in all eight stories are the familiar lonely-hearts and malcontents, most of them of a certain age (let's avoid the 't'-word) and with responsible, or at least interesting, jobs (let's avoid the 'y'-word): Breckie is a surgeon, Zoe teaches American history, Odette is a poet, Harry is a playwright. Most of these people are either locked into unhappy, fitful, unsatisfying relationships, or at least wish they were: 'One of these days, she knew, she would have to give up dating. She had practised declarations in the mirror. "I don't date. I'm sorry. I just don't date." '

This, of course, has been the staple diet of middlebrow American culture—Woody and his (author) sisters—for a long time now. Perhaps 'highbrow pop' is a more exact categorisation. ***Like Life,*** however, is much, much more than simply 'When Harry Met Lorrie'. For starters, Moore's language, her deceptively casual arrival at a beautifully skewed phrase, is above and beyond the call of Highbrow Pop duty: 'Dennis was always kicking himself on a phone, not an easy thing, the tricky ouch of it.' And in this volume, as in ***Self-Help,*** the author looks consistently and successfully for new clothes in which to dress her themes. [**"Like Life"**], for example, is a bleakly impressive work of romantic science-fiction, just as sharp as the rest of her work but with apocalyptic trimmings.

But most of all, Lorrie Moore is funny—funnier than just about anyone operating in this territory, including the director of the hilarious *Interiors* and *September.* While Zoe and Jane and Odette grapple with life, the tricky ouch of it, they produce thousands of wry, self-deprecating, apparently effortless one-liners or they become embroiled in dumb, hilarious, confused conversations with dumb, hilarious men. Zoe's meeting with Earl at a Hallowe'en party, he dressed as a naked woman, she with a bone through her head, he desperate to talk about love and marriage and relationships, is particularly memorable.

It is easy for a man to fall in love with these women, with their wit and their insecurities and their tendernesses, and by childish extension with their creator. Lorrie Moore is the post-feminist woman that post-feminist men are looking for in their non-predatory way. . . . You don't have to feel that way to love ***Like Life,*** however: Lorrie Moore's stories are still the most fun you can have between hard covers.

Nick Hornby, "The Tricky Ouch of It," in The Listener, *Vol. 124, No. 3181, September 6, 1990, p. 27.*

Camille Paglia

1947-

American nonfiction writer.

Paglia has initiated widespread critical controversy with her first published work, *Sexual Personae: Art and Decadence from Nefertiti to Emily Dickinson* (1990). A critical history of Western art and culture from ancient Egypt to the nineteenth century, this study intends, in Paglia's words, "to demonstrate the unity and continuity of Western culture" in opposition to "the modernist idea that culture has collapsed into meaningless fragments." Paglia contends that paganism has flourished alongside Christianity in civilizations from early to modern times, lending a cohesiveness and sense of permanence to Western culture that has often been denied or ignored by humanist scholars. Describing her method as "a form of sensationalism," Paglia emphasizes the emotive rather than the cerebral aspects of sexuality and decadence in art, culture, and literature.

Born into an Italian-American family in New York state, Paglia was inspired to spurn conventional protocol by her father, a professor of Romance Languages at the Jesuit Le-Moyne College in Syracuse, New York. She received her undergraduate degree at the State University of New York in Binghamton before pursuing graduate studies at Yale University in the 1960s under the supervision of noted critic Harold Bloom, who encouraged her to develop her own aesthetic. Paglia began working on *Sexual Personae* while teaching at various universities in the 1970s and completed the work after becoming a professor of humanities at the Philadelphia College of the Arts in 1980. Despite difficulties in finding a publisher, the book appeared in 1990, a delay Paglia attributed to the book's assaults on the "politically correct" ideas of liberal academics.

In addition to attacking leftist standards, *Sexual Personae* also offended conservative literary scholars and critics by critiquing the prevalent deconstructionist notion that experience is determined by cultural forces, particularly language, and that culture can be read as a series of texts. Paglia further incited conservative ire by elevating the works of such "decadent" writers and artists as the Marquis de Sade and Gustave Moreau above more traditional favorites; by upholding the male homosexual artist as "one of the great forgers of Western absolutist identity"; and by discerning elements of sadomasochism and perverse sexuality in the works of revered figures in Western art and literature, including the poet Emily Dickinson, whom Paglia refers to as "Amherst's Madame de Sade." While numerous critics have impugned Paglia for generalizations, sensationalism, and oversimplification, many concur with the opinion of Lillian Faderman: "Paglia seems often bent on astounding the reader. Thus her literary interpretations are sometimes fascinating fictions of their own instead of elucidations of a work. . . . As infuriating as Paglia often is, one must be awed by her vast energy, erudition and wit."

Heated debate has also surrounded Paglia's intention to demonstrate in *Sexual Personae* "the truth in sexual stereotypes and the biologic basis in sex differences." Liberal and feminist critics have expressed anger over Paglia's theory that revolutionary accomplishments in art and science belong exclusively to men. Males, according to Paglia, are compelled by the need to escape the feminine powers of sex and nature, which she refers to as "chthonic," or earthbound forces, and to overcome nature and social convention in the process of creating new forms of art. Correspondingly, Paglia believes that women "lack the violent aggression to change, to revolutionize," and thus create: "If civilization had been left in female hands we would still be living in grass huts." Arguing that rape and murder are historical constants, Paglia derides attempts to eradicate sexual stereotypes as offering women "a sanitized, censored view of human psychology and sexual relations." Identifying herself with such early feminists as Simone de Beauvoir and Jane Harrison, Paglia attacks a modern feminist tendency to blame men for the historical situation of women, and she professes her goal to "bring back the prewar feminism that stresses self-reliance—not blaming other people for your problems." Some reviewers have commended Paglia's unfettered examination of feminism, liberalism, and other totems of academia; others, however, have found her work ignorant of contemporary feminist scholarship and assert that her ideas on the biological basis of sexual stereotypes are derivative of the works of such nineteenth-century scientific writers as Sigmund Freud and Charles Darwin.

Lillian Faderman

"Prison dreams of a self-incarcerated sadomasochist," "a virtuoso of sadomasochistic realism," "brutality that would stop a truck." Algernon Charles Swinburne? Jean Genet? William Burroughs? No. The reclusive poet of Amherst, Emily Dickinson. In [***Sexual Personae: Art and Decadence from Nefertiti to Emily Dickinson,*** a] voluminous, baroque study of decadence in literature, art and society, Camille Paglia leans always towards such dark insights that have eluded more "naive" scholars.

Wedding Freud to J. G. Frazer (*The Golden Bough*), Paglia examines the amorality, aggression, sadism and pornography in "great art" from ancient Egypt to the major 19th-century American writers. Her thesis is that there is a unity and continuity in Western culture that has little to do with the forces of Judeo-Christianity. That unity is aligned instead with paganism, which flourished not only in antiquity but also in the Renaissance and Romantic eras and continues to flourish in pop culture today. It is as inescapable as the unconscious, she suggests, where nature reigns and where there is no law but sex and cruelty. Her method in illustrating her thesis is, as she admits, a form of sensationalism. She tries to flesh out intellect with emotion, and to induce a wide range of emotion from the reader. In this latter goal Paglia is remarkably successful. It is impossible to read this outrageous, fascinating, politically incorrect book with calm or quietude.

Paglia is provocative and provoking whether she discusses society or art. Feminists may find ***Sexual Personae*** the book they most love to hate. Paglia believes there is indeed a basis for sexual stereotypes that is biological and firmly rooted in the unconscious. She criticizes feminists who seek to drive power relations out of sex as having "set themselves against nature." One is reminded in such assertions of the 19th-century sexologists who dubbed feminists "unnatural." But readers would have to go to the most obsessive misogynists such as Strindberg to find her equal: "If civilization had been left in female hands," she declares, "we would still be living in grass huts." One suspects that she is often trying to get a rise out of the reader. Are we really meant to take seriously such an edifying observation as "male urination really *is* a kind of accomplishment, an arc of transcendance. A woman merely waters the ground she stands on"?

But Paglia does not stop at outraging feminists. She seems to strive to include something to offend almost everyone. The naivete of liberals comes under particular attack. She scoffs at the liberals' idea of history being progress, their refusal to see the dark side of human nature, their conviction that what is really innate perversity can be eradicated by plastic bandages. Yet despite the seeming conservative bent of many of her views, conservatives will be no more comfortable with ***Sexual Personae*** than liberals. Just as they are thinking that they and Paglia share a wave length she will zap them with something like her aesthetic defense of man-boy love and her objection that men are pilloried today for something that was considered rational and honorable at the height of western civilization.

Perhaps the seeming contradictions in her views can be explained by a comparison from literary history. Like the aesthete writers on whom Paglia spends the latter half of her book, she is fascinated with the decadent. The aesthetes, slaves to their baptism (they were largely "fallen away" Catholics), could not overcome their guilt about their involvement with the forbidden. Their fascination with it was invariably overlaid with the most traditional views of "sin" and "evil." Paglia betrays the same kind of moral ambivalence. ***Sexual Personae*** is a voyeuristic and often lurid immersion in the universe of decadence where great art flourishes and human nature is dubbed polymorphously and shockingly perverse.

Literary works are judged in this book by the degree to which they demonstrate decadence. Mark Twain, for example, Paglia finds "hateful" because his folksiness and Wordsworthian benevolence strike her as counterfeit. Wordsworth himself is "sexless," having spent a lifetime editing "the brute reality" out of his poetry. He is taken to task especially for leading the more "daemonic" Coleridge astray. "The Rime of the Ancient Mariner" fails, Paglia asserts, when, after Coleridge's magnificent penetration of the daemonic realm of barbaric energy he retreats to conventional emotion by having the mariner bless the water snakes. Coleridge thus "surrenders to Wordsworth and Christianity" and blows the poem.

Her fascination with "perversity" in literature brings her to some startling interpretations. William Blake she sees as "Sade's British brother," a title that might be convincing when illustrated by some of the poems in *Songs of Experience.* However, Paglia chooses to show the chthonian ["of the earth"]—the term she prefers to the more traditional Dionysiac—in Blake's *Songs of Innocence* as well. For example, although Blake's sweet and simple "Infant Joy" indicates no gender whatsoever, she hears "homoerotic intensities" in it. The baby's innocence in the poem demonstrates "provocative vulnerability," a "purity that sucks filth into its wake."

Like the 19th-century decadents she admires, whose ambition was to *epater le bourgeois,* Paglia seems often bent on astounding the reader. Thus her literary interpretations are sometimes fascinating fictions of their own instead of elucidations of a work. Not infrequently, however, she strikes with a glorious insight that seduces even the most reluctant or argumentative reader. Her discussion of the sexual ambiguities and obsessions that critics have ignored or minimized in major American writers is especially compelling. American romanticism, Paglia points out, is really Decadent Late Romanticism and represents America's first internal critique of its optimistic over-idealizations. She illustrates this point with readings not only of Poe, but also Hawthorne, Melville, James and, most notably, Dickinson.

In her interpretation of Dickinson, Paglia makes us into tourists in Madame Tussaud's Chamber of Horrors as she shows us all the instruments of torture Dickinson employs in her poetry. We may be initially repelled by her characterization of Dickinson's poems as betraying an "unrecognized appetite for murder and mayhem," but Paglia's overwhelming documentation of images that depict maelstroms lapping up navies, tigers feasting on men, spirits stabbed and ravished by "dirks of melody" ultimately convinces. One can never read Dickinson again without a suspicion of her "sweet tooth for sadomasochistic horror," as Paglia describes it.

This is a remarkable book, at once outrageous and compelling, fanatical and brilliant. As infuriating as Paglia often is, one must be awed by her vast energy, erudition and wit. At the least, ***Sexual Personae*** seldom fails to be amusing.

Lillian Faderman, "Emily Dickinson and Other Slaves of Passion," in Book World—The Washington Post, *February 18, 1990, p. 5.*

Walter Kendrick

Camille Paglia doesn't care for lesbians. They "seem more interested in softball than art and artifice," she says. Paglia loves art and artifice. She loves gay men, too: "The male homosexual is one of the great forgers of absolutist western identity." From other lips, that might be poisoned praise, but Paglia *loves* "the glamourous, striving, separatist ego," "the hard, cold separatism of Western personality." It has engendered Western culture, she says, and she dotes on Western culture. So much so that she's written ***Sexual Personae: Art and Decadence from Nefertiti to Emily Dickinson,*** 673 pages of fierce wacky homage to that unfashionable idol. And this is only volume one!

Paglia's entire argument is fueled by her disgust at female bodies. Even straight men, she says, have to be tricked by hormones into going after the "spongy," "billowy," "bulging" things. Female genitals, says Paglia, "are lurid in color, vagrant in contour, and architecturally incoherent"; men's may "risk ludicrousness by their rubbery indecisiveness," but at least they have a "rational mathematical design, a syntax." Hence the George Washington Bridge and everything else men have built: "If civilization had been left in female hands, we would still be living in grass huts."

Not that Paglia hates women. It's nature she hates; women are merely pitiful in their helpless bondage to "the chthonian" (Paglia's favorite word), while men strive to break away and build cultures. You think there's beauty in nature? Grow up! "See nature spuming and frothing, its mad spermatic bubbles endlessly spilling out and smashing in that inhuman round of waste, rot, and carnage." See nature's "bloody open mouth," her "impacted, putrefying womb"! See and be afraid: "Never send to know for whom the belle tolls. She tolls for thee."

The first two chapters of ***Sexual Personae*** (from which I took those quotations) read like the inventory of an unusually cerebral fortune-cookie mill: a cosmic claim in every sentence, all in the oracular mode. Once she gets Delphi out of her system, Paglia cools down a bit. The rest of the book is a quirky, sometimes outrageous, but on the whole rather conventional tour of Western culture's high points, from Egypt in the 14th century B.C. to 19th century Amherst. On the way, we visit Classical Greece, Renaissance Italy, Spenser, Shakespeare, the English Romantics, the French Decadents, and various other well-known attractions.

Paglia relies throughout on the nature-culture opposition she sets up at the start. She whips it up into female-male, Dionysian-Apollonian, soft-hard, and lots more; she's also fecund with what she calls "personae," tossing off a good two dozen as she trots along. There's Teiresias, "a category of androgyne, the nurturant male or male mother." Then there's the "beautiful boy," Paglia's special pet. She finds this cutie every time culture is thriving: in ancient Greece, of course, but also in Shakespeare's sonnets, Pre-Raphaelite painting, [Herman Melville's] *Billy Budd,* and [Cuchino Visconti's] *Death in Venice.* He is art's ultimate protest against the "chthonian miasma" of nature, and Paglia adores him.

She's a maniacal classifier, dicing and chopping wherever she goes, but in the end her "personae" don't amount to much. They all represent artistic efforts to transgress natural sex distinctions; they're all extremely artificial, therefore Paglia likes them. The most interesting thing about ***Sexual Personae,*** except for Paglia's zaniness, is what she chooses to leave out—[Milton's] *Paradise Lost,* for instance, and the whole tradition of the "social novel," which she gets rid of in six disdainful pages. Hardly any androgynes there, you see.

Paglia also elevates Coleridge above Wordsworth (a good idea) and bestows high praise on the Marquis de Sade, though she admits he can make you queasy ("Don't read Sade before lunch!"). She's trying to bend the canon without breaking it, and most of the time her efforts provoke thought if not agreement. Perhaps unwisely in such a bulky book, the peak of ***Sexual Personae*** comes at the end—detailed, subtle readings of [Oscar Wilde's] *The Picture of Dorian Gray* and *The Importance of Being Earnest* and a delicious hatchet job on Emily Dickinson, whom Paglia reads as "that autoerotic sadist," "Amherst's Madame de Sade."

Trashing Emily's image brings out the best in Paglia: She gets to say things like "The brutality of this belle of Amherst would stop a truck," in her choicest leaning-on-a-lamppost style. The second volume of ***Sexual Personae*** will probably contain much more guytalk, when Paglia reaches Rita Hayworth ("the modern *Galatea*") and "the sibylline comedienne Gracie Allen." If you cherish namby-pamby ideas about Mommy Nature, Paglia may raise your blood pressure a few points. But if you relax and let her rave, she'll show you a down-and-dirty good time.

Walter Kendrick, in a review of "Sexual Personae: Art and Decadence from Nefertiti to Emily Dickinson," in VLS, *No. 83, March, 1990, p. 7.*

Elizabeth Wilson

[***Sexual Personae***] should be enough to disprove single-handed all recent theories of fragmentation in the post-modern world and the breakdown of the "grand narratives" of history. This is a grand narrative and a half: Oswald Spengler rewritten by Barbara Cartland, an exhaustive journey through the whole of western art, from the "chthonian" ("of the earth") origins of western civilisation to Emily Dickinson, with a companion volume promised on film, TV, sports and rock music. Indeed, the author's stated purpose is to reject "the modernist idea that culture has collapsed into meaningless fragments", and she admits her largest ambition is to "fuse Frazer with Freud". I was under the impression that Freud had done a bit of that himself, but never mind.

The most attractive characteristic of this book is its enormous enthusiasm. Camille Paglia comes fresh to some of the most discussed writers of the western canon, including Shakespeare and the currently fashionable Baudelaire, and communicates to the reader her own love of and fascination with their works. Her main theme appears to be the persistence of certain "pagan" themes throughout western art, despite the influence of Christianity.

Part of the value that Camille Paglia gives to this "paganism" is its aristocratic hierarchism. For example, she compares Chaucer to Edmund Spenser: "Chaucer's comic persona resembles that of Charlie Chaplin's Little Tramp, whom I seem to be alone in loathing." The populism of Chaucer makes "my skin crawl", whereas Spenser has grandeur and recognises what Paglia sees as the operatic nature of sexual attraction and sexual identity or "persona". Unlike poor Chaucer's *Canterbury Tales, The Faerie Queen* is full of "sex and glamour".

She traces the persistence of androgynous romantic ideals through the centuries, and her book is full of interesting insights. For example, she describes the ending of Theophile Gautier's novel *Mademoiselle Maupin* as "an autoerotic elopement". Her discussion of the theme of transvestism here leads down the byway of female transvestism in film, with value judgments such as that the cross dressing of Garbo and Dietrich is "merely titillating", a "Hollywood transplant of Weimar perversity". As in a stream of consciousness, we then find ourselves contemplating the fetishism of male transvestites. The whole passage never clarifies how "Weimar perversity" is different from and inferior to the grand romanticism of 19th century androgyny.

In a strange way the whole book appears caught in a time warp. Paglia seems unfamiliar with the critical work that has been done on film, while Michel Foucault is conspicuous by his absence. Presumably she would radically disagree with his emphasis on historicity, but to ignore his work gives an impression of critical naivety. On the other hand, Harold Bloom, Leslie Fiedler and others from an earlier generation do seem to have influenced Paglia. As I read I felt at times transported back to a distant era, the late fifties perhaps, when a mixture of Freudianism and gloomy urban romanticism created an aesthetic similar to that found here.

Reminiscent of that period is the oversimplification of the grand theory, which brings writers from every place and period under the general umbrella of a "decadence" never defined with sufficient clarity or accuracy. In some ways Paglia's assessment of Dickinson, for example, is powerful. Her emphasis on the sadistic and mechanical imagery with which the poems abound I found very interesting, but is it really helpful to liken her to "a homosexual cultist draping himself in black leather and chains"? Such disregard for historical specificity ends up seeming sensationalist.

What I found most irritating about this enormous curate's egg was the author's unselfconscious romanticism. She goes on about the "dark power" of sex and its "primitive urges". Liberalism in general and feminism in particular are castigated as futile in trying to tame the sexual "daemons" to which we are all in thrall. As with so much else in the book, there is a grain of truth in her criticism of some feminist strategies, but it would have been much sharper had she bothered to work through her insights instead of splurging it all out in the arrogance of her unjustified claims to originality. The feminism of s/m lesbians, for instance, would be quite in harmony with some of her views; her comments on Baudelaire would have benefited had she paid attention to the recent engagement with his work of post-modern critics.

Perhaps my points seem petty, part of my resistance to the whole enterprise of using "sensationalism" to rescue western literature from the library. In her own terms, though, Paglia's theory rests on an unresolved tension. The androgynous/homoerotic/lesbian figure is placed as the high point of western "Appollonian" (a very Spenglerian term) art in a perennial effort to overcome the earthy Great Mother, the all-engulfing womb. Is this a deep insight into the ultimate truth of western culture? Or is it a monumental cliché? I really don't know.

Elizabeth Wilson, "Sex and Destiny," in New Statesman & Society, *Vol. 3, No. 94, March 30, 1990, p. 32.*

Harriett Hawkins

[***Sexual Personae***] is the first volume of a monumental study tracing major themes, character-types and forms of decadence (voyeurism, narcissism, sado-masochism, gender-bending) from ancient Egypt to Hollywood. In the Bacchic energies of a rock concert, as in its display of beautiful boys and nymphets, popular culture is heir to the past. Likewise, Hollywood stars embody forces and types comparable with those associated with their celestial counterparts: Monroe is clearly of the genus Venus. Illustrations show successive personifications of virtually identical types of ideal beauty. Nefertiti's elegance is always in *Vogue.* The beautiful young man as defined in Greek art is illustrated by the strikingly similar profiles of Lord Byron and the young Elvis Presley, whose early deaths enhanced their mythic status and whose positions in the collective affections of their admirers are also comparable. Other types include the boy with the beauty of an angel who is also often doomed, or whose beauty dooms his adorers, from the young Antinous to Billy Budd, Dorian Gray, Tadzio, and (one might add) Sebastian Flyte. Arguably, a mythic persona or a new combination of sacred types seems necessary to ensure stardom, even as Madonna appears in differing personifications—'like a virgin', like a Magdalen, like a maenad, like a Marilyn.

An excerpt from *Sexual Personae*

Sex is a far darker power than feminists have ever been willing to admit. Feminists grossly oversimplify the problem of sex when they reduce it to a matter of social convention; readjust society, they say, eliminate sexual inequality, purify sex roles, and happiness and harmony will reign. Here feminism, like all liberal movements of the past 200 years, is heir to Rousseau.

Rousseau's idea of man's innate goodness led to social environmentalism, now the dominant ethic of American human services, penal codes, and behaviorist therapies. It assumes that aggression, violence, and crime come from social deprivation—a poor neighborhood, a bad home.

Thus feminism blames rape on pornography and smugly interprets outbreaks of sadism as a backlash against itself. But rape and sadism have existed throughout history and in all cultures. Aggression is innate. Society is not the criminal but the force that keeps crime in check. Feminists, whose goal is to remove power relations from sex, have set themselves against nature. For sex is a subset of nature. Sex is the natural in man.

What seems most noteworthy about the works, authors and characters surveyed here is that, like the superstars of popular culture, they all combine traits usually thought of in binary opposition to each other: childlike innocence and sexual experience (Monroe); threat and tenderness (Presley); cynicism and idealism (Bogart in *Casablanca*); strength and vulnerability (Garbo). Over and over, the most potent of sexual personae challenge past and present assumptions about gender: the males are as often gentle as tough; the women as often active and spirited as passive and compliant. Shakespeare's most glamorous *femme fatale,* Cleopatra, is the least conventionally feminine of all his heroines. Thus, both in art and life, 'charisma' as defined by Paglia is 'the radiance produced by the interaction of male and female elements in a gifted personality'. The greatest male and female stars and characters likewise draw heterosexuals 'into a bisexual response' and are equally popular with men and women.

The wide range of types discussed here, from Spenser's brave Britomart to Shakespeare's witty Rosalind and Brontë's wild, passionate Cathy, would seem to suggest that members of both sexes share, to a greater or lesser degree, a comparable spectrum of diverse traits, all of which may be necessary for individual survival as well as for the survival of the species as a whole. They certainly suggest that there is no intellectual or psychological trait demonstrably exclusive to men or to women.

Seen from this angle, Paglia's is a liberating book. For instance, as it were in refutation of the dire equation between masochism and femininity in pornographic and psychoanalytic fictions, the masochistic men outnumber the masochistic women involved in the major works surveyed here, and so suggest that the statistical proportion of women who enjoy being physically and emotionally abused in real life is probably no higher than the number of men who do.

Yet this reading of the evidence is dialectically opposed to the psychoanalytic premise of this book. In chapter after chapter Paglia insists that art and science are male efforts to escape from the earth-mother whose chthonic force condemns them to lifelong sexual anxiety. Even as the Greeks tried to turn their female Furies into 'Kindly Ones', the Romantic idealists, Rousseau and Wordsworth, tried to make the mother-goddess a benevolent force. In reaction, the Marquis de Sade and Coleridge stressed the essential cruelty of nature/sex. As opposed to female 'nature', male art is a heroic, unending and ultimately doomed (nature always wins) attempt to impose Apollonian control on what cannot be controlled. This premise leads to genuine insights. But if ever a book needed a rational Apollonian check on its chthonic energies, it is this one.

From the very first chapter, the reader's credulity is strained by sweeping assertions about sexual determinism that range from the risible to the irresponsible. For instance: 'This is one reason why, in America, so many gay men are reed-thin, while so many gay women are fat. When women stop trying to please the harsh male eye, the female body just drifts back to oceanic nature.' 'Visionary idealism is a male art form', thus 'the lesbian aesthete does not exist': 'as a group in America, lesbians seem more interested in softball than in art and artifice'. The double standard governing heterosexual relationships is intellectually as well as biologically based: whereas promiscuity in men may 'sharpen thought', the 'promiscuous woman is incapable of clear ideas'. Contrariwise, however, the more a 'woman thinks with Apollonian clarity, the more she participates in the historical negation of her sex'. A female who excels in mathematics does so 'in a system devised by men for the mastery of nature'; likewise, a 'contemporary woman clapping on a hard hat merely enters a conceptual system invented by men'. Men, not women, 'are anatomically designed to be projectors': 'construction is a sublime male poetry'. When Paglia crosses the George Washington Bridge, she thinks: '*men* have done this.' By contrast, 'if civilisation had been left in female hands we would still be living in grass huts'. The 'biologic' reason for this discrepancy is that women don't have to project either artistically or intellectually because their creativity is internally based.

In aetiological assertions no responsible clinician would

make, Paglia cites fringe-group homosexual experiments as signs of the 'cycle of excess that led to AIDS'. Freedom is the 'most overrated' of modern ideals, for 'whenever sexual freedom is sought or achieved, sado-masochism will not be far behind': 'Happy are the periods when marriage and religion are strong.' Isn't there as much historical evidence of sado-masochism in repressive religious orders and societies and family situations as in permissive ones?

The dubious generalisations that exhaust the reader's patience throughout the 671 pages of Volume 1 of ***Sexual Personae*** should have been deleted. Because they defy credulity, they constantly distract attention from the far more valid and often strikingly original insights in a book that might be twice as good, if it were half as long.

Harriett Hawkins, "Venus Genus," in The Listener, *Vol. 123, No. 3159, April 5, 1990, p. 30.*

Helen Vendler

Camille Paglia's ***Sexual Personae*** is an attempt (non-feminist) at telling the story of the androgyne from ancient Egypt to the *fin de siècle;* this book bears an enthusiastic comment from Harold Bloom, once Paglia's dissertation adviser at Yale. Paglia's tour takes us from Spenser's Belphoebe and Britomart to Wilde's Cecily and Gwendolyn, with stops along the way for various writers and painters, and many examples of the beautiful boy syndrome. Paglia's conception of the androgyne in history is broad enough to produce the present subtitle: *Art and Decadence from Nefertiti to Emily Dickinson.* This would be a joke if it were not seriously intended.

Paglia's book raises the question of what counts as evidence in literary argument. The value of evidence has been called into question by the assumption, shared by both Marxist and postmodernist critics, that values are masks for vested interests, and that "taste" and "judgment" are coercive elitist gestures. The asserted relativism of literary value, bolstered by well-worn examples of historically fallible critical taste (actually minor in comparison to the sustained historical agreement on the talent of canonical authors) relieves such critics from the burden of evidence. Their conclusions are simply naked claims for their own interests—made, in Paglia's case, for seven hundred pages. "My method," says Paglia, "is a form of sensationalism," and her argument is that "Judeo-Christianity never did defeat paganism, which still flourishes in art, eroticism, astrology, and pop culture" (on which a second volume is promised). Cruelty (as in Sade) is a running theme through the book: Paglia asserts the necessity of cruelty (an intensified form of Apollonian art-order) to hold back the "chthonian" forces embodied in Nature and "her" surrogate, woman.

When Paglia has a congenial subject, as she does in her chapter on *The Importance of Being Earnest,* she can be enlightening and entertaining, revealing [Oscar] Wilde's two impeccably poised heroines as the ultimate representations of personality subsumed entirely into form. But when the subject demands more than appreciation of images and (preferably violent) stories, Paglia fails. She rhapsodizes on the androgynous and impregnable female image (as in Spenser's "glamorous androgynes") but she is utterly indifferent to Spenser's verse. While Spenser is describing sex or rape, he has Paglia's rapt attention, but as soon as ideas enter the picture she yawns: "Belphoebe . . . is given to rather dull speeches. Eloquence belongs to evil characters. . . . " Paglia's emphasis on the theatrical, the visual, and the abstract lets her revel in the Marquis de Sade's most mechanical arrangements, like his rosary of sexually linked nuns. "A hundred nuns linked by dildos! The style of Busby Berkeley or the Radio City Rockettes," she exclaims, as Sade "organizes Dionysian experience into Apollonian patterns. . . . "

To Paglia, women writers remain "chthonic," earthbound, and swamp-like, unable to rise to such inventive Apollonian designs. She reaches the climax of her conceptual invention when she arrives at serial murder:

> Serial or sex murder, like fetishism, is a perversion of male intelligence. . . . It is the asocial equivalent of philosophy, mathematics, and music. There is no female Mozart because there is no female Jack the Ripper.

Paglia's impatience with the sentimentality of feminism blinds her to her own sentimentality toward the masculine, Jack the Ripper and all. Men have, she says, "concentration and projection," symbolized by their splendid capacity for projectile urination:

> Male urination really *is* a kind of accomplishment, an arc of transcendance [*sic*]. A woman merely waters the ground she stands on. . . . To piss is to criticize. John Wayne urinated on the shoes of a grouchy director in full view of cast and crew. This is one genre of self-expression women will never master. A male dog marking every bush on the block is a graffiti artist, leaving his rude signature with each lift of the leg. Women, like female dogs, are earthbound squatters.

The question begging of such a passage (What is transcendent about pissing? How is a dog an artist?) apparently does not bother Paglia; she goes on as if assertion were its own evidence. The most telling clue to Paglia's mind is her paragraph style: the sentences lack connection and syntactic subordination; they lie on the page like so many mutually repellent atoms, incapable of forming a molecular structure.

Northrop Frye once said that he didn't believe in any of the ways of dividing up literature under thematic titles—women's writing, gay writing, black writing, and so on. Literature makes its own verbal universe, and its fundamental organizing structures are not documentary, thematic, or ideological ones. The lifting of the documentary into the symbolic, of the thematic into the syntactic, is the task of art. Disregarding its most fundamental transformations does it poor service. Perhaps that is why books that round up literature behind thematic fences—religion, politics, women, sexual personae—are usually reductive of the genres they treat.

The skittish imagination mocks these attempts to bind it

down; language's fertile misrule mocks such feeble taxonomies. The imp of the perverse, the Muse of the unpredictable next line, laughs, of course, at us all. But while criticism tags her footsteps, it needs to follow her with at least some respect for accuracy and evidence and considered judgment. It needs to understand the reworking of (and disregard for) the documentary that is necessary to literature's symbolic intent. Criticism might also aim for concepts and language that do not violate the supple aims of imaginative work. More highly evolved feminist criticism may be on the way, but it will have to go beyond its current practitioners' innocence about how the imagination works, and what it does. (p.25)

Helen Vendler, "Feminism and Literature," in The New York Review of Books, *Vol. XXXVII, No. 9, May 31, 1990, pp. 19-25.*

Mark Edmundson

What would it mean to create an "erotics of art"? That, you may remember, is what Susan Sontag called for at the close of her famous 1964 essay "Against Interpretation." Most of that piece was given over to a polemic against the so-called depth analysis dominant in contemporary criticism. Sontag, whose own critical sensibility has always been rather remote, gave little indication then or later of what such an "erotics" would be like.

Enter, after more than twenty-five years, Camille Paglia. ***Sexual Personae*** is an erotic history of Western literature and visual art; written in a style both erotic and aggressive, it's the sort of criticism Sontag prophesied but didn't produce. Surely the time is right for such a book. Much academic criticism today is dominated by two interlocked and vulnerable assumptions: first, that human experience is largely determined by cultural forces; and second, that all cultural productions can be read as texts. These, to Paglia, are illusions, humanistic pieties. They deny the crucial role that nature plays in making us what we are, and compel us to encounter art—and life—in a falsely abstract way. For Paglia the best Western art, written works included, is compellingly visual, "eye intense." The current academic fixation on language (one can speak now of reading a painting, a film, a TV commercial, not just a book) is culture's attempt to domesticate the erotic and violent energies of art.

In ***Sexual Personae***'s stunning second chapter, Paglia locates the birth of Western visual culture not in Greece, as art historians conventionally have, but in Egypt. "The Egyptians invented *elegance,*" she writes. "Elegance is reduction, simplification, condensation. It is spare, stark, sleek. Elegance is cultivated abstraction." Egyptian high culture has been underestimated, Paglia goes on,

> because of the moralistic obsession with language that has dominated modern academic thought. Words are not the only measure of mental development. To believe that they are is a very Western or Judeo-Christian illusion. It stems from our invisible God, who talks creation into existence. . . . The most ancient conflict in Western culture, between Jew and Egyptian, continues today: Hebrew word-worship versus pagan imagism, the great unseen versus the glorified thing.

The Egyptian fixation on the image culminates in the glamorous, erotically charged world of the movies. To Paglia, all art worthy of the name aspires to the condition of cinema.

Is Paglia right? One test lies in her power to resuscitate art that has been shut up in the dry air of humanistic commentary. Here is H. W. Janson, one of the deans of contemporary art history, describing Donatello's bronze *David:*

> The Middle Ages would surely have condemned it as an idol. . . . Nudity, clearly, is his natural state, although he resembles a classical statue only in his beautifully poised contrapposto. Donatello has chosen to model an adolescent boy, not a full-grown youth like the athletes of Greece, so that the skeletal structure here is less fully enveloped in swelling muscles; nor does he articulate the boy's torso according to the classical pattern.

Note the effort to place the statue with reference to the Middle Ages, Greece, classical art. Janson doesn't see *David* as an object of intrinsic fascination; rather, he "reads" it as a sort of signifier in the text of art history. The work gets con*text*ualized. Whatever pleasure the piece might yield is quickly refined away by the academic discipline.

Might it not in fact be one of the social functions of historical criticism to discipline aesthetic pleasures? Do art history and literary criticism frequently strain to make us address in an exclusively rational way works aimed to incite our passion? Such questions don't usually turn up on the exam. Next slide, please.

Now Paglia on *David:*

> David's contrapposto is languorously Hellenistic. The hand on hip and cocked knee create an air of sexual solicitation. From the side, one is struck by the peachy buttocks, bony shoulderblades, and petulantly protruding boy-belly. The combination of child's physique with female body language is perverse and pederastic. . . . The David's shimmery, slithery bronze is a frozen wet dream.

For this, someone—though probably not H. W. Janson—might go a little out of his or her way to visit the museum.

Donatello's *David* is an image of the beautiful boy, one of the sexual personae Paglia identifies. These personae are erotic archetypes, figures that compel sexual fascination from all perceivers, whatever their professed erotic preferences. Paglia gets no little pleasure out of naming her personae: There's the male heroine (epitomized by Coleridge's ancient mariner); the vampire/*femme fatale* (Mona Lisa, Spenser's Duessa, Coleridge's Geraldine); the androgyne of manners (all of the "young lovers" in *The Importance of Being Earnest,* and naturally Wilde himself); the court hermaphrodite; the English epicene; the

Gorgon; the Great Mother; the android; the manufactured object; Mercurius; and the Pythoness.

The personae are art's proper material, the primary colors with which Western artists work. It's up to artists of every age to recast the personae to respond to (and create) fresh human desires. Thus, the classical period uses the androgyne as a symbol for the contriving mind. Later, "the Renaissance recasts the androgyne in alchemical terms to represent intuition and the spiritualization of matter. Romanticism uses [it] to symbolize imagination, the creative process, and poetry itself."

But what, exactly, are the sexual personae in themselves? They're culture's variations on nature's incessant biological themes. Paglia buys Freud's dictum that "anatomy is destiny" and believes that male and female identities are pretty much given by nature. The glory of art lies in its power to extemporize fictive identities—the personae—that swerve away from biology's literal insistence on what we are. To Paglia, strong personality, as it is manifest in both art and life, is the highest cultural achievement.

Sexual Personae is more than a random quest for charisma, though. Paglia also has a grand plot to unravel, a plot that reaches its climax in the contention between two visions of nature, what one might call the sublimely nurturing and the sadomasochistic. Until the Romantic period, Paglia believes, Western culture sustained a salutary fear of nature's destructive, chthonian powers. Through antiquity and into the Renaissance, art acknowledged and propitiated nature. With Rousseau and Wordsworth everything changed.

Both Romantics saw nature as unremittingly benevolent. To Paglia that means they repressed its darker side. "This repression, approaching depressiveness, accounts for Wordsworth's lack of appeal to young readers, who are drawn to energy, not to mention lust." Wordsworth never sees nature as it is, never throws off the weight of repression; but Coleridge, Wordsworth's collaborator and friend, captures, or is captured by, the chthonian. His "Christabel" teems with all the forces Wordsworth denied: lust, perversion, sadomasochism, vampirism. From Coleridge descends the decadent line in Western art: Paglia follows with chapters on, among others, Byron; Shelley and Keats; Balzac; Gautier, Baudelaire and Huysmans; Swinburne and Pater; and Wilde, all leading up to Dickinson, who is designated—worshipers of the virginal poetess be forewarned—Amherst's Madame de Sade.

On the subject of decadence, Paglia is at her best:

> Romantic imagination broke through all limits. Decadence, burdened by freedom, invents harsh new limits, psychosexual and artistic. . . . Art supplants nature. The objet d'art becomes the center of fetishistic connoisseurship. Person is transformed into beautiful thing, beyond the law. Decadence . . . is drenched in sex, but sex as thought rather than action.

The decadent sensibility, Paglia implies, is authentic in part because it refuses to idealize nature. It reworks and refines the forces that Wordsworthian nature-worship unleashed in the West. Decadence never loses sight of the fact that giving up to nature means unconditionally surrendering to the erotic and the destructive drives. To Paglia, as to the later Freud, sexual desire is always bound up with the desire to dominate or to submit. Decadence ritualizes, and thus subdues, erotic violence.

The style of ***Sexual Personae*** is, in its own terms, decadent. Paglia's prose is an Apollonian recasting of chthonian truths. It's witty, pointed, aphoristic, swift and usually attractively aware of its own status as hypercivilized artifice: her voice descends, in other words, from Wilde. Paglia's first objective is provocation: She's out to seduce or inspire. But if that doesn't work, she's also happy to provoke scorn, derision, envy or disgust—anything to unsettle the torpid high regard that those who participate in intellectual culture so often sustain for themselves and for their prized canon of great works. Paglia says her method "is a form of sensationalism."

"Sensationalism" may not be all that bad a method, particularly when you compare it with the others now thriving in the critical marketplace. The latest Lacanian revision of the post-Marxist critique of culture is likely to be both derivative and opaque, an anxious collaboration between Echo and the Sphinx, to steal an insult from Coleridge. Paglia, at her epigrammatic best, relays her pleasure in perception and discovery, relays her remarkable energy of mind. The book is a dramatic monologue; the overheard voice is funny, resourceful, wonderfully associative. If there are deserts in the book—I disliked almost all of her material on American writers, though that may be because my idealizations of some of them are unconquerable—there are also lush bowers and ornate pleasure domes: the chapters on Egypt, Apollo and Dionysus, Italian art, de Sade, Coleridge, Byron and Wilde are brilliant.

Yet it's also true that this book works as, in Saul Bellow's indispensable phrase, a "contrast gainer." It's a red comet in a smog-filled sky. Paglia is right, I think, to say that Western criticism has systematically repressed the visual and the erotic in favor of somber meditations on the Word. And she's right that critics have too often submerged their own personalities into a weary and wearisome corporate voice, the better to accrue some momentary cultural authority. ("Art," Paglia optimistically quotes Wilde, "springs from personality, so it is only to personality that it can be revealed.") But Paglia's contention that vision and nature matter almost exclusively is as reductive as the claim by contemporary critics that almost everything boils down to language and culture.

Paglia, in other words, has found a part of the story that no one is telling. It's a splendid and exhilarating find, and makes for a brilliant book. But if everyone followed the lead of Paglia's sex-and-vision thesis (which they won't), in twenty years it would be time for an exhilarating, brilliant book on how it all actually comes down to language and culture.

Part of the pleasure of reading Paglia is akin to the pleasure of watching sports: suddenly everything is reduced to the play of two passionate but opposed forces. Complexities exist, but within a context that is always clear and simple. So in Paglia it's Apollo versus Dionysus, the celestial against the chthonian, and so on. But art does have a conceptual and linguistic dimension—even a moral one—and an account that ignores those, though it may well carry splendid shock effect, is likely to lack staying power.

It is probably worth remembering that the critical focus on the text and insistence on the open-endedness of every interpretation grew in part out of a general horror among postwar intellectuals at the popular fixation on glamorous images that was so central to fascism. To interpret an image—to "read" it as a text—is one way to avoid being mesmerized by it. Surely, it's ludicrous to conceive of every cultural phenomenon exclusively as a text, as many literary intellectuals have come to do; but it's also opportunistic not to see the measure of integrity still alive in that view.

Does criticism need dramatic reductions like the ones Paglia and the textualists practice? Does it need to translate experience exclusively into "reading," in the exalted sense that Derrida and others have conferred on that term, or into Sontag's and Paglia's "erotics"? This kind of allegorizing tends to take place, I think, when critics become convinced that criticism is the central genre of the age, something like what the novel was to the Victorians and the crisis lyric to the Romantics. Critical mythmaking occurs, in other words, when critics believe they have to encompass—and encompass overtly—everything that matters. Whether criticism, or any living critic, is up to so exalted a task is, to say the least, an open question. (pp. 897-99)

Mark Edmundson, "Art and Eros," in The Nation, *New York, Vol. 250, No. 25, June 25, 1990, pp. 897-99.*

Terry Teachout

Camille Paglia, who clearly believes that big books should start with a big bang, makes the following pronouncements on the first page of ***Sexual Personae: Art and Decadence From Nefertiti to Emily Dickinson***: "***Sexual Personae*** seeks to demonstrate the unity and continuity of western culture." "The book accepts the canonical western tradition and rejects the modernist idea that culture has collapsed into meaningless fragments." "My stress on the truth in sexual stereotypes and on the biologic basis of sex differences is sure to cause controversy." "My method is a form of sensationalism."

That's quite a laundry list, even for a 700-page book. Still, Ms. Paglia manages to keep most of her promises. Ostensibly a critical study of the representation of human sexuality in Western art, ***Sexual Personae*** is also a scorched-earth attack on the underlying philosophical assumptions of liberalism and feminism. Such attacks are not taken lightly in the academy these days, and Ms. Paglia is doubtless being picketed at this very moment by a gang of irate undergraduates. But Ms. Paglia, an associate professor of humanities at Philadelphia College of the Performing Arts, is no conservative, either, and any canon-loving traditionalist who takes the trouble to read her book from cover to cover is more than likely to join the picket lines.

"[*Sexual Personae*] is all too clearly the work of a humorless, lapel-grabbing fanatic with a universal theory to hawk. Ms. Paglia's elaborate schema of sexual symbolism, impressive though it may sound in the telling, has led her to construct a bizarre anticanon of decadence in which earnest dullards like Charles Dickens and Henry James are shoved aside in favor of that old fraud, the Marquis de Sade."

—Terry Teachout

The argument of ***Sexual Personae*** runs roughly as follows: Nature is barbarous and violent, though people choose to pretend that it is benevolent rather than succumb to utter despair. Art can be either Apollonian, camouflaging the "dehumanizing brutality" of nature, or Dionysian, accepting and celebrating it. The Apollonian striving for order is central to the Judeo-Christian tradition, which is responsible for "western personality and western achievement." Western culture nonetheless contains a Dionysian dimension (Ms. Paglia prefers the term "chthonic") that liberal humanists prefer not to acknowledge. In art, the chthonic realities of nature are typically represented by sexual symbolism, which is usually violent and compulsive. "The amorality, aggression, sadism, voyeurism, and pornography in great art," Ms. Paglia argues, "have been ignored or glossed over by most academic critics." To this end, ***Sexual Personae*** serves as an illustrated catalogue of the pagan sexual symbolism that Ms. Paglia believes to be omnipresent in Western art; a sequel devoted to popular culture is in the works.

All of this may sound rather conventional, if not actually stodgy, but Ms. Paglia heats things up considerably by drawing a flashy assortment of extreme conclusions from her basic premises. Not only does she praise "the spectacular glory of male civilization," she flatly rejects Rousseau's vision of "benign Romantic nature" and its offspring, "the progressivist strain in nineteenth-century culture, for which social reform was the means to achieve paradise on earth." Feminism, she claims, is "heir to Rousseau" in that it "sees every hierarchy as repressive, a social fiction; every negative about woman is a male lie designed to keep her in her place. Feminism has exceeded its proper mission of seeking political equality for women and has ended by rejecting contingency, that is, human limitation by nature or fate. . . . If civilization had been left in female hands, we would still be living in grass huts."

Ms. Paglia's aggressive antiliberalism is deceptive, however. While she pays lip service to traditional Western values ("Happy are those periods when marriage and religion are strong." "The banning of pornography, rightly sought by Judeo-Christianity, would be a victory over the west's stubborn paganism"), her incessant assaults on liberalism and feminism are in fact profoundly anticonservative. Far from merely arguing for the significance of the chthonian dimension of Western art, Ms. Paglia positively wallows in it. A self-styled "advocate of aestheticism and Decadence," she seems to believe that decadent art is great precisely because it is decadent—that is, because it offers a truer vision of "the amorality of the instinctual life" and thus provides Apollonian civilization with a necessary catharsis for its chthonic fears and fantasies. "We may have to accept an ethical cleavage between imagination and reality," she says happily, "tolerating horrors, rapes, and mutilations in art that we would not tolerate in society."

The ability to infuriate both antagonists in an ideological struggle is often a sign of a first-rate book. ***Sexual Personae*** will undoubtedly antagonize the vast majority of its readers, and it contains patches of real brilliance, but Ms. Paglia is constantly tripping over her own pretentiousness. "My largest ambition," she says at the outset, "is to fuse Frazer with Freud." The pages of ***Sexual Personae*** are littered with equally prideful little packages of self-regard. ("Chaucer's comic persona resembles that of Charlie Chaplin's Little Tramp, whom I seem to be alone in loathing." "Unlike older scholars, some of us find *King Lear* boring and obvious, and we dread having to teach it to resentful students."

Ms. Paglia's esthetic judgment is as erratic as her self-esteem is healthy. Her standard gimmick, endlessly repeated, is the high-low cultural comparison: Lord Byron and the Beach Boys, Coleridge and Rod Serling, Sir Frederick Ashton's ballets and *The Avengers.* Some of these yokings are so ludicrous as to seem almost campy: "Patrick Dennis' *Auntie Mame* (1955) is the American *Alice in Wonderland* and in my view more interesting and important than any 'serious' novel after World War II." But there is nothing intentionally funny about ***Sexual Personae,*** which is all too clearly the work of a humorless, lapel-grabbing fanatic with a universal theory to hawk. Ms. Paglia's elaborate schema of sexual symbolism, impressive though it may sound in the telling, has led her to construct a bizarre anticanon of decadence in which earnest dullards like Charles Dickens and Henry James are shoved aside in favor of that old fraud, the Marquis de Sade.

Sade, to be sure, is not without his significance. Mario Praz and Edmund Wilson, to name only two critics of distinction, recognized and acknowledged his noxious influence on various key figures in the Romantic movement. But Ms. Paglia is not merely interested in Sade—she admires him. She is, in fact, the latest of the Sade cultists who have been haunting the fringes of serious literary criticism for decades. Like the rest of her fellow Sadeans, she complains that her idol is underrated and ignored, "the most unread major writer in western literature. . . . No education in the western tradition is complete without Sade." Comparison with Sade, not surprisingly, is the ultimate superlative in her critical vocabulary: "William Blake is the British Sade, as Emily Dickinson is the American Sade."

After reading ***Sexual Personae,*** one rather expects Camille Paglia to turn up, whip in hand, as a character in David Lodge's next novel, locking horns with Morris Zapp at a Modern Language Association convention. Ms. Paglia is quite real, though, and she is also a conspicuously gifted writer. She is an exciting (if purple) stylist and an admirably close reader with a hard core of common sense. For all its flaws, her first book is every bit as intellectually stimulating as it is exasperating. But ***Sexual Personae*** is tainted with the kind of symbol-mongering reductionism that sees one thing in everything, and despite its considerable virtues, it left me thinking of Earl Long's pithy appraisal of Henry Luce and his notoriously single-minded magazines: "Mr. Luce is like a man that owns a shoe store and buys all the shoes to fit himself. Then he expects other people to buy them."

Terry Teachout, "Siding with the Men," in The New York Times Book Review, *July 22, 1990, p. 7.*

Anne Williams

[The jacket of ***Sexual Personae***] features a dramatic and troubling photograph of a hybrid face—half Nefertiti, half Emily Dickinson. Seldom does a cover so aptly signal what lies within—bizarre juxtapositions, startling insights, and a bright, sometimes lurid critical vision. (Dickinson is characterized in the last chapter as "Amherst's Madame de Sade.") Camille Paglia's aim in ***Sexual Personae*** is "to fuse Frazer with Freud," to "demonstrate the unity and continuity of western culture—something that has inspired little belief since the period before World War I."

Paglia argues that the continuity of Western art can be traced in the "sexual personae" evident from ancient Egypt, which saw the birth of the "western eye," through nineteenth-century America. (A second volume will explore the twentieth century, including rock music and film.) These personae or "masks" include such characters as the Amazon, the beautiful boy, the Gorgon, the Great Mother, the lesbian, the male heroine, the vampire, the virago, and others. They appear throughout the Western tradition—in Ovid and Donatello, Spenser and Shakespeare, Leonardo, Blake, Balzac, Gautier, Baudelaire, Huysmans, Coleridge. Like the Western canon Paglia's list is dominated by men; the only two women discussed at length, Emily Brontë and Dickinson, apparently gain admittance by their capacity for "male" cruelty. Thus *Wuthering Heights* is "a catalog of chthonian horrors," and Dickinson "in her hidden inner life . . . was a male genius and visionary sadist."

What is the source of these personae? Paglia, believing Sade was right and Rousseau was wrong, argues that "Sex and nature are brutal pagan forces" and that civilization is an illusion we create to disguise "our humiliating passivity to nature." As a response to nature's cruel violence, art at its best is necessarily violent and cruel: "Nature is waiting at society's gates to dissolve us in her chthonian bosom. Out with stereotypes, feminism proclaims. But stereotypes are the west's stunning sexual personae, the vehicles of art's assault against nature."

Paglia's interpretation of the sexual personae is based on her uncritical acceptance of dualism: mind and nature, male and female, are essentially different, hostile, and irreconcilable. She believes in "the truth in sexual stereotypes and the biologic basis of sex differences." In the first chapter ("Sex and Violence, or Nature and Art") Paglia argues that nature is horrible, and sex is inherently "daemonic" and ghost-ridden as a consequence of the family romance. Further, sex is sadistic and intrinsically concerned with dominance. According to ***Sexual Personae,*** men are transcendent, women fundamentally identified with nature: "Nature's cycles are woman's cycles. . . . She does not have to become but only to be." Paglia reasons that since the human fetus "becomes female unless it is steeped in male hormone," biology itself bestows male transcendence. The male imagination creates culture in order to escape the terrible power of the Mother (whether "Mother Nature" or the woman who gave him birth), and it follows that the array of Terrible Mothers, Fatal Women, and female vampires in Western art are "real," "authentic," and "true" manifestations of the "nature" of woman.

Paglia quite rightly points out that violence, perversity, and voyeurism pervade high culture; Spenser is as gory as Stephen King, though the poet's academic critics seldom ponder this affinity. In this respect, ***Sexual Personae*** explores a topic that others have, if not quite repressed, at least avoided. Yet Paglia's assumptions about sexual difference are precisely those patriarchal fantasies that Simone de Beauvoir exposed over forty years ago in *The Second Sex.* And like Freud, a profound influence on this book, Paglia equates cultural constructs with universal principles of human nature.

Camille Paglia has quite deliberately written an antifeminist book, one regarding contemporary feminism as a deluded inheritor of Rousseau's unrealistic ideas. (For instance, "Modern feminism's most naive formulation is its assertion that rape is a crime of violence but not of sex. . . . ") In her opening chapter, I counted eighteen generalizations about feminist positions on topics ranging from prehistory to rape, so I am especially troubled to note that the book contains no evidence Paglia has read what contemporary feminists have said about nature and culture, the "Western eye," art and violence—indeed, about our culture's "sexual personae." Some of the most compelling feminist arguments of recent years have challenged the old premises upon which Paglia founds her argument. For instance, in *Speculum of the Other Woman* (1974) Luce Irigaray analyzes "the Western eye"—and focuses on its blind spots. Dorothy Dinnerstein's *The Mermaid and the Minotaur: Sexual Arrangements and Human Malaise* (1976) examines other "sexual personae" from a feminist viewpoint. Paglia might have considered Julia Kristeva's thesis in *Powers of Horror* (1980) that such powers are rooted in pre-Oedipal separation from the mother, and thus makes dubious the assumption that "horror" is self-evidently manifest in nature's processes. In *Pornography and Silence: Culture's Revenge Against Nature* (1981) Susan Griffin challenges the assumption, crucial to Paglia's argument, that cruelty and violence are a necessary concommitant of great art. And Nancy Chodorow's influential book, *The Reproduction of Mothering* (1978), contends that those qualities Paglia associates with the "transcendent" male imagination actually spring from the conditions of patriarchal culture: the son defines himself in his difference from the mother and all that the culture considers feminine, including "nature" itself and psychological capacities such as empathy.

Paglia has silently assented to the common belief that the male point of view is *the* point of view. (Significantly, she tends to dismiss those writers, such as Wordsworth, who propose that human beings may live in harmony with nature.) Paglia has given us a compelling discussion of *patriarchy's* sexual personae, but in her ambitious catalogue of violence and cruelty, she has unintentionally provided feminists with further evidence of their belief that the chief continuity in Western culture is a fundamental, virulent misogyny. (pp. 528-30)

Anne Williams, in a review of "Sexual Personae: Art and Decadence from Nefertiti to Emily Dickinson," in The Georgia Review, *Vol. XLIV, No. 3, Fall, 1990, pp. 528-30.*

Francesca Stanfill

Sexual Personae: Art and Decadence From Nefertiti to Emily Dickinson was published by Yale University Press in February 1990 and has sparked violent reaction ever since. Surging with startling ideas, the book—like its author—is essentially without a niche, which may explain why Paglia has been called everything from a "feminist academic prankster" to an "idea machine reminiscent of Marshall McLuhan." Widely disdained in academia, the book has been championed by many in the literary Establishment, some of whom have seized on it as a powerful if idiosyncratic weapon against modish thinking. Some also construe the success of ***Sexual Personae,*** now in its third printing, as the sign of a burgeoning backlash against academic feminism and what Paglia, in her warrior way, has called the "neo-Fascism of the left."

"[*Sexual Personae*] is provocative, it is stimulating, it is brilliant, it is original, and it compels one to rethink the entire question of the literary representation of human sexuality. . . . Camille will never be politically correct, and they will blackball her everywhere. Eventually, she will have the strength on the basis of her writings to win. But she's going to have a hard time making her way."

—Harold Bloom

Sexual Personae also constitutes a personal triumph for its author. Although Paglia had once despaired of ever being published, she has succeeded in trumpeting her message from a relatively obscure outpost: Philadelphia's University of the Arts, a college for dancers, actors, and visual artists—virtual academic exile to Ivy League elitists. An associate professor of the humanities, Paglia has become, within the past year, the school's most notorious faculty member.

Says literary agent Lynn Nesbit, who does not represent Paglia, "Her message is often controversial, and there's no question she enjoys being an agent provocateur. But what she does is to restore to women their unique power and vibrant potency." "A fine, disturbing book," Anthony Burgess has written. "Each sentence jabs like a needle."

Unlike most scholarly books, ***Sexual Personae*** has also succeeded in crossing the moat from an otherwise politically correct academia to the roiling landscape of the real world. It was nominated for a National Book Critics Circle award. Paperback rights have been bought by Vintage for a rumored $65,000 (an unusually high amount for a university-press book). In addition, it has been optioned for television by producers Kenneth Atchity and Daphna Edwards, who hope to make Paglia a demonic female alternative to the late Joseph Campbell—whose "Pollyannaish" approach Paglia herself "despises."

The controversy over ***Sexual Personae*** has been intensified by Paglia's increasing visibility as a fearless assailant of the feminist-academic orthodoxy. In December, her essay on Madonna-as-real-feminist appeared in the New York *Times* ("Madonna the producer may have chosen the chain, but Madonna the sexual persona is alternately the cross-dressing dominatrix and a slave of male desire"). In January, *Newsday* published Paglia's piece on date rape, in which she attacked feminists for what she sees as their limited and puritanical view of sexual violence ("Women will always be in sexual danger"). The March issue of *Harper's* features her lively discussion on pop culture and television with New York University's Neil Postman [see Further Reading]. (pp. 22, 24)

These assaults—with their colorful, accessible language—partly explain Paglia's impact on the extra-academic world. Yet Paglia's articles are relatively minor sensations compared with ***Sexual Personae*** itself, with its 673 axiom-packed pages and wildly eclectic index (Hermione Gingold, for example, is sandwiched between André Gide and Giorgione). In style, genre, and ideology, the book blasts every trend.

It celebrates the exemplars of high Western culture at a time when it is fashionable to denigrate them. It extols the literary canon—"the great books"—at a moment when this "elitist" concept is being questioned by the deconstructionist-mobbed Academy. It dwells on the personality of the artist when today's critics have dismissed this as irrelevant. Even its epic form and sweeping, impasto brush strokes are considered anachronistic at a time when literary criticism tends toward fashionable petit point. (A paper at a recent Modern Language Association convention was entitled "The Pea That Duty Locks: Clitoral Imagery and Masturbation in Emily Dickinson.")

Above all, Paglia's conclusions about the eternal cruelty of sexual warfare and how this has influenced male domination of art—these alone have made her the prime target of the entrenched feminist orthodoxy.

The pagliaization of western culture is strong stuff. (One British reviewer said reading ***Sexual Personae*** was "a bit like being mugged.") Within the turbulent continuum of history, Paglia investigates the unresolvable struggle between two opposing forces: the rational and the primal, the Apollonian will-to-order and the chthonic urge to chaos, the latter associated with nature and its "blind grinding of subterranean force," its "dehumanizing brutality of biology and geology."

Paglia's view of "chthonic" nature—with its "ugliness," its squalor, and its random brutality—collides with the legacy of Rousseau (which sees nature as benign and society as the corrupter). Sex, as a denizen of nature, is the beast in the jungle: irrational, amoral, violent, and wounding.

Men, according to Paglia, must fight against nature to construct what she so admires: Western civilization, with its art and literature, its cult of personality, its elaborate masks of sexual personae. Men must also fight against nature's earthbound representative: woman herself, with her mysterious, dual nature. From the moment men are wrested from the womb, claims Paglia, they are propelled by a love-hate ambivalence toward the mother who bore them. And it is this fear of woman's frightening procreative force that fuels men's will-to-power and their aggressive urge to make art.

No wonder, then, that most feminists view Paglia derisively—as a politically incorrect Athena sprung full-blown from the head of Bloom. They shudder at her statements. "Male fear of woman's self-containment is written all over mythology and culture," she writes, setting forth the core of her theory. (Note the use of "fear," not "oppression.") "Let us abandon the pretense of sexual sameness and admit the terrible duality of gender." "There is no female Mozart because there is no female Jack the Ripper."

Feminists, however, are not Paglia's only detractors. Others argue that the book's "sensational" quality, much praised by Bloom, is precisely its great weakness—that its lurid emphasis oversexes Western culture and that its "bizarre" comparisons exemplify a particularly distasteful form of literary exhibitionism. (In the Marquis de Sade chapter, for instance, Paglia comments on a randy Bolognese convent: "A hundred nuns linked by dildos! The style of Busby Berkeley or the Radio City Rockettes.") Says Roger Kimball of the neoconservative *New Criterion,* "One cannot help applauding Paglia for her energy, her perverse originality, and above all her choice of enemies. Unfortunately, her extreme dualism leads her to a revulsion of sexuality—and indeed of nature itself—that is as distorted in its own way as the wimpish liberalism of her enemies."

"Camille has a long way to go before she can become the pariah of her profession in her own generation," Harold Bloom says. "But she has made an excellent start. I am not yet ready to pass on the banner to her, but she looks to me like the best candidate around for that inevitable moment when the aged Bloom must totter off the mountain and cast the mantle of Elijah on the next person.

"Let me tell you a story, my dear," Bloom continued.

"Mr. Henry Schwab [of the Bookhaven bookstore in New Haven] told me that a week after ***Sexual Personae*** was published, two young ladies—one a faculty member, the other a graduate student—who had purchased it and begun to read it were so deeply offended that they came back, gave the book to him, said it was ideologically unacceptable, and demanded their money back, which he cheerfully refunded."

If Paglia's ideology were not jolting enough for what art critic Robert Hughes calls "*bien pensant* feminists," there is her baroque style, with its unrelenting epigrams and volcanic tide of digressions. "Paglia is also the supreme master of the subordinate clause," says Jenijoy LaBelle, a professor of literature at the California Institute of Technology, who wryly goes on to quote from Paglia's lengthy chapter on the Marquis de Sade: " 'Sodomized as she rapes her mother, the ingénue Eugénie cheerfully cries. . . . ' Who could not finish such a sentence?"

Intrinsic to this style is also a pulsating "Nelly-I-*am*-Heathcliff" fervor that some consider more appropriate to *Wuthering Heights* than to scholarship. ("I believe I understand this with every atavistic fiber of my being," she writes while discussing the "darkly archaic" Italian imagination.) It is this passionate quality that lends ***Sexual Personae*** the cast of an autobiographical, belletristic novel. Coupled with the omnisexuality gurgling through its pages, this fever prompts the reader to wonder not only who Paglia is but *what* she is, and how she evolved her own complex, sharp-edged persona.

These are the tartlettes—the whores of Babylon," she says, indicating the poster from the movie *Scandal* on one wall of her Philadelphia campus office. It features the actresses who portray Christine Keeler and Mandy Rice-Davies, posing buttock-to-buttock in strapless, skintight lace. I mention having seen the movie about the Profumo affair, though not the unrated version.

"Too bad," she says briskly. "It was very erotic." She goes on to announce that she is pro-pornography and pro-prostitution ("artisans and skilled laborers," she calls prostitutes). "I hate it when they drag prostitutes on to the talk shows and have them go on endlessly about how they've been abused by their johns." A pause, exquisitely timed, before the requisite punch line: "In any profession, you can find people who are unhappy."

Amused by her opening lines and equally aware that she is sizing up the audience, I am also struck by her gait: a swagger edged by a slight awkwardness, like that of an adolescent not fully at home in her body.

We move to the back of the fluorescent-lit office, which is divided into four cubicles, all crammed with books. The last, with its posters of Madonna and Maria Callas, is Paglia's. After commenting on the unruffled desk, I learn that she mostly works out of her rented attic apartment in the suburban town of Swarthmore. "A lair of one's own," she calls it (and she subsequently refuses to let me—or anyone else, apparently—visit it).

We continue to talk—Paglia at characteristic lightning speed—as I scrutinize her face and her outfit. Fair game, I think, as she herself has said, "Physical appearance is not trivial." She is small and not uncurvaceous, with a memorable head: high cheekbones, a hint of the Etruscan about the eyes and mouth, and long, pearly teeth. Her clothes are studiously sedate—a pale-gray turtleneck with matching skirt and pumps—as if to offset the stream of verbal coloratura. (pp. 24-5)

I inquire about the childhood that produced this little girl with a "pornographic mind," as she herself had put it.

At first glance, her Italian-American background seems surprisingly conventional. Her mother, Lydia, was born in Ceccano, south of Rome, and immigrated to the United States as a child. Her father, Pasquale, who died recently of cancer, was born in the U.S. of Italian parents. He was a professor of Romance languages at the Jesuit LeMoyne College, in Syracuse, New York, and is recalled by others as a commanding, cerebral paterfamilias who trained his daughter to defy convention.

Paglia was born upstate, in Endicott, in 1947, and was an only child until the age of fourteen, when her sister, Lenora, now an art conservator, was born. "I got my intellectuality, studiousness, and severity from my father," she tells me. "And I got my energy, optimism, and practicality from my mother. And from both I got the Italian capacity for hard work and the ancient Roman genius for organization."

But nothing in Paglia's life escapes her mythologizing tendencies. Her own childhood, with the "goddesslike figures" of her grandmothers, is no exception. "Part of the confidence of my personality came from the fact that I had the undivided attention of my grandmothers. My mother stayed home for a few years and then went to work. But I didn't have a day-care center—I had my grandmothers, in their homes. And we never talked, never—never, never, never conversation. Everything was, like, *'Mange!,'* *'Dorme!,'* or 'Get up!'—like that. Their pace was not this frenetic pace of the modern career woman. It was mythological time." (pp. 25-6)

From this silent, slow-motion chrysalis, then, evolved this frenetically verbal creature with an omnivorous eye for the physical world and for art. She tells how her father returned from a trip to Paris with a book about the art treasures of the Louvre.

"I'm five at this point, right? So I remember leafing through these pictures—like *The Sabine Women,* where Romulus is standing there totally nude. He has this shield and then the scabbard covering his genitals. And the women are all exposing their breasts. Here I'm like this tiny child, and thinking, What's all this nudity thing? Meanwhile, my parents are telling me, 'Cover up' and 'Don't do this.' There are certain things they don't want to talk about, certain forms of behavior that are forbidden."

A similar message lurked among the "erotic" icons and rituals of the Roman Catholic Church, those "pagan" elements that would eventually make their way into ***Sexual Personae*** (elements she sees everywhere in the work of her "kindred spirit" Madonna).

Among Paglia's favorites were the polychrome statue of Saint Sebastian dripping with blood and "voluptuously pierced with arrows" and Saint Michael the Archangel, with his sword and shield, "trampling the dragon." "That, to me, is one of the first things I identified with," she says, "the angel and the demonic. I don't identify with humans."

Nor did she identify with the playthings of most little girls in the fifties. She rejected dolls for swords and preferred knights in armor to princesses. Her choice of Halloween costumes was anything but suburban: the toreador from *Carmen* (age six), a Roman soldier (seven), Napoleon (eight), and Hamlet (nine). (p. 26)

At puberty, she explains, she seemed to "erupt" with a vengeance into "this rowdy personality," as she calls it, thrashing against the constraints of her gender. She began the quest for the independent-thinking female mentor—Amelia Earhart, for one, whose life she researched with such fanatic zeal that the local newspaper wrote about it. "Camille always had the most interesting obsessions," says Helen Vermeychuk, her best friend. (Paglia also had a collection of 599 photographs of Elizabeth Taylor.) Then, at age sixteen, came Simone de Beauvoir and the stupefying impact of *The Second Sex.* "One of the most learned women who ever lived," says Paglia of Jean-Paul Sartre's companion, "the last major thinker in sex. Her work is at such a high level that you do not need all these other minor [feminist] figures."

At the State University of New York at Binghamton, Paglia continued her intense confrontation with life—in her studies and in her personal life. "She was strongly controversial, unbelievably plucky, even at college," says her childhood friend and college classmate Bruce Benderson, who remembers Paglia looking "Napoleonic" in mannish jackets, hip-huggers, and boots. He also recalls Paglia bashing in the face of a drunken stranger who had pawed her female companion one evening, as he does her withering remarks to "whining, needy" women.

After college, Paglia pursued her graduate studies in English at Yale, a period notable for both the beginning of the dissertation (supervised by Harold Bloom) that would evolve into ***Sexual Personae*** and the beginning of her disenchantment with the late-sixties women's movement.

"From the moment the feminist movement was born, it descended into dogma," she says in her fiercest voice. "They stifled any kind of debate, any kind of dissent. Okay, it's Yale, it's New Haven in '69, I am a rock fanatic, okay. . . . So I was talking about taste to these female rock musicians, and I said the Rolling Stones were the greatest rock band and that just set them off. They said, 'The Rolling Stones are sexist, and it's bad music because it's sexist.' I said, 'But wait a minute. You can't make judgments about art on the basis of whether it fits into some dogma.' And now they're yelling, screaming, saying that nothing that demeans women can be art.

"You see, right from the start it was impossible for me to be taken into the feminist movement, okay? The only art they will permit is art that gives a positive image of women. I said, 'That's like the Soviet Union; that is the demagogic, propagandistic view of art.' "

Interrupting her—as I am frequently forced to do—I ask what she thinks of Arianna Stassinopoulos Huffington's recent biography of Picasso, which suggested that he was less than a great artist because his degrading attitude toward women was reflected in his painting.

"Absolutely *ridiculous,*" she scoffs. "My attitude is, I don't care whether Picasso put out cigarettes on people's arms. My attitude is that if Picasso took a machine gun and cut down a line of grandmothers, okay, it would not affect my opinion of his art. My theory of the artist, anyway, is that he is hostile and aggressive, so his attitude toward women is actually directly related to the art. Because part of my theory, okay, is that the artist is swerving from women's power and dominance." (pp. 26-7)

[She] begins to hurl through her years of teaching at Bennington College (1972 to 1980), a period she describes as "a series of psychodramas, all grand opera and El Greco storm clouds. My Amazon-feminist period. But we parted amicably."

There she acquired a reputation for headlong confrontations: with the dean over a college newsletter (which published announcements that she found discriminated against "the sexually nonconforming") and with men whose behavior she felt was demeaning to women. Despite these frequent contretemps, she is recalled fondly by former Bennington colleagues and her students, many of whom consider Paglia an emboldening influence, if a sometimes exhausting friend.

This was the crucible period during which she tested the limits of liberal sixties ideals, exercised her own "talent for chaos," and realized that she would find no female mentor among the intellectual Establishment. She recalls with a mixture of humor and bitterness her profoundly disillusioning meeting with Susan Sontag in 1973: "I was stunned because I thought she was going to be this major intellectual."

In one famous incident, Paglia set out to wreak revenge on a male student who had insulted her. "I called up Gail Parker [the young president of Bennington at the time]," she recalls, "and I said, 'I'm going to kick him in the ass.' And she said, 'Yeah, you're right, he should be kicked in the ass.' Now, see, as a Wasp, she thought I was using a metaphor, okay." She shrugs. "As an Italian, when I say I'm going to kick someone in the ass, I *mean* kick them in the ass."

So Paglia did exactly that, creating one of the many furors that punctuated her Bennington career, which culminated in another imbroglio, a fistfight at a dance involving several female students—an episode she doesn't much want to elaborate on. "People get obsessed with me," she says obliquely. "They're madly attracted to me or they loathe me." It seems the appropriate moment to ask about her own sexual persona, or personae. I do so, noticing for the first time a slight hesitance amid the braggadocio, which I attribute to the concern of any good Italian-American girl with What Mama Will Think.

"My experience has been dual," she tells me slowly, dodging the question. "I've gone through various phases of sexual identity during my adult life." Then she comes forth with this worked-out statement: "I consider myself neither gay nor straight, neither male nor female, and neither human nor animal." Later, she will call with still another one-liner: "I'm all lit up, but my plug fits no human sockets."

"I used my militant-Amazon thing as a way to make men take me seriously," she continues, "for men not to relate to me purely sexually." She laughs slightly, referring to her own "voluptuous" body. "It's amazing," she says at once girlishly and cynically, "men's Pavlovian response to an overflowing bosom.

"Unlike other women, I don't *need* to be liked. But I do need to be respected intellectually. So there was a period when I did *not* date men, because of the power politics."

She returns with characteristic intensity to the post-Bennington period, when she also learned that "I have to conceal myself. I have to be in hiding. So since Bennington, that's what I've done." Then Paglia quotes James Joyce: " 'Silence, exile, cunning.' "

Indeed, exile followed—a year at Wesleyan, then back to Yale, where she continued to teach part-time. Having only an unpublished manuscript in hand and no specialty, she found the job market tough, if not impenetrable. "I believed that when you're looking for a candidate for a job, you want the best candidate, the strongest candidate. Right? *No!* That was one of my biggest illusions about life, okay. Colleges and universities do *not* want the strongest. They want a colleague who will fit into the already existing power structure."

(Eventually, in 1984, she responded to an advertisement for a post in the humanities department of what was then the Philadelphia College of the Performing Arts. She arrived for an interview and, according to faculty member Kent Christensen, impressed the department with her "wide range of interests" and her "dazzling" teaching skills. She has taught there since and is expected to receive tenure and become a full professor.)

In the meantime, ***Sexual Personae*** was rejected by seven New York publishers, an experience that left her scornful of the "trendy, amoral world of New York publishing." Burdened by research and clerical expenses, she went heavily into debt.

"I had assumed [the book] wasn't going to be published in my lifetime," she says convincingly. "When I was out of graduate school, in the seventies, I sought recognition and acclaim. Then, in the eighties, I began to understand who these [judgmental] people were; then I no longer wanted recognition from them. I knew how good my work was—I *knew* it, you see. The example of Emily Dickinson was extremely inspiring to me—she also tried to get published but couldn't. And I look at the example, over the last 200 years, of so many artists: Van Gogh, Melville, Poe. Because I study history, because I study the past, this inspires me. I have this ability to psych myself up.

"So in the last ten years, I assumed it would not be published, and I was preparing my revenge, my posthumous revenge." She sits up quite straight, almost primly, in the late-afternoon light of the restaurant. "I have this great ability to look at myself posthumously.

"I would triumph over all my contemporaries," she says simply, with a small archaic smile. "I said to myself, 'Okay, my ideas are too original for my own time.' That's not why I've written it, to receive awards, but because I have such an interest in history, in ideas. I can also see the future. I mean, my best sentences are written as if this is going to be the only thing left, *just one sentence.* Two thousand years from now, it's all that will be left. Someone will find this one sentence, and in that one sentence you should be able to re-create it all. It's very Italian."

It's very tombstone-oriented, I interject—very much in the vein of what nineteenth-century Swiss critic Jakob Burckhardt called *Italienische Volksgeist* ("spirit of the Italian people").

"It *is,*" she concurs. "It's like Dante. He puts all his enemies in hell, and then, as his final revenge, people study him when he's dead. Burckhardt says that Italians are very memorious. They remember things in gratitude, things done for them, and they remember insults."

Indeed, she does remember things in gratitude, such as veteran editor Ellen Graham's decision to buy ***Sexual Personae*** for Yale University Press in 1985. But in those intervening years, Paglia has also sharpened her revenge against the feminist academic Establishment, deriding its members for what she construes as the prism of oppression through which they view literature; for what she sees as their politically correct rigidity of thought; for their way of "blaming men for all female failures"; for their "mawkish, incompetent scholarship"; and for their "ignorance of history."

"Feminism from the start closed itself against free thought," she says. "My idea is that every human question remains open and needs constant discussion, constant introduction of new evidence. But young women today—the *boldest* young women—are being funneled into these feminist-theory courses where they're being forced to read this crap, okay. Tenth-rate crap by mediocre women. Because it's *contemporary.* Because it's politically correct. It's embarrassing, unreadable bullshit to anyone who is a conservatively trained, *rigorously* trained person.

"The thing now is that the world began in 1969—nothing is worth reading before 1969. And that's ridiculous," she continues. "The [literary] canon is simply the group of great books, and the dispute is whether education should remain focused on that. And so you've got the feminists and leftists saying, 'Throw out the great books. The books by Dead White European Males.' These people deny the idea of greatness. They say that greatness is something that's simply a conspiracy by white males to preserve European hegemony."

I ask her about Saul Bellow's famous remark—"Who is the Tolstoy of the Zulus? I'd be glad to read him"—which some consider racist. She answers, "For me, both the Zulus and Tolstoy are essential for basic education. It *is* true, however, that the Western genres of novel and tragedy are supreme constructions, without parallel in world culture. In my book, I try to explain this by saying that all the psychological ambiguities and tensions of Western culture lead to very complex artworks and very complex novels.

"So right now you have people who are saying, 'Well, let's find' "—she mimics a goody-goody intonation—" 'a work by a woman, a work by a black, a work by a Chinese person, a work by a Native American, okay, and that will be education. Because anything else—Plato, Montaigne, and Nietzsche—oh, these are Dead White European Males.' " She reassumes her savage tone. "This is stupid. This is *ridiculous.*"

"See, I believe in greatness," she says in her most fervent voice, leaning forward. "I *seek* it. I admire it. In my upcoming *Arion* piece, I address the graduate students. I appeal to them to turn away from this crap. I say, 'You become greater by a humility toward great things.' " (pp. 27-8)

"Women *know* they're women, because they have their period," Paglia says. "They don't have to *prove* they're women. But for a boy to become a man, other men must say that you're a man. So you have to do something to prove your manhood, which often involves cruelty toward women or violence toward women. And that's what women have to wake up to, that women will never be able to protect themselves against rape, for instance, until they wake up to what's going on with male identity, okay. Until they understand the anxiety of male identity."

In this way, she says, feminism has misled, even deluded, women by saying women can "do anything, wear anything, go anywhere." Her contention is that they simply cannot—that women's power to incite men sexually is simply too potent, and that the rituals of courtship (does "no" *always* mean "no"?) are and always will be dangerously loaded with ambiguity.

"It's a state of delusion, this liberal education women are getting. They're receiving a sanitized, censored view of human psychology and sexual relations. I feel feminism is encouraging a kind of arrogant, reckless behavior."

But if women are so complex and exude such "cosmic" power, how does she explain those outrageous, even belittling statements in the book? (Among them: "If civilization had been left in female hands, we would still be living in grass huts.")

"Men are biologically impelled outward," she says, "to flee from woman. To make a world separate from woman. That is the basis of civilization. And it is male compensation, in a way, too, for his lack of innate biological creativity in his body. Even if women don't have children—as I don't—they know they have the *ability* to produce them.

"Women are content with things as they are. Women lack the violent aggression to change, to revolutionize. They don't like causing pain. They are happy when the people around them are happy; otherwise, they are emotionally parched. To be revolutionary, you have to be willing to destroy. And this is the explanation why there are no great female artists. Because every great artist must be willing to kill the father. Women have always followed in the tradition created by others. They've done great with it—Jane Austen, the Brontës, and so on. But very rarely do you have an Emily Brontë doing something new within the novel form.

"To advance civilization means causing the destruction of nature—men chop all the trees down, they get the metals out of the ground, they forge them. Men are impelled from the hearthfire, away from woman—'Get away from her, for Christ's sake. Get away from the suffocating emotionalism of women.'

"Everything here—every single damn thing here, okay, from the silverware to the network that has brought the food to the table—this whole thing is a creation of men. And the feminists are really deluded, with their heads up their ass, if they don't know this." She lapses into her singsongy, nature-is-benevolent Rousseauist voice. "They say, 'Ooh, patriarchal culture, so oppressive' "—then, sharply, "What the hell do they see as an alternative?

"The feminists are stuck on the idea that we are being victimized, right? In fact, male energy has been used by women for everything. Women are repressing, women are blocking, the nature of their indebtedness to men. I feel very free as a modern woman, but I began to understand, to my horror, that my freedom was purchased at the price of male labor. Men have created the world that allows me to be free and allows me to write this book. I think strong women can admit the strength of men. It's only weak women who deny it."

She continues to rail against the "resentful, whining" strain of mainstream feminism. "I identify with the prewar feminists," she says. "I want to bring back the prewar feminism that stresses self-reliance—not blaming other people for your problems."

She would also restore another element to American feminism—a "pagan" respect for beauty and pleasure, as opposed to "androgyny in action." "We have a very puritanical kind of feminism here that hates and fears beauty and pleasure," she claims. "They consider art the servant of political correctness. But for me, art and beauty are eternal and above politics. Of course, feminists are not interested in art, they have no eye. And that's one of the things that has made feminism collapse, see."

I ask about the current cult of physical fitness—so many "bulging" Venus of Willendorfs beating themselves into Apollonian tautness, to use a Pagliaism. "The body becomes this thing that *does* something," she says at once. "It's tense. Conscious and alert. There's nothing about it that's sensual or approachable. It's more of the new Puritanism. The body is now full of imperatives: 'Got to get down there to that aerobics class. Got to get those thighs looking trim.' This exercise fanaticism is typically American. The Europeans, the French, don't punish themselves like that."

The French, however, are responsible for exporting deconstructionism—which Paglia "loathes"—and her take on the literary theory is symbolized by her "despised trinity": Jacques Lacan, Jacques Derrida, and Michel Foucault. For the next few minutes, she does her amusing language-is-an-infinite-number-of-subjectivities deconstructionist skit. "This idea that *language* is the only thing that exists!" she cries. "This idea that there is no such thing as personality, no such thing as character. Now, this is just insane. I see how powerful personality is! It's ridiculous, the whole thing is insane, one of the stupidest scams ever in the history of academia. And these people who fell for it are ignorant fools, ignorant of dance, ignorant of the visual arts, ignorant of music. It's just folly, madness, and this is why college teaching in the Ivy League has gotten more and more full of b.s." (pp. 28-9)

Having survived Paglia's Blitzkrieg, including her own assessment of her significance (i.e., successor to Simone de Beauvoir and the great British scholar Jane Harrison), I found it interesting to hear how others view her. In the end, the spectrum of reactions—a churning sea of nearly merging opposites—eerily reflects Paglia's view of sexuality.

Some damn the book as "dangerous," others find it "brilliant," and still others respond with irony to the idiosyncratic voice and its despairing humor. "From the quotations I've read, [***Sexual Personae***] sounds like Myra Breckinridge on a roll," Gore Vidal told me. "I have no higher praise." A top editor at a New York publishing house, currently reading the polemical woman-as-cosmic-power chapters, told me half jokingly, "It's made me afraid of my wife."

Among other things, Paglia's detractors fault her grandiose, even "dotty" and "unsubstantiated," statements ("Mother Nature turns us all to eunuchs"). They refuse to take seriously a book that finds in male urination a symbolic "arc of transcendence." Says Leon Wieseltier, literary editor of *The New Republic,* "Her reduction of all things to sex is as ugly and as coarse as the erasure of sex that it sets out to criticize."

Most women in academia believe ***Sexual Personae*** out-Blooms Harold Bloom and is thus to be avoided. They see the book as weird, anachronistic, and irrelevant, somewhat like eye of newt. Harvard's Helen Vendler—who has characterized the book as "so many mutually repellent atoms, incapable of forming a molecular structure"—refused to comment.

Many feminists seem astonished that a book they have dismissed as "trivial" should be widely discussed beyond the ivory towers. "The strangeness of the book is such that I would not have expected it to be a subject of debate," remarks Sandra Gilbert, a professor of English at the University of California at Davis. "It has the quality [of the work] of an idiot savant."

Some feminists, however, say Paglia's findings are rooted in outmoded scholarship (Sir James Frazer, Freud, Darwin) and are totally ignorant of current feminist theories. "This is old, old stuff," said Riane Eisler, author of *The Chalice and the Blade.* "It's really fascinating how the system manages to inculcate women with a dominator ideology and then reinforces that ideology with various permutations of the same theme: that men are superior, that men are more creative than women."

What these critics find most dangerous are Paglia's conclusions about women and creativity—in particular, her view that genius is invincible. ("I am convinced that, even without restrictions, there still would have been no female Pascal, Milton, or Kant," she writes.) This theory is understandably abhorrent to feminists and, indeed, disturbing to any creative woman. "Women have only had access to secular education for a little over 100 years," says Eisler. "That is *nothing.* Nothing."

Other feminist thinkers point out that Paglia is railing against a monolithic feminism—an imaginary beast banished by current enlightened thinking. "It's such a completely shallow understanding of what feminism is," says the novelist Mary Gordon, who adds, "It certainly isn't the feminism I identify with."

Paglia's admirers in the literary and academic Establishment praise her for her verve, her incandescent self-reliance, and her daring—a surge of hemoglobin into the listless bloodstream of current literary criticism, which many see as rendered anemic by depressive, labyrinthine deconstructionist jargon. "She is a superb reader of literature," says Richard Poirier, a Rutgers English professor and the chairman of the Library of America. "She has a talent for tending to language—though her temperament drives her on occasion to excess." Robert Hughes finds the opening chapters of ***Sexual Personae*** "extraordinarily suggestive and very courageous. No one can say Paglia hasn't done her research." Others cite Paglia's formidable ability to articulate the impact of the visual, her unforgettable way of explicating things as disparate as Botticelli's *Primavera* and a cat (that "least Christian inhabitant of the average home").

Amid this cacophony, everyone agrees on one thing—that the book has a "Bloomian" quality. In the words of one scholar, "Camille is the perfect daughter to her iconoclastic mentor."

And what of the venerable Bloom, he of the biblical cadence, with its hint of lamentation? "Camille is in the grand old mode of great academic critics and professors," he says. "She is in her way a great formalist. She's very fierce. She's also fiercely loyal, as I am to her." Then, elegiacally: "Camille has a dark nature, and there is a lot of sorrow in it. I think she's more Freudian than she knows. I think for her, Eros and the death drive are dangerously allied."

I begin to ask about the politically correct feminism that Paglia associates with the Ivy League.

"The Ivy League? Why the Ivy League?" he asks, interrupting me, with an expression both weary and furious. "It is a many-headed hydra; its tentacles are everywhere. It's much hotter out in the boondocks than it is now in the Ivy League, where everybody's sick to death of it. It's very hot in Peoria." He signs. "How can you have dialogue with these people? My dear, they are totalitarians, they are sanctimonious, they are self-righteous. They are, in fact, truly illiterate people. They are *careerists.*

"I stick by what I said on the dust jacket," he says. "It's a remarkable book. It doesn't mean that I agree with everything in it. But that's not the point. It is provocative, it is stimulating, it is brilliant, it is original, and it compels one to rethink the entire question of the literary representation of human sexuality.

"Camille, in terms of the achievement of ***Sexual Personae,*** " he continues, "belongs at a place like Yale or Harvard or Princeton or Chicago or Berkeley. But they will not have her. One of the many, many signs of the incredible decadence of our academic institutions is that someone as brilliant, as learned, as talented, and as ferociously burning an intellect as Camille Paglia is much less likely to win conferment at one of our major universities than any of these humdrum bureaucrats of resentment who are appointed by others in the network because they are politically correct. Camille will never be politically correct, and they will blackball her everywhere. Eventually, she will have the strength on the basis of her writings to win. But she's going to have a hard time making her way."

I left Bloom's apartment that January afternoon, my head reeling with the Pandora's box of epithets—angel, demon, idiot, oracle—that had been applied to Paglia in the space of several weeks. I suddenly recalled one moment of our epic interview. . . . I had asked Paglia if she was ever lonely. "Lonely?" she had replied, looking almost shocked. "Like when I'm *alone?*" Yes, I had said. She was never lonely, she went on to insist, alluding to her great "self-love." Then came the one-liner: "There's Tristan and Iseult, Romeo and Juliet, me and me."

I asked her whether she identified with the only two women writers to whom she had devoted whole chapters: the solitary Emilys—Brontë and Dickinson—both gender-conflicted, living cloistral existences as they spun hallucinatory literature. "Amherst's Madame de Sade," she calls Dickinson in that last controversial chapter. Did she think of herself, then, as a suburban Madame de Sade? In response, Paglia merely smiled.

Or—having told me that she identified with the "monastic tradition"—did she think of herself as a nun? "A lecherous nun," she told me. "In my *mind.*"

Or is she, as Kenneth Atchity has suggested, an "intellectual Joan of Arc, willing to be burned at the stake"?

"An intellectual Joan of Arc, willing to burn *others* at the stake," came her swift rebuke. Then, with a look of chilling resoluteness: "No victim am I." (pp. 29-30)

Francesca Stanfill, "Woman Warrior: Sexual Philosopher Camille Paglia Jousts with the Politically Correct," in New York *Magazine, Vol. 24, No. 9, March 4, 1991, pp. 22, 24-30.*

FURTHER READING

Paglia, Camille A. "Oscar Wilde and the English Epicene." *Raritan* 4, No. 3 (Winter 1985): 85-109.

Study in which Paglia designates Oscar Wilde "the premiere documenter of a sexual persona which I call the Androgyne of Manners" and explores his influence on Lewis Carroll.

———. "Ninnies, Pedants, Tyrants and Other Academics." *The New York Times Book Review* (5 May 1991): 1, 29, 33.

Controversial essay in which Paglia attacks what she perceives to be "the dullness and ineptitude of . . . 20th century criticism."

Postman, Neil, and Paglia, Camille. "Dinner Conversation: She Wants Her TV! He Wants His Book!" *Harper's* 282, No. 1690 (March 1991): 44-51, 54-5.

Debate in which Paglia and Postman, a professor of communication arts at New York University, address the "argument that has vexed nearly everyone in this century—the struggle for preeminence between words and pictures, today between books and television."

Sagan, Dorion, and others. "Give Us a Break, Ms. Paglia." *The New York Times Book Review* (2 June 1991): 36.

Letters to the editors of the *New York Times Book Review* attacking and praising Paglia's essay "Ninnies, Pedants, Tyrants and Other Academics" (see above).

Dorothy Parker

1893-1967

(Born Dorothy Rothschild; also wrote under the pseudonym Constant Reader) American short story writer, poet, critic, playwright, and screenwriter.

During the 1920s and 1930s Parker was a literary celebrity whose often-quoted witticisms were as well known as her poetry and short fiction. Her verse, modeled on such traditional forms as the lyric, ballad, and sonnet, frequently addressed women's issues and the starkness of urban life through irony, paradox, and hyperbole. Her short stories examine the social mores of the middle-class, often through bitterly cynical portrayals of stagnant marriages and unhappy love affairs. Despite her flamboyant reputation, Parker regarded herself as a social satirist rather than a humorist and often wrote from a liberal sensibility alternating between outrage and sentimentality. She used her sardonic wit to attack hypocrisy and intolerance, and was sympathetic toward victims of sexual and racial oppression, once remarking: "[There] are things that never have been funny, and never will be. And I know that ridicule may be a shield, but it is not a weapon."

Parker grew up in New York City, the fourth child of a wealthy Jewish garment manufacturer and a Protestant woman who died shortly after her daughter's birth. Parker resented her father's authoritarian personality and disliked his second wife, also a Protestant, whom she regarded as a religious fanatic. Throughout her life Parker felt ashamed of her mixed ethnic and religious background and later stated that if she had written an autobiography she would have entitled it *Mongrel.* Her early schooling took place at the Blessed Sacrament Convent where, according to Parker, the nuns "taught me only that if you spit on a pencil eraser, it will erase ink." She was eventually expelled from the convent for describing the Immaculate Conception as "spontaneous combustion" and was sent by her parents to an exclusive finishing school. After graduation, Parker joined the staff of *Vogue* magazine as a copywriter in 1916. Her editor was impressed by her work and soon appointed her drama critic of the fashionable magazine *Vanity Fair.* Parker was eventually fired from this post—allegedly because of a sarcastic review of a play starring the wife of one of the magazine's financial backers—but went on to earn favorable recognition as the pseudonymous literary critic "Constant Reader," with her most notable commentary appearing in *The New Yorker*'s book review column. Although she was sometimes accused of judging authors and their intentions instead of the works themselves, Parker nonetheless garnered attention for her insistence on quality and excellence in literature: "It is the first job of a writer who demands rating among the great, or even among the good, to write well."

During the 1920s, Parker became well known in New York literary and theatrical societies as a member of the Algonquin Round Table, which also included writers Robert Benchley, Alexander Woollcott, Franklin Pierce Adams, and George S. Kaufman. This group met regularly at the Algonquin Hotel and became famous when newspaper columnists reported their activities and quoted their conversations. Parker earned notoriety as one of the most daring of the Round Table wits; some of her remarks, such as "Men seldom make passes / At girls who wear glasses," became catchphrases of the day. After winning acclaim for her poetry, Parker retired from magazine work to concentrate on writing verse, short fiction, screenplays, and dramas. She would later dismiss the Round Table phenomenon as pretentious and shallow: "[It] *was* the twenties and we had to be smarty. I *wanted* to be cute. That's the terrible thing. I should have had more sense."

Parker's first collection of poetry, *Enough Rope,* became a national best-seller shortly after its publication in 1926. Throughout the volume Parker explored the disappointment and loneliness of lost love and exposed the hypocrisy and sentimentality of romantic jargon. In "Unfortunate Coincidence," for example, Parker warns: "By the time you swear you're his, / Shivering and sighing, / And he vows his passion is / Infinite, undying—/ Lady, make a note of this: / One of you is lying." Parker's second volume of verse, *Sunset Gun,* also won widespread popular acclaim. In this collection Parker continued to chastise vows and false promises she associated with love, and experimented with traditional literary forms, including a cycle of epigrams known as "A Pig's Eye View of Literature." With *Death and Taxes,* Parker's verse became increasingly pessimistic and introspective; Franklin P. Adams called it "her saddest and her best book." This volume contains such sardonic poems as "The Flaw in Paganism," in which Parker urges people to "Drink and dance and laugh and lie, / Love, the reeling midnight through, / For tomorrow we shall die!", then dryly adds "(But, alas, we never do.)" By the time her collected poetry was published in 1936 under the title *Not So Deep as a Well,* Parker had turned almost exclusively to writing prose. Her uniquely candid explorations of the absurdity of human behavior have continually received attention regardless of the fact that Parker herself believed her verse to be "terribly dated." Alexander Woollcott maintained: "[I suspect] that another generation will not share the confusion into which Mrs. Parker's poetry throws so many of her contemporaries, who, seeing that much of it is witty, dismiss it patronizingly as 'light' verse, and do not see that some of it is thrilling poetry of a piercing and rueful beauty."

Parker's early short fiction frequently appeared in *The New Yorker,* marked by the precise, economical language and simple plot structures often associated with that magazine's style. Focusing on the emotional idiosyncrasies of anxious, narcissistic women in the midst of tragicomical crises, Parker demonstrated her belief that self-absorption hampers communication and leads to emotional isolation. Parker's first short story collection, *Laments for the Living,* comprised of thirteen narratives previously published in *The New Yorker* and other periodicals, was simultaneously praised for its satiric prose and sensitivity and faulted for its reliance on dialogue and recurrent themes. "Big Blonde," widely regarded as the most fully developed story of the collection, is an empathetic portrayal of Hazel Morse—a woman emotionally and economically dependent on men—who emerges as a legitimate tragic figure. Like many of the protagonists in *Laments for the Living,* the female characters in Parker's second volume, *After Such Pleasures,* are often socialites who attempt to hide their insecurities behind grandiloquent language and pompous behavior. Parker again sought to expose the superficiality of such individuals, but some commentators noted that with this collection Parker also began to demonstrate a deeper understanding of interpersonal relationships and human emotion. Parker's two volumes of collected stories, *Here Lies* and *The Viking Portable Dorothy Parker,* contain only eight previously unpublished works, including "Cousin Larry" and "The Lovely Leave." While reviewers continued to praise Parker's incisive humor, sense of pathos, and her more serious attempts at satire, most found her explorations of gender roles and romantic relationships the most significant and lasting facet of her short fiction.

Parker's personal life was punctuated by heavy drinking, depression, numerous love affairs, and attempted suicide. Parker's most enduring relationship was with her second husband, actor Alan Campbell, whom she married in 1933, divorced in 1947, and remarried in 1950. They lived in California for most of their married life and collaborated on sixteen filmscripts, their most notable effort being *A Star Is Born,* which was later nominated for an Academy Award. Despite her success, Parker disliked what she considered Hollywood superficiality and became increasingly involved with such political organizations as the American Screen Writers Guild and the Anti-Nazi League. Her association with these left-wing groups impelled the House Un-American Activities Committee (HUAC) to investigate her as a possible Communist subversive during the 1950s. She refused to cooperate with the investigation, but no charges were filed against her. During this time Parker also wrote two plays, *The Coast of Illyria* and *The Ladies of the Corridor,* the latter being an account of two embittered old women living in a disreputable hotel in mid-Manhattan. Although she called *The Ladies of the Corridor* "the only thing I have ever done in which I had great pride," neither it nor *The Coast of Illyria* were popular successes. Finding it increasingly difficult to write because of ill health, Parker only published an occasional book review during the 1960s. She died in 1967 and willed her entire estate to civil rights leader Dr. Martin Luther King, Jr.

Parker's literary reputation rests primarily on what W. Somerset Maugham called her "gift for seeing something to laugh at in the bitterest tragedies of the human animal," but in her later years she longed to be considered a serious and disciplined writer and believed that her reputation as a Algonquin Round Table wit prevented readers and critics from recognizing that her talents extended far beyond sarcastic repartee and whimsical quips. While her work has sometimes been described as melodramatic, sentimental, and trivial because of its acerbic humor, many critics have noted that Parker's complex use of irony and satire enabled her to explore the contradictory nature of human behavior. Marie Luhrs observed: "Parker has her own particular field of frank American humor. She is slangy, vulgar, candid, and withal subtle, delicate, and sparkling. The soul of wit distinguishes most of her pieces. . . . For all their pertness and bravado they mirror, in most cases, quite genuine and profound experiences."

(See also *CLC,* Vol. 15; *Short Story Criticism,* Vol. 2; *Contemporary Authors,* Vols. 17-20 rev. ed., Vols. 25-28 [obituary]; *Contemporary Authors Permanent Series,* Vol. 2; and *Dictionary of Literary Biography,* Vols. 11, 45, 86.)

PRINCIPAL WORKS

POETRY

Enough Rope 1926
Sunset Gun 1928
Death and Taxes 1931
Not So Deep as a Well 1936; also published as *The Collected Poetry of Dorothy Parker,* 1944

SHORT STORY COLLECTIONS

Laments for the Living 1930
After Such Pleasures 1933

Here Lies: Collected Stories 1939; published as *The Collected Stories of Dorothy Parker,* 1942
The Viking Portable Library Dorothy Parker 1944; published as *The Indispensable Dorothy Parker,* 1944; republished as *The Collected Dorothy Parker,* 1973; revised and enlarged as *The Portable Dorothy Parker, Revised and Enlarged Edition,* 1973

PLAYS

Chauve-Souris [Parker et al.] 1922
Close Harmony; or The Lady Next Door [with Elmer Rice] 1924
Round the Town 1924
Shoot the Works 1931
The Coast of Illyria [with Ross Evans] 1949
Ladies of the Corridor [with Arnaud d'Usseau] 1954

SCREENPLAYS

Here is My Heart 1934
Big Broadcast of 1936 1935
Hands Across the Table 1935
Mary Burns, Fugitive 1935
One Hour Late 1935
Paris in Spring 1935
Lady, Be Careful [with Alan Campbell and Harry Ruskin] 1936
The Moon's Over Our Home 1936
Suzy [with Alan Campbell, Horace Jackson, and Lenore Coffee] 1936
Three Married Men [with Alan Campbell] 1936
A Star is Born [with Alan Campbell and Robert Carson] 1937
Sweethearts [with Alan Campbell] 1938
Trade Winds [with Alan Campbell and Frank R. Adams] 1938
Weekend for Three [with Alan Campbell] 1941
Saboteur [with Peter Viertel and Joan Harrison] 1942
Smash Up: The Story of a Woman [with Frank Cavett] 1947
The Fan [with Walter Reisch and Ross Evans] 1949

CRITICISM

Constant Reader 1970; also published as *A Month of Sundays,* 1971

Edmund Wilson

Mrs. Dorothy Parker began her poetic career as a writer of humorous verse of the school of Franklin P. Adams. There are specimens of her early vein in [***Enough Rope***]: a comic roundel, a rondeau redoublé "(and scarcely worth the trouble, at that)" and a parody of some verses of Gilbert. Mrs. Parker's special invention (aside from her vers libre "hymns of hate," unrepresented here), was a kind of burlesque sentimental lyric which gave the effect, till you came to the end, of a typical magazine filler, perhaps a little more authentically felt and a little better written than the average: the last line, however, punctured the rest with incredible ferocity. Thus, to quote only a comparatively mild example included in this book, the old, old gate wreathed with lilacs where the lady waits with yearning in the gloaming turns out, at the end of the poem, to be "the gate her true love gave her."

Mrs. Parker has had scarcely a rival in the contrivance of these loaded cigars, these squirting boutonnières and these pigs-in-clover puzzles of literature; and she could have put together a most amusing book of them. Her present book is, however, quite different. During the last two or three years, Dorothy Parker—though still in the pages of *Life* and the *New Yorker*—has emerged as a distinguished and interesting poet. It is true that, in America just now, we do not lack distinguished woman poets: there are so many women who write creditable lyrics that we have come to take them more or less for granted and are no longer very much excited over the appearance of another promising apprentice of the school of Elinor Wylie or Edna Millay. But Mrs. Parker seems somehow to stand a little apart from this group. It is true that she sometimes echoes Mrs. Wylie and, more frequently, Miss Millay; yet, on the whole, her poems give the impression of differing from those of many of her sisters in being a good deal less "literary"—that is, they have the appearance of proceeding, not merely from the competent exercise of an attractive literary gift, but from a genuine necessity to write. We may be conscious that there are at least thirty women in the country who would have been incapable of spoiling an excellent epigram with such a final couplet as this,

> Inertia rides and riddles me;
> The which is called Philosophy

or who would never have commenced another as follows,

> Oh, both my shoes are shiny new
> And pristine is my hat

—we may be conscious, I say, that there are perhaps thirty expert poets who would have known why "pristine" and "the which" were impossible. But we feel, also, that a sound instinct for style has here merely been betrayed by the bad habits of humorous versifying. And, in a similar way, we are convinced that her addiction to the idiom of Miss Millay is less an evidence of imitative weakness than an accidental and probably passing phase, due to the fact that Mrs. Parker has only just begun to attempt serious poetry and that, of all the poets who are read just now, Miss Millay's temperament, in certain of its aspects, has most affinity with her own. It is on the side of bareness and sharpness that Mrs. Parker most resembles Miss Millay, but the edged and acrid style which emerges in her book is unmistakably individual.

And the personality which reveals itself in Mrs. Parker's poems is quite different from that of Miss Millay: Mrs. Parker has her own complex of emotions, her own philosophy of love. Take the sonnet of which the octet begins as follows,

> If you should sail for Trebizond, or die,
> Or cry another name in your first sleep,
> Or see me board a train, and fail to sigh,
> Appropriately, I'd clutch my breast and weep.

Here she has caught precisely the idiom of Edna Millay; yet Miss Millay would never have drawn the same moral:

> Therefore the mooning world is gratified,
> Quoting how prettily we sigh and swear;
> And you and I, correctly side by side,
> Shall live as lovers when our bones are bare;
> And though we lie forever enemies,
> Shall rank with Abélard and Héloïse.

This is not one of Mrs. Parker's most satisfactory poems: it is, on the contrary, one of her most derivative; yet, at the same time, it is interesting precisely because of a certain originality of accent and of point of view. Perhaps few poems in this book are completely successful: they tend, on the one hand, as I have already suggested, to become a little cheapened in the direction of ordinary humorous verse and, on the other, to become too deeply saturated with the jargon of ordinary feminine poetry, to go in too much for plaintive Aprils, for red stains on velvet gowns and for "pretty maids" and "likely lads." But her best work is extraordinarily vivid: it has a peculiar intensity and frankness which, when they appear in poetry, seem to justify any style or method, no matter how strange to literary convention. Dorothy Parker's unprecedented feat has been to raise to the dignity of poetry the "wise-cracking" humor of New York: she has thus almost invented a new kind of epigram: she has made the comic anti-climax tragic. With the publication of this volume, her figure becomes distinct and her voice unmistakable: in her satires, in her short stories, in her play, we had long been aware of her as somebody and something in particular; and from now on, she must command our attention. We have never before had anything quite like:

> Oh, life is a glorious song,
> A medley of extemporanea;
> And love is a thing that can never go wrong;
> And I am Marie of Roumania.

any more than anything like:

> That a heart falls tinkling down,
> Never think it ceases.
> Every likely lad in town
> Gathers up the pieces.
> If there's one gone whistling by
> Would I let it grieve me?
> Let him wonder if I lie;
> Let him half believe me.

We have nothing quite like the hard dark crystals of Dorothy Parker's irony: they do not spark with prismatic colors and a great many of them are imperfect, but they are beginning to become valuable.

Edmund Wilson, "Dorothy Parker's Poems," in The New Republic, *Vol. XLIX, No. 633, January 19, 1927, p. 256.*

Garreta Busey

Although Miss Parker gives us in [***Sunset Gun***], among other charming fantasies, what she calls a "Pig's-Eye View of Literature," the book itself could never be described as a pig's-eye view of life. There is no luxurious wallowing here (except, perhaps, in misery), no sloppiness, no slothful obesity. The poems are lean and quick as a snake. One might say they represented a porcupine's-eye view of life if Miss Parker had not written that **"Parable of a Certain Virgin,"** beginning:

> Oh, ponder, friend, the porcupine;
> Refresh your recollection,
> And sit a moment, to define
> His means of self-protection.

She goes on to describe those means in swift rhythm and comic rhyme until:

> Or should pursuers press him hot,
> One scarcely needs to mention
> His quick and cruel barbs that got
> Shakespearean attention;
>
> Or driven to his final ditch,
> To his extremest thicket,
> He'll fight with claws and molars (which
> Is not considered cricket).
>
> How amply armored, he, to fend
> The fear of chase that haunts him!
> How well prepared our little friend!—
> And who the devil wants him?

Well, we want Miss Parker and are willing to pursue her. As a matter of fact, I myself went through a great deal just to get the loan of ***Enough Rope*** which is no better book than this, although it is a bit thicker. We are willing to pursue Miss Parker to her extremest thicket in spite of, or rather for the sake of, her quick and cruel barbs.

One of the chief reasons why we like her is that most of us were taught in our childhood that we mustn't "sass back" or thumb our noses, and Miss Parker does these things so well for us. She sasses back at Life, or the Universe, or God, or What Have You, in nimble and absurd rhyme such as we never in the world could have thought of ourselves. And besides, we like her because she laughs at herself. We always like people to laugh at themselves. It takes their attention away from us.

The poems are not all impudent. **"Fair Weather,"** for instance, is an excellent serious sonnet. But in her milder verses there are phrases that recall Housman and rhythms that are Millaysian, as this:

> The day that I was christened—
> It's a hundred years, and more!
> A hag came and listened
> At the white church door.

We listen to her more gleefully when she is bad tempered, shocking, macabre. We like it when she makes us gasp by coming out neatly with this:

> Dear dead Victoria
> Rotted cosily;
> In excelsis gloria,
> And R. I. P.

These three letters sound so reckless and indecent! Or—but we ought not to quote any more. That would be giving away too much of what is really the property of the author and her publishers, and we don't want Miss Parker to starve to death.

Garreta Busey, "A Porcupine's View," in New York Herald Tribune Books, *July 15, 1928, p. 7.*

Henry Seidel Canby

The times are choked and cluttered with disillusion—a sticky disillusion, an adolescent petulance, solemn and unreasonable, that pours itself out in dull, formless novels dealing with ugly people who should have been stepped upon at birth, if indeed they were really as mudgy and disagreeable as the writers make them out—which is most improbable. We are blared at and saxophoned by a tinny sophistication that means nothing, and is nothing but the restlessness of smart people who think they are not appreciated, or the shallow bawdry of children educated beyond their characters. Cynicism leaves the sincerity of a tub for the suspicious publicity of a night club, and a "hard" generation patronizes in the comic strips cruel jokes and a sentimental Tarzan using bad medieval English, without a breath's pause between.

We look for a bitterness that can still be gay, and a witty sorrow, and a disillusion that can thumb its nose at the old one who makes lives "gang agley," and find little salt of that savor in contemporary prose, but some, thank heaven! still in poetry. In verse of a Horatian lightness, with an exquisite certainty of technique, which, like the lustre on a Persian bowl, is proof that civilization is itself a philosophy, Dorothy Parker is writing poetry deserving high praise. If I compare her to Horace and Martial I do so largely, since I am no Latinist, and can better describe the perfection of her admirable lyrics [in ***Death and Taxes***] by a comparison with that almost forgotten humorist, Thomas Hood, who had a gift of beauty second only to his contemporary, Keats, and yet could twist a stanza into laughter with one deft, inimitable line. Hood was a romantic, and when in his vein of sentiment was too much the slave of his mood to lift out into wit. He wrote one of Dorothy Parker's finest poems (**"Requiescat"**) in an epigram—the same figure, the same twist, but all made into farce. And in his serious poems, the last line, in which Mrs. Parker stabs sorrow with a jest, is to be found not in the verse but in the pathetic commentaries of his letters. Dorothy Parker has, it seems to me, perfected his art—

Drink and dance and laugh and lie,
  Love, the reeling midnight through,
For tomorrow we shall die!
  (But, alas, we never do.)

This is slight; her powers are better expressed in **"The Evening Primrose"**

You know the bloom, unearthly white,
That none has seen by morning light—
The tender moon alone, may bare
Its beauty to the secret air.
Who'd venture past its dark retreat
Must kneel, for holy things and sweet.
That blossom, mystically blown,
No man may gather for his own
Nor touch it, lest it droop and fall. . . .
Oh, I am not like that at all!

A lesser humorist would have overstressed the virginal beauty, a lesser poet would have failed to make the last line poignant as well as pungent.

We are easily thrown off by lightness and good humor, for pain and a burning heart may be taken, that way, in homeopathic doses. The river of criticism rolls muddy and splashing about difficult metaphysical poetry which grunts and wheezes unintelligibilities, like a Chinese poet speaking through the mouth of a hippopotamus, while we forget the perfect poems, so lucid as to seem simple, so simple in theme as to seem obvious, yet with three quarters of what matters packed in their lines—

Ah, what avails the sceptered race!
  Ah, what the form divine!
What every virtue, every grace!
  Rose Aylmer, all were thine.

Rose Aylmer, whom these wakeful eyes
  May weep, but never see,
A night of memories and sighs
  I consecrate to thee.

Yet I suspect that one should quote Latin rather than English to parallel the edged fineness of Dorothy Parker's verse. This *belle dame sans merci* has the ruthlessness of the great tragic lyricists whose work was allegorized in the fable of the nightingale singing with her breast against a thorn. It is disillusion recollected in tranquility where the imagination has at last controlled the emotions. It comes out clear, and with the authentic sparkle of a great vintage. I attempt no real criticism here, but I do assert that [the poems in ***Death and Taxes***] deserve criticism and appraisal far more than many much bewritten books of more pretentious cerebration, yet with less beauty of technique and far less depth of emotion.

Henry Seidel Canby, "Belle Dame sans Merci," in The Saturday Review of Literature, *Vol. VII, No. 47, June 13, 1931, p. 891.*

Mark Van Doren

Mrs. Parker's two volumes of prose, ***Laments for the Living*** and ***After Such Pleasures,*** contain twenty-four stories and sketches which pursue the theme or themes already made familiar by her poetry. Some of these sketches are so slight as to seem little more than poems "transprosed," if I may borrow a term from the seventeenth century. The monologues in particular are sharpened to an excessively fine point; everything is eliminated that would obscure or complicate the mood, and the mood, as I have said, comes over without change from the verse. In the earlier volume there are two telephone monologues, **"New York to Detroit"** and **"A Telephone Call,"** which carry on the subject of the cooling lover. In each sketch a woman reveals how little her own feelings have changed and how hopelessly the absent man has moderated with the passage of time. Mrs. Parker seems to know just how to give her women in this predicament that tone of voice, that inflection of the imagination, which will betray, up to the point of hysteria, their desperation. To the extent that their emotions are unrelieved they are, in fact, hysterical; yet the brevity of the tales saves us in the end. The later volume contains four further monologues, one of which, **"Sentiment,"** still harps upon the fading swain. In this case, however, as the title indicates, the distress of the woman who speaks is mixed with her consciousness that she is being sentimental, so that the pathos of the piece, while no less in quantity, represents an improvement in quality upon that of the monologues which preceded it in the same mode. The effect, that is to say, is more complex; Mrs. Parker is learning to play upon a second string; though she returns to one minor note in **"The Waltz"** and **"The Little Hours,"** the note becoming now a peevish one, petulant against discomfort.

More interesting, because more ambitious, are the eight dialogues which Mrs. Parker has distributed through her two volumes. Of these **"The Last Tea"** and **"Dusk before Fireworks"** continue with the lady who has lost her man, yet with the complicating circumstance in one case that she touchingly invents a second man of whom the late lover might be jealous, though he is not, and in the other case that she rails as lengthily as wittily against him. **"Dusk before Fireworks"** is one of Mrs. Parker's wittiest stories; the predicament of the lady-killer, whose telephone insists on bringing him messages which he does not want his Wednesday-evening sweetheart to overhear, is riotously developed to the music of much anger and more laughter. The remaining six dialogues permit us to be eavesdroppers at the lonely conversations of young couples in speakeasies, on trains, in hotel lobbies, and wherever it is that modern young couples meet to hold hands and quarrel. Drunk or sober, angry or affectionate, stupid or inspired, these people of Mrs. Parker's speak with an accent we immediately recognize and relish. Mrs. Parker has listened to her contemporaries with as sharp a pair of ears as anyone has had in the present century, unless, to be sure, [Ring] Lardner is to be considered, as he probably is, without a rival in this field. Mrs. Parker is more limited than Lardner; she is expert only with sophisticates, or at any rate with persons who are somehow up to date, whereas he extracted the savor from barber shops and baseball diamonds as well as from living rooms and resort hotels. But she does her lesser job quite perfectly, achieving as she does it a tone half-way between satire and sympathy. And since it is observation we get in these dialogues, along with a varied world which has many people in it, we get at the same time a more important kind of fiction than the monologues could ever be, successful as they are in their restricted way.

In still another form Mrs. Parker has further enlarged her vision. This is the conventional form of the short story itself. Her best work, whether in prose or in verse, is certainly to be found in ten short stories, where, for the most part, she has been content to compete with living masters. She is not a master even here, since she does not deal with any very great or significant area of life; yet she deals with life, and to the utmost of her ability discloses its complexity. In a majority of the stories in question she is a satirist, engaged in the business of slaying fools and knaves. . . . Again it is only Ring Lardner who can be compared with her in the matter of hatred for stupidity, cruelty, and weakness. Her concentrated loathing for the smug adulterer, the selfish old man, the dominating mother, the society woman who patronizes Negro artists, the tamely frigid wife, and the heartlessly curious friend by the private sickbed—this loathing is given full and brilliant expression in **"Mr. Durant," "The Wonderful Old Gentleman," "Little Curtis," "Arrangement in Black and White," "Too Bad,"** and **"Lady with a Lamp,"** respectively. Such stories, by teaching us how to hate the vices which are really evil, the vices of hypocrisy and coldness, have a salutary, a cleansing power; and I suspect that Mrs. Parker is nowhere more valuable than she is in these contemptuous pages.

Yet it is questioned whether she has not done something still more valuable in those pitiless tales which have for heroines women who through homeliness, advancing age, or the mere brutality of fortune have become both tragic and grotesque. The horse-faced nurse in **"Horsie,"** the faded beauty of the stage in **"Glory in the Daytime,"** and the perfectly harmless woman, punished beyond her deserts by calumniating Time, in **"Big Blonde,"** are created at full length in colors so hard and true that their creator is to be accused neither of callousness nor of sentimentality as she works. Her fault has frequently been one or the other of these things. Here, however, she transcends even the temptation to commit them; for she has learned in her stories how to look directly at people, missing nothing about their appearance but at the same time seeing almost everything of importance beneath the surface. Because these stories have scope and truth they promise something of significance in Mrs. Parker's future as a writer. So far she has been slight when she might have been solid, she has been clever when it was too easy to be nothing else. She has enough talent—in prose if not in poetry—to make her one of the most feared and admirable of American satirical novelists. It is the hope of all her followers that she will use this talent. (pp. 540-43)

Mark Van Doren, "Dorothy Parker," in English Journal, *Vol. XXIII, No. 7, September, 1934, pp. 535-43.*

Louis Kronenberger

It is just ten years since Mrs. Parker first made plain that the world is safe enough for girls who wear glasses, but reasonably precarious for most others. It is ten years or thereabouts since people began to repeat at dinner tables those bright sayings of hers which could not always have been repeated in print. She achieved, as she deserved, the title of wit; and here [in ***Not So Deep as a Well***] are her three volumes of poetry, now collected into one, to reassert her claim. Here is, I think, much the best light verse of our day which is highly personal in tone, which gains its effects through describing some one *in* a situation; and over and over again it is the same effect, one that can be vulgarly described as "The joke's on me."

If that is the formula for so much of this verse, it must yet not be dismissed as simply a device, for behind it lies a settled point of view—the immemorial, rueful, frostbitten laughter of women who, yearning for love, cry out not only because they are frustrated of the lovers they want, but also because they are bored with the lovers they have. For every door that will not open to Mrs. Parker's fluttering knock, there is another that she slams behind her. For every cadenced sob in her book, there is a rhythmical grimace. These verses are, indeed, the record of a constant shuttling between sentimentality and cynicism, of romanticism forever plucked hastily from the stalk, but never uprooted from the soil, of instinct at war with experience and at least half the time victorious.

After ten years Mrs. Parker strikes me as having achieved—as one so often puts it in the case of "weightier" writers—a kind of historical significance. These poems of hers remind us irresistibly of the era during which they were for the most part composed—the frantic Twenties, when people went gathering rosebuds with almost comic intensity and far too much self-consciousness: the frantic Twenties, when it was so imperative to be "honest" that most people became so at the cost of being insincere. No age, so shoulder-shrugging on the surface, was ever more uneasy underneath; and no age, forever denouncing the melodramatic, ever dramatized itself more constantly. The age gave birth to Hemingway, who remains the classic—indeed, the overworked—example of a man who misrepresented his emotions. As everybody now agrees, he was forever insisting that he was hardboiled to conceal the fact that he was hopelessly sentimental. Mrs. Parker played the cynic in much the same spirit of dissimulation. And no one has ever made clearer than she how inseparable from sentimentality cynicism is, just as no one has ever made sentimentality more outrageous by simply juxtaposing it to laughter.

On the serious side, therefore, there is no emotional balance in her poetry, just as there was no emotional balance in the age that produced it. There is equally no emotional relaxation: when Mrs. Parker is not ostentatiously prostrated, she is ostentatiously unmoved. Almost all her serious poems strike a false or self-conscious note: the emotion that transpires is inconsistent with the situation that determined it. Further, the high technical polish of her sentimental poems makes them artificial; there is nothing more incongruous than studied heartbreak. Indeed, between emotional expression that is very simple and artless and emotion operating at white heat under the sovereign control of a deeply poetic mind, every intermediate stage is in danger of a discrepancy between meaning and manner—the two do not coincide; and Mrs. Parker seldom outwits that danger. In her case there is perhaps the additional drawback that she is sometimes derivative; the ghosts of Housman, Millay and Elinor Wylie, to name no others, too often direct her imagination.

One comes back to Mrs. Parker's light verse with the greatest pleasure; with its sharp wit, its clean bite, its perfectly conscious—and hence delightful—archness, it stands re-reading amply. Here her high technical polish has great virtue; sometimes cracking out a surprise effect with an absolute minimum of wind-up, sometimes achieving a foreseen effect by means so dexterous it is exhilarating to watch them. Mrs. Parker can extend anticlimax to irresistible bathos by altering the pitch of her language (from the high-flown to the highly colloquial) at the exact moment she alters her meaning. But what, of course, is more important is the sense of personality that converts what might otherwise be merely a witty idea into a dramatic, however cockeyed, situation; a sense of personality that gives us not cynicism in the abstract but laughter applied to an objective. There is no one else in Mrs. Parker's special field who can do half as much. I suspect that she will survive not only as the author of some first-rate light verse but also as a valuable footnote to the Twenties, out of whose slant on existence that light verse sprang. (pp. 2, 28)

Louis Kronenberger, "The Rueful, Frostbitten Laughter of Dorothy Parker," in The New York Times, *December 13, 1936, pp. 2, 28.*

"My verses are no damn good. Let's face it, honey, my verse is terribly dated—as anything once fashionable is dreadful now. I gave it up, knowing it wasn't getting any better, but nobody seemed to notice my magnificent gesture."

—Dorothy Parker, in a 1956 interview.

Ruth McKenney

I think the legend of Dorothy Parker, the wit and the funmaker, should be settled for once and for all, with the publication of her [***Here Lies: Collected Stories***]. Humorists are all very well in their place but I think a great and serious talent should not be debased by reminiscent chuckles of laughter. For all I know Dostoievsky kept his intimates in stitches. Dorothy Parker is no more a public wit than the bitter Russian.

For Mrs. Parker strips our society down to its festering bones, rips aside the sheltering curtains of the cruel and respectable. I suppose the technical name for Mrs. Parker's writing is "satire"—and yet it seems a faltering word for the passionate and caustic tales set down in this book. Mrs. Parker has pity and indignation and a terrible, almost painful warmth, so that tragedy underlies the acid.

I know that there is a large and weighty school of thought which finds Mrs. Parker very *fin de siècle,* very decadent, as well as very great and very expert. I don't understand that at all. There is not a story in the new book which does not ring with protest, and a few of them are written in fire. The violence of **"The Custard Heart"** is almost frightening—it assaults the reader with its rage, and I cannot see how a moderately sensitive person can live through the story of the lady who was wistful even in her bathroom and not feel like yelling for the tumbrils.

Naturally every Dorothy Parker reader has favorites among the famous stories. I like least the facile tales of the gentlemen recovering from hangovers, the dialogues in speakeasies. The savage stories of **"Little Curtis"** and **"Clothe the Naked"** and **"Wonderful Old Gentleman"** make the slighter tales seem a little faded. Mrs. Parker writes of the Negro with especial power—her Negro characters have strength and dignity; their fate is suggested with real ferocity.

The story on Spain requires, I think, special mention. **"Soldiers of the Republic"** employs a very different technique from even the most powerful of the other stories. Here the attack is turned on the narrator—and by implication on all bystanders in all great human struggles. **"Soldiers of the Republic"** must be uncomfortable reading for anyone who did not and does not stand ready to give himself for truth and justice. I believe it is Mrs. Parker's finest short story, because it is the most direct and the most passionate.

I am always impatient with critics who set up great cheers about a writer's "style." The best style is of course the least noticeable—style is only a means to an end. And yet no comment on Mrs. Parker's short stories can be complete without stating the flat fact that no other . . . writer uses the short story form so perfectly. Mrs. Parker's short stories are not stunted novels, chopped-off tales that should have grown and prospered. Their economy is inherent in the material itself—an extra paragraph, even an extra word, would destroy the whole design.

Under a single cover, now, is the best prose work of one of the important writers of the period. The only major fault I can find, after reading the collected stories, is their number. Most writers, even the very good ones, overwork themselves. But Mrs. Parker should be locked in her study and fed bread and water until she produces twice again as many stories as she has in her new volume.

Ruth McKenney, "Satire and Tragedy," in The Saturday Review of Literature, *Vol. XX, No. 1, April 29, 1939, p. 7.*

Edmund Wilson

Rereading Dorothy Parker [in ***The Viking Portable Library Dorothy Parker***] has affected me, rather unexpectedly, with a distinct attack of nostalgia. Her poems do seem a little dated. . . . Her prose, however, is still alive. It seems to me as sharp and as funny as in the years when it was first coming out. If Ring Lardner outlasts our day, as I do not doubt that he will, it is possible that Dorothy Parker will, too.

But the thing that I have particularly felt is the difference between the general tone, the psychological and literary atmosphere, of the period—the twenties and the earlier thirties—when most of these pieces of Mrs. Parker's were written, and the atmosphere of the present time. It was suddenly brought home to me how much freer people were—in their emotion, in their ideas, and in expressing themselves. In the twenties they could love, they could travel, they could stay up late at night, as extravagantly as they pleased; they could think or say or write whatever seemed to them amusing or interesting. There was a good deal of irresponsibility, and a lot of money and energy wasted, and the artistic activities of the time suffered somewhat from its general vices, but it was a much more favorable climate for writing than the period we are in now. (p. 67)

It is a relief and a reassurance, in reading her soliloquies and dialogues—her straight short stories, which are sometimes sentimental, do not always wear quite so well—to realize how recklessly clever it used to be possible for people to be, and how personal and how direct. All her books had funereal titles, but the eye was always wide open and the tongue always quick to retort. Even these titles were sardonic exclamations on the part of an individual at the idea of her own demise; the idea of the death of a society had not yet fallen on people to paralyze their responses to experience.

But the literary movement of the twenties showed a tendency to break down and peter out which we never should have expected at that time, when it seemed to us that American writing had just had a brilliant rebirth. It was a shock to know that Scott Fitzgerald, who had seemed to be still on his way to fulfilling the promise of imperfect books, was suddenly and prematurely dead, and we soon found that this imperfect work had almost the look of a classic: its value had been heightened by its rarity, since there was not going to be any more of it either by him or by anyone else. And we find, when we take up this new volume, which contains Dorothy Parker's completed published works, that a similar shift of feeling occurs. Mrs. Parker is not yet dead, nor has she altogether ceased writing: there are several new stories in this volume, and they hold up with the earlier ones. But she nowadays produces little, and she has suffered, to our disappointment, one of the dooms of her generation. A decade or more ago she went to Hollywood and more or less steadily stayed there, and, once away from her natural habitat, New York, she succumbed to the expiatory mania that has become epidemic with film writers and was presently making earnest appeals on behalf of those organizations which talked about being "progressive" and succeeded in convincing their followers that they were working for social revolution, though they had really no other purpose than to promote the foreign policy of Stalin. She ought, of course, to have been satirizing Hollywood and sticking pins into fellow-travellers; but, so far as my observation goes, she has never written a word about either. There are among the new pieces here a couple that deal with the war—**"The Lovely Leave"** and **"Song of the Shirt, 1941"** (the first of these especially good)—but this collection mostly makes you feel that you are reliving a vanished era. Except for one sketch of the Spanish War, the story seems to break off abruptly sometime in the early thirties.

But it, too, this collected volume, has a value derived from rarity—a rarity like that of steel penknives, good erasers, and real canned sardines, articles of which the supply has almost given out and of which one is only now beginning to be aware of how excellent the quality was. It seems to me, though I shall name no names, that it has been one of the features of this later time that it produces imitation books. There are things of which one cannot really say that they are either good books or bad books; they are really not books at all. When one has bought them, one has only got paper and print. When one has bought Dorothy Parker, however, one has really got a book. She is not Emily Brontë or Jane Austen, but she has been at some pains to write well, and she has put into what she has written a voice, a state of mind, an era, a few moments of human experience that nobody else has conveyed. (pp. 67-8)

Edmund Wilson, "A Toast and a Tear for Dorothy Parker," in The New Yorker, *Vol. XX, No. 14, May 20, 1944, pp. 67-8.*

W. Somerset Maugham

[It] is not the case that I do not know what to say about Dorothy Parker, but that I do not know what new I can say. It is as difficult to say anything about her that has not been said a thousand times before as it is about the Venus of Milo. Who has not praised her wit, her stories and her verse? Her witticisms are famous. With equal efficacy she can wield the bludgeon of an angry cop and the rapier of the gallant D'Artagnan. Helen could make a scholar immortal with a kiss; she can make a fool immortal with a jibe. Wit must have a butt and is ill-constituted to paddle in the milk of human kindness; but I should do her an injustice if I gave the impression that hers is cruel; it can be, but also it can be lambent, as harmless as summer lightning, and tender; it is then the natural expression of her rueful and exuberant delight in the absurdity of the universe. Most humorists require an audience; sometimes in their company you will see by the sudden twinkle in their eye that a joke has occurred to them, and then you become aware that they have decided to keep it for a more favorable occasion. Not so with Dorothy Parker. Her humor bubbles up and overflows and if there is no one there to enjoy it, it makes no matter. She can no more help being amusing than a peach tree can help bearing peaches. Most of us become writers because we can never think of the apt thing to say till the moment to say it has past. One of the charming things about Dorothy Parker is that when the door of opportunity flies open she is there on the threshold ready to make the most of the God-given moment. She seems to carry a hammer in her handbag to hit the appropriate nail on the head. She has a rare quickness of mind. (pp. 11-12)

In her stories Dorothy Parker has a sense of form which in these days, to my old-fashioned mind, is all too rare. Whether in a sketch or a story she knows exactly where to begin and where to end and when you have done reading it you have no questions to ask (What happened next? Why did he do that?) for she has told you all you need to know. She has a tidy mind and leaves no loose ends. She has a wonderfully delicate ear for human speech and with a few words of dialogue, chosen you might think haphazardly, will give you a character complete in all its improbable plausibility. Her style is easy without being slipshod and cultivated without affectation. It is a perfect instrument for the display of her many-sided humor, her irony, her sarcasm, her tenderness, her pathos. Perhaps what gives her writing its peculiar tang is her gift for seeing something to laugh at in the bitterest tragedies of the human animal. It is a devastating truth that she has discovered, and a salutary one, that there is something irresistibly comic in our most heartfelt woes. Who can but laugh wryly when he reads **"A Telephone Call,"** that heart-rending monologue, for which of us has not thus awaited with agonizing suspense a call on the phone, a telegram, a letter or a visit? Only a nitwit—but what a happy nitwit he! I do not want to go through these stories one by one, pointing out the peculiar excellence of each, for here they are for the reader to read and the reader is for himself the only judge that matters. He is silly if he lets anyone else, however well qualified, judge for him. In [***The Viking Portable Library Dorothy Parker***] he will find stories aimed only to make him laugh, and a very good aim too, too seldom attempted and less seldom achieved; he will find stories that are cruel, moving, sardonic, tragic, funny, sometimes separately and sometimes all together. But I should like to single out **"The Standard of Living"** for its humorous and tender handling of those two little stenographers as they wander up Fifth Avenue looking into the shop windows. They have all the charm, the impertinence, the pathos and the absurdity of youth.

If you are going to judge an author at all he has the right to demand that you shall judge him by his best. **"Big Blonde"** has all the earmarks of a masterpiece. It is worthy to take its place with the short stories, and very few they are, that men have retained in their memories for many, many years. It displays to perfection all Dorothy Parker's enviable gifts. There are few things more difficult than to write a short story the events of which take place over a long period of time, and yet maintain that unity of effect which is the essence of the short story. In **"Big Blonde"** Dorothy Parker has succeeded with peculiar skill in doing just this so that notwithstanding the passage of years you have the same poignancy as is generally only possible to achieve in the narration of a single incident. I think it is done by a determined concentration on the pathetic, feckless, hopeless, tragic, sloppy wanton who is Hazel Morse. People don't often realize how much luck comes into the writing of a good story. A lot of things have to go right. The heaven-sent idea is waiting at the street corner but you must chance to pass that way to pick it up; it is only by a fluke that you come across the persons who will suggest the characters you need; you have to be in the right mood; time and place must be auspicious. It is no wonder that few good stories are written; it is only a wonder that as many are. In **"Big Blonde"** Dorothy Parker had all the luck on her side.

Only a very mediocre writer is always at his best, and Dorothy Parker is not a mediocre writer. Sometimes things don't go so well with one as they might and in such case one can do nothing about it. A carping critic of these stories might suggest that their author on occasion shows an inclination to imitate Dorothy Parker but I as an admiring friend would answer stoutly that she could not have a better model. (pp. 14-16)

W. Somerset Maugham, "Variations on a Theme," in Dorothy Parker, *The Viking Press, 1944, pp. 11-18.*

James Gray

There cannot be much doubt about it now. Dorothy Parker is one of the few writers of our time who is destined for immortality. It is nice for us who have always cherished her gift to know that in centuries to come she will represent the sad, cocky, impudent mood of our tragic era. Waking from our graves five hundred years from now, we shall be pleased to see Dorothy Parker strolling Olympus, perhaps in the company of Marguerite of Navarre and Madame de Sévigné. Proudly we shall say, "We knew her when she was just a quick-witted girl who kidded around with Robert Benchley and wrote pieces for the *New Yorker.*"

This slightly oracular prediction is suggested by the fact that a neat new portmanteau volume [***The Viking Portable Library Dorothy Parker***] is crowded with most of Dorothy Parker's best stories and verses. A handful of them are brand new, though no point need be made of that. There is novelty enough in the oldest and most frequently reprinted of them, like **"You Were Perfectly Fine"** and the verse about how women and elephants never forget.

Dorothy Parker has a kind of admirer whose praise must make as shrewd and fastidious a person as her work shows her to be wish actively that she had never been born. This misguided enthusiast assumes that Mrs. Parker feels a devastating contempt for the human race, and that her scorn is directed in particular toward the half of the race that belongs to her own sex.

It must often depress the author of these deft sketches and poems to realize how superficially her irony has been read. Mrs. Parker does not belong among the haters. Only inferior talents can be prostituted, year after year, to the expression of merely negative feeling. The responsible satirist never uses his weapon to demonstrate his own skill at inflicting pain, but rather to punish a pretension that has too long masqueraded as innocent and winsome grace.

Dorothy Parker's sketch called **"Arrangement in Black and White"** is typical of her method. It introduces a fatuous woman who pretends to be ever so magnificently unprejudiced when she consents to meet a fine Negro artist at a social occasion. But her babble, as she praises her own superior sensibility, exposes a mind that is callow and callous, inept and vicious. With a deft and unobtrusive hand Dorothy Parker lifts the disguise to expose the Nazi mentality. If this character could become independently sentient and aware of her creator, she wouldn't know that she had been hurt by these attentions. Yet a reader cannot fail to perceive the point. That is art.

But even when she is operating on folly with her most uncompromising surgical completeness, Mrs. Parker seldom seems vindictive toward her subject. The sketch called **"From the Diary of New York Lady"** exposes the tawdry private emotions of a complete parasite. Nothing concerns the diarist except her program of pleasures and the tragedy of what an inept manicurist has done to her nails. But she does not exist, like the vicious women of Clare Boothe's plays, in a moral vacuum. Subtly, Mrs. Parker is able to show that already the shrill, insensitive temperament of this creature has alienated all normal people, that she is alone, and that her destiny is a bleak one. It is this

An excerpt from "Big Blonde"

She fell readily into the habit of tears during the first year of her marriage. Even in her good sport days, she had been known to weep lavishly and disinterestedly on occasion. Her behavior at the theatre was a standing joke. She could weep at anything in a play—tiny garments, love both unrequited and mutual, seduction, purity, faithful servitors, wedlock, the triangle.

"There goes Haze," her friends would say, watching her. "She's off again."

Wedded and relaxed, she poured her tears freely. To her who had laughed so much crying was delicious. All sorrows became her sorrows; she was Tenderness. She would cry long and softly over newspaper accounts of kidnapped babies, deserted wives, unemployed men, strayed cats, heroic dogs. Even when the paper was no longer before her, her mind revolved upon these things and the drops slipped rhythmically over her plump cheeks.

"Honestly," she would say to Herbie, "all the sadness there is in the world when you stop to think about it!"

"Yeah," Herbie would say.

She missed nobody. The old crowd, the people who had brought her and Herbie together, dropped from their lives, lingeringly at first. When she thought of this at all, it was only to consider it fitting. This was marriage. This was peace.

But the thing was that Herbie was not amused.

For a time, he had enjoyed being alone with her. He found the voluntary isolation novel and sweet. Then it palled with a ferocious suddenness. It was as if one night, sitting with her in the steam-heated living room, he would ask no more; and the next night he was through and done with the whole thing.

He became annoyed by her misty melancholies. At first, when he came home to find her softly tired and moody, he kissed her neck and patted her shoulder and begged her to tell her Herbie what was wrong. She loved that. But time slid by, and he found that there was never anything really, personally, the matter.

"Ah, for God's sake," he would say. "Crabbing again. All right, sit here and crab your head off. I'm going out."

And he would slam out of the flat and come back late and drunk. . . .

Each time he left the place in a rage, he threatened never to come back. She did not believe him, nor did she consider separation. Somewhere in her head or her heart was the lazy, nebulous hope that things would change and she and Herbie settle suddenly into soothing married life. Here were her home, her furniture, her husband, her station. She summoned no alternatives.

respect for poetic justice and this acknowledgment of a set of positive values which are being violated, that give Mrs. Parker's satire its point.

Her gifts include, beside the satirist's insight, the poet's imagination and the high-spirited person's love of improvisation. She says of a chic and lovely woman, "her body streamed like a sonnet." Into the mind of a girl whose dancing partner is apelike and insistent and whose name she doesn't even know, she puts the thought, "Jukes would be my guess from the look in his eyes. How do you do, Mr. Jukes? And how is that dear little brother of yours, with the two heads?"

But it is not this glittering gift that makes her work worth reading and re-reading. Rather it is the fact that Dorothy Parker has a mature mind and a will to protect the dignity of man from the assaults of the insensitive. (pp. 197-99)

James Gray, "Dream of Unfair Women," in his On Second Thought, *University of Minnesota Press, 1946, pp. 184-200.*

Henry Hewes

"The Ladies of the Corridor" takes its title from a line in T. S. Eliot's "Sweeney Erect." It also borrows from that distinguished poet his habit of looking at life as the pathetic and useless thing it has become for some groups in our society. What it fails to carry over is Mr. Eliot's verse inventions, which make his later plays skate along smoothly over some fairly profound mysteries. This is unfortunate, for Dorothy Parker and Arnaud D'Usseau have chosen a wonderful subject for their elegy. Their examination has been thorough and unflinching. And they have come up with some clever lines with which to relieve the gloominess. However, they keep sinking back to the level of the lonely hotelized ladies' drab existences.

There are: Lulu Ames, a fiftyish widow transplanted from Akron to New York who sums up her married life with "the days were slow, but the years went quickly"; the arthritic Mrs. Nichols, who describes her husband as "sweet, not strong, but—sweet"; Mildred Tynan, an alcoholic in her thirties whose dream husband turned out to have a list of "call girls, and whips in the closet"; Mrs. Gordon, a kleptomaniac at Woolworth's who believes "there's never any good behind those 'Do Not Disturb' signs on the door"; and Mrs. Lauterbach, whose major crises in life are whether or not she'll be invited to her son-in-law's for Thanksgiving and deciding whether the coffee is better at the Normandie or at the Esquire.

There is one other lady who dwells at the Hotel Marlowe, but she cannot be described as a lady of the corridor. She has had a happy and functional married life with healthy outside interests. When her husband died she went back to work. Her viewpoint is practical and courageous—"Life doesn't treat me fine; life and I go dutch"—and obviously the authors point to her as an example of what the others might have been. In fact Lulu Ames, as a newcomer, has the choice of emulating this contemporary specimen of Shaw's "unwomanly woman" or of joining the other domiciled derelicts. As one of them says to her, "Keep going as long as you can, dear, but remember we're here waiting for you."

There are two younger men (*circa* forty) involved. One, Mrs. Nichols's son, who must spend all his time taking care of his invalid mother except for a daily visit to the zoo for a communion with his caged brothers; the other, a bookstore proprietor who has an affair with Mrs. Ames despite the fact that she is his senior by at least a decade. . . .

While the results are as relentlessly grim as a Lillian Hellman third act, and accurate enough so that thousands of women will see a part of themselves in these hallway harpies, one is apt to miss much celebration of their suffering. Amanda in *The Glass Menagerie* is just as miserable and deluded, but yet we feel a real soul struggling there. Tennessee Williams's enemy is not the human being but the conventions that drive her into a dim and nasty life. In ***Ladies of the Corridor*** we feel that these women are almost deliberately responsible for their own condition. They have committed the sin of devoting themselves blindly and completely to their husbands and to their children without attempting to find larger and more useful interests for themselves. Their husbands and their children do not want such all-exclusive devotion and resent the obligation it puts them under. Since it is demonstrated that these mistakes are occasionally avoided, ***The Ladies of the Corridor*** is an object lesson for those who can still escape becoming one.

There is also a lesson for Marxists, as the authors poke fun at them with an amusing scene in which a stodgy husband, shocked at the fact that a widow might spend his hard-earned money with another man, advocates the East-Indian custom of burning the widow on the funeral pyre of the deceased husband. "Why not just burn the money?" quips the realistic woman. The suggestion is not anticapitalistic, but merely a plea for fuller and less incestuous living. (p. 32)

Henry Hewes, "Gloom Service," in The Saturday Review, *New York, Vol. XXXVI, No. 45, November 7, 1953, pp. 32-3.*

Dorothy Parker [Interview with Marion Capron]

[*Capron*]: *It's a popular supposition that there was much more communication between writers in the twenties. The Round Table discussions in the Algonquin, for example.*

[Parker]: I wasn't there very often—it cost too much. Others went. Kaufman was there. I guess he was sort of funny. Mr. Benchley and Mr. Sherwood went when they had a nickel. Franklin P. Adams, whose column was widely read by people who wanted to write, would sit in occasionally. And Harold Ross, the *New Yorker* editor. He was a professional lunatic, but I don't know if he was a great man. He had a profound ignorance. On one of Mr. Benchley's manuscripts he wrote in the margin opposite "Andromache," "Who he?" Mr. Benchley wrote back, "You keep out of this." The only one with stature who came to the Round Table was Heywood Broun.

What was it about the twenties that inspired people like yourself and Broun?

Gertrude Stein did us the most harm when she said, "You're all a lost generation." That got around to certain people and we all said, "Whee! We're lost." Perhaps it suddenly brought to us the sense of change. Or irresponsibility. But don't forget that, though the people in the twenties seemed like flops, they weren't. Fitzgerald, the rest of them, reckless as they were, drinkers as they were, they worked damn hard and all the time.

Did the "lost generation" attitude you speak of have a detrimental effect on your own work?

Silly of me to blame it on dates, but so it happened to be. Dammit, it *was* the twenties and we had to be smarty. I *wanted* to be cute. That's the terrible thing. I should have had more sense.

And during this time you were writing poems?

My verses. I cannot say poems. Like everybody was then, I was following in the exquisite footsteps of Miss Millay, unhappily in my own horrible sneakers. My verses are no damn good. Let's face it, honey, my verse is terribly dated—as anything once fashionable is dreadful now. I gave it up, knowing it wasn't getting any better, but nobody seemed to notice my magnificent gesture.

Do you think your verse writing has been of any benefit to your prose?

Franklin P. Adams once gave me a book of French verse forms and told me to copy their design, that by copying them I would get precision in prose. The men you imitate in verse influence your prose, and what I got out of it was precision, all I realize I've ever had in prose writing.

How did you get started in writing?

I fell into writing, I suppose, being one of those awful children who wrote verses. I went to a convent in New York—The Blessed Sacrament. Convents do the same things progressive schools do, only they don't know it. They don't teach you how to read; you have to find out for yourself. At my convent we *did* have a textbook, one that devoted a page and a half to Adelaide Ann Proctor; but we couldn't read Dickens; he was vulgar, you know. But *I* read him and Thackeray, and I'm the one woman you'll ever know who's read every word of Charles Reade, the author of *The Cloister and the Hearth.* But as for helping me in the outside world, the convent taught me only that if you spit on a pencil eraser it will erase ink. And I remember the smell of oilcloth, the smell of nuns' garb. I was fired from there, finally, for a lot of things, among them my insistence that the Immaculate Conception was spontaneous combustion.

Have you ever drawn from those years for story material?

All those writers who write about their childhood! Gentle God, if I wrote about mine you wouldn't sit in the same room with me.

What, then, would you say is the source of most of your work?

Need of money, dear.

And besides that?

It's easier to write about those you hate—just as it's easier to criticize a bad play or a bad book.

What about **"Big Blonde"**? *Where did the idea for that come from?*

I knew a lady—a friend of mine who went through holy hell. Just say I knew a woman once. The purpose of the writer is to say what he feels and sees. To those who write fantasies—the Misses Baldwin, Ferber, Norris—I am not at home.

That's not showing much respect for your fellow women, at least not the writers.

As artists they're rot, but as providers they're oil wells; they gush. Norris said she never wrote a story unless it was fun to do. I understand Ferber whistles at her typewriter. And there was that poor sucker Flaubert rolling around on his floor for three days looking for the right word. I'm a feminist, and God knows I'm loyal to my sex, and you must remember that from my very early days, when this city was scarcely safe from buffaloes, I was in the struggle for equal rights for women. But when we paraded through the catcalls of men and when we chained ourselves to lamp posts to try to get our equality—dear child, we didn't foresee *those* female writers. Or Clare Boothe Luce, or Perle Mesta, or Oveta Culp Hobby.

You have an extensive reputation as a wit. Has this interfered, do you think, with your acceptance as a serious writer?

I don't want to be classed as a humorist. It makes me feel guilty. I've never read a good tough quotable female humorist, and I never was one myself. I couldn't do it. A "smartcracker" they called me, and that makes me sick and unhappy. There's a hell of a distance between wisecracking and wit. Wit has truth in it; wisecracking is simply calisthenics with words. I didn't mind so much when they were good, but for a long time anything that was called a crack was attributed to me—and then they got the shaggy dogs.

How about satire?

Ah, satire. That's another matter. They're the big boys. If I'd been called a satirist there'd be no living with me. But by satirist I mean those boys in the other centuries. The people we call satirists now are those who make cracks at topical topics and consider themselves satirists—creatures like George S. Kaufman and such who don't even know what satire is. Lord knows, a writer should show his times, but not show them in wisecracks. Their stuff is not satire; it's as dull as yesterday's newspaper. Successful satire has got to be pretty good the day after tomorrow.

And how about contemporary humorists? Do you feel about them as you do about satirists?

You get to a certain age and only the tried writers are funny. I read my verses now and I ain't funny. I haven't been funny for twenty years. But anyway there aren't any humorists any more, except for Perelman. There's no need for them. Perelman must be very lonely.

Why is there no need for the humorist?

It's a question of supply and demand. If we needed them, we'd have them. The new crop of would-be humorists doesn't count. They're like the would-be satirists. They write about topical topics. Not like Thurber and Mr. Benchley. Those two were damn well read and, though I hate the word, they were cultured. What sets them apart is that they both had a point of view to express. That is important to all good writing. It's the difference between Paddy Chayefsky, who just puts down lines, and Clifford Odets, who in his early plays not only sees but has a point of view. The writer must be aware of life around him. Carson McCullers is good, or she used to be, but now she's withdrawn from life and writes about freaks. Her characters are grotesques.

Speaking of Chayefsky and McCullers, do you read much of your own, or the present generation of writers?

I will say of the writers of today that some of them, thank God, have the sense to adapt to their times. Mailer's *The Naked and the Dead* is a great book. And I thought William Styron's *Lie Down in Darkness* an extraordinary thing. The start of it took your heart and flung it over there. He writes like a god. But for most of my reading I go back to the old ones—for comfort. As you get older you go much farther back. I read *Vanity Fair* about a dozen times a year. I was a woman of eleven when I first read it—the thrill of that line "George Osborne lay dead with a bullet through his head." Sometimes I read, as an elegant friend of mine calls them, "who-did-its." I love Sherlock Holmes. My life is so untidy and he's so neat. But as for living novelists, I suppose E. M. Forster is the best, not knowing what that is, but at least he's a semi-finalist, wouldn't you think? Somerset Maugham once said to me, "We have a novelist over here, E. M. Forster, though I don't suppose he's familiar to you." Well, I could have kicked him. Did he think I carried a papoose on my back? Why, I'd go on my hands and knees to get to Forster. He once wrote something I've always remembered: "It has never happened to me that I've had to choose between betraying a friend and betraying my country, but if it ever does so happen I hope I have the guts to betray my country." Now doesn't that make the Fifth Amendment look like a bum?

Could I ask you some technical questions? How do you actually write out a story? Do you write out a draft and then go over it or what?

It takes me six months to do a story. I think it out and then write it sentence by sentence—no first draft. I can't write five words but that I change seven.

How do you name your characters?

The telephone book and from the obituary columns.

Do you keep a notebook?

I tried to keep one, but I never could remember where I put the damn thing. I always say I'm going to keep one tomorrow.

How do you get the story down on paper?

I wrote in longhand at first, but I've lost it. I use two fingers on the typewriter. I think it's unkind of you to ask. I know so little about the typewriter that once I bought a new one because I couldn't change the ribbon on the one I had.

You're working on a play now, aren't you?

Yes, collaborating with Arnaud d'Usseau. I'd like to do a play more than anything. First night is the most exciting thing in the world. It's wonderful to hear your words spoken. Unhappily, our first play, ***The Ladies of the Corridor,*** was not a success, but writing that play was the best time I ever had, both for the privilege and the stimulation of working with Mr. d'Usseau and because that play was the only thing I have ever done in which I had great pride.

How about the novel? Have you ever tried that form?

I wish to God I could do one, but I haven't got the nerve.

And short stories? Are you still doing them?

I'm trying now to do a story that's purely narrative. I think narrative stories are the best, though my past stories make themselves stories by telling themselves through what people say. I haven't got a visual mind. I hear things. But I'm not going to do those *he-said she-said* things any more, they're over, honey, they're over. I want to do the story that can only be told in the narrative form, and though they're going to scream about the rent, I'm going to do it.

Do you think economic security an advantage to the writer?

Yes. Being in a garret doesn't do you any good unless you're some sort of a Keats. The people who lived and wrote well in the twenties were comfortable and easy-living. They were able to find stories and novels, and good ones, in conflicts that came out of two million dollars a year, not a garret. As for me, I'd like to have money. And I'd like to be a good writer. These two can come together, and I hope they will, but if that's too adorable, I'd rather have money. I hate almost all rich people, but I think I'd be darling at it. At the moment, however, I like to think of Maurice Baring's remark: "If you would know what the Lord God thinks of money, you have only to look at those to whom he gives it." I realize that's not much help when the wolf comes scratching at the door, but it's a comfort. (pp. 74-80)

How about your political views? Have they made any difference to you professionally?

Oh, certainly. Though I don't think this "blacklist" business extends to the theater or certain of the magazines, in Hollywood it exists because several gentlemen felt it best to drop names like marbles which bounced back like rubber balls about people they'd seen in the company of what they charmingly called "commies." You can't go back thirty years to Sacco and Vanzetti. I won't do it. Well, well, well, that's the way it is. If all this means something to the good of the movies, I don't know what it is. Sam Goldwyn said, "How'm I gonna do decent pictures when all my good writers are in jail?" Then he added, the infallible Goldwyn, "Don't misunderstand me, they all ought to be hung." Mr. Goldwyn didn't know about "hanged." That's all there is to say. It's not the tragedies that kill us, it's the messes. I can't stand messes. I'm not being a smartcracker. You know I'm not when you meet me—don't you, honey? (p. 82)

> *Dorothy Parker and Marion Capron, in an interview in* Writers at Work: The "Paris Review" Interviews, *edited by Malcolm Cowley, The Viking Press, 1958, pp. 69-82.*

Norris W. Yates

In her early years, Miss Parker often appeared as an "orthodox" humorist—that is, a sensible person who chose the middle way and avoided extremes. . . . (p. 265)

Even after the development of her social conscience, Miss Parker could not be called a "proletarian" writer in the doctrinaire sense of Jack Conroy, Albert Maltz, Albert Halper, Mary Heaton Vorse, and Grace Lumpkin. Miss Parker was no sectarian when literature was concerned. She called Upton Sinclair "one of the American great," but she disagreed with his criticisms of American authors for not always writing of "sweatshops and child-labor, of mill-slaves and strikes and wages," and in her own stories her acidity bit most often into the gilt and brass of a certain type of American personality, the self-absorbed female snob. This happened to be a type she knew best in its middle-class manifestations. Ring Lardner—whom she admired as second only to Hemingway among contemporary American writers—dissected the "idle common man," the middle-class male who, having climbed part way up the economic ladder, devotes his increased leisure time to the pursuit and enjoyment of status symbols that will ease the inadequacy he dimly feels because his real self does not match his inflated self-image. Miss Parker invites comparison with Lardner in her focus on the female companion of Lardner's idle middle-class man, also in her frequent use of the diary form, the monologue, and trivial dialogue. Sometimes her idle, middle-class females are smug and aggressive; sometimes they are pathetic like Lardner's "victims"; sometimes both. Occasionally they are more amusing than anything else.

The "woman with the pink velvet poppies" in **"Arrangement in Black and White,"** and Mrs. Ewing in **"Clothe the Naked,"** both of whom showily patronize Negroes, are examples of the aggressive sort. So are the doll-like Mrs. Lanier of **"The Custard Heart"**; the aristocratic Mrs. Matson of **"Little Curtis"**; and the **"Lady with a Lamp"** who drives a nervous patient into hysteria by saying exactly the wrong things about the girl's having been jilted by her lover. The monologue of this woman especially reminds one of Lardner's egocentric males:

> Well—if that's the way you want to be to me, that's the way you want to be. I won't say anything more about it. Only I do think you might have let me know that you had—well, that you were so *tired,* if that's what you want me to say. Why, I'd never have known a word about it if I hadn't run bang into Alice Patterson and she told me she'd called you up and that maid of yours said you had been sick in bed for ten days. Of course, I'd thought it rather funny I hadn't heard from you, but you know how you are—you simply let people go, and weeks can go by like, well, like *weeks,* and never a sign from you. Why, I could have been dead over and over again, for all you'd know. Twenty times over. Now, I'm not going to scold you when you're sick, but frankly and honestly, Mona, I said to myself this time, "Well, she'll have a good wait before I call her up. I've given in often enough, goodness knows. Now she can just call me first." Frankly and honestly, that's what I said!

This person belongs with the girl who broke up the marriage of **"Cousin Larry,"** and with the **"New York Lady"** who, in her diary, records her pursuit of pleasure **"During Days of Horror, Despair, and World Change."** (In form, the latter story resembles Anita Loos's *Gentlemen Prefer Blondes,* but the scorn with which Miss Parker infused her portrait is largely absent from Miss Loos's lighthearted sketches of 1926.) Equally smug and self-absorbed are the couple who make fun of the homely spinster tending their children in **"Horsie,"** and the wealthy Mrs. Martindale of **"Song of the Shirt, 1941,"** whose attempts at sewing hospital bandages are so completely a pose of *noblesse oblige* that she ignores the needs of a seamstress with a crippled child, to whom she could just as well have given the work for pay.

Women who are mainly pathetic include Mona in **"Lady with a Lamp,"** little Mrs. Murdock in **"Glory in the Daytime,"** the jilted girl who sits hopefully by the telephone in **"A Telephone Call,"** the girl in a similar plight who finally does call her boyfriend—unfortunately—in **"New York to Detroit,"** and Hazel Morse, the **"Big Blonde"** who has neither the will nor the self-consciousness even to reflect on her difficulties with men, much less to solve them.

Pathos and folly, or at least inadequacy, are mixed in varying ratios in several other women, among them the girl in **"Sentiment"** who wallows in self-pity as she relives certain tender moments while riding in a cab down "Sixty-Third" street. The language of her reverie is a parody of Elinor Glyn and other sentimental novelists, and perhaps also a mocking of the sentimentality which Miss Parker could often have found in her own work without looking very far:

> And I waiting for him in the dusk, thinking he would never come; and yet the waiting was lovely, too. And then when I opened the door to him—Oh, no, no, no! Oh, no one could bear this. No one, no one.
>
> Ah, why, why, why must I be driven through here? What torture could there be so terrible as this? It will be better if I uncover my eyes and look. I will see our tree and our house again, and then my heart will burst and I will be dead. I will look, I will look.

Her sentimentality has heretofore kept her from looking, but when she does uncover her eyes, she finds that the street is Sixty-Fifth, not Sixty-Third. Pathetic in their inadequacy are the Weldons of **"Too Bad,"** whose marriage has gone on the rocks from sheer boredom even as the marriage of the Taylors in Lardner's "Anniversary" was going; pathetic in their self-absorption are the wife in **"The Banquet of Crow"** who is encouraged by a quack lay-analyst to believe that it is merely change of life that causes her husband to walk out on her after eleven years of stale marriage, and the wife of the World War II pilot in **"The Lovely Leave"** whose possessiveness ruins what few hours she and her husband can have together. In all of these cases, the "victims" are largely self-victimized.

Amusement overbalances pathos in **"The Sexes,"** where a pair of sweethearts quarrel and make up—but show promise of quarreling again at the drop of a hatpin. Amusement is also the dominant effect of **"The Standard of Living,"** in which two office girls pretend they have a million dollars to spend instead of their tiny salaries, and of **"Just a Little One,"** in which a flapper in a speakeasy insists on only one drink at first but gradually gets tanked and begs her date to let them "go out and get a horsie, Freddie—just a little one, darling, just a little one." There is much humor and little pathos in **"Here We Are,"** a scene in which a newly wedded couple unknowingly foreshadow their married life by quarreling suddenly over trifles and making up just as fast (the possibility of tears in the future is hinted at, of course). There is even less pathos in **"The Waltz,"** in which a girl keeps on dancing with a tangle-footed lout while inwardly abusing him and wondering " . . . why I didn't tell him I was tired," or " . . . why I didn't suggest going back to the table." Equally light is **"The Little Hours,"** in which a female night-owl for once goes to bed at ten o'clock. The result—creeping insomnia, but like the girl in **"The Waltz,"** she is not so miserable that she can't mock at herself. . . . The darker vein is never entirely absent however, even in **"The Waltz"** and **"The Little Hours,"** where the two main characters are self-victimized by their own giddiness and lack of perspective. "A humorist, I think, is just balancing on the edge of the dumps," Miss Parker said in 1936. Even her most playful pieces hint at this view.

Occasionally Miss Parker shifts her spotlight to a Little Man somewhat like Benchley's or Thurber's. Once in a long while, she portrays this man as morally sound and mentally equipped with a share of common sense, though ridiculous and/or pathetic in other ways. (pp. 265-69)

More often Miss Parker's males are nondescripts and function chiefly as the victims or exploiters of her females, than whom, as a group, they are no more sympathetic. The fellow who is bewildered at being actually married (in **"Here We Are"**) is comparatively amusing; somewhat less so is the man who cuts embarrassing capers when he gets oiled (**"You Were Perfectly Fine"**). The colorless fellows who victimize the **"Big Blonde,"** and the passive gigolo in **"Dusk before Fireworks"** are fair samples of Miss Parker's more "aggressive" men. An unusually weak and selfish seducer is "Mr. Durant," an "immovably married man of forty-nine" who, despite his insipidity, manages to have his way with a secretary in the office.

In the concern for status of many of her characters, the author shows an interest in class conflict as an influence on character and action. "Mr. Durant was assistant manager of the rubber company's credit department; his wife was wont to refer to him as one of the officers of the company" (the specification of the company's product is a nice touch, considering the sexual activities of Mr. D.). His middle-class outlook is closely related to his predatory amours: when he decides that Rose should have an abortion, his envy and misunderstanding of the upper class aid him in rationalizing that she ought not to mind—"New York society women, he understood, thought virtually nothing of it." When the operation is over, he says to himself, "Well, that's that," because this expression has "something stylish about it; it was the sort of things you would expect to hear used by men who wore spats and swung canes without self-consciousness." Thus he tries to play the role of a type socially "above" him; on the other hand, he makes use of his small prestige as a low-ranking executive in the company hierarchy to seduce Rose, who, as a secretary, looked up to him.

Miss Parker's women too are often preoccupied with status. This is true not only of such specimens of the leisure class as Mrs. Lanier of **"The Custard Heart,"** Mrs. Martindale of **"Song of the Shirt, 1941,"** and Mrs. Whittaker of **"The Wonderful Old Gentleman,"** but of the white-collar girls in **"Standard of Living."** When the loafers whistle at Annabel and Midge, these office girls hold their heads high "and set their feet with exquisite precision, as if they stepped over the necks of peasants." The nub of the story consists in their discovery of how much the maintenance of upper-class prestige really costs—they knew a double rope of pearls could cost as much as a thousand dollars, but the actual price—a quarter of a million—takes their breath away.

Even where class-consciousness is not explicitly a topic, it runs just under the surface. When the boyfriend in **"The Sexes"** refers to the girl as "snotty," she says, "I'm really not in the habit of hearing language like that," and he has to apologize. The girl in **"The Waltz"** is dancing with a free-spender who is ready to give the orchestra twenty dollars to keep on playing. Surely this lavishness has something to do with her assurance that "I'd simply adore to go on waltzing."

In **"Clothe the Naked,"** class conflict and the poverty that underlies it are shown as interrelated with white condescension to Negroes. Class-consciousness is also important in **"Little Curtis,"** where Mrs. Matson's pretensions to upper-rung status recall George Ade's idle matrons and the wives of Lardner's Guillible and of the narrator in *The Big Town.* Mrs. Matson is proud that " . . . she had been Miss Laura Whitmore, of the Drop Forge and Tool Works Whitmores," and she refrains from wearing new clothes "for every day," although she can well afford it, because " . . . there was an unpleasant suggestion of extravagance and riotous living in the practice. The working classes, who, as Mrs. Matson often explained to her friends, went and bought themselves electric ice-boxes and radios the minute they got a little money, did such things." The middle-class ethic of Ben Franklin thus drives her into conspicuous thrift—conspicuous consumption in reverse.

Her stinginess is also associated with frigidity; the Matsons have no children and it is suggested that they have little taste for "carnal intimacy." Moreover, they are obsessed with the notion that predatory relatives are after their money, and partly to foil these, they adopt a little boy. Mrs. Matson scolds him for playing with "a furnaceman's child" and in other ways tries to bring him up according to her notions of propriety, but he shows his hopelessly asocial boyishness by laughing when one of his foster-mother's tea guests, who is a little deaf, drops her speaking-tube. (pp. 270-72)

Miss Parker does for these idle women what Don Marquis had done for their daughters in *Hermione* and what Lardner did for their husbands and sons. (p. 272)

Lardner's satire was motivated by no strong urge for social reform, whereas Miss Parker's indignation and guilt feelings led her into social crusades and into praise for the fighting peasants of loyalist Spain (in **"Soldiers of the Republic"**), whom she depicted with an emphasis on simplicity, courtesy, and selflessness that seldom appears in her profiles of idle Americans. Yet, in subject matter and in technique, the fiction of Lardner and Miss Parker shows enough mutual resemblance to raise the question of the relationship between satire and social reform—a part of the larger question of how humor and satire are related to values in general and what values, if any, are peculiarly conducive to humor. (p. 273)

Norris W. Yates, "Dorothy Parker's Idle Men and Women," in his The American Humorist: Conscience of the Twentieth Century, *Iowa State University Press, 1964, pp. 262-73.*

"A humorist, I think, is just balancing on the edge of the dumps."

—Dorothy Parker, 1936.

Ross Labrie

For some reason, the writings of Dorothy Parker have been for the most part overlooked by critics in spite of the fact that her work continues to sell well and to go into fresh editions. Part of the reason is doubtlessly the general feeling that her writing belongs to the twenties and thirties and cannot easily be transplanted, even though in fact she continued to publish until the end of the fifties. Rereading Dorothy Parker in 1944, for example, Edmund Wilson was nostalgically reminded of the freedom of the twenties which made her writings so "personal and direct." In many ways she was a child of the twenties with her mixture of wit and scepticism, her uneven taste, and her concern with the American myths of glamour and success.

Among those writing in the twenties, she especially admired the work of Hemingway, Anderson, and Lardner. Hemingway she regarded as the "greatest living writer of short stories," and she imitated his style in an unusually sober short story called **"Soldiers of the Republic"** (1938) which was written following her reporting of the Spanish Civil War. The imagistic reportage and the linear, yet repetitive syntax all recall the Hemingway manner. The influence of Ring Lardner is visible in all of the monologues and in short stories like **"Mrs. Hofstadter on Josephine Street"** (1934) and **"Cousin Larry"** (1934) with their Lardner-like *mélange* of garrulousness and malice. In an essay titled **"Hero Worship,"** she praised Lardner for his "unparallelled ear and eye, his strange, bitter pity, his utter sureness of characterization, his unceasing investigation, his beautiful economy," all qualities which she emulated in her own work. The influence of Sinclair Lewis can be seen in Dorothy Parker's tendency to focus on middle-class stereotypes, like Mrs. Matson in **"Little Curtis"** (1927). She found contagious both Lardner's and Lewis' fondness for stereotypes, and this tended to thin out some of her sketches, such as **"The Waltz"** (1933), **"The Sexes"** (1927), **"The Mantle of Whistler"** (1928), **"A Young Woman in Green Lace"** (1932), and **"Arrangement in Black and White"** (1927).

In a structural sense, nearly all of Dorothy Parker's stories are arrangements in black and white, bold juxtapositions of beauty and plainness, meekness and tyranny, grace and awkwardness, dullness and liveliness, generosity and narrowness. In this respect, she obviously has much in common with Lewis. She found Lewis too facile and prolix, though, noting on one occasion that "it is our national joy to mistake for the first rate, the fecund rate." She preferred Hemingway's ability to discard details "with a magnificent lavishness." She worked assiduously for tightness, and felt finally that she had achieved "precision in prose," having shunned the "plethora of words" and the "philosophizing" of writers like Dreiser. The issue went beyond matters of style. She liked Sherlock Holmes, for example, because her own life was so "untidy" and he was so "neat." "It's not the tragedies that kill us," she reflected ruefully on one occasion, "it's the messes."

She wrote fastidiously, each phrase carefully distilled: "I, after the creative labors involved in composing a telegram to the effect that I won't be able to come to dinner Thursday on account of a severe cold, have to go and lie down for the rest of the day." Her stories are models of precision, often opening with a sharp visualized action which, even if ludicrous or futile in itself, gathers a kind of grace through the cool orderliness of the prose. The opening of **"Arrangement in Black and White"** is a good example:

> The woman with the pink velvet poppies turned round the assisted gold of her hair, traversed the crowded room at an interesting gait combining a skip with a sidle, and clutched the lean arm of her host.

The atmosphere of the passage conveys a sense of awkwardness and self-consciousness, whereas the tone is bemused and curious, the contrast leading to a tautness which is characteristic of Dorothy Parker's writing. The urbanity of the point of view recalls her remark that the words "naive" and "annoying" were synonyms in her lexicon.

Visually, the passage is tightly bound through the underlying image of the show horse, a sign that her writing appealed more to the eye, was less exclusively auditory than she thought. The stories bristle with arresting images. In **"Here We Are"** (1930), for example, a sketch about a rather unoriginal honeymoon couple, the woman, complete in her new wardrobe, is described as looking as "new as a peeled egg." In one of the late stories, **"I Live on Your Visits"** (1955), a dutiful son visits his querulous mother, whose virulent disposition is conveyed to the reader through a description of her jewelry. On her wrists there are "bands and chains of dull silver, from some of which hung amulets of discolored ivory, like rotted fangs." In **"Horsie"** (1932), the prosaic Miss Wilmarth is struck into eloquence by the homage proferred to her new employer: "She had never known a patient to receive so many flowers, or such uncommon ones; yellow violets and strange lilies and little white orchids poised like a bevy of delicate moths along green branches." The image is of course Dorothy Parker's, not Miss Wilmarth's. The impression of an overriding narrative voice is common in the sketches and stories, just as it was in the great tradition of English satirists whom Dorothy Parker so much admired, confessing on one occasion that she read *Vanity Fair* over and over.

She shared with the great satirists an inclination to reveal her characters through their possessions, assuring us in one of her short stories that from a "young man's coat, more surely than from his palm, might be read the ingredients of his character." In **"The Wonderful Old Gentleman"** (1926), two middle-aged sisters converse quietly in the living-room while their father is dying in a room above them. The old gentleman is never seen; instead, his character is relayed through the comments of his daughters and through his contributions to the decor of the living-room. These include a steel engraving of the Crucifixion, "lavish of ghastly detail," together with two other melancholy artifacts: a "painting in oil of two lost sheep, huddled hopelessly together in the midst of a wild blizzard," and a "colored print, showing a railroad crossing, with a train flying relentlessly toward it, a low, red automobile trying to dash across the track before the iron terror shattered it into eternity." The decor is so illustrative of the man that his physical presence is made to seem redundant.

The prevailing theme in the stories is the disintegration of American culture, the petrifying meretriciousness of modern American life, seen almost exclusively in terms of the American woman. **"The Standard of Living"** (1941) epitomizes this theme. The story concerns a game played by two young office workers, Annabel and Midge, in their spare time. Although the two women are physically different, nevertheless they look alike in "their movements, their style, and their adornments." Although the males around them change from time to time, the newcomers are "scarcely distinguishable from their predecessors." The game which they play is a variation on 'what-would-you-do-if-you-had-a-million-dollars,' the essential rule being that "you must spend every nickel of the money on yourself." Furthermore, the money must be a bequest from an "eccentric" who was "not anybody you loved, or, for the matter of that, anybody you even knew." The rule ensures that the recipient can clear her life of all human attachments so that she can concentrate on the money.

As in Dreiser, Fitzgerald, and Dos Passos, the characters are attracted not only to money in a charismatic manner but also vicariously attach themselves to those who are rich and famous. **"Glory in the Daytime"** (1933) concerns an emotionally starved housewife in search of "the glamour and beauty and romance of living." The central character, Mrs. Murdock, fortuitously receives an opportunity to meet the celebrated actress, Lily Wynton. She sets out with her imagination brimming, her memory stirred by the recollection of a chance encounter with another famous actress, "a wonder of sable and violets and round red curls that seemed to tinkle on the air." Lily Wynton hovers in Mrs. Murdock's consciousness, a "tall and slow and silvery" presence. Unhappily, Lily turns out to be not only past her prime but a drunk as well. While she wears the appropriate black satin dress and long white gloves, Mrs. Murdock notices timidly that there were "delicate streaks of grime in the folds of her gloves, and down the shining length of her gown there were small, irregularly shaped dull patches; bits of food or drops of drink, or perhaps both." The scene recalls one of Dorothy Parker's garish memories of Hollywood. In Beverly Hills she had seen a "Cadillac about a block long, and out of the side window was a wonderfully slinky mink, and an arm, and at the end of the arm a hand in a white suede glove wrinkled around a wrist, and in the hand was a bagel with a bite out of it."

As with Fitzgerald and others interested in the failure of the American dream, Dorothy Parker became absorbed by the relationship between beauty, wealth, and evil. She was ambivalent about this, as was Fitzgerald. Her scepticism was articulated through a character in her play, ***Ladies of the Corridor*** (1953), who reflects soberly on the "beauty that makes you imagine there is a heaven. And the mean heart, the tiny mind, the arrogant, vicious, greedy body that makes you know there is a hell." The impunity of beauty is expressed in the well-formed young man in **"Dusk before Fireworks"** (1932) who cracks the whip over a number of distraught lovers who live together in a city of the damned. In **"Lolita"** (1955), the statuesque hero, John Marble, appears "as if he had just alighted from the chariot of the sun." He gives the impression of wealth as well, "for he had the best room at the Wade Hampton Inn and he drove a low, narrow car with a foreign name, a thing of grace and power." Somewhat unexpectedly, instead of choosing from among the swarm of attractive women who pursue him, he selects Lolita, who is "of no color at all" and who has "insistent knobs at the ends of her bones" together with straight hair "so fine that it seemed sparse." Lolita's greatest asset is her deep and enduring silence, which allows her beautiful lover to cultivate his narcissistic relationship with himself in the company of the most perfect of audiences. During the courtship, the only sound which emanates from the porch swing is that of "John Marble's voice flowing easily along."

The idol of beauty can be studied as well in the person of the fragrant Camilla Cruger in **"Horsie."** Camilla, whose name symbolizes the romantic mawkishness which Dorothy Parker loathed, is surrounded by a devoted husband and solicitous friends, who gather "adoring, about the apricot chaise-lounge" where Camilla is convalescing after having given birth to her first child. The child has been thrust into the arms of a live-in nurse, Miss Wilmarth, whose unfortunate face gives the story its name. While pressing Camilla's "limp, fragrant hand against his mouth," Gerald Cruger makes it abundantly clear that the infant will not interfere with his devotion to his wife, announcing briskly at one point that if "that brat ever calls you 'Mummy' . . . I'll turn her out in the snow." Just as it is an exclusively urban world, so too is Dorothy Parker's world for grown-ups only.

The soft figure of Camilla is set off repeatedly against the starchy presence of Miss Wilmarth—beauty and the beast:

> She had big, trustworthy hands, scrubbed and dry, with nails cut short and so deeply cleaned with some small sharp instrument that the ends stood away from the spatulate finger-tips. Gerald Cruger, who nightly sat opposite her, at his own dinner table, tried not to see her hands. It irritated him to be reminded by their sight that they must feel like straw matting and smell of white soap.

Miss Wilmarth's coiffure inspires little more confidence. Dressed festively on the one occasion when she is invited to socialize with her employers, her hair is "crimped and loosened, and ends that had escaped the tongs were already sliding from their pins." Covered in "coarse, bright white talcum," she chooses a rather severe frock of dark blue taffeta, wrapping her ankles in "roughened gray silk and her feet in black casket-shaped slippers, upon which little bows quivered as if in lonely terror at the expanse before them."

Her most distinctive and fatal attribute is her uncanny resemblance to the horse, not simply in physiological detail but particularly in her expression, a look which inevitably arouses in Gerald Cruger feelings of baffled hilarity and disdain. He is observant enough to notice that her equine appearance is strongest when she has occasion to open the "shiny white boxes" and to lift out the "exquisite, scentless blossoms" sent to Camilla, so much so that on these occasions "he thought of proferring her an apple." Gerald observes but fails to understand Miss Wilmarth's chameleon-like behavior as well as the moral basis of the story. The reader perceives that Miss Wilmarth's oddity increases in proportion to her rejection by others. The sight of the concern and attention lavished upon Camilla throws her own drab isolation into relief, and has the effect of intensifying her ugliness. The moral design is confirmed at the end of the story when she is offhandedly given a box of flowers by Gerald Cruger, who is greatly relieved to be finally getting rid of her. Ironically, as she is driven away, no one notices that her resemblance to the horse had faded beneath the softening of her features brought about by her gratitude:

> Miss Wilmarth's strange resemblance was not apparent, as she looked at her flowers. They were her flowers. A man had given them to her. She had been given flowers. They might not fade for days. And she could keep the box.

The vulnerability of women who have never had or who have lost their beauty and therefore their ticket to survival is a persistent, sardonic theme in Dorothy Parker. Such a woman is Hazel Morse, Dorothy Parker's **"Big Blonde"** (1929). The story was a favorite of Somerset Maugham's who liked its poignancy and its mastery of the technical problem of presenting the whole of a woman's life within the narrow frame of the short story. Physically attractive as a young woman, Hazel Morse becomes accustomed to trading sex for security, a characteristic exchange it appears to her, within her society: "Men liked her, and she took it for granted that the liking of many men was a desirable thing. Popularity seemed to her to be worth all the work that had to be put into its achievement." Discarded by a succession of increasingly inferior men as age cuts into her beauty, she resorts to alcohol, and eventually attempts a suicide which rather cruelly doesn't come off. In spite of the triteness and vulgarity of Hazel's situation, Dorothy Parker breathes enough life into her to separate her from the blur of women in the story who are "stout, broad of shoulder and abundantly breasted, with faces thickly clothed in soft, high-colored flesh." Hazel confronts life with generosity and even-tempered stoicism, holding on it spite of the fact that her "heart felt tight and sore in her breast, and her mind turned like an electric fan." The image places her squarely within the dehumanized context of the American technocracy which has molded her.

Nevertheless, there is a depth to Hazel's suffering which transcends her supine existence, partly based upon her strength and partly upon the fact that Dorothy Parker clearly cares about her. The caring is not unlike Fitzgerald's sympathy with Gatsby, but it is probably closer to Dorothy Parker's unexpectedly warm response to Isadora Duncan who, in spite of her outlandishness, was the real thing, heightened by her "great, torn, bewildered, foolhardy soul."

In Dorothy Parker's view, the plight of American women is that their social roles cause them to be "trapped like a trap in a trap," as the rather self-conscious narrator of **"The Waltz"** puts it. Although a feminist all her life, Dorothy Parker portrayed women as not only victims of an insensitive and predatory male sex, but, inasmuch as women welcome the roles which society has ordained for them, as gullible destroyers of themselves. The quiet desperation of Mrs. Weldon in **"Too Bad"** (1933) is a case in point. Mrs. Weldon finally exits from a marriage which is slowly suffocating her. Driven throughout her life by the social stereotypes which pertain to her sex, she moves about her apartment in bewilderment at her role. Unlike Ibsen's Nora, Mrs. Weldon wants dearly to live in a doll's house, having "dreamed of herself as moving softly about her new dwelling, deftly moving a vase here or straightening a flower, and thus transforming it from a house to a home." Mrs. Weldon's daily rearranging, another instance in American culture of the investing of the mechanical with magical properties, fails to turn her house into a home, and she gropes her way through marriage with the humiliating sense that the failure of the marriage is somehow a lapse of her special "duty" as a woman. Fumbling in her attempt to float the sort of lively conversation which she thinks might bring her marriage around, she has the "feeling a hostess has when her party is going badly, when her guests sit in corners and refuse to mingle." The analogy is revealing, indicating Mrs. Weldon's conception of marriage as a public ordeal, even if, as the story brings out, the outside world knows little of the Weldons' buried life. Mrs. Weldon finds herself in the peculiar position of feeling freer, more relaxed, and more candid with others than with her husband, because at least the public world makes no pretension of speaking to her deeper and personal needs.

If Dorothy Parker felt gloomy about the proclivity of people like Mrs. Weldon to wither within the confines of shallow marriages, she was equally sceptical about those women who were still capable of feeling. The monologues and short stories are replete with lovesick and neurotic women who seem to illustrate the point that, if emotion is the particular province of women—as it seems to be in Dorothy Parker's world—then theirs is indeed a cursed sex. **"The Lovely Leave"** (1943) concerns a young woman's disappointment when her soldier husband's leave is unexpectedly shortened. The outpourings of the woman's heart are set off against the baffled commonsense response of her husband, who quickly accepts the inevitable: "You see," he complains, "I don't know what to say, when you start talking about showing me glimpses of your heart, and all that."

A number of the stories focus almost obsessively on the

Caricature of Parker by Hirschfeld.

desultory emotions of distraught women—among them **"The Last Tea"** (1926), **"New York to Detroit"** (1928), **"Lady with a Lamp"** (1932), **"Dusk before Fireworks"** (1932), **"Sentiment"** (1933), and **"The Banquet of Crow"** (1957). The confessions of these unhappy women are usually blunted for the reader by a quality of *déja vu* which recalls Dorothy Parker's stricture: "Poets alone should kiss and tell." Typical is the narrator of **"Sentiment,"** a characteristic Parker heroine who is tormented by the recollection of the "beauty" and "cruelty" of a past lover. She becomes convinced that her taxi is taking her through the street where she and her lover had been happy together, and, increasingly stirred by images from the past, she wonders tenderly "why it's wrong to be sentimental." Ostensibly striving for self-control, she resolves to keep her "poor heart still," to conform to the behaviour of the "little, mean, dry-souled people who are proud not to remember." The satire is completed when she realizes in confusion that she is on the wrong street.

Amidst such pathos, Dorothy Parker has her eye unflinchingly on the potential cruelty of the ardent woman, in addition of course to the obvious self-indulgence. One of her most celebrated sketches in this respect is **"A Telephone Call"** (1928), a monologue involving a young woman who unquietly awaits a conciliatory call from her lover, a call which never comes:

> Maybe he isn't going to call—maybe he's coming straight up here without telephoning. He'll be cross if he sees I've been crying. They don't like you to cry. He doesn't cry. I wish to God I could make him cry and tread the floor and feel his heart heavy and big and festering in him. I wish I could hurt him like hell.

The perversity of the heart was not a theme restricted to women in love. **"Song of the Shirt, 1941"** offers a caustic view of women on the home front during the second world war. The title of the story was drawn from Thomas Hood's well known poem about the miserable living conditions of London seamstresses during the first half of the nineteenth century, and as a piece of social criticism the story has a sharp cutting edge. The heroine, Mrs. Martindale, is an attractive and affluent middle-aged woman whose full heart is especially stirred by the thought of young American soldiers fighting for their country. She decides to share in the national ordeal by joining a volunteer organization, and she is given the excruciating task of sewing together coarse pieces of cloth in order to make hospital shirts. She throws herself into the work in spite of her ineptitude with needle and thread and her phobia about using a sewing machine. The perseverance of this tall, graceful woman whose "body streamed like a sonnet" is a fascinating study in self-discipline.

While the other well-to-do volunteers disperse for the summer, Mrs. Martindale takes a pile of the distasteful work home with her. During this period, she is asked by an acquaintance to think of an employer for a seamstress with a crippled daughter who is in desperate need of work. Instead of turning over her own aching work to the woman, and thus doing two good deeds at once, Mrs. Martindale bends over her painful sewing, having "racked her brains" to come up with a solution for the unfortunate seamstress.

The story appears to have been inspired by Dorothy Parker's astonished observation that a number of American women seemed to have the ingenuous idea that World War II was to be "conducted like a charity bazaar":

> I knew a woman who sent to the U.S. Employment Service and let it be known that she wished to do a job for the war. She explained that she was a peerless driver and had considered placing herself on call with a volunteer motor corps unit. They were happy to hear of her driving ability. There was an appalling shortage of bus drivers in that city, so they told her to pitch right in and drive a bus. "Oh," she cried, recoiling daintily, "but that's a *paid* job."

In a similar manner, Mrs. Martindale anxiously avoids the opportunity of hiring the unemployed seamstress because although this would relieve her of the disagreeable sewing, it would also rob her of the emotional opportunity to experience the sensation of sharing in the war effort along with the brave young men. Without the strain of this sacrifice, the story makes clear, her "big heart" would not have been appeased.

The idolatry of catering to the whims of the female heart is epitomized in **"The Custard Heart"** (1939). The principal character, Mrs. Lanier, is a wealthy beauty who has an agreeably absent husband and who is surrounded by a coterie of young male admirers, none of whom is permitted to overtax her wistful heart. As with Pope's Belinda, who appears to have served as a model for Dorothy Parker's heroine, Mrs. Lanier is depicted in her boudoir, which is both a sanctuary from the world's harshness and a temple for the rites of pride. . . . Oblivious of the torments of those around her, including those borne by her maid, Gwennie, Mrs. Lanier soulfully shuns all manifestations of the ugly, from beggars on the street to her aged chauffeur whose face had unfortunately become "lined and dry" so that she "could stand the sight of him no longer" and was reluctantly forced to dismiss him. While the texture of the story is airy and genial, as in Pope, the social critique is sharply felt, as it is in the **"Song of the Shirt, 1941."** Harmlessly shallow in themselves, perhaps, Mrs. Lanier and Mrs. Martindale symbolize power within American society, power which is contained in their wealth and beauty and which is capriciously used to serve the demands of pampered hearts and indulged enthusiasms. For those women in Dorothy Parker who manage to survive the withering effects of their social roles, then, either through the freedom of affluence or through unusual individual energy and resilience, there is the rule of emotion, generally childlike and always peremptory—a law unto itself. This is made to seem inevitable in a civilization which is obsessed with success and with things and which is fundamentally uninterested in the interior life.

Paradoxically, in spite of her satires against American women in this respect, Dorothy Parker's personal struggle with runaway emotion is uncomfortably apparent in some of her work, as it was even more uncomfortably apparent in her life. The slope towards sentimentality was always to be reckoned with. Her verse seems particularly vulnerable at times: "Love is woman's moon and sun," she writes with chagrin, while man "has other forms of fun." (pp. 48-55)

On the whole, the stories appear to have been a sort of antidote to the poems, urbanely sceptical even when dealing with the most poignant autobiographical experience, as in **"The Lovely Leave,"** for example. While the stories generally exhibit a fine poise, there are exceptions. **"Clothe the Naked"** (1938), for instance, pulls out all the stops. A blind, poor, and illegitimate black boy is cut down by a complacent, racist society, personified in the WASPish matron who provides little Raymond with the cast-off winter coat which makes him an object of ridicule within the ghetto. One of the more heartwarming notes in a story that reeks of pathos is the characterization of black tenement dwellers banding together to protect little Raymond from the tentacles of white institutionalism. Had anyone come to take Raymond away to an institution for the blind, we are assured, "the neighbors would have fought for him with stones and rails and boiling water." Thus, Raymond grows up unaware of "anything but good." The glossing over of the daily abrasiveness of ghetto life was the result both of Dorothy Parker's eager leftism and of that incipient banality which lurks in much of her work, but which is fortunately suppressed in most of it.

Ripening amidst the fecundity and informality of the twenties, she was drawn towards vividness and candor, but fortunately also towards the austerities of form—a tendency towards an almost severe symmetry in structuring and a salty economy in phrasing. As the bracing vitality of her work continues to attract new readers, one feels inclined to speculate on the sources of her brittle, satiric vision. Apart from the desultory pattern of her life, which seems an obvious source, an answer can perhaps be found in her poem, **"Godmother,"** in which she depicts the formation of her character. Along with the civilizing traits which are bestowed upon her by her "kith and kin," the last and most decisive gift is brought to her by an unearthly hag who is seen waiting at the "white church door":

> I give her sadness,
> And the gift of pain,
> The new moon madness,
> And the love of rain.

(pp. 55-6)

Ross Labrie, "Dorothy Parker Revisited," in Canadian Review of American Studies, *Vol. VII, No. 1, Spring, 1976, pp. 48-56.*

Deirdre Neilen

Dorothy Parker remains the legendary lady of the Algonquin's round table; we read her stories and poems, yes, but stay fixated on the cruel wit and unkind genius who gave simultaneous pain and pleasure with all her bon mots. To discover the more contemplative Parker, we can turn to ***The Coast of Illyria,*** a play she co-authored with her lover, Ross Evans.

Illyria tells the story of Charles and Mary Lamb during a six-week period when Charles is hoping to marry a stage actress, Fanny Kelly. Charles' love story is played out against the far darker background of his sister Mary's mental instability. Ten years earlier during one of her "episodes," Mary stabbed their mother to death. In order to prevent her permanent exile to the asylum at Bedlam, Charles has had to promise to be her guardian, a role which has allowed him no other attachment.

Charles has never complained about this; brother and sister share a fierce and mutual love for one another. They write together, and Mary has kept house for him and his friends for years. When she feels the madness beginning its inexorable descent, she simply tells Charles, and he walks her to the asylum where they "treat" her until she can cope.

Parker found the biographical facts a true mother lode for her creativity. The Lambs, after all, were the center of an important circle of literati: Coleridge, Hazlitt, DeQuincey all appear during this play, alternately delighting and destroying their hosts. Parker's wit makes us laugh aloud.

What is most interesting, however, is the play's timeliness. Underneath all the brilliant talk and careless cruelties, ***Illyria*** grapples with our own age's fascination with drugs and substance abusers. All these artists find themselves prisoners of their own obsessions with opium, laudanum, brandy, and whiskey. They are terrified that without the stuff, they'll no longer write and think as well, yet they recognize that their lives are in a shambles because of their pursuits.

Charles and Mary in our day would be stamped "codependents" and strongly urged to separate in order to become well. As Charles says, "Oh, what a couple we are! She in her constant danger, driving me to this; I with my stinking drunkenness sending her quicker to her hells. Two shipwrecked souls." But this is the late nineteenth century, and all must be forgiven those who write the poetry of the age.

Parker's first act describes Charles' fevered preparations to announce his engagement and to welcome his sister home from the hospital. He is nervous about what his news might do to Mary and must also fear how this set of wild friends will affect his far more traditional fiancee. Above all this, however, runs Parker's own obsessions with estrangement and abandonment: the always uncertain position of the gifted woman in a patriarchal world.

Act Two is a riotous retelling of one of the Lambs' Thursday evenings, the night they set aside for their friends to come and eat (and drink) and talk. This particular Thursday, Mary has invited Fanny's scrupulously pious and bigoted mother in the hopes of winning her to Charles and Fanny's side. The evening is of course total disaster as one famous person after another comes through and commits philosophical outrage upon Mrs. Kelly's conservative sensibilities. The poor woman tries to agree with Mary that "geniuses" deserve a little extra leeway, but Coleridge's recitation of "Kublai Khan" frightens her even as DeQuincey's assertion that murder is an art form repulses her. Discovering that her future son-in-law has written an article "Confessions of a Drunkard" (we see how our own time's interest in *People*'s confessional articles is nothing new) is truly the last straw.

Act Three begins with a drunken Charles bitterly bewailing his destiny: no Fanny, Mary always to worry about, these friends of his to defend. At first, it appears that life may offer him a second chance; Fanny comes back and says she still loves him. Charles promises anew to reform and begins to dream of his life as a loving husband. Parker, however, never did believe in the happy ending. Mary's realization that she will lose her brother's singular devotion precipitates another emotional crisis. We see Fanny forced to realize Charles can never have a "normal" life as he leads his sister back to Bedlam.

Illyria has wonderful speeches and powerful characters. We laugh and yet are stricken by the emotional and psychic carnage we witness. (p. 4)

Deirdre Neilen, "Dynamic Duo for Stage," in New Letters Review of Books, *Vol. 3, No. 5, Autumn, 1990, pp. 4-5.*

FURTHER READING

Cooper, Wyatt. "Whatever You Think Dorothy Parker Was Like, She Wasn't." *Esquire* LXX, No. 1 (July 1968): 56-7, 61, 110-14.

Reminiscences about Parker by a friend who knew her chiefly in Hollywood during the 1930s.

Frewin, Leslie. *The Late Mrs. Dorothy Parker.* New York: Macmillan, 1986, 345 p.

Detailed biography of Parker drawn from interviews with a number of her friends and colleagues.

Hellman, Lillian. "Dorothy Parker." In her *An Unfinished Woman,* pp. 212-28. Boston: Little, Brown and Company, 1969.

Revealing personal account of the noted playwright's relationship with Parker.

Keats, John. *You Might As Well Live: The Life and Times of Dorothy Parker.* New York: Simon and Schuster, 1970, 319 p.

First full-length biography of Parker. Subjective in tone, it characterizes her life as "pretty much of a mess."

Kinney, Arthur F. "Dorothy Parker's Letters to Alexander Woollcott." *The Massachusetts Review* XXX, No. 3 (Autumn 1989): 487-515.

Contains numerous letters Parker wrote to Woollcott from 1926 to 1942. Parker discusses her stay in Switzerland, her relationshp with her family, and Ernest Hemingway.

O'Hara, John. "Dorothy Parker, Hip Pocket Size." *New York Times Book Review* (28 May 1944): 5, 29.

Favorable review of *The Viking Portable Library Dorothy Parker.*

Kirkpatrick Sale

1937-

(Full name J. Kirkpatrick Sale) American nonfiction writer, journalist, and editor.

In his nonfiction works, Sale frequently focuses on political, economic and ecological problems of contemporary society, proposing novel—and often controversial—solutions. He also explores environmental and sociological issues from both historical and modern perspectives. Born in Ithaca, New York, Sale inherited a rebellious nature from his father, who taught English at Cornell University and often defied the school's administration. Sale later attended Cornell, where he edited the daily student newspaper and, in 1958, led what he considers to be "the first American student demonstration." After graduating from college, Sale became an associate editor for the leftist magazine *New Leader.* His later work as a foreign correspondent led to a fascination with Africa's political situation and in 1961 he traveled to South Africa, convinced that a revolution would soon occur. He eventually became a lecturer in history at the University of Ghana, Legon, where he worked for several years. Sale's first nonfiction volume, *The Land and People of Ghana,* describes his experiences in Africa. After returning to the United States and resuming his journalistic career, Sale decided to become a full-time nonfiction writer in 1968.

Sale's first work to gain critical note, *SDS,* is a sympathetic analysis of the Students for a Democratic Society movement of the 1960s. Reviewers were impressed with Sale's exhaustive research and meticulous attention to detail, and the book is still considered one of the most respected studies of the SDS movement to date. Sale's following work, *Power Shift: The Rise of the Southern Rim and Its Challenge to the Eastern Establishment,* centers on the political climate of the 1970s and argues that since World War II the bureaucratic power of the United States has been situated in the "Southern Rim"—a coastal area stretching from North Carolina to California. Sale believes that the Rim has been the principle beneficiary of the dominant economic and political trends in America. The first half of the work documents Southern growth, expansion, and power; the second discusses postwar presidential administrations. Although many reviewers praised Sale's dissection of the Nixon cabinet, *Power Shift* was largely criticized for factual inaccuracies and unsubstantiated generalizations. Sale's next book, *Human Scale,* an attack on the enormity and industrialization of contemporary society, is one of his best-known and most highly regarded works. Sale believes that because of large-scale technology and urbanization, human beings have lost touch with their instincts and are no longer in harmony with themselves or with nature. To replace the pressures of fast-paced, over-crowded, technologically complex lifestyles, Sale proposes a return to the smaller and more humane social systems of the past, units that would be "rooted in local circumstances and guided by local institutions." Sale has won consistent praise for the well-reasoned, convincing argument and optimistic tone of *Human Scale.*

In *Dwellers in the Land: The Bioregional Vision,* Sales focuses upon the environmental concept of "bioregionalism," a philosophy of ecological politics which maintains that people should return to their biological roots and live only on resources obtained within their geographic regions. For example, only people living in areas producing citrus fruits would drink orange juice. According to Sale, the earth's ecological problems began when the natural world was viewed as merely something to be controlled and used for human purposes. Sale's radical ecological views in *Dwellers in the Land* were regarded as utopian and overly simplistic by some, but the majority of critics commended Sale's efforts, aware that he intended to provoke thought and debate on an important subject. Environmental concerns also surface in *The Conquest of Paradise: Christopher Columbus and the Columbian Legacy,* a revisionist biography of Christopher Columbus in which Sale reassesses both the explorer and his achievements. The work, which Edward Parks described as "scholarly, ambitious, meticulous and angry," portrays Columbus as a greedy, embittered man whose "discovery" and claim of the already inhabited West Indies personified his egocentric character. The true tragedy of Columbus's discovery, according to Sale, was his complete disregard for the native Indians and their ability to live harmoniously with nature.

(See also *Contemporary Authors,* Vols. 13-16, rev. ed. and *Contemporary Authors New Revision Series,* Vol. 10.)

PRINCIPAL WORKS

NONFICTION

The Land and People of Ghana 1963; revised edition, 1972
SDS 1972
Power Shift: The Rise of the Southern Rim and Its Challenge to the Eastern Establishment 1975
Human Scale 1980
Dwellers in the Land: The Bioregional Vision 1983
The Conquest of Paradise: Christopher Columbus and the Columbian Legacy 1990

Wilson C. McWilliams

Students for a Democratic Society (SDS) was the epitome of a decade of confident turbulence. The "best and the brightest" were outsiders as well as insiders, and both were sustained by the conviction that America contained both a knowledge of the good and the means to make it effective. Students protested "hypocrisy" as often as they did because they refused to allow parents and society the excuse of moral ignorance or the plea of inability. But SDS, like its opponents and counterparts in the Kennedy and Johnson Administrations, has submerged in a sea of defeat and recrimination, new-felt weakness and self-doubt. And America proved emptier than was supposed: "Bye-Bye Miss American pie / Drove my Chevy to the levee, but the levee was dry." But despair has its own illusions. SDS, like its official adversaries, may have looked for the river of national moral strength in the wrong place.

Kirkpatrick Sale—journalist, former magazine editor, one-time teacher in Ghana—has written [*SDS*], the most detailed and the best documented history of SDS to date, moved by the sense that the remembrance of these things past may be vital to the present and future. Sale shares the hope of the founders of SDS in 1960 for an *American* left, free from precast, European ideologies like the Marxism to which SDS eventually turned in a kind of desperation. His concern is evident in the maze of names, conferences and factions, which studs his account of the development of SDS from protest to resistance to revolution. The rise of Maoist-oriented Progressive Labor (P.L.), which resulted in the final split in SDS, runs through his book like a classical nemesis. In both detail and concern, Sale's book is a major service; compared to it, Alan Adelson's *SDS: A Profile* (1971) is a bad joke. Sale deserves special thanks from today's students; effectively, SDS died in 1969, and on the campus four years is a generation and a decade is an epoch. Sale has provided students with a guide to their own recent past.

Not that Sale is an ideal historian. It hardly inspires confidence that he declares, when describing the leftward shift in SDS in 1964-65, that "the most convincing" explanation of Kennedy's assassination "suggested the complicity of the CIA, the Dallas police force, and Lyndon Johnson." And where I have some personal knowledge of SDS (in its early years), Sale often seems bemused or idiosyncratic. Since my friends regarded the formal link between SDS and the League for Industrial Democracy as only a way to get hold of LID money, I find his notion of a lineal relation between SDS and a series of Socialist-sponsored youth organizations going back to 1905 debatable at least. . . .

Too, I suspect that Sale's slighting treatment of the National Student Association—where so many early SDS leaders met and where so many ideas germinated—is due more to the later discovery of CIA funding of NSA than to a sense of history. But these are comparatively minor points.

It is far more serious that Sale, even when he inscribes the letter, misses too much of the spirit. Possibly because disillusionment has touched him too deeply, his own partisan rhetoric—and in SDS, rhetoric was always crucial—is flat, a ritualistic rodomontade like those rote-learned sectarian formulas which Sale detests. Too, his account seems to me too much concerned with formal documents and records, inadequately concerned with the personal relations between early SDS leaders especially. These were, on the whole, very lonely spirits who found joy and support in one another, and their personal ties—and even their rivalries—built relationships and understandings which gave SDS the solidarity to survive, in its early years, despite the lack of doctrine or discipline—in fact, such doctrine as SDS had was the product *of* personal interaction.

The importance of personal bonds became clear when SDS membership expanded massively between 1965 and 1967, growing to 10 times its original size. The new members were outside that structure of interpersonal understandings. Recruited largely by media coverage of SDS, they were not "more committed," as Sale asserts; they were more vehement verbally and more militant stylistically because their relation to the organization was symbolic, moralistic and quasi-ideological. Without the old personal bonds, as the event demonstrated, SDS could not survive without structure and ideological discipline.

Of course, it also could not survive *with* it because, as Sale points out, student life remained local, bound to particular chapters and campuses. And while Sale is right in arguing that campus "issues" were only signs of a deeper discontent, those problems were frequently essential in order to mobilize students at all. Since the "campus issue" was most often the result of administration tropism, SDS had a powerful interest in the stupidity of college presidents; campus reform—and increased administrative cunning—has been powerful in stifling protest.

SDS never had access to very deep commitments, the

media aside. As Sale observes, it was General Hershey's decision to end student exemptions which brought the war "home" to students. For Sale, the antiwar movement was a lost opportunity to create a permanent American left, lost because SDS hesitated to become involved in a "single-issue" campaign. But if it can be argued that SDS might have given a broader dimension to protest, the fact that the end of the draft and the cooling of zeal march hand in hand at least suggests that the roots of rebellion were shallow.

Moreover, it is doubtful if SDS was ready to lead. So much a product of mid-century America, SDS members shared too many of the basic assumptions of American culture to understand themselves, let alone lead others well. Sale describes the tensions, between SDS *as* the left and SDS as part of the left, between the university and the community, between thought and action, that racked SDS from the beginning. But most revealing is the penchant for seeking "connections" which Sale calls "the beginning of wisdom." Perhaps it is, but it also reflects a belief in order, and a very intellectual unwillingness to regard any problem as insoluble, any human dilemma as permanent and inescapable.

Wilson C. McWilliams, "A Guide for Students to Their Own Recent Past: 'SDS'," in The New York Times Book Review, *May 6, 1973, p. 3.*

Trudy Rubin

SDS is the first thorough history of the best known radical student group of the 1960's. That thoroughness may be the book's biggest problem, but readers who persist will find that ***SDS*** has a tragic and necessary story to tell.

Mr. Sale uses 750 pages, including footnotes and appendices, to chronicle the history of Students for a Democratic Society. He shows how the SDS grew out of a group of idealistic students (mostly from top-notch eastern and midnorthern universities), who were radicalized by the civil rights movements of the '60's. Their thankless years of grueling work on reform projects in the ghettoes gave way to important roles in campus rebellions, draft resistance, anti-war marches, until finally frustration and government crackdowns split the movement into dogmatic Marxists and violent Weathermen.

What SDS had needed was to develop a strategy for social change free of the old left's dogmatism. In this way it could have appealed to the vast numbers of Americans who genuinely wanted change. But instead the SDS retreated more and more into itself, ultimately grasping orthodox Marxism.

Even though they worked without pay in the ghetto, most SDS members were unable to rouse the black community and later they were rejected by the black power movement. Trying not to exclude any interested leftist, SDS was no match for the disciplined Maoist Progressive Labor Party cadres which infiltrated it and helped to destroy it. Struggling to organize working class youth, the SDS only confused and angered them. And turning in the end to bombings, it destroyed its own leadership.

Mr. Sale has based his history of the movement on 75 boxes of SDS letters, internal memos, minutes of meetings and copies of the SDS newspaper. And, although he also interviewed many past members of the SDS, his book often bogs down in superfluous details of SDS meetings—and could profit from more biographical insights into SDS members.

Mr. Sale tends to overestimate SDS's legacy. The group was never the spearhead of the anti-war movement or of the movement for social change, but as the only national "new left" organization it did become the symbol of the '60's whose membership rose as student anger grew. SDS's greatest influence was on its own members, acting as a training ground for a generation of activists. Though many former members are still politically active, they are all scattered now.

Except for a few PLP fragments calling themselves SDS, the organization has ended. On politically apathetic campuses it is hard to believe that it ever existed. Perhaps in ten years' time we shall know whether the SDS'ers have made any lasting impression on their country.

Trudy Rubin, "SDS: Shattered from Within," in The Christian Science Monitor, *May 23, 1973, p. 11.*

Richard Todd

[In ***SDS***] Kirkpatrick Sale recounts the history of the Students for a Democratic Society year by year, from the organization's beginnings in 1960, to *The Port Huron Statement* in 1962—which gave voice to discontents that hardly knew of their own existence—and on to the end of the decade, when the movement collapsed into legions of the disillusioned, packs of bombers. This chronological approach makes sense; it is virtually impossible to speak of SDS without placing it in time. The movement, spinning on the outside of the merry-go-round, changed faster than the society it sought to transform.

Sale has been remarkably diligent in reconstructing this story, and he takes pains to share his methodology: has read every issue of *New Left Notes,* interviewed scores; everything here derives from interviews or from documents, nothing is fictionalized. This is all admirable, and so is Sale's straightforward identification of his sympathies: he was not a member but a deep believer in the goals of the early organization. Work shines on every page of this book, but unhappily work doesn't prove to be sufficient.

The trouble in part derives from Sale's role, which has left him with neither the detachment of an observer nor the intimacy of an insider, and which seems instead to have imposed a romantic solemnity on him. The young men and women, whose lives were being shaped by the movement they led, stride through this chronicle as if they were prematurely old statesmen. Sale is well aware of the fascinating social history that produced SDS-ers (children of the old left—"Red-diaper babies"—as well as sons and daughters of the suburban upper middle class). And he's aware of the personal revolutions that occurred. But, though he alludes to all of this, he fails to evoke it.

The most engaging part of the book is the one least under Sale's control, his account of the last years of the movement and the formation of its factions: the Revolutionary Youth Movement, Progressive Labor, and the Weathermen. It is the sheer stuff of this period that is fascinating: the desperate efforts at willed community, the absurdist Days of Rage, the attempts to elide classes and causes. Sale feels evident moral ambivalence about these days. He alternately scowls and sighs at the sight of the high-minded ideas of the past crystallizing into rigid ideology and violence. He knows better than to forgive all on grounds of the government's actions—and yet he wants to do so nonetheless, and so we have such sonorous and queasy sentences as ". . . President Nixon intervened to order 'a new crackdown' on those who would use bombs five thousand miles away from Vietnam."

It may well be true, as Sale hopes, that SDS left a "legacy" from which "will evolve a new organization and a new leftward spirit." In any event, in the organization that recently existed extraordinary human drama occurred, but much of it has slipped through Sale's fingers. (p. 98)

Richard Todd, "Left, Right, Gonzo!" in The Atlantic Monthly, *Vol. 232, No. 1, July, 1973, pp. 97-101.*

Robert Lekachman

Like other native New Yorkers, I grew up fully confident that the only human force in my land more powerful than one Rockefeller was two, or several, Rockefellers. As New York sullenly declines, what are true believers like me to make of a situation in which the nation's appointed President presumes to ignore the pleas not alone of that Rockefeller whom he selected as Vice President, but also of the sibling who manages the family bank down at Chase Manhattan Plaza? Is there no respect? Don't the big rich run things any more?

Kirkpatrick Sale's striking new book [***Power Shift***] conveys a message of reassurance. True, the rich are doing worse in their traditional Eastern habitat but they are faring very well indeed elsewhere in the United States. The Eastern Establishment's difficulty in contriving a Washington rescue of New York City and its premier financial institutions can be interpreted as a natural reflection of a power shift of seismic dimensions from the East and Midwest that, since 1870, have manipulated national investment, dictated the Presidential choices of the major parties, and shaped Congressional policy to their own regional benefit.

In the last 30 years, as Kevin Phillips among others has argued, this power has been flowing in the direction of the Southern Rim. Writing from the left, Sale two years ago produced a massively documented history of SDS of interest to a rather specialized audience of radicals and radical watchers. ***Power Shift,*** which attests to its author's continuing effort to analyze the culture in which political and economic domination flourishes, is a much more important and much more successful interpretation of a generation of turbulent change in the American political economy. In Sale's political geography the Southern Rim of the country stretches southward along the Atlantic coast from North Carolina, turns west along the Gulf Coast, dips inland to Tennessee, Arkansas, Oklahoma, New Mexico, Arizona and the southern tip of Nevada, and terminates in golden California. It is a region, according to Sale, unified by a "climatic, historical, and cultural cohesiveness, that serves to set this broad band off from the rest of the country in many ways." In the three decades since the end of World War II, the Southern Rim's population has doubled from 40 to 80 million souls, a growth much more rapid than that of the remainder of the nation. Its rich economy has been favored by six rapidly developing sectors: oil, leisure industries, defense, advanced technology, agribusiness and real estate.

If the Southern Rim were an independent nation, its Gross National Product would exceed that of any other country except the Soviet Union. Save again for the Russians, the citizens of the Rim drive more cars on more miles of paved highway, speak over more telephones in more housing units and own more television sets than the denizens of less favored lands. On the average, since 1945, 650,000 people have migrated from dourer Northern states to the sunbelt. Naturally the cities of the area have doubled, trebled and quadrupled in population. (p. 1)

As Sale demonstrates in lively detail, the Southern sun shines on a culture especially hospitable to unbridled avarice. The dominant cult of individual achievement measured in dollars and pursued at any cost and by any method, legal or otherwise, is abetted by right wing Protestant fundamentalism, virulent anti-Communism, rampant anti-unionism and militant patriotism. The Rim's far right politics are buttressed by the enduring racism of a society historically allied to slavery.

The political consequences of this economic phenomenon are spectacular. After each census, additional seats in the House of Representatives accrue to the Southern Rim at the expense of older population centers. Next year it is entirely possible that the Rim will supply the candidates of both major parties, plus George Wallace. Ronald Reagan will be the Republican standard bearer if Ford continues to falter. Among the Democratic contenders, Fred Harris, Jimmy Carter, Lloyd Bentsen and Morris Udall all hail from Rim states.

If these possibilities of a muddled campaign year materialize as political reality, they will do no more than accentuate a trend toward Southern Rim control of the Presidency which begins with Lyndon Johnson and continues with Richard Nixon. Sale interprets the latter's Southern strategy as much more than a mere reward for hard-core, reactionary types like Strom Thurmond who in 1968 guaranteed Nixon's nomination by warding off Ronald Reagan. Nixon acted out of a rational assessment of the shifting locale of economic power.

Some of the best pages in ***Power Shift*** anatomize Johnson-Nixon coddling of the Rim's interests and prejudices. Faltering defense contractors like Litton and Lockheed were bailed out. New space and defense installations congested the Texas landscape. Nixon made a specialty of conscientiously sabotaging the civil rights statutes of the 1960's.

Two concluding chapters examine the Yankee counterattack against Nixon and the cowboy economics of the Rim. (pp. 1-2)

Sale expected Nelson Rockefeller to play a far more effective role as protector of Eastern finance and industry than, as the universe now perceives, he was able to achieve. His defeat might be credited (or debited) to the Reagan wing except that a principal beneficiary, Donald Rumsfeld, is a Midwesterner and the principal loser, James Schlesinger, has been a firm partisan of the escalating defense expenditures that primarily enrich the Southern Rim. . . .

This is a convenient place to note the flaws, small and substantial, that mar a generally impressive inquiry into American political economy. Minor but annoying inaccuracies of detail are fairly common. Robert Dole of Kansas is no Easterner. Banfield's first name is Edward, not Arthur, Robert Mayo and David Kennedy are bankers, not economists (the economists are doing badly enough on their own without undeserved recruits). Gerald Ford has numerous faults but he definitely played on the Michigan varsity, not the second team, as Sale erroneously asserts. And so on.

At the top of his form, as in much of his discussion of Nixon, Sale writes clear, vivid, sometimes eloquent prose. But the opening pages in particular are damaged by neologisms, awkward grammatical constructions and endless sentences whose parts are connected by triads of dots. Considerably more serious is a tendency to strain argument beyond evidence. No doubt the far right kookery of the Rim flourishes on the oil millions furnished by the Frawleys and Hunts. But as Sale's own listings of prominent Southern politicians attest, it is possible for Populists like Harris to be elected in Oklahoma, racial moderates of the Askew-Carter-Sanford-Bumpers variety to become Senators and Governors, and orthodox Northern liberals like Alan Cranston and John Tunney to surmount southern California's preferences for the reactionary right. At the least, Southern politics are less monolithic than Sale often implies.

The momentum of his strong thesis tempts Sale into occasional personal as well as regional injustice. It is convenient but less than fair to lump together Lyndon Johnson and Richard Nixon and to sneer at Johnson's commitment to racial equality and the war on poverty. Johnson seems at his political peak to have been a dominant enough President simultaneously to represent Texas oil interests and to heed out of genuine personal emotion the claims of the poor and the black. Sale, who manifestly detests Johnson as much as Nixon, skates longingly around a MacBird theory of the Kennedy assassination. Asking *quo bono,* he lists as the beneficiaries of John Kennedy's elimination defense contractors, the chieftains of organized crime, and, inevitably, Lyndon Johnson. Central to this argument is the still controversial proposition that at the time of his death, Kennedy had decided to withdraw from Vietnam, explore détente with Cuba and China, and reduce Pentagon appropriations and influence.

As Sale, not quite often enough, reminds himself, the cowboy mentality is a state of mind not confined by geographical location. Cowboys seem to be at work in Alaska, Saudi Arabia, Iran, Kuwait and elsewhere. Nevertheless, its excesses and other defects aside, ***Power Shift*** holds the field as the most serious investigation available into the implications of a genuine power shift. Overall it is a powerful and persuasive polemic, a handy weapon for both the political left and respectable members of the old, beleaguered Eastern Establishment. (p. 2)

Robert Lekachman, "Cowboys versus Yankees," in The New York Times Book Review, *November 30, 1975, pp. 1-2.*

James Fallows

Nearly three years ago, when Richard Nixon's happy days were coming to an end, Kirkpatrick Sale published an article in *The New York Review of Books.* Its title was **"The World behind Watergate,"** and its thesis was that the men around Nixon, far from being agents of an unguided immorality, represented a precise geographical interest. "The Nixonian bedfellows, the people whose creed the President expresses," were, said Sale, "the economic sovereigns of America's Southern Rim, the 'sunbelt' that runs from Southern California, through Arizona and Texas, down to the Florida keys." They rose on the postwar strength of the space industry, high technology, defense, and oil; with their rise came the relative decline of the Yankees, the old-money titans of the industrial Northeast.

With the inevitability of a natural cycle, the provocative article has become the misconceived book. But in the creation of ***Power Shift*** something more than the usual padding process has been at work. As one of the most vulgarly oversimplified works of recent political analysis, the book squanders an abundance of rich material; and, as a sneering, nasty diatribe, it inadvertently explains some of the free-floating ill will now abroad in the land.

The riches appear in the first quarter of the book, when Sale describes the processes which have allowed the Rim to dominate American politics. . . . [The] traditional manufacturing and financial centers of the North have, since World War II, seen capital, innovation, people, and, finally, political power flow south, toward the sun. Houston had a population of 400,000 at the beginning of World War II; now it is pushing 2 million. From the electronics industries of the San Francisco Bay to the resort towns of Florida, the South and West rest securely on what Sale calls the six pillars of the Rim economy—defense contracting, agriculture (mainly corporate farms), the technology businesses (such as computers), real estate (in continual boom), the leisure industries, and, it need hardly be said, oil. The evidence is tantalizing, and if Sale had foresworn his vendetta he might have gone on to examine it with the thoroughness and complexity it requires.

Instead, the book careens off into political interpretations that are insulting when not wholly implausible. To put his case crudely, but not much more crudely than the author himself does, Sale argues that the economic power of the Rim has led to a steady increase in political power, until the "Cowboys" have come to dominate the national arena. After a twenty-year climb, the Cowboy ascendancy lasted nearly eleven years, from November 22, 1963, when a Texas assassination created a Texan President, until August 9, 1974, when the "Yankee counterattack" drove Nixon and his ranch hands back to San Clemente. The successful completion of this campaign not only installed Gerald Ford—a "Yankee" in Sale's scheme—but also ushered in the man Sale cleverly fingers as the real power behind the throne, Nelson Rockefeller.

As in most of Sale's arguments, there is a partial truth buried here: Southern politicians and Southern Presidents have had their recent heyday. But Sale's explanations of the beginning and the end of the Cowboy regime illustrate how the partial truth can be torpedoed by his exaggerated argumentation. In his treatise on Dallas, as elsewhere in the book, Sale slips in a one-line disclaimer, for "objectivity's" sake, before driving on to his loaded conclusion:

> No doubt the truth about the assassination of Jack Kennedy will be a long time coming, if ever, but there is an old legal principle that can stand us in temporary stead in the meantime: *cui bono*—to whose advantage?—the idea that probable responsibility for an act lies with those with something to gain. *Cui bono* Dallas? A confluence of forces including organized crime (especially its Southern branch), the defense industry (especially its Texas components), the oil industry (especially its newer and Texas-based elements), the Far Right (especially its Texas and Floridian branches), and beyond doubt Lyndon Johnson, thirty-sixth President of the United States. Or, to put it in three words, the Southern Rim.

Sale fills in the picture even more tidily in describing Nixon's last days. Most of those who stood by the embattled cowboy were, logically enough, men from the Rim . . . says Sale, "not an Ivy Leaguer among them." But an apparent exception crops up—the hired gun from Boston, James St. Clair. Sale hardly breaks stride as he gives the obvious explanation—that St. Clair was "brought in for window dressing to deceive and deflect the Yankee intensity." Even Leon Jaworski was part of the scheme. When he came up from Houston, capital of the Rim, to serve as special prosecutor, Nixon found him to be "if not exactly a subservient lackey, which he never expected, a man who had a rough identity with Richard Nixon and a lifelong attachment to exactly the same interests . . . and who could be expected to be as minimal a prosecutor as possible. Nixon was not disappointed." Again, there may once have been an insight here, but by the time Sale has finished smashing it with the flatiron of his analysis, it is distorted beyond recognition.

Other questions arise about this theory—about the categories themselves, for a start. Since the time of Sale's first article, the Rim seems to have grown; it now includes practically everything south of a line between San Francisco and the southern border of Virginia, and about a third of the country's population. Now and then Sale admits an exception to his simple scheme, but more often his relentless geographical determinism leads to [bizarre and indiscriminate agglomerations]. . . . (pp. 76, 80)

Sale bulldozes . . . bothersome details out of the way. Of all the Cowboys who have come to Washington since the war, Earl Warren, that son of California, might be thought to be one of the most important. But because he won't fit Sale's one-dimensional scheme, he is never mentioned by name in this book (his commission does come in for criticism of its investigations in Dallas). Abe Fortas, on the other hand, crops up several times as a representative Cowboy malefactor, in contexts such as this: "The only member of the United States Supreme Court in its 200-year history ever to resign in the face of public scandal, and thereby escape impeachment charges, was Abe Fortas, from Tennessee—appointed by Lyndon Johnson, from Texas." Here is a man who has spent nearly every moment of his adult life in the Northeast; yet Sale makes him a Cowboy, because he was born in Tennessee.

All this is irritating, and there is irritation, too, in Sale's style, with its sentences strung together with ellipses, its ugly neologisms (*Rimian, pantokratorial*), and its misuse of words (e.g., *enormity* to mean large size). But the truly noxious aspect of the book is its patent hatred for the culture of the Rim. The purpose of ***Power Shift*** is not to delineate the different cultures in this country, nor to make a stab at understanding them through their values and premises, but rather to prove that one of the cultures is bad, bad, bad.

Here I should, perhaps, lay my own cards on the table. I am a Californian by upbringing, but I was educated in, and assimilated by, the very bosom of the Yankee motherland. If forced to choose tomorrow, I would probably cast my spiritual lot with the Yankees rather than the Cowboys, though with full awareness that each regional culture is a quite mixed blessing. Despite that, my hackles rise as Sale performs his heavy-handed denunciation of the three Rs on which Rim culture is based—"Rightism, Racism, and Repression." Indeed, the worst effect of this book may be that it provokes the reader into an equally simple-minded game of "So's your old man." When Sale talks about the rigid conservatism of the Rim ("Like the shotgun in the closet, it makes the Southern Rim a perpetual threat in American politics"), one's thoughts turn to Robert Welch in Massachusetts, the Wallace vote in Michigan, the rampaging hardhats of New York. When Sale proclaims that "for moral obtuseness, there is no place like Texas," such names as Annapolis, Jersey City, and Cook County come to mind. When Sale cites the brutal violence of Southern football as an explanation for the sins of our Cowboy Presidents ("In the last ten years, under the guidance of two Southern Rim Presidents, repression has stalked a national path. This cannot be a coincidence"), one thinks of Woody Hayes, Vince Lombardi, and the football crowds of Pittsburgh and Green Bay. Throughout his analysis, Sale strains to find the representative Rim figure; after toying with Johnson and Nixon, he seems to favor Bebe Rebozo. With equal subtlety and fair-mindedness, one might paint a picture of Northeastern culture featuring dope fiends and welfare chiselers, its representative citizens being Boss Tweed, Richard Speck, and Lucky Luciano.

The loaded comparisons reach an extreme of sorts when Sale contrasts the dignified tranquillity of the Canadian border with the seamy corruption of life along the Rio Grande. One can only wonder at this point which of two explanations is true: that Sale is unaware of the difference between fat and happy Canada, and Mexico, with its severe unemployment and its marijuana fields—or that he simply decided not to mention it.

"Can it only be a coincidence," Sale asks after describing the terror in Vietnam and the crackdown on dissent at home, "that these processes were concurrent with the emergence of the Southern Rim on the national scene? . . . That the last two elected Presidents, who brought political morality to its dimmest point in generations, were from the Southern Rim?" Indeed, it may be more than coincidence; for while many of the traits Sale denounces are human traits, and others are merely national, a few of them may have some special relation to the South and its peculiarities. For example, the difficulties of the outsider, when plunged into the metropolis, has been one of the constant themes of our culture, not only in dealings between East and West, but also in the relationship between America and Europe. Henry James had his Isabel Archer; William Faulkner had his Quentin Compson; in his recent biography of Bernard DeVoto, Wallace Stegner painted the classic portrait of a Westerner who was never permitted to forget his origins while living in the East.

No one who has read the chronicles of the two Cowboy administrations can doubt that both Johnson and Nixon, in their different ways, had their psyches twisted and their policies shaped by the difficulty of coming to terms with the world of John Kennedy and McGeorge Bundy. There may even be something specific in the California air that produces Nixons, Haldemans, Mansons, and worse. But no one will come close to figuring out these forces, or anything else about the national culture, as long as understanding gives way to these vulgar broadsides. Sale's analysis—not only of Nixon and Johnson, but of Southern religion, Southern business, Southern people—is motivated by nothing but contempt, and the results are in keeping with the intention.

The tragedy of this contempt is that it has recently been reciprocated. There is anxiety in Washington when George Wallace denounces the government pointy-heads, and despair in New York when Middle America rejoices in its fall. As long as books like ***Power Shift*** exist, the mindless hatred can be no mystery. George Wallace and Kirkpatrick Sale may be talking past each other, but they are speaking the same language. (pp. 80, 82)

James Fallows, "South against North," in Harper's, *Vol. 252, No. 1509, February, 1976, pp. 76, 80, 82.*

Chilton Williamson, Jr.

Philosophically and aesthetically, ***Power Shift*** is a negligible book. It has none of the solidity and comprehensiveness of another Sale opus—***SDS,*** the history of that unsavory alphabet society—and some of its defects, most particularly a crippling refusal to engage in pragmatic empathy with the unconverted, which bars its author from making sense of the great American political divides. . . .

In tone ***Power Shift*** is at once journalistically slick and radically "authentic"; it drops many a cliché and indulges in numerous stylistic gimmickries; and it represents the fantastic simplification of an already simple proposition that is not even original to Kirkpatrick Sale. Most of what Sale has to say has been said before. . . . ***Power Shift*** is another excellent indication that the recent "no-growth" philosophy is as applicable to publishing as to California: its development ought to have been terminated when it reached the rosy amplitude of a bouncing magazine article.

Simply put—there is no other way to state it—Sale's thesis is that the Southern Rim, "the broad band of America that stretches from Southern California through the Southwest and Texas, into the Deep South and down to Florida," has since 1945 been the principal and unfailing beneficiary of the predominant trends—demographic, economic, and political—prevailing in the United States. Nourished by the tiger's milk of an imperial economy, the Rim has attained to power and to an influence so overweening as to allow it first to challenge and then to dominate—through the Nixon Administration, its most poisonously succulent fruit—the traditional Northeastern Establishment. Sale describes the southward shifting of the population toward a climate fit for suckling brats and cranky septuagenarians; he describes how certain favorable geographic factors (most especially, an abundance of physical space) have caused many new industries (particularly the technological, aerospace, and defense industries) to birth themselves within the Rim; he describes the (to him) Byzantine favors, mainly pecuniary, that Congress lavishes upon these industries in return for the protection of the country against the machinations of Russian polytechnic grads; the offers of encouragement to the oil and natural gas industries and "agribusiness," all of which keep the United States supplied with things that make even socialists happy; and the gradual ascendancy of the "Rimians" on Capitol Hill, as well as the multiplying possibilities available to them for the extension of the sway of their *Weltanschauung* over the rest of us.

The Southern Rim is, for Sale, a study in political and economic pathology. . . . He regards it as a vast stew of Ku Klux Klanners, venal mobile home salesmen, loaded-dice Mafiosi, limousined Baptist preachers, washermen who take in greenbacks, red-baiting politicos, hit men, and tycoons whose snot is oil: a land where "can do" parades itself as a respectable ethical system, where ignorance is bliss, and where theological and political fundamentalism is reducible to a sort of quasi-sadism. At the heart of this pathology is "the still-potent frontier experience of most of the Southern Rim," a powerful expression of which is "the attachment to the *land,* especially the emphasis upon property and its inviolability, to be defended with a shotgun if necessary." The sort of society that this mentality produces, Sale argues, can

> grow up anywhere, at almost any time. In the last quarter of the nineteenth century, that society was to be found in the Northeast, where a culture of rapid growth produced . . . the whole stinking swill of nineteenth-century capitalism out of which the current Northeastern Estab-

> lishment has risen. In the middle of the twentieth century, that society was to be found in the Southern Rim.

Sale's great nightmare is that before the Northeast—that recently and only partially enlightened area—can socialize the Rim, the Rim will rebarbarize the Northeast.

What is of greater interest than the book's two principal theses (that the South is increasing in both prosperity and influence . . .) is the disapproval with which Sale regards the phenomena to which he has addressed himself: a disapproval which appears to cause him much unhappiness and which, I suspect, his recent researches for his book [***The Land and People of Ghana***] did nothing to alleviate.

For it is unlikely that Sale would agree with Pat Moynihan that socialism is better at distributing wealth in a developed society than it is at creating it in an underdeveloped one; and much of what Sale is pleased to call the Southern Rim has, for a century, been an underdeveloped society. But since World War II the South, for years laughed at as "the hookworm and pellagra" and "nocturnal emissions belt," has been bestirring itself, has begun to contribute its share to the national welfare; concomitantly, the Southwest is seeking to divest itself of its reputation as the nation's tubercle and spittle zone. Civilization in America, once relegated to the Northeast, is backing up against the national boundaries like water in a plugged tub. Sale and his ilk, watching the process, are horrified to observe that this force is proceeding according to the mores of a frontier society: underneath it all they espy what Sale himself calls an "anti-democratic current." And yet that current is quite palpably less anti-democratic in its thrust than it is Jacksonian-democratic—redolent of the spirit of an editorial written in 1847 by Walt Whitman, then a newspaper editor:

> Under a proper organization, and even to a great extent as things are, the wealth and happiness of the citizens could hardly be touched by government, could neither be retarded nor advanced. . . . In this wide and naturally rich country, the best government is indeed 'that which governs least.'

If you want to talk about corrupt infringement *in practice* upon that philosophy, that's another matter entirely.

Thus it is that Mr. Sale appears to have arrived, since his days as a member of SDS, at a reappraisal of the elitist Northeastern Establishment, where Whitman is better known for his homosexuality than for his political theory. One gets the impression that, were Nelson Rockefeller's Maine villa, with Mr. Rockefeller aboard it, sawn away from the New England coast and left to drift into the North Atlantic, Kirkpatrick Sale might well be persuaded to run with Rocky's minions. No enemy to the north of Nashville! (pp. 225-26)

Chilton Williamson, Jr., "Zapping the Spittle Zone," in National Review, *New York, Vol. 28, March 5, 1976, pp. 225-26.*

William C. Harvard

Ever since the beginnings of the Southern defection from the Democratic Party in 1948, political observers have been speculating about the possible breakup of the New Deal coalition. And since sectionalism has been one of the constants in the history of partisan alignment in American politics, much of this speculation has focused on the possible emergence of new regional party alliances. The recent reversal (since 1960) of the older electoral pattern in which the Northeast consistently provided the strongest basis of support for the Republicans and the South furnished the highest proportions of votes for the Democrats in presidential elections lends support to the possibility that a realignment is under way. The appearance in 1969 of Kevin Phillips's *The Emerging Republican Majority* not only stimulated debate on the issue but, by combining analysis with advocacy in the advancement of the theory of an incipient conservative coalition among the "Sun Belt" states, reinforced the plausibility of the Southern Strategy among the members of the then dominant wing of the Republican Party.

Kirkpatrick Sale's bold leap into this political thicket affirms, with some alterations, the Phillips thesis on the emergence of a Southern-Southwestern political bloc, [which Sale refers to as the Southern Rim], but the central purpose of ***Power Shift*** is to provide an ideological refutation of Phillips's assumption that this potential new geographical locus of pivotal electoral power is a good thing for the country. (p. 712)

According to Sale, the economic growth of the Southern Rim is based on six basic "pillars": agribusiness, defense, advanced technology, oil and gas, real estate and construction, and tourism and leisure. Since World War II, developments in these industries have "tilted" the country southward in terms of population growth, economic expansion, and political power, largely at the expense of the Northeast, with its older, slower-growth economy based on financial institutions and basic manufacturing industries. Although the major portion of the first half of the book is devoted to a sometimes questionable quantitative documentation of the shift, the essence of the book is the contrast drawn between the two "cultures" posited by Sale. And on that count Senator Goldwater's suggestion that the Northeast ought to be detached from the rest of the country and floated out to sea was a mild solution to the problem as he saw it compared with what the author of ***Power Shift*** must have in mind for the Southern Rim on the basis of his unrelieved indictment of everybody and everything in the United States south of the 37th parallel.

The author has a penchant for cute turns of phrase, *e.g.,* "oilionaires", "moondoggle", and "rococonutty" (the adjective applied to Miami Beach). And he has a mean talent for invective. One would have thought, for example, that it would have been sufficient to brand George Wallace ". . . a racist, a demagogue, a crude, vindictive, repressive, power hungry bigot," but with the insensitivity of a malicious and morally unrestrained child, Sale goes on to describe him as "a tiny man whose body is half useless now and confined to a wheelchair, the governor of a nationally insignificant state. . . . " But this is no more than one might expect from a moralizer who is prepared to condemn an entire (sub?) "culture" and all of its people for "rightism," "racism," and "repression," and who rather indiscriminately flings the degrading term "rednecks" around, while being over-solicitous (as obviously befits an Eastern educated person of high culture) about the terminological characterization of those social classes and groups to which he has extended absolution.

Sale's consummate descriptive phrase for the Southern Rim, however, is the "Cowboy Culture," a term he applies so repeatedly, so chauvinistically, and with such a complete disregard for internal differences in the area that it loses all sardonic bite and simply becomes boring. That the latest "New South" tendencies have some relation both to the frontier expansionism of historic memory and the urban-industrial expansiveness of the developing Southwest is not in question. And it is even possible that the Sun Belt political alignment may be a factor in whatever geographical redistribution of political party strength may be under way in the United States. But strain as he will, Sale cannot override all the historical differences that prevent the immediate homogenization of either of the two cultural regions he attempts to identify, any more than he can totally dissociate the entreprenurial spirit, the political spoilsmanship, and the aggressive upward mobility of the emerging South and the Southwest from their national antecedents in the Gilded Age, McKinleyism, and Business Progressivism, all of which were prominent in the earlier annals of the Northeast, and are perhaps not entirely eradicated even today. But if he cannot override all internal distinctions or totally disconnect the Southern Rim's extravagant social behavior from its sources in national experience, he does ignore such challenges to the comprehensiveness of his thesis to the extent possible, and when he cannot ignore them he apologizes them away.

For Sale, the Southern Rim has reached a stage of total degradation. All of the evils of contemporary American society can be traced to the patterns of behavior associated with the Cowboy Culture, including the military-industrial establishment, Vietnam, racism, and crime (the politics of organized crime resembles that of the Cowboy Culture because both dislike interference by the federal government). (pp. 713-15)

The sum of the matter is that Sale pushes a thesis which has limited validity at best to the point of absurdity. But there is a more insidious side to ***Power Shift.*** Muckraking has long been a semi-respectable form of American journalism, but recently we have witnessed a trend that goes beyond muckraking and becomes a total critique of society or of some social class, segment, or section of society. Heavy-handedly sensationalist, as in the case of the book at hand, this genre (if it can be called that) evokes a Manichean version of morals and politics in which good and evil are absolute, and are absolutely identifiable by authorial ascription. This type of writing plays on and exaggerates existing divisions in society by denying the existence of common values (and common problems) that might make it possible to reconcile the divisions. It is ironic that in the obvious concentration on saleability those examples of this literature which may be identified with the left blatantly display the complicity of their authors in the capitalistic excesses they so roundly condemn.

If one were in a defensive mood, many of Sale's arguments could be answered on their own level by reference to such snappy retorts as that contained in the country music song, "I Wouldn't Live in New York City if You Gave Me the Whole Dang Town," or in the suggestion by Carleton Putnam (the last exponent of classically orthodox arguments supporting racial segregation, and non-Southerner who now lives in the South) that those who regard Southern whites as degenerate should take a ride on a New York subway and give their fellow passengers a close scrutiny for comparative purposes. But I prefer a more direct response from the Gallic sector of the Cowboy Culture. For years a revue entitled the "Fudge Ripple Follies" ran in New Orleans (it may still be playing there). Its sub-title, "Nobody Likes a Smart Ass," seems particularly applicable here. (pp. 716-17)

William C. Harvard, "Power Is Where Power Goes," in The Virginia Quarterly Review, *Vol. 52, No. 4, Autumn, 1976, pp. 712-17.*

Walt Anderson

[***Human Scale*** is an] important book for several reasons. One is its position that a thinking environmentalist in the 1980s must go beyond the specific issues first identified with the movement and begin to deal with larger issues of politics and the world's future. The energy crisis and its literature have been taking us in that direction: Amory Lovins' hard and soft paths, for example, are not only antithetical energy strategies but also fundamentally different images of progress. As categories of political thought, they are more useful and timely in many ways than the more traditional right and left.

One big difference between the hard and the soft paths in Lovins' writings is not the fuel source: it is the mode of organization that the technology calls into being—one a large centralized organization, the other a decentralized system of smaller units. ***Human Scale*** picks up this idea and applies it across a wide range of policy matters, from health to industrial productivity.

The book's front cover announces that it "examines a nation in the grips of growth-mania and presents the ways to shape a more efficient and livable society." The terms "efficient" and "livable" sum up the key arguments, which are (1) that smaller systems do a better job of producing whatever social or economic outputs they were intended for, and (2) that they are more humane, providing richer satisfactions for those involved in them.

So this is in part a refutation of the "economies of scale" argument that is trotted out wherever large-vs.-small issues become politicized—as, for example, in the celebrated controversy over the 160-acre limit on farms that may irrigate with water from federal reclamation projects. It is also a welcome introduction of real and important *human* questions that are all too often left out of economic debates. Sale argues that smaller farms are generally more productive—a position he supports with a mountain of evidence—and also that they are more energy-efficient, less ecologically destructive and more conducive to community interaction. Regions with smaller farms are found to be economically healthier and to have local political and social institutions that are much more vigorous than the ones in comparable regions dominated by large agribusiness holdings.

The two prospective futures Sale envisions involve choices between bigness and smallness. One is a future of "large-scale institutions, multinational corporations, centralized governments, high-technology machinery, large cities, high-rise buildings, luxury cars, and all that is implied in the American ethic of unimpeded growth." The other is a move toward "the decentralization of institutions and the devolution of power, with the slow dismantling of all the large-scale systems that one way or another have created or perpetuated the current crises, and their replacement by smaller, more controllable, more efficiently people-sized units, rooted in local circumstances and guided by local citizens."

This may sound like too much emphasis on the single factor of size, but Sale argues persuasively that the size of any system is a central variable affecting such characteristics as its degree of authoritarianism, the personal rewards it provides to the people engaged in it, its capacity for socially responsible behavior, its flexibility and its ecological impacts. This thesis is a challenge to rethink some of the ideas behind the major political and economic decisions that have been made since the concept of "manifest destiny" first assumed that a bigger nation would inevitably be a better and happier one. Sale believes, in fact, that a major scaling-down—and eventual phasing-out—of the nation-state as a political institution is in order.

One weakness of the book is a certain ambiguity about whether it is an argument for a small-scale future or a program for how to get there. Sometimes it seems to be one, sometimes the other. As a program it is pretty feeble, especially since it fails entirely to confront the issue of population growth, which is carrying us headlong toward an urbanized, angry, hungry and crowded world that will have little room or patience for the amiable ecotopias Sale envisions.

Another weakness is that ***Human Scale*** has a case of the very disease it seeks to stamp out—this is a large book (558 pages). Also, some of its deficiencies—especially its lapses into hurried argumentation in which a large conclusion is drawn from one piece of evidence, and an occasional tendency to hit the reader over the head with the point—are, I suspect, concessions to current ideas of commercial appeal. (pp. 63-5)

[***Human Scale***] is an environmental book. It challenges us to raise our vision once in a while from the current necessary preoccupation with trying to inject a little environmental protection into an environmentally malignant system, and to think about how to make political and economic systems that would be environmentally sound without depending on the protection of huge bureaucracies and without being eternally vulnerable to shifts in the political wind.

Getting there will not be easy. But we cannot function without models of progress, and that is what ***Human Scale*** is—a well-reasoned reassessment of ideas about what a desirable future world might be like. It offers an image of an economically and ecologically stable global society composed of many diverse, self-governing and relatively independent subsystems. This is a concept that should be examined thoroughly and kept at the very center of political discussion. Kirkpatrick Sale deserves our gratitude for having produced a work that fleshes out the small-scale argument so fully and provides a useful resource with which to explore one of the important issues of our time. (p. 65)

Walt Anderson, "A Look into a Smaller Future," in Sierra, *Vol. 66, No. 2, March-April, 1981, pp. 63-5.*

"I write my books to help save society and the planet; I'm actually trying to influence the public psychology and policy of this and other industrial societies, before it's too late. That's very different from what a novelist does: he's trying to create a work of art, which he'd love to see become a bestseller but which he would write anyway. It's very important to me that my books be read, not for reputation or money, but because of what I'm trying to do—influence people in a profound way."

—Kirkpatrick Sale, 1990

Andrew Hacker

[In ***Human Scale***] Kirkpatrick Sale lists the afflictions that beset our time: "loneliness, powerlessness, insecurity, anxiety, anomie, boredom, bewilderment, alienation, rudeness, suicide, mental illness, alcoholism, drug usage, divorce, violence, sexual dysfunction." Another list—he has many—mentions Three Mile Island, *Hustler,* and the square tomato. A poll reveals 53 percent agreeing that "something is deeply wrong with America." And what is wrong, Sale says, is that we allow too much to happen, events rush by too fast, we are called upon to take in more than we can absorb. Most critical of all, we have let the world grow too large for what the human body can bear. If we wish mental and moral health, we must return to circumscribed lives, consonant with our capacities. So ***Human Scale*** proposes

> dismantling all the large-scale systems that one way or another have created or perpetuated our current crises, and their replacement by smaller, more controllable, more efficient, people-sized units, rooted in local circumstances and guided by local situations.

Like Jefferson and Rousseau, Sale would have us living in settings

> of such a size as can be comprehended by a single individual, known at least by acquaintance by all others, where the problems of life are thus kept to manageable proportions, and security is the natural outcome of association.

On this reckoning, no community will number more than several hundred people. Sale feels such a life can be fully satisfying. On the material side, local workshops will fill our immediate needs, and communities will keep in touch with one another by exchanging products and ideas. Simplicity need not be stultifying. Even in a small village, variety will flourish if its inhabitants are encouraged to develop all their faculties. Indeed, only in small-scale settings can humanity be whole. So we will see, Sale says, the "ascendance of womanly virtues: spontaneity, permissiveness, sexuality, emotion, softness, cooperation, lovingness."

Sale bases his prescription on a biological premise. The human constitution can stand only so much strain. Past a certain point, crowding and complexity begin to take a toll. The effects are more than physical: mental health deteriorates and moral standards falter. The problem is that our species, unlike others, will not acknowledge its limits in the social sphere. Ants keep the hills they build to proportions they can manage. Human beings, unhappily, have lost touch with their instincts. Hence the all too common assumption that we can adapt to whatever we create. This overreaching attitude, in Sale's view, underlies the faith in technological progress. Synthetic fuels and genetic splicing are seen as challenges to our ingenuity; so is living with nuclear fission and a chemical-laden climate. Sale calls all this the "techno-fix" mentality; if progress brings more problems, then cure them with more progress. He could have carried the argument further, for it is one that has been with us since Prometheus played with fire.

For the metaphysic of technology, mankind's mission is to improve on nature, transmuting what we find by means of our intelligence. We can curb flood, famine, and disease, building an ever better life from the elements around us. Technology liberates humanity by expanding opportunities. Nature awaits to be developed; our battle for its bounty has only just begun.

To all this Sale, and those sharing his view, must reply that human interventions have reached the point where nature is so violated that it is itself in peril. It is not enough to say that pesticides, for example, can upset a natural balance. Nature is never in equilibrium, and upheavals wrought this planet prior to man's arrival. It must be argued, rather, that we are causing changes as no species ever has; and if we do not stop our surroundings will rebel. Fluorocarbon sprays could so damage the ozone layer as to make this continent a desert. Acid rain can turn the weather against us in ways impervious to control. So the case against technology must be that we are not as clever as we think. The sciences man creates are no better than his intellect, at best a bounded instrument, never made to master the natural world. Mount St. Helens may have been sending us a message. Others may be on the way.

Sale is also anti-city. Once in our rural renaissance, we will "not have need for cities bulging with two, three, or seven million people." For several thousand years, cities have been luring people from the land. Of course much of this migration was not a matter of choice, but resulted from crop failures, changes in land tenure, and less need for rural labor. Even so, there have always been people who, once there, found urban life to their liking. Persons of all classes have spent their entire lives in cities and would not have it any other way. The pleasures surpass the problems in their personal calculations. So when Sale says we will not "need" cities, he seems to be suggesting that while several million people claim they actually like being pushed against one another, efforts should be made to persuade them to another, better way.

Human Scale calls to mind Jefferson, who called cities "pestilential to the morals, the health, and liberties of man." The charge, in Jefferson's time as now, is that many city-dwellers fail to realize how their health and morals have undergone erosion. What passes for urban tolerance, for example, may reveal a weakening of character. Sale really ought to say whether his down-scaled world will disperse cities for their residents' own good. A perennial problem for Utopias is what to do with citizens who seem bent on harming themselves. Rousseau at least grasped this nettle: those who remain misguided will have "to be forced to be free."

In one unintended way, ***Human Scale*** makes a very convincing case. The book weighs in at 558 pages, bulging with quotations and statistics, summaries of studies and paragraph-long lists. Some readers may feel they lack the stamina for a book of this scale. Yet it may be that Sale feels he needs all these facts and figures to reach his audience, who would dismiss a terser essay as much too simple-minded. If that is the case, it shows we have become captive to the premises of an overscaled society: that in a world grown so complex, analysis must be elaborate to offer comprehension. That is why the social sciences have evolved in tandem with contemporary technology. If the latter can be checked, then the former can fade away. (p. 12)

Andrew Hacker, "Up for Grabs," in The New York Review of Books, *Vol. XXVIII, No. 7, April 30, 1981, pp. 8, 10-12, 14, 16.*

Kirkus Reviews

[Kirkpatrick Sale's ***Dwellers in the Land: The Bioregional Vision*** is an] introduction to "bioregionalism," the philosophy at the heart of the worldwide movement of ecological politics known by the sobriquet "Green."

Bioregionalists, like most environmentalists, use the language of ecology to deplore the current state of the environment and contend that modern technology—the megacity, nuclear power, etc.—have put a vast psychic distance between people and the natural world. Where they part ways with conventional environmentalism is in the belief that federal regulation, presidential dispensation and other band-aid approaches imposed from above cannot avert the coming ecological crisis; nothing short of a cognitive shift will suffice. The scientific world view that has ruled the Western mind since the Renaissance must be dethroned by an ecological one which puts technology at the behest of nature rather than at loggerheads with it. Slowly but inexorably, through grass-roots efforts to make humans more sensitive to their "bioregions"—the natural geographic regions defined by their flora and fauna, landforms and watersheds—a new way of economic, cultural and political life would evolve.

Though Sale does a good job of describing the broad outlines of the bioregional concept, he's less adept at exploring its implications: How, exactly, would an economy based not on simple-minded growth but rather biological sustainability through self-reliant bioregions operate? And why has the Green movement blossomed in places like Germany but not here, when much of the groundwork for "steady state" economics, for instance, has been laid by American economists like Herman Daly?

All this sounds hopelessly utopian, but Sale claims it is rooted in historical realities and "patterns of the present," such as regional planning and local cuisine and the belief in self-reliance and town-meeting democracy at the heart of traditional American, or at least Jeffersonian, values.

Anyone interested in the arcane eddies of environmental thought will find this a serviceable first stab at an American Green manifesto. (pp. 947-48)

A review of "Dwellers in the Land: The Bioregional Vision," in Kirkus Reviews, *Vol. LIII, No. 17, September 1, 1985, pp. 947-48.*

Rosalind Williams

[***Dwellers in the Land***] is a radical book—it says that most of us should give up orange juice for breakfast. According to the bioregionalist philosophy, the world should be divided not according to the artificial boundaries of nation-states, but according to natural regions defined by landforms and life-forms. Each region would be self-governing and self-sufficient—so people in non-citrus-growing regions would have to find other sources of vitamin C.

Although Kirkpatrick Sale, the author of ***SDS, Human Scale,*** and ***Power Shift: The Rise of the Southern Rim and Its Challenge to the Eastern Establishment,*** is proposing some radical ideas, he doesn't want to sound radical, far-out or utopian. Indeed, ***Dwellers in the Land*** sounds like inspirational literature. Its basic theme is mythological or even religious. Mr. Sale begins by singing the praises of Gaea, the primordial earth mother of Greek mythology. This one true mother-god was abandoned when "somewhere, somehow, the poisons crept in." Humankind turned to a false scientific god and became obsessed with dictating to the environment rather than heeding its dictates. We have constructed an unhappy civilization based on the "industrio-scientific paradigm": large-scale organizations, a competitive and exploitative economic system, centralized and hierarchical politics and a polarized, violent society.

But now the end of the world is nigh, for "an ecological crisis of some magnitude seems to be at hand." The only salvation lies in returning to ancient Gaean wisdom. We must reconstruct society according to the "bioregional paradigm" of local and regional scale, a conservationist economy, decentralized politics and social diversity. The bioregional vision sees a future of scattered villages loosely linked in regional federations, growing their own food, running their own dispersed industries, using solar energy and recycling paper while rejecting chemical fertilizers and flush toilets.

Mr. Sale would be the first to admit we've heard it before. He cites a string of ecologists, economists, sociologists and the like who have developed similar ideas, especially Americans like Frederick Jackson Turner, Lewis Mumford and Howard Washington Odum, who stressed the particular significance of regionalism in this country. However, Mr. Sale does not mention the most obvious source of bioregionalism, the philosophical anarchism of the Russian thinker Peter Kropotkin, an eminent geographer who lived in English exile around the turn of the century. Mr. Sale's vision mirrors Kropotkin's in nearly every detail, down to a reliance on biological and tribal evidence of humanity's capacity for "mutual aid."

A prime benefit of ***Dwellers in the Land*** is the presentation of a brief, coherent, up-to-date version of philosophical anarchism, which has long sought to find a "third way" other than socialism or capitalism. The ideas of the third way tradition are good, in the sense that we would probably be happier if we lived by them. Its ideas are even practical, as Mr. Sale keeps pleading, if we are considered as biological and tribal beings. But this kind of theoretical analysis omits whole realms of reality—the realities of the daily newspaper, the stock market, the Pentagon, Bloomingdale's, the citrus growers' lobby. Mr. Sale assumes all this can be circumvented rather than confronted. He wants to see the bioregional vision flower into a bioregional movement, a nonpartisan version of contemporary Green politics that can win the loyalty of liberals and conservatives alike. . . .

On a practical level, bioregionalism will probably have far less effect than the old-fashioned lobbying efforts of the Sierra Club, which published Mr. Sale's book. At least Kropotkin, a professed revolutionary, understood that the bioregional vision must confront immensely powerful institutions as well as other, maybe far less desirable, visions. But this vision itself has serious limitations. Maybe we need to increase our environmental consciousness, but we are also creatures of our racial, linguistic, religious, class and historical consciousness. These other sources of our identity by no means fall along geographic lines. It's an old, old dream that a return to nature will simplify and clarify human affairs. But to make geography the basis of society is to oversimplify vastly the complexity of human nature.

Rosalind Williams, "Earth Mother Knows Best," in The New York Times Book Review, *October 6, 1985, p. 15.*

Robert W. Glasgow

[***Dwellers in the Land***] is an audacious proposal to transform radically the way mankind uses and lives on the Earth. To call it radical is an understatement, since parts of the proposal are all over the ideological spectrum. To implement the author's proposal would require, among many other things, redrawing international boundaries, dissolution of traditional sovereignties, eliminating most political and economic institutions—and a dependence upon universal human qualities only rarely demonstrated by history.

Author Kirkpatrick Sale is a familiar figure to many conservationists as an articulate writer and zealous polemicist active in various environmental frays of the last decade. His proposal here would come under the broad rubric of the Green political movement that thus far has flourished principally in Europe. But environmentalists are hardly a homogenous programmatic group, and this book is as likely to provoke argument among them as among political traditionalists. Clearly, that is one of Sale's purposes.

Sale's proposal for saving the Earth from what he presently regards as an inevitable fate of chaos is designated the "bioregional" vision. Because of the encompassing proportions of this vision, it is difficult to summarize it without making it sound bizarre—which I don't think it is. To make summary intelligible, it might be best to start with Sale's beginning.

Sale asserts that the grave threat to the environment began about 400 years ago, with the origination of science and the prompt development of a "world scientific view." This view regarded the natural world as some lifeless abstract to be controlled and used for solely human ends, with humans acting in Descartes' phrase as "masters and possessors of nature."

This solipsist perspective replaced a world view hitherto shared by the early Greeks and many preliterate cultures in which the Earth was a central deity and mankind sought to live in propitiative harmony with sacred nature. (The bioregional vision, as I interpret it, would resacralize the Earth or Mother Nature.)

Sale argues that the new scientific world view provided the intellectual substructure and the practical mechanism for the rise of the nation-state, for the European choice of mercantilism and industrial capitalism and the enterprise of global colonialism and exploitation. One contemporary consequence of such a world view has been critical depletion of natural resources worldwide and terrifying political instability—all to the point where the world is headed for near-apocalyptic chaos.

Now, while some environmental extremists believe this destructive process has already reached a point of no return, Sale is not among them. Professing to be an optimist, he sees the way out as worldwide adoption of the bioregional vision.

Even among traditional environmentalists, bioregionalism is hardly a household word and presently is embraced by a splinter group to which Sale belongs. And as he presents bioregionalism, it appears to be an eclectic amalgam of numerous ecological perspectives, steady-state economic theories and communitarian utopianism.

Bioregionalism starts with the premise that the face of the Earth is organized not into artificial man-made states but by natural regions of tremendously varying sizes. Determined by natural characteristics rather than human dictates, bioregions are distinguished by particular attributes of flora, fauna, water, climate, soils, land-forms and human settlements and cultures that these natural attributes have given rise to.

It is within these natural regions and their smaller units—such as, say, the Ozark Plateau and within it the White River watershed—that the general social community would be organized, rather than within the man-made boundaries that have evolved through political mandate and military conquest. Within these natural regions people, employing scientific technology that is environmentally efficient and by treating the environment with reverent respect and use, could live efficiently and be self-sufficient. Of course, the standard of living would be different. The economic emphasis would be shifted from growth and consumerism to sustaining economic stability.

Since modern governments, whether capitalist or socialist, have been remarkably insensitive to ecological problems, the bioregion would require a new kind of policy. The bioregional policy would seek diffusion of power and decentralization of institutions, with all authority flowing upward incrementally from the smallest political unit to the largest. Basic political and economic decisions would be made at village or small-town levels. (Cities are not a part of the bioregional vision and presumably would wither away as a result of their inefficient use of natural resources.)

The foregoing description is the barest of bones of the bioregional vision. And while Sale acknowledges the insuperable task of implementing such a vision, he professes to believe that it can be done. To support his optimism, he cites various trends toward regionalism and decentralization. As for human acceptance of such mind-boggling changes, he relies on behavioral analysis of contemporary and preliterate cultures to suggest it is not impossible.

With bioregionalism presently such an obscure and complex proposal, Sale and his adherents hardly constitute a movement. But the aim of this book clearly is to provoke public dialogue, and that is how political movements most often begin.

Robert W. Glasgow, in a review of "Dwellers in the Land: The Bioregional Vision," in Los Angeles Times Book Review, *October 20, 1985, p. 5.*

Edwards Park

We can expect a spate of books dealing with Columbus as the Quincentennial of the Discovery approaches—now only two years away. . . . [***The Conquest of Paradise***] is an early one—scholarly, ambitious, meticulous and angry. Sale lives in New York, writes for *The New York Times, The Village Voice, The Nation, The New Leader* and other publications and also teaches history and political science. He's a straight-out, no-holds-barred, 1960s-type ecologist and from where he stands, the discovery of the New World comes off as an ecological disaster.

The Europe that Columbus left in August 1492, was, says Sale, primed for the end of the world, "not as a metaphor or theological trope, but as a somber, terrifying prediction based solidly on . . . biblical prophecy and felt experience of daily life." Violence was even worse than today's; famine was routine; the plague almost halved the population of Catalonia alone between 1365 and 1497.

The New World that Columbus reached two months later seemed to him "an intimation of Paradise." Here were tall, richly foliaged trees and fruits of every kind instead of the parched, thin-soiled fields of a Europe where forests had long been ravaged. Here were friendly, handsome, naked, trusting natives instead of the Inquisition's priests. Here was a warm, welcoming beauty, totally strange to medieval Europeans who instinctively viewed Nature as the great enemy of Man.

In a masterly passage on this European attitude, Sale reminds us that to 15th-century adults, as well as children, mountains were "places of dread," dark forests held such fantasies as "the Wild Man—a huge, powerful, hairy figure, carrying a wooden club, with large genitals exposed, draped with strands of rank foliage . . . slave to natural desires and passions uncontrolled . . . All animals were fearsome."

In 1492, simple sailors from a world beset by these terrors looked upon the New World as Eden, and following their "civilized" European instincts, set about taming it. And now the author beats his drum—the slow beat of a funeral march—for the subjugation of Nature, the rape of the virginal environment and the eventual death or slavery of its inhabitants.

In expressing his outrage at what Europe did to America, Sale seems oddly astonished. That distresses me, mostly, perhaps, because it indicates my age. I was raised in total innocence of the word "ecology," and I zestfully subjugated Nature in various ways, for I lived mostly in the country and was taught by deed as well as by the literature of my youth that one must hack one's own corner out of God's world, and vigilantly maintain it. That was the American way.

Of course the early explorers and settlers exploited the land, hunted the animals and birds, searched out the minerals, despoiled the waters and forests, slew the natives—and prospered. That's what we were all about. Now that we see the horrors that we have been committing, we can be thankful for the ecologists and certainly heed their warnings. But we can't do much about the past—about the conquest of Paradise.

So the author's ecological handwringing blots his attempt to build a new and more accurate Columbus story. He determinedly sticks to nothing but the facts, all that he can mine from the musty, self-serving sources that remain: Columbus's Journal, doctored to please his sponsors, Ferdinand and Isabella, and three 16th-century historians who had to rely on hazy memories. Sale does wonderfully well with these cloudy views of an event so wrapped in folklore. He trots out every detail he can find of the Columbus voyages, and fashions a good story. But his persistent irritation at the wrong-headedness of the times colors it.

It even taints his judgment. Early in his book Sale establishes his revisionism by taking his first shot at Samuel Eliot Morison for "fantasy put forward as fact" in *Admiral of the Ocean Sea.* I must admit to feeling the twitch of rising hackles at that heresy. Morison's was a sailor's book about the voyages—which he resailed himself (with a friend of mine on his crew). He most skillfully intertwined known fact and obvious fantasy (often switching into the present tense to signal the latter) gained from his own experience. The result won the Pulitzer Prize.

Edwards Park, "There Goes the Neighborhood," in Book World—The Washington Post, *October 7, 1990, p. 5.*

Caryl Phillips

By 1892, when America celebrated the 400th anniversary of Columbus' discovery of the New World, the obsessive explorer's name had become synonymous with progress, even virtue. In New York City, a five-day celebration featured a lavish, nighttime parade, while in Chicago, an exhibition brought together the finest American artists from around the world. And throughout America, rivers, bridges, parks, mountains, colleges, squares, lakes and streets bore the name "Columbus." Only George Washington's name, in fact, had been more pervasive.

A century later, "Columbus" continues to dominate the geopolitical map of the United States, although today, a minority has come to view the man as a symbol of racial guilt and environmental destruction.

In his recent essay, "Columbus and the Origins of Racism in the Americas," historian Jan Carew describes the arrival of Columbus in the New World as a "Holocaust which . . . has been glossed over, ignored and rationalized as an 'inevitable' phenomenon in the exotica of European expansionism." This same "holocaust," other revisionist historians have pointed out, sought to replace a people who respected, in fact worshiped, nature with a people for whom nature represented little more than land to be excavated in the search for mineral wealth, or trees to be razed if they dared to stand in the way of "progress."

This is not to say that ours is the first age to cast doubts on the benevolence of the Columbian legacy: In 1768, for example, Cornelius Depauw, a Massachusetts industrialist turned philosopher, wrote that "the discovery of the New World has been the most disastrous event in the history of mankind." He was referring to the resurgence of slavery brought on by the Spanish and started, for all intents and purposes, by Columbus himself.

But as we approach the 1992 quincentennial of his first voyage to America, the debate no doubt will intensify.

Hero or villain? Clearly Kirkpatrick Sale's ***The Conquest***

of Paradise is just one of what promises to be a veritable rain forest of books on the life and achievements of this most enigmatic of men. Columbus toys with both those who adore him and those who loathe him, evoking the most wildly contentious responses from historians who are otherwise noted for their sobriety of judgment. Carew, in his anti-Columbus essay, argues the point that "Columbus was a genius at navigation." Bjorn Landstrom, another respected historian, has claimed that Columbus "was convinced until the very end that he had reached India, and did not realize that he had discovered a New World." Hardly the hallmark of navigational genius.

Setting off in the "spirit of reassessment," Sale journeys with Columbus on his first voyage in 1492, and travels with him until his death in Spain about 14 years later. As his subtitle, *Christopher Columbus and the Columbian Legacy,* informs us, his goal is to reassess both Columbus the man and the legacy of the Columbian achievement.

The narrative employed is a fusion of authorial voice, italicized passages of historical scene-setting, and brief extracts from the admiral's logs. This triple narrative is heavily annotated with asterisked footnotes, and numbered references to notes at the back of the book. Clearly, this is a work of considerable research, drawing together the evidence of countless previous biographies and histories, and aiming to unravel the lies, myths and half-truths before attempting to weave a clearer and more authoritative tapestry. But does Sale's "reassessment" throw any new light on the man named Columbus? Does it, indeed, help us to understand his legacy?

The reassessment is dogged by a number of obstacles, some of which have caused other writers to stumble and fall, but a few of which are clearly of the author's own making. That we know so little about Columbus' life presents an almost-insuperable problem for the would-be biographer. Sale admits that in the last century alone there have been 253 scholarly articles and books on the relatively straightforward question of Columbus' birthplace.

Rival claims range from Poland to France, Majorca to Greece. Most agree on Genoa, but by no means all. Furthermore, before Columbus began to petition the Spanish majesties in about 1486 (when one might reasonably suppose Columbus to have been a man in his middle 30s), there is hardly anything extant about his life.

Incredibly enough, even the explorer's name is subject to debate. Born (presumably) in Genoa with the name "Cristoforo Colombo" or "Christofferus De Columbo," he became either "Christobal Colom" or "Christovam Colombo" in Portugal, and then "Cristobal Colon" in Spain. The riddle of the origins of Columbus—his early years, his adolescence, his youth and his hopes and fears as a young man—defeats Sale as it has defeated many before him. He blandly suggests that Columbus was "a man truly without a past that he could define, without a home, or roots, or family, without even a sense of love, of place."

In order to obviate the lack of reliable information on Columbus' life, Sale resorts to extensive scene-setting. We are treated to a chapter about violence, disease and famine, and yet another on everything from the flora and fauna of the late Middle Ages to the tendency toward 'technophilia' in 15th-Century Europe. As compelling as well-written as much of this information is, one cannot help but suspect that its inclusion at such length does little but weaken the central narrative drive of the book. When the author returns to Columbus and his journeys, the tempo picks up, but sadly the style often fails. The tone becomes flip, the prose slack.

"Very well: landfall. The much-sought prize. The question is—the first question, anyway, directly related to the nagging one about their intended destination—where did they suppose they were?"

When Sale describes Columbus' later, incident-packed, dramatic years, however, the book moves easily and swiftly.

On his first trip to the New World, Columbus was convinced that he had found heaven on Earth. He had read in Pierre D'Ailly's *Imago Mundi* that the Garden of Eden had to be in a warm climate on the other side of the Equator, and so was enraptured by everything he saw from the moment he arrived. "They are very gentle," he wrote of the indigenous population, "and know nothing of evil." When he returned a year later to find that the settlement and crew he left behind had been wiped out by the local chiefs, however, his dream darkened. The same people who, as he wrote in 1492, "loved their neighbors as they loved themselves," he began to call "cruel and hostile savages."

(In his book *The Tears of the White Man,* French journalist Pascal Bruckner suggests that Columbus' disappointment was especially deep because the religious texts that guided him led him to expect a new Garden of Eden. "The Caribbean Indian was a blank slate upon which the Conquistadors drew a picture of the Christian revelation," Bruckner wrote. "They were given the formidable privilege of being perfect, but because of this were in danger of being designated savages if they failed in their mission.")

Thus began Columbus' battles not only with the local population but with his own crew—battles that led Spain's King Ferdinand and Queen Isabella to strip Columbus of his administrative powers. Refusing to obey the newly appointed governor, Columbus eventually was taken back to Spain in chains. Seeing the king and queen upon his return, Columbus, still in shackles, fell on his knees and burst into tears.

Columbus pleaded for a chance to undertake a fourth voyage, certain that he was on the verge of discovering the gold he promised the monarchs he would discover. But this final voyage was a disaster, due to inclement weather, the admiral's stubborn unwillingness to follow the royal instructions to sail south, and to his own failing health. Columbus returned to Spain, where he died a wealthy but somewhat bitter man. His contemporaries never fully acknowledged his true stature, but there is evidence to show that Columbus was aware of the magnitude and import of his achievements.

Sale's reassessment of Columbus is most valuable for shedding sensible light on the veracity of the claims and counterclaims of previous historians and scholars. He dismisses some wrongheaded propositions, such as Simon Wiesenthal's argument that Columbus was one of the Jews expelled from Spain in 1492. Beyond this, however, he has little new to say about Columbus, and his diversions into historical scene-setting and unenlightening extracts from Columbus' logs fail to breathe life into his portrait of the great explorer.

With regard to the "Columbian Legacy", the author does not so much "reassess" as reconfirm the suspicion that Americans' opinion of Columbus reflects what they think of themselves. A century ago, Columbus was a hero. To the overwhelming majority, he remains a hero today. This is hardly surprising, for the nascent colonial power of 1892 that was the United States of America, has, in the intervening century, grown up and replaced Europe as the world's great colonizer. To such a people, Columbus will always cut a heroic figure.

Sale sees Columbus' first voyage in 1492 as

> the journey that began the long process by which a single culture came to dominate as never before all the other cultures in the world, to impose its language in their mouths, its clothes on their backs, its values in their hearts, and to accumulate to itself the power that now enables it to determine nothing less than the destiny of the world.

Really? Africa, China, the Gulf—in fact, the whole of the Islamic world—may wish to take issue with Sale's rather chauvinistic summary of the Columbian achievement.

Columbus the man emerges as enigmatic a character at the end of this book as he was at the beginning. Sale concludes his narrative of Columbus' life by tracing his remains to both Seville in the Old World and Santo Domingo in the New. The irony no doubt would have amused the self-mythologizing man of the sea, who not only knew the full import of his life's work but also knew how to tease generations of would-be historians and scholars onto the rocks of mere speculation. (pp. 4, 8)

Caryl Phillips, "The Errant Enigma from Genoa," in Los Angeles Times Book Review, *October 7, 1990, pp. 4, 8.*

Sale on the politics of place:

Out of [the history of Christopher Columbus] I would suggest some lessons for the present. And the future, if there is to be one.

The only political vision that offers any hope of salvation is one based on an understanding of, a rootedness in, a deep commitment to, and a resacralization of, *place.* Here is where any strategy of resistance to the industrial monolith and its merchants of death must begin; here is where any program of restoration and revitalization must be grounded. It is the only way we can effectively counterpose ourselves to the state and the ridiculous forms of acquiescence and co-optation that it calls politics. It is the only way we can build a politics that can spread the message that Western civilization itself, shot through with a denial of place and a utilitarian concept of nature, must be transformed. By making an awareness of, and attachment to, locality the centerpiece of our philosophy and practice, we can directly and decisively challenge that civilization and its monstrosities, can specifically and creatively offer an alternative.

Such a politics, based, as the original peoples of the Americas had it, upon love of place, also implies the place of love. For ultimately love is the true cradle of politics, the love of the earth and its systems, the love of the particular bioregion we inhabit, the love of those who share it with us in our communities, and the love of that unnameable essence that binds us together with the earth, and provides the water for the roots we sink.

Kirkpatrick Sale, in The Nation, *October 22, 1990.*

William H. McNeill

Anticipating the quincentenary of Christopher Columbus's famous first voyage to the Caribbean, Kirkpatrick Sale offers us in ***The Conquest of Paradise*** a learned, lopsided account of the discoverer's career, and of what he calls the "Columbian legacy" of environmental destructiveness. Convinced that altering the natural environment is wicked, and attributing the vast changes that have come to American landscapes since 1492 to Columbus's example, he has set out to destroy the heroic image that earlier writers have transmitted to us. Mr. Sale makes Columbus out to be cruel, greedy and incompetent (even as a sailor), and a man who was perversely intent on abusing the natural paradise on which he intruded.

Greed and cruelty were indeed characteristics of the first European adventurers who invaded the New World, and Mr. Sale, the author of five previous books and an environmental activist, has combed the relevant documents and secondary literature to show that Columbus shared these traits with those who came after him. No doubt this is a useful corrective to the hero-worship Columbus has often been accorded. But uncritical adulation and the lambasting that Mr. Sale administers are both unhistorical, in the sense that they select from the often cloudy record of Columbus's actual motives and deeds what suits the researcher's 20th-century purposes. That sort of history caricatures the complexity of human reality by turning Columbus into either a bloody ogre or a plaster saint, as the case may be.

The book falls into four distinct parts. The first eight chapters, representing a little over half the entire work, describe Columbus's career in the Americas from 1492 to his death, putting rather more emphasis on his unhappy efforts at governing the new lands than on his seamanship and discoveries. In the next three chapters Mr. Sale describes the transmission of Columbus's bad habits to England and to the English colonists of what became the United States. In this way he plants the "Columbian legacy" of environmental destruction squarely in our own backyard. Then he devotes a chapter to lyrical praise of the natural, environmentally sound life led by the millions of Indians who inhabited the New World before Columbus arrived. Finally, he concludes with a very interesting chapter on the way Columbus's reputation has altered across the centuries.

This last chapter was, to my taste, by far the best part of the book. It is learned and, as far as I can tell, unbiased. It shows how poets, publicists, politicians and historians have twisted the figure of Columbus to suit their different purposes (just as Mr. Sale himself has done). A conspicuously Roman Catholic seaman from Genoa who served the Spaniards was an odd hero for the new American republic to latch onto in the 1780's, yet that is when Columbus entered our national iconography. In our own century he has become the patron saint of Italian-American ethnicity. Mr. Sale summarizes the surprising sea changes Columbus has endured, but says little about why he was chosen for such roles, or why the record lends itself so well to radical, protean reshapings like the one he himself has perpetrated.

The most ridiculous passages of the book are concentrated in Chapter 12, which purports to show how American Indian society, technology, religion and ethics were all superior to their European counterparts. Mr. Sale treats the varied ways of life that actually prevailed in the Americas as if all Indians were the same, and confuses time as well by quoting late-20th-century Indian spokesmen as though their words applied universally to every tribe and people. . . .

Silly remarks and callow, sweeping judgments disfigure the rest of the book as well, and tend to obscure a few worthwhile challenges to received opinions that Mr. Sale scatters through his pages. On the positive side, I was struck, for instance, by his argument that Columbus recognized that he had in fact discovered a new continent in the course of his fourth (and final) voyage, and by the importance Mr. Sale gives to the discovery of a lode of gold-bearing ore in Hispaniola in 1499.

Yet there is no ignoring the negative side. Consider the following characterization of European agriculture:

> Cultivated lands were harvested over and over, often with four and five crops a year, and although fallow systems and manuring were in general use everywhere, yields were perennially inadequate, harvest failures frequent, and crop efficiencies low. . . . In the aftermath of both over-farming and overgrazing, the thin soils gave themselves quickly to erosion by both wind and water, and despite subsequent reclamation in the nineteenth century the legacy still can be seen today throughout the Mediterranean and in much of France and Germany.

Europe's devastation, according to Mr. Sale, collided with a New World "as close to Paradise as noncelestial existence has," with the sad result that we are all now banished from Eden and can only clamber back inside the Garden if we are willing to go to the Indians and learn from their environmental wisdom. "It was salvation then, it might possibly be salvation now. Certainly there is no other." Thus speaketh the Prophet Kirkpatrick Sale, whose saving message requires him to rewrite the past so as to change the future—perhaps.

William H. McNeill, "Debunking Columbus," in The New York Times Book Review, *October 7, 1990, p. 28.*

John F. Baker

Kirkpatrick Sale comes to his *Publishers Weekly* interview at a Chelsea restaurant in Manhattan on his bicycle. It's partly a statement—the vehicle is, after all, on a human scale, is nonpolluting and, in Sale's hands, nonaggressive, for he swears he stops at red lights. It is also highly practical, for this busy, dedicated writer must be off, the moment lunch is over, to a key meeting of PEN, of which he is a board member.

The occasion for the meeting with Kirk Sale (his full name is seldom employed in conversation) is the publication . . . of his most ambitious book among the five he has written: ***The Conquest of Paradise: Christopher Columbus and the Columbian Legacy.*** It is an extensively researched, carefully written—and considered—revisionist history of the man who "discovered" the New World and, more importantly to Sale, turned a society where man lived in harmony and balance with nature into one where man exploited nature—and ultimately exported that concept of domination throughout the world. Its picture of Columbus himself, drawn from a careful rereading of primary source material in the explorer's own journals and contemporary documents, is an oddly poignant one of a rootless man, subject to mystical delusions, never adequately appreciated for his accomplishments in his lifetime, and who died in utter obscurity.

"I find it ironic that a man so rootless himself should have helped create such a rootless society," Sale muses. He is an intense, focused man with flashes of self-mockery, who delights in the absurd, and whose chapter about preparations the nation and the world are making for the quincentenary of Columbus's first voyage would have delighted Mark Twain.

The creation of a book about Columbus and his legacy is the natural outcome of many of Sale's deepest interests. He studied history at Cornell in the late '50s, but, as the editor of the daily student newspaper, was more interested in journalism. "I spent most of my time on that and, writing an editorial every day, I learned to write perforce." His father was a professor of English at the university, and from him, Sale says, "I became aware of the limits of academic life, and knew I didn't want to go into it." His father, as a scholar, had also questioned authority, and a rebel spark animated Sale early on. "I led what I'm convinced was the first American student demonstration, in 1958." He was struck then, he says, by a "disenchantment with conventional politics," and when he left school to become a journalist it was to the leftist *New Leader* that he went. There, he recalls wryly, he edited, "sometimes severely," a column by Reinhold Niebuhr, father of Elisabeth Sifton, who was to become Sale's own editor at Knopf nearly 30 years later.

In 1961 Sale went to Africa, convinced that the decade would belong to that continent and, he says with self-derision, "so astute that I confidently predicted revolution in South Africa would come within 10 years." In Ghana he lectured, studied African cultures, even edited a scholarly journal for a time but, ultimately convinced he could not penetrate the African mind, returned and went to work for the *New York Times Magazine,* "hoping to bore from within."

These were the early years of the Vietnam War, and Sale, as an old campus rebel, became deeply interested in the student protest movement that began to gather force during the mid-'60s. When, in 1968, he decided to become a full-time writer ("and there's been no job with a boss in it ever since"), his first book was ***SDS,*** which he calls a "sympathetic but critical" study of that movement. . . . Its writing, says Sale, "further radicalized me in a way, beyond where I'd been." And looking around him at the political scene in the '70s, he began to observe, as others were to do later, that the balance of power in the country was shifting, via politicians like Nixon and his entourage, away from the Northeast and to the South and West. Hence his second book, ***Power Shift.*** . . . (p. 41)

Another movement gaining force at this time was one centering on the work of E. F. Schumacher, whose *Small Is Beautiful* preached a return to small-scale human society and activities, away from the gigantism of nation-states and large corporations. Sale, spurred also by Leopold Kehr's earlier *Breakdown of Nations,* became convinced that only in such a drawing in of man's ever-expanding ambitions could human society become sane and whole again. He worked five years on ***Human Scale,*** published in 1980 and still probably the book by which he is best known—though he feels that a hostile review in the *New York Times Book Review* helped kill what he hoped would be a paperback version that would have reached a larger readership. Described as "an encyclopedia for the decentralist movement," the book . . . [eventually did become a paperback], but by then, Sale feels, the country's mood, in the Reagan years, had changed.

His had not, however, and he continued to refine his notions, coming to focus on "bioregionalism"—a concept of humankind returning to a context defined by earth's biology and geography, its rivers, mountains and forests, rather than trying for endless expansion and development. This, Sale felt, was a possible solution to the environmental crisis that he regards as the major intellectual issue facing the world, now and for the foreseeable future: "It's a question of saving the world from itself, and it means nothing less than the survival of civilization." A speech he gave on the subject in 1983 was developed into a book, ***Dwellers in the Land,*** published by the Sierra Club two years later—still, claims Sale, "the only work that defines bioregionalism."

And the Columbus book? Sale, pondering the nature of Western civilization, came upon an essay about Christopher Columbus that made him think about the impact of Europe upon the essentially peaceful, earth-centered Indian societies of the New World. He prepared a speech on the subject and was reading it to his wife (Faith Sale is v-p and executive editor at Putnam) when she suggested it would make a good book. Kirk agreed, but thought at first it would take a historian to do it justice. "Eventually," he adds drily, "I thought I'd better do it myself."

Without even an advance, he spent a year—"which I could ill afford"—on research. He learned how to get into the Spanish archives and, although "I'm no expert in 15th-century Spanish," struggled to translate all the documents himself—something, he says, that has not been done for some time by historians writing about Columbus. "I'm asked, did I uncover new documents? No. I carefully read the old ones—the same method that I. F. Stone used so successfully in his studies of the workings of Washington." (pp. 41-2)

He didn't intend to deconstruct Columbus, he says, though that is certainly the effect of much of the material he presents. "I found out things that are not generally known, or stressed, about him: his obsession with gold; the imperial side of him; and the mystical, millennarian madness that led him to believe he'd found Paradise, and was somehow chosen by God."

As for the Indians Columbus encountered, and who within a few generations had been decimated and enslaved by succeeding waves of European invaders, "I make no plea for the innate superiority of the major nation groups like the Mayas and the Aztecs; but the smaller societies were genuinely benign, adjusted to each other and to nature. They could serve as a model for the possibility of harmonious human life." Sale wishes that the Columbus quincentenary would not be used so much as an occasion for celebration, and more as an opportunity to look, as his book does, at what the legacy of the Conquest has been for the rest of the world, "to look for the elements worth preserving in our civilization, elements that won't destroy nature; because the ways we are following will certainly lead to the destruction of the planet."

There are book projects Sale would love to become involved in, but feels he cannot

> while the world is in such a mess, and it needs writing about. I write my books to help save society and the planet; I'm actually trying to influence the public psychology and policy of this and other industrial societies, before it's too late. That's very different from what a novelist does: he's trying to create a work of art, which he'd love to see become a bestseller but which he would write anyway. It's very important to me that my books be read, not for reputation or money, but because of what I'm trying to do—influence people in a profound way.

In furtherance of that ambition, Sale's only venture into fiction so far, a novel under way, is a piece of fiction set 30 years in the future, after world civilization has collapsed, which shows life in an "ecostery"—a word Sale has coined to describe an ecological monastery, where a handful of people in tune with their environment keep sanity alive in the way the monasteries preserved classical learning during the Dark Ages. He plans, if he finishes it in time, to submit it to the $500,000 contest TV magnate Ted Turner has organized for an optimistic novel set in the future—"though," he grins, "I'm not sure it would be considered sufficiently optimistic."

A book he would passionately love to write but has sternly set aside is an examination of the lyrics of the great American popular song writers of this century. "I'd like to do for the lyricists what Alec Wilder did for the composers." A more immediate prospect, but one he has so far failed to sell to a publisher, is for a small luxury gift edition of what he calls "the first piece of Americana": Columbus's letter to the Spanish Court about his first voyage, in facsimile, with a new translation and Sale's own extensive annotations. Oddly, the only known copy of this document in the world is in the New York Public Library.

Sale wants to stay closely involved with the Columbus celebrations until 1992 is over. He has signed as secretary of a group called Encounter, which plans to turn the tables on Europe by sending three sailing ships with inhabitants of the New World—Mexicans, actually—to "discover" Spain, carrying with them documents on the rights of indigenous peoples. "We cast aside the idea of them 'claiming' Spain; it's not something Indians do," chuckles Sale. He also wants to make himself available as a speaker in a range of Columbus seminars to provide "a minority view."

Other activities include being a co-founder of the New York Green Party, and involvement in a group called the Wetlands Restoration Project, which has a plan to turn part of the lower Manhattan waterfront—currently occupied by rusting piers and planned for high-rise development by people who, Sale says, can no longer get up the necessary money—back into the tidal marsh it once was, with biking and hiking trails but no other development.

Thus cheerfully shouldering a number of burdens, and thankfully clutching the first copy of ***The Conquest of Paradise*** to come off the press, Sale pedals off to PEN. (p. 42)

John F. Baker, "Kirkpatrick Sale," in Publishers Weekly, *Vol. 237, No. 42, October 19, 1990, pp. 41-2.*

Garry Wills

Sale's book [***The Conquest of Paradise***] has a comic-epic audacity of its own. He is on to something when he makes Columbus the deadest whitest male now offered for our detestation. If any historical figure can appropriately be loaded up with all the heresies of our time—Eurocentrism, phallocentrism, imperialism, elitism, and all-bad-things-generally-ism—Columbus is the man. But in pursuit of this dead-male white whale, Sale has developed fixations of an Ahab dimension. It is not enough to say that Columbus initiated genocide for Tainos and Aztecs and Incas; he infected the entire world. He stands guilty of *lèse-nature.* He raped the globe. He brought to the idyllic world outside Europe's dread itch for control "an ancient phobia against the forces of nature and the earth goddesses." He had an "ecohybris" to which we can trace all the disturbances of our time. Like all Europeans, he hated forests and mountains. He is the best example of European man's "obsessive will to try 'subduing nature'."

This description of Europe, though given new vehemence by recent developments, is oddly familiar. Though Sale ranges far and wide in his hunt for ammunition in this take-no-prisoners assault on the imprisoning of the earth by Europe, he neglects the author he most resembles. It was [Oswald] Spengler, after all, who, [in *The Decline of the West*], called European culture Faustian, and used Columbus as a symbol of its desire to reduce even space to a function of the will, of our "spiritual will-to-power."

> The bent of the Faustian Culture, therefore, was overpoweringly towards extension, political, economic or spiritual. It overrode all geographical-material bounds. It sought—without any practical object, merely for the Symbol's own sake—to reach the North Pole and South Pole.

In short, it raped the globe.

The Faustian culture has an "adamantine will to overcome and break all resistances of the visible." And Spengler, like Sale, connects this desire for control to the norms and methods of modern capitalism—to reductive accounting procedures and the substitution of money for value.

There is a striking resemblance between Spengler's "Magian culture" and the animistic world of earth-goddesses Sale finds in the pre-Columbian Americas. The Magian culture is healing, uniting, and at rest, as opposed to the driving and dividing restlessness of Faustian man. It incloses and includes as in a womb-cavern. "The Magian man, with his spiritual kind of being, is only *a part of a pneumatic 'We'* that, descending from above, is at one and the same in all believers." So, in Sale's rosy reconstruction of Native Americans' "pre-contact" life, people coaxed food from a cooperating nature, rather than compelling it from a resisting soil. They tickled crops from the earth with a planting stick rather than wounding their mother with the trenches of a plow. This loving treatment was actually more efficient since

> they had learned (how? by wounding experiments on their own?) that opening up and turning over whole fields would only decrease nutrients and increase erosion, or because their thought-world would not have allowed such disregardful violence.

When (rarely) the precontact natives had to kill something, they did it with nonpolluting bow and arrow, "far easier, faster, and safer than the musket." Their healthy regime and holistic medicine preserved themselves as well as the environment—so successfully that

> There is only one way to live in America, and there can be only one way, and that is as Americans—the original Americans—for that is what the earth of America demands. We have tried for five centuries to resist that simple truth. . . .

Spengler's views are treated with a merited disdain these days. His mental schemata fit imperfectly if at all the cultures he tried to force them down on; but at least he knew that historical cultures have limits, and did not think one could be called up again at will, to replace its own replacement. Nor did he judge all other cultures by the standard of any one of the four he invented. Sale is as guilty of "precontactism" as are his enemies of Eurocentrism—with the additional disadvantage that his precontact culture is so heavily the product of wishful thinking.

Sale's book is regrettable because it may tempt some to see in the coming controversies over Columbus a mere hatred for "the West," a kind of catch-all leftist grumbling. But there are grave doubts and fears to be entertained when we call to mind what Columbus has meant for our past. It is not a simplistic, or even a left-wing, reaction to take these matters seriously. In fact, one of the great questioners of Columbus's value to his descendants was that pious Tory Samuel Johnson. Sale mentions other critics of Columbus, but neglects the sustained polemic of Dr. Johnson against the European conquest of the Americas.

One would expect an ardent Christian like Johnson to praise the taking of the gospel to a new part of the globe. But he sees the conquest more as opportunities for Christians to sin against their own religion than to share it with others. Writing in 1759 of the explorers encouraged by King Henry the Navigator, he said:

> Much knowledge has been acquired, and much cruelty been committed; the belief of religion has been very little propagated, and its laws have been outrageously and enormously violated. The Europeans have scarcely visited any coast but to gratify avarice, and extend corruption; to arrogate dominion without right, and practise cruelty without incentive. Happy had it then been for the oppressed if the designs of Henry had slept in his bosom, and surely more happy for the oppressors.

(pp. 8-10)

Johnson wrote about Henry the Navigator during his country's war with the French and Indians for their North American colony. He ridiculed England's "right" to the country taken from its original inhabitants. He called his nation's presence there a usurpation, "the dispossession of the natural lords and original inhabitants," more despicable when it made pretense of treaties:

> And indeed what but false hope, or resistless terror can prevail upon a weaker nation to invite a stronger into their country, to give their lands to strangers whom no affinity of manners, or similitude of opinion can be said to recommend, to permit them to build towns from which the natives are excluded, to raise fortresses by which they are intimidated, to settle themselves with such strength, that they cannot afterwards be expelled, but are for ever to remain the masters of the original inhabitants, the dictators of their conduct, and the arbiters of their fate? . . . It cannot be said, that the Indians originally invited us to their coasts; we went uncalled and unexpected to nations who had no imagination that the earth contained any inhabitants so distant and so different from themselves. We astonished them with our ships. . . . To this influence, and to this only, are to be attributed all the cessions and submissions of the Indian princes, if indeed any such cessions were ever made, of which we have no witness but those who claim from them, and there is no great malignity in suspecting, that those who have robbed have also lied.

Almost twenty years after writing that passage, Johnson connected the conquest of the Americas with its original conqueror, Columbus, who was

> under the necessity of travelling from court to court, scorned and repulsed as a wild projector, an idle promiser of kingdoms in the clouds: nor has any part of the world yet had reason to rejoice that he found at last reception and employment.
>
> In the same year (1498), in a year hitherto disastrous to mankind, by the Portuguese was discovered the passage of the Indies, and by the Spaniards the (mainland) coast of America.

So the National Council of Churches is in good company when it officially deplores the sinful conquests by which Europe came to these shores. Whatever the wilder claims of people like Kirkpatrick Sale, it is hard to impeach the moral witness of Dr. Johnson. He was an anti-imperialist when the Empire was young and growing, when he had to strain very hard to find an ally:

> I love the University of Salamanca; for when the Spaniards were in doubt as to the lawfulness of their conquering America, the University of Salamanca gave it as their opinion that it was unlawful.

(p. 10)

Garry Wills, "Goodbye, Columbus," in The New York Review of Books, *Vol. XXXVII, No. 18, November 22, 1990, pp. 6-10.*

FURTHER READING

Gitlin, Todd. "Maybe You Need a Weatherman After All." *The Village Voice* XVIII, No. 42 (18 October 1973): 29-31.
Laudatory review of *SDS.*

McMurtry, Larry. "How the West Was Won or Lost." *The New Republic* 203, No. 17 (22 October 1990): 32-8.
Castigates the lack of imagination and creativity in most revisionist histories but praises Sale's *The Conquest of Paradise.*

Sale, Kirkpatrick. "What Columbus Discovered." *The Nation,* New York 251, No. 13 (22 October 1990): 444-46.
Discusses Columbus's journey to the New World and Europe's subsequent "conquest of Paradise," stressing the importance of place in politics and civilization.

Charles Simic

1938-

Yugoslavian-born American poet, translator, nonfiction writer, and editor.

Simic writes inventive verse in which he blends surrealist and imagist techniques and employs elements of East European folklore and mysticism as well as American jazz and blues music. Simic's perception of the subjective and intuitive natures of language is revealed in works that display a variety of influences, including those of German philosopher Martin Heidegger, Yugoslavian poet Vasko Popa, and American poet Theodore Roethke. Many of Simic's poems feature commonplace objects that are rendered abstractly through frequently ominous images and metaphors presented in a series of phenomenological reductions. In such poems as "The Spoon," "Fork," and "Knife," Simic scrutinizes dining utensils with such intensity that they become imbued with primordial significance. The "Fork," for example, is a "strange thing [that] must have crept / right out of hell. / It resembles a bird's foot / Worn around the cannibal's neck." Mark Strand noted: "Charles Simic's poems reveal with an essential clarity the shape and properties of a world that we invent in secret, that marks our lives at their most intense, and that we too often deny because it is more real than anything we know. There is a sense in his work that images precede objects, that the world is a creation of myth, that nothing is what we thought it to be, but somehow always suspected it might be."

Simic experienced the Nazi occupation of his homeland during his early childhood in Yugoslavia. Following World War II, his family emigrated to Paris, France, and then to the United States, where they lived in New York City before settling in Chicago. Selections from his early volumes, *What the Grass Says* and *Somewhere among Us a Stone Is Taking Notes,* were later collected in *Dismantling the Silence* in 1971. Critics praised the poems in the latter collection for Simic's thematic application of simple diction and sentence structures. The frequently anthologized "Stone," for instance, instructs the reader to "Go inside a stone / That would be my way. / Let somebody else become a dove / Or gnash with a tiger's tooth. / I am happy to be a stone." In his introduction to *Dismantling the Silence,* Richard Howard stated: [This volume] reinstates an ancient wisdom, as well as an ancient fooling, which, by its presence, we suddenly realize has been absent from recent American verse—a gnomic utterance, convinced in accent, collective in reference, original in impulse."

While some critics detect little development in Simic's continued use of the conversational voice and sinister images in the six collections published from the 1974 to 1986, most acknowledge that these books contain passages that evidence fertile imagination and technical skill. These works also evidence Simic's increasing use of ironic humor, details of urban life, his European heritage, and historical concerns. In *Unending Blues,* Simic attempts to expand his scope to accommodate more personal themes and rural settings. His contrast of foreboding and playful tones in *Unending Blues,* underscored by his continued inclusion of violent and comic details from recent history, prompted Robert B. Shaw to note: "[Simic's] poems oscillate between two dominant moods—one of ritualistic dread evoked in austere, enigmatic scenes, and one of antic exuberance with touches of surrealism and black humor."

Simic was awarded the Pulitzer Prize in 1990 for his collection of prose poems *The World Doesn't End.* Simic's stylistic exploration in this work is enriched through conversational references to figures from history, religion, and philosophy, including Freidrich Nietzsche, Sigmund Freud, and Jesus Christ. John Ash noted that *The World Doesn't End* is "a beautifully designed box of verbal fireworks, or, to put it another way, a seamless fusion of wild jazz and delicate, moonstruck, European chamber music." Other critics discerned favorable similarities between Simic's work and the prose poems of French poets Arthur Rimbaud and Charles Baudelaire. Discussing the differences between his lyric and prose poetry, Simic said,

"Nothing ever happens in a lyric poem. It's a great acknowledgement of the present moment. In a prose sentence, however, things *do* happen. A prose poem is a dialectic between the two. You write in sentences, and tell a story, but the piece is like a poem because it circles back on itself." In many of the poems collected in his subsequent collection, *The Book of Gods and Devils,* Simic depicts New York City as a place populated by mythological creatures and figures as varied as jazz pianist Theolonius Monk, St. Theresa of Avila, and a bag lady who believes she is Venus, the goddess of Love. While some of the pieces retain the terse style of his earlier poetry, the remaining poems are longer and display a more loose and relaxed approach.

(See also *CLC,* Vols. 6, 9, 22, 49; *Contemporary Authors,* Vols. 29-32, rev. ed.; *Contemporary Authors New Revision Series,* Vols. 12, 33; and *Contemporary Authors Autobiography Series,* Vol. 4.)

PRINCIPAL WORKS

POETRY

What the Grass Says 1967
Somewhere among Us a Stone Is Taking Notes 1969
Dismantling the Silence 1971
White 1972; revised edition, 1980
Return to a Place Lit by a Glass of Milk 1974
Charon's Cosmology 1977
Classic Ballroom Dances 1980
Austerities 1982
Weather Forecast for Utopia and Vicinity 1983
Selected Poems, 1963-1983 1985
Unending Blues 1986
The World Doesn't End 1989
The Book of Gods and Devils 1990

OTHER

The Uncertain Certainty: Interviews, Essays, and Notes on Poetry 1985
Wonderful Words, Silent Truth (essays) 1990

Charles Simic [Interview with Philip Dacey]

[*The interview excerpted below was originally published in the journal* Crazy Horse *(Summer 1972).*]

[*Dacey*]: *We like to begin our interviews by having the poet give us a sketch of his life up to the present time. Would you do that?*

[Simic]: No, I hate biographies. What matters ought to be in the poems. The rest is boredom—dates, jobs, schools. If I tried, I would have to reduce it to trivia. Each time I'm forced to do just that I experience an immense sadness. So please forgive me if I can't bring myself to do it.

You were once quoted as saying, "Poetry is no longer a matter of choice for me." Would you care to elaborate on that?

When I said that I had in mind the obsessive nature of this activity. By temperament I'm an absolutist. Everything or nothing. From the greedy "I want" it became over the years "I have no choice." Basho said, "A poet doesn't make a poem, something in him naturally becomes a poem." As you reach that stage, there is a moment of surprise as you realize that what you are doing is extremely serious, that it involves your life and your destiny. In other words, you become more conscious of yourself and your poetry.

If we asked you—as we're doing—to name a half-dozen or so poets who've influenced you most, who would you name and why would you choose them?

I wouldn't know where to begin. There are so many debts. I read everything I can get my hands on. Gary Snyder told me recently that he was influenced by Vachel Lindsay in the beginning. Incredible, so was I! Then came the surrealists. They satisfied my hunger for adventure, risk. I wanted to leap out of the familiar, invent new worlds. The energy I brought to it was almost religious. Give us our daily portion of the miraculous! There were countless other poets, of course. I'd like to name Chaucer, Blake, Villon, Whitman, Rimbaud, and Rilke. I go back to them each time I feel unsure about my own work. Shouldn't forget Roethke, though. He offered me some particular solutions which I don't think are very difficult to detect in my poems. And then there was David Ignatow . . .

I suppose this question is really impossible to answer with any degree of precision. All I know is that what I love in poetry is a kind of devastating simplicity and empathy, and that fortunately can be found equally in Shakespeare and in so-called primitive poetries.

You mention the influence of Roethke on your work. Maybe I'm distracted by the superficial differences between your work, but at the moment I don't quite feel that connection there. Would you explain it somewhat?

I'd say "The Lost Son" and "Praise to the End" were most important to me. Attacking a subject from different angles, juxtaposing with great freedom, making unexpected imaginative leaps and then arranging the whole poem cyclically, struck me at the time as an ideal way to avoid obvious narrative development. Also, Roethke's care for sharply observed detail, the primeval imagery and the simplicity of language, seemed to offer a way out of abstractions with which my early poetry was cluttered. Finally, he is responsible for my interest in nursery rhymes, fairy tales, riddles, proverbs, magic formulas, jump-rope rhymes and folklore in general. I still draw strength from that kind of material.

Would you talk at some length about the relationship between your European background and your own poetry?

Again, I couldn't tell you exactly how it manifests itself, but I'm sure it does. I spent the Second World War in Yugoslavia and had the usual number of terrifying war experiences. That was long ago, though. Inevitably something of that enters my poetry. The form that allows me to create is not mine, it belongs to that memory and probably to my ancestors. At the same time, I'm aware that there are experiences which, if I had been born in this country, I would have had, and which are consequently forever denied to me. So what is one to do?

On the other hand, I've lived here almost twenty-five years, so that in any other country I feel like a perfect alien, not to speak of my first language, Serbo-Croatian, in which I find myself thoroughly uncomfortable. Frankly, the problem doesn't occupy me much anymore. I do what I can.

We're particularly struck by the motif of violence that runs through so many of your poems ("**Ax,**" "**Butcher Shop,**" "**Hearing Steps,**" *and many more). Would you speculate as to why that motif seems to appear so strongly in your work?*

I was astonished when I first detected it while writing the poems. All the violence. And I thought of myself as meek. But there it was, no doubt about it. Violence is a kind of pathetic, perverted attempt to feel. The poems try to understand its origins, to see its consequences, to exorcise its demons. I hope nobody gets the impression that I'm glorifying it.

I think Robert Bly—as well as others, of course—believes very strongly in the importance of solitude and silence for a poet, and I have the feeling from certain of your poems that use solitude and silence as materials that you, too, would make the connection between them and the writing of poetry. Would you care to comment on that?

Silence, solitude, what is more essential to the human condition? "Maternal silence" is what I like to call it. Life before the coming of language. That place where we begin to hear the voice of the inanimate. Poetry is an orphan of silence. The words never quite equal the experience behind them. We are always at the beginning, eternal apprentices, thrown back again and again into that condition. There is a complexity which demands its equivalent in words. Of course, it is impossible to do it justice. I say *Yes* to the impossible—therefore poetry.

This is what we all share, a condition where both the content and the form are one. The deeper a voice calls from that maternal silence, the wider is its echo. Occasionally people think of silence as of something negative, passive. For me silence is the spiritual energy. Of course, the paradox is that neither is there such a thing as silence nor is one ever alone. But then I don't mind admitting that I believe in God.

Many of your poems deal with common objects: knife, hand, stone, shoes, needle. Could you talk about—as you see it—the tradition for using such objects as the subjects for poems? Clearly, they have not at all times and in all places been so used. It's a matter I'd be very interested in your exploring.

Well, the interest in objects came out of a period of creative crisis. I owe it to the U.S. Army. I was discharged in 1963. During the two years I was playing soldier I wrote very little. What I did, though, is to slowly destroy all my early poems. When confronted with the life I was leading at the time, they struck me as no more than literary vomit. In any case, I found myself all of a sudden completely empty. I had nothing. Life and its intensity had conquered. At the same time, I yearned to discover something which was truly my own, which was real and which I understood passionately. And so I looked around. It's not easy to speak of what you love. It took time. I sought a precision—words to be used each as an erotic act. I was led by the belief that the incredible was right under our noses and also that there must be life in each thing. To deny that meant dividing the universe into dead matter and so-called living organisms. The children and the savages never make that error. No wonder Christ sent his disciples to consult little children.

If it took a long time to write these poems, it's because considerable humility was required. You don't get very far with your ego in the presence of a stone. What I wrote in the end had nothing deliberate about it. It came simply out of an openness to metaphorical suggestions to which I was obedient. You can call it an act of faith. A part of myself first had to become a knife or an ax. In addition, this appeared to be the proper way of building my own cosmology, of discovering my own identity.

You referred earlier to "primitive" poetry and just spoke about the vision of children and savages. To what extent would you call yourself a primitivist? Is there a limit beyond which you wouldn't want to go, a danger point, so to speak, where primitivism turns into something primarily destructive of culture and tradition? Or is that a false danger?

Not easy to define briefly. I suppose when I say "primitive" I mean that which came first. It has to do with a certain quality of existence, psychological unity with nature, the impulse for which lies dormant in every human being. I'd like to touch on only one aspect of the problem. For example, what is curious to me is that we are no longer astonished at being alive. Wonder is getting to be a rare emotion. It's not surprising, therefore, that the recent scientific discoveries remain for most of us meaningless. Awe is what could translate them for us, but we have forgotten the taste of it as we have forgotten so much else. Our nakedness, for instance. That all we truly possess is the reality of our bodies. "Culture," "tradition," are for me interesting abstractions. Once one asks oneself what one really knows for oneself, once one begins to be guided by that sense, well then one starts discovering relatives in all cultures and centuries. Or, in other words, one naked man is in the same psychological situation as another.

When Richard Howard says of your poems that "they come to us, then, from an enormous otherness," he's putting his finger on a quality I'm sure most of your readers feel. The poems are somehow magic, and impersonal, and not-in-time, and universal, etc. Given that, would you talk about why you feel, if you do, that your work should nevertheless be labeled "American"?

This is a hard question. Let me say first that I don't attribute the gift to myself. This is not phony humility. It's simply that I cannot believe I wrote it. The successful poem is strangely anonymous. Each one of us is a part of the drama that takes the guise of poetry. I seek a poem in which other men are admitted. My home but with many, many guests. Shall I be labeled "American"? I don't see how it could be avoided. I proceed from a particular experience in this time and place. My landlord bugs me and I tell him to go and fuck himself—in English.

Has there been a particular goal (or goals) over the years in your poetry that you've wanted very hard to achieve, a goal you've been consciously striving for, or is each new poem pretty much a new ball game?

I yearn for coherence, simplicity. This situation is difficult. It's possible to delude oneself with strategies, to wallow in a kind of nostalgia for the mythical. The danger of setting oneself a goal and the deliberateness that goes with it, is that it displaces our attention from the experience at hand and its own intimate requirements. I hope to remain open, experiment as much as I can, even make an ass of myself from time to time. The only thing that makes me afraid is bitterness, bile accompanied with certitude that now, at last, I have figured everything out. (pp. 3-8)

I'm not sure where this question will lead, if anywhere, but I think I'll try it on you. What would you say is the greatest—worst, most harmful, I mean—myth about poetry that has been perpetrated upon the readers of poetry?

It must be the idea that a poem can be fully explicated, and in prose. I sense an immense terror behind that need. Get rid of mystery, out with complexity and imagination! A totalitarian impulse. You notice that dictators never jail literary critics. Reason minus feeling which yearns to eliminate the paradox. . . . As if the universe can be explained. I can't think of a greater stupidity. What they forget is that a poem is an instant of lucidity in which the entire organism participates. It sees. What it sees may not make shopkeeper's sense. This is our situation, the condition of the real—between possibility and that which is actually there. To avoid that paradox is to falsify the situation, to impoverish our lives. The danger really arises when people attempt to write poems out of that critical blindness. If poetry embodies a vision, then why shouldn't criticism? But there are good critics, Gaston Bachelard, for example. (p. 9)

Charles Simic and Philip Dacey, in an interview in The Uncertain Certainty: Interviews, Essays, and Notes on Poetry *by Charles Simic, The University of Michigan Press, 1985, pp. 3-9.*

Charles Simic [Interview with Sherod Santos]

[*The interview excerpted below was originally published in the* Missouri Review *(Vol. 7, no. 3, 1984).*]

[*Santos*]: *I don't want to sound overly psychological, but there is in your work that peculiar element which blends so naturally horror and fun. Do you think it had its origin* [*during the Nazi occupation of your homeland?*]

[Simic]: Very probably. I'm the product of chance, the baby of ideologies, the orphan of history. Hitler and Stalin conspired to make me homeless. Well, then, is my situation tragic? No. There's been too much tragedy all around for anyone to feel like a Hamlet. More likely my situation is comic. It's "the amazement of the thinking spirit at itself" and its predicament—or so said Schlegel. One just has to laugh at the extent of our stupidity.

So what happened after 1945?

Well, from 1945 to 1948 it was just poverty. I remember being very, very hungry, and my mother crying because she had nothing to give me. Still later, it became clear to my mother that if I was ever going to become an American poet, we'd better get moving. That's Phil Levine's theory. Actually, my father was already in the United States working for the same telephone company he had worked for in Yugoslavia before the war. Anyway, we ended up in Chicago, and my father took me out one day to hear Coleman Hawkins. You could say the kid was hooked. Jazz made me both an American and a poet.

What was it about jazz that seemed to you so distinctly American?

I heard in it, experienced in it, what it feels like to be sad or happy in America. Or more idiomatically: how to raise hell, or how to break someone's heart and make beautiful music in the process. I mean, it's fine to read the great lyric poets of the past, but one also has to know how the people in the language you're writing in sing.

Is there an identifiable influence jazz has made on your work? I'm wondering, for example, if you see surrealism in any way as a literary equivalent to jazz?

The poet is really not much different from that tenor player who gets up in a half-empty, smoke-filled dive at two in the morning to play the millionth rendition of "Body and Soul." Which is to say that one plays with the weight of all that tradition, but also to entertain the customers and to please oneself. One is both bound and free. One improvises but there are constraints, forms to obey. It's the same old thing which is always significantly different.

As for surrealism, I think there's more of it in the blues. The early stuff, especially. Most people know Bessie Smith and perhaps Robert Johnson, but there are many others. Incredible verbal invention. What one would call "jive," but also eroticism, the tragic sense of life. If the blues were French, we'd be studying it at Yale. As it is, hardly anyone knows my heroes, people like Cripple Clarence Lofton, Frankie Jaxon, or Bessie Jackson, who also called herself Lucille Bogan. They are our Villons.

Anyway, blues taught me a number of things. How to tell a story quickly, economically. The value of gaps, ellipses, and most importantly, the virtues of simplicity and accessibility.

That erotic element, since you mention it, is an important part of your work as well; and now that I think about it, you use it in ways that are actually quite similar to the ways it's used in the blues. The last two stanzas of your poem "Breasts" is a good example:

O my sweet, my wistful bagpipes.
Look, everyone is asleep on the earth.
Now, in the absolute immobility
Of time, drawing the waist
Of the one I love to mine,

I will tip each breast

Like a dark heavy grape
Into the hive
Of my drowsy mouth.

I don't know if I still care for the ending of that poem. "Wistful bagpipes" is awful. Also, the pace of these stanzas is awkward. The earlier ones are better, I think.

As for eroticism, isn't it synonymous with imagination? Eros as the cause of logos, and that sort of thing. The one lying in the dark and trying to visualize the loved one is at the mercy of both. . . . There's not much more that I can say. . . . (pp. 68-70)

The more I read your work, the more I think of you as a poet of the city—in that particular way one thinks of poets like Baudelaire or Eliot or Auden or even Lowell—not so much in the landscape itself as in the way the city functions, both internally and externally, as a symbol of modernity.

When I close my eyes I go into cities. Others, I suppose, sail the ocean blue. The rat is my totem animal, the cockroach my wood thrush. My mother is calling my name out of a tenement window. She keeps calling and calling. My entire psychic life is there.

I'm sure you're familiar with The Book of Laughter and Forgetting. *At the end of that book Kundera, who also comes from an East European background, draws a pretty sad picture of the West, sad because it seems to him rather soulless.*

That's a version of the old "suffering ennobles" argument. I suppose the more political repression one experiences, the greater one's chances are for spiritual growth. The guys in the gulags are overflowing with soul. Stalin was like Buddha. The problem with us is that we don't shoot poets. Meanwhile, millions have been running in our direction. It's one-way traffic. You don't find anyone going the other way to embrace all that soulfullness. (p. 73)

To what extent do you think poetry is able to engage . . . issues?

I never liked the term "political poetry." It implies a cause, partisanship, petitions for this or that, and finally propaganda, regardless of how worthy the reason. On the other hand, the world is mean, stupid, violent, unjust, cruel. I read in the *Times* this morning that forty thousand children die every day in the world from hunger and disease. Well, what do you say to that? And you must say something. A poet who ignores the world is contemptible. I find the narcissism of so much recent poetry obscene. I don't mind people talking about themselves—we all do—but *all* the time! Mao had the right idea. Send the crybabies to dig turnips. I'm kidding, of course. The Chairman wouldn't find my poems so amusing either. Too many tyrants and torture chambers in them. I make sure the executioners are included. Obviously, I'm uncomfortable with poetry which just keeps telling me how wonderful nature is, or how much the author is misunderstood. (pp. 75-6)

In your essay, ***"Some Thoughts About the Line,"*** you say, "In the end, I'm always at the beginning. Silence—an endless mythical condition." Obviously you mean by silence something more than just that condition out of which poems grow.

I call silence what precedes language: the world and the sense of oneself existing. I always thought, if you will, that speaking is a bit like whistling in the dark. The universe, in my humble opinion, doesn't require my saying anything. When I'm attentive and silent I seem to be closer to the way things are. A number of my early poems are attempts to make that predicament into a myth of origins.

What is it then that makes you break that silence?

To speak as the translator of silence rather than its opposer. I think Thoreau said something like that, seeing language as but a minor ripple on the great pool of wordless silence, which, I agree, is our true environment.

In that same essay you say, "To see the word for what it is, one needs the line. . . . For me the sense of the line is the most instinctive aspect of the entire process of writing." One of the noticeable features of your lines is how often they are end-stopped; how often a sentence is a line by itself, or if not a line, then a stanza. Is that done to further emphasize the silence?

Yes, the line is the unit of measure, the unit of attention. It's the way one slows down and speeds up the language, the place for the "counterpoint of eye and ear," as Robert Morgan says. I'm still learning how to do it right.

Could you describe the particular way in which an image functions within your poems?

Olga Freidenberg, Pasternak's aunt, says in their correspondence: "A poetic metaphor is an image functioning as a concept." I agree with that. In my poetry images think. My best images are smarter than I am.

Your work has always stood somewhere outside the narrative mode, but do you ever find yourself drifting in that direction?

I hope not. Most of the so-called narrative poems just plod. They have no sense of the line, nor do they imagine well.

When poets forget what imagination can do they get into these linear, prosy, redundant, long-winded poems. It's possible to tell a story, the whole story, in twenty lines. The art consists of making a few details and images say everything. They should study Strand's "The Untelling." There's a masterpiece for you.

But don't most poems of any kind just plod? I was really wondering about the exceptional few. Or are you saying that at some point the imagination and the narrative are antithetical?

No. Imagination and narrative go fine together. Consider myths, fairy tales, prose poems, etc. However, most narrative poems I see operate largely in the framework of realism.

I notice in reading reviews of your books that critics at times have a tendency to read your poems as parables. Is that the result of your working beyond the framework of realism?

I don't know. I don't write parables. If I say "rats in diapers" that's to be taken literally.

Then do you think of your poems as having a clearly communicative function, on rational or cognitive levels?

I don't know about "clearly communicative" and "cognitive," but the point of writing a poem, actually the need to do so, is to give, pass on, relate to someone something of value. I don't want to waste people's time. It matters to me (I mean, what goes on in the poem), and I want them to know about it. One can't always make it simple because many things are not simple, but it's worth trying.

You read a good deal of philosophy, and, I'm told, have a particular interest in Heidegger.

I always read philosophy. I suppose I'm a bit envious of that kind of disciplined thinking. Also, I am curious what human beings have been thinking for the last three thousand years about the nature of things. As for Heidegger, I admire the phenomenological impulse to reexamine the simplest, the long-taken-for-granted things. That's what a poet is supposed to do, too.

Is that the most important thing a poet is supposed to do?

No! You must have a pencil handy when the Muse barges in. My father told me that many poems came to him in his lifetime but just in those moments when he couldn't find anything to write with. Otherwise, it's pointless to say what a poem should do. Someone always comes along and does the opposite, and it's perfectly fine. What all good poetry has in common is the use of the imagination. Imagination, on the other hand, is like the universe of which only a small part has been explored. (pp. 76-9)

> *Charles Simic and Sherod Santos, in an interview in* The Uncertain Certainty: Interviews, Essays, and Notes on Poetry *by Charles Simic, The University of Michigan Press, 1985, pp. 68-79.*

Bruce Bond

In Charles Simic's poetry, we glimpse human suffering from a strangely detached perspective, often lending hardship an aura of wonder. This detachment continues to irritate some readers who see in it remnants of a reclusive modernist excess, a failure to let the self become vulnerable, fit for responsible action. As further testimony to Simic's retreat into an invulnerable persona, critics point to his frequent ambiguities, his failure to commit himself to the humane task of communicating. His austere language sounds less like a man speaking to men than a man speaking to himself. And a rhetoric which rarely accommodates itself to a reader not only mirrors but also creates a sense of isolation. What, we may ask, can be the value of such verse? But to refer to Simic's poetry merely as "detached" is simplistic. We cannot help but feel emotionally confronted by the scenes of suffering in his poems. While maintaining a quiet, understating rhetoric, Simic's poems simultaneously dramatize the most pressing needs. Thus, he creates a complex tone of detached involvement. That realm of experience which seems closest, most urgent, most charged by suffering, also feels strangely out of reach. No language can accommodate it. And rather than lapsing into a complacency with the imperfections of words, his poems express a desire for words to be more than arbitrary, to be disciplined by attentiveness. Such verse communicates in ways that poetry best communicates, by drawing attention to its failures but nevertheless attempting an effectively inclusive version of consciousness, "three-dimensional" rather than linear, full of our own sad and marvelous contraries. To attempt this with sensitivity is to recognize both the shortcomings and appeals of mimesis. It is to resist linguistic limits and human insularity, with the knowledge that such resistance is a painful, irresolvable, and constant source of wonder.

Simic refers to the immanent realm unyielding to language as "silence." Consciousness of the incommunicable nature of silence brings with it consciousness of solitude:

> Silence, solitude, what is more essential to the human condition? "Maternal silence" is what I would like to call it. Life before the coming of language. That place where we begin to hear the voice of the inanimate. Poetry is an orphan of silence. The words never quite equal the experience behind them.

We may puzzle over the implications of Simic's metaphor: if poetry is the "orphan of silence," then what can it tell us of its beginnings? Is the notion of prelinguistic experience little but a marvelous afterthought locked with us in our prisonhouse of language? Because consciousness cannot fully account for itself, such questions make their final appeal to awareness rather than consciousness, seeing rather than thinking. Since the advent of Derridean and other post-modern challenges to the notion of linguistic origin, it has become increasingly unpopular to allow undifferentiating awareness a role in informing the process of differentiation, of consciousness. Simic is aware that he holds a minority view:

> I'm one of those who believes that there is something that precedes language. The usual view is that there is some kind of equivalence between thought and language, that you can't verbalize it if you can't think it. I've always felt that there is a stage that precedes verbalization, a complexity of experience that consists of things not yet brought to consciousness, not yet existing as language but as some sort of inner pressure.

A sympathetic understanding of such pressure and its failure to find adequate expression enriches our context for reading Simic's verse. Silence, according to Simic's description, is generative, but it cannot generate its own likeness. This matters insofar as silence demands that it matter. In such a model of mind, language, though imperfect, is nevertheless responsibly bound to something outside itself. We are not in an intellectually dominated, self-referential world comprised of only signs. The body, for instance, demands a quality of attentiveness peripheral to the chatter of signification. Our hands become intimate with spoons and forks in a way that our language cannot. Or, stunned by significant loss, we may sense a gap between our tragic awareness and what can be said. Silence may offer an enlarged version of experience, the liberating sense of a spacious setting for our house of language, but it also burdens us with its impossible task. For Schöenberg's Moses in *Moses and Aaron,* this task is explicitly religious. Moses must try to communicate the Word of God to his people. For Simic, the sense of urgency comes not from the burden of divine authority but from that of human suffering, the most demanding physical and emotional needs.

Despite Simic's confrontation with human suffering, we may be tempted into a narcosis of wonder attracted to the otherworldliness of his poem-world. We may look on the bald realities of mutilation and poverty with a voyeuristic fascination. Simic's understating rhetoric and folk-tale settings often invite this. Voyeuristic fascination appears to be a central part of Simic's experience. But this fascination is coupled with a simultaneous sense of terrifying immanence. Simic remembers his childhood in Yugoslavia:

> There was a church which had a large yard, and there were dead German soldiers there, and so we'd go over there and we'd take from the German soldiers the belts, the ammo-belts, helmets, war-junk such as kids can play with . . . I don't have any nightmares about it. It was all part of this wonderful game we had . . . if you were writing a poem about it, one really has to capture that complicated game. That innocence . . . There was something there, which I can't quite name, but I felt touched and disturbed. But it wasn't any of the obvious things: that here was a dead man, that this was War.

Simic's poem **"Pastoral,"** from the book ***Dismantling the Silence,*** creates a similarly complex feeling of detachment and disturbance. Whatever innocence we detect in Simic's unflinching rhetoric is tainted. In keeping with other pastorals, the poem explores through its setting a style of passion which is at once celebrative and sad, a mood which translates the idyllic into mortal terms. Nature's consolations become reminders of loss. Silence, like flesh, is grass:

> I came to a meadow
> Where the grass was silence
> And flowers
> Words
>
> I saw they were both
> Of flesh and blood
> And that they sense and fear
> The wind like a knife

The poem uses a veneer of simplicity to convey its complex tone. Simic's syntax is bare; his diction, flat as the pavement. Little effort is made to persuade by dazzling. But to call the language "unrhetorical" is to discount the seductive weirdness of its surface. The speaker's quiet lack of astonishment is itself strange given the strangeness of his world. He is the deadpan observer of his own vastly unexplained condition. He does not actively seek out a meadow. He "comes" to it as though incidentally. But this incidental setting then turns into hypersensitized flesh and blood, neurotic imagery which asserts the pre-eminence of emotional life. Silence and language become embodied, humanized, vulnerable. Even the metaphor of the flesh is complicated by contrary feelings: little is more intimate than our own bodies, but little is more mysterious. The speaker then links together a causal chain of private events with apparent self-assurance:

> So I sat between the word *truth*
>
> And the word *gallows*
> Took out my tin can
> And spoon
>
> Whistled for the word *love*
> And she answered me
> By and by in her sleep
>
> There were also many other things
> For which there was no word
> Only a breath now and then

Even the distance which the speaker experiences between himself and the anonymous woman is mitigated by an unaccountable intimacy. Her groggy, milk-toast responsiveness and the withholding of her identity contribute to our sense of her as remote. But the ambiguous pronoun "she" cuts two ways. While withholding her identity, it also suggests that the speaker is already familiar with her. She needs no introduction. It is as though we have been dropped into the middle of an ongoing relation which might make more complete sense if we could only trace it back to its beginnings. But the poem's resistance, its eclipsed origins, make it all the better model of consciousness.

The speaker asks the woman, not for love, but for the word "love." Given the poem's climate of fear, we might expect a request for the "real thing." But the word "love" turns out to be the choice most consistent with the poem's tone. The request for the word "love" is a request for a token rather than an emotional commitment. This particular word, "love," may signify human involvement, but we experience in the speaker's prevailing sense of isolation the gap between word and referent.

To complicate things further, love, though it may signify a form of human involvement, not only tolerates but thrives on isolation and ambiguity. Ambiguity becomes a source of love's wonder, a dark place for the amorous imagination to play. In his essay on the poetry of Benjamin Peret, Simic says:

> If Peret has a "metaphysics," it has to do with the interdependence of love and the marvelous. Each of his images is as earthbound as the act of love. No longing here for the Absolute, only an appetite for multiplicity . . . Peret is the purest practitioner of Keats's negative capability. No one is more patient with the absurd, the inexplicable.

Thus the act of love is an act of faith in the absurd: it draws its mystique and vitality from the very isolation and ambiguity its rituals set out to overcome. Words are the mythemes in such rituals. Rather than representing experience, they express a desire to represent it. Words do not overcome a sense of isolation. They express a desire to overcome it. Thus they are gestures of longing rather than vestiges of truth. And, as such, they become perennial sources of the marvelous.

In **"Pastoral,"** words, like flesh, take on an odd material reality apart from the speaker himself. They, like the body, have a quality of immanent distance, being essential to the experience of self yet spatially apart. Separate from the stuff of his identity, the speaker is strangely anonymous, a self without a self. In his essay **"Images and 'Images',"** Simic writes, "To be conscious is to experience a distancing. One is neither the World, nor Language, nor Self. One *is* and one *is not.*" The self which is not the self is the self-neglecting observer, a point of view which cannot account for its own perspective. Such an observer, in some measure independent from what the self has to lose, resembles an invulnerable voyeur, a persona similar to the Yugoslavian child who sleeps untroubled by nightmares.

Such an invulnerable self is best identified by what it lacks. It is an absence, but paradoxically present in the sense that it is nevertheless experienced. We may recognize in Simic's notion of the self-which-is-not-the-self traces of Husserl's concept of the transcendental ego. Simic frequently nods to the German phenomenological tradition as influential. The transcendental ego (as opposed to the *concept* of the transcendental ego) does not deconstruct since it never "constructs" in the first place. It lies on the periphery of the play of differentiation. The deconstructionist view allows no room for an unconstructed self behind language. The term "ego" may be misleading since this ego is not an organizing center. It is more like a field, something closer to the silent meadow in Simic's poem. In an interview, Simic recalls Heidegger's metaphor of open spaces:

> I've always felt that inside each of us there is profound anonymity . . . whatever you meet, it is not yours though you enclose it . . . [Heidegger] describes the division between the world as nothing, as what he calls the "open," and any act of conceptualizing. Many of his texts are longings to experience that anonymity, the condition where we don't have an "I" yet. It is as if we were in a room from which, paradoxically, we were absent.

If we were to literalize what it is to be half-missing, we might wind up with a pathetic cripple. This is precisely whom we meet in Simic's poem **"Great Infirmities"** from ***Classic Ballroom Dances.*** We may recognize a characteristic economy and quietness to the rhetoric, the correlative to innocence playing its complicated game in a desperate situation:

> Everyone has only one leg.
>
> So difficult to get around,
> So difficult to climb the stairs
> Without a cane or crutch to our name.
>
> And only one arm. Impossible contortions
> Just to embrace the one you love,
> To cut the bread on the table,
> To put a coat on in a hurry.
>
> I should mention that we are almost blind,
> and a little deaf in both ears.
> Perilous to be on the street.
> Among the congregations of the afflicted.

The phrase "I should mention" on the surface implies urgency but functions conversationally as a prelude to an afterthought. The joke, of course, is that we might expect more than a postscript to talk about our near-blindness. Simic has a knack for grim humor, another strategy of emotional distancing which thrives on its simultaneous ability to disturb. In the above poem, Simic alternates between hyperbole—"Everyone has only one leg"—and litotes—"So difficult to get around." Such wildly modulating humor encourages us to take pleasure in ambiguity.

The poem also risks a small pun: "Without a cane or a crutch to our name." The phrase "a crutch to our name" suggests a crutch reaching to our name, a crutch for our name. As in **"Pastoral,"** words are made flesh, halve-able. The pun opens up a reading of the poem as a meditation on living in two worlds, the "sayable" and the "unsayable." Our missing halves complicate things horribly. Language offers no closure, no sense of, not only truth-telling, but sufficiency. To name is to embrace with one arm.

The poem's final stanza plays tricks on our depth perception to dramatize such frustrated desire. To draw close is to withdraw:

> An immense stillness everywhere
>
> With the trees always bare,
> The raindrops coming down only halfway,
> Coming so close and giving up.

The trees are bare for want of what never arrives. What is most desired fades as it approaches like a small object in a blur over the eyes. The result is absolute isolation. To name is to experience a distancing. No attentive effort can overcome this distance.

Finally, we may remain unconvinced that physical hardship is appropriately cast in Simic's terms. It may strike some as trivializing to concern ourselves with the limits of language when subsistence is at stake. By placing language in a state of crisis, Simic's poems suggest the fundamental nature of imaginative need. As Stevens tells us, it is the imagination which makes the world into something we can love. But imaginative need can never be equivalent to physical need. Though our world is shaped by a desire for imaginative flight, game playing, jokes, all the pleasures of abstraction and ambiguity, such marvels cannot overcome physical hardship. Simic's verse swings broadly between the miraculous and the hard. Both contribute to his spacious version of us as immanent and distant, as being in the flesh and being conscious of ourselves in the flesh. Rather than trivializing human need, Simic's verse gives us a model for the quality of inner attentiveness which breeds respect for human range, an expanse extending beyond the sacramental gesturings of language. A world in which words are given like bread involves us deeply because in it we recognize the unresolved dissonance in our own imaginations, rude, venerating, straining our eyes. (pp. 89-95)

Bruce Bond, "Immanent Distance: Silence and the Poetry of Charles Simic," in Mid-America Review, *Vol. VIII, No. 1, 1988, pp. 89-96.*

Jim Elledge

From the time of his initial book, published in 1967, until now, Simic's career has been characterized by chance taking. His ninth collection [***The World Doesn't End***], a group of prose poems, is further evidence of the author's verve. Full of spunk and sass, the book's 67 pieces attempt to redefine human experience and to reveal in the process how odd, even absurd, the everyday is. In one prose poem, a student working on algebra problems at a blackboard is haunted by the equations' *X*'s and imagines them to be crosses in a graveyard at night. In another, Hermes, messenger of the gods in Greek mythology, is metamorphosed into a twentieth-century mailman who, like his ancient counterpart, steals the letters he is to deliver. In others, a week-long vacation is spent in a glass paperweight, people are kidnapped by UFOs, plants speak to their mirrored reflections, and police dogs are dressed up as children. Freewheeling and humorous, Simic's latest is a much-needed reprieve from the tedium that marks far too many current and "safe" volumes of U.S. poetry. Unreservedly recommended.

Jim Elledge, in a review of "The World Doesn't End," in Booklist, *Vol. 85, No. 13, March 1, 1989, p. 1087.*

John Ash

[Reading] Charles Simic's delightful collection of prose poems, ***The World Doesn't End,*** I was struck by the words, "The time of minor poets is coming. Good-by Whitman, Dickinson, Frost," but thankfully, Simic's poems don't put one in a valedictory or regretful mood. This is a beautifully designed box of verbal fireworks, or, to put it another way, a seamless fusion of wild jazz and delicate, moonstruck, European chamber music.

No doubt the word "surreal" will be wielded by reviewers in a hurry, but Simic's marvelously fresh and witty prose-fantasies deserve to escape that dusty pigeon-hole. We learn of a "beautiful lost girl" who is addressed in polite French by lizards in ecclesiastical costume; we get to spend "a week long holiday in a glass paperweight bought at Coney Island"; elsewhere we find "Margaret . . . copying a recipe for 'saints roasted with onions,' " and Dr. Freud falls in love with a pair of shoes.

As Simic himself modestly admits, one of the greatest charms of these waking dreams is the fact that they "can be so easily dismissed as preposterous." And yet they stick in the memory and have the power to disturb. At one point the speaker of the poems remembers dozing off in the shade, dreaming that the rustling trees around him "were my many selves explaining themselves all at the same time so that I could not make out a single word. My life was a beautiful mystery on the verge of understanding, always on the verge! Think of it!"

By turns funny and poignant, whimsical and down-to-earth, ***The World Doesn't End*** is a flawless performance by a poet at the height of his powers. Young poets everywhere should read it attentively. They might learn to write as if they were young.

John Ash, "The Shock of the New," in Book World—The Washington Post, *May 7, 1989, p. 10.*

Kevin Hart

[In] a recent collection of interviews, notes, and essays, ***The Uncertain Certainty,*** Simic offers a philosophical vocabulary which seems to illuminate his poetic project—a vocabulary drawn largely from phenomenology in general and from Heidegger in particular . . . . Simic is, thus far, virtually untouched by criticism. Unclaimed by this or that school, Simic's poetry is not read with specific critical vocabularies in mind. We can therefore approach the theoretical questions which will interest us all the more quickly; and besides, there is also the pleasure of introducing a poetic *œuvre* which deserves more attention.

Exactly what attracts a writer to one philosopher, or kind of philosopher, is not easy to determine in any systematic way. Certainly, though, Heidegger features more prominently in the conversation and writings of poets than, for example, G. E. Moore or A. J. Ayer; and one reason for this would be Heidegger's analysis of ultimate human concerns—the discussion of *Dasein* as "Being-towards-death," of Care and Concern, all of the issues (so one often hears, sometimes unfairly) that analytic philosophers bypass in favour of logical and grammatical puzzles. Philosophers can be influential in two ways: they can exercise fellow philosophers, and they can touch people who have nothing to do with the academic profession of philosophy. Heidegger belongs to that small group that holds sway in both senses, which is not to say that his influence is evenly distributed or that everyone means the same thing by "Martin Heidegger." It is not hard to imagine one writer who prizes the early Heidegger, the author of *Being and Time,* with all his pathos for the human situation, and another who values the later Heidegger, the sage of *Time and Being,* with his no less alluring gnomic simplicity.

There are, after all, poets such as Paul Celan, Yves Bonnefoy, and Mark Strand whose work resonates with the early Heidegger or, more accurately, with a particular reading of the early Heidegger; but Charles Simic is not one of them. His poetry does not derive its power from a rhetoric of crisis but from an abstention from that rhetoric, from a desire to hollow out the self in favour of the other, whether animate or inanimate. What attracts Simic to Heidegger is the latter's patient attention to "the things themselves," as is suggested by the titles of early poems such as **"Stone," "Fork," "Knife," "My Shoes,"** and **"Brooms."** (In this sense, there is perhaps more fellow feeling between Simic and Ponge than, say, between Simic and Bonnefoy.) "I've always felt that inside each of us there is profound anonymity," Simic remarks in an interview [with Rick Jackson and Michael Panori published in ***The Uncertain Certainty***], then says, "This is where Heidegger is very interesting to me. He describes the division between the world as nothing, as what he calls the 'open,' and any act of conceptualizing which restores the world in a particular way. Many of his texts are longings to experience that anonymity, the condition where we don't have an 'I' yet". And in a later interview [with Sherod Santos, also collected in ***The Uncertain Certainty,***] the point is approached from another angle: "As for Heidegger, I admire the phenomenological impulse to reexamine the simplest, the long-taken-for-granted things. That's what a poet is supposed to do, too".

On the kind of evidence supplied in Simic's prose writings, it would be naive to insist upon too close a connection between the poet and the thinker, to argue that Simic is a "Heideggerian." Yet it is not too much to say that he is a phenomenologist; after all, the label is in no way reserved for philosophers—and who is to say that phenomenology is best done within academic philosophy? By the same token, we cannot readily dismiss Simic's interest in philosophy, what he calls the "philosophical, or rather epistemological, preoccupation that haunts my work", let alone his respect for prominent phenomenologists, Husserl and Bachelard, as well as Heidegger. This is not to crowd out, by an appeal to a more cognitively respectable discourse, the host of poets who have doubtless influenced Simic, poets as varied as Crane, Popa, and Péret, not to mention all the blues lyricists and anonymous riddlers and jesters who figure in his development. The issue, rather, is how to give due weight to a poet's avowed interest in someone or something ostensibly outside literature and literary history; or more generally, to work out the rights of one context over another in reading a poet's work. For example, should we read Simic from within the context of Yugoslav poetry—Lalic, Milhkovic, Pavic, Popa, and Simovic, to list only some of those he has translated? Or from within the context of modern American poetry—including Dickinson, Roethke, Stevens, and Williams? Or yet again, is it more profitable to break with literary canons altogether and read Simic as a phenomenologist, as speaking in the name of phenomenology, of Husserl and Heidegger, or of "the things themselves"?

No text can command a particular context, since nothing can prevent a text from being detached from one context and quoted in another. This is not to say, however, that all contexts have equal value or equal interest; and what intrigues me in Simic's prose writings is that they draw attention to a framework which seems natural to the writer but has escaped his readers' attention. It is quite possible—I have done it myself—to read Simic entirely within the context of contemporary poetry, as a discursive space where Eastern European folk poetry, French Surrealism, and American Transcendentalism converge and are made into something else again, something quite unique. At one point in an interview, Rod Steier pauses and says to Simic, "*You must sometimes finish an interview and say to yourself, 'I wish somebody had asked me that question.' Are there any questions you'd like to be asked?*" A rare, unguarded moment, as interviews go, and one which prompts a similarly unguarded response by Simic: "Well, the question that people have not asked me much, and I'm partially happy that they haven't because I don't know exactly how to answer it, is about philosophy." To which Steier responds, predictably enough, "*Do you want to talk about philosophy?*" and Simic replies, "That's a very dangerous thing to be talking about. Ideally, if there's any kind of intellectual content or thought in my work, I have attempted to digest it and absorb it into the experience the poem is describing. It's very difficult to separate. It's very difficult to talk about it. Poetry doesn't state ideas. At best, it causes them. It's thought-provoking".

Or as Williams said earlier in the century, "no ideas but in things." It is a formula which Simic discusses along philosophical rather than literary lines: "At issue here is an attempt to re-create experience which preceded thought and to uncover its phenomenological ground. To allow phenomena to speak for itself [sic]. 'To let that which shows itself be seen from itself in the very way in which it shows itself from itself' (Heidegger)". Yet even though Simic's "philosophical preoccupation" may be deeply encoded within the poems, within the poetic experience, and in experience generally, once we are alerted that it *is* a preoccupation, there begins a process of decoding the poems which is motivated by this concern. One looks again at all those early poems which describe ordinary things, a poem such as **"Fork":**

This strange thing must have crept
Right out of hell.
It resembles a bird's foot
Worn around the cannibal's neck.

As you hold it in your hand,
As you stab with it into a piece of meat,
It is possible to imagine the rest of the bird:
Its head which like your fist
Is large, bald, beakless and blind.

Faced with this poem, one's first impulse is to read it as an exercise in defamiliarisation: the whole point is to see a quotidian object as *strange.* How this occurs is easy enough to work out. First, the fork is pictured as a devil's pitchfork; then the context rapidly changes and it becomes a bird's foot; and, finally, the poem plays with the idea of context. The reader has already had to acknowledge a parallel between himself or herself and the cannibal (stressed by the crude phrasing of "you stab with it into a piece of meat"), but now the problem becomes to imagine a possible world in which there *are* large, bald, beakless, and blind birds. Under a formalist reading such as this the poem becomes vulnerable to Stevens's charge that Surrealism invents but never discovers a world. Yet if, after reading Simic's observations on writing, we regard the poem as a "phenomenological interrogation," a quite different interpretation offers itself.

If a formalist reading bids us follow the poem's formal logic, a phenomenological reading insists that the poem explores an experience which has a logic of its own. Both readings turn on the phrase "It is possible to imagine"; yet the second does not invite a flight from experience but a shift to a radically experiential viewpoint. **"Fork"** starts from the experience of eating, specifically eating meat, and it attempts to grasp an underlying principle, an *eidos,* of that experience. By varying the perspective from hell, to a cannibal, to a scene of eating, the poem enables us to grasp the phenomenon of eating meat. The imagination here works to separate the *eidos* from the surrounding facts, so that, in the end, we are not left with something purely imagined, outside the world of possible experience, but with something *seen.* Strange as it is, the image of the bird with which the poem closes helps us to grasp what is at issue in eating flesh. The bird is at once vulnerable and frightening; more to the point, in being "beakless and blind" it is obscenely defaced. Such birds need not exist for the reader to experience a mixture of compassion and repugnance in reading the image. What is strange, finally, is not the fork but people's complaisance in allowing animals to be killed in order to eat meat. The poem ultimately works in the service of clarity, not strangeness.

To grasp a poem's *eidos* is not to reduce it to a determinate meaning, but only to uncover the intelligibility of the experience described in the poem. At this point we could pass from a consideration of the structure of an experience to the reader's experience of the poem, and this would immediately involve us in issues of determinacy and indeterminacy. Already, though, this would return us to the familiar arena in which literary language confronts philosophy. Derrida has shown, in *Speech and Phenomena,* the problems which the sign poses for Husserl's theory of the imagination, but these can be set aside for now. We need not concern ourselves with Simic's theory of the imagination (if he has one), only with the use to which he puts phenomenology in writing poems. Imagination, for Simic, is certainly a capacity, something which precedes an experience and allows one to hit upon an *eidos* which, after the fact, can be seen to structure the poem. Yet it is also a way of writing poems, what Husserl called "the method of imaginary variation," a leaping from viewpoint to viewpoint which enables an *eidos* to be grasped.

None of this is to deny that Simic holds particular views about philosophy. There is a suspicion of metaphysics, for instance, a fear of totalisation and "a horror of abstractions" which occasionally finds expression in poems. **"Madonnas Touched Up with a Goatee"** is an example:

> Most ancient Metaphysics, (poor Metaphysics!)
> All decked up in imitation jewelry.
> We went for a stroll, arm in arm, smooching in public
> Despite the difference in ages.
>
> It's still the 19th century, she whispered.
> We were in a knife-fighting neighbourhood
> Among some rundown relics of the Industrial Revolution.
> Just a little further, she assured me,
> In the back of a certain candy store only she knew about,
> The customers were engrossed in the *Phenomenology of the Spirit.*
>
> It's long past midnight, my dove, my angel!
> We'd better be careful, I thought.
> There were young hoods on street corners
> With crosses and iron studs on their leather jackets.
> They all looked like they'd read Darwin and that madman Pavlov,
> And were about to ask us for a light.

Hardly a flattering picture of metaphysics, this, with its images of "imitation jewelry" and of Hegelian scholarship having to take place in "the back of a certain candy store." The era of great philosophical systems has passed, the poem tells us, and we live in its shadow, the age of science and technology. The "young hoods" loitering on the street corners are a result of social Darwinism and social conditioning alike. Despite its cheeky title, the poem does not devalue ideas. Quite the opposite in fact: the dangerous situation in which the speaker finds himself as the poem closes answers directly to the ideas of Darwin and Pavlov. The fact that metaphysical systems have little credibility in the twentieth century does not mean that past metaphysical systems do not still have great force and consequence.

Once we become aware of a new context in which to read a writer it becomes difficult to determine where the context actually begins and ends. To realise that one can justify a phenomenological reading of Simic quickly leads, as we have seen, to a reading of poems which use or mention the names of philosophers. **"Madonnas Touched Up with a Goatee"** refers us to Hegel, while other poems cite the names Parmenides, Plato, Descartes, Pascal, and Nietzsche. Yet perhaps we can cover more distance if we turn to a poem which does not quote a philosopher's proper name or, for that matter, appear to engage in any philosophical issues at all. In doing so, however, we cannot forget what Simic has told us, that he has a "philosophical preoccupation," and so we must always be attuned to the *possibility* of philosophical issues in the poem, perhaps encoded so deeply that they resist all attempts to be decoded even while they simultaneously direct and organise the poem. The risk taken, of course, is that to admit such a deep and thorough encoding is, for all intents and purposes, to concede that the issues may not be in the poem. What if Simic has overstated or feigned his "preoccupation" and sits back, even now, smiling to himself at someone earnestly searching through his poems to see how philosophy may have helped them be written? Does Simic write in the name of philosophy, in the name of Heidegger or phenomenology, of "the things themselves"? Can we read those names in the poems? And in using a philosophical vocabulary to discuss the poem will we be discussing the poem at all? Is there, indeed, a proper vocabulary to use when discussing literature? (pp. 200-05)

"[We] cannot forget what Simic has told us, that he has a "philosophical preoccupation," and so we must always be attuned to the *possibility* of philosophical issues in the poem, perhaps encoded so deeply that they resist all attempts to be decoded even while they simultaneously direct and organise the poem."

—Kevin Hart

For [Harold] Bloom and others, literature and philosophy are already two distinct and readily identifiable subject areas. But what if there is nothing proper to literature or poetry? The question takes hold at several levels.

One of the things most evident in reading Simic, for example, is his avoidance of the proper: names of cities and persons, dates of events and poems, seldom feature in his poems. Many of his poems could be titled, as one is, **"Rough Outline"**; and even when he does introduce proper names, as in "Charles Simic," it is characteristic that the name becomes a riddle. To avoid proper names in the interest of the archetype or experience itself is to allow each reader to be addressed by the poem. Which is not to say that the reader is free to identify with the speaker or persons in the poems—very often they simply do not exist, or cannot be recovered in any detail. Again, many of Simic's poems could pass under the title he gives to one of them, **"Austerities."** We are not talking here about the reader's freedom to imagine and enter a poetic scene but of the ways in which a poem can position the reader. In a fairly clear sense, the reader is always produced by the text, placed and displaced by rhetorical moves, narrative stances, the speaker's tone, and so forth. And not just the reader but also the author, whose shifting image is projected by those same elements and procedures. In the event of reading, neither reader nor author absolutely precedes the poem, making that event an economy, a site of various negotiations and exchanges.

In the same way, Simic's poems are not so much receipts of "philosophy" that have been placed in the hands of "literature." A poem such as **"Northern Exposure"** produces a configuration of philosophy and literature as it is read, not so much as clear and distinct areas but as images which can displace the ideas of "philosophy" and "literature" with which we approach the poem. In other words, "philosophy" and "literature" are produced as problems, not as things in themselves. To say that Heidegger, for example, provides us with the proper vocabularly for reading Simic would be to beg the question. **"Northern Exposure"** is many things—a mystery, a puzzle, a pleasure—but at one level it debates how it should be read, inviting readers (and readers within a reader) to make trade-offs in their critical practices. The exchange can never be absolutely finalized because a text is always open to the possibility of being repeated outside its original context or configuration of contexts. As Simic says in the poem **"Elementary Cosmogony,"** the final law is the "submission to chance". It might seem natural and inevitable to take poetry and philosophy as contexts for reading Simic's poems; yet—who knows?—just as there is a surprise in discovering Simic's abiding interest in phenomenology, one which forcibly introduces a new context for reading his work, so may there be many surprises in store for readers of Simic. After all, we have only just begun to read Charles Simic: the future is still very much an open book. (pp. 211-12)

Kevin Hart, "Writing Things: Literary Property in Heidegger and Simic," in New Literary History, *Vol. 21, No. 1, Autumn, 1989, pp. 199-214.*

Charles Simic

Notes on Poetry and Philosophy

> It is the hardship of the times that before an artist can fashion an icon he must compose the theology that his icon will reinforce.
>
> *Harold Rosenberg*

Some sort of Academy of Fine Arts from which they stole the bust of the philosopher Socrates so he might accompany them on what was to be a night of serious drinking.

It was heavy. The two of them had to lug it together. They went from tavern to tavern like that. They'd make Socrates sit in his own chair. When the waiter came, they'd ask for three glasses. Socrates sat over his drink looking wise.

Later, in a low dive where gypsies were playing, a couple of drunken women joined them. They loved their "friend." They kept kissing Socrates and trying to make him drink wine. His mouth turned red. He could have been bleeding.

They left Socrates, as the day was breaking, at a streetcar stop. The number two would arrive full of sleepy factory workers, the doors would open, and there'd be the Greek Philosopher with his blind gaze and his bloodied mouth, waiting on the sidewalk to be taken up.

Knights of Sorrowful Countenance
Sitting Late Over Dog-Eared Books

That was my father's story. Philosophy intrigued him all his life. He loved it. He made fun of it. He was the one who gave me Heidegger's *Being and Time.* We read its most difficult passages together and discussed the book endlessly.

"Amateur philosophers, the worst kind!" he used to say about us.

I continued to read Heidegger as his various works became available in English. The attraction was strong for a Surrealist—which is what I considered myself in those days. "Avant-garde is revolt and metaphysics," says Rosenberg. You cannot have great poetry without at least an attempt at one. That's how I understood the legacy of Rimbaud and Stevens. Heidegger made my own intuitions about the philosophical ambitions of modern poetry clearer to me.

The other appeal of Heidegger was his attack on subjectivism, his idea that it is not the poet who speaks through the poem but the work itself. This has always been my experience. The poet is at the mercy of his metaphors. Everything is at the mercy of the poet's metaphors—even Language who is their Lord and master.

Kevin Hart's essay and his fine reading of my poems give me an opportunity to say more on the subject.

"O Paradiso!" My Pop Sang in the Shower

The twentieth-century poet is "a metaphysician in the dark," according to Wallace Stevens.

That sounds to me like a version of that old joke about chasing a black cat in a dark room. The room today is more crowded than ever. In addition to Poetry, Theology is also there, and so are various representatives of Western and Eastern Philosophies. There's a lot of bumping of heads in the dark. The famous kitty, however, isn't there . . . Still, the poets continue to cry from time to time: "We got her folks!"

Unless, of course, it's the Devil himself they've got by the tail instead!

The Fish Is Sphinx to the Cat

There is a major misunderstanding in literary criticism as to how ideas get into poems. The poets, supposedly, proceed in one of these two ways: They either state their ideas directly or they find equivalents for them. What is usually called philosophical poetry seems to be either a poetry of heightened eloquence or some variety of symbolism. In each case the assumption is that the poet knows beforehand what he or she wishes to say, and that the writing of the poem is the search for the most effective means of gussying up these ideas.

If this were correct, poetry would simply repeat what has been thought and said before. There would be no poetic thinking in the way Heidegger conceives of it. There would be no hope for poetry having any relation to truth.

In a Head This Old There's a Blind Hen which Occasionally Finds a Kernel of Corn and Her Name Is Love

My poems (in the beginning) are like a table on which one places interesting things one has found on one's walks: a pebble, a rusty nail, a strangely shaped root, a corner of a torn photograph, etc. . . . where after months of looking at them and thinking about them daily, certain surprising relationships which hint at meanings begin to appear.

These *objets trouvé* of poetry are, of course, bits of language. The poem is the place where one hears what the language is really saying, where the full meaning of words begins to emerge.

That's not quite right! It's not so much what the words mean that is crucial, but rather what they show and reveal. The literal leads to the figurative, and inside every poetic figure of value there's a theater where a play is in progress. The play is about gods and demons and the world in its baffling presence and variety.

In its essence an interesting poem is an epistemological and metaphysical problem for the poet.

The Way a Child Studies the Minute Hand of His Watch

Back in 1965 I sent some of my object poems (**"Fork"** among them) to a literary magazine. They came back with a letter which said something like this:

"Dear Mr. Simic . . . you're obviously a sensible young man, so why do you waste your time by writing about knives, spoons, and forks?"

I guess the editor's premise was that there were things worthy of poetry and that the fork in my hand was not one of them. In other words, serious subjects and serious ideas make serious poems, etc. He was just trying to give me kindly advice.

I was surprised by the resistance some people had to these poems. "Back to things themselves," said Husserl, and the Imagist had the same idea. An object is the irreducible itself, a convenient place to begin, it seemed to me.

What interested me, too, was the discipline, the attention required, and the dialectics that went with it. You look and you don't see. It's so familiar that it is invisible, etc. I mean, anybody can tell when you're faking it. Everybody is an expert when it comes to forks.

Plus, all genuine poetry in my view is anti-poetry.

Like a Barber College Haircut

> Poets think they're pitchers when they're really catchers.
>
> *Jack Spicer*

Everything would be very simple if we could will our metaphors. We cannot.

This is true of poems, too. We may start believing that we are recreating an experience, that we are making an attempt at mimesis, but then the language takes over. Suddenly the words have a mind of their own.

It's like saying, I wanted to go to church but the poem took me to the dog races.

When it first happened I was horrified. It took me years to admit that the poem is smarter than I am. Now I go where it wants to go.

A Short Order Cook Peeling Metaphysical Onions

Heidegger says that we will never understand properly what poetry is until we understand what thinking is. Then he says, most interestingly, that the nature of thinking is something other than thinking, something other than willing.

It's this "other" that poetry sets traps for.

Eternity, the Present Moment, Playing with Each Other

My hunch has always been that our deepest experiences are wordless. There may be images, but there are no words to describe the gap between seeing and saying, for example. The labor of poetry is finding ways through language to point to what cannot be put into words.

Robert Duncan [in *Bending the Bow,* 1968] had this to say about the pronoun "it," which for him was the most interesting word in the language as it is for me: "The gnostics and magicians claim to know or would know Its real nature, which they believe to be miswritten or cryptically written in the text of the actual world. But Williams is right in his *no ideas but in things;* for It has only the actual universe to realize Itself. We ourselves in our actuality, as the poem in its actuality, its thingness, are facts, factors, in which It makes Itself real."

Duncan is speaking out of the Romantic and occult tradition, but here he's close to Heidegger who speaks of the "It" which gives Being, the "It" which gives Time.

The poem that thinks is a place where we open to "It." The poem's difficulty is that it presents an experience language cannot get at. Being cannot be represented or uttered—as poor realists foolishly believe—but only hinted at. Writing is always a rough translation from wordlessness into words.

Very Quiet. Pssst.

We cannot say what reality is, only what it seems like to us.

Gaston Bachelard

Every new metaphor is a new thought, a fragment of a new myth of reality.

Metaphor is a part of the not-knowing aspect of art, and yet, I'm firmly convinced that it is the supreme way of searching for truth. How can this be? I don't know. I have never been able to figure it out to my satisfaction.

Poetry attracts me because it makes trouble for thinkers.

To Understand, Is That Against Nature, Against God?

I like a poem which understates, which leaves out, breaks off, remains open-ended. A poem as a piece of the unutterable whole. To "complete," to pretend that it is possible to do so (and here, too, I'm following Heidegger), is to set arbitrary boundaries to what is boundless.

Emily Dickinson's poems do that for me. Her ambiguities are philosophical. She lives with uncertainties, even delights in them. To the great questions she remains "unshielded," as Heidegger would say. The nature of presence itself is her subject. The awe of . . . the supreme mystery of consciousness watching itself.

Ideally then, a poem which speculates, is full of mirrors . . . which measures the gap between words and what they presume to name . . . the gap between being and being-said.

Like Those Beautiful Women Asleep a Hundred Years?

Something must be for something to be said.

Paul Ricoeur

The world was going up in flames and I was making screeching noises on my violin. The baby Nero. Once walking to a violin lesson I saw people in a ditch with their throats cut. Then I got lice wearing a German helmet.

This used to be a famous story in my family. I remember those cold, hungry winters just after the war, with everybody huddled around the coal stove, talking and worrying late into the night. Sooner or later, inevitably, someone would bring up my German helmet full of lice as a comic relief. Old people would have tears of laughter in their eyes. A kid dumb enough to walk around with a German helmet full of lice. They were crawling all over it! A blind man could see them!

I sat there saying nothing, pretending to be equally amused, nodding my head in agreement while thinking to myself, what a bunch of idiots! They, of course, had no idea how I got the helmet, and I wasn't about to tell them.

It was the day after the liberation of Belgrade. I was up in the fair grounds by St. Mark's church with a few older boys, kind of snooping around. Then, all of a sudden, we saw them! Two German soldiers, obviously dead, stretched out on the ground. We drew closer to take a better look. They had no more weapons. Their boots were gone, but there was a helmet that had fallen off to the side. I don't remember what the others did, but I went for the helmet. I tiptoed so as not to wake the dead men. I also kept my eyes averted. I never saw their faces, even if sometimes I think I did. Everything else about that moment is still intensely clear to me.

Giuseppe Verdi, the Famous Chinese-American Ventriloquist . . .

Poetry is not just "a verbal universe that looks inwardly on itself," as someone said. Neither is poetry merely a recreation of experience. "It was and it was not," is how the old storytellers used to begin their tales. It lies to tell the truth.

Mallarmé thought there were two kinds of language: *Parole brute* which names things and *parole essentielle* which distances us from things. One serves representation and the other the allusive, fictive world of poetry. He's wrong. It's not that clear cut. If anything, it's both. Poetry is impure. I don't think Heidegger understands this either.

The poem is an attempt at self-recovery, self-recognition, self-remembering, the marvel of being again. That this happens at times, happens in poems in many different and contradictory ways, is as great a mystery as the mystery of being itself and cause for serious thought. (pp. 215-21)

Charles Simic, "Notes on Poetry and Philosophy," in New Literary History, *Vol. 21, No. 1, Autumn, 1989, pp. 215-21.*

Molly McQuade

Charles Simic is Yugoslav and American, skeptic and believer, a poet convinced, as he once wrote, that "writing is always a rough translation from wordlessness into words." Poetry "attracts me because it makes trouble for thinkers," he has declared. "Poetry is an orphan of silence. The words never quite equal the experience behind them. We are always at the beginning, eternal apprentices, thrown back again and again into that condition."

In his new collection, ***The Book of Gods and Devils,*** Simic also returns to a "beginning" of another kind: his early years (1958-1961) in New York City. In **"The Initiate"** he writes, "In that whole city you could hear a pin drop. / Believe me, / I thought I heard a pin drop and I went looking for it." The poetry's locale is 14th Street, Hell's Kitchen and the old Fourth Avenue booksellers' row, where readers find the figure of a young man pursuing "the great secret which kept eluding me: / knowing who I am . . . "

"I came to New York in August of 1958, and it was amazingly simple," Simic recalls. "I would work at some place for a few months, and quit. I'd live the life of a bohemian. Then I'd realize I was running out of money, and I'd get a haircut—and a new job. I had all sorts of office jobs. I got to be pretty good at bookkeeping. I went to school at NYU; it took me 10 years to get a B.A. at night. All that seemed perfectly fine. It was great to be in New York and have a job and buy records and go to movies and jazz clubs. All those street scenes, sights, made a tremendous impression on my mind—I have an endless anthology of them.

"I was aware, in writing ***The Book of Gods and Devils,*** of an almost pagan impulse," he continues. "Pagans would invent gods or demons for any place where people had had intense experiences. A big city is a home of multiple gods, not just the obvious religions. There are things one worships and things one is afraid of. I have a certain pessimism about history that is very Balkan; I'm suspicious of attempts to idealize human beings. We are not noble savages, not kind, good, wholesome. But I don't think the demons are very strong in the book; there is a lot of humor, and there are a lot of gods."

What he calls "the shock, the newness" of New York helped make Simic what he is. So did his solitude there. As his poem **"The Immortal"** tells it, "You had your own heartbeat to listen to. / You were perfectly alone and anonymous. / It would have taken months for anyone / To begin to miss you."

He elaborates, sitting at the dining room table of his house in Strafford, N.H. "You're lonely, you're figuring out everything from scratch. You're broke. I used to spend evenings on long walks, looking at store windows, watching people. But it was a great feeling. I drifted in the most pleasant fashion. It was a time of purity. Cities are places of sphinxes, enigmas. Even though you may think about them for the rest of your life, you'll never come to the bottom. You're the sum of everything you don't understand."

A tall, pale, exuberant and excitable man, Simic has lived with his wife, Helen, for many years in the New Hampshire woods and admits happily to his "peasant" heritage, but his relish for things urban is vigorously evident when he says, "You could smell a certain high lunacy in New York. And there's always been an element of the grotesque in my work; much in ***The Book of Gods and Devils*** seems totally surrealist. Yet it's based on the most factual stuff imaginable." Moreover, he argues, he is "a realist *and* a surrealist, always drawn between the two." By way of example, he invokes **"The Fourteenth Street Poem,"** set in "a long block / Favored by doomsday prophets," and where an obstreperous bag lady holds court. It is "real," but to a heightened degree.

"There is a story to this lady which I couldn't tell," he confides in a rumblingly resonant voice. Simic does not just talk—he groans, whoops and whispers, offering heavily accented phrases that twist and slide with American slang.

"The first time I saw her, I was crossing Washington Square Park late one night. This woman comes up to me, of uncertain age, with flying hair, an older version of the homeless person. And she says to me, 'I'm Venus, the goddess of love. If you don't give me a dollar, I'm gonna curse you, and you'll be unhappy in love.' " Simic laughs ringingly and uproariously at the absurdity of his predicament. "So I said to her, 'Beat it!' And I told myself, 'I'm cursed. There's nothing I can do.'

"A couple of months went by. I was at Barnes & Noble. It's late afternoon, I'm getting some book, I look up and there she is! So I just sort of blurt out, 'You're Venus, the goddess of love!' And she says [and Simic assumes sotto voce], 'How did you *know?*' " (p. 56)

"I don't feel in any way Yugoslavian," insists Simic, who has visited the Eastern Bloc before and since its democratization. "Sometimes this comes to me with some regret. But the first literature I knew was American literature. Most of the important things in my life happened to me in this country. There's no question that many of my outlooks are completely Slavic: Hitler and Stalin fought over my soul, my destiny. Yet I'm never classified among the exiled writers. I really could not go back now. I see things differently. And the language you write in, you have to hear."

Simic was a painter first, not a poet. In his essay collection ***Wonderful Words, Silent Truth,*** published this year by the University of Michigan Press in its Poets on Poetry series, he writes, "One day, two of my friends confessed that they wrote poetry. I asked them to show it to me. I wasn't impressed with what I saw. I went home and wrote some poems myself in order to demonstrate to them how it's supposed to be done. At first, the act of writing and the initial impression were exhilarating. Then, to my astonishment, I realized that my poems were as stupid as theirs were. I couldn't figure it out . . . [but] in the process of writing, I discovered a part of myself, an imagination and a need to articulate certain things, that I could not afterwards forget."

His first published poems appeared in the winter 1959 issue of the *Chicago Review.* Simic enthusiastically accepted many influences—Edgar Lee Masters, Vachel Lindsay, Ezra Pound, Walt Whitman, Hart Crane. But while serving in the U.S. Army in 1962, he destroyed his work to date and started over again. As he explained in a 1972 interview, "When confronted with the life I was leading at the time, [the poems] struck me as no more than literary vomit. . . . Life and its intensity had conquered."

The struggle that followed was difficult and prolonged. The results led Simic to join "a generation of writers who are committed to experimentalism, so much so that I'm struck by the timidity and predictability of a lot of writing today. I read books and get mad. In American poetry at the moment, 75% of American experience is invisible." Simic's first book, ***What the Grass Says,*** was published by Kayak Press in 1967. "It had a tremendous circulation—something like 27 reviews," and was followed by ***Somewhere Among Us a Stone Is Taking Notes,*** also a Kayak release. . . .

Simic has also translated more than half a dozen volumes of poetry, among these the work of Ivan Lalic, Vasko Popa ("an enormous influence on me") and Tomaz Salamun. "In order to do a translation, you have to be a kind of a shaman—you have to pretend, for a moment, that you're somebody else. You realize that the other person is very different from you—*disgustingly* different. That's fascinating." . . .

"***The World Doesn't End*** happened without too much deliberation," Simic maintains, marveling at winning the Pulitzer "lottery." What did the prose poem form offer him that poetry had not? "A lyric impulse is an impulse in which everything stands still," he replies. "It's like a song that repeats. Nothing ever happens in a lyric poem. It's a great acknowledgment of the present moment. In a prose sentence, however, things *do* happen. A prose poem is a dialectic between the two. You write in sentences, and tell a story, but the piece is like a poem because it circles back on itself.

"Books of poems—it takes a long time for the writer to really understand what's inside them," he admits. "It's like being in a period of your life." Simic reflects on the version of himself that appears in ***The Book of Gods and Devils.*** "It's amusing to see oneself at that distance. It isn't personal anymore. As you get older, the subject of a poem is astonishment at what is before you. It's almost a religious experience, one of standing apart and seeing yourself in awe before the world." (p. 57)

Molly McQuade, "Charles Simic," in Publishers Weekly, *Vol. 237, No. 44, November 2, 1990, pp. 56-7.*

David Kirby

Currently there is a schism in American letters between the presence of humor in poetry and the failure of reviewers to comment on that presence. It is hard to think of a poet today who does not sample in some way the widely varying comic tones, from subtle to raucous, that are first heard in the poems of Walt Whitman and Emily Dickinson and then echoed by writers as different as William Carlos Williams, Marianne Moore and Allen Ginsberg. Yet, while reviewers argue theme and technique in great detail, when it comes to humor they seem to have a collective tin ear. If humor is noticed at all, it is often dismissed as simply slick or clever.

Lately, this schism seems all the more remarkable, given the eagerness of a new generation of reviewers, fresh from graduate seminars, to buttress their arguments with references to Jacques Derrida, Mikhail Bakhtin and other formidable European intellects. Has none of them remarked the witty mischief in Derrida's deconstructive strategies or Bakhtin's assertion, in his book on Rabelais, that laughter has "a deep philosophical meaning"?

Three splendid books [***The Book of Gods and Devils*** by Charles Simic, *Body Traffic* by Stephen Dobyns, and *Westward* by Amy Clampitt] illustrate some of the ways in which humor functions not as a mere stylistic quality but as a mode of perception. Typically, a Charles Simic poem starts with a sentence fragment, an ungainly image crash-landing at the feet of a speaker who was expecting something else entirely. Thus the characters in his poems are often like the protagonists of fairy tales—farmers or fishermen who in the course of their labors come across a talking fox or a lamp with a genie inside. These characters begin as rather ordinary types and end as heroes, their bemusement turning to amusement as they regain control over their interrupted lives.

Mr. Simic was born in Yugoslavia in 1938, and his family moved to Chicago in 1954; perhaps there is a Central European sensibility at work in his poems. His colors are fairy-tale colors: where his world is not sooty, it is splashed with reds and whites. And in many of his poems, a simple, lighthearted fellow succeeds against a harsh world. It is as though Thumbling found himself on State Street rather than his father's farm.

Fairy tales tell us that things will work out, that little people like ourselves are capable of great heroism. In ***The Book of Gods and Devils*** the speaker of **"Windy Evening,"** in which this cheap stage set of an earth seems to be falling to pieces, can say, with confidence: "Better grab hold of that tree, Lucille. . . . / I'll hold the barn." In Mr. Simic's world, action is everything.

Besides, thinking is too hard—"I get sad when I think," confides the speaker of **"A Letter."** Thought is sad because it simply leads to more thought, whereas action is the royal road to life's goofy splendors. In **"Evening Talk,"** the speaker tells a friend he shouldn't have wasted his time worrying about someone who didn't show up. Instead,

> You should have crossed the street
> And followed that obviously demented woman
> With the long streak of blood-red hair
> Which the sky took up like a distant cry.

Fortunately, most of Mr. Simic's hero-next-door types are more resolute. They speak to every fox, rub every magic lamp. And they are the ones who are invited, as it says in **"Heights of Folly,"**

> To breakfast on slices of watermelon
> In the company of naked gods and goddesses
> On a patch of last night's snow.

David Kirby, "Life's Goofy Splendors," in The New York Times Book Review, *December 23, 1990, p. 16.*

Anthony Thwaite

Whitmanesque unstoppability has never been a danger in Charles Simic's poems. Rather, he has inclined to the ***Austerities*** of one of his earlier books, taking his lead from such poets as Vasco Popa (Simic moved from Yugoslavia to the United States in his teens) and Miroslav Holub, wry and cryptic Eastern Europeans. In ***The Book of Gods and Devils,*** his mysterious simplicities and humorous bleaknesses sometimes sound like very good translations, as in **"Babylon":**

> Every time I prayed
> The universe got bigger,
> And I got smaller.
>
> My wife almost stepped on me.
> I saw her huge legs
> Rising to dizzying heights.
> The hair between them
> Glistened like a god's beard.
> She looked Babylonian.
>
> "I'm getting smaller every minute,"
> I yelled, but she could not hear me
> Among the winged lions and ziggurats,
> The mad astrologers of her painted eyes.

Simic is adept at such runic inscriptions, fragments of dislodged civilizations, the shards of universal disjunction and poignant ruin. But such universality spells out its own limitations, in the way Simic's inventions lack much verbal color. It's the situation—the "experience," if you like—that has to carry the fully weight of the poem; and what this means is that one often gets a momentary pleased shock from the invention, but nothing much actually stays in one's head.

Anthony Thwaite, "Poems and Experiences," in Book World—The Washington Post, *December 30, 1990, p. 8.*

David Starkey

It will come as no surprise to anyone who has read Charles Simic's ***The World Doesn't End*** that the book won the Pulitzer Prize for poetry. This collection of untitled prose poems may well be the poet's strongest to date, not the least of its charm being, as he writes in one poem, that it "can be so easily dismissed as preposterous." Indeed, it is in the prose poem that Simic appears to have found the most fluid vehicle for his poetry.

Since he first began publishing his neo-surrealist work in the mid-1960s, Simic has always possessed the ability to startle his readers with new ways of viewing the world. "Go inside a stone / That would be my way," he says in the frequently anthologized **"Stone,"** and in fact one of Simic's great powers is his ability to scrutinize the sort of seemingly mundane objects and situations which we often overlook in everyday life and find wonders hidden in them. In ***The World Doesn't End,*** the poet continues his investigations of these ordinary mysteries in prose which is so lovely, so non-*prosaic* that it will surprise anyone who has dismissed the prose poem as "anti-poetry."

The book is divided into three sections of prose poems, each part dotted with several free verse miniatures or epigrams like **"History Lesson"**—"The roaches look like / Comic rustics / In serious dramas"—and **"My Secret Identity Is"**—"The room is empty, / And the window is open[.]" The prose poems are typically based on a surrealistic premise which is described in precise, domestic detail. . . . The poems range in length from nearly a full page to single whimsical sentences like, "O the great God of Theory, he's just a pencil stub with a worn eraser at the end of a huge scribble." And they range in tone from extremely playful—"At least four or five Hamlets on this block alone"—to very dark. "The stone is a mirror which works poorly," Simic writes in one poem which seems to reject the optimism of **"Stone."** "Nothing in it but dimness. Your dimness or its dimness, who's to say? In the hush your heart sounds like a black cricket."

Simic, who emigrated to the United States from Yugoslavia in 1949 when he was eleven years old, has frequently countered arguments that his poems are full of wild, impossible images by replying that the world of his poems actually existed, that he saw it as a boy in World War II. And, clearly, a number of the poems in Part I are "autobiographical" in that they describe the terrors of war as they must have appeared to a child: "My mother was a braid of black smoke. She bore me swaddled over the burning cities." "We were so poor I had to take the place of the bait in the mousetrap." "The city had fallen. We came to the window of a house drawn by a madman. The setting sun shone on a few abandoned machines of futility."

The second and third sections include a variety of meditations on everything from art and philosophy to the tenor of the century (it is a "century of gathering clouds. Ghost ships arriving and leaving"), but all the poems attempt to bring contradictory ideas and images together and, if not resolve them, at least point to the comedy or tragedy behind the poems' incongruities: "It's so quiet in the world. One can hear the old river, which in its confusion sometimes forgets and flows backwards." Appropriately, "Let's waltz the rumba" (a song lyric by Fats Waller) is the epigraph to ***The World Doesn't End.***

If there is one fault in this lovely book it is the lack of poem titles, which have always been one of Simic's fortes. **"Concerning My Neighbors the Hittites," "Baby Pictures of Famous Dictators," "My Weariness of Epic Proportions,"** and **"Early Evening Algebra"** are only a few examples of his past inventiveness. Granted, the collection may be more coherent as a book without titles, but surely a number of gems have been lost.

However, the fact that the chief complaint against a book is that it has no titles should indicate the book's excellence. Future critics will have the final say, but it may not be an exaggeration to assert that ***The World Doesn't End*** can stand with any other book of prose poems since Baudelaire's *Paris Spleen,* the volume which more or less defined the genre. The French poet had asked, "Which one of us, in his moments of ambition, has not dreamed of the miracle of a poetic prose, musical, without rhythm and without rhyme, supple enough to adapt itself to the lyrical impulses of the soul, the undulations of reverie, the jibes of conscience?" Certainly Charles Simic has had just such a dream, and if he has not fulfilled it entirely, it may not be our place to ask that any poet come much closer to perfection. (pp. 101-02)

David Starkey, in a review of "The World Doesn't End," in The Southern Humanities Review, *Vol. XXV, No. 1, Winter, 1991, pp. 101-02.*

David Dooley

If ease of publication, ready acceptance by peers, and receipt of grants and awards, including the Pulitzer Prize, mean good fortune, then Charles Simic has been a supremely lucky poet. His Pulitzer Prize-winning ***The World Doesn't End*** has now been followed by a newly enlarged version of his ***Selected Poems: 1963-1983.*** The Pulitzer award to ***The World Doesn't End*** aroused considerable controversy, at least in part because most of the poems are in prose. This objection is difficult to understand, since prose poems have been part of the European poetic tradition since Baudelaire and Rimbaud. . . . Furthermore, those who administer the Pulitzer surely have the right to reward whomever they choose, just as the rest of us have the right to discuss the wisdom of that choice.

The World Doesn't End does contain five short poems in verse, all of them feeble. **"History Lesson"** may be marginally the best:

The roaches look like
Comic rustics
In serious dramas.

Mildly amusing, perhaps; definitely slight. The prose poems are superior, even if they rarely rise above the level of amusing squibs. Often they begin engagingly—"The stone is a mirror which works poorly"; "He held the Beast of the Apocalypse by its tail, the stupid kid!"; "A dog with a soul, you've got that?"—but fail to develop. To be sure, Simic writes out of the surrealist tradition, which denies development and organic form, but lays the burden on the poet of being consistently entertaining from one image or sentence to the next. The best poem in the book, **"Everything's foreseeable,"** uses a surreal framework in which to write about ordinary life. The narrator's grandmother "says there's no god, only an eye here and there that sees clearly. The neighbors are too busy watching TV to burn her as a witch."

That Simic's newer work is slight could not surprise anyone who has read his selected poems. Galway Kinnell, a poet of considerable range, confined his selected poems to 148 pages; Simic, a poet of limited range, now feels compelled to issue a selected poems of 229 pages. Simic has risked much less and accomplished much less than Wright or Hall. Whereas Wright and Hall continually questioned how to write a poem, Simic has been content to drift with the tide. Over the years he has been influenced by most of the quasi-surreal trends that came along. He has written deep image poems ("I am happy to be a stone"). He has written the three kinds of poems Robert Peters in *The Great American Poetry Bake-Off* described as "catatonic surrealism": instruction or recipe poems (**"Dismantling the Silence"**—a period title if there ever was one), poems which resemble fairy tales (**"The Chicken Without a Head"**), and paranoid quasi-narratives (**"Begotten of the Spleen"**). Simic's best work has affinities with Gary Larson's *Far Side* cartoons—for instance, the fanciful accounts of ordinary objects considered as having lives of their own (**"Brooms," "Fork," "Knife"**). **"Eyes Fastened with Pins"** imagines Death as an ordinary worker with a wife at home ironing his laundry. Simic sometimes descends to E-Z 2 Rite surrealism—e.g., "Wintry pallor and ire. / Wind's rabies. Pitchy heavens. // Apes with rice-powdered asses. / Monday moving its dentures." In ***The World Doesn't End*** Simic also includes deliberately nondiscursive poems in which the nondiscursiveness becomes in effect the subject of the poem as well as a fashion statement ("A century of gathering clouds" and "I knew a night owl," for instance). Poets like Simic may not tell us much about human beings or the world they live in, or about language or craftsmanship, but they do tell us a great deal about period taste. (pp. 157-59)

David Dooley, in a review of "The World Doesn't End" and "Selected Poems: 1963-1983," in The Hudson Review, *Vol. XLIV, No. 1, Spring, 1991, pp. 157-59.*

W. D. Snodgrass

1926-

(Full name William De Witt Snodgrass; has also written under the pseudonym S. S. Gardons) American poet, translator, critic, essayist, and editor.

Snodgrass is considered a seminal figure in the Confessional school of poetry. He is credited with helping to initiate the Confessional movement with the publication of his first work, *Heart's Needle,* a highly influential volume of autobiographical poems that received praise for its direct and brutally honest examination of intensely emotional and painful experiences. Writing about topics of personal importance in a candid, straightforward voice, Snodgrass rejected what he termed the modernist tradition of "obscure and symbol-laden language on 'significant' subjects: the loss of myth in our time, the decay of civilization," viewing his work as a reaction against impersonal intellectual poetry. His work greatly influenced other poets often called Confessionalists, including his mentor, Robert Lowell, as well as Sylvia Plath and Anne Sexton. Snodgrass, however, dislikes the label of Confessional poet: "So far as I can see, my poems aren't confessional. That has to imply that one is talking about some kind of forbidden activity and doing it in a rather lurid way—like a confessional magazine or something like that." Writing primarily in terse, tightly rhymed metrical patterns, Snodgrass is instead concerned with a poem's authenticity and sincerity, asserting that hope for his generation lies in the poet's ability to ask, "Am I writing what I *really* think? Not what I think is acceptable; not what my favorite intellectual would think in this situation; nor what I wish I felt. Only what I cannot help thinking."

Born in Wilkinsburg, Pennsylvania, into a Quaker household, Snodgrass was expected to join his family's accounting firm but entertained hopes for a career in music. He attended Geneva College in Beaver Falls, Pennsylvania, before being drafted into the United States Navy during World War II. After the war, he married Lila Jean Hank and transferred to the University of Iowa, initially intending to study playwriting. At the Iowa Writer's Workshop he became interested in poetry and received instruction from such writers as John Berryman, Paul Engel, Joe Langland, Robert Lowell, and Karl Shapiro. Through therapy sessions in which he described his marital woes, and through the influence of the work of Robert Shelley, a fellow student who committed suicide before fully developing his straightforward free verse style, Snodgrass realized the appropriateness of frankly discussing one's emotions in a poem. His instructors disapproved of his overt description of what critic David McDuff later termed "the repressed, violent feelings that often lurk beneath the seemingly placid surface of everyday life." Snodgrass, however, rebelled against T. S. Eliot's objective approach to poetry, which he felt unnecessarily obscured the extremely personal nature of the elder poet's work. In 1955, two years after divorcing his first wife, Snodgrass began teaching college classes to help finance his writing career, and, in 1960, he earned a Pulitzer Prize for *Heart's Needle.* Published the same year as Lowell's *Life Studies* (1959), Snodgrass's volume, considered one of the most important works of its decade, helped to distinguish the evolving confessional tradition.

References to alienation, isolation, and loss are common in Snodgrass's early work. The poems in *Heart's Needle,* which takes its title from an Irish folktale equating the loss of an only daughter with a needle puncturing the heart, primarily deal with Snodgrass's reentry into American society following World War II, his divorce from Lila Jean and remarriage to Janice Marie Ferguson Wilson, and, in the book's title sequence, his separation from his daughter, Cynthia, as a result of the divorce. Snodgrass's use of compact and lyrical lines in this volume present a means of ordering and examining chaotic experience. Paul L. Gaston noted that the "artfulness of each constituent poem, the obvious care and skill which have animated its development, insist that it conveys not raw experience itself but the evaluation and understanding of experience."

Nearly a decade elapsed before Snodgrass published his second work, *After Experience: Poems and Translations.*

During this time, Snodgrass strove to refine his style, which had been imitated by many poets of the 1960s. In *After Experience,* Snodgrass continues to emphasize the themes of loss and separation, relating them to the failure of his second marriage and the emotional distance growing between him and his daughter. In "The First Leaf," for example, Snodgrass writes of his daughter: "Next year we'll hardly know you; / Still all the blame endures. / This year you will live at our expense; we have a life at yours." Considered less lyrical but more dramatic than *Heart's Needle, After Experience* also represents Snodgrass's attempt to distance himself from purely subjective experience; the book's latter half is comprised of a series of translations of poems by Rainer Maria Rilke and Arthur Rimbaud as well as poems based on such famous paintings as Monet's *Les Nymphéas* and Van Gogh's *Starry Night.*

Snodgrass's next work, *Remains,* represents a return to the themes of alienation and despair found in *Heart's Needle* and the first half of *After Experience.* The poems in this volume, however, concern the death of his sister and its effect on his parents. Snodgrass states that he published the collection under the pseudonymous anagram S. S. Gardons because it contains unflattering descriptions of his parents, whose overprotectiveness, Snodgrass implies, prevented his shy, asthmatic sister from enjoying life. In his ensuing works, Snodgrass examines the relationship between poetry and other art forms first explored in *After Experience.* While reflecting his background in music through his attention to rhyme and meter and his interest in multiple voices, such volumes as *The Death of Cock Robin, The Kinder Capers,* and *W. D.'s Midnight Carnival* also explore poetry's connections to the visual arts. Snodgrass juxtaposes the poems in these books with DeLoss McGraw's paintings, which critics often consider integral to each work's overall meaning. William M. Chace has noted that *The Death of Cock Robin* also reflects Snodgrass's belief in relativism and common bonds of humanity, for the character W. D., who appears in most of these poems, represents "the creation of the painter and the voice of the poet, the voice of anyone who, looking on pain and defeat, asks for help and for explanation."

The Führer Bunker: A Cycle of Poems in Progress, which has been performed on stage, grew out of Snodgrass's interest in events that took place in Nazi Germany during World War II. The volume is based upon historical facts presented in literature about the Nazis, including H. R. Trevor-Roper's nonfiction work *The Last Days of Hitler* (1947) and Henri Coulette's *The War of the Secret Agents and Other Poems* (1966). The book is also informed by Snodgrass's belief "that every important act in our lives is both propelled and governed by the darker, less visible areas of emotion and personality." In *The Führer Bunker,* Snodgrass presents a series of monologues spoken by Adolf Hitler, his mistress Eva Braun, and such high-ranking Nazis as Joseph Goebbels and Wilhelm Göring. Orating from Hitler's bunker in April of 1945, each character speaks in a specific poetic form indicative of personality and moral outlook. Although Snodgrass has been accused of humanizing and eliciting sympathy for the Nazis, Laurence Goldstein asserted that he simply "tried to disinfect our imagination by use of the so-called 'Jewish science' of psychoanalysis, showing how one can apprehend the Nazis as forms of Everyman and yet move beyond such a generous recognition to a mature, and politically urgent, judgment of their twisted natures." Snodgrass himself maintains that these historical figures *were* indeed human as well as representative of some aspect of every individual, stressing that the aim of his historically inaccurate collection, which has never been printed in its entirety, "is a step, I hope, much further into relativism."

(See also *CLC,* Vols. 2, 6, 10, 18; *Contemporary Authors* Vols. 1-4, rev. ed.; *Contemporary Authors New Revision Series,* Vol. 6; and *Dictionary of Literary Biography,* Vol. 5.)

PRINCIPAL WORKS

POETRY

Heart's Needle 1959
After Experience: Poems and Translations 1968
Remains [as S. S. Gardons] 1970
The Führer Bunker: A Cycle of Poems in Progress 1977
If Birds Build with Your Hair 1979
**The Kinder Capers* 1986
A Locked House 1986
Selected Poems, 1957-1987 1987
**W. D.'s Midnight Carnival* 1988
**The Death of Cock Robin* 1989

OTHER

In Radical Pursuit: Critical Essays and Lectures (essays) 1975

*With art work by DeLoss McGraw.

William Heyen

S. S. Gardons. All right. There are reasons for his existence and now, we are told, his disappearance, and there are reasons that, to some, he should not be known. To say that the voice in the Gardons poems is too close to the voice of the author's other work and does not justify or necessitate a pseudonym, as one critic insists, is to miss the whole point. The familial love-hate relationships [in ***Remains***] bear too close a resemblance to persons living and dead, and the poet's vision is inexorable. Could your parents possibly understand how you could describe the "Eyeshadow like a whore" on your dead sister's face? How could you say that? How could you remember her in that way?

The world of this sequence is a spider web which **"The Mother"** has woven and on which "her mates, her sapless young" are black shapes that hang precariously "Where she moves by habit, hungering and blind." The father is here, too, a diplomat who will not take sides. His mission is to "remain a balance / of power in the family, the firm, this whole world through" **("Diplomacy: The Father").**

The atmosphere is poisonous and complex. Gardon's feelings in some of these poems are so multiple and elusive that it is good and even surprising that he survived, escaped, remained negatively capable. We need only compare **"Fourth of July"** here with remarks the poet made about his dead sister in the Spring, 1959 *Partisan Review:* "To die on Independence Day seemed an act of terrible and destructive blamefulness, yet this may have been, in its way, the easiest solution of her dilemma. . . . " Looking back, he doesn't know whether to blame her for refusing to live or to whisper a fond farewell to her and to forgive her passivity and weakness. . . . [The] potential for bathos is certainly here, but the metrical control and hard rhymes, because the employment of conscious technique always implies the poet is attempting to control highly emotional matter by mind, stop the voice from breaking, stave off the purely melodramatic. And there is, again, an undercurrent of rage here and throughout ***Remains,*** the hate and fury of a disciplined athlete. Many a game has been won that hate started and control finished.

The eight poems that make up this sequence **("The Mother," "Diplomacy: The Father," "The Mouse," "Viewing the Body," "Fourth of July," "Disposal," "The Survivors," "To a Child")** bring us in to witness the residues of experience, the artifacts built on memories that will not subside. Returning home out of a morbid curiosity rather than out of any love or devotion for his parents, the poet finds, in **"The Survivors,"** that nothing has changed in the year since his sister died. His parents have survived. He has survived. But when are the living, in any true sense, no more alive than the dead?—this is the question posed by several of these poems. In **"The Survivors,"** as their property runs down around them, members of the family pass one another like zombies unable to acknowledge their own existence: "At any time they come / To pass, they drop their eyes." The idea of Family now has no more meaning than does the lottery to the inhabitants of Shirley Jackson's village. Even evening togetherness and entertainment is rote and deadly:

> Only at night they meet.
> By voiceless summoning
> They come to the living room; each repeats
> Some words he has memorized; each takes his seat
> In the hushed, expectant ring
> By the television set.
> No one can draw his eyes
> From that unnatural, cold light. They wait.
> The screen goes dim and they hunch closer yet,
> As the image dies.
>
> (pp. 253-54)

And take the gruesome joke that surfaces earlier in the same poem. Though addressing his stanzas to his dead sister, the poet is not afraid to draw an ironic parallel—if the poem does not make this explicit, it is impossible to avoid hearing this—between his sister and an unwanted but protected fruit:

> On the tree they still protect
> From the ungoverned gang
> Of neighbor boys,—eaten with worms, bird-pecked,
> But otherwise uncared-for and unpicked,
> The bitter cherries hang,
> Brown and soft and botched.
> The ground is thick with flies.

Decorum and good taste are not in question here. We must, at least, talk honestly to the dead. And there is no avoiding the fact that what remains, after experience, is a need for expression as urgent as air or food. (pp. 254-55)

[In **"Viewing the Body,"** the] sister, plain and hidden, "gray as a mouse," asthmatic, "slept / Alone in the dim bedcovers." She is dull and dim and gray until she dies, "Till the obscene red folds / Of satin close down on her." Only when dead does she become the center of all eyes. And this red that folds down on her is lurid, bizarre. In **"Disposal"** she "lies boxed in satin / Like a pair of party shoes / That seemed to never find a taker." I don't know which way to twist my face. No one else is as good at these macabre effects as Gardons. W. D. Snodgrass, in ***Heart's Needle,*** wrote a slightly longer sequence with the same grace and control exhibited in ***Remains,*** but Gardons touches nerves that are more exposed, probes a subject matter (parents and dead sister as opposed to wife and child) somehow deeper, more explosive, less public.

If we suppose, as I suspect we may, that the "Prefatory Note on the Author" was written by the author himself, then we can suppose that the deadly serious businesses of sublimation, exhumation, and exorcism going on in ***Remains*** have been, at least for now, transcended, that the poems helped the poet maintain his balance, and that now that all or most of the poems about it have been written, he can even laugh at his grotesque past. The author invented Gardons because Gardons could be made to appear when needed and disappear when not. The first biographical notes on him in periodicals and anthologies were briefer, perhaps plausible. He may first have been an alter ego, a wish-fulfilling second half, a member of the author's SS, *Schutzstaffel,* protective echelon, who left academia. But now, to complete a process of separation, he has become a sort of redneck-hippie-James Dean-mechanic-musician-dropout, someone who couldn't possible have written these poems.

> S. S. Gardons lived most of his life in and near Red Creek, Texas. For years he worked as a gas station attendant, although he took a few university classes in Houston, and later became an owner of a cycle shop. Also a musician, he played lead guitar in the well-known rock group, Chicken Gumbo. : : This sequence of poems was collected by his friends after his disappearance on a hunting trip in the mountains. From the condition of his abandoned motorcycle, it was impossible to determine whether he suffered foul play, was attacked by animals, merely became confused and lost, or perhaps fell victim to amnesia. At present, the case is listed as unsolved.

This is good. The poet's struggle has been, although his experience has taught him that love is at least as destructive as it is creative, to endure and hope. In **"To a Child"** he says that "Without love we die; / With love we kill each other." But the poem ends: "I tell you love is possible. / We have to try." It is good that Gardons himself can be put to rest now, at least for a time. God knows the life was maddening.

It seems to me that this sequence is at least as fine as Snodgrass' **"Heart's Needle,"** and as such deserves high praise indeed. It may be, in fact, that its effect is even stronger. And it is fine that now, for a time, the poet can comically dismiss Gardons. I'm reminded here of John Berryman's Henry as he leaves us in "Dream Song 77": "it is a wonder that, with in each hand / one of his own mad books and all, / ancient fires for eyes, his head full / & his heart full, he's making ready to move on." Gardons may never, as did Henry, come back from the dead, but then he may not have to come that far. His case is unsolved, and I have a hunch that if he is needed—and there are some gaps in the sequence, certainly, that could be filled in with poems—he will show up again, maybe even change his name. (pp. 255-56)

William Heyen, "A Note on S. S. Gardons," in Western Humanities Review, *Vol. XXV, No. 3, Summer, 1971, pp. 253-56.*

W. D. Snodgrass [Interview with Paul L. Gaston]

[*The interview excerpted below took place on January 2, 1977, at Snodgrass's home near Erieville, New York.*]

[*Gaston*]: *It seems that* [*in* **The Führer Bunker**] *you have deliberately selected a subject which is by its nature far more objective than the highly personal subjects for which your early work is so well known.*

[Snodgrass]: That is certainly true. I did the pseudonymous book [***Remains***] very much with the idea that it would be the last thing I would do in that style. Of course, ***After Experience*** has some poems that are like the first book [***Heart's Needle***]. That seemed like normal growth, that you wouldn't change altogether overnight and be completely different. On the other hand, there would be a certain amount of change. But when I got through with the pseudonymous book, I felt, OK, that's enough of that. I really don't want to do that anymore. (pp. 295-96)

What first prompted your idea of a series of poems based upon the last days of the Third Reich?

Well, I don't think I can tell you much about the things that come from my personality, about what drove me personally. All I know is that I was very much interested in this period. As soon as the war was over, I began reading the Nazi books and memoirs. I really wanted to know what the hell could somebody think, or feel, that would make them feel those acts were necessary. How could they even think they were possible?

But it's a long way from such historical curiosity to the conception of a poem on the subject.

Yes. Well, I started by trying to write a play [—*The Last Days of Hitler*] based on all of the Trevor-Roper stuff. That was within two or three years of the end of the war. That didn't work. I had rather poor teachers, and I wasn't very good. I don't know whether it ever would've got going. Then, gradually, three or four years ago, maybe more, my ideas began to take the shape of monologues. The Braun poem and the first Speer poem (the one which, split up, became the three in the book) were the first two. The material began to take the shape of dramatic monologues, and it has been sort of growing and spreading, "metastasizing," ever since.

Are there particular dramatic monologues that you found influential?

The thing that hits me right off is *The War of the Secret Agents,* by Henri Coulette. You have a World War II situation, in which a whole bunch of British secret agents were sent to France and all caught by the Germans and killed. The British betrayed them. They were sent there to be caught, so that real secret agents wouldn't be noticed. Coulette's cycle of poems about these people and about talking to people, trying to get back to the historical actuality, very much interested me. All the different voices! It seems to me that the most interesting poems of the last fifteen years have all been poly-voiced poems. Like *The Waste Land.* Like some of Bob Hayden's. Like [Henry Reed's] "The Naming of Parts," where you have several voices combating each other. And like the poems I have been doing along that line, where you have two voices or more.

As in the poems on paintings in **After Experience?**

Yes, the last two of those, especially. There are some other dramatic monologues which have probably affected me. Some of Browning's are very strong for me: "Mr. Sludge, 'The Medium,' " "Bishop Blougram's Apology." I think of these right away, though there are a lot of other poems which are dramatic monologues, though you don't tend to file them under that term. You *think* the poet is speaking in his own voice, so you don't call it a dramatic monologue. But, of course, it *is.* Just because the speaker carries the name "Robert Browning" doesn't mean it is any less an artificial creation than the thing that is called "Bishop Blougram."

Do you think that principle applies to the earlier poems by W. D. Snodgrass?

I would think so. Sure. There is always a kind of invented persona. Though one isn't aware of the ways in which this persona differs from one's self, it is at best a distillation of one's self. You surely aren't getting the whole complete richness of your psyche into any one poem. The poem isn't long enough to do that. So I guess one of the ways you try to do that is to write something like ***The Führer Bunker,*** where you have a whole lot of voices and hope to get in even more angles of yourself. (pp. 298-99)

Let's consider the standards implicit in your early poems and how they may still apply. It does seem to me that while **The Führer Bunker** *is at least half a world apart from* **Heart's Needle,** *"the depth of its sincerity," which you once established as the crucial criterion for a poem, is clear in at least two respects. One is the sense of authenticity and candor we get from the voices of the speakers, the speakers dramatized in the poem. We don't at any point have the sense that these speakers are posing, misrepresenting themselves. To that extent you are successful in creating characters who are consistent and effective.*

I hope you're right. That is at least partly because they are not talking to anyone outside themselves. That does come from the dramatic monologue. If we were dealing with dialogue, many of these things could not be said.

We are allowed to overhear them.

Right.

And the second respect in which the idea of "depth of sincerity" seems to apply is that you have, in imagining these characters on the basis of your historical knowledge, insisted that your imagination be faithful to how you must *conceive of them, rather than to how you might* want *to conceive of them. I'm paraphrasing a line from your essay,* ***"Finding a Poem."***

Right. How you *must* see it, rather than how you'd *like* to. I sure would buy that. I remember an introduction I once read to an edition of the *Iliad.* What the man said was that such men as Homer—I would feel this is also true, say, of Rembrandt—have made a vocation of justice of vision. That's a very poor paraphrase. In other words, they wanted to make their vision just. *Is* that the way the world is? *Is* that the way I experience the world? (Which is to say the same thing in different words.) So, in talking about ***The Führer Bunker,*** it seems to me that, instead of talking about "sincerity," it is much better to ask, "Does it *feel* authentic?" Does it feel like the way the world feels? The first thing I felt about Henri Coulette's book, before I ever analyzed it at all, was, yes, that feels right, that's the way the world feels. Then I later found to my great horror that those things had literally happened. At the time I read the book, I didn't know it was based on fact. It seems to me that your word, "authenticity," when applied to this kind of poem, means the same thing that "sincerity" meant in that earlier piece I wrote. It is a lot easier to use.

You mention that your experience of The War of the Secret Agents *fell into two stages. My experience of* **The Führer Bunker** *has been similar. I read your poem and thought to myself, these are real people speaking. I'm not sure I ever wanted to hear them! A sense of authenticity. Then I received your letter, and you said that nearly everything in the poem can be documented. That kind of discovery can provide a second, distinct experience, it seems to me. Perhaps it would be ideal if everyone reading either book, yours or Coulette's, could experience it in this way.*

Well, that is one of the reasons that we, having written an essay explaining how much of it *is* documentable, have decided that maybe we ought not print that and let that sort of thing happen in interviews or something of the sort. We haven't really decided. (pp. 300-01)

One of the really amazing things, when I look at it, is that all the facts that are outrageous, horrifying, and unbelievable are the ones that are documented. The episodes I made up are all rather commonplace. And very believable. But, you know, if you're a writer, you're supposed to be believable. Reality doesn't feel those constraints. And the world at that time (and a lot of other times) was full of a lot of realities that were very, very hard to believe.

The reality of your poem, however, is that, even if none of its details were documentable, it still should be able to convince.

If it is a successful poem, that would have to be true.

One could never argue for it on the basis of its—

No. Absolutely not. A true fact which doesn't feel true in the poem is no good at all. The poem has to feel authentic. That is much more important than anything so shallow as documentary evidence.

Yet isn't there the danger that in any "authentic" first-person narrative, poetic or fictional, the mere presence of the speaker's voice may win him more sympathy than his actions deserve? I am wondering how you would respond to the charge, were it ever levelled against you, that you have made Hitler and Goebbels and Speer more sympathetic than they should be, simply by having them speak in their own voices.

Well, now, this sort of thing has come up. I read the poems in Philadelphia, and somebody jumped up and accused me of glorifying the Nazis. The rest of the audience sort of howled him down and said that wasn't so at all. Later, the man wrote me a letter, reasserting most of the same charges. But now he said I was *humanizing* the Nazis. This was very upsetting to me, I must say, and I have been inventing answers to him ever since. If I had answered him, one of the things I would have said is, "You know, you can't blame *me* for humanizing the Nazis. God did that. They *were* human." If you desire to believe that they were *not* human, then you are guilty of exactly their worst crime, which is what they tried to do to the Jews, to believe that they were not human. They started out with the belief that the Jews were very different and less human. That made it possible for them to take the acts against the Jews they wanted to take, to make them *seem* less human by putting them in the camps and bestializing them and brutalizing them and working them until they were ready to drop, until they had no resources left that could make them seem like capable, sensitive, decent human beings. Then you could feel that you were justified in doing those awful things to them. The more you beat them up, the less they looked like something that shouldn't be beaten up.

But your desire to believe the Nazis were not human makes you guilty of their technique. It seems to me that what is involved here is one of the real, basic, terrible paradoxes of being alive, that your enemy *is* human and not so different from you. If Fegelein were here, and I had a revolver, I know what I would do. But that doesn't mean that I can absolutely guarantee that if I had been raised in his place at that time, under those conditions, that I would have resisted those things he didn't resist. I can't be absolutely positive, though I *hope* so. I hope I am different. But to admit that you're not much better than the man you're killing is a pretty fearful thing to have to look at. But there is a strong possibility that it is true. I suppose that is one of the things the poem is trying to get at, ultimately.

Like most people, I am strung out between absolute and relative. Although I try to be as relativistic as possible, I also have some leanings the other way, of course, having been raised with such feelings. But it seems to me that the aim of a work of art surely is to stretch the reader's psyche, to help him to identify with more people, with more life than he normally does. He is only going to be able to do that if you get him past his beliefs about right and wrong which keep him from seeing what ways in which he is like certain other people. And, of course, he is going to object to that when you do it. Picasso said that all art is an aggression against the reader, or against the observer, the listener, or whatever. In some sense, that certainly is true. It certainly is an act of aggression against the reader's narrow definitions of himself and what he believes and what he thinks—which keep him from seeing an awful lot of things. Naturally, that is one of the things behind the complaint of that man in Philadelphia, who was so upset at me for writing the poem. But he was accusing me in just exactly the way the Nazis liked to accuse people, without any regard for the justice of the accusation, with only the desire to make himself seem morally superior. If the work of art *doesn't* bring the observer to see more of himself than he was aware of before, what use does it have to exist? What's it for?

You use the word "relativity." In **The Führer Bunker,** *you do establish a relative universe for the reader, one in which he is on his own. Hearing different voices of different speakers, even different voices in particular monologues, the reader must be on guard, must make judgments and revise them. You have placed a great weight of responsibility on the reader's shoulders. You must feel that's not a dangerous thing to do in this case.*

Well, I suppose it *is.* To give anybody power is dangerous. But any power or any freedom is the freedom to make a mistake. If that isn't included in it, it isn't free. The work of art, it seems to me, ought to be free and freeing. At the same time it involves the possibility that, for instance, you might choose Nazism.

Would you tell me about some of these different voices in the poem? And about the different forms?

Some of the poems use old-fashioned verse forms. Some of the speakers make up their own. I think I had in mind the sort of thing that happened in the very first cycle, the "Heart's Needle" cycle, in which each poem, almost, is in a different kind of verse form. The same way here. Each speaker has a kind of verse form that is typical of his or her personality.

Goebbels always speaks in those tight little waspish couplets. In a way, he was much like Pope, although, of course, much more vicious. But, basically, both of them were crippled, so that perfection of form becomes terribly important in a poem or statement. And both of them really do have a kind of waspish humor about them.

Magda [Goebbels] speaks in villanelles and other fancy French forms. I think I was looking for a compendium of verse forms.

The Hitler poems tend to become more compressed. That partly has to do with the dramatic problem of trying to get a grip on his mind. It seems to me that, above everything, he had a mind that was exceedingly brutal and powerful, but crude, really crude. One of the ways I was trying to catch that was by letting him be much more elliptical—using chunks of language like a hammer, with less worry about the civilized side of language, grammar and syntax and so forth—letting him have the kind of simple, brutal language which a child might have. He becomes much, much more elliptical because of that. I was trying to get my own voice out of the poem, my more civilized side out of the poem. When I read the first version of the first Hitler poem, a couple of years ago, down in Virginia at William and Mary, one of the people there said he was terribly interested in the poem but didn't think it was Hitler's voice. And Camille [Snodgrass's wife] said the same thing, that it wasn't as brutal and crude as his mind ought to be. So I tried to get something much more crude and brutal and direct. I became less concerned with making sentences fit together in a civilized order.

Would you explain the structural principle involved in the Speer poems? What is the significance of the inverted pyramids?

I think I meant those to be a sort of easy imitation of his compulsion for growth, for size. Quite regardless of the logic of speech and thought, the poems have a kind of continual lengthening of the line that keeps happening over and over again, compulsively. In a way, this is a compulsion in opposition to what he is saying about limits. Like his compulsion for size in his buildings, he was maintaining the compulsion to grow, to grab everybody around, that Germany had. But then, something strange: as his conscience begins to catch up with him, that compulsion breaks down. The poems begin swimming around very formlessly.

I might also say that the pyramids are related to other things, like the steps Speer is going down and coming up in the poem. A pyramid is an arrangement of steps, as far as that goes.

The pyramid pattern breaks down. First it goes into a little block on the page. Then it breaks up completely, and you get a kind of swimming form all over the page. Later, as his self-justifications begin to come back, the little triangles get started again, but he doesn't let them go as far. (pp. 301-05)

You do think of **The Führer Bunker** *as a poem, don't you?*

Oh yes. Oh yes. I hope that ultimately it will feel like *a* poem, yes. The first cycle, the "Heart's Needle" poems, seemed to me to be a poem. They call it a cycle of poems, but the larger poem also has a unity. I would want this one to have such unity. They don't have that now. (p. 306)

How do you see these poems as fitting into the context of contemporary American poetry?

My hope is that they don't.

That is my impression, that they don't. That there is nothing around—

Wonderful. I mean, one's natural *hubris* says, why don't we just rewrite the history of American poetry. You hope you're doing something that will be different enough and

"Like most people, I am strung out between absolute and relative. Although I try to be as relativistic as possible, I also have some leanings the other way, of course, having been raised with such feelings. But it seems to me that the aim of a work of art surely is to stretch the reader's psyche, to help him to identify with more people, with more life than he normally does. He is only going to be able to do that if you get him past his beliefs about right and wrong which keep him from seeing what ways in which he is like certain other people. And, of course, he is going to object to that when you do it. Picasso said all art is an aggression against the reader, or against the observer, the listener, or whatever. In some sense, that certainly is true. It certainly is an act of aggression against the reader's narrow definitions of himself and what he believes and what he thinks—which keep him from seeing an awful lot of things. . . . If the work of art *doesn't* bring the observer to see more of himself than he was before, what use does it have to exist? What's it for?"

—W. D. Snodgrass

big enough to—that is certainly what I was trying to do with the first book. You feel that this is big enough, so that if it is bad, it'll be *really* bad. You're not going to be playing it safe. I remember that when I was working on the "Heart's Needle" poems, Robert Lowell really was concerned for me. He liked me and my work but said, "Oh, my gosh, you just can't do these things." Later, he came to love the poems and did everything for them. You really want to do something that you figure is big enough to really change the direction of things. Not *in order* to change the direction of things but, rather, just because you want to do something that nobody but you could do. (p. 307)

[*Truman Capote has described* In Cold Blood] *as a "nonfiction novel." It seems inevitable that some critic is going to describe what you have done as nonfiction poetry, as the imaginative ordering of the historical record.*

I imagine there is something to that. But, generally speaking, those distinctions have been breaking down. It seems to me that they should break down, that they are artificial distinctions and don't really have to do with the nature of art. You have something rather like this at the beginning of art. When Homer wrote, did he think that he was writing about real people? I don't think we know whether anybody by the name of Achilles ever lived. He surely didn't believe in the gods, in the way that one speaks of believing in gods. I'm pretty sure of that. On the other hand, you get, fairly early, *The Persians,* by Aeschylus. He is dealing with the enemies of his state within thirty or forty years of their demise. Later on, that seems to become an impossible kind of poem. People want to separate history and poetry. Or history and drama. I think that the art doesn't demand that separation.

In the same way, there has been a great tendency for poetry to become separated from song. The historical process has grown more and more hardened, until now you have most of the people writing free verse. They've gotten clear away from the conventional forms which began in songs, forms where the stanza is necessary. Just because the way the civilization has developed has tended to make a split between dance and drama, drama and poetry, poetry and song doesn't mean you have to accept those splits. At least at one time, these things were all conceived of together.

Or history and poetry?

Yes. Surely, the people who wrote the sagas thought they were writing history. If you want to do something new, usually the best way to do that is to go back and do something very old.

So you think that you are *in a sense writing history?*

Yes, in a sense, although I have made up some episodes. I have put things in that I don't believe happened. Or in some cases I have accepted an interpretation of a character which I do not believe to be historical fact. For instance, I have accepted some historians' views that Magda Goebbels laid around a whole lot. I am not certain that that is the fact. *After* her marriage to Goebbels. I'm not certain that she had an affair with anyone other than Karl Hanke. She had affairs earlier. As to why I accept this view—the easy answer is that it's more dramatic if she has had a lot of affairs. After all, I am writing about betrayal, so I wanted her to betray a lot of people. There is also a sense in which I am probably more interested in our perception of these people than in whether they did a particular thing or not. In some way it may be true that what we think those people did is truer than what they did. (pp. 308-09)

W. D. Snodgrass and Paul L. Gaston, in an interview in Papers on Language & Literature, *Vol. 13, No. 3, Summer, 1977, pp. 295-311.*

Richard Gilman

The play [***The Führer Bunker***]—or theater piece or dramatic poem, as it more properly should be called—is constructed from [***The Führer Bunker: A Cycle of Poems in Progress***] by W. D. Snodgrass, a book published in 1977. In his program notes, Snodgrass writes that his purpose isn't to provide a historically accurate dramatic account of what went on in the Berlin bunker during the last days of the Third Reich, although much of what does occur on stage is drawn from documentary sources. (The one historical discrepancy is that neither Himmler nor Goering, both prominent figures in the piece, were in the bunker at all; the "bunker," one assumes, is to be taken as a metaphor or organizing image.) "My aim," Snodgrass writes, "is to investigate the thoughts and feelings behind the public facade" of the Nazi leaders and such consorts as Eva Braun and Magda Goebbels. "My poems, then, must include voices they would hide from others and even themselves."

The thoughts and feelings revealed here aren't quite so surprising as Snodgrass assumes, but they're vivid and disturbing enough. Hitler, for example, is shown in that mode of horrifying resentment at his "betrayal" by the German people with which we became familiar through Albert Speer's memoirs. Himmler defends himself, as we know he did, by a harrowing division of consciousness: "To kill so many and still remain happy, upright and idealistic—that is something." Goebbels, the incarnation of emptiness, is malevolently intelligent and "poetic": "I come back to my first ideal, the vacancy that's always real." Bormann writes maudlin letters to his wife and schemes to take power. And Goering, appearing at one point in an enormous pair of beige silk drawers, speaks of himself as a "slab of blubber," preening and mincing in false, knowing self-abasement.

The problem with this interesting material is that since there's almost no dialogue—the characters voicing their "hidden" thoughts at considerable distances from one another in shorter or longer soliloquies—the piece immediately falls under the handicap of all works of this kind: it's intrinsically undramatic. I don't mean it isn't "expressive" or affecting at times but it isn't knit together, doesn't constitute a unified field of action or a process of interaction. Unlike a work such as Grotowski's *Acropolis,* also a play about the Nazi horror, it doesn't offer a coherent new vision so much as fragments of response—sharp and disquieting, but fragments nevertheless. (p. 803)

Richard Gilman, in a review of "The Fuehrer Bunker," in The Nation, *New York, Vol. 232, No. 25, June 27, 1981, pp. 803-04.*

Dana Gioia

Critics moralized endlessly about W. D. Snodgrass' last book, ***The Führer Bunker,*** asking whether a poet should write with such obvious fascination about Hitler and his *ungemütlich* gang. They seemed surprised as schoolgirls that poets could be fascinated with evil. (Does no one read Milton or Marlowe seriously any more?) This critical breast-beating was touching to behold, but it mainly served to deflect attention from the underlying literary issue of how a writer as good as Snodgrass could have written poems generally so lax and ineptly sentimental. After this macabre romp with Adolph and Eva, I hesitated in picking up ***If Birds Build with Your Hair*** from Nadja, but I am happy to say that this new collection shows Snodgrass at his best again—witty, wise, and endlessly inventive.

The poems in ***If Birds Build with Your Hair*** are contemporary pastorals. Owls, barns, cherry trees, and dying elms may not be the subjects one would expect from a poet who has become famous writing on Matisse, Goebbels, and professorial lust, but then Snodgrass has never been predictable. Writing about country life, he manages to avoid the stereotypes of nature poetry and addresses his subjects with fresh intelligence and humor. A discursive poet at heart, Snodgrass occasionally has given two or even three images where one might do, but this indecisiveness is often part of his charm—as in **"Old Apple Trees,"** which despite its fancifulness contains the most realistic apple orchard I know:

> Like battered old millhands, they stand in the orchard—
> Like drunk legionnaires, heaving themselves up,
> Lurching to attention. Not one of them wobbles
> The same way as another. Uniforms won't fit them—
> All those cramps, humps, bulges. Here, a limb's gone;
> There, rain and corruption have eaten the whole core.
> They've all grown too tall, too thick, or too something.
> Like men bent too long over desks, engines, benches.
> Or bent under mailsacks, under loss.
> They've seen too much history and bad weather, grown
> Around rocks, into high winds, diseases, grown
> Too long to be willful, too long to be changed.

This passage shows why one returns to Snodgrass' best work with such pleasure. It is not simply because he is so clever and entertaining, but because he is so true to experience. (pp. 492-93)

Dana Gioia, "Poetry and the Fine Presses," in The Hudson Review, *Vol. XXXV, No. 3, Autumn, 1982, pp. 483-98.*

Gavin Ewart

On the evidence of his ***Selected Poems, 1957-1987,*** W. D. Snodgrass is one of the six best poets now writing in English—though who the other five are would be arguable. He writes mainly in rhymed stanzas, a technique that has never entirely gone out of fashion in Britain but which has been ridiculed in certain quarters in the United States. British and American literary cultures are not exactly in synch, but they do overlap. In Britain, Anthony Hecht and Richard Wilbur are as easily appreciated as W. H. Auden. Mr. Snodgrass, whose Pulitzer Prize-winning first book, ***Heart's Needle,*** was published in England in 1960, only one year after its American appearance, is certainly one of the poets who can make the Atlantic crossing easily.

It is a measure of Mr. Snodgrass's traditionalism and accessibility that his quality can often be defined by comparing him with poets of the past. ***Heart's Needle*** contributes 17 of its 30 poems to this volume, and these are still among the best by Mr. Snodgrass. The resemblances to other poets are striking (conscious or not). In **"Ten Days Leave"** we have Wilfred Owen:

> He steps down from the dark train, blinking; stares
> At trees like miracles. He will play games
> With boys or sit up all night touching chairs.
> Talking with friends, he can recall their names.

There's a hint of Donne in **"Riddle"**:

> If they act as a microscope
> Of mounted powers it shall be magnified
> Like an airy globe or beach ball that expands
> Between them so vast they could never hope
> To grasp it without all four of their hands
> Opened wide.

Lines like "You have the damnedest friends and seem to think / You have some right to think" are everyday speech like that of Donne. Even A. E. Housman seems a ghostly presence:

> I go out like a ghost,
> nights, to walk the streets
> I walked fifteen years younger—
> seeking my old defeats,
> devoured by the old hunger.

And, just as Housman, in unguarded moments, could seem trite, so can Mr. Snodgrass: "The blossoms snow down in my hair; / The trees and I will soon be bare."

These similarities do no harm to the poems. This is still an American scene, rural Frost rather than Housman, though, when Orpheus is singing of "That flowered bride cut down in Spring, / Struck by the snake, your underling," the formal rhyming and exactitude bring Marvell to mind. In a much later satirical poem there are conscious echoes of Marlowe and Tennyson. Well, Auden and Louis MacNeice literally quoted Shakespeare in "serious" verse.

Although not all of the ***Heart's Needle*** poems are rhyming lyrics, the approximate rhyming of some of them (meter/motors, hills/still, sergeants/bargain) reminds one of Auden's practice in the 1930's—except for the rhyming of singulars with plurals—and so does their fluidity, the sense flowing on easily from stanza to stanza. A phrase like "Heaven's vault" reminds us that this is, in some respects, a very old-fashioned kind of verse—but outstandingly successful in such poems as **"Riddle," "Home Town," "A Cardinal"** and **"The Campus on the Hill."** And the 80 Thomas Hardy-like stanzas of **"Heart's Needle"** itself contain memorable lines:

> Like nerves caught in a graph,
> the morning-glory vines
> frost has erased by half
> still scrawl across their rigid twines.
> Like broken lines
>
> of verses I can't make.

Mr. Snodgrass's next book, ***Remains,*** had its share of moving poems. Of those included here **"The Mouse"** and **"Viewing the Body"** work as a pair. **"The Survivors"** gives a true, unsentimental description of bereavement. **"The Boy Made of Meat"** is a poem for children, about the revolt of a vegetarian child too often stuffed with steak; the poem is very nicely done, relaxed, humorous, pleasant.

Of the 40 poems in ***After Experience,*** a record of disillusion, 24 are here, including 8 that are first class. The most remarkable are **"The Examination"** a surrealist dissection of the American eagle, and **"A Flat One,"** which is about keeping a patient alive to no purpose. Others, in freer forms, concern paintings; a poem about Van Gogh, **"The Starry Night,"** is the most interesting. But Van Gogh's last words (*"Zoo heen kan gaan"*) need a note, as they have in the Oxford edition of ***After Experience,*** in which we are told that the phrase can mean "This is the way to go," "I'd like to die like this" or "I want to go home."

"The Führer Bunker" is a long sequence in which the Nazi leaders and Eva Braun take turns at dramatic monologues. It is extraordinarily effective and inventive. Himmler speaks like a machine with the voice of one of the Daleks in the *Dr. Who* television series. Eva Braun sings "Tea for Two" (she used to annoy Hitler by singing such songs). Magda Goebbels gives cyanide to her six children, in a "This-is-the-house-that-Jack-built" nursery rhyme:

> This is the needle that we give
> Soldiers and children when they live
> Near the front in primitive
> Conditions or real dangers;
> This is the spoon we use to feed
> Men trapped in trouble or in need,
> When weakness or bad luck might lead
> Them to the hands of strangers. . . .
>
> Open wide, now, little bird;
> I who sang you your first word
> Soothe away every sound you've heard
> Except your Leader's voice.

A sinister quotation from Goebbels stands as an epigraph: "Even if we lose this war, we still win, for our spirit will have penetrated the hearts of our enemies."

All the poems from ***If Birds Build With Your Hair*** are here, giving us contemporary life in a traditional setting ("Some say better not get involved; / Send Hallmark if you care"), with the bonus of imagination, mostly verbal, as in "Bees hum / Through these branches like lascivious intentions" and:

> Polish ciocias, toothless flirts
> Whose breasts dangle down to there
> Triple sea-hags say: headaches if
> Birds build with your hair.

Selected from ***A Locked House*** are several poems about people breaking up—**"Mutability,"** a rather hesitant villanelle; **"The Last Time,"** which is about the absent-minded caress of a loved one before the breakup of a marriage, and the best poem in this section; **"A Locked House"**; and **"A Seashell." "Old Jewelry"** has an obsession with the emotional significance of things that is very reminiscent of Hardy and Philip Larkin. The most inventive work is **"The Death of Cock Robin"** from ***Kinder Capers.*** Fantasy tribes—the Brutish, the Merkans, the Ruffians, the Youmans—appear and one character, "W. D.," is almost equivalent to "Henry" in John Berryman's "Dream Songs."

The last section, "Darkling," has one supreme poem—**"The Poet Ridiculed by Hysterical Academics,"** including the lines:

> Where are the beard, the bongo drums,
> Tattered T-shirt and grubby sandals,
> As who, released from Iowa, comes
> To tell of wondrous scandals?

Mr. Snodgrass has a pleasant kind of mind, great originality and a terrific talent for verse that is not-quite-for-children; but in general the poems here that are unhappy, rather than playful, are the best.

Gavin Ewart, "One Poet, Many Voices," in The New York Times Book Review, *September 13, 1987, p. 52.*

Snodgrass on the demands made of poetry:

Robert Frost once asserted that, for a problem which has an answer, we go to medicine and laws; for a problem with none, we go to poetry. And it may be worth asking whether, if it has an answer, it really is a problem. If Frost was right, it surely follows that the poem will side with the multiplicity of our feelings and perceptions, not the simplifications of our system-building. It is natural enough that present-day Americans, after decades of empire, demand that their lives be made freer, simpler, more pleasant—regardless of the cost to the rest of the world or to their own development. And it follows that they would demand that poetry, too, should not only be easy for everyone to write (as if free verse were not immeasurably more difficult!) but that it should prove reality manageable and comfy. As William Empson wrote, "You don't want chaos and the whole thing there."

The poem does not make the world simpler or easier; Auden was right: "poetry makes nothing happen." Except that, if we can persuade our minds to wake up every three weeks or so, the poem can make us more aware of, and so better able to deal with, our world's and our own complexities.

W. D. Snodgrass in "Against Your Beliefs," 1990.

Larry Levis

Long after Modernism perished, it lived on as a worshipped deity in the institutionalized altars of academia. And the work of Snodgrass [as presented in ***Selected Poems, 1957-1987***] begins with his apostasy at one of its cathedrals, the University of Iowa in the late 1950s. In retrospect, even his heresy has within it a kind of in-dwelling American iconoclasm and revisionary puritanism:

> I remember when I was in school, we were all taught to write obscure, brilliant, highly symbolized poems about the loss of myth in our time, and, you know, it suddenly began to occur to me that I didn't care about the loss of myth in our time; frankly, I was glad to be rid of the stuff. . . . But we were all writing poems about what we thought *The Waste Land* was about. None of us had bothered to find out that *The Waste Land* isn't about that at all. We thought it was about that because you could make doctoral dissertations by talking about all the learned allusions in *The Waste Land* and how it was about, you know, the need for a "meaningful myth" in our lives; nobody had noticed it was about Eliot's insane wife and his frozen sex life. He had helped disguise this, with Pound's assistance, by his editing of the poem. We believed people's doctoral statements about the poem. We believed Frost and Eliot when they said their poems were about other things than their own sex lives, and we can now look at the poems and see that that just isn't so at all.

The intimation, of course, is that Snodgrass understands the Modernists' real concerns, however they may be masked by mythical method, and so, in a curious appropriation of them via his own obsessions, he has created a new allegiance with that sexuality which the priesthood of Modernism had either ignored or censored. He is not rebelling against the Modernists (whom he elsewhere has called "definitive") so much as he is adopting them, in all their repressed, censored splendor, as grandparents. His struggle will be against those priests who have gelded them and locked them in the sacristy of New Criticism.

And yet part of his unbridled attack depends upon a reversal, for, as Paul Gaston has noted, in Snodgrass's art an older form is used, a durational and spoken lyrical form, in which the content is new. In Modernism, new forms were created to house the "treasure-trove" of the past. At least some of Snodgrass's work is involved in demythologizing, dismantling, a clearing away of what, after the War, must have felt suddenly archaic and false, a mode which in itself had become "a tyrant in a varnished car" and which had spread into the outlying culture like some contagious sleep, one in which all sleepers are alike. It is appropriate that **"Fourth of July"** is placed in ***Remains,*** Snodgrass's [first] collection published under the pseudonym S. S. Gardons and in a limited edition. For the speaker is both anonymous and representative of what most inhabitants feel about the "monolithic piety," or living falsehood, of their culture. What is more intriguing is the phenomenon of a Confessional poet traveling under an assumed name, for it suggests that the future of Confessional work lies in another direction, as if the exhibitionist had become an agoraphobic, a transformation not uncommon, in life or in art:

> Hearing some politician fume;
> Someone leads out a blonde schoolgirl to crown
> Queen of this war-contract factory town;
> Skyrockets and the last guns boom.
>
> I keep my seat and wonder where,
> Into what ingrown nation has she gone
> Among a people silent and withdrawn;
> I wonder in the stifling air
>
> Of what deprived and smoked-filled town
> They brush together and do not feel lust,
> Hope, rage, love; within what senseless dust
> Is she at home to settle down;
>
> Where do they know her, and the dead
> Meet in a vacancy of shared disgrace,
> Keep an old holiday of blame and place
> Their tinsel wreath on her dark head?
>
> We tramp home through the sulfurous smoke
> That is my father's world. Now we must
> Enter my mother's house of lint and dust
> She could not breathe; I wheeze and choke.
>
> It is an evil, stupid joke:

My wife is pregnant; my sister's in her grave.
We live in the home of the free and of the brave.
No one would hear me, even if I spoke.

It is, and it has always been, Snodgrass's willingness to make what Camus in *The Plague* would call a complete "condemnation of things as they are" that distinguishes this poet; it is also part of what his power comes from, for no one transgresses a taboo, which in this case was a rebellion against the kind of poem his mentors prescribed, without releasing a certain amount of psychic energy. Yet Snodgrass's "condemnation" is not quite or not yet nihilism; nihilism knows it needn't wait to see if things improve, and nihilism, as George P. Eliot maintained years ago, doesn't care so much about getting the rhymes right. Snodgrass cares, and waits. And the value that rushes into the poetry of Confessionalism, this most identifiably American of all Post-Modernist modes, is simply life itself, the detailing and almost Flaubertian observation of it whether it occurs in a threadbare zoo in Iowa City where a father and daughter go to see the raccoons, or in the smell of a linen chest at 91 Revere Street. After wholesale genocide and nuclear death, it can almost be said that what one experiences with his senses and mind is a value *per se,* and that the record each "poor, passing fact" makes of such an impoverished world and culture is the only wealth that anyone might expect. But it is not the only value that can be posited, or striven for: "I tell you love is possible. We have to try," Snodgrass adds.

It is this very domesticity and representativeness that makes ***Heart's Needle,*** and, I would argue, ***Remains,*** American classics of our time, just as these qualities are what will make Lowell endure any present chorus of critical jackals who seem themselves victims of that "monolithic piety" of American culture. Yet the usual ethical charge against any poet of the Confessional mode had to do with what appeared as an indecent display of private disclosures of their own lives, of unalleviated obsessions, of an almost pathological introversion or public manicness. The subjects it took up, after all, were madness, divorce, cruelty, violence, suicide, even homicidal impulses, and the general reading public, who, as Leslie Fiedler pointed out, is not interested in enjoying poetry so much as it feels obligated to judge it, or to judge the poet or the life of the poet, probably wondered why they couldn't all be kindly old soothsayers like the Frost they had so mistaken for a kindly old soothsayer. Certainly they had trouble with a druggie like Poe or a Fascist like Pound. And yet in all fairness it seems now that it was the imitators of Lowell, Sexton, Plath, Berryman and Snodgrass, followers and mediocre talents who displayed each psychic scar they could find, and who held up their traumas like medals, and who chanted a rosary of petty complaints until their very stridency passed for hysteria, and who then made a shrine of hysteria or of an irresponsible cruelty they mistook for masculinity, who made the mode repugnant by sensationalizing and sentimentalizing it. The eventual result of their vanity, of their whole effort, is this: I cannot remember even one of their names.

And yet it appears true, as Yeats observed, that "All that is merely personal soon rots, unless it is packed in salt or ice." And What Lowell called the "perfect little stanzas" of the ***Heart's Needle*** sequence is exactly that salt, that ice. The new content, the intimacy of its disclosure, is distilled into variations upon some very old forms of English prosody. What might have become "merely personal" is never idiosyncratic; it is representative not only of the pain of an absentee father but also of the entire impoverishment of a culture. It is the tenacity of the father with his obsessive love that matters and that mirrors his larger community; it is his love's embarrassing persistence that makes him representative, that throws the values of America into relief by displaying their dispossession. Furthermore, this fellow walking hand in hand with his daughter on her weekend visit will not be nice about it, will not shut up and go away, will not adjust, will not even adopt, for appearances, the correct, liberal attitudes. All this is emphasized in the poem's close, which is its recapitulative *coda,* complete with its diminished Lear and innocent Cordelia in their confinement:

In full regalia, the pheasant cocks
  march past their dubious hens;
the porcupine and the lean, red fox
  trot around their bachelor pens

and the miniature painted train
  wails on its oval track:
you said, I'm going to Pennsylvania!
  and waved. And you've come back.

If I loved you, they said I'd leave
  and find my own affairs.
Well, once again this April, we've
  come around to the bears;

punished and cared for, behind bars,
  the coons on bread and water
stretch thin black fingers after ours.
  And you are still my daughter.

Still; my; to pack in salt or ice means what I hear as that slight variation of the trimeter in the last line: not three iambs but two iambs followed by a spondee, the possessive "my" rising up a little against the recumbency of the iambic pattern, its accommodation. For everything else has been wrested away from the speaker here but this knowledge, this "still" and "my" by which his feeling continues. These too, he might have been tricked out of, or might have given up in the foolish acceptance of neighborly good advice. But to "concede" *that* is to concede (an important word in the sequence) all that this father is, all that he feels. And as J. D. McClatchy argues in his brilliant essay on Snodgrass, "The Mild, Reflective Art," Snodgrass's ". . . controlling concerns—identity and choice—are existential in nature, and confessional in revelation. . . ." But in Snodgrass, that which is "confessional in revelation" often confesses to a hard-won self-knowledge. In **"April Inventory"** his aggression is a kind of self-preservation, and therefore it is a value, perhaps the oldest value, one always accompanied by its faithful antagonist, the *thanatos* of every *eros:*

I taught myself to name my name,
To bark back, to loosen love and crying;
To ease my woman so she came,
To ease an old man who was dying.
I have not learned how often I
Can win, can love, but choose to die.

And yet the joyous knowledge of the poem's final stanza depends upon a change of pronoun and point of view; the "we" and its discovery of *loveliness* is necessary as counterpoint to the isolated "I" and its self-destructive nature; a "we" that is possible only through the wizening of age that occurs in the penultimate stanza and that affords the seer-like, almost gleefully posthumous tonal change:

> Though trees turn bare and girls turn wives,
> We shall afford our costly seasons;
> There is a gentleness survives
> That will outspeak and has its reasons.
> There is a loveliness exists,
> Preserves us, not for specialists.

If the whole poem had not cautioned us with its ironies, this stanza would be one that could only be spoken by an imposter, a Polonius, a spokesperson for "monolithic piety." But because they exist against a panorama of confessional revelations of lust, professional irresponsibility, and all sorts of dalliance and pleasures in life, they plead their case from seasoned experience, experience in which a decent amount of fun and the offensive laziness necessary for every poet has been emphasized, and vindicated.

But this "we" is a change that is indicative of larger changes to come in Snodgrass's work. Although the Confessional mode remains prominent in the first half of ***After Experience,*** and although these poems do not disappoint me, they lack the vital, and sometimes aggressive, energy of the earlier work. Curiously, the most powerful poem in their order centers not upon the poet's life, but upon the man, Old Fritz, dying in a hospital as the poet, who at that time was a young orderly, contemplates the subject in **"A Flat One."** After the inevitable slow death, it is his meditation that seems, characteristically again, representative in the kind of choice he makes in the final reversal of the closure:

> They'd say this was a worthwhile job
> Unless they tried it. It is mad
> To throw our good lives after bad;
> Waste time, drugs, and our minds, while
> strong
> Men starve. How many young men did we rob
> To keep you hanging on?
>
> I can't think we did *you* much good.
> Well, when you died, none of us wept.
> You killed for us, and so we kept
> You, because we have to earn our pay.
> No. We'd still have to help you try. We would
> Have killed for you today.

Old Fritz is a veteran, has "killed for us," and although Snodgrass is willing to rebel against any suspect piety of the past, he cannot wholly rebel against that culture which has, after all, so inevitably become a part of him. Here, he chooses what he can only believe is the last decency available.

The sequence of poems on paintings and painters that concludes ***After Experience*** is abruptly abstract in mode rather than Confessional; it attempts to confront, in one of its most haunting manifestations, the principles aswirl beneath all action, that *eros* that is unjudgeably constant as occasioned by Monet's *Les Nymphéas:*

> And I am shared out. I become these things:
> These lillies, if these things are lillies
> Which are dancers growing dim across no floor;
> These mayflies; whirled dust orbiting in the
> sun;
> This blossoming diffused as rushlights; galactic
> vapors;
> Fluorescence into which we pass and pene
> trate;
> O soft as the thighs of women;
> O radiance, into which I go on dying . . .

The attempt by Snodgrass to enlarge the focus of his lens in ***Heart's Needle,*** to suggest that the personal *agon* of the poem is in some way reciprocally reflected by the contemporaneous Korean War, that there is some causal connection or even synchronous connection between the private and public war, is what M. L. Rosenthal considers a major flaw in the poem; but if it is, Snodgrass's tenacity in a later historical cycle might come to be seen as a gesture in which such a flaw is recuperated, relieved and even explained by the later revisionary work, ***The Führer Bunker,*** for his tenacity is a reflex of his desire for overall coherence and unity over a life's work in a variety of modes, and certainly in a range of different voices.

Nothing in the poet's work so far has aroused more controversy than this unfinished poem-in-progress. Only fifteen of over seventy poems are included in this collection, and yet these have been enough to stir up trouble, and no wonder given the stigma of its *dramatis personae:* Goebbels, Goering, Himmler, Hitler, Eva Braun and Magda Goebbels. Perhaps the most obvious casual source for the poems is H. R. Trevor-Roper's account, *The Last Days of Hitler;* certainly the most obvious prior model for a formal source is the long syllabic sequence by Henri Coulette, *The War of the Secret Agents,* although it is clear that Coulette's poem is valuable not for its use of syllabics so much as its larger formal method, in which various *personae* speak, are displaced by other speakers, then return and speak again from altered circumstances a reader must surmise on his own from the clues given. Paul Gaston in *W. D. Snodgrass* identifies a further source of the poem's origins.

> The most immediate impetus for ***The Führer Bunker*** may have come, however, from two experiences Snodgrass had while participating in panel discussions. As a member of one panel, he found himself with Allen Ginsberg and LeRoi Jones (now Imamu Amiri Baraka). Snodgrass recalls the experience vividly: "They were calling me every filthy name and talking about what a rotten fascist I was and how dreadful and horrible." When the moderator interrupted to restore order by asking the panel what they thought was wrong with American civilization, Jones pointed to Snodgrass and said, "He's what's wrong with American civilization." Snodgrass's reaction? "What a compliment!" "I started thinking about that and decided: if only it were true! If one could identify with all that evil, he ought to be one hell of a poet. And I suppose the ***Bunker*** is one way to try that."

The large, thematic question that the poem confronts is apparent from its two epigraphs. The first is from Joseph Goebbels: "Even if we lose this war, we still win, for our spirit will have penetrated the hearts of our enemies." The second is attributed and unidentified: "Mother Theresa, asked when she first began her work of relief and care for abandoned children, replied, 'On the day I discovered I had a Hitler inside me.' " In these poems, Gaston argues that the sincerity of the earlier work has been replaced by "authenticity" in a far more objective mode. (pp. 9-12)

So the authenticity of the Confessional mode *is* a presence in ***The Führer Bunker.*** But here, there is a bristling thicket of speakers, a density of texture and formal experimentation that resembles more the quest of a Modernist sensibility than a Post-Modernist one—with this exception: the subject of the poem is recent history, not myth, and every attempt by any *personae* in the poem at self-mythologizing is restricted and admonished by the whole context, which, as Snodgrass argues, leaves these Nazis with only their appallingly realistic selves. The final prophecy of Goebbels is hardly the tragedy he refers to, and Snodgrass shrewdly displays him in what Hannah Arendt terms "the banality of evil":

> The rest is silence. Left like sperm
> In a stranger's gut, waiting its term,
> Each thought, each step lies; the roots spread.
> They'll believe in us when we're dead:
> When we took "Red Berlin" we found
> We always worked best underground.
> So; the vile body turns to spirit
> That speaks soundlessly. They'll hear it.

It is Goebbels's illogic as he rushes to a conclusion of his argument that perjures him here. And it is difficult not to suppose that the "sperm / In a stranger's gut" will come to be only another stranger, or nothing at all given the circumstances, the final "silence" of such evil. For the notion of evil in the poem is not modern at all, but is essentially a Renaissance notion. It wears well through the centuries, and here it is, at least in some of the poem, renewed and amazing, especially in the voices of Magda Goebbels as she kills her children and in that of Eva Braun just after her hurried wedding to Hitler. For the nature of evil in this poem, as in tragedy, is to devour its Host, which is the order of the world, until it has nothing left to feed upon but itself, and then to devour itself. It is, in itself, nothing at all, and can have only its representation as nothing for a goal. (p. 13)

Ironically, it is marriage to Hitler that deprives Eva Braun suddenly of both her innocence and her ignorance. Of the extant poems, hers is ironically the most incriminating and compelling testimony to the nature of evil. It is all the more frightening because it is also the nature of her husband.

> And even if He came, He
> would be missing; He
> would not hear me. I
> could look through Him
> like a worn-out lantern slide. The priest
> held up the monstrance
> they said held the Host
> before the people, right and left,
> while we cast down our eyes. But one day I
> crept up in the empty chapel,
> to the holy case. There
> the sacred vestments, the gold
> chains, the monstrance
> rayed out gleaming
> like the May sun. And in the
> center, the tiny glass bead?
> I could see nothing.
> Nothing.
>
> And yet I have these albums, these
> pictures proving it all so.
> We danced together; we
> sat together over tea; even
> the wedding ceremony . . .

On this day of her wedding and of her suicide, she speculates on her ring, "this ring torn off some Jew's hand," and goes on to say:

> I am the Black Bride that will be
> devoured, that will pass
> down into Him like used water
> down a drain, a film stuck,
> burning through, or reeling
> back into itself.

Such is the sudden representation of evil, which, in Snodgrass's art, seeks to devour all things, even itself, and, in doing so, deprives itself of any possible mythology.

It is unfair to attempt to evaluate a poem that remains mostly unpublished, but both its scale and the questions posed by the poem are large and worth investigating. The central danger of the poem is the problem of drama itself. Characters must be interesting enough to compel our attention, and the reader must not be allowed to ignore them as mere monsters; if the dramatic element of the poem cycle fails, then one is left, unfortunately, with an assembly that comprises only "the banality of evil"—and not its tragedy. (pp. 13-14)

Larry Levis, "Not Life So Proud to Be Life: Snodgrass, Rothenberg, Bell, and The Counter-Revolution," in The American Poetry Review, *Vol. 18, No. 1, January-February, 1989, pp. 9-20.*

William M. Chace

[Many] artists begin alone, trusting nothing but their own impulses, the rhythms in which they are first comfortable. Only with maturity and experience do they come by the knowledge and the pleasure of how the self can be expanded through the incorporation of new modes of expression. In the career of W. D. Snodgrass, for instance, what began in the 1950s as a painfully intense scrutiny of the singular self has now (in the 1970s and 1980s) become the depiction of a crowded landscape of multiple selves, characters in opposition—the many rather than the one. In ***Heart's Needle*** (1959), his first book of poems, "Snodgrass is walking through the universe" but is doing so, make no mistake about it, *alone.* When he remarks in that volume that "I carry a scared silence / with me like my smell," he reveals an essential truth about the narrow conventions in which he was writing at the time. The vogue of "confessional poetry" inaugurated by ***Heart's Needle*** (and, to a lesser extent, by Robert Lowell's *Life Studies*) drew exclusively on the singularity of one speaker; it spoke of the ravages of *his* existence and suggested that the rest of life was mere background to that tragedy.

But Snodgrass did not remain in the small room of confessional poetry. Moving beyond the claustrophobia of selfhood, Snodgrass published ***After Experience*** (1968) and thereby gave notice both to himself and his readers that he had achieved considerable distance from personal travail. He was now prepared to explore terrain that was unfamiliar because it was not of his own making. Poems about his daughter, about his failing marriage, about the dislocations of his academic existence, make up but part of the volume. The voice of fragility and vulnerability is still present. But poems like **"Planting a Magnolia"** announce that Snodgrass is no longer speaking about his own puniness, but about human puniness in general. The planted tree represents all those forces superior in strength to the strength of humankind; it is not the poet alone who is insignificant when compared to the "mystery" and the "obscene blunt beauty" of that tree. Hence the use of the first-person *plural* pronoun: it is "we" who are belittled by the presence of the magnolia and its ancient roots, and it is "we" who will die before the tree does.

But the real departures in ***After Experience*** do not come with the new positions Snodgrass can assume in the face of his weakness and the superior force of the universe, but with his discovery of an art form not his own: painting. Owing to a series of pedagogical accidents, the poet is suddenly made to confront Matisse, Monet, Vuillard, Manet, and Van Gogh. And, with that confrontation, the sensibility and the art of the poet undergo an extraordinary change. One art, "tending" toward another, is transformed.

Snodgrass's essay about the discovery of the five painters and their paintings, **"Poems about Paintings,"** reveals the seductive power possessed by something beyond him and other than him. Talking about Claude Monet's *Les Nymphéas,* he says:

> Sitting before it for long hours at the museum, I often had the sensation that if I did not get up and leave the room, the guards might well come in and find me missing. . . . I, trying to absorb this picture—might be absorbed by it.

Such fear of disappearance was, in turn, connected with another sensation provided by the painting—the sensation of liberation. [**"MONET: Les Nymphéas"**] was for Snodgrass "about the effort to break down the armoring of the self and its beliefs and ideas; one might become an energy among energies, open to the flux of experience, absorbing and being absorbed by sensation." These profound alterations in Snodgrass's way of looking at himself and at the world, alterations caused by the impact of another form of art on his own, are summed up by his recognition that the five paintings all involved a theme—incarceration and liberation—that he now knew was central to his development as a poet: "an extremely ambivalent feeling toward a womblike containment: on the one hand a fierce desire to escape; on the other, a desire to be captured and contained."

That recognition changed Snodgrass as a poet. And it illustrates the great power the forms and expressions of one art can have on those of another. After the five "poems about paintings" in ***After Experience,*** Snodgrass moved to a more active involvement with the problems of translation (translation itself being a departure from selfhood into the sensibility of another). Then, in ***The Führer Bunker: A Cycle of Poems in Progress*** (1977), he moved to an imaginative recreation of an entire chorus of tortured voices, each with its own inflections, accent, and willfulness. ***The Führer Bunker*** is, in fact, about the power of will and the associated power of individual autonomy, themes close to Snodgrass all his career, but now enacted by characters drawn out of the darkest and most disturbed pages of this century's history. In a singularly ambitious demonstration of the artistic facility John Keats called "negative capability," Snodgrass lets his own mind and imagination drift free so that he can enter the driven and poisoned minds of Adolf Hitler and those close to him in the final days of the Third Reich. Rant, song, dream and nightmare, proclamation, and idle talk—all fill the page as they fill the reader's mind. The diversity of the individuals present in the bunker is made manifest by the range of poetic forms selected for them: everything from couplet to villanelle. And lurking behind all the presences is the mind of Hitler: total will imprisoned by absolute obsession.

After the dark world of ***The Führer Bunker,*** Snodgrass has moved to a world quite different, a world seemingly lighter and more playful in tone, a world whose music and rhythm are supplied by a nursery rhyme, a fabulous world of animals and birds. And, most interesting to anyone tracing Snodgrass's career, this transformation has come directly from the power of a painter: DeLoss McGraw.

Perhaps the first observation to be made about the impact of McGraw on Snodgrass's work is that the painter proved to be an excellent reader of poetry and showed that the poet in time could become an excellent reader of visual creations. In first writing to Snodgrass in 1982, McGraw said that he had seen a "childlike attitude toward death" in the poet's work. That perception, the kind of insight between two artists that Nathaniel Hawthorne once called "the shock of recognition," was the beginning of the shared understanding that was later to unite the work of the two men.

The Death of Cock Robin, the result of that union, wholly fuses the energies of two artists. It is not paintings "about" poems any more than it is poems about certain paintings. It is instead the product of one artist (whether painter or poet) enlivened and strengthened by the work of another (the painter, forty years of age, and the poet, some twenty years older, become exact contemporaries in that fusion). Neither artist nor art takes the upper hand in this relationship, for each of them gets to see ways in which the limitations of his art can be pushed back and opened up. And each artist reserves the right, an ultimate privilege, of *mis*-reading the work of the other. Snodgrass has said, "We both often find that we've misunderstood each other," but he adds, "Those misreadings nearly always prove fertile."

The ground on which the poet and the painter have found themselves is the buried past of childhood. The vehicle of their artistic association is a childish rhyme, "The Death of Cock Robin," about the death of an innocent. Like many such rhymes, its apparent naïveté disguises the violence and pain residing beneath the surface of the story. In the world of nursery rhymes trauma is anesthetized by simple verbal beats and syncopation, thus revealing the wonderful power of children to assimilate pain by giving it pattern and making it playful.

The nursery rhyme "Cock Robin," ostensibly about the regrettable death of a bird, is in fact about the complicity of many living things in the world of death. The sparrow has killed the robin, and everyone else, from beetle to owl to dove, thrush, and bull, seems glad to play a part in all the traditional rites—from mourning to burial. For that reason, the rhyme gained popularity in the mid-eighteenth century as an Aesopian way of explaining the fall of Robert Walpole's ministry under George III of England. It became, then, a rhyme about intrigue and deceit.

And that is the very subject of the paintings/poems titled ***The Death of Cock Robin.*** Like the nursery rhyme, this unified work feigns jocularity to focus on the dark business of interrogation, accusation, betrayal, and intrigue. The noxious smell of complicity is everywhere. The poem begins with "charges," it portrays fear and persecution, and it ends with death. Cock Robin is the victim of forces moving implacably against him. Unlike the nursery rhyme, however, the work includes a character who is part friend to Cock Robin, part his alter ego, and part witness to his destruction. That character is "W. D.," whose name, interestingly enough, happens not to have been the invention of the poet, but of the painter. "W. D." comforts Cock Robin and provides him safe haven while he studies the plight faced by the bird. More thoughtful and analytical than Cock Robin, "W. D." is at once the creation of the painter and the voice of the poet, the voice of anyone who, looking on pain and defeat, asks for help and for explanation. "W. D.," then, is *us* as we read the poem. It is the device used by the painter and the poet to lure us into their joint enterprise and its drama.

But the power of that enterprise does not issue from just this device. Rather, the poems, limited by their confinement in words, crucially depend on the way they become defined and expanded by the work of DeLoss McGraw. By the same token, McGraw's work, confined in shape and color, becomes defined and "voiced" by its relationship to those poems. The wonder of the relationship is that it is perfectly reciprocal; artist answers to artist, each provoking, surprising, and challenging the other. The paintings are thus organically a part of ***The Death of Cock Robin*** and not at all its "illustration." (pp. 85-9)

From their partnership, Snodgrass and McGraw say to those who see and read their work that the annihilation stored up for Cock Robin—and indeed for all of us—will hardly be bleak. It will be filled with animation, color, song, and some good company. The vision the painter and the poet share is revealed in, for instance, **"W. D. Assists in the Protection of Cock Robin's Roost,"** where W. D.'s solicitude is represented by his plural selves floating and working everywhere in the air. There is no sense in either the poem or the painting of loneliness or despair but rather splendid flashes of energy and dynamic determination. Look, for example, at **"W. D. Picks a Bouquet for Cock Robin but Cannot Separate the Thorns from the Flowers"** (many of the paintings sharing titles with poems came first from the inspiration of the painter, not from the poet). Here the tone of McGraw's work, surprisingly enough, is placid. Instead of the isolated despair of introspection, a genuine stability and poise in color and design and in rhyme scheme predominate. The painter and the poet seem vigorously involved in an effort to repudiate depression by euphoria, ruination by construction. Theirs is that most admirable and rare of creations: a joint project in the artistic resurrection of the human spirit. (p. 90)

[***The Death of Cock Robin***], open to the eye and mind, is an enormously handsome fusion of the best work of two practiced and original artists. Our eyes and minds are strengthened in encountering that work, and we are in the presence of a triumphant doubling of creative power. (p. 91)

William M. Chace, in an afterword to The Death of Cock Robin *by W. D. Snodgrass, University of Delaware Press, 1989, pp. 83-91.*

Snodgrass on the relationship between poets, poetry, and reality:

The poem does not drive out chaos; it thumbs its nose at it. How better to confirm its almost overwhelming presence? Ideas, chess, the arts—they offer us forms of play, outlets for mental energies which yearn, desperately, to tie up the world and pull its teeth. No matter; the world does not read the rules; whatever our tactics, we will lose. Only the arts admit—no; proclaim—that despite whatever prowess we may achieve, we're still at the mercy of our mortality, of our frequently foolish passions.

No wonder artists are disliked. Revelling in mastery over the world's details, they show us, finally, our helplessness before its totality—not just that we have the wrong ideas but that there are no right ones. If it had an answer, it wouldn't be a problem.

My father, like Plato, thought the artist dangerous because he keeps mentioning matters, like his own passions and perceptions, which the society wants to ignore. I thought the artist valuable for the same reason. The chances are, both of us were worse, each more wrong than the other.

W. D. Snodgrass in "After-Images: Autobiographical Sketches," 1988.

William Logan

The Muses are cruel devils, and never crueler than when they whisper, "Why haven't we seen *your* Selected Poems?" They offer the only contract they know, the one they offered Faust: No poet who selects his own work believes he will betray it.

A book of selected poems is a monument to middle age. It may revive a flagging career or embalm an overvalued one. As a sign of respectability, or merely as a device to return to print poems long out of it, a selected poems is an unendurable temptation for poets who have not received their due (and even great poets live in fear that they have not received their due). Though a clever poet can obscure his old sins or alter his alliances (early Yeats, in our standard texts, is often late Yeats in sheep's clothing), revising with a liver-spotted hand the radical errors of his youth, these monumental designs usually falter, like those of public statuary, between ingratiation and ingratitude. Many poets ought to rest on their laurels, or their old reviews.

[As revealed in his ***Selected Poems, 1957-1987***], W. D. Snodgrass has given few hostages to ingratiation. Of the important poets of his generation, none except James Merrill has pursued such eccentric obsessions, and none has suffered so peculiar a history of publication. The obsessions are not entirely responsible for the difficulties of this career. Among our contemporaries, Snodgrass is the shining—or tarnished—example of a poet whose gifts, lavishly bestowed and then prodigally diffused, have only benefited him under rare conditions. The cloak of invisibility, or power, has under other conditions become Nessus's toxic shirt.

Heart's Needle (1959) is a work of imaginative maturity, of concentrated and informed feeling rare in any poet, and particularly rare in a first book. (p. 72)

Much of its force is the force of repetition. In their stringent focus the early poems offer two movements, from ignorance outward to knowledge and experience, and from observation inward to revelation. The first usually moves from sleep to the shock of consciousness; the second from the mirror of nature to the shock of recognition. The symbolic range of the first is spiritual; the second psychological. From these mechanisms of argument, so obviously complementary, ***Heart's Needle*** derives its unity and governing momentum, also its constriction. Snodgrass is not a poet who can take any joy in a mastering knowledge, or even in the humbling that attends a deep look in the mirror. He would not describe himself, as Newton did, as a child picking up seashells. In the early poems, there are always horrors to be woken to, and recognitions that become afflictions:

Observe the cautious toadstools
  still on the lawn today
though they grow over-evening;
  sun shrinks them away.
Pale and proper and rootless,
  they righteously extort
their living from the living.
  I have been their sort.

("Song")

Even an account of mushrooms serves a scathing self-denunciation, but then no symbol is innocent to the psychological eye. The repetitions are not just mental but formal. Snodgrass is one of the mid-century masters of formal verse, and as restless as Hardy: Every poem throws on a new verse form like a new shirt. He is as restless as Hardy, but more calculating in his clumsiness, as the wandering rhythms and impure rhymes above may reveal. Singly, these poems have the virtues of their responsibilities; but the concentration of those responsibilities comes only in the notorious title sequence.

Though the poems of ***Heart's Needle*** may now form a rusty piece of stage machinery, one more exhibit in the museum devoted to the conflict between free verse and form, they retain the original pathos, the pathos of a violent tenderness. In ten sections of a verse always decorous but often distraught, the poet addresses his young daughter, from whom he is divided by marital separation and then divorce. Verse so formally elaborate rarely gives the impression of such simplicity:

Child of my winter, born
When the new fallen soldiers froze
In Asia's steep ravines and fouled the snows,
When I was torn

By love I could not still,
By fear that silenced my cramped mind
To that cold war where, lost, I could not find
My peace in my will,

All those days we could keep
Your mind a landscape of new snow
Where the chilled tenant-farmer finds, below,
His fields asleep. . . .

("Heart's Needle"—1)

This complicated and mastered rhetoric, extending over half a dozen stanzas in one sinuous sentence, argues the poet's high claims but also his self-absorption. That the rhetoric is not *fully* mastered (the precise adverbial function of *All those days* is obscure without emphasis on *those*) suggests how much difficulty can be concealed by such elaborations. The construction is involute, but the diction has been willed into monosyllables, a mouthful of monosyllables. Snodgrass's innovation was to borrow the battery of formal method from Lowell, Wilbur, and the poets of the early Fifties who came out of Wilbur's coat, but not the encrustations of manner. He imposed upon complex stanzas a direct and even blunt emotional statement that often comes perilously close to prose.

In the poet's self-involvement, the Korean War provides no more than a symbolic gratification, a landscape littered with dead fetal figures, for the "cold war" in himself. After this apostrophe invoking the winter of the child's birth, the sequence properly begins in the spring before the couple's estrangement, when the child is three, and advances season by season for two years, until another winter finally yields to spring. Each season is primly commemorated with a poem. (pp. 73-4)

The symbolic climate of these seasons marks the poems' strict management, and the progress of seasons forms a motif as studied as the recurring references to poems written and unwritten. The poems have a deceptively easy manner, and depend on incidents absurdly commonplace: the child planting seeds, or sweating with fever, or masquerading as a fox one Halloween. The normal incidents have abnormal force: The poet imposes on the child's simplest gesture a metaphysical burden (one may want to invoke Donne as the ghostly presence behind those complex stanzas). For her father, every sign is a sign of loss:

Here in the scuffled dust
  is our ground of play.
I lift you on your swing and must
  shove you away,
see you return again,
  drive you off again, then

stand quiet till you come.
  You, though you climb
higher, farther from me, longer,
  will fall back to me stronger.
Bad penny, pendulum,
  you keep my constant time

to bob in blue July
  where fat goldfinches fly
over the glittering, fecund
  reach of our growing lands.
Once more now, this second,
  I hold you in my hands.

("Heart's Needle"—7)

The colloquial manner, stripped of most demands upon figurative language, often marries its rhythms barely within a meter, acknowledging but never quite cooperating with the severity such form demands. The sentences maintain their tenuous dignity only by adhering to the scaffolding of form. As prose all their suppressed mawkishness would leak out.

In what does Snodgrass's formality lie? Chiefly in a highly modulated iambic line that subsides, by subtle degrees, from a carefully crafted monotony to a superbly varied and flexible instrument which takes advantage of liberal substitutions and inversions, and which finally slips into accentual verse. Much of his poetry (including the passages just quoted) approaches the condition, if not the conviction, of pure accentuals, though he never quite finds the rhythms of hesitation, or of conscience, in, say, Yeats's "Easter 1916." It is difficult to be certain of Snodgrass's convictions, or even his intents, since he permits himself small formal deviations—when composing syllabics (which he does less often than many critics think) he counts about as accurately as Marianne Moore. That may be as much to say, he will not spoil the line for the sake of fulfilling the form, he will not let meter get in the way of the meaning.

Snodgrass is heavily dependent on rhyme for his formal architecture: Most poets take rhythm as architecture and rhyme as adornment, more rarely as flying buttress. It unites his disparate rhythms, dispels (for the most part) the threat of prose. He can be quite unfaithful, nevertheless; he will change patterns stanza by stanza, corrupt a pure rhyme or correct an impure one. He is, in other words, wholly shameless in exploiting formal possibilities, though the poems are not deeply enough dyed by their variety, and the forms they acquire risk seeming merely miscellaneous. (pp. 75-6)

The decorum of Snodgrass's early verse signifies the emotion withheld, and the power of that emotion may be measured by the formal bonds required to restrain it. I don't think it has often been noted how much brutality lies behind the force of this feeling. One poem refers to a tug of possession that dislocated the child's wrist (the incident is less innocent than it is meant to be). What masquerades as sorrow in Snodgrass is often self-regard, and the love hides more than a little loathing. Such a mixed issue is of course resonant as long as it is unrecognized; a reader might still be forgiven from flinching, or expecting the child to flinch, from such attentions.

The poems diagnose a man painfully wrapped in his own embrace: Aside from the daughter, other people are scarcely mentioned, and if mentioned scarcely disclosed. That claustrophobic fascination with the self made ***Heart's Needle*** so radically different from other books of the period, and so corrosively influential.

Heart's Needle was the determining twin of *Life Studies.* Older poets are so rarely influenced by younger that one may forget the revivifying nature of this reversal—the effect of the young Ezra Pound on W. B. Yeats was surely less dangerous than the monkey glands or vasectomy Yeats later experimented with. Lowell's *Life Studies* and Snodgrass's ***Heart's Needle*** appeared within days of each other in April, 1959, the cruellest month. The next year they divided the awards between them, Lowell receiving the National Book Award and Snodgrass the Pulitzer Prize. Snodgrass had been Lowell's student at Iowa in 1950 and 1953. It was perhaps natural to ascribe to the teacher the directness of feeling common to both books, but Lowell was not so sure: "(Snodgrass) did these things before I did, though he's younger than I am and had been my student. He may have influenced me, though people have suggested the opposite."

Snodgrass found, in the inner life and the broken family, a poetry of great pathos and formal character that insulated itself in its period and the demands of period. Lowell's concern for heritage, literary posture, and political indispositions seems rudely up to date—it is not the aptitudes but the attitudes that are fresh, and freshening. Snodgrass takes the conventions of the time to their conclusion, gaining force but not a value; Lowell's disruptive intelligence is bleaker, more damaged, and less susceptible to the solicitudes of pity.

What has dated Snodgrass's early poems is their diction, not their delineations. They sound now like the outpourings of a man heartbroken, but a little vain and priggish, even overweening ("I taught myself to name my name, / . . . To ease my woman so she came," he says in **"April Inventory"**). Poems that so knowingly and so eagerly take advantage of the rueful idiom could not have these manners without the example of Eliot. They are Prufrock *after experience,* after a bite of the peach. Snodgrass is often too calculating, too fond of the well-made, symbolically governed poem—the careful roughness can't conceal it. But in the aftermath of that school so condescendingly called confessional, the simple declaratives of Snodgrass were more imitated than Lowell's gaudy mannerism. We have lived through three decades of pure prose in consequence.

Not all confessions are meant to be overheard. Snodgrass once claimed to have been deeply influenced by the poet S. S. Gardons, who in the early Sixties published a few poems in *Hudson Review* and in the second selection of *New Poets of England and America.* They seem to draw uncannily from, or belatedly to prefigure, the rhythms and stanzas of ***Heart's Needle.*** Gardons was given an implausible biography in the anthology ("Works as a gas station attendant in Fort Worth"), and it was not until 1970 that eight poems ascribed to him were published in an elegant limited edition called ***Remains.***

Among poets their real authorship was an open secret, but it was discreetly concealed until the death of the poet's parents. The pseudonym ("Snodgrass spelled sideways," the poet once remarked) protected him from the consequences of his rage:

> She stands in the dead center like a star;
> They form around her like her satellites
> Taking her energies, her heat, light
> And massive attraction on their paths, however
> far.
>
> Born of her own flesh; still, she feels them drawn
> Into the outer cold by dark forces;
> They are in love with suffering and perversion,
> With the community of pain. Thinking them
> gone,
>
> Out of her reach, she is consoled by evil
> In neighbors, children, the world she cannot
> change,
> That lightless universe where they range
> Out of the comforts of her disapproval.

("The Mother")

It is hard not to find this all very odd psychologically, perhaps odder than it really is: the guilty concealment of the poems (how difficult to claim what is already ours), the judgments masked by formal dispassion and a formulary sympathy. The spleen is contained, controlled, and even denied by the dignity of the diction that channels it, and is the more shocking for that. Wound within a metaphysical conceit, the anger invites the division of self which does not violate Snodgrass's most disturbing work, but is its very heart (how often in his poems he speaks as "we" and addresses "you").

Remains is a ghoulish title, or could be thought so (the innocence is an innocence assumed). Trailing after ***Heart's Needle*** like a bitter epilogue, the poems are some of his most bitterly accomplished. Most of them trace the aftermath of his sister's death, and as a group they compose a family pathology:

> Flowers like a gangster's funeral;
> Eyeshadow like a whore.
> They all say isn't she beautiful.
> She, who never wore
>
> Lipstick or such a dress,
> Never got taken out,
> Was scarcely looked at, much less
> Wanted or talked about;
>
> Who, gray as a mouse, crept
> The dark halls at her mother's
> Or snuggled, soft, and slept
> Alone in the dim bedcovers.
>
> Today at last she holds
> All eyes and a place of honor
> Till the obscene red folds
> Of satin close down on her.

("Viewing the Body")

The grotesque masquerade (which mocks the grotesque mask of Gardons) savages the usual proprieties of death, the proprieties poets observe in their elegies. This cool autopsy, so empty of the expected comforts and petty compassions, does not allow the reader to avert his gaze. The reader is that all too unwilling voyeur; but the poet a little too much relishes the abrogation of decency. Snodgrass's moral understandings derive a purity of observation from an impure response. The modestly optimistic note that ends a final poem to his daughter ("I tell you love is possible. / We have to try.") is betrayed by the failures of compassion evident elsewhere; but it is those failures that have made confession necessary.

After Experience (1968) lacks the thematic compression, the gravity of an obsession, of ***Heart's Needle.*** Since unity of impulse is part of a Romantic preference, the poems have been undervalued if not ignored. Their subjects are frequently trivial without triumphing over triviality—Snodgrass finds few Grecian urns in the wreckage of his household and his marriages. (pp. 77-80)

The selection from ***After Experience*** (twenty-three of the original forty poems, not counting the translations, which have been excluded) seriously misrepresents the quality of the book, which is a less stirring but also less restricted achievement than ***Heart's Needle.*** Many of the poems of marital discord have been discarded in favor of alkaline subjects given alkaline treatments (**"Looking," "The Lovers Go Fly a Kite," "Regraduating the Lute"**) or poems symbolically fantastic or overwrought (**"The Examination," "Flash Flood"**). If ***Selected Poems*** had no other flaw, it would be suspect for the omission of **"Leaving Ithaca," "Takeoff," "The Platform Man," "Autumn Scene," "Point Pelee in March," "Edmund to Gloucester," "A Visitation,"** and **"The Men's Room in the College Chapel,"** all poems of formal and syntactic ambition. (pp. 81-2)

The most astringent poems of ***After Experience,*** so many of which have been excluded, moderate the earlier angers into a wryness and moral suspicion reminiscent of Larkin's, though without his smug and sour resignation. If this strain in Snodgrass had been developed, the poetry of the last two decades might have been enriched. Whatever blinded him to its potential then has apparently blinded him since. Included in this selection instead are the poems after paintings by Manet, Monet, Matisse, Vuillard, and Van Gogh. These are artfully contrived, each poem with its different rhythm and method of attack (a set of instructions for a visit, a lyric effusion), and each utterly parasitical on its visual inspiration. Only the Manet achieves a dramatic Impressionism on its own terms. Elizabeth Bishop wrote two striking poems about paintings; but they were bad paintings, and as in so much of her work the observer became the subject of the thing observed. Snodgrass's observations are utterly impersonal. These suppressions of personality, and the search for adventitious inspiration from visual art or foreign poetry, shadow some philosophical argument with the self over the name and nature of poetry. In the grandiose projects of his maturity that argument was not won or lost: It turned into melodrama. (pp. 82-3)

[***The Führer Bunker*** (1977)] is still in progress, and though Snodgrass released a score of poems initially, and has added to them in two limited editions, fewer than half of the seventy composed have been published. The cycle is a series of dramatic monologues by most of the major Nazis and a flock of the minor ones, limited to the last month of Adolf Hitler's life, when he had entered the bunker in Berlin. Each character in this Götterdämmerung claims a different poetic form: Goebbels speaks in tetrameter couplets, Himmler in alphabetical acrostics written out on graph paper, Hitler in prosaic free verse. When Göring fattens on his own riddles, or Goebbels plays the leering poseur, the monologues swell with operatic viciousness:

> Stand back, make way, you mindless scum,
> Squire Voland the Seducer's come—
> Old Bock from Babelsberg whose tower
> Falls silent now, whose shrunken power
> For lies or lays comes hobbling home
> Into this concrete catacomb.
>
> Here's Runty Joe, the cunt collector
> Who grew to greatness, first erector
> Of myths and missions, fibs and fables,
> Who pulled the wool then turned the tables:
> He piped the tunes and called the dance
> Where shirtless countries lost their pants.

Half a dozen poems might have exhausted this absurdist strain of invention; half a dozen dozen creates a tyranny of them. The monologues neither humanize this gang of assassins nor offer insight into their particular derangements. It may be of service to know, or to imagine, that Hitler was a closet coprophage; but no poetic invention can make the truth more malign, or more comprehensible. The poems instead risk turning the Nazis into stand-up comedians, closer to pratfall than politics. Only the women's voices deserve their measure of pathetic sympathy, and in Magda Goebbels the poet has created a voice and a verse form that perhaps fulfill his intentions. . . .

The cycle is otherwise preposterous and interminable, vitiated by its crude psychology, fulsome irony, and irrelevant fiction. One doesn't expect bad men to be good poets.

The Führer Bunker makes one think kindly—I would have thought it impossible—of Hardy's attempt to versify the Napoleonic Wars. Poets resent having to repeat their successes, perhaps even resent having successes to repeat. I can spare no more charitable thought for a poet who has found a way—an ugly, dispiriting, ingenious way—of exhausting the complications of his talent on such crackpot material. It's like hearing that Bobby Fischer has spent the last decade in California flophouses poring over anti-Semitic religious tracts.

Snodgrass's other recent project, ***Kinder Capers,*** has been no less driven, or deranged: a cycle of poems related to, and frequently borrowing their titles from, the paintings of DeLoss McGraw. The paintings, if one produced on the jacket of ***Selected Poems*** is representative, are colorful and childlike, by Miró out of Mickey Mouse, and frequently portray the antics of a cartoonlike figure named W. D. The inter-referentiality of this *folie à deux* is obvious, and the poems encourage in Snodgrass an infantile strain that has rarely been allowed to surface (the most grating poem in ***Heart's Needle*** used the refrain, "Snodgrass is walking through the universe"). The poems range from nursery rhyme:

> My hat leaps up when I behold
> A rhino in the sky;
> When crocodiles upon the wing
> Perch on my windowsill to sing
> All my loose ends turn blue and cold;
> I don't know why.
> **("W. D., Don't Fear That Animal")**

to political satire:

> The Brutish are coming; the Brutish;
> The Rude-Coats with snares and bum-drumming!
> The Skittish and Prudish
> The Brattish and Crude
> Who'll check on your morals
> And find your songs lewd. . . .
> **("W. D. Tries to Warn Cock Robin")**

A vague narrative concerns **"The Death of Cock Robin,"** the title of the cycle's first section. The buffoonish figure of W. D. ("Hot on my track still, / But I tricked 'em; / Now who's your criminal; / Where's your victim? / *Dee-flee-a-beadle-tweedle free!*") oversees an anthology of clumsy effects and witless humor. If Snodgrass's Goebbels had written for children, he would have written these poems; but he would have called them lite verse.

Both ***Kinder Capers*** and ***The Führer Bunker*** retreat from the unendurable tensions of the early poems, as if those tensions could be avoided only by childish fantasy or deformed monologue, a hyperventilation of personality or a suppression of it. They are the dream poems of a fascist Disneyland. One of the strongest poets of the period has thus been reduced to writing in a manner poisonous to his talent. As Hazlitt said of Shelley, he has a maggot in his brain.

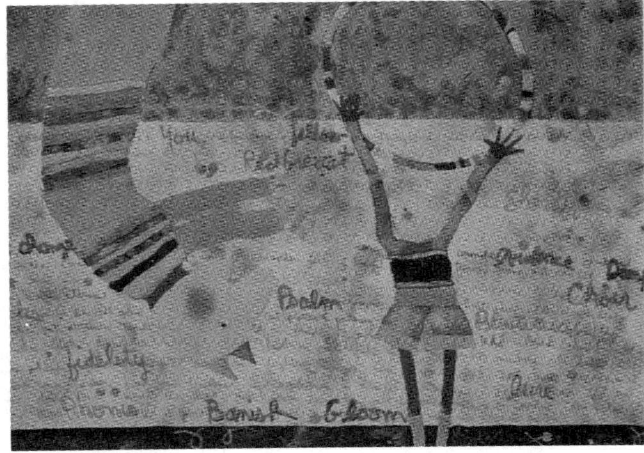

DeLoss McGraw's W.D. Creates a Device for Inverting Mr. Evil, *a companion in* The Death of Cock Robin.

Amid the confused welter of ***Kinder Capers*** lies one delicate lullaby, its subtlety at odds with the surroundings. Beyond these claustrophobic cycles, there have been a dozen or more poems in the old style, collected here from the two limited editions in which almost all of them appeared, ***If Birds Build with Your Hair*** (1979) and ***A Locked House*** (1986). Though the methods of warding off the pain of the early poems even affect some of these, half a dozen requite the old Roman restraint in the face of loss.

I'd known them, each one—weighed in hand,
  Rubbed, bargained, and then with my love,
Pinned each one on for her, to stand
  In fickle times for emblems of

What lasts—just as they must have once
  For someone long dead. Love that dies
Can still be wrung out for quick funds;
  No doubt someone would pay the price.

("Old Jewelry")

The graceless rhythms here and elsewhere betray a talent too long in disuse; but **"Cherry Saplings," "Owls," "An Elm Tree,"** and **"Coming Down from the Acropolis"** rank in their autumnal passion among the better, if not the best, of his work. On the other hand, **"D. D. Byrde Callyng Jennie Wrenn"** seems to have been composed in Middle English baby talk.

More sampler than selection, and not always well-sampled at that, ***Selected Poems*** distorts the achievement of a poet who has deserved his sublimity as well as his ridicule. I do not value—I cannot find the means of valuing—his recent work; but his early poetry is a distinctive and sometimes brilliant elaboration of a condition, the condition of introspection within suffering. (pp. 83-6)

William Logan, "Natural Selections," in Parnassus: Poetry in Review, *Vol. 16, No. 1, 1990, pp. 72-86.*

FURTHER READING

Boyers, Robert. "W. D. Snodgrass: An Interview." In *Contemporary Poetry in America: Essays and Interviews,* edited by Robert Boyers, pp. 174-88. New York: Schocken Books, 1974.

Examines Snodgrass's views on contemporary poetry.

Gaston, Paul L. *W. D. Snodgrass.* Boston: Twayne Publishers, 1978, 173 p.

Provides analyses of *Heart's Needle, Remains, After Experience,* and *The Führer Bunker.*

———. "W. D. Snodgrass and *The Führer Bunker:* An Interview." *Papers on Language and Literature* 13, No. 4 (Fall 1977): 401-12.

Examines origins, forms, and philosophy of *The Führer Bunker.*

Goldstein, Laurence. "*The Führer Bunker* and the New Discourse About Nazism." *The Southern Review* 24, No. 1 (Winter 1988): 100-14.

Classifies *The Führer Bunker* as an attempt to demythologize Nazi leaders of World War II.

Howard, Richard. "W. D. Snodgrass: 'There's Something Beats the Same in Opposed Hearts.' " In his *Alone with America: The Art of Poetry in the United States Since 1950.* pp. 471-84. London: Thames and Hudson, 1970.

Asserts that Snodgrass's early poetry collections describe a universe "divided against itself."

Phillips, Robert. "W. D. Snodgrass and the Sad Hospital of the World." In his *The Confessional Poets,* pp. 45-72. Carbondale: Southern Illinois University Press, 1973.

Examines how the sincerity of Snodgrass's work stems from an "urgency [that] touches the urgency of the readers."

Raisor, Philip. "Framing Portraits: An Interview with W. D. Snodgrass." *The Southern Review* 26, No. 1 (January 1990): 65-80.

Discusses "the role and importance of form in [Snodgrass's] work, and . . . the kind of art to which he is faithful."

Snodgrass, W. D. "After-Images: Autobiographical Sketches." *Salmagundi,* No. 78-79 (Spring/Summer 1988): 176-204.

Humorous account of the influences Snodgrass's parents, grandparents, and the Pulitzer Prize had on his work.

Spires, Elizabeth. "W. D. Snodgrass: An Interview," *The American Poetry Review* 19, No. 4 (July/August 1990): 38-46.

Interview providing a comprehensive overview of Snodgrass's career.

Philippe Soupault

1897-1990

French poet, novelist, critic, playwright, and journalist.

Soupault, along with André Breton, Louis Aragon, and Paul Eluard, is credited as one of the founders of Surrealism, a highly influential literary and artistic movement dedicated to examining the irrational, paranormal, and subconscious aspects of the human mind. Soupault and Breton coauthored *Les champs magnétiques* (*The Magnetic Fields*), a poetic discourse that is widely considered the first major Surrealist text. Although Soupault wrote several volumes of verse, as well as novels, criticism, and autobiographical writings, few of his works have been translated into English, and his role in French literature has often been ignored by critics. Throughout his career, Soupault rejected social and political systems that attempted to restrain individual freedom. In his fiction, he often exposed the hypocrisy and insensitivity of the middle and upper classes, and later championed authors who, like himself, opposed personal and creative oppression. Soupault was awarded the Grand Prix de Poésie of the Academie française in 1972 and the Grand Prix National des Lettres in 1977.

Soupault was raised in a bourgeois family in Chaville, France, and served in the French artillery during World War I. Following his military service he sought out the friendship and tutelage of the poet Guillaume Apollinaire, who influenced much of his later work. Soupault commented: "Many of the young prewar writers had been killed, and among the survivors Guillaume Apollinaire seemed to me to be the only poet who refused to conform and wished to explore a new world." In 1917, at one of Apollinaire's regular Tuesday gatherings at the Café de Flore in Paris, Soupault met Breton, a medical student at the time, with whom he would establish the Surrealist movement. The two writers shared an interest in the poets Arthur Rimbaud and Comte de Lautréamont, and were intrigued by the Dada movement headed by Tristan Tzara and others in Zurich. Although Soupault contributed to a Dada anthology, he soon rejected the movement's nihilistic tenets in favor of more positive explorations that might lead to a "superior reality."

In 1919, along with Breton and Aragon, Soupault founded *Littérature,* the journal which became the first voice of Surrealism. The same year Soupault and Breton coauthored *The Magnetic Fields,* serializing the work in *Littérature* before publishing it in book form the following year. Soupault commented on the volume, which has alternately been labeled poetry, a novel, and a play: "In the course of our researches we established that the mind, liberated from all critical pressures and academic habits, offered not logical propositions but images, and that if we accepted what the psychiatrist Pierre Janet had called 'automatic writing' we could obtain texts which would describe a hitherto unexplored universe. Breton and I therefore decided to spend a fortnight writing a work in collaboration which we would publish without correcting or erasing anything. . . . From [*The Magnetic Fields*] was born what we at first prudently called a method, and which we then baptised Surrealism." *The Magnetic Fields* was followed by two plays, *S'il vous plaît* (*If You Please*) and *Vous m'oublierez,* also cowritten by Soupault and Breton. Both plays utilize nonsequential dialogue and disregard dramatic conventions. Although these volumes are regarded as influential in establishing surrealist methods, later critics often note that the works appear traditional when compared to subsequent surrealist texts. While Breton insisted that he expelled Soupault from the surrealist group in 1926 for being mercenary, Soupault contended that he left of his own accord due to his disapproval of the group's political views and increasing dogmatism. According to Herbert S. Gershman, Soupault left because "literature in the traditional sense was his (as it was Apollinaire's) primary goal, his career." Soupault then traveled extensively throughout Europe, the United States, and the Soviet Union, and concentrated his literary activities on prose, criticism, and political analysis.

Initially a dedicated member of the tightly knit Surrealist

group, Soupault displayed in his poetry stronger similarities to his predecessors Apollinaire, Arthur Rimbaud, Pierre Reverdy, and Lautréamont than to his fellow Surrealists. In the long, confessional poem *Westwego,* for example, Soupault emphasized sustained atmosphere and conscious personal exploration in favor of abandonment to the subconscious. Thus, his structured poetic language, as evidenced in *Westwego* and his next volume, *Georgia,* does not resemble the experimental verse of his contemporaries. J. H. Matthews observed: "[Upon] the surface, the poems of *Georgia* present a paradox: one of the initiators of the revolutionary poetic method from which surrealism took its point of departure appears, in his later writing, lacking in boldness in comparison with those who had joined surrealism meanwhile." Aragon also found fault with this volume, published shortly after Soupault left the group. In a well-known commentary published in 1926 in the magazine *La révolution surréaliste,* he stated: "There is no one who believes in the power of words as much as I do. And [*Georgia*] is a book that made me think how weak words can be. . . . Is it the poems, or was it the heaviness in the air? I suddenly believed that I could touch the weakness of words. This book is like the signs that precede a storm. When every blade of grass has become aware of the sky." Verse from throughout Soupault's career is included in *Poèmes et poésies, 1917-1973.* Often deviating from the introspection of *Georgia* and *Westwego,* his later pieces are considered more concrete and less self-centered than his earlier poetry.

Soupault's novels display his rejection of restrictive systems; for example, *Les frères Durandeau,* which was a runner-up for the Prix Goncourt, paints a negative picture of French bourgeois lifestyles. Many of Soupault's contemporary critics have noted that these novels reflected the directionlessness of youth of the post-World War I era. Henry-Jacques Dupuy summarized Soupault's fiction: "Philippe Soupault's novels? Spacious works of prose, each of which is less a narrative than a lyrical sequence through which wide-eyed creatures pass, social misfits without any apparent depth who pretend to act and then slip away feverishly toward a strange nowhere. The last chapter does not, strictly speaking, lead to a conclusion. Like life." In *Les dernières nuits de Paris* (*Last Nights of Paris*), Soupault's only novel to be translated into English, a disorganized group of characters ruminate on crimes in Paris, and the narrator, who may be Soupault himself, casually observes murders in the city by night. A. Flores elaborated: "In *Last Nights of Paris* a world palpitates—an autonomous and singular world, as impossible to summarize as the 'story' of our own cosmos. Only that Soupault's is more beautiful than ours because it is so dehumanized, so triumphantly absurd."

In 1938, Soupault established and became director of press and radio services in Tunis, the capital of the French protectorate of Tunisia, but was dismissed in 1940 by the Vichy government and given a six-month prison sentence in 1942 for his anti-Nazi views. His experiences in the Tunis prison inform his memoir, *Le temps des assassins, histoire du détenu no. 1234* (*Age of Assassins; The Story of Prisoner No. 1234*). Following forty-five days of solitary confinement, Soupault circulated amongst his fellow prisoners, hearing their recollections of dreams and observing the intense feeling of comaraderie that developed between inmates. According to Henry-Jacques Dupuy: "With a modesty that does him credit, Soupault did not wish to have the book published in France when he returned, feeling that his six months in prison were almost nothing compared to the boundless martyrdom of thousands of men in Nazi concentration camps." Although some critics similarly dismissed *Age of Assassins* as trivial when compared to other war memoirs, many praised Soupault for his honest account of prison experiences.

(See also *Contemporary Authors,* Vols. 116, 131 [obituary].)

PRINCIPAL WORKS

POETRY

Aquarium 1917
**Les champs magnétiques* [with André Breton] 1920
[*The Magnetic Fields,* 1985]
Rose des vents 1920
Westwego 1922
Georgia 1926
Poésies complètes: 1917-1937 1937
Ode à Londres bombardée 1944
[*Ode to Bombed London,* 1944]
Chansons 1949
Poèmes et poésies: 1917-1973 1973
I'm Lying: Selected Translations of Philippe Soupault 1985

NOVELS

Le bon apôtre 1923
Les frères Durandeau 1924
En jouel 1925
Le grand homme 1925
Le nègre 1927
Les dernières nuits de Paris 1928
[*Last Nights of Paris,* 1929]
Les moribonds 1934

OTHER

S'il vous plaît (play) 1920
[*If You Please,* published in *Modern French Plays,* 1964]
Vous m'oublierez 1920
William Blake (criticism) 1928
[*William Blake,* 1928]
Souvenirs de James Joyce (memoir) 1943
Le temps des assassins, histoire du détenu no. 1234 (memoirs) 1945
[*Age of Assassins; The Story of Prisoner No. 1234,* 1946)
Essai sur la poésie (essays) 1950
Vingt mille et un jours: Entretiens avec Serge Fauchereau (interviews) 1980

*This work was originally published in the magazine *Littérature* in 1919.

Virgilia Peterson

Philippe Soupault, a veteran of the first world war and a member, for a time, of Aragon's nucleus of Surréalistes writers in France, was arrested in 1942 in Tunis by the Vichy police because of his anti-Nazi activities. [***Age of Assassins***] is his personal record of the half year he spent in jail.

In the preface, M. Soupault declares that too little has been written by prisoners about the peculiar experience of being behind bars and that most of the accounts have gone unheeded by the rest of the world. This indifference, he maintains, is partly because much of the writing has been done by amateurs striving for literary effect, "under the false impression that all writing must be eloquent, picturesque, tragic, moving." Implying that neither eloquence nor emotion is essential to a description of suffering, he goes on to say that "in order not to 'make literature,' it is important to know what literature is and to despise it as only an honest writer can."

Theoretically, perhaps, sincerity of purpose should suffice; fidelity to the truth should, in itself, rouse the readers' imagination. Yet an obviously literary piece of work such as Oscar Wilde's *De Profundis,* while its sincerity has sometimes been questioned, still lives, along with the books by the highly articulate prisoners Verlaine and Dostoievski, as a classic of this kind of experience. Even the contemporary accounts of imprisonment by Arthur Koestler and Hans Habe, to name outstanding examples, though a certain amount of artifice has gone into their dramatization, make a sharper impact upon those of us who have never been in prison than M. Soupault's unquestionably honest but rambling report.

More moving than the actual contents of the book is his motive for having written it. Filled, as he had been since the armistice of 1940, with contempt for the meanness, mediocrity and utter cowardice engendered in many of his countrymen by the Vichy regime, Soupault, still looking for men who loved liberty more than life, found them where no liberty existed save in the mind: he found them in prison. For these men, his companions in the north cell block of the Tunis prison, for these outcasts from a weasel-hearted society, more than for his own sake, M. Soupault set down his prison experience.

During his six months as prisoner No. 1234 in the Vichy-controlled jail, neither the author nor his fellow inmates underwent the kind of torture familiar to victims of the Gestapo, nor did the magistrate, the warden, or the guards exhibit more sadism than is common to many such officials wherever they have human lives at their mercy. The record deals, therefore, not with extraordinary suffering, but with the ordinary lot of incarcerated men: the high, barred window, the locked door, the watery food, the heat, the cramped space, the lack of exercise, the sleepless nights, the exacerbation of nerves, the routine humiliations, and above all the intolerable sameness which is enough to kill the soul. These are the hooks on which M. Soupault hangs his psychological observations. These are the miseries which, piled one upon another, drove the men around him to groan aloud and sometimes to go mad. Because such living was almost more than they could endure, they became, as he explains, profoundly suspicious of every one, ready to burst into violence, haunted by rumor and fear, and each one sought in desperation, in the self-conjured, wild improbability of his dreams, to escape from fact.

In the block of cells where M. Soupault was imprisoned there were not only men serving time for theft or murder, but also political prisoners like himself, called "dissidents," because they had refused or were said to have refused to collaborate with Pétain's "National Revolution." Some were awaiting trial for treason, some had been sentenced for life, a few had been condemned to die. Together, they were considered the most dangerous group in the prison.

M. Soupault, older than the others and the only "intellectual" among them, received more food and cigarettes from the outside, more visits from his wife, more attention from his lawyer, and, especially precious to him, plenty of books of his own choosing. Thus he was somewhat set apart. Yet he managed to make friends with most of the prisoners in his group—even with such alien men as Curly, the convict from an African battalion who had paid a price for becoming a "tough guy," and Amor, the gazelle-eyed Arab youth whose reprieved sentence was worse than death. But most of all, M. Soupault learned what it means to forge friends in common misery and to draw from such friendship his needed strength.

Age of Assassins, another testimonial to human suffering, lacks neither dignity nor conviction, but it is a repetitious, formless book. Had M. Soupault been willing to employ the skill of the artist in setting down his tale it might have become an abiding record and commanded a hearing for prisoners throughout the world.

Virgilia Peterson, "A Weasel-Hearted Vichy," in New York Herald Tribune Weekly Book Review, *April 28, 1946, p. 10.*

W. McNeil Lowry

One of the bitterest legacies of war is the host of men and women who have spent months or years as prisoners, those millions who are struggling now beneath the burdens which confinement has levied upon mind, body and spirit.

One of these, the French poet, novelist and journalist, Philippe Soupault, has chosen to report upon his six months as a political prisoner in Tunis at the hands of the government of Vichy and, by so doing, "to awaken some interest in the state of mind of returned prisoners." ***Age of Assassins*** is not the only book M. Soupault could have written from his experience. He could, in his words, have "made literature" of it; instead he has elected to follow the advice of Charles Péguy: "Tell the truth, the whole truth, nothing but the truth. Tell the stupid truth stupidly, the dull truth dully, the sad truth sadly."

Inevitably, M. Soupault puts Péguy's maxim to a severe test. At first he deals chronologically with his own gradual assumption of the consciousness and the habits of a prisoner. Since there is here a unity of impression and a continuity of action, even though psychological in character, M. Soupault "makes literature" at what would seem to be no cost to "telling the truth." Later, however, when generalizing about the prisoner's typical being, through his observations of his cellmates, he does present some "dull truth dully."

The total effect of ***Age of Assassins*** is yet far from dull. After all, M. Soupault is a writer, and when the matter that lends itself to good writing comes to hand he makes excellent use of it. Perhaps the best is in his treatment of the psychological and moral influences of prison life. He reveals to us, for example, the mental workings, the psychological preparation for death, of men who believe they have been chosen as hostages. He tells us of the art of dreams which the imprisoned man must cultivate. And through the days spent in listening to the dreams retailed by his cellmates, he thinks he discovers richer visions possessed by innocent or ignorant men. "The nature, form, color and development of the dreams almost never correspond with the character of the dreamer."

In its account of the moral influences of prison life, ***Age of Assassins*** strikes a positive note of hope and of direction in the lives of those millions of men and women who have emerged from behind the bars. "We were learning," M. Soupault says, "the value of anger, hope, indignation. Our prison was more than a shelter against the rising flood of corruption, against the storm of claptrap, the typhoon of cowardice beyond the walls: it was a school for wrath and rebellion." Without the feeling of solidarity with one's fellows which prison life also developed, the lessons of revolt might only have added to the individual prisoner's burdens. Taken together, the two attitudes made for strength. "I had learned that the only way to survive is not to take things lying down, . . . that rebellion is never futile."

Age of Assassins has grown out of Philippe Soupault's consciousness of what freedom-loving men and women have suffered and learned at the hands of other men. He cannot forget, and he wants us to remember.

W. McNeil Lowry, "Moral Influences of Prison Life," in The New York Times, *April 28, 1946, p. 26.*

Arthur M. Schlesinger, Jr.

The twentieth century has done more than its share to sustain [the flow of prison literature] by putting writers behind bars (though modern penal methods have managed to choke off many witnesses before release). Philippe Soupault's ***Age of Assassins*** is a minor but thoughtful addition to the contemporary literature of incarceration.

Soupault, French poet and novelist, active in the early days of the surrealist movement, was one of the writers drawn into government work in the thirties. From 1938 on he was director of press and radio services in Tunis. Vichy took over in North Africa after the 1940 armistice; and, when Britain survived the summer and the Free French began to gather behind Charles de Gaulle, small centers of resistance sprang up spontaneously all over Tunisia. The Vichy police set out to break up these centers. Soupault's name was on an early list of suspects because of his well-known contempt for Pétain and for Hitler, and on March 12, 1942 the order was given to arrest him.

Age of Assassins is a story of prison, not of resistance. Soupault was picked up, given preliminary questioning, and then thrown into the Tunis military prison. He was confined to the north cell block, among the "dissidents"—political prisoners—and spent forty-five days in solitary. Then he was allowed to mingle with the other prisoners. He heard their stories, probed into their inner lives, observed the healing work of comradeship and the simple, passionate desire for freedom. After six months he was released, and two months later the Allies landed in North Africa.

As a writer, an older man (he was forty-five), the only prisoner to wear a necktie, Soupault occupied a special place among the inmates. They confided much in him, and he is particularly interesting in describing the mechanisms of psychological adjustment to prison life, especially the compulsive dreaming.

> The life within prison walls, the lack of exercise, and the insistence on silence, all encourage men to dream. . . . Dreams were not only an escape—they were life on a larger plane, more free even than life outside of the prison. None of them struggled against it; they all abandoned themselves voluptuously to the current that led to the unknown.

Perhaps too these explorations into the shadows were given "not as a means of escape, nor even to give us a sense of freedom, but rather to allow us every night to take our own form of revenge."

As more political prisoners came into the cell block, as favorable war news filtered through, as Vichy's demoralization became more unmistakable, the prisoners were brought together in solidarity against the rotten regime which had taken away their liberty. "Prison compelled us to know each other better, comradeship forced each man to develop his most genuine qualities, loyalty and natural generosity." Outside the prison men were being turned into slaves, and the prisoners felt closer to freedom than those who had been bribed or frightened into submission. Far from breaking the will to resist, imprisonment solidified it, gave life and freedom new meanings.

It is obvious that Soupault's experience was by current standards mild. Even in solitary he could call for what books he liked; the regimen of the prison was not intolerable, the food was apparently edible, physical torture was practically non-existent; and the prison staff, infected by the corruption and panic of Vichy, sought increasingly to insure itself against Allied victory by playing up to the prisoners. However unpleasant for a sensitive person, the material conditions did not conspire against the foundations of moral existence. You had none of the agonizing horrors of Buchenwald and Dachau, where Nazi diabolism triumphed in creating an atmosphere of degradation which made martyrdom meaningless and set prisoners fighting each other for the privilege of maintaining internal discipline on behalf of the SS. You did not even have conditions as grim as those in the camps run by the French for anti-Nazi refugees.

That is why I would call ***Age of Assassins*** a minor addition to prison literature. Its theme is disgust rather than terror. But, as Soupault writes, "an experience of half a year in jail seems short, especially to those who have never been in jail." One advantage of the short term is that sensations are not dulled; and Soupault's record has the precision and immediacy of one who never became fully accustomed to the life. "I never stopped being surprised during the whole period of my detention. I could not then, and I cannot even yet, accept or resign myself to it."

His book is an honest and sensitive account which, if neither very powerful nor very profound, yet supplies sympathetic insights into a predicament which the war against the Axis has not solved. In an age in which the dominant question is getting to be whether you believe in the police state or not, we should all know at least what we are being asked to accept.

Arthur M. Schlesinger, Jr., "Prisoner with a Necktie," in The Saturday Review of Literature, *Vol. 29, No. 18, May 4, 1946, p. 13.*

J. H. Matthews

Whenever ***Les Champs magnétiques*** is mentioned as the first specifically surrealist text, serialized in the magazine *Littérature* in 1919 before separate publication the following year, the name of Philippe Soupault is mentioned also, [along with that of André Breton], as its co-author. As a result, Soupault is one of the surrealists best known to the general public. He has a place reserved in the history of surrealism even though his participation in the activities of the Paris group was of comparatively short duration, ending in 1927. Ironically, he is remembered when other writers, faithful to surrealist principles for longer than he, are forgotten. And he is remembered as having written, with Breton, a book cited by many but read by few. Meanwhile, his other surrealist publications have not been subjected to scrutiny. This is not only an injustice to Soupault but to surrealism as well, since, before parting company with Breton's followers, Philippe Soupault published poems which no one wishing to acquaint himself with the first poetic trends of surrealism can afford to ignore. [In a footnote, Matthews adds that the "early poems of Soupault were reprinted in his ***Poésies complètes: 1917-1937.*** Thirty years later, they were still in print, readily available at a price which suggests that Soupault has been forgotten even by the bibliophiles."] (p. 17)

Of those whom history will record as surrealists Soupault was the first to show publicly how much he owed [Guillaume] Apollinaire. His book of verse, ***Aquarium,*** provided the most conclusive proof of indebtedness literature can offer—imitation. . . . [This volume] deserves mention as evidence of how soon the young poet fell under Apollinaire's spell. Soupault's next collection of poems, ***Rose des vents,*** appeared in 1920. By that time Dada had found in him an active defender. In spite of this, as though to emphasize that the aesthetic focus of his poetry continued to be the same as in ***Aquarium,*** Soupault dedicated to Apollinaire the first poem of ***Rose des vents,*** **"Souffrance."** Only in verses celebrating faraway places can some technical and emotional evolution be noticed. These are poems expressing the young poet's wanderlust while at the same time betraying a sharpened sense of nostalgia. The finest of them **"La grande mélancolie d'une avenue,"** is dedicated to Giorgio de Chirico, the painter who so magnificently found inspiration in the anguish of waiting and departure. Even in this poem, Soupault looks to the author of *Calligrammes* for guidance in matters of form, and gives little sign of the iconoclasm of Dada, despite his association with Tristan Tzara whose arrival in Paris in 1920 marked the beginning of organized Dada activities in France.

Soupault's next publication was the long poem ***Westwego,*** written during the period spanning the years 1917-1922. Like ***Rose des vents, Westwego*** supplies no clue suggesting that Dada exerted as great an influence upon its composition as did Apollinaire. No one who has read it can question its author's acquaintance with Apollinaire's "L'Emigrant de Landor Road." Nor can he doubt that ***Westwego*** has its place in the tradition of the confessional poem, whose survival into the twentieth century was guaranteed in French poetry by Apollinaire's mastery of the form.

Westwego has a resonance, markedly Apollinairian, which is revealed more in the music and tone of the poem than in the sentiments it expresses:

> All the cities in the world
> oases of our boredom dead of hunger
> offer fresh drink
> to the memoirs of solitary men of cranks
> and of sedentary people

Nothing here reminds us that its author shared in writing ***Les champs magnétiques.*** Nothing shows, either, that ***Westwego*** was composed during the years when surrealist ideas were beginning to take form around the theme of automatism. Instead, we see a poem characterized by a remarkable unity of tone. We are dealing, in fact, with a poet less interested in abandoning himself to the meandering flow of uncensored thought than in emulating Apollinaire's skill at creating and sustaining a mood, by means which can hardly be said to exclude conscious control.

Linguistically, ***Westwego*** presents no striking innovatory features. The same is true of ***Georgia.*** Appearing after Breton's manifesto, in 1926, ***Georgia*** was published at a time when Soupault was actively engaged in the surrealist venture. Nevertheless, one would search its pages without success for evidence of verbal experimentation like that of Desnos, Leiris, or Vitrac. It is positively timid by the side of the poems Aragon was writing during the same period. Hence, upon the surface, the poems of ***Georgia*** present a paradox: one of the initiators of the revolutionary poetic method from which surrealism took its point of departure appears, in his later writing, lacking in boldness in comparison with those who had joined surrealism meanwhile.

Looking only at the language of his poems, we might be tempted to wonder whether Soupault's reputation within the surrealist group was not fated to decline. A glance at Aragon's review of ***Georgia*** in the seventh issue of *La Rév-*

olution surréaliste reassures us and suffices to show that it would be a major error to conclude that this could be so. Although Aragon did not have occasion to praise it for formal inventiveness, he called ***Georgia,*** "This book that is like the premonitory signs of a storm." Examination of the poems it brings together leads to the conclusion that ***Georgia*** merits a place among the revolutionary works inspired by surrealist principles above all because, in fulfilling the promise of ***Westwego,*** it reveals a poet successfully dedicated to the presentation of the *moderne.*

A notable feature of ***Westwego*** is the manner in which Soupault's mood induces sensitivity to aspects of the world about him to which he attributes private significance. Here, especially, encouragement comes from Apollinaire, as the young poet writes:

> I was walking about in London one summer
> my feet burning my heart in my eyes
> near the black walls near the red walls
> near the big docks
> where the giant policemen
> are dotted like question marks

In likening policemen to question marks, Soupault comes particularly close to the fancy of Apollinaire who, in "Zone," referred to the Eiffel Tower as a shepherdess watching over her sheep, the bridges of the Seine. As is the case with Aragon crying, "Oh top hats! For a whole week you had, for me, the black appearance of a question mark," Soupault's responsiveness to external reality—"le cœur dans les yeux"—is governed and controlled by emotion. The consequence is the projection of feeling upon the outside world in a way which makes even dock police reflect the poet's interrogatory glance.

The free play of emotional forces bears witness in ***Westwego*** to the influence of the Apollinairian maxim "J'émerveille." Soupault's encounter with the surrealist marvelous is effected by the poetic experience of viewing the urban landscape through the filter of feeling. In a foreign city, London, his sense of estrangement—real or imaginary, it makes no difference—provides elements poetically developed by the combination of nostalgia for Paris with hypersensitivity to an unfamiliar environment. The effect is to impose upon successive, mainly visual, impressions of reality a tonality largely emotive in character. This makes references to the sense of mystery typical of popular film serials (especially the series devoted to Nick Carter "et son chapeau melon"), no more out of place in ***Westwego*** than is the motif of the derby hat in the painting of Magritte:

> I have only my hat
> key to the fields key to dreams
> father of memories
> have I ever left Paris
> but tonight I am in that city
> behind each tree on the avenues
> a memory lies in wait for me as I pass by

Here the hat is explicitly identified with escape from constraining reality (*La Clé des Champs,* significantly, is the title of the volume of essays Breton published in 1953) and with the mystery of poetic experience. The same mystery provides a leitmotif throughout ***Westwego.*** It owes its presence in the poem to a quality of vision which earned Soupault the respect of his fellow surrealists, one of whom, Jacques-André Boiffard, called him in the fourth number of *La Révolution surréaliste* an "elf with breath of opium."

Expression of this quality antedated ***Westwego.*** It is possible to see in ***Rose des vents*** that, under the influence of Apollinaire, Soupault's sensitivity to the world about him is heightened by promptings from within. In **"Antipodes"** he writes, "The breath of a thought makes the illuminated world map revolve," and declares "To abandon one's claim / A desire sweeps away dead thoughts." Thoughts left behind by the past are swept away by desire anticipating the future, as Soupault observes in **"Haines,"** "Against the wall hopes creep." He concludes in **"Marche":**

> On the way back everything is changed
> I have broken my immobile ideas
> My stained memories I have sold

When the poet talks of change, of breaking immobile ideas, and of selling his stained memories, he quite definitely, if without ostentation, gives precedence to his desires. Throughout ***Rose des vents*** he grants them victory over the material universe supplying their background as, in a poem dedicated to Tristan Tzara, he writes beneath the title **"Horizon":**

> The whole city has come into my room
> the trees disappear
> and the evening clings to my fingers
> The houses become deckchairs
> the sound of the sea has risen to me

A feeling of freedom, associated emotionally with the sea and with a sea voyage, is achieved without evasion by the imaginative transformation of the urban milieu, obliged here to submit to the poet's longing, powerful enough to transform houses into deckchairs for the enjoyment of his voyage.

After ***Rose des vents, Westwego*** adds its testimony to Soupault's ability to escape the restrictions of the material world without dismissing it entirely from sight. Here is an aspect of surrealist modernity no one has presented more successfully than he. His power to subject reality to modulation in accord with his inner needs is amply demonstrated in a remarkable passage:

> the sun rise like a flower
> they call I think dandelion
> the great mechanical vegetations
> which were waiting only to be encouraged
> climb and make their way
> faithfully
> one no longer knows whether to compare them
> to ivy
> or to grasshoppers

As great mechanical vegetations present themselves, encouraged by the poet's sensibility, the reasoning mind would expect to have no difficulty in selecting from two such widely differing alternatives as ivy and grasshoppers the image more appropriate to completing the comparison. Soupault's incapacity to do so may be taken as a sign of his commitment to a view of the real in which familiar scales of value no longer have meaning, and reason has no role to play. He explains his attitude in the first issue of *La Révolution surréaliste* (December, 1924): "Life is a dream, they say. I have no proof of what they claim. I am content with these revelations which are, to say the least, sensational, and remain absolutely public."

His emphasis upon the public nature of poetic revelation helps situate Soupault in relation to surrealist aspirations, since in the poem **"Say it with Music"** in ***Georgia*** he writes:

On each floor is it a friend waiting for me
is it a thief
is it me

Soupault's fascination with the double, revealed in these lines, is the expression of the sense of the mysterious haunting him during his years as a surrealist. Breton has reported an act of his which may be regarded as indicative of Soupault's involvement in something quite different from romantic posturing. In the first surrealist manifesto we learn that Soupault would knock on doors at random to ask if Philippe Soupault was at home. Breton assures us that his friend would not have been surprised at an affirmative answer. Meanwhile Soupault himself has commented, "I wanted to bring a little poetry into my life." The conclusion of his poem **"Say it with Music"** is apposite:

but my red blood my dear red blood
courses through my veins
sweeping before it the memories of the present
but my thirst is too great
I stop once more and I wait for
the light
Paradise paradise paradise

A statement like the last, with its reference to sweeping away memories of the present and to the poet's passionate need for light, raises this question: Is the surrealist paradise attainable? According to many detractors of surrealism this question uncovers the principal stumbling block of surrealist theory. They forget they do not formulate the problems of poetic destiny in the same way as the surrealists when they claim to have discovered, here, a fundamental weakness in surrealist reasoning. A surrealist does not need to have assurances of the successful attainment of his goals before he can regard his ambitions as well-founded. All surrealist poets need in order to have a poetic vocation sufficient to guide their efforts is the conviction that, whether promised ultimate success or not, their aspirations are leading to a view of existence other than the one to which we would have to resign ourselves in their absence. Soupault shared in this conviction. It colors his poems. Thus he talks in **"Autre Fois"** of a non-existent fire, present nonetheless:

all that does not exist
and which is there
once again
then once more

Soupault presents us with the example of **"Le Pirate"**—"He roams the seas in search of the invisible axis of the world"—shown to be dedicated to a cause no less compelling in its attraction because it is without precise definition: "But his eyes gaze at another star / lost in the crowd." No one can comprehend the scope of the surrealist venture without being responsive to the excitement that is in ***Georgia,*** impelling Soupault further and further toward the unattainable goal which gives significance to surrealist poetry. Modestly entitled **"Stumbling,"** one poem in particular catches the poet's mood of exultation, as it asserts faith in the need to push onward beyond the bounds of the so-called real:

Tomorrow is a city
more beautiful more red than the others
in which departure is arrival
and rest a tomb
The line of the horizon
shines
like a bar of steel
like a thread that we must cut
so as not to rest
ever

Associating departure with arrival and likening rest to death, drawn onward by the shining horizon, Soupault gives voice to his excitement as he affirms, in this poem, "There exists only my heart / and all awaits me." He realizes the privilege that is his when he feels "in his heart / desire that is a bell." As is shown in **"Larmes de soleil,"** the heart assumes power to govern the whole universe and brings the poet in contact with other men:

Everything sleeps and everything awakes
my heart becomes an ocean
my arms hang down
and my hands reach out
to catch hold of other hands

Now his vision takes a form similar to the one we shall find Eluard adopting, as Soupault writes in **"Comrade":**

I read in the stars my friends' goodwill
in a river I love a hand
I listen to the flowers sing
There is the farewell of birds
A cry falls like a fruit

and at the end of **"Médaille d'or":**

The sky will fall on our heads
We await the wind
which today is to be blue
like a flag

As flowers sing, cries fall like fruit and the wind, not the sky, is blue like a flag, nature is transformed, assuming unwonted aspect and shades; and not just because Soupault sees himself changed. In **"Le nageur"** he explains clearly enough when he announces, "in the eyes of mirrors and in the laughter of the wind / I recognize a stranger who is me." So we find in his later surrealist texts a noteworthy evolution in the confessional poem. Here the impulse to imitate Apollinaire gives way to the need to explore the self in relation to the real and to the surreal. Soupault makes plain what he wishes to accomplish, in **"Comrade":**

It is not enough to speak of sun
of stars
of sea and of rivers
of blood eyes hands
It is necessary very often

to speak of other things

As it becomes necessary to speak of other things than nature puts before our eyes, popular images of mysterious power—one thinks especially of Fantômas and Nick Carter—take on a new dimension of significance, thanks to surrealist aspirations. Projecting himself into the world surrounding him, in **"Le nageur"** the poet universalizes his message of regenerative change:

I stop to know again if the summer is red
in my veins
and my shadow revolves about me
in the direction of the hands of a watch

Deeply sensitive to the mystery around us, making each man's shadow revolve clockwise about him, Soupault expressed in his surrealist verse a need to know more than our eyes can see and confidence that it is not beyond our capabilities to do so. Precisely because this is so, Aragon could be accused of making neither a mistake nor a concession when he saluted in ***Georgia*** the forewarnings of a storm, presented in the form of poetic prophecy.

"Dernières cartouches," with its prediction of revolutionary force for arms, is hardly characteristic. Much more representative of Soupault's approach to man and to society and a more permanent, more original contribution to surrealism in poetry are texts in which, without display of violence, he quietly affirms belief in the presence of another world that the universe around us cannot be expected to hide indefinitely. The poem **"Larmes de soleil,"** for example, is representative of Soupault's legacy to surrealism. It permits us to see how serious was the surrealists' loss when mistrust for political involvement and fear of the consequences of too restrictive a codification of surrealist aims led Soupault to sever his connections with Breton:

I close my eyes simply
the better to see
my country
my kingdom
There is no longer anything around me
my country of sleep
which I discover feeling my way

Those who infer that, because Soupault speaks of closing his eyes simply to see his own kingdom better, his message to his fellow surrealists was one of evasion, and who thus would fail to recognize the most significant aspect of Apollinaire's influence upon him, are advised to examine the poem with which ***Georgia*** comes to a close. Called **"Cruz Alta,"** it ends with this positive assertion, proving conclusively Soupault's right to be remembered among the poets of surrealism:

All is ready
a man
a cross
it is the Night answering
Land land
another hour
we hear breathing
another hour
it is day
it is sunlight
Land land
We are coming ashore

(pp. 19-30)

At the Centrale Surréaliste in 1924. Soupault is third from the right; Breton is fourth from the left.

[The] message expressed elliptically in these lines is the message surrealist poetry is meant to communicate. (p. 30)

J. H. Matthews, "Philippe Soupault (1897-)," in his Surrealist Poetry in France, *Syracuse University Press, 1969, pp. 17-30.*

The Times Literary Supplement

This collected edition of Philippe Soupault's poetry [***Poèmes et poésies (1917-1973)***], which brings the ***Poésies complètes*** of 1937 up to date by doubling it in size and including all his further work in verse up to and including the unpublished ***Crépuscules*** (1960-71), is very welcome.

Soupault is famous above all as a founding apostle of André Breton's Surrealist True Church, and for his collaboration with Breton on ***Les champs magnétiques,*** usually regarded as the first major Surrealist text. Though he speedily fell from apostolate to excommunication, and left the movement for ever in 1927, it is as a Surrealist that he is mainly thought of. It is true that for a long time his style hardly varied from those early days, when Breton praised him for his modernism. It is also true that as a poet he is much overshadowed by Éluard. But this new collected edition is an appropriate moment to wonder if a reassessment is not due.

Soupault's early collections are frankly imitative: the voices of two far greater poets, Apollinaire and Pierre Reverdy, are unmistakable, not merely because of the subject matter but also because of the manner. His other most characteristic vein is a childlike, humorous fantasy, but this appears only rarely. There is a poem dedicated to himself (as befits a man who went around knocking on strange doors asking if Philippe Soupault lived there), but little else, if one excludes the delicate ***Chansons*** (1921-37).

By the mid-1920s Soupault has managed to assimilate the influence of Apollinaire and Reverdy into a plaintive and delicate melody of his own. This remains his characteristic voice up to the Second World War, when the effort to write Resistance verse sometimes forces his gentle accents to assume a stridency quite foreign to them.

His best moments as a poet come perhaps after the War, when the fantasy of the nursery rhyme combines with black humour and wistful melancholy to produce an amalgam not unlike that of Jean Tardieu. . . .

This [type of poem] dates from the early 1950s. But Soupault is, at all periods, quite without emotional obscurity; he is a tender and melancholy, but always imaginative and rewarding poet.

"Puffs of Cloud," in The Times Literary Supplement, *No. 3717, June 1, 1973, p. 610.*

J. H. Matthews

[Tristan] Tzara was shortly to leave Zurich when Breton informed him on Friday, December 26, 1919, "I have just finished with Soupault a play in four acts." A couple of weeks later, this first announcement was elaborated on Wednesday, January 14, 1920—only three days before Tzara's arrival in Paris: "I have just finished a play in collaboration with Soupault: ***If You Please*** a drama in 4 acts. We are trying to get it staged next spring."

Three things merit notice before we go any further. First, Breton and Soupault did not have to wait until Tzara had joined them before feeling the urge to write their first play or even before thinking of having it staged. Second, they had previously worked side by side on a significant series of texts that time would justify acknowledging as a landmark in the history of the emergence of the surrealist spirit. These texts, ***Les champs magnétiques (The Magnetic Fields),*** were written in the summer of 1919, serialized in *Littérature,* and published in book form at the end of May 1920. It is advisable therefore to examine the first Breton-Soupault play, written so soon afterward, for possible signs of tendencies that finally will divert the theatre from the track to which Dada had committed it, setting it upon another, which will be given direction by surrealist principles. Third, the comments that critics and literary historians have made on ***S'il vous plaît (If You Please)*** are, generally speaking, unreliable. Henri Béhar, it is true, avoids serious distortion by taking refuge in vagueness. He situates the play "on the border of dadaism." Martin Esslin, though, dismisses it summarily as "bizarre and largely improvised" [in his *The Theatre of the Absurd* (1961)], while [Michel] Sanouillet inaccurately dates it from January 1920.

Sanouillet notes correctly that ***S'il vous plaît*** was performed at the Salle Berlioz on March 27, 1920, beside *La Première Aventure céleste de Monsieur Antipyrine* and *Le Serin muet.* He points out that Breton and Soupault both took part, as did Mlle L. Moyon, Paul and Gala Éluard, Théodore Fraenkel, Henry Cliquennois, and Georges Ribemont-Dessaignes. Béhar lists the same participants. (pp. 87-8)

Simply stated, the purpose underlying [***S'il vous plaît***] appears to be to demonstrate the ineffectuality of conventional theatrical forms in two acts that, rationally speaking, lead nowhere, before traditional modes are combated more vigorously in an innovative third act. The fourth and final act makes no attempt to render Act Three palatable to any spectator who may not have found it to his taste.

Act One opens as though its authors have every intention of abiding by the usages of bourgeois drama. Hinting broadly at the existence of a love triangle, the first scene lets us hear Paul ("40 years old, moustache in the American style") speaking passionately to a young woman. Scene Two brings on Valentine's husband, François, who announces his intention of leaving Paris on a trip to Geneva that his wife has urged him to take. At this stage, Breton and Soupault seem content to borrow stock situation and predictable effect. With unconscious irony, François says to his wife, "I hope you are not going to be bored," and tells Paul, "Try to keep her amused. I'm counting on you, old friend." A similar use of conventional material can be observed in Robert Desnos' film script *Midi à quatorze heures.* As is the case with Desnos' use of cinematographic clichés, conventionality at first lulls our suspicions in ***S'il vous plaît.*** In *Midi à quatorze heures,* conventional beginnings lead to unaccountable mysterious developments. In the play by Breton and Soupault, psychological motivation is totally disregarded, thus offering no acceptable explanation for the violent gesture bringing the opening act to an end.

As in *Midi à quatorze heures,* in ***S'il vous plaît*** outworn situation initially seems to function as a shortcut to apprehension of the authors' meaning. Spectators are deluded into thinking themselves on familiar ground, and so entitled to adopt their accustomed posture vis-à-vis the drama being enacted before them. Eventually, however, they discover that the elements of the spectacle in which they have come to place confidence are the least capable of justifying what takes place in the end. With François safely out of the house, Paul can take advantage of his friend's absence. But he does not make love to Valentine, as his amorous language earlier led us to anticipate that he would. In direct contradiction with the pompous commonplace he delivered at the start of the third scene ("A door closes and our life begins"), he murders her with a revolver carried in his pocket.

It is reasonable to assume that the second act of ***S'il vous plaît*** is going to help elucidate the first. However, instead of meeting expectations, Act Two develops quite independently of Act One. Set in a business office run by Létoile ("40 years old, clean shaven, Legion of Honor, tortoise-shell glasses"), it presents a mysterious figure—played by Breton—engaged in a bewildering variety of activities, some of them rather exotic.

Létoile "enjoys the same faculties as God," observes a man who asks him to help recover stolen jewelry—only to be referred to the police. In every situation that would appear to have been designed to illustrate his powers and uncover his motivation, Létoile's actions are just as paradoxical. When two ladies come to appeal for funds "in a good cause," he generously gives them a large sum. Then he promptly has the police summoned to arrest them for stealing. Learning now that they have a license for what they are doing, he reclaims his money and calmly burns it before their eyes. Next, when a veiled lady consults him on her marital difficulties, this supposed marriage counselor seems far more disposed than she to insist upon divorce. After her departure, Létoile proceeds to dictate a notice of reward for information about the whereabouts of two women (the fund raisers?) whom he accuses of stealing the jewelry we heard him decline to recover. Then, as marriage broker, he follows truisms on the joys of conjugal life with an order to two policemen to arrest his latest client "for the murder of his mistress, Madame Valentine Saint-Cervan." Is this, at last, the connection between Act Two and Act One? If it is, then why is the man Létoile accuses visibly younger than Paul, and why does he have a curly blond moustache?

A delegation of employees arrives to present grievances. "It's hard to give wallets back," they point out. Also, "The other day we disguised ourselves separately upon your orders, and you had us follow one another." Létoile is firm, however: "I owe no explanation. If you are not satisfied, I'll not detain you." Arrival of a police inspector who talks of charges that remain unspecified (he is impersonated by Ribemont-Dessaignes) leaves Létoile unperturbed as the act comes to an end:

> THE INSPECTOR. You are charged . . .
>
> LETOILE What difference do you think that makes to me?

Observing that ***S'il vous plaît*** is composed of "a series of playlets constructed according to the best rules of dramatic art but perfectly incoherent," Michel Sanouillet gives Breton and Soupault less than their due. Carefully put together according to established dramatic methods, the individual sections making up the first two acts of this play do not achieve total incoherence, and are not intended to do so. This, in fact, is what frustrates the spectator whom the application of familiar techniques has persuaded to believe he is witnessing theatre of a kind he knows well: like Act One, Act Two almost succeeds in making sense to him. Apparently, though, as a result of some lapse that he finds unaccountable, each time the playwrights fall just short of accomplishing something he thought they wished to do.

In both of the first two acts, the degree of technical competence displayed is far from negligible. Thus to give full credit to the experiment carried out in ***S'il vous plaît*** one must start by admitting that its authors had enough skill, should they have cared to do this, to make sure of erecting the second act upon the foundation laid in the first. Intention, not incompetence, therefore underlies the incoherent plot structure of the first half of their four-act drama. In aggressive fashion, Breton and Soupault demonstrate how proven ingredients can be arranged in a manner that shakes the stability of dramatic convention. Outward respect for form merely conceals, temporarily, their lack of respect for the unity from which formal considerations traditionally draw both purpose and value. Being deprived of purpose, form guarantees nothing in ***S'il vous plaît.*** Thus it loses significance, so increasing the audience's exasperation as time goes by, instead of alleviating it. To anyone inclined to leave his seat, after the second act, the playwrights have nothing to add to the words used by Létoile, when declining to detain those looking to him for an explanation of his conduct.

But what of those spectators—or readers—who persevere? It should come as no surprise to them to find the third act, set in a café where two men are playing cards at three in the afternoon, without any observable connection with what it follows. However, this new sequence does more than confirm that ***S'il vous plaît*** is wilfully discontinuous. Focusing attention on a young man about thirty and a prostitute, it lets us in on a strange conversation. Beside this one, the amorous dialogue involving Paul and Valentine earlier appears a model of clarity. Act Three contrasts even more sharply with the second act. And of course it sounds nothing at all like a conventionally realistic conversation between a streetwalker and a prospective client.

Although interrupted here and there by commonplaces, the words exchanged between Maxime and Gilda represent a violent challenge to theatrical language in the naturalistic vein. True, their conversation closes with a direct attack upon idealism (Gilda: "Don't insist, my dear. You'd regret it. I have the pox"). Yet for the most part it is pitched at a level that sets the third act quite apart from the rest of ***S'il vous plaît:***

> GILDA. The instinct to please resembles a well. Believe me, rings are nothing. There is in Paris on the big boulevards such a slight incline that almost no one has managed to avoid slipping on it.
>
> MAXIME. The most touching maps of the world are the silvered globes in which the café waiter from time to time puts a serviette away. Caged birds like these little shining spheres. It all comes down to the same thing, singing with the street, or the sewing machine.
>
> GILDA. I know liberty through certain finer attachments.
>
> MAXIME. The kingdom of heaven is peopled with assassins. There is a swing awaiting you higher up. Do not lift your head yet.

No explanation comes from any of the Dada writings of Tzara for such dialogue as we have just sampled. Nor does any statement, inspired by Dada principles, coming from some other writer, help account for it. Not until Breton's *Manifeste du Surréalisme* appears in 1924 does one encounter comments offering guidance to an understanding of why Maxime and Gilda talk as they do.

Declaring that the forms of surrealist language are best adapted to dialogue, Breton notes in his first surrealist manifesto that, in dialogue, two thoughts confront one another, the one reacting to the other. The important factor here is the nature of that reaction, he believes: "My attention, prey to a solicitation it cannot decently reject, treats the opposing thought as an enemy." Hence when one talks to someone, he can turn the other person's thought "to account" in a reply that "distorts" it, or, more exactly (Breton employs the verb *dénaturer*) "changes its nature." Emphasizing this point with the assistance of examples furnished by pathological states of mind, "in which sensorial disturbances takes the patient's complete attention," Breton asserts that something of this disorder passes into every conversation, despite our effort to be sociable. The important thing is that, in the examples of echolalia ("How old are you?"—"You.") and Gasner syndrome ("What is your name?"—"Forty-five houses.") offered in [Breton's] *Le Manifeste du Surréalisme,* the patient has the advantage, because "he imposes himself through his replies upon the examining doctor's attention—and is not the person asking questions."

Breton's 1924 text goes on to explain that, to date, poetic surrealism has applied itself to establishing dialogue "in absolute truth" once again, by "freeing both interlocutors from the obligations of politeness." As a consequence, each one simply pursues his own soliloquy, "without seeking to derive any special dialectical pleasure from it or to impose in the least upon his neighbor." Statements uttered under these conditions do not serve to present a thesis, nor even to develop a consecutive theme. As for the replies they bring forth, these, "theoretically," have nothing to do with the vanity of the speaker. "Words and images offer themselves as springboards to the mind of the listener," Breton explains: "This is how, in ***Les champs magnétiques,*** the first purely surrealist work, those pages grouped under the title *Barrières* must present themselves. There Soupault and I show ourselves to be those impartial interlocutors."

Glancing down a page of "Barrières," we have the impression that Breton and Soupault respect logical progression in arranging statements we anticipate finding rationally acceptable. However, an attempt to read the page, which one would expect to confirm this impression, denies it validity. Instead, we find grammatical structure—generally most carefully respected in surrealist writing—to be a trap.

Our habitual responsiveness to a familiar grammatical sequence evidences inculcated prejudice in favor of a rational order that surrealists seek to overthrow. Thus in the extract below, stress falls upon things seen, against common sense and in no reasonably perceptible order. What we are made to see is brought to our attention in a manner that reproves the principle of cause and effect, which, incidentally, makes grammatical structure seem authoritative:

> "The rivers are not mirrors, much better ones have been made in the past ten years. With a stone I can break all the mirrors in the city where we live and insects smaller than the cries of infants voluptuously burrow into the foundations of skyscrapers."
>
> "No doubt, and yet we are not witnessing central pillaging. You are wrong in thinking that our voices serve to fill spaces that signify. We were not born very long ago."
>
> "Alas! A friend of the family gave me an octopus and, so that this respectable animal should not know hunger, a green liqueur that contained liquid metal polish. The invertebrate wasted away before our eyes and when, two days after its death, we cleaned out the bowl, we had the joy of discovering a mauve shell which was called chalcedony."
>
> "That's happened before. I myself could tell you of an embellishment which followed the visit by the President of the Republic. From a bunch of keys he had placed under glass was born an official clock that struck the hour of restorations."

We need read no further to appreciate how the confidence engendered by the reassuringly logical succession of introductory phrases ("No doubt," "Alas!," "That's happened before"), identifiable when the page is merely scanned, collapses upon close examination of the text.

In the dialogued passage entitled "Barrières," each response is less of a reply to what goes before than a new departure. The underlying idea, Breton has explained, was to "Take to the highest point the misunderstanding of conversation. This is what results. One of the interlocutors writes a few phrases very quickly. The other reads them very quickly without really getting to know them. He continues in the same way." Thus to varying degrees each response finds impetus in the statement preceding it. Yet in no case is development reasonably controlled by what came first. As a consequence, the reader is made aware of gathering imaginative momentum, while at the same time becoming increasingly conscious of the speakers' disrespect for logical sequence. Indeed, where one is most aware of a consecutive order, the imaginative content seems to have been diluted, as when mention of "a magnificent doorway" elicits the pedestrian response: "The most magnificent doorways are those behind which one reads 'Open in the name of the law!' " This means that "Barrières" impresses most when it lends substance to the assertion that Breton boldly makes in his first surrealist manifesto: "Surrealism does not permit those who devote themselves to it to forsake it when they please. There is every reason to believe it acts upon the mind in the manner of narcotics; like these it creates a certain state of need and can impel man to terrible revolts."

The elements giving "Barrières" its characteristic quality are the very ones that we find to be present in the dialogue between Gilda and Maxime. It is worth noticing, therefore, that Alain Jouffroy has reported, when presenting a reprint of ***Les champs magnétiques,*** "It was André Breton himself who wished, at the time when he gave his approval for a reprinting of the original surrealist text, that these two plays [***S'il vous plaît*** and ***Vous m'oublierez***] be included [. . .]" Clearly, toward the end of his life Breton was eager to direct attention to features that those plays had in common with ***Les champs magnétiques.*** Although the *Manifeste du Surréalisme* does not cite ***S'il vous plaît*** as an example of poetic surrealism, it is possible—thanks to ***Les champs magnétiques***—to grasp an essential fact, evidenced as early as the first play that Breton and Soupault wrote together. At a time when he was still dedicated to the cause of Dada, Breton already had begun to look out of "a new window." It was a window he had had to find for himself, Tzara having proved incapable of directing him to its location.

To talk of ***Les champs magnétiques*** is to open the question of automatic writing and its role in surrealism. This, in turn, means discussing the relationship of surrealism to Dada. (pp. 89-96)

It is Miss [Anna] Balakian's contention that surrealist automatic writing should be viewed in a "strictly scientific context" [see Further Reading list]. She insists that it was thanks to his medical studies, not to Dada, that Breton became acquainted with the phenomenon of automatic writing, and argues that he tried to practice it as a scientific device. . . . In automatism practiced within a scientific context, Miss Balakian comments elsewhere, what is irrational is "the effect produced on the observer when the mind is, in the process, unburdened of the overwhelming armor of patterns which are called 'rational' because of collective, social agreement." (p. 96)

[Balakian] performs the useful service of indicating how different is the role of automatism to the surrealist leader from the role reserved for it in Dada. Whether justifiably or not, from the medical standpoint, inspiration from [Dr. Pierre] Janet did contribute to helping Breton make of automatic writing, as Miss Balakian goes on to say, "not a device for the vilification of the human image, or the satirical representation of man's linguistic inefficacies, but rather a resource for the release of the latent powers of words."

We shall return to this question shortly. For the time being, we may readily forgive a reader of *Littérature*'s September-October 1920 number (in which the first three acts of ***S'il vous plaît*** were published) for being quite insensitive to the differences Miss Balakian helps us identify between automatic writing in Dada and automatism as practiced during the composition of the third act of the Breton-Soupault play. A note informed him abruptly, "The authors of ***If You Please*** wish the text of the fourth act not to be published," so leaving him to speculate about its content and to wonder whether Act Four might have furnished the all-embracing explanation he was now denied. [Michel] Benedikt's deduction—made, as it happens, in ignorance of what takes place in the fourth act—is that the note after Act Three (and which he translates incorrectly, by the way) is one of "many outward signs of the then contemporary movement, Dada." No doubt those acquainted with as much of ***S'il vous plaît*** as *Littérature* made accessible would have concurred in this judgment. What is more, consultation with someone who had seen the play performed would surely have strengthened their impression.

During the final act, the house lights are lowered but not extinguished entirely. On stage, two "insignificant characters" stop in a street by a doorway. Consulting his watch, X says he is leaving. Y remains, walking up and down, looking upward, brushing off his sleeve, blowing his nose. From the auditorium comes the question, "That's all?" On stage, Y looks surprised, but says nothing. A second member of the audience intervenes, despite efforts to silence him: "I don't understand anything. It's stupid." Presumably encouraged by another spectator who cries "If only it were amusing!" Spectator No. 2 stands on his seat and delivers the following speech, to the accompaniment of applause:

> I repeat that I don't understand anything. It's probable that I'm not the only one. For some time now, on the pretext of originality and independence, our fine art has been sabotaged by a gang, increasing in number every day, who are, for the most part, only agitators, lazy fellows or practical jokers.

The curtain comes down. Undeterred, Spectator No. 2 goes on:

> It is easier to get yourself talked about in this fashion than to attain real glory at the cost of hard work. Are we going to put up with the most contradictory ideas and aesthetic theories, the beautiful and the ugly, talent and force without style, being placed on the same footing, from now on? I appeal to our traditional good sense. It shall not be said that the sons of Montaigne, Voltaire, Renan . . .

At this moment yet another spectator, one who earlier questioned No. 2's right to say what he thought ("You have the right to leave"), interrupts: "Throw him out. Continue." The fourth act now begins once again, causing No. 2 to lose patience altogether. He and his wife leave, but not before he has exclaimed, "It's shameful," shaking his fist at the stage. In the ensuing hubbub the cries "*Vive la France*" and "Continue" can be distinguished. The call "Author" brings on two actors, in place of Breton and Soupault, and the curtain comes down for good.

Only hindsight can offer clarification where it would have been difficult, around 1920, for Breton and his friends to see clearly all that their efforts implied. It is plain, today, that the argument put forward by Ribemont-Dessaignes in *Déjà Jadis* uses inadmissible simplification of facts so as to cast Breton in the role of unsavory opportunist. "The truth is," declares Ribemont-Dessaignes, "that Breton no doubt never had anything of the dadaist about him and that he used Dada to draw the vague idea he had of Surrealism with difficulty from its matrix, and to appear afterward as the chief of a conscious and organized group." It is quite unjust to suggest, as Ribemont-Dessaignes does, that, in allowing ***S'il vous plaît*** and ***Vous m'oublierez*** (***You Will Forget Me***) to be presented within the framework of Dada spectacles, Breton and Soupault were knowingly guilty of passing surrealism off as Dada. Indeed the former has confessed in his *Entretiens,* "Soupault and I, for instance, got no little satisfaction from the fact that a sketch of ours [***Vous m'oublierez***], at the Salle Gaveau, earned us a bombardment of eggs, tomatoes, and beefsteak that the spectators precipitately went out for during the intermission. What the public thought of us we thought in return, a hundredfold." The end of ***S'il vous plaît*** ridicules the kind of objections voiced during and after Dada demonstrations. Nothing in the text of the fourth act, printed for the first time in 1967 from a copy Breton had retained, gives us to understand that, when bringing their drama to a close, the playwrights wished to appear in any guise other than that of Dada activists.

In the long run, though, the point at issue is not whether Breton and Soupault could be accused of being surrealists masquerading as dedicated members of the Dada movement. The negative aspects of their theatre were unquestionable and unquestioned credentials for admission to the Dada circle. But this does not alter the fact that, in retrospect, the most striking feature of their first play, written while they were in contact with Dada, emerges better when it is considered in the perspective appropriate to surrealism. What matters, really, is that, already alarmed at seeing Dada "fighting the Battle of *Hernani* every month" and complacently using "the same stereotyped tactics," Breton and Soupault, however little they realized this, were advancing through Dada scandal toward something more positive, in which Tzara clearly had no interest.

When ***S'il vous plaît*** and ***Vous m'oblierez*** are examined in conjunction, the parallel observable between the language used in the third act of the former and the dialogued section of ***Les champs magnétiques*** takes on particular significance for anyone concerned with the early manifestation of the surrealist spirit in the theatre. [In a footnote, Matthews adds: "It is not without significance that Anna Balakian has reported, with regard to ***Les champs magnétiques,*** 'When the work was finished, neither poet made any attempt to identify publicly which part belonged to him, and the impression of continuity is expertly maintained. However, in discovering on a marked copy who wrote what in the collaboration, I was able to observe the dialogue character of much of it, which makes the automatism appear like a game of ping-pong' " (*André Breton*).] Considered side by side, these plays certainly merit a better fate than the one reserved for them by Anna Balakian, who writes them off as "dramatic fragments which today are of no more than documentary interest."

All the same, what Sanouillet has to tell us of ***Vous m'oublierez,*** when commenting on the Festival Dada that saw its performance, invites us to give it scant attention. Preoccupied with proving that Dada "was getting out of breath already," rather than with giving ***Vous m'oublierez*** its due, Sanouillet mentions the second Breton-Soupault play after the first as proof of repetitiveness in Dada ideas. Another critic adopts a less sympathetic attitude. Citing Breton's complaint in *Entretiens* about the monotony of Dada tactics and his slighting references to "the n%St%Sh *Celestial Adventure of Monsieur Antipyrine,*" Béhar remarks, "one could say as much of the plays of Breton and Soupault, acted by their friends. Between ***S'il vous plaît*** and ***Vous m'oublierez*** there is very little difference, and the latter sketch could be added to the preceding play, as fourth act, without its being apparent, so much does the dislocation of rules of composition authorize additions or cuts." Reluctant to entertain the idea that Breton and Soupault may have been even the slightest bit more inventive than Tzara, neither Béhar nor Sanouillet considers the possibility that the authors of ***Vous m'oublierez*** might have taken a step forward, for which writing ***S'il vous plaît*** had prepared them.

Sanouillet affirms that ***Vous m'oublierez*** "has real theatrical value," but without specifying whether this quality guarantees or denies the text value as an expression of

Soupault (upper left) with Paul Eluard, André Breton, and Théodore Fraenkel in a performance of Vous m'oublierez.

Dada. Whatever he wishes us to conclude, his remark bears little relationship to the significance that ***Vous m'oublierez*** assumes in the light of surrealism.

From where the surrealists stand, there seems no reason at all why, as theatre, this play should demonstrate any improvement over its predecessor. Technical competence has no bearing upon the standards by which surrealists evaluate writing for the stage. Recognition of this fact promotes responsiveness to the second play authored by Breton and Soupault as, from the surrealist viewpoint, complementary to the drama it followed. To these playwrights it seemed less important to break new ground than to continue in the direction they had begun exploring in the third act of their first stage play.

It is not difficult to detect in ***S'il vous plaît***'s third act an armature of consecutive dialogue, beneath apparently inconsequential language denoting a striking departure from familiar theatrical usage. ***Vous m'oublierez,*** however, dispenses with a rational substructure of this sort, which becomes redundant in a sketch that brings together Robe de Chambre ("Dressing Gown," played by Philippe Soupault), Parapluie ("Umbrella," impersonated by André Breton), Machine à Coudre ("Sewing Machine," acted by Paul Éluard even though it is a female role), and an unknown man (Théodore Fraenkel). Pursuing ends peculiarly their own, the authors are willing now to relax dramatic structure totally. In fact the vestiges of conventional drama that do survive in ***Vous m'oublierez*** are reduced to such ridiculously restricted proportions that their presence can have no function other than an ironic one. At one point, for example, a remark by Sewing Machine seems intended to introduce a theme of proven theatrical vitality: "You know Flag, don't you? You know he does not forgive. If I fall into his claws I am lost" (Scene 2). But neither Umbrella nor Dressing Gown pays serious attention. On the contrary, by a process typical of this sketch, conversational links are soon severed. Before long Sewing Machine is crying, "Umbrella, listen to me, I have nothing to tell you!"

Sustained and consecutive dialogue has no place in a play that allows Umbrella to take time to write up a ludicrous multiplication sum on a blackboard and to offer a description of Paris straight out of a guide book. No attempt is made, meanwhile, to interest the audience in what the grotesquely named people on stage do, or in their relations with one another. On the contrary, discontinuity is the governing principle throughout. Umbrella whispers in Sewing Machine's ear, "The virgin is ready? Not everything can be sung to the tune of impatient stamping feet, if the yellow daisies whirl around, lottery flowers, in the place of closing eyes" (Scene 2). Sewing Machine's reply shows that she admits no obligation to *respond,* in the accepted sense of the word. Rather, she claims the same privilege to follow her own thoughts as was granted the unidentified speakers in "Barrières": "Do you want string or oranges? My fine boss made me a present of a pair of suspenders and that is not all. Department store elephants, come running with your dark lanterns. The sun has not set. Dressing Gown! Are you there, dear?"

Between the composition of the first Breton-Soupault play and that of the second, the authors' conception of the nature of communication has evolved. Instead of rehearsing the familiar, language is now called upon to pioneer more boldly exploration of the unknown in the direction at which Anna Balakian has hinted. Increasingly, logical incoherence opens the door on poetry.

Two points call for stress, here, to dispel confusion regarding poetry as surrealists speak of it, and poetry of the kind advocated by Tzara and those whose ambitions were circumscribed, like his, by Dada principles. The emphasis upon impeccable grammatical structure so noticeable in ***Les champs magnétiques*** shows well enough that, as cofounders of surrealism, Breton and Soupault were by no means inclined to agree with Tzara over the poetic virtue of "words in liberty." Meanwhile, comparison of ***Vous m'oublierez*** with Ribemont-Dessaignes's *Le Serin muet* highlights in the former another fundamental departure from Dada practice.

It is by no means true that, as Béhar affirms when discussing Riquet's conversations with Barate, in *Le Serin muet* "each of the two characters pursues his own monologue, without attending to the other's words." Each listens, albeit with no more attention than is necessary to make it possible for him to try diverting the other's monologue to a direction more congenial to himself. In ***Vous m'oublierez*** we face something more complex. To explain it, we have to be aware of influences upon Breton and Soupault to which Tzara and Ribemont-Dessaignes were quite impervious.

Béhar seems to believe he has caught Breton and Soupault out, as though he had detected some unconfessed crime. He talks accusingly of "aesthetic preoccupations" as being "all too evident" in their ***Vous m'oublierez.*** Apparently, he has not noticed that in *Entretiens,* with no sign at all of reluctance, Breton's recollections of his period of association with Dada give prominence to a sense of tradition that, we are told, was important to "at least two or three" of those who participated in Dada activities. Being a literary tradition that extended back into the nineteenth century, it could hold little appeal for a Tristan Tzara. All the same, it exerted a strong enough attraction over Breton and Soupault, at the time they were writing their second play, to make ***Vous m'oublierez*** less than fully comprehensible unless we realize how fervently it pays tribute to Lautréamont.

In *Entretiens* also we find Breton speaking openly of the violence of certain "imperatives" to which, around 1920, Lautréamont's *Les Chants de Maldoror* submitted him and a few close friends. In this connection, he comments upon the preoccupation they all shared with "the *lyrical* phenomenon in poetry," explaining his understanding of lyricism in these terms: "that which constitutes going in some sort of spasmodic way beyond controlled expression." The best definition of lyricism as he saw it then, he recalls, is the fourth *Chant,* with its remarkable comparisons, of which the most celebrated in surrealist circles is, "Beautiful as the chance encounter, on a dissecting table, of a sewing machine and an umbrella." What clearer indication could one have than the presence on stage of Machine à Coudre and Parapluie that, writing ***Vous***

m'oublierez, Breton and Soupault had Lautréamont in mind?

To estimate how deep was the loyalty that Breton and his friends came to feel for Lautréamont, one has only to open *Entretiens,* which reproduces a statement by Soupault that Breton says he would gladly have countersigned: "It is not my place, or anyone else's (do you hear, Gentlemen, who wishes to receive my seconds?) to judge the Count. One does not judge M. de Lautréamont. One recognizes him as he passes and one bows to the ground. I will give my life to the person, man or woman, who will ever make me forget him." What is important is that the surrealist attitude with regard to Lautréamont was, from the first, fiercely defensive and strongly proprietory in nature. This is why in ***Vous m'oublierez*** the general public's ignorance about his work was not merely anticipated but actually turned to account in keeping the audience at a distance. When Sewing Machine pleads, "Explain to me, Umbrella, and I will leave," Dressing Gown replies sharply, "No explanations" (Scene 2).

Presentation of ***Vous m'oublierez*** in the course of a Dada show has had the consequence of encouraging everyone to assess this play exclusively in relation to Dada. Thus attention has gone naturally to aspects of the Breton-Soupault text that seem typical of the iconoclastic approach favored in Dada. These include Sewing Machine's question to Umbrella, which presents no novelty to those who have sat through certain other Dada plays before hearing ***Vous m'oublierez:*** "Is this comedy going to come to an end?" (Scene 2). They include too conversations like the following, in which Umbrella's interpretation of Sewing Machine's word *temps* as "weather," not "time," disrupts logical sequence in a manner that, apparently, does not trouble Sewing Machine at all:

> SEWING MACHINE. Umbrella, for pity's sake, answer me, where do we stand with time?
>
> UMBRELLA. Variable. (*Correcting himself*) Set fair.
>
> SEWING MACHINE. You love me.

Better acquaintance with the writings of Lautréamont might have redressed the balance, making it possible for public and commentators alike to appreciate that Breton and Soupault were not content with merely engaging in Dada provocation. They were reaching out for something that lay beyond Dada and would have long-range consequences of the most profound significance for surrealism.

That both Breton and Soupault were in the process of turning away from Dada is evident once we consider the structure and function of dialogue in their second theatrical experiment.

Whereas the Dada dialogue of Tzara shocked by its disjunctive nature, by the anti-rational juxtaposition of words, the language of surrealism would aim at seducing reason, at persuading the imagination to surrender before the enticing images of the marvelous. In the course of explaining why he had taken over the direction of the magazine *La Révolution surréaliste,* Breton wrote in its fourth number (July 15, 1925) of "the conviction we all share here, that is to say, that we are living in the very midst of modern society on such a serious compromise that it justifies every audacity on our part." He continued, "Who speaks of having us at his disposal, of making us contribute to the abominable comfort of this world? We want, we will have the beyond in our time. All we need for that is to listen to our impatience and to remain, without any reticence at all, at the disposal of the marvelous."

Occupying an intermediary position between Dada and surrealism, ***Vous m'oublierez*** offers pertinent evidence that Anna Balakian might well have included when presenting her thesis that Dada "had proved only to be a cry of freedom *from* certain stilted conventions of living and communication," while Breton "stressed freedom *for.*" In its typical form, the Dada playwright's sense of responsibility—and this is as true of Ribemont-Dessaignes as it is of Tzara—had consisted in declining to accept the obligation to meet his audience on their ground. For the surrealist, ***Vous m'oublierez*** warned, responsibility would lie, rather, in luring spectators into magnetic fields (*champs magnétiques*) where they would no longer be able to find customary bearings.

The theatre inspired exclusively by Dada aims at challenging the audience to protest by refusing to provide what the public felt entitled to expect of a play. Its practitioner could congratulate himself when he had turned the tables on his audience. Recalling the Salle Gaveau demonstration, Tzara exclaimed with pride in *Le Surréalisme et l'Après-Guerre,* "The spectacle was in the auditorium, we were assembled on stage and watched the public unleashed." But while negation was the mainspring of Dada, it was to be for the surrealists a key to effects in which their convictions led them to see positive value. Hence, in the perspective soon to be formally adopted by those listed as advocates of surrealism in the *Manifeste du Surréalisme* of 1924, it was less important to worry over the literary air that ***Vous m'oublierez*** had, next to *La deuxième aventure céleste de Monsieur Antipyrine,* than to recognize what prospect of release it offered from the impasse of Dada.

Vous m'oublierez begins on an interrogative note. It closes without having provided rationally acceptable answers to the questions it has raised, either among the characters on stage or in the minds of the audience. Although posed three times, Robe de Chambre's query elicits no response, even when he opens a window to shout it to the world—"Tell me: what then is that tree, that young leopard which I caressed the other day when I came home?" (Scene 1). As for the answer supplied by Parapluie to a question he himself has asked—"a dead animal under a piece of furniture"—it makes no more sense whether we read the question *"Qu'est-ce que l'acacia?"* as "What is acacia?" or as "What is gum arabic?" (Scene 2). In ***Vous m'oublierez*** we are denied the right to protest in the name of reason, when hearing Robe de Chambre give the very same answer to two questions that he in turn raises: "What is honor?" and "What is the future?" (Scene 2). Robe de Chambre could evidently say, "My role is to establish nothing," just as Parapluie does before remarking, "I am twenty-four years old and wear glasses" (Scene 2). To the authors of this play, stating the obvious (Breton, who wore spectacles, was twenty-four at the time ***Vous m'oublierez*** was staged) establishes nothing. They prefer therefore to challenge our reluctance to be guided by anything but reason, which, in the world of pedestrian reality, presides despotically over the ordering of verifiable facts.

The question-and-answer technique as employed in ***Vous m'oublierez*** is a means of confronting the public with the inadequacies of reason. It betokens an inclination that later works for the stage will show to be characteristic of surrealism, expressive of an abiding impulse to divert the theatre from dramatic to poetic ends, as surrealists define and pursue these. Needless to say, then, poetry as surrealists speak of it is not compatible with theatre, as it is in the case of the plays of Maeterlinck, but at variance with theatrical usage. Thus, in contrast with the informative style of pointless guide-book descriptions of Paris to be found in ***Vous m'oublierez,*** remarks like the following, by Machine à Coudre, stand out sharply defined: "My hair leans over the river and my lips are long venomous fish" (Scene 2).

Recurrently in ***Vous m'oublierez*** statements of this nature are isolated at the expense of dialogue continuity. Their poetic appeal is thus set off by their gratuitousness, which undermines theatrical unity. Remarks like Parapluie's—"I told you so: a bowl of camomile-colored sky has a less sweet taste than your little niece's glance" (Scene 1)—have that "fairly bizarre quality" that held Breton's attention, one evening just before he fell asleep, in a phrase that presented itself to his consciousness without his being able to explain its origin. In the Breton-Soupault play we come across a significant number of remarks of this kind, reminiscent of the spontaneously generated phrase that prompted Breton to investigate automatic writing in the hope of accumulating statements no less disturbing to reason than the first one to have impressed him: "There is a man cut in two by the window." Speaking of the products of automatism in his first surrealist manifesto, Breton declared, "Poetically speaking, they strike us thanks to a very high degree of *immediate absurdity,* the characteristic of this absurdity being, upon closer scrutiny, to give way to everything that is admissible, legitimate in the world: the disclosure of a certain number of properties and facts no less objective, in the final analysis, than the others."

This explains why, in ***Vous m'oublierez,*** the right to question what others say is forfeited by everyone present:

> SEWING MACHINE. Pretty white days, necklace of nights, distant clouds, flowers of boredom.
>
> DRESSING GOWN. What?
>
> SEWING MACHINE. Nothing, rattle-mechanism. (*Silence.*)

The role of dialogue in surrealism is anything but the reconciliation of poetry, as surrealists refer to it, with reason. The principle underlying its use favors extending to the maximum the distance between question and answer, statement and response. As a result, dialogue presents significant analogies with the process of image-making described in the *Manifeste du Surréalisme:* "It is false, in my opinion, to claim that 'the mind has grasped the relationship' between two realities facing one another. To begin with, it has grasped nothing consciously. It is from the somewhat fortuitous linking of the two terms that a particular light has sprung, *the light of the image,* to which we are infinitely sensitive." Thus the value of the image "depends on the beauty of the spark obtained; it is in consequence a function of the difference in potential between the two conductors." In the rarefied atmosphere of surrealist automatism, images "alone steer the mind," which "is convinced little by little of the supreme reality of these images."

Gratuitousness necessarily heightens the degree of immediate absurdity in images born of automatism. In surrealist dialogue, it is a direct result of neglect of causal links between statement and response. (pp. 96-107)

"Le dialogue en 1928" and "Le dialogue en 1934" present findings resulting from a typical surrealist form of word game that, André Breton has remarked, "has always seemed to us poetically the most fabulous source of *undiscoverable* images." The adjective underlined by Breton points to the most vital link between dialogue resulting from the arbitrary confrontation of question and answer and the dialogue of ***Vous m'oublierez,*** upon which automatism has left an indelible mark. In both instances we are provided with evidence of fidelity to the program outlined by Breton when he spoke of "giving language back its full purpose," that of "making cognition take a big step forward." It is by recognizing how much importance both Breton and Soupault already attached to rationally undiscoverable images that with least delay we can relate ***Vous m'oublierez*** to a belief that finds expression through *Les Pas perdus,* in the course of an essay on *Les Chants de Maldoror,* by the way: "We know now that poetry must lead somewhere."

At the end of ***Vous m'oublierez,*** Parapluie reports that, although he can recall in detail visiting one of the castles on the Loire, he now finds it impossible to evoke memories that last as long as his two-hour visit. Recollected experience is less than adequate, then. Much more satisfying, we infer, are anticipated sights, unprecedented in past experience but foreshadowed by undiscoverable images of the sort in which Breton and Soupault seek to interest us. Just before the curtain comes down, these are given the right of way, as Parapluie advances to the proscenium, waving a red flag like the ones used by railroad crossing-keepers to halt traffic of one kind, going in one direction, so that another kind of traffic, heading somewhere else, may take precedence. (p. 108)

J. H. Matthews, "André Breton and Philippe Soupault," in his Theatre in Dada and Surrealism, *Syracuse University Press, 1974, pp. 85-108.*

Kirby Olson

Philippe Soupault, Louis Aragon, and Andre Breton were described in Roger Shattuck's *The Banquet Years* as the three storm centers of Surrealism. At first they were simply tempestuous poets, playing pranks on the city. Gradually they became didactic. ***Last Nights of Paris,*** by Soupault, *Nightwalker,* by Aragon, and *Nadja,* by Breton, were all first published in the mid 1920s. . . . All three books simply follow their authors' drifts: personal philosophy is sandwiched in between lyrical descriptions of women, buildings, and flowers. Breton's is the most marvelous novel: it is written in an even, elevated style, it also contains the most interesting situations.

Soupault's atmosphere is like a mist in which chance has the upper hand over logic. Soupault gets second place in this walk-around-Paris-at-night and write a novel about it competition. Though Soupault's book [***Last Nights of Paris***] contains some bogus metaphysics, and not much of a story (though it seems to play off the mystery genre), it is worth reading for three reasons. First, it is interesting to read a book that W. C. Williams translated at the outset of his career. Second, it is interesting for the comparison it gives to *Nadja* and *Nightwalker.* Third, it is worth reading for the strangely enchanted atmosphere Soupault gives to the Paris underworld in the wee hours of the 1920s.

Soupault's milieu is that of a disorganized crime syndicate. They meet in cafes to gossip about absent members of the group, Georgette, and murders that have been committed and by whom. The characters are flat, with the exception of Soupault. The few thieves, a literary man who makes a couple of jarring intrusions into the dreamy narrative, a sailor who decides to become a butcher, a commonplace girl named Georgette who becomes at night a professional femme fatale, and Soupault himself make up the entire cast. Only Soupault himself is developed as a character. There is a series of axe murders which may have been good fun then, but which since have become, due to their monstrous regularity, merely third-page news articles. These murders create little suspense because Soupault's solipsistic imagination does not go out in sympathy to anyone but himself. Soupault himself is never in any danger, walking clear across Paris in the middle of the night observing murders and such as if he were an invisible man. Williams' quick speech rhythms over Soupault's lugubrious thought makes the prose vaguely giddy at times. This contributes to the lack of suspense: . . .

> "My name is Georgette."
>
> There's an astounding name, makes one think of a needle, a hem, a spot of grease. This name without beginning or end, calls to mind the grandeur of thrones, or the moon in a mist.
>
> To utter that name is enough to bring back the memory of a toothache or a couple of good smacks in the face.
>
> I kept these reflections to myself, being content to summarize them under the simple adjective which says, by the way, a plenty:
>
> "Charming."
>
> I had scarcely finished the last syllable when the dog stood up and made himself pleasant by sticking out his tongue. Then the strangest events of the evening began to unfold. . . .

Soupault is a vivid personality. In his youth he played tennis, engaged in food fights, had constant love affairs. His splendid constitution is reflected in this book when he describes walking across Paris *sans* fatigue. In the Surrealist set photos, he stands a head taller than the others. He had a classic '20s face, like F. Scott Fitzgerald. Soupault is still alive at the age of 87 and still writing. After this novel he was expelled from the Surrealist order by Breton. Soupault's writing was mercenary, Breton felt. Once this happened, Soupault's stay in the Surrealist limelight was over. He wrote many more books which reflect his early preoccupation with chance and fate.

This is the only one of Soupault's novels which is available in an English translation. It is also the only novel William Carlos Williams ever translated. Despite his expulsion (or withdrawal, whichever story you prefer) from the Surrealist group, Soupault remains one of the founding members of the movement, and this one of his most memorable texts.

Kirby Olson, in a review of "Last Nights of Paris," in San Francisco Review of Books, *November-December, 1984, p. 18.*

Jack Byrne

Last Nights of Paris, published in Paris in 1928, has the authentic ring of that memorable decade, the 1920s, the decade referred to on the back cover as "the magic 1920's." One need only refer to 1922 for evidence to support that phrase: Joyce's *Ulysses* and Eliot's *The Waste Land.* Furthermore, it is for English-speaking readers "a rare collaboration between literary geniuses of two different cultures: Soupault, the brilliant young French Dada/Surrealist, and Williams, the great American poet." And finally, this edition has a 1980 preface by Soupault, **"William Carlos Williams: By Day and by Night,"** in which the author, with brilliant hindsight, in 1980, recreates the atmosphere of the Paris Williams saw when the two of them walked the streets of the City of Light "at night in the deserted streets and the quais along the Seine. Sometimes we sat down on a bench to admire the moonlight and the vagabonds who preferred night to the light of day. For reasons he easily guessed."

It is these vagabonds about whom Soupault writes in ***Last Nights,*** a work, according to the author, incorrectly subtitled "novel." For him it is "my 'testimony' . . . describing the atmosphere of the Parisian nights." Soupault's characters, other than the narrator (who just might be Soupault, the "young, anticonformist French poet"), belong to what are often called apaches, ruffians of the Paris streets: Most important are Georgette the prostitute—"In each little street she knew some gloomy small hotel"—and her brother Octave, the experimenter, who goes from putting his milk and coffee in his soup "to know what this mixture will taste like" to burning himself to a cinder in an attempt to set fire to Paris. The rest are a melange of hoodlum types who gather at the "blue café," pilgrims of a sort, a ship of fools who afford the narrator the opportunity to tell his tale with Paris as his nocturnal stage.

Jack Byrne, in a review of "Last Nights of

Paris," *in* The Review of Contemporary Fiction, *Vol. VII, No. 1, Spring, 1987, p. 185.*

FURTHER READING

Balakian, Anna. *André Breton: Magus of Surrealism.* New York: Oxford University Press, 1971, 289 p.

Critical study of Breton's life and career containing references to Soupault's relationship to and collaborations with Breton.

Biron, Lionel A. "Philippe Soupault's Early Contact with Zurich Dada: A Gracious Butterfly Flirting with Dada in *Les champs magnétiques.*" *Rackham Literary Studies,* No. 6 (1975): 41-9.

Argues that Soupault was involved with and influenced by Dadaism before coauthoring *The Magnetic Fields.*

Josephson, Matthew. *Life among the Surrealists.* New York: Holt, Rinehart and Winston, 1962, 403 p.

Memoir of Josephson's experiences with the Surrealists that includes several anecdotes about Soupault's activities in the 1920s and his subsequent expulsion from the group.

Jean Stafford

1915-1979

(Full name Jean Wilson Stafford) American novelist, short story writer, essayist, critic, nonfiction writer, and author of children's books.

Stafford believed that writers should strive to vividly present the truth without moral judgment. Throughout her career she drew upon her personal life in her fiction, which was praised for its vivid characterizations, strong attention to detail, and elegiac tone. Many of the characters in her novels and short stories are adolescents who struggle to find and assert their personal identity, or who must cope with the traumas of alienation and shattered innocence. Elizabeth Janeway asserted: "There is no one else writing today whose people speak more truly, and more surprisingly. This is something finer than 'having an ear.' It is the mark of a writer whose perceptions are so immediate and exact that she can use dialogue not just for color or plausibility or character drawing, but to embody and convey the very heart of her intentions."

Stafford was born in Covina, California, the youngest of four children. Her father, John, owned a successful walnut ranch, but was forced to move his family in 1921 after he went bankrupt playing the stock market. The family never knew financial security after leaving California and relocating in Boulder, Colorado. Obsessed with the idea of being an author, John wrote a pulp Western novel, *When Cattle Kingdom Fell,* and spent the rest of his life writing and revising manuscripts that were never published. The family worked odd jobs to make ends meet, and Stafford's mother, Ethel, alienated her already distant daughter by taking in sorority girls as boarders. Always individualistic, Stafford was exasperated with her family from an early age and grew more aloof from them during her adolescence. A gawky, bookish tomboy, she resented her older sisters, Marjorie and Mary Lee, who were pretty and well-mannered, and her mother, whom she regarded as her father's obedient servant. She was close only to her brother, Dick. After graduating from high school, Stafford attended the University of Colorado, where she met Lucy and Andrew Cooke, a couple who strongly influenced her by introducing her to a bohemian way of life and making her aware, for the first time, of her sexuality. During Stafford's senior year, Lucy killed herself, and the unexplained suicide affected Stafford enormously. For years she had difficulty coping with this loss, and elements of Lucy's death and the Cookes' unorthodox lifestyle would recur in much of her fiction. After graduating in 1936, Stafford traveled to Germany to study philology on a yearlong fellowship at the University of Heidelberg. The Nazi fervor in Germany astounded Stafford, but she later admitted that the experience helped her to understand the naivete that allowed Nazism to prosper.

Returning to Colorado a year later, Stafford was asked to act as secretary for a writer's conference at the University. There she met Robert Lowell, then a 22-year-old Harvard dropout and aspiring poet. He was immediately smitten and asked her to keep in touch, but Stafford was preoccupied with her own career. Determined to become a writer but also desperately in need of a job, she applied for numerous teaching positions throughout the country. She accepted her only offer from Stephens College in Columbia, Missouri, but was soon disappointed with the institution, which was more of a finishing school than a university. She quit after a discouraging year and moved to New York City in 1938. After finally being offered a contract with the Boston publishing firm Atlantic Monthly, Stafford moved again, to Concord, Massachusetts, and began writing a novel. During this time, Lowell, who had been wooing Stafford by mail from Kenyon College, returned to Boston to visit his family. Although his genteel parents strongly disapproved of Stafford, Lowell proposed to her. She was unsure, however, and hesitated to answer him. Several days after Lowell's marriage proposal, the couple was involved in a serious automobile accident. Lowell, who had poor vision and was driving while intoxicated, was unhurt, but Stafford suffered massive head injuries, a crushed nose, and a fractured skull and jaw. The painful surgery and months of hospitalization she endured became the basis for her acclaimed short story "The Interior Castle."

Stafford ultimately accepted Lowell's marriage proposal, and the couple wed in 1940. The relationship was stressful from the start, punctuated by clashing creative temperaments, professional jealousy, and Lowell's zealous practice of Catholicism, to which he had recently converted. He took a vow of celibacy soon after he and Stafford were married; she later told friends that the marriage was never consummated. After six years, the couple separated and Stafford spent much of 1947 in New York's Payne-Whitney Clinic recuperating from a nervous breakdown. She was married twice more, briefly to *Time* magazine writer Oliver Jensen, and later to *New Yorker* writer A. J. Liebling, who died in 1963. Stafford's last fifteen years were spent in relative seclusion on Long Island, although she continued to see friends and write short stories well into her sixties. *The Collected Stories of Jean Stafford,* published in 1969, won a Pulitzer Prize. In 1979, after several unproductive writing years marked by eccentric behavior and heavy drinking, Stafford died of complications following a stroke, and willed her entire estate to her cleaning woman.

Stafford's first novel, *Boston Adventure,* was both a popular and critical success. The protagonist, a young woman named Sonie Marburg, grows up in a poor suburb of Boston longing for a better life for herself. Her dream comes true when she becomes the secretary of Miss Lucy Pride, an upper-class Bostonian, and moves into her house on Beacon Hill. Sonie realizes, however, that the elite have problems too, and soon yearns to escape this world as well. Although some critics found *Boston Adventure* melodramatic, most praised Stafford's highly condensed style. Howard Mumford Jones observed: "I have read no modern novel of late which so truly compelled me to think of the concentrated emotional power of the Brontës. [Stafford] has a trick of making time stand still while she wrings every conceivable value, whether of comedy or horror, out of successive episodes in her tale." Stafford's second novel, *The Mountain Lion,* was even more successful than *Boston Adventure,* and is generally considered her finest work. Stafford herself regarded it as her favorite. A tale of the end of innocence, *The Mountain Lion* revolves around Ralph and Molly Fawcett, two young children who live with their two older sisters and widowed mother in California. Neglected by their mother and alienated from their peers because of their homeliness and poor health, Ralph and Molly cling to each other for support and love. After spending several summers on their grandfather's Colorado ranch, Ralph begins to ignore Molly as he becomes more comfortable with the onset of adolescence. At the novel's end, Ralph goes hunting and, unconsciously burdened by Molly's love and her inability to mature, mistakes his sister for the mountain lion he has been tracking and "accidentally" kills her. In addition to viewing *The Mountain Lion* as a exploration of lost innocence, some critics interpret it as a statement on the unjust social roles of women and a resistance of traditional gender initiation. Bruce Bawer maintained: "*The Mountain Lion* is one of the most admirable short novels of its time—elegantly structured, deftly composed, and sensitively imagined. . . . Stafford captures the world of childhood in masterly fashion, rendering details, dialogue, and thoughts for pages on end without a misstep."

The Catherine Wheel was largely unsuccessful when first published but received positive notice in 1982 when Ecco Press included the novel in its "Neglected Books of the Twentieth Century" series. Described by James Wolcott as "a novel so sensuously deft that it makes most writers look as if they were slapping words on the page with their elbows," *The Catherine Wheel* chronicles the loneliness and frustration of Andrew Shipley, a twelve-year-old boy who is spending a dismal summer in Maine with his insufferable twin sisters and his eccentric, unmarried Aunt Katharine. In alternate chapters, Stafford focuses on Katharine's sadness and disappointments to illustrate the fundamental egocentrism of individuals: neither Andrew nor Katharine is ever aware of each other's problems. Katharine, a 38-year-old virgin, has been in unrequited love with Andrew's father for twenty years, and lives with the futile hope that the man will one day divorce his wife to be with her. The book's title refers to the spiked torture wheel on which St. Catherine was tortured and also to the giant pinwheel firework with which Katharine is ultimately burned to death. Such overt symbolism was one cause for the novel's initial failure, but recent critics have focused on Stafford's precise characterizations.

Stafford's short stories share many themes with her novels. Similarly autobiographical in content, they often feature comic irony and emphasize character rather than plot; most of her fully developed, poignant protagonists are children and adolescents. In a review of Stafford's first short story collection, *Children Are Bored on Sunday,* Gene Baro noted: "Reading Jean Stafford's short stories, one does not remain outside of them; rather, one is caught up into their rich emotional and physical texture. First, one participates in the individual, created worlds of Miss Stafford; later, upon reflection, one can begin to speculate upon, to analyze and to wonder at Miss Stafford's artistry." Throughout *Children Are Bored on Sunday* as well as her following short story collections, *The Interior Castle* and *Bad Characters,* Stafford contrasts unpleasant situations with eloquent narration to portray individuals attempting to maintain their shaky identities in peculiar, alienating surroundings. In "Children Are Bored on Sunday," for example, two acquaintances whose lives have been ravaged by alcohol confront each other in the Metropolitan Museum of Art and attempt to help each other. In "The Philosophy Lesson," college student Cora Savage rebels against convention by posing nude for a Life Drawing class. During one sitting, she listens to the class gossip about a fellow student's suicide and realizes it was a boy with whom she was infatuated. While remaining completely silent and immobile, Cora comes to terms with her grief, confusion, and feelings of loss. Polly Bay, in "The Liberation," endures her life in a similarly steadfast manner. Although she is an adult—and a college instructor—Polly lives as a veritable prisoner in the stifling home of her aunt and uncle. Her impending marriage promises an escape, but her fiance is tragically killed on the eve of their wedding. Polly still leaves, but in panic and trepidation rather than triumph. This story's ironic twist of fate is an element in much of Stafford's fiction; many critics trace the nature of the plot device to the death of Stafford's beloved brother Dick, which occurred shortly before her first novel was published.

Stafford's previously published short works were later compiled in the Pulitzer Prize-winning volume *The Collected Stories of Jean Stafford* and arranged geographically in sections titled "The Innocents Abroad," "The Bostonians and Other Manifestations of the American Scene," "Cowboys and Indians, and Magic Mountains," and "Manhattan Island." These titles, borrowed from Stafford's favorite authors, Mark Twain and Henry James, indicate her affinity for their works; she once remarked that she felt allied to their sense of place and dislocation. In the years following the publication of *The Collected Stories* until her death in 1979, Stafford was largely unproductive, publishing *A Mother in History,* a seriocomic nonfiction work about the mother of assassin Lee Harvey Oswald, and several short stories in *The New Yorker.* Stafford's last *New Yorker* story, "An Influx of Poets," published only a few months before her death, clearly showed that her wit and shrewdness were undiminished. A thinly disguised chronicle of her years with Robert Lowell and a sarcastic attack on his religious affectations, "An Influx of Poets" won an O. Henry Award for Best Short Story. Although her later years were plagued by illness and alcoholism, Stafford's stylistic brilliance, her psychological insight, and her ability to interpret the many levels of human experience remained with her throughout her career. In an early review of Stafford's short fiction, Gene Baro wrote: "[Though] Miss Stafford's is essentially an intellectual vision, it does not overwhelm or needlessly complicate her materials. This is to say that Miss Stafford's intelligence serves her art. There is no ornament here, but rather the appropriate psychological and physical elements, richly detailed. This is life, created in its evocative variety with surpassing skill. And along with the wealth of images in these stories, the often brilliant prose, there is—true to life—humor, rage, faith, skepticism, irony, and an abiding human tenderness."

(See also *CLC,* Vols. 4, 7, 19; *Contemporary Authors,* Vols. 1-4, rev. ed., Vols. 85-88 [obituary]; *Contemporary Authors New Revision Series,* Vol. 3; *Dictionary of Literary Biography,* Vol. 2; and *Something about the Author,* Vol. 22.)

PRINCIPAL WORKS

NOVELS

Boston Adventure 1944
The Mountain Lion 1947
The Catherine Wheel 1952

SHORT FICTION COLLECTIONS

Children Are Bored on Sunday 1953
The Interior Castle 1953
Bad Characters 1964
The Collected Stories of Jean Stafford 1969

OTHER

Elephi, the Cat with a High I.Q. (children's book) 1962
A Mother in History (nonfiction) 1966

Howard Mumford Jones

It is no compliment to ***Boston Adventure*** to say that it is a striking and original novel in a poor season; it would be a striking and original novel in any season. It is full-blooded. Its style is condensed, old-fashioned in its dignity, highly accurate as a report on the sensibilities of the "I" who tells the story. Its events, made credible by the style and by a kind of indignant pleasure in experience, are memorable and haunting, even when they are grotesque.

There are, I suppose, two points of view from which to approach this book. The title is a challenge to that part of Boston which, in the words of the author, begins somewhere on Beacon Hill and concludes abruptly with the end of Commonwealth Avenue, and "*Boston*" in this sense is bound to debate the sociological and psychological accuracy of the portrait for which it has unwittingly posed. The verdict is likely to be that we can't be as bad as all that, but the verdict will be tangential to the real merit of the work.

The other point of view, and as I think the right one, is to consider ***Boston Adventure*** as imaginative experience; and as imaginative experience it is a powerful and disturbing book. The tale is the autobiography of Sonie Marburg, daughter of a German shoemaker and a Russian wife, who ends in captivity as amanuensis to Miss Pride, the embodiment of that lust for personal control which gives vitality to the Brahmins. The work is in two parts; or rather the imaginative picture is in two panels: Boston as seen in the dreams of the young and growing girl, living in macabre surroundings in a poor suburb; and Boston as discovered by the same girl after she has been taken up by Miss Pride. In part one, ["Boston"], the father deserts his family, but not until he has engendered an epileptic son. After the boy's death, the mother goes steadily mad, and has to be shut up in an asylum. But there is a kind of queer beauty in the mother's dementia, just as there is a beauty of horror in the brief life and death of the little boy.

The second panel, entitled "Pinckney Street," is the maturing woman's experience of the outward decorum and inward decay of "Boston"; and if this section lacks some of the more powerful moments of the earlier part, it has its unforgettable episodes, such as the marriage of a rebellious daughter of the aristocrats to a young doctor in order to conceal her pregnancy, and her suicide. The "adventure" consists, I suppose, in the high hopes with which the heroine approached what seemed to be earthly felicity, and the numbing discovery that the madness from which she thought she had escaped lies about her in the well-bred purlieus of Pinckney Street.

The "I" of the story is a curious and tantalizing figment of the imagination, timeless and changeless, a devouring and pitiless register of emotion, sensibility, place, and person. If the tale traces the life of Sonie from the time she is a little girl until the time she is helplessly entrapped by

"Boston," the teller of the story never develops, for the queer reason that she does not seem to need to develop. She is born old. Emerson has somewhere a phrase about becoming a transparent eyeball; this is the achievement of Miss Stafford. I have read no modern novel of late which so truly compelled me to think of the concentrated emotional power of the Brontës. She has a trick of making time stand still while she wrings every conceivable value, whether of comedy or horror, out of successive episodes in her tale.

To be sure, the book is uneven. Some of the characters are cartoons; some of the episodes are merely tawdry or melodramatic. The writing is not always at the high level of its better parts, and the construction of the book, particularly in part two, is indefinite, as if portions had been cut away and the remainder joined awkwardly together. It is puzzling to know whether Sonie Marburg is simply a recorder or the heroine of her own story. The "Boston" section is in this respect especially confused, inasmuch as Sonie is thrust aside by the rebellious daughter of the Puritans, fantastically named Hopestill Mather.

Somehow these things do not matter. No big book (and especially no big first book) in the tradition of English fiction but has radical flaws sufficient to ruin a work of lesser magnitude. But the book is bigger than its mistakes, and so is ***Boston Adventure.*** Miss Stafford is a commanding talent, who writes in the great tradition of the English novel; and unless her first work is a flash in the pan (and Heaven send it be not), American letters have been enriched by a unique, vigorous, and remarkable artist.

Howard Mumford Jones, "The Artistry of Jean Stafford," in The Saturday Review of Literature, *Vol. XXVII, No. 39, September 23, 1944, p. 10.*

Ernest Jones

The Catherine Wheel is the most engrossing unsuccessful novel I have read for a very long time. It is unsuccessful because it tries to do too much and because Miss Stafford's attitude toward her subject or subjects is ambiguous. Sometimes she marshals her awareness to achieve a density comparable to that which marked the fine opening chapter of ***Boston Adventure.*** Sometimes she clutters her writing with a multiplicity of matters ineptly crowded together.

The central symbol, for example, is beautifully worked out. The wheel of Saint Catherine was an instrument of torture named for that Egyptian martyr who was subjected to it. Here it represents the long, virginal, imperceptive, and imperceptible torment of Katharine Congreve. She is thirty-eight in the summer of the novel. Nothing has really happened to her since her heart was most conventionally broken twenty years earlier. She is rapidly approaching entire collapse. Her chief nervous symptoms are a feeling which recurs with increasing frequency of being whirled about, wheeling and helpless; and a desire for death. Yet her outer life is serene. Watched over by "her faithful servants," her beauty untouched by any flame, she presides as chatelaine of a great Maine summer house, adorned, from cellar to garret, with objects chosen by generations endowed with impeccable taste.

The everyday Catherine wheel is a kind of fireworks which gushes upward, circles about in brief splendor, and then splutters out. Like it, Katharine's "rarified world" is an ephemeral pyrotechnical display. When, during a show of fireworks, she is burned to death, one of our last sights of her is as she "ran by herself in a widening circle, fanning the fire until it reached her waist."

But the novel is also about the initiation of her twelve-year-old cousin, Andrew Shipley, into a knowledge of the frailty of human ties. Miss Stafford is very good at recapturing what goes on in the minds of children—***The Mountain Lion*** displays this power—but Andrew's difficulties are a distraction never really incorporated into the novel. And he, in turn, has twin sisters, whose blossoming, though intended as a contrast to the sterility of Katharine's life, is a further distraction.

On another level ***The Catherine Wheel*** is a daydream brought to a violent conclusion. The ordered life of a great house, the objects which adorn it, the way this woman lives are, in their fashion, desirable. Miss Stafford loves them all. Yet she weighs them also with a meaningless irony and, after displaying them lovingly, destroys them with meaningless violence. She seems to be saying that the nerves and the senses *will* have their destructive way. When she destroys what she has so tenderly re-created—her earlier novels end in similar, inconclusive, senseless catastrophes—rage rather than knowledge possesses her during the cold ceremonial preparations to kill, tritely, the thing she loves.

Occasionally she over-writes. But Miss Stafford's elegant sentences, except when they fall into lists of rare objects connoting vanished elegance, are, unlike most contemporary ornate writing, organic to what one guesses was a large design. They are the sometimes fanciful garment of intentions and perceptions which are never quite successfully organized into a whole because she never knows exactly what she thinks and feels about her subject and also, probably, because private feelings, irrelevant to her purpose, will intrude upon her fiction. She creates, constantly, the impression of seeing clear through everything she writes about to nothing at all. (pp. 136-37)

Ernest Jones, "The Widening Circle," in The Nation, *New York, Vol. 174, No. 6, February 9, 1952, pp. 136-37.*

Gene Baro

Reading Jean Stafford's short stories, one does not remain outside of them; rather, one is caught up into their immediate reality, into their rich emotional and physical texture. First, one participates in the individual, created worlds of Miss Stafford; later, upon reflection, one can begin to speculate upon, to analyze and to wonder at Miss Stafford's artistry.

Character is most important in [the stories in ***Children Are Bored on Sunday***], but character does not play out a drama of isolated sensibility. Instead, Miss Stafford's people are seen, as it were, in a full round of experience, are set with their problems and conflicts in a milieu that is vital and charged both with intimate and external meaning. To an unusual degree, there is significant rapport and reciprocal influence between these characters and their environments, and from this ability of Miss Stafford's to relate aspects of character with the details of scene and situation comes a major strength of these stories, their compelling believability.

For example, in **"A Summer Day,"** the loneliness of Jim Littlefield, the eight-year-old orphan Indian boy, colors and is colored by the empty, barren and lonely Oklahoma landscape to which he has come from his green, sheltered home in Missouri. Symbol and reality are one and the same, and when Jim at last falls asleep on the bare ground in the courtyard of the Reservation School, he has begun to accept and take comfort from the world of his misery, which is in fact the world of all the dispossessed, whether it sits in the arid heat of the Oklahoma plain or is elsewhere upon the rude, indifferent earth.

There is a great variety of theme, character and locale in these stories. **"The Interior Castle"** takes us into the cold, antiseptic atmosphere of a hospital, where the heroine, recovering from a near-fatal automobile accident, retreats from her ruined body into the terrible sterility of her mind. **"The Home Front"** tells most eloquently of the conflict between a refugee doctor in an American defense plant town and his landlady and her family, a moral battle which is an ironic component of the issues of the last war, indeed, of every war, and in which the innocent, here a bird and a cat, suffer the full measure of the human antagonists' rage and guilt. The title story, **"Children are Bored on Sunday"** explores the warped intellectual and artistic life of New York, when one of its exiles fears to meet another she knows in the galleries of the Metropolitan Museum of Art.

But such descriptions can do no justice to these pieces or their six fellows. Their meaning overflows the mere outlines of Miss Stafford's stories, for these are interpretations of experience that have relevance beyond the confines of a tale. Or at least this is true of most of the matter Miss Stafford offers here. More often, the human situation is widely revealed, even through what may appear to be the most circumscribed situation or problem of individual character.

And though Miss Stafford's is essentially an intellectual vision, it does not overwhelm or needlessly complicate her materials. This is to say that Miss Stafford's intelligence serves her art. There is no ornament here, but rather the appropriate psychological and physical elements, richly detailed. This is life, created in its evocative variety with surpassing skill. And along with the wealth of images in these stories, the often brilliant prose, there is—true to life—humor, rage, faith, skepticism, irony and an abiding human tenderness.

Gene Baro, "The Several Worlds of Jean Stafford," in New York Herald Tribune Book Review, *May 10, 1953, p. 3.*

Elizabeth Janeway

In arranging [***The Collected Stories***] for publication, Jean Stafford has divided them into four groups by their geographical settings: "The Innocents Abroad"; "The Bostonians and Other Manifestations of the American Scene"; "Cowboys and Indians, and Magic Mountains"; and "Manhattan Island." She seems indisputably right in doing so, for the stories in each group are related by mood and by range as well as by setting. "In a sense," Miss Stafford writes in her introductory note, "the geographical grouping is arbitrary"; but in another sense it is not, and she acknowledges this when she speaks of Mark Twain and Henry James, whose titles she has borrowed as "two of my favorite American writers to whose dislocation and whose sense of place I feel allied." Nor can the reader ignore the hovering presence of these and of others who earlier considered American isolation, American awkwardness, American fantasies, and the price of American innocence.

In a way Miss Stafford's themes are archaic as well as indigenous, for they are older than today, and they will be newer tomorrow. They are, however, re-examined very thoroughly. If Miss Stafford is still on the side of her "Innocents Abroad," she does not take her stand there unequivocally. Innocence can be rather silly, can be adulterated with ignorance and lack of imagination. These qualities shadow the young girls who are the heroines of **"Maggie Meriwether's Rich Experience"** and **"The Echo and the Nemesis,"** two of the first group of stories. Reading them some years ago one felt a shock in them that has since been lost, and now one identifies less easily with the shocked heroine. It is a tribute to Miss Stafford's skill that the stories are not dated by this, but instead are changed and deepened. Our present doubts about American innocence, and our uneasy feeling that it contains the seeds of moral irresponsibility, existed already in these stories.

Another of Miss Stafford's strengths can be seen even in a rather slight story like **"The Children's Game"**—that is, her ability to tell us exactly what is happening and nevertheless to deepen the mystery of why her people behave as they do. (p. 136)

The Western stories, and most of those laid in New York too, fall into a different mood. "The Innocents Abroad" can go home again, but the children and young people caught in the provinces hate their homes and live there as despairing prisoners, aching to leave a world so small and mean it cramps the spirit. Again, this is an archaic American theme, a part (one might say) of the Matter of America, as Arthur and Gawain and Tristan belong to the Matter of Britain. Not only Mark Twain but Sherwood Anderson, Dreiser, and Willa Cather have dealt with it. Miss Stafford's story **"In the Zoo"** creates magnificently that emotion of waste, impotence, self-pity, self-contempt, and angry hopelessness that we refer to when we say "alienation" but that has never really been named. It haunts the Great Plains, and the slopes of the Rockies, as it haunted the thickets and the steppes of Chekhov's Russia. It is a way station on the road to paranoia. Even in happy later life, the children who breathed that atmosphere can suffer recurrences of distrust and despair, remembering their years of servitude to a foster-mother worse than Cinderella's. Indeed the "Gran" of **"In the Zoo"** is less a person than a local deity, mean as a Snopes but without Snopesian ambition, a Mrs. Grundy of the home, an injustice collector of genius. There are two of her in **"The Liberation,"** and in other stories, like **"Bad Characters," "A Reading Problem,"** and **"The Healthiest Girl in Town,"** one feels her unseen presence driving desperate children to look for refuge in the exhilarating, anarchic world of real outsiders instead of accepting the shabby community where Gran rules.

It is in the New England stories that one finds an alternative to Gran's world, and that is why they seem to me the most interesting. From the time she created Sonie Marburg of ***Boston Adventure*** twenty-five years ago Miss Stafford has regularly sent forth inquiring and ardent explorers of the one indisputable high culture which the United States has achieved. . . . What is it that we made there, in New England? Miss Stafford asks, and it is not a regional or a dated question, but an invitation to study the American identity through its quintessential social artifacts and, perhaps, to divine from these the American destiny.

Here come the outsiders, like Sonie Marburg and Rose Fabrizio in the story **"The Bleeding Heart,"** drawn by a vision of order and of a civilization worthy of willing obedience. What fires must burn within to have produced the balanced and convoluted perfection without! Sonie sees Miss Pride as a replacement for her mad witch-mother. Rose imagines the handsome stranger she sees reading in the library as a foster-father. Then each penetrates the citadel. Rose finds madness and rot. Sonie's participation in the rites of civilization is not as priestess but as sacrificial victim. Of the creative fire that once burned, nothing remains but a spark like a maggot in the brain, or an incestuous flame that licks the last hickory logs on the hearth, which will blacken and die if they are separated.

And yet something was there, and something lingers, distorted and eccentric but incontestable. The best story in the book (no easy judgment on a collection containing **"Bad Characters," "In the Zoo,"** and that marvelously controlled tale **"The Interior Castle"**) is a Boston story, **"Life Is No Abyss,"** which is published here for the first time. It is about eighty-year-old Isobel Carpenter, who has taken up residence in the poorhouse, to the horror of her rich relatives, and who refuses to leave. It is also about the nature of reality, and the value of confronting it, for reality is where Isobel dwells—or, rather, where she reigns—even though her motives for settling herself there are malice and spite. Cousin Will invested her fortune for her after her father, the Judge, died at the age of 103, invested it (says Isobel) "in banana plantations in Winnipeg," and immediately lost every penny. Horrified, Will invited her to share his home and his purse (and so did half a dozen others of the cousinage). A lesser woman might have done so, and spent her declining years in luxury and conscientious nagging. But Isobel is capable of the grand gesture. "Will put me in the poorhouse," she declared, and thither she departed.

There she has been for eighteen months on the day that pretty twenty-year-old Lily comes to call in place of poor Cousin Will, who has come down with bronchitis. Lily has been protected up to now from the sight of Isobel in the squalor of her surroundings, but she is warm-hearted and kind, and eager to help Will bear the burden which Isobel's revenge has thrust on him, for Lily too is penniless, orphaned by her parents' death in an accident, and dependent on Will's generosity. It is through her eyes that we see the three-bed ward which Isobel shares with mad, gentle Viola and a series of old women who arrive only to die. The food is awful. Isobel is clothed in a gruesome print uniform. Her arthritis is untreated. A radio plays incessantly, poor Viola croons, a disc jockey jokes. And here Isobel chooses to stay!

She is not crazy, for she judges her surroundings accurately and speaks her mind about them. She's neither lost her wit nor gained humility by living in conditions which only a saint could endure—and enduring them. Vicious-tongued, opinionated, unkind, Isobel is still alive and awake, for she has preserved the basic right of the individual, the right to choose. It may be a poor choice, Hobson's choice, but she is where she is by her own will and for her own continuing purpose, which is more than Lily can claim, or rich Cousin Augusta either, who is also calling to offer Isobel her hospitality. And whether she knows it or not—quite possibly she does not, but she may—there is a great deal to be said for her choice, for the poorhouse is where life is. After eighty years under the Judge's wing Isobel has found the gritty margin of experience where nerves react to real stimuli, where the senses transmit messages from outside, and the mind finds its vocation as an instrument of salvation. Whether or not Isobel will gain a reward for the sufferings she has chosen to endure, whether one can reach sainthood by way of fury and spite, *we* gain, reading the story of one who is neither an innocent nor yet corrupt.

I must not close without saying how moving these stories are, more austere than Miss Stafford's novels, but able at

The opening of *Boston Adventure*

Because we were very poor and could not buy another bed, I used to sleep on a pallet made of old coats and comforters in the same room with my mother and father. When I played wishing games or said "Starlight, starbright," my first wish always was that I might have a room of my own, and the one I imagined was Miss Pride's at the Hotel Barstow which I sometimes had to clean when my mother, the chambermaid, was not feeling well. I knew its details so thoroughly that I had only to say to myself the words "Miss Pride's room" and at once my feet stood on the tawny rug with its hugh faded peonies, and before me was the window seat covered with flat, flowered cushions, at one end of which was a folded afghan, at the other, three big soft pillows on which cherubs floated amongst blue daisies, holding up in their dimpled hands a misty picture of a castle. And I could gaze through the windows which overlooked the bay. On a clear morning, looking across the green, excited water, littered with dories and lobster-pots and buoys, I could see Boston and its State House dome, gleaming like a golden blister.

their best to reach as far and point as precisely. A particular grace is the dialogue. There is no one else writing today whose people speak more truly, and more surprisingly. This is something finer than "having an ear." It is the mark of a writer whose perceptions are so immediate and exact that she can use dialogue not just for color or plausibility or character drawing, but to embody and convey the very heart of her intentions. (pp. 136-38)

Elizabeth Janeway, "The Worlds of Jean Stafford," in Atlantic Monthly, *Vol. 223, No. 3, March, 1969, pp. 136-38.*

Barbara White

In her lifetime Jean Stafford published several collections of short stories and three novels: ***Boston Adventure*** (1944), ***The Mountain Lion*** (1947), and ***The Catherine Wheel*** (1952). Although her novels were very favorably reviewed and her ***Collected Stories*** (1969) won a Pulitzer Prize, Stafford is not well known. There are relatively few critical studies of her work, and in the many recent books and articles on female writers she is seldom mentioned. It may be that critics have been diverted by her reputation as a writer of "well-made" short stories. At any rate, Stafford is an important novelist whose work has been undeservedly neglected. Her fiction is not, as the label "well-made" can imply, detached from broad social concerns. It has much to say about cherished American myths, especially myths about women, the West, and the ritual of the hunt.

Stafford should also be of interest to students of the *Bildungsroman,* for she is above all a chronicler of adolescence. All three of her novels are about initiation into adulthood. ***Boston Adventure*** is the story of a young girl's growth to womanhood, while the youth in ***The Catherine Wheel*** is a boy whose growing pains have an impact on the older woman who befriends him. In ***The Mountain Lion,*** the subject of this essay, there are two young protagonists, one female and one male, who face initiation.

The plot of ***The Mountain Lion*** is simple. The protagonists, Molly and Ralph Fawcett, are introduced at ages nine and eleven, respectively, and taken to ages thirteen and fifteen. At the beginning of the novel they live with their widowed mother and older sisters in California and are very much under the influence of two grandfathers. Their home is a shrine to Mrs. Fawcett's deceased father, Grandfather Bonney, who was a genteel merchant; each year they receive a visit from her stepfather Kenyon, a crude rancher. After Grandfather Kenyon dies, Ralph and Molly spend several summers at his son Claude's ranch. Here Ralph is gradually initiated into adulthood and Molly refuses initiation. At the end of the novel Ralph kills Molly in a hunting "accident."

The reviewers and critics who have discussed ***The Mountain Lion*** agree in their basic interpretation of the novel. They see two symbolic schemes. First, Grandfather Bonney and the Fawcett home over which his image presides stand for everything bourgeois and stifling. Ralph and Molly reject the Bonney world for that represented by Grandfather Kenyon and Uncle Claude's ranch—a natural world of freedom. The second set of contrasting symbols is formed by Ralph and Molly themselves. They supposedly represent two different ways of reacting to adulthood, the ways of alienation and integration; Ralph illustrates acceptance, while Molly is a symbol of resistance to growth. The novel concludes appropriately because Ralph is symbolically rejecting childhood when he not-so-accidentally kills Molly. Molly's end is also fitting because if she won't grow up she must die.

Within this general outline there is some room for disagreement. What is the symbolic meaning of the mountain lion Ralph misses as he shoots Molly? What values are to be assigned Molly's refusal of adulthood and Ralph's acceptance of it? Should one stress Molly's nobility in the face of a society which rejects "misfits" and "freaks," or should one dismiss Molly as a hopeless neurotic and emphasize Ralph's successful growth to "maturity"? There is no limit to speculation because the answers depend on readers projecting their own attitudes on the worth of the society the initiate faces.

The problem is that the novel itself does not focus on these questions. It does not simply assume x, an adolescent resistant to initiation, and y, an adolescent accepting of initiation, and move on to other matters. Stafford is primarily concerned with portraying why it is that one adolescent rejects what the other can accept. Why is Molly a misfit and Ralph a candidate for initiation? Although the gender of the two protagonists has been ignored, it is essential in the novel that Molly is female and Ralph male. As we shall see, the action of the book would not make sense if the protagonists were two boys. Stafford shows us clearly that because Molly and Ralph are of different sexes, the conditions of their lives and the fates which they may expect are also different.

It is generally assumed that Molly and Ralph start out the same and only later grow apart. They are ugly, sickly, and precocious children who do not get along with other people. They band together against the rest of the world and are so close they suffer nosebleeds at the same time. Both children resist the prospect of adulthood; for example, they refuse knowledge of sexual intercourse—schoolmates "had said things and hinted at others so awful that Ralph and Molly had to fight them." In one sense they are treated similarly by their mother. She obviously prefers her two older daughters, who are attractive and well-behaved, and denies Molly and Ralph love.

Even at the beginning of the book, however, there are important differences in Ralph's and Molly's views and in the treatment afforded them. Mrs. Fawcett may withhold affection from both children, but she is less harsh with Ralph. When Ralph offends her and Molly stands up for him, she sends Ralph from the room but slaps Molly's face and locks her in the closet. Mrs. Fawcett sees Ralph as more significant than Molly and as deserving of some respect just because he is a boy. When the neighbors are sympathizing with her after Grandfather Kenyon's death, she says, "First my father, then my husband, and now Mr. Kenyon. But I have my son." Because only men count, Ralph is "all I have left in the world."

Even Ralph at age eleven is aware of his superior position. Molly may be his best friend, but she is not an equal. (pp. 194-96)

Not only is Molly made aware of the inferior status of women but she is also instructed in the types of things women are expected to do. It is Molly, not Ralph, who is sent on household errands and made to sew and cook. Ralph is enthusiastic about dogs, prizefights, and beards. The children's areas of activity have already been marked out for them. Molly tries to copy Ralph, for she sees his world as more worthwhile than that of her mother and sisters. The sisters, Leah and Rachel, seem to step from the pages of a nineteenth-century young ladies' conduct book. They are considered beautiful because of their golden hair, their fair skin (which Mrs. Fawcett carefully protects from sunburn and freckles), their delicate oval faces, and their small-boned bodies. Leah and Rachel are always polite, prefer the company of grownups, and are "perfect ladies." Although Molly sometimes envies her sisters' good looks, she basically dislikes the "femininity" which they represent; she refers to them contemptuously as "Elsie Dinsmores."

The low status of women and their typical pursuits is already evident to Molly. Ralph may be a "freak" also, but he is aware of his "superiority" in gender; he is preferred by his mother, he is not unfavorably compared to his sisters, and he is held out, even before adolescence, the possibility of a fate different from Molly's. Certainly the implications of accepting or rejecting initiation into adulthood are different when we begin not just with x and y but with a girl who has an inkling of belonging to an inferior group and being accorded an unwanted fate and a boy who may have to give up some things to become an adult but is conscious of a more palatable destiny.

Just as Molly and Ralph have been seen as tokens symbolizing two opposing reactions to adulthood, so have their Bonney and Kenyon heritages been regarded as contrasting symbols. The theory is that when Ralph and Molly visit Claude Kenyon's ranch they are entering an environment superior to their Bonney-dominated home, an environment which is freer and thus gives the children a chance to develop and be initiated into adulthood. The Kenyon ranch supposedly offers great opportunities of which only Ralph takes advantage, while Molly proves herself a "true freak" who can fit into neither world. There are two assumptions here which need to be examined: one that the Kenyon world is opposite from and superior to the Bonney world, and the other that entrance into the Kenyon world provides Ralph and Molly with equal opportunity for development. (pp. 196-97)

[Gradually] Stafford makes it clear that Grandfather Kenyon's world, the West, is no Eden. The Bonney home is indeed associated with deadness (Mrs. Fawcett wants to poison the children's cat and [her friend] Reverend Follansbee's hobby is taxidermy), but it is hard to support the contention that the Kenyon world is vital in comparison. The Western towns near Claude's ranch are described as "exactly the same." The buildings are faded and the streets filled with undernourished dogs. There are ghost towns with "sagging, rotten" houses and saloons and gambling dens "as haggard as death itself." The names of the saloons—"The Golden Horn," "The Silver Dollar," etc.—have become ironic. When Ralph goes driving with Uncle Claude, he sees "dreary, unpainted farmhouses that stood here and there along the road, unprotected by any tree, bleak and dusty in a grassless field."

If this is not the Romantic "West," neither are the inhabitants Natty Bumppos and Chingachgooks. The men are freer than the Bonney types only in the sense that they are externally more lawless. They get drunk with abandon, "behaving exactly as drunk people in the movies did," and they get drunk every Saturday night. Molly is quick enough to perceive the conventionality of their behavior, and Stafford continues from her point of view the movie analogy previously introduced by the narrative voice.

> Uncle Claude had bought a lot of grain alcohol and rotgut (rotgut! People ought to be put in jail for using words like that) and kept saying that they would all 'get stinko and then I'm gonna trim every jack man of you at Red Dog.' It was not hard to imagine. They would all pile up to the gallery and clank their silver dollars together, acting as if they were in a movie.

The Westerners follow their own internal laws, which are different from Grandfather Bonney's, but just as stringent.

Stafford includes in ***The Mountain Lion*** two descriptions of dinner conservations, one a typical Bonney dinner conversation and the other a Kenyon one. Mrs. Fawcett recalls nostalgically dinners with Grandfather Bonney, where he "directed table talk as adroitly and interestingly as a professional forum leader. . . . They talked of everything under the sun, often examining such concepts as 'justice," 'charity,' and 'truth.' Some of Mrs. Fawcett's most cherished values had been developed at that table." The satiric thrust of this passage is obvious, but supper at the Kenyon ranch is hardly presented as superior. There are some advantages; for instance, table talk is not presided over by a forum leader. Yet conversation is so undirected that no one pays any heed to anyone else; each man speaks when he feels like it and no one listens. While the subject matter is not intellectually and ethically pretentious, it is limited and unvaried—the men give their opinions on hunting, drinking, breeding bulls, and auctioning horses.

It seems that in many ways there is not much difference between the Kenyon and Bonney worlds after all. The ranchers gossip as much and are as concerned with appearances and one-upmanship as the Follansbees and other Bonney types. Only the topics are different, so that while the Bonneys criticize people's table manners the Westerners gossip about who can drink more, what so-and-so did when he was drunk, who has the best horses, and who cheated whom out of a horse. One of the outstanding defects of the Bonney world is hypocrisy; the Kenyonites are masters of the lie direct (Ralph is disillusioned when he discovers that many of his cherished Grandfather Kenyon stories were tall tales). While the Bonneyites make a pretense of caring about other people, the Kenyons openly don't care—they are frankly more interested in animals. There is a parallel between Mrs. Fawcett's being over-solicitous of Ralph's health and Uncle Claude's making him give up wearing his glasses. Neither one is considering Ralph's own welfare.

Perhaps readers have ignored Stafford's presentation of the West in non-idyllic terms because they have focused on the way Ralph sees it through most of the book. Ralph sets up a dichotomy between the Kenyon and Bonney worlds:

> Looking at the portrait of his Grandfather Bonney, Ralph read into his face vacuity and self-pride; he saw the plump hands as indolent and useless and believed that in a handclasp they would be flaccid. . . . He decided that the world was made up of two groups of people. The first he called the 'Kenyon men' and this included those who, like Uncle Claude, knew the habits of animals and subjected themselves to the government of the seasons and who, with age, became neither fat and bald like Grandfather Bonney nor boney and ragged like Mr. Follansbee. The other group he called 'Bonney merchants' and this included everyone he had ever known with the exception of the people at the Bar K, Grandpa, and Molly. The fundamental distinction between the two groups was, he thought, their attitude toward horses and, vice versa, the attitude of horses toward them.

We must note that this is Ralph's perception and that when he makes his observation, he is twelve or thirteen years old; even if he were an adult one might ask whether type of handshake and attitude toward horses are the best criteria for judging people.

Moreover, as Ralph grows older and becomes more intimately acquainted with Kenyon life, his perceptions change. He still prefers Kenyon over Bonney but he no longer idolizes the Kenyon men. He is troubled by Uncle Claude's scornful reaction to a sick bull, and he sees in Claude's face "a certain ponderous stupidity, a sort of virile opacity, an undeviating dedication to the sickness and health and the breeding of animals." If Claude has contempt for a sick bull, what would be his reaction to an infirm person? When Ralph is greeted by Claude on his last trip to the ranch, he "distrusts the enthusiasm in his uncle's voice, so boy-like that it actually cracked." Uncle Claude, the epitome of the Kenyon man, now seems more like a boy. Previously Ralph had considered him the most independent person in the world. Now he realizes that Uncle Claude demands company on his hunting and fishing expeditions because he can't stand to be alone. Ralph has a new understanding of the noble hunt for the mountain lion: "He (Uncle Claude) had never grown up and his hunt for Goldilocks was a childhood game; his men indulged and protected him like an innocent. They wanted him to be happy and so they wanted him to have the mountain lion."

It is not surprising that American literary critics could overlook the childishness of Kenyon men when young Ralph finally comes to recognize it. We can speculate that critics are as caught up as anyone else in American myths, and it is especially difficult to treat very objectively an American novel which juxtaposes civilized and relatively uncivilized worlds and which includes a boy's hunt for a wild animal. We are under the shadow of Huck Finn escaping from Aunt Polly and Ike McCaslin hunting bear. (pp. 197-99)

In ***The Mountain Lion*** the only women at the Kenyon ranch are Mrs. Brotherman and her daughter, Winifred. Mrs. Brotherman is the housekeeper; she performs services for the men that they would prefer not to do themselves. Winifred, when she is not waiting on the men at the dinner table, is a "tomboy"; she doesn't look or act like a "girl." The only concerns of the ranchers are the traditionally male ones of animal breeding, hunting, drinking, and gambling; their values are knowledge of the above activities, aggressiveness, and physical courage. Since the Kenyon world is uncivilized in comparison to the Bonney world and is heavily masculine, it is easy to see it as "idyllic," another "mythicized rural hinterland," until one realizes that Stafford is debunking rather than following the myth. (p. 199)

If we examine Ralph's attitude toward adulthood, we will see that, like many adolescents in modern novels, he is in conflict about becoming an adult. He does not want to be treated as a child, and he craves the privileges of adulthood. Yet he sees that he will have to compromise his integrity, will have to give in to and perhaps even become the things he hates about the Follansbees and Grandfather Bonney. In the beginning of the novel Ralph has a pact with Molly that they will not compromise themselves—they will always "hate the right ones." Ralph even wants an operation to drain off his Bonney blood. What is it about the Kenyon world that makes Ralph change his mind, while Molly continues to refuse initiation?

We know that "the vitality and freedom of the Kenyon ranch" is not an accurate answer because the Kenyon world is presented as only different from, not more vital and free than, the Bonney world. As we have also noted, however, the Kenyon ranch is masculine; it is free from women and what are considered female concerns and values. It is the masculinity of the Kenyon world and the implications of this masculinity which allow Ralph to accept adulthood.

We have seen that Ralph is not subjected to the discrimination Molly is and that, even before he makes his first trip to the ranch, he has begun to recognize the superior position of his sex. He is also beginning to show an interest in growing up which, as critics have noted, expresses itself in his resentment of Molly's copying him. But this desire for independence is specifically independence from Molly, for Ralph has begun to seek out male companionship. (p. 200)

Stafford points up Ralph's concern with masculinity by using . . . terms strongly suggesting masculinity whenever he thinks of his grandfather or Uncle Claude. So when Grandfather Kenyon arrives Ralph thinks he makes the family chauffeur look small and "somehow womanly." Ralph believes it impossible that Mr. Kenyon had ever kissed anyone, and when he shakes hands and greets Ralph, Ralph feels "personally, privately addressed, man to man." After Grandfather Kenyon dies of a heart attack

(Ralph worries that his collapse is unmanly), Ralph transfers his attentions to Uncle Claude, whom he also views as masculine. Claude looks like his father and has "massive, bullish" shoulders and heavy arms which terminate in the biggest hands Ralph has ever seen. Ralph is embarrassed about his "sissy life" in front of this animal-like man and is determined to win his respect.

Ralph's first necessity is to detach himself as much as possible from Molly. He convinces himself that Molly is "going crazy" and accepts Uncle Claude's invitation to the ranch only for himself, because "maybe something is going to happen to Molly." (This suggests, of course, that he wants something to happen to her, and foreshadows the ending of the book.) Although Ralph cannot prevent Molly's being sent to the ranch with him, he can completely separate himself from her at the ranch. For the next few years, then, Ralph is intimate with Molly at home while ignoring her at the Bar K. He intends that Molly and Winifred be friends so that he can more conveniently spend all his time with Uncle Claude. Ralph understands that Molly is supposed to be taking Winifred as a female "role model" just as he is taking Uncle Claude as a male one. Although he pities Molly when he looks at Winifred and notes Molly's comparative plainness (she may not be able to successfully imitate Winifred), he believes he can live up to Uncle Claude. Late in the novel Ralph recalls that his friendship with Uncle Claude began with a look. His first evening at the ranch he saw Claude looking at him and "read the look as a question of his worth or of his manliness." Ralph has learned to equate worth and manliness.

Claude Kenyon may have little to teach Ralph about becoming an adult (if Ralph himself comes to perceive Uncle Claude as childish), but Claude can initiate his nephew into male activities. Ralph learns to work "like a grown man"; he learns to ride and to shoot and to butcher animals. On Claude's suggestion he stops wearing his glasses, even though he is sick for a while and can never see as well without them. Although Claude at first laughs at Ralph's blunders, he occasionally praises him so that his confidence grows. Finally they become constant companions, spending their free time talking of hunting and horses. Through Uncle Claude, Ralph also comes to knowledge of sex. Earlier he had joined with Molly in refusing such knowledge. Now when Claude takes him to see a cow calving, he feels a "painful exultation." Although he knows it to be "bad," he gets a warm feeling.

By the time Ralph is fourteen and preparing to spend his last year on the ranch he has begun to view his mother and older sisters in a different way, that is, as sexual objects. He is so conscious of his sisters' sexuality that he is frequently overcome by the desire to kiss their necks, and he has sexual daydreams about them. He can see nothing but their physical beauty: "Looking at his older sisters with their fine, tender faces, their shining hair, their dresses of flowered pongee, catching their clean, delicious smell of soap and talcum powder, he wished Molly had never been born." Since he has reached adolescence Ralph's attitudes have changed so much that whereas before he admired Molly and was contemptuous of his other sisters, he now scorns Molly instead. Ralph shows how thoroughly he has absorbed the values of his society in the way he judges female beauty. He covets Leah and Rachel because of their whiteness and blondness: he appreciates their faces because they are "doll-like and china-white." (pp. 200-02)

[Ralph is able to grow up in ***The Mountain Lion***], while Molly cannot, for two reasons. First, he receives positive reinforcement from adults. Claude praises and encourages him, and the more Ralph learns about manhood at the ranch the better things are for him at home. Mrs. Fawcett approves Ralph's having "normal interests" and admits that "it was right for him to enjoy the company of a grown man—and, moreover, he was beginning to look . . . well, to put it bluntly, to look like a human being." She now considers him worthy of love and makes affectionate gestures.

Secondly, although he may have a few reservations, Ralph likes what he has discovered manhood will mean. He is pleased when his mother and sisters receive libidinous stares; while he feels some guilt, he likes the fact of women being prey. (One wonders whether he wishes increasingly that Molly didn't exist because he feels sorry for her or because she, in not accepting womanhood, is a threat to the existing order.) Ralph has learned that men have power and, even though he won't be able to exercise Claude's power in the Bonney world, where external violence is subdued, he has at least been promised the role of "man of the family" as he gets his college education in the East.

In many ways Ralph's initiation process at the Kenyon ranch resembles boys' initiation as it has taken place in primitive cultures. Stafford presents Ralph as being separated from women and having a male sponsor who takes the novice into his circle. (pp. 202-03)

The sequence of ordeals the youth goes through is supposed to establish the authority of the elders. . . . The ordeals Ralph meets range from his learning to go without glasses to his conquering his fear of horses and guns, and finally culminate in his actually hunting the mountain lion.

In the hunt of the mountain lion Stafford is drawing not only upon the extensive practice of trial by hunting in primitive cultures but also upon this practice as it has been presented as a motif in American literature. American initiation stories often include ritual trappings, as in Faulkner's "The Bear," and they presuppose the same values implied in the primitive practice of trial by hunting. Most American initiation stories involving a hunt have as an unstated premise that physical courage is the prime value and that it determines "masculinity," a requirement for maturity. Francis MacComber, for example, "comes of age" or gains maturity by becoming a "man" in mastering his physical cowardice. Thus it is quite natural that, just as they followed traditional American literary patterns in assuming a neat polarity between the Kenyon and Bonney worlds, critics should place positive value on Ralph's hunt for the mountain lion. The killing of the mountain lion would be a final trophy for Ralph, a symbolic indication that he has come to adulthood.

But Stafford treats the hunt ironically. As in the case of

the East versus the West, or the Bonney versus Kenyon worlds, she is departing from the traditional romantic pattern. As we have already seen, Claude's obsession with the hunt is finally viewed as childish. Instead of a deadly serious adult ritual in which an innocent youth is allowed to partake, the hunt is a "childhood game" in which Claude, the supposed initiator, is himself an "innocent." Nor does Uncle Claude serve as an intermediary between the boy and nature, like Sam Fathers. His only power is secular (he reserves the lion for himself by threatening to fire any of his men who shoot at it), and his natural integrity is called into question when he, like Ralph, breaks their pact that neither should hunt the lion when alone. Stafford not only questions the assumption that the hunt determines maturity, but she also makes explicit other premises of the hunt as an initiation ritual, that the hunt is an exclusively male activity and that it involves an assertion of power over the female.

Only men hunt at the Kenyon ranch (Ralph thinks it "natural" that girls would be uninterested in hunting). We are not allowed to forget, however, that the hunted, the mountain lion, is female. Claude names her "Goldilocks" because she is "blond as a movie star." Both Claude and Ralph never fail to refer to the lion as a "she" or a "bitch." (pp. 203-04)

In many initiation stories involving the hunt the protagonist destroys a "feminine principle" (perhaps in himself or perhaps a part of nature conceived of as feminine). As in the case of "The Short Happy Life of Francis MacComber" and Walter Van Tilburg Clark's *The Track of the Cat,* the hero thus proves his fitness to dominate an actual woman. In ***The Mountain Lion*** the pattern is so exaggerated that Ralph's hunt leads to the killing of the mountain lion as the symbol of femininity, the loss of any "feminine principle" within himself, and the death of Molly. If Ralph's initiation is costly to himself, in that his becoming thoroughly masculinized entails denying part of his humanity, its effect on Molly is to destroy her altogether.

At first Molly is as happy as Ralph to escape her Bonney home and visit Uncle Claude's ranch. But, as we have seen, the Kenyon ranch turns out to be a male refuge, where the role of women is to be silent hardworking servants to the men. The housekeeper, Mrs. Brotherman, hates the West and can hardly wait to return to New England; Mrs. Brotherman's predecessor, Mrs. Fawcett, "buried herself alive" for ten years keeping house while Grandfather Kenyon travelled; Mrs. Fawcett's predecessor, Grandmother Bonney-Kenyon, was "humorless," "beaten," and "unhappy." Other women in the West are worse off than the Bar K women. When Ralph and Molly travel to the ranch, they always see a number of gaunt young women with several small children. "Years of hard work and bad food had given the women a canine look in the mouth and eyes." They have teeth which have rotted and fallen out and hair like dirty strings, and they always leave the train at some "bleak, treeless town."

Whereas Uncle Claude enthusiastically takes on the role of Ralph's initiator, he gives Molly the same kind of treatment she received at home. He considers her "bookish and unhealthy" and is offended by her ironic comments on the "ride 'em cowboy" behavior of the ranch men. At first Molly makes an effort to win Uncle Claude's favor. She too stops wearing glasses, but her eyes are worse than Ralph's and she is almost blind without them. Finally, as Ralph recognizes, Claude is "so mean to Molly" that she avoids their outings and stays inside to write.

Although Molly initially continues her adoration of Ralph, taking vicarious pleasure in his accomplishments, they grow further and further apart. Molly blames Uncle Claude and life at the ranch in general for destroying her close relationship with her brother, the only person with whom she has been able to communicate. She pours acid on her hand when she realizes that Ralph is repudiating her in favor of Claude. Molly is no longer sure that she prefers the ranch to home. She gradually changes her mind about the superiority of the Kenyon world and revises her list of heroic figures to include only her father and Grandfather Kenyon, who are both dead.

Home life, while it gets better for Ralph, becomes worse for Molly as she enters her teens. Mrs. Fawcett thinks ranch life has improved Ralph, but she considers Molly more of a freak than ever. Although she makes affectionate gestures to Ralph, she remembers to stroke Molly only "as a sop to her conscience." Molly has never completely relinquished her desire to gain attention and love from her mother. The acid-pouring incident should probably be seen as an attempt to gain Mrs. Fawcett's attention as well as to punish Ralph for his defection. However, it becomes increasingly difficult for Molly to win her mother's favor because, as an adolescent, she is supposed to become more "feminine" in her appearance and behavior. When she refuses to conform to this expectation, she seems more and more eccentric to those around her.

Much of Mrs. Fawcett's new approval of Ralph is involved simply with looks. He has begun to look "like a human being" to her while Molly appears the same as she did when she was eight. The growing discrepancy in the protagonists' looks has been seen [by Stuart Burns in "The Novel of Adolescence"] as a "motif to point up their respective movements toward integration and alienation." Actually the motif reveals the differences in what is expected of them according to their sex. It is significant that Ralph and Molly look much alike: they have the same coarse, straight hair, heavy eyebrows, and prominent nose, but, as Ralph notes, "in a girl such ruggedness was not handsome as it was in him and Uncle Claude." It makes little difference what type of hair and features Ralph has so long as he is healthy and strong. But Molly is doomed because the ideal for girls is curly golden hair and delicate, rather than prominent, features.

It is clear that Molly actually hates herself as much as she hates all her "enemies" at home and at the ranch. We must remember, however, that when Molly adds her own name to her list of unforgivable people, she is looking at herself in the mirror. She cries and cries as she watches herself "getting uglier and uglier until she looked like an Airedale." (She does not look like a cat, the golden mountain lion.) It would be surprising if Molly did not hate herself, considering the overriding importance placed on good looks in women. (pp. 204-06)

[Girls] growing up are often told what Molly is told, that beauty is supreme and intellectual attainments are worthless. Molly's predominant virtue, her sharp intelligence, counts for nothing in both the Bonney and Kenyon worlds. Reverend Follansbee ridicules intelligence in women, while Mrs. Fawcett is ashamed of Molly's interest in books and embarrassed by her bright comments. "Everyone said that she had the brains of the family, but as Mrs. Fawcett was not interested in brains, she thought this a handicap rather than otherwise and often told Molly that there were other things in life besides books." At the ranch it is even worse for Molly because no one there reads. In the Bonney world intellectual attainments are valued in a man (Grandfather Bonney's knowledge of literature is a plus), but in the Kenyon world intellectual attainments are not valued at all. As for Ralph, when he and Molly were younger he admired her quickness and learning; when he becomes an adolescent he begins to resent her greater intelligence. (p. 206)

Molly manages to withstand public criticism of her interests and abilities without turning her anger on herself until she loses Winifred as a model. Winifred is one of the few bright spots in Molly's vacations at the ranch. Molly greatly admires this "tomboy" who wears blue jeans with dung on them. But when Ralph and Molly arrive at the ranch for their last stay, they discover that Winifred has changed:

> She was plump now and so mature and feminine that Ralph could not recognize in her the shooting companion of earlier summers, that rather negative and taciturn person who, without playing a role, had seemed like another boy. Now she was a positive creature, self-assured, beautiful and glowing with an interior smile.

Stafford with fellow writers Peter Taylor (left) and Robert Lowell in Louisiana around 1940. Taylor saw this photograph again thirty years later and noted that "Jean looks like the keeper of two nuts."

The terms "negative" and "positive" indicate that Ralph is pleased with Winifred's transformation (she has become prey, like his sisters, and he has sexual daydreams about her too), but for Molly the change is a disaster. Because Winifred remained a "tomboy" through her early teens, Molly was given hope that she herself could grow up without becoming like her sisters. Now at sixteen or seventeen, Winifred is suddenly "demure" and "soft-spoken," wearing upon her lips an "enchanting" and "mysterious" smile. The new Winifred is pleased when Ralph tells her he heard she was a good dancer; when Molly counters by praising her ability to read Latin, Winifred frowns and casts down her eyes "as though her character had been impugned."

Molly is disillusioned but does not give up on Winifred until Winifred writes back from college that "my sorority sisters are griped because I'm the only pledge who is dated up for the junior prom." Molly had thought that Winifred went to college to study Cicero's essays. Stafford makes the content and style of Winifred's letter deliberately parallel to an earlier letter their sister sent Molly and Ralph when she left on a trip. Leah wrote of her engagement:

> Mother made me promise not to tell but she can't do anything now since by the time you read this I will be on my way to China!!!!! On the third finger of my left hand, I am now the proud wearer of a diamond ring! . . . The Donor of the Famous Engagement Ring is named Robert Appleton and he is a senior at Dartmouth. I'd give anything to see your faces when you read this.

Molly's reaction was to pretend she was going to vomit. Throughout the book she has been sickened by Leah's vapidity, and now Winifred, as evidenced by her letter from college, has become another Leah. It is not surprising that Winifred leaves college after her first year in order to get married. (pp. 206-07)

Molly's distaste for the female roles prescribed for her explains the fact that she resists knowledge of sex. She refers to sex as "all that tommyrot with which people are trying to ruin my life." When Ralph tells her about the cows calving, she calls him a liar and has a nosebleed. She insists that stallions and geldings are two different breeds of horses. Although this behavior could be interpreted as evidence that Molly is "crazy," as Ralph believes, other female adolescent protagonists, like Frankie Addams of Carson McCullers's *The Member of the Wedding* (1946), fear sex also; they connect sexual intercourse with male domination. Ralph learned to accept sex when he realized he would have power as a man. It is probably not the act of sex itself which repulses Molly, but the fact that it reminds her of her inferior role.

Molly's elaborate preparations for her bath show that she is at least unconsciously aware of the implications of her physical development. She locks herself in the bathroom, blocks the keyhole, puts on her wrapper while she removes her underclothes, and gets into her bathing suit for the bath. She hates the word "body" and prefers to think of herself as a "long wooden box with a mind inside." Her maturing body is relentless proof that she is becoming a woman. Related to Molly's denial of her body is her obsession with fatness. She decides she hates the people she does because they are all fat. Since "fat" does not refer only to physical makeup, as people can say "fat" things to her, it would seem that she associates "fat" with "sexual." In this case Molly's attitude resembles that of many young girls who react to the growth of their breasts and the rounding out of their bodies by glorifying thinness. It is not unusual for adolescent girls to diet excessively or, in some cases, to refuse to eat at all. This behavior is sometimes interpreted as showing fear of pregnancy; a more fundamental explanation is that the girls are resisting the signs of their sexual maturity.

However "crazy" one may consider her, Molly has many other characteristics similar to "normal" girls her age. She would like to live up to the feminine ideal (for example, be beautiful, be approved by others) and at the same time reject it. Yet whatever types of rebellion she tries are essentially passive and even, as in the case of the acid incident, masochistic. Molly views herself, in part correctly, as helpless. When she and Ralph were younger their attempts to exercise control over their environment took the form of childish rituals; they would print Reverend Follansbee's name seven times on a piece of paper and then set fire to it in their Buddha incense burner. Ralph outgrows his belief in magic, not because it automatically disappears when he reaches adolescence but because he learns that he himself has power. Molly, on the other hand, uses the incense burner at the end of the novel just as she did at the beginning. As she sees fewer and fewer possibilities for action, she retreats into a dream world and isolates herself from those around her. She is like Sonie Marburg in Stafford's ***Boston Adventure,*** whose desire for a room of her own is thwarted until she imagines her own room and resorts to living in fantasy.

Because one can envision no viable alternatives for her, it seems as inevitable that Molly perish as it is that the mountain lion be killed. That Molly and Goldilocks are somehow linked is suggested by their simultaneous death at the end of the novel. Molly identifies with the mountain lion, which has its own special meaning for her. She envies the lion for its freedom, beauty, and golden hair, but she hates it for being hunted. That is to say, the mountain lion has qualities of a mythical female selfhood which Molly dreams of: it is independent, beautiful, virginal, and untamed; yet in reality it is not free—it is hunted by man and will ultimately be destroyed. Molly and the lion are both prey.

The mountain lion may seem to be a goddess, a Diana roaming the woods, but it is a false god, one with limited power. While it is undeniably a dangerous animal, it is also like the bull-roarer, a sacred object found in many primitive initiation rituals. The bull-roarer when attached to a string and whirled about makes terrifying noises which are supposed to represent the voice of the Sky God. When the male novice is initiated, he discovers that the bull-roarer is really harmless, and he is thus set apart from the women and children who fear it. (pp. 207-09)

The revelation that "adult men" have the "real power" is the key to initiation in ***The Mountain Lion.*** As we have seen, it is Ralph's recognition of this fact which leads him to overcome his repugnance to adulthood. But in Molly's case the dialectic between desire for adult status and resistance to it is weighted heavily to one side. The inducements for her to grow up are few because becoming an adult woman would mean accepting a state of powerlessness and, in fact, affirming her own "inferiority." It is thus misleading to discuss initiation in general terms of entrance to "adulthood," for adulthood has traditionally conferred a different status on men and women. Stafford does portray in her novel two adolescents reacting in opposite ways to the prospect of initiation. Her more central concern, however, is the *meaning* of initiation, which is different for each character. Ralph accepts initiation because manhood gives him privileges. Molly resists not growth in general, but growth to womanhood, a devalued state. (p. 209)

Barbara White, "Initiation, the West, and the Hunt in Jean Stafford's 'The Mountain Lion'," in Essays in Literature, *Vol. IX, No. 2, Fall, 1982, pp. 194-210.*

Mary Ellen Williams Walsh

In the Pultizer Prize-winning ***The Collected Stories of Jean Stafford,*** Stafford groups ten stories under the heading, "Cowboys and Indians, and Magic Mountains." The heading, which suggests a romantic, mythic West of the past filled with red men and white men in conflict, ironically comments on the contemporary, restricted lives of the characters in Stafford's stories who grow up overshadowed by that myth. For Stafford's central characters are girls and young women and a small Indian boy. They live in a modern West, most of them in one small town, a vantage point from which they get only occasional glimpses of the glorious West that was. They are, for the most part, separated both by time and by sex from the expansive Western tradition which provides a sharp contrast to their cramped and painful lives.

Seven of the stories are set in Adams, Colorado. In the "Author's Note" to ***The Collected Stories,*** Stafford writes that her "roots remain" in this semi-fictitious town. Adams, Colorado, is in an important sense Stafford's Yoknapatawpha. The stories she sets there strongly define her perception of the reality of the lives of girls and young women in the West. Adams is a quiet college town in the foothills of the Rockies. For each of Stafford's characters, however, the geography of the town is more narrowly defined than in this generalization. For most, the geography is rather bleak; for some, grotesque. The restrictions on their lives are exemplified in how they see where they live. (p. 230)

For Kitty Winstanley, in **"The Tea Time of Stouthearted Ladies,"** Adams is a world of near bankrupt boarding houses where her mother and other boarding house keepers rest their swollen feet and their "tumid hands mutilated by work" in kitchens such as the Winstanley's—"a room all skin and bones: a coal-oil range with gaunt Queen Anne legs, a Hoosier cabinet ready to shudder into pieces, a linoleum rug worn down to gummy blackness save in the places that were inaccessible to feet and still showed forth its pattern of glossy bruises." . . . The narrator of **"In the Zoo"** and her sister Daisy, who also grew up in the geography of the boarding houses, remember Adams as an "ugly town" with a "dreary park," "mongrel . . . churches," a "high school shaped like a loaf of bread." For them, the college campus was "an oasis of which (they) had no experience except to walk through it now and then." . . .

For Cora Savage, in **"The Philosophy Lesson,"** the college is not an oasis, but a place where she poses nude and immobile for a life drawing class, three mornings a week for three hours at a stretch, ignored by the other students except as she is an object which they paint or draw. Although Polly Bay, in **"The Liberation,"** teaches at the college, her Adams is reduced to a city block, lined by the ancestral homes of the Bays, a place which induces in her a feeling of claustrophobia. The homes are in various stages of dismantling, which suggest the decay of the Bay family. One has become a museum, one has been made into apartments, and one has been torn down. The fourth is the one in which she lives with her widowed aunt and widowed uncle, a house so "gorged with furniture and with garnishments and clumps and hoards of artifacts of Bays, you had no sense of space . . . and felt cornered and nudged and threatened." . . .

Emily Vanderpool, the narrator of **"Bad Characters"** and **"A Reading Problem,"** inhabits yet another Adams. While her own home is a "normal" middle-class household, her travels around Adams take her to the "bedlam" of a Woolworth's, where old men "look as if they were walking over their own dead bodies"; to the library, where the librarian wears a yellow wig; to the lobby of a hotel whose permanent residents are querulous old men; to the waiting room of the jail where she overhears obscenities shouted by drunken moonshiners; and finally to a roadside campground where the single occupants are a traveling evangelist-bootlegger and his daughter.

The Adams, Colorado, in which these girls and young women live is, then, collectively a place of illness, poverty, stasis, and grotesquerie. In this landscape, they are allowed little freedom of action. For months, [nine-year-old Jessie, in **"The Healthiest Girl in Town"**] is forced to spend several afternoons a week enduring boredom and harassment as the captive playmate of the children of her widowed mother's employer, so that her mother will not lose her job. Throughout the deadly afternoons the sickly Butler children lovingly caress their illnesses and deride Jessie's healthiness. The sisters in **"In the Zoo"** are equally trapped. None of their movements goes undetected or untaunted by their foster mother. She does not object to their visits to their one childhood friend, a gentle, drunken Irishman who lives by the railroad tracks with two capuchin monkeys and several other animals, because these visits allow her to heap verbal abuse on Mr. Murphy. Her greatest triumph over the sisters and their friend is turning the gentle dog given to the girls by Mr. Murphy into a killer that destroys one of his beloved capuchins.

Emily Vanderpool, whose family and social class at least allow her the freedom of choosing her own friends and moving with relative ease about the town, is nonetheless not shielded from painful and grotesque human situations, which come to her in the persons of Lottie Jump and Opal Gerlash. Emily bewails her "bad character" which causes her to alienate all her friends. Lottie Jump, whom Emily first encounters as a thief in the Vanderpool home, is a hardened, eleven-year-old criminal, "evilly ugly," dressed in filthy, ill-fitting clothes. She is a real "bad character," the extension in all details of Emily's somewhat refined fears. Similarly, Emily's "reading problem" is parodied by the situation of Opal Gerlash. When Emily finally finds a place where she can read and memorize the names of the books of the Bible, Opal and her father intrude upon Emily's peace. Opal, a twelve-year-old con artist who assists her father in selling hell-fire-and-brimstone religion and an alcohol-based liver medicine, recites by rote some of her religious spiel.

The actions of Emily, Jessie, and the sisters in **"In the Zoo"** are limited partly because they are children. The actions of the older young women in the other Adams stories are, however, equally limited. Cora Savage and Kitty Winstanley are both students at Nevilles College. That they are educating themselves suggests a possible means for them to achieve greater freedom and eventually to escape their current situations. It is important, however, that neither do they consciously consider this point nor does Stafford imply it, other than by portraying them as college students. In fact, in the most stunning image of restriction in the stories, Cora is literally immobile throughout the episode of **"The Philosophy Lesson."** She poses nude, only her eyes and her mind active, enduring the psychological pain of becoming an object and servant to her fellow students and the harsh physical pain of her straining muscles. Kitty, like Cora, is restricted to the role of servant to her fellow students each evening in her mother's boarding house. Each summer she escapes to the comparative freedom of a dude ranch, where as a hired servant she is in a less ambiguous position than she is in at home, but where she exists at the whim of the dudes and her employers and where her day is circumscribed by chores from 5 a.m. to 9 p.m. (pp. 231-33)

The family situations of the girls and young women in the Adams stories contribute to their powerlessness. Most of the characters are in fact either orphans or the children of invalid fathers. Thus, early in their lives they have experienced the deep emotional loss caused by the death or lingering illness of a parent and the resulting psychological and physical deprivation. While Emily Vanderpool's parents are both very much alive, the distortions in the lives of her alter egos are at least partially explained by missing or disabled parents. Opal Gerlash's mother had died a year before Emily encounters her. Lottie Jump's father was slowly dying of tuberculosis. Although Cora Savage fondly remembers some childhood experiences with her father, he is absent from her reflections on the present. It is only her "anxious United Presbyterian" mother whom she has had to reassure about her posing nude. Kitty Winstanley's father has lost a lung. His inability to find work and the constant fear and bitterness of his wife as they live "hand to mouth, one jump ahead of the sheriff" unman him, in the eyes of Kitty, who hates him for his weakness and hates her mother "for her injustice" and hates "herself for hating in them what they could not help."

The other characters are true orphans. Jessie, in all her health, is "possessed with the facts of dying and of death," especially by the memory of her father's death from gangrene. While she retains the consolation of a "valiant, pretty" mother, the two of them are subject because of her father's death to having to please people like the Butlers so that they may live. The deaths of both their parents place the sisters in **"In the Zoo"** in the hands of the paranoiac Mrs. Placer, herself the widow of a tubercular husband. Griefstricken for their parents and with no responsible relatives to offer them comfort, the girls are left to grow up "like worms," in a house "steeped in . . . mists of accusation and hidden plots and double meanings." . . .

Both Polly Bay's parents are also dead. Her mother died when she was a child. Her father's death, seven years prior to the action of **"The Liberation,"** has placed her at the mercy of her aunt and uncle: "Both widowed and both bereft of their heartless children, (they) had cajoled her and played tricks upon her will until she had consented to go and live with them. It was not so much because she was weak as it was because they were so extremely strong that she had at last capitulated out of fatigue." . . .

Orphaned or near-orphaned, caught like insects in amber in restricted situations, living in a nightmarish landscape, the girls and young women cope with their situations, but they do not resolve them. Jessie is unable to free herself from spending the obligatory afternoons with the Butler children. She does however defy them with her vitality and frees herself from the feeling they had imposed on her that her health was a "disgrace." In a purging of fear and anguish and as a reaction to their torture, she admits she has lied about her father's dying of leprosy. She exultantly exclaims: " 'He got shot out hunting, if you want to know. . . . My father was as tall as this room. The district nurse told Ma that I am the healthiest girl in town. Also I have the best teeth.' "

The sisters in **"In the Zoo"** cope by adapting their behavior to the suspicions of Mrs. Placer, living "in a mesh of lies and evasions, baffled and mean, like rats in a maze." As adults, they wonder why they had not fled their situation as soon as they were old enough to work. They realize, the narrator concludes, that Mrs. Placer had "held us trapped by our sense of guilt. We were vitiated, and we had no choice but to wait, flaccidly, for her to die." The sisters as adults feel themselves at last free of the "succubus" who had preyed on them. Their farewell remarks to each other, however, reveal that they have been permanently damaged by the suspicion and hostility toward other people that Mrs. Placer ingrained in them, even to the point of their unconsciously using her favorite phrase, "I had to laugh," to preface their spiteful remarks about the narrator's fellow passengers.

Polly Bay is awakened to her situation when she falls in love and begins planning to leave her aunt and uncle. She begins to understand how she had coped. She sees, "appalled and miserably ashamed of herself, that she had never once insisted on her own identity in this house. She had dishonestly, supinely (thinking, however, that she was only being polite), allowed her aunt and uncle to believe that she was contented in their house, in sympathy with them, and keenly interested in the minutiae that preoccupied them. . . . She had never disagreed with them." . . . She counts herself lucky that unlike Aunt Lacy, her uncle's wife, she had not had to die to free herself of the Bays. In an outrageous irony, her fiancé does die. Nonetheless, her love for him and the realization that her love has brought to her about her life continue the impetus for her "liberation." She leaves Adams, not triumphantly as she has expected, but fleeing, taking with her only the clothes she is wearing. (pp. 233-36)

Cora Savage's body remains frozen in a pose, but her active mind seeks release. The avenues she finds remove her farther from, rather than connect her to, humanity. First she glories in the falling snow, because it dematerializes the studio and conceals "the harshness of the world." Then she reflects on Bishop Berkeley's philosophy and concludes that "she would be at peace forever if she could believe that she existed only for herself and possibly for a superior intelligence and that no one existed for her save when he was tangibly present." Finally, she considers the ultimate dematerialization of self, the possibility of suicide.

Emily Vanderpool, who seems to lead a life that Jessie and Mrs. Placer's foster children would long for, cannot control or resolve by herself the bizarre situations into which she falls. Lottie Jump mesmerizes her. She is afraid that Lottie will "get revenge" on her if she does not join Lottie in the shoplifting venture. Finally, it is she, not Lottie, who is punished when they are caught. (pp. 236-37)

As the powerless often do, many of these characters turn their frustration inward and begin to hate themselves. Jessie begins to loathe her own health. She sees herself as a "pariah" and begins to be ashamed, she says, "not only of myself but of my mother, who was crassly impervious to disease. . . . I felt left out, not only in the Butler's house but in this town of consumptive confederates." In a terrible irony, she longs to be as ill as her tormentors. Under the tutelage of Mrs. Placer, the orphaned sisters develop a suspicion of themselves which makes them "mope and weep and grimace with self-judgment." As Mrs. Placer destroys their friendship with Mr. Murphy, they wish they were dead and wish they were "something besides kids! Besides girls." Kitty Winstanley hates herself for hating her parents. Cora Savage's thoughts of suicide reveal her self-loathing. Polly Bay feels "an ebbing away of self-respect" and under her uncle's harassment doubts "the testimony of her own eyes, the judgments of her own intellect." Even Emily Vanderpool says, "My badness never gave me half the enjoyment Jack and Stella thought it did. A good deal of the time I wanted to eat lye."

The backdrop against which the lives of these characters are played out is the West of "cowboys and Indians, and magic mountains." None of them, however, participates in the heroic West. Polly Bay comes closest. Her family had migrated to Colorado in a covered wagon in the 1840's, and her senile great-grandmother had talked "without pause of red Indians and storms on the plains," chastising her descendants by saying, "Not a one of you knows the sensation of having a red Indian arrow whiz by your sunbonnet with wind enough to make the ribbons wave." The family's pride in its forebears has calcified to a defense of all things Western, and a hatred of all things Eastern. As Polly contemplates her escape to the East, she realizes the Bays have been "too busy defending the West even to look at it. For all their pride in their surroundings, they had never contemplated them at all but had sat with the shades drawn, huddled under the steel engravings." She looks forward to a time after the deaths of her aunt and uncle when the young Bays may return, free to view the landscape, when "in their mouths there would not be a trace of the dust of the prairies where, as on a treadmill, Great-grandfather Bay's oxen plodded on and on into eternity."

For Emily Vanderpool, the heroic West is reduced to a collection of "seedy" souvenirs in the lobby of the hotel: "a rusted, beat-up placer pan with samples of ore in it, some fossils and some arrowheads, a tomahawk, a powder horn, and the shellacked tail of a beaver that was supposed to have been trapped by a desperado named Mountain Jim Nugent, who had lived in Estes Park in the seventies." This West has no meaning for Emily except that the collection is the source of an argument between the old men at the hotel that ultimately forces Emily from her reading place.

Other characters have made westward treks which parody the pioneering of the Bays and the tarnished glory of the souvenirs in the hotel. The pastor who sends the orphaned sisters west to their foster home talks to them "of Indians and of buffaloes," trying to use the romance of the West to quiet them. Jessie moves west with her mother "because there were enough (sick) people there to need her (mother's) services and therefore to keep a roof over our heads and shoes on our feet." Kitty Winstanley's family has sought a new life in the West because of her father's health. The same is true of Lottie Jump's family. The situation in **"The Philosophy Lesson"** suggests the same is true for Cora Savage's family. For these families, with absent or invalid fathers, there is no possibility that the West will yield riches from a placer pan or a trap line or glory from a brush with the Indians.

The image of the young female in the West that emerges in the Adams stories is that of a human being who is powerless, who has few defenses, who exhibits some degree of self-hatred, who lives in a confined psychological and physical space, and whose actions are restricted to surviving in that space, rather than redefining it. Stafford herself fled the West. "As soon as I could," she says, "I hotfooted it across the Rocky Mountains and across the Atlantic Ocean." She was pursued no doubt by the smothering image that she presents in the Adams stories. Stafford does give us glimpses of girls and women whose lives do not seem as circumscribed as the lives of her central characters. Cora Savage and Kitty Winstanley go to school with young women who enjoy all the advantages of wealth. The Butler children can control, not be controlled by, Jessie. Mrs. Butler holds a Phi Beta Kappa key, was a student of Professor Kittredge, and writes plays. It is important to recognize, however, that the lives Stafford chooses to reveal fully *are* circumscribed. The stories also make clear that had she examined the lives of these others, she probably would have found that they too have little freedom. Polly Bay, after all, is a member of a wealthy, prominent family. Emily Vanderpool suffers no economic or physical deprivation.

The other three Western stories in the ***Collected Stories*** further develop the idea of the West as a place from which romance and heroism have vanished and as a place which is antithetical to young women. **"A Summer Day"** is set in the Indian territory, in the capital of the Cherokee nation. Jim Littlefield, the eight-year-old orphan who follows his own trail of tears to Oklahoma, symbolizes the diminished stature of the red man in the West. He and his fellow Cherokees, adults and children alike, are wards of Uncle Sam. He is placed in an orphanage, where most of the children are sick, and one has died, as a result of drinking bad water, because the bureaucrats in Washington have failed to provide an adequate septic tank for the orphanage. While Jim enters the orphanage with plans to escape as soon as night falls, he is overpowered by his experiences of the day—by the heat, the isolation, the bureaucracy, the sickness—and decides to delay his escape. As he falls asleep, outside in the heat, alone and unprotected, lying on the "sickly grass," he sees himself "growing smaller and smaller and lying in a bureau drawer." Jim's sense of himself as diminished, his inability to carry out his escape, his confinement in an institution which is riddled by disease—all re-enact the fate of the conquered Indian nations. It is perhaps no accident that Stafford portrays the powerlessness of Jim Littlefield, an Indian, in terms very similar to those she uses to describe the lives of young women in the Adams stories.

Judy, the narrator and central character of **"The Mountain Day,"** has all the advantages that the Adams characters lack. She is a student at Bryn Mawr, engaged to a handsome and intelligent Harvard student. Her family is loving and wealthy. Vacationing in Colorado with her family, Judy, in this summer of her love, finds the West more beautiful than it has ever been: "The aspen leaves were more brilliant . . . , the upland snow was purer, the pinewoods were more redolent, and the gentle winds in them were more mellifluous; the berries I ate for breakfast came from the bushes of Eden." The same landscape holds danger, however. Huge turtles and hellbenders live in the heart-shaped lake which lies between her father's cabin and her grandmother's house. While Judy is protected from these and other dangers, the young Irish maids who work for her grandmother are not. When they capsize a canoe in the lake, they drown and their bodies are mutilated by the turtles and hellbenders. Thus, against Judy's "storybook summertime romance," Stafford juxtaposes the stark image of the corpses of two young women, "their lovely faces and their work-swollen hands" eaten away, an image of what can happen to women in the West infinitely more powerful than the happy ending suggested for Judy.

The last of the ten Western stories, **"The Darkening Moon,"** is emblematic of Stafford's portrayal of the young girl in the West. Ella, the central character, is eleven years old. Her father has been dead for one year. She lives in a small, nameless mining town. Her story takes place completely at night. When we first see her, she is "alone beneath the black firmament and between the blacker mountains that (loom) up to the right and to the left of her like the blurred figures of fantastic beasts." She makes a trip she often makes, riding her brother's horse several miles through the dark to babysit at an isolated farm on the other side of town. Sometimes she dreads the trip because the horse tries to throw her if it is frightened by the sight of the high bluffs along the highway. Once it had tossed her in the path of a bus and left her to walk a mile and a half home in the cold. Tonight she has the added danger of carrying through town ten pounds of elk meat her brother has poached. She postpones her arrival at the farm as long as she dares, knowing that this will be like all the other evenings she has spent there: "Afraid to move lest by moving she make a noise that would obscure another noise . . . , she would sit motionless all evening in a big pink wing chair. . . . By midnight, she would be wringing wet with sweat, although it was cold and she had let the fire go out. And yet, as soon as she had mounted for the ride back, her fear had changed its focus and she was not anxious to get home, but only to get Squaw safely past the bluff." This night is like the others, except that Ella endures the additional horror of an eclipse of the moon.

Stripped of its narrative particulars, this story embodies Stafford's version of the mythic journey possible to young girls in the West. An orphaned child travels through a dark landscape riding a steed which she has difficulty controlling because the landscape itself threatens the beast. Her destination is a place where she sits paralyzed by fear. She is released from her place of paralysis only to travel once again through the threatening landscape and to return to where she began. This is not the triumphant journey of a hero. Her dark night of the soul does not release her finally into the light of new perceptions and new possibilities. Instead, it is a journey which she is doomed to repeat. The repetition and the willingness with which the young girl reenters her state of paralysis distinguish the horror of her situation. She has accepted the journey as normality.

The stories in the ***Collected Stories*** do not provide us with a means of comparing the lives of the central female characters with those of boys and young men in similar settings and situations. Stafford's western novel, ***The Mountain Lion,*** does. Stafford places Molly and Ralph Fawcett, a young sister and brother, in exactly the same situations, makes them equally misfit, and has them share an emotional bond which makes them the male and female sides of the same coin. Their destinies, however, are very different. Molly, unlike the characters in the stories, does not cope and is unable to accept the limited life open to her as a female. Consequently, she must die. (pp. 237-41)

The female characters in Stafford's stories do not have to make Molly Fawcett's ultimate sacrifice to the myth of the West. What is clear from the stories, however, is that the myth equally excludes them. The reality of their lives denies the ideas in the myth of boundless individual opportunity, of freedom and open spaces, of the chance to form one's own destiny. Instead, the dominant images are repressive ones: girls and young women trapped inside unpleasant houses, frozen in immobile positions, surrounded by the trappings of illness and death, often harassed by grotesque people. The uncomfortable truth suggested by the stories is that the initiation ritual for these young women is learning to accept their condition—to live with fear and pain and restraint as a normal consequence of their being female. (p. 242)

Mary Ellen Williams Walsh, "The Young Girl in the West: Disenchantment in Jean Stafford's Short Fiction," in Women and Western American Literature, *edited by Helen Winter Stauffer and Susan J. Rosowski, The Whitston Publishing Company, 1982, pp. 230-43.*

On Fame

"It is hard to convey, without sounding hypocritical or grotesquely eccentric, how little I like the small fame I have acquired. I feel what I have always felt, 'If only they knew what I'm really like, if only they knew what a fraud I am, they would not flatter me in this way'."

—Jean Stafford, 1948

Melody Graulich

Of the few critics who have written about Jean Stafford, a Pulitzer Prize winner in 1970, most begin their essays, as I do, with a comment about the lack of critical attention her fine work has received. This neglect seems especially surprising among feminists, for much of Stafford's fiction explores the consequences of rigid sex roles. In her three novels, ***Boston Adventure*** (1944), ***The Mountain Lion*** (1947), and ***The Catherine Wheel*** (1952), and in some of her best stories, she shows the price women pay for wearing enforced social masks which deface their inner selves. Pressured to be attentive (**"Beatrice Trueblood's Story"**), proper (**"Polite Conversation"**), thin (**"The Echo and the Nemesis"**), and beautiful (**"The End of a Career"**), Stafford's women rebel only indirectly, and often self-destructively. Although their needs for authority and a measure of free will cause the fictions' conflicts, these heroines are often too self-effaced to assert a self apart from social norms. They assent to their prescribed identities because they can find no social space for their real selves, which they nurture in a private world of alienation Stafford called **"The Interior Castle."**

While Stafford's women have learned to conform, her girls

hold on as long as they can to their rebellion. Two of these adolescent rebels, Molly Fawcett, the heroine of the critically neglected ***The Mountain Lion,*** and Emily Vanderpool, the narrator of the title story in ***Bad Characters*** (1964), struggle to escape from conventional definitions of masculine and feminine behavior so powerful that they cannot be challenged without consequences. While Molly's refusal to conform leads to her violent death, Emily "grows up" by compromising her sense of self. In these two stories, Stafford suggests that girls cannot escape stereotyped women's roles, that the young female rebel should give up on the possibility of becoming Huckleberry Finn and accept that she must be an Elsie Dinsmore. (Elsie Dinsmore is the child heroine of a series of pious books for little girls, written by Martha Farquharson Finley (1828-1909). Molly calls her sisters "Elsie Dinsmores").

Molly and Emily, Stafford has hinted, possess much of her own childhood character. Like their creator, the two girls are raised in the West, the setting for the masculine themes of escape and rebellion which have dominated the American literary canon from Cooper to Fiedler, where masculinity and femininity have become so stripped down and antithetical that they are reduced, depending on one's point of view, to myths or to clichés: the never-changing book jacket image of the freedom-loving, identity-seeking man and his sidekick leaving behind the fences, houses, and churches of the dogma-spouting, civilizing woman. Stafford makes the West a major theme in both fictions in order to explore the pressures of growing up in a world dominated by such myths, and her stories' autobiographical nature helps illuminate her struggles as a woman writer using male conventions and writing within a male tradition. I will look at how she describes the influence of her own western childhood, and how she recreates it in these two pieces of fiction to question the sex role expectations within the American literary tradition.

In her short preface to ***The Collected Stories*** (1969), Stafford humorously emphasizes the lingering effect of her western childhood.

> By the time I knew him, my father was writing Western stories under the *nom de plume* Jack Wonder, or, occasionally, Ben Delight. But before that, before I was born, he wrote under his own name and he published a novel called *When Cattle Kingdom Fell.* The other principal book in my family . . . was by my first cousin once removed on my mother's side, Margaret Lynn, and this was *A Stepdaughter of the Prairie,* a reminiscence of her girlhood in frontier days in Kansas. To my regret, I have read neither of these books, so I cannot say that they influenced me. However, their titles influenced me . . . and I wrote about twisters on the plains, stampedes when herds of longhorns were being driven south of the border. All of the foremen of all the ranches had steely blue eyes to match the barrels of their Colt .45's. With this kind of heritage and early practice, I might have been expected to become a regional writer, but my father's wicked West and Cousin Margaret's noble West existed only in memory, and I could not wait to quit my tamed-down native grounds . . . but my roots remain in the semi-fictitious town of Adams, Colorado.
>
> (pp. 39-41)

In bare outline, ***The Mountain Lion*** is a classic western fable: a youngster leaves behind "the sissy life he had to lead" with his refined mother for the "Ride 'em, cowboy" world of his Uncle Claude's Colorado ranch, where he hunts a golden mountain lion, whose death will initiate him into the mysteries of nature and sexuality, while proving his superior power, his manhood. But the fable goes awry when, at the anticipated climax, Ralph "accidentally" kills not "Goldilocks," but his sister Molly, with whom he has shared such a close relationship that the two had felt "themselves . . . split in half." Through Ralph's story, Stafford implies that the fable of the wicked West is predicated on the destruction of the feminine, in nature and within the masculine self. But Molly's story is as important as Ralph's, and it shows that the wicked West welcomes only male misfits; that to those women who, for whatever reasons, dream the American dream of rebellion and escape from the noble world of social integration, the frontier and its "liberating" myths have always been closed.

In the novel, Stafford creates two sets of contrasting images that echo her distinction between noble and wicked Wests and satirize "archetypal" thematic pairings in American literature: civilization / wilderness; conformity / rebellion; East / West; culture / nature; feminine / masculine. The story shifts between two points of view, female and male, sister and brother, both of whom are obsessed with two patriarchal symbols: the long-dead Grandfather Bonney, an effeminate man who represents the civilized world of the city, so cultured that he orchestrates dinner table conversations about Tennyson, wears "a pink carnation in the lapel of his morning coat; a silk hat and a gold-headed stick, a black Chesterfield and a pair of white gloves," and after dying reposes not in the earth but in an urn on the mantlepiece; and Grandpa Kenyon, a tall-tale-telling rancher who looks like an Indian, dresses like Jesse James, and is so connected to freedom that he reminds Ralph of a "big river." Subsequent generations take on the symbolic—and hilariously clichéd—values of these forefathers. Mrs. Fawcett, née Bonney, talks about "our sort of people" (who don't own cows or linoleum), appreciates elevated conversations, and gets sick headaches, while her half-brother Claude Kenyon, who rides and shoots with authority, tries to eat his sherbet out of his fingerbowl and reads gun catalogues. The extroverted, well-finished older Fawcett daughters, Leah and Rachel, with their golden hair, eastern schooling, and social graces, are interchangeable copies of their mother; unlike the Kenyons, she prefers Leah and Rachel to "hot-tempered and rebellious" Ralph and Molly, violators of all social proprieties. This dichotomy is further drawn through the story's two settings. Mrs. Fawcett creates a cultural enclave at Covina, California, which is *not,* Grandpa Kenyon says, the *real* West. Life there is mannered and controlled, defined by what one is "not allowed" to do, and dominated by the reprehensible Reverend Follansbee, whose hobby is taxidermy. At Claude's "Bar K," "lawlessness seemed natural." Ralph responds to his dichotomized world by categorizing everyone as either "Bonney merchants" or "Kenyon men," the "fundamental distinction (being) their attitude toward horses and vice versa, the attitude of horses toward them."

By reducing the two worlds in her novel of growing up to rigid male and female stereotypes, as cluttered with comic cultural symbols as the Grangerford house [in *Huckleberry Finn*], Stafford mocks gender expectations frozen into cultural myths. In ***The Mountain Lion,*** the wicked and noble worlds are absolutely antithetical, and no character manages to bridge them permanently. Like Miss Watson and Pap, the adult representatives of both worlds try to make the children over in their own images. Ralph can choose membership in either world; he can be, in effect, Huck Finn or Tom Sawyer. There are numerous instances which show that his mother favors him, despite his bad character, simply because he is a boy, and it is significant, of course, that patriarchal figures head *both* worlds. While Ralph might feel that "manly" (his word, oft-repeated) men reject social convention, those who choose not to, like Grandfather Bonney and Reverend Follansbee, take over positions of power.

But although Molly and Ralph are alike in almost every way and copy each other throughout their childhood, *her* basic identity is unacceptable, denied, in both worlds. Independent, alienated, outspoken, and ugly, she is everything a "noble" woman should not be. Her very presence produces social awkwardness. Even her strengths become weaknesses: "Everyone said that she had the brains of the family, but as Mrs. Fawcett was not interested in brains, she thought this a handicap rather than otherwise." Mr. Follansbee "chuckles" at her for being a "rugged individualist." Molly's rebellious individualism would seem to make her a natural candidate for membership in the wicked West. And yet again—over and over again—she is rejected:

> Uncle Claude occasionally praised (Ralph) and his confidence grew, but he was so mean to Molly ("You set on that bench like a sack of potatoes," he would say to her) that she seldom went with them but stayed at home to help in the garden or to write.

Mrs. Fawcett hopes that Molly doesn't tag along with Ralph and Claude, but she needn't worry because their bond is based, in part, on her exclusion.

Of course Molly, rebel that she is, searches not for conformity in either world, but for acceptance and camaraderie, which Ralph finds in his intense relationship with Claude. She does not find them. She sees the ranch's limitations (it is she who sums it up in the single satiric phrase "Ride 'em, cowboy"), and she rejects its communication-by-non-sequitur, its brutality and violence, and its major symbols: hunting and riding. Mrs. Fawcett has forbidden these activities, and that Molly, for once, goes along with her mother's rules underscores her attraction to many "traditional" female attitudes. But it is impossible for her to straddle two such antagonistic and narrowly-defined worlds, as Stafford shows (among many other ways) through her portrayal of Mrs. Brotherman, Claude's housekeeper, and her daughter Winifred. Mrs. Brotherman, whose name hints at her place, is so cultured that she hails from Boston. Molly likes her and especially her flower garden. Despite being "so unflowerlike . . . she loved flowers," even though her mother had allowed her to pick only the "harsh, scentless" ones, saving the delphiniums and roses for Leah and Rachel. With Mrs. Brotherman she plans to grow roses, a sad and ironic symbol of cultivated womanhood, beauty, and romance for thorny Molly. At the ranch, where "the public library was too far away," Mrs. Brotherman also helps feed Molly's hunger for culture. But she is no role model, only an absurd island of refinement with no power, no voice, no wit. Removed from civilization, she has no character at all.

When the children first met Winifred, she is a "tomboy" with "dung" on her jeans. Smart, capable, and independent, she embodies what Molly most admires in the West: a lack of hypocrisy and artificiality. But by the story's end, the "pretty" Winifred has become "boy crazy," and takes on these very qualities, turning into a copy of Molly's sisters. . . . One of the cowboys links Winifred to the long-hunted lion, whom Claude and Ralph perceive, for no stated reason, as female, and name Goldilocks because she reminds them of a film star:

> I wouldn't think you'd have to go into the mountains to hunt that kind of game. What's the matter with the little lady settin' here? Settin' right here with all us big grown men?

Ralph also sees his golden-haired sisters as prey, and he even turns Molly into a sexual object by asking her to tell him all the dirty words she knows. Only after Winifred's defection does Molly realize that "if only she had yellow hair . . . she would be an entirely different kind of person." Indeed. Both worlds recognize the value of the golden girl. But rebellious Molly wants to act, not simply be, and she will not find a role in the wicked West except as civilizing antagonist or sexual prey. Although she reads *The Pathfinder,* canonized American authors (in 1947 and today) have not granted her, a girl, a culturally sanctioned myth of rebellion; they grant one to Ralph, but force him, in repayment, to destroy his feminine side, to kill to be a man.

It is difficult to understand why most critics have overlooked Stafford's not-so-subtle and very funny mockery of sexual stereotyping and gender expectations. ***The Mountain Lion*** is filled with examples. Stafford, for instance, suggests that Ralph is offered more "room" in both worlds when he misunderstands a patriotic description of America as "O Beautiful for Spacious Guys." . . . Stafford also ironically exposes the flexibility of physical standards for men but not for women. Although both kids have always been ugly, Ralph mysteriously gets more attractive as he gets older.

> It was curious that she bore so close a resemblance to him. She had the same coarse, straight black hair, the same heavy eyebrows, and the same prominent nose that looked as solid and unbreakable as a stone. But in a girl such ruggedness was not handsome as it was in him and Uncle Claude.

And she persistently mocks themes associated with the

wicked West. Ralph, like Claude, is so far gone on male bonding that he "was glad that his horse and his uncle's had a pure masculine friendship and that they ran away from Winifred's mare whenever she came near." The attitudes expressed in these examples, characterizing both masculine and feminine worlds, suggest why Ralph comes increasingly to accept his strength and power as a man; his future is "spacious." But Molly finds her horizon contracting. (pp. 43-7)

Both children have been repressed (especially sexually), and their natural characters have been distorted by their social roles. What began as humorous satire becomes blacker as Stafford chronicles their gradual and painful estrangement. Under the pressure to be a man, Ralph worries that he has "abandoned" Molly for his friendship with Claude. He recognizes that his close relationship with her jeopardizes his masculinity. After touching Molly in sympathy, he "looked at Uncle Claude and saw that he was watching them inquisitively; he read the look as a question of his worth or of his manliness." And under the pressure to *avoid* becoming a woman, Molly defensively rejects Ralph when he reveals his sexual confusion. A natural symbol which Ralph finds and gives to Molly suggests the nature of their relationship: he finds "the skulls of two deer with horns so tightly interlocked that he could not get them apart" and imagines them "being joined as one, toppling into the water to drown, still struggling to get free."

Like the mountain lion itself, this wilderness symbol is partly ironic, consistent with Stafford's satire of the wicked West myth. Although it clearly refers to Molly and Ralph, female and male "joined as one," the two deer are, of course, bucks fighting for supremacy. The competition between Ralph and Claude to kill Goldilocks, another female, causes Molly's death, freeing Ralph to live. This act of freeing himself from his sister is co-existent with the myth's rite of manhood. There is nothing "natural" about this total estrangement of female and male, no sense that it is a necessary acceptance of adulthood and sexuality, as some critics have said. It is the unnatural confusion about "Kenyon men" and "little ladies" that leads to the horrible climax, no more accidental than the death of Cyrus Bourne in Hawthorne's "Roger Malvin's Burial." Recognizing her role and her limitations—" 'I know I'm ugly. I know everybody hates me. I wish I were dead' "—Molly remains rebellious, and Stafford, feeling "deep . . . remorse for what (she) had done to (her) heroine," kills her because she is a misfit who has no wilderness, no territory, to run to. Ralph's end, too, is sadly ironic. Having begun to recognize that Claude "had never grown up and his hunt for Goldilocks was a childhood game," Ralph is trapped in a myth so rigid that he has to kill the symbol of his own female nature. Stafford lets Ralph see beyond Claude's "virile opacity," but she does not let him escape the quintessential American plot.

In her violent ending, Stafford makes one further point about the presentation of female images in the wicked West. At the moment that Ralph kills Molly, Claude kills Goldilocks. As lovely and valuable in the natural world as the Fawcett golden girls are in the social world, the mountain lion is a symbol of the female in nature. As critics . . . have argued, the American hero often escapes from a civilizing woman into a feminized natural landscape (a conventional image which still bears questioning), which he masters either because he has superior power or because it is naturally nurturant and compliant, responding to love but making no demands. In Stafford's version of the hunt, men seek power simultaneously over women and over nature. Women are threatening not only because they are civilizers, but also because they are, like Claude's black cook Magdalene (whom Molly fears might be her "real" mother), so very primitive, so mysteriously powerful in their fertile nature, that they must be dominated.

Stafford must have felt remorse for what she did to Molly, for she rewrote her story with a "happier" ending. In **"Bad Characters,"** she creates another girl "outlaw" who finds her way out of a dilemma very similar to Molly's by compromising her sense of self for inclusion in the social world. Emily Vanderpool, whose skin Stafford says in an author's note she "often occupied," learns a lesson in western con artistry that allows her to manipulate the conventions of the noble and wicked Wests. Emily's realization helps readers to understand Stafford's struggles with the dominant myths of her "tamed-down" childhood and the ways she would use them in her writing. (pp. 47-9)

Emily has a tendency to feel crowded. Her talent, her "awful tongue," alienates her from her buddies who already possess the noble team spirit.

> Up until I learned my lesson in a very bitter way, I never had more than one friend at a time, and my friendships, though ardent, were short. When they ended and I was sent packing in unforgetting indignation, it was always my fault; I would swear vilely in front of a girl I knew to be pious and prim (by the time I was eight, the most grandiloquent gangster could have added nothing to my vocabulary—I had an awful tongue), or I would call a Tenderfoot Scout a sissy or make fun of athletics to the daughter of the high school coach. These outbursts came without plan; I would simply one day . . . be possessed with a passion to be by myself and my lips instantly and without warning would accommodate me. My friend was never more surprised than I was when this irrevocable slander, this terrible, talented invective, came boiling out of my mouth.

Like Molly, Emily wants to merge the roles offered her by the wicked and noble Wests. She cannot restrain her defiance, her need to be free from the conformity and hypocrisy of group behavior, and yet she longs for a feeling of community. She learns her lesson from Lottie Jump; they are the story's outlaws, the "bad characters" who "hold up the dime store." From Lottie, the con artist, Emily learns that she can manipulate her social relations, that she can hide, or preserve, her "bad character" behind social masks.

Throughout her fiction Stafford frequently uses cats as symbols of women's inner characters. Emily's siblings perpetually remind her of her alienation and rebelliousness through malicious cat nicknames. They call her "Kitty," claiming she is kin to the family cat, Muff, an ugly "ill-natured cat" who "loathed all human beings except, significantly (Emily). . . . She bit and scratched the hands that fed her, arched her back like a Halloween cat if someone kindly tried to pet her, she hissed, laid her ears flat to her skull, growled, fluffed up her tail into a great bush and flailed it like a bullwhip." Muff is no blunderer, as her name might imply, but she consistently acts "contrary to orders."

More odious to Emily is her related nickname, "Polecat," an old western epithet. Both literally and in western metaphor, polecats are lesser outlaws, chicken thieves. Like that of the ostracized skunk, Emily's own "poisonous" nature damns her, she thinks, to be a loner. Her outbursts lead to the rapid departure of anyone in the vicinity—and the consequences linger. By accepting her family's view that she has an "evil disposition," Emily has come to believe that she stinks.

She does resemble Muff: she is independent and cantankerous. Honest and unrehearsed, her insults are hilarious challenges to propriety, expressing her uncontrollable desire for freedom from the capitulations of communal behavior. And yet Emily's tamed-down West is dominated by the values of the noble West, inhabited by widows and judges, and she believes she must be self-sacrificing, conventional, and docile to deserve the sense of belonging she yearns for. She feels that she is a "black-hearted villain" when she robs her savings box, "the one in the shape of a church, which held (her) Christmas Sunday School offering," her "mite for the poor widow." She imagines that her "hardness of heart and evil of intention" cause the hemorrhage of the selfless old woman, a member of the Eastern Star, whom her mother nurses. Having been threatened with arrest by Virgil Meade, whose deputy marshal father she called a bootlegger, she envisions her ultimate punishment: Judge Bay, her father's friend and the keeper of communal morality, coming toward her with a double-barrelled shotgun to enforce justice. Accepting the dialectical western clichés as she does, Emily can neither deny her "bad character" nor escape guilt for failing to fit into the noble world: "My badness never gave me half the enjoyment Jack and Stella (the siblings) thought it did." Stuck, like Molly, between wicked and noble, outlaw or civilized, Lottie or her siblings, Emily can find no way to affirm both her rebellion and her humanity.

What she needs is a sidekick, a companion as outrageous and rebellious as she is, and for a time she finds one. Lottie, who had "plainly . . . gone it alone for a long time and could go it alone for the rest of her life" and whom Emily expects to arrive with a "black handkerchief over the lower part of her face . . . or a Jesse James waistcoat," impresses Emily with her acceptance of her lonely independence and outlawry, traits which cause "Polecat" agony and guilt. Having escaped from any indoctrination by the noble West, Lottie mocks all those in authority: her teacher (who had a "head shaped like a pine cone and who had killed several people with her ruler"); her father (a "big piece of cheese," who is still worth quoting because he calls tapioca "fish eyes . . . and floating island horse spit"); religion (" 'I should worry if it's a sin or not' "); and the law (" 'They'll never put a smart old whatsis like *me* in jail. It's fun, stealing is—it's a picnic' "). Sharing none of Emily's ambivalence, the confident Lottie is a familiar character in western literature: she's a con "man." She even "slobbers a little" when playing deaf and dumb, like her literary forefather, the Duke of Bilgewater.

Emily quickly notices that Lottie, caught in the act of stealing a cake, tells a "prodigious lie," and yet the girl's "gaudy, cynical talk" "mesmerizes" her. The two reveal their shared fascination with words when they exchange names: each finds the sound of the other's name ludicrous but fails to find any humor in her own. Lottie's run-on anecdotal stories overflow with bizarre, distorted details, unlikely images, and colorful language. Emily is so impressed with the languge possibilities which Lottie shows her that she almost reveals their plan to Stella, who exclaims, " 'Where'd you get *that* kind of talk?' " Stafford packs the story with humorous references to the "talk" theme which emphasize that Emily, always trying to repress her own verbal acrobatics, finds Lottie's tall tales more attractive than her anti-social acts.

Emily shares Lottie's fascination with the liberating possibilities of uninhibited western word-play, but she won't be a petty crook like Lottie; she aspires to be Huck Finn, not the King. Breaking with Lottie and backing out of the robbery, she accepts some of the values of the noble West and rejects Lottie's kind of outlawry. Lottie may be free, but with such a fluid character she possesses no genuine self, no honest relations with others. Inescapably honest (until the story's end), Emily discovers that she rebels more in word than in deed, and yet she recognizes that rebellion defines her very character. When Judge Bay ends his "long declamation" with the warning, "I want you to search and seek in the innermost concerns of your consciousness and root out every bit of badness," Emily thinks, "Oh, him! Why listen, if I'd rooted out all the badness in me, there wouldn't have been anything left of me."

Emily parts company with Lottie in Woolworth's through another attack of her "talented invective." Although she rejects being a "polecat," her "awful tongue" ironically once again gets her in trouble and causes her "mother (to cry) for days because she had nurtured an outlaw." Lottie, the verbal wizard, shows Emily the value of shutting up, of pretending to be what you are not. When they are caught, Lottie, instead of trying to talk her way out as Emily does, "never said a word but kept making signs with her fingers, ad-libbing the whole thing. They tested her hearing by shooting off a popgun right in her ear and she never batted an eyelid." After the authorities pat "the poor afflicted child" on the shoulder and let her go, they send Emily to Judge Bay.

Like most con artists, Lottie shows how easily society can be duped, how easily its expectations and stereotypes can be exploited. Emily learns to keep quiet about her "terrible need to be alone" in order to con her way into acceptance in the noble world. She shuts up and joins the Camp Fire Girls, a "wilderness" group that shapes young women's values. Unlike Lottie, who delights in deception, she will con to fit in, preserving her ambivalent feelings, still alienated but pretending not to be. Perpetually dislocated, detached from whatever community she "joins," she recognizes the separation between genuine and social self, as do Stafford's women, who invariably "shut up" about their inner lives. When Emily puts on her mask and joins the crowd, she accepts her role as an adult woman, a point Stafford comically insists upon in the story's last line: Muff "grew up and started having literally millions of kittens." (pp. 49-52)

Joanna Russ begins her influential feminist essay, "What Can a Heroine Do? or Why Women Can't Write," with two plot summaries which parody women's exclusion from the myths of the wicked West: "1. Two strong women battle for supremacy in the early West. 2. A young girl in Minnesota finds her womanhood by killing a bear." The absurdity of her recast plots suggests to Russ that "authors do not make their plots up out of thin air. . . . These very familiar plots simply will not work (because) they are tales for heroes, not heroines, and one of the things that handicaps women writers in our—and every other—culture is that there are so very few stories in which women can figure as protagonists."

As a western child and an American fiction writer, Stafford was raised on these male myths, with their rigid definitions of masculine and feminine roles. [Howard Moss notes in "Jean: Some Fragments" that, like] many other women, she was attracted to the wilderness, to the escape and rebellion themes, but in the stories available to her, girls are given not the independence of orphanhood, not Fitzgerald's "fresh, green breast" of New World possibility, not soulful camaraderie under the stars, but family obligations, churches, social contracts, Camp Fire groups, the Eastern Star. Torn between "the outlandish and the decorous," like her heroines, she "paid great respect to the civilized, but something ingrained and western in her mocked it at the same time." This "mockery" allows Stafford to overcome—partially—what Russ describes as the "handicap" for women writers. She simultaneously employs the myths and conventions of her literary tradition and undermines them. She certainly could not escape them.

The classic story Stafford recasts with female protagonists was written by one of her two favorite writers, Mark Twain. The struggles of Molly and Emily with their bad characters echo those of the "wicked and low-down and onery" Huck Finn. Disreputable outsiders, the three share an instinctive mistrust of authority and a sorrowful loneliness. Like the girls, Huck is stuck with extremes: he runs away from the violent and anti-social Pap, but also from Miss Watson, whose unquestioning conformity and moral blindness he associates with being "civilized." "Brung up wicked," Huck knows what Emily learns, that he can manipulate others by creating multiple selves, by pretending to be what he is not, but Twain preserves for him opportunities for emotional honesty and integrity through his relationship with Jim and with the natural world and through the promise of an escape to the Territory. Huck's is an anti-success story, a mockery of the orphan-rags-to-riches plot of Horatio Alger. He gains stature through avoiding assimilation into a corrupt world, and the reader hopes that he will never again turn into Tom Sawyer.

Perhaps Stafford was attracted to Twain because Huck may well be the most androgynous of the sons of Bumppo, because he searches, ironically, for a community and values usually associated with women, the family. Within her fiction, however, Stafford cannot recreate Huck's opportunities for her heroines. In his introduction to ***The Mountain Lion,*** William T. Pilkington makes a comment which reveals Stafford's dilemma: "By the end of the novel it is no longer possible to think of Molly as a female Huck Finn; she has been transformed into a young Miss Watson, complete with exacting Victorian morality." Influenced as we all are by the narrow views of women in the American literary tradition, it is possible to react positively to Molly only so long as she is a "female" boy, a role she cannot sustain. As she grows up to resist not just the social world but also the wicked West and its sexual stereotypes, she is "transformed" into an obstacle to someone else's freedom. Her anti-success story is realizable only through her death.

Although the western hero derives his moral force from his alienation, from his "wickedness," the wicked West offers Emily only petty outlawry, only the hypocrisy of the confidence game, itself a manipulation of social roles and values. Searching for Jim, for the androgynous outsider-as-sidekick, Emily finds only the Duke, whose exploits make Huck ashamed of the whole human race. With no one to go to hell for, Emily covers up her badness, and she measures her success, unlike the western hero and anti-hero, by the acceptance of civilization.

Of course, Huck's creator ended up in a feudal manor in Hartford, Connecticut, and Stafford is too tough-minded to accept his wistful fantasy of escape. And yet she denies to Molly and to Emily Huck's promised freedom not because it is "unrealistic," but because they are girls, because the myths Twain relied upon and helped to create denied it to her. Although Stafford acknowledges that both women and men suffer from these rigid roles, when female and male "joined as one" are separated, it is woman's identity, woman's individuality, woman's free will that is totally effaced: it is Molly who dies. Although she wrote that the story plot, "The Drive to Be a Misfit and Its Reward," was "meant . . . for" her, Stafford could find no acceptance within the western fable for a woman's rebellion. She must have found that the western myths effaced her own identity, that they did not allow room for or correspond to her own character and experiences, as did critic Dawn Lander, who has written persuasively [in "Eve among the Indians"] about the stereotype of the civilizing woman and its effect on her own growth as a western child.

> I did not identify myself with houses, churches, and fences. I loved to be outdoors. I loved the space, energy, and passion of the landscape. . . . Repeatedly, however, I could find no place for myself and for my pleasure in the wilderness in the traditionally recorded images of (the woman) on the frontier. . . . She is celebrated because she stoically transcended a situation she never would have freely chosen. She submits to the wilderness just as—supposedly—she submits to sex. But she needn't enjoy it, and her whole posture is in rigid opposi-

> tion to the wilderness experience: to the land, to the Indians. Her glory, we are told, is that she carried the family, religion, fences, the warmth of the hearth and steaming washtubs inviolate to the (West).

Lander describes my own experiences as a well-read western "tomboy," but as I have grown older, I have recognized, as did Stafford, that my rebellious identification with the male virtues has led me to underestimate "the warmth of the hearth." Both wicked and noble myths express universal *human* dreams, American dreams: the western male archetype offers *boys* heroism in return for rebellion and nonconformity, while the female archetype promises happiness and community through a recognition of human obligation and interdependence. But with women and their "noble" virtues presented within our literary canon as Miss Watsons, as antagonists and destroyers, it is small wonder that Molly, Emily, Stafford, Lander, and I hungered to be Huck.

In *The Resisting Reader,* Judith Fetteringly explores the "powerlessness" of the female reader of "classic American literature," who "is asked to identify with a selfhood that defines itself in opposition to her. . . .Our literature neither leaves women alone nor allows them to participate. It insists on its universality at the same time that it defines that universality in specifically male terms." As an author, Stafford "resisted" the very themes that she employed, themes that demanded that she identify against herself, and her work demonstrates the effect of such powerlessness on the female American. She achieves some measure of power herself through her mockery of these themes, but irony is, after all, another kind of mask. Both Molly, who plans to be a writer, and Emily, who tells her own story, share Stafford's sarcastic voice and fascination with words; especially in these autobiographical works, Stafford's wry wit and detached tone seem to me to "mask" the kind of pain and alienation Molly feels when she finally adds her own name to her "unforgiveable" list. Stafford may have been a misfit with no chance to be a hero, but by resisting the destructive sexual stereotypes that deny us all our full humanity, she proved herself a rebel in the best American tradition. (pp. 52-5)

Melody Graulich, "Jean Stafford's Western Childhood: Huck Finn Joins the Camp Fire Girls," in The Denver Quarterly, *Vol. 18, No. 1, Spring, 1983, pp. 39-55.*

William Leary

On November 11, 1935, the Boulder (Colorado) *Daily Camera* carried a front-page story of a college girl's suicide. Under the column head GIRL STUDENT / SHOT HERSELF / LATE SATURDAY, the report told the reader that Mrs. Lucy McKee Cooke, age twenty-three, a senior in the Colorado University law school, and wife of Andrew Cooke, also a law senior, died at Community hospital Saturday night at ten o'clock of a self-inflicted bullet wound.

In the very full account that followed, running over to two inner pages, a dramatic narrative unfolded. Lucy Cooke had been visiting friends in Denver during the afternoon of Saturday, November 9. When she returned to Boulder on the bus, she was met at the depot by her husband, Andrew. On the way back to their home, at 962 Ninth Street, the couple appear to have had an argument. Later, during dinner with their friend, Jeane (*sic*) Stafford, who lived with them, Mrs. Cooke got up from the table saying she was not hungry and left the house. When she returned an hour later her appearance and manner so alarmed Miss Stafford that she went to the phone to call a physician. While Miss Stafford was at the phone and Mr. Cooke was in the bathroom, Mrs. Cooke went to the kitchen and there shot herself in the left temple with a twenty-five caliber revolver. (p. 389)

In keeping with its tradition of factual reporting, the police record does not speculate on the cause of the suicide. But the *Daily Camera* offers this second-hand conjecture: "Friends attribute Mrs. Cooke's act to ill health rather than the quarrel, which they said was over a minor matter." Apparently the authorities felt it unnecessary to seek any other explanation, for the newspaper account goes on to say "Sheriff Richart and Coroner Howe decided no inquest would be necessary."

Such, then, are the publicly reported and recorded facts concerning a suicide that, according to her own repeated testimony, would haunt Jean Stafford for years. Her efforts to come to terms with this experience took various forms.

Not surprisingly, she sometimes talked about it to sympathetic and interested listeners. On one notable occasion she told the whole story to Robert Lowell, then her husband, and their friend, Delmore Schwartz. The two poets, impressed by both the story and her telling it, urged her to make it the centerpiece of a novel about her college days in the thirties. They thought she should write it down word for word as she had told it to them. While she was trying to follow this advice, she told the story again, this time to John Berryman. Perhaps because of his own inordinate sensitivity to suicide—his father had taken his own life and years later Berryman would follow the same pattern of despair—he urged Stafford to lay the novel aside and work on something else.

References to the suicide appear in Stafford's letters as well. One of these contains a startling revelation of the effects of trauma on the artistic sensibility. Writing in 1946 to a former classmate who had left the university sometime before Lucy Cooke shot herself, Stafford not only confirms his surmises concerning the identity of the principals but makes an astonishing disclosure concerning the effects of this shocking experience on both her conscious and unconscious mind.

> P.S. Yes, you are right about Andrew; he was Lucy's husband. And Lucy, of course, is the one who killed herself, but one particular is wrong: you say, "for no reason anyone could fathom." After almost eleven years I think I understand it now. It has lain in my consciousness without ever departing although it has sometimes blessedly submerged itself. I am almost ready to write about it, although I have really written about nothing else ever. Hopestill in my book is Lucy.

> Miss Pride (and I did not connect these things until the other day) is named Lucy. [Stafford to Joe Chay, 27 February 1946; Stafford Collection; Special Collections; University of Colorado Library]

If one knows (or is told) that Hopestill Mather was the neurotically tormented rich girl whose suicide was a pivotal episode in Stafford's first novel, ***Boston Adventure,*** and that her aunt, Miss Pride, was a wealthy Boston patrician whose proffers of help to impoverished Sonie Marburg, the novel's heroine, had a vicious way of transforming themselves into conditions resembling bondage, the revelations in Stafford's letter are very suggestive. Now if to this we add the information that one of Lucy Cooke's contemporaries recalls her as rich, a reckless driver, and an early hippie who won Stafford's admiration, in part because she wrote "true romances" for the slick confession magazines, and that another contemporary remembers Jean Stafford's once telling him that Lucy Cooke deliberately tried to corrupt her, then the parallels between fact and fiction begin to suggest something very like Jamesian horror.

Jean Stafford spoke and wrote publicly as well as privately about Lucy Cooke's suicide and its effect on her. On at least three occasions she publicly discussed her failure to transform this real life episode into a literary experience. The first time was in 1950 in the course of a lecture on the place of autobiography in fiction which she delivered to Wellesley College students (**"Observations on the Uses of Autobiography in Fiction,"** the Sophie Hart Lecture, delivered at Wellesley College, 17 April 1950). A little more than a year after that, she published an article in *Harper's Bazaar* in which she detailed eloquently and exhaustively her failure to metamorphose the fact of Lucy's suicide into acceptable fiction (**"Truth and the Novelist,"** *Harper's Bazaar,* August 1951). Then fifteen years later, in 1966, she returned to this event and this theme in a *Library Journal* piece titled **"Truth in Fiction"** (*Library Journal,* 1 October 1966).

The burden of these three public confessions is always the same. Stafford tells her listeners or readers, "Six years after I had seen a life go up in gun-smoke, I had written the whole thing down in a long story which was a failure since I did not know what it was about and had no idea what my own feeling toward the characters in it was." That failed effort was made in 1941. Starting over again in 1946, she labored for "the next three and a half years . . . accumulated twenty pounds of manuscript and destroyed an equal amount . . . completed two versions, one in the first person and one in the third," then despairing of what she had wrought, she "burned it up, leaving no word of it behind." She continues:

> As the last feather of smoke curled up my chimney, I underwent a profound shock that lasted for several days. But when it had passed, I knew from my euphoria that I had performed one of the most intelligent acts of my life.

That intelligent act had been prompted by her sudden discovery one day of the reason she could not write this novel.

> It was ever so simple—I hated my material. The years I had elected to write about had not been happy ones for me or for any of my characters . . . (and) I still *resented* them and in consequence, all of us emerged a sorry lot, humorless, morbid, given to collecting injustices.

These public confessions spanned a period from 1950 to 1966. Yet, in 1948, two years before Stafford had discovered that she could not sufficiently distance her morbid memories so as to convert them into plausible fiction, she revealed just how morbid and intense these memories were. She did so in yet another letter to the classmate who had earlier inquired about the identity of the principals in the suicide. This time he appears to have been urging her to meet him for a reunion in Boulder, and, on receiving her refusal to return to this scene of her unhappiness, had accused her of attempting to run away from her past. Stafford's reply answers this charge and at the same time reveals the intensity of her feeling toward Lucy Cooke who now appears in a lurid light.

> I object to your saying that I "can't run away much longer" from the past. Alas, alas, I live within it and if I *could* run away, it would be ever so much better for me. I daresay I have been unhappy all my life but I was never so wretched before I knew that terrible girl and her terrifying *modus vivendi* and her limp, disreputable entourage. [Stafford to Joe Chay, 3 July 1948, Stafford Collection]

Thirty-three years after Lucy Cooke's suicide, and twenty years after writing the letter revealing her view of the dead girl's unsavory character, Jean Stafford, now a celebrated writer, confronted a task more difficult than the one she had failed in before. Earlier her problem had been one of metamorphosis. Now it was one of genesis. For by 1968 Stafford, as a writer of fiction, appeared to have dried up. She had not published a novel since 1952 nor a short story since 1964. True, she still displayed rare ability to write accomplished prose, but since 1964 this had taken the form of journalism exclusively.

Still, if others had given up on her, Robert Giroux, her publisher, had not. In the summer of 1968 he issued a contract to Stafford for a new novel, avowedly autobiographical, which bore the tentative title *The Parliament of Women.* This provocative title was unmistakably an echo of Chaucer's dream allegory, *The Parlement of Fowles.* Perhaps Giroux thought he detected some parallels between the principal actors in the Chaucerian poem and persons who had figured large in the colorful life of his wickedly funny author. He may thus have seen in her suggested title a good augury: if Stafford could unleash the Chaucerian wit and irony he knew she possessed in this new novel, then all would be well.

Giroux must have been encouraged when by the fall of 1968 Stafford produced **"The Philosophy Lesson,"** and he must have been exhilarated when that story was accepted for publication by *The New Yorker.* (pp. 390-93)

A close reading of this story will disclose that it is vintage Stafford—a mosaic of cunningly wrought details, vivid imagery, buried ironies, startling juxtaposition of both action and rhythm, and, at the end, an epiphany whose meaning is hinted at in the story's title. Like so many of Stafford's best stories, this one invites a thoughtful rereading and rewards the reader who accepts the invitation. Besides possessing the structural and textural qualities of Stafford's best short fiction, **"The Philosophy Lesson"** captures one of the dominant tones of the thirties—the tone of despair turned morbid. Stafford knew this tone as well as she knew the events of that decade that contributed to it. . . . It is time to give this story the close reading it deserves.

On the narrative level alone, **"The Philosophy Lesson"** seems a simple enough little story. Cora Savage is a young, first-year student in a unnamed Colorado university who, three mornings a week, poses nude as a model before twenty-seven art students in a Life class. We discover that she possesses an almost inhuman ability to remain motionless for nearly an hour at a time, resting only twice during the nine-to-twelve class sessions. She has, apparently, developed several strategies for achieving and holding this state of immobility. Sometimes she fixes her attention on the top of the cottonwood tree that she alone can see outside the studio window from her vantage point on the dais. Transfixed, she memorizes and thus possesses every detail of leaf, twig, and bough, of the bark's sheen in both sun and rain, of the coming and going of birds and squirrels, in fact of everything concerning this treetop that swims into her ken. Alternatively, and more mechanically, she counts slowly to one hundred every five minutes until she can be released when she reaches one thousand. And, when these strategies fail her, she engages in retrospection concerning events in her earlier life, the details of which are often prompted by something taking place in her present environment, like today's first snowfall of the season.

We learn, too, that she pays a high price for this thrice-weekly *tour de force:* she suffers from a variety of physical pains; she completely dissociates herself from her fellow students; and, half-consciously, she assumes the potentially dangerous arrogance of a transcendentalist, someone who feels herself superior to mundane reality.

On the morning of our story, we find ourselves Cora's mental companions as she practices all three of these strategies, but chiefly the retrospective musing that takes her back to a snowy Christmas during her childhood in Missouri, then to other, later snow scenes during her girlhood in Adams (Boulder), Colorado and, finally, to her Introduction to Philosophy class, where she has recently become aware of the powerful attraction of Bishop Berkeley's philosophical idealism, in which she discerns a sublimity that seems capable of dismantling her world of unpleasant reality.

Suddenly her trancelike state is disrupted by the panicky arrival of a latecomer who blurts out the shocking news that "somebody has just committed suicide on the Base Line." We learn that a second-year medical student named Bernie Allen had driven his car to the outskirts of the town two hours before, had left the car at a railroad crossing with the motor still running, and had later been found run over and hideously dismembered by the morning mail train from Denver.

The rest of Stafford's story is divided between a candid account of the shocked behavior of the art students, set forth with the objectivity and accuracy of a good court reporter, and the private thoughts of Cora presented as an interior monologue. It is from these private musings that the story's meaning emerges. Cora had been, it seems, in love with the dead boy but was compelled to remain hopelessly remote from him because of his wealth and his attachment to Maisie Perrine, a rich girl who lived in the boarding house next door to Cora's, from where she had painfully observed the comings and goings of this glamorous pair. Now, momentarily, Cora gives way to the seductive notion that only she understands the "terror of ultimate hopelessness" that had driven Bernie to take his life. This private insight fuels her sense of superiority. For a few seconds the story and its heroine remain in a state of dangerous equilibrium, teetering between the claims of common humanity and isolating solipsism. Then Cora rescues herself. She recognizes and accepts her interdependence with her fellow students, credits them with a moral sensibility as great as, if different from, her own, and turning once more to view the falling snow, sees it as a kind of benison that "forgave them all." (pp. 394-96)

It is an indication of Stafford's stature in the literary world that, from the very beginning, commentators discussing her novels and short stories invariably invoked the names of such literary giants as Proust, James, Dostoevski, Austen, Flaubert, and Joyce. She was both the gainer and the loser from these comparisons, which were, inevitably, both flattering and invidious. But a reminder of their frequency serves our immediate purpose—to demonstrate what a conscious literary artist Jean Stafford always was, and how this is made evident in **"The Philosophy Lesson."**

Starting with the double meaning of her title, with its literal reference to the classroom lesson on Bishop Berkeley, and its metaphoric reference to the epiphany by means of which Cora preserves her humanity, Stafford works with the lapidary cunning of a poet to achieve enriched meanings at every possible juncture. For example, the image of the falling snow envelopes the entire story since it is the subject of both its opening and its closing sentences. Again, Stafford establishes Cora's isolation in a variety of ways. At the outset she places the art studio in a tower that is "exorbitantly Gothic and had nothing to do with the other buildings on the campus, which were serene and low and Italian Renaissance." Then we are successively told of "her inhuman ability to remain motionless so long," and of the students who "chattered about it among themselves as if she had no ears to hear," and of the instructor, named Mr. Steele, who spent most of his time reading that master of everyday realism, Trollope, and of how Cora, following the ten-minute breaks, "turned herself to stone" when the bell signaling the resumption of class rang again. Perhaps most effective of all, we watch Cora discover, when she examines the work of the students after they have left the classroom, that the "representations of her face were, nearly invariably, the faces of the authors of the work. Her complete anonymity to them at once enraged and fascinated her." This frightening feeling of isolation invites comparable reactions in the reader.

There is more. The image of the falling snow, established in the first sentence, enters and re-enters the story until it threatens to envelope and muffle Cora and both her inner and outer worlds. Early on we are told, "When the snow came the studio was dematerialized." Next, referring to Cora's inner thoughts while posing, Stafford writes, "she drifted in a charming ease, a floating, as if she hovered, slowly winding, like the flakes themselves." And, respecting Cora's memories of her childhood, we discover that "when she had first heard of heaven, she had thought it would be a place where snow was forever falling and forever concealing the harshness of the world." The snow image even fuses with her enthusiasm for Berkeley's philosophical idealism: "Cora was pleased that probably she alone in the studio had seen what was happening outside. . . . The snow was a private experience; perhaps everything at this moment proceeded from her own mind."

Then Truth breaks in with all its matter-of-fact about the suicide, and for a time we are caught up in a world of ordinary people talking in ordinary language about an extraordinary event: the mystery of the suicide of a man who had everything but the will to live. Predictably, "Cora no longer listened." Instead she raised disturbing questions: "And what was the misery that had brought the boy to suicide? Rich, privileged, in love, he and his girl had seemed the paradigm of joy. Why had he done it?" At this moment Cora nearly succumbs to the twin evils of self-pity and pride. Sorrowing for herself, she reflects: "And yet, why not? Why did not she, who was seldom happy, do it herself? A darkness beat her like the wings of an enormous bird and frantic terror of the ultimate hopelessness shook her until the staff she held slipped and her heart seemed for a moment to fail." Even more dangerous thoughts follow. Looking at the students "still talking of the death this morning, (she) could tell by their faces that none of them had been thinking her thoughts, that she alone, silent and stationary there on the dais, had shared Bernard Allen's experience and had plunged with him into sightlessness." Yet, at the last moment, Cora, recognizing like Shakespeare's youthful Claudio her own frail humanity, will not be "absolute for death." "No, wait a minute. Each mortal in the room must, momentarily, have died. But just as the fledgling artists put their own faces on their canvases, so they had perished in their own particular ways. The snow was a benison. It forgave them all." (pp. 396-98)

[With **"The Philosophy Lesson,"** Stafford] had apparently recovered her powers of invention. More than that, she had also apparently exorcised the ghost of Lucy Cooke whose suicide she had tried unavailingly to write about. And she had done so in the time-honored manner of the seasoned fiction writer—by departing from the truth and telling lies. Stafford was seemingly following her own advice, the advice she had long ago given to the readers of *Harper's Bazaar:*

> It is not fair to buttonhole our reader with an exegesis of ourselves if there is the slightest risk of his being bored or offended: and while I have no objection to the use of autobiography—for in a sense all writing is of necessity autobiographical—I should counsel any beginner to winnow carefully and to add a good portion of lies, the bigger the better.

Stafford's strategy of lies in **"The Philosophy Lesson"** seems clear enough. For the suicide of a young woman, she substitutes the suicide of a young man. Instead of a smoking revolver, the suicide weapon is a speeding train. Rather than closeting her three principals in the confines of a house, she scatters them in three widely separated parts of town, Cora in a Life class on the campus, Bernie at the Base Line railroad crossing on the outskirts of town, and Maisie presumably at the boarding house where her lover had left her in the early hours of the morning. And, significantly, instead of a tale of two women and a man who knew each other well and lived under the same roof, we read of a poor female outsider who yearned from afar for the attention of a rich young man and envied his lover, a rich young woman, neither of whom suspected her feelings if, indeed, they were aware of her existence.

It sounds for all the world like a clear instance of a writer's discovering at last how to distance her recalcitrant material and create a literary experience that till then had eluded her because she had insisted on standing too close, attempting to mirror exactly what had happened to her. Now, by exercising artistic license, she had written a story instead of a clinical case study of human despair.

Still, appearances were deceiving. All the hopes raised by the publication of **"The Philosophy Lesson"** were to be disappointed. Instead of serving as a harbinger of more stories to come, this story was destined to look like a desert island in a sea of silence. Stafford's readers would have to wait another ten years before once again seeing any fiction of hers in print. Then, when two final stories did appear, one of them, **"An Influx of Poets,"** was issued as late as November of 1978, only five months before her death; the other, **"Woden's Day,"** was published posthumously. (pp. 398-99)

How—the question forms itself—did a writer who appears to have been barren of fiction both before and after producing this story, come to conceive it so swiftly following the signing of a contract to deliver a new, and autobiographical, novel? The answer until now was Stafford's secret, one that she kept from even her editor and her publisher and carried to her grave. As befits a writer whose vision of life was more often than not unhappy and was invariably ironic, the explanation is both ironic and a little sad.

When she published **"The Philosophy Lesson"** in November of 1968, Stafford had not in fact recovered her powers of invention. Instead, she had simply reworked an episode from an unfinished novel that she had begun writing in the thirties when she was in college and considered herself "a secret writer." This incomplete novel, which bears the title *In the Snowfall,* survives as a jumble of fascinating fragments, many of which are repetitive. These fragments, when assembled like the shards of an archaeologist, yield both a barely coherent outline and the partial contents of an interesting fictional account of Stafford's first three years of college, from 1932 to 1935, when it breaks off. Curiously, these fragments include no fewer than four versions of Bernie Allen's suicide as we have it in **"The Philosophy Lesson."** Even more curious, one of these four versions is intertwined with the Lucy Cooke story.

To keep matters clear, we shall sort out the real-life players and their fictional counterparts. Lucy is identified in the novel as Maisie, Andrew Cooke is called Cecil, and Jean Stafford is, alternatively, Joyce Batholomew or Cora Savage. In the episode that reflects Lucy's suicide, Jean appears as Joyce. In this meld of stories, Stafford presents both Maisie (unfaithful to Cecil) and Joyce as in love with Bernie Allen. The unhealthy relationship of these two young women is highlighted by a suicide contract into which they have entered and which Maisie, in an episode clearly modeled after Lucy Cooke's own story, acts out. Prior to this climactic act, the reader is treated to scenes right out of Clara Bow movies in which a decadent Maisie humiliates unsophisticated Joyce while Bernie appears as at once the infatuated slave of Maisie and a kind of big brother to Joyce. Cecil is the most forlorn figure. As the presumably cuckolded husband, he insists that Maisie love only him.

That Stafford, despite the bravado she displayed when she declared that she had burned mountains of manuscript concerning Lucy's suicide, recognized the potential power of *In the Snowfall* is demonstrated in several ways. First, she did not destroy it. Second, she extracted the fragment from it which became **"The Philosophy Lesson."** Third, sometime in 1948 she showed it to Henry A. Murray, a well-known psychologist and a distinguished literary amateur. Murray in 1949 achieved a kind of limited fame as the author of an "Introduction" to Melville's most Freudian novel, *Pierre.* This essay has ever since been regarded as a penetrating piece of Melvillian criticism.

Murray's relationship with Stafford appears to have begun in 1948 when he sent her an eloquent fan letter praising her recently published second novel, ***The Mountain Lion,*** and inviting her to lunch. Although both writers frequently leave their letters undated, it is not difficult to establish from topical references that they corresponded several times during 1948 and 1949. Stafford was then at the height of her artistic powers but was still fragile psychologically following her sequestration of many months in 1947 in the Payne-Whitney Clinic of New York Hospital. . . .

To form an association at this moment with a distinguished psychologist who was also an extraordinarily astute reader of fiction must have been both exhilarating and reassuring. Sometime in 1948 Stafford showed Murray the bits and pieces that make up *In the Snowfall.* They elicited this extraordinary response,

> This foreshadow of your work is tremendously moving, more powerful, even in its present sketchy form, than anything you have created so far. (A worshipper of your genius so faithful as I, could scarcely be more superlative in praising.) You know, surely with what enthusiasm I embrace and still cleave to ***Boston Adventure*** and ***The Mountain Lion.*** *In the Snowfall* will surpass both. It has the same miraculous insight, subtlety, and peerless expression, and in addition it has passion.
>
> Knowing next to nothing about art and the artist I shall not venture to discuss the basic structure of the book. . . . a pet, amateurish, and unpopular hypothesis of mine being that a work of art should covertly represent a parable, pertinent to a stage of development, a station of the cross on the path to salvation. What you have set forth here is a segment of disintegrated Society, a loose clique of wasters, with Maisie as its exhibitionist anima. Out of this futile suicidal maelstrom of nervous sensations each individual must ascend as best he can, creating for himself a credible mythology of evolutionary love, synthesis, and integration. [Henry Murray to Stafford, undated, 1948, Stafford Collection]

This is very startling praise. But Stafford's response to it is equally startling. Perhaps if it had been offered back in the late thirties when the many promising fragments that make up *In the Snowfall* were composed, Stafford might not have abandoned this manuscript. But by 1948 she knew her own powers and had twice demonstrated their full extent in her first two novels. Probably that explains why, in the face of this ecstatic praise from an unusually perceptive reader, she could now keep her head. She quietly put the fragments of *In the Snowfall* back into the filing cabinet where she kept unpublished—and perhaps unpublishable—work. Subsequent events have proved her right. A summary of these events will provide an illuminating epiloque to this account of factual and fictional suicides.

Henry Murray is still living in Boston, and only the other day Forrest Robinson, who is writing his biography, asked him what he could recall of Jean Stafford as she appeared during the year he knew her. He replied that she appealed to him then as a forlorn young woman who possessed a wonderful beauty and sensitivity and a girlish quality but who seemed to him as someone lost and removed from reality.

Knowing what Jean Stafford had gone through during the two previous years—the terrible dissolution of her marriage to Lowell, and her self-imposed confinement in the Payne-Whitney Clinic—it is not difficult to understand Murray's impression of her in 1948. But what this literature-loving psychologist appears not to have understood was the remarkable ability of his artist friend to preserve an inner core of great strength and purity even when her outer self suggested chaos. Jean Stafford may have seemed to Henry Murray lost and far removed from reality, but at the same time her artistic judgment was like the "ever-fixed mark" of the north star "that looks on tempests and is never shaken." Even when she needed all the confidence she could get from the good opinions of others, she did not permit this need to impair her criticial judgment. She correctly interpreted Murray's praise of *In the Snowfall* as excited hyperbole and resolutely laid that parcel of fascinating fragments permanently aside.

All but one. Twenty years later she plucked out the fragment that today appears as **"The Philosophy Lesson"** and submitted it to *The New Yorker.* That they published it even though eleven years had passed since a story of hers had appeared in their pages testifies to Stafford's sureness of judgment in extracting that particular fragment from her unfinished novel of the thirties.

Of course, at this time it was important for Stafford to be able to provide her publisher with an installment on the proposed autobiographical novel she had promised to deliver some day. But it is just possible that another reason may have guided her choice. **"The Philosophy Lesson"** 's governing image of falling snow was also the thematic image of the unfinished novel, as its title *In the Snowfall* makes explicit. It is, moreover, an appropriate image of the peace that passeth all understanding, the peace that Jean Stafford so often desperately sought during many moments of her turbulent life. Maybe, to echo Henry Murray, out of the futile suicidal maelstrom of nervous sensations that characterized so much of her life in the thirties Jean Stafford did create for herself a credible mythology of evolutionary love, synthesis, and integration. If so, **"The Philosophy Lesson"** was one of the important stations of the cross on her journey.

But I doubt if Jean Stafford ever thought this. Taken all in all, even when she appeared outwardly to be most stricken, she was a lot more durable than many of her concerned friends suspected. If she were alive today, I think she would be neither surprised nor dashed to learn that forty years after their meeting and his flattering praise of her work, Henry Murray does not recall ever reading an unfinished novel titled *In the Snowfall.* (pp. 399-403)

William Leary, "The Suicidal Thirties: Jean Stafford's 'The Philosophy Lesson'," in Southwest Review, *Vol. 72, No. 3, Summer, 1987, pp. 389-403.*

"I'm a rather slow person. Experience has to sink in for years before I can use it. . . . I have to let impressions and experience age within me until they become integrated into my whole life and perceptions before I can use them as materials for fiction."

—Jean Stafford, 1951

Bruce Bawer

[*In the following essay, which is excerpted from a review of David Roberts's* Jean Stafford: A Biography *(1988), Bawer examines Stafford's strongest themes and their ties to her "strangely tormenting childhood" and difficult adult life.*]

[Any essay about Jean Stafford] should probably begin with her parents, her family, and her strangely tormenting childhood. She was born in Covina, California, in 1915, the youngest of four children. Her father, John Stafford, was himself a writer of sorts—a genuine obsessive whose career peaked early with the publication of an obscure hack Western novel, *When Cattle Kingdom Fell.* From there it was straight downhill: selling his Covina walnut ranch in 1921, he promptly lost the proceeds in the stock market and moved his family to Colorado, where he spent the last forty years of his life writing and rewriting a bizarre magnum opus . . . on the perils of the American economy. His wife, Ethel, was the practical-minded one, a pleasant former schoolteacher whom Jean resented for her conventional domestic preoccupations, and who, once the increasingly destitute family had found its way to the city of Boulder, earned her daughter's resentment for taking in her sorority-girl classmates as boarders.

Stafford's life with this hapless couple—and with her beloved brother, Dick, and her remoter sisters, Marjorie and Mary Lee—had deep and lasting effects. [After moving to Colorado], her feelings about both her parents would be a heady compound of love and shame, pity and resentment; and many of her actions, during her undergraduate years at the University of Colorado and thereafter, strike one primarily as desperate attempts to remove herself from the world of her parents, and to forge a distinctive identity. For instance, the young Stafford—universally described as fragile, shy, and sexually naïve—shocked her fellow students by becoming the nude model for a life-drawing class, and by idolizing, befriending, and moving in with Lucy and Andrew Cooke, a notorious artsy couple. The Cookes seem to have symbolized sex and freedom to Stafford, but their wild, bohemian demimonde was shattered when Lucy committed suicide during Jean's senior year; long afterward, a still-devastated Stafford remarked of Lucy's suicide that "I am almost ready to write about it, although I have really written about nothing else ever." Indeed, though she never published anything explicitly based on her life with the Cookes, Stafford did give the names Lucy and Andrew to major characters in two of her novels, and dealt with her friends' memory in various subtler ways throughout her fiction.

Lucy's death did not put an end to Stafford's search for a separate identity. After her graduation from college, she studied philology for a year at Heidelberg, and had barely returned home before she began writing bitterly condescending letters about her parents and country. "I *can't* stay in America next year," she wrote a friend, "until I completely repudiate the whole past and live in some foreign quarter." She didn't belong here, she insisted: "I have realized suddenly to my horror that I'm an artist + have to be with my fellow beings." (p. 61-2)

[Stafford was very much against marriage]. The principal reason why she didn't want to marry, she explained to an early beau, was that marriage would turn her into a conventional wife, a philistine: "eventually we would be Mother and Dad." So unsure was she . . . of her identity as Jean Stafford, writer, that the only consequence of marriage she was able to envision was a gradual metamorphosis into a version of Ethel McKillop Stafford, housewife.

And yet when Stafford did take a husband, in 1940, she assumed the role of thankless helpmeet almost immediately. Of the man in question—Robert Lowell—she wrote that he "does what I have always needed to have done to me and that is that he dominates me." Lowell, of course, was not just any domineering man; the prep-school educated scion of a distinguished Boston family, he was the very personification of wealth, breeding, and Easternness, all of which intimidated her. He was also, alas, spoiled, irresponsible, and mentally unbalanced. In the spring of 1938, with Stafford in the passenger seat of his car and a quantity of alcohol in his blood, Lowell plowed into a wall at the end of a road in Cambridge, Massachusetts; while he escaped unscathed, Stafford's face suffered extraordinary damage. By all accounts, Lowell was less than remorseful over the incident; according to a friend, he regarded it as "just an accident, and he didn't feel responsible particularly. He looked up, there was a dead end. It was not his fault." Yet the accident was a crucial event in Stafford's life; though surgeons managed to restore her to relatively normal appearance, the accident had done permanent damage to both her looks and her health, and the fact of it hovered tragically over the eight-year marriage to Lowell.

That marriage was, from the start, an ambiguous enterprise. Once Stafford and Lowell had set up house together—first in Baton Rouge (where Lowell attended graduate school at LSU), then in New York, Tennessee, and Maine—she apparently lost no time in becoming, like her mother, the subservient spouse of an obsessive artist. While Lowell wrote poems, Stafford performed secretarial work and housekeeping chores; a fanatical convert to Catholicism, Lowell insisted, during their stay in New York, that she also do "Catholic work," and so she spent much of her free time folding papers at the offices of the *Catholic Worker.* (Lowell himself had a job—as a copy editor at Sheed and Ward—for a total of nine months during the marriage.) Even when she did find a few moments to sit at her typewriter, she often had to spend it typing Lowell's work rather than writing her own. (pp. 62-3)

In sum, Stafford seems to have given a great deal in her marriage and received very little in return. It is hard to escape the conclusion that, in marrying such a man as Lowell and in maintaining so self-abnegating a spousal role, she was essentially forsaking, for the time being at least, the hope of an independent identity, and capitulating to her own seemingly unshakable inner sense of identity with her much-despised mother.

It was in 1944 that Stafford—who before that year had published only one short story—became a best-selling novelist. ***Boston Adventure*** was not her first attempt at a novel; over the years she had worked on several different manuscripts, some of which she had abandoned, and some of which had been turned down by various editors. To any reader familiar with Stafford's later, superior fiction, her graceful, charming, but thoroughly stylized first novel reads like an out-and-out capitulation to the demands of the marketplace. It reads, as a matter of fact, like the work of someone with a weak sense of authorial identity, someone afraid to reveal a distinctive sensibility. . . . In essence, ***Boston Adventure*** is one of those capacious, old-fashioned, atmosphere-heavy affairs, mostly decorous but with perhaps a touch of the risqué, that used to be written for respectable middlebrow ladies by such authors as Anya Seton, Margaret Goudge, Daphne du Maurier, and Nancy Hale; the chief difference is that Stafford is a far more stylish and intelligent writer than most of these women.

Like many novels of its kind, ***Boston Adventure*** concerns the dramatically improving fortunes, over a period of years, of an attractive young female—in this case, Sonie Marburg. The smart, well-read, endlessly put-upon daughter of a poor Chichester, Massachusetts, immigrant couple, Sonie spends her childhood and early youth working in a hotel and entertaining a secret pipe dream—that she might one day live with Miss Lucy Pride, a wealthy Boston lady who summers at the hotel and who, to Sonie, is the very embodiment of breeding and culture. Miraculously, Sonie's dream comes to pass: she becomes Miss Pride's secretary, and takes her place among the fashionable young folk of Boston society. Yet life on Beacon Hill proves to have its own sorrows, and by novel's end Sonie is dreaming of liberation from Miss Pride as fervently as she once dreamed of escape from her parents.

To read ***Boston Adventure*** is, among other things, to be reminded of Oscar Wilde's remark that one would have to have a heart of stone to contemplate the fate of Little Nell without laughing. Sonie is no Little Nell, to be sure, but she is almost ridiculously long-suffering, and the travails she must endure before the nearly five-hundred-page opus winds to a close are legion: her father abandons the family, her younger brother dies, her mother goes insane. Through all this, Sonie seems never to stop worrying, to stop working, to enjoy so much as an hour of her life; even once she arrives in Boston there seems to be astonishingly little light or beauty in her grim world. Nor does she really *do* much of anything; instead, she lets things happen to her. If she is to be compared to the protagonists of great novels, it is not to anyone from James or Proust but rather to such figures as Maggie Tulliver in George Eliot's *The Mill on the Floss,* Hardy's Tess, and Dickens's rags-to-riches boy heroes; for in many ways, Sonie Marburg is an English Victorian heroine in modern American dress.

She is also, in a sense, her author in disguise. Like the young Stafford, Sonie longs for a world more sophisticated than that of her parents. If Stafford's authorial ambitions seem to have been fueled, in part, by her pained awareness of her father's thwarted hopes for literary glory, so Sonie's attraction to life on Beacon Hill seems to be related to her own father's frustrated hopes for success in America as a shoemaker. If Stafford's father was an author of Zane Gray-style Western stories who spent his last forty years endlessly rewriting the same book, so Sonie's father is a perpetual re-reader of *The Riders of the Purple Sage;* and if Stafford thought she had found a new family in Lucy Cooke, and later in her blue-blooded Bostonian husband, so Sonie thinks she has found a new family in the person of the blue-blooded Bostonian Lucy Pride. Read in purely biographical terms, ***Boston Adventure*** comes across both as a plea for pity by an author who is intent upon mythifying her childhood troubles, and as an unsettling fantasy of childhood liberation—for after her brother's death, her father's departure, and the onset of her mother's insanity, Sonie is to all intents and purposes an orphan. (pp. 63-4)

Remarkably, however, for all the autobiographical parallels, ***Boston Adventure*** has an extremely fabricated quality. It is, one might say, a masterpiece of false emotion. For a reader in search of something escapist, to be sure, it's a good read—an engaging, well-bred novel that is almost never rude enough to confront one with the shock of recognition. There are moments of wit, insight, and realistic dialogue, but nothing, really, that would offend or challenge a *Saturday Evening Post* subscriber. The characters, sentiments, and plot turns are all familiar—not from life, but from other books. The tone is lofty—sometimes almost absurdly so, as when Sonie (who serves double duty as protagonist and narrator) describes a dog-and-cat fight: "I saw the dreadful slaughter: the dog's eyes popping as he rent and strangled the creature, spittle mingled with blood, and I heard the cat's single wail of entreaty." When a neighbor remarks that Sonie seems pleased with her newborn brother, we are told that "immediately the words were out, a leaven commenced to resolve my wonder into the emotion the woman had assumed in me and my pity became protective." The Jean Stafford of ***Boston Adventure,*** in short, is an author who doesn't write "was ill" when she can write "ailed." Still, the novel does contain a handful of real-seeming episodes, most of which involve children; Stafford's insight into the sensibilities of the young, and her superb ear for their conversation, are evinced in a number of small, seemingly incidental touches:

> Betty Brunson, who rarely addressed me, was embracing a young elm tree near the door and swinging round it, her head appearing now on one side, now on another. "Hi, Sonie Marburg, whatcha going to do this aft?"

Stafford never again wrote anything as long or as popular as ***Boston Adventure*** (which was one of the three best-selling novels of 1944). Yet her second novel, ***The Mountain Lion*** (1947), marked an advance in every important way. Like its predecessor, ***The Mountain Lion*** is a story of childhood—specifically, of Ralph . . . [and Molly Fawcett], who after a bout of scarlet fever have health problems that draw them extremely close to each other and set them apart from their school mates. (Like other characters in Stafford's fiction, Ralph and Molly feel superior to others on account of their delicate health.) They live in California with their mother and two stuck-up older sisters, all of whom revere the memory of Grandfather Bonney, a stuffed shirt who peppered his conversation with Latin epigrams and (as he continually reminded everyone) had once met Grover Cleveland; Ralph and Molly, for their part, prefer their mother's stepfather, the down-to-earth rancher Grandfather Kenyon. (As in ***Boston Adventure,*** then, there is an emphatic contrast between hight-toned types and simple folk.) But it is not till after Grandfather Kenyon's death, early in the novel, that Ralph and Molly meet Kenyon's son Claude and begin to spend summers at the family's Colorado ranch; it is there, during their pubescence, that Ralph's health improves and he and Molly grow apart, the boy becoming attached to his uncle and learning to shoot, the girl—an aspiring author—withdrawing into her writing and developing an icy hatred for virtually everyone around her.

The novel's turning point comes when Ralph and Molly are on a train which is, not incidentally, passing through a tunnel. Ralph, who has recently experienced a disturbing sexual attraction toward his sister Leah, takes a seat beside Molly, who despite her intelligence and curiosity retains a childlike innocence that he feels slipping away from him. . . . . [Something]—namely, the hormonal urge that accompanies the onset of manhood—compels him to despoil the purity that Molly represents. Aware that he is "weakening and ready to fall," Ralph whispers to his sister: "Molly, tell me all the dirty words you know." Before she can respond, the train emerges into the light of day, and the chapter concludes:

> Ralph's childhood and his sister's expired at that moment of the train's entrance into the surcharged valley. It was a paradox, for now they should be going into a tunnel with no end, now that they had heard the devil speak.

It is only a matter of time before the division between Ralph and Molly reaches its tragic apotheosis. Ralph, who has been eager to kill a mountain lion rumored to be in the vicinity of the Kenyon ranch, sees and fires at the lion one day in the underbrush—but, instead, accidentally kills Molly.

Here, as in ***Boston Adventure,*** the parallels to Stafford's own life appear meaningful. Molly and Ralph are clearly based on Stafford and her brother, Dick, to whom she felt very close (and who had died in an automobile accident soon after the publication of ***Boston Adventure***); the children's older sisters are based on Stafford's sisters. Like Sonie Marburg's mother, moreover, Mrs. Fawcett reflects, to a considerable degree, Stafford's view of her own mother: she is a foolish, vain, and superficial woman whose dearest wish is that her son become a "gentleman" like Grandfather Bonney and that her daughters be proper "ladies." As for the father, if in ***Boston Adventure*** Stafford removed Mr. Marburg from the scene after a few chapters, in ***The Mountain Lion*** she kills off the children's father before the novel even begins. Though the bulk of the novel is told from Ralph's point of view, it is Molly with whom the author plainly identifies, and who gradually becomes the center of interest. The girl is bright, introverted, obnoxious, and frighteningly eccentric; but the principal fact about her is that, as she approaches adulthood, she is—by virtue of her identity as an aspiring artist, a budding intellectual, and a sickly girl whose innocence refuses to die—increasingly alienated from the robust, physical, masculine environment of the ranch, and even from Ralph, who is fast growing into an altogether average young man. Plainly, Stafford's second novel can be read as a symbolic rendering of the author's own sense of isolation from her family—and, indeed, from the world—and its ending can be understood as a means of sacrificing her own life, in fiction, to save her brother's.

But of course it is not the novel's autobiographical subtext that makes it valuable; to overemphasize such matters, in fact, is to divert attention from the book's aesthetic import. And the fact is that ***The Mountain Lion*** is one of the most admirable short novels of its time—elegantly structured, deftly composed, and sensitively imagined. It is as taut and well constructed as a short novel by Henry James, as free of superfluities as ***Boston Adventure*** was swimming in them; its prose, furthermore, is as lean and temperate as that of Stafford's first novel was mannered. All of the characters are artfully drawn, but it is the portrayal of the children that qualifies the novel as a *tour de force.* For Stafford captures the world of childhood in masterly fashion, rendering details, dialogue, and thoughts for pages on end without a noticeable misstep. To recapture the way one's own mind worked at the age of eight or ten or twelve is among the most difficult of challenges for a writer, and in ***The Mountain Lion*** Stafford accomplishes this feat magnificently. Like Truman Capote's *Other Voices, Other Rooms* (which would appear a year later), ***The Mountain Lion*** is an emblematic account of the death of childhood, the end of innocence. If it has a failing, it is that the ending feels more than a bit contrived; yet there is, at the same time, a symbolic appropriateness and inevitability about it that makes it work.

The last of Stafford's three published novels, ***The Catherine Wheel*** (1953), presents us with yet another child. Twelve-year-old Andrew Shipley is spending the summer at the New England country house of his cousin Katharine Congreve, a beautiful, charming Boston spinster in her early forties whose intimate tie with Andrew's parents is regarded as "the most winning friendship in Boston." Andrew's story—which takes place entirely during this one summer—is reminiscent in many ways of ***The Mountain Lion.*** Like Molly, Andrew is a sensitive, imaginative isolato. Just as Molly comes to feel rejected by her brother, so Andrew feels abandoned by his only friend in the world, Victor Smithwick, the son of his cousin's seamstress; just as Molly's brother is busy hero-worshipping his uncle, so Andrew's friend is preoccupied with his older brother, a Navy man whom he idolizes, and who is at home with a serious illness. Like Molly, too, Andrew has a pair of silly, conventional sisters and a mother who is much closer to them than to him; and just as Molly's mother leaves her at the family ranch while she circles the globe with her older daughters, so Andrew's parents leave him at Katharine's country house while they spend their summer in Europe.

Andrew is not, strictly speaking, the only protagonist of ***The Catherine Wheel.*** Chapter by chapter, Stafford alternately focuses on Andrew, who secretly pines for Victor and hopes that the boy's brother will either die or recover and leave, and Cousin Katharine, who has her own secret preoccupation: she's been conducting a clandestine romance with Andrew's father, whom she has loved for twenty years, and is waiting to hear whether he will divorce his wife. Neither Andrew nor Katharine is aware of the other's hidden torment; each nervously interprets the other's occasional show of anxiety as evidence that his own deepest thoughts have been perceived. Together they agonize alone, neither receiving an ounce of comfort from the other. This situation persists until the end of the summer—and of the novel—when Katharine is burned to death in a fireworks accident.

The Catherine Wheel is an unusual novel—and, in many ways, a satisfying one. The principal characters are vividly imagined, and the prose is as finely crafted as in ***The Mountain Lion***; the central dramatic situation, moreover, is skillfully and often wittily managed, and Stafford's central point—namely, that we all live in individual worlds, obsessed, in spite of our best intentions, with our private dilemmas—certainly comes through clearly. Ultimately, though, the novel is less effective than Stafford must have hoped it would be. A large part of the reason is the ending. Like ***The Mountain Lion, The Catherine Wheel*** concludes in a burst of symbolism. Significantly, the fireworks device that kills Katharine is a Catherine wheel—a rapidly spinning wheel of colored fire, also known as a pinwheel, which is typically nailed to a tree; this, the novel's main symbol, serves much the same function as the mountain lion in Stafford's second book. We are told that when Katharine first fell in love with Andrew's father—who on that same night fell in love with his wife-to-be—there was a Catherine wheel spinning; we are reminded that the wheel is the symbol of the martyr Catherine ("They tied her to a thing like that and set it spinning, but it broke before it killed her and then they chopped off her head"); and we are informed that Katharine has ordered an image of the wheel carved into her own gravestone.

A comparison of the endings of this novel and ***The Mountain Lion*** is highly instructive. ***The Mountain Lion*** ends with the appearance of the eponymous feline and the death of Molly; ***The Catherine Wheel*** concludes with the appearance of the eponymous wheel and the death of Katharine. As critics have noted, both endings involve a *deus ex machina* and are thus less than completely pleasing; but there is a clear difference between them. For, despite its artificiality, the conclusion of ***The Mountain Lion*** manages to be quite affecting, and indeed feels somehow *right*—partly because the story is so symbolic in tone to begin with, and perhaps also in part because the conclusion represents an expert tapping into the reader's unconscious storehouse of myths and emotions relating to childhood, family, and growing up. Besides, whereas it is the fire from the Catherine wheel that kills Katharine, it is not the lion but her brother who kills Molly. And the act is a direct—if hardly an inevitable—consequence of the changes that both children in ***The Mountain Lion*** have undergone: Molly has increasingly kept to her own company, prowling quietly around the ranch and examining the local fauna (which would explain her sudden appearance in the brush); her brother has become more of a "man," incautiously gun-happy. Hence the killing of Molly has both credibility and import. The conclusion of ***The Catherine Wheel,*** by contrast—for all of Stafford's skilled foreshadowing—has a facile, phony quality; Katharine's death comes off as a freak accident, and the image of the Catherine wheel has no more resonance than a naughty limerick.

By the time ***The Catherine Wheel*** was published, Stafford's life had changed enormously. As her marriage to Lowell disintegrated, Stafford's life fell into a grim routine of insomnia, heavy drinking, and nervous breakdowns; after Lowell left her in 1946 she broke down completely and spent most of the following year as a patient at the Payne-Whitney Clinic of New York Hospital. . . . When, some time after their estrangement, Lowell expressed the hope that she would be recognized as the best novelist of her generation, she replied that such a turn of events "would mean to me absolutely *nothing.* It could not happen and even if it could, it would not make the days here less long nor would my loss of you be made up for." The truth seems to be that without the dominating figure of Lowell in her life Stafford was lost, directionless; that his rejection of her was so destructive of her mental stability seems to have been a measure not only of her love for him but of her continued insecurity, her inadequate sense of self—which, even after the financial success of ***Boston Adventure*** and the artistic triumph of ***The Mountain Lion,*** seems not to have been altered substantially.

Stafford's second and third experiments with wedlock were more conservative than her first. Following a brief marriage, in the early Fifties, to Oliver Jensen—a *Time* magazine writer who would later co-found *American Heritage*—Stafford wed *New Yorker* writer A. J. Liebling, to whom she remained married until his death in 1963. Both of these men provided a measure of stability (and Liebling, by her own testimony, brought her considerable happiness), but Stafford's life continued, for the most part, to be an emotional roller coaster. Though she lived until 1979, passing her last fifteen years in relative seclusion on Long Island—as much of an isolato as Molly Fawcett or Andrew Shipley—she never completed another novel after ***The Catherine Wheel.*** Why? Perhaps part of the explanation is that once she had satisfied herself that she'd *made* it—in other words, that she had accomplished what her father had never done—her driving motivation to write was gone. For Stafford seems oddly to have been driven, at once, to show up her father, to vindicate him, and to duplicate his long, pathetic, unproductive decline. In fact, in a manner eerily reminiscent of her father's decades of work on his economic manifesto, Stafford spent many of her last years laboring over a novel, entitled *The Parliament of Women,* that would never be published. (pp. 64-8)

More importantly, Stafford continued to write short stories well into the mid-Sixties. Indeed, as her novels faded in the reading public's memory, she began to be known primarily for her work in that field, and, in particular, as one of the most celebrated practitioners of the controversial genre known as the *New Yorker* story. Stafford's short fiction, most of which was assembled in various volumes during the Fifties and Sixties and brought together in the Pulitzer Prize-winning ***Collected Stories*** (1969), represents one of the finest moments of the American short story. Witty, luminous, and impeccably crafted, her contributions to the genre are crowded with people named Otis and Meriwether and Fairweather, with troubled children and snobby society women, and with garden-party conversations reported word for word. Extremely long sentences abound, and the vocabulary is unusually rich: a single page of the story **"A Modest Proposal"** contains the words *concupiscently, nares, sybarite, mufti,* and *cereus.* Yet Stafford succeeds in fashioning a lucid, well-upholstered style into which such words fit very gracefully.

To read ***The Collected Stories*** is to note the recurrence of certain themes, many of which recall the preoccupations of Stafford's life as well as the plots of her novels. The book abounds in protagonists who are, to some extent, Sonie Marburgs—unsatisfied with their lot and eager to be taken into someone else's world. In **"The Bleeding Heart,"** for instance, "a Mexican girl from the West" named Rose Fabrizio longs to be adopted by a mysterious elderly man who visits the New England library where she works; but her illusions about the man are soon shattered. The most prominent of Stafford's themes, indeed, may well be the shattering of illusions—the illusions of Americans about Europe, of Westerners about the Eastern seaboard, of poor people about the rich, of naïve young people about the *beau monde.* One story after another seems to derive in some way from the young Stafford's encounter with Lucy Cooke's bohemia, with the *Kultur* of Heidelberg, or with Robert Lowell's Boston. In **"Maggie Meriwether's Rich Experience,"** a girl from Nashville on her first trip abroad is intimidated into silence by a host of rich and titled folk at a garden party in France; in **"The Echo and the Nemesis,"** Sue Ledbetter, an American student in Heidelberg, feels painfully inferior to the more worldly Ramona Dunn; in **"The Healthiest Girl in Town,"** a girl named Jessie is made to feel *déclassé* by two well-to-do schoolmates who regard their delicate health as a sign of privilege. (Like Ralph and Molly Fawcett, they're *proud* of their illness.) Time and again, however, sophistication is revealed to be a mask for vulnerability, for failure, for loneliness, for a history of personal tragedy. And tragedy is certainly plentiful in these stories. Just as Stafford lost her brother immediately prior to the appearance of her first novel, so some of her characters are struck by tragedy on the threshold of their greatest joy. In the deeply haunting story **"The Liberation,"** for instance, Polly Bay—who has been saved from a life of eternal spinsterhood in her aunt and uncle's tomblike Colorado house by a proposal of marriage from a wonderful young Harvard professor—learns just before her would-be triumphal departure that her fiancé has died.

Naturally, some of Stafford's stories are more impressive than others. Aside from the ones I have named, Stafford's strongest stories include **"A Country Love Story," "The Interior Castle,"** and **"An Influx of Poets."** But even her weakest stories are a joy to read, if only because their prose is so lovely. The deficiencies that they do manifest are, for the most part, those which are notoriously characteristic of *New Yorker* short stories in general. For instance, like many a fiction writer associated with that illustrious magazine, Stafford places a good deal less emphasis on plot than on character. This is, to be sure, not always a weakness, but it is hard to read the ***Collected Stories*** in sequence without eventually becoming irritated by their mostly ambiguous, well-nigh pretentious endings; one has the feeling that the author doesn't want to push too far, doesn't want to face the difficult choices attendant upon reaching the conclusion of a story, doesn't want to risk sentimentality or conventionality or melodrama. The contrast with the emphatic sense of closure achieved in ***The Mountain Lion*** and ***The Catherine Wheel*** is striking; and the result is too often a denouement that feels dry to the point of heartlessness and pat to the point of meaninglessness. Another *New Yorker*ish problem is that the stories tend to be cluttered up with gratuitous details—inventories of clothes, furnishings, meals, and the like, with a frequent emphasis on the hoity-toity.

A failing more specific to Stafford's stories is that her sarcasm toward a character sometimes overwhelms her sympathy. This is true, for instance, of **"Polite Conversation,"** in which a recently married young woman is forced to endure a visit to her new home by a rich lady who lives nearby. The only apparent point of the story is to make fun of the lady, who in her fatuity, condescension, and bigotry is rather too easy a target—not to mention a very familiar one, whose like (in male and female form) may be found throughout Stafford's fiction. These stories, then, are not without serious flaws; to compare them to the short fiction of John Cheever—and especially to that of Eudora Welty and Peter Taylor—is to notice, on Stafford's part, a relative want of sympathy and narrowness of range. Cheever's stories are more inventive than hers, Welty's more playful and abundant, Taylor's more thoughtful; Welty's and Taylor's stories, moreover, seem markedly *realer* than Stafford's, more significant, more profoundly human. Yet the very fact that one is compelled to speak of Stafford in the company of such masters is to acknowledge that her achievement in the genre is of a very high order indeed. (pp. 68-70)

Bruce Bawer, "Jean Stafford's Triumph," in The New Criterion, *Vol. VII, No. 3, November, 1988, pp. 61-72.*

FURTHER READING

Gelfant, Blanche H. "Revolutionary Turnings: *The Mountain Lion* Reread." *The Massachusetts Review* XX, No. 1 (Spring 1979): 117-25.

Focuses on the abundance of moral and verbal satire in *The Mountain Lion.* A revised version of the essay excerpted in *CLC,* Vol. 7, pp. 459-60.

Leary, William. "Grafting onto Her Roots: Jean Stafford's 'Woden's Day'." *Western American Literature* XXIII, No. 2 (August 1988): 129-39.

Explores the interspersion of fact and fiction in "Woden's Day," a story that traces Stafford's family history.

———. "Jean Stafford: The Wound and the Bow." *The Sewanee Review* XCVIII, No. 3 (Summer 1990): 333-49.

Compares the similar autobiographical elements in the stories "And Lots of Solid Color" and "The Tea Time of Stouthearted Ladies," especially Stafford's resentment toward her family and her urgency to escape them.

———. "Native Daughter: Jean Stafford's California." *Western American Literature* XXI, No. 3 (November 1986): 195-205.

Traces Stafford's early childhood in Covina, California and her feelings of alienation as they are reflected in *The Mountain Lion.*

Leary, William G. "Checkmate: Jean Stafford's 'A Slight Maneuver'." *Western American Literature* XXI, No. 2 (August 1986): 99-109.

Discusses the circumstances behind the writing of "A Slight Maneuver," as well as the story's irony, action, and resolution.

———. "A Tale of Two Titles: Jean Stafford's 'Caveat Emptor'." *The South Atlantic Quarterly* 85, No. 2 (Spring 1986): 123-33.

Speculates as to why Stafford often changed the titles of published stories, focusing chiefly on how the farcical plot and style of "Caveat Emptor" reflects Stafford's playful attitude toward fiction.

Mann, Jeanette W. "Toward New Archetypal Forms: *Boston Adventure.*" *Studies in the Novel* VIII, No. 3 (Fall 1976): 291-303.

Asserts that critical neglect of Stafford's works is due to her presentation of "a new kind of truth," which the critic must comprehend by formulating "new structures and a new vocabulary." Excerpted in *CLC,* Vol. 7, pp. 458-59.

Oates, Joyce Carol. "*The Interior Castle:* The Art of Jean Stafford's Short Fiction." *Shenandoah* 30, No. 3 (1979): 61-4.

Notes that Stafford's strengths as a writer include her elegiac tone, subdued dramatic tension, and sharp impressions.

Roberts, David. *Jean Stafford: A Biography.* London: Chatto & Windus, 1988, 494 p.

Detailed work includes critical commentary of Stafford's writings, personal reminiscences of her life, numerous photographs, and an extensive bibliography.

Straus, Dorothea. "Jean Stafford." *Shenandoah* 30, No. 3 (1979): 85-91.

Revealing personal tribute written by a close friend following Stafford's death.

Viera, Carroll. "'In the Zoo' and *The Mill on the Floss.*" *American Notes and Queries* XX, Nos. 3 & 4 (November-December 1981): 53-4.

Correlates the symbolic use of polar bears in Stafford's story and George Eliot's novel.

Wolcott, James. "Blowing Smoke into the Zeitgeist." *Harper's* 266, No. 1597 (June 1983): 57-9.

Castigates the lack of popular and critical attention toward Stafford's writings and comments on her life, her novels *The Mountain Lion* and *The Catherine Wheel,* and several short stories.

David Wingrove

1954-

(Full name David John Wingrove) English novelist, editor, and nonfiction writer.

Wingrove attracted critical attention with *Chung Kuo: The Middle Kingdom, Book One* and *The Broken Wheel: Chung Kuo II,* the first two volumes of his projected eight-volume epic, *Chung Kuo.* In this series, Wingrove creates a futuristic world in which the Chinese, led by seven emperors called the T'ang, have gained control of a society made up of peoples of diverse nationalities, whose population numbers almost forty billion. Set in the twenty-second and twenty-third centuries, *Chung Kuo* explores the conflict between the T'ang's attempt to maintain peace through order and stability and the Westerners' desire for change. Wingrove delineates the highly stratified society both professionally, with Europeans developing new technology and the Chinese filling leadership positions, and geographically, with the lower classes living on the ground, or "Clay," level and the T'ang inhabiting the uppermost layer of "Ice," a synthetic material from which several stories of living space are built above the earth. Charles de Lint commented on *Chung Kuo*'s first volume: "*The Middle Kingdom* is an absorbing and elaborate work, reading more like the best kind of historical or fantasy novel than like science fiction. Yet its view of the future, and its fascinating speculations about all aspects of this future world, are the very lifeblood of [science fiction] at its bravest."

Chung Kuo chronicles the activities of dozens of characters, particularly focusing on a group of individuals from the upper echelons of the "Ice" who are introduced as children in *The Middle Kingdom* and become the Dispersionists—ruthless rebels who fight the T'ang in the second book. Although many critics have noted that *Chung Kuo* is occasionally imitative, recalling the works of such science fiction novelists as Frank Herbert, Philip K. Dick, and Brian Aldiss, several commentators observed that the series is unique because it impartially presents both sides of the conflict between the Dispersionists and the T'ang. Vance Anderson noted: "None of Wingrove's characters remain black and white stereotypes; all are shades of gray; constantly growing and changing. The ease with which Wingrove circumvents the classic good versus evil formula makes the future volumes of *Chung Kuo* that much more intriguing."

PRINCIPAL WORKS

NONFICTION

Apertures: A Study of the Writings of Brian W. Aldiss (with Brian Griffin) 1984
The Science Fiction Sourcebook (editor) 1984
The Science Fiction Film Source Book (editor) 1985
Trillion Year Spree: The History of Science Fiction (with Brian Aldiss) 1986

NOVELS

Chung Kuo: The Middle Kingdom, Book One 1990
The Broken Wheel: Chung Kuo II 1991

Michael Dirda

In ***Chung Kuo: The Middle Kingdom*** David Wingrove inaugurates a seven-volume science-fiction epic about the world at the end of the 22nd century, a strange and wondrous place dominated by the Chinese, where most of the population lives on vast decks built high above the surface of the earth.

As in Dante's *Purgatorio* (itself the middle volume of a noted sf trilogy), status is determined by one's level. At the tippy-top live the T'ang—no relation to the orange drink—in a realm of order, beauty and changeless ritual; these are the rulers, seven of them, who govern with brotherly harmony the nearly 40 billion who teem uneasily on the decks below. Also enjoying exceptional comfort, high on the social pyramid, are the big businessmen, senior security officials, upper-echelon bureaucrats. Mostly concerned with profits, new inventions and special perks, a few churlish members of this elite have nonetheless embraced the Dispersionist cause and are beginning to advocate the radical, indeed outlawed, doctrine of Change.

On lower levels, below the Net (the Net? don't ask), matters have gotten a little out of hand. Crime lords rule, martial artists compete in gladiatorial contests to the death, very young girls are sold into sing-song houses and nearly everyone is looking for a way to move on up. Few make it. Those who don't have a good chance of ending down on the Clay.

The Clay, the actual terra firma to which the earth's superstructure of decks is anchored, has become a no-man's land, bleak and savage. Imagine "The Road Warrior" after all the cars have run out of gas. Things are so bad that people eat the only food they can find—each other.

Given such a global vision of things to come, Wingrove needs to generate enough plot material to fuel seven fat volumes. With admirable profligacy, the youngish British author sets in motion love affairs, bizarre scientific experiments, dynastic struggles. His dramatis personae include assassins, traitors, clones, replicants, androids, genetic monsters, Rambo-like soldiers, peasants and princes. The action ranges from the building of a generation starship to the discovery of the earth's true history, with pit stops for sexual torture, matricide and ritual murder. With such operatic excess a novel could easily lose its way, but Wingrove makes sure that everything circles around a single main plot: the Dispersionist cabal to overthrow the T'ang, a conspiracy that leads inexorably to the world-shattering "War of Two Directions."

Now in most science fiction the heroes tend to be freebooters and freethinkers, opposed to the iron-fisted oppression of the local galactic empire. But in what seems, at least so far, to be a conservative, almost Thatcherite thriller, the Dispersionists possess virtually no saving graces. Their cause may look just, since clearly the world has grown stagnant and over-populated, but these freedom fighters prove as venal, ruthless and sadistic as the Seven are noble, kindly and forebearing. Plato himself couldn't have imagined more ideal statesmen. When Gen. Tolonen, the T'ang's trusted military adviser, orders a dozen men killed to protect his sovereign, he reflects mournfully on military necessity. When Maj. DeVore, the mastermind of the Dispersionist strategies, murders, he does so with lip-smacking relish.

As the projected septet (to be published over the next six years) will cover roughly half a century, the main characters of the sequence are now little more than children. Around this handful of the preternaturally gifted and talented will swirl the many battles to come. Li-Yuan, T'ang apparent, is a young David—wise beyond his years. He loves the beautiful Fei-Yen, a girl of flower-petal perfection. No doubt she will be threatened, with rape or worse, by the villainous albino Stefan Lehmann, protege of DeVore. Three other preteens, basically sympathetic characters so far, will certainly become major players: Kim, a scientific genius who has been saved from a short, brutish life on the Clay; the schizophrenic Ben, possessor of an unnerving artistic sensitivity; and Jelka, Tolonen's high-spirited daughter.

Having studied the myths surrounding the birth of heroes, Wingrove endows nearly all these characters with some kind of genetic or sexual mystery. Li-Yuan is untimely ripped from his dead mother's womb. Ben believes himself a clone of one of his ancestors; his sister adores him with an unhealthy passion. Kim is the product of his Clay mother's rape by a mysterious visitor from Above. Stefan Lehmann is, in a sense, of no woman born. Jelka's mother had been her father's ward, and he now looks on his daughter with tinges of more than paternal affection. Yet another young character sleeps with a prostitute who reminds him of his sister. Incest, the poet Shelley once observed, is a very poetical circumstance. In ***Chung Kuo*** it may turn out to be a very political one as well.

As a thriller ***Chung Kuo*** is certainly exciting, despite rather colorless prose. Structurally, Wingrove organizes his book like a match of Wei-Chi, the game of encirclement usually known as Go. Short chapters pick up characters and place them, like stones on a board, around some climactic event: a marriage, an assassination, a police raid. Circles interpenetrate circles.

For many readers, then, ***Chung Kuo*** will be superb gung-ho entertainment, a "Tinker, Tailor, Soldier, Spaceman." But science fiction fans may find it somewhat disturbing. David Wingrove, coauthor (with Brian Aldiss) of the standard history of sf, ***Trillion Year Spree,*** knows every plot, villain and hero in the genre. Unfortunately, a lot of them are in his novel. ***Chung Kuo*** leans most heavily on Frank Herbert's *Dune* and the gritty industrial vision of Philip K. Dick, but too many scenes also recall William Gibson, Fritz Leiber, Bruce Sterling, Ursula Le Guin, Isaac Asimov or Jack Vance, among others. I'd also bet that Wingrove has read at least one poem by Philip Larkin. As a result of all this influence, ***Chung Kuo*** simply lacks imaginative originality. The plot turns may be exciting but they're only occasionally surprising.

Wingrove may not deserve any real blame for this: He may have simply planned to fix up a good commercial novel. Still, ***Chung Kuo*** seems entirely characteristic of too much current science fiction. Sf appears to have entered a post-modern period of decadence in which many of its practitioners are either slavishly imitating or coyly parodying the work of the past. This is hardly what we expect from a genre that, at its best, should deliver the shock of the new. (pp. 5, 7)

Michael Dirda, "The War of Two Directions," in Book World—The Washington Post, *December 31, 1989, pp. 5, 7.*

Vance Anderson

Set at the turn of the 23rd Century, at a time when China has come to dominate the world, ***Chung Kuo: The Middle***

Kingdom is an historical epic in the tradition of Tolstoy. The vast wheel of history is turning and a change in the dynastic cycle seems imperative. At these crucial times, everyone and everything is swept up in the dynamic of possible change. This first of seven planned volumes introduces the initial set of characters and their children who seem destined to resolve the conflicts set into motion. The current government has regressed back to the trappings of traditional Confucian standards. Appearances are paramount. Truth is a commodity reserved for the elite and for most it entails responsibility and guilt. The opposition focuses on change and technological development at the expense of the security of tradition. Overpopulation guarantees that any type of change will result in massive starvation and death. Who is right?

Wingrove masterfully plays both sides. Initially, the reader is led to sympathize with the Dispersionists (rebels) against the Seven (dictators) which literally mandate at which level people live, from the bestiality of the Clay—the ground level of the massive cities—to the royalty at the apex, and every shade in between. Slowly, doubts creep in; questionable activities, from the involvement of a sinister albino billionaire to the brutal rape of a peasant, reveal the amoral nature of the rebel opposition. Do the ends justify the means? Will a new regime mean a better life for the masses? Towards the end of the book the sincerity of The Seven as leaders trying to deal with apparently insurmountable pressures is explored. The awe with which a new Prince faces his baptism of understanding is truly touching.

Chung Kuo: The Middle Kingdom has the quality of a soap opera and carries with it both the strengths and weaknesses of this format. One strength is the personal involvement of the reader. One cares for the individual victories and losses of the characters. However, a classic soap opera weakness is also on display: the stereotypical characterizations. There's the embittered old general, the gladiator turned assassin, the coy yet conniving princess, and the computer-like whiz kid named Kim. Fortunately, Wingrove doesn't remain within the bounds of his stereotypes. The length of the novel (and the series) means that the stereotypical and seemingly obvious situations take so long to develop that the reader makes a false assumption of predictability. Actually this couldn't be further from the truth; constant change is the rule. As soon as Kim realizes some insights into the world situation and his own existence, conditions change so quickly that his insights become meaningless.

Wingrove artfully complicates matters by juxtaposing different characters' understanding of society and history. Which one is most accurate? It's a mystery that lasts hundreds of pages. Considering that six more books of equal length are planned, it seems likely that the revelations of the first book will not remain constant through the last.

The technology of the 22nd century is a relatively minor theme. Ice, a molecule as light as air yet as strong as titanium—and the basic assumption underlying the many-layered high-rise cities—is not explained until page 258. The cities cover the earth like glaciers, housing 40 billion people. Technological innovation—yes. Answer to overpopulation—no. The cities have reached the saturation point. With a magical element like ice it would seem that living space shouldn't be a problem. Continuing to build higher should give everyone plenty of room. However, crowding occurs on almost every level, especially the lowest level, the Clay. Logically, food rather than space should be the defining factor in supporting such a large population.

The technological elements of the next volume seem similarly simplistic. In a summary of ***Chung Kuo: The Broken Wheel,*** it is revealed that Li Yuan, the innocent young Prince of ***Chung Kuo: The Middle Kingdom,*** is working to electronically wire the entire population in order to observe and control them. The Bureaucracy is the one institution that has never changed throughout China's history. Dynasties have fallen, foreigners have invaded and through it all the taxes have been collected. The clerks at the DMV consider Mao's little red tape book their Bible. Thus it makes complete sense that the monolithic Chinese bureaucracy would attempt to implement a bureaucratic nightmare like complete surveillance. But, the point is that this idea has been written about hundreds of times in the science fiction genre. Technology-oriented readers will be disappointed with the simplicity of ***Chung Kuo's*** design.

Throughout the context of change Wingrove seamlessly weaves the details of Chinese society. Wingrove has done his homework, passing with flying colors, by utilizing historically accurate references where other authors would have opted for fictional embroiderings. He avoids a common error by not making these interesting tidbits a focal point of the plot (usually employed by the lazy author to prove the novel's "Chineseness"). Two examples of this detailing come to mind.

The first is the well-known folk tale of Yu the archer. Ten suns scorched the Earth in ancient times. Yu shot down the nine extra suns thereby saving China. He returns home to find that while he was away his wife drank too much of the elixir of life which protected Yu from the suns. Yu's wife's greedy attempt to gain immortality resulted in her transformation into a toad and banishment to the dark side of the moon. In ***Chung Kuo: The Middle Kingdom*** a wise man dreams that Li Yuan is Yu. Prince Li Yuan at first revels at the idea of being a hero like Yu. However, perhaps this dream means that he will be betrayed by his wife. Many Chinese folk-tales have this intentional double meaning. Wingrove reveals the augury just the way a traditional Chinese scholar would have interpreted it. He captures the richness of an important Chinese tradition in which nothing is clear-cut. Some modern scholars believe that the *Shang* priests actually controlled the empire through their interpretation of the way a turtle bone cracks. Their answers to the Emperor's questions often dictated his response to a crisis.

The second example is a passing reference to the theory behind the obscure spitting bronze vase. Joseph Needham in *Science and Civilization in China* documents this curious flat bronze. When it is filled with water and the rim is rubbed with a wet palm, water squirts three inches to three feet above the rim. This application of dynamic wave mechanics indicates an early understanding of the theories of motion. Wingrove borrows these scientific principles as the basis for all-purpose ice weavers. These spider-like machines emit a small hum as they operate which corresponds to the wet palm rubbing the rim. This time-bridging leap of imagination is truly remarkable. Wingrove's embroidery deserves high praise: *qing chu yu lan, er sheng yu lan* (Literally: the color navy comes from blue, but it's even better than blue. Meaning: the student learns from the teacher and in practice becomes superior to the teacher).

While Wingrove's interpretation of specific historical references is *virtuoso,* the harmonics of the larger cultural traits are slightly out of tune. One of the most important and difficult to translate cultural aspects of ancient China is that of face. While he does not define it as such, Wingrove's use of face is akin to military honor: loyalty and respect to the Emperor with the twist of self-sacrifice when the Emperor's honor has been insulted. This seems more reminiscent of the Japanese *bushido* as characterized in its modern reincarnation of *kamikaze.* The Confucian concept of face has more personal, ascetic, and familial overtones. The act of striving for success in business as opposed to scholarly endeavors leads to a loss of face. Wingrove's characters talk of honor and respect but the reader does not experience the intake of breath and personal feeling of insult that should occur upon a serious loss of face. Instead of distilling this subtle yet powerful cultural context, Wingrove opts for the more easily obtainable sledgehammer shock-value reminiscent of Wes Craven. From brainwashed replicant assassins with bombs housed in their chests to perfectly crafted *go* pieces made of human bone, these excesses seem out of place when rendered in Wingrove's sparse, lyric style. However, this gore does add to the compelling nature of the plot's soap opera tenor.

Another Asian concept which Wingrove does not adequately embody through his prose is that of *guanxi. Guanxi* is a sense of responsibility or a debt which is owed for favors done in the past; *guanxi* is a powerful actualization of the folk saying "I'll wash your back if you wash mine." However, the folk saying does not do justice to the actual emotion. The debt must be repaid in such a way that shows the debtor's generosity and honor. The immediacy of this emotion is related to face in that failure to fulfill a debt of *guanxi* results in a serious loss of face, while paying back this debt in a greater amount than necessary can add to one's face. The shame of unreturned *guanxi,* even if no one else knows about it, is debilitating. *Guanxi* is time sensitive. A simple little unrequited favor can blossom into a full-blown neurosis. China's communal sense is so strong that if the neighborhood learns about a *guanxi* debt or a loss of face, they will all share the sense of responsibility and dishonor. This will result in immense peer pressure to repay the debt or if the loss of face is too great, the individual will be ostracized from the group: a fate worse than death to most of the community-oriented people in traditional China. The closest Wingrove comes to following the unwritten rules for the *guanxi* system is with the character Karr, a gladiator turned assassin, and his loyalty to his benefactor General Tolonen. Once again this is closer to a sense of military honor or in anthropological terms a patron-client relationship. This is quite different from the *guanxi* which permeates all facets of Chinese society and everyday life. (pp. 61-2)

The understated historical and cultural references prove to be the gems amidst the seemingly soap-operaish plot [in ***Chung Kuo: The Middle Kingdom***]. None of Wingrove's characters remain black and white stereotypes; all are shades of gray; constantly growing and changing. The ease with which Wingrove circumvents the classic good versus evil formula makes the future volumes of ***Chung Kuo*** that much more intriguing. The complexity of characters and events is the strength of this novel. The strength of the series will rely on Wingrove's ability to continue his successful theme of constant change. (p. 63)

Vance Anderson, in a review of "Chung Kuo: The Middle Kingdom," in Science Fiction Eye, *Vol. 2, No. 1, February 1990, pp. 61-3.*

Gerald Jonas

[***Chung Kuo: The Middle Kingdom***]—the first of a projected seven-volume series—reads like a historical novel that took a wrong turn and wandered into the future. Set in the 22d and 23d centuries, it looks back to the glories of pre-19th-century China, when all-powerful emperors ruled a vast civilization from within the Forbidden City. The premise of David Wingrove's tale is that the Chinese somehow regained their sense of purpose in the latter half of the 21st century and went on to conquer the entire world. By the year 2190, when the action begins, the population of the earth has grown to 34 billion, spread among seven continent-sized cities, each ruled by a Chinese king, or T'ang; the only counterbalance to the rule of the T'angs is a sort of world parliament dominated by restive Europeans whose real power derives from their control of huge corporations.

The plot centers on the efforts of the T'angs to preserve the status quo, lest humanity destroy itself (and their heirs face unemployment). To this end, technological progress has been inhibited and history has been rewritten so that everyone—including the European rebels—believes that China has ruled the world since its decisive victory over the Roman Empire. The resulting world order is grim indeed; the T'angs take for granted that peace can be maintained only by unremitting repression, and their adversaries are no less ruthless. Virtually all the principal players, even the youngest children, come across as arrogant, self-satisfied and, when their ambitions are thwarted, downright nasty.

Mr. Wingrove—a Hugo Award-winning nonfiction writer now living in North London—has taken some trouble to re-create the customs and attitudes of a bygone imperial China in the futuristic world known as Chung Kuo. There is much bowing and scraping to the T'angs, many references to the importance of family ties and hierarchical status and the subservience of women, and a Chinese expression on almost every page (with a brief glossary of Mandarin terms in the back of the book). At the same time, the plot bristles with the apparatus of superscience, from all-but-indestructible plastics to androids that mimic human behavior to near perfection. Out of these disparate materials Mr. Wingrove has fashioned a lively but ultimately unsatisfying hybrid of historical fiction and science fiction.

For all the novel's authenticated trappings, his vision of a Chinese-dominated future seems arbitrary, ungrounded in historical process, intended not as a vehicle for speculating on the shape of things to come or commenting on things as they are but solely to sustain a fast-moving entertainment. Indeed, Mr. Wingrove is so busy keeping all the subplots straight and planting seeds that will undoubtedly mature in succeeding volumes that he has no time to deal with some of the fascinating questions raised by his own narrative strategy. For example, what status would an android—an artificially created human being—be accorded in a rigidly stratified society?

Readers who couldn't care less about exploring such matters will find sufficient distractions in the conspiracies, assassinations, betrayals, rapes and torture scenes that crowd the pages of ***Chung Kuo.*** Even when the action pauses for a bit of palaver, someone is bound to keep the hot pot stirring with lines like these: " 'Maybe you're right, Soren. Maybe he is what you say. But my feelings tell me otherwise. I don't trust him. And if he's here, I'd wager he's up to something.' He paused, then turned, looking back at the pagoda. 'In fact, I'd stake my life on it.' "

Gerald Jonas, "In a Bygone World of the Future," in The New York Times Book Review, *March 4, 1990, p. 30.*

Nicholas Bradbury

My first thought was that British writer David Wingrove had spent a long time—too long a time—in Beijing. All of us who have endured the experience know the struggle for sanity, or at least perspective, that it requires. What else but a desire to exorcize the soul of festering sinophilic frustration could prompt someone to embark on a seven-volume cycle of novels exploring the "grand conflict between the Western idea of progress and the Eastern belief in stability," of which ***Chung Kuo: The Middle Kingdom,*** is the first 600-page chunk?

It is hard to say. Wingrove has not, it would appear, spent time in China. So it is all the more curious that his book displays a fair understanding, in as much as a Westerner can have any, of Chinese culture. Many incidents in the book are reminiscent of Chinese classics such as *The Water Margin, The Romance Of The Three Kingdoms* and *The Dream Of Red Mansions.* The role of "face," the controlling force of the Chinese society and psyche, permeates every scene. Particularly well observed is the political tenor—the almost instinctive obedience to a higher authority, above considerations of petty morality and the Byzantine intrigues between powerful families, that characterize Chinese politics as much now as in Imperial times.

But the middle kingdom of the story is not the past or present, but the future. Wingrove has created a fantasy world in which the Chinese, having allied themselves with northern Europeans, have taken control of a world that was being destroyed by Western technology. After eliminating other races, the Han continue their alliance with the Europeans, harnessing their technology for the benevolent aim of establishing a Peace of Ten Thousand Years, a state run according to New Confucian principles. It is strictly hierarchical. At the apex are the seven T'ang who rule like a joint emperor. Beneath them are the 29 families of the minor nobility and numerous Han officials.

The Europeans are left to run the technological and commercial enterprises, as well as the army. Below are the mainly Han subjects of the T'ang who live very controlled, simple lives. The new society occupies cities that are huge hive-like structures above the land mass. Most of the Earth itself is turned into a vast plantation where peasants harvest food for the Above. In a nether world called the Clay some remnants of the destroyed civilizations such as England eke out a barbaric existence.

It is a highly civilized society in the Chinese mold. It is also highly artificial, the great cities raised on stilts and sealed off from the Earth symbolic of man divorced from nature in every sense. As such, the novel seems to imply, it is a flawed perfection. The restless forces within man are threatening to break this desiccated harmony. These crystallize in the person of DeVore, an army major who secretly plots the overthrow of the T'angs and succeeds in securing the assassination of the T'ang of Europe's heir.

The T'ang represent the logical extension of the Confucian ruler—benevolent and cruel beyond personal interest and steeped in an education devoted entirely to the ruling of men. DeVore, by contrast, epitomizes the Western (one should perhaps say Greek) reduction of man to an abstract entity, of life as a game to be played. To both men, therefore, people are abstracted, but for the T'ang they are to be guided so as to live together in harmonious hierarchy, but to DeVore they exist purely to further his own, as yet unclear, goals.

Heady stuff. But it would be a mistake to suppose that this is a dry treatise on political economy. ***Chung Kuo*** reads rather like an adventure fantasy—often an embarrassingly cheap one considering the serious ideas it attempts to tackle. The dialogue is peculiar. It is surely not enough justification that the protagonists are all Han and northern European for their speech so often to sound like a poor translation from Swedish or Chinese. Wingrove's powers of description are also apt to fail him on occasion. There are a number of action sequences, such as barbaric fighters sparring to the death, where we are treated to hackneyed descriptions of broad chests and proud looks.

Rather than concentrating on sharpening his ideas, the author might have spent a little more time honing his prose. For all that, this is an enjoyable novel, of interest for its thesis and for its understanding of the Chinese mind. I hope someone buys the film rights. It would make a splendid film.

Nicholas Bradbury, "An Adventure Fantasy," in Toronto Star, *April 21, 1990, p. M10.*

David Wingrove [correspondence with *Contemporary Literary Criticism* **]**

[CLC]: *Comment on the process of writing* ***Chung Kuo,*** *including the amount of time it took to complete, your writing habits, the process of revision, and significant editorial input.*

[Wingrove]: Work began on this project in December, 1983. It originated as a simple short story, "A Spring Day at the Edge of the World," and developed into a novel, which, from mid-1985 onward, was revised and enlarged, becoming several volumes, the final one of which was the original work. From January, 1986 onward this project took up most of my writing time and energies (interspersed with looking after my children three days a week). During this period my writing methods changed quite radically and it was not until early 1987 that I found the proper way of telling and structuring my (by now) vast story. There was no editorial input at this stage, though I relied quite heavily upon writer friends commenting upon the various drafts of the work.

Relate the terms of any background research you conducted.

Background research for ***Chung Kuo*** has been intense from mid-1985 onwards. Basically, it entails finding source material on China and things Chinese. Most useful amongst these have been the *Cambridge History of China* (Volumes 1, 3, 7, 10, and 11), C. P. Fitzgerald's *China: A Short Cultural History, The Shorter Science and Civilization in China* (Colin A. Ronan and Joseph Needham), and the writings of Reginald Johnston, Edgar Snow, William Huston, Jonathan Spence, Derk Bodde, and Alastair Clayre. Add to this a list of some further three hundred volumes.

How is your own experience incorporated into your fiction?

Like a great number of authors, I tend to place parts of myself into various characters, exaggerating my own character traits and building fictional people from such exaggerations. Furthermore, the structure of my great continent-spanning city in ***Chung Kuo*** is an extrapolation of something experienced in my early youth: having seen war-damaged parts of the London dockside area being replaced by vast high-rises. Many incidents I've heard about or seen or directly experienced, find their way—in a fictional and non-autobiographical form—into the work.

Was there a particular event or person that inspired you to compose this work?

No. There was a "moment" when I saw—clearly and in its entirety—the short story from which it all came. Otherwise it has been a process of growth; very organic—though there have been moments along the way where I've sat down and imposed an order or structure on things.

What do you hope to accomplish through your writing?

I hope to create an awareness in my readers—by dramatizing certain situations—that there are healthy and unhealthy ways of living in the world; also that it is an error to look at things in a simplistic "Us or Them" way. Which is to say, I suppose, that I'm a very moralistic writer, and I guess that's true. Like Dickens, I have my "touchstone" characters, by which all else is ultimately judged.

"I hope to create an awareness in my readers—by dramatizing certain situations—that there are healthy and unhealthy ways of living in the world; also that it is an error to look at things in a simplistic 'Us or Them' way. Which is to say, I suppose, that I'm a very moralistic writer, and I guess that's true."

—David Wingrove

As you write, do you have a particular audience in mind or an ideal reader?

The ideal reader is one who rereads the work, not only because they enjoyed it first time round, but because they discerned that there were other levels and they wanted to investigate and get to grips with them. But as I'm writing, I'm conscious only of trying to please myself. To *satisfy* my desire for story.

Whom do you consider your primary literary influences, and why?

(1) D. H. Lawrence: because—within limits—I share a great deal of his worldview. I've adopted the thematic dialectic of *The Rainbow* (sun/moon, inwardness/outwardness) in my own **"War of the Two Directions."**

(2) Thomas Mann: his structuring of material (in *Buddenbrooks* and *Joseph and His Brothers*) lies behind the form of ***Chung Kuo,*** as does his use of *leitmotif.*

(3) Philip K. Dick: his fascination with reality and the artificial constructs of our modern world *permeate* my own work. Indeed, I'd go so far as to say that ***Chung Kuo*** would not exist had Dick not cleared the ground beforehand.

Describe any works-in-progress.

Five more volumes of ***Chung Kuo,*** to complete an eight-volume work covering sixty years of a society two hundred years from now.

The Dark Ages. A novel begun in 1983, about a mute Irish blacksmith living in Northumberland in the year 932 A.D.

The Apple Tree. A novel begun in 1982, about a young woman's experience of contemporary life, and her quest to find out the truth about her parents' past.

Martin Morse Wooster

David Wingrove's ***The Broken Wheel: Chung Kuo II*** is a series novel of the second type. As editor of ***The Science Fiction Source Book*** and Brian Aldiss's collaborator on ***Trillion Year Spree,*** Wingrove has shown a keen appreciation of sf 's past masters; his reading is reflected in his writing, for ***Chung Kuo*** is an amalgam of the works of Aldiss, Michael Moorcock and Frank Herbert.

It is the 22nd century, and the Chinese have taken over the world, burying Western civilization in the rubble of giant world cities. It is a world where bureaucracy is the dominant social, political and cultural form, and where most of the novel's 124 characters are scheming to be at the top of the pile. Can a small band of revolutionaries topple the existing order? Can the seven aging members of the council that rules the world survive until volume three without being assassinated by rival clans?

Wingrove's goal is to produce a novel as dense and complex as the game of *go;* one character, for example, is described as "a mere counter, played by some being greater than himself in a game the scale of which his tiny human mind could scarcely comprehend."

But to achieve this vast complexity, Wingrove has to sacrifice characterization and depth; most of the heroes and villains in ***The Broken Wheel: Chung Kuo II,*** like the black and white stones used in a *go* game, are simply pieces to be moved. For most of the first 250 pages, the plot consists of little more than machinations, in which sex and violence alternate as regularly as a metronome. For those who may not have read volume one (***Chung Kuo: The Middle Kingdom***), these machinations make little sense.

The last third of ***The Broken Wheel: Chung Kuo II*** is a sharp improvement over the first two thirds, as Wingrove focuses on tormented artist Ben Shepard. While Wingrove has many thoughtful comments on the nature and purposes of art, these musings are buried in the endless battles and bedroom scenes.

Chung Kuo is a work in progress. When complete, it may well be one of the masterpieces of the decade. But it is at least as likely that Wingrove will be unable to sustain a multi-volume narrative, resulting in a colossal ruin in which pages of brilliance occasionally can be found in the rubble.

Martin Morse Wooster, "New Worlds and Old Dreams," in Book World—The Washington Post, *March 31, 1991, p. 9.*

K. V. Bailey

[In ***The Broken Wheel: Chung Kuo II,*** action] extends over the year 2206-7. It perpetuates the endemic palace machinations, barrack-room rivalries, and bedroom and brothel manoevers of David Wingrove's anti-utopian, world-spanning sino-city. Though repetitive of the kind of incidents to be found in Book I (eight books are now projected), these episodes do graphically characterize a pervading corruption and articulate the complex story of mutually suspicious factions striving the regime of the Seven, the continent ruling T'ang. Focal centres of conspiracy are on Mars and in the Alpine "wilderness" (locations exercising Wingrove's library talent for landscape description); but undercover operations penetrate all of the interconnected levels of City Earth.

Impossible here to detail the plot; sufficient to say that pressures and strategies successfully weaken the vulnerable hegemony. By whom this is achieved, and at whose expense, is made much clearer by a now provided comprehensive and annotated cast list. If the successions of knife-fight, assassination, bribery and rape make for a somewhat routine sameness, there is also a more positively aspected iteration—that which restates and elaborates the large symbolic dimensions of the work. The moves of the game of *wei chei* model those of the global antagonists; and the dichotomy of a concealed past and a fraudulent official version of it keeps open the fundamental official version of it keeps open the fundamental question of whether the heritages are "true". (A descent from the warrens, walkways and malls of Oxford Canton to historic Oxford's ruins, hidden on the lowest "Clay" level, is potent metaphor.) Above all, there is the opposition of freedom and manipulation, represented most vividly by contrasts of life within the City and in privileged enclaves outside the ice of its towering walls, and this depicted mainly notably in two "romantic" interludes, one pastoral, the other nordic. The other is the brother-sister idyll played out along the sunlit Tamar estuary; the other is Jelka Tolonen's retreat to her origins, islanded and tower-sequestered off the stormy coast of Finland.

Within the City certain role-assigned characters question the reactionary ethos of its oligarchy. These are not so much the revolutionaries, who use much the same terrorist tactics as their enemies, as the outsiders—Ben Shepherd, the artist, and Kim, the Clayborn intuitive scientist. Scenes such as Shepherd's encounter with the funerary "Oven Man" and Kim's holistic vision in the Heilbronn observatory, are imaginally positive, and balance those many negative scenes of brutality, so many as eventually rather to diminish their dramatic impact—though admittedly they are integral to the novel's structure. The *yin-yang* elements in the structuring of the series constitute a dimension which intriguingly transcends dystopian confines.

K. V. Bailey, in a review of "The Broken Wheel: Chung Kuo II," in Vector, *No. 159, February-March, 1991, p. 24.*

□ Contemporary Literary Criticism Indexes

Literary Criticism Series
  Cumulative Author Index
Cumulative Nationality Index
Title Index, Volume 68

This Index Includes References to Entries in These Gale Series

Children's Literature Review includes excerpts from reviews, criticism, and commentary on works of authors and illustrators who create books for children.

Classical and Medieval Literature Criticism offers excerpts of criticism on the works of world authors from classical antiquity through the fourteenth century.

Contemporary Authors series encompasses five related series. ***Contemporary Authors*** provides biographical and bibliographical information on more than 97,000 writers of fiction, nonfiction, poetry, journalism, drama, and film. ***Contemporary Authors New Revision Series*** provides completely updated information on active authors covered in previously published volumes of *CA*. ***Contemporary Authors Permanent Series*** consists of updated listings for deceased and inactive authors removed from the original volumes 9-36 when those volumes were revised. ***Contemporary Authors Autobiography Series*** presents specially commissioned autobiographies by leading contemporary writers. ***Contemporary Authors Bibliographical Series*** contains primary and secondary bibliographies as well as analytical bibliographical essays by authorities on major modern authors.

Contemporary Literary Criticism presents excerpts of criticism on the works of novelists, poets, dramatists, short story writers, scriptwriters, and other creative writers who are now living or who have died since 1960.

Dictionary of Literary Biography comprises three related series. ***Dictionary of Literary Biography*** furnishes illustrated overviews of authors' lives and works and places them in the larger perspective of literary history. ***Dictionary of Literary Biography Documentary Series*** illuminates the careers of major figures through a selection of literary documents, including letters, interviews, and photographs. ***Dictionary of Literary Biography Yearbook*** summarizes the past year's literary activity and includes updated and new entries on individual authors. A cumulative index to authors and articles is included in each new volume. ***Concise Dictionary of Literary Biography,*** a six-volume series, collects revised and updated sketches on major American authors that were originally presented in *Dictionary of Literary Biography.*

Drama Criticism provides excerpts of criticism on the works of playwrights of all nationalities and periods of literary history.

Literature Criticism from 1400 to 1800 compiles significant passages from the most noteworthy criticism on authors of the fifteenth through the eighteenth centuries.

Nineteenth-Century Literature Criticism offers significant passages from criticism on authors who died between 1800 and 1899.

Poetry Criticism presents excerpts of criticism on the works of poets from all eras, movements, and nationalities.

Short Story Criticism combines excerpts of criticism on short fiction by writers of all eras and nationalities.

Something about the Author series encompasses three related series. ***Something about the Author*** contains well-illustrated biographical sketches on authors and illustrators of juvenile and young adult literature from all eras. ***Something about the Author Autobiography Series*** presents specially commissioned autobiographies by prominent authors and illustrators of books for children and young adults. ***Authors & Artists for Young Adults*** provides high school and junior high school students with profiles of their favorite creative artists.

Twentieth-Century Literary Criticism contains critical excerpts by the most significant commentators on poets, novelists, short story writers, dramatists, and philosophers who died between 1900 and 1960.

Yesterday's Authors of Books for Children contains heavily illustrated entries on children's writers who died before 1961. Complete in two volumes.

Literary Criticism Series Cumulative Author Index

This index lists all author entries in the Gale Literary Criticism Series and includes cross-references to other Gale sources. References in the index are identified as follows:

AAYA: *Authors & Artists for Young Adults,* Volumes 1-6
CAAS: *Contemporary Authors Autobiography Series,* Volumes 1-13
CA: *Contemporary Authors* (original series), Volumes 1-133
CABS: *Contemporary Authors Bibliographical Series,* Volumes 1-3
CANR: *Contemporary Authors New Revision Series,* Volumes 1-33
CAP: *Contemporary Authors Permanent Series,* Volumes 1-2
CA-R: *Contemporary Authors* (revised editions), Volumes 1-44
CDALB: *Concise Dictionary of American Literary Biography,* Volumes 1-6
CLC: *Contemporary Literary Criticism,* Volumes 1-68
CLR: *Children's Literature Review,* Volumes 1-24
CMLC: *Classical and Medieval Literature Criticism,* Volumes 1-7
DC: *Drama Criticism,* Volume 1
DLB: *Dictionary of Literary Biography,* Volumes 1-107
DLB-DS: *Dictionary of Literary Biography Documentary Series,* Volumes 1-8
DLB-Y: *Dictionary of Literary Biography Yearbook,* Volumes 1980-1988
LC: *Literature Criticism from 1400 to 1800,* Volumes 1-17
NCLC: *Nineteenth-Century Literature Criticism,* Volumes 1-33
PC: *Poetry Criticism,* Volumes 1-3
SAAS: *Something about the Author Autobiography Series,* Volumes 1-12
SATA: *Something about the Author,* Volumes 1-65
SSC: *Short Story Criticism,* Volumes 1-8
TCLC: *Twentieth-Century Literary Criticism,* Volumes 1-42
YABC: *Yesterday's Authors of Books for Children,* Volumes 1-2

Author Index

Author Index

Author Index

Author Index

Author Index

Author Index

CLC Cumulative Nationality Index

Nationality Index

Nationality Index

CLC-68 Title Index

ISBN 0-8103-4442-4